THE MODERN LIBRARY
of the World's Best Books

>>

TWELVE FAMOUS PLAYS
OF THE RESTORATION AND
EIGHTEENTH CENTURY

>>>

The publishers will be pleased to send, upon request, an illustrated folder setting forth the purpose and scope of THE MODERN LIBRARY, *and listing each volume in the series. Every reader of books will find titles he has been looking for, handsomely printed, in unabridged editions. and at an unusually low price.*

>>>

TWELVE FAMOUS
PLAYS
OF THE RESTORATION AND
EIGHTEENTH CENTURY

>>

Introduction by
PROFESSOR CECIL A. MOORE
of the University of Minnesota

>>

BENNETT A. CERF · DONALD S. KLOPFER
THE MODERN LIBRARY
NEW YORK

THE MODERN LIBRARY

IS PUBLISHED BY

RANDOM HOUSE, INC.

BENNETT A. CERF · DONALD S. KLOPFER · ROBERT K. HAAS

Manufactured in the United States of America
Printed by Parkway Printing Company   *Bound by H. Wolff*

822

CONTENTS

7262

CONTENTS

INTRODUCTION

WHEN Charles II came to the throne (1660), the London theatres had been closed for about eighteen years—since the puritans, in 1642, had ordered that actors in all "Stage Plays, Interludes, or other common Plays" were to be "punished as Rogues, according to Law." On August 21, 1660, the new king issued letters patent to Thomas Killigrew and Sir William D'Avenant for the incorporation of two companies of players. By this official act the theatrical interregnum was brought to an end, and the stage, now protected by royal patronage, was safe from the attacks of its puritan enemies.

Londoners who recalled the last performances allowed under Charles I were to find conditions greatly altered in the new theatre. In former times, says a writer of 1664, the theatre was "but plain and simple, with no other Scenes, nor Decorations of the Stage, but only old Tapestry, and the Stage strew'd with Rushes, (with their Habits accordingly) whereas ours now for Cost and ornament are arriv'd to the heighth of Magnificence." If this is extravagant praise, at least the illusion of drama was greatly enhanced by the addition of movable scenery. Actually in many cases the scenic effects were very elaborate. Much greater use was made of music, too, and—most important of all —female parts, which formerly had been played by boys, were now regularly performed by actresses. Another difference soon began to be evident, at least to the more discerning patrons. With the restoration of the stage had come also a new type of drama, plays of a much more sophisticated type than those to which they had been accustomed. Sir Philip Sidney had deplored the formlessness of Elizabethan drama and had urged playwrights to improve their art by an imitation of classical drama. The advice went unheeded in his time, and, with the sole exception of Ben Jonson, no English dramatist of the later period had tried seriously to compose "regular" plays upon the model of the ancients. During the interregnum in England, the classical ideal had been generally adopted in France and loudly proclaimed. Largely through the influence of French example and criticism, the English began after 1660 to set their own house in order, and thus inaugurated the Age of Classicism.

vii

As the cult of correctness gained ground, Elizabethan plays were regarded with increasing disfavor. Not that they were neglected or that the national tradition had been severed. Indeed, as one may see from the lists of offerings at the King's and the Duke's, their repertory consisted largely of plays written by Shakespeare, Jonson, and Beaumont and Fletcher. But, Jonson alone excepted, none of them were considered as authoritative exemplars of dramatic art, and seldom were any of their tragedies or comedies put upon the boards until they had undergone drastic revision. No doubt existed that some of the Elizabethans and Jacobeans were men of great native genius; but, unhappily, they had not acquired that refinement of manner demanded in an age of politeness. Though sufficient for a rude and barbarous generation, they "could charm an understanding age no more." To be acceptable now, they had to be reshaped into conformity with the three unities and the other prescriptions of the neo-classic code as it was being constantly elaborated by Gallic doctrinaires. Within limits, the attitude was thoroughly defensible; beyond question, many of the old plays are inexcusably loose in structure, some of them marred by downright crudeness. The process of remodeling the elder poets began with the Restoration and continued without abatement for fully a hundred years.

Although the effort to moderate "the generous splendour and faulty exuberance of adventurous youth" sometimes resulted in sheer mutilation, it is not to be denied that a few of the adaptations were better than the originals for the purpose of the stage. Only one of them, however, has found a permanent place in English literature, Dryden's *All for Love* (1677), and his success was only partial. None but a prejudiced critic would question that Dryden's *All for Love* is a better piece of dramaturgy than Shakespeare's *Antony and Cleopatra,* and no producer would hesitate in his preference for the later version; but only an insensitive critic would fail to perceive that the gain in dramatic technique has been secured at the expense of human appeal. The loss is felt especially in the character of Cleopatra herself; the well-known criticism is just, that Shakespeare's wily "serpent of old Nile" has dwindled into a conventional courtesan of the Merry Monarch's *ménage.* The redactor himself knew that, while he was reforming the artless original according to the ancients and Mr. Rymer's rules, he had allowed much of the human essence to escape. With the good sense and candor which seldom, though occasionally, failed him, Dryden expresses the modest hope that by imitating the "divine Shakespeare" he has managed to rise above himself.

The same characterization is applicable, indeed, to most of the original tragedy of the new era; it excels in technique, but is lacking in true passion. The astonishing fact is that for more than a century after the Restoration, only two tragedies of lasting worth were composed—Otway's *The Orphan* (1680) and *Venice Preserv'd* (1682). The explanation sometimes given for the dearth is too simple to be true. It will not suffice to say that the Muse of Tragedy was suffocated by an artificial code. No doubt the neo-classic prescription in its extreme form tended to destroy naturalness of expression and thus to inhibit genuine tragedy. Of this danger Englishmen of the Restoration were not unaware. There was never a time when the invasion of England by the French critics was not resented in some quarters and a plea being made that the English playwright assert his independence of the foreign dictators. Rymer might, if he liked, call *Othello* a "bloody farce" because Shakespeare had neglected the proprieties; but Rymer was the extreme rigorist in England. His bigotry is less typical of critical opinion than are the protests he evoked from saner men, those who believed that the doctrine of correctness was salutary only when applied in moderation and that a dramatist must have regard for the peculiarities of his public. When ample allowance has been made for the sterilizing effects of the new dramatic rules, the sickly state of English tragedy has not been explained. That Addison's *Cato* (1713)— the one correct tragedy produced in England, according to Voltaire—is devoid of passion is no proof that a play may not be both correct and impassioned. If the typical tragedy of the classical period is a perfect body without a soul, the true explanation seems to be that the age itself was deficient in spiritual quality.

While the theatre remained under the immediate control of a dissolute and cynical court, as it was during the twenty-five years of Charles II's rule, the dramatist had slight incentive to provide his audience with anything better than rhetoric and splendor. The beginning of rhymed tragedy, the so-called Heroic Play, was attributed largely to the French taste of the monarch, but it accumulated absurdities for which certainly France cannot be held responsible. The Heroic Play is the most exotic and unreal of all the drama the English people have ever tolerated in the name of tragedy. Dryden's *Conquest of Granada* (1670), a thoroughly representative specimen of the *genre*, was not designed to move the audience with pity or terror. The superhuman deeds of Almanzor ("that great trumpet-blower" Taine calls him) place him at a remote distance from human sympathy or comprehension. The poet laureate's purpose was rather to dazzle the audience and excite "admiration." Dryden endeavored, says Johnson, "to glut the publick with dramatick wonders; to exhibit in its highest elevation a theatrical meteor of incredible love and impossible valour, and to leave no room for a wilder flight to the extravagance of posterity." There is ample evidence in *The Rehearsal* (1671) that the absurdities of the type were fully understood by contemporary wits; but the existence of the fashion remains a damning commentary on the low state of dramatic taste.

Against this background of artificiality, the tragedies of Thomas Otway appear strangely anachronistic; they are probably more out of place in the reign of the Merry Monarch than they would appear at any other moment in the history of English drama. A testimony to the indestructible genuineness of the poet's character, they testify also to the inspiration which was still to be derived from the "giant race before the flood." Wherever tragedy takes on the semblance of life in the age of passionless rhetoric, it will be found that the dramatist has derived his inspiration, as Otway did, from the fountainhead of Elizabethan drama. Much of Otway's early work is in the conventional manner of his time. He, too, has written plays in which "Declamation roars while Passion sleeps"; but in *The Orphan* and *Venice Preserv'd* are heard once more the accents of genuine feeling. There is a tradition that the pathos woven into the parts of Belvidera and Monimia is the effect partly of Otway's hopeless love for Mrs. Barry, the mistress of Lord Rochester, for whom the parts were written. In the conception of these two characters, at least, Otway has earned a right of comparison to Shakespeare. Dryden had once spoken of his rival as "a barren illiterate man," but afterwards acknowledged his greatness in terms of true understanding. "The motions which are studied," he says, "are never so natural as those which break out in the height of a real passion. Mr. Otway possessed this part as thoroughly as any of the ancients or moderns." Goldsmith thought Otway was "next to Shakespeare the greatest genius England has ever produced in tragedy." A generation later Scott went so far as to say that Otway not only rivals, but in some respects surpasses, the master himself, and that "more tears have been shed probably for the sorrows of Belvidera and Monimia than for those of Juliet and Desdemona."

Undoubtedly Otway has been over-praised, largely because his two tragedies are the one oasis in a dreary desert. Theatrical conditions improved later, and drama became less artificial than it had been during the heroic age of the Restoration, partly in response to Otway's own example. Still, no single specimen of pronounced worth had been produced before Scott wrote. So far as tragedy is concerned, Dryden's characterization was still applicable:

> Our age was cultivated thus at length;
> But what we gained in skill we lost in strength.
> Our builders were with want of genius curst,
> The second temple was not like the first.

The Augustan Ages were richly endowed to produce a literature of knowledge, as DeQuincey calls it, but not a literature of power.

Out of these very conditions which all but extinguished tragedy came the impulse for a vigorous comedy—comedy, too, of a new kind. Charles II was fond of "a very merry play." This well-known taste of the sovereign's was an invitation not to be neglected by the wits in his kingdom. The writing of comedy became at once the most lucrative and fashionable kind of literary work. Dryden, Charles's poet laureate, complained pathetically that in order to succeed a writer had to compose comedies whether he liked or not, or whether indeed he had the necessary skill. No English men of letters have ever had a richer field for the exercise of their talent in satire or a more generous license for their practice. The life of the time—brilliant, but corrupt and cynical—provided admirable copy for satiric portraiture, and the artist was allowed to reproduce it without let or hindrance. It is to this peculiar combination of circumstances that we are indebted for what is by common consent the most scintillating of all English comedy. If Lamb meant that the satirist was not drawing his material from actual conditions, he was clearly wrong. Hazlitt insists, rightly, that the truthfulness of the portrait is what accounts for the vigor of Restoration comedy and its fascination for the contemporary public. No one supposes that the loose morals exhibited on the Restoration stage are those of a whole people or indeed any considerable portion of it; but they are, emphatically, the manners of that modish world centering in Whitehall—and in the Restoration theatre no one else counted. Let anyone read such private records of court life as have survived—Pepys's *Diary* and Grammont's *Memoirs* if nothing else —and then ask himself if the dramatist needed great gift of invention to people his stage with a motley group of fops, gallants, libertines, coquettes, and courtesans or to provide them with their amorous intrigues. The characters are as real as the familiar scenes through which they pass—the Rose, Hyde Park, Spring Gardens, the New Exchange; some of the scandalous episodes are transcripts from life. Gathered in the Duke's or the King's, haunts of pleasure where no puritanic censor would think of appearing, was a more homogeneous audience than had ever before assembled in an English theatre or was likely to assemble again. The men and women who composed it came to see themselves mirrored to the life, to laugh over their follies, and to applaud the wit inspired by their frailties. The picture is, of course, selective, as satirical portraiture always is. It has the exaggeration of any composite. Vice and Folly are, speaking in terms of art, idealized. But the elements are indigenous, and the degree of exaggeration is actually slighter than comic realism usually requires. To think of this drama as "a speculative scene of things, which has no reference whatever to the world that is" is to mistake the only possible explanation of its existence. The reality of the scene accounts for both the strength and the weakness of the *genre*. As soon as the comic writer confines himself to a study of a shallow-minded group of aristocratic rakes, he limits his art to a small part of the comic field and gives an incomplete report of the human comedy. This is merely to say that the Restoration Comedy of Manners is not the Human Comedy of Shakespeare; but in its kind it is supreme.

The main tendencies of the new comedy of manners are reflected in the character of its founder, Sir George Etherege. "Easy Etherege" was a clever and dissolute man of fashion who, like many other royalists, had spent most of his time in Paris during the dark days of puritan rule. After he had returned to help the king enjoy his own and make up for the lean years of exile, he was to be found with his fellow-wits at the Mulberry Garden and the other haunts of the *beau monde*. Among his intimate friends were Rochester, Buckingham, and Sedley. His first play, *Love in a Tub* (1664), provides scarcely more than the rough outlines of the pattern he was to develop afterwards in *She Wou'd if She Cou'd* (1668) and *The Man of Mode* (1676). It was part of the gentleman's creed that the Muse should never be taxed. Sir Fopling Flutter, speaking with slight exaggeration for Etherege himself, declares that writing is "a mechanic part of wit" and that "a gentleman should never go beyond a song or a ballet." Etherege astonished the Town with the brilliant wit of three comedies; then he laid his pen aside and spent the remaining years of his life *à la mode*. Meanwhile, John Dryden, unquestionably the greatest literary figure of the age, was producing comedy after comedy, but never quite succeeded in attaining the "fashionable cut." Even *Marriage à la Mode* (1672), though witty enough and licentious enough, fails to catch the easy nonchalance requisite for perfection. The explanation Etherege himself gave Dryden is probably the true one: the poet laureate was too serious, he lacked that "noble laziness of the mind" in which the king had set the example.

It is a striking fact that only those writers succeeded who had Etherege's attitude of the gentleman amateur. His friend Sir Charles Sedley produced *The Mulberry Garden* in 1668; after a silence of nineteen years it was followed by *Bellamira* (1687), and nothing more is heard of Sedley the dramatist. Wycherley's four comedies—*Love in a Wood, The Gentleman Dancing Master, The Country Wife,* and *The Plain Dealer*— were first acted between 1671 and 1676. "Manly" Wycherley lived long enough to become the friend and adviser of Pope; but, once he had found favor at court (through the influence of one of the royal mistresses, the Duchess of Cleveland) and thus established his claim to gentility, he idled away the remainder of his life. Congreve, that "splendid Phœbus Apollo of the Mall" who was destined to give the comedy of manners its final perfection of epigrammatic splendor and delicate artistry, ran true to form. When his first play, *The Old Bachelor,* was produced, in 1693, he was only twenty-three years old. It was followed in swift succession by *The Double Dealer* (1693), *Love for Love* (1695), and *The Way of the World* (1700). If there had been any suspicion that he was merely a drudging professional, the misconception was now to be removed. His meteoric flight concluded as suddenly as it had begun. The most scintillating wit of the whole tribe buried his talent, content to live upon such sinecures as he could obtain and devote himself to the business of being a gentleman. Sir John Vanbrugh "descended into authorship" as an avocation in the intervals he could spare from architecture and other business. His only original comedies were *The Relapse* (1696) and *The Provok'd Wife* (1697). The last twenty years of his life were spent in retirement with nothing to show for them except the unfinished manuscript of a comedy afterwards completed by Colley Cibber—*The Provok'd Husband* (1728).

Any form of literary art as definitely identified with a peculiar set of social conventions as the Restoration comedy of manners was could count upon its existence only so long as those conventions prevailed. "By what I've heard," says Wycherley's Hippolita, " 'tis a pleasant, well-bred, complaisant, free, frolic, good-natured, pretty age: and if you do not like it, leave it to us that do." This was all well enough when *The Gentleman Dancing Master* was first played. The Merry Monarch was on the throne; his subjects could live and love as he did; if there were others who still had old-fashioned notions about the sinfulness of sin or the sacredness of matrimony or the heinousness of adultery, let them stay away from the theatre and enjoy the luxury of a good conscience in private. But this flippant answer gradually lost authority after the last of the Stuart kings had withdrawn from Whitehall. The Gardens of Epicurus were no longer sacred from the intrusion of the vulgar. The moral opinion of the conventional middle classes could not be brushed aside with a laugh from the wits. Under the rule of William and Mary there was an emphatic demand for reform, one patronized by the rulers. The Society for the Reformation of Manners was organized. Strict laws were made for the suppression of drunkenness, profanity, and debauchery, and the stage came in for specific consideration. Jeremy Collier's *Profaneness and Immorality of the English Stage* (1698) was not the first protest of its kind; it is significant mainly as the embodiment of a public conscience which was no longer to be denied. By an irony of history he was a High Churchman, a non-juror; the strength of his protest lay largely in the fact that by restating, in modified form, the argument of Prynne and other puritan opponents of the stage, he became the mouthpiece of the puritanic section of society. Dryden, now approaching the end of his busy life, acknowledged that the parson's complaint was, on the whole (though not in all details), a just reproof and promised to mend his ways. The truth is, Dryden, never quite of the fraternity, had made a confession thirteen years earlier in a spirit of contrition which ought to have satisfied even Collier:

> O gracious God! how far have we
> Profan'd thy heav'nly gift of poesy!
> Made prostitute and profligate the Muse,
> Debas'd to each obscene and impious use,
> Whose harmony was first ordain'd above
> For tongues of angels, and for hymns of love!
> O wretched we! why were we hurried down
>   This lubric and adult'rous age,
>   (Nay, added fat pollutions of our own)
> T' increase the steaming ordures of the stage.

The younger wits, some of them just entering upon their careers in the drama, adopted a very different tone. They undertook to argue the matter with the clergyman. From the outset they were doomed to defeat. They were hopelessly lost the moment they began contradicting him, as Congreve did, or asserting, as Vanbrugh did, that his plays were worthy of a place in a lady's library next to her Bible. It required more ingenuity than even the brilliant Mr. Congreve possessed to prove that Restoration comedy was not indecent according to the recognized conventions of decorum; the most courageous apologists of the *genre* have had to admit that the wits were guilty of obscenity and nastiness. Congreve fared almost as badly when he fell back upon his second line of defense and contended that, even if the Muse had occasionally overstepped the bounds of propriety, the indiscretion was atoned for by the salutary moral inculcated in the conclusion. His antagonist needed only to remind him of (what he had apparently forgotten) the morals enforced in the final lines of *The 'Old Bachelor* and *Love for Love!* Modern critics who have undertaken the cause have succeeded no better than Congreve did. It is futile to impute to Etherege and his followers the noble design of reforming a frivolous and vicious society. That certain kinds of hypocrisy and depravity are rendered odious is true enough. But the Cavalier wits have one trait, if no other, in common with their sanctimonious opponents; they

> Compound for sins they are inclined to
> By damning those they have no mind to.

They can be severe enough upon the faults of ill-breeding and vulgarity or monstrous vices that a man of fashion would abhor, but they have more than a sneaking kindness for the modish vices. The only sin they recognize is the sin of dullness. Much of the merriment of their comedies arises from the humorous contrast between themselves and their conventional neighbors. They have no greater desire to remake fashionable London than Pope has when he writes *The Rape of the Lock*. Their plays, like his mock-epic, idealize the very follies they expose. It is not as if they were spectators standing apart and viewing the pageant of folly; they themselves are a part of the picture they paint, and, though keenly conscious of the absurdities in their snug little world, they find it, on the whole, a very agreeable one, not in spite of but because of, its absurdities, for these are material for wit. Most of the characters in Etherege's plays were identified with members of his own group. Usually he himself was considered the original for Sir Fopling Flutter, and Dean Lockier says that he "designed Dorimant the genteel rake of wit for his own picture." The Wit's Creed is ideally summarized by Bellmour in the opening scene of Congreve's first play: "Come, come, leave business to idlers, and wisdom to fools: they have need of 'em: wit, be my faculty, and pleasure my occupation; and let father Time shake his glass." Only a quixotic apologist will undertake to enthrone these graceless wags among the great English moralists, and they would be amused to find themselves there. Vanbrugh wrote for gentlemen, hoping "to

divert (if possible) some part of their spleen in spite of their
wives and their taxes." Diversion was their object, wit was their
faculty, and nothing else mattered.

Various critics have remarked that Congreve might have made
an effective reply to Collier if he had not consented to argue the
case on the parson's own terms; he might, that is, have stood
upon his right as an artist, insisting that Art justifies the means
it employs and is not to be tried by the conventions of the
moralist. But the observation, however sound, is irrelevant in a
discussion of Congreve's quarrel. Such language would not have
been understood by Collier or any of his contemporaries. No
doubt, wit, like virtue, is its own reward; and great was the
reward of Congreve and his fellows in the satisfaction of an
artistic taste. It is doubtful, however, if they themselves ever
definitely put the credo of art for art's sake into words. By rare
good fortune, Etherege and Wycherley were at work during the
brief and unique period in the history of England when wit was
its own apology for being. So long as they could turn off sparkling
epigrams they were asked no questions by a moral censor. It is
to be remembered, however, that the license granted to them
was based, not upon any modern æsthetic doctrine, but solely
upon the moral indifference of their judges. There was no relaxa-
tion of the theory that satire must perform a moral function;
the comic dramatists themselves were perpetually reiterating the
truism. Congreve and Vanbrugh had the misfortune to be born
an age too late. When called to account, they had no choice of
weapon. The time was still distant when a philosophy of an
independent æsthetic would be formulated, to say nothing of
the remoteness of the time when the doctrine would affect public
taste. Congreve used the only argument available, and, inevitably,
the artist lost in the controversy with the parson.

The moral prejudice aroused by the Restoration wits was not
the only obstacle to be confronted by comic writers of the eighteenth century, nor the most formidable. A more insidious opposition arose from the comedy of sensibility and tears—what Goldsmith calls a "bastard tragedy." In January of 1696, there was
performed at Drury Lane a play by Colley Cibber called *Love's
Last Shift, or The Fool in Fashion*. Those who attended the
performance, expecting merely to be diverted as usual, had the
novel experience of weeping over virtue in distress through four
acts and then of rejoicing virtuously in the happy deliverance of
the heroine from all her sorrows. Hints of the sentimental view
of life are to be found in plays preceding this; but Cibber had
founded a new type of drama. Sir John Vanbrugh was quick

to sense the presence of a dangerous foe. Cibber's play was offensive to him because of its tears, still more because of the unsound moral philosophy it inculcated. The assumption that the virtuous Amanda could permanently reform her libertine husband, a typical Restoration figure, by appealing to his feelings and reducing him to tears was ridiculous. In the following December Vanbrugh was ready with a witty sequel, *The Relapse,* in which the converted rake returns to his vices, and the world, stripped of sentimental gloss, is shown in its true colors—the world as it had been depicted in the honest comedies of the Restoration.

There is reason for suspecting that if Cibber did not become an innovator by mere chance at least he did not grasp the full significance of what he had done or foresee the results. He was not by nature a propagandist. Evidently he felt no resentment towards Vanbrugh, for he played one of the principal parts in *The Relapse.* The work of exploiting the discovery was left to Richard Steele. By nature a sentimentalist and also an incorrigible reformer, Steele realized that here was a golden opportunity for him in his dual rôle. His initial play, *The Funeral, or Grief à la Mode,* acted in 1701, gives a bare hint of what was to follow a little later. In *The Lying Lover* (1703) he converts the pure comedy of Corneille's *Le Menteur* into a solemn and lachrymose disquisition upon the evils of dueling and other fashionable vices. The transformation itself is an important historical phenomenon, for it prefigures the mangling of many genuine comedies by the purveyors of sentimental morality. The prologue notifies the Drury Lane audience that *The Lying Lover* they are to witness will offer no gross vices to their sight, for it has been fashioned

> With just regard to a reforming age.

But the complete doctrine is reserved for the epilogue:

> Our too advent'rous author soared to-night
> Above the little praise, mirth to excite,
> And chose with pity to chastise delight.
> For laughter's a distorted passion, born
> Of sudden self-esteem and sudden scorn;
> Which, when 'tis o'er, the men in pleasure wise,
> Both them that moved it and themselves despise;
> While generous pity of a painted woe
> Makes us ourselves both more approve and know.

It is astonishing that a theatrical audience could have been preached to in this solemn fashion within three years of Congreve's *Way of the World*. Strangest of ironies, the sentimentalist is now levying upon the philosophy of Hobbes, rationalist and cynic, for a theory of laughter to be used against the cynics of the Restoration! There is pleasure in reflecting that Steele did not quite carry the day; he himself reported, with some exaggeration, that this play was "damned for its piety." But he had not failed, and he was not to be discouraged. After he had produced another comedy, *The Tender Husband* (1705), he continued the campaign in his essays, by teaching his readers "what to think" of the gallant writers of the former age. *The Man of Mode*, they are told, is "a perfect contradiction of good manners, good sense, and common honesty"; but this is not Etherege's gravest offense—"I know but one who has professedly writ a play upon the basis of the desire of multiplying our species, and that is the polite Sir George Etherege; if I understand what the lady would be at in the play called *She Would if She Could*." Finally, returning to the stage, Steele brought out *The Conscious Lovers* (1722). This, according to Parson Adams, is the only play fit for a Christian to see; indeed, he adds, it has some things in it "almost solemn enough for a sermon." What Steele did was of vast and ominous significance: he brought about a firm alliance of morality and sensibility to the prejudice of true comedy. He is significant most of all perhaps as the forerunner of Richardson and the other apostles of sentiment in the mid-century.

The conflicting counsels of the time and the resulting confusion are nowhere more clearly reflected than in the work of George Farquhar. Though placed by Leigh Hunt in the group of Restoration wits, with whom he has obvious relations, he is distinctly a transitional figure. An author by profession and wholly dependent upon his work for an income, he was under the necessity of consulting public taste as well as his own literary ideals. His work falls into three distinct periods. In his earliest plays—*Love and a Bottle* (1699), *The Constant Couple* (1699), and *Sir Harry Wildair* (1701)—his aim was to write comedy of manners and to recommend his productions by outdoing, occasionally at least, his models in profligacy. If Collier and his friends had any doubt concerning his attitude towards them, they could have found further evidence of his defiance in the *Discourse upon Comedy* (1702). There he proves that the comedy so offensive to the reformer is "a well-form'd tale handsomely told as an agreeable vehicle for counsel or reproof"; its monsters are used for edification as the lion, the fox, the hare, and the ass are employed by Æsop. Then suddenly came a complete reversal. Farquhar apparently thought it wise to placate a dangerous enemy. *The Inconstant* and *The Twin-Rivals*, both of 1702, are dramatic

sermons written avowedly for a moral purpose and pointedly intended to comply with Collier's design of purifying the stage. In
his final period, when he has ceased to be an opportunist, *The
Recruiting Officer* (1706) and *The Beaux' Stratagem* (1707)
reveal dramatic genius of a high order. The first thing that must
strike a reader familiar with seventeenth-century comedy is that
the Muse has now deserted the drawing-room for the country,
and that many charmingly fresh types of character have been
brought in to replace the endless parade of fops and coquettes.
There is a prophecy here of the English country scenes in *Tom
Jones* and of the whimsical characters in the comedies of Goldsmith. Comedy has outgrown the narrow bounds of social satire,
and humor has again found a place. Farquhar was not able to
realize fully the possibilities within his grasp, and it is not certain that he greatly influenced the immediate course of literature; but he had provided the most effective answer so far given
to the rebellious moralists and the sentimentalists.

The struggle between the two ideals in comedy was waged,
throughout the eighteenth century, with no decisive result. Although the two types constantly intermingle, the issue was clear-
cut. It is defined as sharply in the novels of Richardson and Fielding as it is on the stage. Nor was it merely another "battle of the
books." At the root of the literary quarrel was a fundamental
difference in ethical philosophy, which had a definite bearing on
social and political theory. Since the Comic Muse had to give a
good moral account of herself, most of the comedy produced is
satire directed at actual abuses of the time, the dramatic counter-
part of Pope's *Satires* and *Epistles* and Young's *Universal Passion*.
The comedy of humor could not flourish in this drily didactic
atmosphere; the fashion still was one of wit. The connection between the stage and the popular dissipations and follies is so
close that the social life is imbedded in the comic literature as
it is in the satirical prints of Hogarth. The supply of wit is constantly replenished by recourse to the Restoration writers. In
spite of all the objections urged against the immorality of the
old comedies, they had not been abandoned. In many instances
they underwent considerable expurgation or complete revision.
The Country Wife reappears in Garrick's adaptation as *The
Country Girl*. To the same story Sheridan was indebted for the
germ of his plot in *The School for Scandal*. These are but typical
instances of a widespread practice. Still, the new plays themselves
are by no means free from the licentiousness of their predecessors.
One has only to read the comedies of Fielding, for example, to
realize that public taste has undergone no thorough revolution.

It is a significant commentary on the merits of the controversy between the two schools of dramatists that not one of the eighteenth-century comedies of sensibility has survived as a part of permanent literature. The only dramatic pieces of the time that have really lasted are examples of pure comedy.

The year 1728 is important in the history of comedy for two reasons. First, the Comic Muse appeared in the novel dress of *The Beggar's Opera*. John Gay, the most dependent but the luckiest of poets, had been advised by his friend Swift to try his hand at a "Newgate Pastoral." The hint bore fruit, though not precisely what Swift had in mind. With some suggestions from Buckingham's *Rehearsal*, a model he had consulted when writing *The What-d'ye-call-it* (1715), Gay turned out the most sensational dramatic hit of the eighteenth century. His ballad opera, produced at Lincoln's Inn Fields by Rich, took London by storm. It "made Gay rich and Rich gay." Addison and others had labored in vain to laugh or argue the fashionable set out of their affected taste for Italian opera. Neither ridicule nor appeal to patriotism had had any effect. Gay's rollicking burlesque accomplished more in three hours of fun than all the critics had done to expose the absurdities of opera and also the false sentiment of weeping comedy. In his exposure of the corrupt political methods of Sir Robert Walpole he opened up virtually a new field for dramatic satire. His experience soon proved, however, that it was safer to ridicule opera and the vicious manners of the polite world than to capitalize the character of Bob Booty. Walpole was so offended that when Gay was about to bring out a sequel, *Polly*, he was refused permission to put it on the stage, and had to content himself with the handsome profits from the sale of his book. The year of *The Beggar's Opera* witnessed also the beginning of Henry Fielding's career as a playwright. It is true that none of the twenty-five comedies he composed within the following decade rise above mediocrity, and that they were completely overshadowed by his later work in the novel. Nevertheless, Fielding's connection with the theatre was more important in the cause of sanity than Gay's one brilliant achievement. His slashing comedies and burlesques did more than anything else in the next ten years to stem the current of maudlin sentiment. Once engaged, Fielding never gave up the fight. His defense of comedy as an ally of virtue proceeded from a sincere conviction that the doctrine of innate goodness, upon which all sentimental literature is founded, was the most insidious enemy morality had to encounter, and that the antidote was to be found in a merciless satire of the delusion. The Fielding of these comedies is the inexperienced young man who afterward was to employ all the force of his satiric genius against the false ideal of Richardson's *Pamela*.

The hostility of the two factions in comedy came to a climax during the early years of George III's reign when David Garrick —actor, playwright, and manager—was at the height of his power. Being a shrewd manager, Garrick produced the plays which he thought would fill his house, and it is evident that the tide was turning definitely towards the drama of tears. But that he himself preferred genuine comedy is clear from the favorite parts he played, his adaptations from Restoration drama, and his own dramatic compositions. *The Clandestine Marriage* (1766), in which he collaborated with George Colman, is an excellent comedy of manners, and probably would be better known if it had not been excelled within a few years by Sheridan's work. The critical intention and the general tone are sufficiently indicated by saying that the principal *motif* was derived from Hogarth's *Marriage-à-la-Mode*. Except for its more wholesome atmosphere, it is a typical Restoration play. The ancestry of Lord Ogleby goes back through various well-known intermediaries to Etherege's Lord Foppington. Mrs. Heidelberg is good enough to suggest kinship on one side with Fielding's Mrs. Slipslop and on the other with Sheridan's Mrs. Malaprop. *The Clandestine Marriage* is especially noteworthy in the history of the period as being one of an extremely small number of plays indicating that the spark of comedy had not been quite extinguished before the arrival of Goldsmith and Sheridan.

It is somewhat strange that the most determined opposition to the drama of sensibility should have come from Oliver Goldsmith, author of *The Deserted Village* and *The Vicar of Wakefield*. His critical rôle seems hardly in keeping even with his own comedies, *The Good Natur'd Man* (1768) and *She Stoops to Conquer* (1773). Goldsmith was not an enemy of sentiment; what he was attacking was an extreme form of humorless sentimentality. Long before he himself became a dramatist—in his first publication, *An Enquiry into the Present State of Polite Learning* (1759)—he expressed contempt for what he calls the "genteel comedy" at that time rapidly coming into fashion. In its perfected form, this was a borrowing from the French sentimentalists and was even more objectionable than anything the English had produced. Goldsmith protested against it on two grounds. He despised it, first, because it excluded humor and substituted sentiment, professing, as he says, to teach men by depicting them, not as they actually are, but as they should be. Secondly he objected even more violently to the rule that no "low characters" should be admitted into comedy. If the native comedy of sentiment had erred from the truth, at least it had not fallen into this absurdity; humor had been permitted in some scenes of the sentimental comedy, and for this purpose free use had been made of "low characters." A glance at Goldsmith's plays will make it clear why he found this second article of the new creed especially obnoxious. It is to be remembered, then, that he was directing his criticism at the faults of sentimentalism as they now appeared in English imitations of the correct *comédie larmoyante*. By an evil accident *The Good Natur'd Man* had to compete for popular favor with a perfect specimen of this artificial type, Hugh Kelly's *False Delicacy*. Kelly was already very popular, and it was understood that a test was now being made to determine the relative merits of the two schools. Johnson declared that *The Good Natur'd Man* was the best comedy that had been produced in England since the appearance of *The Provok'd Husband* in 1728. But the public was of another mind; *False Delicacy* was highly successful, and *The Good Natur'd Man* was soon withdrawn. Goldsmith's disappointment helps explain the energy he threw into his essay written to expose the absurdities of "bastard tragedy." The reception accorded his second comedy, *She Stoops to Conquer,* was so much more favorable that he had some reason to think he had improved public taste. Part of the explanation is that it is really a much better play than his first; but even here the technique is faulty, especially in comparison with the careful execution in Garrick's and Sheridan's plays. Goldsmith's comedies are delightful mainly as a reflection of his own rich and genial nature. Though opposed to the lachrymose tribe, he owes much of his appeal to a vein of sentiment which was a part of the man himself and is never absent long from his writing. What endears him most perhaps is a kindly and sympathetic humor. Though not without wit, he had little in common with the Restoration wits and, by virtue of a distinctive humor, stands apart from his contemporaries. As he himself was well aware, the ancestor of his kind of comedy was *The Beaux' Stratagem*.

Goldsmith and Sheridan are inseparably linked through their common interest in the restoration of true comedy; yet they are derived from different strains. Sheridan, like Garrick, comes of the Restoration stock. He remade Vanbrugh's *Relapse* into *A Trip to Scarborough*. *The Critic* flays sentimental literature as *The Rehearsal* had ridiculed the Heroic Play. It is impossible to read Sheridan without constantly detecting the influence of Congreve in character, situation, and cleverness of dialogue. If any of the "graceless wits" could have come to life, they would have recognized Sheridan as the inheritor of their comic ideals and genius. They would have been surprised, perhaps a little disappointed, in his regard for the proprieties; but the manners of Londoners living under George III, though coarse enough, were not so free as they had been a century earlier. Besides, Jeremy Collier and William Law and other moral censors had lived in the interim, and it was necessary now for wit to come to terms with virtue. His ancestors would undoubtedly have noted also, with some concern, that even Sheridan had not wholly escaped the general infection of sentiment. But essentially he is of their kind—the last and in some respects the greatest. He is almost as witty as Congreve, and a much superior dramatist. He had what Congreve lacked, a thorough knowledge of the stage, and his plays act as well as they read. His work reaches a high plane of excellence in *The Rivals* (1775), and comes to its climax in *The School for Scandal* (1777). "Sheridan brought the comedy of manners to the highest perfection," says Sir Henry Irving, "and *The School for Scandal* remains to this day the most popular comedy in the English language."

C. A. MOORE.

UNIVERSITY OF MINNESOTA,
February, 1933.

THE COUNTRY WIFE

by

WILLIAM WYCHERLEY

PROLOGUE

SPOKEN BY MR. HART

POETS, like cudgelled bullies, never do
At first or second blow submit to you;
But will provoke you still, and ne'er have done,
Till you are weary first with laying on.
The late so baffled scribbler of this day,
Though he stands trembling, bids me boldly say,
What we before most plays are used to do,
For poets out of fear first draw on you;
In a fierce prologue the still pit defy,
And, ere you speak, like Castril give the lie.
But though our Bayes's battles oft I've fought,
And with bruised knuckles their dear conquests bought;
Nay, never yet feared odds upon the stage,
In prologue dare not hector with the age;
But would take quarter from your saving hands,
Though Bayes within all yielding countermands,
Says, you confederate wits no quarter give,
Therefore his play shan't ask your leave to live.
Well, let the vain rash fop, by huffing so,
Think to obtain the better terms of you;
But we, the actors, humbly will submit,
Now, and at any time, to a full pit;
Nay, often we anticipate your rage,
And murder poets for you on our stage:
We set no guards upon our tiring-room,
But when with flying colours there you come,
We patiently, you see, give up to you
Our poets, virgins, nay, our matrons too.

THE COUNTRY WIFE

ACT I

Scene I.—Horner's *Lodging*

Enter Horner, *and* Quack *following him at a distance.*

Horn. [*Aside.*] A quack is as fit for a pimp, as a midwife for a
bawd; they are still but in their way, both helpers of nature.—
[*Aloud.*] Well, my dear doctor, hast thou done what I desired?

Quack. I have undone you for ever with the women, and reported you throughout the whole town as bad as an eunuch, with
as much trouble as if I had made you one in earnest.

Horn. But have you told all the midwives you know, the orange
wenches at the playhouses, the city husbands, and old fumbling
keepers of this end of the town? for they'll be the readiest to
report it.

Quack. I have told all the chambermaids, waiting-women, tire-
women, and old women of my acquaintance; nay, and whispered
it as a secret to 'em, and to the whisperers of Whitehall; so that
you need not doubt 'twill spread, and you will be as odious to the
handsome young women as——

Horn. As the small-pox. Well——

Quack. And to the married women of this end of the town,
as——

Horn. As the great one; nay, as their own husbands.

Quack. And to the city dames, as aniseed Robin, of filthy and
contemptible memory; and they will frighten their children with
your name, especially their females.

Horn. And cry, Horner's coming to carry you away. I am only
afraid 'twill not be believed. You told 'em it was by an English-
French disaster, and an English-French chirurgeon, who has given
me at once not only a cure, but an antidote for the future against
that damned malady, and that worse distemper, love, and all other
women's evils?

Quack. Your late journey into France has made it the more
credible, and your being here a fortnight before you appeared in
public, looks as if you apprehended the shame, which I wonder

you do not. Well, I have been hired by young gallants to belie 'em t'other way; but you are the first would be thought a man unfit for women.

Horn. Dear Mr. Doctor, let vain rogues be contented only to be thought abler men than they are, generally 'tis all the pleasure they have; but mine lies another way.

Quack. You take, methinks, a very preposterous way to it, and as ridiculous as if we operators in physic should put forth bills to disparage our medicaments, with hopes to gain customers.

Horn. Doctor, there are quacks in love as well as physic, who get but the fewer and worse patients for their boasting; a good name is seldom got by giving it one's self; and women, no more than honour, are compassed by bragging. Come, come, Doctor, the wisest lawyer never discovers the merits of his cause till the trial; the wealthiest man conceals his riches, and the cunning gamester his play. Shy husbands and keepers, like old rooks, are not to be cheated but by a new unpractised trick: false friendship will pass now no more than false dice upon 'em; no, not in the city.

Enter Boy.

Boy. There are two ladies and a gentleman coming up. [*Exit.*

Horn. A pox! some unbelieving sisters of my former acquaintance, who, I am afraid, expect their sense should be satisfied of the falsity of the report. No—this formal fool and women!

Enter Sir JASPER FIDGET, Lady FIDGET, *and* Mrs. DAINTY FIDGET.

Quack. His wife and sister.

Sir Jasp. My coach breaking just now before your door, sir, I look upon as an occasional reprimand to me, sir, for not kissing your hands, sir, since your coming out of France, sir; and so my disaster, sir, has been my good fortune, sir; and this is my wife and sister, sir.

Horn. What then, sir?

Sir Jasp. My lady, and sister, sir.—Wife, this is Master Horner.

Lady Fid. Master Horner, husband!

Sir Jasp. My lady, my Lady Fidget, sir.

Horn. So, sir.

Sir Jasp. Won't you be acquainted with her, sir?—[*Aside.*] So, the report is true, I find, by his coldness or aversion to the sex, but I'll play the wag with him.—[*Aloud.*] Pray salute my wife, my lady, sir.

Horn. I will kiss no man's wife, sir, for him, sir; I have taken my eternal leave, sir, of the sex already, sir.

Sir Jasp. [*Aside.*] Ha! ha! ha! I'll plague him yet.—[*Aloud.*] Not know my wife, sir?

Horn. I do know your wife, sir; she's a woman, sir, and consequently a monster, sir, a greater monster than a husband, sir.

Sir Jasp. A husband! how, sir?

Horn. So, sir; but I make no more cuckolds, sir. [*Makes horns.*

Sir Jasp. Ha! ha! ha! Mercury! Mercury!

Lady Fid. Pray, Sir Jasper, let us be gone from this rude fellow.

Mrs. Dain. Who, by his breeding, would think he had ever been in France?

Lady Fid. Foh! he's but too much a French fellow, such as hate women of quality and virtue for their love to their husbands. Sir Jasper, a woman is hated by 'em as much for loving her husband as for loving their money. But pray let's be gone.

Horn. You do well, madam; for I have nothing that you came for. I have brought over not so much as a bawdy picture, no new postures, nor the second part of the *Ecole des Filles;* nor——

Quack. Hold, for shame, sir! what d'ye mean? you'll ruin yourself for ever with the sex——   [*Apart to* HORNER.

Sir Jasp. Ha! ha! ha! he hates women perfectly, I find.

Mrs. Dain. What pity 'tis he should!

Lady Fid. Ay, he's a base fellow for't. But affectation makes not a woman more odious to them than virtue.

Horn. Because your virtue is your greatest affectation, madam.

Lady Fid. How, you saucy fellow! would you wrong my honour?

Horn. If I could.

Lady Fid. How d'ye mean, sir?

Sir Jasp. Ha! ha! ha! no, he can't wrong your ladyship's honour, upon my honour. He, poor man—hark you in your ear—a mere eunuch.   [*Whispers.*

Lady Fid. O filthy French beast! foh! foh! why do we stay? let's be gone: I can't endure the sight of him.

Sir Jasp. Stay but till the chairs come; they'll be here presently.

Lady Fid. No.

Sir Jasp. Nor can I stay longer. 'Tis, let me see, a quarter and half quarter of a minute past eleven. The council will be sat; I must away. Business must be preferred always before love and ceremony with the wise, Mr. Horner.

Horn. And the impotent, Sir Jasper.

Sir Jasp. Ay, ay, the impotent, Master Horner; hah! hah! hah!

Lady Fid. What, leave us with a filthy man alone in his lodgings?

Sir Jasp. He's an innocent man now, you know. Pray stay, I'll hasten the chairs to you.—Mr. Horner, your servant; I should be glad to see you at my house. Pray come and dine with me, and play at cards with my wife after dinner; you are fit for women at that game yet, ha! ha!—[*Aside.*] 'Tis as much a husband's prudence to provide innocent diversion for a wife as to hinder her unlawful pleasures; and he had better employ her than let her employ herself.—[*Aloud.*] Farewell.

Horn. Your servant, Sir Jasper.   [*Exit* Sir JASPER.

Lady Fid. I will not stay with him, foh!——

Horn. Nay, madam, I beseech you stay, if it be but to see I can be as civil to ladies yet as they would desire.

Lady Fid. No, no, foh! you cannot be civil to ladies.

Mrs. Dain. You as civil as ladies would desire?

Lady Fid. No, no, no, foh! foh! foh!

[*Exeunt* Lady FIDGET *and* Mrs. DAINTY FIDGET.

Quack. Now, I think, I, or you yourself, rather, have done your business with the women.

Horn. Thou art an ass. Don't you see already, upon the report, and my carriage, this grave man of business leaves his wife in my lodgings, invites me to his house and wife, who before would not be acquainted with me out of jealousy?

Quack. Nay, by this means you may be the more acquainted with the husbands, but the less with the wives.

Horn. Let me alone; if I can but abuse the husbands, I'll soon disabuse the wives. Stay—I'll reckon you up the advantages I am like to have by my stratagem. First, I shall be rid of all my old acquaintances, the most insatiable sort of duns, that invade our lodgings in a morning; and next to the pleasure of making a new mistress is that of being rid of an old one, and of all old debts. Love, when it comes to be so, is paid the most unwillingly.

Quack. Well, you may be so rid of your old acquaintances; but how will you get any new ones?

Horn. Doctor, thou wilt never make a good chemist, thou art so incredulous and impatient. Ask but all the young fellows of the town if they do not lose more time, like huntsmen, in starting the game, than in running it down. One knows not where to find 'em; who will or will not. Women of quality are so civil, you can hardly distinguish love from good breeding, and a man is often mistaken: but now I can be sure she that shows an aversion to me loves the sport, as those women that are gone, whom I warrant to be right. And then the next thing is, your women of honour, as you call 'em, are only chary of their reputations, not their persons; and 'tis scandal they would avoid, not men. Now may I have, by the reputation of an eunuch, the privileges of one, and be seen in a lady's chamber in a morning as early as her husband;

kiss virgins before their parents or lovers; and may be, in short, the *passe-partout* of the town. Now, doctor.

Quack. Nay, now you shall be the doctor; and your process is so new that we do not know but it may succeed.

Horn. Not so new either; *probatum est,* doctor.

Quack. Well, I wish you luck, and many patients, whilst I go to mine.   [*Exit.*

Enter HARCOURT *and* DORILANT.

Har. Come, your appearance at the play yesterday has, I hope, hardened you for the future against the women's contempt, and the men's raillery; and now you'll abroad as you were wont.

Horn. Did I not bear it bravely?

Dor. With a most theatrical impudence, nay, more than the orange-wenches show there, or a drunken vizard-mask, or a great-bellied actress; nay, or the most impudent of creatures, an ill poet; or what is yet more impudent, a second-hand critic.

Horn. But what say the ladies? have they no pity?

Har. What ladies? The vizard-masks, you know, never pity a man when all's gone, though in their service.

Dor. And for the women in the boxes, you'd never pity them when 'twas in your power.

Har. They say 'tis pity but all that deal with common women should be served so.

Dor. Nay, I dare swear they won't admit you to play at cards with them, go to plays with 'em, or do the little duties which other shadows of men are wont to do for 'em.

Horn. What do you call shadows of men?

Dor. Half-men.

Horn. What, boys?

Dor. Ay, your old boys, old *beaux garçons,* who, like superannuated stallions, are suffered to run, feed, and whinny with the mares as long as they live, though they can do nothing else.

Horn. Well, a pox on love and wenching! Women serve but to keep a man from better company. Though I can't enjoy them, I shall you the more. Good fellowship and friendship are lasting, rational, and manly pleasures.

Har. For all that, give me some of those pleasures you call effeminate too; they help to relish one another.

Horn. They disturb one another.

Har. No, mistresses are like books. If you pore upon them too much, they doze you, and make you unfit for company; but if used discreetly, you are the fitter for conversation by 'em.

Dor. A mistress should be like a little country retreat near the town; not to dwell in constantly, but only for a night and away, to taste the town the better when a man returns.

Horn. I tell you, 'tis as hard to be a good fellow, a good friend, and a lover of women, as 'tis to be a good fellow, a good friend, and a lover of money. You cannot follow both, then choose your side. Wine gives you liberty, love takes it away.

Dor. Gad, he's in the right on't.

Horn. Wine gives you joy; love, grief and tortures, besides surgeons. Wine makes us witty; love, only sots. Wine makes us sleep; love breaks it.

Dor. By the world he has reason, Harcourt.

Horn. Wine makes——

Dor. Ay, wine makes us—makes us princes; love makes us beggars, poor rogues, egad—and wine——

Horn. So, there's one converted.—No, no, love and wine, oil and vinegar.

Har. I grant it; love will still be uppermost.

Horn. Come, for my part, I will have only those glorious manly pleasures of being very drunk and very slovenly.

Enter Boy.

Boy. Mr. Sparkish is below, sir.   [*Exit.*

Har. What, my dear friend! a rogue that is fond of me only, I think, for abusing him.

Dor. No, he can no more think the men laugh at him than that women jilt him; his opinion of himself is so good.

Horn. Well, there's another pleasure by drinking I thought not of,—I shall lose his acquaintance, because he cannot drink: and you know 'tis a very hard thing to be rid of him; for he's one of those nauseous offerers at wit, who, like the worst fiddlers, run themselves into all companies.

Har. One that, by being in the company of men of sense, would pass for one.

Horn. And may so to the short-sighted world; as a false jewel amongst true ones is not discerned at a distance. His company is as troublesome to us as a cuckold's when you have a mind to his wife's.

Har. No, the rogue will not let us enjoy one another, but ravishes our conversation; though he signifies no more to't than Sir Martin Mar-all's gaping, and awkward thrumming upon the lute, does to his man's voice and music.

Dor. And to pass for a wit in town shows himself a fool every night to us, that are guilty of the plot.

Horn. Such wits as he are, to a company of reasonable men, like rooks to the gamesters; who only fill a room at the table, but are so far from contributing to the play, that they only serve to spoil the fancy of those that do.

Dor. Nay, they are used like rooks too, snubbed, checked, and abused; yet the rogues will hang on.

Horn. A pox on 'em, and all that force nature, and would be still what she forbids 'em! Affectation is her greatest monster.

Har. Most men are the contraries to that they would seem. Your bully, you see, is a coward with a long sword; the little humbly-fawning physician, with his ebony cane, is he that destroys men.

Dor. The usurer, a poor rogue, possessed of mouldy bonds and mortgages; and we they call spendthrifts, are only wealthy, who lay out his money upon daily new purchases of pleasure.

Horn. Ay, your arrantest cheat is your trustee or executor; your jealous man, the greatest cuckold; your churchman the greatest atheist; and your noisy pert rogue of a wit, the greatest fop, dullest ass, and worst company, as you shall see; for here he comes.

Enter SPARKISH.

Spark. How is't, sparks? how is't? Well, faith, Harry, I must rally thee a little, ha! ha! ha! upon the report in town of thee, ha! ha! ha! I can't hold i'faith; shall I speak?

Horn. Yes; but you'll be so bitter then.

Spark. Honest Dick and Frank here shall answer for me; I will not be extreme bitter, by the universe.

Har. We will be bound in a ten thousand pound bond, he shall not be bitter at all.

Dor. Nor sharp, nor sweet.

Horn. What, not downright insipid?

Spark. Nay then, since you are so brisk, and provoke me, take what follows. You must know, I was discoursing and rallying with some ladies yesterday, and they happened to talk of the fine new signs in town——

Horn. Very fine ladies, I believe.

Spark. Said I, I know where the best new sign is.—Where? says one of the ladies.—In Covent Garden, I replied.—Said another, In what street?—In Russel Street, answered I.—Lord, says another, I'm sure there was never a fine new sign there yesterday. —Yes, but there was, said I again; and it came out of France, and has been there a fortnight.

Dor. A pox! I can hear no more, prithee.

Horn. No, hear him out; let him tune his crowd a while.

Har. The worst music, the greatest preparation.

Spark. Nay, faith, I'll make you laugh.—It cannot be, says a third lady.—Yes, yes, quoth I again.—Says a fourth lady——

Horn. Look to't, we'll have no more ladies.

Spark. No—then mark, mark, now. Said I to the fourth, Did you never see Mr. Horner? he lodges in Russel Street, and he's a sign of a man, you know, since he came out of France; ha! ha! ha!

Horn. But the devil take me if thine be the sign of a jest.

Spark. With that they all fell a-laughing, till they bepissèd themselves. What, but it does not move you, methinks? Well, I see one had as good go to law without a witness, as break a jest without a laughter on one's side.—Come, come, sparks, but where do we dine? I have left at Whitehall an earl, to dine with you.

Dor. Why, I thought thou hadst loved a man with a title, better than a suit with a French trimming to't.

Har. Go to him again.

Spark. No, sir, a wit to me is the greatest title in the world.

Horn. But go dine with your earl, sir; he may be exceptious. We are your friends, and will not take it ill to be left, I do assure you.

Har. Nay, faith, he shall go to him.

Spark. Nay, pray, gentlemen.

Dor. We'll thrust you out, if you won't; what, disappoint anybody for us?

Spark. Nay, dear gentlemen, hear me.

Horn. No, no, sir, by no means; pray go, sir.

Spark. Why, dear rogues——

Dor. No, no.   [*They all thrust him out of the room.*

All. Ha! ha! ha!

Re-enter SPARKISH.

Spark. But, sparks, pray hear me. What, d'ye think I'll eat then with gay shallow fops and silent coxcombs? I think wit as necessary at dinner as a glass of good wine; and that's the reason I never have any stomach when I eat alone.—Come, but where do we dine?

Horn. Even where you will.

Spark. At Chateline's?

Dor. Yes, if you will.

Spark. Or at the Cock?

Dor. Yes, if you please.

Spark. Or at the Dog and Partridge?

Horn. Ay, if you have a mind to't; for we shall dine at neither.

Spark. Pshaw! with your fooling we shall lose the new play; and I would no more miss seeing a new play the first day, than I would miss sitting in the wit's row. Therefore I'll go fetch my mistress, and away. [*Exit.*

Enter PINCHWIFE.

Horn. Who have we here? Pinchwife?

Pinch. Gentlemen, your humble servant.

Horn. Well, Jack, by thy long absence from the town, the grumness of thy countenance, and the slovenliness of thy habit, I should give thee joy, should I not, of marriage?

Pinch. [*Aside.*] Death! does he know I'm married too? I thought to have concealed it from him at least.—[*Aloud.*] My long stay in the country will excuse my dress; and I have a suit of law that brings me up to town, that puts me out of humour. Besides, I must give Sparkish to-morrow five thousand pounds to lie with my sister.

Horn. Nay, you country gentlemen, rather than not purchase, will buy anything; and he is a cracked title, if we may quibble. Well, but am I to give thee joy? I heard thou wert married.

Pinch. What then?

Horn. Why, the next thing that is to be heard, is thou'rt a cuckold.

Pinch. Insupportable name! [*Aside.*

Horn. But I did not expect marriage from such a whoremaster as you; one that knew the town so much, and women so well.

Pinch. Why, I have married no London wife.

Horn. Pshaw! that's all one. That grave circumspection in marrying a country wife, is like refusing a deceitful pampered Smithfield jade, to go and be cheated by a friend in the country.

Pinch. [*Aside.*] A pox on him and his simile!—[*Aloud.*] At least we are a little surer of the breed there, know what her keeping has been, whether foiled or unsound.

Horn. Come, come, I have known a clap gotten in Wales; and there are cousins, justices' clerks, and chaplains in the country, I won't say coachmen. But she's handsome and young?

Pinch. [*Aside.*] I'll answer as I should do.—[*Aloud.*] No, no; she has no beauty but her youth, no attraction but her modesty: wholesome, homely, and huswifely; that's all.

Dor. He talks as like a grazier as he looks.

Pinch. She's too awkward, ill-favoured, and silly to bring to town.

Har. Then methinks you should bring her to be taught breeding.

Pinch. To be taught! no, sir, I thank you. Good wives and private soldiers should be ignorant—I'll keep her from your instructions, I warrant you.

Har. The rogue is as jealous as if his wife were not ignorant.
[*Aside.*

Horn. Why, if she be ill-favoured, there will be less danger here for you than by leaving her in the country. We have such variety of dainties that we are seldom hungry.

Dor. But they have always coarse, constant, swingeing stomachs in the country.

Har. Foul feeders indeed!

Dor. And your hospitality is great there.

Har. Open house; every man's welcome.

Pinch. So, so, gentlemen.

Horn. But prithee, why shouldst thou marry her? If she be ugly, ill-bred, and silly, she must be rich then.

Pinch. As rich as if she brought me twenty thousand pound out of this town; for she'll be as sure not to spend her moderate portion, as a London baggage would be to spend hers, let it be what it would: so 'tis all one. Then, because she's ugly, she's the likelier to be my own; and being ill-bred, she'll hate conversation; and since silly and innocent, will not know the difference betwixt a man of one-and-twenty and one of forty.

Horn. Nine—to my knowledge. But if she be silly, she'll expect as much from a man of forty-nine, as from him of one-and-twenty. But methinks wit is more necessary than beauty; and I think no young woman ugly that has it, and no handsome woman agreeable without it.

Pinch. 'Tis my maxim, he's a fool that marries; but he's a greater that does not marry a fool. What is wit in a wife good for, but to make a man a cuckold?

Horn. Yes, to keep it from his knowledge.

Pinch. A fool cannot contrive to make her husband a cuckold.

Horn. No; but she'll club with a man that can: and what is worse, if she cannot make her husband a cuckold, she'll make him jealous, and pass for one: and then 'tis all one.

Pinch. Well, well, I'll take care for one. My wife shall make me no cuckold, though she had your help, Mr. Horner. I understand the town, sir.

Dor. His help! [*Aside.*

Har. He's come newly to town, it seems, and has not heard how things are with him. [*Aside.*

Horn. But tell me, has marriage cured thee of whoring, which it seldom does?

Har. 'Tis more than age can do.

Horn. No, the word is, I'll marry and live honest: but a marriage vow is like a penitent gamester's oath, and entering into bonds and penalties to stint himself to such a particular small sum at play for the future, which makes him but the more eager; and not being able to hold out, loses his money again, and his forfeit to boot.

Dor. Ay, ay, a gamester will be a gamester whilst his money lasts, and a whoremaster whilst his vigour.

Har. Nay, I have known 'em, when they are broke, and can lose no more, keep a fumbling with the box in their hands to fool with only, and hinder other gamesters.

Dor. That had wherewithal to make lusty stakes.

Pinch. Well, gentlemen, you may laugh at me; but you shall never lie with my wife: I know the town.

Horn. But prithee, was not the way you were in better? is not keeping better than marriage?

Pinch. A pox on't! the jades would jilt me, I could never keep a whore to myself.

Horn. So, then you only married to keep a whore to yourself. Well, but let me tell you, women, as you say, are like soldiers, made constant and loyal by good pay, rather than by oaths and covenants. Therefore I'd advise my friends to keep rather than marry, since too I find, by your example, it does not serve one's turn; for I saw you yesterday in the eighteenpenny place with a pretty country-wench.

Pinch. How the devil! did he see my wife then? I sat there that she might not be seen. But she shall never go to a play again. [*Aside.*

Horn. What! dost thou blush, at nine-and-forty, for having been seen with a wench?

Dor. No, faith, I warrant 'twas his wife, which he seated there out of sight; for he's a cunning rogue, and understands the town.

Har. He blushes. Then 'twas his wife; for men are now more ashamed to be seen with them in public than with a wench.

Pinch. Hell and damnation! I'm undone, since Horner has seen her, and they know 'twas she. [*Aside.*

Horn. But prithee, was it thy wife? She was exceeding pretty: I was in love with her at that distance.

Pinch. You are like never to be nearer to her. Your servant, gentlemen. [*Offers to go.*

Horn. Nay, prithee stay.

Pinch. I cannot; I will not.

Horn. Come, you shall dine with us.

Pinch. I have dined already.

Horn. Come, I know thou hast not: I'll treat thee, dear rogue; thou sha't spend none of thy Hampshire money to-day.

Pinch. Treat me! So, he uses me already like his cuckold.

[*Aside.*

Horn. Nay, you shall not go.

Pinch. I must; I have business at home.

Har. To beat his wife. He's as jealous of her as a Cheapside husband of a Covent Garden wife.

Horn. Why, 'tis as hard to find an old whoremaster without jealousy and the gout, as a young one without fear, or the pox:—

> As gout in age from pox in youth proceeds,
> So wenching past, then jealousy succeeds;
> The worst disease that love and wenching breeds.

[*Exeunt.*

ACT II

Scene I.—*A Room in* Pinchwife's *House*

Mrs. Margery Pinchwife *and* Alithea. Pinchwife
peeping behind at the door.

Mrs. Pinch. Pray, sister, where are the best fields and woods to walk in, in London?

Alith. [*Aside.*] A pretty question!—[*Aloud.*] Why, sister, Mulberry Garden and St. James's Park; and, for close walks, the New Exchange.

Mrs. Pinch. Pray, sister, tell me why my husband looks so grum here in town, and keeps me up so close, and will not let me go a-walking, nor let me wear my best gown yesterday.

Alith. O, he's jealous, sister.

Mrs. Pinch. Jealous! what's that?

Alith. He's afraid you should love another man.

Mrs. Pinch. How should he be afraid of my loving another man, when he will not let me see any but himself?

Alith. Did he not carry you yesterday to a play?

Mrs. Pinch. Ay; but we sat amongst ugly people. He would not let me come near the gentry, who sat under us, so that I could not see 'em. He told me, none but naughty women sat there, whom they toused and moused. But I would have ventured, for all that.

Alith. But how did you like the play?

Mrs. Pinch. Indeed I was weary of the play; but I liked hugeously the actors. They are the goodliest, properest men, sister!

Alith. O, but you must not like the actors, sister.

Mrs. Pinch. Ay, how should I help it, sister? Pray, sister, when my husband comes in, will you ask leave for me to go a-walking?

Alith. A-walking! ha! ha! Lord, a country-gentlewoman's pleasure is the drudgery of a footpost; and she requires as much airing as her husband's horses.—[*Aside.*] But here comes your husband: I'll ask, though I'm sure he'll not grant it.

Mrs. Pinch. He says he won't let me go abroad for fear of catching the pox.

Alith. Fy! the small-pox you should say.

Enter PINCHWIFE.

Mrs. Pinch. O my dear, dear bud, welcome home! Why dost thou look so fropish? who has nangered thee?

Pinch. You're a fool.   [Mrs. PINCHWIFE *goes aside, and cries.*

Alith. Faith, so she is, for crying for no fault, poor tender creature!

Pinch. What, you would have her as impudent as yourself, as arrant a jilflirt, a gadder, a magpie; and to say all, a mere notorious town-woman?

Alith. Brother, you are my only censurer; and the honour of your family will sooner suffer in your wife there than in me, though I take the innocent liberty of the town.

Pinch. Hark you, mistress, do not talk so before my wife.— The innocent liberty of the town!

Alith. Why, pray, who boasts of any intrigue with me? what lampoon has made my name notorious? what ill women frequent my lodgings? I keep no company with any women of scandalous reputations.

Pinch. No, you keep the men of scandalous reputations company.

Alith. Where? would you not have me civil? answer 'em in a box at the plays, in the drawing-room at Whitehall, in St. James's Park, Mulberry Garden, or——

Pinch. Hold, hold! Do not teach my wife where the men are to be found: I believe she's the worse for your town-documents already. I bid you keep her in ignorance, as I do.

Mrs. Pinch. Indeed, be not angry with her, bud, she will tell me nothing of the town, though I ask her a thousand times a day.

Pinch. Then you are very inquisitive to know, I find?

Mrs. Pinch. Not I indeed, dear; I hate London. Our place-house in the country is worth a thousand of't: would I were there again!

Pinch. So you shall, I warrant. But were you not talking of plays and players when I came in?—[*To* ALITHEA.] You are her encourager in such discourses.

Mrs. Pinch. No, indeed, dear; she chid me just now for liking the playermen.

Pinch. [*aside*]. Nay, if she be so innocent as to own to me her liking them, there is no hurt in't.—[*Aloud.*] Come, my poor rogue, but thou likest none better than me?

Mrs. Pinch. Yes, indeed, but I do. The playermen are finer folks.

Pinch. But you love none better than me?

Mrs. Pinch. You are my own dear bud, and I know you. I hate a stranger.

Pinch. Ay, my dear, you must love me only; and not be like the naughty town-women, who only hate their husbands, and love every man else; love plays, visits, fine coaches, fine clothes, fiddles, balls, treats, and so lead a wicked town-life.

Mrs. Pinch. Nay, if to enjoy all these things be a town-life, London is not so bad a place, dear.

Pinch. How! if you love me, you must hate London.

Alith. The fool has forbid me discovering to her the pleasures of the town, and he is now setting her agog upon them himself.

[*Aside.*

Mrs. Pinch. But, husband, do the town-women love the playermen too?

Pinch. Yes, I warrant you.

Mrs. Pinch. Ay, I warrant you.

Pinch. Why, you do not, I hope?

Mrs. Pinch. No, no, bud. But why have we no playermen in the country?

Pinch. Ha!—Mrs. Minx, ask me no more to go to a play.

Mrs. Pinch. Nay, why, love? I did not care for going: but when you forbid me, you make me, as 'twere, desire it.

Alith. So 'twill be in other things, I warrant. [*Aside.*

Mrs. Pinch. Pray let me go to a play, dear.

Pinch. Hold your peace, I wo' not.

Mrs. Pinch. Why, love?

Pinch. Why, I'll tell you.

Alith. Nay, if he tell her, she'll give him more cause to forbid her that place. [*Aside.*

Mrs. Pinch. Pray why, dear?

Pinch. First, you like the actors; and the gallants may like you.

Mrs. Pinch. What, a homely country girl! No, bud, nobody will like me.

Pinch. I tell you yes, they may.

Mrs. Pinch. No, no, you jest—I won't believe you: I will go.

Pinch. I tell you then, that one of the lewdest fellows in town, who saw you there, told me he was in love with you.

Mrs. Pinch. Indeed! who, who, pray who was't?

Pinch. I've gone too far, and slipped before I was aware; how overjoyed she is! [*Aside.*

Mrs. Pinch. Was it any Hampshire gallant, any of our neighbours? I promise you, I am beholden to him.

Pinch. I promise you, you lie; for he would but ruin you, as he has done hundreds. He has no other love for women but that; such as he look upon women, like basilisks, but to destroy 'em.

Mrs. Pinch. Ay, but if he loves me, why should he ruin me? answer me to that. Methinks he should not, I would do him no harm.

Alith. Ha! ha! ha!

Pinch. 'Tis very well; but I'll keep him from doing you any harm, or me either. But here comes company; get you in, get you in.

Mrs. Pinch. But, pray, husband, is he a pretty gentleman that loves me?

Pinch. In, baggage, in. [*Thrusts her in, and shuts the door.*

Enter SPARKISH *and* HARCOURT.

What, all the lewd libertines of the town brought to my lodging by this easy coxcomb! 'sdeath, I'll not suffer it.

Spark. Here, Harcourt, do you approve my choice?—[*To* ALITHEA.] Dear little rogue, I told you I'd bring you acquainted with all my friends, the wits and—— [HARCOURT *salutes her.*

Pinch. Ay, they shall know her, as well as you yourself will, I warrant you.

Spark. This is one of those, my pretty rogue, that are to dance at your wedding to-morrow; and him you must bid welcome ever, to what you and I have.

Pinch. Monstrous! [*Aside.*

Spark. Harcourt, how dost thou like her, faith? Nay, dear, do not look down; I should hate to have a wife of mine out of countenance at anything.

Pinch. Wonderful! [*Aside.*

Spark. Tell me, I say, Harcourt, how dost thou like her? Thou hast stared upon her enough, to resolve me.

Har. So infinitely well, that I could wish I had a mistress too, that might differ from her in nothing but her love and engagement to you.

Alith. Sir, Master Sparkish has often told me that his acquaintance were all wits and raillieurs, and now I find it.

Spark. No, by the universe, madam, he does not rally now; you may believe him. I do assure you, he is the honestest, worthiest, true-hearted gentleman—a man of such perfect honour, he would say nothing to a lady he does not mean.

Pinch. Praising another man to his mistress!   [*Aside.*

Har. Sir, you are so beyond expectation obliging, that——

Spark. Nay, egad, I am sure you do admire her extremely; I see't in your eyes.—He does admire you, madam.—By the world, don't you?

Har. Yes, above the world, or the most glorious part of it, her whole sex: and till now I never thought I should have envied you, or any man about to marry, but you have the best excuse for marriage I ever knew.

Alith. Nay, now, sir, I'm satisfied you are of the society of the wits and raillieurs, since you cannot spare your friend, even when he is but too civil to you; but the surest sign is, since you are an enemy to marriage,—for that I hear you hate as much as business or bad wine.

Har. Truly, madam, I was never an enemy to marriage till now, because marriage was never an enemy to me before.

Alith. But why, sir, is marriage an enemy to you now? because it robs you of your friend here? for you look upon a friend married, as one gone into a monastery, that is, dead to the world.

Har. 'Tis indeed, because you marry him; I see, madam, you can guess my meaning. I do confess heartily and openly, I wish it were in my power to break the match; by Heavens I would.

Spark. Poor Frank!

Alith. Would you be so unkind to me?

Har. No, no, 'tis not because I would be unkind to you.

Spark. Poor Frank! no gad, 'tis only his kindness to me.

Pinch. Great kindness to you indeed! Insensible fop, let a man make love to his wife to his face!   [*Aside.*

Spark. Come, dear Frank, for all my wife there, that shall be, thou shalt enjoy me sometimes, dear rogue. By my honour, we men of wit condole for our deceased brother in marriage, as much as for one dead in earnest: I think that was prettily said of me, ha, Harcourt?—But come, Frank, be not melancholy for me.

Har. No, I assure you, I am not melancholy for you.

Spark. Prithee, Frank, dost think my wife that shall be there, a fine person?

Har. I could gaze upon her till I became as blind as you are.

Spark. How as I am? how?

Har. Because you are a lover, and true lovers are blind, stock blind.

Spark. True, true; but by the world she has wit too, as well as beauty: go, go with her into a corner, and try if she has wit; talk to her anything, she's bashful before me.

Har. Indeed, if a woman wants wit in a corner, she has it nowhere.

Alith. Sir, you dispose of me a little before your time——

[*Aside to* SPARKISH.

Spark. Nay, nay, madam, let me have an earnest of your obedience, or—go, go, madam——

[HARCOURT *courts* ALITHEA *aside.*

Pinch. How, sir! if you are not concerned for the honour of a wife, I am for that of a sister; he shall not debauch her. Be a pander to your own wife! bring men to her! let 'em make love before your face! thrust 'em into a corner together, then leave 'em in private! is this your town wit and conduct?

Spark. Ha! ha! ha! a silly wise rogue would make one laugh more than a stark fool, ha! ha! I shall burst. Nay, you shall not disturb 'em; I'll vex thee, by the world.

[*Struggles with* PINCHWIFE *to keep him from* HARCOURT *and* ALITHEA.

Alith. The writings are drawn, sir, settlements made; 'tis too late, sir, and past all revocation.

Har. Then so is my death.

Alith. I would not be unjust to him.

Har. Then why to me so?

Alith. I have no obligation to you.

Har. My love.

Alith. I had his before.

Har. You never had it; he wants, you see, jealousy, the only infallible sign of it.

Alith. Love proceeds from esteem; he cannot distrust my virtue: besides, he loves me, or he would not marry me.

Har. Marrying you is no more sign of his love than bribing your woman, that he may marry you, is a sign of his generosity. Marriage is rather a sign of interest than love; and he that marries a fortune covets a mistress, not loves her. But if you take marriage for a sign of love, take it from me immediately.

Alith. No, now you have put a scruple in my head; but in short, sir, to end our dispute, I must marry him, my reputation would suffer in the world else.

Har. No; if you do marry him, with your pardon, madam, your reputation suffers in the world, and you would be thought in necessity for a cloak.

Alith. Nay, now you are rude, sir.—Mr. Sparkish, pray come hither, your friend here is very troublesome, and very loving.

Har. Hold! hold!——   [*Aside to* ALITHEA.

Pinch. D'ye hear that?

Spark. Why, d'ye think I'll seem to be jealous, like a country bumpkin?

Pinch. No, rather be a cuckold, like a credulous cit.

Har. Madam, you would not have been so little generous as to have told him.

Alith. Yes, since you could be so little generous as to wrong him.

Har. Wrong him! no man can do't, he's beneath an injury: a bubble, a coward, a senseless idiot, a wretch so contemptíble to all the world but you, that——

Alith. Hold, do not rail at him, for since he is like to be my husband, I am resolved to like him: nay, I think I am obliged to tell him you are not his friend.—Master Sparkish, Master Sparkish!

Spark. What, what?—[*To* HARCOURT.] Now, dear rogue, has not she wit?

Har. Not so much as I thought, and hoped she had.

          [*Speaks surlily.*

Alith. Mr. Sparkish, do you bring people to rail at you?

Har. Madam——

Spark. How! no; but if he does rail at me, 'tis but in jest, I warrant: what we wits do for one another, and never take any notice of it.

Alith. He spoke so scurrilously of you, I had no patience to hear him; besides, he has been making love to me.

Har. True, damned tell-tale woman!   [*Aside.*

Spark. Pshaw! to show his parts—we wits rail and make love often, but to show our parts: as we have no affections, so we have no malice, we——

Alith. He said you were a wretch below an injury——

Spark. Pshaw!

Har. Damned, senseless, impudent, virtuous jade! Well, since she won't let me have her, she'll do as good, she'll make me hate her.   [*Aside.*

Alith. A common bubble——

Spark. Pshaw!

Alith. A coward——

Spark. Pshaw, pshaw!

Alith. A senseless, drivelling idiot——

Spark. How! did he disparage my parts? Nay, then, my honour's concerned, I can't put up that, sir, by the world—brother, help me to kill him—[*Aside*] I may draw now, since we have the odds of him:—'tis a good occasion, too, before my mistress——

[*Offers to draw.*

Alith. Hold, hold!

Spark. What, what?

Alith. [*Aside.*] I must not let 'em kill the gentleman neither, for his kindness to me: I am so far from hating him, that I wish my gallant had his person and understanding. Nay, if my honour——

Spark. I'll be thy death.

Alith. Hold, hold! Indeed, to tell the truth, the gentleman said after all, that what he spoke was but out of friendship to you.

Spark. How! say, I am, I am a fool, that is, no wit, out of friendship to me?

Alith. Yes, to try whether I was concerned enough for you; and made love to me only to be satisfied of my virtue, for your sake.

Har. Kind, however.   [*Aside.*

Spark. Nay, if it were sô, my dear rogue, I ask thee pardon; but why would not you tell me so, faith?

Har. Because I did not think on't, faith.

Spark. Come, Horner does not come; Harcourt, let's be gone to the new play.—Come, madam.

Alith. I will not go, if you intend to leave me alone in the box, and run into the pit, as you use to do.

Spark. Pshaw! I'll leave Harcourt with you in the box to entertain you, and that's as good; if I sat in the box, I should be thought no judge but of trimmings.—Come away, Harcourt, lead her down.   [*Exeunt* SPARKISH, HARCOURT, *and* ALITHEA.

Pinch. Well, go thy ways, for the flower of the true town fops, such as spend their estates before they come to 'em, and are cuckolds before they're married. But let me go look to my own freehold.—How!

Enter LADY FIDGET, MRS. DAINTY FIDGET, *and* MRS. SQUEAMISH.

Lady Fid. Your servant, sir: where is your lady? We are come to wait upon her to the new play.

Pinch. New play!

Lady Fid. And my husband will wait upon you presently.

Pinch. [*Aside.*] Damn your civility.—[*Aloud.*] Madam, by no means; I will not see Sir Jasper here, till I have waited upon him at home; nor shall my wife see you till she has waited upon your ladyship at your lodgings.

Lady Fid. Now we are here, sir?

Pinch. No, Madam.

Mrs. Dain. Pray, let us see her.

Mrs. Squeam. We will not stir till we see her.

Pinch. [*Aside.*] A pox on you all!—[*Goes to the door, and returns.*] She has locked the door, and is gone abroad.

Lady Fid. No, you have locked the door, and she's within.

Mrs. Dain. They told us below she was here.

Pinch. [*Aside.*] Will nothing do?—[*Aloud.*] Well, it must out then. To tell you the truth, ladies, which I was afraid to let you know before, lest it might endanger your lives, my wife has just now the small-pox come out upon her; do not be frightened; but pray be gone, ladies; you shall not stay here in danger of your lives; pray get you gone, ladies.

Lady Fid. No, no, we have all had 'em.

Mrs. Squeam. Alack, alack!

Mrs. Dain. Come, come, we must see how it goes with her; I understand the disease.

Lady Fid. Come!

Pinch. [*Aside.*] Well, there is no being too hard for women at their own weapon, lying, therefore I'll quit the field.   [*Exit.*

Mrs. Squeam. Here's an example of jealousy!

Lady Fid. Indeed, as the world goes, I wonder there are no more jealous, since wives are so neglected.

Mrs. Dain. Pshaw! as the world goes, to what end should they be jealous?

Lady Fid. Foh! 'tis a nasty world.

Mrs. Squeam. That men of parts, great acquaintance, and quality, should take up with and spend themselves and fortunes in keeping little playhouse creatures, foh!

Lady Fid. Nay, that women of understanding, great acquaintance, and good quality, should fall a-keeping too of little creatures, foh!

Mrs. Squeam. Why, 'tis the men of quality's fault; they never visit women of honour and reputation as they used to do; and have not so much as common civility for ladies of our rank, but use us with the same indifferency and ill-breeding as if we were all married to 'em.

Lady Fid. She says true; 'tis an arrant shame women of quality should be so slighted; methinks birth—birth should go for something; I have known men admired, courted, and followed for their titles only.

Mrs. Squeam. Ay, one would think men of honour should not love, no more than marry, out of their own rank.

Mrs. Dain. Fy, fy, upon 'em! they are come to think cross

breeding for themselves best, as well as for their dogs and horses.

Lady Fid. They are dogs and horses for't.

Mrs. Squeam. One would think, if not for love, for vanity a little.

Mrs. Dain. Nay, they do satisfy their vanity upon us sometimes; and are kind to us in their report, tell all the world they lie with us.

Lady Fid. Damned rascals, that we should be only wronged by 'em! To report a man has had a person, when he has not had a person, is the greatest wrong in the whole world that can be done to a person.

Mrs. Squeam. Well, 'tis an arrant shame noble persons should be so wronged and neglected.

Lady Fid. But still 'tis an arranter shame for a noble person to neglect her own honour, and defame her own noble person with little inconsiderable fellows, foh!

Mrs. Dain. I suppose the crime against our honour is the same with a man of quality as with another.

Lady Fid. How! no sure, the man of quality is likest one's husband, and therefore the fault should be the less.

Mrs. Dain. But then the pleasure should be the less.

Lady Fid. Fy, fy, fy, for shame, sister! whither shall we ramble? Be continent in your discourse, or I shall hate you.

Mrs. Dain. Besides, an intrigue is so much the more notorious for the man's quality.

Mrs. Squeam. 'Tis true that nobody takes notice of a private man, and therefore with him 'tis more secret; and the crime's the less when 'tis not known.

Lady Fid. You say true; i'faith, I think you are in the right on't: 'tis not an injury to a husband, till it be an injury to our honours; so that a woman of honour loses no honour with a private person; and to say truth——

Mrs. Dain. So, the little fellow is grown a private person——
with her—— [*Apart to* Mrs. SQUEAMISH.

Lady Fid. But still my dear, dear honour——

Enter Sir JASPER FIDGET, HORNER, *and* DORILANT.

Sir Jasp. Ay, my dear, dear of honour, thou hast still so much honour in thy mouth——

Horn. That she has none elsewhere. [*Aside.*

Lady Fid. Oh, what d'ye mean to bring in these upon us?

Mrs. Dain. Foh! these are as bad as wits.

Mrs. Squeam. Foh!

Lady Fid. Let us leave the room.

Sir Jasp. Stay, stay; faith, to tell you the naked truth——

Lady Fid. Fy, Sir Jasper! do not use that word naked.

Sir Jasp. Well, well, in short I have business at Whitehall, and cannot go to the play with you, therefore would have you go——

Lady Fid. With those two to a play?

Sir Jasp. No, not with t'other, but with Mr. Horner; there can be no more scandal to go with him than with Mr. Tattle, or Master Limberham.

Lady Fid. With that nasty fellow! no—no.

Sir Jasp. Nay, prithee, dear, hear me.

[*Whispers to* Lady FIDGET.

Horn. Ladies——

[HORNER *and* DORILANT *draw near* Mrs. SQUEAMISH *and* Mrs. DAINTY FIDGET.

Mrs. Dain. Stand off.

Mrs. Squeam. Do not approach us.

Mrs. Dain. You herd with the wits, you are obscenity all over.

Mrs. Squeam. And I would as soon look upon a picture of Adam and Eve, without fig-leaves, as any of you, if I could help it; therefore keep off, and do not make us sick.

Dor. What a devil are these?

Horn. Why, these are pretenders to honour, as critics to wit, only by censuring others; and as every raw, peevish, out-of-humoured, affected, dull, tea-drinking, arithmetical fop, sets up for a wit by railing at men of sense, so these for honour, by railing at the court, and ladies of as great honour as quality.

Sir Jasp. Come, Mr. Horner, I must desire you to go with these ladies to the play, sir.

Horn. I, sir?

Sir Jasp. Ay, ay, come, sir.

Horn. I must beg your pardon, sir, and theirs; I will not be seen in women's company in public again for the world.

Sir Jasp. Ha, ha, strange aversion!

Mrs. Squeam. No, he's for women's company in private.

Sir Jasp. He—poor man—he—ha! ha! ha!

Mrs. Dain. 'Tis a greater shame amongst lewd fellows to be seen in virtuous women's company, than for the women to be seen with them.

Horn. Indeed, madam, the time was I only hated virtuous women, but now I hate the other too; I beg your pardon, ladies.

Lady Fid. You are very obliging, sir, because we would not be troubled with you.

Sir Jasp. In sober sadness, he shall go.

THE COUNTRY WIFE

Dor. Nay, if he wo' not, I am ready to call upon the ladies, and I think I am the fitter man.

Sir Jasp. You, sir! no, I thank you for that. Master Horner is a privileged man amongst the virtuous ladies, 'twill be a great while before you are so; he! he! he! he's my wife's gallant; he! he! he! No, pray withdraw, sir, for as I take it, the virtuous ladies have no business with you.

Dor. And I am sure he can have none with them. 'Tis strange a man can't come amongst virtuous women now, but upon the same terms as men are admitted into the Great Turk's seraglio. But heavens keep me from being an ombre player with 'em!—But where is Pinchwife?   [*Exit.*

Sir Jasp. Come, come, man; what, avoid the sweet society of womankind? that sweet, soft, gentle, tame, noble creature, woman, made for man's companion——

Horn. So is that soft, gentle, tame, and more noble creature a spaniel, and has all their tricks; can fawn, lie down, suffer beating, and fawn the more; barks at your friends when they come to see you, makes your bed hard, gives you fleas, and the mange sometimes. And all the difference is, the spaniel's the more faithful animal, and fawns but upon one master.

Sir Jasp. He! he! he!

Mrs. Squeam. O the rude beast!

Mrs. Dain. Insolent brute!

Lady Fid. Brute! stinking, mortified, rotten French wether, to dare——

Sir Jasp. Hold, an't please your ladyship.—For shame, Master Horner! your mother was a woman—[*Aside.*] Now shall I never reconcile 'em.—[*Aside to* Lady FIDGET.] Hark you, madam, take my advice in your anger. You know you often want one to make up your drolling pack of ombre players, and you may cheat him easily; for he's an ill gamester, and consequently loves play. Besides, you know you have but two old civil gentlemen (with stinking breaths too) to wait upon you abroad; take in the third into your service. The other are but crazy; and a lady should have a supernumerary gentleman-usher as a supernumerary coach-horse, lest sometimes you should be forced to stay at home.

Lady Fid. But are you sure he loves play, and has money?

Sir Jasp. He loves play as much as you, and has money as much as I.

Lady Fid. Then I am contented to make him pay for his scurrility. Money makes up in a measure all other wants in men.—Those whom we cannot make hold for gallants, we make fine.
    [*Aside.*

Sir Jasp. [*Aside.*] So, so; now to mollify, wheedle him.—[*Aside to* Horner.] Master Horner, will you never keep civil company? methinks 'tis time now, since you are only fit for them. Come, come, man, you must e'en fall to visiting our wives, eating at our tables, drinking tea with our virtuous relations after dinner, dealing cards to 'em, reading plays and gazettes to 'em, picking fleas out of their smocks for 'em, collecting receipts, new songs, women, pages, and footmen for 'em.

Horn. I hope they'll afford me better employment, sir.

Sir Jasp. He! he! he! 'tis fit you know your work before you come into your place. And since you are unprovided of a lady to flatter, and a good house to eat at, pray frequent mine, and call my wife mistress, and she shall call you gallant, according to the custom.

Horn. Who, I?

Sir Jasp. Faith, thou sha't for my sake; come, for my sake only.

Horn. For your sake——

Sir Jasp. Come, come, here's a gamester for you; let him be a little familiar sometimes; nay, what if a little rude? Gamesters may be rude with ladies, you know.

Lady Fid. Yes; losing gamesters have a privilege with women.

Horn. I always thought the contrary, that the winning gamester had most privilege with women; for when you have lost your money to a man, you'll lose anything you have, all you have, they say, and he may use you as he pleases.

Sir Jasp. He! he! he! well, win or lose, you shall have your liberty with her.

Lady Fid. As he behaves himself; and for your sake I'll give him admittance and freedom.

Horn. All sorts of freedom, madam?

Sir Jasp. Ay, ay, ay, all sorts of freedom thou canst take. And so go to her, begin thy new employment; wheedle her, jest with her, and be better acquainted one with another.

Horn. [*Aside.*] I think I know her already; therefore may venture with her my secret for hers.

[Horner *and* Lady Fidget *whisper.*

Sir Jasp. Sister cuz, I have provided an innocent playfellow for you there.

Mrs. Dain. Who, he?

Mrs. Squeam. There's a playfellow, indeed!

Sir Jasp. Yes sure.—What, he is good enough to play at cards, blindman's-buff, or the fool with, sometimes!

Mrs. Squeam. Foh! we'll have no such playfellows.

Mrs. Dain. No, sir; you shan't choose playfellows for us, we thank you.

Sir Jasp. Nay, pray hear me. .   [*Whispering to them.*

Lady Fid. But, poor gentleman, could you be so generous, so truly a man of honour, as for the sakes of us women of honour, to cause yourself to be reported no man? No man! and to suffer yourself the greatest shame that could fall upon a man, that none might fall upon us women by your conversation? but, indeed, sir, as perfectly, perfectly the same man as before your going into France, sir? as perfectly, perfectly, sir?

Horn. As perfectly, perfectly, madam. Nay, I scorn you should take my word; I desire to be tried only, madam.

Lady Fid. Well, that's spoken again like a man of honour: all men of honour desire to come to the test. But, indeed, generally you men report such things of yourselves, one does not know how or whom to believe; and it is come to that pass, we dare not take your words no more than your tailor's, without some staid servant of yours be bound with you. But I have so strong a faith in your honour, dear, dear, noble sir, that I'd forfeit mine for yours, at any time, dear sir.

Horn. No, madam, you should not need to forfeit it for me; I have given you security already to save you harmless, my late reputation being so well known in the world, madam.

Lady Fid. But if upon any future falling-out, or upon a suspicion of my taking the trust out of your hands, to employ some other, you yourself should betray your trust, dear sir? I mean, if you'll give me leave to speak obscenely, you might tell, dear sir.

Horn. If I did, nobody would believe me. The reputation of impotency is as hardly recovered again in the world as that of cowardice, dear madam.

Lady Fid. Nay, then, as one may say, you may do your worst, dear, dear sir.

Sir Jasp. Come, is your ladyship reconciled to him yet? have you agreed on matters? for I must be gone to Whitehall.

Lady Fid. Why, indeed, Sir Jasper, Master Horner is a thousand, thousand times a better man than I thought him. Cousin Squeamish, sister Dainty, I can name him now. Truly, not long ago, you know, I thought his very name obscenity; and I would as soon have lain with him as have named him.

Sir Jasp. Very likely, poor madam.

Mrs. Dain. I believe it.

Mrs. Squeam. No doubt on't.

Sir Jasp. Well, well—that your ladyship is as virtuous as any she, I know, and him all the town knows—he! he! he! therefore now you like him, get you gone to your business together, go, go to your business, I say, pleasure, whilst I go to my pleasure, business.

Lady Fid. Come, then, dear gallant.

Horn. Come away, my dearest mistress.

Sir Jasp. So, so; why, 'tis as I'd have it.   [*Exit.*

Horn. And as I'd have it.

Lady Fid. Who for his business from his wife will run,
      Takes the best care to have her business done.
                                         [*Exeunt.*

ACT III

Scene I.—*A Room in* Pinchwife's *House*

Enter Alithea *and* Mrs. Pinchwife.

Alith. Sister, what ails you? you are grown melancholy.

Mrs. Pinch. Would it not make any one melancholy to see you go every day fluttering about abroad, whilst I must stay at home like a poor lonely sullen bird in a cage?

Alith. Ay, sister; but you came young, and just from the nest to your cage: so that I thought you liked it, and could be as cheerful in't as others that took their flight themselves early, and are hopping abroad in the open air.

Mrs. Pinch. Nay, I confess I was quiet enough till my husband told me what pure lives the London ladies live abroad, with their dancing, meetings, and junketings, and dressed every day in their best gowns; and I warrant you, play at nine-pins every day of the week, so they do.

Enter Pinchwife.

Pinch. Come, what's here to do? you are putting the town-pleasures in her head, and setting her a-longing.

Alith. Yes, after nine-pins. You suffer none to give her those longings you mean but yourself.

Pinch. I tell her of the vanities of the town like a confessor.

Alith. A confessor! just such a confessor as he that, by forbidding a silly ostler to grease the horse's teeth, taught him to do't.

Pinch. Come, Mrs. Flippant, good precepts are lost when bad examples are still before us: the liberty you take abroad makes her hanker after it, and out of humour at home. Poor wretch! she desired not to come to London; I would bring her.

Alith. Very well.

Pinch. She has been this week in town, and never desired till this afternoon to go abroad.

Alith. Was she not at a play yesterday?

Pinch. Yes; but she ne'er asked me; I was myself the cause of her going.

Alith. Then if she ask you again, you are the cause of her asking, and not my example.

Pinch. Well, to-morrow night I shall be rid of you; and the next day, before 'tis light, she and I'll be rid of the town, and my dreadful apprehensions.—Come, be not melancholy; for thou sha't go into the country after to-morrow, dearest.

Alith. Great comfort!

Mrs. Pinch. Pish! what d'ye tell me of the country for?

Pinch. How's this! what, pish at the country?

Mrs. Pinch. Let me alone; I am not well.

Pinch. O, if that be all—what ails my dearest?

Mrs. Pinch. Truly, I don't know: but I have not been well since you told me there was a gallant at the play in love with me.

Pinch. Ha!——

Alith. That's by my example too!

Pinch. Nay, if you are not well, but are so concerned, because a lewd fellow chanced to lie, and say he liked you, you'll make me sick too.

Mrs. Pinch. Of what sickness?

Pinch. O, of that which is worse than the plague, jealousy.

Mrs. Pinch. Pish, you jeer! I'm sure there's no such disease in our receipt-book at home.

Pinch. No, thou never met'st with it, poor innocent.—Well, if thou cuckold me, 'twill be my own fault—for cuckolds and bastards are generally makers of their own fortune.   [*Aside.*

Mrs. Pinch. Well, but pray, bud, let's go to a play to-night.

Pinch. 'Tis just done, she comes from it. But why are you so eager to see a play?

Mrs. Pinch. Faith, dear, not that I care one pin for their talk there; but I like to look upon the player-men, and would see, if I could, the gallant you say loves me: that's all, dear bud.

Pinch. Is that all, dear bud?

Alith. This proceeds from my example!

Mrs. Pinch. But if the play be done, let's go abroad, however, dear bud.

Pinch. Come, have a little patience and thou shalt go into the country on Friday.

Mrs. Pinch. Therefore I would see first some sights to tell my neighbours of. Nay, I will go abroad, that's once.

Alith. I'm the cause of this desire too!

Pinch. But now I think on't, who, who was the cause of Horner's coming to my lodgings to-day? That was you.

Alith. No, you, because you would not let him see your handsome wife out of your lodging.

Mrs. Pinch. Why, O Lord! did the gentleman come hither to see me indeed?

Pinch. No, no.——You are not the cause of that damned question too, Mistress Alithea?——[*Aside.*] Well, she's in the right of it. He is in love with my wife——and comes after her——'tis so——but I'll nip his love in the bud; lest he should follow us into the country, and break his chariot-wheel near our house, on purpose for an excuse to come to't. But I think I know the town.

Mrs. Pinch. Come, pray, bud, let's go abroad before 'tis late; for I will go, that's flat and plain.

Pinch. [*Aside.*] So! the obstinacy already of the town-wife; and I must, whilst she's here, humour her like one.——[*Aloud.*] Sister, how shall we do, that she may not be seen or known?

Alith. Let her put on her mask.

Pinch. Pshaw! a mask makes people but the more inquisitive, and is as ridiculous a disguise as a stage-beard: her shape, stature, habit will be known. And if we should meet with Horner, he would be sure to take acquaintance with us, must wish her joy, kiss her, talk to her, leer upon her, and the devil and all. No, I'll not use her to a mask, 'tis dangerous; for masks have made more cuckolds than the best faces that ever were known.

Alith. How will you do then?

Mrs. Pinch. Nay, shall we go? The Exchange will be shut, and I have a mind to see that.

Pinch. So——I have it——I'll dress her up in the suit we are to carry down to her brother, little Sir James; nay, I understand the town-tricks. Come, let's go dress her. A mask! no——a woman masked, like a covered dish, gives a man curiosity and appetite; when, it may be, uncovered, 'twould turn his stomach: no, no.

Alith. Indeed your comparison is something a greasy one: but I had a gentle gallant used to say, A beauty masked, like the sun in eclipse, gathers together more gazers than if it shined out.

[*Exeunt.*

Scene II.—*The New Exchange*

Enter HORNER, HARCOURT, *and* DORILANT.

Dor. Engaged to women, and not sup with us!

Horn. Ay, a pox on 'em all!

Har. You were much a more reasonable man in the morning,

and had as noble resolutions against 'em as a widower of a week's liberty.

Dor. Did I ever think to see you keep company with women in vain?

Horn. In vain: no—'tis since I can't love 'em, to be revenged on 'em.

Har. Now your sting is gone, you looked in the box amongst all those women like a drone in the hive; all upon you, shoved and ill-used by 'em all, and thrust from one side to t'other.

Dor. Yet he must be buzzing amongst 'em still, like other beetle-headed liquorish drones. Avoid 'em, and hate 'em, as they hate you.

Horn. Because I do hate 'em, and would hate 'em yet more, I'll frequent 'em. You may see by marriage, nothing makes a man hate a woman more than her constant conversation. In short, I converse with 'em, as you do with rich fools, to laugh at 'em and use 'em ill.

Dor. But I would no more sup with women, unless I could lie with 'em, than sup with a rich coxcomb, unless I could cheat him.

Horn. Yes, I have known thee sup with a fool for his drinking; if he could set out your hand that way only, you were satisfied, and if he were a wine-swallowing mouth, 'twas enough.

Har. Yes, a man drinks often with a fool, as he tosses with a marker, only to keep his hand in use. But do the ladies drink?

Horn. Yes, sir; and I shall have the pleasure at least of laying 'em flat with a bottle, and bring as much scandal that way upon 'em as formerly t'other.

Har. Perhaps you may prove as weak a brother among 'em that way as t'other.

Dor. Foh! drinking with women is as unnatural as scolding with 'em. But 'tis a pleasure of decayed fornicators, and the basest way of quenching love.

Har. Nay, 'tis drowning love, instead of quenching it. But leave us for civil women too!

Dor. Ay, when he can't be the better for 'em. We hardly pardon a man that leaves his friend for a wench, and that's a pretty lawful call.

Horn. Faith, I would not leave you for 'em, if they would not drink.

Dor. Who would disappoint his company at Lewis's for a gossiping?

Har. Foh! Wine and women, good apart, together are as nauseous as sack and sugar. But hark you, sir, before you go, a little of your advice; an old maimed general, when unfit for action, is fittest for counsel. I have other designs upon women than eating and drinking with them; I am in love with Sparkish's mistress, whom he is to marry to-morrow: now how shall I get her?

Enter SPARKISH, *looking about.*

Horn. Why, here comes one will help you to her.

Har. He! he, I tell you, is my rival, and will hinder my love.

Horn. No; a foolish rival and a jealous husband assist their rival's designs; for they are sure to make their women hate them, which is the first step to their love for another man.

Har. But I cannot come near his mistress but in his company.

Horn. Still the better for you; for fools are most easily cheated when they themselves are accessaries: and he is to be bubbled of his mistress as of his money, the common mistress, by keeping him company.

Spark. Who is that that is to be bubbled? Faith, let me snack; I han't met with a bubble since Christmas. 'Gad, I think bubbles are like their brother woodcocks, go out with the cold weather.

Har. A pox! he did not hear all, I hope.   [*Apart to* HORNER.

Spark. Come, you bubbling rogues you, where do we sup?— Oh, Harcourt, my mistress tells me you have been making fierce love to her all the play long: ha! ha!—But I——

Har. I make love to her!

Spark. Nay, I forgive thee, for I think I know thee, and I know her; but I am sure I know myself.

Har. Did she tell you so? I see all women are like these of the Exchange; who, to enhance the prize of their commodities, report to their fond customers offers which were never made 'em.

Horn. Ay, women are apt to tell before the intrigue, as men after it, and so show themselves the vainer sex. But hast thou a mistress, Sparkish? 'Tis as hard for me to believe it, as that thou ever hadst a bubble, as you bragged just now.

Spark. O, your servant, sir: are you at your raillery, sir? But we are some of us beforehand with you to-day at the play. The wits were something bold with you, sir; did you not hear us laugh?

Horn. Yes; but I thought you had gone to plays, to laugh at the poet's wit, not at your own.

Spark. Your servant, sir: no, I thank you. 'Gad, I go to a play as to a country treat; I carry my own wine to one, and my own wit to t'other, or else I'm sure I should not be merry at either. And the reason why we are so often louder than the players, is, because we think we speak more wit, and so become the poet's rivals in his audience: for to tell you the truth, we hate the silly rogues; nay, so much, that we find fault even with their bawdy upon the stage, whilst we talk nothing else in the pit as loud.

Horn. But why shouldst thou hate the silly poets? Thou hast too much wit to be one; and they, like whores, are only hated by each other: and thou dost scorn writing, I'm sure.

Spark. Yes; I'd have you to know I scorn writing: but women, women, that make men do all foolish things, make 'em write songs too. Everybody does it. 'Tis even as common with lovers, as playing with fans; and you can no more help rhyming to your Phillis, than drinking to your Phillis.

Har. Nay, poetry in love is no more to be avoided than jealousy.

Dor. But the poets damned your songs, did they?

Spark. Damn the poets! they have turned 'em into burlesque, as they call it. That burlesque is a hocus-pocus trick they have got, which, by the virtue of *Hictius doctius topsy turvy,* they make a wise and witty man in the world, a fool upon the stage you know not how: and 'tis therefore I hate 'em too, for I know not but it may be my own case; for they'll put a man into a play for looking asquint. Their predecessors were contented to make serving-men only their stage-fools: but these rogues must have gentlemen, with a pox to 'em, nay, knights; and, indeed, you shall hardly see a fool upon the stage but he's a knight, And to tell you the truth, they have kept me these six years from being a knight in earnest, for fear of being knighted in a play, and dubbed a fool.

Dor. Blame 'em not, they must follow their copy, the age.

Har. But why shouldst thou be afraid of being in a play, who expose yourself every day in the play-houses, and at public places?

Horn. 'Tis but being on the stage, instead of standing on a bench in the pit.

Dor. Don't you give money to painters to draw you like? and are you afraid of your pictures at length in a playhouse, where all your mistresses may see you?

Spark. A pox! painters don't draw the small-pox or pimples in one's face. Come, damn all your silly authors whatever, all books and booksellers, by the world; and all readers, courteous or un-courteous!

Har. But who comes here, Sparkish?

Enter PINCHWIFE *and* MRS. PINCHWIFE *in man's clothes,*
ALITHEA *and* LUCY.

Spark. Oh, hide me! There's my mistress too.
[SPARKISH *hides himself behind* HARCOURT.

Har. She sees you.

Spark. But I will not see her. 'Tis time to go to Whitehall, and I must not fail the drawing-room.

Har. Pray, first carry me, and reconcile me to her.

Spark. Another time. Faith, the king will have supped.

Har. Not with the worse stomach for thy absence. Thou art one of those fools that think their attendance at the king's meals as necessary as his physicians, when you are more troublesome to him than his doctors or his dogs.

Spark. Pshaw! I know my interest, sir. Prithee hide me.

Horn. Your servant, Pinchwife.—What, he knows us not!

Pinch. Come along.   [*To his* Wife *aside.*

Mrs. Pinch. Pray, have you any ballads? give me sixpenny worth.

Bookseller. We have no ballads.

Mrs. Pinch. Then give me "Covent Garden Drollery," and a play or two—Oh, here's "Tarugo's Wiles," and "The Slighted Maiden"; [1] I'll have them.

Pinch. No; plays are not for your reading. Come along; will you discover yourself?   [*Apart to her.*

Horn. Who is that pretty youth with him, Sparkish?

Spark. I believe his wife's brother, because he's something like her: but I never saw her but once.

Horn. Extremely handsome; I have seen a face like it too. Let us follow 'em.

[*Exeunt* PINCHWIFE, MRS. PINCHWIFE, ALITHEA, *and* LUCY; HORNER *and* DORILANT *following them.*

Har. Come, Sparkish, your mistress saw you, and will be angry you go not to her. Besides, I would fain be reconciled to her, which none but you can do, dear friend.

Spark. Well, that's a better reason, dear friend. I would not go near her now for her's or my own sake; but I can deny you nothing: for though I have known thee a great while, never go, if I do not love thee as well as a new acquaintance.

Har. I am obliged to you indeed, dear friend. I would be well with her, only to be well with thee still; for these ties to wives

---

[1] "Covent Garden Drolery, Or a Colection of all the Choice Songs, Poems, Prologues, and Epilogues (Sung and Spoken at Courts and Theaters) never in Print before. Written by the refined'st Witts of the Age. And Collected by R[ichard] B[rome] Servant to His Majestie. London, Printed for James Magnes neer the Piazza in Russel-Street, 1672."— *Tarugo's Wiles, or the Coffee House;* a comedy by Sir Thomas St. Serle, produced in 1668.—*The Slighted Maid,* a comedy by Sir Robert Stapleton, produced in 1663.

usually dissolve all ties to friends. I would be contented she should enjoy you a-nights, but I would have you to myself a-days as I have had, dear friend. •

Spark. And thou shalt enjoy me a-days, dear, dear friend, never stir: and I'll be divorced from her, sooner than from thee. Come along.

Har. [*aside*]. So, we are hard put to't, when we make our rival our procurer; but neither she nor her brother would let me come near her now. When all's done, a rival is the best cloak to steal to a mistress under, without suspicion; and when we have once got to her as we desire, we throw him off like other cloaks.

[*Exit* SPARKISH, HARCOURT *following him.*

Re-enter PINCHWIFE *and* MRS. PINCHWIFE. •

Pinch. [*to* ALITHEA]. Sister, if you will not go, we must leave you.—[*Aside.*] The fool her gallant and she will muster up all the young saunterers of this place, and they will leave their dear sempstresses to follow us. What a swarm of cuckolds and cuckold-makers are here!—Come, let's be gone, Mistress Margery.

Mrs. Pinch. Don't you believe that; I han't half my bellyful of sights yet.

Pinch. Then walk this way.

Mrs. Pinch. Lord, what a power of brave signs are here! stay— the Bull's-Head, the Ram's-Head, and the Stag's-Head, dear——

Pinch. Nay, if every husband's proper sign here were visible, they would be all alike.

Mrs. Pinch. What d'ye mean by that, bud?

Pinch. 'Tis no matter—no matter, bud.

Mrs. Pinch. Pray tell me: nay, I will know.

Pinch. They would be all Bulls, Stags, and Rams-heads.

[*Exeunt* PINCHWIFE *and* MRS. PINCHWIFE.

Re-enter SPARKISH, HARCOURT, ALITHEA, *and* LUCY, *at the other side.*

Spark. Come, dear madam, for my sake you shall be reconciled to him.

Alith. For your sake I hate him.

Har. That's something too cruel, madam, to hate me for his sake.

Spark. Ay indeed, madam, too, too cruel to me, to hate my friend for my sake.

Alith. I hate him because he is your enemy; and you ought to hate him too, for making love to me, if you love me.

Spark. That's a good one! I hate a man for loving you! If he did love you, 'tis but what he can't help; and 'tis your fault, not his, if he admires you. I hate a man for being of my opinion! I'll n'er do't, by the world.

Alith. Is it for your honour, or mine, to suffer a man to make love to me, who am to marry you to-morrow?

Spark. Is it for your honour, or mine, to have me jealous? That he makes love to you, is a sign you are handsome; and that I am not jealous, is a sign you are virtuous. That I think is for your honour.

Alith. But 'tis your honour too I am concerned for.

Har. But why, dearest madam, will you be more concerned for his honour than he is himself? Let his honour alone, for my sake and his. He! he has no honour——

Spark. How's that?

Har. But what my dear friend can guard himself.

Spark. O ho——that's right again.

Har. Your care of his honour argues his neglect of it, which is no honour to my dear friend here. Therefore once more, let his honour go which way it will, dear madam.

Spark. Ay, ay; were it for my honour to marry a woman whose virtue I suspected, and could not trust her in a friend's hands?

Alith. Are you not afraid to lose me?

Har. He afraid to lose you, madam! No, no——you may see how the most estimable and most glorious creature in the world is valued by him. Will you not see it?

Spark. Right, honest Frank, I have that noble value for her that I cannot be jealous of her.

Alith. You mistake him. He means, you care not for me, nor who has me.

Spark. Lord, madam, I see you are jealous! Will you wrest a poor man's meaning from his words?

Alith. You astonish me, sir, with your want of jealousy.

Spark. And you make me giddy, madam, with your jealousy and fears, and virtue and honour. 'Gad, I see virtue makes a woman as troublesome as a little reading or learning.

Alith. Monstrous!

Lucy. Well, to see what easy husbands these women of quality can meet with! a poor chambermaid can never have such lady-like luck. Besides, he's thrown away upon her. She'll make no use of her fortune, her blessing, none to a gentleman, for a pure cuckold; for it requires good breeding to be a cuckold.   [*Aside.*

Alith. I tell you then plainly, he pursues me to marry me.

Spark. Pshaw!

Har. Come, madam, you see you strive in vain to make him

jealous of me. My dear friend is the kindest creature in the world to me.

Spark. Poor fellow!

Har. But his kindness only is not enough for me, without your favour, your good opinion, dear madam: 'tis that must perfect my happiness. Good gentleman, he believes all I say: would you would do so! Jealous of me! I would not wrong him nor you for the world.

Spark. Look you there. Hear him, hear him, and do not walk away so.   [ALITHEA *walks carelessly to and fro.*

Har. I love you, madam, so——

Spark. How's that? Nay, now you begin to go too far indeed.

Har. So much, I confess, I say, I love you, that I would not have you miserable, and cast yourself away upon so unworthy and inconsiderable a thing as what you see here.

[*Clapping his hand on his breast, points at* SPARKISH.

Spark. No, faith, I believe thou wouldst not: now his meaning is plain: but I knew before thou wouldst not wrong me, nor her.

Har. No, no, Heavens forbid the glory of her sex should fall so low, as into the embraces of such a contemptible wretch, the least of mankind—my friend here—I injure him!

[*Embracing* SPARKISH

Alith. Very well.

Spark. No, no, dear friend, I knew it.—Madam, you see he will rather wrong himself than me, in giving himself such names

Alith. Do not you understand him yet?

Spark. Yes: how modestly he speaks of himself, poor fellow!

Alith. Methinks he speaks impudently of yourself, since—before yourself too; insomuch that I can no longer suffer his scurrilous abusiveness to you, no more than his love to me.

[*Offers to go.*

Spark. Nay, nay, madam, pray stay—his love to you! Lord, madam, has he not spoke yet plain enough?

Alith. Yes, indeed, I should think so.

Spark. Well then, by the world, a man can't speak civilly to a woman now, but presently she says, he makes love to her. Nay, madam, you shall stay, with your pardon, since you have not yet understood him, till he has made an eclaircissement of his love to you, that is, what kind of love it is. Answer to thy catechism, friend; do you love my mistress here?

Har. Yes, I wish she would not doubt it.

Spark. But how do you love her?

Har. With all my soul.

Alith. I thank him, methinks he speaks plain enough now.

Spark. [*To* ALITHEA.] You are out still.—But with what kind of love, Harcourt?

Har. With the best and the truest love in the world.

Spark. Look you there then, that is with no matrimonial love, I'm sure.

Alith. How's that? do you say matrimonial love is not best?

Spark. 'Gad, I went too far ere I was aware. But speak for thyself, Harcourt, you said you would not wrong me nor her.

Har. No, no, madam, e'en take him for Heaven's sake.

Spark. Look you there, madam.

Har. Who should in all justice be yours, he that loves you most.

[*Claps his hand on his breast.*

Alith. Look you there, Mr. Sparkish, who's that?

Spark. Who should it be?—Go on, Harcourt.

Har. Who loves you more than women titles, or fortune fools,

[*Points at* SPARKISH.

Spark. Look you there, he means me still, for he points at me.

Alith. Ridiculous!

Har. Who can only match your faith and constancy in love.

Spark. Ay.

Har. Who knows, if it be possible, how to value so much beauty and virtue.

Spark. Ay.

Har. Whose love can no more be equalled in the world, than that heavenly form of yours.

Spark. No.

Har. Who could no more suffer a rival, than your absence, and yet could no more suspect your virtue, than his own constancy in his love to you.

Spark. No.

Har. Who, in fine, loves you better than his eyes, that first made him love you.

Spark. Ay—Nay, madam, faith, you shan't go till——

Alith. Have a care, lest you make me stay too long.

Spark. But till he has saluted you; that I may be assured you are friends, after his honest advice and declaration. Come, pray, madam, be friends with him.

Re-enter PINCHWIFE *and* MRS. PINCHWIFE.

Alith. You must pardon me, sir, that I am not yet so obedient to you.

Pinch. What, invite your wife to kiss men? Monstrous! are you not ashamed? I will never forgive you.

Spark. Are you not ashamed. that I should have more confidence in the chastity of your family than you have? You must not teach me, I am a man of honour, sir, though I am frank and free; I am frank, sir——

Pinch. Very frank, sir, to share your wife with your friends.

Spark. He is an humble, menial friend, such as reconciles the differences of the marriage bed; you know man and wife do not always agree; I design him for that use, therefore would have him well with my wife.

Pinch. A menial friend!—you will get a great many menial friends, by showing your wife as you do.

Spark. What then? It may be I have a pleasure in't, as I have to show fine cloths at a play-house, the first day, and count money before poor rogues.

Pinch. He that shows his wife or money, will be in danger of having them borrowed sometimes.

Spark. I love to be envied, and would not marry a wife that I alone could love; loving alone is as dull as eating alone. Is it not a frank age? and I am a frank person; and to tell you the truth, it may be, I love to have rivals in a wife, they make her seem to a man still but as a kept mistress; and so good night, for I must to Whitehall.—Madam, I hope you are now reconciled to my friend; and so I wish you a good night, madam, and sleep if you can: for to-morrow you know I must visit you early with a canonical gentleman. Good night, dear Harcourt. [*Exit.*

Har. Madam, I hope you will not refuse my visit to-morrow, if it should be earlier with a canonical gentleman than Mr. Sparkish's.

Pinch. This gentlewoman is yet under my care, therefore you must yet forbear your freedom with her, sir.

[*Coming between* ALITHEA *and* HARCOURT.

Har. Must, sir?

Pinch. Yes, sir, she is my sister.

Har. 'Tis well she is, sir—for I must be her servant, sir.— Madam——

Pinch. Come away, sister, we had been gone, if it had not been for you, and so avoided these lewd rake-hells, who seem to haunt us.

Re-enter HORNER *and* DORILANT.

Horn. How now, Pinchwife!

Pinch. Your servant.

Horn. What! I see a little time in the country makes a man turn wild and unsociable, and only fit to converse with his horses, dogs, and his herds.

Pinch. I have business, sir, and must mind it; your business is pleasure, therefore you and I must go different ways.

Horn. Well, you may go on, but this pretty young gentle-man——   [*Takes hold of* Mrs. PINCHWIFE.

Har. The lady——

Dor. And the maid——

Horn. Shall stay with us; for I suppose their business is the same with ours, pleasure.

Pinch. 'Sdeath, he knows her, she carries it so sillily! yet if he does not, I should be more silly to discover it first.   [*Aside.*

Alith. Pray, let us go, sir.

Pinch. Come, come——

Horn. [*To* Mrs. PINCHWIFE.] Had you not rather stay with us? —Prithee, Pinchwife, who is this pretty young gentleman?

Pinch. One to whom I'm a guardian.—[*Aside.*] I wish I could keep her out of your hands.

Horn. Who is he? I never saw anything so pretty in all my life.

Pinch. Pshaw! do not look upon him so much, he's a poor bashful youth, you'll put him out of countenance.—Come away, brother.   [*Offers to take her away.*

Horn. O, your brother!

Pinch. Yes, my wife's brother.—Come, come, she'll stay supper for us.

Horn. I thought so, for he is very like her I saw you at the play with, whom I told you I was in love with.

Mrs. Pinch. [*Aside.*] O jeminy! is that he that was in love with me? I am glad on't, I vow, for he's a curious fine gentleman, and I love him already, too.—[*To* PINCHWIFE.] Is this he, bud?

Pinch. Come away, come away.   [*To his* Wife.

Horn. Why, what haste are you in? why won't you let me talk with him?

Pinch. Because you'll debauch him; he's yet young and innocent, and I would not have him debauched for anything in the world.—[*Aside.*] How she gazes on him! the devil!

Horn. Harcourt, Dorilant, look you here, this is the likeness of that dowdy he told us of, his wife; did you ever see a lovelier creature? The rogue has reason to be jealous of his wife, since she is like him, for she would make all that see her in love with her.

Har. And, as I remember now, she is as like him here as can be.

Dor. She is indeed very pretty, if she be like him.

Horn. Very pretty? a very pretty commendation!—she is a glorious creature, beautiful beyond all things I ever beheld.

Pinch. So, so.

Har. More beautiful than a poet's first mistress of imagination.

Horn. Or another man's last mistress of flesh and blood.

Mrs. Pinch. Nay, now you jeer, sir; pray don't jeer me.

Pinch. Come, come.—[*Aside.*] By Heavens, she'll discover herself!

Horn. I speak of your sister, sir.

Pinch. Ay, but saying she was handsome, if like him, made him blush.—[*Aside.*] I am upon a rack!

Horn. Methinks he is so handsome he should not be a man.

Pinch. [*Aside.*] O, there 'tis out! he has discovered her! I am not able to suffer any longer.—[*To his* Wife.] Come, come away, I say.

Horn. Nay, by your leave, sir, he shall not go yet.—[*Aside to them.*] Harcourt, Dorilant, let us torment this jealous rogue a little.

Har. Dor. How?

Horn. I'll show you.

Pinch. Come, pray let him go, I cannot stay fooling any longer; I tell you his sister stays supper for us.

Horn. Does she? Come then, we'll all go to sup with he and thee.

Pinch. No, now I think on't, having stayed so long for us, I warrant she's gone to bed.—[*Aside.*] I wish she and I were well out of their hands.—[*To his* Wife.] Come, I must rise early to-morrow, come.

Horn. Well then, if she be gone to bed, I wish her and you a good night. But pray, young gentleman, present my humble service to her.

Mrs. Pinch. Thank you heartily, sir.

Pinch. [*Aside.*] 'Sdeath, she will discover herself yet in spite of me.—[*Aloud.*] He is something more civil to you, for your kindness to his sister, than I am, it seems.

Horn. Tell her, dear sweet little gentleman, for all your brother there, that you have revived the love I had for her at first sight in the playhouse.

Mrs. Pinch. But did you love her indeed, and indeed?

Pinch. [*Aside.*] So, so.—[*Aloud.*] Away, I say.

Horn. Nay, stay.—Yes, indeed, and indeed, pray do you tell her so, and give her this kiss from me. [*Kisses her.*

Pinch. [*Aside.*] O Heavens! what do I suffer? Now 'tis too plain he knows her, and yet——

Horn. And this, and this—— [*Kisses her again.*

Mrs. Pinch. What do you kiss me for? I am no woman.

Pinch. [*Aside.*] So, there, 'tis out.—[*Aloud.*] Come, I cannot, nor will stay any longer.

Horn. Nay, they shall send your lady a kiss too. Here Harcourt, Dorilant, will you not?   [*They kiss her.*

Pinch. [*Aside.*] How! do I suffer this? Was I not accusing another just now for this rascally patience, in permitting his wife to be kissed before his face? Ten thousand ulcers gnaw away their lips.—[*Aloud.*] Come, come.

Horn. Good night, dear little gentleman; madam, good night; farewell, Pinchwife.—[*Apart to* HARCOURT *and* DORILANT.] Did not I tell you I would raise his jealous gall?

[*Exeunt* HORNER, HARCOURT, *and* DORILANT.

Pinch. So, they are gone at last; stay, let me see first if the coach be at this door.   [*Exit.*

Re-enter HORNER, HARCOURT, *and* DORILANT.

Horn. What, not gone yet? Will you be sure to do as I desired you, sweet sir?

Mrs. Pinch. Sweet sir, but what will you give me then?

Horn. Anything. Come away into the next walk.

[*Exit, haling away* Mrs. PINCHWIFE.

Alith. Hold! hold! what d'ye do?

Lucy. Stay, stay, hold——

Har. Hold, madam, hold, let him present him—he'll come presently; nay, I will never let you go till you answer my question.

Lucy. For God's sake, sir, I must follow 'em.

[ALITHEA *and* LUCY, *struggling with* HARCOURT *and* DORILANT.

Dor. No, I have something to present you with too, you shan't follow them.

Re-enter PINCHWIFE.

Pinch. Where?—how—what's become of?—gone!—whither?

Lucy. He's only gone with the gentleman, who will give him something, an't please your worship.

Pinch. Something!—give him something, with a pox!—where are they?

Alith. In the next walk only, brother.

Pinch. Only, only! where, where?

[*Exit and returns presently, then goes out again.*

Har. What's the matter with him? why so much concerned? But, dearest madam——

Alith. Pray let me go, sir; I have said and suffered enough already.

Har. Then you will not look upon, nor pity, my sufferings?

Alith. To look upon 'em, when I cannot help 'em, were cruelty, not pity; therefore, I will never see you more.

Har. Let me then, madam, have my privilege of a banished lover, complaining or railing, and giving you but a farewell reason why, if you cannot condescend to marry me, you should not take that wretch, my rival.

Alith. He only, not you, since my honour is engaged so far to him, can give me a reason why I should not marry him; but if he be true, and what I think him to me, I must be so to him. Your servant, sir.

Har. Have women only constancy when 'tis a vice, and are, like Fortune, only true to fools?

Dor. Thou sha't not stir, thou robust creature; you see I can deal with you, therefore you should stay the rather, and be kind.

[*To* LUCY, *who struggles to get from him.*

Re-enter PINCHWIFE.

Pinch. Gone, gone, not to be found! quite gone! ten thousand plagues go with 'em! Which way went they?

Alith. But into t'other walk, brother.

Lucy. Their business will be done presently sure, an't please your worship; it can't be long in doing, I'm sure on't.

Alith. Are they not there?

Pinch. No, you know where they are, you infamous wretch, eternal shame of your family, which you do not dishonour enough yourself you think, but you must help her to do it too, thou legion of bawds!

Alith. Good brother——

Pinch. Damned, damned sister!

Alith. Look you here, she's coming.

Re-enter MRS. PINCHWIFE *running, with her hat full of oranges and dried fruit under her arm,* HORNER *following.*

Mrs. Pinch. O dear bud, look you here what I have got, see!

Pinch. And what I have got here too, which you can't see.

[*Aside, rubbing his forehead.*

Mrs. Pinch. The fine gentleman has given me better things yet.

Pinch. Has he so?—[*Aside.*] Out of breath and coloured!—I must hold yet.

Horn. I have only given your little brother an orange, sir.

Pinch. [*to* HORNER]. Thank you, sir.—[*Aside.*] You have only squeezed my orange, I suppose, and given it me again; yet I must have a city patience.—[*To his* Wife.] Come, come away.

Mrs. Pinch. Stay, till I have put up my fine things, bud.

Enter Sir Jasper Fidget.

Sir Jasp. O, Master Horner, come, come, the ladies stay for you; your mistress, my wife, wonders you make not more haste to her.

Horn. I have stayed this half hour for you here, and 'tis your fault I am not now with your wife.

Sir Jasp. But, pray, don't let her know so much; the truth on't is, I was advancing a certain project to his majesty about—I'll tell you.

Horn. No, let's go, and hear it at your house. Good night, sweet little gentleman; one kiss more, you'll remember me now, I hope.
[*Kisses her.*

Dor. What, Sir Jasper, will you separate friends? He promised to sup with us, and if you take him to your house, you'll be in danger of our company too.

Sir Jasp. Alas! gentlemen, my house is not fit for you; there are none but civil women there, which are not for your turn. He, you know, can bear with the society of civil women now, ha! ha! ha! besides, he's one of my family—he's—he! he! he!

Dor. What is he?

Sir Jasp. Faith, my eunuch, since you'll have it; he! he! he!
[*Exeunt* Sir Jasper Fidget *and* Horner.

Dor. I rather wish thou wert his or my cuckold. Harcourt, what a good cuckold is lost there for want of a man to make him one? Thee and I cannot have Horner's privilege, who can make use of it.

Har. Ay, to poor Horner 'tis like coming to an estate at three-score, when a man can't be the better for't.

Pinch. Come.

Mrs. Pinch. Presently, bud.

Dor. Come, let us go too.—[*To* Alithea.] Madam, your servant.—[*To* Lucy.] Good night, strapper.

Har. Madam, though you will not let me have a good day or night, I wish you one; but dare not name the other half of my wish.

Alith. Good night, sir, for ever.

Mrs. Pinch. I don't know where to put this here, dear bud, you shall eat it; nay, you shall have part of the fine gentleman's good things, or treat, as you call it, when we come home.

Pinch. Indeed, I deserve it, since I furnished the best part of it.
[*Strikes away the orange.*

The gallant treats presents, and gives the ball;
But 'tis the absent cuckold pays for all. [*Exeunt.*

ACT IV

SCENE I.—PINCHWIFE's *House in the morning*

Enter ALITHEA *dressed in new clothes, and* LUCY.

Lucy. Well—madam, now have I dressed you, and set you out with so many ornaments, and spent upon you ounces of essence and pulvillio; and all this for no other purpose but as people adorn and perfume a corpse for a stinking second-hand grave: such, or as bad, I think Master Sparkish's bed.

Alith. Hold your peace.

Lucy. Nay, madam, I will ask you the reason why you would banish poor Master Harcourt for ever from your sight; how could you be so hard-hearted?

Alith. 'Twas because I was not hard-hearted.

Lucy. No, no; 'twas stark love and kindness, I warrant.

Alith. It was so; I would see him no more because I love him.

Lucy. Hey day, a very pretty reason!

Alith. You do not understand me.

Lucy. I wish you may yourself.

Alith. I was engaged to marry, you see, another man, whom my justice will not suffer me to deceive or injure.

Lucy. Can there be a greater cheat or wrong done to a man than to give him your person without your heart? I should make a conscience of it.

Alith. I'll retrieve it for him after I am married a while.

Lucy. The woman that marries to love better, will be as much mistaken as the wencher that marries to live better. No, madam, marrying to increase love is like gaming to become rich; alas! you only lose what little stock you had before.

Alith. I find by your rhetoric you have been bribed to betray me.

Lucy. Only by his merit, that has bribed your heart, you see, against your word and rigid honour. But what a devil is this honour! 'tis sure a disease in the head, like the megrim or falling-sickness, that always hurries people away to do themselves mischief. Men lose their lives by it; women, what's dearer to 'em, their love, the life of life.

Alith. Come, pray talk you no more of honour, nor Master Harcourt; I wish the other would come to secure my fidelity to him and his right in me.

Lucy. You will marry him then?

Alith. Certainly, I have given him already my word, and will my hand too, to make it good, when he comes.

Lucy. Well, I wish I may never stick pin more, if he be not an arrant natural, to t'other fine gentleman.

Alith. I own he wants the wit of Harcourt, which I will dispense withal for another want he has, which is want of jealousy, which men of wit seldom want.

Lucy. Lord, madam, what should you do with a fool to your husband? You intend to be honest, don't you? then that husbandly virtue, credulity, is thrown away upon you.

Alith. He only that could suspect my virtue should have cause to do it; 'tis Sparkish's confidence in my truth that obliges me to be so faithful to him.

Lucy. You are not sure his opinion may last.

Alith. I am satisfied, 'tis impossible for him to be jealous after the proofs I have had of him. Jealousy in a husband—Heaven defend me from it! it begets a thousand plagues to a poor woman, the loss of her honour, her quiet, and her——

Lucy. And her pleasure.

Alith. What d'ye mean, impertinent?

Lucy. Liberty is a great pleasure, madam.

Alith. I say, loss of her honour, her quiet, nay, her life sometimes; and what's as bad almost, the loss of this town; that is, she is sent into the country, which is the last ill-usage of a husband to a wife, I think.

Lucy. [*Aside*.] O, does the wind lie there?—[*Aloud*.] Then of necessity, madam, you think a man must carry his wife into the country, if he be wise. The country is as terrible, I find, to our young English ladies, as a monastery to those abroad; and on my virginity, I think they would rather marry a London jailer, than a high sheriff of a county, since neither can stir from his employment. Formerly women of wit married fools for a great estate, a fine seat, or the like; but now 'tis for a pretty seat only in Lincoln's Inn Fields, St. James's Fields, or the Pall Mall.

Enter SPARKISH, *and* HARCOURT, *dressed like a* Parson.

Spark. Madam, your humble servant, a happy day to you, and to us all.

Har. Amen.

Alith. Who have we here?

Spark. My chaplain, faith—O madam, poor Harcourt remembers his humble service to you; and, in obedience to your last commands, refrains coming into your sight.

Alith. Is not that he?

Spark. No, fy, no; but to show that he ne'er intended to hinder our match, has sent his brother here to join our hands. When I

get me a wife, I must get her a chaplain, according to the custom;
that is his brother, and my chaplain.

Alith. His brother!

Lucy. And your chaplain, to preach in your pulpit then——
                                                    [*Aside.*

Alith. His brother!

Spark. Nay, I knew you would not believe it.—I told you, sir,
she would take you for your brother Frank.

Alith. Believe it!

Lucy. His brother! ha! ha! he! he has a trick left still, it seems.
                                                    [*Aside.*

Spark. Come, my dearest, pray let us go to church before the
canonical hour is past.

Alith. For shame, you are abused still.

Spark. By the world, 'tis strange now you are so incredulous.

Alith. 'Tis strange you are so credulous.

Spark. Dearest of my life, hear me. I tell you this is Ned Harcourt of Cambridge, by the world; you see he has a sneaking college look. 'Tis true he's something like his brother Frank; and
they differ from each other no more than in their age, for they
were twins.

Lucy. Ha! ha! ha!

Alith. Your servant, sir; I cannot be so deceived, though you
are. But come, let's hear, how do you know what you affirm so
confidently?

Spark. Why I'll tell you all. Frank Harcourt coming to me this
morning to wish me joy, and present his service to you, I asked
him if he could help me to a parson. Whereupon he told me, he
had a brother in town who was in orders; and he went straight
away, and sent him, you see there, to me.

Alith. Yes, Frank goes and put on a black coat, then tells you
he is Ned; that's all you have for't.

Spark. Pshaw! pshaw! I tell you, by the same token, the midwife put her garter about Frank's neck, to know 'em asunder,
they were so like.

Alith. Frank tells you this too?

Spark. Ay, and Ned there too:.nay, they are both in a story.

Alith. So, so; very foolish.

Spark. Lord, if you won't believe one, you had best try him
by your chambermaid there; for chambermaids must needs know
chaplains from other men, they are so used to 'em.

Lucy. Let's see: nay, I'll be sworn he has the canonical smirk,
and the filthy clammy palm of a chaplain.

Alith. Well, most reverend doctor, pray let us make an end of this fooling.

Har. With all my soul, divine heavenly creature, when you please.

Alith. He speaks like a chaplain indeed.

Spark. Why, was there not soul, divine, heavenly, in what he said?

Alith. Once more, most impertinent black coat, cease your persecution, and let us have a conclusion of this ridiculous love.

Har. I had forgot, I must suit my style to my coat, or I wear it in vain. [*Aside.*

Alith. I have no more patience left; let us make once an end of this troublesome love, I say.

Har. So be it, seraphic lady, when your honour shall think it meet and convenient so to do.

Spark. 'Gad, I'm sure none but a chaplain could speak so, I think.

Alith. Let me tell you, sir, this dull trick will not serve your turn; though you delay our marriage, you shall not hinder it.

Har. Far be it from me, munificent patroness, to delay your marriage; I desire nothing more than to marry you presently, which I might do, if you yourself would; for my noble, good-natured, and thrice generous patron here would not hinder it.

Spark. No, poor man, not I, faith.

Har. And now, madam, let me tell you plainly nobody else shall marry you; by Heavens! I'll die first, for I'm sure I should die after it.

Lucy. How his love has made him forget his function, as I have seen it in real parsons!

Alith. That was spoken like a chaplain too? now you understand him, I hope.

Spark. Poor man, he takes it heinously to be refused; I can't blame him, 'tis putting an indignity upon him, not to be suffered; but you'll pardon me, madam, it shan't be; he shall marry us; come away, pray, madam.

Lucy. Ha! ha! he! more ado! 'tis late.

Alith. Invincible stupidity! I tell you, he would marry me as your rival, not as your chaplain.

Spark. Come, come, madam. [*Pulling her away.*

Lucy. I pray, madam, do not refuse this reverend divine the honour and satisfaction of marrying you; for I dare say, he has set his heart upon't, good doctor.

Alith. What can you hope or design by this?

Har. I could answer her, a reprieve for a day only, often revokes a hasty doom. At worst, if she will not take mercy on me, and let me marry her, I have at least the lover's second pleasure, hindering my rival's enjoyment, though but for a time.   [*Aside.*

Spark. Come, madam, 'tis e'en twelve o'clock, and my mother charged me never to be married out of the canonical hours. Come, come; Lord, here's such a deal of modesty, I warrant, the first day.

Lucy. Yes, an't please your worship, married women show all their modesty the first day, because married men show all their love the first day.   [*Exeunt.*

SCENE II.—*A Bedchamber in* PINCHWIFE's *House*

PINCHWIFE *and* Mrs. PINCHWIFE *discovered.*

Pinch. Come, tell me, I say.

Mrs. Pinch. Lord! han't I told it a hundred times over?

Pinch. [*aside*]. I would try, if in the repetition of the ungrateful tale, I could find her altering it in the least circumstance; for if her story be false, she is so too.—[*Aloud.*] Come, how was't, baggage?

Mrs. Pinch. Lord, what pleasure you take to hear it sure!

Pinch. No, you take more in telling it I find; but speak, how was't?

Mrs. Pinch. He carried me up into the house next to the Exchange.

Pinch. So, and you two were only in the room!

Mrs. Pinch. Yes, for he sent away a youth that was there, for some dried fruit, and China oranges.

Pinch. Did he so? Damn him for it—and for——

Mrs. Pinch. But presently came up the gentlewoman of the house.

Pinch. O, 'twas well she did; but what did he do whilst the fruit came?

Mrs. Pinch. He kissed me a hundred times, and told me he fancied he kissed my fine sister, meaning me, you know, whom he said he loved with all his soul, and bid me to be sure to tell her so, and to desire her to be at her window, by eleven of the clock this morning, and he would walk under it at that time.

Pinch. And he was as good as his word, very punctual; a pox reward him for't.   [*Aside.*

Mrs. Pinch. Well, and he said if you were not within, he would come up to her, meaning me, you know, bud, still.

Pinch, [*Aside.*] So—he knew her certainly; but for this confession, I am obliged to her simplicity.—[*Aloud*.] But what, you stood very still when he kissed you?

Mrs. Pinch. Yes, I warrant you; would you have had me discovered myself?

Pinch. But you told me he did some beastliness to you, as you call it; what was't?

Mrs. Pinch. Why, he put——

Pinch. What?

Mrs. Pinch. Why, he put the tip of his tongue between my lips, and so mousled me—and I said, I'd bite it.

Pinch. An eternal canker seize it, for a dog!

Mrs. Pinch. Nay, you need not be so angry with him neither, for to say truth, he has the sweetest breath I ever knew.

Pinch. The devil! you were satisfied with it then, and would do it again?

Mrs. Pinch. Not unless he should force me.

Pinch. Force you, changeling! I tell you, no woman can be forced.

Mrs. Pinch. Yes, but she may sure, by such a one as he, for he's a proper, goodly, strong man; 'tis hard, let me tell you, to resist him.

Pinch. [*Aside*.] So, 'tis plain she loves him, yet she has not love enough to make her conceal it from me; but the sight of him will increase her aversion for me and love for him; and that love instruct her how to deceive me and satisfy him, all idiot as she is. Love! 'twas he gave women first their craft, their art of deluding. Out of Nature's hands they came plain, open, silly, and fit for slaves, as she and Heaven intended 'em; but damned Love— well—I must strangle that little monster whilst I can deal with him.—[*Aloud*.] Go fetch pen, ink, and paper out of the next room.

Mrs. Pinch. Yes, bud. [*Exit.*

Pinch. Why should women have more invention in love than men? It can only be, because they have more desires, more soliciting passions, more lust, and more of the devil.

Re-enter Mrs. PINCHWIFE.

Come, minx, sit down and write.

Mrs. Pinch. Ay, dear bud, but I can't do't very well.

Pinch. I wish you could not at all.

Mrs. Pinch. But what should I write for?

Pinch. I'll have you write a letter to your lover.

Mrs. Pinch. O Lord, to the fine gentleman a letter!

Pinch. Yes, to the fine gentleman.

Mrs. Pinch. Lord, you do but jeer: sure you jest.

Pinch. I am not so merry: come, write as I bid you.

Mrs. Pinch. What, do you think I am a fool?

Pinch. [*Aside.*] She's afraid I would not dictate any love to him, therefore she's unwilling.—[*Aloud.*] But you had best begin.

Mrs. Pinch. Indeed, and indeed, but I won't, so I won't.

Pinch. Why?

Mrs. Pinch. Because he's in town; you may send for him if you will.

Pinch. Very well, you would have him brought to you; is it come to this? I say, take the pen and write, or you'll provoke me.

Mrs. Pinch. Lord, what d'ye make a fool of me for? Don't I know that letters are never writ but from the country to London, and from London into the country? Now he's in town, and I am in town too; therefore I can't write to him, you know.

Pinch. [*Aside.*] So, I am glad it is no worse; she is innocent enough yet.—[*Aloud.*] Yes, you may, when your husband bids you, write letters to people that are in town.

Mrs. Pinch. O, may I so? then I'm satisfied.

Pinch. Come, begin:—"Sir"—— [*Dictates.*

Mrs. Pinch. Shan't I say, "Dear Sir?"—You know one says always something more than bare "Sir."

Pinch. Write as I bid you, or I will write whore with this pen-knife in your face.

Mrs. Pinch. Nay, good bud—"Sir"—— [*Writes.*

Pinch. "Though I suffered last night your nauseous, loathed kisses and embraces"—Write!

Mrs. Pinch. Nay, why should I say so? You know I told you he had a sweet breath.

Pinch. Write!

Mrs. Pinch. Let me but put out "loathed."

Pinch. Write, I say!

Mrs. Pinch. Well then. [*Writes.*

Pinch. Let's see, what have you writ?—[*Takes the paper and reads.*] "Though I suffered last night your kisses and embraces"—Thou impudent creature! where is "nauseous" and "loathed?"

Mrs. Pinch. I can't abide to write such filthy words.

Pinch. Once more write as I'd have you, and question it not, or I will spoil thy writing with this. I will stab out those eyes that cause my mischief. [*Holds up the penknife.*

Mrs. Pinch. O Lord! I will.

Pinch. So—so—let's see now.—[*Reads.*] "Though I suffered last night your nauseous, loathed kisses and embraces"—go on—

"yet I would not have you presume that you shall ever repeat them"—so—— [*She writes.*

Mrs. Pinch. I have writ it.

Pinch. On, then—"I then concealed myself from your knowledge, to avoid your insolencies."—— [*She writes.*

Mrs. Pinch. So——

Pinch. "The same reason, now I am out of your hands"—— [*She writes.*

Mrs. Pinch. So——

Pinch. "Makes me own to you my unfortunate, though innocent frolic, of being in man's clothes"—— [*She writes.*

Mrs. Pinch. So——

Pinch. "That you may for evermore cease to pursue her, who hates and detests you"—— [*She writes on.*

Mrs. Pinch. So—heigh! [*Sighs.*

Pinch. What, do you sigh?—"detests you—as much as she loves her husband and her honour."

Mrs. Pinch. I vow, husband, he'll ne'er believe I should write such a letter.

Pinch. What, he'd expect a kinder from you? Come, now your name only.

Mrs. Pinch. What, shan't I say "Your most faithful humble servant till death?"

Pinch. No, tormenting fiend!—[*Aside.*] Her style, I find, would be very soft.—[*Aloud.*] Come, wrap it up now, whilst I go fetch wax and a candle; and write on the backside, "For Mr. Horner." [*Exit.*

Mrs. Pinch. "For Mr. Horner."—So, I am glad he has told me his name. Dear Mr. Horner! but why should I send thee such a letter that will vex thee, and make thee angry with me?—Well, I will not send it.—Ay, but then my husband will kill me—for I see plainly he won't let me love Mr. Horner—but what care I for my husband?—I won't, so I won't, send poor Mr. Horner such a letter —But then my husband—but oh, what if I writ at bottom my husband made me write it?—Ay, but then my husband would see't —Can one have no shift? ah, a London woman would have had a hundred presently. Stay—what if I should write a letter, and wrap it up like this, and write upon't too? Ay, but then my husband would see't—I don't know what to do.—But yet evads I'll try, so I will—for I will not send this letter to poor Mr. Horner, come what will on't.

"Dear, sweet Mr. Horner"—[*Writes and repeats what she writes.*]—so—"my husband would have me send you a base, rude, unmannerly letter; but I won't"—so—"and would have me forbid you loving me; but I won't"—so—"and would have me say to you, I hate you, poor Mr. Horner; but I won't tell a lie for him"—there—"for I'm sure if you and I were in the country at cards together"—so—"I could not help treading on your toe under the table"—so—"or rubbing knees with you, and staring in your face, till you saw me"—very well—"and then looking down, and blushing for an hour together"—so—"but I must make haste before my husband comes: and now he has taught me to write letters, you shall have longer ones from me, who am, dear, dear, poor, dear Mr. Horner, your most humble friend, and servant to command till death,—Margery Pinchwife."

Stay, I must give him a hint at bottom—so—now wrap it up just like t'other—so—now write "For Mr. Horner"—But oh now, what shall I do with it? for here comes my husband.

Re-enter PINCHWIFE.

Pinch. [*aside*]. I have been detained by a sparkish coxcomb, who pretended a visit to me; but I fear 'twas to my wife—[*Aloud.*] What, have you done?

Mrs. Pinch. Ay, ay, bud, just now.

Pinch. Let's see't: what d'ye tremble for? what, you would not have it go?

Mrs. Pinch. Here—[*aside.*] No, I must not give him that: so I had been served if I had given him this.

[*He opens and reads the first letter.*]

Pinch. Come, where's the wax and seal?

Mrs. Pinch. [*aside*]. Lord, what shall I do now? Nay, then I have it—[*aloud*]. Pray let me see't. Lord, you will think me so arrant a fool, I cannot seal a letter; I will do't, so I will.

[*Snatches the letter from him, changes it for the other, seals it, and delivers it to him.*]

Pinch. Nay, I believe you will learn that, and other things too, which I would not have you.

Mrs. Pinch. So, han't I done it curiously?—[*Aside.*] I think I have; there's my letter going to Mr. Horner, since he'll needs have me send letters to folks.

Pinch. 'Tis very well; but I warrant, you would not have it go now?

Mrs. Pinch. Yes, indeed, but I would, bud, now.

Pinch. Well, you are a good girl then. Come, let me lock you up in your chamber, till I come back; and be sure you come not within three strides of the window when I am gone, for I have a spy in the street.—[*Exit* Mrs. PINCHWIFE, PINCHWIFE *locks the door.*] At least, 'tis fit she think so. If we do not cheat women, they'll cheat us, and fraud may be justly used with secret enemies, of which a wife is the most dangerous; and he that has a handsome one to keep, and a frontier town, must provide against treachery, rather than open force. Now I have secured all within, I'll deal with the foe without, with false intelligence.

[*Holds up the letter. Exit.*

SCENE III.—HORNER'S *Lodging*

Enter HORNER *and* QUACK.

Quack. Well, sir, how fadges the new design? have you not the luck of all your brother projectors, to deceive only yourself at last?

Horn. No, good domine doctor, I deceive you, it seems, and others too; for the grave matrons, and old, rigid husbands think me as unfit for love, as they are; but their wives, sisters, and daughters know, some of 'em, better things already.

Quack. Already!

Horn. Already, I say. Last night I was drunk with half-a-dozen of your civil persons, as you call 'em, and people of honour, and so was made free of their society and dressing-rooms for ever hereafter; and am already come to the privileges of sleeping upon their pallets, warming smocks, tying shoes and garters, and the like, doctor, already, already, doctor.

Quack. You have made good use of your time, sir.

Horn. I tell thee, I am now no more interruption to 'em, when they sing, or talk bawdy, than a little squab French page who speaks no English.

Quack. But do civil persons and women of honour drink, and sing bawdy songs?

Horn. O, amongst friends, amongst friends. For your bigots in honour are just like those in religion; they fear the eye of the world more than the eye of Heaven; and think there is no virtue, but railing at vice, and no sin, but giving scandal. They rail at a poor, little, kept player, and keep themselves some young, modest pulpit comedian to be privy to their sins in their closets, not to tell 'em of them in their chapels.

Quack. Nay, the truth on't is, priests, amongst the women now, have quite got the better of us lay-confessors, physicians.

Horn. And they are rather their patients; but——

Enter Lady FIDGET, *looking about her.*

Now we talk of women of honour, here comes one. Step behind the screen there, and but observe, if I have not particular privileges with the women of reputation already, doctor, already.

[QUACK *retires.*

Lady Fid. Well, Horner, am not I a woman of honour? you see, I'm as good as my word.

Horn. And you shall see, madam, I'll not be behind-hand with you in honour; and I'll be as good as my word too, if you please but to withdraw into the next room.

Lady Fid. But first, my dear sir, you must promise to have a care of my dear honour.

Horn. If you talk a word more of your honour, you'll make me incapable to wrong it. To talk of honour in the mysteries of love, is like talking of Heaven or the Deity, in an operation of witchcraft, just when you are employing the devil: it makes the charm impotent.

Lady Fid. Nay, fy! let us not be smutty. But you talk of mysteries and bewitching to me; I don't understand you.

Horn. I tell you, madam, the word money in a mistress's mouth, at such a nick of time, is not a more disheartening sound to a younger brother, than that of honour to an eager lover like myself.

Lady Fid. But you can't blame a lady of my reputation to be chary.

Horn. Chary! I have been chary of it already, by the report I have caused of myself.

Lady Fid. Ay, but if you should ever let other women know that dear secret, it would come out. Nay, you must have a great care of your conduct; for my acquaintance are so censorious (oh, 'tis a wicked, censorious world, Mr. Horner!), I say, are so censorious, and detracting, that perhaps they'll talk to the prejudice of my honour, though you should not let them know the dear secret.

Horn. Nay, madam, rather than they shall prejudice your honour, I'll prejudice theirs; and, to serve you, I'll lie with 'em all, make the secret their own, and then they'll keep it. I am a Machiavel in love, madam.

Lady Fid. Oh, no, sir, not that way.

Horn. Nay, the devil take me, if censorious women are to be silenced any other way.

Lady Fid. A secret is better kept, I hope, by a single person than a multitude; therefore pray do not trust anybody else with it, dear, dear Mr. Horner.   [*Embracing him.*

Enter Sir JASPER FIDGET

Sir Jasp. How now!

Lady Fid. [*Aside.*] O my husband!—prevented—and what's almost as bad, found with my arms about another man—that will appear too much—what shall I say?—[*Aloud.*] Sir Jasper, come hither: I am trying if Mr. Horner were ticklish, and he's as ticklish as can be. I love to torment the confounded toad; let you and I tickle him.

Sir Jasp. No, your ladyship will tickle him better without me, I suppose. But is this your buying china? I thought you had been at the china-house.

Horn. [*Aside.*] China-house! that's my cue, I must take it.—[*Aloud.*] A pox! can't you keep your impertinent wives at home? Some men are troubled with the husbands, but I with the wives; but I'd have you to know, since I cannot be your journeyman by night, I will not be your drudge by day, to squire your wife about, and be your man of straw, or scarecrow only to pies and jays, that would be nibbling at your forbidden fruit; I shall be shortly the hackney gentleman-usher of the town.

Sir Jasp. [*Aside.*] He! he! he! poor fellow, he's in the right on't, faith. To squire women about for other folks is as ungrateful an employment, as to tell money for other folks.—[*Aloud.*] He! he! he! be'n't angry, Horner.

Lady Fid. No, 'tis I have more reason to be angry, who am left by you, to go abroad indecently alone; or, what is more indecent, to pin myself upon such ill-bred people of your acquaintance as this is.

Sir Jasp. Nay, prithee, what has he done?

Lady Fid. Nay, he has done nothing.

Sir Jasp. But what d'ye take ill, if he has done nothing?

Lady Fid. Ha! ha! ha! faith, I can't but laugh however; why, d'ye think the unmannerly toad would come down to me to the coach? I was fain to come up to fetch him, or go without him, which I was resolved not to do; for he knows china very well, and has himself very good, but will not let me see it, lest I should beg some; but I will find it out, and have what I came for yet.

Horn. [*Apart to* Lady FIDGET, *as he follows her to the door.*] Lock the door, madam.—[*Exit* Lady FIDGET, *and locks the door.*] —[*Aloud.*] So, she has got into my chamber and locked me out. Oh the impertinency of woman-kind! Well, Sir Jasper, plain-dealing is a jewel; if ever you suffer your wife to trouble me again here, she shall carry you home a pair of horns; by my lord mayor she shall; though I cannot furnish you myself, you are sure, yet I'll find a way.

Sir Jasp. Ha! ha! he!—[*Aside.*] At my first coming in, and finding her arms about him, tickling him it seems, I was half jealous, but now I see my folly.—[*Aloud.*] He! he! he! poor Horner.

Horn. Nay, though you laugh now, 'twill be my turn ere long.

Oh women, more impertinent, more cunning, and more mischievous than their monkeys, and to me almost as ugly!—Now is she throwing my things about and rifling all I have; but I'll get in to her the back way, and so rifle her for it.

Sir Jasp. Ha! ha! ha! poor angry Horner.

Horn. Stay here a little, I'll ferret her out to you presently, I warrant.   [*Exit at the other door.*

    [Sir JASPER *talks through the door to his* Wife, *she answers from within.*

Sir Jasp. Wife! my Lady Fidget! wife! he is coming into you the back way.

Lady Fid. Let him come, and welcome, which way he will.

Sir Jasp. He'll catch you, and use you roughly, and be too strong for you.

Lady Fid. Don't you trouble yourself, let him if he can.

Quack. [*Aside.*] This indeed I could not have believed from him, nor any but my own eyes.

Enter Mrs. SQUEAMISH.

Mrs. Squeam. Where's this woman-hater, this toad, this ugly, greasy, dirty sloven?

Sir Jasp. [*Aside.*] So, the women all will have him ugly: methinks he is a comely person, but his wants make his form contemptible to 'em; and 'tis e'en as my wife said yesterday, talking of him, that a proper handsome eunuch was as ridiculous a thing as a gigantic coward.

Mrs. Squeam. Sir Jasper, your servant: where is the odious beast?

Sir Jasp. He's within in his chamber, with my wife; she's playing the wag with him.

Mrs. Squeam. Is she so? and he's a clownish beast, he'll give her no quarter, he'll play the wag with her again, let me tell you: come, let's go help her.—What, the door's locked?

Sir Jasp. Ay, my wife locked it.

Mrs. Squeam. Did she so? let's break it open then.

Sir Jasp. No, no, he'll do her no hurt.

Mrs. Squeam. [*Aside.*] But is there no other way to get in to 'em? whither goes this? I will disturb 'em.

                    [*Exit at another door.*

Enter Old Lady SQUEAMISH.

Lady Squeam. Where is this harlotry, this impudent baggage, this rambling tomrigg? O Sir Jasper, I'm glad to see you here; did you not see my vile grandchild come in hither just now?

Sir Jasp. Yes.

Lady Squeam. Ay, but where is she then? where is she? Lord, Sir Jasper, I have e'en rattled myself to pieces in pursuit of her: but can you tell what she makes here? they say below, no woman lodges here.

Sir Jasp. No.

Lady Squeam. No! what does she here then? say, if it be not a woman's lodging, what makes she here? But are you sure no woman lodges here?

Sir Jasp. No, nor no man neither, this is Mr. Horner's lodging.

Lady Squeam. Is it so, are you sure?

Sir Jasp. Yes, yes.

Lady Squeam. So; then there's no hurt in't, I hope. But where is he?

Sir Jasp. He's in the next room with my wife.

Lady Squeam. Nay, if you trust him with your wife, I may with my Biddy. They say, he's a merry harmless man now, e'en as harmless a man as ever came out of Italy with a good voice, and as pretty, harmless company for a lady, as a snake without his teeth.

Sir Jasp. Ay, ay, poor man.

Re-enter Mrs. SQUEAMISH.

Mrs. Squeam. I can't find 'em.—Oh, are you here, grandmother? I followed, you must know, my Lady Fidget hither; 'tis the prettiest lodging, and I have been staring on the prettiest pictures——

Re-enter Lady FIDGET *with a piece of china in her hand, and* HORNER *following.*

Lady Fid. And I have been toiling and moiling for the prettiest piece of china, my dear.

Horn. Nay, she has been too hard for me, do what I could.

Mrs. Squeam. Oh, lord, I'll have some china too. Good Mr. Horner, don't think to give other people china, and me none; come in with me too.

Horn. Upon my honour, I have none left now.

Mrs. Squeam. Nay, nay, I have known you deny your china before now, but you shan't put me off so. Come.

Horn. This lady had the last there.

Lady Fid. Yes indeed, madam, to my certain knowledge, he has no more left.

Mrs. Squeam. O, but it may be he may have some you could not find.

Lady Fid. What, d'ye think if he had had any left, I would not have had it too? for we women of quality never think we have china enough.

Horn. Do not take it ill, I cannot make china for you all, but I will have a roll-waggon for you too, another time.

Mrs. Squeam. Thank you, dear toad.

Lady Fid. What do you mean by that promise?

[*Aside to* HORNER.

Horn. Alas, she has an innocent, literal understanding.

[*Aside to* Lady FIDGET.

Lady Squeam. Poor Mr. Horner! he has enough to do to please you all, I see.

Horn. Ay, madam, you see how they use me.

Lady Squeam. Poor gentleman, I pity you.

Horn. I thank you, madam: I could never find pity, but from such reverend ladies as you are; the young ones will never spare a man.

Mrs. Squeam. Come, come, beast, and go dine with us; for we shall want a man at ombre after dinner.

Horn. That's all their use of me, madam, you see.

Mrs. Squeam. Come, sloven, I'll lead you, to be sure of you.

[*Pulls him by the cravat.*

Lady Squeam. Alas, poor man, how she tugs him! Kiss, kiss her; that's the way to make such nice women quiet.

Horn. No, madam, that remedy is worse than the torment; they know I dare suffer anything rather than do it.

Lady Squeam. Prithee kiss her, and I'll give you her picture in little, that you admired so last night; prithee do.

Horn. Well, nothing but that could bribe me: I love a woman only in effigy, and good painting as much as I hate them.—I'll do't, for I could adore the devil well painted.

[*Kisses* Mrs. SQUEAMISH.

Mrs. Squeam. Foh, you filthy toad! nay, now I've done jesting.

Lady Squeam. Ha! ha! ha! I told you so.

Mrs. Squeam. Foh! a kiss of his——

Sir Jasp. Has no more hurt in't than one of my spaniel's.

Mrs. Squeam. Nor no more good neither.

Quack. I will now believe anything he tells me.   [*Aside.*

Enter PINCHWIFE.

Lady Fid. O lord, here's a man! Sir Jasper, my mask, my mask! I would not be seen here for the world.

Sir Jasp. What, not when I am with you?

Lady Fid. No, no, my honour—let's be gone.

Mrs. Squeam. Oh grandmother, let's be gone; make haste, make haste, I know not how he may censure us.

Lady Fid. Be found in the lodging of anything like a man!— Away.

[*Exeunt* Sir JASPER FIDGET, Lady FIDGET, Old Lady SQUEAMISH, *and* Mrs. SQUEAMISH.

Quack. What's here? another cuckold? he looks like one, and none else sure have any business with him.   [*Aside.*

Horn. Well, what brings my dear friend hither?

Pinch. Your impertinency.

Horn. My impertinency!—why, you gentlemen that have got handsome wives, think you have a privilege of saying anything to your friends, and are as brutish as if you were our creditors.

Pinch. No, sir, I'll ne'er trust you any way.

Horn. But why not, dear Jack? why diffide in me thou know'st so well?

Pinch. Because I do know you so well.

Horn. Han't I been always thy friend, honest Jack, always ready to serve thee, in love or battle, before thou wert married, and am so still?

Pinch. I believe so, you would be my second now, indeed.

Horn. Well then, dear Jack, why so unkind, so grum, so strange to me? Come, prithee kiss me, dear rogue: gad, I was always, I say, and am still as much thy servant as——

Pinch. As I am yours, sir. What, you would send a kiss to my wife, is that it?

Horn. So, there 'tis—a man can't show his friendship to a married man, but presently he talks of his wife to you. Prithee, let thy wife alone, and let thee and I be all one, as we were wont. What, thou art as shy of my kindness as a Lombard Street alderman of a courtier's civility at Locket's!

Pinch. But you are over-kind to me, as kind as if I were your cuckold already; yet I must confess you ought to be kind and civil to me, since I am so kind, so civil to you, as to bring you this: look you there, sir.   [*Delivers him a letter.*

Horn. What is't?

Pinch. Only a love-letter, sir.

Horn. From whom?—how! this is from your wife—hum— and hum—   [*Reads.*

Pinch. Even from my wife, sir: am I not wondrous kind and civil to you now too?—[*Aside.*] But you'll not think her so.

Horn. Ha! is this is a trick of his or hers?   [*Aside.*

Pinch. The gentleman's surprised I find.—What, you expected a kinder letter?

Horn. No faith, not I, how could I?

Pinch. Yes, yes, I'm sure you did. A man so well made as you are, must needs be disappointed, if the women declare not their passion at first sight or opportunity.

Horn. [*aside*]. But what should this mean? Stay, the post-script.—[*Reads aside.*] "Be sure you love me, whatsoever my husband says to the contrary, and let him not see this, lest he should come home and pinch me, or kill my squirrel."—It seems he knows not what the letter contains.

Pinch. Come, ne'er wonder at it so much.

Horn. Faith, I can't help it.

Pinch. Now, I think I have deserved your infinite friendship and kindness, and have showed myself sufficiently an obliging kind friend and husband; am I not so, to bring a letter from my wife to her gallant?

Horn. Ay, the devil take me, art thou, the most obliging, kind friend and husband in the world, ha! ha!

Pinch. Well, you may be merry, sir; but in short I must tell you, sir, my honour will suffer no jesting.

Horn. What dost thou mean?

Pinch. Does the letter want a comment? Then, know, sir, though I have been so civil a husband, as to bring you a letter from my wife, to let you kiss and court her to my face, I will not be a cuckold, sir, I will not.

Horn. Thou art mad with jealousy. I never saw thy wife in my life but at the play yesterday, and I know not if it were she or no. I court her, kiss her!

Pinch. I will not be a cuckold, I say; there will be danger in making me a cuckold.

Horn. Why, wert thou not well cured of thy last clap?

Pinch. I wear a sword.

Horn. It should be taken from thee, lest thou shouldst do thyself a mischief with it; thou art mad, man.

Pinch. As mad as I am, and as merry as you are, I must have more reason from you ere we part. I say again, though you kissed and courted last night my wife in man's clothes, as she confesses in her letter——

Horn. Ha!   [*Aside.*

Pinch. Both she and I say, you must not design it again, for you have mistaken your woman, as you have done your man.

Horn. [*aside*]. O—I understand something now—[*Aloud.*] Was that thy wife! Why wouldst thou not tell me 'twas she? Faith, my freedom with her was your fault, not mine.

Pinch. Faith, so 'twas.   [*Aside.*

Horn. Fy! I'd never do't to a woman before her husband's face, sure.

Pinch. But I had rather you should do't to my wife before my face, than behind my back; and that you shall never do.

Horn. No—you will hinder me.

Pinch. If I would not hinder you, you see by her letter she would.

Horn. Well, I must e'en acquiesce then, and be contented with what she writes.

Pinch. I'll assure you 'twas voluntarily writ; I had no hand in't you may believe me.

Horn. I do believe thee, faith.

Pinch. And believe her too, for she's an innocent creature, has no dissembling in her: and so fare you well, sir.

Horn. Pray, however, present my humble service to her, and tell her, I will obey her letter to a tittle, and fulfil her desires, be what they will, or with what difficulty soever I do't; and you shall be no more jealous of me, I warrant her, and you.

Pinch. Well then, fare you well; and play with any man's honour but mine, kiss any man's wife but mine, and welcome.

[*Exit.*

Horn. Ha! ha! ha! doctor.

Quack. It seems, he has not heard the report of you, or does not believe it.

Horn. Ha! ha!—now, doctor, what think you?

Quack. Pray let's see the letter—hum—"for—dear—love you——" [*Reads the letter.*

Horn. I wonder how she could contrive it! What say'st thou to't? 'tis an original.

Quack. So are your cuckolds too originals: for they are like no other common cuckolds, and I will henceforth believe it not impossible for you to cuckold the Grand Signior amidst his guards of eunuchs, that I say.

Horn. And I say for the letter, 'tis the first love-letter that ever was without flames, darts, fates, destinies, lying and dissembling in't.

Enter SPARKISH *pulling in* PINCHWIFE.

Spark. Come back, you are a pretty brother-in-law, neither go to church nor to dinner with your sister bride!

Pinch. My sister denies her marriage, and you see is gone away from you dissatisfied.

Spark. Pshaw! upon a foolish scruple, that our parson was not in lawful orders, and did not say all the common-prayer; but 'tis her modesty only I believe. But let all women be never so modest the first day, they'll be sure to come to themselves by night, and I shall have enough of her then. In the meantime, Harry Horner, you must dine with me: I keep my wedding at my aunt's in the Piazza.

Horn. Thy wedding! what stale maid has lived to despair of a husband, or what young one of a gallant?

Spark. O, your servant, sir—this gentleman's sister then,—no stale maid.

Horn. I'm sorry for't.

Pinch. How comes he so concerned for her? [*Aside.*

Spark. You sorry for't? why, do you know any ill by her?

Horn. No, I know none but by thee; 'tis for her sake, not yours, and another man's sake that might have hoped, I thought.

Spark. Another man! another man! what is his name?

Horn. Nay, since 'tis past, he shall be nameless.—[*Aside.*] Poor Harcourt! I am sorry thou hast missed her.

Pinch. He seems to be much troubled at the match. [*Aside.*

Spark. Prithee, tell me—Nay, you shan't go, brother.

Pinch. I must of necessity, but I'll come to you to dinner.
[*Exit.*

Spark. But, Harry, what, have I a rival in my wife already? But with all my heart, for he may be of use to me hereafter; for though my hunger is now my sauce, and I can fall on heartily without, the time will come when a rival will be as good sauce for a married man to a wife, as an orange to veal.

Horn. O thou damned rogue! thou hast set my teeth on edge with thy orange.

Spark. Then let's to dinner—there I was with you again. Come.

Horn. But who dines with thee?

Spark. My friends and relations, my brother Pinchwife, you see, of your acquaintance.

Horn. And his wife?

Spark. No, 'gad, he'll ne'er let her come amongst us good fellows; your stingy country coxcomb keeps his wife from his friends, as he does his little firkin of ale, for his own drinking, and a gentleman can't get a smack on't; but his servants, when his back is turned, broach it at their pleasures, and dust it away, ha! ha! ha!—'Gad, I am witty, I think, considering I was married to-day, by the world; but come——

Horn. No, I will not dine with you, unless you can fetch her too.

Spark. Pshaw! what pleasure canst thou have with women now, Harry?

Horn. My eyes are not gone; I love a good prospect yet, and will not dine with you unless she does too; go fetch her there-fore, but do not tell her husband 'tis for my sake.

Spark. Well, I'll go try what I can do; in the meantime, come away to my aunt's lodging, 'tis in the way to Pinchwife's.

Horn. The poor woman has called for aid, and stretched forth her hand, doctor; I cannot but help her over the pale out of the briars.   [*Exeunt.*

SCENE IV.—*A Room in* PINCHWIFE'S *House*

Mrs. PINCHWIFE *alone, leaning on her elbow.—A table, pen, ink, and paper.*

Mrs. Pinch. Well, 'tis e'en so, I have got the London disease they call love; I am sick of my husband, and for my gallant. I have heard this distemper called a fever, but methinks 'tis like an ague; for when I think of my husband, I tremble, and am in a cold sweat, and have inclinations to vomit; but when I think of my gallant, dear Mr. Horner, my hot fit comes, and I am all in a fever indeed; and, as in other fevers, my own chamber is tedious to me, and I would fain be removed to his, and then methinks I should be well. Ah, poor Mr. Horner! Well, I cannot, will not stay here; therefore I'll make an end of my letter to him, which shall be a finer letter than my last, because I have studied it like anything. Oh sick, sick!   [*Takes the pen and writes.*

Enter PINCHWIFE, *who seeing her writing, steals softly behind her and looking over her shoulder, snatches the paper from her.*

Pinch. What, writing more letters?

Mrs. Pinch. O Lord, bud, why d'ye fright me so?

[*She offers to run out; he stops her, and reads.*

Pinch. How's this? nay, you shall not stir, madam:—"Dear, dear, dear Mr. Horner"—very well—I have taught you to write letters to good purpose—but let us see't. "First, I am to beg your pardon for my boldness in writing to you, which I'd have you to know I would not have done, had not you said first you loved me so extremely, which if you do, you will never suffer me to lie in the arms of another man whom I loathe, nauseate, and detest."—Now you can write these filthy words. But what fol-lows?—"Therefore, I hope you will speedily find some way to free me from this unfortunate match, which was never, I assure you, of my choice, but I'm afraid 'tis already too far gone; how-ever, if you love me, as I do you, you will try what you can do; but you must help me away before to-morrow, or else, alas! I shall be for ever out of your reach. for I can defer no longer our—

our——" what is to follow "our"?—speak, what—our journey into the country I suppose—Oh woman, damned woman! and Love, damned Love, their old tempter! for this is one of his miracles; in a moment he can make those blind that could see, and those see that were blind, those dumb that could speak, and those prattle who were dumb before; nay, what is more than all, make these dough-baked, senseless, indocile animals, women, too hard for us their politic lords and rulers, in a moment. But make an end of your letter, and then I'll make an end of you thus, and all my plagues together. [*Draws his sword.*

Mrs. Pinch. O Lord, O Lord, you are such a passionate man, bud!

Enter SPARKISH.

Spark. How now, what's here to do?

Pinch. This fool here now!

Spark. What! drawn upon your wife? You should never do that, but at night in the dark, when you can't hurt her. This is my sister-in-law, is it not? ay, faith, e'en our country Margery [*pulls aside her handkerchief*]; one may know her. Come, she and you must go dine with me; dinner's ready, come. But where's my wife? is she not come home yet? where is she?

Pinch. Making you a cuckold; 'tis that they all do, as soon as they can.

Spark. What, the wedding-day? no, a wife that designs to make a cully of her husband will be sure to let him win the first stake of love, by the world. But come, they stay dinner for us: come, I'll lead down our Margery.

Pinch. No—sir, go, we'll follow you.

Spark. I will not wag without you.

Pinch. This coxcomb is a sensible torment to me amidst the greatest in the world. [*Aside.*

Spark. Come, come, Madam Margery.

Pinch. No; I'll lead her my way: what, would you treat your friends with mine, for want of your own wife?—[*Leads her to the other door, and locks her in and returns.*] I am contented my rage should take breath—— [*Aside.*

Spark. I told Horner this.

Pinch. Come now.

Spark. Lord, how shy you are of your wife! but let me tell you, brother, we men of wit have amongst us a saying, that cuckolding, like the small-pox, comes with a fear; and you may keep your wife as much as you will out of danger of infection, but if her constitution incline her to't, she'll have it sooner or later, by the world, say they.

Pinch. [*Aside.*] What a thing is a cuckold, that every fool can make him ridiculous!—[*Aloud.*] Well, sir—but let me advise you, now you are come to be concerned, because you suspect the danger, not to neglect the means to prevent it, especially when the greatest share of the malady will light upon your own head, for

> Hows'e'er the kind wife's belly comes to swell,
> The husband breeds for her, and first is ill.

[*Exeunt.*

ACT V

SCENE I.—PINCHWIFE'S *House*

Enter PINCHWIFE *and* MRS. PINCHWIFE. *A table and candle.*

Pinch. Come, take the pen and make an end of the letter, just as you intended; if you are false 'in a tittle, I shall soon perceive it, and punish you as you deserve.—[*Lays his hand on his sword.*] Write what was to follow—let's see—"You must make haste, and help me away before to-morrow, or else I shall be for ever out of your reach, for I can defer no longer our"—What follows "our"?

Mrs. Pinch. Must all out, then, bud?—Look you there, then.
[Mrs. PINCHWIFE *takes the pen and writes.*

Pinch. Let's see—"For I can defer no longer our—wedding—Your slighted Alithea."—What's the meaning of this? my sister's name to't? speak, unriddle.

Mrs. Pinch. Yes, indeed, bud.

Pinch. But why her name to't? speak—speak, I say.

Mrs. Pinch. Ay, but you'll tell her then again. If you would not tell her again——

Pinch. I will not:—I am stunned, my head turns round.—Speak.

Mrs. Pinch. Won't you tell her, indeed, and indeed?

Pinch. No; speak, I say.

Mrs. Pinch. She'll be angry with me; but I had rather she should be angry with me than you, bud; and, to tell you the truth, 'twas she made me write the letter, and taught me what I should write.

Pinch. [*Aside.*] Ha! I thought the style was somewhat better than her own.—[*Aloud.*] Could she come to you to teach you, since I had locked you up alone?

Mrs. Pinch. O, through the key-hole, bud.

Pinch. But why should she make you write a letter for her to him, since she can write herself?

Mrs. Pinch. Why, she said because—for I was unwilling to do it——

Pinch. Because what—because?

Mrs. Pinch. Because, lest Mr. Horner should be cruel, and refuse her; or be vain afterwards, and show the letter, she might disown it, the hand not being hers.

Pinch. [*Aside.*] How's this? Ha!—then I think I shall come to myself again.—This changeling could not invent this lie: but if she could, why should she? she might think I should soon discover it.—Stay—now I think on't too, Horner said he was sorry she had married Sparkish; and her disowning her marriage to me makes me think she has evaded it for Horner's sake: yet why should she take this course? But men in love are fools; women may well be so—[*Aloud.*] But hark you, madam, your sister went out in the morning, and I have not seen her within since.

Mrs. Pinch. Alack-a-day, she has been crying all day above, it seems, in a corner.

Pinch. Where is she? let me speak with her.

Mrs. Pinch. [*Aside.*] O Lord, then she'll discover all!—[*Aloud.*] Pray hold, bud; what, d'ye mean to discover me? she'll know I have told you then. Pray, bud, let me talk with her first.

Pinch. I must speak with her, to know whether Horner ever made her any promise, and whether she be married to Sparkish or no.

Mrs. Pinch. Pray, dear bud, don't, till I have spoken with her, and told her that I have told you all; for she'll kill me else.

Pinch. Go then, and bid her come out to me.

Mrs. Pinch. Yes, yes, bud.

Pinch. Let me see—— [*Pausing.*

Mrs. Pinch. [*Aside.*] I'll go, but she is not within to come to him: I have just got time to know of Lucy her maid, who first set me on work, what lie I shall tell next; for I am e'en at my wit's end. [*Exit.*

Pinch. Well, I resolve it, Horner shall have her: I'd rather give him my sister than lend him my wife; and such an alliance will prevent his pretensions to my wife, sure. I'll make him of kin to her, and then he won't care for her.

Re-enter Mrs. PINCHWIFE.

Mrs. Pinch. O Lord, bud! I told you what anger you would make me with my sister.

Pinch. Won't she come hither?

Mrs. Pinch. No, no. Lack-a-day, she's ashamed to look you in the face: and she says, if you go in to her, she'll run away downstairs, and shamefully go herself to Mr. Horner, who has promised her marriage, she says; and she will have no other, so she won't.

Pinch. Did he so?—promise her marriage!—then she shall have no other. Go tell her so; and if she will come and discourse with me a little concerning the means, I will about it immediately. Go.—[*Exit* Mrs. PINCHWIFE.] His estate is equal to Sparkish's, and his extraction as much better than his, as his parts are; but my chief reason is, I'd rather be akin to him by the name of brother-in-law than that of cuckold.

Re-enter Mrs. PINCHWIFE.

Well, what says she now?

Mrs. Pinch. Why, she says, she would only have you lead her to Horner's lodging; with whom she first will discourse the matter before she talks with you, which yet she cannot do; for alack, poor creature, she says she can't so much as look you in the face, therefore, she'll come to you in a mask. And you must excuse her, if she make you no answer to any question of yours, till you have brought her to Mr. Horner; and if you will not chide her, nor question her, she'll come out to you immediately.

Pinch. Let her come: I will not speak a word to her, nor require a word from her.

Mrs. Pinch. Oh, I forgot: besides, she says she cannot look you in the face, though through a mask; therefore would desire you to put out the candle.

Pinch. I agree to all. Let her make haste.—There, 'tis out.— [*Puts out the candle. Exit* Mrs. PINCHWIFE.] My case is something better: I'd rather fight with Horner for not lying with my sister, than for lying with my wife; and of the two, I had rather find my sister too forward than my wife. I expected no other from her free education, as she calls it, and her passion for the town. Well, wife and sister are names which make us expect love and duty, pleasure and comfort; but we find 'em plagues and torments, and are equally, though differently, troublesome to their keeper; for we have as much ado to get people to lie with our sisters as to keep 'em from lying with our wives.

Re-enter Mrs. PINCHWIFE *masked, and in hoods and scarfs, and a night-gown and petticoat of* ALITHEA'S.

What, are you come, sister? let us go then.—But first, let me lock up my wife. Mrs. Margery, where are you?

Mrs. Pinch. Here, bud.

Pinch. Come hither, that I may lock you up: get you in.—
[*Locks the door.*] Come, sister, where are you now?

[Mrs. PINCHWIFE *gives him her hand; but when he lets her*
go, she steals softly on to the other side of him, and is
led away by him for his Sister, ALITHEA.

SCENE II.—HORNER'S *Lodging*

HORNER *and* QUACK.

Quack. What, all alone? not so much as one of your cuckolds
here, nor one of their wives! They use to take their turns with
you, as if they were to watch you.

Horn. Yes, it often happens that a cuckold is but his wife's
spy, and is more upon family duty when he is with her gallant
abroad, hindering his pleasure, than when he is at home with her
playing the gallant. But the hardest duty a married woman imposes upon a lover is keeping her husband company always.

Quack. And his fondness wearies you almost as soon as hers.

Horn. A pox! keeping a cuckold company, after you have had
his wife, is as tiresome as the company of a country squire to
a witty fellow of the town, when he has got all his money.

Quack. And as at first a man makes a friend of the husband to
get the wife, so at last you are fain to fall out with the wife to
be rid of the husband.

Horn. Ay, most cuckold-makers are true courtiers; when once
a poor man has cracked his credit for 'em, they can't abide to
come near him.

Quack. But at first, to draw him in, are so sweet, so kind, so
dear! just as you are to Pinchwife. But what becomes of that
intrigue with his wife?

Horn. A pox! he's as surly as an alderman that has been bit;
and since he's so coy, his wife's kindness is in vain, for she's a
silly innocent.

Quack. Did she not send you a letter by him?

Horn. Yes; but that's a riddle I have not yet solved. Allow
the poor creature to be willing, she is silly too, and he keeps her
up so close——

Quack. Yes, so close, that he makes her but the more willing,
and adds but revenge to her love; which two, when met, seldom
fail of satisfying each other one way or other.

Horn. What! here's the man we are talking of, I think.

Enter PINCHWIFE, *leading in his* Wife *masked, muffled,*
and in her Sister's *gown.*

Pshaw!

Quack. Bringing his wife to you is the next thing to bringing a love-letter from her.

Horn. What means this?

Pinch. The last time, you know, sir, I brought you a love-letter; now, you see, a mistress; I think you'll say I am a civil man to you.

Horn. Ay, the devil take me, will I say thou art the civilest man I ever met with; and I have known some. I fancy I understand thee now better than I did the letter. But, hark thee, in thy ear——

Pinch. What?

Horn. Nothing but the usual question, man: is she sound, on thy word?

Pinch. What, you take her for a wench, and me for a pimp?

Horn. Pshaw! wench and pimp, paw words; I know thou art an honest fellow, and hast a great acquaintance among the ladies, and perhaps hast made love for me, rather than let me make love to thy wife.

Pinch. Come, sir, in short, I am for no fooling.

Horn. Nor I neither: therefore prithee, let's see her face presently. Make her show, man: art thou sure I don't know her?

Pinch. I am sure you do know her.

Horn. A pox! why dost thou bring her to me then?

Pinch. Because she's a relation of mine——

Horn. Is she, faith, man? then thou art still more civil and obliging, dear rogue.

Pinch. Who desired me to bring her to you.

Horn. Then she is obliging, dear rogue.

Pinch. You'll make her welcome for my sake, I hope.

Horn. I hope she is handsome enough to make herself welcome. Prithee let her unmask.

Pinch. Do you speak to her; she would never be ruled by me.

Horn. Madam—— [Mrs. PINCHWIFE *whispers to* HORNER.] She says she must speak with me in private. Withdraw, prithee.

Pinch. [*Aside.*] She's unwilling, it seems, I should know all her indecent conduct in this business.—[*Aloud.*] Well then, I'll leave you together, and hope when I am gone, you'll agree; if not, you and I shan't agree, sir.

Horn. What means the fool? if she and I agree 'tis no matter what you and I do.

[*Whispers to* Mrs. PINCHWIFE, *who makes signs with her hand for him to be gone.*

Pinch. In the meantime I'll fetch a parson, and find out Sparkish, and disabuse him. You would have me fetch a parson, would you not? Well then—now I think I am rid of her, and shall have no more trouble with her—our sisters and daughters, like usurers' money, are safest when put out; but our wives, like their writings, never safe, but in our closets under lock and key. [*Exit.*

Enter Boy.

Boy. Sir Jasper Fidget, sir, is coming up.   [*Exit.*
Horn. Here's the trouble of a cuckold now we are talking of. A pox on him! has he not enough to do to hinder his wife's sport, but he must other women's too?—Step in here, madam.
                              [*Exit* Mrs. PINCHWIFE

Enter Sir JASPER FIDGET.

Sir Jasp. My best and dearest friend.
Horn. [*Aside to* QUACK.] The old style, doctor.—[*Aloud.*] Well, be short, for I am busy. What would your impertinent wife have now?
Sir Jasp. Well guessed, i'faith; for I do come from her.
Horn. To invite me to supper! Tell her, I can't come: go.
Sir Jasp. Nay, now you are out, faith; for my lady, and the whole knot of the virtuous gang, as they call themselves, are resolved upon a frolic of coming to you to-night in masquerade, and are all dressed already.
Horn. I shan't be at home.
Sir Jasp. [*Aside.*] Lord, how churlish he is to women!— [*Aloud.*] Nay, prithee don't disappoint 'em; they'll think 'tis my fault: prithee don't. I'll send in the banquet and the fiddles. But make no noise on't; for the poor virtuous rogues would not have it known, for the world, that they go a-masquerading; and they would come to no man's ball but yours.
Horn. Well, well—get you gone; and tell 'em, if they come, 'will be at the peril of their honour and yours.
Sir Jasp. He! he! he!—we'll trust you for that: farewell.
                                        [*Exit.*
Horn. Doctor, anon you too shall be my guest,
          But now I'm going to a private feast.   [*Exeunt.*

SCENE III.—*The Piazza of Covent Garden*

Enter SPARKISH *with a letter in his hand,* PINCHWIFE *following.*

Spark. But who would have thought a woman could have been false to me? By the world, I could not have thought it.
Pinch. You were for giving and taking liberty: she has taken it

only, sir, now you find in that letter. You are a frank person, and so is she, you see there.

Spark. Nay, if this be her hand—for I never saw it.

Pinch. 'Tis no matter whether that be her hand or no; I am sure this hand, at her desire, led her to Mr. Horner, with whom I left her just now, to go fetch a parson to 'em at their desire too, to deprive you of her for ever; for it seems yours was but a mock marriage.

Spark. Indeed, she would needs have it that 'twas Harcourt himself, in a parson's habit, that married us; but I'm sure he told me 'twas his brother Ned.

Pinch. O, there 'tis out; and you were deceived, not she: for you are such a frank person. But I must be gone.—You'll find her at Mr. Horner's. Go, and believe your eyes. [*Exit*.

Spark. Nay, I'll to her, and call her as many crocodiles, sirens, harpies, and other heathenish names, as a poet would do a mistress who had refused to hear his suit, nay more, his verses on her.—But stay, is not that she following a torch at t'other end of the Piazza? and from Horner's certainly—'tis so.

Enter ALITHEA *following a torch, and* LUCY *behind.*

You are well met, madam, though you don't think so. What, you have made a short visit to Mr. Horner? but I suppose you'll return to him presently, by that time the parson can be with him.

Alith. Mr. Horner and the parson, sir!

Spark. Come, madam, no more dissembling, no more jilting; for I am no more a frank person.

Alith. How's this?

Lucy. So, 'twill work, I see. [*Aside*.

Spark. Could you find out no easy country fool to abuse? none but me, a gentleman of wit and pleasure about the town? But it was your pride to be too hard for a man of parts, unworthy false woman! false as a friend that lends a man money to lose; false as dice, who undo those that trust all they have to 'em.

Lucy. He has been a great bubble, by his similes, as they say.
                                                                    [*Aside*.

Alith. You have been too merry, sir, at your wedding-dinner, sure.

Spark. What, d'ye mock me too?

Alith. Or you have been deluded.

Spark. By you.

Alith. Let me understand you.

Spark. Have you the confidence (I should call it something else, since you know your guilt) to stand my just reproaches?

you did not write an impudent letter to Mr. Horner? who I find now has clubbed with you in deluding me with his aversion for women, that I might not, forsooth, suspect him for my rival.

Lucy. D'ye think the gentleman can be jealous now, madam?
[*Aside.*

Alith. I write a letter to Mr. Horner!

Spark. Nay, madam, do not deny it. Your brother showed it me just now; and told me likewise, he left you at Horner's lodging to fetch a parson to marry you to him: and I wish you joy, madam, joy, joy; and to him too, much joy; and to myself more joy, for not marrying you.

Alith. [*Aside.*] So, I find my brother would break off the match; and I can consent to't, since I see this gentleman can be made jealous.—[*Aloud.*] O Lucy, by his rude usage and jealousy, he makes me almost afraid I am married to him. Art thou sure 'twas Harcourt himself, and no parson, that married us?

Spark. No, madam, I thank you. I suppose, that was a contrivance too of Mr. Horner's and yours, to make Harcourt play the parson; but I would as little as you have him one now, no, not for the world. For, shall I tell you another truth? I never had any passion for you till now, for now I hate you. 'Tis true, I might have married your portion, as other men of parts of the town do sometimes: and so, your servant. And to show my unconcernedness, I'll come to your wedding, and resign you with as much joy, as I would a stale wench to a new cully; nay, with as much joy as I would after the first night, if I had been married to you. There's for you; and so your servant, servant. [*Exit.*

Alith. How was I deceived in a man!

Lucy. You'll believe then a fool may be made jealous now? for that easiness in him that suffers him to be led by a wife, will likewise permit him to be persuaded against her by others.

Alith. But marry Mr. Horner! my brother does not intend it, sure: if I thought he did, I would take thy advice, and Mr. Harcourt for my husband. And now I wish, that if there be any overwise woman of the town, who, like me, would marry a fool for fortune, liberty, or title, first, that her husband may love play, and be a cully to all the town but her, and suffer none but Fortune to be mistress of his purse; then, if for liberty, that he may send her into the country, under the conduct of some huswifely mother-in-law; and if for title, may the world give 'em none but that of cuckold.

Lucy. And for her greater curse, madam, may he not deserve it.

Alith. Away, impertinent! Is not this my old Lady Lanterlu's?

Lucy. Yes, madam.—[*Aside.*] And here I hope we shall find Mr. Harcourt.   [*Exeunt.*

SCENE IV.—HORNER'S *Lodging. A table, banquet, and bottles*

Enter HORNER, Lady FIDGET, Mrs. DAINTY FIDGET, *and* Mrs. SQUEAMISH.

Horn. A pox! they are come too soon—before I have sent back my new mistress. All that I have now to do is to lock her in, that they may not see her.   [*Aside.*

Lady Fid. That we may be sure of our welcome, we have brought our entertainment with us, and are resolved to treat thee, dear toad.

Mrs. Dain. And that we may be merry to purpose, have left Sir Jasper and my old Lady Squeamish quarrelling at home at backgammon.

Mrs. Squeam. Therefore let us make use of our time, lest they should chance to interrupt us.

Lady Fid. Let us sit then.

Horn. First, that you may be private, let me lock this door and that, and I'll wait upon you presently.

Lady Fid. No, sir, shut 'em only, and your lips for ever; for we must trust you as much as our women.

Horn. You know all vanity's killed in me; I have no occasion for talking.

Lady Fid. Now, ladies, supposing we had drank each of us two bottles, let us speak the truth of our hearts.

Mrs. Dain. and Mrs. Squeam. Agreed.

Lady Fid. By this brimmer, for truth is nowhere else to be found—[*aside to* HORNER] not in thy heart, false man!

Horn. You have found me a true man, I'm sure.

      [*Aside to* Lady FIDGET.

Lady Fid. [*Aside to* HORNER.] Not every way.—But let us sit and be merry.   [*Sings.*

> Why should our damned tyrants oblige us to live
> On the pittance of pleasure which they only give?
>   We must not rejoice
>   With wine and with noise:
> In vain we must wake in a dull bed alone,
> Whilst to our warm rival the bottle they're gone.
>   Then lay aside charms,
>   And take up these arms.
> 'Tis wine only gives 'em their courage and wit;
> Because we live sober, to men we submit.

If for beauties you'd pass,
   Take a lick of the glass,
'Twill mend your complexions, and when they are gone,
   The best red we have is the red of the grape:
Then, sisters, lay't on,
   And damn a good shape.

Mrs. Dain. Dear brimmer! Well, in token of our openness and plain-dealing, let us throw our masks over our heads.

Horn. So, 'twill come to the glasses anon.   [*Aside.*

Mrs. Squeam. Lovely brimmer! let me enjoy him first.

Lady Fid. No, I never part with a gallant till I've tried him. Dear brimmer! that makest our husbands short-sighted.

Mrs. Dain. And our bashful gallants bold.

Mrs. Squeam. And, for want of a gallant, the butler lovely in our eyes.—Drink, eunuch.

Lady Fid. Drink, thou representative of a husband. Damn a husband!

Mrs. Dain. And, as it were a husband, an old keeper.

Mrs. Squeam. And an old grandmother.

Horn. And an English bawd, and a French surgeon.

Lady Fid. Ay, we have all reason to curse 'em.

Horn. For my sake, ladies?

Lady Fid. No, for our own; for the first spoils all young gallants' industry.

Mrs. Dain. And the other's art makes 'em bold only with common women.

Mrs. Squeam. And rather run the hazard of the vile distemper amongst them, than of a denial amongst us.

Mrs. Dain. The filthy toads choose mistresses now as they do stuffs, for having been fancied and worn by others.

Mrs. Squeam. For being common and cheap.

Lady Fid. Whilst women of quality, like the richest stuffs, lie untumbled, and unasked for.

Horn. Ay, neat, and cheap, and new, often they think best.

Mrs. Dain. No, sir, the beasts will be known by a mistress longer than by a suit.

Mrs. Squeam. And 'tis not for cheapness neither.

Lady Fid. No; for the vain fops will take up druggets and embroider 'em. But I wonder at the depraved appetites of witty men; they used to be out of the common road, and hate imitation. Pray tell me, beast, when you were a man, why you rather chose to club with a multitude in a common house for an entertainment. than to be the only guest at a good table.

Horn. Why, faith, ceremony and expectation are unsufferable to those that are sharp bent. People always eat with the best stomach at an ordinary, where every man is snatching for the best bit.

Lady Fid. Though he get a cut over the fingers.—But I have heard, that people eat most heartily of another man's meat, that is, what they do not pay for.

Horn. When they are sure of their welcome and freedom; for ceremony in love and eating is as ridiculous as in fighting: falling on briskly is all should be done on those occasions.

Lady Fid. Well, then, let me tell you, sir, there is nowhere more freedom than in our houses; and we take freedom from a young person as a sign of good breeding; and a person may be as free as he pleases with us, as frolic, as gamesome, as wild as he will.

Horn. Han't I heard you all declaim against wild men?

Lady Fid. Yes; but for all that, we think wildness in a man as desirable a quality as in a duck or rabbit: a tame man! foh!

Horn. I know not, but your reputations frightened me as much as your faces invited me.

Lady Fid. Our reputation! Lord, why should you not think that we women make use of our reputation, as you men of yours, only to deceive the world with less suspicion? Our virtue is like the statesman's religion, the quaker's word, the gamester's oath, and the great man's honour; but to cheat those that trust us.

Mrs. Squeam. And that demureness, coyness, and modesty, that you see in our faces in the boxes at plays, is as much a sign of a kind woman, as a vizard-mask in the pit.

Mrs. Dain. For, I assure you, women are least masked when they have the velvet vizard on.

Lady Fid. You would have found us modest women in our denials only.

Mrs. Squeam. Our bashfulness is only the reflection of the men's.

Mrs. Dain. We blush when they are shamefaced.

Horn. I beg your pardon, ladies, I was deceived in you devilishly. But why that mighty pretence to honour?

Lady Fid. We have told you; but sometimes 'twas for the same reason you men pretend business often, to avoid ill company, to enjoy the better and more privately those you love.

Horn. But why would you ne'er give a friend a wink then?

Lady Fid. Faith, your reputation frightened us, as much as ours did you, you were so notoriously lewd.

Horn. And you so seemingly honest.

Lady Fid. Was that all that deterred you?

Horn. And so expensive—you allow freedom, you say.

Lady Fid. Ay, ay.

Horn. That I was afraid of losing my little money, as well as my little time, both which my other pleasures required.

Lady Fid. Money! foh! you talk like a little fellow now: do such as we expect money?

Horn. I beg your pardon, madam, I must confess, I have heard that great ladies, like great merchants, set but the higher prices upon what they have, because they are not in necessity of taking the first offer.

Mrs. Dain. Such as we make sale of our hearts?

Mrs. Squeam. We bribed for our love? foh!

Horn. With your pardon, ladies, I know, like great men in offices, you seem to exact flattery and attendance only from your followers; but you have receivers about you, and such fees to pay, a man is afraid to pass your grants. Besides, we must let you win at cards, or we lose your hearts; and if you make an assignation, 'tis at a goldsmith's, jeweller's, or china-house; where for your honour you deposit to him, he must pawn his to the punctual cit, and so paying for what you take up, pays for what he takes up.

Mrs. Dain. Would you not have us assured of our gallants' love?

Mrs. Squeam. For love is better known by liberality than by jealousy.

Lady Fid. For one may be dissembled, the other not.—[*Aside.*] But my jealousy can be no longer dissembled, and they are telling ripe.—[*Aloud.*]—Come, here's to our gallants in waiting, whom we must name, and I'll begin. This is my false rogue.
                                        [*Claps him on the back.*

Mrs. Squeam. How!

Horn. So, all will out now.   [*Aside.*

Mrs. Squeam. Did you not tell me, 'twas for my sake only you reported yourself no man?   [*Aside to* HORNER.

Mrs. Dain. Oh, wretch! did you not swear to me, 'twas for my love and honour you passed for that thing you do?
                                        [*Aside to* HORNER.

Horn. So, so.

Lady Fid. Come, speak, ladies: this is my false villain.

Mrs. Squeam. And mine too.

Mrs. Dain. And mine.

Horn. Well then, you are all three my false rogues too, and there's an end on't

Lady Fid. Well then, there's no remedy; sister sharers, let us not fall out, but have a care of our honour. Though we get no presents, no jewels of him, we are savers of our honour, the jewel of most value and use, which shines yet to the world unsuspected, though it be counterfeit.

Horn. Nay, and is e'en as good as if it were true, provided the world think so; for honour, like beauty now, only depends on the opinion of others.

Lady Fid. Well, Harry Common, I hope you can be true to three. Swear; but 'tis to no purpose to require your oath, for you are as often forsworn as you swear to new women.

Horn. Come, faith, madam, let us e'en pardon one another; for all the difference I find betwixt we men and you women, we forswear ourselves at the beginning of an amour, you as long as it lasts.

Enter Sir JASPER FIDGET, *and* Old Lady SQUEAMISH.

Sir Jasp. Oh, my Lady Fidget, was this your cunning, to come to Mr. Horner without me? but you have been nowhere else, I hope.

Lady Fid. No, Sir Jasper.

Lady Squeam. And you came straight hither, Biddy?

Mrs. Squeam. Yes, indeed, lady grandmother.

Sir Jasp. 'Tis well, 'tis well; I knew when once they were thoroughly acquainted with poor Horner, they'd ne'er be from him: you may let her masquerade it with my wife and Horner, and I warrant her reputation safe.

Enter Boy.

Boy. O, sir, here's the gentleman come, whom you bid me not suffer to come up, without giving you notice, with a lady too, and other gentlemen.

Horn. Do you all go in there, whilst I send 'em away; and, boy, do you desire 'em to stay below till I come, which shall be immediately.

[*Exeunt* Sir JASPER FIDGET, Lady FIDGET, Lady SQUEAM-
ISH, Mrs. SQUEAMISH, *and* Mrs. DAINTY FIDGET.

Boy. Yes, sir. [*Exit.*

[*Exit* HORNER *at the other door, and returns with* Mrs.
PINCHWIFE.

Horn. You would not take my advice, to be gone home before your husband came back, he'll now discover all; yet pray, my dearest, be persuaded to go home, and leave the rest to my management; I'll let you down the back way.

Mrs. Pinch. I don't know the way home, so I don't.

Horn. My man shall wait upon you.

Mrs. Pinch. No, don't you believe that I'll go at all; what, are you weary of me already?

Horn. No, my life, 'tis that I may love you long, 'tis to secure my love, and your reputation with your husband; he'll never receive you again else.

Mrs. Pinch. What care I? d'ye think to frighten me with that? I don't intend to go to him again; you shall be my husband now.

Horn. I cannot be your husband, dearest, since you are married to him.

Mrs. Pinch. O, would you make me believe that? Don't I see every day at London here, women leave their first husbands, and go and live with other men as their wives? pish, pshaw! you'd make me angry, but that I love you so mainly.

Horn. So, they are coming up—In again, in, I hear 'em.—— [*Exit* Mrs. PINCHWIFE.] Well, a silly mistress is like a weak place, soon got, soon lost, a man has scarce time for plunder; she betrays her husband first to her gallant, and then her gallant to her husband.

Enter PINCHWIFE, ALITHEA, HARCOURT, SPARKISH, LUCY, *and a* Parson.

Pinch. Come, madam, 'tis not the sudden change of your dress, the confidence of your asseverations, and your false witness there, shall persuade me I did not bring you hither just now; here's my witness, who cannot deny it, since you must be confronted.— Mr. Horner, did not I bring this lady to you just now?

Horn. Now must I wrong one woman for another's sake,— but that's no new thing with me, for in these cases I am still on the criminal's side against the innocent. [*Aside.*

Alith. Pray speak, sir.

Horn. It must be so. I must be impudent, and try my luck; impudence uses to be too hard for truth. [*Aside.*

Pinch. What, you are studying an evasion or excuse for her! Speak, sir.

Horn. No, faith, I am something backward only to speak in women's affairs or disputes.

Pinch. She bids you speak.

Alith. Ah, pray, sir, do, pray satisfy him.

Horn. Then truly, you did bring that lady to me just now.

Pinch. O-ho!

Alith. How, sir?

Har. How, Horner?

Alith. What mean you, sir? I always took you for a man of honour.

Horn. Ay, so much a man of honour, that I must save my mistress, I thank you, come what will on't. [*Aside*

Spark. So, if I had had her, she'd have made me believe the moon had been made of a Christmas pie.

Lucy. Now could I speak, if I durst, and solve the riddle, who am the author of it. [*Aside*

Alith. O unfortunate woman! A combination against my honour! which most concerns me now, because you share in my disgrace, sir, and it is your censure, which I must now suffer that troubles me, not theirs.

Har. Madam, then have no trouble, you shall now see 'tis possible for me to love too, without being jealous; I will not only believe your innocence myself, but make all the world believe it.—[*Aside to* HORNER.] Horner, I must now be concerned for this lady's honour.

Horn. And I must be concerned for a lady's honour too.

Har. This lady has her honour, and I will protect it.

Horn. My lady has not her honour, but has given it me to keep, and I will preserve it.

Har. I understand you not.

Horn. I would not have you.

Mrs. Pinch. What's the matter with 'em all?
[*Peeping in behind*

Pinch. Come, come, Mr. Horner, no more disputing; here's the parson, I brought him not in vain.

Har. No, sir, I'll employ him, if this lady please.

Pinch. How! what d'ye mean?

Spark. Ay, what does he mean?

Horn. Why, I have resigned your sister to him, he has my consent.

Pinch. But he has not mine, sir; a woman's injured honour no more than a man's, can be repaired or satisfied by any but him that first wronged it; and you shall marry her presently, or——
[*Lays his hand on his sword*

Re-enter Mrs. PINCHWIFE.

Mrs. Pinch. O Lord, they'll kill poor Mr. Horner! besides, he shan't marry her whilst I stand by, and look on; I'll not lose my second husband so.

Pinch. What do I see?

Alith. My sister in my clothes!

Spark. Ha!

Mrs. Pinch. Nay, pray now don't quarrel about finding work for the parson, he shall marry me to Mr. Horner; or now, I believe, you have enough of me.   [*To* PINCHWIFE.

Horn. Damned, damned loving changeling!   [*Aside.*

Mrs. Pinch. Pray, sister, pardon me for telling so many lies of you.

Horn. I suppose the riddle is plain now.

Lucy. No, that must be my work.—Good sir, hear me.

    [*Kneels to* PINCHWIFE, *who stands doggedly with his hat over his eyes.*

Pinch. I will never hear woman again, but make 'em all silent thus——   [*Offers to draw upon his* Wife.

Horn. No, that must not be.

Pinch. You then shall go first, 'tis all one to me.

    [*Offers to draw on* HORNER, *but is stopped by* HARCOURT.

Har. Hold!

Re-enter Sir JASPER FIDGET, Lady FIDGET, Lady SQUEAMISH, Mrs. DAINTY FIDGET, *and* Mrs. SQUEAMISH.

Sir Jasp. What's the matter? what's the matter? pray, what's the matter, sir? I beseech you communicate, sir.

Pinch. Why, my wife has communicated, sir, as your wife may have done too, sir, if she knows him, sir.

Sir Jasp. Pshaw, with him! ha! ha! he!

Pinch. D'ye mock me, sir? a cuckold is a kind of a wild beast; have a care, sir.

Sir Jasp. No, sure, you mock me, sir. He cuckold you! it can't be, ha! ha! he! why, I'll tell you, sir——

    [*Offers to whisper.*

Pinch. I tell you again, he has whored my wife, and yours too, if he knows her, and all the women he comes near; 'tis not his dissembling, his hypocrisy, can wheedle me.

Sir Jasp. How! does he dissemble? is he a hypocrite? Nay, then—how—wife—sister, is he a hypocrite?

Lady Squeam. A hypocrite! a dissembler! Speak, young harlotry, speak, how?

Sir Jasp. Nay, then—O my head too!—O thou libidinous lady!

Lady Squeam. O thou harloting harlotry! hast thou done't then?

Sir Jasp. Speak, good Horner, art thou a dissembler, a rogue? hast thou——

Horn. So!

Lucy. I'll fetch you off, and her too, if she will but hold her tongue.   [*Apart to* HORNER.

Horn. Canst thou? I'll give thee——   [*Apart to* LUCY.

Lucy. [*To* PINCHWIFE.] Pray have but patience to hear me, sir, who am the unfortunate cause of all this confusion. Your wife is innocent, I only culpable; for I put her upon telling you all these lies concerning my mistress, in order to the breaking off the match between Mr. Sparkish and her, to make way for Mr. Harcourt.

Spark. Did you so, eternal rotten tooth? Then, it seems, my mistress was not false to me, I was only deceived by you. Brother, that should have been, now man of conduct, who is a frank person now, to bring your wife to her lover, ha?

Lucy. I assure you, sir, she came not to Mr. Horner out of love, for she loves him no more——

Mrs. Pinch. Hold, I told lies for you, but you shall tell none for me, for I do love Mr. Horner with all my soul, and nobody shall say me nay; pray, don't you go to make poor Mr. Horner believe to the contrary; 'tis spitefully done of you, I'm sure.

Horn. Peace, dear idiot.   [*Aside to* Mrs. PINCHWIFE.

Mrs. Pinch. Nay, I will not peace.

Pinch. Not till I make you.

Enter DORILANT *and* QUACK.

Dor. Horner, your servant; I am the doctor's guest, he must excuse our intrusion.

Quack. But what's the matter, gentlemen? for Heaven's sake, what's the matter?

Horn. Oh, 'tis well you are come. 'Tis a censorious world we live in; you may have brought me a reprieve, or else I had died for a crime I never committed, and these innocent ladies had suffered with me; therefore, pray satisfy these worthy, honourable, jealous gentlemen—that——   [*Whispers.*

Quack. O, I understand you, is that all?—Sir Jasper, by Heavens, and upon the word of a physician, sir——

    [*Whispers to* Sir JASPER.

Sir Jasp. Nay, I do believe you truly.—Pardon me, my virtuous lady, and dear of honour.

Lady Squeam. What, then all's right again?

Sir Jasp. Ay, ay, and now let us satisfy him too.

    [*They whisper with* PINCHWIFE.

Pinch. An eunuch! Pray, no fooling with me.

Quack. I'll bring half the chirurgeons in town to swear it.

Pinch. They!—they'll swear a man that bled to death through his wounds. died of an apoplexy.

Quack. Pray, hear me, sir—why, all the town has heard the report of him.

Pinch. But does all the town believe it?

Quack. Pray, inquire a little, and first of all these.

Pinch. I'm sure when I left the town, he was the lewdest fellow in't.

Quack. I tell you, sir, he has been in France since; pray, ask but these ladies and gentlemen, your friend Mr. Dorilant. Gentlemen and ladies, han't you all heard the late sad report of poor Mr. Horner?

All the Ladies. Ay, ay, ay.

Dor. Why, thou jealous fool, dost thou doubt it? he's an arrant French capon.

Mrs. Pinch. 'Tis false, sir, you shall not disparage poor Mr. Horner, for to my certain knowledge——

Lucy. O, hold!

Mrs. Squeam. Stop her mouth!   [*Aside to* Lucy.

Lady Fid. Upon my honour, sir, 'tis as true——

[*To* Pinchwife.

Mrs. Dain. D'ye think we would have been seen in his company?

Mrs. Squeam. Trust our unspotted reputations with him?

Lady Fid. This you get, and we too, by trusting your secret to a fool.   [*Aside to* Horner.

Horn. Peace, madam.—[*Aside to* Quack.] Well, doctor, is not this a good design, that carries a man on unsuspected, and brings him off safe?

Pinch. Well, if this were true—but my wife——   [*Aside*.

[Dorilant *whispers with* Mrs. Pinchwife.

Alith. Come, brother, your wife is yet innocent, you see; but have a care of too strong an imagination, lest, like an over-concerned timorous gamester, by fancying an unlucky cast, it should come. Women and fortune are truest still to those that trust 'em.

Lucy. And any wild thing grows but the more fierce and hungry for being kept up, and more dangerous to the keeper.

Alith. There's doctrine for all husbands, Mr. Harcourt.

Har. I edify, madam, so much, that I am impatient till I am one.

Dor. And I edify so much by example, I will never be one.

Spark. And because I will not disparage my parts, I'll ne'er be one.

Horn. And I, alas! can't be one.

Pinch. But I must be one—against my will to a country wife, with a country murrain to me!

Mrs. Pinch. And I must be a country wife still too, I find; for I can't, like a city one, be rid of my musty husband, and do what I list. [*Aside.*

Horn. Now, sir, I must pronounce your wife innocent, though I blush whilst I do it; and I am the only man by her now exposed to shame, which I will straight drown in wine, as you shall your suspicion; and the ladies' troubles we'll divert with a ballad.— Doctor, where are your maskers?

Lucy. Indeed, she's innocent, sir, I am her witness; and her end of coming out was but to see her sister's wedding; and what she has said to your face of her love to Mr. Horner, was but the usual innocent revenge on a husband's jealousy—was it not, madam, speak?

Mrs. Pinch. [*aside to* LUCY *and* HORNER]. Since you'll have me tell more lies—[*Aloud.*] Yes, indeed, bud.

Pinch. For my own sake fain I would all believe;
    Cuckolds, like lovers, should themselves deceive.
    But—— [*Sighs.*
    His honour is least safe (too late I find)
    Who trusts it with a foolish wife or friend.

A Dance of Cuckolds.

Horn. Vain fops but court and dress, and keep a pother,
    To pass for women's men with one another;
    But he who aims by women to be prized,
    First by the men, you see, must be despised. [*Exeunt.*

EPILOGUE

SPOKEN BY MRS. KNEP

Now you the vigorous, who daily here
O'er vizard-mask in public domineer,
And what you'd do to her, if in place where;
Nay, have the confidence to cry, "Come out!"
Yet when she says, "Lead on!" you are not stout;
But to your well-dressed brother straight turn round,
And cry, "Pox on her, Ned, she can't be sound!"
Then slink away, a fresh one to engage,
With so much seeming heat and loving rage,
You'd frighten listening actress on the stage;
Till she at last has seen you huffing come,
And talk of keeping in the tiring-room,
Yet cannot be provoked to lead her home.
Next, you Falstaffs of fifty, who beset
Your buckram maidenheads, which your friends get;
And whilst to them you of achievements boast,
They share the booty, and laugh at your cost.
In fine, you essenced boys, both old and young,
Who would be thought so eager, brisk, and strong,
Yet do the ladies, not their husbands wrong;
Whose purses for your manhood make excuse,
And keep your Flanders mares for show not use;
Encouraged by our woman's man to-day,
A Horner's part may vainly think to play;
And may intrigues so bashfully disown,
That they may doubted be by few or none;
May kiss the cards at picquet, ombre, loo,
And so be taught to kiss the lady too;
But, gallants, have a care, faith, what you do.
The world, which to no man his due will give,
You by experience know you can deceive,
And men may still believe you vigorous,
But then we women—there's no cozening us.

ALL FOR LOVE

by

JOHN DRYDEN

ALL FOR LOVE

OR, THE WORLD WELL LOST

by

JOHN DRYDEN

TO THE RIGHT HONOURABLE
THOMAS, EARL OF DANBY

Viscount Latimer, and Baron Osborne of Kiveton, in Yorkshire;
Lord High Treasurer of England, one of His Majesty's Most
Honourable Privy Council, and Knight of the Most Noble Order
of the Garter.

MY LORD,—The gratitude of poets is so troublesome a virtue
to great men, that you are often in danger of your own benefits:
for you are threatened with some epistle, and not suffered to do
good in quiet, or to compound for their silence whom you have
obliged. Yet, I confess, I neither am nor ought to be surprised
at this indulgence; for your lordship has the same right to favour
poetry, which the great and noble have ever had—

> *Carmen amat, quisquis carmine digna gerit.*

There is somewhat of a tie in nature betwixt those who are
born for worthy actions, and those who can transmit them to
posterity; and though ours be much the inferior part, it comes
at least within the verge of alliance; nor are we unprofitable members of the commonwealth, when we animate others to those
virtues, which we copy and describe from you.

It is indeed their interest, who endeavour the subversion of
governments, to discourage poets and historians; for the best
which can happen to them, is to be forgotten. But such who, under
kings, are the fathers of their country, and by a just and prudent
ordering of affairs preserve it, have the same reason to cherish
the chroniclers of their actions, as they have to lay up in safety
the deeds and evidences of their estates; for such records are
their undoubted titles to the love and reverence of after ages.
Your lordship's administration has already taken up a considerable part of the English annals; and many of its most happy years
are owing to it. His Majesty, the most knowing judge of men,

and the best master, has acknowledged the ease and benefit he
receives in the incomes of his treasury, which you found not only
disordered, but exhausted. All things were in the confusion of a
chaos, without form or method, if not reduced beyond it, even
to annihilation; so that you had not only to separate the jarring
elements, but (if that boldness of expression might be allowed
me) to create them. Your enemies had so embroiled the management of your office, that they looked on your advancement as the
instrument of your ruin. And as if the clogging of the revenue,
and the confusion of accounts, which you found in your entrance,
were not sufficient, they added their own weight of malice to the
public calamity, by forestalling the credit which should cure it.
Your friends on the other side were only capable of pitying, but
not of aiding you; no further help or counsel was remaining to
you, but what was founded on yourself; and that indeed was
your security; for your diligence, your constancy, and your
prudence, wrought most surely within, when they were not disturbed by any outward motion. The highest virtue is best to be
trusted with itself; for assistance only can be given by a genius
superior to that which it assists; and it is the noblest kind of debt,
when we are only obliged to God and nature. This then, my lord,
is your just commendation, that you have wrought out yourself
a way to glory, by those very means that were designed for your
destruction. You have not only restored but advanced the rev-
enues of your master, without grievance to the subject; and, as
if that were little yet, the debts of the exchequer, which lay
heaviest both on the crown, and on private persons, have by your
conduct been established in a certainty of satisfaction. An action
so much the more great and honourable, because the case was
without the ordinary relief of laws; above the hopes of the afflicted
and beyond the narrowness of the treasury to redress, had it been
managed by a less able hand. It is certainly the happiest, and
most unenvied part of all your fortune, to do good to many, while
you do injury to none; to receive at once the prayers of the
subject, and the praises of the prince; and, by the care of your
conduct, to give him means of exerting the chiefest (if any be
the chiefest) of his royal virtues, his distributive justice to the
deserving, and his bounty and compassion to the wanting. The
disposition of princes towards their people cannot be better discovered than in the choice of their ministers; who, like the animal
spirits betwixt the soul and body, participate somewhat of both
natures, and make the communication which is betwixt them.
A king, who is just and moderate in his nature, who rules according
to the laws, whom God has made happy by forming the temper

of his soul to the constitution of his government, and who makes us happy, by assuming over us no other sovereignty than that wherein our welfare and liberty consists; a prince, I say, of so excellent a character, and so suitable to the wishes of all good men, could not better have conveyed himself into his people's apprehensions, than in your lordship's person; who so lively express the same virtues, that you seem not so much a copy, as an emanation of him. Moderation is doubtless an establishment of greatness; but there is a steadiness of temper which is likewise requisite in a minister of state; so equal a mixture of both virtues, that he may stand like an isthmus betwixt the two encroaching seas of arbitrary power, and lawless anarchy. The undertaking would be difficult to any but an extraordinary genius, to stand at the line, and to divide the limits; to pay what is due to the great representative of the nation, and neither to enhance, nor to yield up, the undoubted prerogatives of the crown. These, my lord, are the proper virtues of a noble Englishman, as indeed they are properly English virtues; no people in the world being capable of using them, but we who have the happiness to be born under so equal, and so well-poised a government;—a government which has all the advantages of liberty beyond a commonwealth, and all the marks of kingly sovereignty, without the danger of a tyranny. Both my nature, as I am an Englishman, and my reason, as I am a man, have bred in me a loathing to that specious name of a republic; that mock appearance of a liberty, where all who have not part in the government, are slaves; and slaves they are of a viler note, than such as are subjects to an absolute dominion. For no Christian monarchy is so absolute, but it is circumscribed with laws; but when the executive power is in the law-makers, there is no further check upon them; and the people must suffer without a remedy, because they are oppressed by their representatives. If I must serve, the number of my masters, who were born my equals, would but add to the ignominy of my bondage. The nature of our government, above all others, is exactly suited both to the situation of our country, and the temper of the natives; an island being more proper for commerce and for defence, than for extending its dominions on the Continent; for what the valour of its inhabitants might gain, by reason of its remoteness, and the casualties of the seas, it could not so easily preserve. And, therefore, neither the arbitrary power of One, in a monarchy, nor of Many, in a commonwealth, could make us greater than we are. It is true, that vaster and more frequent taxes might be gathered, when the consent of the people was not asked or needed; but this were only by conquering abroad, to be poor at home; and the examples of our neighbours teach us, that they are not always the happiest subjects, whose kings extend their dominions farthest. Since therefore we cannot win by an offensive war, at least a land war, the model of our government seems naturally contrived for the defensive part; and the consent of a people is easily obtained to contribute to that power which must protect it. *Felices nimium, bona si sua nôrint, Angligenæ!* And yet there are not wanting malcontents among us, who, surfeiting themselves on too much happiness, would persuade the people that they might be happier by a change. It was indeed the policy of their old forefather, when himself was fallen from the station of glory, to seduce mankind into the same rebellion with him, by telling him he might yet be freer than he was; that is more free than his nature would allow, or, if I may so say, than God could make him. We have already all the liberty which freeborn subjects can enjoy, and all beyond it is but licence. But if it be liberty of conscience which they pretend, the moderation of our church is such, that its practice extends not to the severity of persecution; and its discipline is withal so easy, that it allows more freedom to dissenters than any of the sects would allow to it. In the meantime, what right can be pretended by these men to attempt innovation in church or state? Who made them the trustees, or to speak a little nearer their own language, the keepers of the liberty of England? If their call be extraordinary, let them convince us by working miracles; for ordinary vocation they can have none, to disturb the government under which they were born, and which protects them. He who has often changed his party, and always has made his interest the rule of it, gives little evidence of his sincerity for the public good; it is manifest he changes but for himself, and takes the people for tools to work his fortune. Yet the experience of all ages might let him know, that they who trouble the waters first, have seldom the benefit of the fishing; as they who began the late rebellion enjoyed not the fruit of their undertaking, but were crushed themselves by the usurpation of their own instrument. Neither is it enough for them to answer, that they only intend a reformation of the government, but not the subversion of it: on such pretence all insurrections have been founded; it is striking at the foot of power, which is obedience. Every remonstrance of private men has the seed of treason in it; and discourses, which are couched in ambiguous terms, are therefore the more dangerous, because they do all the mischief of open sedition, yet are safe from the punishment of the laws. These, my lord, are considerations, which I should not pass so lightly over, had I room to manage them as they deserve; for no man can be so inconsiderable in a nation, as not to have a share in the welfare of it; and if he be a true Englishman, he must at the same time be fired with indignation, and revenge himself as he can on the disturbers of his country. And to whom could I more fitly apply myself than to your lordship, who have not only an inborn, but an hereditary loyalty? The memorable constancy and sufferings of your father, almost to the ruin of his estate, for the royal cause, were an earnest of that which such a parent and such an institution would produce in the person of a son. But so unhappy an occasion of manifesting your own zeal, in suffering for his present majesty, the providence of God, and the prudence of your administration, will, I hope, prevent; that, as your father's fortune waited on the unhappiness of his sovereign, so your own may participate of the better fate which attends his son. The relation which you have by alliance to the noble family of your lady, serves to confirm to you both this happy augury. For what can deserve a greater place in the English chronicle, than the loyalty and courage, the actions and death, of the general of an army, fighting for his prince and country? The honor and gallantry of the Earl of Lindsey is so illustrious a subject, that it is fit to adorn an heroic poem; for he was the proto-martyr of the cause, and the type of his unfortunate royal master.

Yet after all, my lord, if I may speak my thoughts, you are happy rather to us than to yourself; for the multiplicity, the cares, and the vexations of your employment, have betrayed you from yourself, and given you up into the possession of the public. You are robbed of your privacy and friends, and scarce any hour of your life you can call your own. Those, who envy your fortune, if they wanted not good-nature, might more justly pity it; and when they see you watched by a crowd of suitors, whose importunity it is impossible to avoid, would conclude, with reason, that you have lost much more in true content, than you have gained by dignity; and that a private gentleman is better attended by a single servant, than your lordship with so clamorous a train. Pardon me, my lord, if I speak like a philosopher on this subject; the fortune which makes a man uneasy, cannot make him happy; and a wise man must think himself uneasy, when few of his actions are in his choice.

This last consideration has brought me to another, and a very seasonable one for your relief; which is, that while I pity your want of leisure, I have impertinently detained you so long a time. I have put off my own business, which was my dedication, till it is so late, that I am now ashamed to begin it; and therefore I will say nothing of the poem, which I present to you, because I know not if you are like to have an hour, which, with a good conscience, you may throw away in perusing it; and for the author, I have only to beg the continuance of your protection to him, who is, my lord, your lordship's most obliged, most humble, and most obedient servant,

JOHN DRYDEN.

PREFACE

The death of Antony and Cleopatra is a subject which has been treated by the greatest wits of our nation, after Shakespeare; and by all so variously, that their example has given me the confidence to try myself in this bow of Ulysses amongst the crowd of suitors; and, withal, to take my own measures, in aiming at the mark. I doubt not but the same motive has prevailed with all of us in this attempt; I mean the excellency of the moral. For the chief persons represented were famous patterns of unlawful love; and their end accordingly was unfortunate. All reasonable men have long since concluded, that the hero of the poem ought not to be a character of perfect virtue, for then he could not, without injustice, be made unhappy; nor yet altogether wicked, because he could not then be pitied. I have therefore steered the middle course; and have drawn the character of Antony as favourably as Plutarch, Appian, and Dion Cassius would give me leave; the like I have observed in Cleopatra. That which is wanting to work up the pity to a greater height, was not afforded me by the story; for the crimes of love, which they both committed, were not occasioned by any necessity, or fatal ignorance, but were wholly voluntary; since our passions are, or ought to be, within our power. The fabric of the play is regular enough, as to the inferior parts of it; and the unities of time, place, and action, more exactly observed, than perhaps the English theatre requires. Particularly, the action is so much one, that it is the only of the kind without episode, or underplot; every scene in the tragedy conducing to the main design, and every act concluding with a turn of it. The greatest error in the contrivance seems to be in the person of Octavia; for, though I might use the privilege of a poet, to introduce her into Alexandria, yet I had not enough considered, that the compassion she moved to herself and children was destructive to that which I reserved for Antony and Cleopatra; whose mutual love being founded upon vice, must lessen the favour of the audience to them, when virtue and innocence were oppressed by it. And, though I justified Antony in some measure, by making Octavia's departure to proceed wholly from herself; yet the force of the first machine still remained; and the dividing of pity, like the cutting of a

river into many channels, abated the strength of the natural
stream. But this is an objection which none of my critics have
urged against me, and therefore I might have let it pass, if I
could have resolved to have been partial to myself. The faults
my enemies have found are rather cavils concerning little and
not essential decencies; which a master of the ceremonies may
decide betwixt us. The French poets, I confess, are strict observers of these punctilios. They would not, for example, have
suffered Cleopatra and Octavia to have met; or, if they had
met, there must have only passed betwixt them some cold civilities, but no eagerness of repartee, for fear of offending against
the greatness of their characters, and the modesty of their sex.
This objection I foresaw, and at the same time contemned; for
I judged it both natural and probable, that Octavia, proud of
her new-gained conquest, would search out Cleopatra to triumph
over her; and that Cleopatra, thus attacked, was not of a spirit
to shun the encounter. And it is not unlikely, that two exas-
perated rivals should use such satire as I have put into their
mouths; for, after all, though the one were a Roman, and the
other a queen, they were both women. It is true, some actions,
though natural, are not fit to be represented; and broad ob-
scenities in words ought in good manners to be avoided: expressions therefore are a modest clothing of our thoughts, as breeches
and petticoats are of our bodies. If I have kept myself within
the bounds of modesty, all beyond, it is but nicety and affectation;
which is no more but modesty depraved into a vice. They betray
themselves who are too quick of apprehension in such cases, and
leave all reasonable men to imagine worse of them, than of the
poet.

Honest Montaigne goes yet further: *Nous ne sommes que
cérémonie; la cérémonie nous emporte, et laissons la substance
des choses. Nous nous tenons aux branches, et abandonnons le
tronc et le corps. Nous avons appris aux dames de rougir, oyans
seulement nommer ce qu'elles ne craignent aucunement à faire:
Nous n'osons appeller à droit nos membres, et ne craignons pas de
les employer à toute sorte de débauche. La cérémonie nous défend
d'exprimer par paroles les choses licites et naturelles, et nous l'en
croyons; la raison nous défend de n'en faire point d'illicites et
mauvaises, et personne ne l'en croit.* My comfort is, that by this
opinion my enemies are but sucking critics, who would fain be
nibbling ere their teeth are come.

Yet, in this nicety of manners does the excellency of French
poetry consist. Their heroes are the most civil people breathing;
but their good breeding seldom extends to a word of sense; all

their wit is in their ceremony; they want the genius which ani-
mates our stage; and therefore it is but necessary, when they
cannot please, that they should take care not to offend. But as
the civilest man in the company is commonly the dullest, so these
authors, while they are afraid to make you laugh or cry, out of
pure good manners make you sleep. They are so careful not to
exasperate a critic, that they never leave him any work; so busy
with the broom, and make so clean a riddance that there is little
left either for censure or for praise. For no part of a poem is
worth our discommending, where the whole is insipid; as when
we have once tasted of pallid wine, we stay not to examine it
glass by glass. But while they affect to shine in trifles, they are
often careless in essentials. Thus, their Hippolytus is so scrupulous in point of decency, that he will rather expose himself to
death, than accuse his stepmother to his father; and my critics
I am sure will commend him for it. But we of grosser apprehensions are apt to think that this excess of generosity is not practicable, but with fools and madmen. This was good manners with
a vengeance; and the audience is like to be much concerned at
the misfortunes of this admirable hero. But take Hippolytus out
of his poetic fit, and I suppose he would think it a wiser part
to set the saddle on the right horse, and choose rather to live
with the reputation of a plain-spoken, honest man, than to die
with the infamy of an incestuous villain. In the meantime we may
take notice, that where the poet ought to have preserved the
character as it was delivered to us by antiquity, when he should
have given us the picture of a rough young man, of the Ama-
zonian strain, a jolly huntsman, and both by his profession and
his early rising a mortal enemy to love, he has chosen to give
him the turn of gallantry, sent him to travel from Athens to
Paris, taught him to make love, and transformed the Hippolytus
of Euripides into Monsieur Hippolyte. I should not have troubled
myself thus far with French poets, but that I find our *Chedreux*
critics wholly form their judgments by them. But for my part,
I desire to be tried by the laws of my own country; for it seems
unjust to me, that the French should prescribe here, till they
have conquered. Our little sonneteers, who follow them, have
too narrow souls to judge of poetry. Poets themselves are the
most proper, though I conclude not the only critics. But till some
genius, as universal as Aristotle, shall arise, one who can penetrate
into all arts and sciences, without the practice of them, I shall
think it reasonable, that the judgment of an artificer in his own
art should be preferable to the opinion of another man; at least
where he is not bribed by interest, or prejudiced by malice. And

this, I suppose, is manifest by plain inductions. For, first, the crowd cannot be presumed to have more than a gross instinct, of what pleases or displeases them. Every man will grant me this; but then, by a particular kindness to himself, he draws his own stake first, and will be distinguished from the multitude, of which other men may think him one. But, if I come closer to those who are allowed for witty men, either by the advantage of their quality, or by common fame, and affirm that neither are they qualified to decide sovereignly concerning poetry, I shall yet have a strong party of my opinion; for most of them severally will exclude the rest, either from the number of witty men, or at least of able judges. But here again they are all indulgent to themselves; and every one who believes himself a wit, that is, every man, will pretend at the same time to a right of judging. But to press it yet further, there are many witty men, but few poets; neither have all poets a taste of tragedy. And this is the rock on which they are daily splitting. Poetry, which is a picture of nature, must generally please; but it is not to be understood that all parts of it must please every man; therefore is not tragedy to be judged by a witty man, whose taste is only confined to comedy. Nor is every man, who loves tragedy, a sufficient judge of it; he must understand the excellences of it too, or he will only prove a blind admirer, not a critic. From hence it comes that so many satires on poets, and censures of their writings, fly abroad. Men of pleasant conversation (at least esteemed so), and endued with a trifling kind of fancy, perhaps helped out with some smattering of Latin, are ambitious to distinguish themselves from the herd of gentlemen, by their poetry—

> *Rarus enim fermè sensus communis in illâ Fortunâ.*

And is not this a wretched affectation, not to be contented with what fortune has done for them, and sit down quietly with their estates, but they must call their wits in question, and needlessly expose their nakedness to public view? Not considering that they are not to expect the same approbation from sober men, which they have found from their flatterers after the third bottle. If a little glittering in discourse has passed them on us for witty men, where was the necessity of undeceiving the world? Would a man who has an ill title to an estate, but yet is in possession of it; would he bring it of his own accord, to be tried at Westminster? We who write, if we want the talent, yet have the excuse that we do it for a poor subsistence; but what can be urged in their defence, who, not having the vocation of poverty to scribble, out of mere wantonness take pains to make themselves ridiculous? Horace was certainly in the right where he said, "That no man is satisfied with his own condition." A poet is not pleased, because he is not rich; and the rich are discontented,. because the poets will not admit them of their number. Thus the case is hard with writers. If they succeed not, they must starve; and if they do, some malicious satire is prepared to level them, for daring to please without their leave. But while they are so eager to destroy the fame of others, their ambition is manifest in their concernment; some poem of their own is to be produced, and the slaves are to be laid flat with their faces on the ground, that the monarch may appear in the greater majesty.

Dionysius and Nero had the same longings, but with all their power they could never bring their business well about. 'Tis true, they proclaimed themselves poets by sound of trumpet; and poets they were, upon pain of death to any man who durst call them otherwise. The audience had a fine time on't, you may imagine; they sat in a bodily fear, and looked as demurely as they could: for it was a hanging matter to laugh unseasonably; and the tyrants were suspicious, as they had reason, that their subjects had them in the wind; so, every man, in his own defence, set as good a face upon the business as he could. It was known beforehand that the monarchs were to be crowned laureates; but when the show was over, and an honest man was suffered to depart quietly, he took out his laughter which he had stifled, with a firm resolution never more to see an emperor's play, though he had been ten years a-making it. In the meantime the true poets were they who made the best markets: for they had wit enough to yield the prize with a good grace, and not contend with him who had thirty legions. They were sure to be rewarded, if they confessed themselves bad writers, and that was somewhat better than to be martyrs for their reputation. Lucan's example was enough to teach them manners; and after he was put to death, for overcoming Nero, the emperor carried it without dispute for the best poet in his dominions. No man was ambitious of that grinning honour; for if he heard the malicious trumpeter proclaiming his name before his betters, he knew there was but one way with him. Mæcenas took another course, and we know he was more than a great man, for he was witty too: but finding himself far gone in poetry, which Seneca assures us was not his talent, he thought it his best way to be well with Virgil and with Horace; that at least he might be a poet at the second hand; and we see how happily it has succeeded with him; for his own

bad poetry is forgotten, and their panegyrics of him still remain.
But they who should be our patrons are for no such expensive
ways to fame; they have much of the poetry of Mæcenas, but
little of his liberality. They are for persecuting Horace and
Virgil, in the persons of their successors; for such is every man
who has any part of their soul and fire, though in a less degree.
Some of their little zanies yet go further; for they are persecutors
even of Horace himself, as far as they are able, by their ignorant
and vile imitations of him; by making an unjust use of his
authority, and turning his artillery against his friends. But how
would he disdain to be copied by such hands! I dare answer for
him, he would be more uneasy in their company, than he was
with Crispinus, their forefather, in the Holy Way; and would
no more have allowed them a place amongst the critics, than he
would Demetrius the mimic, and Tigellius the buffoon;

> ———— *Demetri, teque, Tigelli,*
> *Discipularum inter jubeo plorare cathedras.*

With what scorn would he look down on such miserable trans-
lators, who make doggerel of his Latin, mistake his meaning,
misapply his censures, and often contradict their own? He is
fixed as a landmark to set out the bounds of poetry—

> ———— *Saxum antiquum, ingens,—*
> *Limes agro positus, litem ut discerneret arvis.*

But other arms than theirs, and other sinews are required, to
raise the weight of such an author; and when they would toss
him against enemies—

> *Genua labant, gelidus concrevit frigore sanguis.*
> *Tum lapis ipse viri, vacuum per inane volatus,*
> *Nec spatium evasit totum, nec pertulit ictum.*

For my part, I would wish no other revenge, either for myself,
or the rest of the poets, from this rhyming judge of the twelve-
penny gallery, this legitimate son of Sternhold, than that he
would subscribe his name to his censure, or (not to tax him
beyond his learning) set his mark. For, should he own himself
publicly, and come from behind the lion's skin, they whom he
condemns would be thankful to him, they whom he praises would
choose to be condemned; and the magistrates, whom he has
elected, would modestly withdraw from their employment, to
avoid the scandal of his nomination. The sharpness of his satire,
next to himself, falls most heavily on his friends, and they ought
never to forgive him for commending them perpetually the wrong
way, and sometimes by contraries. If he have a friend, whose
hastiness in writing is his greatest fault, Horace would have

taught him to have minced the matter, and to have called it readiness of thought, and a flowing fancy; for friendship will allow a man to christen an imperfection by the name of some neighbour virtue—

> *Vellem in amicitiâ sic erraremus; et isti*
> *Errori nomen virtus posuisset honestum.*

But he would never have allowed him to have called a slow man hasty, or a hasty writer a slow drudge, as Juvenal explains it—

> —— *Canibus pigris, scabieque vetustâ*
> *Lævibus, et siccæ lambentibus ora lucernæ,*
> *Nomen erit, Pardus, Tigris, Leo; si quid adhuc est*
> *Quod fremit in terris violentius.*

Yet Lucretius laughs at a foolish lover, even for excusing the imperfections of his mistress—

> *Nigra* μελίχροος *est, immunda et fœtida* ἄκοσμος.
> *Balba loqui non quit,* τραυλίζει; *muta pudens est,* etc.

But to drive it *ad Æthiopem cygnum* is not to be endured. I leave him to interpret this by the benefit of his French version on the other side, and without further considering him, than I have the rest of my illiterate censors, whom I have disdained to answer, because they are not qualified for judges. It remains that I acquaint the reader, that I have endeavoured in this play to follow the practice of the ancients, who, as Mr. Rymer has judiciously observed, are and ought to be our masters. Horace likewise gives it for a rule in his art of poetry—

> —— *Vos exemplaria Græca*
> *Nocturnâ versate manu, versate diurnâ.*

Yet, though their models are regular, they are too little for English tragedy; which requires to be built in a larger compass. I could give an instance in the *Œdipus Tyrannus*, which was the masterpiece of Sophocles; but I reserve it for a more fit occasion, which I hope to have hereafter. In my style, I have professed to imitate the divine Shakespeare; which that I might perform more freely, I have disencumbered myself from rhyme. Not that I condemn my former way, but that this is more proper to my present purpose. I hope I need not explain myself, that I have not copied my author servilely. Words and phrases must of necessity receive a change in succeeding ages; but it is almost a miracle that much of his language remains so pure; and that he who began dramatic poetry amongst us, untaught by any, and as Ben Jonson tells us, without learning, should by the force of his own genius perform so much, that in a manner he has left no praise for any who come after him. The occasion is fair, and the subject would be pleasant to handle the difference of styles betwixt him and Fletcher, and wherein, and how far they are both to be imitated. But since I must not be over-confident of my own performance after him, it will be prudence in me to be silent. Yet, I hope, I may affirm, and without vanity, that, by imitating him, I have excelled myself throughout the play; and particularly, that I prefer the scene betwixt Antony and Ventidius in the first act, to anything which I have written in this kind.

PROLOGUE

WHAT flocks of critics hover here to-day,
As vultures wait on armies for their prey,
All gaping for the carcase of a play!
With croaking notes they bode some dire event,
And follow dying poets by the scent.
Ours gives himself for gone; y' have watched your time:
He fights this day unarmed,—without his rhyme;--
And brings a tale which often has been told;
As sad as Dido's; and almost as old.
His hero, whom you wits his bully call,
Bates of his mettle, and scarce rants at all:
He's somewhat lewd; but a well-meaning mind;
Weeps much; fights little; but is wond'rous kind.
In short, a pattern, and companion fit,
For all the keeping Tonies of the pit.
I could name more: a wife, and mistress too;
Both (to be plain) too good for most of you:
The wife well-natured, and the mistress true.

Now, poets, if your fame has been his care,
Allow him all the candour you can spare.
A brave man scorns to quarrel once a-day;
Like Hectors in at every petty fray.
Let those find fault whose wit's so very small,
They've need to show that they can think at all;
Errors, like straws, upon the surface flow;
He who would search for pearls, must dive below.
Fops may have leave to level all they can;
As pigmies would be glad to lop a man.
Half-wits are fleas; so little and so light,
We scarce could know they live, but that they bite.
But, as the rich, when tired with daily feasts,
For change, become their next poor tenant's guests;
Drink hearty draughts of ale from plain brown bowls,
And snatch the homely rasher from the coals:
So you, retiring from much better cheer,
For once, may venture to do penance here.
And since that plenteous autumn now is past,
Whose grapes and peaches have indulged your taste,
Take in good part, from our poor poet's board,
Such rivelled fruits as winter can afford.

DRAMATIS PERSONÆ

MARK ANTONY.
VENTIDIUS, his General.
DOLABELLA, his Friend.
ALEXAS, the Queen's Eunuch.
SERAPION, Priest of Isis.
MYRIS, another Priest.
Servants to Antony.

CLEOPATRA, Queen of Egypt.
OCTAVIA, Antony's Wife.
CHARMION, ⎱ Cleopatra's Maids.
IRAS, ⎰
Antony's two little Daughters.

SCENE—ALEXANDRIA.

ALL FOR LOVE

ACT I

Scene I.—*The Temple of Isis*

Enter Serapion, Myris, Priests of Isis.

Serap. Portents and prodigies have grown so frequent,
That they have lost their name. Our fruitful Nile
Flowed ere the wonted season, with a torrent
So unexpected, and so wondrous fierce,
That the wild deluge overtook the haste
Even of the hinds that watched it: Men and beasts
Were borne above the tops of trees, that grew
On the utmost margin of the water-mark.
Then, with so swift an ebb that flood drove backward,
It slipt from underneath the scaly herd:
Here monstrous phocæ panted on the shore;
Forsaken dolphins there with their broad tails,
Lay lashing the departing waves: hard by them,
Sea horses floundering in the slimy mud,
Tossed up their heads, and dashed the ooze about them.

Enter Alexas *behind them.*

Myr. Avert these omens, Heaven!
Serap. Last night, between the hours of twelve and one,
In a lone aisle of the temple while I walked,
A whirlwind rose, that, with a violent blast,
Shook all the dome: the doors around me clapt;
The iron wicket, that defends the vault,
Where the long race of Ptolemies is laid,
Burst open, and disclosed the mighty dead.
From out each monument, in order placed,
An armed ghost starts up: the boy-king last
Reared his inglorious head. A peal of groans
Then followed, and a lamentable voice
Cried, Egypt is no more! My blood ran back,
My shaking knees against each other knocked;
On the cold pavement down I fell entranced,
And so unfinished left the horrid scene.

Alex. And dreamed you this? or did invent the story,

                              [Showing himself.

To frighten our Egyptian boys withal,
And train them up, betimes, in fear of priesthood?
    Serap. My lord, I saw you not,
Nor meant my words should reach your ears; but what
I uttered was most true.
    Alex. A foolish dream,
Bred from the fumes of indigested feasts,
And holy luxury.
    Serap. I know my duty:
This goes no further.
    Alex. 'Tis not fit it should;
Nor would the times now bear it, were it true.
All southern, from yon hills, the Roman camp
Hangs o'er us black and threatening, like a storm
Just breaking on our heads.
    Serap. Our faint Egyptians pray for Antony;
But in their servile hearts they own Octavius.
    Myr. Why then does Antony dream out his hours,
And tempts not fortune for a noble day,
Which might redeem what Actium lost?
    Alex. He thinks 'tis past recovery.
    Serap. Yet the foe
Seems not to press the siege.
    Alex. Oh, there's the wonder.
Mæcenas and Agrippa, who can most
With Cæsar, are his foes. His wife Octavia,
Driven from his house, solicits her revenge;
And Dolabella, who was once his friend,
Upon some private grudge, now seeks his ruin:
Yet still war seems on either side to sleep.
    Serap. 'Tis strange that Antony, for some days past,
Has not beheld the face of Cleopatra;
But here, in Isis' temple, lives retired,
And makes his heart a prey to black despair.
    Alex. 'Tis true; and we much fear he hopes by absence
To cure his mind of love.
    Serap. If he be vanquished,
Or make his peace, Egypt is doomed to be
A Roman province; and our plenteous harvests
Must then redeem the scarceness of their soil.
While Antony stood firm, our Alexandria
Rivalled proud Rome (dominion's other seat),

And Fortune striding, like a vast Colossus,
Could fix an equal foot of empire here.

Alex. Had I my wish, these tyrants of all nature,
Who lord it o'er mankind, should perish,—perish,
Each by the other's sword; but, since our will
Is lamely followed by our power, we must
Depend on one; with him to rise or fall.

Serap. How stands the queen affected?

Alex. Oh, she dotes,
She dotes, Serapion, on this vanquished man,
And winds herself about his mighty ruins;
Whom would she yet forsake, yet yield him up,
This hunted prey, to his pursuer's hands,
She might preserve us all: but 'tis in vain—
This changes my designs, this blasts my counsels,
And makes me use all means to keep him here,
Whom I could wish divided from her arms,
Far as the earth's deep centre. Well, you know
The state of things; no more of your ill omens
And black prognostics; labour to confirm
The people's hearts.

Enter VENTIDIUS, *talking aside with a* Gentleman *of* ANTONY'S.

Serap. These Romans will o'erhear us.
But, who's that stranger? By his warlike port,
His fierce demeanour, and erected look,
He's of no vulgar note.

Alex. Oh 'tis Ventidius,
Our emperor's great lieutenant in the East,
Who first showed Rome that Parthia could be conquered.
When Antony returned from Syria last,
He left this man to guard the Roman frontiers.

Serap. You seem to know him well.

Alex. Too well. I saw him at Cilicia first,
When Cleopatra there met Antony:
A mortal foe he was to us, and Egypt.
But,—let me witness to the worth I hate,—
A braver Roman never drew a sword;
Firm to his prince, but as a friend, not slave.
He ne'er was of his pleasures; but presides
O'er all his cooler hours, and morning counsels:
In short the plainness, fierceness, rugged virtue,
Of an old true-stampt Roman lives in him.
His coming bodes I know not what of ill

To our affairs. Withdraw to mark him better;
And I'll acquaint you why I sought you here,
And what's our present work.

> [*They withdraw to a corner of the stage; and* VENTIDIUS,
> *with the other, comes forward to the front.*

Vent. Not see him, say you?
I say, I must, and will.
    Gent. He has commanded,
On pain of death, none should approach his presence.
    Vent. I bring him news will raise his drooping spirits,
Give him new life.
    Gent. He sees not Cleopatra.
    Vent. Would he had never seen her!
    Gent. He eats not, drinks not, sleeps not, has no use
Of anything, but thought; or if he talks,
'Tis to himself, and then 'tis perfect raving:
Then he defies the world, and bids it pass;
Sometimes he gnaws his lip, and curses loud
The boy Octavius; then he draws his mouth
Into a scornful smile, and cries, "Take all,
The world's not worth my care."
    Vent. Just, just his nature.
Virtue's his path; but sometimes 'tis too narrow
For his vast soul; and then he starts out wide,
And bounds into a vice, that bears him far
From his first course, and plunges him in ills:
But, when his danger makes him find his fault,
Quick to observe, and full of sharp remorse,
He censures eagerly his own misdeeds,
Judging himself with malice to himself,
And not forgiving what as man he did,
Because his other parts are more than man.—
He must not thus be lost.

> [ALEXAS *and the* Priests *come forward.*

    Alex. You have your full instructions, now advance;
Proclaim your orders loudly.
    Serap. Romans, Egyptians, hear the queen's command.
Thus Cleopatra bids: Let labour cease;
To pomp and triumphs give this happy day,
That gave the world a lord: 'tis Antony's.
Live, Antony; and Cleopatra live!
Be this the general voice sent up to heaven,
And every public place repeat this echo.
    Vent. Fine pageantry!   [*Aside.*

Serap. Set out before your doors
The images of all your sleeping fathers,
With laurels crowned; with laurels wreathe your posts,
And strew with flowers the pavement; let the priests
Do present sacrifice; pour out the wine,
And call the gods to join with you in gladness.

Vent. Curse on the tongue that bids this general joy!
Can they be friends of Antony, who revel
When Antony's in danger? Hide, for shame,
You Romans, your great grandsires' images,
For fear their souls should animate their marbles,
To blush at their degenerate progeny.

Alex. A love, which knows no bounds, to Antony,
Would mark the day with honours, when all heaven
Laboured for him, when each propitious star
Stood wakeful in his orb, to watch that hour,
And shed his better influence. Her own birthday
Our queen neglected like a vulgar fate,
That passed obscurely by.

Vent. Would it had slept,
Divided far from this; till some remote
And future age had called it out, to ruin
Some other prince, not him!

Alex. Your emperor,
Though grown unkind, would be more gentle, than
To upbraid my queen for loving him too well.

Vent. Does the mute sacrifice upbraid the priest?
He knows him not his executioner.
Oh, she has decked his ruin with her love,
Led him in golden bands to gaudy slaughter,
And made perdition pleasing: She has left him
The blank of what he was.
I tell thee, eunuch, she has quite unmanned him.
Can any Roman see, and know him now,
Thus altered from the lord of half mankind,
Unbent, unsinewed, made a woman's toy,
Shrunk from the vast extent of all his honours,
And crampt within a corner of the world?
O Antony!
Thou bravest soldier, and thou best of friends!
Bounteous as nature; next to nature's God!
Couldst thou but make new worlds, so wouldst thou give them.
As bounty were thy being! rough in battle,
As the first Romans when they went to war;

Yet after victory more pitiful
Than all their praying virgins left at home!
   Alex. Would you could add, to those more shining **virtues,**
His truth to her who loves him.
   Vent. Would I could not!
But wherefore waste I precious hours with thee!
Thou art her darling mischief, her chief engine,
Antony's other fate. Go, tell thy queen,
Ventidius is arrived, to end her charms.
Let your Egyptian timbrels play alone,
Nor mix effeminate sounds with Roman trumpets.
You dare not fight for Antony; go pray
And keep your cowards' holiday in temples.
                      [*Exeunt* ALEXAS, SERAPION.

       Re-enter the Gentleman *of* M. ANTONY.

   2 *Gent.* The emperor approaches, and commands,
On pain of death, that none presume to stay.
   1 *Gent.* I dare not disobey him.   [*Going out with the other.*
   Vent. Well, I dare.
But I'll observe him first unseen, and find
Which way his humour drives: The rest I'll venture.
                            [*Withdraws.*

Enter ANTONY, *walking with a disturbed motion before he
                    speaks.*

   Ant. They tell me, 'tis my birthday, and I'll keep it
With double pomp of sadness.
'Tis what the day deserves, which gave me breath.
Why was I raised the meteor of the world,
Hung in the skies, and blazing as I travelled,
Till all my fires were spent; and then cast downward,
To be trod out by Cæsar?
   Vent. [*Aside.*] On my soul,
'Tis mournful, wondrous mournful!
   Ant. Count thy gains.
Now, Antony, wouldst thou be born for this?
Glutton of fortune, thy devouring youth
Has starved thy wanting age.
   Vent. How sorrow shakes him!   [*Aside.*
So, now the tempest tears him up by the roots,
And on the ground extends the noble ruin.
           [ANTONY *having thrown himself down.*
Lie there, thou shadow of an emperor;

The place thou pressest on thy mother earth
Is all thy empire now: now it contains thee;
Some few days hence, and then 'twill be too large,
When thou'rt contracted in thy narrow urn,
Shrunk to a few cold ashes; then Octavia
(For Cleopatra will not live to see it),
Octavia then will have thee all her own,
And bear thee in her widowed hand to Cæsar;
Cæsar will weep, the crocodile will weep,
To see his rival of the universe
Lie still and peaceful there. I'll think no more on't.

    Ant. Give me some music: look that it be sad:
I'll soothe my melancholy, till I swell,
And burst myself with sighing.—   *[Soft music.*
'Tis somewhat to my humour: stay, I fancy
I'm now turned wild, a commoner of nature;
Of all forsaken, and forsaking all;
Live in a shady forest's sylvan scene,
Stretched at my length beneath some blasted oak,
I lean my head upon the mossy bark,
And look just of a piece as I grew from it;
My uncombed locks, matted like mistletoe,
Hang o'er my hoary face; a murmuring brook
Runs at my foot.

    Vent. Methinks I fancy
Myself there too.

    Ant. The herd come jumping by me,
And, fearless, quench their thirst, while I look on,
And take me for their fellow-citizen.
More of this image, more; it lulls my thoughts.

                        [Soft music again.

    Vent. I must disturb him; I can hold no longer.

                        [Stands before him.

    Ant. [*starting up*]. Art thou Ventidius?

    Vent. Are you Antony?
I'm liker what I was, than you to him
I left you last.

    Ant. I'm angry.

    Vent. So am I.

    Ant. I would be private: leave me.

    Vent. Sir, I love you,
And therefore will not leave you.

    Ant. Will not leave me!
Where have you learnt that answer? Who am I?

Vent. My emperor; the man I love next Heaven:
If I said more, I think 'twere scarce a sin:
You're all that's good, and god-like.
  Ant. All that's wretched.
You will not leave me then?
  Vent. 'Twas too presuming
To say I would not; but I dare not leave you:
And, 'tis unkind in you to chide me hence
So soon, when I so far have come to see you.
  Ant. Now thou hast seen me, art thou satisfied?
For, if a friend, thou hast beheld enough;
And, if a foe, too much.
  Vent. Look, emperor, this is no common dew. [*Weeping.*
I have not wept this forty years; but now
My mother comes afresh into my eyes;
I cannot help her softness.
  Ant. By heaven, he weeps! poor good old man, he weeps!
The big round drops course one another down
The furrows of his cheeks.—Stop them, Ventidius,
Or I shall blush to death: they set my shame,
That caused them, full before me.
  Vent. I'll do my best.
  Ant. Sure there's contagion in the tears of friends:
See, I have caught it too. Believe me, 'tis not
For my own griefs, but thine.—Nay, father!
  Vent. Emperor.
  Ant. Emperor! Why, that's the style of victory;
The conqu'ring soldier, red with unfelt wounds,
Salutes his general so: but never more
Shall that sound reach my ears.
  Vent. I warrant you.
  Ant. Actium, Actium! Oh!—
  Vent. It sits too near you.
  Ant. Here, here it lies; a lump of lead by day,
And, in my short, distracted, nightly slumbers,
The hag that rides my dreams.——
  Vent. Out with it; give it vent.
  Ant. Urge not my shame.
I lost a battle,——
  Vent. So has Julius done.
  Ant. Thou favour'st me, and speak'st not half thou think'st;
For Julius fought it out, and lost it fairly:
But Antony——
  Vent. Nay, stop not.

Ant. Antony,—
Well, thou wilt have it—like a coward, fled,
Fled while his soldiers fought; fled first, Ventidius.
Thou long'st to curse me, and I give thee leave.
I know thou cam'st prepared to rail.
    Vent. I did.
    Ant. I'll help thee.—I have been a man, Ventidius.
    Vent. Yes, and a brave one; but——
    Ant. I know thy meaning.
But I have lost my reason, have disgraced
The name of soldier, with inglorious ease.
In the full vintage of my flowing honours,
Sat still, and saw it prest by other hands.
Fortune came smiling to my youth, and wooed it,
And purple greatness met my ripened years.
When first I came to empire, I was borne
On tides of people, crowding to my triumphs;
The wish of nations, and the willing world
Received me as its pledge of future peace;
I was so great, so happy, so beloved,
Fate could not ruin me; till I took pains,
And worked against my fortune, chid her from me,
And turned her loose; yet still she came again.
My careless days, and my luxurious nights,
At length have wearied her, and now she's gone,
Gone, gone, divorced for ever. Help me, soldier,
To curse this madman, this industrious fool,
Who laboured to be wretched: Pr'ythee, curse me.
    Vent. No.
    Ant. Why?
    Vent. You are too sensible already
Of what you've done, too conscious of your failings;
And, like a scorpion, whipt by others first
To fury, sting yourself in mad revenge.
I would bring balm, and pour it in your wounds,
Cure your distempered mind, and heal your fortunes.
    Ant. I know thou would'st.
    Vent. I will.
    Ant. Ha, ha, ha, ha!
    Vent. You laugh.
    Ant. I do, to see officious love
Give cordials to the dead.
    Vent. You would be lost, then?
    Ant. I am.

Vent. I say you are not. Try your fortune.

Ant. I have, to the utmost. Dost thou think me desperate,
Without just cause? No, when I found all lost
Beyond repair, I hid me from the world,
And learnt to scorn it here; which now I do
So heartily, I think it is not worth
The cost of keeping.

Vent. Cæsar thinks not so;
He'll thank you for the gift he could not take.
You would be killed like Tully, would you? do,
Hold out your throat to Cæsar, and die tamely.

Ant. No, I can kill myself; and so resolve.

Vent. I can die with you too, when time shall serve;
But fortune calls upon us now to live,
To fight, to conquer.

Ant. Sure thou dream'st, Ventidius.

Vent. No; 'tis you dream; you sleep away your hours
In desperate sloth, miscalled philosophy.
Up, up, for honour's sake; twelve legions wait you,
And long to call you chief: By painful journeys
I led them, patient both of heat and hunger,
Down from the Parthian marches to the Nile.
'Twill do you good to see their sunburnt faces,
Their scarred cheeks, and chopt hands: there's virtue in them.
They'll sell those mangled limbs at dearer rates
Than yon trim bands can buy.

Ant. Where left you them?

Vent. I said in Lower Syria.

Ant. Bring them hither;
There may be life in these.

Vent. They will not come.

Ant. Why didst thou mock my hopes with promised aids,
To double my despair? They're mutinous.

Vent. Most firm and loyal.

Ant. Yet they will not march
To succour me. O trifler!

Vent. They petition
You would make haste to head them.

Ant. I'm besieged.

Vent. There's but one way shut up: How came I hither?

Ant. I will not stir.

Vent. They would perhaps desire
A better reason.

Ant. I have never used

My soldiers to demand a reason of
My actions. Why did they refuse to march?
   Vent. They said they would not fight for Cleopatra.
   Ant. What was't they said?
   Vent. They said they would not fight for Cleopatra.
Why should they fight indeed, to make her conquer,
And make you more a slave? to gain your kingdoms,
Which, for a kiss, at your next midnight feast,
You'll sell to her? Then she new-names her jewels,
And calls this diamond such or such a tax;
Each pendant in her ear shall be a province.
   Ant. Ventidius, I allow your tongue free licence
On all my other faults; but, on your life,
No word of Cleopatra: she deserves
More worlds than I can lose.
   Vent. Behold, you Powers,
To whom you have intrusted humankind!
See Europe, Afric, Asia, put in balance,
And all weighed down by one light, worthless woman!
I think the gods are Antonies, and give,
Like prodigals, this nether world away
To none but wasteful hands.
   Ant. You grow presumptuous.
   Vent. I take the privilege of plain love to speak.
   Ant. Plain love! plain arrogance, plain insolence!
Thy men are cowards; thou, an envious traitor;
Who, under seeming honesty, hast vented
The burden of thy rank, o'erflowing gall.
O that thou wert my equal; great in arms
As the first Cæsar was, that I might kill thee
Without a stain to honour!
   Vent. You may kill me;
You have done more already,—called me traitor.
   Ant. Art thou not one?
   Vent. For showing you yourself,
Which none else durst have done? but had I been
That name, which I disdain to speak again,
I needed not have sought your abject fortunes,
Come to partake your fate, to die with you.
What hindered me to have led my conquering eagles
To fill Octavius' bands? I could have been
A traitor then, a glorious, happy traitor,
And not have been so called.
   Ant. Forgive me, soldier;

I've been too passionate.

    Vent. You thought me false;
Thought my old age betrayed you: Kill me, sir,
Pray, kill me; yet you need not, your unkindness
Has left your sword no work.

    Ant. I did not think so;
I said it in my rage: Pr'ythee, forgive me.
Why didst thou tempt my anger, by discovery
Of what I would not hear?

    Vent. No prince but you
Could merit that sincerity I used,
Nor durst another man have ventured it;
But you, ere love misled your wandering eyes,
Were sure the chief and best of human race,
Framed in the very pride and boast of nature;
So perfect, that the gods, who formed you, wondered
At their own skill, and cried—A lucky hit
Has mended our design. Their envy hindered,
Else you had been immortal, and a pattern,
When Heaven would work for ostentation's sake
To copy out again.

    Ant. But Cleopatra—
Go on; for I can bear it now.

    Vent. No more.

    Ant. Thou dar'st not trust my passion, but thou may'st;
Thou only lov'st, the rest have flattered me.

    Vent. Heaven's blessing on your heart for that kind word!
May I believe you love me? Speak again.

    Ant. Indeed I do. Speak this, and this, and this.

                                          [*Hugging him*
Thy praises were unjust; but, I'll deserve them,
And yet mend all. Do with me what thou wilt;
Lead me to victory! thou know'st the way.

    Vent. And, will you leave this——

    Ant. Pr'ythee, do not curse her,
And I will leave her; though, Heaven knows, I love
Beyond life, conquest, empire, all, but honour;
But I will leave her.

    Vent. That's my royal master;
And, shall we fight?

    Ant. I warrant thee, old soldier.
Thou shalt behold me once again in iron;
And at the head of our old troops, that beat
The Parthians, cry aloud—Come, follow me!

Vent. Oh, now I hear my emperor! in that word
Octavius fell. Gods, let me see that day,
And, if I have ten years behind, take all:
I'll thank you for the exchange.
   Ant. O Cleopatra!
   Vent. Again?
   Ant. I've done: In that last sigh she went.
Cæsar shall know what 'tis to force a lover
From all he holds most dear.
   Vent. Methinks, you breathe
Another soul: Your looks are more divine;
You speak a hero, and you move a god.
   Ant. Oh, thou hast fired me; my soul's up in arms,
And mans each part about me: Once again,
That noble eagerness of fight has seized me;
That eagerness with which I darted upward
To Cassius' camp: In vain the steepy hill
Opposed my way; in vain a war of spears
Sung round my head, and planted on my shield;
I won the trenches, while my foremost men
Lagged on the plain below.
   Vent. Ye gods, ye gods,
For such another honour!
   ✗ *Ant.* Come on, my soldier!
Our hearts and arms are still the same: I long
Once more to meet our foes; that thou and I,
Like Time and Death, marching before our troops,
May taste fate to them; mow them out a passage,
And, entering where the foremost squadrons yield,
Begin the noble harvest of the field. ✗   [*Exeunt.*

ACT II

Scene I

Enter Cleopatra, Iras, *and* Alexas.

✝ *Cleo.* What shall I do, or whither shall I turn?
Ventidius has o'ercome, and he will go.
   Alex. He goes to fight for you.
   Cleo. Then he would see me, ere he went to fight:
Flatter me not: If once he goes, he's lost,
And all my hopes destroyed.
   Alex. Does this weak passion

Become a mighty queen?

 Cleo. I am no queen:
Is this to be a queen, to be besieged
By yon insulting Roman, and to wait
Each hour the victor's chain? These ills are small:
For Antony is lost, and I can mourn
For nothing else but him. Now come, Octavius,
I have no more to lose! prepare thy bands;
I'm fit to be a captive: Antony
Has taught my mind the fortune of a slave.

 Iras. Call reason to assist you.

 Cleo. I have none,
And none would have: My love's a noble madness,
Which shows the cause deserved it. Moderate sorrow
Fits vulgar love, and for a vulgar man:
But I have loved with such transcendent passion,
I soared, at first, quite out of reason's view,
And now am lost above it. No, I'm proud
'Tis thus: Would Antony could see me now
Think you he would not sigh, though he must leave me?
Sure he would sigh; for he is noble-natured,
And bears a tender heart: I know him well.
Ah, no, I know him not; I knew him once,
But now 'tis past.

 Iras. Let it be past with you:
Forget him, madam.

 Cleo. Never, never, Iras.
He once was mine; and once, though now 'tis gone,
Leaves a faint image of possession still.

 Alex. Think him inconstant, cruel, and ungrateful.

 Cleo. I cannot: If I could, those thoughts were vain.
Faithless, ungrateful, cruel, though he be,
I still must love him.

Enter CHARMION.

Now, what news, my Charmion?
Will he be kind? and will he not forsake me?
Am I to live, or die?—nay, do I live?
Or am I dead? for when he gave his answer,
Fate took the word, and then I lived or died.

 Char. I found him, madam——

 Cleo. A long speech preparing?
If thou bring'st comfort, haste, and give it me,
For never was more need.

Iras. I know he loves you.

Cleo. Had he been kind, her eyes had told me so,
Before her tongue could speak it: Now she studies,
To soften what he said; but give me death,
Just as he sent it, Charmion, undisguised,
And in the words he spoke.

Char. I found him, then,
Encompassed round, I think, with iron statues;
So mute, so motionless his soldiers stood,
While awfully he cast his eyes about,
And every leader's hopes or fears surveyed:
Methought he looked resolved, and yet not pleased.
When he beheld me struggling in the crowd,
He blushed, and bade make way.

Alex. There's comfort yet.

Char. Ventidius fixed his eyes upon my passage
Severely, as he meant to frown me back,
And sullenly gave place: I told my message,
Just as you gave it, broken and disordered;
I numbered in it all your sighs and tears,
And while I moved your pitiful request,
That you but only begged a last farewell,
He fetched an inward groan; and every time
I named you, sighed, as if his heart were breaking,
But, shunned my eyes, and guiltily looked down;
He seemed not now that awful Antony,
Who shook an armed assembly with his nod;
But, making show as he would rub his eyes,
Disguised and blotted out a falling tear.

Cleo. Did he then weep? And was I worth a tear?
If what thou hast to say be not as pleasing,
Tell me no more, but let me die contented.

Char. He bid me say,—He knew himself so well,
He could deny you nothing, if he saw you;
And therefore——

Cleo. Thou wouldst say, he would not see me?

Char. And therefore begged you not to use a power,
Which he could ill resist; yet he should ever
Respect you, as he ought.

Cleo. Is that a word
For Antony to use to Cleopatra?
O that faint word, *respect!* how I disdain it!
Disdain myself, for loving after it!
He should have kept that word for cold Octavia.

Respect is for a wife: Am I that thing,
That dull, insipid lump, without desires,
And without power to give them?
  Alex. You misjudge;
You see through love, and that deludes your sight;
As, what is straight, seems crooked through the water:
But I, who bear my reason undisturbed,
Can see this Antony, this dreaded man,
A fearful slave, who fain would run away,
And shuns his master's eyes: If you pursue him,
My life on't, he still drags a chain along
That needs must clog his flight.
  Cleo. Could I believe thee!——
  Alex. By every circumstance I know he loves.
True, he's hard prest, by interest and by honour;
Yet he but doubts, and parleys, and casts out
Many a long look for succour.
  Cleo. He sends word,
He fears to see my face.
  Alex. And would you more?
He shows his weakness who declines the combat,
And you must urge your fortune. Could he speak
More plainly? To my ears, the message sounds——
Come to my rescue, Cleopatra, come;
Come, free me from Ventidius; from my tyrant:
See me, and give me a pretence to leave him!——
I hear his trumpets. This way he must pass.
Please you, retire a while; I'll work him first,
That he may bend more easy.
  Cleo. You shall rule me;
But all, I fear, in vain.   [*Exit with* CHARMION *and* IRAS.
  Alex. I fear so too;
Though I concealed my thoughts, to make her bold;
But 'tis our utmost means, and fate befriend it! [*Withdraws.*

Enter LICTORS *with Fasces; one bearing the Eagle; then enter*
 ANTONY *with* VENTIDIUS, *followed by other* Commanders.

  Ant. Octavius is the minion of blind chance,
But holds from virtue nothing.
  Vent. Has he courage?
  Ant. But just enough to season him from coward.
Oh, 'tis the coldest youth upon a charge,
The most deliberate fighter! if he ventures
(As in Illyria once, they say, he did,

To storm a town), 'tis when he cannot choose;
When all the world have fixt their eyes upon him;
And then he lives on that for seven years after;
But, at a close revenge he never fails.

Vent. I heard you challenged him.

Ant. I did, Ventidius.
What think'st thou was his answer? 'Twas so tame!—
He said, he had more ways than one to die;
I had not.

Vent. Poor!

Ant. He has more ways than one;
But he would choose them all before that one.

Vent. He first would choose an ague, or a fever.

Ant. No; it must be an ague, not a fever;
He has not warmth enough to die by that.

Vent. Or old age and a bed.

Ant. Ay, there's his choice,
He would live, like a lamp, to the last wink,
And crawl upon the utmost verge of life.
O Hercules! Why should a man like this,
Who dares not trust his fate for one great action,
Be all the care of Heaven? Why should he lord it
O'er fourscore thousand men, of whom each one
Is braver than himself?

Vent. You conquered for him:
Philippi knows it; there you shared with him
That empire, which your sword made all your own.

Ant. Fool that I was, upon my eagle's wings
I bore this wren, till I was tired with soaring,
And now he mounts above me.
Good heavens, is this—is this the man who braves me?
Who bids my age make way? Drives me before him,
To the world's ridge, and sweeps me off like rubbish?

Vent. Sir, we lose time; the troops are mounted all.

Ant. Then give the word to march:
I long to leave this prison of a town,
To join thy legions; and, in open field,
Once more to show my face. Lead, my deliverer.

Enter ALEXAS.

Alex. Great emperor,
In mighty arms renowned above mankind,
But, in soft pity to the opprest, a god;
This message sends the mournful Cleopatra

To her departing lord.

 Vent. Smooth sycophant!

 Alex. A thousand wishes, and ten thousand prayers,
Millions of blessings wait you to the wars;
Millions of sighs and tears she sends you too,
And would have sent
As many dear embraces to your arms,
As many parting kisses to your lips;
But those, she fears, have wearied you already.

 Vent. [*Aside.*] False crocodile!

 Alex. And yet she begs not now, you would not leave her;
That were a wish too mighty for her hopes,
Too presuming
For her low fortune, and your ebbing love;
That were a wish for her more prosperous days,
Her blooming beauty, and your growing kindness.

 Ant. [*Aside.*] Well, I must man it out:—What would the
  queen?

 Alex. First, to these noble warriors, who attend
Your daring courage in the chase of fame,—
Too daring, and too dangerous for her quiet,—
She humbly recommends all she holds dear,
All her own cares and fears,—the care of you.

 Vent. Yes, witness Actium.

 Ant. Let him speak, Ventidius.

 Alex. You, when his matchless valour bears him forward,
With ardour too heroic, on his foes,
Fall down, as she would do, before his feet;
Lie in his way, and stop the paths of death:
Tell him, this god is not invulnerable;
That absent Cleopatra bleeds in him;
And, that you may remember her petition,
She begs you wear these trifles, as a pawn,
Which, at your wished return, she will redeem
      [*Gives jewels to the* Commanders.
With all the wealth of Egypt:
This to the great Ventidius she presents,
Whom she can never count her enemy,
Because he loves her lord.

 Vent. Tell her, I'll none on't;
I'm not ashamed of honest poverty;
Not all the diamonds of the east can bribe
Ventidius from his faith. I hope to see
These and the rest of all her sparkling store,

Where they shall more deservingly be placed.

Ant. And who must wear them then?

Vent. The wronged Octavia.

Ant. You might have spared that word.

Vent. And he that bribe.

Ant. But have I no remembrance?

Alex. Yes, a dear one;

Your slave the queen——

Ant. My mistress.

Alex. Then your mistress;

Your mistress would, she says, have sent her soul,
But that you had long since; she humbly begs
This ruby bracelet, set with bleeding hearts,
The emblems of her own, may bind your arm.

          [Presenting a bracelet.

Vent. Now, my best lord,—in honour's name, I ask you,
For manhood's sake, and for your own dear safety,—
Touch not these poisoned gifts,
Infected by the sender; touch them not;
Myriads of bluest plagues lie underneath them,
And more than aconite has dipt the silk.

Ant. Nay, now you grow too cynical, Ventidius:
A lady's favours may be worn with honour.
What, to refuse her bracelet! On my soul,
When I lie pensive in my tent alone,
'Twill pass the wakeful hours of winter nights,
To tell these pretty beads upon my arm,
To count for every one a soft embrace,
A melting kiss at such and such a time:
And now and then the fury of her love,
When——And what harm's in this?

Alex. None, none, my lord,
But what's to her, that now 'tis past for ever.

Ant. [*Going to tie it.*] We soldiers are so awkward—help me
  tie it.

Alex. In faith, my lord, we courtiers too are awkward
In these affairs: so are all men indeed:
Even I, who am not one. But shall I speak?

Ant. Yes, freely.

Alex. Then, my lord, fair hands alone
Are fit to tie it; she, who sent it can.

Vent. Hell, death! this eunuch pander ruins you.
You will not see her?

      [ALEXAS *whispers an* Attendant, *who goes out.*

Ant. But to take my leave.

Vent. Then I have washed an Æthiop. You're undone;
Y' are in the toils; y' are taken; y' are destroyed:
Her eyes do Cæsar's work.

Ant. You fear too soon.
I'm constant to myself: I know my strength;
And yet she shall not think me barbarous neither,
Born in the depths of Afric: I am a Roman,
Bred in the rules of soft humanity.
A guest, and kindly used, should bid farewell.

Vent. You do not know
How weak you are to her, how much an infant:
You are not proof against a smile, or glance;
A sigh will quite disarm you.

Ant. See, she comes!
Now you shall find your error.—Gods, I thank you:
I formed the danger greater than it was,
And now 'tis near, 'tis lessened.

Vent. Mark the end yet.

Enter Cleopatra, Charmion, *and* Iras.

Ant. Well, madam, we are met.

Cleo. Is this a meeting?
Then, we must part?

Ant. We must.

Cleo. Who says we must?

Ant. Our own hard fates.

Cleo. We make those fates ourselves.

Ant. Yes, we have made them; we have loved each other,
Into our mutual ruin.

Cleo. The gods have seen my joys with envious eyes;
I have no friends in heaven; and all the world,
As 'twere the business of mankind to part us,
Is armed against my love: even you yourself
Join with the rest; you, you are armed against me.

Ant. I will be justified in all I do
To late posterity, and therefore hear me.
If I mix a lie
With any truth, reproach me freely with it;
Else, favour me with silence.

Cleo. You command me,
And I am dumb.

Vent. I like this well; he shows authority.

Ant. That I derive my ruin
From you alone——
    Cleo. O heavens! I ruin you!
    Ant. You promised me your silence, and you break it
Ere I have scarce begun.
    Cleo. Well, I obey you.
    Ant. When I beheld you first, it was in Egypt.
Ere Cæsar saw your eyes, you gave me love,
And were too young to know it; that I settled
Your father in his throne, was for your sake;
I left the acknowledgment for time to ripen.
Cæsar stept in, and, with a greedy hand,
Plucked the green fruit, ere the first blush of red,
Yet cleaving to the bough. He was my lord,
And was, beside, too great for me to rival;
But, I deserved you first, though he enjoyed you.
When, after, I beheld you in Cilicia,
An enemy to Rome, I pardoned you.
    Cleo. I cleared myself——
    Ant. Again you break your promise.
I loved you still, and took your weak excuses,
Took you into my bosom, stained by Cæsar,
And not half mine: I went to Egypt with you,
And hid me from the business of the world,
Shut out inquiring nations from my sight,
To give whole years to you.
    Vent. Yes, to your shame be't spoken.   [*Aside.*
    Ant. How I loved.
Witness, ye days and nights, and all ye hours,
That danced away with down upon your feet,
As all your business were to count my passion!
One day passed by, and nothing saw but love;
Another came, and still 'twas only love:
The suns were wearied out with looking on,
And I untired with loving.
I saw you every day, and all the day;
And every day was still but as the first,
So eager was I still to see you more.
    Vent. 'Tis all too true.
    Ant. Fulvia, my wife, grew jealous
(As she indeed had reason), raised a war
In Italy, to call me back.
    Vent. But yet
You went not.

Ant. While within your arms I lay,
The world fell mouldering from my hands each hour,
And left me scarce a grasp—I thank your love for't.

Vent. Well pushed: that last was home.

Cleo. Yet may I speak?

Ant. If I have urged a falsehood, yes; else, not.
Your silence says, I have not. Fulvia died
(Pardon, you gods, with my unkindness died);
To set the world at peace, I took Octavia,
This Cæsar's sister; in her pride of youth,
And flower of beauty, did I wed that lady,
Whom blushing I must praise, because I left her.
You called; my love obeyed the fatal summons:
This raised the Roman arms; the cause was yours.
I would have fought by land, where I was stronger;
You hindered it: yet, when I fought at sea,
Forsook me fighting; and (O stain to honour!
O lasting shame!) I knew not that I fled;
But fled to follow you.

Vent. What haste she made to hoist her purple sails!
And, to appear magnificent in flight,
Drew half our strength away.

Ant. All this you caused.
And, would you multiply more ruins on me?
This honest man, my best, my only friend,
Has gathered up the shipwreck of my fortunes;
Twelve legions I have left, my last recruits.
And you have watched the news, and bring your eyes
To seize them too. If you have aught to answer,
Now speak, you have free leave.

Alex. [*Aside.*] She stands confounded:
Despair is in her eyes.

Vent. Now lay a sigh in the way to stop his passage:
Prepare a tear, and bid it for his legions;
'Tis like they shall be sold.

Cleo. How shall I plead my cause, when you, my judge,
Already have condemned me? Shall I bring
The love you bore me for my advocate?
That now is turned against me, that destroys me;
For love, once past, is, at the best, forgotten;
But oftener sours to hate: 'twill please my lord
To ruin me, and therefore I'll be guilty.
But, could I once have thought it would have pleased you,
That you would pry, with narrow searching eyes,

Into my faults, severe to my destruction,
And watching all advantages with care,
That serve to make me wretched? Speak, my lord,
For I end here. Though I deserved this usage,
Was it like you to give it?
   Ant. Oh, you wrong me,
To think I sought this parting, or desired
To accuse you more than what will clear myself,
And justify this breach.
   Cleo. Thus low I thank you;
And, since my innocence will not offend,
I shall not blush to own it.
   Vent. After this,
I think she'll blush at nothing.
   Cleo. You seemed grieved
(And therein you are kind), that Cæsar first
Enjoyed my love, though you deserved it better:
I grieve for that, my lord, much more than you;
For, had I first been yours, it would have saved
My second choice: I never had been his,
And ne'er had been but yours. But Cæsar first,
You say, possessed my love. Not so, my lord:
He first possessed my person; you, my love:
Cæsar loved me; but I loved Antony.
If I endured him after, 'twas because
I judged it due to the first name of men;
And, half constrained, I gave, as to a tyrant,
What he would take by force.
   Vent. O Syren! Syren!
Yet grant that all the love she boasts were true,
Has she not ruined you? I still urge that,
The fatal consequence.
   Cleo. The consequence indeed,
For I dare challenge him, my greatest foe,
To say it was designed: 'tis true, I loved you,
And kept you far from an uneasy wife,—
Such Fulvia was.
Yes, but he'll say, you left Octavia for me;—
And, can you blame me to receive that love,
Which quitted such desert, for worthless me?
How often have I wished some other Cæsar,
Great as the first, and as the second young,
Would court my love, to be refused for you!
   Vent. Words, words; but Actium, sir; remember Actium.

Cleo. Even there, I dare his malice. True, I counselled
To fight at sea; but I betrayed you not.
I fled, but not to the enemy. 'Twas fear;
Would I had been a man, not to have feared!
For none would then have envied me your friendship,
Who envy me your love.

    Ant. We are both unhappy:
If nothing else, yet our ill fortune parts us.
Speak: would you have me perish by my stay?

    Cleo. If, as a friend, you ask my judgment, go;
If, as a lover, stay. If you must perish——
'Tis a hard word—but stay.

    Vent. See now the effects of her so boasted love!
She strives to drag you down to ruin with her;
But, could she 'scape without you, oh, how soon
Would she let go her hold, and haste to shore,
And never look behind!

    Cleo. Then judge my love by this. [*Giving* ANTONY *a writing*.
Could I have borne
A life or death, a happiness or woe,
From yours divided, this had given me means.

    Ant. By Hercules, the writing of Octavius!
I know it well: 'tis that proscribing hand,
Young as it was, that led the way to mine,
And left me but the second place in murder.——
See, see, Ventidius! here he offers Egypt,
And joins all Syria to it, as a present;
So, in requital, she forsake my fortunes,
And join her arms with his.

    Cleo. And yet you leave me!
You leave me, Antony; and yet I love you,
Indeed I do: I have refused a kingdom;
That is a trifle;
For I could part with life, with anything,
But only you. Oh, let me die but with you!
Is that a hard request?

    Ant. Next living with you,
'Tis all that Heaven can give.

    Alex. He melts; we conquer.   [*Aside*.

    Cleo. No; you shall go: your interest calls you hence;
Yes; your dear interest pulls too strong, for these
Weak arms to hold you here.   [*Takes his hand*.
Go; leave me, soldier
(For you're no more a lover): leave me dying:

Push me, all pale and panting, from your bosom,
And, when your march begins, let one run after,
Breathless almost for joy, and cry—She's dead.
The soldiers shout; you then, perhaps, may sigh,
And muster all your Roman gravity:
Ventidius chides; and straight your brow clears up,
As I had never been.

   Ant. Gods, 'tis too much; too much for man to bear.

   Cleo. What is't for me then,
A weak, forsaken woman, and a lover?—
Here let me breathe my last: envy me not
This minute in your arms: I'll die apace,
As fast as e'er I can, and end your trouble.

   Ant. Die! rather let me perish; loosened nature
Leap from its hinges, sink the props of heaven,
And fall the skies, to crush the nether world!
My eyes, my soul, my all!   [*Embraces her.*

   Vent. And what's this toy,
In balance with your fortune, honour, fame?

   Ant. What is't, Ventidius?—it outweighs them all;
Why, we have more than conquered Cæsar now:
My queen's not only innocent, but loves me.
This, this is she, who drags me down to ruin!
"But, could she 'scape without me, with what haste
Would she let slip her hold, and make to shore,
And never look behind!"
Down on thy knees, blasphemer as thou art,
And ask forgiveness of wronged innocence.

   Vent. I'll rather die, than take it. Will you go?

   Ant. Go! whither? Go from all that's excellent?
Faith, honour, virtue, all good things forbid,
That I should go from her, who sets my love
Above the price of kingdoms! Give, you gods,
Give to your boy, your Cæsar,
This rattle of a globe to play withal,
This gewgaw world, and put him cheaply off:
I'll not be pleased with less than Cleopatra.

   Cleo. She's wholly yours. My heart's so full of joy,
That I shall do some wild extravagance
Of love, in public; and the foolish world,
Which knows not tenderness, will think me mad.

   Vent. O women! women! women! all the gods
Have not such power of doing good to man,
As you of doing harm.   [*Exit.*

Ant. Our men are armed:—
Unbar the gate that looks to Cæsar's camp:
I would revenge the treachery he meant me;
And long security makes conquest easy.
I'm eager to return before I go;
For, all the pleasures I have known beat thick
On my remembrance.—How I long for night!
　That both the sweets of mutual love may try,
　And triumph once o'er Cæsar ere we die.　　　　[*Exeunt*

ACT III

Scene I

At one door enter Cleopatra, Charmion, Iras, *and* Alexas, *
　Train of Egyptians: *at the other* Antony *and* Romans
　The entrance on both sides is prepared by music; the trum
　pets first sounding on Antony's *part: then answered b*
　timbrels, etc., on Cleopatra's. Charmion *and* Iras *hol*
　a laurel wreath betwixt them. A Dance of Egyptians. *Afte*
　the ceremony, Cleopatra *crowns* Antony.

　Ant. I thought how those white arms would fold me in,
And strain me close, and melt me into love;
So pleased with that sweet image, I sprung forwards,
And added all my strength to every blow.
　Cleo. Come to me, come, my soldier, to my arms!
You've been too long away from my embraces;
But, when I have you fast, and all my own,
With broken murmurs, and with amorous sighs,
I'll say, you were unkind, and punish you,
And mark you red with many an eager kiss.
　Ant. My brighter Venus!
　Cleo. O my greater Mars!
　Ant. Thou join'st us well, my love!
Suppose me come from the Phlegræan plains,
Where gasping giants lay, cleft by my sword,
And mountain-tops paired off each other blow,
To bury those I slew. Receive me, goddess!
Let Cæsar spread his subtle nets; like Vulcan,
In thy embraces I would be beheld
By heaven and earth at once;
And make their envy what they meant their sport.
Let those, who took us, blush; I would love on,

With awful state, regardless of their frowns,
As their superior gods.
There's no satiety of love in thee:
Enjoyed, thou still art new; perpetual spring
Is in thy arms; the ripened fruit but falls,
And blossoms rise to fill its empty place;
And I grow rich by giving.

Enter VENTIDIUS, *and stands apart.*

Alex. Oh, now the danger's past, your general comes!
He joins not in your joys, nor minds your triumphs;
But, with contracted brows, looks frowning on,
As envying your success.

Ant. Now, on my soul, he loves me; truly loves me:
He never flattered me in any vice,
But awes me with his virtue: even this minute,
Methinks, he has a right of chiding me.
Lead to the temple: I'll avoid his presence;
It checks too strong upon me.   [*Exeunt the rest.*
     [*As* ANTONY *is going,* VENTIDIUS *pulls him by the robe.*
Vent. Emperor!
Ant. 'Tis the old argument; I pr'ythee, spare me.
                                         [*Looking back.*
Vent. But this one hearing, emperor.
Ant. Let go
My robe; or, by my father Hercules——
Vent. By Hercules' father, that's yet greater,
I bring you somewhat you would wish to know.
Ant. Thou see'st we are observed; attend me here,
And I'll return.   [*Exit.*
Vent. I am waning in his favour, yet I love him;
I love this man, who runs to meet his ruin;
And sure the gods, like me, are fond of him:
His virtues lie so mingled with his crimes,
As would confound their choice to punish one,
And not reward the other.

Enter ANTONY.

Ant. We can conquer,
You see, without your aid.
We have dislodged their troops;
They look on us at distance, and, like curs
'Scaped from the lion's paws, they bay far off.
And lick their wounds, and faintly threaten war.

Five thousand Romans, with their faces upward,
Lie breathless on the plain.
    Vent. 'Tis well; and he,
Who lost them, could have spared ten thousand more.
Yet if, by this advantage, you could gain
An easier peace, while Cæsar doubts the chance
Of arms——
    Ant. Oh, think not on't, Ventidius!
The boy pursues my ruin, he'll no peace;
His malice is considerate in advantage.
Oh, he's the coolest murderer! so staunch,
He kills, and keeps his temper.
    Vent. Have you no friend
In all his army, who has power to move him?
Mæcenas, or Agrippa, might do much.
    Ant. They're both too deep in Cæsar's interests.
We'll work it out by dint of sword, or perish.
    Vent. Fain I would find some other.
    Ant. Thank thy love.
Some four or five such victories as this
Will save thy further pains.
    Vent. Expect no more; Cæsar is on his guard:
I know, sir, you have conquered against odds;
But still you draw supplies from one poor town,
And of Egyptians: he has all the world,
And, at his beck, nations come pouring in,
To fill the gaps you make. Pray, think again.
    Ant. Why dost thou drive me from myself, to search
For foreign aids?—to hunt my memory,
And range all o'er a waste and barren place,
To find a friend? The wretched have no friends,
Yet I had one, the bravest youth of Rome,
Whom Cæsar loves beyond the love of women:
He could resolve his mind, as fire does wax,
From that hard rugged image melt him down,
And mould him in what softer form he pleased.
    Vent. Him would I see; that man, of all the world;
Just such a one we want.
    Ant. He loved me too;
I was his soul; he lived not but in me:
We were so closed within each other's breasts,
The rivets were not found, that joined us first.
That does not reach us yet: we were so mixt,
As meeting streams, both to ourselves were lost;

We were one mass; we could not give or take,
But from the same; for he was I, I he.
 Vent. He moves as I would wish him.   [*Aside.*
 Ant. After this,
I need not tell his name;—'twas Dolabella.
 Vent. He's now in Cæsar's camp.
 Ant. No matter where,
Since he's no longer mine. He took unkindly,
That I forbade him Cleopatra's sight,
Because I feared he loved her: he confessed,
He had a warmth, which, for my sake, he stifled;
For 'twere impossible that two, so one,
Should not have loved the same. When he departed,
He took no leave; and that confirmed my thoughts.
 Vent. It argues, that he loved you more than her,
Else he had stayed; but he perceived you jealous,
And would not grieve his friend: I know he loves you.
 Ant. I should have seen him, then, ere now.
 Vent. Perhaps
He has thus long been labouring for your peace.
 Ant. Would he were here!
 Vent. Would you believe he loved you?
I read your answer in your eyes, you would.
Not to conceal it longer, he has sent
A messenger from Cæsar's camp, with letters
 Ant. Let him appear.
 Vent. I'll bring him instantly.
[*Exit* VENTIDIUS, *and re-enters immediately with* DOLABELLA.
 Ant. 'Tis he himself! himself, by holy friendship!
        [*Runs to embrace him.*
Art thou returned at last, my better half?
Come, give me all myself!
Let me not live,
If the young bridegroom, longing for his night,
Was ever half so fond.
 Dola. I must be silent, for my soul is busy
About a nobler work: she's new come home,
Like a long-absent man, and wanders o'er
Each room, a stranger to her own, to look
If all be safe.
 Ant. Thou hast what's left of me;
For I am now so sunk from what I was,
Thou find'st me at my lowest water-mark.
The rivers that ran in, and raised my fortunes,

Are all dried up, or take another course:
What I have left is from my native spring;
I've still a heart that swells, in scorn of fate,
And lifts me to my banks.
    Dola. Still you are lord of all the world to me.
    Ant. Why, then I yet am so; for thou art all.
If I had any joy when thou wert absent,
I grudged it to myself; methought I robbed
Thee of thy part. But, O my Dolabella!
Thou hast beheld me other than I am.
Hast thou not seen my morning chambers filled
With sceptred slaves, who waited to salute me?
With eastern monarchs, who forgot the sun,
To worship my uprising?—menial kings
Ran coursing up and down my palace-yard,
Stood silent in my presence, watched my eyes,
And, at my least command, all started out,
Like racers to the goal.
    Dola. Slaves to your fortune.
    Ant. Fortune is Cæsar's now; and what am I?
    Vent. What you have made yourself; I will not flatter.
    Ant. Is this friendly done?
    Dola. Yes; when his end is so, I must join with him;
Indeed I must, and yet you must not chide;
Why am I else your friend?
    Ant. Take heed, young man,
How thou upbraid'st my love: The queen has eyes,
And thou too hast a soul. Canst thou remember,
When, swelled with hatred, thou beheld'st her first,
As accessary to thy brother's death?
    Dola. Spare my remembrance; 'twas a guilty day,
And still the blush hangs here.
    Ant. To clear herself,
For sending him no aid, she came from Egypt.
Her galley down the silver Cydnus rowed,
The tackling silk, the streamers waved with gold;
The gentle winds were lodged in purple sails:
Her nymphs, like Nereids, round her couch were placed;
Where she, another sea-born Venus, lay.
    Dola. No more; I would not hear it.
    Ant. Oh, you must!
She lay, and leant her cheek upon her hand,
And cast a look so languishingly sweet,
As if, secure of all beholders' hearts,

Neglecting, she could take them: boys, like Cupids,
Stood fanning, with their painted wings, the winds,
That played about her face. But if she smiled,
A darting glory seemed to blaze abroad,
That men's desiring eyes were never wearied,
But hung upon the object: To soft flutes
The silver oars kept time; and while they played,
The hearing gave new pleasure to the sight;
And both to thought. 'Twas heaven, or somewhat more:
For she so charmed all hearts, that gazing crowds
Stood panting on the shore, and wanted breath
To give their welcome voice.
Then, Dolabella, where was then thy soul?
Was not thy fury quite disarmed with wonder?
Didst thou not shrink behind me from those eyes
And whisper in my ear—Oh, tell her not
That I accused her with my brother's death? ✓
    Dola. And should my weakness be a plea for yours?
Mine was an age when love might be excused,
When kindly warmth, and when my springing youth
Made it a debt to nature. Yours——
    Vent. Speak boldly.
Yours, he would say, in your declining age,
When no more heat was left but what you forced,
When all the sap was needful for the trunk,
When it went down, then you constrained the course,
And robbed from nature, to supply desire;
In you (I would not use so harsh a word)
'Tis but plain dotage.
    Ant. Ha!
    Dola. 'Twas urged too home.——
But yet the loss was private, that I made;
'Twas but myself I lost: I lost no legions;
I had no world to lose, no people's love.
    Ant. This from a friend?
    Dola. Yes, Antony, a true one;
A friend so tender, that each word I speak
Stabs my own heart, before it reach your ear.
Oh, judge me not less kind, because I chide!
To Cæsar I excuse you.
    Ant. O ye gods!
Have I then lived to be excused to Cæsar?
    Dola. As to your equal.
    Ant. Well, he's but my equal:

While I wear this he never shall be more.

Dola. I bring conditions from him.

Ant. Are they noble?
Methinks thou shouldst not bring them else; yet he
Is full of deep dissembling; knows no honour
Divided from his interest. Fate mistook him;
For nature meant him for an usurer:
He's fit indeed to buy, not conquer kingdoms.

Vent. Then, granting this,
What power was theirs, who wrought so hard a temper
To honourable terms?

Ant. It was my Dolabella, or some god.

Dola. Nor I, nor yet Mæcenas, nor Agrippa:
They were your enemies; and I, a friend,
Too weak alone; yet 'twas a Roman's deed.

Ant. 'Twas like a Roman done: show me that man,
Who has preserved my life, my love, my honour;
Let me but see his face.

Vent. That task is mine,
And, Heaven, thou know'st how pleasing.   [*Exit* VENTIDIUS

Dola. You'll remember
To whom you stand obliged?

Ant. When I forget it,
Be thou unkind, and that's my greatest curse.
My queen shall thank him too.

Dola. I fear she will not.

Ant. But she shall do it: The queen, my Dolabella!
Hast thou not still some grudgings of thy fever?

Dola. I would not see her lost.

Ant. When I forsake her,
Leave me my better stars! for she has truth
Beyond her beauty. Cæsar tempted her,
At no less price than kingdoms, to betray me;
But she resisted all: and yet thou chidest me
For loving her too well. Could I do so?

Dola. Yes; there's my reason.

Re-enter VENTIDIUS, *with* OCTAVIA, *leading* ANTONY'S *two
little* Daughters.

Ant. Where?—Octavia there!   [*Starting back*

Vent. What, is she poison to you?—a disease?
Look on her, view her well, and those she brings:
Are they all strangers to your eyes? has nature
No secret call, no whisper they are yours?

Dola. For shame, my lord, if not for love, receive them
With kinder eyes. If you confess a man,
Meet them, embrace them, bid them welcome to you.
Your arms should open, even without your knowledge,
To clasp them in; your feet should turn to wings,
To bear you to them; and your eyes dart out
And aim a kiss, ere you could reach the lips.

Ant. I stood amazed, to think how they came hither.

Vent. I sent for them; I brought them in unknown
To Cleopatra's guards.

Dola. Yet, are you cold?

Octav. Thus long I have attended for my welcome;
Which, as a stranger, sure I might expect.
Who am I?

Ant. Cæsar's sister.

Octav. That's unkind.
Had I been nothing more than Cæsar's sister,
Know, I had still remained in Cæsar's camp:
But your Octavia, your much injured wife,
Though banished from your bed, driven from your house,
In spite of Cæsar's sister, still is yours.
'Tis true, I have a heart disdains your coldness,
And prompts me not to seek what you should offer;
But a wife's virtue still surmounts that pride.
I come to claim you as my own; to show
My duty first; to ask, nay beg, your kindness:
Your hand, my lord; 'tis mine, and I will have it.

                              [*Taking his hand.*

Vent. Do, take it; thou deserv'st it.

Dola. On my soul,
And so she does: she's neither too submissive,
Nor yet too haughty; but so just a mean
Shows, as it ought, a wife and Roman too.

Ant. I fear, Octavia, you have begged my life.

Octav. Begged it, my lord?

Ant. Yes, begged it, my ambassadress!
Poorly and basely begged it of your brother.

Octav. Poorly and basely I could never beg:
Nor could my brother grant.

Ant. Shall I, who, to my kneeling slave, could say,
Rise up, and be a king; shall I fall down
And cry,—Forgive me, Cæsar! Shall I set
A man, my equal, in the place of Jove,
As he could give me being? No; that word,

Forgive, would choke me up,
And die upon my tongue.

   Dola. You shall not need it.

   Ant. I will not need it. Come, you've all betrayed me,—
My friend too!—to receive some vile conditions.
My wife has bought me, with her prayers and tears;
And now I must become her branded slave.
In every peevish mood, she will upbraid
The life she gave: if I but look awry,
She cries—I'll tell my brother.

   Octav. My hard fortune
Subjects me still to your unkind mistakes.
But the conditions I have brought are such,
You need not blush to take: I love your honour,
Because 'tis mine; it never shall be said,
Octavia's husband was her brother's slave.
Sir, you are free; free, even from her you loathe;
For, though my brother bargains for your love,
Makes me the price and cement of your peace,
I have a soul like yours; I cannot take
Your love as alms, nor beg what I deserve.
I'll tell my brother we are reconciled;
He shall draw back his troops, and you shall march
To rule the East: I may be dropt at Athens;
No matter where. I never will complain,
But only keep the barren name of wife,
And rid you of the trouble.

   Vent. Was ever such a strife of sullen honour!
Both scorn to be obliged.

   Dola. Oh, she has touched him in the tenderest part;
See how he reddens with despite and shame,   *Apart*
To be outdone in generosity!

   Vent. See how he winks! how he dries up a tear,
That fain would fall!

   Ant. Octavia, I have heard you, and must praise
The greatness of your soul;
But cannot yield to what you have proposed:
For I can ne'er be conquered but by love;
And you do all for duty. You would free me,
And would be dropt at Athens; was't not so?

   Octav. It was, my lord.

   Ant. Then I must be obliged
To one who loves me not; who, to herself,
May call me thankless and ungrateful man:—

I'll not endure it; no.

Vent. I am glad it pinches there.   [*Aside.*

Octav. Would you triumph o'er poor Octavia's virtue?
That pride was all I had to bear me up;
That you might think you owed me for your life,
And owed it to my duty, not my love.
I have been injured, and my haughty soul
Could brook but ill the man who slights my bed.

Ant. Therefore you love me not.

Octav. Therefore, my lord,
I should not love you.

Ant. Therefore you would leave me?

Octav. And therefore I should leave you—if I could.

Dola. Her soul's too great, after such injuries,
To say she loves; and yet she lets you see it.
Her modesty and silence plead her cause.

Ant. O Dolabella, which way shall I turn?
I find a secret yielding in my soul;
But Cleopatra, who would die with me,
Must she be left? Pity pleads for Octavia;
But does it not plead more for Cleopatra?

Vent. Justice and pity both plead for Octavia;
For Cleopatra, neither.
One would be ruined with you; but she first
Had ruined you: The other, you have ruined,
And yet she would preserve you.
In everything their merits are unequal.

Ant. O my distracted soul!

Octav. Sweet Heaven compose it!—
Come, come, my lord, if I can pardon you,
Methinks you should accept it. Look on these;
Are they not yours? or stand they thus neglected,
As they are mine? Go to him, children, go;
Kneel to him, take him by the hand, speak to him;
For you may speak, and he may own you too,
Without a blush; and so he cannot all
His children: go, I say, and pull him to me,
And pull him to yourselves, from that bad woman.
You, Agrippina, hang upon his arms;
And you, Antonia, clasp about his waist:
If he will shake you off, if he will dash you
Against the pavement, you must bear it, children;
For you are mine, and I was born to suffer.

                    [*Here the* Children *go to him, etc.*

Vent. Was ever sight so moving?——Emperor!
Dola. Friend!
Octav. Husband!
Both Child. Father!
Ant. I am vanquished: take me,
Octavia; take me, children; share me all.   [*Embracing them.*
I've been a thriftless debtor to your loves,
And run out much, in riot, from your stock;
But all shall be amended.
Octav. O blest hour!
Dola. O happy change!
Vent. My joy stops at my tongue;
But it has found two channels here for one,
And bubbles out above.
Ant. [*to* OCTAVIA]. This is thy triumph; lead me where
    thou wilt;
Even to thy brother's camp.
Octav. All there are yours.

Enter ALEXAS *hastily.*

Alex. The queen, my mistress, sir, and yours——
Ant. 'Tis past.——
Octavia, you shall stay this night: To-morrow,
Cæsar and we are one.
    [*Exit leading* OCTAVIA; DOLABELLA *and the* Children *follow.*
Vent. There's news for you; run, my officious eunuch,
Be sure to be the first; haste forward:
Haste, my dear eunuch, haste.   [*Exit.*
Alex. This downright fighting fool, this thick-skulled hero,
This blunt, unthinking instrument of death,
With plain dull virtue has outgone my wit.
Pleasure forsook my earliest infancy;
The luxury of others robbed my cradle,
And ravished thence the promise of a man.
Cast out from nature, disinherited
Of what her meanest children claim by kind,
Yet greatness kept me from contempt: that's gone.
Had Cleopatra followed my advice,
Then he had been betrayed who now forsakes.
She dies for love; but she has known its joys:
Gods, is this just, that I, who know no joys,
Must die, because she loves?

Enter CLEOPATRA, CHARMION, IRAS, *and* Train.

O madam, I have seen what blasts my eyes!
Octavia's here.

   Cleo. Peace with that raven's note.
I know it too; and now am in
The pangs of death.

   Alex. You are no more a queen;
Egypt is lost.

   Cleo. What tell'st thou me of Egypt?
My life, my soul is lost! Octavia has him!——
O fatal name to Cleopatra's love!
My kisses, my embraces now are hers;
While I——But thou hast seen my rival; speak,
Does she deserve this blessing? Is she fair?
Bright as a goddess? and is all perfection
Confined to her? It is. Poor I was made
Of that coarse matter, which, when she was finished,
The gods threw by for rubbish.

   Alex. She is indeed a very miracle.

   Cleo. Death to my hopes, a miracle!

   Alex. A miracle;   [*Bowing.*
I mean of goodness; for in beauty, madam,
You make all wonders cease.

   Cleo. I was too rash:
Take this in part of recompense. But, oh!   [*Giving a ring.*
I fear thou flatterest me.

   Char. She comes! she's here!

   Iras. Fly, madam, Cæsar's sister!

   Cleo. Were she the sister of the thunderer Jove,
And bore her brother's lightning in her eyes,
Thus would I face my rival.

       [*Meets* OCTAVIA *with* VENTIDIUS. OCTAVIA *bears up to*
         her. Their Trains come up on either side.

   Octav. I need not ask if you are Cleopatra;
Your haughty carriage——

   Cleo. Shows I am a queen:
Nor need I ask you, who you are.

   Octav. A Roman:
A name, that makes and can unmake a queen.

   Cleo. Your lord, the man who serves me, is a Roman.

   Octav. He was a Roman, till he lost that name,
To be a slave in Egypt; but I come
To free him thence.

   Cleo. Peace, peace, my lover's Juno.
When he grew weary of that household clog,

He chose my easier bonds.

    Octav. I wonder not
Your bonds are easy: you have long been practised
In that lascivious art: He's not the first
For whom you spread your snares: Let Cæsar witness.

    Cleo. I loved not Cæsar; 'twas but gratitude
I paid his love: The worst your malice can,
Is but to say the greatest of mankind
Has been my slave. The next, but far above him
In my esteem, is he whom law calls yours,
But whom his love made mine.

    Octav. I would view nearer   [*Coming up close to her.*
That face, which has so long usurped my right,
To find the inevitable charms, that catch
Mankind so sure, that ruined my dear lord.

    Cleo. Oh, you do well to search; for had you known
But half these charms, you had not lost his heart.

    Octav. Far be their knowledge from a Roman lady,
Far from a modest wife! Shame of our sex,
Dost thou not blush to own those black endearments,
That make sin pleasing?

    Cleo. You may blush, who want them.
If bounteous nature, if indulgent Heaven
Have given me charms to please the bravest man,
Should I not thank them? Should I be ashamed,
And not be proud? I am, that he has loved me;
And, when I love not him, Heaven change this face
For one like that.

    Octav. Thou lov'st him not so well.

    Cleo. I love him better, and deserve him more.

    Octav. You do not; cannot: You have been his ruin.
Who made him cheap at Rome, but Cleopatra?
Who made him scorned abroad, but Cleopatra?
At Actium, who betrayed him? Cleopatra.
Who made his children orphans, and poor me
A wretched widow? only Cleopatra.

    Cleo. Yet she, who loves him best, is Cleopatra.
If you have suffered, I have suffered more.
You bear the specious title of a wife,
To gild your cause, and draw the pitying world
To favour it: the world condemns poor me.
For I have lost my honour, lost my fame,
And stained the glory of my royal house,
And all to bear the branded name of mistress.

There wants but life, and that too I would lose
For him I love.

 Octav. Be't so, then; take thy wish. [*Exit with her Train.*

 Cleo. And 'tis my wish,
Now he is lost for whom alone I lived.
My sight grows dim, and every object dances,
And swims before me, in the maze of death.
My spirits, while they were opposed, kept up;
They could not sink beneath a rival's scorn!
But now she's gone, they faint.

 Alex. Mine have had leisure
To recollect their strength, and furnish counsel,
To ruin her, who else must ruin you.

 Cleo. Vain promiser!
Lead me, my Charmion; nay, your hand too, Iras.
My grief has weight enough to sink you both.
Conduct me to some solitary chamber,
And draw the curtains round;
Then leave me to myself, to take alone
My fill of grief:
 There I till death will his unkindness weep;
 As harmless infants moan themselves asleep. [*Exeunt.*

ACT IV

Scene I

Enter Antony *and* Dolabella.

 Dola. Why would you shift it from yourself on me?
Can you not tell her, you must part?

 Ant. I cannot.
I could pull out an eye, and bid it go,
And t'other should not weep. O Dolabella,
How many deaths are in this word, *Depart!*
I dare not trust my tongue to tell her so:
One look of hers would thaw me into tears,
And I should melt, till I were lost again.

 Dola. Then let Ventidius;
He's rough by nature.

 Ant. Oh, he'll speak too harshly;
He'll kill her with the news: Thou, only thou.

 Dola. Nature has cast me in so soft a mould,
That but to hear a story, feigned for pleasure,

Of some sad lover's death, moistens my eyes,
And robs me of my manhood. I should speak
So faintly, with such fear to grieve her heart,
She'd not believe it earnest.

    Ant. Therefore,—therefore
Thou only, thou art fit: Think thyself me;
And when thou speak'st (but let it first be long),
Take off the edge from every sharper sound,
And let our parting be as gently made,
As other loves begin: Wilt thou do this?

    Dola. What you have said so sinks into my soul,
That, if I must speak, I shall speak just so.

    Ant. I leave you then to your sad task: Farewell.
I sent her word to meet you. [*Goes to the door, and comes back.*
I forgot;
Let her be told, I'll make her peace with mine:
Her crown and dignity shall be preserved,
If I have power with Cæsar.——Oh, be sure
To think on that.

    Dola. Fear not, I will remember.

          [ANTONY *goes again to the door, and comes back.*

    Ant. And tell her, too, how much I was constrained;
I did not this, but with extremest force:
Desire her not to hate my memory,
For I still cherish hers;——insist on that.

    Dola. Trust me, I'll not forget it.

    Ant. Then that's all.   [*Goes out, and returns again.*
Wilt thou forgive my fondness this once more?
Tell her, though we shall never meet again,
If I should hear she took another love,
The news would break my heart.—Now I must go;
For every time I have returned, I feel
My soul more tender; and my next command
Would be, to bid her stay, and ruin both.   [*Exit.*

    Dola. Men are but children of a larger growth;
Our appetites as apt to change as theirs,
And full as craving too, and full as vain;
And yet the soul, shut up in her dark room,
Viewing so clear abroad, at home sees nothing;
But, like a mole in earth, busy and blind,
Works all her folly up, and casts it outward
To the world's open view: Thus I discovered,
And blamed the love of ruined Antony;
Yet wish that I were he, to be so ruined.

Enter VENTIDIUS *above.*

Vent. Alone, and talking to himself? concerned too?
Perhaps my guess is right; he loved her once,
And may pursue it still.
    Dola. O friendship! friendship!
Ill canst thou answer this; and reason, worse:
Unfaithful in the attempt; hopeless to win;
And if I win, undone: mere madness all.
And yet the occasion's fair. What injury
To him, to wear the robe which he throws by!
    Vent. None, none at all. This happens as I wish,
To ruin her yet more with Antony.

Enter CLEOPATRA, *talking with* ALEXAS; CHARMION,
IRAS *on the other side.*

Dola. She comes! What charms have sorrow on that face!
Sorrow seems pleased to dwell with so much sweetness;
Yet, now and then, a melancholy smile
Breaks loose, like lightning in a winter's night,
And shows a moment's day.
    Vent. If she should love him too! her eunuch there?
That porc'pisce bodes ill weather. Draw, draw nearer,
Sweet devil, that I may hear.
    Alex. Believe me; try
        [DOLABELLA *goes over to* CHARMION *and* IRAS; *seems to*
            talk with them.
To make him jealous; jealousy is like
A polished glass held to the lips when life's in doubt;
If there be breath, 'twill catch the damp, and show it.
    Cleo. I grant you, jealousy's a proof of love,
But 'tis a weak and unavailing medicine;
It puts out the disease, and makes it show,
But has no power to cure.
    Alex. 'Tis your last remedy, and strongest too:
And then this Dolabella, who so fit
To practise on? He's handsome, valiant, young,
And looks as he were laid for nature's bait,
To catch weak women's eyes.
He stands already more than half suspected
Of loving you: the least kind word or glance
You give this youth, will kindle him with love:
Then, like a burning vessel set adrift,
You'll send him down amain before the wind,

To fire the heart of jealous Antony.

 Cleo. Can I do this? Ah, no; my love's so true,
That I can neither hide it where it is,
Nor show it where it is not. Nature meant me
A wife; a silly, harmless, household dove,
Fond without art, and kind without deceit;
But Fortune, that has made a mistress of me,
Has thrust me out to the wide world, unfurnished
Of falsehood to be happy.

 Alex. Force yourself.
The event will be, your lover will return,
Doubly desirous to possess the good
Which once he feared to lose.

 Cleo. I must attempt it;
But oh, with what regret!

      [*Exit* ALEXAS. *She comes up to* DOLABELLA.

 Vent. So, now the scene draws near; they're in my reach.

 Cleo. [*to* DOL.]. Discoursing with my women! might not I
Share in your entertainment?

 Char. You have been
The subject of it, madam.

 Cleo. How! and how?

 Iras. Such praises of your beauty!

 Cleo. Mere poetry.
Your Roman wits, your Gallus and Tibullus,
Have taught you this from Cytheris and Delia.

 Dola. Those Roman wits have never been in Egypt;
Cytheris and Delia else had been unsung:
I, who have seen——had I been born a poet,
Should choose a nobler name.

 Cleo. You flatter me.
But, 'tis your nation's vice: All of your country
Are flatterers, and all false. Your friend's like you.
I'm sure, he sent you not to speak these words.

 Dola. No, madam; yet he sent me——

 Cleo. Well, he sent you——

 Dola. Of a less pleasing errand.

 Cleo. How less pleasing?
Less to yourself, or me?

 Dola. Madam, to both;
For you must mourn, and I must grieve to cause it.

 Cleo. You, Charmion, and your fellow, stand at distance.—
Hold up, my spirits. [*Aside*]——Well, now your mournful
  matter!

For I'm prepared, perhaps can guess it too.

Dola. I wish you would; for 'tis a thankless office,
To tell ill news: And I, of all your sex,
Most fear displeasing you.

Cleo. Of all your sex,
I soonest could forgive you, if you should.

Vent. Most delicate advances! Women! women!
Dear, damned, inconstant sex!

Cleo. In the first place,
I am to be forsaken; is't not so?

Dola. I wish I could not answer to that question.

Cleo. Then pass it o'er, because it troubles you:
I should have been more grieved another time.
Next, I'm to lose my kingdom——Farewell, Egypt!
Yet, is there any more?

Dola. Madam, I fear
Your too deep sense of grief has turned your reason.

Cleo. No, no, I'm not run mad; I can bear fortune:
And love may be expelled by other love,
As poisons are by poisons.

Dola. You o'erjoy me, madam,
To find your griefs so moderately borne.
You've heard the worst; all are not false like him.

Cleo. No; Heaven forbid they should.

Dola. Some men are constant.

Cleo. And constancy deserves reward, that's certain.

Dola. Deserves it not; but give it leave to hope.

Vent. I'll swear, thou hast my leave. I have enough:
But how to manage this! Well, I'll consider.   [*Exit.*

Dola. I came prepared
To tell you heavy news; news, which I thought
Would fright the blood from your pale cheeks to hear:
But you have met it with a cheerfulness,
That makes my task more easy; and my tongue,
Which on another's message was employed,
Would gladly speak its own.

Cleo. Hold, Dolabella.
First tell me, were you chosen by my lord?
Or sought you this employment?

Dola. He picked me out; and, as his bosom friend,
He charged me with his words.

Cleo. The message then
I know was tender, and each accent smootn,
To mollify that rugged word, *Depart.*

Dola. Oh, you mistake: He chose the harshest words;
With fiery eyes, and with contracted brows,
He coined his face in the severest stamp;
And fury shook his fabric, like an earthquake;
He heaved for vent, and burst like bellowing Ætna,
In sounds scarce human—"Hence away for ever,
Let her begone, the blot of my renown,
And bane of all my hopes!"

> [*All the time of this speech,* CLEOPATRA *seems more and*
> *more concerned, till she sinks quite down.*

"Let her be driven, as far as men can think,
From man's commerce! she'll poison to the centre."
    Cleo. Oh, I can bear no more!
    Dola. Help, help!—O wretch! O cursed, cursed wretch!
What have I done!
    Char. Help, chafe her temples, Iras.
    Iras. Bend, bend her forward quickly.
    Char. Heaven be praised,
She comes again.
    Cleo. Oh, let him not approach me.
Why have you brought me back to this loathed being,
The abode of falsehood, violated vows,
And injured love? For pity, let me go;
For, if there be a place of long repose,
I'm sure I want it..My disdainful lord
Can never break that quiet; nor awake
The sleeping soul, with hollowing in my tomb
Such words as fright her hence.—Unkind, unkind!
    Dola. Believe me, 'tis against myself I speak;   [*Kneeling.*
That sure desires belief; I injured him:
My friend ne'er spoke those words. Oh, had you seen
How often he came back, and every time
With something more obliging and more kind,
To add to what he said; what dear farewells;
How almost vanquished by his love he parted,
And leaned to what unwillingly he left!
I, traitor as I was, for love of you
(But what can you not do, who made me false?)
I forged that lie; for whose forgiveness kneels
This self-accused, self-punished criminal.
    Cleo. With how much ease believe we what we wish!
Rise, Dolabella; if you have been guilty,
I have contributed, and too much love
Has made me guilty too.

The advance of kindness, which I made, was feigned,
To call back fleeting love by jealousy;
But 'twould not last. Oh, rather let me lose,
Than so ignobly trifle with his heart.

   Dola. I find your breast fenced round from human reach,
Transparent as a rock of solid crystal;
Seen through, but never pierced. My friend, my friend,
What endless treasure hast thou thrown away;
And scattered, like an infant, in the ocean,
Vain sums of wealth, which none can gather thence!

   Cleo. Could you not beg
An hour's admittance to his private ear?
Like one, who wanders through long barren wilds
And yet foreknows no hospitable inn
Is near to succour hunger, eats his fill,
Before his painful march;
So would I feed a while my famished eyes
Before we part; for I have far to go,
If death be far, and never must return.

VENTIDIUS with OCTAVIA, behind.

   Vent. From hence you may discover—oh, sweet, sweet!
Would you indeed? The pretty hand in earnest?

   Dola. I will, for this reward.   [*Takes her hand.*
Draw it not back.
'Tis all I e'er will beg.

   Vent. They turn upon us.

   Octav. What quick eyes has guilt!

   Vent. Seem not to have observed them, and go on.

They enter.

   Dola. Saw you the emperor, Ventidius?

   Vent. No.
I sought him; but I heard that he was private,
None with him but Hipparchus, his freedman.

   Dola. Know you his business?

   Vent. Giving him instructions,
And letters to his brother Cæsar.

   Dola. Well,
He must be found.   [*Exeunt* DOLABELLA *and* CLEOPATRA.

   Octav. Most glorious impudence!

   Vent. She looked, methought,
As she would say—Take your old man, Octavia;
Thank you, I'm better here.——

Well, but what use
Make we of this discovery?

   Octav. Let it die.

   Vent. I pity Dolabella; but she's dangerous;
Her eyes have power beyond Thessalian charms,
To draw the moon from heaven; for eloquence,
The sea-green Syrens taught her voice their flattery;
And, while she speaks, night steals upon the day,
Unmarked of those that hear: Then she's so charming,
Age buds at sight of her, and swells to youth:
The holy priests gaze on her when she smiles;
And with heaved hands, forgetting gravity,
They bless her wanton eyes: Even I, who hate her,
With a malignant joy behold such beauty;
And, while I curse, desire it. Antony
Must needs have some remains of passion still,
Which may ferment into a worse relapse,
If now not fully cured. I know, this minute,
With Cæsar he's endeavouring her peace.

   Octav. You have prevailed:——But for a further purpose
                                    [Walks off.

I'll prove how he will relish this discovery.
What, make a strumpet's peace! it swells my heart:
It must not, shall not be.

   Vent. His guards appear.
Let me begin, and you shall second me.

               Enter ANTONY.

   Ant. Octavia, I was looking you, my love:
What, are your letters ready? I have given
My last instructions.

   Octav. Mine, my lord, are written.

   Ant. Ventidius.   *[Drawing him aside.*

   Vent. My lord?

   Ant. A word in private.——
When saw you Dolabella?

   Vent. Now, my lord,
He parted hence; and Cleopatra with him.

   Ant. Speak softly.——'Twas by my command he went,
To bear my last farewell.

   Vent. It looked indeed   *[Aloud.*
Like your farewell.

   Ant. More softly.——My farewell?
What secret meaning have you in those words

Of—My farewell? He did it by my order.

Vent. Then he obeyed your order. I suppose   [*Aloud.*
You bid him do it with all gentleness,
All kindness, and all——love.

Ant. How she mourned,
The poor forsaken creature!

Vent. She took it as she ought; she bore your parting
As she did Cæsar's, as she would another's,
Were a new love to come.

Ant. Thou dost belie her;   [*Aloud.*
Most basely, and maliciously belie her.

Vent. I thought not to displease you; I have done.

Octav. You seemed disturbed, my lord.   [*Coming up.*

Ant. A very trifle.
Retire, my love.

Vent. It was indeed à trifle.
He sent——

Ant. No more. Look how thou disobey'st me;   [*Angrily.*
Thy life shall answer it.

Octav. Then 'tis no trifle.

Vent. [*to* Octav.]. 'Tis less; a very nothing: You too saw it,
As well as I, and therefore 'tis no secret.

Ant. She saw it!

Vent. Yes: She saw young Dolabella——

Ant. Young Dolabella!

Vent. Young, I think him young,
And handsome too; and so do others think him.
But what of that? He went by your command,
Indeed 'tis probable, with some kind message;
For she received it graciously; she smiled;
And then he grew familiar with her hand,
Squeezed it, and worried it with ravenous kisses;
She blushed, and sighed, and smiled, and blushed again;
At last she took occasion to talk softly,
And brought her cheek up close, and leaned on his;
At which, he whispered kisses back on hers;
And then she cried aloud—That constancy
Should be rewarded.

Octav. This I saw and heard.

Ant. What woman was it, whom you heard and saw
So playful with my friend?
Not Cleopatra?

Vent. Even she, my lord.

Ant. My Cleopatra?

Vent. Your Cleopatra;
Dolabella's Cleopatra; every man's Cleopatra.

Ant. Thou liest.

Vent. I do not lie, my lord.
Is this so strange? Should mistresses be left,
And not provide against a time of change?
You know she's not much used to lonely nights.

Ant. I'll think no more on't.
I know 'tis false, and see the plot betwixt you.—
You needed not have gone this way, Octavia.
What harms it you that Cleopatra's just?
She's mine no more. I see, and I forgive:
Urge it no further, love.

Octav. Are you concerned,
That she's found false?

Ant. I should be, were it so;
For, though 'tis past, I would not that the world
Should tax my former choice, that I loved one
Of so light note; but I forgive you both.

Vent. What has my age deserved, that you should think
I would abuse your ears with perjury?
If Heaven be true, she's false.

Ant. Though heaven and earth
Should witness it, I'll not believe her tainted.

Vent. I'll bring you, then, a witness
From hell, to prove her so.—Nay, go not back;
          [*Seeing* ALEXAS *just entering, and starting back.*
For stay you must and shall.

Alex. What means my lord?

Vent. To make you do what most you hate,—speak truth.
You are of Cleopatra's private counsel,
Of her bed-counsel, her lascivious hours;
Are conscious of each nightly change she makes,
And watch her, as Chaldeans do the moon,
Can tell what signs she passes through, what day.

Alex. My noble lord!

Vent. My most illustrious pander,
No fine set speech, no cadence, no turned periods,
But a plain homespun truth, is what I ask:
I did, myself, o'erhear your queen make love
To Dolabella. Speak; for I will know,
By your confession, what more passed betwixt them;
How near the business draws to your employment;
And when the happy hour.

Ant. Speak truth, Alexas; whether it offend
Or please Ventidius, care not: Justify
Thy injured queen from malice: Dare his worst.

Octav. [*Aside.*] See how he gives him courage! how he fears
To find her false! and shuts his eyes to truth,
Willing to be misled!

Alex. As far as love may plead for woman's frailty,
Urged by desert and greatness of the lover,
So far, divine Octavia, may my queen
Stand even excused to you for loving him
Who is your lord: so far, from brave Ventidius,
May her past actions hope a fair report.

Ant. 'Tis well, and truly spoken: mark, Ventidius.

Alex. To you, most noble emperor, her strong passion
Stands not excused, but wholly justified.
Her beauty's charms alone, without her crown,
From Ind and Meroe drew the distant vows
Of sighing kings; and at her feet were laid
The sceptres of the earth, exposed on heaps,
To choose where she would reign:
She thought a Roman only could deserve her,
And, of all Romans, only Antony;
And, to be less than wife to you, disdained
Their lawful passion.

Ant. 'Tis but truth.

Alex. And yet, though love, and your unmatched desert,
Have drawn her from the due regard of honour,
At last Heaven opened her unwilling eyes
To see the wrongs she offered fair Octavia,
Whose holy bed she lawlessly usurped.
The sad effects of this improsperous war
Confirmed those pious thoughts.

Vent. [*Aside.*] Oh, wheel you there?
Observe him now; the man begins to mend,
And talk substantial reason.—Fear not, eunuch;
The emperor has given thee leave to speak.

Alex. Else had I never dared to offend his ears
With what the last necessity has urged
On my forsaken mistress; yet I must not
Presume to say, her heart is wholly altered.

Ant. No, dare not for thy life, I charge thee dare not
Pronounce that fatal word!

Octav. Must I bear this? Good Heaven, afford me patience.
                                          [*Aside.*

Vent. On, sweet eunuch; my dear half-man, proceed.

Alex. Yet Dolabella
Has loved her long; he, next my god-like lord,
Deserves her best; and should she meet his passion,
Rejected, as she is, by him she loved——

Ant. Hence from my sight! for I can bear no more:
Let furies drag thee quick to hell; let all
The longer damned have rest; each torturing hand
Do thou employ, till Cleopatra comes;
Then join thou too, and help to torture her!

[*Exit* ALEXAS, *thrust out by* ANTONY.

Octav. 'Tis not well,
Indeed, my lord, 'tis much unkind to me,
To show this passion, this extreme concernment,
For an abandoned, faithless prostitute.

Ant. Octavia, leave me; I am much disordered:
Leave me, I say.

Octav. My lord!

Ant. I bid you leave me.

Vent. Obey him, madam: best withdraw a while,
And see how this will work.

Octav. Wherein have I offended you, my lord,
That I am bid to leave you? Am I false,
Or infamous? Am I a Cleopatra?
Were I she,
Base as she is, you would not bid me leave you;
But hang upon my neck, take slight excuses,
And fawn upon my falsehood.

Ant. 'Tis too much.
Too much, Octavia; I am pressed with sorrows
Too heavy to be borne; and you add more:
I would retire, and recollect what's left
Of man within, to aid me.

Octav. You would mourn,
In private, for your love, who has betrayed you.
You did but half return to me: your kindness
Lingered behind with her. I hear, my lord,
You make conditions for her,
And would include her treaty. Wondrous proofs
Of love to me!

Ant. Are you my friend, Ventidius?
Or are you turned a Dolabella too,
And let this fury loose?

Vent. Oh, be advised,

Sweet madam, and retire. ·

Octav. Yes, I will go; but never to return.
You shall no more be haunted with this Fury.
My lord, my lord, love will not always last,
When urged with long unkindness and disdain:
Take her again, whom you prefer to me;
She stays but to be called. Poor cozened man!
Let a feigned parting give her back your heart,
Which a feigned love first got; for injured me,
Though my just sense of wrongs forbid my stay,
My duty shall be yours.
To the dear pledges of our former love
My tenderness and care shall be transferred,
And they shall cheer, by turns, my widowed nights:
So, take my last farewell; for I despair
To have you whole, and scorn to take you half.   [*Exit.*

Vent. I combat Heaven, which blasts my best designs:
My last attempt must be to win her back;
But oh! I fear in vain.   [*Exit.*

Ant. Why was I framed with this plain, honest heart,
Which knows not to disguise its griefs and weakness,
But bears its workings outward to the world?
I should have kept the mighty anguish in,
And forced a smile at Cleopatra's falsehood:
Octavia had believed it, and had stayed.
But I am made a shallow-forded stream,
Seen to the bottom: all my clearness scorned,
And all my faults exposed.—See where he comes,

Enter DOLABELLA.

Who has profaned the sacred name of friend,
And worn it into vileness!
With how secure a brow, and specious form
He gilds the secret villain! Sure that face
Was meant for honesty; but Heaven mismatched it,
And furnished treason out with nature's pomp,
To make its work more easy.

Dola. O my friend!

Ant. Well, Dolabella, you performed my message?

Dola. I did, unwillingly.

Ant. Unwillingly?
Was it so hard for you to bear our parting?
You should have wished it.

Dola. Why?

Ant. Because you love me.
And she received my message ·with as true,
With as unfeigned a sorrow as you brought it?
 Dola. She loves you, even to madness.
 Ant. Oh, I know it.
You, Dolabella, do not better know
How much she loves me. And should I
Forsake this beauty? This all-perfect creature?
 Dola. I could not, were she mine.
 Ant. And yet you first
Persuaded me: How come you altered since?
 Dola. I said at first I was not fit to go:
I could not hear her sighs, and see her tears,
But pity must prevail: And so, perhaps,
It may again with you; for I have promised,
That she should take her last farewell: And, see,
She comes to claim my word.

Enter CLEOPATRA.

 Ant. False Dolabella!
 Dola. What's false, my lord?
 Ant. Why, Dolabella's false,
And Cleopatra's false; both false and faithless.
Draw near, you well-joined wickedness, you serpents,
Whom I have in my kindly bosom warmed,
Till I am stung to death.
 Dola. My lord, have I
Deserved to be thus used?
 Cleo. Can Heaven prepare
A newer torment? Can it find a curse
Beyond our separation?
 Ant. Yes, if fate
Be just, much greater: Heaven should be ingenious
In punishing such crimes. The rolling stone,
And gnawing vulture, were slight pains, invented
When Jove was young, and no examples known
Of mighty ills; but you have ripened sin,
To such a monstrous growth, 'twill pose the gods
To find an equal torture. Two, two such!—
Oh, there's no further name,—two such! to me,
To me, who locked my soul within your breasts,
Had no desires, no joys, no life, but you;
When half the globe was mine, I gave it you
In dowry with my heart; I had no use,

No fruit of all, but you: A friend and mistress
Was what the world could give. O Cleopatra!
O Dolabella! how could you betray
This tender heart, which with an infant fondness
Lay lulled betwixt your bosoms, and there slept,
Secure of injured faith?

Dola. If she has wronged you,
Heaven, hell, and you revenge it.

Ant. If she has wronged me!
Thou wouldst evade thy part of guilt; but swear
Thou lov'st not her.

Dola. Not so as I love you.

Ant. Not so? Swear, swear, I say, thou dost not love her.

Dola. No more than friendship will allow.

Ant. No more?
Friendship allows thee nothing: Thou art perjured—
And yet thou didst not swear thou lov'st her not;
But not so much, no more. O trifling hypocrite,
Who dar'st not own to her, thou dost not love,
Nor own to me, thou dost! Ventidius heard it;
Octavia saw it.

Cleo. They are enemies.

Ant. Alexas is not so: He, he confessed it;
He, who, next hell, best knew it, he avowed it.
Why do I seek a proof beyond yourself?   [*To* DOLABELLA.
You, whom I sent to bear my last farewell,
Returned, to plead her stay.

Dola. What shall I answer?
If to have loved be guilt, then I have sinned;
But if to have repented of that love
Can wash away my crime, I have repented.
Yet, if I have offended past forgiveness,
Let not her suffer: She is innocent.

Cleo. Ah, what will not a woman do, who loves?
What means will she refuse, to keep that heart,
Where all her joys are placed? 'Twas I encouraged,
'Twas I blew up the fire that scorched his soul,
To make you jealous, and by that regain you.
But all in vain; I could not counterfeit:
In spite of all the dams my love broke o'er,
And drowned my heart again: fate took the occasion;
And thus one minute's feigning has destroyed
My whole life's truth.

Ant. Thin cobweb arts of falsehood;

Seen, and broke through at first.

Dola. Forgive your mistress.

Cleo. Forgive your friend.

Ant. You have convinced yourselves.
You plead each other's cause: What witness have you,
That you but meant to raise my jealousy?

Cleo. Ourselves, and Heaven.

Ant. Guilt witnesses for guilt. Hence, love and friendship!
You have no longer place in human breasts,
These two have driven you out: Avoid my sight!
I would not kill the man whom I have loved,
And cannot hurt the woman; but avoid me:
I do not know how long I can be tame;
For, if I stay one minute more, to think
How I am wronged, my justice and revenge
Will cry so loud within me, that my pity
Will not be heard for either.

Dola. Heaven has but
Our sorrow for our sins; and then delights
To pardon erring man: Sweet mercy seems
Its darling attribute, which limits justice;
As if there were degrees in infinite,
And infinite would rather want perfection
Than punish to extent.

Ant. I can forgive
A foe; but not a mistress and a friend.
Treason is there in its most horrid shape,
Where trust is greatest; and the soul resigned,
Is stabbed by its own guards: I'll hear no more;
Hence from my sight for ever!

Cleo. How? for ever!
I cannot go one moment from your sight,
And must I go for ever?
My joys, my only joys, are centred here:
What place have I to go to? My own kingdom?
That I have lost for you: Or to the Romans?
They hate me for your sake: Or must I wander
The wide world o'er, a helpless, banished woman,
Banished for love of you; banished from you?
Ay, there's the banishment! Oh, hear me; hear me,
With strictest justice: For I beg no favour;
And if I have offended you, then kill me,
But do not banish me.

Ant. I must not hear you.

I have a fool within me takes your part;
But honour stops my ears.
   Cleo. For pity hear me!
Would you cast off a slave who followed you?
Who crouched beneath your spurn?—He has no pity!
See, if he gives one tear to my departure;
One look, one kind farewell: O iron heart!
Let all the gods look down, and judge betwixt us,
If he did ever love!
   Ant. No more: Alexas!
   Dola. A perjured villain!
   Ant. [*To* Cleo.] Your Alexas; yours.
   Cleo. Oh, 'twas his plot; his ruinous design,
To engage you in my love by jealousy.
Hear him; confront him with me; let him speak.
   Ant. I have; I have.
   Cleo. And if he clear me not——
   Ant. Your creature! one, who hangs upon your smiles!
Watches your eye, to say or to unsay,
Whate'er you please! I am not to be moved.
   Cleo. Then must we part? Farewell, my cruel lord!
The appearance is against me; and I go,
Unjustified, for ever from your sight.
How I have loved, you know; how yet I love,
My only comfort is, I know myself:
I love you more, even now you are unkind,
Than when you loved me most; so well, so truly
I'll never strive against it; but die pleased,
To think you once were mine.
   Ant. Good heaven, they weep at parting!
Must I weep too? that calls them innocent.
I must not weep; and yet I must, to think
That I must not forgive.——
Live, but live wretched; 'tis but just you should,
Who made me so: Live from each other's sight:
Let me not hear you meet. Set all the earth,
And all the seas, betwixt your sundered loves:
View nothing common but the sun and skies.
Now, all take several ways;
   And each your own sad fate, with mine, deplore;
   That you were false, and I could trust no more.
                   [*Exeunt severally.*

ACT V

Scene I

Enter CLEOPATRA, CHARMION, *and* IRAS.

Char. Be juster, Heaven; such virtue punished thus,
Will make us think that chance rules all above,
And shuffles, with a random hand, the lots,
Which man is forced to draw.
    Cleo. I could tear out these eyes, that gained his heart,
And had not power to keep it. O the curse
Of doting on, even when I find it dotage!
Bear witness, gods, you heard him bid me go;
You, whom he mocked with imprecating vows
Of promised faith!——I'll die; I will not bear it.
You may hold me——
        [*She pulls out her dagger, and they hold her.*
But I can keep my breath; I can die inward,
And choke this love.

Enter ALEXAS.

    Iras. Help, O Alexas, help!
The queen grows desperate; her soul struggles in her
With all the agonies of love and rage,
And strives to force its passage.
    Cleo. Let me go.
Art thou there, traitor!—O,
O for a little breath, to vent my rage,
Give, give me way, and let me loose upon him.
    Alex. Yes, I deserve it, for my ill-timed truth.
Was it for me to prop
The ruins of a falling majesty?
To place myself beneath the mighty flaw,
Thus to be crushed, and pounded into atoms,
By its o'erwhelming weight? 'Tis too presuming
For subjects to preserve that wilful power,
Which courts its own destruction.
    Cleo. I would reason
More calmly with you. Did not you o'errule,
And force my plain, direct, and open love,
Into these crooked paths of jealousy?
Now, what's the event? Octavia is removed;
But Cleopatra's banished. Thou, thou villain,
Hast pushed my boat to open sea: to prove,

At my sad cost, if thou canst steer it back.
It cannot be; I'm lost too far; I'm ruined:
Hence, thou impostor, traitor, monster, devil!—
I can no more: Thou, and my griefs, have sunk
Me down so low, that I want voice to curse thee.

    Alex. Suppose some shipwrecked seaman near the shore,
Dropping and faint with climbing up the cliff,
If, from above, some charitable hand
Pull him to safety, hazarding himself,
To draw the other's weight; would he look back,
And curse him for his pains? The case is yours;
But one step more, and you have gained the height.

    Cleo. Sunk, never more to rise.

    Alex. Octavia's gone, and Dolabella banished.
Belive me, madam, Antony is yours.
His heart was never lost, but started off
To jealousy, love's last retreat and covert;
Where it lies hid in shades, watchful in silence,
And listening for the sound that calls it back.
Some other, any man ('tis so advanced),
May perfect this unfinished work, which I
(Unhappy only to myself) have left
So easy to his hand.

    Cleo. Look well thou do't; else——

    Alex. Else, what your silence threatens.—Antony
Is mounted up the Pharos; from whose turret,
He stands surveying our Egyptian galleys,
Engaged with Cæsar's fleet. Now death or conquest!
If the first happen, fate acquits my promise;
If we o'ercome, the conqueror is yours. [*A distant shout within.*

    Char. Have comfort, madam: Did you mark that shout?
                       [*Second shout nearer.*

    Iras. Hark! they redouble it.

    Alex. 'Tis from the port.
The loudness shows it near: Good news, kind heavens!

    Cleo. Osiris make it so!

                Enter SERAPION.

    Serap. Where, where's the queen?

    Alex. How frightfully the holy coward stares
As if not yet recovered of the assault,
When all his gods, and, what's more dear to him,
His offerings, were at stake.

    Serap. O horror, horror!

Egypt has been; our latest hour has come:
The queen of nations, from her ancient seat,
Is sunk for ever in the dark abyss:
Time has unrolled her glories to the last,
And now closed up the volume.

    Cleo. Be more plain:
Say, whence thou comest; though fate is in thy face,
Which from thy haggard eyes looks wildly out,
And threatens ere thou speakest.

    Serap. I came from Pharos;
From viewing (spare me, and imagine it)
Our land's last hope, your navy——

    Cleo. Vanquished?

    Serap. No:
They fought not.

    Cleo. Then they fled.

    Serap. Nor that. I saw,
With Antony, your well-appointed fleet
Row out; and thrice he waved his hand on high,
And thrice with cheerful cries they shouted back:
'Twas then false Fortune, like a fawning strumpet,
About to leave the bankrupt prodigal,
With a dissembled smile would kiss at parting,
And flatter to the last; the well-timed oars,
Now dipt from every bank, now smoothly run
To meet the foe; and soon indeed they met,
But not as foes. In few, we saw their caps
On either side thrown up; the Egyptian galleys,
Received like friends, passed through, and fell behind
The Roman rear: And now, they all come forward,
And ride within the port.

    Cleo. Enough, Serapion:
I've heard my doom.—This needed not, you gods:
When I lost Antony, your work was done;
'Tis but superfluous malice.—Where's my lord?
How bears he this last blow?

    Serap. His fury cannot be expressed by words:
Thrice he attempted headlong to have fallen
Full on his foes, and aimed at Cæsar's galley:
Withheld, he raves on you; cries,—He's betrayed.
Should he now find you——

    Alex. Shun him; seek your safety,
Till you can clear your innocence.

    Cleo. I'll stay.

Alex. You must not; haste you to your monument,
While I make speed to Cæsar.

Cleo. Cæsar! No,
I have no business with him.

Alex. I can work him
To spare your life, and let this madman perish.

Cleo. Base fawning wretch! wouldst thou betray him too?
Hence from my sight! I will not hear a traitor;
'Twas thy design brought all this ruin on us.—
Serapion, thou art honest; counsel me:
But haste, each moment's precious.

Serap. Retire; you must not yet see Antony.
He who began this mischief,
'Tis just he tempt the danger; let him clear you:
And, since he offered you his servile tongue,
To gain a poor precarious life from Cæsar,
Let him expose that fawning eloquence,
And speak to Antony.

Alex. O heavens! I dare not;
I meet my certain death.

Cleo. Slave, thou deservest it.—
Not that I fear my lord, will I avoid him;
I know him noble: when he banished me,
And thought me false, he scorned to take my life;
But I'll be justified, and then die with him.

Alex. O pity me, and let me follow you.

Cleo. To death, if thou stir hence. Speak, if thou canst,
Now for thy life, which basely thou wouldst save;
While mine I prize at—this! Come, good Serapion.

[*Exeunt* CLEOPATRA, SERAPION, CHARMION, *and* IRAS.

Alex. O that I less could fear to lose this being,
Which, like a snowball in my coward hand,
The more 'tis grasped, the faster melts away.
Poor reason! what a wretched aid art thou!
For still, in spite of thee,
These two long lovers, soul and body, dread
Their final separation. Let me think:
What can I say, to save myself from death?
No matter what becomes of Cleopatra.

Ant. Which way? where?   [*Within.*
Vent. This leads to the monument.   [*Within.*

Alex. Ah me! I hear him; yet I'm unprepared:
My gift of lying's gone;
And this court-devil, which I so oft have raised,

Forsakes me at my need. I dare not stay;
Yet cannot far go hence.　　　　　　　　　　　　　　[*Exit.*

Enter ANTONY *and* VENTIDIUS.

Ant. O happy Cæsar! thou hast men to lead:
Think not 'tis thou hast conquered Antony;
But Rome has conquered Egypt. I'm betrayed.
　Vent. Curse on this treacherous train!
Their soil and heaven infect them all with baseness:
And their young souls come tainted to the world
With the first breath they draw.
　Ant. The original villain sure no god created;
He was a bastard of the sun, by Nile,
Aped into man; with all his mother's mud
Crusted about his soul.
　Vent. The nation is
One universal traitor; and their queen
The very spirit and extract of them all.
　Ant. Is there yet left
A possibility of aid from valour?
Is there one god unsworn to my destruction?
The least unmortgaged hope? for, if there be,
Methinks I cannot fall beneath the fate
Of such a boy as Cæsar.
The world's one half is yet in Antony;
And from each limb of it, that's hewed away,
The soul comes back to me.
　Vent. There yet remain
Three legions in the town. The last assault
Lopt off the rest; if death be your design,—
As I must wish it now,—these are sufficient
To make a heap about us of dead foes,
An honest pile for burial.
　Ant. They are enough.
We'll not divide our stars; but, side by side,
Fight emulous, and with malicious eyes
Survey each other's acts: So every death
Thou giv'st, I'll take on me, as a just debt,
And pay thee back a soul.
　Vent. Now you shall see I love you. Not a word
Of chiding more. By my few hours of life,
I am so pleased with this brave Roman fate,
That I would not be Cæsar, to outlive you.
When we put off this flesh, and mount together,

I shall be shown to all the ethereal crowd,—
Lo, this is he who died with Antony!

Ant. Who knows, but we may pierce through all their troops,
And reach my veterans yet? 'tis worth the 'tempting,
To o'erleap this gulf of fate,
And leave our wandering destinies behind.

Enter ALEXAS, *trembling.*

Vent. See, see, that villain!
See Cleopatra stamped upon that face,
With all her cunning, all her arts of falsehood!
How she looks out through those dissembling eyes!
How he sets his countenance for deceit,
And promises a lie, before he speaks!
Let me despatch him first.   [*Drawing.*

Alex. O spare me, spare me!

Ant. Hold; he's not worth your killing.—On thy life,
Which thou may'st keep, because I scorn to take it,
No syllable to justify thy queen;
Save thy base tongue its office.

Alex. Sir, she is gone,
Where she shall never be molested more
By love, or you.

Ant. Fled to her Dolabella!
Die, traitor! I revoke my promise! die!   [*Going to kill him.*

Alex. O hold! she is not fled.

Ant. She is: my eyes
Are open to her falsehood; my whole life
Has been a golden dream of love and friendship;
But, now I wake, I'm like a merchant, roused
From soft repose, to see his vessel sinking,
And all his wealth cast over. Ungrateful woman!
Who followed me, but as the swallow summer,
Hatching her young ones in my kindly beams,
Singing her flatteries to my morning wake:
But, now my winter comes, she spreads her wings,
And seeks the spring of Cæsar.

Alex. Think not so:
Her fortunes have, in all things, mixed with yours.
Had she betrayed her naval force to Rome,
How easily might she have gone to Cæsar,
Secure by such a bribe!

Vent. She sent it first,
To be more welcome after.

Ant. 'Tis too plain;
Else would she have appeared, to clear herself.
    Alex. Too fatally she has: she could not bear
To be accused by you; but shut herself
Within her monument; looked down and sighed;
While, from her unchanged face, the silent tears
Dropt, as they had not leave, but stole their parting.
Some indistinguished words she inly murmured;
At last, she raised her eyes; and, with such looks
As dying Lucrece cast——
    Ant. My heart forebodes——
    Vent. All for the best:—Go on.
    Alex. She snatched her poniard,
And, ere we could prevent the fatal blow,
Plunged it within her breast; then turned to me:
Go, bear my lord, said she, my last farewell;
And ask him, if he yet suspect my faith.
More she was saying, but death rushed betwixt.
She half pronounced your name with her last breath,
And buried half within her.
    Vent. Heaven be praised!
    Ant. Then art thou innocent, my poor dear love,
And art thou dead?
O those two words! their sound should be divided:
Hadst thou been false, and died; or hadst thou lived,
And hadst been true—But innocence and death!
This shows not well above. Then what am I,
The murderer of this truth, this innocence!
Thoughts cannot form themselves in words so horrid
As can express my guilt!
    Vent. Is't come to this? The gods have been too gracious;
And thus you thank them for it!
    Ant. [*To* ALEX.] Why stayest thou here?
Is it for thee to spy upon my soul,
And see its inward mourning? Get thee hence;
Thou art not worthy to behold, what now
Becomes a Roman emperor to perform.
    Alex. He loves her still:
His grief betrays it. Good! the joy to find
She's yet alive, completes the reconcilement.
I've saved myself, and her. But, oh! the Romans!
Fate comes too fast upon my wit,
Hunts me too hard, and meets me at each double. [*Aside. Exit.*
    Vent. Would she had died a little sooner, though!

Before Octavia went, you might have treated:
Now 'twill look tame, and would not be received.
Come, rouse yourself, and let's die warm together.
 Ant. I will not fight: there's no more work for war.
The business of my angry hours is done.
 Vent. Cæsar is at your gates.
 Ant. Why, let him enter;
He's welcome now.
 Vent. What lethargy has crept into your soul?
 Ant. 'Tis but a scorn of life, and just desire
To free myself from bondage.
 Vent. Do it bravely.
 Ant. I will; but not by fighting. O Ventidius!
What should I fight for now?—my queen is dead.
I was but great for her; my power, my empire,
Were but my merchandise to buy her love;
And conquered kings, my factors. Now she's dead,
Let Cæsar take the world,—
An empty circle, since the jewel's gone
Which made it worth my strife: my being's nauseous;
For all the bribes of life are gone away.
 Vent. Would you be taken?
 Ant. Yes, I would be taken;
But, as a Roman ought,—dead, my Ventidius:
For I'll convey my soul from Cæsar's reach,
And lay down life myself. 'Tis time the world
Should have a lord, and know whom to obey.
We two have kept its homage in suspense,
And bent the globe, on whose each side we trod,
Till it was dented inwards. Let him walk
Alone upon't: I'm weary of my part.
My torch is out; and the world stands before me,
Like a black desert at the approach of night:
I'll lay me down, and stray no farther on.
 Vent. I could be grieved,
But that I'll not outlive you: choose your death;
For, I have seen him in such various shapes,
I care not which I take: I'm only troubled,
The life I bear is worn to such a rag,
'Tis scarce worth giving. I could wish, indeed,
We threw it from us with a better grace;
That, like two lions taken in the toils,
We might at last thrust out our paws, and wound
The hunters that inclose us.

Ant. I have thought on it.
Ventidius, you must live.

    Vent. I must not, sir.

    Ant. Wilt thou not live, to speak some good of me?
To stand by my fair fame, and guard the approaches
From the ill tongues of men?

    Vent. Who shall guard mine,
For living after you?

    Ant. Say, I command it.

    Vent. If we die well, our deaths will speak themselves
And need no living witness.

    Ant. Thou hast loved me,
And fain I would reward thee. I must die;
Kill me, and take the merit of my death,
To make thee friends with Cæsar.

    Vent. Thank your kindness.
You said I loved you; and in recompense,
You bid me turn a traitor: Did I think
You would have used me thus?—that I should die
With a hard thought of you?

    Ant. Forgive me, Roman.
Since I have heard of Cleopatra's death,
My reason bears no rule upon my tongue,
But lets my thoughts break all at random out.
I've thought better; do not deny me twice.

    Vent. By Heaven I will not.
Let it not be to outlive you.

    Ant. Kill me first,
And then die thou; for 'tis but just thou serve
Thy friend before thyself.

    Vent. Give me your hand.
We soon shall meet again. Now, farewell, emperor!—[*Embrace*
Methinks that word's too cold to be my last:
Since death sweeps all distinctions, farewell, friend!
That's all——
I will not make a business of a trifle;
And yet I cannot look on you, and kill you;
Pray turn your face.

    Ant. I do: strike home, be sure.

    Vent. Home as my sword will reach.   [*Kills himself*

    Ant. Oh, thou mistak'st;
That wound was not of thine; give it me back;
Thou robb'st me of my death.

    Vent. I do indeed;

But think 'tis the first time I e'er deceived you,
If that may plead my pardon.—And you, gods,
Forgive me, if you will; for I die perjured,
Rather than kill my friend.   [*Dies.*

  Ant. Farewell! Ever my leader, even in death!
My queen and thou have got the start of me,
And I'm the lag of honour.—Gone so soon?
Is Death no more? he used him carelessly,
With a familiar kindness: ere he knocked,
Ran to the door, and took him in his arms,
As who should say—You're welcome at all hours,
A friend need give no warning. Books had spoiled him;
For all the learned are cowards by profession.
'Tis not worth
My further thought; for death, for aught I know,
Is but to think no more. Here's to be satisfied.
                              [*Falls on his sword.*
I've missed my heart. O unperforming hand!
Thou never couldst have erred in a worse time.
My fortune jades me to the last; and death,
Like a great man, takes state, and makes me wait
For my admittance.——   [*Trampling within.*
Some, perhaps, from Cæsar:
If he should find me living, and suspect
That I played booty with my life! I'll mend
My work, ere they can reach me.   [*Rises upon his knees.*

          Enter CLEOPATRA, CHARMION, *and* IRAS.

  Cleo. Where is my lord? where is he?
  Char. There he lies,
And dead Ventidius by him.
  Cleo. My fears were prophets; I am come too late.
O that accursed Alexas!   [*Runs to him.*
  Ant. Art thou living?
Or am I dead before I knew, and thou
The first kind ghost that meets me?
  Cleo. Help me seat him.
Send quickly, send for help!   [*They place him in a chair.*
  Ant. I am answered.
We live both. Sit thee down, my Cleopatra:
I'll make the most I can of life, to stay
A moment more with thee.
  Cleo. How is it with you?
  Ant. 'Tis as with a man

Removing in a hurry; all packed up,
But one dear jewel that his haste forgot;
And he, for that, returns upon the spur:
So I come back for thee.

 Cleo. Too long, ye heavens, you have been cruel to me:
Now show your mended faith, and give me back
His fleeting life!

 Ant. It will not be, my love;
I keep my soul by force.
Say but, thou art not false.

 Cleo. 'Tis now too late
To say I'm true: I'll prove it, and die with you.
Unknown to me, Alexas feigned my death:
Which, when I knew, I hasted to prevent
This fatal consequence. My fleet betrayed
Both you and me.

 Ant. And Dolabella——

 Cleo. Scarce
Esteemed before he loved; but hated now.

 Ant. Enough: my life's not long enough for more.
Thou say'st, thou wilt come after: I believe thee;
For I can now believe whate'er thou sayest,
That we may part more kindly.

 Cleo. I will come:
Doubt not, my life, I'll come, and quickly too:
Cæsar shall triumph o'er no part of thee.

 Ant. But grieve not, while thou stayest,
My last disastrous times:
Think we have had a clear and glorious day
And Heaven did kindly to delay the storm,
Just till our close of evening. Ten years' love,
And not a moment lost, but all improved
To the utmost joys,—what ages have we lived?
And now to die each other's; and, so dying,
While hand in hand we walk in groves below,
Whole troops of lovers' ghosts shall flock about us,
And all the train be ours.

 Cleo. Your words are like the notes of dying swans,
Too sweet to last. Were there so many hours
For your unkindness, and not one for love?

 Ant. No, not a minute.—This one kiss—more worth
Than all I leave to Cæsar.   [*Dies.*

 Cleo. O tell me so again,
And take ten thousand kisses for that word.

My lord, my lord! speak, if you yet have being;
Sign to me, if you cannot speak; or cast
One look! Do anything that shows you live.
 Iras. He's gone too far to hear you;
And this you see, a lump of senseless clay,
The leavings of a soul.
 Char. Remember, madam,
He charged you not to grieve.
 Cleo. And I'll obey him.
I have not loved a Roman, not to know
What should become his wife; his wife, my Charmion!
For 'tis to that high title I aspire;
And now I'll not die less. Let dull Octavia
Survive, to mourn him dead: My nobler fate
Shall knit our spousals with a tie, too strong
For Roman laws to break.
 Iras. Will you then die?
 Cleo. Why shouldst thou make that question?
 Iras. Cæsar is merciful.
 Cleo. Let him be so
To those that want his mercy: My poor lord
Made no such covenant with him, to spare me
When he was dead. Yield me to Cæsar's pride?
What! to be led in triumph through the streets,
A spectacle to base plebeian eyes;
While some dejected friend of Antony's,
Close in a corner, shakes his head, and mutters
A secret curse on her who ruined him!
I'll none of that.
 Char. Whatever you resolve,
I'll follow, even to death.
 Iras. I only feared
For you; but more should fear to live without you.
 Cleo. Why, now, 'tis as it should be. Quick, my friends,
Despatch; ere this, the town's in Cæsar's hands:
My lord looks down concerned, and fears my stay,
Lest I should be surprised;
Keep him not waiting for his love too long.
You, Charmion, bring my crown and richest jewels;
With them, the wreath of victory I made
(Vain augury!) for him, who now lies dead:
You, Iras, bring the cure of all our ills.
 Iras. The aspics, madam?
 Cleo. Must I bid you twice? [*Exit* CHARMION *and* IRAS.

'Tis sweet to die, when they would force life on me,
To rush into the dark abode of death,
And seize him first; if he be like my love,
He is not frightful, sure.
We're now alone, in secrecy and silence;
And is not this like lovers? I may kiss
These pale, cold lips; Octavia does not see me:
And, oh! 'tis better far to have him thus,
Than see him in her arms.—Oh, welcome, welcome!

Enter CHARMION *and* IRAS.

Char. What must be done?
Cleo. Short ceremony, friends;
But yet it must be decent. First, this laurel
Shall crown my hero's head: he fell not basely,
Nor left his shield behind him.—Only thou
Couldst triumph o'er thyself; and thou alone
Wert worthy so to triumph.
Char. To what end
These ensigns of your pomp and royalty?
Cleo. Dull, that thou art! why 'tis to meet my love;
As when I saw him first, on Cydnus' bank,
All sparkling, like a goddess: so adorned,
I'll find him once again; my second spousals
Shall match my first in glory. Haste, haste, both,
And dress the bride of Antony.
Char. 'Tis done.
Cleo. Now seat me by my lord. I claim this place;
For I must conquer Cæsar too, like him,
And win my share of the world.—Hail, you dear relics
Of my immortal love!
O let no impious hand remove you hence:
But rest for ever here! Let Egypt give
His death that peace, which it denied his life.—
Reach me the casket.
Iras. Underneath the fruit
The aspic lies.
Cleo. Welcome, thou kind deceiver! [*Putting aside the leaves.*
Thou best of thieves; who, with an easy key,
Dost open life, and, unperceived by us,
Even steal us from ourselves; discharging so
Death's dreadful office, better than himself;
Touching our limbs so gently into slumber,
That Death stands by, deceived by his own image,

And thinks himself but sleep.
 Serap. The queen, where is she?   [*Within.*
The town is yielded, Cæsar's at the gates.
 Cleo. He comes too late to invade the rights of death.
Haste, bare my arm, and rouse the serpent's fury.
     [*Holds out her arm, and draws it back.*
Coward flesh,
Wouldst thou conspire with Cæsar to betray me,
As thou wert none of mine? I'll force thee to it,
And not be sent by him,
But bring, myself, my soul to Antony.
     [*Turns aside, and then shows her arm bloody.*
Take hence; the work is done.
 Serap. Break ope the door,   [*Within.*
And guard the traitor well.
 Char. The next is ours.
 Iras. Now, Charmion, to be worthy
Of our great queen and mistress. [*They apply the aspics.*
 Cleo. Already, death, I feel thee in my veins:
I go with such a will to find my lord,
That we shall quickly meet.
A heavy numbness creeps through every limb,
And now 'tis at my head: My eyelids fall
And my dear love is vanquished in a mist.
Where shall I find him, where? O turn me to him,
And lay me on his breast!—Cæsar, thy worst;
Now part us, if thou canst.   [*Dies.*
  [IRAS *sinks down at her feet, and dies;* CHARMION *stands*
   behind her chair, as dressing her head.

Enter SERAPION, *two* Priests, ALEXAS *bound,* Egyptians.

 Priest. Behold, Serapion,
What havoc death has made!
 Serap. 'Twas what I feared.—
Charmion, is this well done?
 Char. Yes, 'tis well done, and like a queen, the last
Of her great race: I follow her. [*Sinks down: dies.*
 Alex. 'Tis true,
She has done well: Much better thus to die,
Than live to make a holiday in Rome.
 Serap. See how the lovers sit in state together,
As they were giving laws to half mankind!
The impression of a smile, left in her face,
Shows she died pleased with him for whom she lived,

And went to charm him in another world.
Cæsar's just entering: grief has now no leisure.
Secure that villain, as our pledge of safety,
To grace the imperial triumph.—Sleep, blest pair,
Secure from human chance, long ages out,
While all the storms of fate fly o'er your tomb;
   And fame to late posterity shall tell,
   No lovers lived so great, or died so well.   [*Exeunt.*

EPILOGUE

POETS, like disputants, when reasons fail,
Have one sure refuge left—and that's to rail.
Fop, coxcomb, fool, are thundered through the pit;
And this is all their equipage of wit.
We wonder how the devil this difference grows,
Betwixt our fools in verse, and yours in prose:
For, 'faith, the quarrel rightly understood,
'Tis civil war with their own flesh and blood.
The threadbare author hates the gaudy coat;
And swears at the gilt coach, but swears afoot:
For 'tis observed of every scribbling man,
He grows a fop as fast as e'er he can;
Prunes up, and asks his oracle, the glass,
If pink or purple best become his face.
For our poor wretch, he neither rails nor prays;
Nor likes your wit just as you like his plays;
He has not yet so much of Mr. Bayes.
He does his best; and if he cannot please,
Would quietly sue out his *writ of ease*.
Yet, if he might his own grand jury call,
By the fair sex he begs to stand or fall.
Let Cæsar's power the men's ambition move,
But grace you him who lost the world for love!
Yet if some antiquated lady say,
The last age is not copied in his play;
Heaven help the man who for that face must drudge,
Which only has the wrinkles of a judge.
Let not the young and beauteous join with those;
For should you raise such numerous hosts of foes,
Young wits and sparks he to his aid must call;
'Tis more than one man's work to please you all.

VENICE PRESERV'D
by
THOMAS OTWAY

EPISTLE DEDICATORY TO HER GRACE THE DUTCHESS

OF PORTSMOUTH

MADAM,

Were it possible for me to let the World know how entirely your Graces Goodness has devoted a poor man to your service; were there words enough in speech to express the mighty sense I have of your great bounty towards me; surely I should write and talk of it for ever: But your Grace has given me so large a Theam, and laid so very vast a foundation, that Imagination wants stock to build upon it. I am as one dumb when I would speak of it, and when I strive to write, I want a scale of thought sufficient to comprehend the height of it. Forgive me then, Madam, if (as a poor Peasant once made a Present of an Apple to an Emperor) I bring this small Tribute, the humble growth of my little Garden, and lay it at your feet. Believe it is paid you with the utmost gratitude, believe that so long as I have thought to remember, how very much I owe your generous Nature, I will ever have a heart that shall be gratefull for it too: Your Grace, next Heaven, deserves it amply from me; That gave me life, but on a hard condition, till your extended favour taught me to prize the gift, and took the heavy burthen it was clogg'd with from me: I mean hard Fortune: When I had enemies, that with malitious power kept back and shaded me from those Royal Beams, whose warmth is all I have, or hope to live by; Your noble pity and compassion found me, where I was far cast backward from my blessing; down in the rear of Fortune, call'd me up, plac'd me in the shine, and I have felt its comfort. You have in that restor'd me to my native Right, for a steady Faith, and Loyalty to my Prince, was all the Inheritance my Father left me and however hardly my ill Fortune deal with me, 'tis what I prize so well that I ne'r pawn'd it yet, and hope I ne'r shall part with it. Nature and Fortune were certainly in league when you were born, and as the first took care to give you beauty enough to enslave the hearts of all the World, so the other resolv'd to doe its merit Justice, that none but a Monarch, fit to rule that World, should e'r possess it, and in it he had an Empire. The Young Prince you have given him, by his blooming Vertues, early declares the mighty stock he came from; and as you have taken all the pious care of a dear Mother and a prudent Guardian to give him a noble and generous education; may it succeed according to his merits and your wishes: May he grow up to be a Bulwark to his illustrious Father, and a Patron to his Loyal Subjects, with Wisedom and Learning to assist him, whenever call'd to his Councils, to defend his right against the encroachments of Republicans in his Senates, to cherish such men as shall be able to vindicate the Royal Cause, that good and fit servants to the Crown, may never be lost for want of a Protectour. May He have courage and conduct, fit to fight his Battels abroad, and terrifie his Rebells at home; and that all these may be yet more sure, may He never, during the Spring-time of his years, when those growing Vertues ought with care to be cherish'd, in order to their ripening; may he never meet with vitious Nature, or the tongues of faithless, sordid, insipid Flatterers, to blast 'em: To conclude; may He be as great as the hand of Fortune (with his Honour) shall be able to make him: And may your Grace, who are so good a Mistress, and so noble a Patroness, never meet with a less gratefull Servant, than,

Madam,

Your Graces entirely
Devoted Creature,

THOMAS OTWAY.

PROLOGUE

In these distracted times, when each man dreads
The bloudy stratagems of busie heads;
When we have fear'd three years we know not what,⎫
Till Witnesses begin to die o'th' rot,⎬
What made our Poet meddle with a Plot?⎭
Was't that he fansy'd, for the very sake
And name of Plot, his trifling Play might take?
For there's not in't one Inch-board Evidence,⎫
But 'tis, he says, to reason plain and sense,⎬
And that he thinks a plausible defence.⎭
Were Truth by Sense and Reason to be tri'd,
Sure all our Swearers might be laid aside:
No, of such Tools our Author has no need,
To make his Plot, or may his Play succeed;
He, of black Bills, has no prodigious Tales,
Or Spanish Pilgrims cast a-shore in Wales;
Here's not one murther'd Magistrate at least,
Kept rank like Ven'son for a City feast,
Grown four day stiff, the better to prepare
And fit his plyant limbs to ride in Chair:
Yet here's an Army rais'd, though under ground,
But no man seen, nor one Commission found;
Here is a Traitour too, that's very old,
Turbulent, subtle, mischievous and bold,
Bloudy, revengefull, and to crown his part,
Loves fumbling with a Wench, with all his heart;
Till after having many changes pass'd,
In spight of Age (thanks Heaven) is hang'd at last:
Next is a Senatour that keeps a Whore,
In Venice none a higher office bore;
To lewdness every night the Letcher ran,⎫
Shew me, all London, such another man,⎬
Match him at Mother Creswolds if you can.⎭
Oh Poland, Poland! had it been thy lot,
T' have heard in time of this Venetian Plot,
Thou surely chosen hadst one King from thence,
And honour'd them as thou hast England since.

DRAMATIS PERSONÆ

DUKE OF VENICE	Mr. D. Williams
PRIULI, *Father to Belvidera, a Senatour* . .	Mr. Boman
ANTONIO, *A fine Speaker in the Senate* . . .	Mr. Leigh
JAFFEIR	Mr. Betterton
PIERRE	Mr. Smith
RENAULT	Mr. Wilshire
BEDAMAR	Mr. Gillo
SPINOSA	Mr. Percival

THEODORE
ELIOT
REVILLIDO
DURAND   *Conspiratours*
MEZZANA
BRAMVEIL
TERNON
BRABE
RETROSI

BELVIDERA	Mrs. Barry
AQUILINA	Mrs. Currer

TWO WOMEN, *Attendants on Belvidera*
TWO WOMEN, *Servants to Aquilina*
THE COUNCIL OF TEN
OFFICER
GUARDS
FRIAR
EXECUTIONER AND RABBLE

VENICE PRESERV'D;

or,

A Plot Discovered

ACT I

Scene I

Enter Priuli *and* Jaffeir.

Priu. No more! I'le hear no more; begone and leave.
Jaff. Not hear me! by my sufferings but you shall!
My Lord, my Lord; I'm not that abject wretch
You think me: Patience! where's the distance throws
Me back so far, but I may boldly speak
In right, though proud oppression will not hear mee!
  Priu. Have you not wrong'd me?
  Jaff.   Could my Nature e're
Have brook'd Injustice or the doing wrongs,
I need not now thus low have bent my self,
To gain a Hearing from a Cruel father!
Wrong'd you?
  Priu. Yes! wrong'd me, in the nicest point:
The Honour of my House; you have done me wrong;
You may remember: (For I now will speak,
And urge its baseness:) When you first came home
From Travell, with such hopes, as made you lookt on
By all men's Eyes, a Youth of expectation;
Pleas'd with your growing Virtue, I receiv'd you;
Courted, and sought to raise you to your Merits:
My House, my Table; nay my Fortune too,
My very self, was yours; you might have us'd me
To your best service; like an open friend,
I treated, trusted you, and thought you mine;
When in requital of my best Endeavours,
You treacherously practis'd to undo me,
Seduc'd the weakness of my Age's Darling,

185

My only Child, and stole her from my bosome:
Oh Belvidera!

   Jaff. 'Tis to me you owe her,
Childless you had been else, and in the Grave,
Your name extinct, nor no more Priuli heard of.
You may remember, scarce five years are past,
Since in your Brigandine you fail'd to see
The Adriatick wedded by our Duke,
And I was with you: Your unskilfull Pilot
Dash't us upon a Rock; when to your Boat
You made for safety; entred first your self;
The affrighted Belvidera following next,
As she stood trembling on the Vessel side,
Was by a Wave washt off into the Deep,
When instantly I plung'd into the Sea,
And Buffeting the Billows to her rescue,
Redeem'd her Life with half the loss of mine,
Like a rich Conquest in one hand I bore her,
And with the other dasht the sawcy Waves,
That throng'd and prest to rob me of my prize:
I brought her, gave her to your despairing Arms:
Indeed you thank't me; but a nobler gratitude
Rose in her soul: for from that hour she lov'd me,
Till for her Life she paid me with her self.

   Priu. You stole her from me, like a Theif you stole her,
At dead of night; that cursed hour you chose
To rifle me of all my Heart held dear.
May all your Joys in her prove false like mine;
A steril Fortune, and a barren Bed,
Attend you both: Continual discord make
Your Days and Nights bitter and grievous: Still
May the hard hand of a vexatious Need
Oppress, and grind you; till at last you find
The Curse of Disobedience all your Portion.

   Jaff. Half of your Curse you have bestow'd in vain,
Heav'n has already crown'd our faithfull Loves
With a young Boy, sweet as his mothers Beauty:
May he live to prove more gentle than his Grandsire,
And happier than his Father!

   Priu. Rather live
To bait thee for his bread, and din your ears
With hungry Cries: Whilst his unhappy Mother
Sits down and weeps in bitterness of want.

   Jaff. You talk as if it would please you.

Priu. 'Twould by Heav'n.
Once she was dear indeed; the Drops that fell
From my sad heart, when she forgot her Duty,
The fountain of my Life was not so pretious:
But she is gone, and if I am a man
I will forget her.
    Jaff. Would I were in my Grave.
    Priu. And she too with thee;
For, living here, you're but my curs'd Remembrancers
I once was happy.
    Jaff. You use me thus, because you know my soul
Is fond of Belvidera: You perceive
My Life feeds on her, therefore thus you treat me;
Oh! could my Soul ever have known satiety:
Were I that Theif, the doer of such wrongs
As you upbraid me with, what hinders me,
But I might send her back to you with Contumely,
And court my fortune where she wou'd be kinder!
    Priu. You dare not do't.—
    Jaff. Indeed, my Lord, I dare not.
My heart that awes me is too much my Master:
Three years are past since first our Vows were plighted,
During which time, the World must bear me witness,
I have treated Belvidera like your Daughter,
The Daughter of a Senator of Venice;
Distinction, Place, Attendance and Observance,
Due to her Birth, she always has commanded;
Out of my little Fortune I have done this;
Because (though hopeless e're to win your Nature)
The World might see, I lov'd her for her self,
Not as the Heiress of the great Priuli.—
    Priu. No more!
    Jaff. Yes! all, and then adieu for ever.
There's not a Wretch that lives on common Charity
But's happier than me: for I have known
The Luscious Sweets of Plenty; every night
Have slept with soft content about my head,
And never waked but to a joyfull morning,
Yet now must fall like a full Ear of Corn,
Whose blossom scap'd, yet's withered in the ripening.
    Priu. Home and be humble, study to retrench;
Discharge the lazy Vermin of thy Hall,
Those Pageants of thy Folly,
Reduce the glittering Trappings of thy Wife

To humble Weeds, fit for thy little state;
Then to some suburb Cottage both retire;
Drudge, to feed loathsome life: Get Brats, and Starve—
Home, home, I say—   [*Exit* PRIULI.

Jaff. Yes, if my heart would let me—
This proud, this swelling heart: Home I would go,
But that my Dores are hatefull to my eyes,
Fill'd and damm'd up with gaping Creditors,
Watchfull as Fowlers when their Game will spring;
I have now not 50 Ducats in the World,
Yet still I am in love, and pleas'd with Ruin.
Oh Belvidera! oh she's my Wife—
And we will bear our wayward Fate together,
But ne're know Comfort more.

Enter PIERRE.

Pierr. My friend, good morrow!
How fares the honest Partner of my Heart?
What, melancholy! not a word to spare me?
Jaff. I'm thinking Pierre, how that damn'd starving Quality
Call'd Honesty, got footing in the World.
Pierr. Why, pow'rfull Villainy first set it up,
For its own ease and safety: Honest men
Are the soft easy Cushions on which Knaves
Repose and fatten: Were all mankind Villains,
They'd starve each other; Lawyers wou'd want practice,
Cut-Throats Rewards: Each man would kill his Brother
Himself, none would be paid or hang'd for Murder:
Honesty was a Cheat invented first
To bind the hands of bold deserving Rogues,
That Fools and Cowards might sit safe in Power,
And lord it uncontroul'd above their Betters.
Jaff. Then Honesty is but a Notion.
Pierr. Nothing else,
Like wit, much talkt of, not to be defin'd:
He that pretends to most too, has least share in't;
'Tis a ragged Virtue: Honesty! no more on't.
Jaff. Sure thou art Honest?
Pierr. So indeed men think me:
But they're mistaken Jaffeir: I am a Rogue
As well as they;
A fine gay bold fac'd Villain, as thou seest me;
'Tis true, I pay my debts when they'r contracted;
I steal from no man; would not cut a Throat

To gain admission to a great man's purse,
Or a Whores bed; I'de not betray my Friend,
To get his Place or Fortune: I scorn to flatter
A Blown-up Fool above me, or Crush the wretch beneath me,
Yet, Jaffeir, for all this, I am a Villain!
   Jaff. A Villain—
   Pierr. Yes a most notorious Villain:
To see the suffrings of my fellow Creatures,
And own my self a Man: To see our Senators
Cheat the deluded people with a shew
Of Liberty, which yet they ne'r must taste of;
They say, by them our hands are free from Fetters,
Yet whom they please they lay in basest bonds;
Bring whom they please to Infamy and Sorrow;
Drives us like Wracks down the rough Tide of Power,
Whilst no hold's left to save us from Destruction;
All that bear this are Villains; and I one,
Not to rouse up at the great Call of Nature,
And check the Growth of these Domestick spoilers,
That makes us slaves and tells us 'tis our Charter.
   Jaff. Oh Aquilina! Friend, to lose such Beauty,
The Dearest Purchase of thy noble Labours;
She was thy Right by Conquest, as by Love.
   Pierr. Oh Jaffeir! I'de so fixt my heart upon her,
That wheresoe're I fram'd a Scheme of Life
For time to come, she was my only Joy
With which I wish't to sweeten future Cares;
I fancy'd pleasures, none but one that loves
And dotes as I did can Imagine like 'em:
When in the Extremity of all these Hopes,
In the most Charming hour of Expectation,
Then when our Eager Wishes soar the highest,
Ready to stoop and grasp the lovely Game,
A Haggard Owl, a Worthless Kite of Prey,
With its foul wings sayl'd in and spoyl'd my Quarry.
   Jaff. I know the Wretch, and scorn him as thou hat'st him.
   Pierr. Curse on the Common Good that's so protected,
Where every slave that heaps up wealth enough
To do much Wrong, becomes a Lord of Right:
I, who beleiv'd no Ill could e're come near me,
Found in the embraces of my Aquilina
A Wretched old but itching Senator;
A wealthy Fool, that had bought out my Title,
A Rogue, that uses Beauty like a Lambskin,

Barely to keep him warm: That filthy Cuckoo too
Was in my absence crept into my Nest,
And spoyling all my Brood of noble Pleasure.
    Jaff. Didst thou not chace him thence?
    Pierr. I did, and drove
The rank old bearded Hirco stinking home:
The matter was complain'd of in the Senate,
I summon'd to appear, and censur'd basely,
For violating something they call priviledge—
This was the Recompence of my service:
Would I'd been rather beaten by a Coward!
A Souldier's Mistress Jaffeir 's his Religion,
When that's prophan'd, all other Tyes are broken,
That even dissolves all former bonds of service,
And from that hour I think my self as free
To be the Foe as e're the Friend of Venice—
Nay, Dear Revenge, when e're thou call'st I am ready.
    Jaff. I think no safety can be here for Virtue,
And grieve my friend as much as thou to live
In such a wretched State as this of Venice;
Where all agree to spoil the Publick Good,
And Villains fatten with the brave man's Labours.
    Pierr. We have neither safety, Unity, nor Peace,
For the foundation's lost of Common Good;
Justice is lame as well as blind amongst us;
The Laws (corrupted to their ends that make 'em)
Serve but for Instruments of some new Tyranny,
That every day starts up to enslave us deeper:
Now could this glorious Cause but find out friends
To do it right! oh Jaffeir! then might'st thou
Not wear these seals of Woe upon thy Face,
The proud Priuli should be taught humanity,
And learn to value such a son as thou art.
I dare not speak! But my heart bleeds this moment!
    Jaff. Curst be the Cause, though I thy friend be part on't:
Let me partake the troubles of thy bosom,
For I am us'd to misery, and perhaps
May find a way to sweeten't to thy spirit.
    Pierr. Too soon it will reach thy knowledg—
    Jaff. Then from thee
Let it proceed. There's Virtue in thy Friendship
Would make the saddest Tale of sorrow pleasing,
Strengthen my Constancy, and welcome Ruin.
    Pierr. Then thou art ruin'd!

Jaff. That I long since knew,
I and ill Fortune have been long Acquaintance.
   Pierr. I past this very moment by thy dores,
And found them guarded by a Troop of Villains;
The sons of public Rapine were destroying:
They told me, by the sentence of the Law
They had Commission to seize all thy fortune,
Nay more, Priuli's cruel hand hath sign'd it.
Here stood a Ruffian with a horrid face
Lording it o're a pile of massy Plate,
Tumbled into a heap for publick sale:
There was another making villainous jests
At thy undoing; he had ta'ne possession
Of all thy antient most domestick Ornaments,
Rich hangings, intermixt and wrought with gold;
The very bed, which on thy wedding night
Receiv'd thee to the Arms of Belvidera,
The scene of all thy Joys, was violated
By the course hands of filthy Dungeon Villains,
And thrown amongst the common Lumber.
   Jaff. Now thanks Heav'n—
   Pierr. Thank Heav'n! for what?
   Jaff. That I am not worth a Ducat.
   Pierr. Curse thy dull Stars, and the worse Fate of Venice,
Where Brothers, Friends, and Fathers, all are false;
Where there's no trust, no truth; where Innocence
Stoop's under vile Oppression; and Vice lords it:
Hadst thou but seen, as I did, how at last
Thy Beauteous Belvidera, like a Wretch
That's doom'd to Banishment, came weeping forth,
Shining through Tears, like April Sun's in showers
That labour to orecome the Cloud that loads 'm,
Whilst two young Virgins, on whose Arms she lean'd,
Kindly lookt up, and at her Grief grew sad,
As if they catch't the Sorrows that fell from her:
Even the lewd Rabble that were gather'd round
To see the sight, stood mute when they beheld her;
Govern'd their roaring throats and grumbled pity:
I cou'd have hugg'd the greazy Rogues: They pleas'd me.
   Jaff. I thank thee for this story from my soul,
Since now I know the worst that can befall me:
Ah Pierre! I have a Heart, that could have born
The roughest Wrong my Fortune could have done me:
But when I think what Belvidera feels.

The bitterness her tender spirit tasts of,
I own my self a Coward: Bear my weakness,
If throwing thus my Arms about thy Neck,
I play the Boy, and blubber in thy bosome.
Oh! I shall drown thee with my Sorrows!
 Pierr. Burn!
First burn, and Level Venice to thy Ruin,
What starve like Beggars Brats in frosty weather,
Under a Hedge, and whine our selves to Death!
Thou, or thy Cause, shall never want assistance,
Whilst I have blood or Fortune fit to serve thee;
Command my heart: Thou art every way its master.
 Jaff. No: there's a secret Pride in bravely dying.
 Pierr. Rats die in Holes and Corners, Dogs run mad;
Man knows a braver Remedy for sorrow:
Revenge! the Attribute of Gods, they stampt it
With their great Image on our Natures; dye!
Consider well the Cause that calls upon thee:
And if thou art base enough, dye then: Remember
Thy Belvidera suffers: Belvidera!
Dye—Damn first—what be decently interr'd
In a Church-yard, and mingle thy brave dust
With stinking Rogues that rot in dirty winding sheets,
Surfeit-slain Fools, the common Dung o'th Soyl.
 Jaff. Oh!
 Pierr. Well said, out with't, Swear a little—
 Jaff. Swear!
By Sea and Air! by Earth, by Heaven and Hell,
I will revenge my Belvidera's Tears!
Heark thee my Friend—Priuli—is—a Senator!
 Pierr. A Dog!
 Jaff. Agreed.
 Pierr. Shoot him.
 Jaff. With all my heart.
No more: Where shall we meet at Night?
 Pierr. I'l tell thee;
On the Ryalto every Night at Twelve
I take my Evening's walk of Meditation,
There we two will meet, and talk of pretious
Mischief—
 Jaff. Farewell.
 Pierr. At Twelve.
 Jaff. At any hour, my plagues
Will keep me waking.   *[Exit* PIERR.

Tell me why, good Heav'n,
Thou mad'st me what I am, with all the Spirit,
Aspiring thoughts and Elegant desires
That fill the happiest Man? Ah! rather why
Did'st thou not form me sordid as my Fate,
Base minded, dull, and fit to carry Burdens?
Why have I sence to know the Curse that's on me?
Is this just dealing, Nature? Belvidera!

Enter BELVIDERA.

Poor Belvidera!
    Belvid. Lead me, lead me my Virgins!
To that kind Voice. My Lord, my Love, my **Refuge!**
Happy my Eyes, when they behold thy Face:
My heavy heart will leave its doleful beating
At sight of thee, and bound with sprightful joys.
Oh smile, as when our Loves were in their Spring,
And cheer my fainting Soul.
    Jaff. As when our Loves
Were in their Spring? has then my Fortune chang'd?
Art thou not Belvidera, still the same,
Kind, good, and tender, as my Arms first found thee?
If thou art alter'd, where shall I have harbour?
Where ease my loaded Heart? Oh! where complain?
    Belv. Does this appear like Change, or Love decaying?
When thus I throw my self into thy bosom,
With all the resolution of a strong Truth:
Beat's not my heart, as 'twou'd alarm thine
To a new Charge of bliss; I joy more in thee,
Than did thy Mother when she hugg'd thee first,
And bless'd the Gods for all her Travel past.
    Jaff. Can there in Woman be such glorious Faith?
Sure all ill stories of thy Sex are false;
Oh Woman! lovely Woman! Nature made thee
To temper Man: We had been Brutes without you,
Angels are Painted fair, to look like you;
There's in you all that we believe of Heav'n,
Amazing Brightness, Purity and Truth,
Eternal Joy, and everlasting Love.
    Belv. If Love be Treasure, wee'l be wondrous rich:
I have so much, my heart will surely break with't;
Vows cannot express it, when I wou'd declare
How great's my Joy, I am dumb with the big thought;
I swell, and sigh, and labour with my longing.

Oh lead me to some Desart wide and wild,
Barren as our Misfortunes, where my Soul
May have its vent: Where I may tell aloud
To the high Heavens, and every list'ning Planet,
With what a boundless stock my bosom's fraught;
Where I may throw my eager Arms about thee,
Give loose to Love with kisses, kindling Joy,
And let off all the Fire that's in my Heart.

    Jaff. Oh Belvidera! double I am a Begger,
Undone by Fortune, and in debt to thee;
Want! worldly Want! that hungry meager Fiend
Is at my heels, and chaces me in view;
Can'st thou bear Cold and Hunger? Can these Limbs,
Fram'd for the tender Offices of Love,
Endure the bitter Gripes of smarting Poverty?
When banisht by our miseries abroad,
(As suddenly we shall be) to seek out
(In some far Climate where our Names are strangers)
For charitable succour; wilt thou then,
When in a Bed of straw we shrink together,
And the bleak winds shall whistle round our heads;
Wilt thou then talk thus to me? Wilt thou then
Hush my Cares thus, and shelter me with Love?

    Belv. Oh I will love thee, even in Madness love thee:
Tho my distracted Senses should forsake me,
I'd find some intervals, when my poor heart
Should swage it self and be let loose to thine.
Though the bare Earth be all our Resting-place,
It's Root's our food, some Clift our Habitation,
I'l make this Arm a Pillow for thy Head;
As thou sighing ly'st, and swell'd with sorrow,
Creep to thy Bosom, pour the balm of Love
Into thy Soul, and kiss thee to thy Rest;
Then praise our God, and watch thee 'till the Morning.

    Jaff. Hear this you Heavens, and wonder how you made her
Reign, reign ye Monarchs that divide the World,
Busy Rebellion ner'e will let you know
Tranquility and Happiness like mine;
Like gawdy Ships, th' obsequious Billows fall
And rise again, to lift you in your Pride;
They wait but for a storm and then devour you:
I, in my private Bark, already wreck't,
Like a poor Merchant driven on unknown Land,
That had by chance packt up his choicest Treasure

In one dear Casket, and sav'd only that:
  Since I must wander further on the shore,
  Thus hug my little, but my precious store;
  Resolv'd to scorn, and trust my Fate no more.   [*Exeunt.*

ACT II

Enter PIERRE *and* AQUILINA.

Aquil. By all thy Wrongs, thou art dearer to my Arms
Than all the Wealth of Venice: Prithee stay,
And let us love to night.
  Pierr. No: There's Fool,
There's Fool about thee: When a Woman sells
Her Flesh to Fools, her Beauty's lost to me;
They leave a Taint, a sully where th'ave past,
There's such a baneful Quality about 'em,
Even spoyls Complexions with their own Nauseousness,.
They infect all they touch; I cannot think
Of tasting any thing a Fool has pall'd.
  Aqui. I loath and scorn that Fool thou mean'st, as much
Or more than thou can'st; But the Beast has Gold
That makes him necessary: Power too,
To qualifie my Character, and poise me
Equal with peevish Virtue, that beholds
My Liberty with Envy: In their Hearts
Are loose as I am; But an ugly Power
Sits in their Faces, and frights Pleasures from 'em.
  Pierr. Much good may't do you, Madam, with your Senator.
  Aquil. My Senator! why, can'st thou think that Wretch
I're fill'd thy Aquilina's Arms with Pleasure?
Think'st thou, because I sometimes give him leave
To soyle himself at what he is unfit for;
Because I force my self to endure and suffer him,
Think'st thou I love him? No, by all the Joys
Thou ever gav'st me, his Presence is my Pennance;
The worst thing an old Man can be 's a Lover,
A meer *Memento Mori* to poor woman.
I never lay by his decrepit side,
But all that night I ponder'd on my Grave.
  Pierr. Would he were well sent thither.
  Aqui. That's my wish too:
For then, my Pierre, I might have cause with pleasure
To play the Hypocrite: Oh! how I could weep

Over the dying Dotard, and kiss him too,
In hopes to smother him quite; then, when the time
Was come to pay my Sorrows at his Funeral,
For he has already made me Heir to Treasures,
Would make me out-act a real Widows whining:
How could I frame my face to fit my mourning!
With wringing hands attend him to his Grave,
Fall swooning on his Hearse: Take mad possession,
Even of the Dismal Vault, where he lay bury'd,
There like the Ephesian Matron dwell, till Thou,
My lovely Soldier, comest to my Deliverance;
Then throwing up my Veil, with open Armes
And laughing Eyes, run to new dawning Joy.

    Pierr. No more! I have Friends to meet here to night,
And must be private. As you prize my Friendship
Keep up your Coxcomb: Let him not pry nor listen,
Nor fisk about the House as I have seen him,
Like a tame mumping Squirrel with a bell on;
Currs will be abroad to bite him, if you do.

    Aquil. What Friends to meet? may I not be of your Council?
    Pierr. How! a Woman ask Questions out of Bed?
Go to your Senator, ask him what passes
Amongst his Brethren, hee'l hide nothing from you;
But pump not me for Politicks. No more!
Give order that whoever in my name
Comes here, receive Admittance: so good night.

    Aquil. Must we ne're meet again! Embrace no more!
Is Love so soon and utterly forgotten!

    Pierr. As you hence-forward treat your Fool, I'le think on't
    Aquil. Curst be all Fools, and doubly curst my self,
The worst of Fools—I die if he forsakes me;
And now to keep him, Heav'n or Hell instruct me.   [*Exeunt*

Scene.—*The Ryalto*

Enter Jaffeir.

    Jaff. I am here, and thus, the Shades of Night around me
I look as if all Hell were in my Heart,
And I in Hell. Nay, surely 'tis so with me;—
For every step I tread, methinks some Fiend
Knocks at my Breast, and bids it not be quiet:
I've heard, how desperate Wretches, like my self,
Have wander'd out at this dead time of Night
To meet the Foe of Mankind in his walk:

Sure I am so Curst, that, tho' of Heav'n forsaken,
No Minister of Darkness cares to Tempt me.
Hell! Hell! why sleepest thou?

Enter PIERRE.

Pierr. Sure I have stay'd too long:
The Clock has struck, and I may lose my Proselyte.
Speak, who goes there?
    Jaff. A Dog, that comes to howl
At yonder Moon: What's he that asks the Question?
    Pierr. A Friend to Dogs, for they are honest Creatures,
And ne're betray their Masters; never Fawn
On any that they love not: Well met, Friend:
Jaffeir!
    Jaff. The same. Oh Pierre! Thou art come in season,
I was just going to Pray.
    Pierr. Ah that's Mechanick,
Priests make a Trade on't, and yet starve by it too:
No Praying, it spoils Business, and time's precious;
Where's Belvidera?
    Jaff. For a Day or two
I've lodg'd her privately, 'till I see farther
What Fortune will do with me? Prithee, Friend,
If thou would'st have me fit to hear good Council,
Speak not of Belvidera—
    Pierr. Speak not of her.
    Jaff. Oh no!
    Pierr. Nor name her. May be I wish her well.
    Jaff. Who well?
    Pierr. Thy Wife, thy lovely Belvidera,
I hope a man may wish his Friends Wife well,
And no harm done!
    Jaff. Y'are merry Pierre!
    Pierr. I am so:
Thou shalt smile too, and Belvidera smile;
We'll all rejoyce, here's something to buy Pins,
Marriage is Chargeable.
    Jaff. I but half wisht
To see the Devil, and he's here already.
Well!
What must this buy, Rebellion, Murder, Treason?
Tell me which way I must be damn'd for this.
    Pierr. When last we parted, we had no qualms like these,
But entertain'd each others thoughts like Men,

Whose Souls were well acquainted. Is the World
Reform'd since our last meeting? What new miracles
Have happen'd? Has Priuli's heart relented?
Can he be honest?

    Jaff. Kind Heav'n! let heavy Curses
Gall his old Age; Cramps, Aches, rack his Bones;
And bitterest disquiet wring his Heart;
Oh let him live 'till Life become his burden!
Let him groan under't long, linger an Age
In the worst Agonies and Pangs of Death,
And find its ease, but late.

    Pierr. Nay, could'st thou not
As well, my Friend, have stretcht the Curse to all
The Senate round, as to one single Villain?

    Jaff. But Curses stick not: Could I kill with Cursing,
By Heav'n I know not thirty Heads in Venice
Should not be blasted; Senators should rot
Like Dogs on Dunghills; but their Wives and Daughters
Dye of their own diseases. Oh for a Curse
To kill with!

    Pierr. Daggers, Daggers, are much better!

    Jaff. Ha!

    Pierr. Daggers.

    Jaff. But where are they?

    Pierr. Oh, a Thousand
May be dispos'd in honest hands in Venice.

    Jaff. Thou talk'st in Clouds.

    Pierr. But yet a Heart half wrong'd
As thine has bin, would find the meaning, Jaffeir.

    Jaff. A thousand Daggers, all in honest hands;
And have not I a Friend will stick one here?

    Pierr. Yes, if I thought thou wert not to be cherisht
To a nobler purpose, I'd be that Friend.
But thou hast better Friends, Friends, whom thy Wrongs
Have made thy Friends; Friends, worthy to be call'd so;
I'l trust thee with a secret: There are Spirits
This hour at work. But as thou art a Man,
Whom I have pickt and chosen from the World,
Swear, that thou wilt be true to what I utter,
And when I have told thee, that which only Gods
And Men like Gods are privy to, then swear,
No Chance or Change shall wrest it from thy Bosom.

    Jaff. When thou would'st bind me, is there need of Oaths
(Green-sickness Girls lose Maiden-heads with such Counters

For thou art so near my heart, that thou may'st see
Its bottom, sound its strength, and firmness to thee:
Is Coward, Fool, or Villain, in my face?
If I seem none of these, I dare believe
Thou would'st not use me in a little Cause,
For I am fit for Honour's toughest task;
Nor ever yet found fooling was my Province;
And for a villainous inglorious enterprize,
I know thy heart so well, I dare lay mine
Before thee, set it to what Point thou wilt.
    Pierr. Nay, It's a Cause thou wilt be fond of Jaffeir.
For it is founded on the noblest Basis,
Our Liberties, our natural Inheritance;
There's no Religion. no Hypocrisie in't;
Wee'l do the Business, and ne'r fast and pray for't:
Openly act a deed, the World shall gaze
With wonder at, and envy when it is done.
    Jaff. For Liberty!
    Pierr. For Liberty, my Friend:
Thou shalt be freed from base Priuli's Tyranny,
And thy sequestred Fortunes heal'd again.
I shall be freed from opprobrious Wrongs,
That press me now, and bend my Spirit downward:
All Venice free, and every growing Merit
Succeed to its just Right: Fools shall be pull'd
From Wisdoms Seat; those baleful unclean Birds,
Those Lazy-Owls, who (perch'd near Fortunes Top)
Sit only watchful with their heavy Wings
To cuff down new fledg'd Virtues, that would rise
To nobler heights, and make the Grove harmonious.
    Jaff. What can I do?
    Pierr. Cans't thou not kill a Senator?
    Jaff. Were there one wise or honest, I could kill him
For herding with that nest of Fools and Knaves;
By all my Wrongs, thou talk'st as if revenge
Were to be had, and the brave Story warms me.
    Pierr. Swear then!
    Jaff. I do, by all those glittering Stars,
And yond great Ruling Planet of the Night!
By all good Pow'rs above, and ill below!
By Love and Friendship, dearer than my Life!
No Pow'r or Death shall make me false to thee.
    Pierr. Here we embrace, and I'l unlock my Heart.
A Councel's held hard by, where the destruction

Of this great Empire's hatching: There I'l lead thee!
But be a Man, for thou art to mix with Men
Fit to disturb the Peace of the World,
And rule it when it's wildest—
    Jaff. I give thee thanks
For this kind warning: Yes, I will be a Man,
And charge thee, Pierre, when er'e thou see'st my fears
Betray me less, to rip this Heart of mine
Out of my Breast, and shew it for a Cowards.
Come, let's begone, for from this hour I chase
All little thoughts, all tender humane Follies
Out of my bosom: Vengeance shall have room:
Revenge!
    Pierr. And Liberty!
    Jaff. Revenge! Revenge—   [*Exeunt.*

The SCENE *changes to* AQUILINA'S *house, the Greek Curtezan*

Enter RENAULT.

Renault. Why was my choice Ambition, the first ground
A Wretch can build on? it's indeed at distance
A good Prospect, tempting to the View,
The Height delights us, and the Mountain Top
Looks beautiful, because it's nigh to Heav'n,
But we ne're think how sandy's the Foundation,
What Storm will batter, and what Tempest shake us!
Who's there?   *Enter* SPINOSA.

Spino. Renault, good morrow! for by this time
I think the Scale of Night has turn'd the ballance,
And weighs up Morning: Has the Clock struck Twelve?
    Rena. Yes, Clocks will go as they are set: But Man,
Irregular Man's ne're constant, never certain:
I've spent at least three pretious hours of darkness
In waiting dull attendance; 'tis the Curse
Of diligent Virtue to be mixt like mine,
With giddy Tempers, Souls but half resolv'd.
    Spin. Hell seize that Soul amongst us, it can frighten.
    Rena. What's then the cause that I am here alone?
Why are we not together?

Enter ELIOT.

O Sir, welcome!
You are an Englishman: When Treason's hatching
One might have thought you'd not have been behind hand.

In what Whore's lap have you been lolling?
Give but an Englishman his Whore and ease,
Beef and a Sea-coal fire, he's yours for ever.
 Eliot. Frenchman, you are sawcy.
 Rena. How!

Enter BEDAMAR *the Embassador,* THEODORE, BRAMVEIL, DURAND,
 BRABE, REVILLIDO, MEZZANA, TERNON, RETROSI, *Conspirators.*

 Bedam. At difference, fy.
Is this a time for quarrels? Thieves and Rogues
Fall out and brawl: Should Men of your high calling,
Men separated by the Choice of Providence,
From the gross heap of Mankind, and set here
In this great assembly as in one great Jewel,
T'adorn the bravest purpose it er'e smil'd on;
Should you like Boys wrangle for trifles?
 Ren. Boys!
 Beda. Renault, thy Hand!
 Ren. I thought I'd given my Heart
Long since to every Man that mingles here;
But grieve to find it trusted with such Tempers,
That can't forgive my froward Age its weakness.
 Beda. Eliot, thou once had'st Vertue, I have seen
Thy stubborn Temper bend with godlike Goodness,
Not half thus courted: 'Tis thy Nations Glory,
To hugg the Foe that offers brave Alliance.
Once more embrace, my Friends—wee'l all embrace—
United thus, we are the mighty Engin
Must twist this rooted Empire from its Basis!
Totters it not already?
 Eliot. Would it were tumbling.
 Bed. Nay it shall down: This Night we Seal its ruine.
    Enter PIERRE.
Oh Pierre! thou art welcome!
Come to my breast, for by its hopes thou look'st
Lovelily dreadful, and the Fate of Venice
Seems on thy Sword already. Oh my Mars!
The Poets that first feign'd a God of War
Sure prophesy'd of thee.
 Pierr. Friends! was not Brutus,
I mean that Brutus, who in open Senate
Stabb'd the first Cæsar that usurp'd the World)
 Gallant Man?

Rena. Yes, and Cateline too;
Tho story wrong his Fame: for he conspir'd
To prop the reeling Glory of his Country:
His Cause was good.
    Beda. And ours as much above it,
As Renault thou art Superior to Cethegus,
Or Pierre to Cassius.
    Pierr. Then to what we aim at
When do we start? or must we talk for ever?
    Beda. No Pierre, the Deed's near Birth: Fate seems to have set
The Business up, and given it to our care,
I hope there's not a heart nor hand amongst us
But is firm and ready.
    All. All!
Wee'l die with Bedamore.
    Beda. Oh Men,
Matchless, as will your Glory be hereafter.
The Game is for a Matchless Prize, if won;
If lost, disgraceful Ruine.
    Ren. What can lose it?
The publick Stock's a Beggar; one Venetian
Trusts not another: Look into their Stores
Of general safety; Empty Magazines,
A tatter'd Fleet, a murmuring unpaid Army,
Bankrupt Nobility, a harrast Commonalty,
A Factious, giddy, and divided Senate,
Is all the strength of Venice: Let's destroy it;
Let's fill their Magazines with Arms to awe them,
Man out their Fleet, and make their Trade maintain it;
Let loose the murmuring Army on their Masters,
To pay themselves with plunder; Lop their Nobles
To the base Roots, whence most of 'em first sprung;
Enslave the Rowt, whom smarting will make humble,
Turn out their droning Senate, and possess
That Seat of Empire which our Souls were fram'd for.
    Pierr. Ten thousand men are Armed at your Nod,
Commanded all by Leaders fit to guide
A Battle for the freedom of the World;
This wretched State has starv'd them in its service,
And by your bounty quicken'd, they're resolv'd
To serve your Glory, and revenge their own!
Th' have all their different Quarters in this City,
Watch for th' Alarm, and grumble 'tis so tardy.
    Beda. I doubt not Friend, but thy unweary'd diligence

Has still kept waking, and it shall have ease;
After this Night it is resolv'd we meet
No more, 'till Venice own us for her Lords.

Pierr. How lovely the Adriatique Whore,
Drest in her Flames, will shine! devouring Flames!
Such as shall burn her to the watery bottom
And hiss in her Foundation.

Beda. Now if any
Amongst us that owns this glorious Cause,
Have friends or Interest, hee'd wish to save,
Let it be told, the general Doom is Seal'd;
But I'de forgo the Hopes of a Worlds Empire,
Rather than wound the Bowels of my Friend.

Pierr. I must confess you there have toucht my weakness,
I have a Friend; hear it, such a Friend!
My heart was ner'e shut to him: Nay, I'l tell you,
He knows the very Business of this Hour;
But he rejoyces in the Cause, and loves it,
W' have chang'd a Vow to live and die together,
And He's at hand to ratify it here.

Ren. How! all betray'd?

Pierr. No—I've dealt nobly with you;
I've brought my All into the publick Stock;
I had but one Friend, and him I'l share amongst you!
Receive and Cherish him: Or if, when seen
And searcht, you find him worthless, as my Tongue
Has lodg'd this Secret in his faithful Breast,
To ease your fears I wear a Dagger here
Shall rip it out again, and give you rest.
Come forth, thou only Good I er'e could boast of.

Enter JAFFEIR *with a Dagger.*

Beda. His Presence bears the show of Manly Vertue.

Jaff. I know you'l wonder all, that thus uncall'd,
I dare approach this place of fatal Councels;
But I am amongst you, and by Heav'n it glads me,
To see so many Vertues thus united,
To restore Justice and dethrown Oppression.
Command this Sword, if you would have it quiet,
Into this Breast; but if you think it worthy
To cut the Throats of reverend Rogues in Robes,
Send me into the curs'd assembl'd Senate;
It shrinks not, tho I meet a Father there;
Would you behold this City Flaming? Here's

A hand shall bear a lighted Torch at noon
To the Arsenal, and set its Gates on fire.

Ren. You talk this well, Sir.

Jaff. Nay—by Heav'n I'l do this.

Come, come, I read distrust in all your faces,
You fear me a Villain, and indeed it's odd
To hear a stranger talk thus at first meeting,
Of matters, that have been so well debated;
But I come ripe with Wrongs as you with Councels;
I hate this Senate, am a Foe to Venice;
A Friend to none, but Men resolv'd like me,
To push on Mischief: Oh did you but know me,
I need not talk thus!

Beda. Pierre! I must embrace him,
My heart beats to this Man as if it knew him.

Rena. I never lov'd these huggers.

Jaff. Still I see
The cause delights me not. Your Friends survey me,
As I were dang'rous—but I come Arm'd
Against all doubts, and to your trust will give
A Pledge, worth more than all the World can pay for.
My Belvidera! Ho! my Belvidera!

Beda. What wonder next?

Jaff. Let me entreat you,
As I have henceforth hopes to call ye friends,
That all but the Ambassador, this
Grave Guide of Councels, with my friend that owns me,
Withdraw a while to spare a Womans blushes.

[*Exit all but* BEDA., RENA., JAFF., PIERR

Beda. Pierre, whither will this Ceremony lead us?

Jaff. My Belvidera! Belvidera!

Belvid. Who?

Enter BELVIDERA.

Who calls so lowd at this late peacefull hour?
That Voice was wont to come in gentler whispers,
And fill my Ears with the soft breath of Love:
Thou hourly Image of my Thoughts, where art thou?

Jaff. Indeed 'tis late.

Belv. Oh! I have slept, and dreamt,
And dreamt again: Where hast thou been, thou **Loyterer?**
Tho my Eyes clos'd, my Arms have still been open'd;
Stretcht every way betwixt my broken slumbers,
To search if thou wert come to crown my Rest;

There's no repose without thee: Oh the day,
Too soon will break, and wake us to our sorrow;
Come, come to bed, and bid thy Cares good Night.
     Jaff. Oh Belvidera! we must change the Scene
In which the past Delights of Life were tasted:
The poor sleep little, we must learn to watch
Our labours late, and early every Morning,
Midst winter Frosts, then clad and fed with sparing,
Rise to our toils, and drudge away the day.
     Belv. Alas! where am I! whither is't you lead me!
Methinks I read distraction in your face!
Something less gentle than the Fate you tell me:
You shake and tremble too! your blood runs cold!
Heavens guard my Love, and bless his heart with Patience.
     Jaff. That I have Patience, let our Fate bear witness,
Who has ordain'd it so, that thou and I
(Thou the divinest God man e're possest,
And I the wretched'st of the Race of Man)
This very hour, without one tear, must part.
     Belv. Part! must we part? Oh! am I then forsaken?
Will my Love cast me off? have my misfortunes
Offended him so highly, that hee'l leave me?
Why dragg you from me? whither are you going?
My Dear! my Life! my Love!
     Jaff. Oh Friends!
     Belv. Speak to me.
     Jaff. Take her from my heart,
Shee'l gain such hold else, I shall ner'e get loose.
I charge thee take her, but with tender'st care,
Relieve her Troubles and asswage her sorrows.
     Ren. Rise, Madam! and Command amongst your Servants!
     Jaff. To you, Sirs, and your Honours, I bequeath her,
And with her this, when I prove unworthy—   [*Gives a dagger.*
You know the rest:—Then strike it to her heart;
And tell her, he, who three whole happy years
Lay in her Arms, and each kind Night repeated
The passionate Vows of still encreasing Love,
Sent that Reward for all her Truth and Sufferings.
     Belv. Nay, take my Life, since he has sold it cheaply;
Or send me to some distant Clime your slave,
But let it be far off, lest my complainings
Should reach his guilty Ears, and shake his peace.
     Jaff. No Belvidera, I've contriv'd thy honour,
Trust to my Faith, and be but Fortune kind

To me, as I'l preserve that faith unbroken,
When next we meet, I'l lift thee to a height,
Shall gather all the gazing World about thee,
To wonder what strange Virtue plac'd thee there.
But if we ner'e meet more—
    Belv. Oh thou unkind one,
Never meet more! have I deserv'd this from you?
Look on me, tell me, tell me, speak thou dear deceiver,
Why am I separated from thy Love?
If I am false, accuse me; but if true,
Don't, prithee don't in poverty forsake me.
But pitty the sad heart, that's torn with parting.
Yet hear me! yet recall me—
                    [*Exit* RENA., BEDA., *and* BELV.

    Jaff. Oh my Eyes!
Look not that way, but turn your selves awhile
Into my heart, and be wean'd all together.
My Friend, where art thou?
    Pierr. Here, my Honour's Brother.
    Jaff. Is Belvidera gone?
    Pierr. Renault has led her
Back to her own Apartment: but, by Heav'n!
Thou must not see her more till our work's over.
    Jaff. No.
    Pierr. Not for your life.
    Jaff. Oh Pierre, wert thou but she,
How I could pull thee down into my heart,
Gaze on thee till my Eye-strings crackt with Love,
Till all my sinews with its fire extended,
Fixt me upon the Rack of ardent longing;
Then swelling, sighing, raging to be blest,
Come like a panting Turtle to thy Breast,
On thy soft Bosom, hovering, bill and play,
Confess the cause why last I fled away;
    Own 'twas a fault, but swear to give it or'e,
And never follow false Ambition more.   [*Exit ambo*

ACT III

Enter AQUILINA *and her* MAID.

Aquil. Tell him I am gone to bed: Tell him I am not at home
tell him I've better Company with me, or any thing; tell him
in short I will not see him, the eternal, troublesome, vexatious

Fool: He's worse Company than an ignorant Physitian—I'l not be disturb'd at these unseasonable hours.

Maid. But Madam! He's here already, just enter'd the doors.

Aquil. Turn him out agen, you unnecessary, useless, giddy-brain'd Asse! if he will not begone, set the house a fire and burn us both: I had rather meet a Toad in my dish than that old hideous Animal in my Chamber to Night.

Enter ANTONIO.

Ant. Nacky, Nacky, Nacky—how dost do Nacky? Hurry durry. I am come, little Nacky; past eleven a Clock, a late hour; time in all Conscience to go to bed, Nacky—Nacky did I say? Ay Nacky; Aquilina, lina, lina, quilina, quilina, quilina, Aquilina, Naquilina, Naquilina, Acky, Acky, Nacky, Nacky, Queen Nacky—come let's to bed—you Fubbs, you Pugg you—you little Puss—Purree Tuzzey—I am a Senator.

Aquil. You are a Fool, I am sure.

Anto. May be so too sweet-heart. Never the worse Senator for all that. Come Nacky, Nacky, lets have a Game at Rump, Nacky.

Aquil. You would do well Signior to be troublesome here no longer, but leave me to my self, be sober and go home, Sir.

Anto. Home Madona!

Aquil. Ay home, Sir. Who am I?

Anto. Madona, as I take it you are my—you are—thou art my little Nicky Nacky—that's all!

Aquil. I find you are resolv'd to be troublesome, and so to make short of the matter in few words, I hate you, detest you, bath you, I am weary of you, sick of you—hang you, you are an Old, silly, Impertinent, impotent, sollicitous Coxcomb, Crazy in your head, and lazy in your Body, love to be medling with every thing, and if you had not Money, you are good for nothing.

Anto. Good for nothing! Hurry durry, I'l try that presently. Sixty one years Old, and good for nothing; that's brave. [*To the* MAID.] Come, come, come, Mistress fiddle-faddle, turn you out for a season; go turn out I say, it is our will and pleasure to be private some moments—out, out when you are bid too.— *Puts her out and locks the door*.] Good for nothing you say.

Aquil. Why what are you good for?

Anto. In the first place, Madam, I am Old, and consequently very wise, very wise, Madona, d'e mark that? in the second place take notice, if you please, that I am a Senator, and when I think it can make Speeches Madona. Hurry durry, I can make a speech in the Senate-house now and then—wou'd make your hair stand an end, Madona.

Aquil. What care I for your Speeches in the Senate-house, if you wou'd be silent here, I should thank you.

Anto. Why, I can make make Speeches to thee too, my lovely Madona; for Example—my cruel fair one—[*Takes out a Purse of Gold, and at every pawse shakes it.*] Since it is my Fate, that you should with your Servant angry prove; tho late at Night— I hope 'tis not too late with this to gain reception for my Love— there's for thee, my little Nicky Nacky—take it, here take it— I say take it, or I'l throw it at your head—how now, rebel!

Aquil. Truly, my Illustrious Senator, I must confess your Honour is at present most profoundly eloquent indeed.

Anto. Very well: Come, now let's sit down and think upon't a little—come sit I say—sit down by me a little, my Nicky Nacky, hah—[*Sits down.*] Hurry durry—good for nothing—

Aquil. No Sir, if you please I can know my distance and stand.

Anto. Stand: How? Nacky, up and I down! Nay then let me exclaim with the Poet:

> *Shew me a case more pitiful who can,*
> *A standing Woman, and a falling Man.*

Hurry durry—not sit down—see this ye Gods— You won't sit down?

Aquil. No Sir.

Anto. Then look you now, suppose me a Bull, a Basan-Bull, the Bull of Bulls, or any Bull. Thus up I get and with my brows thus bent—I broo, I say I broo, I broo, I broo. You won't sit down will you?—I broo—

> [*Bellows like a Bull, and drives her about*

Aquil. Well, Sir, I must endure this. Now your honour has been a Bull, pray what Beast will your Worship please to be next?

> [*She sits down*

Anto. Now I'l be a Senator agen, and thy Lover, little Nicky Nacky! [*He sits by her.*] Ah toad, toad, toad, toad! spit in my Face a little, Nacky—spit in my Face prithee, spit in my Face never so little: spit but a little bit—spit, spit, spit, spit, when you are bid I say; do, prithee spit—now, now, now, spit: what you won't spit, will you? Then I'l be a Dog.

Aquil. A Dog my Lord?

Anto. Ay a Dog—and I'l give thee this to'ther purse to let me be a Dog—and to use me like a Dog a little. Hurry durry— will—here 'tis.—

> [*Gives the Purse*

Aquil. Well, with all my heart. But let me beseech your Dogship to play your tricks over as fast as you can, that you ma come to stinking the sooner, and be turn'd out of dores as you deserve.

Anto. Ay, ay—no matter for that—that [*he gets under the Table*] shan't move me— Now, bough, waugh, waugh, bough waugh—   [*Barks like a Dog.*

Aquil. Hold, hold, hold Sir, I beseech you: what is't you do: If Curs bite, they must be kickt, Sir. Do you see, kickt thus.

Anto. Ay with all my heart: do kick, kick on, now I am under the Table, kick agen—kick harder—harder yet, bough waugh waugh, waugh, bough—'odd, I'le have a snap at thy shins— bough waugh wough, waugh, bough—'odd she kicks bravely.—

Aquil. Nay then I'l go another way to work with you: and I think here's an Instrument fit for the purpose. [*Fetches a Whip and Bell.*] What, bite your Mistress, sirrah! out, out of dores, you Dog, to kennel and be hang'd—bite your Mistress by the Legs, you rogue.—   [*She Whips him.*

Anto. Nay prithee Nacky, now thou art too loving: Hurry durry, 'odd I'l be a Dog no longer.

Aquil. Nay none of your fawning and grinning: But be gone, or here's the discipline: What, bite your Mistress by the Legs you mungril? out of dores—hout hout, to kennel sirra! go.

Anto. This is very barbarous usage Nacky, very barbarous: look you, I will not go—I will not stir from the dore, that I resolve—hurry durry, what, shut me out?   [*She Whips him out.*

Aquil. Ay, and if you come here any more to night I'l have my Foot-men lug you, you Curr: What, bite your poor Mistress Nacky, sirrah!

Enter MAID.

Maid. Heav'ns Madam! Whats the matter?
                        [*He howls at the dore like a Dog.*
Aquil. Call my Foot-men hither presently.

Enter two FOOT-MEN.

Maid. They are here already Madam, the house is all alarm'd with a strange noise, that no body knows what to make of.

Aquil. Go all of you and turn that troublesome Beast in the next room out of my house—If I ever see him within these walls again, without my leave for his Admittance, you sneaking Rogues —I'l have you poison'd all, poison'd, like Rats: every Corner of the house shall stink of one of you: Go, and learn hereafter to know my pleasure. So now for my Pierre:

> Thus when Godlike Lover was displeas'd,
> We Sacrifice our Fool and he's appeas'd.

                                          [*Exeunt.*

SCENE *the Second*

Enter BELVIDERA.

Belvid. I'm Sacrific'd! I am sold! betray'd to shame!
Inevitable Ruin has inclos'd me!
No sooner was I to my bed repair'd,
To weigh, and (weeping) ponder my condition,
But the old hoary Wretch, to whose false Care
My Peace and Honour was intrusted, came
(Like Tarquin) gastely with infernal Lust.
Oh thou Roman Lucrece! thou could'st find friends to vindicat
    thy Wrong;
I never had but one, and he's prov'd false;
He that should guard my Virtue, has betray'd it;
Left me! undone me! Oh that I could hate him!
Where shall I go! Oh whither whither wander?

Enter JAFFEIR.

Jaff. Can Belvidera want a resting place
When these poor Arms are open to receive her?
Oh 'tis in vain to struggle with Desires
Strong as my Love to thee; for every moment
I am from thy sight, the Heart within my Bosom
Moans like a tender Infant in its Cradle
Whose Nurse had left it: Come, and with the Songs
Of gentle Love perswade it to its peace.
    Belvid. I fear the stubborn Wanderer will not own me,
'Tis grown a Rebel to be rul'd no longer,
Scorns the Indulgent Bosom that first lull'd it,
And like a Disobedient Child disdains
The soft Authority of Belvidera.
    Jaff. There was a time—
    Belvid. Yes, yes, there was a time,
When Belvidera's tears, her crys, and sorrows,
Were not despis'd; when if she chanc'd to sigh,
Or look but sad;—there was indeed a time
When Jaffeir would have ta'ne her in his Arms,
Eas'd her declining Head upon his Breast,
And never left her 'till he found the Cause,
But let her now weep Seas,
Cry, 'till she rend the Earth; sigh 'till she burst
Her heart asunder; still he bears it all;
Deaf as the Wind, and as the Rocks unshaken.

Jaff. Have I been deaf? am I that Rock unmov'd?
Against whose root, Tears beat and sighes are sent!
In vain have I beheld thy Sorrows calmly!
Witness against me Heav'ns, have I done this?
Then bear me in a Whirlwind back agen,
And let that angry dear one ne're forgive me!
Oh thou too rashly censur'st of my Love!
Could'st thou but think how I have spent this night,
Dark and alone, no pillow to my Head,
Rest in my Eyes, nor quiet in my Heart,
Thou would'st not Belvidera, sure thou would'st not
Talk to me thus, but like a pitying Angel,
Spreading thy wings come settle on my breast,
And hatch warm comfort there e're sorrows freeze it.

Belv. Why, then poor Mourner, in what baleful Corner
Hast thou been talking with that Witch the Night?
On what cold stone hast thou been stretcht along,
Gathering the grumbling Winds about thy Head,
To mix with theirs the Accents of thy Woes!
Oh now I find the Cause my Love forsakes me!
I am no longer fit to bear a share
In his Concernments: My weak female Virtue
Must not be trusted; 'Tis too frail and tender.

Jaff. Oh Porcia! Porcia! What a Soul was thine?

Belv. That Porcia was a Woman, and when Brutus
Big with the fate of Rome, (Heav'n guard thy safety!)
Conceal'd from her the Labours of his Mind,
She let him see, her Blood was great as his,
Flow'd from a Spring as noble, and a Heart
Fit to partake his Troubles, as his Love:
Fetch, fetch that Dagger back, the dreadful dower
Thou gav'st last night in parting with me; strike it
Here to my Heart; and as the Blood flows from it,
Judge if it run not pure as Cato's Daughter's.

Jaff. Thou art too good, and I indeed unworthy,
Unworthy so much Virtue: Teach me how
I may deserve such matchless Love as thine,
And see with what attention I'l obey thee.

Belv. Do not despise me: that's the All I ask.

Jaff. Despise thee! Hear me—

Belv. Oh thy charming Tongue
Is but too well acquainted with my weakness,
Knows, let it name but Love, my melting heart
Dissolves within my Breast; 'till with clos'd Eyes

I reel into thy Arms, and all's forgotten.

Jaff. What shall I do?

Belv. Tell me! be just, and tell me
Why dwells that busy Cloud upon thy face?
Why am I made a stranger? why that sigh,
And I not know the Cause? Why when the World
Is wrapt in Rest, why chooses then my Love
To wander up and down in horrid darkness,
Loathing his bed, and these desiring Arms?
Why are these Eyes Blood shot, with tedious watching?
Why starts he now? and looks as if he wisht
His Fate were finisht? Tell me, ease my fears;
Least when we next time meet, I want the power
To search into the sickness of thy Mind,
But talk as wildly then as thou look'st now.

Jaff. Oh Belvidera!

Belv. Why was I last night deliver'd to a Villain?

Jaff. Hah, a Villain!

Belv. Yes! to a Villain! Why at such an hour
Meets that assembly all made up of Wretches
That look as Hell had drawn 'em into League?
Why, I in this hand, and in that a Dagger,
Was I deliver'd with such dreadful Ceremonies?
"To you, Sirs, and to your Honour I bequeath her,
"And with her this: When e're I prove unworthy,
"You know the rest, then strike it to her Heart?"
Oh! why's that *rest* conceal'd from me? must I
Be made the hostage of a hellish Trust?
For such I know I am; that's all my value!
But by the Love and Loyalty I owe thee,
I'l free thee from the Bondage of these Slaves;
Strait to the Senate, tell 'em all I know,
All that I think, all that my fears inform me!

Jaff. Is this the Roman Virtue! this the Blood
That boasts its purity with Cato's Daughter!
Would she have e're betray'd her Brutus?

Belv. No:
For Brutus trusted her: Wer't thou so kind,
What would not Belvidera suffer for thee?

Jaff. I shall undo my self, and tell thee all.

Belv. Look not upon me, as I am a Woman,
But as a Bone, thy Wife, thy Friend; who long
Has had admission to thy heart, and there
Study'd the Virtues of thy gallant Nature;

Thy Constancy, thy Courage and thy Truth,
Have been my daily lesson: I have learnt them,
Am bold as thou, can suffer or despise
The worst of Fates for thee; and with thee share them.
    Jaff. Oh you divinest Powers! look down and hear
My Prayers! instruct me to reward this Virtue!
Yet think a little, e're thou tempt me further:
Think I have a Tale to tell, will shake thy Nature,
Melt all this boasted Constancy thou talk'st of
Into vile tears and despicable sorrows:
Then if thou should'st betray me!
    Belv. Shall I swear?
    Jaff. No: do not swear: I would not violate
Thy tender Nature with so rude a Bond:
But as thou hop'st to see me live my days,
And love thee long, lock this within thy Breast;
I've bound my self by all the strictest Sacraments,
Divine and humane—
    Belv. Speak!—
    Jaff. To kill thy Father—
    Belv. My Father!
    Jaff. Nay the Throats of the whole Senate
Shall bleed, my Belvidera: He amongst us
That spares his Father, Brother, or his Friend,
Is Damn'd: How rich and beauteous will the face
Of Ruin look, when these wide streets run blood;
I and the glorious Partners of my Fortune
Shouting, and striding o're the prostrate Dead,
Still to new waste; whilst thou, far off in safety
Smiling, shalt see the wonders of our daring;
And when night comes, with Praise and Love receive me.
    Belv. Oh!
    Jaff. Have a care, and shrink not even in thought!
For if thou do'st—
    Belv. I know it, thou wilt kill me.
Do, strike thy Sword into this bosom: Lay me
Dead on the Earth, and then thou wilt be safe:
Murder my Father! tho his Cruel Nature
Has persecuted me to my undoing,
Driven me to basest wants; Can I behold him
With smiles of Vengeance, butcher'd in his Age?
The sacred Fountain of my life destroy'd?
And canst thou shed the blood that gave me being?
Nay, be a Traitor too, and sell thy Country;

Can thy great Heart descend so vilely low,
Mix with hired Slaves, Bravoes, and Common stabbers,
Nose-slitters, Ally-lurking Villains! joyn
With such a Crew, and take a Ruffian's Wages,
To cut the Throats of Wretches as they sleep?

    Jaff. Thou wrong'st me, Belvidera! I've engag'd
With Men of Souls: fit to reform the ills
Of all Mankind: There's not a Heart amongst them,
But's as stout as Death, yet honest as the Nature
Of Man first made, e're Fraud and Vice were fashions.

    Belv. What's he, to whose curst hands last night thou gav'st me?
Was that well done? Oh! I could tell a story
Would rowse thy Lyon Heart out of its Den,
And make it rage with terrifying fury.

    Jaff. Speak on, I charge thee!

    Belv. Oh my Love! if e're
Thy Belvidera's Peace deserv'd thy Care,
Remove me from this place: Last night, last night!

    Jaff. Distract me not, but give me all the Truth.

    Belv. No sooner wer't thou gone, and I alone,
Left in the pow'r of that old Son of Mischief;
No sooner was I laid on my sad Bed,
But that vile Wretch approacht me; loose, unbutton'd,
Ready for violation: Then my Heart
Throbb'd with its fears: Oh how I wept and sigh'd,
And shrunk and trembled; wish'd in vain for him
That should protect me. Thou alas! wert gone!

    Jaff. Patience! sweet Heav'n, till I make vengeance sure.

    Belv. He drew the hideous Dagger forth thou gav'st him,
And with upbraiding smiles he said, *Behold it;*
This is the pledge of a false Husbands love:
And in my Arms then prest, and wou'd 'have clasp'd me;
But with my Cries I scar'd his Coward heart,
'Till he withdrew, and mutter'd vows to Hell.
These are thy Friends! with these thy Life, thy Honour,
Thy Love, all's stakt, and all will go to ruine.

    Jaff. No more: I charge thee keep this secret close;
Clear up thy sorrows, look as if thy wrongs
Were all forgot, and treat him like a Friend,
As no complaint were made. No more, retire,
Retire my Life, and doubt not of my Honour;
I'l heal its failings, and deserve thy Love.

    Belv. Oh should I part with thee, I fear thou wilt
In Anger leave me, and return no more:

Jaff. Return no more! I would not live without thee
Another Night to purchase the Creation.
   Belv. When shall we meet again?
   Jaff. Anon at Twelve!
I'l steal my self to thy expecting Arms!
Come like a Travell'd Dove and bring thee Peace.
   Belv. Indeed!
   Jaff. By all our loves!
   Belv. 'Tis hard to part:
But sure no falsehood e're lookt so fairly.
Farewell—Remember Twelve.   [*Exit* BELVID.
   Jaff. Let Heav'n forget me
When I remember not thy Truth, thy Love.
How curst is my Condition, toss'd and justl'd,
From every Corner; Fortune's Common Fool,
The jest of Rogues, an Instrumental Ass
For Villains to lay loads of Shame upon,
And drive about just for their ease and scorn.

          Enter PIERRE.

   Pierr. Jaffeir!
   Jaff. Who calls!
   Pierr. A Friend, that could have wisht
T'have found thee otherwise imploy'd: what, hunt
A Wife on the dull foil! sure a stanch Husband
Of all Hounds is the dullest: wilt thou never,
Never be wean'd from Caudles and Confections?
What feminine Tale hast thou been listening to,
Of unayr'd shirts; Catharrs and Tooth Ach got
By thin-sol'd shoos? Damnation! that a Fellow
Chosen to be a Sharer in the Destruction
Of a whole People, should sneak thus in Corners
To ease his fulsom Lusts, and Fool his Mind.
   Jaff. May not a Man then trifle out an hour
With a kind Woman and not wrong his calling?
   Pierr. Not in a Cause like ours.
   Jaff. Then Friend, our Cause
Is in a damn'd condition: for I'l tell thee,
That Canker-worm call'd Letchery has toucht it,
'Tis tainted vilely: would'st thou think it, Renault,
(That mortify'd old wither'd Winter Rogue)
Loves simple Fornication like a Priest,
I found him out for watering at my Wife:
He visited her last night like a kind Guardian:

Faith she has some Temptations, that's the truth on't.

 Pierr. He durst not wrong his Trust!

 Jaff. 'Twas something late tho
To take the freedome of a Ladies Chamber.

 Pierr. Was she in bed?

 Jaff. Yes faith in Virgin sheets
White as her bosom, Pierre, disht neatly up,
Might tempt a weaker appetite to taste.
Oh how the old Fox stunk I warrant thee
When the rank fit was on him.

 Pierr. Patience guide me!
He us'd no violence?

 Jaff. No, no! out on't, violence!
Play'd with her neck; brusht her with his Gray-beard,
Struggl'd and towz'd, tickl'd her 'till she squeak'd a little
May be, or so—but not a jot of violence—

 Pierr. Damn him.

 Jaff. Ay, so say I: but hush, no more on't;
All hitherto is well, and I believe
My self no Monster yet: Tho no Man knows
What Fate he's born to? sure 'tis near the hour
We all should meet for our concluding Orders:
Will the Ambassador be here in person?

 Pierr. No; he has sent Commission to that Villain, Renault,
To give the Executing Charge;
I'd have thee be a Man if possible
And keep thy temper; for a brave Revenge
Ne're comes too late.

 Jaff. Fear not, I am cool as Patience:
Had he compleated my dishonour, rather
Than hazard the Success our hopes are ripe for,
I'd bear it all with mortifying Vertue.

 Pierr. He's yonder coming this way through the Hall;
His thoughts seem full.

 Jaff. Prithee retire, and leave me
With him alone: I'l put him to some tryal,
See how his rotten part will bear the touching.

 Pierr. Be careful then.   [*Exit* PIERRE.

 Jaff. Nay never doubt, but trust me.
What, be a Devil! take a Damning Oath
For shedding native blood! can there be a sin
In merciful repentance? Oh this Villain.

Enter RENAULT.

Renault. Perverse! and peevish! what a slave is Man!
To let his itching flesh thus get the better of him!
Dispatch the Tool her Husband—that were well.
Who's there?

Jaff. A Man.

Ren. My Friend, my near Ally!
The hostage of your faith, my beauteous Charge, is very well.

Jaff. Sir, are you sure of that?
Stands she in perfect health? beats her pulse even?
Neither too hot nor cold?

Ren. What means that question?

Jaff. Oh Women have fantastick Constitutions,
Inconstant as their Wishes, always wavering,
And ne're fixt; was it not boldly done
Even at first sight to trust the Thing I lov'd
(A tempting Treasure too!) with Youth so fierce
And vigorous as thine? but thou art honest.

Ren. Who dares accuse me?

Jaff. Curst be him that doubts
Thy virtue, I have try'd it, and declare,
Were I to choose a Guardian of my Honour
I'd put it into thy keeping: for I know thee.

Ren. Know me!

Jaff. Ay know thee: There's no falsehood in thee.
Thou look'st just as thou art: Let us embrace.
Now would'st thou cut my Throat or I cut thine?

Ren. You dare not do't.

Jaff. You lye Sir.

Ren. How!

Jaff. No more.
'Tis a base World, and must reform, that's all.

Enter SPINOSA, THEODORE, ELIOT, REVILLIDO, DURAND, BRAM-
VEIL, *and the rest of the* CONSPIRATORS.

Ren. Spinosa! Theodore!

Spin. The same.

Ren. You are welcome!

Spin. You are trembling, Sir.

Ren. 'Tis a cold Night indeed, I am Aged,
Full of decay and natural infirmities;   [PIERRE *re-enters.*
We shall be warm, my Friend, I hope to morrow.

Pierr. 'Twas not well done, thou shou'd'st have stroakt him
And not have gall'd him.

Jaff. Damn him, let him chew on't.

Heav'n! where am I? beset with cursed Fiends,
That wait to Damn me: What a Devil's man,
When he forgets his nature—hush my heart.

    Ren. My Friends, 'tis late: are we assembled all?
Where's Theodore?

    Theo. At hand.

    Ren. Spinosa.

    Spin. Here.

    Ren. Bramveil.

    Bram. I am ready.

    Ren. Durand and Brabe.

    Dur. Command us,
We are both prepar'd!

    Ren. Mezzana, Revillido,
Ternon, Retrosi; Oh you are Men I find
Fit to behold your Fate, and meet her Summons,
To morrow's rising Sun must see you all
Deckt in your honours! are the Souldiers ready?

    Omn. All, all.

    Ren. You, Durand, with your thousand must possess
St. Marks; You, Captain, know your charge already;
'Tis to secure the Ducal Palace: you
Brabe with a hundred more must gain the Secque.
With the like number Brainveil to the Procuralle.
Be all this done with the least tumult possible,
'Till in each place you post sufficient guards:
Then sheath your Swords in every breast you meet.

    Jaff. Oh reverend Cruelty: Damn'd bloody Villain!

    Ren. During this Execution, Durand, you
Must in the mid'st keep your Battalia fast,
And Theodore be sure to plant the Canon
That may Command the streets; whilst Revellido,
Mezzana, Ternon and Retrosi, Guard you.
(This done!) wee'l give the General Alarm,
Apply Petards, and force the Ars'nal Gates;
Then fire the City round in several places,
Or with our Canon (if it dare resist)
Batter't to Ruin. But above all I charge you
Shed blood enough, spare neither Sex nor Age,
Name nor Condition; if there live a Senator
After to morrow, tho the dullest Rogue
That er'e said nothing, we have lost our ends;
If possible, lets kill the very Name
Of Senator, and bury it in blood.

Jaff. Merciless, horrid slave!—Ay, blood enough!
Shed blood enough, old Renault: how thou charm'st me!
   Ren. But one thing more, and then farewell till Fate
Join us again, or separate us ever:
First, let's embrace, Heav'n knows who next shall thus
Wing ye together: But let's all remember
We wear no Common Cause upon our Swords,
Let each Man think that on his single Virtue
Depends the Good and Fame of all the rest;
Eternal Honour or perpetual Infamy.
Let's remember, through what dreadful hazards
Propitious Fortune hitherto has led us,
How often on the brink of some discovery
Have we stood tottering, and yet still kept our ground
So well, the busiest searchers ne'r could follow
Those subtle Tracks which puzzled all suspition:
You droop Sir.
   Jaff. No: with a most profound attention
I've heard it all, and wonder at thy vertue.
   Ren. Though there be yet few hours 'twixt them and Ruin,
Are not the Senate lull'd in full security,
Quiet and satisfy'd, as Fools are always!
Never did so profound repose forerun
Calamity so great: Nay our good Fortune
Has blinded the most piercing of Mankind;
Strengthen'd the fearfull'st, charm'd the most suspectful,
Confounded the most subtle: for we live,
We live my Friends, and quickly shall our Life
Prove fatal to these Tyrants: Let's consider
That we destroy Oppression, Avarice,
A People nurst up equally with Vices
And loathsome Lusts, which Nature most abhors,
And such as without shame she cannot suffer.
   Jaff. Oh Belvidera, take me to thy Arms
And shew me where's my Peace, for I've lost it.   [*Exit* JAFF.
   Ren. Without the least remorse then let's resolve
With Fire and Sword t'exterminate these Tyrants,
And when we shall behold those curst Tribunals,
Stain'd by the Tears and sufferings of the Innocent,
Burning with flames rather from Heav'n than ours,
The raging furious and unpitying Souldier
Pulling his reeking Dagger from the bosoms
Of gasping Wretches; Death in every Quarter,
With all that sad disorder can produce,

To make a Spectacle of horror: Then,
Then let's call to mind, my dearest Friends,
That there's nothing pure upon the Earth,
That the most valu'd things have most allays,
And that in change of all those vile Enormities,
Under whose weight this wretched Country labours,
The means are only in our hands to Crown them.
   Pierr. And may those Powers above that are propitious
To gallant minds record this Cause, and bless it.
   Ren. Thus happy, thus secure of all we wish for,
Should there my Friends be found amongst us one
False to this glorious Enterprize, what Fate,
What Vengeance were enough for such a Villain?
   Eliot. Death here without repentance, Hell hereafter.
   Ren. Let that be my lott, if as here I stand
Lifted by Fate amongst her darling Sons,
Tho I had one only Brother, dear by all
The strictest ties of Nature; tho one hour
Had given us birth, one Fortune fed our wants,
One only love, and that but of each other,
Still fill'd our minds: Could I have such a Friend
Joyn'd in this Cause, and had but ground to fear
Meant fowl play; may this right hand drop from me,
If I'd not hazard all my future peace,
And stabb him to the heart before you: who
Would not do less? Would'st not thou Pierre the same?
   Pierr. You have singled me, Sir, out for this hard question,
As if 'twere started only for my sake!
Am I the thing you fear? Here, here's my bosom,
Search it with all your Swords! am I a Traytor?
   Ren. No: but I fear your late commended Friend
Is little less: Come Sirs, 'tis now no time
To trifle with our safety. Where's this Jaffeir?
   Spino. He left the room just now in strange disorder.
   Ren. Nay, there is danger in him: I observ'd him,
During the time I took for Explanation,
He was transported from most deep attention
To a confusion which he could not smother.
His looks grew full of sadness and surprize,
All which betray'd a wavering Spirit in him,
That labour'd with reluctancy and sorrow;
What's requisite for safety must be done
With speedy Execution: he remains
Yet in our power: I for my own part wear

A Dagger.

Pierr. Well.

Ren. And I could wish it!

Pierr. Where?

Ren. Bury'd in his heart.

Pierr. Away! w'are yet all friends;
No more of this, 'twill Breed ill blood amongst us.

Spin. Let us all draw our Swords, and search the house,
Pull him from the dark hole where he sits brooding
O're his cold fears, and each man kill his share of him.

Pierr. Who talks of killing? who's he'll shed the blood
That's dear to me? is't you? or you? or you Sir?
What, not one speak how you stand gaping all
On your grave Oracle, your wooden God there;
Yet not a word: Then Sir I'l tell you a secret,
Suspition's but at best a Cowards Virtue!   [*To* REN.

Ren. A Coward—   [*Handles his Sword*

Pierr. Put, put up thy Sword, old Man,
Thy hand shakes at it; come let's heal this breach,
I am too hot: we yet may live Friends.

Spino. 'Till we are safe, our Friendship cannot be so.

Pierr. Again: who's that?

Spino. 'Twas I.

Theo. And I.

Revell. And I.

Eliot. And all.

Ren. Who are on my side?

Spinos. Every honest Sword,
Let's die like men and not be sold like Slaves.

Pierr. One such word more, by Heav'n I'l to the Senate
And hang ye all, like Dogs in Clusters,
Why peep your Coward Swords half out their shells?
Why do you not all brandish them like mine?
You fear to die, and yet dare talk of Killing?

Ren. Go to the Senate and betray us, hasten,
Secure thy wretched life, we fear to die
Less than thou dar'st be honest.

Pierr. That's rank falsehood,
Fear'st not thou death? fy, there's a knavish itch
In that salt blood, an utter foe to smarting.
Had Jaffeir's Wife prov'd kind, he had still been true.
Foh—how that stinks?
Thou dy! thou kill my Friend! or thou, or thou,
Or thou, with that lean wither'd wretched Face!

Away! disperse all to your several Charges,
And meet to morrow where your honour calls you,
I'll bring that man, whose blood you so much thirst for,
And you shall see him venture for you fairly—
Hence, hence, I say.   [*Exit* RENAULT *angrily.*

   Spino. I fear we have been to blame,
And done too much.

   Theo. 'Twas too farr urg'd against the man you lov'd.

   Rev. Here, take our Swords and crush 'em with your feet.

   Spino. Forgive us, gallant Friend.

   Pierr. Nay, now y'have found
The way to melt and cast me as you will:
I'll fetch this Friend and give him to your mercy:
Nay he shall dye if you will take him from me,
For your repose I'll quit my hearts Jewel;
But would not have him torn away by Villains
And spiteful villany.

   Spino. No; may you both
For ever live and fill the world with fame!

   Pierr. Now you are too kind. Whence rose all this discord?
Oh what a dangerous precipice have we scap'd!
How near a fall was all we had long been building!
What an eternal blot had stain'd our glories,
If one the bravest and the best of men
Had fallen a Sacrifice to rash suspicion!
Butcher'd by those whose Cause he came to cherish:
Oh could you know him all as I have known him,
How good he is, how just, how true, how brave,
You wou'd not leave this place till you had seen him;
Humbled your selves before him, kiss'd his feet,
   And gain'd remission for the worst of follies;
Come but to morrow all your doubts shall end,   ⎫
And to your Loves me better recommend,   ⎬
That I've preserv'd your Fame, and, sav'd my Friend. ⎭

                         [*Exeunt omnes.*

ACT IV

Enter JAFFEIR *and* BELVIDERA.

   Jaff. Where dost thou lead me? Every step I move,
Methinks I tread upon some mangled Limb
Of a rack'd Friend: Oh my dear charming ruine!
Where are we wandring?

   Bel. To eternal Honour;

To doe a deed shall Chronicle thy name,
Among the glorious Legends of those few
That have sav'd sinking Nations: thy Renown
Shall be the future Song of all the Virgins,
Who by thy piety have been preserv'd
From horrid violation: Every Street
Shall be adorn'd with Statues to thy honour,
And at thy feet this great Inscription written,
Remember him that prop'd the fall of Venice.
   Jaff. Rather, Remember him, who after all
The sacred Bonds of Oaths and holyer Friendship
In fond compassion to a Womans tears
Forgot his Manhood, Vertue, truth and Honour,
To sacrifice the Bosom that reliev'd him.
Why wilt thou damn me?
   Bel. Oh inconstant man!
How will you promise? how will you deceive?
Do, return back, re-place me in my Bondage,
Tell all thy Friends how dangerously thou lovst me;
And let thy Dagger doe its bloudy office.
Oh that kind Dagger, Jaffeir, how 'twill look
Stuck through my heart, drench'd in my bloud to th' hilts!
Whilst these poor dying eyes shall with their tears
No more torment thee, then thou wilt be free:
Or if thou think'st it nobler, Let me live
Till I am a Victim to the hatefull lust
Of that Infernal Devil, that old Fiend
That's Damn'd himself and wou'd undoe Mankind:
Last night, my Love!
   Jaff. Name, name it not again.
It shews a beastly Image to my fancy.
Will wake me into madness. Oh the Villain!
That durst approach such purity as thine
On terms so vile: Destruction, swift destruction
Fall on my Coward-head, and make my Name
The common scorn of Fools if I forgive him;
If I forgive him, if I not revenge
With utmost rage, and most unstaying fury,
Thy sufferings, thou dear darling of my life, Love.
   Bel. Delay no longer then, but to the Senate;
And tell the dismalst story e'r was utter'd,
Tell 'em what bloudshed, rapines, desolations,
Have been prepar'd, how near's the fatal hour!
Save thy poor Country, save the Reverend bloud

Of all its Nobles, which to morrows Dawn
Must else see shed: Save the poor tender lives
Of all those little Infants which the Swords
Of murtherers are whetting for this moment;
Think thou already hearst their dying screams,
Think that thou seest their sad distracted Mothers
Kneeling before thy feet, and begging pity
With torn dishevel'd hair and streaming eyes,
Their naked mangled breasts besmeared with bloud,
And even the Milk with which their fondled Babes,
Softly they hush'd, dropping in anguish from 'em.
Think thou seest this, and then consult thy heart.
 Jaff. Oh!
 Bel. Think too, If thou lose this present minute,
What miseries the next day bring upon thee.
Imagine all the horrours of that night:
Murther and Rapine, Waste and Desolation,
Confusedly ranging. Think what then may prove
My Lot! the Ravisher may then come safe,
And midst the terrour of the publick ruine
Doe a damn'd deed; perhaps to lay a Train
May catch thy life; then where will be revenge,
The dear revenge that's due to such a wrong?
 Jaff. By all Heavens powers Prophetick truth dwells in thee,
For every word thou speak'st strikes through my heart
Like a new light, and shows it how't has wander'd;
Just what th' hast made me, take me, Belvidera,
And lead me to the place where I'm to say
This bitter Lesson, where I must betray
My truth, my vertue, constancy and friends:
Must I betray my friends? Ah take me quickly,
Secure me well before that thought's renew'd;
If I relapse once more, all's lost for ever.
 Bel. Hast thou a friend more dear than Belvidera?
 Jaff. No, th'art my Soul it self, wealth, friendship, **honour,**
All present joys, and earnest of all future,
Are summ'd in thee: methinks when in thy armes
Thus leaning on thy breast, one minute's more
Than a long thousand years of vulgar hours.
Why was such happiness not given me pure?
Why dash't with cruel wrongs, and bitter wantings?
Come, lead me forward now like a tame Lamb
To Sacrifice, thus in his fatal Garlands,
Deck'd fine and pleas'd. The wanton skips and plays,

Trots by the enticing flattering Priestes side,
And much transported with his little pride,
Forgets his dear Companions of the plain
Till by Her, bound, Hee's on the Altar layn
Yet then too hardly bleats, such pleasure's in the pain.

Enter OFFICER *and* 6 GUARDS.

Offic. Stand, who goes there?
Bel. Friends.
Jaff. Friends, Belvidera! hide me from my Friends,
By Heaven I'd rather see the face of Hell,
Than meet the man I love.
Offic. But what friends are you?
Bel. Friends to the Senate and the State of Venice.
Offic. My orders are to seize on all I find
At this late hour, and bring 'em to the Council,
Who now are sitting.
Jaff. Sir, you shall be obey'd.
Hold, Brutes, stand off, none of your paws upon me.
Now the Lot's cast, and Fate doe what thou wilt.

[*Exeunt guarded.*

SCENE.—*The Senate-house.*

Where appear sitting, the DUKE OF VENICE, PRIULI, ANTONIO
and Eight other SENATORS.

Duke. Antony, Priuli, Senators of Venice,
Speak; why are we assembled here this night?
What have you to inform us of, concerns
The State of Venice, honour, or its safety?
Priu. Could words express the story I have to tell you,
Fathers, these tears were useless, these sad tears
That fall from my old eyes; but there is cause
We all should weep; tear off these purple Robes,
And wrap our selves in Sack-cloth, sitting down
On the sad Earth, and cry aloud to Heaven.
Heaven knows if yet there be an hour to come
E'r Venice be no more!
All Senators. How!
Priu. Nay we stand
Upon the very brink of gaping ruine,
Within this City's form'd a dark Conspiracy,
To massacre us all, our Wives and Children,
Kindred and Friends, our Palaces and Temples

To lay in Ashes; nay the hour too, fixt;
The Swords, for ought I know, drawn even this moment,
And the wild Waste begun: from unknown hands
I had this warning: but if we are men
Let's not be tamely butcher'd, but doe something
That may inform the world in after Ages,
Our Virtue was not ruin'd though we were.
[*A noise without*.] Room, room, make room for some Prisoners—
    2 *Senat*. Let's raise the City.

Enter OFFICER *and* GUARD.

Priu. Speak there, what disturbance?
Offic. Two Prisoners have the Guard seiz'd in the Streets,
Who say they come to inform this Reverend Senate
About the present danger.

Enter JAFFEIR *and* BELVIDERA *guarded*.

All. Give 'em entrance—
Well, who are you?
    Jaff. A Villain.
    Anto. Short and pithy.
The man speaks well.
    Jaff. Would every man that hears me
Would deal so honestly, and own his title.
    Duke. 'Tis rumour'd that a Plot has been contriv'd
Against this State; that you have a share in't too.
If you are a Villain, to redeem your honour,
Unfold the truth and be restor'd with Mercy.
    Jaff. Think not that I to save my life come hither,
I know its value better; but in pity
To all those wretches whose unhappy dooms
Are fix'd and seal'd. You see me here before you,
The sworn and Covenanted foe of Venice.
But use me as my dealings may deserve
And I may prove a friend.
    Duke. The Slave Capitulates,
Give him the Tortures.
    Jaff. That you dare not doe,
Your fears won't let you, nor the longing Itch
To hear a story which you dread the truth of.
Truth with the fear of smart shall ne'r get from me.
Cowards are scar'd with threatenings. Boys are whipt
Into confessions: but a Steady mind
Acts of its self, ne'r asks the body Counsell.

Give him the Tortures. Name but such a thing
Again; by Heaven I'll shut these lips for ever,
Not all your Racks, your Engines or your Wheels
Shall force a groan away—that you may guess at.

 Anto. A bloudy minded fellow I'll warrant;
A damn'd bloudy minded fellow.

 Duke. Name your Conditions.

 Jaff. For my self full pardon,
Besides the lives of two and twenty friends *[Delivers a list.*
Whose names are here inroll'd: Nay, let their Crimes
Be ne'r so monstrous, I must have the Oaths
And sacred promise of this Reverend Council,
That in a full Assembly of the Senate
The thing I ask be ratifi'd. Swear this,
And I'll unfold the secrets of your danger.

 All. Wee'l swear.

 Duke. Propose the Oath.

 Jaff. By all the hopes
Ye have of Peace and Happiness hereafter,
Swear.

 All. We all swear.

 Jaff. To grant me what I've ask'd, Ye swear.

 All. We swear.

 Jaff. And as ye keep the Oath,
May you and your posterity be blest
Or curst for ever.

 All. Else be curst for ever.

 Jaff.—Then here's the list, and with't the full disclose of all
that threatens you. *[Delivers another paper.]* Now Fate thou hast
caught me.

 Anto. Why what a dreadful Catalogue of Cut-throats is here!
I'll warrant you not one of these fellows but has a face like a
Lion. I dare not so much as reade their names over.

 Duke. Give orders that all diligent search be made
To seize these men, their characters are publick,
The paper intimates their Rendevouz
To be at the house of a fam'd Grecian Curtezan
Call'd Aquilina; see that place secur'd.

 Anto. What, my Nicky Nacky,
Hurry Durry, Nicky Nacky in the Plot
—I'll make a Speech.
Most noble Senators,
What headlong apprehension drives you on,
Right noble, wise and truly solid Senators,

To violate the Laws and right of Nations?
The Lady is a Lady of renown.
'Tis true, she holds a house of fair Reception,
And though I say't my self, as many more
Can say as well as I.

   2 Senat. My Lord, long Speeches
Are frivolous here, when dangers are so near us;
We all well know your Interest in that Lady,
The world talks loud on't:

   Anto. Verily I have done,
I say no more.

   Duke. But since he has declar'd
Himself concern'd, Pray, Captain, take great caution
To treat the fair one, as becomes her Character,
And let her Bed-chamber be search'd with decency.
You, Jaffeir, must with patience bear till morning, to be our
Prisoner.

   Jaff. Would the Chains of death
Had bound me fast e'r I had known this minute,
I've done a deed will make my Story hereafter
Quoted in competition with all ill ones:
The History of my wickedness shall run
Down through the low traditions of the vulgar,
And Boys be thought to tell the tale of Jaffeir.

   Duke. Captain, withdraw your Prisoner.

   Jaff. Sir, if possible,
Lead me where my own thoughts themselves may lose me,
Where I may doze out what I've left of life,
Forget my self and this days guilt and falsehood.
Cruel remembrance how shall I appease thee!   [*Exit guarded.*
[*Noise without.*] More Traitors; room, room, make room there.

   Duke. How's this, Guards?
Where are our Guards? shut up the Gates, the Treason's
Already at our Dores.

Enter OFFICER.

   Offic. My Lords, more Traitors:
Seiz'd in the very act of Consultation;
Furnish'd with Arms and Instruments of mischief,
Bring in the Prisoners.

Enter PIERRE, RENAULT, THEODORE, ELIOT, REVILLIDO and other CONSPIRATORS, in fetters, guarded.

   Pierr. You, my Lords and Fathers,
(As you are pleas'd to call your selves) of Venice;

If you sit here to guide the course of Justice,
Why these disgracefull chains upon the limbs
That have so often labour'd in your service?
Are these the wreaths of triumphs ye bestow
On those that bring you Conquests home and Honours?
 Duke. Go on, you shall be heard, Sir.
 Anto. And be hang'd too, I hope.
 Pierr. Are these the Trophies I've deserv'd for fighting
Your battels with confederated Powers,
When winds and Seas conspir'd to overthrow you,
And brought the Fleets of Spain to your own Harbours?
When you, great Duke, shrunk trembling in your Palace,
And saw your Wife, th'Adriatick, plough'd
Like a lew'd Whore by bolder Prows than yours,
Stept not I forth, and taught your loose Venetians
The task of honour and the way to greatness,
Rais'd you from your capitulating fears
To stipulate the terms of su'd for peace,
And this my recompence? If I am a Traitor
Produce my charge; or shew the wretch that's base enough
And brave enough to tell me I am a Traitor.
 Duke. Know you one Jaffeir?
[All the C<small>ONSPIRATORS</small> murmur.
 Pierr. Yes, and know his Vertue.
His Justice, Truth, his general Worth and Sufferings
From a hard father taught me first to love him.

Enter J<small>AFFEIR</small> guarded.

 Duke. See him brought forth.
 Pierr. My friend too bound? nay then
Our Fate has conquer'd us, and we must fall,
Why droops the man whose welfare's so much mine
They're but one thing? these Reverend Tyrants, Jaffeir,
Call us all Traitors, art thou one, my Brother?
 Jaff. To thee I am the falsest, veryest slave
That e'r betray'd a generous trusting friend,
And gave up honour to be sure of ruine.
All our fair hopes which morning was to have crown'd
Has this curst tongue o'rthrown.
 Pierr. So, then all's over:
Venice has lost her freedom; I my life;
No more, farewell.
 Duke. Say; will you make confession
Of your vile deeds and trust the Senates mercy?

Pierr. Curst be your Senate: Curst your Constitution:
The Curse of growing factions and division
Still vex your Councils, shake your publick safety,
And make the Robes of Government, you wear,
Hatefull to you, as these base chains to me.

Duke. Pardon or death?

Pierr. Death, honourable death.

Renault. Death's the best thing we ask or you can give.

All Conspir. No shamefull bonds, but honourable death.

Duke. Break up the Council: Captain, guard your prisoners.
Jaffeir, y' are free, but these must wait for judgment.

            [*Exit all the* SENATORS.

Pierr. Come, where's my Dungeon? lead me to my straw:
It will not be the first time I've lodg'd hard
To doe your Señate service.

Jaff. Hold one moment.

Pierr. Who's he disputes the Judgment of the Senate?
Presumptuous Rebel—on—   [*Strikes* JAFF.

Jaff. By Heaven you stir not.
I must be heard, I must have leave to speak:
Thou hast disgrac'd me, Pierre, by a vile blow:
Had not a dagger done thee nobler justice?
But use me as thou wilt, thou canst not wrong me,
For I am fallen beneath the basest injuries;
Yet look upon me with an eye of mercy,
With pity and with charity behold me;
Shut not thy heart against a friend's repentance,
But as there dwells a God-like nature in thee
Listen with mildness to my supplications.

Pierr. What whining Monk art thou? what holy cheat
That wou'dst encroach upon my credulous ears
And cant'st thus vilely? hence. I know thee not,
Dissemble and be nasty: leave me, Hippocrite.

Jaff. Not know me, Pierre?

Pierr. No, know thee not: what art thou?

Jaff. Jaffeir, thy friend, thy once lov'd, valu'd friend,
Though now deservedly scorn'd, and us'd most hardly.

Pierr. Thou Jaffeir! Thou my once lov'd, valu'd friend!
By Heavens thou ly'st; the man, so call'd, my friend,
Was generous, honest, faithfull, just and valiant,
Noble in mind, and in his person lovely,
Dear to my eyes and tender to my heart:
But thou a wretched, base, false, worthless Coward,
Poor even in Soul, and loathsome in thy aspect,

All eyes must shun thee, and all hearts detest thee.
Prithee avoid, nor longer cling thus round me,
Like something banefull, that my nature's chill'd at.

Jaff. I have not wrong'd thee, by these tears I have not.
But still am honest, true, and hope too, valiant;
My mind still full of thee: therefore still noble,
Let not thy eyes then shun me, nor thy heart
Detest me utterly: Oh look upon me
Look back and see my sad sincere submission!
How my heart swells, as even 'twould burst my bosom;
Fond of its Gaol and labouring to be at thee!
What shall I doe, what say to make thee hear me?

Pierr. Hast thou not wrong'd me? dar'st thou call thy self
Jaffeir, that once lov'd, valued friend of mine,
And swear thou hast not wrong'd me? whence these chains?
Whence the vile death, which I may meet this moment?
Whence this dishonour, but from thee, thou false one?

Jaff.—All's true, yet grant one thing, and I've done asking.

Pierr. What's that?

Jaff. To take thy life on such conditions
The Council have propos'd: Thou and thy friends
May yet live long, and to be better treated.

Pierr. Life! ask my life! confess! record my self
A villain for the privilege to breath,
And carry up and down this cursed City
A discontented and repining spirit,
Burthensome to it self a few years longer,
To lose, it may be, at last in a lewd quarrel
For some new friend, treacherous and false as thou art!
No, this vile world and I have long been jangling,
And cannot part on better terms than now,
When onely men like thee are fit to live in't.

Jaff. By all that's just—

Pierr. Swear by some other powers,
For thou hast broke that sacred Oath too lately.

Jaff. Then by that hell I merit, I'll not leave thee,
Till to thy self at least, thou'rt reconcil'd,
However thy resentment deal with me.

Pierr. Not leave me!

Jaff. No, thou shalt not force me from thee,
Use me reproachfully, and like a slave,
Tread on me, buffet me, heap wrongs on wrongs
On my poor head; I'll bear it all with patience,
Shall weary out thy most unfriendly cruelty,

Ly at thy feet and kiss 'em though they spurn me,
Till, wounded by my sufferings, thou relent,
And raise me to thy armes with dear forgiveness.
   Pierr. Art thou not—
   Jaff. What?
   Pierr. A Traitor?
   Jaff. Yes.
   Pierr. A Villain?
   Jaff. Granted.
   Pierr. A Coward, a most scandalous Coward,
Spiritless, void of honour, one who has sold
Thy everlasting Fame, for shameless life?
   Jaff. All, all, and more, much more: my faults are Numberless.
   Pierr. And wouldst thou have me live on terms like thine?
Base as thou art false—
   Jaff. No, 'tis to me that's granted,
The safety of thy life was all I aim'd at,
In recompence for faith, and trust so broken.
   Pierr. I scorn it more because preserv'd by thee,
And as when first my foolish heart took pity
On thy misfortunes, sought thee in thy miseries.
Reliev'd thy wants, and rais'd thee from thy State
Of wretchedness in which thy fate had plung'd thee,
To rank thee in my list of noble friends;
All I receiv'd in surety for thy truth,
Were unregarded oaths; and this, this dagger,
Given with a worthless pledge, thou since hast stoln,
So I restore it back to thee again,
Swearing by all those powers which thou hast violated,
Never from this curs'd hour to hold communion,
Friendship or interest with thee, though our years
Were to exceed those limited the world.
Take it—farewell—for now I owe thee nothing.
   Jaff. Say thou wilt live then.
   Pierr. For my life, dispose it
Just as thou wilt, because tis what I'm tir'd with.
   Jaff. Oh, Pierre!
   Pierr. No more.
   Jaff. My eyes won't lose the sight of thee,
But languish after thine, and ake with gazing.
   Pierr. Leave me—Nay, then thus, thus, I throw thee from me.
And curses, great as is thy falsehood, catch thee.
   Jaff. Amen.
He's gone, my father, friend, preserver,

And here's the portion he has left me.

> *[Holds the dagger up.*

This dagger, well remembred, with this dagger
 gave a solemn vow of dire importance,
Parted with this and Belvidera together;
Have a care, Mem'ry, drive that thought no farther;
No, I'll esteem it as a friend's last legacy,
Treasure it up in this wretched bosom,
Where it may grow acquainted with my heart,
That when they meet, they start not from each other;
So; now for thinking: A blow, call'd Traitor, Villain,
Coward, dishonourable coward, fogh!
Oh for a long sound sleep, and so forget it!
Down, busie Devil—

Enter BELVIDERA.

Bel. Whither shall I fly?
Where hide me and my miseries together?
There's now the Roman Constancy I boasted?
Sunk into trembling fears and desperation!
Not daring now to look up to that dear face
Which us'd to smile even on my faults, but down
Bending these miserable eyes to earth,
Must move in penance, and implore much Mercy.

Jaff. Mercy, kind Heaven has surely endless stores
Hoarded for thee of blessings yet untasted;
Let wretches loaded hard with guilt as I am,
Bow the weight and groan beneath the burthen,
Creep with a remnant of that strength th' have left,
Before the footstool of that Heaven th'have injur'd.
Oh Belvidera! I'm the wretchedest creature
E'er crawl'd on earth; now if thou hast Vertue help me,
Take me into thy Armes, and speak the words of peace
To my divided Soul, that wars within me,
And raises every Sense to my confusion;
By Heav'n I am tottering on the very brink
Of Peace; and thou art all the hold I've left.

Bel. Alass! I know thy sorrows are most mighty;
I know th'hast cause to mourn; to mourn, my Jaffeir,
With endless cries, and never ceasing wailings,
Th'hast lost—

Jaff. Oh I have lost what can't be counted;
My friend too, Belvidera, that dear friend,
Who, next to thee, was all my health rejoyc'd in,

Has us'd me like a slave; shamefully us'd me;
'Twould break thy pitying heart to hear the story,
What shall I doe? resentment, indignation,
Love, pity, fear and mem'ry, how I've wrong'd him,
Distract my quiet with the very thought on't,
And tear my heart to pieces in my bosome.

    Bel. What has he done?

    Jaff. Thou'dst hate me, should I tell thee.

    Bel. Why?

    Jaff. Oh he has us'd me! yet by Heaven I bear it;
He has us'd me, Belvidera, but first swear
That when I've told thee, thou'lt not loath me utterly,
Though vilest blots and stains appear upon me;
But still at least with charitable goodness,
Be near me in the pangs of my affliction,
Not scorn me, Belvidera, as he has done.

    Bel. Have I then e'r been false that now I am doubted?
Speak, whats the cause I am grown into distrust,
Why thought unfit to hear my Love's complainings?

    Jaff. Oh!

    Bel. Tell me.

    Jaff. Bear my failings, for they are many,
Oh my dear Angel! in that friend I've lost
All my Soul's peace; for every thought of him
Strikes my Sense hard, and deads it in my brains;
Wouldst thou believe it?

    Bel. Speak.

    Jaff. Before we parted,
E'r yet his Guards had led him to his prison,
Full of severest sorrows for his suff'rings,
With eyes o'rflowing and a bleeding heart,
Humbling my self almost beneath my nature;
As at his feet I kneel'd, and su'd for mercy,
Forgetting all our friendship, all the dearness,
In which w'have liv'd so many years together,
With a reproachfull hand, he dash'd a blow,
He struck me, Belvidera, by Heaven, he struck me,
Buffeted, call'd me Traitor, Villain, Coward;
Am I a Coward? am I a Villain? tell me:
Th'art the best Judge, and mad'st me, if I am so.
Damnation; Coward!

    Bel. Oh! forgive him, Jaffeir.
And if his sufferings wound thy heart already,
What will they doe to morrow?

Jaff. Hah!

Bel. To morrow,
When thou shalt see him stretch'd in all the Agonies
Of a tormenting and a shamefull death,
His bleeding bowels, and his broken limbs,
Insulted o'r by a vile butchering villain;
What will thy heart doe then? Oh sure 't will stream
Like my eyes now.

Jaff. What means thy dreadfull story?
Death, and to morrow? broken limbs and bowels?
Insulted o'r by a vile butchering Villain?
By all my fears I shall start out to madness,
With barely guessing if the truth's hid longer.

Bel. The faithless Senators, 'tis they've decree'd it:
They say according to our friends request,
They shall have death, and not ignoble bondage:
Declare their promis'd mercy all as forfeited,
False to their oaths, and deaf to intercession;
Warrants are pass'd for publick death to morrow.

Jaff. Death! doom'd to die! condemn'd unheard! unpleaded!

Bel. Nay, cruel'st racks and torments are preparing,
To force confessions from their dying pangs;
Oh do not look so terribly upon me,
How your lips shake, and all your face disordered!
What means my Love?

Jaff. Leave me, I charge thee leave me—strong temptations
Wake in my heart.

Bel. For what?

Jaff. No more, but leave me.

Bel. Why?

Jaff. Oh! by Heaven I love thee with that fondness
would not have thee stay a moment longer,
Near these curst hands: are they not cold upon thee?
    [*Pulls the dagger half out of his bosom and puts it back agen.*

Bel. No, everlasting comfort's in thy armes,
To lean thus on thy breast is softer ease
Than downy pillows deck'd with leaves of roses.

Jaff. Alas thou thinkest not of the thorns 'tis fill'd with,
Fly e'r they call thee: there's a lurking serpent
Ready to leap and sting thee to thy heart:
Art thou not terrifi'd?

Bel. No.

Jaff. Call to mind
What thou hast done, and whither thou hast brought me.

Bel. Hah!

Jaff. Where's my friend? my friend, thou smiling mischief?
Nay, shrink not, now 'tis too late, thou shouldst have fled
When thy Guilt first had cause, for dire revenge,
Is up and raging for my friend. He groans,
Hark how he groans, his screams are in my ears
Already; see, th' have fixt him on the wheel,
And now they tear him—Murther! perjur'd Senate!
Murther—Oh!—hark thee, Traitress, thou hast done this;
Thanks to thy tears and false perswading love,

                              [*Fumbling for his Dagger*

How her eyes speak! Oh thou bewitching creature!
Madness cannot hurt thee: Come, thou little trembler,
Creep, even into my heart, and there lie safe;
'Tis thy own Cittadel—hah—yet stand off,
Heaven must have Justice, and my broken vows
Will sink me else beneath its reaching mercy;
I'll wink and then 'tis done—

    Bel. What means the Lord
Of me, my life and love, what's in thy bosom,
Thou graspst at so? nay, why am I thus treated?

                    [*Draws the dagger, offers to stab her*

What wilt thou doe? Ah, do not kill me, Jaffeir,
Pity these panting breasts, and trembling limbs,
That us'd to clasp thee when thy looks were milder,
That yet hang heavy on my unpurg'd Soul,
And plunge it not into eternal darkness.

    Jaff. No, Belvidera, when we parted last
I gave this dagger with thee as in trust
To be thy portion, If I e'r prov'd false.
On such condition was my truth believ'd:
But now 'tis forfeited and must be paid for.

                              [*Offers to stab her again*
                                        [*Kneeling*

    Bel. Oh, mercy!
    Jaff. Nay, no strugling.
    Bel. Now then kill me,   [*Leaps upon his neck and kisses him*
While thus I cling about thy cruel neck,
Kiss thy revengeful lips and die in joys
Greater than any I can guess hereafter.

    Jaff. I am, I am a Coward; witness't, Heaven,
Witness it, Earth, and every being witness;
'Tis but one blow yet: by immortal Love,
I cannot longer bear a thought to harm thee,

                    [*He throws away the dagger and embraces he*

The Seal of Providence is sure upon thee.
And thou wert born for yet unheard of wonders:
Oh thou wert either born to save or damn me!
By all the power that's given thee o'r my soul,
By thy resistless tears and conquering smiles,
By the victorious love that still waits on thee;
Fly to thy cruel Father: save my friend,
Or all our future Quiet's lost for ever:
Fall at his feet, cling round his reverend knees;
Speak to him with thy Eyes, and with thy tears,
Melt thy hard heart, and wake dead nature in him,
Crush him in th'Arms, and torture him with thy softness:
Nor, till thy Prayers are granted, set him free,
But conquer him, as thou hast vanquish'd me.   [*Exit Ambo.*

ACT V

Enter PRIULI *solus.*

Priu. Why, cruel Heaven, have my unhappy days
Been lengthen'd to this sad one? Oh! dishonour
And deathless infamy is fall'n upon me.
Was it my fault? Am I a traitour? No.
But then, my onely child, my daughter, wedded;
There my best bloud runs foul, and a disease
Incurable has seiz'd upon my memory,
To make it rot and stink to after ages.
Curst be the fatal minute when I got her;
Or woud that I'd been any thing but man,
And rais'd an issue which wou'd ne'r have wrong'd me.
The miserablest Creatures (man excepted)
Are not the less esteem'd, though their posterity
Degenerate from the vertues of their fathers;
The vilest Beasts are happy in their offsprings,
While onely man gets traitours, whores and villains.
Curst be the names, and some swift blow from Fate
Lay his head deep, where mine may be forgotten.

Enter BELVIDERA *in a long mourning Veil.*

Bel. He's there, my father, my inhumane father,
That, for three years, has left an onely child
Expos'd to all the outrages of Fate,
And cruel ruine—oh!—
     Priu. What child of sorrow

Art thou that com'st thus wrapt in weeds of sadness,
And mov'st as if thy steps were towards a grave?

Bel. A wretch, who from the very top of happiness
Am fallen into the lowest depths of misery,
And want your pitying hand to raise me up again.

Priu. Indeed thou talk'st as thou hadst tasted sorrows;
Would I could help thee.

Bel. 'Tis greatly in your power,
The world too, speaks you charitable, and I,
Who ne'r ask'd almes before, in that dear hope
Am come a begging to you, Sir.

Priu. For what?

Bel. Oh, well regard me, is this voice a strange one?
Consider too, when beggars once pretend
A case like mine, no little will content 'em.

Priu. What wouldst thou beg for?

Bel. Pity and forgiveness;   *[Throws up her Veil.*
By the kind tender names of child and father,
Hear my complaints and take me to your love.

Priu. My daughter?

Bel. Yes, your daughter, by a mother
Vertuous and noble, faithfull to your honour,
Obedient to your will, kind to your wishes,
Dear to your armes; by all the joys she gave you,
When in her blooming years she was your treasure,
Look kindly on me; in my face behold
The lineaments of hers y'have kiss'd so often,
Pleading the cause of your poor cast-off Child.

Priu. Thou art my daughter.

Bel. Yes—And y'have oft told me
With smiles of love and chaste paternal kisses,
I'd much resemblance of my mother.

Priu. Oh!
Hadst thou inherited her matchless vertues
I'd been too bless'd.

Bel. Nay, do not call to memory
My disobedience, but let pity enter
Into your heart, and quite deface the impression;
For could you think how mine's perplext, what sadness,
Fears and despairs distract the peace within me,
Oh, you would take me in your dear, dear Armes,
Hover with strong compassion o'r your young one,
To shelter me with a protecting wing,
From the black gather'd storm, that's just, just breaking.

Priu. Don't talk thus.

Bel. Yes, I must, and you must hear too.
I have a husband.

Priu. Damn him.

Bel. Oh, do not curse him!
He would not speak so hard a word towards you
On any terms, oh! e'r he deal with me.

Priu. Hah! what means my child?

Bel. Oh there's but this short moment
'Twixt me and Fate, yet send me not with curses
Down to my grave, afford me one kind blessing
Before we part: just take me in your armes
And recommend me with a prayer to Heaven,
That I may dye in peace, and when I'm dead—

Priu. How my Soul's catcht!

Bel. Lay me, I beg you, lay me
By the dear ashes of my tender mother.
She would have pitied me, had fate yet spared her.

Priu. By Heaven, my aking heart forebodes much mischief,
Tell me thy story, for I'm still thy father.

Bel. No, I'm contented.

Priu. Speak.

Bel. No matter.

Priu. Tell me.
By you, blest Heaven, my heart runs o'r with fondness.

Bel. Oh!

Priu. Utter't.

Bel. Oh my husband, my dear husband
Carries a dagger in his once kind bosom
To pierce the heart of your poor Belvidera.

Priu. Kill thee?

Bel. Yes, kill me; when he pass'd his faith
And covenant, against your State and Senate,
He gave me up as hostage for his truth,
With me a dagger and a dire commission:
When e'r he fail'd to plunge it through this bosome;
I learnt the danger, chose the hour of love
T'attempt his heart, and bring it back to honour.
Great love prevail'd and bless'd me with success,
He came, confest, betray'd his dearest friends
For promis'd mercy; now they're doom'd to suffer,
Gall'd with remembrance of what then was sworn;
If they are lost, he vows t'appease the Gods
With this poor life, and make my bloud th' attonement.

Priu. Heavens!

Bel. Think you saw what pass'd at our last parting;
Think you beheld him like a raging lion,
Pacing the earth and tearing up his steps,
Fate in his eyes, and roaring with the pain
Of burning fury; think you saw his one hand
Fix't on my throat, while the extended other
Grasp'd a keen threatening dagger, oh 'twas thus,
We last embrac'd, when, trembling with revenge,
He dragg'd me to the ground, and at my bosome
Presented horrid death, cried out, My friends,
Where are my friends? swore, wept, rag'd, threaten'd, lov'd,
For he yet lov'd, and that dear love preserv'd me,
To this last tryal of a father's pity.
I fear not death, but cannot bear a thought
That that dear hand should do th' unfriendly office;
If I was ever then your care, now hear me;
Fly to the Senate, save the promis'd lives
Of his dear friends, e'r mine be made the sacrifice.

Priu. Oh, my hearts comfort!

Bel. Will you not, my father?
Weep not but answer me.

Priu. By Heaven, I will.
Not one of 'em but what shall be immortal.
Canst thou forgive me all my follies past,
I'll henceforth be indeed a father; never,
Never more thus expose, but cherish thee,
Dear as the vital warmth that feeds my life,
Dear as these eyes that weep in fondness o'r thee,
Peace to thy heart. Farewel.

Bel. Go, and remember,
'Tis Belvidera's life her father pleads for.   [*Exit severally.*

Enter ANTONIO.

Anto. Hum, hum, hah,
Seignior Priuli, my Lord Priuli, my Lord, my Lord, my Lord:
Now, we Lords love to call one another by our Titles. My Lord,
my Lord, my Lord—Pox on him, I am a Lord as well as he, And
so let him fiddle—I'll warrant him he's gone to the Senate-house,
and I'll be there too, soon enough for somebody. Odd—here's a
tickling speech about the Plot, I'll prove there's a Plot with a
Vengeance—would I had it without book; let me see—

Most Reverend Senatours,
That there is a Plot, surely by this time, no man that hath eyes or

understanding in his head will presume to doubt, 'tis as plain as the light in the Cowcumber—no—hold there—Cowcumber does not come in yet—'tis as plain as the light in the Sun, or as the man in the Moon, even at noon day. It is indeed a Pumpkin-Plot, which, just as it was mellow, we have gathered, and now we have gathered it, prepar'd and dress'd it, shall we throw it like a pickled Cowcumber out at the window? no: that it is not onely a bloudy, horrid, execrable, damnable and audacious Plot, but it is, as I may say, a sawcy Plot: and we all know, most Reverend Fathers, that what is sawce for a Goose is sawce for a Gander: Therefore, I say, as those bloud-thirsty Ganders of the conspiracy would have destroyed us Geese of the Senate, let us make haste to destroy them, so I humbly move for hanging—hah, hurry durry—I think this will doe, thô I was something out, at first, about the Sun and the Cowcumber.

Enter AQUILINA.

Aquil. Good morrow, Senatour.

Anto. Nacky, my dear Nacky, morrow, Nacky, odd I am very brisk, very merry, very pert, very jovial—ha a-a-a-a—kiss me. Nacky; how dost thou doe, my little Tory, rory Strumpet, kiss me, I say, hussy, kiss me.

Aquil. Kiss me, Nacky, hang you, Sir, Coxcomb, hang you, Sir.

Anto. Hayty tayty, is it so indeed, with all my heart, faith— *Hey then up go we*, faith—*hey then up go we*, dum dum derum dump.   [*Sings*.

Aquil. Seignior.

Anto. Madona.

Aquil. Do you intend to die in your bed—?

Anto. About threescore years hence, much may be done, my dear.

Aquil. You'll be hang'd, Seignior.

Anto. Hang'd, sweet heart, prithee be quiet, hang'd quoth-a, that's a merry conceit, with all my heart; why thou jok'st, Nacky, thou art given to joking, I'll swear; well, I protest, Nacky, nay, I must protest, and will protest that I love joking dearly, man. And I love thee for joking, and I'll kiss thee for joking, and towse thee for joking, and odd, I have a devilish mind to take thee aside about that business for joking too, odd I have, and *Hey then up go we*, dum dum derum dump.   [*Sings*.

Aquil. See you this, Sir?   [*Draws a dagger*.

Anto. O Laud, a dagger! Oh Laud! it is naturally my aversion, I cannot endure the sight on't, hide it, for Heavens sake, I cannot look that way till it be gone—hide it, hide it, oh, oh, hide it!

Aquil. Yes, in your heart, I'll hide it.

Anto. My heart; what, hide a dagger in my heart's bloud!

Aquil. Yes, in thy heart, thy throat, thou pamper'd Devil;
Thou hast help'd to spoil my peace, and I'll have vengeance
On thy cust life, for all the bloody Senate,
The perjur'd faithless Senate: Where's my Lord,
My happiness, my love, my God, my Hero,
Doom'd by thy accursed tongue, amongst the rest,
T' a shamefull wrack? By all the rage that's in me
I'll be whole years in murthering thee.

Anto. Why, Nacky, Wherefore so passionate? what have I
done? what's the matter, my dear Nacky? am not I thy love,
thy Happiness, thy Lord, thy Hero, thy Senatour, and every
thing in the world, Nacky?

Aquil. Thou! thinkst thou, thou art fit to meet my joys;
To bear the eager clasps of my embraces?
Give me my Pierre, or——

Anto. Why, he's to be hang'd, little Nacky,
Trust up for Treason, and so forth, Child.

Aquil. Thou ly'st, stop down thy throat that hellish sentence,
Or 'tis thy last: swear that my Love shall live,
Or thou art dead.

Anto. Ah-h-h-h.

Aquil. Swear to recall his doom,
Swear at my feet, and tremble at my fury.

Anto. I do, now if she would but kick a little bit, one kick
now, Ah-h-h-h.

Aquil. Swear, or——

Anto. I doe, by these dear fragrant foots
And little toes, sweet as, e-e-e-e, my Nacky Nacky Nacky.

Aquil. How!

Anto. Nothing but untie thy shoestring a little faith and troth,
That's all, that's all, as I hope to live, Nacky, that's all.

Aquil. Nay, then——

Anto. Hold, hold, thy Love, thy Lord, thy Hero
Shall be preserv'd and safe.

Aquil. Or may this Poniard
Rust in thy heart.

Anto. With all my soul.

Aquil. Farewell——   [*Exit* Aquil.

Anto. Adieu. Why what a bloudy-minded inveterate termagant,
Strumpet have I been plagu'd with! oh-h-h yet more! nay then
I die, I die—I am dead already.   [*Stretches himself out.*

Enter Jaffeir.

Jaff. Final destruction seize on all the world:
Bend down, ye Heavens, and shutting round this earth,
Crush the Vile Globe into its first confusion;
Scorch it, with Elemental flames, to one curst Cindar,
And all us little creepers in't, call'd men,
Burn, burn to nothing: but let Venice burn
Hotter than all the rest: Here kindle Hell
Ne'r to extinguish, and let souls hereafter
Groan here, in all those pains which mine feels now.

Enter BELVIDERA.

Bel. My Life—   [*Meeting him.*
Jaff. My Plague—   [*Turning from her.*
Bel. Nay then I see my ruine,
If I must die!
Jaff. No, Death's this day too busie,
Thy Father's ill time'd Mercy came too late,
I thank thee for thy labours thô and him too,
But all my poor betray'd unhappy friends
Have Summons to prepare for Fate's black hour;
And yet I live.
Bel. Then be the next my doom.
I see thou hast pass'd my sentence in thy heart,
And I'll no longer weep or plead against it,
But with the humblest, most obedient patience
Meet thy dear hands, and kiss 'em when they wound me;
Indeed I am willing, but I beg thee doe it
With some remorse, and where thou giv'st the blow,
View me with eyes of a relenting love,
And shew me pity, for 'twill sweeten Justice.
Jaff. Shew pity to thee?
Bel. Yes, and when thy hands,
Charg'd with my fate, come trembling to the deed,
As thou hast done a thousand thousand dear times,
To this poor breast, when kinder rage has brought thee,
When our sting'd hearts have leap'd to meet each other,
And melting kisses seal'd our lips together,
When joyes have left me gasping in thy armes,
So let my death come now, and I'll not shrink from't.
Jaff. Nay, Belvidera, do not fear my cruelty,
Nor let the thoughts of death perplex thy fancy,
But answer me to what I shall demand
With a firm temper and unshaken spirit.
Bel. I will when I've done weeping—

Jaff. Fie, no more on't—
How long is't since the miserable day
We wedded first—
    Bel. Oh-h-h.
    Jaff. Nay, keep in thy tears,
Lest they unman me too.
    Bel. Heaven knows I cannot;
The words you utter sound so very sadly
These streams will follow—
    Jaff. Come, I'll kiss 'em dry then.
    Bel. But, 'twas a miserable day?
    Jaff. A curs'd one.
    Bel. I thought it otherwise, and you've oft sworn
In the transporting hours of warmest love
When sure you spoke the truth, you've sworn you bless'd it.
    Jaff. 'Twas a rash oath.
    Bel. Then why am I not curss'd too?
    Jaff. No, Belvidera; by th' eternal truth,
I doat with too much fondness.
    Bel. Still so kind?
Still then do you love me?
    Jaff. Nature, in her workings,
Inclines not with more ardour to Creation,
Than I doe now towards thee; man ne'r was bless'd,
Since the first pair first met, as I have been.
    Bel. Then sure you will not curse me.
    Jaff. No, I'll bless thee.
I came on purpose, Belvidera, to bless thee.
'Tis now, I think, three years w'have liv'd together.
    Bel. And may no fatal minute ever part us,
Till, reverend grown, for age and love, we go
Down to one Grave, as our last bed, together,
There sleep in peace till an eternal morning.
    Jaff. When will that be?   *[Sighing.*
    Bel. I hope long Ages hence.
    Jaff. Have I not hitherto (I beg thee tell me
Thy very fears) us'd thee with tender'st love?
Did e'r my Soul rise up in wrath against thee?
Did I e'r frown when Belvidera smil'd,
Or, by the least unfriendly word, betray
A bating passion? have I ever wrong'd thee?
    Bel. No.
    Jaff. Has my heart, or have my eyes e'r wandred
To any other woman?

Bel. Never, never—
I were the worst of false ones should I accuse thee.
I own I've been too happy, bless'd above
My Sexes Charter.
    Jaff. Did I not say I came to bless thee?
    Bel. Yes.
    Jaff. Then hear me, bounteous Heaven,
Pour down your blessings on this beauteous head,
Where everlasting sweets are always springing,
With a continual giving hand, let peace,
Honour and safety always hover round her,
Feed her with plenty, let her eyes ne'r see
A sight of sorrow, nor her heart know mourning,
Crown all her days with joy, her nights with rest,
Harmless as her own thoughts, and prop her vertue,
To bear the loss of one that too much lov'd,
And comfort her with patience in our parting.
    Bel. How, parting, parting!
    Jaff. Yes, forever parting,
I have sworn, Belvidera; by yon Heaven,
That best can tell how much I lose to leave thee,
We part this hour for ever.
    Bel. Oh, call back
Your cruel blessings, stay with me and curse me!
    Jaff. No, 'Tis resolv'd.
    Bel. Then hear me too, just Heaven,
Pour down your curses on this wretched head
With never-ceasing Vengeance, let despair,
Danger or infamy, nay all surround me,
Starve me with wantings, let my eyes ne'r see
A sight of comfort, nor my heart know peace,
But dash my days with sorrow, nights with horrours
Wild as my own thoughts now, and let loose fury
To make me mad enough for what I lose,
If I must lose him; if I must, I will not.
Oh turn and hear me!
    Jaff. Now hold, heart, or never.
    Bel. By all the tender days we have liv'd together,
By all our charming nights, and joyes that crown'd 'em,
Pity my sad condition, speak, but speak.
    Jaff. Oh-h-h.
    Bel. By these armes that now cling round thy neck,
By his dear kiss and by ten thousand more,
By these poor streaming eyes—

Jaff. Murther! uphold me:
By th'immortal destiny that doom'd me   [*Draws his Dagger.*
To this curs'd minute, I'll not live one longer,
Resolve to let me go or see me fall—
  Bel. Hold, Sir, be patient.
  Jaff. Hark, the dismal Bell   [*Passing-bell towles.*
Towles out for death, I must attend its call too,
For my poor friend, my dying Pierre expects me,
He sent a message to require I'd see him
Before he dy'd, and take his last forgiveness.
Farewell for ever.
  Bel. Leave thy dagger with me
Bequeath me something—Not one kiss at parting?
Oh my poor heart, when wilt thou break?
  Jaff. Yet stay,   [*Going out looks back at her.*
We have a Child, as yet, a tender Infant.
Be a kind mother to him when I am gone,
Breed him in vertue and the paths of Honour,
But let him never know his father's story;
I charge thee guard him from the wrongs my Fate
May doe his future fortune or his name.
Now—nearer yet—   [*Approaching each other.*
Oh that my armes were rivetted
Thus round thee ever! But my friends, my oath!
This and no more.   [*Kisses her.*
  Bel. Another, sure another,
For that poor little one you've ta'n care of,
I'll giv't him truly.
  Jaff. So, now farewell.
  Bel. For ever?
  Jaff. Heaven knows for ever; all good Angels guard thee.
  Bel. All ill ones sure had charge of me this moment,
Curst be my days, and doubly curst my nights,
Which I must now mourn out in widdow'd tears;
Blasted be every herb and fruit and tree,
Curst be the rain that fall upon the earth,
And may the general Curse reach man and beast;
Oh give me daggers, fire or water,
How I could bleed, how burn, how drown the waves
Huzzing and booming round my sinking head,
Till I descended to the peacefull bottome!
Oh there's all quiet, here all rage and fury,
The Air's too thin, and pierces my weak brain,
I long for thick substantial sleep: Hell, Hell,

Burst from the Centre, rage and roar aloud,
If thou art half so hot, so mad as I am.

Enter PRIULI *and* SERVANTS.

Who's there?   [*They seize her.*
    Priu. Run, seize and bring her safely home,
Guard her as you would life: Alas poor creature!
    Bel. What? to my husband then conduct me quickly,
Are all things ready? shall we dye most gloriously?
Say not a word of this to my old father,
Murmuring streams, soft shades, and springing flowers,
Lutes, Laurells, Seas of Milk, and ships of Amber.   [*Exit.*

[*Scene opening discovers a Scaffold and a Wheel prepar'd for
    the executing of* PIERRE; *then enter* OFFICERS, PIERRE *and*
    GUARDS, *a* FRIAR, EXECUTIONER *and a great Rabble.*

    Offic. Room room there—stand all by, make room for the
        Prisoner.
    Pierr. My friend not come yet?
    Father. Why are you so obstinate?
    Pierr. Why you so troublesome, that a poor wretch cannot dye
        in peace?
But you, like Ravens will be croaking round him—
    Fath. Yet, Heaven—
    Pierr. I tell thee Heaven and I are friends,
I ne'r broke Peace with't yet, by cruel murthers,
Rapine, or perjury, or vile deceiving,
But liv'd in moral Justice towards all men,
Nor am a foe to the most strong believers;
How e'r my own short-sighted Faith confine me.
    Fath. But an all-seeing Judge—
    Pierr. You say my conscience
Must be mine accuser: I have search'd that Conscience,
And find no records there of crimes that scare me.
    Fath. 'Tis strange you should want faith.
    Pierr. You want to lead
My Reason blindfold, like a hamper'd Lion,
Check'd of its nobler vigour then, when baited,
Down to obedient tameness, make it couch,
And shew strange tricks which you call signs of **Faith.**
So silly Souls are gull'd and you get money.
Away, no more: Captain, I would hereafter
This fellow write no lyes of my conversion,
Because he has crept upon my troubled hours.

Enter JAFFEIR.

Jaff. Hold: Eyes, be dry;
Heart, strength me to bear
This hideous sight, and humble me, take
The last forgiveness of a dying friend,
Betray'd by my vile falsehood, to his ruine.
Oh Pierre!

Pierr. Yet nearer.

Jaff. Crawling on my knees,
And prostrate on the earth, let me approach thee,
How shall I look up to thy injur'd face,
That always us'd to smile, with friendship, on me?
It darts an air of so much manly virtue,
That I, methinks, look little in thy sight,
And stripes are fitter for me than embraces.

Pierr. Dear to my Armes, though thou hast undone my fame,
I cannot forget to love thee: prithee, Jaffeir,
Forgive that filthy blow my passion dealt thee;
I am now preparing for the land of peace,
And fain would have the charitable wishes
Of all good men, like thee, to bless my journy.

Jaff. Good! I am the vilest creature, worse than e'r
Suffer'd the shamefull Fate thou art going to taste of,
Why was I sent for to be us'd thus kindly?
Call, call me villain, as I am, describe
The foul complexion of my hatefull deeds,
Lead me to the Rack, and stretch me in thy stead,
I've crimes enough to give it its full load,
And doe it credit: Thou wilt but spoil the use on't,
And honest men hereafter bear its figure
About 'em, as a charm from treacherous friendship.

Offic. The time grows short, your friends are dead already.

Jaff. Dead!

Pierr. Yes, dead, Jaffeir, they've all dy'd like men too,
Worthy their Character.

Jaff. And what must I doe?

Pierr. Oh, Jaffeir!

Jaff. Speak aloud thy burthen'd Soul,
And tell thy troubles to thy tortur'd friend.

Pierr. Friend! Could'st thou yet be a Friend, a generous friend,
I might hope Comfort from thy noble sorrows,
Heav'n knows I want a Friend.

Jaff. And I a kind one,

That would not thus scorn my repenting Vertue,
Or think when he is to dye, my thoughts are idle.
   Pierr. No! live, I charge thee, Jaffeir.
   Jaff. Yes, I will live,
But it shall be to see thy fall reveng'd
At such a rate, as Venice long shall groan for.
   Pierr. Wilt thou?
   Jaff. I will, by Heav'n.
   Pierr. Then still thou'rt noble,
And I forgive thee, oh—yet—shall I trust thee?
   Jaff. No: I've been false already.
   Pierr. Dost thou love me?
   Jaff. Rip up my heart, and satisfie thy doubtings.
   Pierr. Curse on this weakness.   *[He weeps.*
   Jaff. Tears! Amazement! Tears!
I never saw thee melted thus before;
And know there's something lab'ring in thy bosom
That must have vent: Though I'm a Villain, tell me.
   Pierr. Seest thou that Engine?   *[Pointing to the Wheel.*
   Jaff. Why?
   Pierr. Is't fit a Souldier who has liv'd with Honour,
Fought Nations Quarrels, and bin Crown'd with Conquest,
Be expos'd a common Carcass on a Wheel?
   Jaff. Hah!
   Pierr. Speak! is't fitting?
   Jaff. Fitting?
   Peirr. Yes, Is't fitting?
   Jaff. What's to be done?
   Pierr. I'd have thee undertake
Something that's Noble, to preserve my Memory
From the disgrace that's ready to attaint it.
   Offic. The day grows late, Sir.
   Pierr. I'll make haste! oh Jaffeir,
Though thou'st betray'd me, doe me some way Justice.
   Jaff. No more of that: Thy wishes shall be satisfi'd,
I have a Wife, and she shall bleed, my Child too
Yield up his little Throat, and all t'appease thee—
             [Going away PIERR. *holds him.*
   Pierr. No—this—no more!   *[He whispers* JAFFEIR.
   Jaff. Hah! is't then so?
   Pierr. Most certainly.
   Jaff. I'll do't.
   Pierr. Remember.
   Offic. Sir.

Pierr. Come, now I'm ready.

> [*He and* JAFFEIR *ascend the Scaffold.*

Captain, you should be a Gentleman of honour,
Keep off the Rabble, that I may have room
To entertain my Fate, and dye with Decency.
Come!

> [*Takes off his Gown.* EXECUTIONER *prepares to bind him.*

Fath. Son!

Pierr. Hence, Tempter.

Offic. Stand off, Priest.

Pierr. I thank you, Sir.
You'll think on't.   [*To* JAFFEIR.

Jaff. 'Twon't grow stale before to morrow.

Pierr. Now, Jaffeir! now I am going. Now—

> [EXECUTIONER *having bound him.*

Jaff. Have at thee,
Thou honest heart, then—here—   [*Stabs him.*
And this is well too.   [*Then stabs himself.*

Fath. Damnable Deed!

Pierr. Now thou hast indeed been faithful.
This was done Nobly—We have deceiv'd the Senate.

Jaff. Bravely.

Pierr. Ha ha ha—oh oh—   [*Dyes.*

Jaff. Now, ye curs'd Rulers,
Thus of the blood y'have shed I have Libation,
And sprinkl't mingling: May it rest upon you,
And all your Race: Be henceforth Peace a stranger
Within your Walls; let Plagues and Famine waste
Your Generations—oh poor Belvidera!
Sir, I have a Wife, bear this in safety to her.
A Token that with my dying breath, I blest her,
And the dear little Infant left behind me.
I am sick—I'm quiet—   [JAFF *dyes.*

Offic. Bear this news to the Senate,
And guard their Bodies till there's farther order:
Heav'n grant I dye so well—   [*Scene shuts upon them.*

[*Soft Musick. Enter* BELVIDERA *distracted, led by two of her*
      WOMEN, PRIULI *and* SERVANTS.

Priu. Strengthen her heart with Patience, pitying Heav'n.

Belv. Come come come come come. Nay, come to bed!
Prithee my Love. The Winds! hark how they whistle!
And the Rain beats: oh how the weather shrinks me!
You are angry now, who cares? pish, no indeed.

Choose then, I say you shall not go, you shall not;
Whip your ill nature; get you gone then! oh,

       [JAFFEIR's *Ghost rises.*

Are you return'd? See, Father, here he's come agen,
Am I to blame to love him! oh thou dear one. [*Ghost sinks.*
Why do you fly me? are you angry still then?
Jaffeir! where art thou? Father, why do you doe thus?
Stand off, don't hide him from me. He's here somewhere.
Stand off I say! what gone? remember't, Tyrant!
I may revenge my self for this trick one day.

    Enter OFFICER *and others.*

I'll do't—I'll do't. Renault's a nasty fellow.
Hang him, hang him, hang him.
 Priu. News, what news?   [OFFIC. *whispers* PRIULI
 Offic. Most sad, Sir.
Jaffeir upon the Scaffold, to prevent
A shamefull death, stab'd Pierre, and next himself:
Both fell together.
 Priu. Daughter.
 Bel. Hah, look there!

 [*The Ghosts of* JAFF. *and* PIERR. *rise together both bloody.*

My Husband bloody, and his friend too! Murther!
Who has done this? speak to me thou sad Vision, [*Ghosts sink.*
On these poor trembling Knees I beg it, Vanisht—
Here they went down; Oh I'll dig, dig the Den up.
You shan't delude me thus. Hoa, Jaffeir, Jaffeir.
Peep up and give me but a look. I have him!
I've got him, Father: Oh now how I'll smuggle him!
My Love! my Dear! my Blessing! help me, help me!
They have hold on me, and drag me to the bottom.
Nay—now they pull so hard—farewell— [*She dyes.*
 Maid. She's dead.
Breathless and dead.
 Priu. Then guard me from the sight on't:
Lead me into some place that's fit for mourning;
Where the free Air, Light and the chearfull Sun
May never enter: Hang it round with Black;
Set up one Taper that may last a day
As long as I've to live: And there all leave me.
Sparing no Tears when you this Tale relate,
But bid all Cruel Fathers dread my Fate.

      [*Curtain falls. Exit omnes.*
    FINIS

EPILOGUE

The Text is done, and now for Application,
And when that's ended pass your Approbation.
Though the Conspiracy's prevented here,
Methinks I see another hatching there;
And there's a certain Faction fain would sway, ⎫
If they had strength enough and damn this Play, ⎬
But this the Author bad me boldly say: ⎭
If any take his plainness in ill part,
He's glad on't from the bottome of his heart;
Poet's in honour of the Truth shou'd write,
With the same Spirit brave men for it fight;
And though against him causeless hatreds rise, ⎫
And dayly where he goes of late, he spies ⎬
The scowles of sullen and revengeful eyes; ⎭
'Tis what he knows with much contempt to bear,
And serves a cause too good to let him fear:
He fears no poison from an incens'd Drabb,
No Ruffian's five-foot-sword, nor Rascal's stab;
Nor any other snares of mischief laid,
Not a Rose-alley Cudgel-Ambuscade,
From any private cause where malice reigns,
Or general Pique all Block-heads have to brains:
Nothing shall daunt his Pen when Truth does call,
No not the [1] *Picture-mangler at Guildhall.*
The Rebel-Tribe, of which that Vermin's one,
Have now set forward and their course begun;
And while that Prince's figure they deface,
As they before had massacred his Name,
Durst their base fears but look him in the face,
They'd use his Person as they've us'd his Fame;
A face, in which such lineaments they reade
Of that great Martyr's, whose rich bloud they shed,
That their rebellious hate they still retain,
And in his Son would murther him again:

---

[1] The Rascal that cut the Duke of York's Picture.

252

With indignation then, let each brave heart,
Rouse and unite to take his injur'd part;
Till Royal Love and Goodness call him home,
And Songs of Triumph meet him as he come;
Till Heaven his Honour and our Peace restore,
And Villains never wrong his Vertue more.

LOVE FOR LOVE
by

WILLIAM CONGREVE

"Nudus agris, nudus nummis paternis,
  *   *   *   *
Insanire parat certa ratione modoque."
HORAT. lib. ii. Sat. 3.[1]

[1] A madman, stripped of your paternal estate, stripped of your money,
 * *   *   *   *   *   *
He will make no more of it, than if he should set about raving by right
reason and rule.

To the Right Honourable

CHARLES, EARL OF DORSET AND MIDDLESEX,

*Lord Chamberlain of His Majesty's household, and Knight
of the most noble Order of the Garter, &c.*

My Lord,

A young poet is liable to the same vanity and indiscretion
with a young lover; and the great man who smiles upon one,
and the fine woman who looks kindly upon t'other, are both of
them in danger of having the favour published with the first
opportunity.

But there may be a different motive, which will a little distinguish the offenders. For though one should have a vanity in
ruining another's reputation, yet the other may only have an
ambition to advance his own. And I beg leave, my Lord, that I
may plead the latter, both as the cause and excuse of this
dedication.

Whoever is king, is also the father of his country; and as
nobody can dispute your Lordship's monarchy in poetry: so all
that are concerned ought to acknowledge your universal patronage; and it is only presuming on the privilege of a loyal subject,
that I have ventured to make this my address of thanks to your
Lordship; which, at the same time, includes a prayer for your
protection.

I am not ignorant of the common form of poetical dedications,
which are generally made up of panegyrics, where the authors
endeavour to distinguish their patrons by the shining characters
they give them above other men. But that, my Lord, is not my
business at this time, nor is your Lordship now to be distinguished.
I am contented with the honour I do myself in this epistle, without the vanity of attempting to add or to explain your Lordship's
character.

I confess it is not without some struggling that I behave myself
in this case as I ought; for it is very hard to be pleased with a
subject, and yet forbear it. But I choose rather to follow Pliny's
precept, than his example, when in his panegyric to the Em-

peror Trajan he says—"Nec minus considerabo quid aures eju
pati possint, quam quid virtutibus debeatur."

I hope I may be excused the pedantry of a quotation, wher
it is so justly applied. Here are some lines in the print (and whicl
your Lordship read before this play was acted) that were omittec
on the stage, and particularly one whole scene in the third Act
which not only helps the design forward with less precipitation
but also heightens the ridiculous character of Foresight, whicl
indeed seems to be maimed without it. But I found myself ir
great danger of a long play, and was glad to help it where I could
Though notwithstanding my care, and the kind reception it hac
from the town, I could hardly wish it yet shorter; but the numbe
of different characters represented in it would have been toc
much crowded in less room.

This reflection on prolixity (a fault for which scarce any on
beauty will atone) warns me not to be tedious now, and detaii
your Lordship any longer with the trifles of, my Lord, you
Lordship's most obedient, and most humble servant,

WILL. CONGREVE.

PROLOGUE

SPOKEN, AT THE OPENING OF THE NEW HOUSE,
BY MR. BETTERTON.[1]

THE husbandman in vain renews his toil,
To cultivate each year a hungry soil;
And fondly hopes for rich and generous fruit,
When what should feed the tree devours the root;
The unladen boughs, he sees, bode certain dearth,
Unless transplanted to more kindly earth.
So, the poor husbands of the stage, who found
Their labours lost upon ungrateful ground,
This last and only remedy have proved,
And hope new fruit from ancient stocks removed.
Well may they hope, when you so kindly aid,
Well plant a soil which you so rich have made.
As Nature gave the world to man's first age,
So from your bounty we receive this stage;
The freedom man was born to you've restored.
And to our world such plenty you afford,
It seems like Eden, fruitful of its own accord.
But since in Paradise frail flesh gave way,
And when but two were made, both went astray;
Forbear your wonder and the fault forgive,
If in our larger family we grieve
One falling Adam, and one tempted Eve.
We who remain would gratefully repay
What our endeavours can, and bring, this day,
The first-fruit offering of a virgin play.
We hope there's something that may please each taste,
And though of homely fare we make the feast,
Yet you will find variety at least.

---

[1] The most celebrated actor of the day—the "phœnix of the stage" (born
1635, died 1710). According to Pepys, he was "the best actor in the world."
The new house was Lincoln's Inn Fields Theatre, built on the site of a
tennis court, by Congreve, Betterton, Mrs. Barry, and Mrs. Bracegirdle,
and opened April 30, 1695, with this comedy. Betterton appears to have
acted the principal part in all of Congreve's plays on their first representation.

There's humour, which for cheerful friends we got,
And for the thinking party there's a plot.
We've something, too, to gratify ill-nature,
(If there be any here) and that is satire;
Though satire scarce dares grin, 'tis grown so mild,
Or only shows its teeth as if it smiled.
As asses thistles, poets mumble wit,
And dare not bite, for fear of being bit.
They hold their pens, as swords are held by fools,
And are afraid to use their own edge-tools.
Since *The Plain Dealer's* scenes of manly rage,
Not one has dared to lash this crying age.
This time the poet owns the bold essay,
Yet hopes there's no ill-manners in his play:
And he declares by me, he has designed
Affront to none, but frankly speaks his mind.
And should the ensuing scenes not chance to hit,
He offers but this one excuse, 'twas writ
Before your late encouragement of wit.

DRAMATIS PERSONÆ

SIR SAMPSON LEGEND, Father of VALENTINE and BEN.
VALENTINE, fallen under his Father's displeasure by his expensive way of living, in love with ANGELICA.
SCANDAL, his Friend, a free speaker.
TATTLE, a half-witted Beau, vain of his amours, yet valuing himself for secrecy.
BEN, SIR SAMPSON's younger Son, half home-bred, and half sea-bred, designed to marry MISS PRUE.
FORESIGHT, an illiterate old fellow, peevish and positive, superstitious, and pretending to understand Astrology, Palmistry, Physiognomy, Omens, Dreams, &c., Uncle to ANGELICA.
JEREMY, Servant to VALENTINE.
TRAPLAND, a Scrivener.
BUCKRAM, a Lawyer.
SNAP, a Bailiff.

ANGELICA, Niece to FORESIGHT, of a considerable Fortune in her own hands.
MRS. FORESIGHT, second Wife of FORESIGHT.
MRS. FRAIL, Sister to MRS. FORESIGHT, a Woman of the Town.
MISS PRUE, Daughter of FORESIGHT by a former Wife, a silly awkward country Girl.
Nurse to MISS PRUE.
JENNY, Maid to ANGELICA.

Stewards, Sailors, and Servants.

SCENE—LONDON.

LOVE FOR LOVE

ACT THE FIRST

Scene I

Valentine's *Lodging*

Valentine *discovered reading,* Jeremy *waiting: several books upon the table.*

Val. Jeremy!

Jer. Sir?

Val. Here, take away; I'll walk a turn, and digest what I have read.

Jer. [*Aside.*] You'll grow devilish fat upon this paper diet.
                                        [*Takes away the books.*

Val. And d'ye hear, you go to breakfast.—There's a page doubled down in Epictetus that is a feast for an emperor.

Jer. Was Epictetus a real cook, or did he only write receipts?

Val. Read, read, sirrah! and refine your appetite; learn to live upon instruction; feast your mind, and mortify your flesh; read, and take your nourishment in at your eyes; shut up your mouth, and chew the cud of understanding; so Epictetus advises.

Jer. O Lord! I have heard much of him, when I waited upon a gentleman at Cambridge. Pray what was that Epictetus?

Val. A very rich man—not worth a groat.

Jer. Humph, and so he has made a very fine feast where there is nothing to be eaten?

Val. Yes.

Jer. Sir, you're a gentleman, and probably understand this fine feeding; but if you please, I had rather be at board-wages. Does your Epictetus, or your Seneca here, or any of these poor rich rogues, teach you how to pay your debts without money? Will they shut up the mouths of your creditors? Will Plato be bail for you? or Diogenes, because he understands confinement, and lived in a tub, go to prison for you? 'Slife, sir, what do you mean? to mew yourself up here with three or four musty books, in commendation of starving and poverty?

Val. Why, sirrah, I have no money, you know it; and therefore resolve to rail at all that have; and in that I but follow the examples of the wisest and wittiest men in all ages; these poets and philosophers whom you naturally hate, for just such another reason, because they abound in sense, and you are a fool.

Jer. Ay, sir, I am a fool, I know it; and yet, Heaven help me, I'm poor enough to be a wit;—but I was always a fool when I told you what your expenses would bring you to; your coaches and your liveries, your treats and your balls; your being in love with a lady that did not care a farthing for you in your prosperity; and keeping company with wits that cared for nothing but your prosperity, and now, when you are poor, hate you as much as they do one another.

Val. Well, and now I am poor I have an opportunity to be revenged on 'em all; I'll pursue Angelica with more love than ever, and appear more notoriously her admirer in this restraint, than when I openly rivalled the rich fops that made court to her; so shall my poverty be a mortification to her pride, and perhaps make her compassionate the love, which has principally reduced me to this lowness of fortune. And for the wits, I'm sure I am in a condition to be even with them.

Jer. Nay, your position is pretty even with theirs, that's the truth on't.

Val. I'll take some of their trade out of their hands.

Jer. Now Heaven, of mercy, continue the tax upon paper! you don't mean to write?

Val. Yes, I do; I'll write a play.

Jer. Hem!—Sir, if you please to give me a small certificate of three lines;—only to certify those whom it may concern, that the bearer hereof, Jeremy Fetch by name, has for the space of seven years, truly and faithfully served Valentine Legend, Esq.; and that he is not now turned away for any misdemeanour, but does voluntarily dismiss his master from any future authority over him.

Val. No, sirrah, you shall live with me still.

Jer. Sir, it's impossible:—I may die with you, starve with you, or be damned with your works; but to live, even three days, the life of a play, I no more expect it, than to be canonised for a Muse after my decease.

Val. You are witty, you rogue! I shall want your help; I'll have you learn to make couplets, to tag the ends of acts; d'ye hear, get the maids to crambo in an evening, and learn the knack of rhyming: you may arrive at the height of a song sent by an unknown hand, or a chocolate-house lampoon.

Jer. But, sir, is this the way to recover your father's favour? why, Sir Sampson will be irreconcilable. If your younger brother should come from sea, he'd never look upon you again. You're undone, sir, you're ruined, you won't have a friend left in the world if you turn poet.—Ah, pox confound that Will's Coffee-house![1] it has ruined more young men than the Royal Oak lottery;—nothing thrives that belongs to't. The man of the house would have been an alderman by this time with half the trade, if he had set up in the city. For my part, I never sit at the door that I don't get double the stomach that I do at a horse-race:—the air upon Banstead downs is nothing to it for a whetter. Yet I never see it, but the spirit of famine appears to me, sometimes like a decayed porter, worn out with pimping, and carrying billets-doux and songs; not like other porters for hire, but for the jest's sake:—now like a thin chairman, melted down to half his proportion with carrying a poet upon tick, to visit some great fortune, and his fare to be paid him, like the wages of sin, either at the day of marriage, or the day of death.

Val. Very well, sir; can you proceed?

Jer. Sometimes like a bilked bookseller, with a meagre terrified countenance, that looks as if he had written for himself, or were resolved to turn author, and bring the rest of his brethren into the same condition:—and lastly, in the form of a worn-out punk,[2] with verses in her hand, which her vanity had preferred to settlements, without a whole tatter to her tail, but as ragged as one of the Muses; or as if she were carrying her linen to the paper-mill, to be converted into folio books of warning to all young maids, not to prefer poetry to good sense, or lying in the arms of a needy wit, before the embraces of a wealthy fool.

Enter SCANDAL.

Scan. What, Jeremy holding forth?

Val. The rogue has (with all the wit he could muster up) been declaiming against wit.

Scan. Ay? why then I'm afraid Jeremy has wit: for wherever it is, it's always contriving its own ruin.

Jer. Why, so I have been telling my master, sir; Mr. Scandal, for Heaven's sake, sir, try if you can dissuade him from turning poet.

Scan. Poet! he shall turn soldier first, and rather depend upon

---

[1] Will's Coffee-house was situated at No. 1, Bow Street, at the corner of Russell Street, and was called after its proprietor William Urwin. It was frequented at this date by gamblers as well as wits.
[2] Prostitute.

the outside of his head, than the lining. Why, what the devil!
has not your poverty made you enemies enough? must you needs
show your wit to get more?

Jer. Ay, more indeed; for who cares for anybody that has more
wit than himself?

Scan. Jeremy speaks like an oracle. Don't you see how worthless great men, and dull rich rogues, avoid a witty man of small
fortune? Why, he looks like a writ of inquiry into their titles and
estates; and seems commissioned by Heaven to seize the better
half.

Val. Therefore I would rail in my writings, and be revenged.

Scan. Rail? at whom? the whole world? Impotent and vain!
who would die a martyr to sense in a country where the religion
is folly? you may stand at bay for a while; but when the full
cry is against you, you shan't have fair play for your life. If you
can't be fairly run down by the hounds, you will be treacherously shot by the huntsmen. No, turn pimp, flatterer, quack,
lawyer, parson, be chaplain to an atheist, or stallion to an old
woman, anything but poet; a modern poet is worse, more servile,
timorous and fawning, than any I have named: without you
could retrieve the ancient honours of the name, recall the stage
of Athens, and be allowed the force of open, honest satire.

Val. You are as inveterate against our poets as if your character had been lately exposed upon the stage.—Nay, I am not
violently bent upon the trade.—[*Knocking at the door.*] Jeremy,
see who's there.—[*Exit* JEREMY.] But tell me what you would
have me do? What does the world say of me, and my forced
confinement?

Scan. The world behaves itself as it uses to do on such occasions; some pity you and condemn your father; others excuse
him and blame you; only the ladies are merciful, and wish you
well; since love and pleasurable expense have been your greatest
faults.

Re-enter JEREMY.

Val. How now?

Jer. Nothing new, sir; I have despatched some half-a-dozen
duns with as much dexterity as a hungry judge does causes at
dinner time.

Val. What answer have you given 'em?

Scan. Patience, I suppose? the old receipt.

Jer. No, faith, sir; I have put 'em off so long with patience
and forbearance, and other fair words, that I was forced now
to tell 'em in plain downright English—

Val. What?

Jer. That they should be paid.

Val. When?

Jer. To-morrow.

Val. And how the devil do you mean to keep your word?

Jer. Keep it! not at all; it has been so very much stretched that I reckon it will break of course by to-morrow, and nobody be surprised at the matter. [*Knocking.*] Again!—Sir, if you don't like my negotiation, will you be pleased to answer these yourself?

Val. See who they are.   [*Exit* JEREMY.

Val. By this, Scandal, you may see what it is to be great; secretaries of state, presidents of the council, and generals of an army, lead just such a life as I do; have just such crowds of visitants in a morning, all soliciting of past promises; which are but a civiler sort of duns, that lay claim to voluntary debts.

Scan. And you, like a true great man, having engaged their attendance, and promised more than ever you intend to perform, are more perplexed to find evasions than you would be to invent the honest means of keeping your word, and gratifying your creditors.

Val. Scandal, learn to spare your friends, and do not provoke your enemies: this liberty of your tongue will one day bring a confinement on your body, my friend.

Re-enter JEREMY.

Jer. O sir, there's Trapland the scrivener, with two suspicious fellows like lawful pads, that would knock a man down with pocket-tipstaves;—and there's your father's steward, and the nurse with one of your children from Twitnam.

Val. Pox on her! could she find no other time to fling my sins in my face? Here, give her this [*Gives money*], and bid her trouble me no more;—a thoughtless, two-handed whore! she knows my condition well enough, and might have overlaid the child a fortnight ago, if she had had any forecast in her.

Scan. What, is it bouncing Margery with my godson?

Jer. Yes, sir.

Scan. My blessing to the boy, with this token of my love.—[*Gives money.*] And, d'ye hear, bid Margery put more flocks in her bed, shift twice a-week, and not work so hard, that she may not smell so vigorously. I shall take the air shortly.

Val. Scandal, don't spoil my boy's milk.—[*To* JEREMY.] Bid Trapland come in. [*Exit* JEREMY.] If I can give that Cerberus a sop, I shall be at rest for one day.

Re-enter JEREMY *with* TRAPLAND.

Val. O Mr. Trapland, my old friend, welcome!—Jeremy, a chair quickly; a bottle of sack and a toast;—fly—a chair first.

Trap. A good morning to you, Mr. Valentine, and to you, Mr. Scandal.

Scan. The morning's a very good morning, if you don't spoil it.

Val. Come sit you down, you know his way.

Trap. [*Sits.*] There is a debt, Mr. Valentine, of fifteen hundred pounds of pretty long standing—

Val. I cannot talk about business with a thirsty palate.—[*To* Jeremy.] Sirrah, the sack.

Trap. And I desire to know what course you have taken for the payment?

Val. Faith and troth, I am heartily glad to see you:—my service to you. [*Drinks.*] Fill, fill, to honest Mr. Trapland, fuller.

Trap. Hold, sweetheart;—this is not to our business. My service to you, Mr. Scandal. [*Drinks.*] I have forborne as long—

Val. T'other glass, and then we'll talk.—Fill, Jeremy.

Trap. No more, in truth.—I have forborne, I say—

Val. [*To* Jeremy.] Sirrah, fill when I bid you.—[*To* Trapland.] And how does your handsome daughter? Come, a good husband to her.   [*Drinks.*

Trap. Thank you.—I have been out of this money—

Val. Drink first.—Scandal, why do you not drink?

[*They drink.*

Trap. And in short, I can be put off no longer.

Val. I was much obliged to you for your supply: it did me signal service in my necessity. But you delight in doing good.—Scandal, drink to me my friend Trapland's health. An honester man lives not, nor one more ready to serve his friend in distress, though I say it to his face. Come, fill each man his glass.

Scan. What, I know Trapland has been a whoremaster, and loves a wench still. You never knew a whoremaster that was not an honest fellow.

Trap. Fy, Mr. Scandal! you never knew—

Scan. What, don't I know?—I know the buxom black widow in the Poultry—eight hundred pounds a-year, jointure, and twenty thousand pounds in money. Aha, old Trap!

Val. Say you so, i'faith? come, we'll remember the widow: I know whereabouts you are; come, to the widow—

Trap. No more, indeed.

Val. What, the widow's health.—[*To* Jeremy.] Give it him—Off with it. [*They drink.*] A lovely girl, i'faith, black sparkling eyes, soft pouting ruby lips; better sealing there than a bond for a million, ha!

Trap. No, no, there's no such thing, we'd better mind our business;—you're a wag.

Val. No, faith, we'll mind the widow's business, fill again.— Pretty round heaving breasts, a Barbary shape, and a jut with her bum would stir an anchorite, and the prettiest foot! Oh, if a man could but fasten his eyes to her feet, as they steal in and out, and play at bo-peep under her petticoats! ah, Mr. Trapland?

Trap. Verily, give me a glass—you're a wag—and here's to the widow.   [*Drinks.*

Scan. [*Aside to* VALENTINE.] He begins to chuckle; ply him close, or he'll relapse into a dun.   [*Exit* JEREMY.

Enter SNAP.

Snap. By your leave, gentlemen.—Mr. Trapland, if we must do our office, tell us: we have half-a-dozen gentlemen to arrest in Pall Mall and Covent Garden; and if we don't make haste, the chairmen will be abroad, and block up the chocolate-houses,[1] and then our labour's lost.

Trap. Udso, that's true.—Mr. Valentine, I love mirth, but business must be done; are you ready to——

Re-enter JEREMY.

Jer. Sir, your father's steward says he comes to make proposals concerning your debts.

Val. Bid him come in.—Mr. Trapland, send away your officer; you shall have an answer presently.

Trap. Mr. Snap, stay within call.   [*Exit* SNAP.

Enter Steward, *who whispers* VALENTINE.

Scan. Here's a dog now, a traitor in his wine; [*To* TRAPLAND] —sirrah, refund the sack.—Jeremy, fetch him some warm water, or I'll rip up his stomach, and go the shortest way to his conscience.

Trap. Mr. Scandal, you are uncivil; I did not value your sack; but you cannot expect it again, when I have drunk it.

Scan. And how do you expect to have your money again, when a gentleman has spent it?

Val. [*To* Steward.] You need say no more, I understand the conditions, they are very hard, but my necessity is very pressing; I agree to 'em. Take Mr. Trapland with you, and let him draw the writing.—Mr. Trapland, you know this man, he shall satisfy you.

---

[1] The chief chocolate-houses were White's, St. James's Street; the Cocoa Tree, Pall Mall; and the Spread Eagle, Covent Garden.

Trap. I am loth to be thus pressing, but my necessity——
Val. No apology, good Mr. Scrivener, you shall be paid.
Trap. I hope you forgive me, my business requires——
                    [*Exeunt* TRAPLAND, Steward, *and* JEREMY.

SCENE II

The Same

VALENTINE *and* SCANDAL *seated.*

Scan. He begs pardon like a hangman at an execution.
Val. But I have got a reprieve.
Scan. I am surprised; what, does your father relent?
Val. No; he has sent me the hardest conditions in the world.
You have heard of a booby brother of mine that was sent to
sea three years ago? this brother my father hears is landed;
whereupon he very affectionately sends me word, if I will make
a deed of conveyance of my right to his estate after his death
to my younger brother, he will immediately furnish me with
four thousand pounds to pay my debts, and make my fortune.
This was once proposed before, and I refused it; but the present
impatience of my creditors for their money, and my own impatience of confinement, and absence from Angelica, force me
to consent.
Scan. A very desperate demonstration of your love to Angelica;
and I think she has never given you any assurance of hers.
Val. You know her temper; she never gave me any great
reason either for hope or despair.
Scan. Women of her airy temper, as they seldom think before
they act, so they rarely give us any light to guess at what they
mean; but you have little reason to believe that a woman of
this age, who has had an indifference for you in your prosperity,
will fall in love with your ill-fortune; besides, Angelica has a
great fortune of her own; and great fortunes either expect another great fortune, or a fool.

Enter JEREMY.

Jer. More misfortunes, sir.
Val. What, another dun?
Jer. No, sir, but Mr. Tattle is come to wait upon you.
Val. Well, I can't help it;—you must bring him up; he knows
I don't go abroad.   [*Exit* JEREMY.
Scan. Pox on him! I'll be gone.
Val. No, prithee stay: Tattle and you should never be asunder;

you are, light and shadow, and show one another; he is perfectly thy reverse both in humour and understanding; and, as you set up for defamation, he is a mender of reputations.

Scan. A mender of reputations! ay, just as he is a keeper of secrets, another virtue that he sets up for in the same manner. For the rogue will speak aloud in the posture of a whisper; and deny a woman's name, while he gives you the marks of her person: he will forswear receiving a letter from her, and at the same time show you her hand in the superscription; and yet perhaps he has counterfeited the hand too, and sworn to a truth; but he hopes not to be believed; and refuses the reputation of a lady's favour, as a doctor says *No* to a bishopric, only that it may be granted him.—In short, he is a public professor of secrecy, and makes proclamation that he holds private intelligence. —He's here.

Enter TATTLE.

Tat. Valentine, good morrow; Scandal, I am yours,—that is, when you speak well of me.

Scan. That is, when I am yours; for while I am my own, or anybody's else, that will never happen.

Tat. How inhuman!

Val. Why, Tattle, you need not be much concerned at anything that he says: for to converse with Scandal, is to play at Losing Loadum: you must lose a good name to him, before you can win it for yourself.

Tat. But how barbarous that is and how unfortunate for him, that the world should think the better of any person for his calumniation!—I thank heaven, it has always been a part of my character to handle the reputation of others very tenderly indeed.

Scan. Ay, such rotten reputations as you have to deal with, are to be handled tenderly indeed. .

Tat. Nay, but why rotten; why should you say rotten, when you know not the persons of whom you speak? how cruel that is!

Scan. Not know 'em? why, thou never hadst to do with anybody that did not stink to all the town.

Tat. Ha! ha! ha! nay, now you make a jest of it indeed; for there is nothing more known, than that nobody knows anything of that nature of me.—As I hope to be saved, Valentine, I never exposed a woman since I knew what woman was.

Val. And yet you have conversed with several.

Tat. To be free with you, I have;—I don't care if I own that; —nay more (I'm going to say a bold word now), I never could meddle with a woman that had to do with anybody else.

Scan. How!

Val. Nay, faith, 'm apt to believe him.—Except her husband, Tattle.

Tat. Oh, that—

Scan. What think you of that noble commoner Mrs. Drab?

Tat. Pooh, I know Madam Drab has made her brags in three or four places, that I said this and that, and writ to her, and did I know not what;—but upon my reputation she did me wrong.— Well, well, that was malice:—but I know the bottom of it. She was bribed to that by one we all know;—a man too—only to bring me into disgrace with a certain woman of quality—

Scan. Whom we all know.

Tat. No matter for that.—Yes, yes, everybody knows—no doubt on't, everybody knows my secret.—But I soon satisfied the lady of my innocence; for I told her—Madam, says I, there are some persons who make it their business to tell stories and say this and that of one and t'other, and everything in the world; and say I, if your grace—

Scan. Grace!

Tat. O Lord! what have I said? my unlucky tongue!

Val. Ha! ha! ha!

Scan. Why, Tattle, thou hast more impudence than one can in reason expect: I shall have an esteem for thee. Well, and, ha! ha! ha! well, go on: and what did you say to her grace?

Val. I confess this is sometheng extraordinary.

Tat. Not a word, as I hope to be saved; an arrant *lapsus linguæ* —Come, let's talk of something else.

Val. Well, but how did you acquit yourself?

Tat. Pooh! pooh! nothing at all, I only rallied with you—a woman of ordinary rank was a little jealous of me, and I told her something or other, faith—I know not what.—Come, let's talk o something else.   [*Hums a song*

Scan. Hang him, let him alone, he has a mind we should inquire

Tat. Valentine, I supped last night with your mistress, and he uncle old Foresight; I think your father lies at Foresight's.

Val. Yes.

Tat. Upon my soul, Angelica's a fine woman.—And so is Mrs Foresight, and her sister Mrs. Frail.

Scan. Yes, Mrs. Frail is a very fine woman; we all know her.

Tat. Oh, that is not fair!

Scan. What?

Tat. To tell.

Scan. To tell what? why, what do you know of Mrs. Frail?

Tat. Who, I? upon honour I don't know whether she be ma

or woman; but, by the smoothness of her chin, and roundness of her hips.

Scan. No!

Tat. No.

Scan. She says otherwise.

Tat. Impossible!

Scan. Yes, faith. Ask Valentine else.

Tat. Why then, as I hope to be saved, I believe a woman only obliges a man to secrecy, that she may have the pleasure of telling herself.

Scan. No doubt on't. Well, but has she done you wrong, or no? you have had her? ha?

Tat. Though I have more honour than to tell first, I have more manners than to contradict what a lady has declared.

Scan. Well, you own it?

Tat. I am strangely surprised!—Yes, yes, I can't deny't, if she taxes me with it.

Scan. She'll be here by-and-by, she sees Valentine every morning.

Tat. How?

Val. She does me the favour, I mean, of a visit sometimes. I did not think she had granted more to anybody.

Scan. Nor I, faith; but Tattle does not use to belie a lady; it is contrary to his character.—How one may be deceived in a woman, Valentine!

Tat. Nay, what do you mean, gentlemen?

Scan. I'm resolved I'll ask her.

Tat. O barbarous! why, did you not tell me—

Scan. No, you told us.

Tat. And bid me ask Valentine?

Val. What did I say? I hope you won't bring me to confess an answer, when you never asked me the question?

Tat. But, gentlemen, this is the most inhuman proceeding—

Val. Nay, if you have known Scandal thus long, and cannot avoid such a palpable decoy as this was, the ladies have a fine time whose reputations are in your keeping.

Re-enter JEREMY.

Jer. Sir, Mrs. Frail has sent to know if you are stirring.

Val. Show her up when she comes.　　　　[*Exit* JEREMY.

Tat. I'll be gone.

Val. You'll meet her.

Tat. Is there not a back way?

Val. If there were, you have more discretion than to give Scandal such an advantage; why, your running away will prove all that he can tell her.

Tat. Scandal, you will not be so ungenerous?—Oh, I shall lose my reputation of secrecy for ever!—I shall never be received but upon public days; and my visits will never be admitted beyond a drawing-room: I shall never see a bedchamber again, never be locked in a closet, nor run behind a screen, or under a table; never be distinguished among the waiting-women by the name of trusty Mr. Tattle more.—You will not be so cruel.

Val. Scandal, have pity on him; he'll yield to any conditions.

Tat. Any, any terms.

Scan. Come, then, sacrifice half-a-dozen women of good reputation to me presently.—Come, where are you familiar?—and see that they are women of quality too, the first quality.

Tat. 'Tis very hard.—Won't a baronet's lady pass?

Scan. No, nothing under a right honourable.

Tat. O inhuman! you don't expect their names?

Scan. No, their titles shall serve.

Tat. Alas! that's the same thing: pray spare me their titles; I'll describe their persons.

Scan. Well, begin then: but take notice, if you are so ill a painter, that I cannot know the person by your picture of her, you must be condemned, like other bad painters, to write the name at the bottom.

Tat. Well, first then—

Enter Mrs. FRAIL.

Tat. O unfortunate! she's come already; will you have patience till another time;—I'll double the number.

Scan. Well, on that condition.—Take heed you don't fail me.

Mrs. Frail. I shall get a fine reputation by coming to see fellows in a morning.—Scandal, you devil, are you here too?—Oh, Mr. Tattle, everything is safe with you, we know.

Scan. Tattle!

Tat. Mum.—O madam, you do me too much honour.

Val. Well, lady galloper, how does Angelica?

Mrs. Frail. Angelica? manners!

Val. What, you will allow an absent lover—

Mrs. Frail. No, I'll allow a lover present with his mistress to be particular;—but otherwise I think his passion ought to give place to his manners.

Val. But what if he has more passion than manners?

Mrs. Frail. Then let him marry and reform.

Val. Marriage indeed may qualify the fury of his passion, but it very rarely mends a man's manners.

Mrs. Frail. You are the most mistaken in the world; there is no creature perfectly civil but a husband. For in a little time he grows only rude to his wife, and that is the highest good breeding, for it begets his civility to other people.—Well, I'll tell you news; but I suppose you hear your brother Benjamin is landed. And my brother Foresight's daughter is come out of the country—I assure you there's a match talked of by the old people.—Well, if he be but as great a sea-beast as she is a land monster, we shall have a most amphibious breed.—The progeny will be all otters; he has been bred at sea, and she has never been out of the country.

Val. Pox take 'em! their conjunction bodes me no good, I'm sure.

Mrs. Frail. Now you talk of conjunction, my brother Foresight has cast both their nativities, and prognosticates an admiral and an eminent justice of the peace to be the issue male of their two bodies.—'Tis the most superstitious old fool! he would have persuaded me, that this was an unlucky day, and would not let me come abroad; but I invented a dream, and sent him to Artemidorus for interpretation, and so stole out to see you. Well, and what will you give me now? come, I must have something.

Val. Step into the next room—and I'll give you something.

Scan. Ay, we'll all give you something.

Mrs. Frail. Well, what will you all give me?

Val. Mine's a secret.

Mrs. Frail. I thought you would give me something that would be a trouble to you to keep.

Val. And Scandal shall give you a good name.

Mrs. Frail. That's more than he has for himself.—And what will you give me, Mr. Tattle?

Tat. I? my soul, madam.

Mrs. Frail. Pooh, no, I thank you, I have enough to do to take care of my own. Well; but I'll come and see you one of these mornings: I hear you have a great many pictures.

Tat. I have a pretty good collection at your service, some originals.

Scan. Hang him, he has nothing but the Seasons and the Twelve Cæsars, paltry copies; and the Five Senses, as ill represented as they are in himself; and he himself is the only original you will see there.

Mrs. Frail. Ay, but I hear he has a closet of beauties.

Scan. Yes, all that have done him favours, if you will believe him.

Mrs. Frail. Ay, let me see those, Mr. Tattle.

Tat. Oh, madam, those are sacred to love and contemplation. No man but the painter and myself was ever blest with the sight.

Mrs. Frail. Well, but a woman—

Tat. Nor woman, 'till she consented to have her picture there too;—for then she's obliged to keep the secret.

Scan. No, no; come to me if you'd see pictures.

Mrs. Frail. You?

Scan. Yes, faith, I can show you your own picture, and most of your acquaintance to the life, and as like as at Kneller's.

Mrs. Frail. O lying creature!—Valentine, does not he lie?—I can't believe a word he says.

Val. No, indeed, he speaks truth now; for as Tattle has pictures of all that have granted him favours, he has the pictures of all that have refused him; if satires, descriptions, characters, and lampoons are pictures.

Scan. Yes, mine are most in black and white;—and yet there are some set out in their true colours, both men and women. I can show your pride, folly, affectation, wantonness, inconstancy, covetousness, dissimulation, malice, and ignorance, all in one piece. Then I can show you lying, foppery, vanity, cowardice, bragging, lechery, impotence, and ugliness in another piece; and yet one of these is a celebrated beauty, and t'other a professed beau. I have paintings too, some pleasant enough.

Mrs. Frail. Come, let's hear 'em.

Scan. Why, I have a beau in a bagnio, cupping for a complexion, and sweating for a shape.

Mrs. Frail. So.

Scan. Then I have a lady burning brandy in a cellar with a hackney coachman.

Mrs. Frail. O devil! Well, but that story is not true.

Scan. I have some hieroglyphics too; I have a lawyer with a hundred hands, two heads, and but one face; a divine with two faces, and one head; and I have a soldier with his brains in his belly, and his heart where his head should be.

Mrs. Frail. And no head?

Scan. No head.

Mrs. Frail. Pooh, this is all invention. Have you ne'er a poet?

Scan. Yes, I have a poet weighing words, and selling praise for praise, and a critic picking his pocket. I have another large piece too, representing a school; where there are huge-proportioned critics, with long wigs, laced coats, Steenkirk cravats,[1] and ter-

---

[1] The fashionable neckcloth of the day, so called from the battle of that name, which was fought August 3, 1692, when the English under William III, were defeated. It was arranged with graceful carelessness, pre-

rible faces; with catcalls in their hands, and horn-books about their necks. I have many more of this kind, very well painted as you shall see.

Mrs. Frail. Well, I'll come, if it be but to disprove you.

Re-enter JEREMY.

Jer. Sir, here's the steward again from your father.

Val. I'll come to him.—Will you give me leave? I'll wait on you again presently.

Mrs. Frail. No, I'll be gone. Come, who squires me to the Exchange? I must call my sister Foresight there.

Scan. I will: I have a mind to your sister.

Mrs. Frail. Civil!

Tat. I will, because I have a *tendre* for your ladyship.

Mrs. Frail. That's somewhat the better reason, to my opinion.

Scan. Well, if Tattle entertains you, I have the better opportunity to engage your sister.

Val. Tell Angelica, I am about making hard conditions to come abroad, and be at liberty to see her.

Scan. I'll give an account of you and your proceedings. If indiscretion be a sign of love, you are the most a lover of anybody that I know: you fancy that parting with your estate will help you to your mistress.—In my mind he is a thoughtless adventurer,

    Who hopes to purchase wealth by selling land,

    Or win a mistress with a losing hand.   [*Exeunt.*

ACT THE SECOND

SCENE I

A Room in FORESIGHT'S *House*

FORESIGHT *and* Servant.

Fore. Heyday! what, are all the women of my family abroad? Is not my wife come home, nor my sister, nor my daughter?

Ser. No, sir.

Fore. Mercy on us, what can be the meaning of it? Sure the moon is in all her fortitudes. Is my niece Angelica at home?

Ser. Yes, sir.

Fore. I believe you lie, sir.

Ser. Sir?

Fore. I say you lie, sir. It is impossible that anything should be

tending to imitate the haste with which the French generals rushed into battle, they not having had time to tie their neckcloths.

as I would have it; for I was born, sir, when the Crab was ascending, and all my affairs go backward.

Ser. I can't tell, indeed, sir.

Fore. No, I know you can't, sir; but I can tell, sir, and foretell, sir.

Enter Nurse.

Fore. Nurse, where's your young mistress?

Nurse. Wee'st heart, I know not, they're none of 'em come home yet. Poor child! I warrant she's fond o' seeing the town;—marry, pray heaven, they ha' given her any dinner.—Good lack-a-day, ha! ha! ha! Oh strange! I'll vow and swear now,—ha! ha! ha! marry, and did you ever see the like?

Fore. Why, how now, what's the matter?

Nurse. Pray Heaven send your worship good luck! marry and amen with all my heart; for you have put on one stocking with the wrong side outward.

Fore. Ha, how? faith and troth I'm glad of it!—And so I have; that may be good luck in troth, in troth it may, very good luck; nay, I have had some omens: I got out of bed backwards too this morning, without premeditation; pretty good that too; but then I stumbled coming down stairs, and met a weasel; bad omens those: some bad, some good, our lives are chequered: mirth and sorrow, want and plenty, night and day, make up our time.—But in troth I am pleased at my stocking; very well pleased at my stocking.—Oh, here's my niece!—Sirrah, go tell Sir Sampson Legend I'll wait on him if he's at leisure; 'tis now three o'clock, a very good hour for business. Mercury governs this hour.

[*Exit* Servant.

Enter ANGELICA.

Ang. Is it not a good hour for pleasure too, uncle? pray lend me your coach, mine's out of order.

Fore. What, would you be gadding too? sure all females are mad to-day. It is of evil portent, and bodes mischief to the master of a family.—I remember an old prophecy written by Messahalah the Arabian, and thus translated by a reverend Buckinghamshire bard.

> "When housewives all the house forsake,
> And leave goodman to brew and bake,
> Withouten guile then be it said,
> That house doth stond upon its head;
> And when the head is set in ground,
> Ne mar'l if it be fruitful found."

Fruitful, the head fruitful;—that bodes horns; the fruit of the head is horns.—Dear niece, stay at home; for by the head of the house is meant the husband; the prophecy needs no explanation.

Ang. Well, but I can neither make you a cuckold, uncle, by going abroad; nor secure you from being one, by staying at home.

Fore. Yes, yes; while there's one woman left, the prophecy is not in full force.

Ang. But my inclinations are in force; I have a mind to go abroad; and if you won't lend me your coach, I'll take a hackney, or a chair, and leave you to erect a scheme, and find who's in conjunction with your wife. Why don't you keep her at home, if you're jealous of her when she's abroad? You know my aunt is a little retrograde (as you call it) in her nature. Uncle, I'm afraid you are not lord of the ascendant, ha! ha! ha!

Fore. Well, jilt-flirt, you are very pert—and always ridiculing that celestial science.

Ang. Nay, uncle, don't be angry;—if you are, I'll rip up all your false prophecies, ridiculous dreams, and idle divinations: I'll swear you are a nuisance to the neighbourhood.—What a bustle did you keep against the last invisible eclipse, laying in provision, as 'twere for a siege! What a world of fire and candle, matches and tinderboxes did you purchase! One would have thought we were ever after to live underground, or at least making a voyage to Greenland, to inhabit there all the dark season.

Fore. Why, you malapert slut!

Ang. Will you lend me your coach, or I'll go on?—Nay, I'll declare how you prophesied popery was coming, only because the butler had mislaid some of the apostle spoons, and thought they were lost. Away went religion and spoonmeat together.—Indeed, uncle, I'll indict you for a wizard.

Fore. How, hussy! was there ever such a provoking minx!

Nurse. O merciful Father, how she talks!

Ang. Yes, I can make oath of your unlawful midnight practices; you and the old nurse there——

Nurse. Marry, Heaven defend!—I at midnight practices!—O Lord, what's here to do!—I in unlawful doings with my master's worship!—Why, did you ever hear the like now?—Sir, did ever I do anything of your midnight concerns—but warm your bed, and tuck you up, and set the candle and your tobacco-box and your urinal by you, and now and then rub the soles of your feet?—O Lord, I?——

Ang. Yes, I saw you together, through the keyhole of the closet, one night, like Saul and the witch of Endor, turning the sieve and shears, and pricking your thumbs to write poor innocent servants' names in blood, about a little nutmeg-grater, which she had forgot in the caudle-cup.—Nay, I know something worse, if I would speak of it.

Fore. I defy you, hussy! but I'll remember this, I'll be revenged on you, cockatrice; I'll hamper you.—You have your fortune in your own hands,—but I'll find a way to make your lover, your prodigal spendthrift gallant, Valentine, pay for all, I will.

Ang. Will you? I care not but all shall out then.—Look to't, nurse; I can bring witness that you have a great unnatural teat under your left arm, and he another; and that you suckle a young devil in the shape of a tabby-cat, by turns, I can.

Nurse. A teat! a teat! I an unnatural teat! O the false, slanderous thing; feel, feel here, if I have anything but like another Christian.   [*Crying.*

Fore. I will have patience, since it is the will of the stars I should be thus tormented.—This is the effect of the malicious conjunctions and oppositions in the third house of my nativity; there the curse of kindred was foretold.—But I will have my doors locked up—I'll punish you, not a man shall enter my house.

Ang. Do, uncle, lock 'em up quickly before my aunt comes home;—you'll have a letter for alimony to-morrow morning,—but let me begone first, and then let no mankind come near the house, but converse with spirits and the celestial signs, the Bull, and the Ram, and the Goat. Bless me! there are a great many horned beasts among the Twelve Signs, uncle;—but cuckolds go to Heaven.

Fore. But there's but one virgin among the twelve signs, spitfire, but one virgin.

Ang. Nor there had not been that one, if she had had to do with anything but astrologers, uncle. That makes my aunt go abroad.

Fore. How? how? is that the reason? Come, you know something: tell me and I'll forgive you; do, good niece.—Come, you shall have my coach and horses;—faith and troth you shall.—Does my wife complain? come, I know women tell one another.—She is young and sanguine, has a wanton hazel eye, and was born under Gemini, which may incline her to society; she has a mole upon her lip, with a moist palm, and an open liberality on the mount of Venus.

Ang. Ha! ha! ha!

Fore. Do you laugh?—Well, gentlewoman, I'll—but come, be a good girl, don't perplex your poor uncle, tell me; won't you speak?—Odd, I'll——

Re-enter Servant.

Ser. Sir Sampson is coming down to wait upon you.

Ang. Good b'w'ye, uncle.—Call me a chair.—[*Exit* Servant.] I'll find out my aunt, and tell her she must not come home. [*Exit.*

Fore. I'm so perplexed and vexed, I am not fit to receive him; I shall scarce recover myself before the hour be past.—Go, nurse, tell Sir Sampson I'm ready to wait on him.

Nurse. Yes, sir. [*Exit.*

Fore. Well—why, if I was born to be a cuckold there's no more to be said—he's here already.

Enter Sir SAMPSON *with a paper.*

Sir Samp. Nor no more to be done, old boy; that's plain.— Here 'tis, I have it in my hand, old Ptolomee; I'll make the ungracious prodigal know who begat him; I will, old Nostrodamus. What, I warrant my son thought nothing belonged to a father but forgiveness and affection; no authority, no correction, no arbitrary power; nothing to be done, but for him to offend, and me to pardon. I warrant you, if he danced till doomsday, he thought I was to pay the piper. Well, but here it is under black and white, *signatum, sigillatum,* and *deliberatum;* that as soon as my son Benjamin is arrived, he is to make over to him his right of inheritance. Where's my daughter that is to be—ha! old Merlin! body o' me, I'm so glad I'm revenged on this undutiful rogue.

Fore. Odso, let me see; let me see the paper.—Ay, faith and troth, here 'tis, if it will but hold. I wish things were done, and the conveyance made. When was this signed, what hour? Odso, you should have consulted me for the time. Well, but we'll make haste.

Sir Samp. Haste, ay, ay; haste enough, my son Ben will be in own to-night.—I have ordered my lawyer to draw up writings of settlement and jointure:—all shall be done to-night. No matter for the time: prithee, Brother Foresight, leave superstition. Pox o' th' time! there's no time but the time present, there's no more to be said of what's past, and all that is to come will happen. If the sun shine by day, and the stars by night, why, we shall know one another's faces without the help of a candle, and that's all the stars are good for.

Fore. How, how, Sir Sampson? that all? Give me leave to contradict you, and tell you, you are ignorant.

Sir Samp. I tell you I am wise; and *sapiens dominabitur astris;* here's Latin for you to prove it, and an argument to confound your ephemeris.—Ignorant!—I tell you, I have travelled, old Fircu, and know the globe. I have seen the antipodes, where the sun rises at midnight, and sets at noonday.

Fore. But I tell you, I have travelled, and travelled in the celestial spheres, know the signs and the planets, and their houses. Can judge of motions direct and retrograde, of sextiles, quadrates, trines, and oppositions, fiery trigons and aquatical trigons. Know whether life shall be long or short, happy or unhappy, whether diseases are curable or incurable. If journeys shall be prosperous, undertakings successful; or goods stolen recovered, I know——

Sir Samp. I know the length of the Emperor of China's foot; have kissed the Great Mogul's slipper, and rid a hunting upon an elephant with the Cham of Tartary.—Body o' me, I have made a cuckold of a king, and the present majesty of Bantam is the issue of these loins.

Fore. I know when travellers lie or speak truth, when they don't know it themselves.

Sir Samp. I have known an astrologer made a cuckold in the twinkling of a star; and seen a conjuror that could not keep the devil out of his wife's circle.

Fore. [*Aside.*] What, does he twit me with my wife too? I must be better informed of this.—[*Aloud.*] Do you mean my wife, Sir Sampson? Though you made a cuckold of the King of Bantam, yet by the body of the sun——

Sir Samp. By the horns of the moon, you would say, brother Capricorn.

Fore. Capricorn in your teeth, thou modern Mandeville! Ferdinand Mendez Pinto was but a type of thee, thou liar of the first magnitude! Take back your paper of inheritance; send your son to sea again. I'll wed my daughter to an Egyptian mummy, ere she shall incorporate with a contemner of sciences, and a defamer of virtue.

Sir Samp. [*Aside.*] Body o'me, I have gone too far;—I must not provoke honest Albumazar.[1]—[*Aloud.*] An Egyptian mummy is an illustrious creature, my trusty hieroglyphic; and may have significations of futurity about him; odsbud, I would my son were an Egyptian mummy for thy sake. What, thou art not angry for a jest, my good Haly?—I reverence the sun, moon, and stars with all heart. What, I'll make thee a present of a mummy: now I think on't, body o'me, I have a shoulder of an Egyptian king, that I purloined from one of the pyramids, powdered with hieroglyphics; thou shalt have it brought home to thy house, and make an entertainment for all the philomaths, and students in physic and astrology, in and about London.

Fore. But what do you know of my wife, Sir Sampson?

Sir Samp. Thy wife is a constellation of virtues; she's the moon, and thou art the man in the moon: nay, she is more illustrious than

[1] A Persian astrologer who has given his name to a play.

the moon; for she has her chastity without her inconstancy; 'sbud, I was but in jest.

Enter JEREMY.

Sir Samp. How now, who sent for you? ha! what would you have? [JEREMY *whispers to* SIR SAMPSON.

Fore. Nay, if you were but in jest—Who's that fellow? I don't like his physiognomy.

Sir Samp. [*To* JEREMY.] My son, sir; what son, sir? my son Benjamin, hoh?

Jer. No, sir; Mr. Valentine, my master.—'Tis the first time he has been abroad since his confinement, and he comes to pay his duty to you.

Sir Samp. Well, sir.

Enter VALENTINE.

Jer. He is here, sir.

Val. Your blessing, sir.

Sir Samp. You've had it already, sir. I think I sent it you to-day in a bill of four thousand pounds.—A great deal of money, Brother Foresight.

Fore. Ay, indeed, Sir Sampson, a great deal of money for a young man; I wonder what he can do with it.

Sir Samp. Body o'me, so do I.—Hark ye, Valentine, if there be too much, refund the superfluity, dost hear, boy?

Val. Superfluity, sir! it will scarce pay my debts. I hope you will have more indulgence, than to oblige me to those hard conditions which my necessity signed to.

Sir Samp. Sir, how, I beseech you, what were you pleased to intimate concerning indulgence?

Val. Why, sir, that you would not go to the extremity of the conditions, but release me at least from some part.

Sir Samp. Oh, sir, I understand you—that's all, ha?

Val. Yes, sir, all that I presume to ask;—but what you, out of fatherly fondness, will be pleased to add shall be doubly welcome.

Sir Samp. No doubt of it, sweet sir, but your filial piety and my fatherly fondness would fit like two tallies.—Here's a rogue, Brother Foresight, makes a bargain under hand and seal in the morning, and would be released from it in the afternoon; here's a rogue, dog, here's conscience and honesty; this is your wit now, this is the morality of your wits! You are a wit, and have been a beau, and may be a—why, sirrah, is it not here under hand and seal?—can you deny it?

Val. Sir, I don't deny it.

Sir Samp. Sirrah, you'll be hanged; I shall live to see you go up Holborn Hill.[1]—Has he not a rogue's face?—Speak, brother, you understand physiognomy, a hanging look to me;—of all my boys the most unlike me; he has a damned Tyburn-face, without the benefit o' the clergy.

Fore. Hum—truly I don't care to discourage a young man. He has a violent death in his face; but I hope no danger of hanging.

Val. Sir, is this usage for your son?—for that old weather-headed fool, I know how to laugh at him; but you, sir—

Sir Samp. You, sir; and you, sir;—why, who are you, sir?

Val. Your son, sir.

Sir Samp. That's more than I know, sir, and I believe not.

Val. Faith, I hope not.

Sir Samp. What, would you have your mother a whore!—Did you ever hear the like! did you ever hear the like! Body o'me—

Val. I would have an excuse for your barbarity and unnatural usage.

Sir Samp. Excuse! impudence! Why, sirrah, mayn't I do what I please? are not you my slave? did not I beget you? and might not I have chosen whether I would have begot you or no? 'Oons who are you? whence came you? what brought you into the world? how came you here, sir? here, to stand here, upon those two legs, and look erect with that audacious face, hah? answer me that. Did you come a volunteer into the world? or did I, with the lawful authority of a parent, press you to the service?

Val. I know no more why I came than you do why you called me. But here I am, and if you don't mean to provide for me, I desire you would leave me as you found me.

Sir Samp. With all my heart: come, uncase, strip, and go naked out of the world as you came into't.

Val. My clothes are soon put off;—but you must also divest me of reason, thought, passions, inclinations, affections, appetites, senses, and the huge train of attendants that you begot along with me.

Sir Samp. Body o'me, what a many-headed monster have I propagated!

Val. I am of myself a plain, easy, simple creature, and to be kept at small expense; but the retinue that you gave me are craving and invincible; they are so many devils that you have raised, and will have employment.

Sir Samp. 'Oons, what had I to do to get children!—can't a private man be born without all these followers?—Why, nothing

[1] Meaning on the way to Tyburn.

under an emperor should be born with appetites.—Why, at this rate, a fellow that has but a groat in his pocket, may have a stomach capable of a ten-shilling ordinary.

Jer. Nay, that's as clear as the sun; I'll make oath of it before any justice in Middlesex.

Sir Samp. Here's a cormorant too.—'S'heart, this fellow was not born with you?—I did not beget him, did I?

Jer. By the provision that's made for me, you might have begot me too:—nay, and to tell your worship another truth, I believe you did, for I find I was born with those same whoreson appetites too that my master speaks of.

Sir Samp. Why, look you there now—I'll maintain it, that by the rule of right reason, this fellow ought to have been born without a palate.—'S'heart, what should he do with a distinguishing taste?—I warrant now he'd rather eat a pheasant than a piece of poor John [1] : and smell now—why, I warrant he can smell, and loves perfumes above a stink.—Why, there's it; and music—don't you love music, scoundrel?

Jer. Yes, I have a reasonable good ear, sir, as to jigs and country dances, and the like; I don't much matter your solos or sonatas; they give me the spleen.

Sir Samp. The spleen, ha! ha! ha! a pox confound you!—solos or sonatas? 'Oons, whose son are you? how were you engendered, muckworm?

Jer. I am by my father the son of a chairman; my mother sold oysters in winter and cucumbers in summer; and I came up-stairs into the world; for I was born in a cellar.

Fore. By your looks, you should go up-stairs out of the world too, friend.

Sir Samp. And if this rogue were anatomised now, and dissected, he has his vessels of digestion and concoction, and so forth, large enough for the inside of a cardinal, this son of a cucumber!— These things are unaccountable and unreasonable.—Body o'me, why was not I a bear? that my cubs might have lived upon sucking their paws. Nature has been provident only to bears and spiders; the one has its nutriment in his own hands, and t'other spins his habitation out of his own entrails.

Val. Fortune was provident enough to supply all the necessities of my nature, if I had my right of inheritance.

Sir Samp. Again! 'Oons, han't you four thousand pounds—if I had it again, I would not give thee a groat.—What, wouldst thou have me turn pelican, and feed thee out of my own vitals?— 'S'heart, live by your wits,—you were always fond of the wits:—

[1] An inferior kind of dried hake.

now let's see if you have wit enough to keep yourself.—Your brother will be in town to-night or to-morrow morning, and then look you, perform covenants, and so your friend and servant.— Come, Brother Foresight.

[*Exeunt* SIR SAMPSON *and* FORESIGHT.

Jer. I told you what your visit would come to.

Val. 'Tis as much as I expected.—I did not come to see him: I came to Angelica; but since she was gone abroad it was easily turned another way; and at least looked well on my side.—What's here? Mrs. Foresight and Mrs. Frail; they are earnest.—I'll avoid 'em.—Come this way, and go and inquire when Angelica will re- turn.

[*Exeunt*

SCENE II

A Room in FORESIGHT'S *House*

Mrs. FORESIGHT *and* Mrs. FRAIL.

Mrs. Frail. What have you to do to watch me! 'slife, I'll do what I please.

Mrs. Fore. You will?

Mrs. Frail. Yes, marry will I.—A great piece of business to go to Covent-Garden square in a hackney-coach, and take a turn with one's friend!

Mrs. Fore. Nay, two or three turns, I'll take my oath.

Mrs. Frail. Well, what if I took twenty?—I warrant if you had been there, it had been only innocent recreation.—Lord, where's the comfort of this life, if we can't have the happiness of conversing where we like?

Mrs. Fore. But can't you converse at home?—I own it, I think there is no happiness like conversing with an agreeable man; I don't quarrel at that, nor I don't think but your conversation was very innocent; but the place is public, and to be seen with a man in a hackney-coach is scandalous: what if anybody else should have seen you alight, as I did?—How can anybody be happy, while they're in perpetual fear of being seen and censured?—Besides, it would not only reflect upon you, sister, but me.

Mrs. Frail. Pooh, here's a clutter!—Why should it reflect upon you?—I don't doubt but you have thought yourself happy in a hackney-coach before now.—If I had gone to Knightsbridge, or to Chelsea, or to Spring Gardens, or Barn Elms, with a man alone —something might have been said.[1]

---

[1] Spring Garden, a favourite haunt of pleasure between St. James's Park and Charing Cross, with butts and bowling-green. After the Restoration the entertainments were removed to the Spring Garden at Lambeth, sub

Mrs. Fore. Why, was I ever in any of those places? what do you mean, sister?

Mrs. Frail. Was I? what do you mean?

Mrs. Fore. You have been at a worse place.

Mrs. Frail. I at a worse place, and with a man!

Mrs. Fore. I suppose you would not go alone to the World's-End.

Mrs. Frail. The world's-end! what, do you mean to banter me?

Mrs. Fore. Poor innocent! you don't know that there's a place called the World's-End? I'll swear you can keep your countenance purely, you'd make an admirable player.

Mrs. Frail. I'll swear you have a great deal of confidence, and in my mind too much for the stage.

Mrs. Fore. Very well, that will appear who has most; you never were at the World's-End?

Mrs. Frail. No.

Mrs. Fore. You deny it positively to my face?

Mrs. Frail. Your face! what's your face?

Mrs. Fore. No matter for that, it's as good a face as yours.

Mrs. Frail. Not by a dozen years' wearing.—But I do deny it positively to your face then.

Mrs. Fore. I'll allow you now to find fault with my face;—for I'll swear your impudence has put me out of countenance:—but look you here now—where did you lose this gold bodkin?—O sister, sister!

Mrs. Frail. My bodkin?

Mrs. Fore. Nay, 'tis yours, look at it.

Mrs. Frail. Well, if you go to that, where did you find this bodkin?—O sister, sister!—sister every way.

Mrs. Fore. [*Aside.*] O devil on't, that I could not discover her without betraying myself!

Mrs. Frail. I have heard gentlemen say, sister, that one should take great care, when one makes a thrust in fencing, not to lie open one's self.

Mrs. Fore. It's very true, sister; well, since all's out, and as you say, since we are both wounded, let us do what is often done in

equently called Vauxhall. We know that Mr. Spectator visited Spring Garden, and how he regretted he found there more strumpets than nightingales. Knightsbridge was then a retired and notorious district, where were two somewhat disreputable taverns, the Swan and the World's End, with gardens attached. Chelsea was also at that date a place of resort much patronised by cockneys; it was noted for its bun-house. Swift writes to Stella about the "r-r-r-r-rare Chelsea buns." Barn Elms had once a fashionable promenade in which Evelyn loved to swagger, but at this time it was more famous for the duels that were fought there.

duels, take care of one another, and grow better friends than before.

Mrs. Frail. With all my heart: ours are but slight flesh wounds, and if we keep 'em from air, not at all dangerous: well, give me your hand in token of sisterly secrecy and affection.

Mrs. Fore. Here 'tis with all my heart.

Mrs. Frail. Well, as an earnest of friendship and confidence, I'll acquaint you with a design that I have. To tell truth, and speak openly one to another, I'm afraid the world have observed us more than we have observed one another. You have a rich husband, and are provided for; I am at a loss, and have no great stock either of fortune or reputation; and therefore must look sharply about me. Sir Sampson has a son that is expected to-night; and by the account I have heard of his education, can be no conjuror; the estate you know is to be made over to him:—now if I could wheedle him, sister, ha? you understand me?

Mrs. Fore. I do; and will help you to the utmost of my power.—And I can tell you one thing that falls out luckily enough; my awkward daughter-in-law, who you know is designed to be his wife, is grown fond of Mr. Tattle; now if we can improve that, and make her have an aversion for the booby, it may go a great way towards his liking you. Here they come together; and let us contrive some way or other to leave 'em together.

Enter TATTLE *and* MISS PRUE.

Prue. Mother, mother, mother, look you here!

Mrs. Fore. Fy, fy, miss! how you bawl.—Besides, I have told you, you must not call me mother.

Prue. What must I call you then? are you not my father's wife?

Mrs. Fore. Madam; you must say madam.—By my soul, I shall fancy myself old indeed, to have this great girl call me mother!—Well, but, miss, what are you so overjoyed at?

Prue. Look you here, madam, then, what Mr. Tattle has given me.—Look you here, cousin, here's a snuff-box; nay, there's snuff in't;—here, will you have any?—Oh good! how sweet it is.—Mr. Tattle is all over sweet, his peruke is sweet, and his gloves are sweet, and his handkerchief is sweet, pure sweet, sweeter than roses.—Smell him, mother, madam, I mean.—He gave me this ring for a kiss.

Tat. O fy, miss! you must not kiss and tell.

Prue. Yes; I may tell my mother.—And he says he'll give me something to make me smell so.—[*To* TATTLE.] Oh pray lend me your handkerchief.—Smell, cousin; he says, he'll give me something that will make my smocks smell this way.—Is not it pure?—

't's better than lavender, mun—I'm resolved I won't let nurse put
ιny more lavender among my smocks—ha, cousin?

Mrs. Frail. Fy, miss! amongst your linen, you must say;—you
must never say smock.

Prue. Why, it is not bawdy, is it, cousin?

Tat. Oh, madam, you are too severe upon miss; you must not find
'ault with her pretty simplicity, it becomes her strangely.—Pretty
miss, don't let 'em persuade you out of your innocency.

Mrs. Fore. Oh, demn you, toad!—I wish you don't persuade her
out of her innocency.

Tat. Who I, madam?—Oh Lord, how can your ladyship have
such a thought—sure you don't know me?

Mrs. Frail. Ah, devil! sly devil!—He's as close, sister, as a confessor.—He thinks we don't observe him.

Mrs. Fore. A cunning cur! how soon he could find out a fresh
harmless creature! and left us, sister, presently.

Tat. Upon reputation—

Mrs. Fore. They're all so, sister, these men:—they love to have
the spoiling of a young thing, they are as fond of it, as of being
first in the fashion, or of seeing a new play the first day.—I warrant it would break Mr. Tattle's heart, to think that anybody else
should be beforehand with him.

Tat. Oh Lord, I swear I would not for the world—

Mrs. Frail. O hang you! who'll believe you?—You'd be hanged
before you'd confess—we know you—she's very pretty!—Lord,
what pure red and white!—she looks so wholesome;—ne'er stir, I
don't know, but I fancy, if I were a man—

Prue. How you love to jeer one, cousin!

Mrs. Fore. Hark ye, sister.—By my soul the girl is spoiled
already—d'ye think she'll ever endure a great lubberly tarpaulin!
—gad, I warrant you, she won't let him come near her, after Mr.
Tattle.

Mrs. Frail. O' my soul, I'm afraid not—eh!—filthy creature,
that smells of all pitch and tar.—[*To* TATTLE.] Devil take you,
you confounded toad!—why did you see her before she was married?

Mrs. Fore. Nay, why did we let him?—My husband will hang
us;—he'll think we brought 'em acquainted.

Mrs. Frail. Come, faith, let us begone.—If my brother Foresight
should find us with them, he'd think so, sure enough.

Mrs. Fore. So he would—but then leaving 'em together is as
bad.—And he's such a sly devil, he'll never miss an opportunity.

Mrs. Frail. I don't care; I won't be seen in't.

Mrs. Fore. Well, if you should, Mr. Tattle, you'll have a world

to answer for;—remember I wash my hands of it.—I'm thorough
innocent.   [*Exeunt* Mrs. FORESIGHT *and* Mrs. FRAI

Prue. What makes 'em go away, Mr. Tattle? what do the
mean, do you know?

Tat. Yes, my dear,—I think I can guess;—but hang me if
know the reason of it.

Prue. Come, must not we go too?

Tat. No, no, they don't mean that.

Prue. No! what then? what shall you and I do together?

Tat. I must make love to you, pretty miss; will you let me mak
love to you?

Prue. Yes, if you please.

Tat. [*Aside.*] Frank, egad, at least. What a pox does Mrs. For
sight mean by this civility? Is it to make a fool of me? or does sh
leave us together out of good morality, and do as she would b
done by?—Gad, I'll understand it so.

Prue. Well; and how will you make love to me? come, I long t
have you begin. Must I make love too? you must tell me how.

Tat. You must let me speak, miss, you must not speak first;
must ask you questions, and you must answer.

Prue. What, is it like the catechism?—come then, ask me.

Tat. D'ye think you can love me?

Prue. Yes.

Tat. Pooh! pox! you must not say yes already; I shan't car
a farthing for you then in a twinkling.

Prue. What must I say then?

Tat. Why, you must say no, or you believe not, or you can't tel

Prue. Why, must I tell a lie then?

Tat. Yes, if you'd be well-bred;—all well-bred persons lie.—
Besides, you are a woman, you must never speak what you think
your words must contradict your thoughts; but your actions ma
contradict your words. So, when I ask you, if you can love me
you must say no, but you must love me too. If I tell you you ar
handsome, you must deny it, and say I flatter you. But you mus
think yourself more charming than I speak you: and like me, fo
the beauty which I say you have, as much as if I had it myself. I
I ask you to kiss me, you must be angry, but you must not refus
me. If I ask you for more, you must be more angry,—but mor
complying; and as soon as ever I make you say you'll cry out, yo
must be sure to hold your tongue.

Prue. O Lord, I swear this is pure!—I like it better than ou
old-fashioned country way of speaking one's mind; and must no
you lie too?

Tat. Hum!—Yes; but you must believe I speak truth.

Prue. O Gemini! well, I always had a great mind to tell lies: but they frighted me, and said it was a sin.

Tat. Well, my pretty creature; will you make me happy by giving me a kiss?

Prue. No, indeed; I'm angry at you.   [*Runs and kisses him.*

Tat. Hold, hold, that's pretty well;—but you should not have given it me, but have suffered me to have taken it.

Prue. Well, we'll do't again.

Tat. With all my heart. Now then, my little angel!   [*Kisses her.*

Prue. Pish!

Tat. That's right—again, my charmer.   [*Kisses her again.*

Prue. O fy! nay, now I can't abide you.

Tat. Admirable! that was as well as if you had been born and bred in Covent Garden. And won't you show me, pretty miss, where your bedchamber is?

Prue. No, indeed, won't I; but I'll run there and hide myself from you behind the curtains.

Tat. I'll follow you.

Prue. Ah, but I'll hold the door with both hands, and be angry; and you shall push me down before you come in.

Tat. No, I'll come in first, and push you down afterwards.

Prue. Will you? then I'll be more angry, and more complying.

Tat. Then I'll make you cry out.

Prue. Oh, but you shan't; for I'll hold my tongue.

Tat. Oh, my dear apt scholar!

Prue. Well, now I'll run, and make more haste than you.

Tat. You shall not fly so fast as I'll pursue.   [*Exeunt.*

ACT THE THIRD

Scene I

The Gallery adjoining Prue's *Bedchamber*

Enter Nurse.

Nurse. Miss! miss! Miss Prue!—mercy on me, marry and amen!—Why, what's become of the child? why, miss? Miss Foresight!—Sure, she has locked herself up in her chamber, and gone to sleep, or to prayers.—Miss! miss! I hear her;—come to your father, child; open the door—open the door, miss!—I hear you cry "Hush!"—O Lord, who's there?—[*Peeps through the keyhole.*]—What's here to do?—O the father! a man with her! —Why, miss, I say! God's my life, here's fine doings towards!— O Lord, we're all undone!—O you young harlotry!—[*Knocks.*]

Od's my life! won't you open the door?—I'll come in the back way. [*Exit.*

SCENE II

PRUE'S *Bedchamber*

TATTLE *and* Miss PRUE.

Prue. O Lord, she's coming!—and she'll tell my father; what shall I do now!

Tat. Pox take her!—if she had stayed two minutes longer, I should have wished for her coming.

Prue. Oh dear, what shall I say? tell me, Mr. Tattle, tell me a lie.

Tat. There's no occasion for a lie; I could never tell a lie to no purpose;—but since we have done nothing, we must say nothing, I think. I hear her; I'll leave you together, and come off as you can. [*Thrusts her back, and shuts the door.*

SCENE III

A Room in FORESIGHT'S *House*

TATTLE, VALENTINE, SCANDAL, *and* ANGELICA.

Ang. You can't accuse me of inconstancy; I never told you that I loved you.

Val. But I can accuse you of uncertainty, for not telling me whether you did or not.

Ang. You mistake indifference for uncertainty; I never had concern enough to ask myself the question.

Scan. Nor good-nature enough to answer him that did ask you; I'll say that for you, madam.

Ang. What, are you setting up for good-nature?

Scan. Only for the affectation of it, as the women do for ill-nature.

Ang. Persuade your friend that it is all affectation.

Scan. I shall receive no benefit from the opinion; for I know no effectual difference between continued affectation and reality.

Tat. [*Coming up.*] Scandal, are you in private discourse? anything of secrecy? [*Aside to* SCANDAL.

Scan. Yes, but I dare trust you! we were talking of Angelica's love for Valentine; you won't speak of it?

Tat. No, no, not a syllable;—I know that's a secret, for it's whispered everywhere.

Scan. Ha! ha! ha!

Ang. What is, Mr. Tattle? I heard you say something was whispered everywhere.

Scan. Your love of Valentine.

Ang. How!

Tat. No, madam, his love for your ladyship.—Gad take me, beg your pardon;—for I never heard a word of your ladyship's passion till this instant.

Ang. My passion! and who told you of my passion, pray, sir?

Scan. [*Aside to* TATTLE.] Why, is the devil in you? did not I tell it you for a secret?

Tat. [*Aside to* SCANDAL.] Gad so, but I thought she might have been trusted with her own affairs.

Scan. Is that your discretion? trust a woman with her self?

Tat. You say true, I beg your pardon;—I'll bring all off.— *Aloud.*] It was impossible, madam, for me to imagine, that a person of your ladyship's wit and gallantry could have so long deceived the passionate addresses of the accomplished Valentine, and yet remain insensible; therefore you will pardon me, if, from a just weight of his merit, with your lady's good judgment, formed the balance of a reciprocal affection.

Val. O the devil! what damned costive poet has given thee this lesson of fustian to get by rote?

Ang. I dare swear you wrong him, it is his own; and Mr. Tattle only judges of the success of others from the effects of his own merit. For certainly Mr. Tattle was never denied anything in his life.

Tat. O Lord! yes, indeed, madam, several times.

Ang. I swear I don't think 'tis possible.

Tat. Yes, I vow and swear I have: Lord, madam, I'm the most unfortunate man in the world, and the most cruelly used by the ladies.

Ang. Nay, now you are ungrateful.

Tat. No, I hope not:—'tis as much ingratitude to own some favours as to conceal others.

Val. There, now it's out.

Ang. I don't understand you now: I thought you had never asked anything but what a lady might modestly grant, and you confess.

Scan. So, faith, your business is done here; now you may go brag somewhere else.

Tat. Brag! O heavens! why, did I name anybody?

Ang. No, I suppose that is not in your power: but you would if you could, no doubt on't.

Tat. Not in my power, madam! what, does your ladyship mean that I have no woman's reputation in my power?

Scan. [*Aside to* TATTLE.] 'Oons, why, you won't own it, will you?

Tat. Faith, madam, you're in the right: no more I have, as I hope to be saved; I never had it in my power to say anything to a lady's prejudice in my life. For, as I was telling you, madam, I have been the most unsuccessful creature living, in things of that nature; and never had the good fortune to be trusted once with a lady's secret, not once.

Ang. No!

Val. Not once, I dare answer for him.

Scan. And I'll answer for him; for I'm sure if he had, he would have told me.—I find, madam, you don't know Mr. Tattle.

Tat. No, indeed, madam, you don't know me at all, I find. For sure my intimate friends would have known—

Ang. Then it seems you would have told, if you had been trusted.

Tat. O pox, Scandal! that was too far put.—Never have told particulars, madam. Perhaps I might have talked as of a third person, or have introduced an amour of my own, in conversation, by way of novel; but never have explained particulars.

Ang. But whence comes the reputation of Mr. Tattle's secrecy, if he was never trusted?

Scan. Why thence it arises: the thing is proverbially spoken; but may be applied to him.—As if we should say in general terms, "He only is secret who never was trusted;" a satirical proverb upon our sex.—There's another upon yours, as "She is chaste who was never asked the question." That's all.

Val. A couple of very civil proverbs truly: 'tis hard to tell whether the lady or Mr. Tattle be the more obliged to you. For you found her virtue upon the backwardness of the men, and his secrecy upon the mistrust of the women.

Tat. Gad, it's very true, madam, I think we are obliged to acquit ourselves; and for my part—but your ladyship is to speak first.

Ang. Am I? well, I freely confess I have resisted a great deal of temptation.

Tat. And, egad, I have given some temptation that has not been resisted.

Val. Good!

Ang. I cite Valentine here, to declare to the court how fruitless he has found his endeavours, and to confess all his solicitations and my denials.

Val. I am ready to plead not guilty for you, and guilty for myself.

Scan. So, why this is fair, here's demonstration with a witness!

Tat. Well, my witnesses are not present. But I confess I have had favours from persons—but as the favours are numberless, so the persons are nameless.

Scan. Pooh, this proves nothing.

Tat. No? I can show letters, lockets, pictures, and rings; and if there be occasion for witnesses, I can summon the maids at the chocolate-houses, all the porters at Pall-Mall and Covent-Garden, the door-keepers at the playhouse, the drawers at Locket's, Pontac's, the Rummer, Spring-Garden;[1] my own land-lady, and valet-de-chambre; all who shall make oath, that I re-ceive more letters than the Secretary's Office; and that I have more vizor-masks to inquire for me than ever went to see the Hermaphrodite, or the Naked Prince. And it is notorious, that in a country church, once, an inquiry being made who I was, it was answered, I was the famous Tattle, who had ruined so many women.

Val. It was there, I suppose, you got the nick-name of the Great Turk.

Tat. True, I was called Turk-Tattle all over the parish.—The next Sunday all the old women kept their daughters at home, and the parson had not half his congregation. He would have brought me into the spiritual court, but I was revenged upon him, for he had a handsome daughter, whom I initiated into the science. But I repented it afterwards, for it was talked of in town; and a lady of quality, that shall be nameless, in a raging fit of jealousy, came down in her coach and six horses, and ex-posed herself upon my account; gad, I was sorry for it with all my heart.—You know whom I mean—you know where we raf-fled—

Scan. Mum, Tattle.

Val. 'Sdeath, are not you ashamed?

Ang. O barbarous! I never heard so insolent a piece of vanity. —Fy, Mr. Tattle!—I'll swear I could not have believed it.—Is this your secrecy?

Tat. Gad so, the heat of my story carried me beyond my dis-cretion, as the heat of the lady's passion hurried her beyond her

---

[1] Noted taverns. Pontac's was a celebrated French eating-house in Ab-church Lane; Locket's, a famous ordinary at Charing Cross, so called from Adam Locket the landlord; the Rummer Tavern was between Whitehall and Charing Cross. It was kept by Sam. Prior, the uncle of Matthew Prior the poet.

reputation.—But I hope you don't know whom I mean; fo
there were a great many ladies raffled.—Pox on't! now could
bite off my tongue.

Scan. No, don't; for then you'll tell us no more.—Come, I'l
recommend a song to you upon the hint of my two proverbs, an
I see one in the next room that will sing it.   [*Exit*

Tat. For Heaven's sake if you do guess, say nothing; gad, I'm
very unfortunate.

Re-enter SCANDAL *with one to sing.*

Scan. Pray sing the first song in the last new play.

SONG.

A nymph and a swain to Apollo once prayed,
The swain had been jilted, the nymph been betrayed:
Their intent was to try if his oracle knew
E'er a nymph that was chaste, or a swain that was true.

Apollo was mute, and had like t'have been posed,
But sagely at length he this secret disclosed:
"He alone won't betray in whom none will confide:
And the nymph may be chaste that has never been tried."

                                                   [*Exit* Singer

Enter Sir SAMPSON, Mrs. FRAIL, Miss PRUE, *and* Servant.

Sir Samp. Is Ben come? odso, my son Ben come? odd I'm
glad on't: where is he? I long to see him.—Now, Mrs. Frail, you
shall see my son Ben.—Body o' me, he's the hopes of my fam
ily.—I han't seen him these three years.—I warrant he's grown
—Call him in, bid him make haste.—[*Exit* Servant.] I'm ready
to cry for joy.

Mrs. Frail. Now, miss, you shall see your husband.

Prue. [*Aside to* Mrs. FRAIL.] Pish, he shall be none of my
husband.

Mrs. Frail. [*Aside to* PRUE.] Hush: well he shan't, leave that
to me.—I'll beckon Mr. Tattle to us.

Ang. Won't you stay and see your brother?

Val. We are the twin-stars, and cannot shine in one sphere
when he rises I must set.—Besides, if I should stay, I don't know
but my father in good-nature may press me to the immediate
signing the deed of conveyance of my estate; and I'll defer it
as long as I can.—Well, you'll come to a resolution?

Ang. I can't. Resolution must come to me, or I shall never
have one.

Scan. Come, Valentine, I'll go with you; I've something in my head to communicate to you.

[*Exeunt* VALENTINE *and* SCANDAL.

Sir Samp. What, is my son Valentine gone? what, is he sneaked off, and would not see his brother? There's an unnatural whelp! there's an ill-natured dog!—What, were you here too, madam, and could not keep him? could neither love, nor duty, nor natural affection, oblige him? Odsbud, madam, have no more to say to him; he is not worth your consideration. The rogue has not a drachm of generous love about him: all interest, all interest; he's an undone scoundrel, and courts your estate: body o' me, he does not care a doit for your person.

Ang. I'm pretty even with him, Sir Sampson; for if ever I could have liked anything in him, it should have been his estate, too: but since that's gone, the bait's off, and the naked hook appears.

Sir Samp. Odsbud, well spoken; and you are a wiser woman than I thought you were: for most young women now-a-days are to be tempted with a naked hook.

Ang. If I marry, Sir Sampson, I'm for a good estate with any man, and for any man with a good estate: therefore if I were obliged to make a choice, I declare I'd rather have you than your son.

Sir Samp. Faith and troth, you're a wise woman, and I'm glad to hear you say so; I was afraid you were in love with the reprobate; odd, I was sorry for you with all my heart: hang him, mongrel; cast him off; you shall see the rogue show himself, and make love to some desponding Cadua of four-score for sustenance. Odd, I love to see a young spendthrift forced to cling to an old woman for support, like ivy round a dead oak: faith I do; I love to see 'em hug and cotton together, like down upon a thistle.

Enter BEN *and* Servant.

Ben. Where's father?

Serv. There, sir, his back's toward you.

Sir Samp. My son Ben! bless thee, my dear boy; body o' me, thou art heartily welcome.

Ben. Thank you, father, and I'm glad to see you.

Sir Samp. Odsbud, and I am glad to see thee; kiss me, boy, kiss me again and again, dear Ben. [*Kisses him.*

Ben. So, so, enough, father.—Mess,[1] I'd rather kiss these gentlewomen.

[1] A survival of the old oath. By the mass!

Sir Samp. And so thou shalt.—Mrs. Angelica, my son Ben.

Ben. Forsooth, if you please.—[*Salutes her.*] Nay, mistress, I'm not for dropping anchor here; about ship i'faith.—[*Kisses* Mrs. FRAIL.] Nay, and you, too, my little cock-boat—so.

[*Kisses* Miss PRUE.

Tat. Sir, you're welcome ashore.

Ben. Thank you, thank you, friend.

Sir Samp. Thou hast been many a weary league, Ben, since I saw thee.

Ben. Ey, ey, been! been far enough, an that be all.—Well father, and how do all at home? how does brother Dick, and brother Val?

Sir Samp. Dick! body o' me, Dick has been dead these two years! I writ you word when you were at Leghorn.

Ben. Mess, that's true; marry, I had forgot. Dick's dead, as you say.—Well, and how? I have many questions to ask you. Well, you ben't married again, father, be you?

Sir Samp. No, I intend you shall marry, Ben; I would not marry for thy sake.

Ben. Nay, what does that signify?—An you marry again—why, then, I'll go to sea again, so there's one for t'other, an that be all.—Pray don't let me be your hindrance; e'en marry a God's name, an the wind sit that way. As for my part, mayhap I have no mind to marry.

Mrs. Frail. That would be a pity, such a handsome young gentleman.

Ben. Handsome! he! he! he! nay, forsooth, an you be for joking, I'll joke with you; for I love my jest, an the ship were sinking, as we say'n at sea. But I'll tell you why I don't much stand toward matrimony. I love to roam about from port to port, and from land to land: I could never abide to be port-bound, as we call it; now, a man that is married has, as it were, d'ye see, his feet in the bilboes, and mayhap mayn't get 'em out again when he would.

Sir Samp. Ben's a wag.

Ben. A man that is married, d'ye see, is no more like another, more than a galley-slave is like one of us free sailors; he is chained to an oar all his life; and mayhap forced to tug a leaky vessel into the bargain.

Sir Samp. A very wag! Ben's a very wag! only a little rough, he wants a little polishing.

Mrs. Frail. Not at all; I like his humour mightily, it's plain and honest; I should like such a humour in a husband extremely.

Ben. Say'n you so, forsooth? Marry, and I should like such a handsome gentlewoman for a bedfellow hugely; how say you, mistress, would you like going to sea? Mess, you're a tight vessel! and well rigged, an you were but as well manned.

Mrs. Frail. I should not doubt that, if you were master of me.

Ben. But I'll tell you one thing, an you come to sea in a high wind, or that lady—you mayn't carry so much sail o' your head.—Top and top-gallant, by the mess.

Mrs. Frail. No, why so?

Ben. Why, an you do, you may run the risk to be overset, and then you'll carry your keels above water, he! he! he!

Ang. I swear, Mr. Benjamin is the veriest wag in nature; an absolute sea-wit.

Sir Samp. Nay, Ben has parts, but, as I told you before, they want a little polishing: you must not take anything ill, madam.

Ben. No, I hope the gentlewoman is not angry; I mean all in good part; for if I give a jest I'll take a jest: and so, forsooth, you may be as free with me.

Ang. I thank you, sir, I am not at all offended.—But methinks, Sir Sampson, you should leave him alone with his mistress.—Mr. Tattle, we must not hinder lovers.

Tat. [*Aside to* Miss Prue.] Well, miss, I have your promise.

Sir Samp. Body o' me, madam, you say true.—Look you, Ben, his is your mistress.—Come, miss, you must not be shamefaced; we'll leave you together.

Prue. I can't abide to be left alone, mayn't my cousin stay with me?

Sir Samp. No, no.—Come, let's away.

Ben. Look you, father, mayhap the young woman mayn't take a liking to me.

Sir Samp. I warrant thee, boy; come, come, we'll be gone; 'll venture that.

[*Exeunt* Sir Sampson, Angelica, Tattle, *and* Mrs. Frail.

Ben. Come, mistress, will you please to sit down? for an you stand astern a that'n, we shall never grapple together.—Come, 'll haul a chair; there, an you please to sit I'll sit by you.

Prue. You need not sit so near one; if you have anything to say can hear you farther off, I an't deaf.

Ben. Why, that's true, as you say; nor I an't dumb; I can e heard as far as another;—I'll heave off to please you.— *Sits farther off.*] An we were a league asunder, I'd undertake o hold discourse with you, an 'twere not a main high wind indeed, nd full in my teeth. Look you, forsooth, I am, as it were, bound or the land of matrimony; 'tis a voyage, d'ye see, that was none f my seeking, I was commanded by father, and if you like of it mayhap I may steer into your harbour. How say you, mistress? The short of the thing is, that if you like me, and I like you, we may chance to swing in a hammock together.

Prue. I don't know what to say to you, nor I don't care to speak with you at all.

Ben. No? I'm sorry for that.—But pray, why are you so scornful?

Prue. As long as one must not speak one's mind, one had better not speak at all, I think, and truly I won't tell a lie for the matter.

Ben. Nay, you say true in that, 'tis but a folly to lie: for to speak one thing, and to think just the contrary way, is, as it were, to look one way and row another. Now, for my part, d'ye see, I'm for carrying things above board, I'm not for keeping anything under hatches,—so that if you ben't as willing as I, say so a' God's name, there's no harm done. Mayhap you may be shamefaced? some maidens, tho'f they love a man well enough, yet they don't care to tell'n so to's face: if that's the case, why silence gives consent.

Prue. But I'm sure it is not so, for I'll speak sooner than you should believe that; and I'll speak truth, though one should always tell a lie to a man; and I don't care, let my father do what he will; I'm too big to be whipped so I'll tell you plainly I don't like you, nor love you at all, nor never will, that's more: so, there's your answer for you; and don't trouble me no more you ugly thing!

Ben. Look you, young woman, you may learn to give good words however. I spoke you fair, d'ye see, and civil.—As for your love or your liking, I don't value it of a rope's end;—and mayhap I like you as little as you do me.—What I said was in obedience to father; gad, I fear a whipping no more than you do. But I tell you one thing, if you should give such language at sea you'd have a cat o' nine-tails laid across your shoulders. Flesh! who are you? You heard t'other handsome young woman speak civilly to me, of her own accord: whatever you think of yourself, gad, I don't think you are any more to compare to her than a can of small beer to a bowl of punch.

Prue. Well, and there's a handsome gentleman, and a fine gentleman, and a sweet gentleman, that was here, that love me, and I love him; and if he sees you speak to me any more he'll thrash your jacket for you, he will, you great sea-calf!

Ben. What, do you mean that fair-weather spark that was here just now? will he thrash my jacket?—let'n—let'n. But an he comes near me, mayhap I may giv'n a salt eel for's supper.

for all that. What does father mean to leave me alone as soon as I come home, with such a dirty dowdy? Sea-calf! I an't calf enough to lick your chalked face, you cheese-curd you!—Marry thee! 'oons, I'll marry a Lapland witch as soon, and live upon selling contrary winds and wrecked vessels.

Prue. I won't be called names, nor I won't be abused thus, so I won't.—If I were a man [*Cries*], you durst not talk at this rate; —no, you durst not, you stinking tar-barrel!

Enter Mrs. FORESIGHT *and* Mrs. FRAIL.

Mrs. Fore. [*Aside to* Mrs. FRAIL.] They have quarreled just as we could wish.

Ben. Tar-barrel? let your sweetheart there call me so if he'll take your part, your Tom Essence, and I'll say something to him; gad, I'll lace his musk doublet for him! I'll make him stink! he shall smell more like a weasel than a civet cat afore I ha' done with 'en.

Mrs. Fore. Bless me, what's the matter, miss? What, does she cry?—Mr. Benjamin, what have you done to her?

Ben. Let her cry: the more she cries, the less she'll—she has been gathering foul weather in her mouth, and now it rains out at her eyes.

Mrs. Fore. Come, miss, come along with me, and tell me, poor child.

Mrs. Frail. Lord, what shall we do? there's my brother Foresight and Sir Sampson coming.—Sister, do you take miss down into the parlour, and I'll carry Mr. Benjamin into my chamber, for they must not know that they are fallen out.—Come, sir, will you venture yourself with me?   [*Looking kindly on him.*

Ben. Venture, mess, and that I will, though 'twere to sea in a storm.   [*Exeunt.*

SCENE IV

The same

Enter Sir SAMPSON *and* FORESIGHT.

Sir Samp. I left 'em together here; what, are they gone? Ben's a brisk boy; he has got her into a corner; father's own son, faith, he'll touzle her, and mouzle her; the rogue's sharp set, coming from sea; if he should not stay for saying grace, old Foresight, but fall to without the help of a parson, ha? Odd, if he should, I could not be angry with him; 'twould be but like me, *a chip of the old block.* Ha! thou'rt melancholic, old prognostication; as melancholic as if thou hadst spilt the salt, or pared thy nails on a Sunday.—Come, cheer up, look about thee: look up, old star-gazer.—[*Aside*.] Now is he poring upon the ground for a crooked pin, or an old horse-nail, with the head towards him.

Fore. Sir Sampson, we'll have the wedding to-morrow morning.

Sir Samp. With all my heart.

Fore. At ten o'clock, punctually at ten.

Sir Samp. To a minute, to a second; thou shalt set thy watch, and the bridegroom shall observe its motions; they shall be married to a minute; go to bed to a minute; and when the alarm strikes, they shall keep time like the figures of St. Dunstan's clock, and *consummatum est* shall ring all over the parish.

Enter SCANDAL.

Scan. Sir Sampson, sad news!

Fore. Bless us!

Sir Samp. Why, what's the matter?

Scan. Can't you guess at what ought to afflict you and him, and all of us more than anything else?

Sir Samp. Body o' me, I don't know any universal grievance but a new tax, or the loss of the Canary fleet. Unless popery should be landed in the west, or the French fleet were at anchor at Blackwall.

Scan. No! undoubtedly Mr. Foresight knew all this, and might have prevented it.

Fore. 'Tis no earthquake.

Scan. No, not yet; nor whirlwind. But we don't know what it may come to.—But it has had a consequence already that touches us all.

Sir Samp. Why, body o' me, out with't.

Scan. Something has appeared to your son Valentine.—He's gone to bed upon't, and very ill.—He speaks little, yet says he has a world to say. Asks for his father and the wise Foresight; talks of Raymond Lully, and the ghost of Lilly. He has secrets to impart I suppose to you two. I can get nothing out of him but sighs. He desires he may see you in the morning, but would not be disturbed to-night, because he has some business to do in a dream.

Sir Samp. Hoity, toity, what have I to do with his dreams or his divinations?—Body o' me, this is a trick to defer signing the conveyance. I warrant the devil will tell him in a dream, that he must not part with his estate; but I'll bring him a parson, to tell him that the devil's a liar; or, if that won't do, I'll bring a lawyer that shall outlie the devil. And so I'll try whether my blackguard or his shall get the better of the day.   [*Exit.*

Scan. Alas, Mr. Foresight! I'm afraid all is not right.—You are a wise man, and a conscientious man; a searcher into obscurity and futurity; and if you commit an error, it is with a great deal of consideration and discretion and caution.

Fore. Ah, good Mr. Scandal—

Scan. Nay, nay, 'tis manifest; I do not flatter you.—But Sir Sampson is hasty, very hasty;—I'm afraid he is not scrupulous enough, Mr. Foresight.—He has been wicked, and Heaven grant he may mean well in his affair with you.—But my mind gives me, these things cannot be wholly insignificant. You are wise, and should not be over-reached, methinks you should not.

Fore. Alas, Mr. Scandal!—*Humanum est errare.*

Scan. You say true, man will err; mere man will err—but you are something more.—There have been wise men; but they were such as you;—men who consulted the stars, and were observers of omens.—Solomon was wise, but how?—by his judgment in astrology:—so says Pineda in his third book and eighth chapter.

Fore. You are learned, Mr. Scandal!

Scan. A trifler—but a lover of art.—And the wise men of the East owed their instruction to a star, which is rightly observed by Gregory the Great in favour of astrology! And Albertus Magnus makes it the most valuable science: because (says he) it teaches us to consider the causation of causes, in the causes of things.

Fore. I protest I honour you, Mr. Scandal:—I did not think you had been read in these matters.—Few young men are inclined—

Scan. I thank my stars that have inclined me.—But I fear this marriage, and making over this estate, this transferring of a rightful inheritance, will bring judgments upon us. I prophesy it, and I would not have the fate of Cassandra, not to be believed. Valentine is disturbed, what can be the cause of that? and Sir Sampson is hurried on by an unusual violence.—I fear he does not act wholly from himself; methinks he does not look as he used to do.

Fore. He was always of an impetuous nature.—But as to this marriage, I have consulted the stars, and all appearances are prosperous.

Scan. Come, come, Mr. Foresight, let not the prospect of worldly lucre carry you beyond your judgment, nor against your conscience:—you are not satisfied that you act justly.

Fore. How?

Scan. You are not satisfied, I say.—I am loath to discourage you—but it is palpable that you are not satisfied.

Fore. How does it appear, Mr. Scandal? I think I am very well satisfied.

Scan. Either you suffer yourself to deceive yourself; or you do not know yourself.

Fore. Pray explain yourself.

Scan. Do you sleep well o' nights?

Fore. Very well.

Scan. Are you certain? you do not look so.

Fore. I am in health, I think.

Scan. So was Valentine this morning; and looked just so.

Fore. How! am I altered any way? I don't perceive it.

Scan. That may be, but your beard is longer than it was two hours ago.

Fore. Indeed! bless me!

Enter Mrs. FORESIGHT.

Mrs. Fore. Husband, will you go to bed? it's ten o'clock.—Mr. Scandal, your servant.

Scan. [*Aside.*] Pox on her! she has interrupted my design:—but I must work her into the project.—[*Aloud.*] You keep early hours, madam.

Mrs. Fore. Mr. Foresight is punctual, we sit up after him.

Fore. My dear, pray lend me your glass, your little looking-glass.

Scan. Pray, lend it him, madam—I'll tell you the reason.—[*She gives him the glass:* SCANDAL *and she talk aside.*] My passion for you is grown so violent, that I am no longer master of myself.—I was interrupted in the morning, when you had charity enough to give me your attention, and I had hopes of finding another opportunity of explaining myself to you;—but was disappointed all this day; and the uneasiness that has attended me ever since, brings me now hither at this unseasonable hour.

Mrs. Fore. Was there ever such impudence! to make love to me before my husband's face! I'll swear I'll tell him.

Scan. Do; I'll die a martyr, rather than disclaim my passion. But come a little farther this way, and I'll tell you what project I had to get him out of the way, that I might have an opportunity of waiting upon you.

Fore. [*Looking in the glass.*] I do not see any revolution here; —methinks I look with a serene and benign aspect—pale, a little pale—but the roses of these cheeks have been gathered many years.—Ha! I do not like that sudden flushing;—gone already! —hem, hem, hem! faintish. My heart is pretty good; yet it beats; and my pulses, ha!—I have none—mercy on me!—hum—yes

here they are—gallop, gallop, gallop, gallop, gallop, gallop, hey!
whither will they hurry me?—Now they're gone again—and now
I'm faint again; and pale again, and, hem; and my, hem!—
breath, hem!—grows short; hem! hem! he, he, hem!

Scan. [*Aside to* Mrs. FORESIGHT.] It takes; pursue it, in the
name of love and pleasure!

Mrs. Fore. How do you do, Mr. Foresight?

Fore. Hum, not so well as I thought I was. Lend me your hand.

Scan. Look you there now—your lady says your sleep has
been unquiet of late.

Fore. Very likely.

Mrs. Fore. O mighty restless; but I was afraid to tell him so.—
He has been subject to talking and starting.

Scan. And did not use to be so?

Mrs. Fore. Never, never, till within these three nights; I cannot say that he has once broken my rest since we have been married.

Fore. I will go to bed.

Scan. Do so, Mr. Foresight, and say your prayers.—He looks
better than he did.

Mrs. Fore. Nurse, nurse!   [*Calls.*

Fore. Do you think so, Mr. Scandal?

Scan. Yes, yes; I hope this will be gone by morning, taking
it in time.

Fore. I hope so.

Enter Nurse.

Mrs. Fore. Nurse, your master is not well; put him to bed.

Scan. I hope you will be able to see Valentine in the morning.
You had best take a little diacodian and cowslip water, and lie
upon your back, may be you may dream.

Fore. I thank you, Mr. Scandal, I will.—Nurse, let me have a
watch-light, and lay *The Crumbs of Comfort* by me.

Nurse. Yes, sir.

Fore. And—hem, hem! I am very faint.

Scan. No, no; you look much better.

Fore. Do I?—[*To* Nurse.] And, d'ye hear, bring me, let me
see—within a quarter of twelve—hem—he, hem!—just upon the
turning of the tide, bring me the urinal. And I hope neither the
lord of my ascendant, nor the moon, will be combust; and then
I may do well.

Scan. I hope so. Leave that to me; I will erect a scheme; and
I hope I shall find both Sol and Venus in the sixth house.

Fore. I thank you, Mr. Scandal, I will.—Nurse, let me have a comfort to me. Hem, hem; good night.   [*Exit with* Nurse.

Scan. Good night, good Mr. Foresight; and I hope Mars and Venus will be in conjunction, while your wife and I are together.

Mrs. Fore. Well, and what use do you hope to make of this project? you don't think that you are ever like to succeed' in your design upon me?

Scan. Yes, faith, I do; I have a better opinion both of you and myself than to despair.

Mrs. Fore. Did you ever hear such a toad? Hark ye, devil! do you think any woman honest?

Scan. Yes, several very honest; they'll cheat a little at cards, sometimes; but that's nothing.

Mrs. Fore. Pshaw! but virtuous, I mean.

Scan. Yes, faith; I believe some women are virtuous too; but 'tis as I believe some men are valiant, through fear. For why should a man court danger, or a woman shun pleasure?

Mrs. Fore. O monstrous! what are conscience and honour?

Scan. Why, honour is a public enemy; and conscience a domestic thief; and he that would secure his pleasure, must pay a tribute to one, and go halves with t'other. As for honour, that you have secured; for you have purchased a perpetual opportunity for pleasure.

Mrs. Fore. An opportunity for pleasure?

Scan. Ay, your husband; a husband is an opportunity for pleasure; so you have taken care of honour, and 'tis the least I can do to take care of conscience.

Mrs. Fore. And so you think we are free for one another.

Scan. Yes, faith, I think so; I love to speak my mind.

Mrs. Fore. Why, then I'll speak my mind. Now, as to this affair between you and me. Here you make love to me; why, I'll confess, it does not displease me. Your person is well enough, and your understanding is not amiss.

Scan. I have no great opinion of myself; but I think I'm neither deformed nor a fool.

Mrs. Fore. But you have a villainous character; you are a libertine in speech as well as practice.

Scan. Come, I know what you would say; you think it more dangerous to be seen in conversation with me, than to allow some other men the last favour. You mistake; the liberty I take in talking is purely affected, for the service of your sex. He that first cries out, *Stop thief!* is often he that has stolen the treasure. I am a juggler, that act by confederacy; and, if you please, we'll put a trick upon the world.

Mrs. Fore. Ay; but you are such a universal juggler, that I'm afraid you have a great many confederates.

Scan. Faith, I'm sound.

Mrs. Fore. O, fy!—I'll swear you're impudent.

Scan. I'll swear you're handsome.

Mrs. Fore. Pish! you'd tell me so, though you did not think so.

Scan. And you'd think so, though I should not tell you so. And now I think we know one another pretty well.

Mrs. Fore. O Lord, who's here?

Enter Mrs. FRAIL *and* BEN.

Ben. Mess, I love to speak my mind; father has nothing to do with me. Nay, I can't say that neither; he has something to do with me. But what does that signify? if so be, that I be'n't minded to be steered by him, 'tis as tho'f he should strive against wind and tide.

Mrs. Frail. Ay, but, my dear, we must keep it secret till the estate be settled; for you know marrying without an estate is like sailing in a ship without ballast.

Ben. He! he! he! why, that's true; just so for all the world it is indeed, as like as two cable-ropes.

Mrs. Frail. And though I have a good portion, you know one would not venture all in one bottom.

Ben. Why, that's true again; for mayhap one bottom may spring a leak. You have hit it indeed, mess, you've nicked the channel.

Mrs. Frail. Well, but if you should forsake me after all, you'd break my heart.

Ben. Break your heart! I'd rather the Marygold should break her cable in a storm, as well as I love her. Flesh, you don't think I'm false-hearted like a landman! A sailor will be honest, tho'f mayhap he has never a penny of money in his pocket.—Mayhap I may not have so fair a face as a citizen or a courtier; but for all that, I've as good blood in my veins, and a heart as sound as a biscuit.

Mrs. Frail. And will you love me always?

Ben. Nay, an I love once, I'll stick like pitch; I'll tell you that. Come, I'll sing you a song for a sailor.

Mrs. Frail. Hold, there's my sister; I'll call her to hear it.

Mrs. Fore. Well, I won't go to bed to my husband to-night; because I'll retire to my own chamber, and think of what you have said.

Scan. Well; you'll give me leave to wait upon you to your chamber door, and leave you my last instructions?

Mrs. Fore. Hold, here's my sister coming towards us.

Mrs. Frail. If it won't interrupt you, I'll entertain you with a song.

Ben. The song was made upon one of our ship's crew's wife; our boatswain made the song; mayhap you may know her, sir. Before she was married, she was called buxom Joan of Deptford.

Scan. I have heard of her.

BEN *sings.*

A soldier and a sailor,
A tinker and a tailor,
Had once a doubtful strife, sir,
To make a maid a wife, sir,
　　Whose name was buxom Joan.
For now the time was ended,
When she no more intended
To lick her lips at men, sir,
And gnaw the sheets in vain, sir,
　　And lie o' nights alone.

The soldier swore like thunder,
He loved her more than plunder;
And showed her many a scar, sir,
That he had brought from far, sir,
　　With fighting for her sake.
The tailor thought to please her,
With offering her his measure.
The tinker too with mettle,
Said he could mend her kettle
　　And stop up every leak.

But while these three were prating,
The sailor slily waiting,
Thought if it came about, sir,
That they should all fall out, sir,
　　He then might play his part.
And just e'en as he meant, sir,
To loggerheads they went, sir,
And then he let fly at her
A shot 'twixt wind and water,
　　That won this fair maid's heart.

If some of our crew that came to see me are not gone, you shall see that we sailors can dance sometimes as well as other folks.— [*Whistles.*] I warrant that brings 'em, an they be within hearing.

Enter Sailors.

O, here they be!—and fiddles along with 'em. Come, my lads, let's have a round, and I'll make one. [*They dance.*

Ben. We're merry folks, we sailors, we han't much to care for. Thus we live at sea; eat biscuit, and drink flip; put on a clean shirt once a quarter—come home and lie with our landladies once a year, get rid of a little money; and then put off with the next fair wind. How d'ye like us?

Mrs. Frail. O you are the happiest, merriest men alive!

Mrs. Fore. We're beholden to Mr. Benjamin for this entertainment.—I believe it's late.

Ben. Why, forsooth, an you think so, you had best go to bed. For my part, I mean to toss a can, and remember my sweetheart, afore I turn in; mayhap I may dream of her.

Mrs. Fore. Mr. Scandal, you had best go to bed and dream too.

Scan. Why faith, I have a good lively imagination; and can dream as much to the purpose as another, if I set about it; but dreaming is the poor retreat of a lazy, hopeless, and imperfect lover; 'tis the last glimpse of love to worn-out sinners, and the faint dawning of a bliss to wishing girls and growing boys.

There's nought but willing, waking love that can
Make blest the ripened maid and finished man.   [*Exeunt.*

ACT THE FOURTH

Scene I

An Ante-room at Valentine's *Lodging*

Scandal *and* Jeremy.

Scan. Well, is your master ready? does he look madly, and talk madly?

Jer. Yes, sir; you need make no great doubt of that; he that was so near turning poet yesterday morning, can't be much to seek in playing the madman to-day.

Scan. Would he have Angelica acquainted with the reason of his design?

Jer. No, sir, not yet;—he has a mind to try, whether his playing the madman won't make her play the fool, and fall in love with him; or at least own that she has loved him all this while and concealed it.

Scan. I saw her take coach just now with her maid; and think I heard her bid the coachman drive hither.

Jer. Like enough, sir, for I told her maid this morning my master was run stark mad only for love of her mistress. I hear a coach stop; if it should be she, sir, I believe he would not see her, till he hears how she takes it.

Scan. Well, I'll try her:—'tis she, here she comes.

Enter ANGELICA *and* JENNY.

Ang. Mr. Scandal, I suppose you don't think it a novelty to see a woman visit a man at his own lodgings in a morning?

Scan. Not upon a kind occasion, madam. But when a lady comes tyrannically to insult a ruined lover, and make manifest the cruel triumphs of her beauty, the barbarity of it something surprises me.

Ang. I don't like raillery from a serious face.—Pray tell me what is the matter?

Jer. No strange matter, madam; my master's mad, that's all: I suppose your ladyship has thought him so a great while.

Ang. How d'ye mean, mad?

Jer. Why, faith, madam, he's mad for want of his wits, just as he was poor for want of money; his head is e'en as light as his pockets; and anybody that has a mind to a bad bargain, can't do better than to beg him for his estate.

Ang. If you speak truth, your endeavouring at wit is very unseasonable.

Scan. [*Aside.*] She's concerned, and loves him.

Ang. Mr. Scandal, you cannot think me guilty of so much inhumanity, as not to be concerned for a man I must own myself obliged to; pray tell me the truth.

Scan. Faith, madam, I wish telling a lie would mend the matter. But this is no new effect of an unsuccessful passion.

Ang. [*Aside.*] I know not what to think.—Yet I should be vexed to have a trick put upon me.—[*Aloud.*] May I not see him?

Scan. I'm afraid the physician is not willing you should see him yet.—Jeremy, go in and inquire.   [*Exit* JEREMY.

Ang. [*Aside.*] Ha! I saw him wink and smile—I fancy 'tis a trick—I'll try.—[*Aloud.*] I would disguise to all the world a failing which I must own to you.—I fear my happiness depends upon the recovery of Valentine. Therefore I conjure you, as you are his friend, and as you have compassion upon one fearful of affliction, to tell me what I am to hope for.—I cannot speak—but you may tell me, for you know what I would ask.

Scan. [*Aside.*] So, this is pretty plain.—[*Aloud.*] Be not too much concerned, madam, I hope his condition is not desperate: an acknowledgment of love from you, perhaps, may work a cure; as the fear of your aversion occasioned his distemper.

Ang. [*Aside.*] Say you so? nay, then I'm convinced; and if I don't play trick for trick, may I never taste the pleasure of revenge!—[*Aloud.*] Acknowledgment of love! I find you have mistaken my compassion, and think me guilty of a weakness I'm a stranger to. But I have too much sincerity to deceive you, and too much charity to suffer him to be deluded with vain hopes. Good-nature and humanity oblige me to be concerned for him; but to love is neither in my power nor inclination; and if he can't be cured without I suck the poison from his wounds, I'm afraid he won't recover his senses till I lose mine.

Scan. [*Aside.*] Hey, brave woman, i'faith!—[*Aloud.*] Won't you see him then, if he desire it?

Ang. What signify a madman's desires? besides, 'twould make me uneasy. If I don't see him, perhaps my concern for him may lessen. If I forget him, 'tis no more than he has done by himself; and now the surprise is over, methinks I am not half so sorry as I was.

Scan. So, faith, good-nature works apace; you were confessing just now an obligation to his love.

Ang. But I have considered that passions are unreasonable and involuntary; if he loves, he can't help it; and if I don't love, I can't help it; no more than he can help his being a man, or I my being a woman; or no more than I can help my want of inclination to stay longer here.—Come, Jenny.

[*Exeunt* ANGELICA *and* JENNY.

Scan. Humph!—An admirable composition, faith, this same womankind!

Re-enter JEREMY.

Jer. What, is she gone, sir?

Scan. Gone? why she was never here; nor anywhere else; nor I don't know her if I see her; nor you neither.

Jer. Good lack! what's the matter now? are any more of us to be mad? Why, sir, my master longs to see her; and is almost mad in good earnest with the joyful news of her being here.

Scan. We are all under a mistake. Ask no questions, for I can't resolve you; but I'll inform your master. In the mean time, if our project succeed no better with his father than it does with his mistress, he may descend from his exaltation of madness into the road of common sense, and be content only to be made a fool with other reasonable people.—I hear Sir Sampson. You know your cue; I'll to your master. [*Exit.*

Enter Sir SAMPSON *and* BUCKRAM.

Sir Samp. D'ye see, Mr. Buckram, here's the paper signed with his own hand.

Buck. Good, sir. And the conveyance is ready drawn in this box, if he be ready to sign and seal.

Sir Samp. Ready, body o' me, he must be ready! his sham-sickness shan't excuse him.—O, here's his scoundrel.—Sirrah, where's your master?

Jer. Ah, sir, he's quite gone.

Sir Samp. Gone! what, he is not dead?

Jer. No, sir, not dead.

Sir Samp. What, is he gone out of town? run away, ha! he has tricked me? speak, varlet.

Jer. No, no, sir, he's safe enough, sir, an he were but as sound, poor gentleman. He is, indeed, here, sir, and not here, sir.

Sir Samp. Heyday, rascal, do you banter me? sirrah, d'ye banter me?—Speak, sirrah, where is he? for I will find him.

Jer. Would you could, sir! for he has lost himself. Indeed, sir, I have almost broke my heart about him—I can't refrain tears when I think of him, sir: I'm as melancholy for him as a passing-bell, sir; or a horse in a pound.

Sir Samp. A pox confound your similitudes, sir!—Speak to be understood, and tell me in plain terms what the matter is with him, or I'll crack your fool's skull.

Jer. Ah, you've hit it, sir! that's the matter with him, sir; his skull's cracked, poor gentleman; he's stark mad, sir.

Sir Samp. Mad!

Buck. What, is he *non compos?*

Jer. Quite *non compos,* sir.

Buck. Why, then all's obliterated, Sir Sampson; if he be *non compos mentis,* his act and deed will be of no effect, it is not good in law.

Sir Samp. 'Oons, I won't believe it! let me see him, sir.—Mad! I'll make him find his senses.

Jer. Mr. Scandal is with him, sir; I'll knock at the door.

[*Goes to the Scene, which opens*

Scene II

Another Room at Valentine's *Lodgings*

Sir Sampson, Valentine, Scandal, Jeremy, *and* Buckram
Valentine *upon a couch, disorderly dressed.*

Sir Samp. How now! what's here to do?

Val. [*Starting.*] Ha! who's that?

Scan. For Heaven's sake softly, sir, and gently! don't provoke him.

Val. Answer me, who is that, and that?

Sir Samp. Gadsobs, does he not know me? Is he mischievous? I'll speak gently.—Val, Val, dost thou not know me, boy? not know thy own father, Val? I am thy own father, and this is honest Brief Buckram the lawyer.

Val. It may be so—I did not know you—the world is full.— There are people that we do know and people that we do not know; and yet the sun shines upon all alike.—There are fathers that have many children; and there are children that have many fathers.—'Tis strange! but I am Truth, and come to give the world the lie.

Sir Samp. Body o' me, I know not what to say to him!

Val. Why does that lawyer wear black?—does he carry his conscience withoutside?—Lawyer, what art thou? dost thou know me?

Buck. O Lord! what must I say?—Yes, sir.

Val. Thou liest, for I am Truth. 'Tis hard I cannot get a livelihood amongst you. I have been sworn out of Westminster-hall the first day of every term—let me see—no matter how long— but I'll tell you one thing; it's a question that would puzzle an arithmetician, if you should ask him, whether the Bible saves more souls in Westminster-Abbey or damns more in Westminster-Hall; for my part, I am Truth, and can't tell; I have very few acquaintance.

Sir Samp. Body o' me, he talks sensibly in his madness! has he no intervals?

Jer. Very short, sir.

Buck. Sir, I can do you no service while he's in this condition; here's your paper, sir—he may do me a mischief if I stay—the conveyance is ready, sir, if he recover his senses.

[*Exit* BUCKRAM.

Sir Samp. Hold, hold, hold, don't you go yet.

Scan. You'd better let him go, sir; and send for him if there be occasion; for I fancy his presence provokes him more.

Val. Is the lawyer gone? 'tis well; then we may drink about without going together by the ears—heigh-ho! What o'clock is 't?— My father here! your blessing, sir.

Sir Samp. He recovers.—Bless thee, Val,—how dost thou do, boy?

Val. Thank you, sir, pretty well—I have been a little out of order—won't you please to sit, sir?

Sir Samp. Ay, boy.—Come, thou shalt sit down by me.

Val. Sir, 'tis my duty to wait.

Sir Samp. No, no, come, come, sit thee down, honest Val; how dost thou do? let me feel thy pulse.—Oh, pretty well now, Val; body o' me, I was sorry to see thee indisposed! but I'm glad thou art better, honest Val.

Val. I thank you, sir.

Scan. Miracle! the monster grows loving. [*Aside.*

Sir Samp. Let me feel thy hand again, Val; it does not shake —I believe thou canst write, Val; ha, boy, thou canst write thy name, Val?—Jeremy, step and overtake Mr. Buckram, bid him make haste back with the conveyance! quick! quick!

[*Whispers to* JEREMY, *who goes out.*

Scan. [*Aside.*] That ever I should suspect such a heathen of any remorse!

Sir Samp. Dost thou know this paper, Val? I know thou'rt honest, and wilt perform articles.

[*Shows him the paper, but holds it out of his reach.*

Val. Pray, let me see it, sir. You hold it so far off, that I can't tell whether I know it or no.

Sir Samp. See it, boy? ay, ay, why thou dost see it—'tis thy own hand, Vally. Why, let me see, I can read it as plain as can be; look you here—[*Reads.*] "The conditions of this obligation" —look you, as plain as can be, so it begins—and then at the bottom—"As witness my hand, Valentine Legend," in great letters; why, 'tis as plain as the nose in one's face; what, are my eyes better than thine? I believe I can read it farther off yet— let me see. [*Stretches out his arm as far as he can.*

Val. Will you please to let me hold it, sir?

Sir Samp. Let thee hold it, sayest thou?—ay, with all my heart.—What matter is it who holds it? what need anybody hold it?—I'll put it in my pocket, Val, and then nobody need hold it.—[*Puts the paper in his pocket.*] There, Val, it's safe enough, boy—but thou shalt have it as soon as thou hast set thy hand to another paper, little Val.

Re-enter JEREMY *and* BUCKRAM.

Val. What, is my bad genius here again! Oh no, it is the lawyer with his itching palm; and he's come to be scratched—my nails are not long enough—let me have a pair of red-hot tongs, quickly! quickly! and you shall see me act St. Dunstan, and lead the devil by the nose.

Buck. O Lord, let me be gone! I'll not venture myself with a madman. [*Exit.*

Val. Ha! ha! ha! you need not run so fast, honesty will not overtake you.—Ha! ha! ha! the rogue found me out to be *in forma pauperis* presently.

Sir Samp. Oons! what a vexation is here! I know not to do or say, or which way to go.

Val. Who's that, that's out of his way! I am Truth, and can set him right.—Hark ye, friend, the straight road is the worst way you can go:—he that follows his nose always, will very often be led into a stink.—*Probatum est*.—But what are you for, religion or politics? There's a couple of topics for you, no more like one another than oil and vinegar; and yet those two beaten together by a state-cook, make sauce for the whole nation.

Sir Samp. What the devil had I to do, ever to beget sons? why did I ever marry?

Val. Because thou wert a monster, old boy; the two greatest monsters in the world are a man and a woman; what's thy opinion?

Sir Samp. Why, my opinion is that those two monsters joined together, make a yet greater, that's a man and his wife.

Val. Aha, old truepenny! sayest thou so? thou hast nicked it. —But, it's wonderful strange, Jeremy.

Jer. What is, sir?

Val. That grey hairs should cover a green head, and I make a fool of my father.—What's here! *Erra Pater,* or a bearded Sibyl? If Prophecy comes, Truth must give place.   [*Exeunt*.

Scene III

An Ante-room at Valentine's *Lodgings*

Enter Sir Sampson, Scandal, Foresight, Mrs. Foresight, *and* Mrs. Frail.

Fore. What says he? what, did he prophesy?—Ha, Sir Sampson, bless us! how are we?

Sir Samp. Are we! a pox o' your prognostication—why, we are fools as we used to be.—Oons, that you could not foresee that the moon would predominate, and my son be mad!—Where's your oppositions, your trines, and your quadrates?—What did your Cardan and your Ptolemy tell you? your Messahalah and your Longomontanus, your harmony of chiromancy with astrology? Ah! pox on't, that I that know the world, and men and manners, that don't believe in a syllable in the sky and stars, and suns, and almanacs, and trash, should be directed by a dreamer, an omen-hunter, and defer business in expectation of a lucky hour! when, body o' me, there never was a lucky hour after the first opportunity.   [*Exit* Sir Sampson.

Fore. Ah, Sir Sampson, Heaven help your head! This is none of your lucky hour! *Nemo omnibus horis sapit.* What, is he gone, and in contempt of science? Ill stars and unconvertible ignorance attend him!

Scan. You must excuse his passion, Mr. Foresight, for he has been heartily vexed.—His son is *non compos mentis,* and thereby incapable of making any conveyance in law; so that all his measures are disappointed.

Fore. Ha! say you so?

Mrs. Frail. [*Aside to* Mrs. Foresight.] What, has my sea-lover lost his anchor of hope then?

Mrs. Fore. Oh, sister, what will you do with him?

Mrs. Frail. Do with him! send him to sea again in the next foul weather.—He's used to an inconstant element, and won't be surprised to see the tide turned.

Fore. Wherein was I mistaken, not to foresee this?

[*Considers*

Scan. [*Aside to* Mrs. Foresight.] Madam, you and I can tell him something else that he did not foresee, and more particularly relating to his own fortune.

Mrs. Fore. [*Aside to* Scandal.] What do you mean? I don't understand you.

Scan. Hush, softly—the pleasures of last night, my dear too considerable to be forgot so soon.

Mrs. Fore. Last night! and what would your impudence infer from last night! last night was like the night before, I think.

Scan. 'Sdeath, do you make no difference between me and your husband?

Mrs. Fore. Not much;—he's superstitious, and you are mad in my opinion.

Scan. You make me mad.—You are not serious;—pray, recollect yourself.

Mrs. Fore. O yes, now I remember, you were very impertinent and impudent,—and would have come to bed to me.

Scan. And did not?

Mrs. Fore. Did not! with what face can you ask the question

Scan. [*Aside.*] This I have heard of before, but never believed I have been told she had that admirable quality of forgetting to a man's face in the morning that she had lain with him a night, and denying that she had done favours with more impudence than she could grant 'em.—Madam, I'm your humble servant, and honour you.—[*Aloud.*] You look pretty well, M Foresight.—How did you rest last night?

Fore. Truly, Mr. Scandal, I was so taken up with broken dreams and distracted visions, that I remember little.

Scan. 'Twas a very forgetting night.—But would you not talk with Valentine, perhaps you may understand him? I'm apt to believe there is something mysterious in his discourses, and sometimes rather think him inspired than mad.

Fore. You speak with singular good judgment, Mr. Scandal, truly.—I am inclining to your Turkish opinion in this matter, and do reverence a man whom the vulgar think mad. Let us go to him.   [*Exeunt* FORESIGHT *and* SCANDAL.

Mrs. Frail. Sister, do you stay with them; I'll find out my lover, and give him his discharge, and come to you.—O' my conscience here he comes.   [*Exit* Mrs. FORESIGHT.

Enter BEN.

Ben. All mad, I think.—Flesh, I believe all the calentures of the sea are come ashore, for my part!

Mrs. Frail. Mr. Benjamin in choler!

Ben. No, I'm pleased well enough now I have found you.—Mess, I have had such a hurricane upon your account yonder!

Mrs. Frail. My account! pray what's the matter?

Ben. Why, father came and found me squabbling with yon chitty-faced thing as he would have me marry,—so he asked what was the matter.—He asked in a surly sort of a way.—It seems brother Val is gone mad, and so that put'n into a passion: but what did I know that, what's that to me?—So he asked in a surly sort of manner,—and glad I answered 'en as surlily; what tho'f he be my father? I ain't bound prentice to 'en:—so faith I told'n in plain terms, if I were minded to marry I'd marry to please myself, not him: and for the young woman that he provided for me, I thought it more fitting for her to learn her sampler and make dirt-pies, than to look after a husband; for my part I was none of her man.—I had another voyage to make, let him take it as he will.

Mrs. Frail. So then, you intend to go to sea again?

Ben. Nay, nay, my mind run upon you,—but I would not tell him so much.—So he said he'd make my heart ache; and if so be that he could get a woman to his mind, he'd marry himself. Gad, says I, an you play the fool and marry at these years, there's more danger of your head's aching than my heart.—He was woundy angry when I gav'n that wipe.—He hadn't a word to say, and so I left'n and the green girl together; may-hap the bee may bite, and he'll marry her himself; with all my heart.

Mrs. Frail. And were you this undutiful and graceless wretcl to your father?

Ben. Then why was he graceless first?—If I am undutifu and graceless, why did he beget me so? I did not get myself.

Mrs. Frail. O impiety! how have I been mistaken! what ar inhuman merciless creature have I set my heart upon! O, I an happy to have discovered the shelves and quicksands that lur beneath that faithless smiling face!

Ben. Hey toss? what's the matter now? why, you ben't angry be you?

Mrs. Frail. O see me no more! for thou wert born amongs rocks, suckled by whales, cradled in a tempest, and whistle to by winds; and thou art come forth with fins and scales, an three rows of teeth, a most outrageous fish of prey.

Ben. O Lord, O Lord, she's mad! poor young woman; lov has turned her senses, her brain is quite overset! Well-a-day, ho shall I do to set her to right?

Mrs. Frail. No, no, I am not mad, monster, I am wise enoug to find you out. Hadst thou the impudence to aspire at bein a husband with that stubborn and disobedient temper?—Yo that know not how to submit to a father, presume to have sufficient stock of duty to undergo a wife? I should have bee finely fobbed indeed, very finely fobbed.

Ben. Hark ye, forsooth; if so be that you are in your righ senses, d'ye see; for aught as I perceive I'm like to be finel fobbed,—if I have got anger here upon your account, and yo are tacked about already.—What d'ye mean, after all your fai speeches and stroking my cheeks, and kissing, and hugging, what would you sheer off so? would you, and leave me aground?

Mrs. Frail. No, I'll leave you adrift, and go which way yo will.

Ben. What, are you false-hearted, then?

Mrs. Frail. Only the wind's changed.

Ben. More shame for you:—the wind's changed! It's an il wind blows nobody good,—mayhap I have a good riddance o you, if these be your tricks. What did you mean all this while to make a fool of me?

Mrs. Frail. Any fool but a husband.

Ben. Husband! gad, I would not be your husband, if yo would have me, now I know your mind, tho'f you had you weight in gold and jewels, and tho'f I loved you never so well.

Mrs. Frail. Why, canst thou love, porpoise?

Ben. No matter what I can do; don't call names,—I don' love you so well as to bear that, whatever I did. I'm glad yo

ıow yourself, mistress.—Let them marry you, as don't know
ou:—gad, I know you too well, by sad experience; I believe
e that marries you will go to sea in a hen-pecked frigate—I
elieve that, young woman—and mayhap may come to an anchor
t Cuckold's-point; so there's a dash for you, take it as you
ill, mayhap you may holla after me when I won't come to.

[*Exit.*

Mrs. Frail. Ha! ha! ha! no doubt on't;—
    [*Sings.*] My true love is gone to sea—

Re-enter Mrs. FORESIGHT.

Mrs. Frail. O sister, had you come a minute sooner, you would
ıve seen the resolution of a lover.—Honest Tar and I are
ırted,—and with the same indifference that we met.—O' my life
am half vexed at the insensibility of a brute that I despised.
Mrs. Fore. What, then, he bore it most heroically?
Mrs. Frail. Most tyrannically,—for you see he has got the
art of me; and I the poor forsaken maid am left complaining
ı the shore. But I'll tell you a hint that he has given me;
r Sampson is enraged, and talks desperately of committing
atrimony himself;—if he has a mind to throw himself away,
e can't do it more effectually than upon me, if we could bring
about.
Mrs. Fore. Oh, hang him, old fox! he's too cunning; besides
e hates both you and me. But I have a project in my head for
ıu, and I have gone a good way towards it. I have almost made
bargain with Jeremy, Valentine's man, to sell his master to us.
Mrs. Frail. Sell him! how?
Mrs. Fore. Valentine raves upon Angelica, and took me for
er, and Jeremy says will take anybody for her that he imposes
ı him. Now I have promised him mountains, if in one of his
ad fits he will bring you to him in her stead, and get you mar-
ed together, and put to bed together; and after consummation,
rl, there's no revoking. And if he should recover his senses, he'll
e glad at least to make you a good settlement.—Here they come:
and aside a little, and tell me how you like the design.

Enter VALENTINE, SCANDAL, FORESIGHT, *and* JEREMY.

Scan. [*To* JEREMY.] And have you given your master a hint
their plot upon him?
Jer. Yes, sir; he says he'll favour it, and mistake her for
ngelica.
Scan. It may make us sport.
Fore. Mercy on us!

Val. Hush!—interrupt me not: I'll whisper prediction to the
and thou shalt prophesy. I am Truth, and can teach thy tongu
a new trick:—I have told thee what's past—now I'll tell what
to come. Dost thou know what will happen to-morrow?—answe
me not—for I will tell thee. To-morrow, knaves will thrive throug
craft, and fools through fortune, and honesty will go as it di
frost-nipped in a summer suit. Ask me questions concernin
to-morrow.

Scan. Ask him, Mr. Foresight.

Fore. Pray, what will be done at court?

Val. Scandal will tell you:—I am Truth, I never come ther

Fore. In the city?

Val. Oh, prayers will be said in empty churches, at the usu
hours. Yet you will see such zealous faces behind the counter
as if religion were to be sold in every shop. Oh, things will g
methodically, in the city; the clocks will strike twelve at noo
and the horned herd buzz in the Exchange at two. Husbands an
wives will drive distinct trades, and care and pleasure separate
occupy the family. Coffee-houses will be full of smoke an
stratagem. And the cropt prentice, that sweeps his master's sho
in the morning, may, ten to one, dirty his sheets before nigh
But there are two things that you will see very strange; whic
are wanton wives with their legs at liberty, and tame cuckol
with chains about their necks.—But hold, I must examine yo
before I go further; you look suspiciously. Are you a husband

Fore. I am married.

Val. Poor creature! is your wife of Covent-garden parish?

Fore. No; St. Martin's-in-the-fields.

Val. Alas, poor man! his eyes are sunk, and his hands shriv
elled; his legs dwindled, and his back bowed; pray, pray, for
metamorphosis. Change thy shape, and shake off age; get the
Medea's kettle, and be boiled anew; come forth with labourin
callous hands, a chine of steel, and Atlas shoulders. Let Taliacoti
trim the calves of twenty chairmen, and make thee pedestals t
stand erect upon, and look matrimony in the face. Ha! ha! ha
that a man should have a stomach to a wedding supper, whe
the pigeons ought rather to be laid to his feet, ha! ha! ha!

Fore. His frenzy is very high now, Mr. Scandal.

Scan. I believe it is a spring-tide.

Fore. Very likely, truly; you understand these matters;—M
Scandal, I shall be very glad to confer with you about the
things which he has uttered—his sayings are very mysteriou
and hieroglyphical.

Val. Oh, why would Angelica be absent from my eyes so long

Jer. She's here, sir.

Mrs. Fore. Now, sister.

Mrs. Frail. O Lord, what must I say?

Scan. Humour him, madam, by all means.

Val. Where is she? oh, I see her;—she comes like riches, wealth, and liberty at once, to a despairing, starving, and abandoned wretch. Oh welcome, welcome.

Mrs. Frail. How d'ye, sir? can I serve you?

Val. Hark ye—I have a secret to tell you—Endymion and the moon shall meet us upon Mount Latmos and we'll be married in the dead of night—but say not a word. Hymen shall put his torch into a dark lantern, that it may be secret; and Juno shall give her peacock poppy-water, that he may fold his ogling tail, and Argus's hundred eyes be shut, ha! Nobody shall know but Jeremy.

Mrs. Frail. No, no, we'll keep it secret, it shall be done presently.

Val. The sooner the better.—Jeremy, come hither—closer—that none may overhear us—Jeremy, I can tell you news; Angelica is turned nun, and I am turning friar, and yet we'll marry one another in spite of the pope. Get me a cowl and beads, that I may play my part; for she'll meet me two hours hence in black and white, and a long veil to cover the project, and we won't see one another's faces, till we have done something to be ashamed of, and then we'll blush once for all.

Enter TATTLE *and* ANGELICA.

Jer. I'll take care, and—

Val. Whisper.

Ang. Nay, Mr. Tattle, if you make love to me, you spoil my design, for I intend to make you my confidant.

Tat. But, madam, to throw away your person, such a person, and such a fortune, on a madman?

Ang. I never loved him till he was mad; but don't tell anybody so.

Scan. [*Aside.*] How's this! Tattle making love to Angelica?

Tat. Tell, madam! alas, you don't know me—I have much ado to tell your ladyship how long I have been in love with you; but encouraged by the impossibility of Valentine's making any more addresses to you, I have ventured to declare the very inmost passion of my heart. Oh, madam, look upon us both; there you see the ruins of a poor decayed creature,—here a complete and lively figure, with youth and health, and all his five senses in perfection, madam; and to all this, the most passionate lover—

Ang. O fy, for shame! hold your tongue; a passionate love and five senses in perfection! when you are as mad as Valentine I'll believe you love me, and the maddest shall take me.

Val. It is enough.—Ha, who's here?

Mrs. Frail. [*Aside to* JEREMY.] O Lord, her coming will spoil all!

Jer. [*Aside to* Mrs. FRAIL.] No, no, madam, he won't know her; if he should, I can persuade him.

Val. Scandal, who are these? foreigners? If they are, I'll tell you what I think.—[*Whispers.*] Get away all the company but Angelica, that I may discover my design to her.

Scan. [*Whispers.*] I will; I have discovered something of Tattle that is of a piece with Mrs. Frail. He courts Angelica; if we could contrive to couple 'em together; hark ye.

Mrs. Fore. He won't know you, cousin, he knows nobody.

Fore. But he knows more than anybody. Oh, niece, he knows things past and to come, and all the profound secrets of time.

Tat. Look you, Mr. Foresight, it is not my way to make many words of matters, and so I shan't say much; but, in short, d'ye see, I will hold you a hundred pounds now, that I know more secrets than he.

Fore. How! I cannot read that knowledge in your face, Mr. Tattle. Pray, what do you know?

Tat. Why, d'ye think I'll tell you, sir? Read it in my face? no, sir, 'tis written in my heart; and safer there, sir, than letter writ in juice of lemon; for no fire can fetch it out. I am no blab, sir.

Val. [*Aside to* SCANDAL.] Acquaint Jeremy with it, he may easily bring it about.—[*Aloud.*] They are welcome, and I'll tell 'em so myself. What, do you look strange upon me? then I must be plain.—[*Coming up to them.*] I am Truth, and hate an old acquaintance with a new face.

[SCANDAL *goes aside with* JEREMY.

Tat. Do you know me, Valentine?

Val. You? who are you? no, I hope not.

Tat. I am Jack Tattle, your friend.

Val. My friend? what to do? I am no married man, and thou canst not lie with my wife; I am very poor, and thou canst not borrow money of me; then what employment have I for a friend?

Tat. Ha! a good open speaker, and not to be trusted with a secret.

Ang. Do you know me, Valentine?

Val. Oh, very well.

Ang. Who am I?

Val. You're a woman,—one to whom Heaven gave beauty, when it grafted roses on a briar. You are the reflection of Heaven in a pond, and he that leaps at you is sunk. You are all white, a sheet of lovely, spotless paper, when you first are born; but you are to be scrawled and blotted by every goose's quill. I know you; for I loved a woman, and loved her so long, that I found out a strange thing; I found out what a woman was good for.

Tat. Ay, prithee, what's that?

Val. Why, to keep a secret.

Tat. O Lord!

Val. O, exceeding good to keep a secret: for though she should tell, yet she is not to be believed.

Tat. Ha! good again, faith.

Val. I would have music.—Sing me the song that I like.

SONG.

I tell thee, Charmion, could I time retrieve,
And could again begin to love and live,
To you I should my earliest offering give;

I know, my eyes would lead my heart to you,
And I should all my vows and oaths renew;
But, to be plain, I never would be true.

For by our weak and weary truth I find,
Love hates to centre in a point assigned;
But runs with joy the circle of the mind:

Then never let us chain what should be free,
But for relief of either sex agree:
Since women love to change, and so do we.

Val. No more, for I am melancholy.   [*Walks musing.*

Jer. [*Aside to* SCANDAL.] I'll do't, sir.

Scan. Mr. Foresight, we had best leave him. He may grow outrageous, and do mischief.

Fore. I will be directed by you.

Jer. [*Aside to* Mrs. FRAIL.] You'll meet, madam? I'll take care everything shall be ready.

Mrs. Frail. Thou shalt do what thou wilt; in short, I will deny thee nothing.

Tat. [*To* ANGELICA.] Madam, shall I wait upon you?

Ang. No, I'll stay with him; Mr. Scandal will protect me.— Aunt, Mr. Tattle desires you would give him leave to wait on you.

Tat. [*Aside*.] Pox on't! there's no coming off, now she has said that.—[*Aloud*.] Madam, you will do me the honour?

Mrs. Fore. Mr. Tattle might have used less ceremony.

[*Exeunt* FORESIGHT, Mrs. FRAIL, Mrs. FORESIGHT, and TATTLE.

Scan. Jeremy, follow Tattle.   [*Exit* JEREMY

Ang. Mr. Scandal, I only stay till my maid comes, and because I had a mind to be rid of Mr. Tattle.

Scan. Madam, I am very glad that I overheard a better reason, which you gave to Mr. Tattle; for his impertinence forced you to acknowledge a kindness for Valentine which you denied to all his sufferings and my solicitations. So I'll leave him to make use of the discovery, and your ladyship to the free confession of your inclinations.

Ang. Oh Heavens! you won't leave me alone with a madman?

Scan. No, madam, I only leave a madman to his remedy.

[*Exit* SCANDAL

Val. Madam, you need not be very much afraid, for I fancy I begin to come to myself.

Ang. [*Aside*.] Ay, but if I don't fit you, I'll be hanged.

Val. You see what disguises love makes us put on: gods have been in counterfeited shapes for the same reason; and the divine part of me, my mind, has worn this mask of madness, and this motley livery, only as the slave of love, and menial creature of your beauty.

Ang. Mercy on me, how he talks! poor Valentine!

Val. Nay, faith, now let us understand one another, hypocrisy apart.—The comedy draws toward an end, and let us think of leaving acting, and be ourselves; and since you have loved me, you must own, I have at length deserved you should confess it.

Ang. [*Sighs*.] I would I had loved you!—for Heaven knows I pity you; and could I have foreseen the bad effects, I would have striven; but that's too late.   [*Sighs*

Val. What bad effects?—what's too late? My seeming madness has deceived my father, and procured me time to think of means to reconcile me to him, and preserve the right of my inheritance to his estate; which otherwise by articles I must this morning have resigned: and this I had informed you of to-day, but you were gone, before I knew you had been here.

Ang. How! I thought your love of me had caused this transport in your soul; which it seems you only counterfeited, for mercenary ends and sordid interest!

Val. Nay, now you do me wrong; for if any interest was

:onsidered it was yours; since I thought I wanted more than
ove to make me worthy of you.

Ang. Then you thought me mercenary.—But how am I deluded
)y this interval of sense, to reason with a madman!

Val. Oh, 'tis barbarous to misunderstand me longer.

Enter JEREMY.

Ang. Oh, here's a reasonable creature—sure he will not have
he impudence to persevere.—Come, Jeremy, acknowledge your
rick, and confess your master's madness counterfeit.

Jer. Counterfeit, madam! I'll maintain him to be as abso-
utely and substantially mad as any freeholder in Bethlehem;
1ay, he's as mad as any projector, fanatic, chemist, lover, or
)oet in Europe.

Val. Sirrah, you lie! I am not mad.

Ang. Ha! ha! ha! you see he denies it.

Jer. O Lord, madam, did you ever know any madman mad
:nough to own it?

Val. Sot, can't you comprehend?

Ang. Why, he talked very sensible just now.

Jer. Yes, madam, he has intervals; but you see he begins
:o look wild again now.

Val. Why, you thick-skulled rascal, I tell you the farce is
lone, and I will be mad no longer.   [*Beats him.*

Ang. Ha! ha! ha! is he mad or no, Jeremy?

Jer. Partly I think—for he does not know his own mind two
1ours.—I'm sure I left him just now in the humour to be mad;
1nd I think I have not found him very quiet at this present!—
[*Knocking at the door.*] Who's there?

Val. Go see, you sot.—[*Exit* JEREMY.] I'm very glad that I
:an move your mirth, though not your compassion.

Ang. I did not think you had apprehension enough to be ex-
:eptious: but madmen show themselves most, by over-pretending
:o a sound understanding; as drunken men do by over-acting
;obriety. I was half-inclining to believe you, till I accidentally
:ouched upon your tender part; but now you have restored me
:o my former opinion and compassion.

Re-enter JEREMY.

Jer. Sir, your father has sent to know if you are any better
yet.—Will you please to be mad, sir, or how?

Val. Stupidity! you know the penalty of all I'm worth must
)ay for the confession of my senses; I'm mad, and will be mad
:o everybody but this lady.

Jer. So;—Just the very backside of truth.—But lying is a figure in speech, that interlards the greatest part of my conversation.—Madam, your ladyship's woman. [*Exit.*

Enter JENNY.

Ang. Well, have you been there?—Come hither.

Jen. [*Aside to* ANGELICA.] Yes, madam, Sir Sampson will wait upon you presently.

Val. You are not leaving me in this uncertainty?

Ang. Would anything but a madman complain of uncertainty? Uncertainty and expectation are the joys of life. Security is an insipid thing, and the overtaking and possessing of a wish, discovers the folly of the chase. Never let us know one another better: for the pleasure of a masquerade is done, when we come to show our faces; but I'll tell you two things before I leave you; I am not the fool you take me for; and you are mad, and don't know it. [*Exeunt* ANGELICA *and* JENNY.

Val. From a riddle you can expect nothing but a riddle. There's my instruction, and the moral of my lesson.

Re-enter JEREMY.

Jer. What, is the lady gone again, sir? I hope you understood one another before she went?

Val. Understood! she is harder to be understood than a piece of Egyptian antiquity, or an Irish manuscript; you may pore till you spoil your eyes, and not improve your knowledge.

Jer. I have heard 'em say, sir, they read hard Hebrew books backwards; may be you begin to read at the wrong end.

Val. They say so of a witch's prayer: and dreams and Dutch almanacs are to be understood by contraries. But there's regularity and method in that; she is a medal without a reverse or inscription, for indifference has both sides alike. Yet while she does not seem to hate me, I will pursue her, and know her if it be possible, in spite of the opinion of my satirical friend, Scandal, who says,

> That women are like tricks by sleight of hand,
> Which, to admire, we should not understand.

[*Exeunt.*

ACT THE FIFTH

Scene I

A Room in Foresight's *House*

Enter Angelica *and* Jenny.

Ang. Where is Sir Sampson? did you not tell me he would be here before me?

Jen. He's at the great glass in the dining-room, madam, setting his cravat and wig.

Ang. How! I'm glad on't.—If he has a mind I should like him, it's a sign he likes me; and that's more than half my design.

Jen. I hear him, madam.

Ang. Leave me; and d'ye hear, if Valentine should come or send, I am not to be spoken with.   [*Exit* Jenny.

Enter Sir Sampson.

Sir Samp. I have not been honoured with the commands of a fair lady, a great while:—odd, madam, you have revived me! —not since I was five-and-thirty.

Ang. Why, you have no great reason to complain, Sir Sampson, that is not long ago.

Sir Samp. Zooks, but it is, madam, a very great while to a man that admires a fine woman as much as I do.

Ang. You're an absolute courtier, Sir Sampson.

Sir Samp. Not at all, madam; odsbud you wrong me; I am not so old neither to be a bare courtier, only a man of words: odd, I have warm blood about me yet, and can serve a lady any way.—Come, come, let me tell you, you women think a man old too soon, faith and troth, you do!—Come, don't despise fifty; odd, fifty, in a hale constitution, is no such contemptible age.

Ang. Fifty a contemptible age! not at all, a very fashionable age, I think.—I assure you, I know very considerable beaux that set a good face upon fifty:—fifty! I have seen fifty in a side-box, by candle-light, out-blossom five-and-twenty.

Sir Samp. Outsides, outsides; a pize take 'em, mere outsides! hang your side-box beaux; no, I'm none of those, none of your forced trees, that pretend to blossom in the fall, and bud when they should bring forth fruit; I am of a long-lived race, and inherit vigour: none of my ancestors married till fifty; yet they begot sons and daughters till fourscore; I am of your patriarchs, I, a branch of one of your antediluvian families, fellows that the flood could not wash away. Well, madam, what are your com-

mands? has any young rogue affronted you, and shall I cut hi
throat? or—

Ang. No, Sir Sampson, I have no quarrel upon my hands—
I have more occasion for your conduct than your courage at thi
time. To tell the truth, I'm weary of living single, and want
husband.

Sir Samp. Odsbud, and 'tis pity you should!—[*Aside.*] Odo
would she would like me, then I should hamper my youn
rogues: odd, would she would; faith and troth she's devilis
handsome!—[*Aloud.*] Madam, you deserve a good husbanc
and 'twere pity you should be thrown away upon any of thes
young idle rogues about the town. Odd, there's ne'er a youn
fellow worth hanging!—that is a very young fellow.—Pize o
'em! they never think beforehand of anything;—and if the
commit matrimony, 'tis as they commit murder; out of a frolic
and are ready to hang themselves, or to be hanged by the law
the next morning:—odso, have a care, madam.

Ang. Therefore I ask your advice, Sir Sampson: I have fortun
enough to make any man easy that I can like; if there were sucl
a thing as a young agreeable man with a reasonable stock o
good-nature and sense.—For I would neither have an absolute
wit nor a fool.

Sir Samp. Odd, you are hard to please, madam; to find a
young fellow that is neither a wit in his own eye, nor a fool ir
the eye of the world, is a very hard task. But, faith and troth
you speak very discreetly; for I hate both a wit and a fool.

Ang. She that marries a fool, Sir Sampson, forfeits the reputa
tion of her honesty or understanding: and she that marries a very
witty man is a slave to the severity and insolent conduct of her
husband. I should like a man of wit for a lover, because I would
have such a one in my power; but I would no more be his wife
than his enemy. For his malice is not a more terrible conse
quence of his aversion than his jealousy is of his love.

Sir Samp. None of old Foresight's Sibyls ever uttered such a
truth. Odsbud, you have won my heart! I hate a wit; I had a
son that was spoiled among 'em; a good hopeful lad, till he
learned to be a wit—and might have risen in the state.—But a
pox on't! his wit run him out of his money, and now his poverty
has run him out of his wits.

Ang. Sir Sampson, as your friend, I must tell you, you are very
much abused in that matter: he's no more mad than you are.

Sir Samp. How, madam! would I could prove it!

Ang. I can tell you how that may be done.—But it is a thing that would make me appear to be too much concerned in your affairs.

Sir Samp. [*Aside.*] Odsbud, I believe she likes me! [*Aloud.*] Ah, madam, all my affairs are scarce worthy to be laid at your feet; and I wish, madam, they were in a better posture, that I might make a more becoming offer to a lady of your incomparable beauty and merit.—If I had Peru in one hand, and Mexico in t'other, and the eastern empire under my feet, it would make me only a more glorious victim to be offered at the shrine of your beauty.

Ang. Bless me, Sir Sampson, what's the matter?

Sir Samp. Odd, madam, I love you!—and if you would take my advice in a husband—

Ang. Hold, hold, Sir Sampson. I asked your advice for a husband, and you are giving me your consent.—I was indeed thinking to propose something like it in jest, to satisfy you about Valentine: for if a match were seemingly carried on between you and me, it would oblige him to throw off his disguise of madness, in apprehension of losing me: for you know he has long pretended a passion for me.

Sir Samp. Gadzooks, a most ingenious contrivance!—if we were to go through with it. But why must the match only be seemingly carried on?—Odd, let it be a real contract.

Ang. O fy, Sir Sampson! what would the world say?

Sir Samp. Say! they would say you were a wise woman and I a happy man. Odd, madam, I'll love you as long as I live, and leave you a good jointure when I die.

Ang. Ay; but that is not in your power, Sir Sampson; for when Valentine confesses himself in his senses, he must make over his inheritance to his younger brother.

Sir Samp. Odd, you're cunning, a wary baggage! faith and troth, I like you the better.—But, I warrant you, I have a proviso in the obligation in favour of myself.—Body o' me, I have a trick to turn the settlement upon issue male of our two bodies begotten. Odsbud, let us find children, and I'll find an estate.

Ang. Will you? well, do you find the estate, and leave the other to me.

Sir Samp. O rogue! but I'll trust you. And will you consent! is it a match then?

Ang. Let me consult my lawyer concerning this obligation; and if I find what you propose practicable, I'll give you my answer.

Sir Samp. With all my heart: come in with me, and I'll lend you the bond.—You shall consult your lawyer, and I'll consult a parson. Odzooks, I'm a young man: odzooks, I'm a young man, and I'll make it appear. Odd, you're devilish handsome: faith and troth, you're very handsome; and I'm very young, and very lusty. Odsbud, hussy, you know how to choose, and so do I;—odd, I think we are very well met. Give me your hand, odd, let me kiss it; 'tis as warm and as soft—as what?—Odd, as t'other hand; give me t'other hand, and I'll mumble 'em and kiss 'em till they melt in my mouth.

Ang. Hold, Sir Sampson: you're profuse of your vigour before your time: you'll spend your estate before you come to it.

Sir Samp. No, no, only give you a rent-roll of my possessions, —ha! baggage!—I warrant you for little Sampson: odd, Sampson's a very good name for an able fellow: your Sampsons were strong dogs from the beginning.

Ang. Have a care, and don't overact your part. If you remember, Sampson, the strongest of the name, pulled an old house over his head at last.

Sir Samp. Say you so, hussy? Come, let's go then; odd, I long to be pulling too, come away.—Odso, here's somebody coming.

[*Exeunt.*

Scene II

The same

Enter Tattle *and* Jeremy.

Tat. Is not that she, gone out just now?

Jer. Ay, sir, she's just going to the place of appointment. Ah, sir, if you are not very faithful and close in this business, you'll certainly be the death of a person that has a most extraordinary passion for your honour's service.

Tat. Ay, who's that?

Jer. Even my unworthy self, sir. Sir, I have had an appetite to be fed with your commands a great while; and now, sir, my former master having much troubled the fountain of his understanding, it is a very plausible occasion for me to quench my thirst at the spring of your bounty. I thought I could not recommend myself better to you, sir, than by the delivery of a great beauty and fortune into your arms, whom I have heard you sigh for.

Tat. I'll make thy fortune; say no more. Thou art a pretty fellow, and canst carry a message to a lady, in a pretty soft kind of phrase, and with a good persuading accent.

Jer. Sir, I have the seeds of rhetoric and oratory in my head; I have been at Cambridge.

Tat. Ay! 'tis well enough for a servant to be bred at a university:

but the education is a little too pedantic for a gentleman. I hope you are secret in your nature, private, close, ha?

Jer. O sir, for that, sir, 'tis my chief talent: I'm as secret as the head of Nilus.

Tat. Ay! who is he, though? a privy counsellor?

Jer. [*Aside.*] O ignorance!—[*Aloud.*] A cunning Egyptian, sir, that with his arms would overrun the country: yet nobody could ever find out his headquarters.

Tat. Close dog! a good whoremaster, I warrant him. The time draws nigh, Jeremy. Angelica will be veiled like a nun; and I must be hooded like a friar; ha, Jeremy?

Jer. Ay, sir, hooded like a hawk, to seize at first sight upon the quarry. It is the whim of my master's madness to be so dressed; and she is so in love with him, she'll comply with anything to please him. Poor lady, I'm sure she'll have reason to pray for me, when she finds what a happy exchange she has made, between a madman and so accomplished a gentleman.

Tat. Ay, faith, so she will, Jeremy; you're a good friend to her, poor creature. I swear I do it hardly so much in consideration of myself as compassion to her.

Jer. 'Tis an act of charity, sir, to save a fine woman with thirty thousand pounds, from throwing herself away.

Tat. So 'tis, faith. I might have saved several others in my time; but egad, I could never find in my heart to marry anybody before.

Jer. Well, sir, I'll go and tell her my master is coming; and meet you in half a quarter of an hour, with your disguise, at your own lodgings. You must talk a little madly, she won't distinguish the tone of your voice.

Tat. No, no, let me alone for a counterfeit; I'll be ready for you.

[*Exit* JEREMY.

Enter Miss PRUE.

Prue. O Mr. Tattle, are you here! I'm glad I have found you; I have been looking up and down for you like anything, 'till I am as tired as anything in the world.

Tat. [*Aside.*] O pox, how shall I get rid of this foolish girl!

Prue. O I have pure news, I can tell you, pure news. I must not marry the seaman now—my father says so. Why won't you be my husband? you say you love me, and you won't be my husband. And I know you may be my husband now if you please.

Tat. O fy, miss! who told you so, child?

Prue. Why, my father. I told him that you loved me.

Tat. O fy, miss! why did you do so? and who told you so, child?

Prue. Who! why, you did; did not you?

Tat. O pox! that was yesterday, miss, that was a great while ago, child. I have been asleep since; slept a whole night, and did not so much as dream of the matter.

Prue. Pshaw! O but I dreamt that it was so though.

Tat. Ay, but your father will tell you that dreams come by contraries, child. O fy! what, we must not love one another now—pshaw, that would be a foolish thing indeed! Fy! fy! you're a woman now, and must think of a new man every morning, and forget him every night.—No, no, to marry is to be a child again, and play with the same rattle always; O fy! marrying is a paw thing.

Prue. Well, but don't you love me as well as you did last night then?

Tat. No, no, child, you would not have me.

Prue. No! yes, but I would though.

Tat. Pshaw! but I tell you, you would not—You forget you're a woman, and don't know your own mind.

Prue. But here's my father, and he knows my mind.

Enter FORESIGHT.

Fore. O, Mr. Tattle, your servant, you are a close man; but methinks your love to my daughter was a secret I might have been trusted with; or had you a mind to try if I could discover it by my art? Hum, ha! I think there is something in your physiognomy that has a resemblance of her; and the girl is like me.

Tat. And so you would infer, that you and I are alike?— [*Aside.*] What does the old prig mean? I'll banter him, and laugh at him, and leave him.—[*Aloud.*] I fancy you have a wrong notion of faces.

Fore. How? what? a wrong notion! how so?

Tat. In the way of art: I have some taking features, not obvious to vulgar eyes; that are indications of a sudden turn of good fortune in the lottery of wives; and promise a great beauty and great fortune reserved alone for me, by a private intrigue of destiny kept secret from the piercing eye of perspicuity; from all astrologers and the stars themselves.

Fore. How? I will make it appear that what you say is impossible.

Tat. Sir, I beg your pardon, I'm in haste—

Fore. For what?

Tat. To be married, sir, married.

Fore. Ay, but pray take me along with you,[1] sir—

Tat. No, sir: 'tis to be done privately. I never make confidants

---

[1] *i.e.* Let me understand you.

Fore. Well, but my consent, I mean.—You won't marry my daughter without my consent.

Tat. Who, I, sir? I'm an absolute stranger to you and your daughter, sir.

Fore. Heyday! what time of the moon is this?

Tat. Very true, sir, and desire to continue so. I have no more love for your daughter than I have likeness of you; and I have a secret in my heart, which you would be glad to know, and shan't know; and yet you shall know it too, and be sorry for it afterwards. I'd have you to know, sir, that I am as knowing as the stars, and as secret as the night. And I'm going to be married just now, yet did not know of it half an hour ago; and the lady stays for me, and does not know of it yet. There's a mystery for you!— I know you love to untie difficulties—or if you can't solve this, stay here a quarter of an hour, and I'll come and explain it to you.

[*Exit.*

Prue. O father, why will you let him go? won't you make him to be my husband?

Fore. Mercy on us! what do these lunacies portend?—Alas, he's mad, child, stark wild.

Prue. What, and must not I have e'er a husband then? What, must I go to bed to nurse again, and be a child as long as she's an old woman? Indeed but I won't; for now my mind is set upon a man, I will have a man some way or other. Oh! methinks I'm sick when I think of a man; and if I can't have one I would go to sleep all my life: for when I'm awake it makes me wish and long, and I don't know for what:—and I'd rather be always asleep, than sick with thinking.

Fore. O fearful! I think the girl's influenced too.—Hussy, you shall have a rod.

Prue. A fiddle of a rod! I'll have a husband: and if you won't get me one I'll get one for myself. I'll marry our Robin the butler; he says he loves me, and he's a handsome man, and shall be my husband: I warrant he'll be my husband, and thank me too, for he told me so.

Enter SCANDAL, MRS. FORESIGHT, *and* Nurse.

Fore. Did he so? I'll dispatch him for it presently; rogue!—Oh, nurse, come hither.

Nurse. What is your worship's pleasure?

Fore. Here take your young mistress, and lock her up presently, till farther orders from me.—Not a word, hussy. Do what I bid you; no reply; away! And bid Robin make ready to give an account of his plate and linen, d'ye hear: begone when I bid you.

Mrs. Fore. What is the matter, husband?

Fore. 'Tis not convenient to tell you now.—Mr. Scandal, heaven keep us all in our senses!—I fear there is a contagious frenzy abroad. How does Valentine?

Scan. O, I hope he will do well again:—I have a message from him to your niece Angelica.

Fore. I think she has not returned since she went abroad with Sir Sampson.—Nurse, why are you not gone? [*Exit* Nurse

Enter BEN.

Mrs. Fore. Here's Mr. Benjamin; he can tell us if his father be come home.

Ben. Who, father? ay, he's come home with a vengeance.

Mrs. Fore. Why, what's the matter?

Ben. Matter! why, he's mad.

Fore. Mercy on us! I was afraid of this.

Ben. And there's the handsome young woman, she, as they say, brother Val went mad for, she's mad too, I think.

Fore. O my poor niece, my poor niece, is she gone too? Well, I shall run mad next.

Mrs. Fore. Well, but how mad? how d'ye mean?

Ben. Nay, I'll give you leave to guess:—I'll undertake to make a voyage to Antegoa—no, hold, I mayn't say so neither—but I'll sail as far as Leghorn, and back again, before you shall guess at the matter, and do nothing else; mess, you may take in all the points of the compass and not hit right.

Mrs. Fore. Your experiment will take up a little too much time.

Ben. Why then I'll tell you: there's a new wedding upon the stocks, and they two are a-going to be married to-night.

Scan. Who?

Ben. My father, and—the young woman. I can't hit of her name.

Scan. Angelica?

Ben. Ay, the same.

Mrs. Fore. Sir Sampson and Angelica: impossible!

Ben. That may be—but I'm sure it is as I tell you.

Scan. 'Sdeath, it's a jest! I can't believe it.

Ben. Look you, friend, it's nothing to me whether you believe it or no. What I say is true, d'ye see; they are married, or just going to be married, I know not which.

Fore. Well, but they are not mad, that is not lunatic?

Ben. I don't know what you may call madness; but she's mad for a husband, and he's horn mad, I think, or they'd ne'er make a match together.—Here they come.

Enter Sir SAMPSON, ANGELICA, *and* BUCKRAM.

Sir Samp. Where is this old soothsayer? this uncle of mine elect?—Aha! old Foresight, Uncle Foresight, wish me joy, Uncle Foresight, double joy, both as uncle and astrologer; here's a conjunction that was not foretold in all your Ephemeris. The brightest star in the blue firmament—is *shot from above in a jelly of love,* and so forth; and I'm lord of the ascendant. Odd, you're an old fellow, Foresight, uncle I mean; a very old fellow, Uncle Foresight; and yet you shall live to dance at my wedding, faith and troth you shall. Odd, we'll have the music of the spheres for thee, old Lilly, that we will, and thou shalt lead up a dance *in via lactea!*

Fore. I'm thunderstruck!—You are not married to my niece?

Sir Samp. Not absolutely married, uncle; but very near it, within a kiss of the matter, as you see.   [*Kisses* ANGELICA.

Ang. 'Tis very true, indeed, uncle; I hope you'll be my father, and give me.

Sir Samp. That he shall, or I'll burn his globes. Body o' me, he shall be thy father, I'll make him thy father, and thou shalt make me a father, and I'll make thee a mother, and we'll beget sons and daughters enough to put the weekly bills out of countenance.

Scan. Death and hell! where's Valentine?   [*Exit.*

Mrs. Fore. This is so surprising—

Sir Samp. How! what does my aunt say? Surprising, aunt! not at all, for a young couple to make a match in winter: not at all.—It's a plot to undermine cold weather, and destroy that usurper of a bed called a warming-pan.

Mrs. Fore. I'm glad to hear you have so much fire in you, Sir Sampson.

Ben. Mess, I fear his fire's little better than tinder: mayhap it will only serve to light up a match for somebody else. The young woman's a handsome young woman, I can't deny it; but, father, if I might be your pilot in this case, you should not marry her. It's just the same thing, as if so be you should sail so far as the Straits without provision.

Sir Samp. Who gave you authority to speak, sirrah? To your element, fish! be mute, fish, and to sea! rule your helm, sirrah, don't direct me.

Ben. Well, well, take you care of your own helm, or you mayn't keep your new vessel steady.

Sir Samp. Why, you impudent tarpaulin! sirrah, do you bring your forecastle jests upon your father? but I shall be even with you, I won't give you a groat.—Mr. Buckram, is the conveyance so worded that nothing can possibly descend to this scoundrel? I would not so much as have him have the prospect of an estate;

though there were no way to come to it but by the north-east passage.

Buck. Sir, it is drawn according to your directions, there is not the least cranny of the law unstopped.

Ben. Lawyer, I believe there's many a cranny and leak unstopped in your conscience.—If so-be that one had a pump to your bosom, I believe we should discover a foul hold. They say a witch will sail in a sieve,—but I believe the devil would not venture aboard o' your conscience. And that's for you.

Sir Samp. Hold your tongue, sirrah!—How now? who's here?

Enter TATTLE *and* Mrs. FRAIL.

Mrs. Frail. O sister, the most unlucky accident!

Mrs. Fore. What's the matter?

Tat. Oh, the two most unfortunate poor creatures in the world we are!

Fore. Bless us! how so?

Mrs. Frail. Ah, Mr. Tattle and I, poor Mr. Tattle and I are—I can't speak it out.

Tat. Nor I—but poor Mrs. Frail and I are—

Mrs. Frail. Married.

Mrs. Fore. Married! How?

Tat. Suddenly—before we knew where we were—that villain Jeremy, by the help of disguises, tricked us into one another.

Fore. Why, you told me just now, you went hence in haste to be married.

Ang. But I believe Mr. Tattle meant the favour to me: I thank him.

Tat. I did, as I hope to be saved, madam; my intentions were good.—But this is the most cruel thing, to marry one does not know how, nor why, nor wherefore.—The devil take me if ever I was so much concerned at anything in my life!

Ang. 'Tis very unhappy, if you don't care for one another.

Tat. The least in the world;—that is, for my part; I speak for myself. Gad, I never had the least thought of serious kindness:—I never liked anybody less in my life. Poor woman! gad, I'm sorry for her, too; for I have no reason to hate her neither; but I believe I shall lead her a damned sort of life.

Mrs. Fore. [*Aside to* Mrs. FRAIL.] He's better than no husband at all—though he's a coxcomb.

Mrs. Frail. [*Aside to* Mrs. FORESIGHT.] Ay, ay, it's well it's no worse.—[*Aloud.*] Nay, for my part I always despised Mr. Tattle of all things; nothing but his being my husband could have made me like him less.

Tat. Look you there, I thought as much!—Pox on't, I wish we could keep it secret! why, I don't believe any of this company would speak of it.

Mrs. Frail. But, my dear, that's impossible; the parson and that rogue Jeremy will publish it.

Tat. Ay, my dear, so they will, as you say.

Ang. O you'll agree very well in a little time; custom will make it easy to you.

Tat. Easy! pox on't! I don't believe I shall sleep to-night.

Sir Samp. Sleep, quotha! no; why you would not sleep o' your wedding night! I'm an older fellow than you, and don't mean to sleep.

Ben. Why, there's another match now, as tho'f a couple of privateers were looking for a prize, and should fall foul of one another. I'm sorry for the young man with all my heart. Look you, friend, if I may advise you, when she's going, for that you must expect, I have experience of her, when she's going, let her go. For no matrimony is tough enough to hold her, and if she can't drag her anchor along with her, she'll break her cable, I can tell you that.—Who's here? the madman?

Enter VALENTINE, SCANDAL, *and* JEREMY.

Val. No; here's the fool; and, if occasion be, I'll give it under my hand.

Sir Samp. How now!

Val. Sir, I'm come to acknowledge my errors, and ask your pardon.

Sir Samp. What, have you found your senses at last then? in good time, sir.

Val. You were abused, sir, I never was distracted.

Fore. How, not mad! Mr. Scandal?

Scan. No, really, sir; I'm his witness, it was all counterfeit.

Val. I thought I had reasons.—But it was a poor contrivance; the effect has shown it such.

Sir Samp. Contrivance! what, to cheat me? to cheat your father? sirrah, could you hope to prosper?

Val. Indeed, I thought, sir, when the father endeavoured to undo the son, it was a reasonable return of nature.

Sir Samp. Very good, sir!—Mr. Buckram, are you ready?— [*To* VALENTINE.] Come, sir, will you sign and seal?

Val. If you please, sir; but first I would ask this lady one question.

Sir Samp. Sir, you must ask me leave first.—That lady! no, sir; you shall ask that lady no questions, till you have asked her blessing, sir; that lady is to be my wife.

Val. I have heard as much, sir; but I would have it from her own mouth.

Sir Samp. That's as much as to say, 'I lie, sir, and you don't believe what I say.

Val. Pardon me, sir. But I reflect that I very lately counterfeited madness; I don't know but the frolic may go round.

Sir Samp. Come, chuck, satisfy him, answer him.—Come, come Mr. Buckram, the pen and ink.

Buck. Here it is, sir, with the deed; all is ready.

[VALENTINE *goes to* ANGELICA

Ang. 'Tis true, you have a great while pretended love to me nay, what if you were sincere; still you must pardon me, if I think my own inclinations have a better right to dispose of my person than yours.

Sir Samp. Are you answered now, sir?

Val. Yes, sir.

Sir Samp. Where's your plot, sir; and your contrivance now sir? Will you sign, sir? come, will you sign and seal?

Val. With all my heart, sir.

Scan. 'Sdeath, you are not mad indeed, to ruin yourself?

Val. I have been disappointed of my only hope; and he tha loses hope may part with anything. I never valued fortune, but a it was subservient to my pleasure; and my only pleasure was t please this lady; I have made many vain attempts, and find at las that nothing but my ruin can effect it; which, for that reason I wi sign to.—Give me the paper.

Ang. [*Aside.*] Generous Valentine!

Buck. Here is the deed, sir.

Val. But where is the bond, by which I am obliged to sign this

Buck. Sir Sampson, you have it.

Ang. No, I have it; and I'll use it, as I would everything that an enemy to Valentine. [*Tears the pape*

Sir Samp. How now!

Val. Ha!

Ang. [*To* VALENTINE.] Had I the world to give you, it coul not make me worthy of so generous and faithful a passion; here my hand, my heart was always yours, and struggled very hard make this utmost trial of your virtue.

Val. Between pleasure and amazement, I am lost.—But on n knees I take the blessing.

Sir Samp. Oons, what is the meaning of this?

Ben. Mess, here's the wind changed again! Father, you and I may make a voyage together now.

Ang. Well, Sir Sampson, since I have played you a trick, I'll advise you how you may avoid such another. Learn to be a good father, or you'll never get a second wife. I always loved your son, and hated your unforgiving nature. I was resolved to try him to the utmost; I have tried you too, and know you both. You have not more faults than he has virtues; and 'tis hardly more pleasure to me, that I can make him and myself happy, than that I can punish you.

Val. If my happiness could receive addition, this kind surprise would make it double.

Sir Samp. Oons, you're a crocodile!

Fore. Really, Sir Sampson, this is a sudden eclipse.

Sir Samp. You're an illiterate old fool, and I'm another! [*Exit.*

Tat. If the gentleman is in disorder for want of a wife, I can spare him mine.—[*To* JEREMY.] Oh, are you there, sir? I'm indebted to you for my happiness.

Jer. Sir, I ask you ten thousand pardons; 'twas an arrant mistake.—You see, sir, my master was never mad, or anything like it:—then how could it be otherwise?

Val. Tattle, I thank you, you would have interposed between me and Heaven; but Providence laid purgatory in your way:—you have but justice.

Scan. I hear the fiddles that Sir Sampson provided for his own wedding; methinks 'tis pity they should not be employed when the match is so much mended.—Valentine, though it be morning, we may have a dance.

Val. Anything, my friend, everything that looks like joy and transport.

Scan. Call 'em, Jeremy.   [*Exit* JEREMY.

Ang. I have done dissembling now, Valentine; and if that coldness which I have always worn before you, should turn to an extreme fondness, you must not suspect it.

Val. I'll prevent that suspicion:—for I intend to dote to that immoderate degree, that your fondness shall never distinguish itself enough to be taken notice of. If ever you seem to love too much, it must be only when I can't love enough.

Ang. Have a care of promises; you know you are apt to run more in debt than you are able to pay.

Val. Therefore I yield my body as your prisoner, and make your best on't.

Re-enter JEREMY.

Jer. The music stays for you.   [*A dance.*

Scan. Well, madam, you have done exemplary justice, in punishing an inhuman father, and rewarding a faithful lover: but
there is a third good work, which I, in particular, must thank you
for; I was an infidel to your sex, and you have converted me.—
For now I am convinced that all women are not like Fortune, blind
in bestowing favours, either on those who do not merit, or who do
not want 'em.

Ang. 'Tis an unreasonable accusation, that you lay upon our
sex: you tax us with injustice, only to cover your own want of
merit. You would all have the reward of love; but few have the
constancy to stay till it becomes your due. Men are generally hypo-
crites and infidels, they pretend to worship, but have neither zeal
nor faith: how few, like Valentine, would persevere even to mar-
tyrdom, and sacrifice their interest to their constancy! In admiring
me you misplace the novelty:—

                The miracle to-day is, that we find
                A lover true: not that a woman's kind.

                                        [*Exeunt omnes.*

EPILOGUE

SURE Providence at first designed this place
To be the player's refuge in distress;
For still in every storm they all run hither,
As to a shed that shields 'em from the weather.
But thinking of this change which last befel us,
It's like what I have heard our poets tell us:
For when behind our scenes their suits are pleading,
To help their love sometimes they show their reading;
And wanting ready cash to pay for hearts,
They top their learning on us and their parts.
Once of philosophers they told us stories,
Whom, as I think, they called—Py—Pythagories;—
I'm sure 'tis some such *Latin* name they give 'em,
And we, who know no better, must believe 'em.
Now to these men (say they) such souls were given,
That after death ne'er went to hell nor heaven,
But lived, I know not how, in beasts; and then,
When many years were passed, in men again.
Methinks, we players resemble such a soul;
That does from bodies, we from houses stroll.
Thus Aristotle's soul, of old that was,
May now be damned to animate an ass;
Or in this very house, for aught we know,
Is doing painful penance in some beau:
And thus, our audience, which did once resort
To shining theatres to see our sport,
Now find us tossed into a tennis-court.
These walls but t'other day were filled with noise
Of roaring gamesters, and your *damn-me* boys;
Then bounding balls and rackets they encompast,
And now they're filled with jests, and flights, and bombast!
I vow, I don't much like this transmigration,
Strolling from place to place by circulation;
Grant, Heaven, we don't return to our first station.

I know not what these think, but, for my part,
I can't reflect without an aching heart,
How we should end in our original, a cart.
But we can't fear, since you're so good to save us
That you have only set us up,—to leave us.
Thus from the past, we hope for future grace
I beg it———
And some here know I have a begging face.
Then pray continue this your kind behaviour.
For a clear stage won't do, without your favour.

THE PROVOK'D WIFE
by
JOHN VANBRUGH

PROLOGUE

Since 'tis the Intent and Business of the Stage,
To Coppy out the Follies of the Age;
To hold to every Man a Faithful Glass,
And shew him of what Species he's an Ass:
I hope the next that teaches in the School,
Will shew our Author he's a scribling Fool.
And that the Satyr may be sure to Bite, ⎫
Kind Heav'n! Inspire some venom'd ⎬
     Priest to Write, ⎪
And grant some Ugly Lady may Indite. ⎭
For I wou'd have him lash'd, by Heav'ns! I would,
Till his presumption swam away in Blood.
Three Plays at once proclaims a Face of Brass, ⎫
No matter what they are! That's not the Case, ⎬
To Write three Plays, ev'n that's to be an Ass. ⎭
But what I least forgive, he knows it too,
For to his Cost he lately has known you.
Experience shews, to many a Writers smart,
You hold a Court where mercy ne're had part;
So much of the old Serpent's Sting you have,
You Love to Damn, as Heav'n Delights to Save.
In Foreign Parts, let a bold Voluntiere, ⎫
For publick Good upon the Stage appear, ⎬
He meets ten thousand Smiles to Dissi- ⎪
    pate his Fear. ⎭
All tickle on, th' adventuring young Beginner,
And only scourge th' incorrigible Sinner;
They touch indeed his Faults, but with a hand
So gentle, that his Merit still may stand:
Kindly they Buoy the Follies of his Pen,
That he may shun 'em when he Writes again.
But 'tis not so, in this good natur'd ⎫
    Town, ⎬
All's one, an Ox, a Poet, or a Crown; ⎬
Old England's play was always knock- ⎪
    ing Down. ⎭

345

DRAMATIS PERSONÆ

CONSTANT	Mr. Verbruggen
HEARTFREE	Mr. Hudson
SIR JOHN BRUTE	Mr. Betterton
TREBLE, *A Singing Master*	Mr. Bowman
RASOR, *Vallet de Chambre to Sir J. B.* . .	Mr. Bowen
JUSTICE OF THE PEACE	Mr. Bright
LORD RAKE ⎫	
COL. BULLY ⎭ *Companions to Sir J. B.*	
CONSTABLE *and* WATCH	
LADY BRUTE	Mrs. Barry
BELLINDA *her Neice*	Mrs. Bracegirdle
LADY FANCYFULL	Mrs. Bowman
MADAMOISELLE	Mrs. Willis
CORNET *and* PIPE, *Servants to Lady Fancyfull*	

THE PROVOK'D WIFE

ACT THE FIRST

Scene.—Sir John Brute's *House*

Enter Sir John, *solus.*

What cloying meat is Love,—when Matrimony's the Sauce to
t. Two years Marriage has debaucht my five Senses. Every thing
see, every thing I hear, every thing I feel, every thing I smell,
nd every thing I taste—methinks has Wife in't.

No Boy was ever so weary of his Tutor; no Girl of her Bib; no
Jun of doing Penance nor Old Maid of being Chast, as I am of be-
ng Married.

Sure there's a secret Curse entail'd upon the very Name of
Wife. My Lady is a young Lady, a fine Lady, a Witty Lady, a
Jirtuous Lady—and yet I hate her. There is but one thing on
Jarth I loath beyond her: That's fighting. Wou'd my Courage
ome up but to a fourth part of my Ill Nature, I'd stand buff to her
Relations, and thrust her out of Doors.

But Marriage has sunk me down to such an Ebb of Resolution,
dare not draw my Sword, tho' even to get rid of my Wife. But
ere she comes.

Enter Lady Brute.

Lady. Do you Dine at home to day, Sir John?

Sir Joh. Why, do you expect I shou'd tell you, what I don't know
ny self?

Lady. I thought there was no harm in asking you.

Sir Joh. If thinking wrong were an excuse for Impertinence,
Jomen might be justifi'd in most things they say or do.

Lady. I'm sorry I have said any thing to displease you.

Sir Joh. Sorrow for things past, is of as little Importance to me,
s my dining at home or abroad ought to be to you.

Lady B. My Enquiry was only that I might have provided what
ou lik'd.

Sir Joh. Six to four you had been in the wrong there again, for
hat I lik'd yesterday I don't like to day, and what I like to day,
is odds I mayn't like to morrow.

347

Lady B. But if I had ask'd you what you lik'd?

Sir Joh. Why then there would have been more asking about it, than the thing was worth.

Lady B. I wish I did but know how I might please you.

Sir Joh. Ay, but that sort of knowledge is not a Wife's Talent.

Lady B. What e'er my Talent is, I'm sure my Will has ever been to make you easie.

Sir Joh. If Women were to have their Wills, the World wou'd be finely govern'd.

Lady B. What reason have I given you to use me as you do of late? It once was otherwise: You married me for Love.

Sir Joh. And you me for Money: So you have your Reward, and I have mine.

Lady B. What is it that disturbs you?

Sir Joh. A Parson.

Lady B. Why, what has he done to you?

Sir Joh. He has married me.　　　　　　　　　[*Exit* SIR JOHN.

LADY BRUTE, *sola.*

The Devil's in the Fellow I think—I was told before I married him, that thus 'twou'd be. But I thought I had Charms enough to govern him; and that where there was an Estate, a Woman must needs be happy; so my Vanity has deceiv'd me, and my Ambition has made me uneasie. But some comfort still; if one wou'd be reveng'd of him, these are good times; a Woman may have a Gallant, and a separate maintenance too—The surly Puppy—yet he's a Fool for't: For hitherto he has been no Monster: But who knows how far he may provoke me? I never lov'd him, yet I have been ever true to him; and that, in spight of all the attacks of Art and Nature upon a poor weak Womans heart, in favour of a Tempting Lover.

Methinks so Noble a Defence as I have made, shou'd be rewarded with a better usage—Or who can tell?—Perhaps a good part of what I suffer from my Husband may be a Judgment upon me for my cruelty to my Lover.—Lord, with what pleasure cou'd I indulge that thought, were there but a possibility of finding Arguments to make it good.—And how do I know but there may?—Let me see—What opposes?—My Matrimonial Vow?—Why, what did I Vow? I think I promis'd to be true to my Husband.

Well; and he promis'd to be kind to me.

But he han't kept his Word—

Why then I'm so absolv'd from mine—ay, that seems clear to me. The Argument's good between the King and the People, why not between the Husband and the Wife? O, but that Condition was not exprest.—No matter, 'twas understood.

Well, by all I see, If I argue the matter a little longer with my self, I shan't find so many Bug-bears in the way, as I thought I shou'd: Lord, what fine notions of Virtue do we Women take up upon the Credit of old foolish Philosophers. Virtue's it's own reward, Virtue's this, Virtue's that;—Virtue's an Ass, and a Gallant's worth forty on't.

Enter BELLINDA.

Lady. Good-morrow, Dear Cousin.

Bel. Good-morrow, Madam; you look pleas'd this morning.

Lady. I am so.

Bel. With what, pray?

Lady. With my Husband.

Bel. Drown Husbands; for your's is a provoking Fellow: As he went out just now, I pray'd him to tell me what time of day 'twas: And he ask'd me if I took him for the Church Clock, that was Oblig'd to tell all the Parish.

Lady B. He has been saying some good obliging things to me too. In short, Bellinda, he has us'd me so barbarously of late, that I cou'd almost resolve to play the down-right Wife,—and Cuckold him.

Bel. That wou'd be down-right indeed.

Lady B. Why, after all, there's more to be said for't than you'd Imagine, Child. I know according to the Strict Statute Law of Religion, I shou'd do wrong: But if there were a Court of Chancery in Heaven, I'm sure I shou'd cast him.

Bel. If there were a House of Lords you might.

Lady B. In either I shou'd infallibly carry my Cause. Why, he is the first Agressor. Not I.

Bel. Ay, but you know, we must return Good for Evil.

Lady B. That may be a mistake in the Translation— Prethee be of my opinion, Bellinda; for I'm positive I'm in the right; and if you'll keep up the Prerogative of a Woman, you'll likewise be positive you are in the right, when ever you do any thing you have a mind to. But I shall play the fool, and jest on till I make you begin to think I'm in Earnest.

Bel. I sha'n't take the liberty, Madam, to think of any thing that you desire to keep a Secret from me.

Lady B. Alas, my Dear, I have no Secrets. My heart cou'd never yet confine my Tongue.

Bel. Your eyes you mean; for I am sure I have seen them gadding, when your Tongue has been lockt up safe enough.

Lady B. My eyes gadding? Prethee after who, Child?

Bel. Why, after one that thinks you hate him, as much as I know you love him.

Lady B. Constant you mean.

Bel. I do so.

Lady B. Lord, what shou'd put such a thing into your head?

Bel. That which puts things into most peoples Heads; Observation.

Lady B. Why, what have you observ'd, in the name of Wonder?

Bel. I have observ'd you blush when you meet him; force your self away from him; and then be out of humour with every thing about you: In a word, never was poor Creature so spurr'd on by desire, and so rein'd in with fear!

Lady B. How strong is Fancy!

Bel. How weak is Woman.

Lady B. Prethee, Neice, have a better opinion of your Aunt's Inclinations.

Bel. Dear Aunt, have a better opinion of your Neice's Understanding.

Lady B. You'll make me Angry.

Bel. You'll make me Laugh.

Lady B. Then you are resolv'd to persist?

Bel. Positively.

Lady B. And all I can say——

Bel. Will signifie nothing.

Lady B. Tho' I shou'd swear 'twere false——

Bel. I shou'd think it true.

Lady B. Then let us both forgive [*kissing her*] for we have both offended. I in making a Secret, you in discovering it.

Bel. Good nature may do much: But you have more reason to forgive one, than I have to pardon t'other.

Lady B. 'Tis true, Bellinda, you have given me so many proofs of your Friendship, that my reserve has been indeed a Crime: But that you may more easily forgive me, Remember, Child, that when our Nature prompts us to a thing, our Honour and Religion have forbid us. We wou'd (were't possible) conceal even from the Soul it self, the knowledge of the Bodies weakness.

Bel. Well, I hope, to make your Friend amends, you'll hide nothing from her for the future, tho' the Body shou'd still grow weaker and weaker.

Lady B. No, from this moment I have no more reserve; and for a proof of my Repentance, I own, Bellinda, I'm in danger. Merit and Wit assault me from without: Nature and Love solicite me within; my Husbands barbarous usage piques me to revenge; and

Sathan catching at the fair occasion, throws in my way that venge-ance, which of all Vengeance pleases Women best.

Bel. 'Tis well Constant don't know the weakness of the Fortifi-cations; for o'my Conscience he'd soon come on to the Assault.

Lady B. Ay, and I'm afraid carry the Town too. But whatever you may have observ'd, I have dissembled so well as to keep him Ignorant. So you see I'm no Coquet, Bellinda: And if you'll follow my advice you'll never be one neither. 'Tis true, Coquettry is one of the main ingredients in the natural Composition of a Woman, and I as well as others, cou'd be well enough pleas'd to see a Crowd of young Fellows, Ogling and Glancing and Watching all occasions to do forty foolish officious things: nay, shou'd some of 'em push on, even to Hanging or Drowning: Why— Faith—if I shou'd let pure Woman alone, I shou'd e'en be but too well pleas'd with't.

Bel. I'll swear 'twoud tickle me strangely.

Lady B. But after all, 'tis a Vicious practice in us, to give the least encouragement but where we design to come to a Conclusion. For 'tis an unreasonable thing, to engage a Man in a Disease which we before-hand resolve we never will apply a Cure to.

Bel. 'Tis true; but then a Woman must abandon one of the supream Blessings of her Life. For I am fully convinc'd, no Man has half that pleasure in possessing a Mistress, as a Woman has in jilting a Gallant.

Lady B. The Happiest Woman then on Earth must be our Neighbour.

Bel. O the Impertinent Composition; she has Vanity and Affec-tation enough to make her a Ridiculous Original, in spight of all that Art and Nature ever furnisht to any of her Sex before her.

Lady B. She concludes all Men her Captives; and whatever Course they take, it serves to confirm her in that opinion.

Bel. If they shun her, she thinks 'tis modesty, and takes it for a proof of their Passion.

Lady B. And if they are rude to her, 'tis Conduct, and done to prevent Town talk.

Bel. When her Folly makes 'em laugh, she thinks they are pleas'd with her Wit.

Lady B. And when her impertinence makes 'em Dull, Concludes they are jealous of her favours.

Bel. All their Actions and their Words, she takes for granted, aim at her.

Lady B. And pities all other Women, because she thinks they envy her.

Bel. Pray, out of pity to our selves, let us find a better Subject, for I am weary of this. Do you think your Husband inclin'd to Jealousie?

Lady B. O, no; he do's not love me well enough for that.

Lord, how wrong Men's Maxims are. They are seldom jealous of their Wives, unless they are very fond of 'em; whereas they ought to consider the Womans Inclinations, for there depends their Fate.

Well, Men may talk; but they are not so Wise as we—that's certain.

Bel. At least in our Affairs.

Lady B. Nay, I believe we shou'd out do 'em in the business of the State too: For me thinks they Do and Undo, and make but mad work on't.

Bel. Why then don't we get into the Intrigues of Government as well as they?

Lady B. Because we have Intrigues of our own, that make us more sport, Child. And so let's in and consider of 'em.   [*Exeunt.*

Scene.—*A Dressing Room*

Enter Lady Fancyfull, Madamoiselle, *and* Cornet.

Lady Fan. How do I look this morning?

Cor. Your Ladyship looks very ill, truly.

Lady Fan. Lard, how ill-natur'd thou art, Cornet, to tell me so, tho' the thing should be true. Don't you know that I have humility enough to be but too easily out of Conceit with my self? Hold the Glass; I dare swear that will have more manners than you have. Madamoiselle, let me have your opinion too.

Madam. My opinion pe, Matam, dat your Ladyship never look so well in your Life.

Lady Fan. Well, the French are the prettiest obliging People; they say the most acceptable, well manner'd things—and never flatter.

Madam. Your Ladyship say great Justice inteed.

Lady Fan. Nay, every thing's Just in my House but Cornet. The very Looking-Glass gives her the *Démenti.* But I'm almost afraid it flatters me, it makes me look so very engaging.

[*Looking affectedly in the Glass.*

Madam. Inteed, Matam, your Face pe hansomer den all de Looking-Glass in tee World, croyiez-moy.

Lady Fan. But is it possible my Eyes can be so languishing—and so very full of fire?

Madam. Matam, if de Glass was burning Glass, I believe your Eyes set de fire in de House.

Lady Fan. You may take that Night-Gown, Madamoiselle; get out of the Room, Cornet; I can't endure you. This Wench methinks does look so unsufferably ugly.   [*Exit* COR.

Madam. Every ting look ugly, Matam, dat stand by your Latiship.

Lady Fan. No really, Madamoiselle, methinks you look mighty prety.

Madam. Ah Matam; de Moon have no Eclat, ven de Sun appear.

Lady Fan. O pretty Expression. Have you ever been in Love, Madamoiselle?

Madam. Ouy, Matam.   [*Sighing.*

Lady Fan. And were you belov'd again?

Madam. No Matam.   [*Sighing.*

Lady Fan. O ye Gods, What an Unfortunate Creature should I be in such a Case. But nature has made me Nice for my own defence; I'm Nice, strangely Nice, Madamoiselle; I believe were the merit of whole mankind bestow'd upon one single Person, I should still think the Fellow wanted something, to make it worth my while to take notice of him: And yet I could Love; nay, fondly Love, were it possible to have a thing made on purpose for me: For I'm not cruel, Madamoiselle, I'm only Nice.

Madam. Ah Matam, I wish I was fine Gentelman for your sake. I do all de ting in de World to get leetel way into your heart. I make Song, I make Verse, I give you de Serenade, I give great many Present to Madamoiselle, I no eat, I no sleep, I be lean, I be mad, I hang my self, drown my self. Ah ma Chere Dame, Que je vous Aimerois.   [*Embracing her.*

Lady Fan. Well, the French have strange obliging ways with 'em; you may take those two pair of Gloves, Madamoiselle.

Madam. Me humbly tanke my sweet Lady.

Enter CORNET.

Cor. Madam, here's a Letter for your Ladyship by the Penny-post.

Lady Fan. Some new Conquest I'll warrant you. For without Vanity I look'd extreamly clear last night, when I went to the Park.

O agreeable. Here's a new Song made of me. And ready set too. O thou Welcome thing. [*Kissing it*] Call *Pipe* hither, she shall Sing it instantly.

Enter PIPE.

Here, Sing me this new Song, Pipe.

SONG

I

Fly, fly, you happy Shepherds, fly,
  Avoid Philira's *Charms;*
The rigour of her heart denies
  The Heaven that's in her Arms.
Ne'er hope to gaze and then retire,
  Nor yielding, to be blest:
Nature who form'd her Eyes of Fire,
  Of Ice Compos'd her Breast.

II

Yet, lovely Maid, this once believe
  A slave, whose Zeal you move:
The Gods Alas, your youth deceive;
  Their Heaven consists in Love.
In spight of all the thanks you owe,
  You may Reproach 'em this,
That where they did their Form bestow
  They have deny'd their Bliss.

Lady Fan. Well, there may be faults, Madamoiselle, but the Design is so very obliging, 'twou'd be a matchless Ingratitude in me to discover 'em.

Madam. Ma foy Matam, I tink de Gentelman's Song tell you de trute. If you never love, you never be Happy—Ah—que j' aime l' amour moy.

Enter SERVANT *with another Letter.*

Serv. Madam, here's another Letter for your Ladyship.

Lady Fan. 'Tis thus I am importun'd every morning, Madamoiselle. Pray how do the French Ladies when they are thus Accablées?

Madam. Matam, dey never Complain. Au Contraire. When one Frense Laty have got hundred Lover—Den she do all she can —to get hundred more.

Lady Fan. Well, strike me dead, I think they have Le gout bon. For 'tis an unutterable pleasure to be ador'd by all the Men, and envy'd by all the Women—Yet I'll swear I'm concerned at the Torture I give 'em. Lard, why was I form'd to make the whole Creation uneasy? But let me read my Letter.   [*Reads.*

"If you have a mind to hear of your faults, instead of being praised for your Virtues, take the pains to walk in the Green walk in St. James's with your Woman an hour hence. You'll there meet one, who hates you for some things, as he cou'd love you for Others, and therefore is willing to endeavour your Reformation.—If you come to the Place I mention, you'll know who I am; if you don't, you never shall, so take your Choice."

This is strangely Familiar, Madamoiselle; now have I a provoking Fancy to know who this Impudent fellow is.

Madam. Den take your Scarf and your Mask, and go to de Rendezvous. De Frense Laty do justement comme çaι

Lady Fan. Rendezvous! What, Rendezvous with a man, Madamoiselle.

Madam. Eh, pourquoy non?

Lady Fan. What? and a man perhaps I never saw in my Life?

Madam. Tant mieux: c'est donc quelque chose de nouveau.

Lady Fan. Why, how do I know what designs he may have? He may intend to Ravish me for ought I know.

Madam. Ravish?—Bagatelle. I would fain see one Impudent Rogue Ravish Madamoiselle; Ouy, je le voudrois.

Lady Fan. O but my Reputation, Madamoiselle, my Reputation, ah ma Chere Reputation.

Madam. Matam;—Quand on l' a une fois perdue—On n'en est plus embarassée.

Lady Fan. Fe Madamoiselle, Fe: Reputation is a Jewel.

Madam. Qui coute bien chere, Matam.

Lady Fan. Why sure you wou'd not Sacrifice your Honour to your Pleasure?

Madam. Je suis Philosophe.

Lady Fan. Bless me how you talk. Why what if Honour be a burden, Madamoiselle, must it not be borne?

Madam. Chaque un a sa façon—quand quelque chose m'incommode moy je m' en defais, Vite.

Lady Fan. Get you gone, you little naughty French woman you, I vow and swear I must turn you out of doors if you talk thus.

Madam. Turn me out of doors?—turn your self out of doors and go see what de Gentleman have to say to you—Tennez. Voila [*giving her her things hastily*] vostre Esharpe, Voila vostre Quoife, Voila vostre Masque, Voila tout.

Hey, Mercure, Coquin; Call one Chair for Matam, and one oder [*calling within*] for me, Va t'en Vite. [*Turning to her*

Lady and helping her on hastily with her things] Alons, Matam; depechez vous donc. Mon Dieu quelles scrupules.

Lady Fan. Well, for once, Madamoiselle I'll follow your Advice, out of the intemperate desire I have to know who this ill bred Fellow is. But I have too much Delicatesse, to make a Practice on it.

Madam. Belle chose Vraiment que la Delicatesse, lors qu'il 'agit de se devertir.—a ça—Vous Voila equipée, partons.—He bien!—qu'avez vous donc?

Lady Fan. J'ay peur.

Madam. J' n'en ay point moy.

Lady Fan. I dare not go.

Madam. Demeurez donc.

Lady Fan. Je suis Poltrone.

Madam. Tant pis pour Vous.

Lady Fan. Curiosity's a wicked Devil.

Madam. C'est une Charmante Sainte.

Lady Fan. It ruin'd our first Parents.

Madam. Elle a bien diverti leurs Enfants.

Lady Fan. L' honneur est contre.

Madam. Le plaisir est pour.

Lady Fan. Must I then go?

Madam. Must you go?—must you eat, must you drink, must you sleep, must you live? De nature bid you do one, de nature bid you do toder. Vous me ferez enrager.

Lady Fan. But when reason corrects nature, Madamoiselle.

Madam. Elle est donc bien Insolente, C'est sa sœur aisnée.

Lady Fan. Do you then prefer your nature to your reason, Madamoiselle?

Madam. Ouy da.

Lady Fan. Pourquoy?

Madam. Because my nature make me merry, my reason make me mad.

Lady Fan. Ah la Mechante Françoise.

Madam. Ah la Belle Angloise.   [*Forcing her Lady off.*

THE END OF THE FIRST ACT

ACT THE SECOND

Scene.—*St. James's Park*

Enter Lady Fancyfull *and* Madamoiselle.

Lady Fanc. Well, I vow, Madamoiselle, I'm strangely impatient to know who this confident Fellow is.

Enter Heartfree.

Look, there's Heartfree. But sure it can't be him; he's a profess'd Woman-hater. Yet who knows what my wicked Eyes may have done?

Madam. Il nous approche, Madame.

Lady Fanc. Yes, 'tis he: Now will he be most intolerably Cavalier, tho' he should be in love with me.

Heartf. Madam, I'm your humble Servant: I perceive you have more Humility and Good-nature than I thought you had.

Lady Fanc. What you attribute to Humility and Good-nature, Sir, may perhaps be only due to Curiosity. I had a mind to know who 'twas had ill manners enough to write that Letter.

[*Throwing him his Letter.*

Heartf. Well, and now, I hope, you are satisfied.

Lady Fanc. I am so, Sir; good b'w'y to ye.

Heartf. Nay, hold there; tho' you have done your Business, I han't done mine: By your Ladiship's leave, we must have one moments prattle together. Have you a mind to be the prettiest Woman about Town, or not? How she stares upon me! What! this passes for an impertinent Question with you now, because you think you are so already.

Lady Fanc. Pray Sir, let me ask you a Question in my turn: By what right do you pretend to examine me?

Heartf. By the same right that the Strong govern the Weak, because I have you in my power; for you cannot get so quickly to your Coach, but I shall have time enough to make you hear every thing I have to say to you.

Lady Fanc. These are strange Liberties you take, Mr. Heartfree.

Heartf. They are so, Madam, but there's no help for it; for know, that I have a Design upon you.

Lady Fanc. Upon me, Sir!

Heartfr. Yes; and one that will turn to your Glory and my Comfort, if you will but be a little wiser than you use to be.

Lady Fanc. Very well, Sir.

Heartf. Let me see,—Your Vanity, Madam, I take to be abou
some eight degrees higher than any Womans in the Town, le
t'other be who she will; and my Indifference is naturally abou
the same pitch. Now, cou'd you find the way to turn this In
difference into Fire and Flames, methinks your Vanity ought t
be satisfied; and this, perhaps, you might bring about upo
pretty reasonable terms.

Lady Fanc. And pray at what rate would this Indifferenc
be bought off, if one should have so deprav'd an Appetite t
desire it?

Heartfr. Why, Madam, to drive a Quaker's Bargain, and mak
but one word with you, if I do part with it,—you must lay m
down—your Affectation.

Lady Fanc. My Affectation, Sir!

Heartf. Why, I ask you nothing but what you may very wel
spare.

Lady Fanc. You grow rude, Sir. Come, Madamoiselle, 'tis hig
time to be gone.

Madam. Alons, alons, alons.

Heartfr. [*Stopping 'em.*] Nay, you may as well stand still
for hear me, you shall, walk which way you please.

Lady Fanc. What mean you, sir?

Heartfr. I mean to tell you, that you are the most ungratefu
Woman upon Earth.

Lady Fanc. Ungrateful! To who?

Heartfr. To Nature.

Lady Fanc. Why, what has Nature done for me?

Heartf. What you have undone by Art. It made you handsom
it gave you Beauty to a Miracle, a Shape without a fault, Wi
enough to make 'em relish, and so turn'd you loose to your ow
Discretion; which has made such Work with you, that you ar
become the Pity of our Sex, and the Jest of your own. There i
not a Feature in your Face, but you have found the way t
teach it some affected Convulsion; your Feet, your Hands, you
very Fingers ends, are directed never to move without som
ridiculous Air or other; and your Language is a suitable Trumpet
to draw Peoples Eyes upon the Raree-show.

Madam. [*Aside.*] Est ce qu'on fais l'amour en Angleterr
comme ça?

Lady Fanc. [*Aside.*] Now could I cry for madness, but tha
I know he'd laugh at me for it.

Heartfr. Now do you hate me for telling you the Truth; bu
that's because you don't believe it is so: for were you onc

onvinc'd of that, you'd reform for your own sake. But 'tis
s hard to perswade a Woman to quit any thing that makes
er ridiculous, as 'tis to prevail with a Poet to see a Fault in
is own Play.

Lady Fanc. Every Circumstance of nice Breeding must needs
ppear ridiculous to one who has so natural an Antipathy to good
Manners.

Heartfr. But suppose I could find the means to convince you,
That the whole World is of my Opinion, and that those who
latter and commend you, do it to no other intent, but to make
ou persevere in your Folly, that they may continue in their
Mirth.

Lady Fanc. Sir, tho' you and all that World you talk of,
hould be so impertinently officious, as to think to perswade me
don't know how to behave my self, I should still have Charity
nough for my own Understanding, to believe my self in the
ight, and all you in the wrong.

Madam. Le voilà mort.

[*Exeunt* LADY FANC. *and* MADAMOISELLE.

Heartfr. [*Gazing after her.*] There her single Clapper has
ublished the sense of the whole Sex.

Well, this once I have endeavour'd to wash the Blackamoor
white; but henceforward I'll sooner undertake to teach Sincerity
o a Courtier, Generosity to an Usurer, Honesty to a Lawyer,
ay, Humility to a Divine, than Discretion to a Woman I see
as once set her Heart upon playing the Fool.

Enter CONSTANT.

'Morrow, Constant.

Const. Good morrow, Jack; What are you doing here this
morning?

Heartfr. Doing! guess if thou canst. Why, I have been en-
eavouring to perswade my Lady Fanciful, that she's the foolish-
st Woman about Town.

Const. A pretty Endeavour truly.

Heartfr. I have told her in as plain English as I could speak,
oth what the Town says of her, and what I think of her. In
hort, I have us'd her as an Absolute King would do Magna
Charta.

Const. And how does she take it?

Heartfr. As Children do Pills; bite 'em, but can't swallow 'em.

Const. But, prithee, what has put it in your Head, of all
Mankind, to turn Reformer?

Heartf. Why, one thing was, the Morning hung upon my

Hands, I did not know what to do with my self. And another was, That as little as I care for Women, I could not see with patience one that Heaven had taken such wondrous pains about, be so very industrious, to make her self the Jack Pudding of the Creation.

Const. Well, now could I almost wish to see my cruel Mistriss make the self-same use of what Heaven has done for her, that so I might be cur'd of a Disease that makes me so very uneasie; for Love, Love is the Devil, Heartfree.

Heartfr. And why do you let the Devil govern you?

Const. Because I have more Flesh and Blood than Grace and Self-denial. My dear, dear Mistriss, 'dsdeath! that so genteel a Woman should be a Saint, when Religion's out of fashion!

Heartfr. Nay, she's much in the wrong truly; but who knows how far Time and Good Example may prevail?

Const. O! they have play'd their Parts in vain already: 'Tis now two Years since that damn'd fellow her Husband invited me to his Wedding; and there was the first time I saw that charming Woman, whom I have lov'd ever since, more than e'er a Martyr did his Soul; but she's cold, my Friend, still cold as the Northern Star.

Heartfr. So are all Women by Nature, which makes 'em so willing to be warm'd.

Const. O, don't prophane the Sex; prithee think 'em all Angels for her sake, for she's virtuous, even to a fault.

Heartf. A Lover's Head is a good accountable thing truly; he adores his Mistriss for being virtuous, and yet is very angry with her, because she won't be lewd.

Const. Well, the only Relief I expect in my Misery, is to see thee some day or other as deeply engag'd as my self, which will force me to be merry in the midst of all my Misfortunes.

Heartfr. That day will never come, be assur'd, Ned: Not but that I can pass a Night with a Woman, and for the time, perhaps, make my self as good sport as you can do. Nay, I can court a Woman too, call her Nymph, Angel, Goddess what you please; but here's the Difference 'twixt you and I: I perswade a Woman she's an Angel; she perswades you she's one.

Prithee let me tell you how I avoid falling in love; that which serves me for Prevention, may chance to serve you for a Cure.

Const. Well, use the Ladies moderately then, and I'll hear you.

Heartfr. That using 'em moderately undoes us all; but I'll use 'em justly, and that you ought to be satisfied with.

I always consider a Woman, not as the Taylor, the Shoo-maker, the Tire-woman, the Sempstress (and which is more than all that), the Poet makes her; but I consider her as pure Nature has contriv'd her, and that more strictly than I should have done our old Grandmother Eve, had I seen her naked in the Garden; for I consider her turn'd inside out. Her Heart well examin'd, I find there Pride, Vanity, Covetousness, Indiscretion, but above all things, Malice; Plots eternally aforging, to destroy one-an-others Reputations, and as honestly to charge the Levity of Mens Tongues with the Scandal; hourly Debates, how to make poor Gentlemen in love with 'em, with no other intent, but to use 'em like Dogs when they have done; a constant Desire of doing more mischief, and an everlasting War, wag'd against Truth and Good-nature.

Const. Very well, Sir, an admirable Composition truly.

Heartfr. Then for her Outside, I consider it meerly as an Out-side; She has a thin Tiffany covering over just such Stuff as you and I are made on.

As for her Motion, her Meen, her Airs, and all those Tricks, I know they affect you mightily. If you should see your Mistriss at a Coronation, dragging her Peacock's Train, with all her state and insolence about her, 'twould strike you with all the awful thoughts that Heaven it self could pretend to from you; whereas I turn the whole matter into a Jest, and suppose her strutting in the self-same stately manner, with nothing on but her Stays, and her under scanty quilted Petticoat.

Const. Hold thy prophane Tongue, for I'll hear no more.

Heartfr. What, you'll love on then?

Const. Yes, to Eternity.

Heartfr. Yet you have no Hopes at all.

Const. None.

Heartfr. Nay, the Resolution may be discreet enough; perhaps you have found out some new Philosophy, That Love's like Virtue, its own Reward: so you and your Mistriss will be as well content at a distance, as others that have less Learning are in coming together.

Const. No; but if she should prove kind at last, my dear Heartfree.   [*Embracing him.*

Heartfr. Nay, prithee don't take me for your Mistriss, for Lovers are very troublesome.

Const. Well, who knows what Time may do?

Heartfr. And just now he was sure Time could do nothing.

Const. Yet not one kind Glance in Two Years, is somewhat strange.

Heartfr. Not strange at all; she don't like you, that's all the business.

Const. Prithee don't distract me.

Heartfr. Nay, you are a good handsome young Fellow, she might use you better: Come, will you go see her? perhaps she may have chang'd her mind; there's some Hopes as long as she's a Woman.

Const. O, 'tis in vain to visit her: sometimes to get a sight of her, I visit that Beast, her Husband, but she certainly finds some Pretence to quit the Room as soon as I enter.

Heartfr. It's much she don't tell him you have made Love to her too, for that's another good-natur'd thing usual amongst Women, in which they have several Ends.

Sometimes 'tis to recommend their Virtues, that they may be lewd with the greater security.

Sometimes 'tis to make their Husbands fight in hopes they may be kill'd, when their Affairs require it should be so. But most commonly 'tis to engage two men in a Quarrel, that they may have the Credit of being fought for; and if the Lover's kill'd in the business, they cry, *Poor Fellow! he had ill Luck.*—And so they go to Cards.

Const. Thy Injuries to Women are not to be forgiven. Look to't if ever thou dost fall into their hands—

Heartfr. They can't use me worse than they do you, that speak well of 'em. O ho! here comes the Knight.

Enter SIR JOHN BRUTE.

Heartfr. Your humble Servant, Sir John.

Sir J. Servant, Sir.

Heartfr. How does all your Family?

Sir J. Pox o' my Family.

Const. How does your Lady? I han't seen her abroad a good while.

Sir J. Do! I don't know how she does, not I; she was well enough yesterday: I ha'n't been at home to night.

Const. What! were you out of Town!

Sir J. Out of Town! no, I was drinking.

Const. You are a true Englishman; Don't you know your own Happiness? if I were married to such a Woman, I would not be from her a Night for all the Wine in France.

Sir J. Not from her!—Oons,—what a time should a man have of that!

Heartfr. Why, there's no Division, I hope?

Sir J. No; but there's a Conjunction, and that's worse; a Pox o' the Parson.—Why the plague don't you two marry? I fansie I look like the Devil to you.

Heartfr. Why, you don't think you have Horns, do you?

Sir J. No; I believe my Wife's Religion will keep her honest.

Heartfr. And what will make her keep her Religion?

Sir. J. Persecution; and therefore she shall have it.

Heartfr. Have a care, Knight, Women are tender things.

Sir J. And yet, methinks, 'tis a hard matter to break their Hearts.

Const. Fie, fie; you have one of the best Wives in the World, and yet you seem the most uneasie Husband.

Sir. J. Best Wives!—the Woman's well enough; she has no Vice that I know of, but she's a Wife, and—damn a Wife; if I were married to a Hogshead of Claret, Matrimony would make me hate it.

Heartfr. Why did you marry then? you were old enough to know your own mind.

Sir J. Why did I marry! I married because I had a mind to lie with her, and she would not let me.

Heartfr. Why did not you ravish her?

Sir. J. Yes, and so have hedg'd my self into forty Quarrels with her Relations, besides buying my Pardon: But more than all that, you must know, I was afraid of being damn'd in those days, for I kept sneaking cowardly Company, Fellows that went to Church, said Grace to their Meat, and had not the least Tincture of Quality about 'em.

Heartfr. But I think you are got into a better Gang now.

Sir J. Zoons, Sir, my Lord Rake and I are Hand and Glove: I believe we may get our Bones broke together to night; Have you a mind to share a Frolick?

Const. Not I truly; my Talent lies to softer Exercises.

Sir. J. What? a Doune-bed and a Strumpet? A Pox of Venery, I say. Will you come and drink with me this Afternoon?

Const. I can't drink to day, but we'll come and sit an hour with you if you will.

Sir J. Phugh, Pox, sit an hour! Why can't you drink?

Const. Because I'm to see my Mistriss.

Sir J. Who's that?

Const. Why, do you use to tell?

Sir. J. Yes.

Const. So won't I.

Sir J. Why?

Const. Because 'tis a Secret.

Sir J. Wou'd my Wife knew it, 'twould be no Secret long.

Const. Why, do you think she can't keep a Secret?

Sir J. No more than she can keep Lent.

Heartfr. Prithee, tell it her to try, Constant.

Sir J. No, prithee don't, that I mayn't be plagu'd with it.

Const. I'll hold you a Guinea you don't make her tell it you.

Sir J. I'll hold you a Guinea I do.

Const. Which way?

Sir J. Why I'll beg her not to tell it me.

Heartfr. Nay, if any thing do's it, that will.

Const. But do you think, Sir?——

Sir J. Oons, Sir, I think a Woman and a Secret, are the two Impertinentest Themes in the Universe. Therefore pray let's hear no more, of my Wife nor your Mistress. Damn 'em both with all my Heart, and every thing else that Daggles a Petticoat, except four Generous Whores, with Betty Sands at the head of 'em, who were drunk with my Lord Rake and I, ten times in a Fortnight. [*Exit* SIR JOHN.

Con. Here's a dainty fellow for you. And the veriest Coward too. But his usage of his Wife makes me ready to stab the Villain.

Heartfr. Lovers are short sighted: All their Senses run into that of feeling. This proceeding of his is the only thing on Earth can make your Fortune. If any thing can prevail with her to accept of a Gallant 'tis his ill usage of her; for Women will do more for revenge than they'll do for the Gospel.

Prethee take heart, I have great hopes for you, and since I can't bring you quite off of her, I'll endeavour to bring you quite on; for a whining lover, is the damn'd'st Companion upon Earth.

Con. My Dear Friend, flatter me a little more with these hopes; for whilst they prevail I have Heaven within me, and cou'd melt with joy.

Heartfr. Pray, no melting yet: let things go farther first. This afternoon perhaps we shall make some advance. In the mean while, let's go Dine at Locket's, and let hope get you a Stomach. [*Exeunt.*

SCENE.—LADY FANCYFULL'S *House*

Enter LADY FANCYFULL *and* MADAMOISELLE.

Lady F. Did you ever see any thing so Importune, Madamoiselle?

Madam. Inteed Matam, to say de trute, he want leetel good breeding.

Lady F. Good breeding? He wants to be cain'd, Madamoiselle: an Insolent Fellow.

And yet let me expose my Weakness, 'tis the only Man on earth I cou'd resolve to dispence my Favours on, were he but a fine Gentleman. Well, did Men but know how deep an Impression a fine Gentleman makes in a Lady's heart, they wou'd reduce all their studies to that of good breeding alone.

Enter CORNET.

Cor. Madam, here's Mr. Treble. He has brought home the Verses your Ladyship made, and gave him to set.
Lady F. O let him come in by all means.
Now, Madamoiselle, am I going to be unspeakably happy.

Enter TREBLE.

So Mr. Treble, you have set my little Dialogue?
Treb. Yes, Madam, and I hope your Ladyship will be pleased with it.
Lady F. O, no doubt on't; for really Mr. Treble, you set all things to a Wonder: But your Musick is in particular Heavenly, when you have my words to cloath in't.
Treb. Your words themselves, Madam, have so much Musick in 'em they inspire me.
Lady F. Nay, now you make me blush, Mr. Treble; but pray let's hear what you have done.
Treb. You shall, Madam.

A Song to be Sung between a Man and a Woman

M. *Ah Lovely Nymph, the World's on Fire:*
   Veil, Veil those cruel Eyes.
W. *The World may then in Flames expire,*
   And boast that so it Dies.
M. *But when all Mortals are destroy'd,*
   Who then shall Sing your Praise?
W. *Those who are fit to be employ'd:*
   The Gods shall Altars raise.

Treb. How do's your Ladyship like it, Madam?
Lady F. Rapture, Rapture, Mr. Treble, I'm all Rapture. O Wit and Art, what power you have when joyn'd. I must needs tell you the Birth of this Little Dialogue, Mr. Treble. It's Father was a Dream, and it's Mother was the Moon. I dreamt that by an unanimous Vote, I was chosen Queen of that Pale World. And that the first time I appear'd upon my Throne,—all my Subjects fell in love with me. Just then I wak'd: and seeing Pen, Ink and Paper

lie idle upon the Table, I slid into my Morning Gown, and writ this *impromptu.*

Treb. So I guess the Dialogue, Madam, is suppos'd to be between your Majesty and your first Minister of State.

Lady F. Just: he as Minister advises me to trouble my head about the wellfare of my Subjects; which I as Soveraign, find a very impertinent proposal. But is the Town so Dull, Mr. Treble, it affords us never another New Song?

Treb. Madam, I have one in my Pocket, came out but yesterday, if your Ladyship pleases to let Mrs. Pipe Sing it.

Lady F. By all means. Here Pipe. Make what Musique you can of this Song, here.

SONG

I

Not an Angel dwells above
Half so fair as her I Love:
   Heaven knows how she'll receive me:
If she smiles, I'm blest indeed;
If she frowns, I'm quickly freed;
   Heaven knows, she ne'er can grieve me.

II

None can Love her more than I,
Yet she ne'er shall make me die.
   If my flame can never warm her,
Lasting Beauty, I'll adore,
I shall never Love her more,
   Cruelty will so deform her.

Lady F. Very well: This is Heartfree's Poetry without question.

Treb. Won't your Ladiship please to sing your self this morning?

Lady F. O Lord, Mr. Treble, my cold is still so Barbarous, to refuse me that pleasure; He he hem.

Treb. I'm very sorry for it Madam: Methinks all Mankind shou'd turn Physicians for the Cure on't.

Lady F. Why truly to give mankind their due, There's few that know me, but have offer'd their Remedy.

Treb. They have reason, Madam, for I know no body Sings so near a Cherubin as your Ladyship.

Lady F. What I do I owe chiefly to your skill and care, Mr Treble. People do flatter me indeed, that I have a voice and a je ne sçai quoy in the Conduct of it, that will make Musick of any thing. And truly I begin to believe so, since what happen'd t'other night: would you think it, Mr. Treble? walking pretty late in the Park, (for I often walk late in the Park, Mr. Treble) A whim took me to sing Chevy-Chase, and would you believe it? Next morning I had three Copies of Verses, and six Billet-doux at my Levée upon it.

Treb. And without all dispute you deserv'd as many more, Madam. Are there any further Commands for your Ladyship's humble Servant?

Lady F. Nothing more at this time, Mr. Treble. But I shall expect you here every morning for this Month, to sing my little matter there to me. I'll reward you for your pains.

Treb. O Lord, Madam.

Lady F. Good morrow, sweet Mr. Treble.

Treb. Your Ladyships most obedient Servant.   [*Exit* TREB.

Enter SERVANT.

Serv. Will your Ladyship please to dine yet?

Lady F. Yes: let 'em serve. [*Exit* SERV.] Sure this Heartfree has bewitch'd me, Madamoiselle. You can't imagine how oddly he mixt himself in my thoughts during my Rapture e'en now. I vow 'tis a thousand pities he is not more polish'd. Don't you think so?

Madam. Matam. I tink it is so great pity, dat if I was in your Ladyship place, I take him home in my House, I lock him up in my Closet, and I never let him go till I teach him every ting dat fine Laty expect from fine Gentelman.

Lady F. Why truly I believe I shou'd soon subdue his Brutality; for without doubt, he has a strange penchant to grow fond of me, in spight of his Aversion to the Sex, else he wou'd ne'er have taken so much pains about me. Lord, how proud wou'd some poor Creatures be of such a Conquest? But I alas, I don't know how to receive as a favour, what I take to be so infinitely my due. But what shall I do to new mould him, Madamoiselle? for till then he's my utter aversion.

Madam. Matam, you must laugh at him in all de place dat you meet him, and turn into de ridicule all he say and all he do.

Lady F. Why truly Satyr has been ever of wonderous use, to reform ill manners. Besides 'tis my particular Talent to ridicule folks. I can be severe; strangely severe, when I will, Madamoiselle. —Give me the Pen and Ink:—I find my self whimsicall—I'll write to him.

—or I'll let it alone, and be severe upon him that way.

[*Siting down to write. Rising up again.*

Yet active severity is better than passive.　　　*[Siting down.*
'Tis as good let alone too, for every lash I give him, perhaps
he'll take for a favour.　　　　　　　　　　　　　　*[Rising.*
Yet 'tis a thousand pities so much　　　　　　　　*[Siting.*
Satyr should be lost.
But if it shou'd have a wrong effect upon him 'twould distract
me.　　　　　　　　　　　　　　　　　　　　　　　*[Rising.*
Well I must write tho' after all.　　　　　　　　　*[Siting.*
Or I'll let it alone which is the same thing.　　　　*[Rising.*
Madam. La Voilà determinée.　　　　　　　　　　*[Exeunt.*

The End of the Second Act

ACT THE THIRD

Scene *Opens.*—Sir John, Lady Brute *and* Bellinda *rising
from the Table*

Sir J. Here, take away the things: I expect Company. But first
bring me a Pipe; I'll smoak.　　　　　　　　*[To a* Servant.

Lady B. Lord, Sir John, I wonder you won't leave that nasty
Custom.

Sir J. Prithee don't be Impertinent.

Bell. [*To* Lady.] I wonder who those are he expects this afternoon?

Lady B. I'd give the World to know: Perhaps 'tis Constant; he
comes here sometimes; if it does prove him, I'm resolved I'll share
the visit.

Bel. We'll send for our Work and sit here.

Lady B. He'll choak us with his Tobacco.

Bel. Nothing will choak us, when we are doing what we have a
mind to.

Enter Lovewell.

Love. Madam.

Lady B. Here; bring my Cousin's work and mine hither.
　　　　　　　　　[*Exit* Love. *and Re-enters with their Work.*

Sir J. Whe! Pox, can't you work somewhere else?

Lady B. We shall be carefull not to disturb you, Sir.

Bel. Your Pipe would make you too thoughtfull, Unkle, if you
were left alone; Our prittle prattle will Cure your Spleen.

Sir J. Will it so, Mrs. Pert? Now I believe it will so increase
it I shall take my own House for a Paper-Mill.
　　　　　　　　　　　　　　　　　　　　[Sitting and smoaking

Lady B. [*To* BEL. *aside.*] Don't let's mind him; let him say what he will.

Sir J. A Woman's Tongue a cure for the Spleen—Oons— [*Aside.*] If a Man had got the Headach, they'd be for applying the same Remedy.

Lady B. You have done a great deal Bellinda, since yesterday.

Bel. Yes, I have work'd very hard; how do you like it?

Lady B. O, 'tis the prettiest Fringe in the World. Well Cousin you have the happiest fancy. Prithee advice me about altering my Crimson Petticoat.

Sir J. A Pox o' your Petticoat; here's such a prating a man can't digest his own thoughts for you.

Lady B. Don't answer him. [*Aside.*] Well, what do you advise me?

Bel. Why really I would not alter it at all. Methinks 'tis very pretty as it is.

Lady B. Ay that's true: But you know one grows weary of the prettiest things in the world, when one has had 'em long.

Sir J. Yes, I have taught her that.

Bel. Shall we provoke him a little?

Lady B. With all my heart. Bellinda, don't you long to be Married?

Bel. Why there are some things in't I could like well enough.

Lady B. What do you think you shou'd dislike?

Bel. My Husband a hundred to one else.

Lady B. O ye wicked wretch: Sure you don't speak as you think '

Bel. Yes I do: Especially if he smoak'd Tobacco.

[*He looks earnestly at 'em.*

Lady B. Why that many times takes off worse smells.

Bel. Then he must smell very ill indeed.

Lady B. So some Men will, to keep their Wives from coming near 'em.

Bel. Then those Wives shou'd Cuckold 'em at a Distance.

[*He rises in a fury, throws his Pipe at 'em and drives 'em out. As they run off,* CONSTANT *and* HEARTFREE *enter.* LADY B. *runs against* CONSTANT.]

Sir J. Oons, get you gone up stairs, you confederating Strumpets you, or I'll Cuckold you with a Vengeance.

Lady B. O Lord, he'll beat us, he'll beat us. Dear, Dear Mr. Constant, save us. [*Exeunt.*

Sir J. I'll Cuckold you with a Pox.

Const. Heavens, Sir John, what's the matter?

Sir J. Sure if Woman had been ready created, the Devil, instead of being kick'd down into Hell, had been Married.

Heart. Why, what new plague have you found now?

Sir J. Why, these two Gentlewomen did but hear me say, I expected you here this afternoon; upon which, they presently resolved to take up the Room, o' purpose to plague me and my Friends.

Const. Was that all? why we shou'd have been glad of their Company.

Sir J. Then I should have been weary of yours. For I can't relish both together. They found fault with my smoking Tobacco too; and said Men stunk. But I have a good mind—to say something.

Const. No, nothing against the Ladies, pray.

Sir J. Split the Ladies. Come, will you sit down? Give us some Wine, Fellow: You won't smoak?

Const. No nor drink neither at this time, I must ask your pardon.

Sir J. What, this Mistress of yours runs in your head; I'll warrant it's some such squeamish Minx as my Wife, that's grown so dainty of late, she finds fault even with a Dirty shirt.

Heart. That a woman may do, and not be very dainty neither.

Sir J. Pox o' the women, let's drink. Come, you shall take one Glass, tho' I send for a Box of Lozenges to sweeten your mouth after it.

Const. Nay if one Glass will satisfy you I'll drink it without putting you to that expence.

Sir J. Why that's honest. Fill some Wine, Sirrah: So, Here's to you Gentlemen—A Wife's the Devil. To your being both married.
                                                                    [*They drink.*

Heart. O your most humble Servant, Sir.

Sir J. Well, how do you like my Wine?

Const. 'Tis very good indeed.

Heart. 'Tis Admirable.

Sir J. Then give us t'other Glass.

Const. No, pray excuse us now. We'll come another time, and then we won't spare it.

Sir J. This one Glass and no more. Come: It shall be your Mistresses health: And that's a great Compliment from me, I assure you.

Const. And 'tis a very obliging one to me: So give us the Glasses.

Sir J. So let her live—   [SIR JOHN *Coughs in the Glass*

Heart. And be kind.

Const. What's the matter? does't go the wrong way?

Sir J. If I had love enough to be jealous, I shou'd take this for an ill Omen. For I never drank my Wifes health in my life, but I puk'd in the Glass.

Const. O she's too Virtuous to make a Reasonable man jealous.

Sir J. Pox of her Virtue. If I could but catch her Adulterating I might be divorc'd from her by Law.

Heart. And so pay her a yearly Pension, to be a distinguish'd Cuckold.

Enter SERVANT.

Serv. Sir, There's my Lord Rake, Colonel Bully, and some other Gentlemen at the *Blew-Posts,* desire your Company.

Sir J. Cods so, we are to Consult about playing the Devil to night.

Heart. Well, we won't hinder business.

Sir J. Methinks I don't know how to leave you tho'. But for once I must make bold—Or look you: may be the Conference mayn't last long; so if you'll wait here half an hour, or an hour; if I don't come then,—why then—I won't come at all.

Heart. [*To* CONST.] A good modest proposition truly! [*Aside.*

Const. But let's accept on't however. Who knows what may happen?

Heart. Well Sir, to shew you how fond we are of your Company we'll expect your return as long as we can.

Sir J. Nay, may be I mayn't stay at all: But business you know must be done. So your Servant—Or hark you: if you have a mind to take a frisk with us, I have an interest with my Lord; I can easily introduce you.

Const. We are much beholding to you, but for my part I'm engaged another way.

Sir J. What! To your Mistress I'll warrant. Prithee leave your nasty Punk to entertain her self with her own Lewd thoughts, and make one with us to Night.

Const. Sir, 'tis business that is to employ me.

Heart. And me; and business must be done you know.

Sir J. Ay, Womens business, tho' the world were consum'd for't. [*Exit* SIR J.

Const. Farewell Beast: And now my Dear Friend, wou'd my Mistress be but as Complaisant as some mens Wives, who think it a piece of good breeding to receive the visits of their Husbands Friends in his absence.

Heart. Why for your sake I could forgive her, tho' she should be so Complaisant to receive something else in his absence. But what way shall we invent to see her?

Const. O ne'er hope it: Invention will prove as Vain as Wishes.

Enter LADY BRUTE *and* BELLINDA.

Heart. What do you think now, Friend?

Const. I think I shall swoon.

Heart. I'll speak first then, whilst you fetch breath.

Lady B. We think our selves oblig'd Gentlemen, to come and return you thanks for your Knight Errantry. We were just upon being devour'd by the Fiery Dragon.

Bell. Did not his fumes almost knock you down, Gentlemen?

Heart. Truly Ladies, we did undergo some hardships, and should have done more, if some greater Heroes than our selves hard by had not diverted him.

Const. Tho' I'm glad of the Service you are pleased to say we have done you, yet I'm sorry we cou'd do it no other way, than by making our selves privy to what you wou'd perhaps have kept a secret.

Lady B. For Sir John's part, I suppose he design'd it no secret since he made so much noise. And for my self, truly I am not much concern'd, since 'tis fallen only into this Gentleman's hands and yours; who I have many reasons to believe, will neither interpret nor report any thing to my disadvantage.

Const. Your good opinion, Madam, was what I feard, I ne'er cou'd have merited.

Lady B. Your fears were vain then, Sir, for I am just to every body.

Heart. Prithee, Constant, what is't you do to get the Ladies good Opinions? for I'm a Novice at it?

Bell. Sir, will you give me leave to instruct you?

Heartfr. Yes, that I will with all my Soul, Madam.

Bell. Why then you must never be slovenly, never be out of humour, fare well and cry Roast-meat; smoak Tobacco, nor drink but when you are a-dry.

Heartfr. That's hard.

Const. Nay, if you take his Bottle from him, you break his Heart, Madam.

Bell. Why, is it possible the Gentleman can love Drinking?

Heartfr. Only by way of Antidote.

Bell. Against what, pray?

Heartfr. Against Love, Madam.

Lady Br. Are you afraid of being in Love, Sir?

Heartfr. I should, if there were any danger of it.

Lady Br. Pray why so?

Heartfr. Because I always had an aversion to being us'd like a Dog.

Bell. Why truly, men in love are seldom us'd better.

Lady Br. But was you never in love, Sir?

Heartfr. No, I thank Heaven, Madam.

Bell. Pray, where got you your Learning then?

Heartfr. From other Peoples Expence.

Bell. That's being a Spunger, Sir, which is scarce honest; if you'd buy some Experience with your own Mony, as 'twould be fairlier got, so 'twould stick longer by you.

Enter FOOTMAN.

Footm. Madam, here's my Lady Fancyfull, to wait upon your Ladiship.

Lady Br. Shield me, kind Heaven, what an inundation of Impertinence is here coming upon us!

Enter LADY FANCYFULL, *who runs first to* LADY BRUTE, *then to* BELLINDA, *kissing 'em.*

Lady Fanc. My dear Lady Brute, and sweet Bellinda! methinks 'tis an Age since I saw you.

Lady Br. Yet 'tis but three days; sure you have pass'd your time very ill, it seems so long to you.

Lady Fanc. Why really, to confess the Truth to you, I am so everlastingly fatigu'd with the Addresses of Unfortunate Gentlemen, that were it not for the extravagancy of the Example, I should e'en tear out these wicked Eyes with my own Fingers, to make both my self and Mankind easie. What think you on't, Mr. Heartfree, for I take you to be my faithful Adviser?

Heartfr. Why truly, Madam—I think—every Project that is for the Good of Mankind, ought to be encourag'd.

Lady Fanc. Then I have your Consent, Sir.

Heartfr. To do whatever you please, Madam.

Lady Fanc. You had a much more limited Complaisance this Morning, Sir. Would you believe it, Ladies? The Gentleman has been so exceeding generous, to tell me of above fifty Faults, in less time than it was well possible for me to commit two of 'em.

Const. Why truly, Madam, my Friend there is apt to be something familiar to the Ladies.

Lady Fanc. He is indeed, Sir; but he's wondrous charitable with it; he has had the Goodness to design a Reformation, even down to my Fingers ends.

[*Opening her Fingers in an awkward manner.*
'Twas thus, I think, Sir, you would have had 'em stand.—My Eyes too he did not like: How was't you would have directed 'em? Thus, I think. [*Staring at him.*] Then there was something amiss in my Gate too: I don't know well how 'twas; but as I take it, he would have had me walk like him. Pray, Sir, do me the Favour

to take a turn or two about the Room, that the Company may see you.—He's sullen, Ladies, and wont: But, to make short, and give you as true an Idea as I can of the matter, I think 'twas much about this Figure in general, he would have moulded me to: But I was an obstinate Woman, and could not resolve to make my self Mistriss of his Heart, by growing as aukward as his Fancy.

[*She walks aukwardly about, staring and looking ungainly, then changes on a sudden to the extremity of her usual Affectation.*]

Heartfr. Just thus Women do, when they think we are in love with 'em, or when they are so with us.

[*Here* CONSTANT *and* LADY BRUTE *talk together apart.*

Lady Fanc. 'Twould however be less Vanity for me to conclude the former, than you the latter, Sir.

Heartfr. Madam, all I shall presume to conclude, is, That if I were in Love, you'd find the means to make me soon weary on't.

Lady Fanc. Not by over-fondness, upon my word, Sir. But pray let's stop here, for you are so much govern'd by Instinct, I know you'll grow brutish at last.

Bell. [*Aside.*] Now am I sure she's fond of him: I'll try to make her jealous.

Well, for my part, I should be glad to find some-body would be so free with me, that I might know my Faults, and mend 'em.

Lady Fanc. Then pray let me recommend this Gentleman to you: I have known him some time, and will be Surety for him, That upon a very limited Encouragement on your side, you shall find an extended Impudence on his.

Heartfr. I thank you Madam, for your recommendation; But hating Idleness, I'm unwilling to enter into a place where I believe there would be nothing to do. I was fond of serving your Lady-ship, because I know you'd find me constant employment.

Lady. Fanc. I told you he'd be rude, Bellinda.

Bell. O, a little Bluntness is a sign of honesty, which makes me always ready to pardon it. So, Sir, if you have no other exceptions to my service, but the fear of being idle in't, You may venture to list your self: I shall find you work I warrant you.

Heartfr. Upon those terms I engage, Madam, and this (with your leave) I take for earnest.   [*Offering to kiss her hand.*

Bell. Hold there, Sir, I'm none of your earnest givers. But if I'm well serv'd, I give good wages and pay punctually.

Lady Fanc. [*Aside.*] I don't like this jesting between 'em—methinks the Fool begins to look as if he were in earnest—but then he must be a Fool indeed.

[HEART. *and* BELL. *seem to continue talking familiarly.*

—Lard, what a difference there is between me and her. [*Looking at* BEL. *scornfully.*] How I should despise such a thing if I were a man.—What a Nose she has—What a Chin—What a Neck— Then her Eyes—And the worst Kissing Lips in the Universe—No, no, he can never like her, that's positive—Yet I can't suffer 'em together any longer. Mr. Heartfree, do you know that you and I must have no Quarrel for all this? I can't forbear being a little severe now and then: But Women you know may be allowed any thing.

Heartfr. Up to a certain age, Madam.

Lady Fanc. Which I am not yet past, I hope.

Heartfr. [*Aside.*] Nor never will, I dare swear.

Lady Fanc. [*To* LADY B.] Come Madam; Will your Ladyship be witness to our Reconciliation?

Lady B. You agree then at last?

Heartfr. [*slightingly.*] We forgive.

Lady Fanc. [*Aside.*] That was a cold, ill-natur'd reply.

Lady B. Then there's no Challenges sent between you?

Heartfr. Not from me I promise. [*Aside to* CONSTANT.] But that's more than I'll do for her, for I know she can as well be damn'd as forbear writing to me.

Const. That I believe. But I think we had best be going lest she should suspect something, and be malicious.

Heartfr. With all my heart.

Const. Ladies, we are your humble Servants. I see Sir John is quite engag'd, 'twould be in vain to expect him. Come, Heartfree.

[*Exit.*

Heartfr. Ladies, your Servant. [*To* BELLINDA.] I hope Madam you won't forget our Bargain; I'm to say what I please to you.

[*Exit* HEARTFREE.

Bel. Liberty of Speech entire, Sir.

Lady Fanc. [*Aside.*] Very pretty truly—But how the Blockhead went out: Languishing at her; and not a look toward me.— Well, Churchmen may talk, but Miracles are not ceas'd. For 'tis more than natural, such a Rude fellow as he, and such a little impertinent as she, shou'd be capable of making a Woman of my sphere uneasy.

But I can bear her sight no longer—methinks she's grown ten times uglier than Cornet. I must go home, and study revenge. [*To* LADY B.] Madam, your humble Servant; I must take my leave.

Lady B. What, going already, Madam?

Lady Fanc. I must beg you'l excuse me this once. For really I

have eighteen visits to return this afternoon, so you see I'm
importun'd by the Women as well as the Men.

Bel. [*Aside*.] And she's quits with 'em both.

Lady Fanc. [*going*.] Nay, you sha'n't go one step out of the
room.

Lady B. Indeed I'll wait upon you down.

Lady Fanc. No, sweet Lady Brute; you know I swoon at Ceremony.

Lady B. Pray give me leave.

Lady Fanc. You know I won't.

Lady B. Indeed I must.

Lady Fanc. Indeed you sha'n't.

Lady B. Indeed I will.

Lady Fanc. Indeed you sha'n't.

Lady B. Indeed I will.

Lady Fanc. Indeed you sha'n't. Indeed, Indeed, Indeed you
    sha'n't.   [*Exit* LADY FANC. *running. They follow.*

Re-enter LADY BRUTE, *sola.*

This impertinent Woman has put me out of humour for a Fortnight.—What an agreeable moment has her foolish visit interrupted—Lord, how like a Torrent Love flows into the Heart when
once the sluce of desire is open'd! Good Gods, what a pleasure
there is in doing what we shou'd not do!

Re-enter CONSTANT.

Ha! here again?

Const. Tho' the renewing my visit may seem a little irregular, I
hope I shall obtain your pardon for it, Madam, when you know
I only left the Room, lest the Lady who was here shou'd have
been as malicious in her Remarks, as she's foolish in her Conduct.

Lady B. He who has discretion enough to be tender of a
Womans Reputation, carries a Virtue about him may atone for
a great many faults.

Const. If it has a Title to atone for any, its pretentions must
needs be strongest, where the Crime is Love. I therefore hope I
shall be forgiven the attempt I have made upon your Heart, since
my Enterprize has been a secret to all the World but your self.

Lady B. Secrecy indeed in sins of this kind, is an Argument of
weight to lessen the Punishment; but nothing's a Plea, for a Pardon entire, without a sincere Repentance.

Const. If Sincerity in Repentance consist in sorrow for offending: No Cloister ever enclosed so true a Penitent as I should be.

But I hope it cannot be reckon'd an offence to Love, where 'tis a duty to adore.

Lady B. 'Tis an offence, a great one, where it wou'd rob a Woman of all she ought to be ador'd for: her Virtue.

Const. Virtue?—Virtue alas is no more like the thing that's call'd so, than 'tis like Vice it self. Virtue consists in Goodness, Honour, Gratitude, Sincerity, and Pity; and not in Peevish, snarling, streightlac'd Chastity. True Virtue whereso'e'er it moves, still carries an intrinsique worth about it, and is in every place, and in each Sex of equal value. So is not Continence, you see: That Phantome of Honour, which men in every Age have so contemn'd, they have thrown it amongst the Women to scrable for.

Lady B. If it be a thing of so very little Value, Why do you so earnestly recommend it to your Wives and Daughters?

Const. We recommend it to our Wives, Madam, because we wou'd keep 'em to our selves. And to our Daughters, because we wou'd dispose of 'em to others.

Lady B. 'Tis then of some Importance it seems, since you can't dispose of 'em without it.

Const. That importance, Madam, lies in the humour of the Country, not in the nature of the thing.

Lady B. How do you prove that, Sir?

Const. From the Wisdom of a neighb'ring Nation in a Contrary Practice. In Monarchies things go by Whimsie, but Commonwealths weigh all things in the Scale of Reason.

Lady B. I hope we are not so very light a People to bring up fashions without some Ground.

Const. Pray what do's your Ladiship think of a powder'd Coat for Deep Mourning?

Lady B. I think, Sir, your Sophistry has all the effect that you can reasonably expect it shou'd have: it puzzles, but don't convince.

Const. I'm sorry for it.

Lady B. I'm sorry to hear you say so.

Const. Pray why?

Lady B. Because if you expected more from it, you have a worse opinion of my understanding than I desire you shou'd have.

Const. [*Aside.*] I comprehend her: She wou'd have me set a value upon her Chastity, that I may think my self the more oblig'd to her, when she makes me a present of it. [*To her.*] I beg you will believe I did but rally, Madam; I know you judge too well of Right and Wrong, to be deceiv'd by Arguments like those. I hope you'll have so favourable an opinion of my Understanding too, to believe the thing call'd Virtue has worth enough with me, to pass for an eternal Obligation where're 'tis sacrific'd.

Lady B. It is I think so great a one, as nothing can repay.

Const. Yes; the making the man you love your everlasting Debtor.

Lady B. When Debtors once have borrow'd all we have to lend, they are very apt to grow very shy of their Creditors Company.

Const. That, Madam, is only when they are forc'd to borrow of Usurers, and not of a Generous Friend. Let us choose our Creditors, and we are seldom so ungrateful to shun 'em.

Lady B. What think you of Sir John, Sir? I was his free choice.

Const. I think he's marri'd, Madam.

Lady B. Do's Marriage then exclude men from your Rule of Constancy?

Const. It do's. Constancy's a Brave, free, haughty, generous Agent, that cannot buckle to the Chains of Wedlock. There's a poor sordid slavery in Marriage, that turns the flowing Tyde of Honour, and sinks us to the lowest ebb of Infamy. 'Tis a corrupted Soil; Ill Nature, Avarice, Sloath, Cowardice and Dirt, are all its product.

Lady B. Have you no exceptions to this General Rule, as well as to t'other?

Const. Yes: I wou'd (after all) be an exception to it my self if you were free in Power and Will to make me so.

Lady B. Compliments are well plac'd, where 'tis impossible to lay hold on 'em.

Const. I wou'd to Heaven 'twere possible for you to lay hold on mine, that you might see it is no Compliment at all. But since you are already dispos'd of beyond Redemption, to one who do's not know the value of the Jewel you have put into his hands: I hope you wou'd not think him greatly wrong'd, tho' it shou'd sometimes be look'd on by a Friend, who knows how to esteem it as he ought.

Lady B. If looking on't alone wou'd serve his turn, the wrong perhaps might not be very great.

Const. Why, what if he shou'd wear it now and then a day, so he gave good Security to bring it home again at night?

Lady B. Small Security I fansie might serve for that. One might venture to take his word.

Const. Then where's the injury to the Owner?

Lady B. 'Tis an injury to him, if he think it one. For if Happiness be seated in the Mind, Unhappiness must be so too.

Const. Here I close with you, Madam, and draw my conclusive

Argument from your own Position: If the injury lie in the fancy, there needs nothing but Secrecy to prevent the Wrong.

Lady B. [*going.*] A surer way to prevent it, is to hear no more Arguments in its behalf.

Const. [*following her.*] But, Madam—

Lady B. But, Sir, 'tis my turn to be discreet now, and not suffer too long a Visit.

Const. [*catching her Hand.*] By Heaven, you shall not stir, till you give me hopes that I shall see you again, at some more convenient Time and Place.

Lady B. I give you just Hopes enough—[*breaking from him*] To get loose from you: And that's all I can afford you at this time.   [*Exit running.*

CONSTANT *Solus.*

Now by all that's Great and Good, she is a charming Woman. In what Extasie of Joy she has left me. For she gave me Hope; Did she not say she gave me Hope?—Hope? Ay; what Hope?—enough to make me let her go—Why, that's enough in Conscience. Or no matter how 'twas spoke; Hope was the word: It came from her, and it was said to me.

Enter HEARTFREE.

Ha, Heartfree: Thou hast done me Noble Service in pratling to the young Gentlewoman without there; come to my Arms, Thou venerable Bawd, and let me squeeze thee [*embracing him eagerly*] as a new pair of stayes do's a Fat Country Girl, when she's carry'd to Court to stand for a Maid of Honour.

Heart. Why what the Devil's all this Rapture for?

Const. Rapture? There's ground for Rapture, man, there's hopes, my Heartfree, hopes, my Friend.

Heart. Hopes? of what?

Const. Why, hopes that my Lady and I together, (for 'tis more than one bodies work) should make Sir John a Cuckold.

Heart. Prithee, what did she say to thee?

Const. Say? what did she not say? she said that—says she—she said—Zoons I don't know what she said: But she look'd as she said every thing I'd have her, and so if thou'lt go to the Tavern, I'll treat thee with any thing that Gold can buy; I'll give all my Silver amongst the Drawers, make a Bonfire before the Door, say the Plenipo's have sign'd the Peace, and the Bank of England's grown honest.   [*Exeunt.*

SCENE *opens.*—LORD RAKE, SIR JOHN, *&c., at a Table drinking.*

All. Huzza.

Lord R. Come, Boys. Charge again.—So—Confusion to all order. Here's Liberty of Conscience.

All. Huzza.

Lord R. I'll Sing you a Song I made this morning to this purpose.

Sir J. 'Tis wicked I hope.

Col. B. Don't my Lord tell you he made it?

Sir J. Well then, let's ha't.

Lord R. [*Sings*.]

I

> *What a Pother of Late*
> *Have they kept in the State*
> > *About setting our Consciences free.*
> *A Bottle has more*
> *Dispensation in Store,*
> > *Than the King and the State can decree.*

II

> *When my Head's full of Wine,*
> *I o'er flow with Design*
> > *And know no penal Laws that can curb me.*
> *What e'er I devise,*
> *Seems good in my Eyes,*
> > *And Religion ne'er dares to disturb me.*

III

> *No saucy remorse*
> *Intrudes in my Course,*
> > *Nor Impertinent notions of Evil:*
> *So there's Claret in store,*
> *In Peace I've my Whore,*
> > *And in Peace I jog on to the Devil.*

All. [*Sing*.] *So there's Claret, &c.*

Lord R. [*Rep*.] *And in Peace I jog on to the Devil.*

Lord R. Well, how do you like it, Gentlemen?

All. O, Admirable.

Sir J. I wou'd not give a fig for a Song that is not full of Si▪ and Impudence.

Lord R. Then my Muse is to your taste. But drink away; Th▪

Night steals upon us; we shall want time to be Lewd in. Hey, Page, sally out, Sirrah, and see what's doing in the Camp; we'll beat up their Quarters presently.

Page. I'll bring your Lordship an Exact account. [*Exit* PAGE.

Lord R. Now let the spirit of Clary go round. Fill me a Brimmer. Here's to our forlorn-hope. Courage Knight; Victory attends you.

Sir J. And Lawrells shall Crown me. Drink away and be damn'd.

Lord R. Again Boys; t'other Glass, and damn Morality.

Sir J. [*Drunk.*] Ay—damn Morality—and damn the Watch. And let the Constable be married.

All. Huzza.

Re-enter PAGE.

Lord R. How are the Streets inhabited, Sirrah?

Page. My Lord, it's Sunday night; they are full of Drunken Citizens.

Lord R. Along then Boys, we shall have a feast.

Col. B. Along Noble Knight.

Sir J. Ay—along Bully; and he that says Sir John Brute is not as Drunk and as Religious as the Drunkenest Citizen of 'em all—is a liar, and the Son of a Whore.

Col. B. Why, that was bravely spoke, and like a free-born Englishman.

Sir J. What's that to you, Sir, whether I am an English man or a French man?

Col. B. Zoons, you are not angry, Sir?

Sir J. Zoons, I am angry, Sir,—for if I am a Free-born English man, what have you to do, even to talk of my Privileges?

Lord R. Why prithee Knight, don't quarrel here; leave private Animosities to be decided by day light; let the night be imployer against the publick Enemy.

Sir J. My Lord, I respect you, because you are a man of Quality: But I'll make that fellow know I am within a hairs breadth as absolute by my Priveleges, as the King of France is by his prerogative. He by his prerogative takes money where it is not his due; I, by my Privelege refuse paying it, where I owe it. Liberty and Property and Old England, Huzza.

[*Exit* SIR J. *reeling, all following him.*

All. Huzza.

Scene.—*A Bed-Chamber*

Enter Lady Brute *and* Bellinda.

Lady B. Sure it's late, Bellinda; I begin to be sleepy.

Bell. Yes, 'tis near twelve. Will you go to Bed?

Lady B. To bed, my Dear? And by that time I'm fallen into a sweet sleep, (or perhaps a sweet Dream which is better and better) Sir John will come home, roaring drunk, and be overjoy'd he finds me in a Condition to be disturb'd.

Bell. O you need not fear him; he's in for all night. The Servants say he's gone to drink with my Lord Rake.

Lady B. Nay, 'tis not very likely indeed, such suitable Company should part presently. What Hogs Men turn, Bellinda, when they grow weary of Women.

Bell. And what Owles they are whilst they are fond of 'em.

Lady B. But that we may forgive well enough, because they are so upon our Accounts.

Bell. We ought to do so indeed: But 'tis a hard matter. For when a man is really in Love, he looks so unsufferably silly, that tho' a Woman lik'd him well enough before, she has then much ado to endure the sight of him. And this I take to be the reason why Lovers are so generally ill used.

Lady B. Well I own now, I'm well enough pleased to see a man look like an Ass for me.

Bell. Ay, I'm pleas'd he should look like an Ass too—That is I'm pleased with my self for making him look so.

Lady B. Nay truly, I think if he'd find some other way to express his Passion, 'twould be more to his advantage.

Bell. Yes; For then a Woman might like his Passion and him too.

Lady B. Yet, Bellinda, after all, A Woman's life would be but a dull business, if 'twere not for Men; And Men that can look like Asses too. We shou'd never blame Fate for the shortness of our days; our time wou'd hang wretchedly upon our hands.

Bell. Why truly they do help us off with a good share on't. For were there no Men in the World, O' my Conscience I shou'd be no longer a dressing than I'm a saying my prayers; Nay tho it were Sunday: For you know that one may go to Church without Stays on.

Lady B. But don't you think Emulation might do something? for every Woman you see desires to be finer than her Neighbour.

Bell. That's only that the men may like her better than her

Neighbour. No: if there were no men, adieu fine Petticoats, we shou'd be weary of wearing 'em.

Lady B. And adieu Plays, we shou'd be weary of seeing 'em.

Bell. Adieu Hide-Park, the Dust wou'd Choak us.

Lady B. Adieu St. James's,. Walking wou'd Tire us.

Bell. Adieu London, the smoak wou'd stifle us.

Lady B. And adieu going to Church, for Religion wou'd ne'er prevail with us.

Both. Ha, ha, ha, ha, ha.

Bell. Our Confession is so very hearty, sure we merit Absolution.

Lady B. Not unless we go through with't, and confess all. So prithee, for the Ease of our Consciences, let's hide nothing.

Bel. Agreed.

Lady B. Why then I confess, That I love to sit in the Forefront of a Box. For if one sits behind, there's two Acts gone perhaps, before one's found out. And when I am there, if I perceive the Men whispering and looking upon me, you must know I cannot for my Life forbear thinking they talk to my Advantage. And that sets a Thousand little tickling Vanities on Foot.—

Bel. Just my Case for all the World; but go on.

Lady B. I watch with Impatience for the next Jest in the Play, that I may laugh and shew my white Teeth. If the Poet has been dull, and the Jest be long a coming, I pretend to whisper one to my Friend, and from thence fall into a little short Discourse, in which I take Occasion to shew my Face in all Humours, Brisk, Pleas'd, Serious, Melancholy, Languishing—Not that what we say to one another causes any of these Alterations. But—

Bel. Don't trouble your self to explain: For if I'm not mistaken, you and I have had some of these necessary Dialogues before now, with the same Intention.

Lady B. Why I'll swear Bellinda, some People do give strange agreeable Airs to their Faces in speaking.

Tell me true!—Did you never practice in the Glass?

Bel. Why, did you?

Lady B. Yes Faith, many a time.

Bel. And I too, I own it. Both how to speak my self, and how to look when others speak; But my Glass and I cou'd never yet agree what Face I shou'd make, when they come blurt out, with a nasty thing in a Play: For all the Men presently look upon the Women, that's certain; so laugh we must not, though our Stays burst for't, Because that's telling Truth, and owning we understand the Jest. And to look serious is so dull, when the whole House is a laughing.

Lady B. Besides, that looking serious, do's really betray our Knowledge in the Matter, as much as laughing with the Company wou'd do. For if we did not understand the thing, we shou'd naturally do like other People.

Bel. For my part I always take that Occasion to blow my Nose.

Lady B. You must blow your Nose half off then at some Plays.

Bel. Why don't some Reformer or other, beat the Poet for't?

Lady B. Because he is not so sure of our private Approbation as of our publick Thanks. Well, sure there is not upon Earth so impertinent a thing as Womens Modesty.

Bel. Yes; Mens Fantasque, that obliges us to it. If we quit our Modesty, they say we lose our Charms, and yet they know that very Modesty is Affectation, and rail at our Hypocrisie.

Lady B. Thus one wou'd think, 'twere a hard Matter to please 'em, Neice. Yet our kind Mother Nature has given us something that makes amends for all. Let our Weakness be what it will, Mankind will still be weaker, and whilst there is a World, 'tis Woman that will govern it.

But prithee one word of poor Constant before we go to Bed, if it be but to furnish Matter for Dreams; I dare swear he's talking of me now, or thinking of me at least, tho' it be in the middle of his Prayers.

Bel. So he ought I think; for you were pleas'd to make him a good round Advance to day, Madam.

Lady B. Why, I have e'en plagu'd him enough to satisfie any reasonable Woman: He has besieg'd me these two Years to no Purpose.

Bel. And if he besieg'd you two Years more, he'd be well enough paid, so he had the plundering of you at last.

Lady B. That may be; but I'm afraid the Town won't be able to hold out much longer; for to confess the Truth to you, Bellinda, the Garrison begins to grow mutinous.

Bel. Then the sooner you capitulate, the better.

Lady B. Yet methinks I wou'd fain stay a little longer, to see you fix'd too, that we might start together, and see who cou'd love longest. What think you if Heartfree shou'd have a Month's Mind to you?

Bel. Why Faith, I cou'd almost be in Love with him, for despising that foolish affected Lady Fancyfull, but I'm afraid he's too cold ever to warm himself by my Fire.

Lady B. Then he deserves to be froze to Death. Wou'd I were a Man for your sake, my dear Rogue.   [*Kissing her.*

Bel. You'd wish your self a Woman again for your own, or the Men are mistaken.

But if I cou'd make a Conquest of this Son of Bacchus, and rival his Bottle: What shou'd I do with him? he has no Fortune; I can't marry him; and sure you wou'd not have me commit Fornication?

Lady B. Why, if you did, Child, 'twou'd be but a good friendly part; if 'twere only to keep me in Countenance whilst I commit —You know what.

Bel. Well, if I can't resolve to serve you that way, I may perhaps some other, as much to your Satisfaction. But pray how shall we contrive to see these Blades again quickly?

Lady B. We must e'en have Recourse to the old way; make 'em an Appointment 'twixt jest and earnest; 'twill look like a Frolick, and that you know's a very good thing to save a Woman's Blushes.

Bel. You advise well; but where shall it be?

Lady B. In Spring-Garden. But they shan't know their Women, till their Women pull off their Masques; for a Surprize is the most agreeable thing in the World: And I find my self in a very good Humour, ready to do 'em any good turn I can think on.

Bel. Then pray write 'em the necessary Billet, without farther Delay.

Lady B. Let's go into your Chamber then, and whilst you say your Prayers, I'll do it, Child.   [*Exeunt.*

THE END OF THE THIRD ACT

ACT THE FOURTH

SCENE.—*Covent-Garden*

Enter LORD RAKE, SIR JOHN, *&c., with Swords drawn.*

Lord R. Is the Dog dead?

Bully. No, damn him, I heard him wheeze.

Lord R. How the Witch his Wife howl'd!

Bully. Ay, she'll alarm the Watch presently.

Lord R. Appear, Knight, then; come, you have a good Cause to fight for, there's a Man murder'd.

Sir John. Is there? Then let his Ghost be satisfied: For I'll sacrifice a Constable to it presently; and burn his Body upon his Wooden Chair.

Enter a TAYLOR, *with a Bundle under his Arm.*

Bully. How now? What have we got here? A Thief?

Taylor. No an't please you; I'm no Thief.

Lord R. That we'll see presently: Here, let the General examine him.

Sir John. Ay, Ay, Let me examine him; and I'll lay a Hundred Pound I find him guilty, in spight of his Teeth—for he looks—like a—sneaking Rascal. Come Sirrah, without Equivocation, or mental Reservation, tell me of what Opinion you are, and what Calling; for by them—I shall guess at your Morals.

Taylor. An't please you, I'm a Dissenting Journeyman Taylor.

Sir John. Then Sirrah, you love Lying by your Religion, and Theft by your Trade. And so, that your Punishment may be suitable to your Crimes,—I'll have you first gagg'd,—and then hang'd.

Taylor. Pray good worthy Gentlemen, don't abuse me; indeed I'm an honest Man, and a good Workman, tho' I say it, that shou'd not say it.

Sir John. No Words, Sirrah, but attend your Fate.

Lord R. Let me see what's in that Bundle.

Taylor. An't please you, it's the Doctor of the Parish's Gown.

Lord R. The Doctor's Gown!—Heark you, Knight, you won't stick at abusing the Clergy, will you?

Sir John. No, I'm drunk, and I'll abuse any thing—but my Wife; and her I name—with Reverence.

Lord R. Then you shall wear this Gown, whilst you charge the Watch. That tho' the Blows fall upon you, the Scandal may light upon the Church.

Sir John. A generous Design—by all the Gods—give it me.

[*Takes the Gown and puts it on.*

Taylor. O dear Gentlemen, I shall be quite undone, if you take the Gown.

Sir John. Retire, Sirrah; and since you carry off your Skin—go home, and be happy.

Taylor [*pausing*]. I think I had e'en as good follow the Gentleman's friendly Advice. For if I dispute any longer, who knows but the whim may take him to Case me. These Courtiers are fuller of Tricks than they are of Money; they'll sooner cut a Man's Throat, than pay his Bill. [*Exit* TAYLOR.

Sir John. So, how d'ye like my Shapes now?

Lord R. This Will do to a Miracle; he looks like a Bishop

going to the Holy War. But to your Arms, Gentlemen, the Enemy appears.

Enter CONSTABLE *and* WATCH.

Watchman. Stand! Who goes there? Come before the Con-stable.

Sir John. The Constable's a Rascal—and you are the Son of a Whore.

Watchman. A good civil Answer for a Parson, truly.

Constable. Methinks Sir, a Man of your Coat might set a better Example.

Sir John. Sirrah, I'll make you know—there are Men of my Coat can set as bad Examples—as you can do, you Dog you.

[SIR JOHN *strikes the* CONSTABLE. *They knock him down,
disarm him and seize him.* LORD R. *&c., run away.*

Constable. So, we have secur'd the Parson however.

Sir John. Blood and Blood—and Blood.

Watchman. Lord have Mercy upon us: How the Wicked Wretch Raves of Blood. I'll warrant he has been murdering some body to Night.

Sir John. Sirrah, There's nothing got by Murder but a Halter: My Talent lies towards Drunkenness and Simony.

Watchman. Why, that now was spoke like a Man of Parts, Neighbours: It's pity he shou'd be so Disguis'd.

Sir John. You Lye,—I am not Disguis'd; for I am Drunk barefac'd.

Watchman. Look you there again—This is a mad Parson, Mr. Constable; I'll lay a Pot of Ale upon's Head, he's a good Preacher.

Constable. Come Sir, out of Respect to your Calling, I shan't put you into the Round-house; but we must Secure you in our Drawing-Room till Morning, that you may do no Mischief. So, Come along.

Sir John. You may put me where you will, Sirrah, now you have overcome me—But if I can't do Mischief, I'll think of Mischief—in spite of your Teeth, you Dog you.   [*Exeunt.*

SCENE.—*A Bed-Chamber*

Enter HEARTFREE, *solus.*

What the Plague Ail's me?—Love? No, I thank you for that; my heart's Rock still.—
Yet 'tis Bellinda that disturbs me; that's positive.

—Well, what of all that? Must I love her for being troublesome?
at that rate, I might love all the Women I meet, I'gad.
But hold!—tho' I don't love her for disturbing me, yet she may
disturb me, because I love her—Ay, that may be, faith.
I have dreamt of her, that's certain—Well, so I have of my
Mother; therefore what's that to the purpose? Ay, but Bellinda
runs in my Mind waking—And so do's many a damn'd thing,
that I don't care a Farthing for—Methinks tho', I would fain
be talking to her, and yet I have no Business.—
Well, am I the first Man that has had a Mind to do an Impertinent thing?

Enter CONSTANT.

Const. How now, Heartfree? What makes you up and Dress'd
so soon? I thought none but Lovers quarrell'd with their Bed;
I expected to have found you snoaring, as I us'd to do.
Heart. Why, faith Friend, 'tis the Care I have of your Affairs,
that makes me so thoughtful; I have been studying all Night,
how to bring your Matter about with Bellinda.
Const. With Bellinda?
Heart. With my Lady, I mean: And faith I have mighty hopes
on't. Sure you must be very well satisfy'd with her Behaviour to
you Yesterday?
Const. So well, that nothing but a Lover's Fears can make me
doubt of Success. But what can this sudden Change proceed
from?
Heart. Why, you saw her Husband beat her, did you not?
Const. That's true: A Husband is scarce to be borne upon
any terms, much less when he fights with his Wife. Methinks
she shou'd e'en have Cuckolded him upon the very spot, to shew
that after the Battel, she was Master of the Field.
Heart. A Council of War of Women would infallibly have
advis'd her to't. But, I confess, so agreeable a Woman as Bellinda,
deserves a better usage.
Const. Bellinda again!
Heart. My Lady, I mean: What a pox makes me blunder so
to day? [*Aside.*] A Plague of this treacherous Tongue.
Const. Prithee look upon me seriously, Heartfree—
Now answer me directly! Is it my Lady, or Bellinda, employs
your careful Thoughts thus?
Heart. My Lady, or Bellinda?
Const. In Love, by this Light in Love.
Heart. In Love?
Const. Nay, ne'er deny it: for thou'lt do it so awkerdly, 'twill

out make the Jest sit heavier about thee. My Dear Friend, I give
hee much Joy.

Heart. Why prithee, you won't perswade me to it, will you?

Const. That she's Mistress of your Tongue, that's plain, and
know you are so honest a Fellow, your Tongue and Heart
always go together.

But how? but how the Devil? Pha, ha, ha, ha—

Heart. Hey day: Why sure you don't believe it in earnest?

Const. Yes, I do; because I see you deny it in jest.

Heart. Nay, but look you, Ned,—a—deny in jest—a—gadzooks, you know I say—a—when a Man denies a thing in jest—
a—

Const. Pha, ha, ha, ha, ha.

Heart. Nay, then we shall have it: What, because a Man
stumbles at a word: Did you never make a Blunder?

Const. Yes, for I am in Love, I own it.

Heart. Then; so am I.—
Now laugh till thy Soul's glutted with Mirth. [*Embracing him.*
But, dear Constant, don't tell the Town on't.

Const. Nay, then 'twere almost pity to laugh at thee, after so
honest a Confession.
But tell us a little, Jack. By what new-invented Arms has this
mighty Stroak been given?

Heart. E'en by that unaccountable Weapon, call'd, je ne sçai
quoy; For every thing that can come within the Verge of Beauty,
I have seen it with Indifference.

Const. So in few words then; the Je ne sçai quoy has been too
hard for the Quilted Petticoat.

Heart. I'gad, I think the Je ne sçai quoy is in the Quilted Petticoat; at least, 'tis certain, I ne'er think on't without—a—a Je
ne sçai quoy in every Part about me.

Const. Well, but have all your Remedies lost their Virtue?
have you turn'd her In-side out yet?

Heart. I dare not so much as think on't.

Const. But don't the two Years Fatigue I have had discourage
you?

Heart. Yes: I dread what I foresee; yet cannot quit the Enterprize. Like some Soldiers, whose Courage dwells more in their
Honour, than their Nature—On they go, tho' the Body trembles
at what the Soul makes it Undertake.

Const. Nay, if you expect your Mistress will use you, as your
Profanations against her Sex deserve, you tremble Justly.
But how do you intend to proceed, Friend?

Heart. Thou know'st I'm but a Novice; be friendly and advise me.

Const. Why look you then; I'd have you—Serenade and a—write a Song—Go to Church; Look like a Fool—Be very Officious: Ogle, Write and Lead out; And who knows, but in a Year or two's time, you may be—call'd a troublesome Puppy and sent about your Business.

Heart. That's hard.

Const. Yet thus it oft falls out with Lovers, Sir.

Heart. Pox on me for making one of the Number.

Const. Have a Care: Say no Saucy things: 'twill but augment your Crime, and if your Mistress hears on't, increase your Punishment.

Heart. Prithee say something then to encourage me; you know I help'd you in your Distress.

Const. Why then to encourage you to Perseverance, that you may be thoroughly ill us'd for your Offences, I'll put you in Mind, That even the coyest Ladies of 'em all are made up of Desires, as well as we; and tho' they do hold out a long time they will Capitulate at last. For that thundering Enginier, Nature, do's make such havock in the Town, they must Surrender at long Run, or Perish in their own Flames.

Enter a FOOTMAN.

Foot. Sir, There's a Porter without with a Letter; he desires to give it into your own Hands.

Const. Call him in.

Enter PORTER.

Const. What, Jo; Is it thee?

Porter. An't please you Sir, I was Order'd to Deliver this into your own Hands, by two well-shap'd Ladies, at the New-Exchange. I was at your Honour's Lodgings, and your Servants sent me hither.

Const. 'Tis well. Are you to carry any Answer?

Porter. No, my noble Master. They gave me my Orders, and whip, they were gone, like a Maiden-head at Fifteen.

Const. Very well; there.   [*Gives him money*

Porter. God bless your Honour.   [*Exit* PORTER

Const. Now let's see what honest, trusty Jo has brought us.

[*Reads.*] *If you and your Play-fellow can spare time from your Business and Devotions, don't fail to be at Spring-Garden about Eight in the Evening. You'll find nothing there but Women, so you need bring no other Arms than what you usually carry about you.*

So, Play-fellow: Here's something to stay your Stomach, till your Mistresses Dish is ready for you.

Heart. Some of our old Batter'd Acquaintance. I won't go, not I.

Const. Nay, that you can't avoid: There's honour in the Case; 'tis a Challenge, and I want a Second.

Heart. I doubt I shall be but a very useless one to you; for I'm so dishearten'd by this Wound Bellinda has given me, I don't think I shall have Courage enough to draw my Sword.

Const. O, if that be all, come along; I'll warrant you find Sword enough for such Enemies as we have to deal withal.

[Exeunt.

Enter CONSTABLE, &c., with SIR JOHN.

Constable. Come along, Sir, I thought to have let you slip this Morning, because you were a Minister; but you are as Drunk and as Abusive as ever. We'll see what the Justice of the Peace will say to you.

Sir John. And you shall see what I'll say to the Justice of the Peace, Sirrah.   *[They knock at the Door.*

Enter SERVANT.

Constab. Pray Acquaint his Worship, we have got an unruly Parson here: We are unwilling to expose him, but don't know what to do with him.

Servant. I'll Acquaint my Master.   *[Exit SERVANT.*

Sir John. You—Constable—What damn'd Justice is this?

Constab. One that will take Care of you, I warrant you.

Enter JUSTICE.

Justice. Well, Mr. Constable; What's the Disorder here?

Constab. An't Please your Worship—

Sir John. Let me speak and be damn'd: I'm a Divine, and can unfold Mysteries better than you can do.

Justice. Sadness, Sadness, a Minister so Over-taken. Pray Sir, Give the Constable leave to speak, and I'll hear you very patiently; I assure you Sir, I will.

Sir John. Sir,—You are a very Civil Magistrate. Your most humble Servant.

Constab. An't Please your Worship then, he has attempted to beat the Watch to Night, and Swore—

Sir John. You Lye.

Justice. Hold, pray Sir, a little.

Sir John. Sir, your very humble Servant.

Constab. Indeed Sir, he came at us without any Provocation, call'd us Whores and Rogues, and laid us on with a great Quarter-Staff. He was in my Lord Rake's Company. They have been playing the Devil to Night.

Justice. Hem—Hem—Pray Sir—May you be Chaplain to my Lord?

Sir John. Sir—I presume—I may if I will.

Justice. My meaning Sir, is—Are you so?

Sir John. Sir,—You mean very well.

Justice. He hem—hem—Under favour, Sir, Pray Answer me directly.

Sir John. Under favour, Sir—Do you use to Answer directly when you are Drunk?

Justice. Good lack, good lack: Here's nothing to be got from him. Pray Sir, may I crave your Name?

Sir John. Sir,—My Name's—   [*He Hycops.*
Hyccop, Sir.

Justice. Hyccop? Doctor Hyccop. I have known a great many Country Parsons of that Name, especially down in the Fenns. Pray where do you live, Sir?

Sir John. Here—and there, Sir.

Justice. Why, what a strange Man is this? Where do you Preach, Sir? Have you any Cure?

Sir John. Sir—I have—a very good Cure—for a Clap, at your Service.

Justice. Lord have mercy upon us.

Sir John. [*Aside.*] This Fellow do's Ask so many Impertinent Questions, I believe I'gad, 'tis the Justice's Wife, in the Justice's Clothes.

Justice. Mr. Constable, I Vow and Protest, I don't know what to do with him.

Constab. Truly, he has been but a troublesome Guest to us all Night.

Justice. I think, I had e'en best let him go about his Business for I'm unwilling to expose him.

Constab. E'en what your Worship thinks fit.

Sir John. Sir,—not to interrupt Mr. Constable, I have a small Favour to ask.

Justice. Sir, I open both my Ears to you.

Sir John. Sir, your very humble Servant. I have a little Urgent Business calls upon me; And therefore I desire the Favour of you, to bring Matters to a Conclusion.

Justice. Sir, If I were sure that Business were not to Commit more Disorders, I wou'd release you.

Sir John. None,—By my Priesthood.

Justice. Then, Mr. Constable, you may Discharge him.

Sir John. Sir, your very humble Servant. If you please to Accept of a Bottle—

Justice. I thank you kindly, Sir; but I never drink in a Morning. Good-buy to ye, Sir, good-buy to ye.

Sir John. Good-buy t'ye, good Sir.   [*Exit* JUSTICE.

So—now, Mr. Constable, Shall you and I go pick up a Whore together.

Constab. No, thank you, Sir; My Wife's enough to satisfie any reasonable Man.

Sir John. [*Aside.*] He, he, he, he, he,—The Fool is Married then. Well, you won't go?

Constab. Not I, truly.

Sir John. Then I'll go by my self; and you and your Wife may be Damn'.   [*Exit* SIR JOHN.

[CONSTABLE *gazing after him.*

Constab. Why God-a-marcy, Parson.   [*Exeunt.*

SCENE.—*Spring-Garden*

CONSTANT *and* HEARTFREE *Cross the Stage. As they go off, Enter*
LADY FANCYFULL *and* MADAMOISELLE, *Mask'd and Dogging 'em.*

Const. So: I think we are about the time appointed; Let us walk up this way.   [*Exeunt.*

Lady Fancy. Good: Thus far I have Dogg'd 'em without being discover'd. 'Tis, infallibly some Intrigue that brings them to Spring-Garden. How my poor Heart is torn and wrackt with Fear and Jealousie. Yet let it be any thing but that Flirt Bellinda, and I'll try to bear it. But if it prove her. All that's Woman in ne shall be employ'd to destroy her.

[*Exeunt after* CONSTANT *and* HEARTFREE.

Re-enter CONSTANT *and* HEARTFREE. LADY FANCYFULL *and*
MADAMOISELLE *still following at a Distance.*

Const. I see no Females yet, that have any thing to say to us. 'm afraid we are banter'd.

Heart. I wish we were; for I'm in no Humour to make either hem or my self merry.

Const. Nay, I'm sure you'll make them merry enough, if I

tell 'em why you are dull. But prithee why so heavy and sad, before you begin to be ill us'd?

Heart. For the same Reason, perhaps, that you are so brisk and well pleas'd; because both Pains and Pleasures are generally more considerable in Prospect, than when they come to pass.

Enter LADY B. *and* BELLINDA, *masked, and poorly dress'd.*

Const. How now, who are these? Not our Game I hope.

Heart. If they are, we are e'en well enough serv'd, to come hunting here, when we had so much better Game in Chase elsewhere.

Lady Fancy. [*To* MADAMOISELLE.] So, those are their Ladies without doubt. But I'm afraid that Doily Stuff is not worn for want of better Cloaths. They are the very Shape and Size of Bellinda and her Aunt.

Madamois. So day be inteed, Matam.

Lady Fancy. We'll slip into this close Arbour, where we may hear all they say.

[*Exeunt* LADY FANCY *and* MADAMOISELLE.

Lady B. What, are you afraid of us, Gentlemen?

Heart. Why truly I think we may, if Appearance don't lye.

Bel. Do you always find Women what they appear to be, Sir?

Heart. No Forsooth; but I seldom find 'em better than they appear to be.

Bel. Then the Outside's best, you think?

Heart. 'Tis the honestest.

Const. Have a care, Heartfree; you are relapsing again.

Lady B. Why, does the Gentleman use to rail at Women?

Const. He has done formerly.

Bel. I suppose he had very good Cause for't: They did not use you so well, as you thought you deserv'd, Sir.

Lady B. They made themselves merry at your Expence, Sir.

Bel. Laugh'd when you Sigh'd.

Lady B. Slept while you were waking.

Bel. Had your Porter beat.

Lady B. And threw your Billet doux in the Fire.

Heart. Hey day, I shall do more than rail presently.

Bel. Why, you won't beat us, will you?

Heart. I don't know but I may.

Const. What the Devil's coming here? Sir John in a Gown?— And drunk I'faith.

Enter SIR JOHN.

Sir John. What a Pox—here's Constant, Heartfree,—and two

Whores I 'gad:—O you covetous Rogues; what, have you never a spare Punk for your Friend?—But I'll share with you.

[*He seizes both the Women.*

Heart. Why, what the Plague have you been doing, Knight?

Sir John. Why, I have been beating the Watch, and scandalizing the Clergy.

Heart. A very good Account, truly.

Sir John. And what do you think I'll do next?

Const. Nay, that no Man can guess.

Sir John. Why, if you'll let me sup with you, I'll treat both your Strumpets.

Lady B. [*Aside.*] O Lord, we are undone.

Heart. No, we can't sup together, because we have some Affairs elsewhere. But if you'll accept of these two Ladies, we'll be so complaisant to you, to resign our Right in 'em.

Bel. [*Aside.*] Lord, what shall we do?

Sir John. Let me see, their Cloaths are such damn'd Cloaths, they won't pawn for the Reckoning.

Heart. Sir John, your Servant. Rapture attend you.

Const. Adieu Ladies, make much of the Gentleman.

Lady B. Why sure, you won't leave us in the Hands of a drunken Fellow to abuse us.

Sir John. Who do you call a drunken Fellow, you Slut you? I'm a Man of Quality; the King has made me a Knight.

[HEART. *runs off.*

Heart. Ay, ay, you are in good Hands! Adieu, adieu.

Lady B. The Devil's Hands: Let me go, or I'll—For Heaven's sake protect us.

[*She breaks from him, runs to* CONSTANT, *twitching off her Mask and clapping it on again.*

Sir John. I'll Devil you, you Jade you. I'll demolish your ugly Face.

Const. Hold a little, Knight, she swoons.

Sir John. I'll swoon her.

Const. Hey, Heartfree.

Re-enter HEARTFREE. BELLINDA *runs to him and shews her Face.*

Heart. O Heavens! My dear Creature, stand there a little.

Const. Pull him off, Jack.

Heart. Hold, mighty Man; look you, Sir, we did but jest with you. These are Ladies of our Acquaintance, that we had a mind to frighten a little, but now you must leave us.

Sir John. Oons, I won't leave you, not I.

Heart. Nay, but you must though; and therefore make no words on't.

Sir John. Then you are a couple of damn'd uncivil Fellows. And I hope your Punks will give you sauce to your Mutton.

[*Exit* SIR JOHN.

Lady B. Oh, I shall never come to my self again, I'm so fright'ned.

Const. 'Twas a narrow 'scape, indeed.

Bel. Women must have Frolicks, you see, whatever they cost 'em.

Heart. This might have prov'd a dear one tho'.

Lady B. You are the more oblig'd to us, for the Risque we run upon your Accounts.

Const. And I hope you'll acknowledge something due to our Knight Errantry, Ladies. This is the second time we have deliver'd you.

Lady B. 'Tis true; and since we see Fate has design'd you for our Guardians, 'twill make us the more willing to trust our selves in your Hands. But you must not have the worse Opinion of us for our Innocent Frolick.

Heart. Ladies, you may command our Opinions in every thing that is to your Advantage.

Bel. Then, Sir, I command you to be of Opinion, that Women are sometimes better than they appear to be.

[LADY BRUTE *and* CONSTANT *talk apart.*

Heart. Madam, you have made a Convert of me in every thing, I'm grown a Fool: I cou'd be fond of a Woman.

Bel. I thank you, Sir, in the Name of the whole Sex.

Heart. Which Sex nothing but your self cou'd ever have aton'd for.

Bel. Now has my Vanity a devilish Itch, to know in what my Merit consists.

Heart. In your Humility, Madam, that keeps you ignorant it consists at all.

Bel. One other Compliment with that serious Face, and I hate you for 'ever after.

Heart. Some Women love to be abus'd: Is that it you wou'd be at?

Bel. No, not that neither: But I'd have Men talk plainly what's fit for Women to hear; without putting 'em either to a real, or an affected Blush.

Heart. Why then, in as plain Terms as I can find to express my self: I cou'd love you even to—Matrimony it self a'most I'gad.

Bel. Just as Sir John did her Ladyship there.

What think you? Don't you believe one Month's time might bring you down to the same Indifference, only clad in a little better Manners, perhaps? Well, you Men are unaccountable things, mad till you have your Mistresses; and then stark mad till you are rid of 'em again. Tell me, honestly, is not your Patience put to a much severer Tryal after Possession, than before?

Heart. With a great many, I must confess, it is, to our eternal Scandal; but I—dear Creature, do but try me.

Bel. That's the surest way indeed, to know, but not the safest. [*To* Lady B.] Madam, are not you for taking a turn in the Great Walk? It's almost dark, no body will know us.

Lady B. Really I find myself something idle, Bellinda; besides, I dote upon this little odd private Corner. But don't let my lazy Fancy confine you.

Const. [*Aside.*] So, she wou'd be left alone with me; that's well.

Bel. Well, we'll take one turn, and come to you again. [*To* Heart.] Come, Sir, shall we go pry into the secrets of the Garden? Who knows what Discoveries we may make?

Heart. Madam, I'm at your Service.

Const. to Heart. [*Aside.*] Don't make too much haste back; for, d'ye hear?—I may be busie.

Heart. Enough.

[*Exit* Bellinda *and* Heartfree.

Lady B. Sure you think me scandalously free, Mr. Constant. I'm afraid I shall lose your good Opinion of me.

Const. My good Opinion, Madam, is like your Cruelty, never to be remov'd.

Lady B. But if I shou'd remove my Cruelty, then there's an end of your good Opinion.

Const. There is not so strict an Alliance between 'em neither. 'Tis certain I shou'd love you then better (if that be possible) than I do now; and where I love, I always esteem.

Lady B. Indeed, I doubt you much: Why, suppose you had a Wife, and she shou'd entertain a Gallant?

Const. If I gave her just Cause, how cou'd I justly condemn her?

Lady B. Ah! but you'd differ widely about just Causes.

Const. But blows can bear no Dispute.

Lady B. Nor Ill Manners much, truly.

Const. Then no Woman upon Earth has so just a Cause as you have.

Lady B. O, but a faithful Wife is a beautiful Character.

Const. To a deserving Husband, I confess it is.

Lady B. But can his Faults Release my Duty?

Const. In Equity without doubt. And where Laws dispense with Equity, Equity should dispense with Laws.

Lady B. Pray let's leave this Dispute; for you Men have as much Witchcraft in your Arguments, as Women have in their Eyes.

Const. But whilst you Attack me with your Charms, 'tis but reasonable I Assault you with mine.

Lady B. The Case is not the same. What Mischief we do, we can't help, and therefore are to be forgiven.

Const. Beauty soon obtains Pardon for the Pain that it gives, when it applies the Balm of Compassion to the Wound; But a fine Face, and a hard Heart, is almost as bad as an ugly Face and a soft one: both very troublesom to many a Poor Gentleman.

Lady B. Yes, and to many a Poor Gentlewoman too, I can assure you. But pray which of 'em is it, that most afflicts you?

Const. Your Glass and Conscience will inform you, Madam. But for Heaven's sake (for now I must be serious) if Pity or if Gratitude can move you. [*Taking her hand.*] If Constancy and Truth have Power to tempt you, If Love, if Adoration can affect you, give me at least some hopes that time may do what you perhaps mean never to perform; 'Twill ease my Sufferings, tho' not quench my Flame.

Lady B. Your Sufferings eas'd, your Flame wou'd soon abate; And that I wou'd preserve, not quench it, Sir.

Const. Wou'd you preserve it, nourish it with favours; for that's the Food it naturally requires.

Lady B. Yet on that Natural Food 'twou'd Surfeit soon, shou'd I resolve to grant all that you wou'd ask.

Const. And in refusing all, you starve it. Forgive me therefore, since my Hunger rages, if I at last grow Wild, and in my frenzy force at least, This from you. [*Kissing her hand.*] Or if you'd have my Flame soar higher still, then grant me this, and this, and this, and Thousands more; [*kissing first her hand, then her neck. Aside.*] for now's the time. She melts into Compassion.

Lady B. [*Aside.*] Poor Coward Vertue, how it shuns the Battle. O heavens! let me go.

Const. Ay, go, ay: Where shall we go, my Charming Angel,— into this private Arbour—Nay, let's lose no time—moments are precious.

Lady B. And Lovers wild. Pray let us stop here; at least for this time.

Const. 'Tis impossible: He that has Power over you, can have none over himself.

[*As he is forcing her into the Arbour,* LADY FANCYFULL
and MADAMOISELLE *bolt out upon them, and Run
over the Stage.*]

Lady B. Ah! I'm lost.

Lady Fancy. Fe, fe, fe, fe, fe.

Madamois. Fe, fe, fe, fe, fe.

Const. Death and Furies, who are these?

Lady B. Oh heavens, I'm out of my Wits; if they knew me,
I'm Ruin'd.

Const. Don't be fright'ned; Ten thousand to One they are
Strangers to you.

Lady B. Whatever they are, I won't stay here a moment longer.

Const. Whither will you go?

Lady B. Home, as if the Devil were in me. Lord, where's this
Bellinda now?

Enter BELLINDA *and* HEARTFREE.

O! it's well you are come: I'm so fright'ned my Hair stands **an**
end. Let's be gone for Heaven's sake.

Bell. Lord, What's the Matter?

Lady B. The Devil's the Matter; we are discover'd. Here's a
Couple of Women have done the most impertinent thing. Away,
Away, Away, Away, Away.   [*Exit running.*

Re-enter LADY FANCYFULL *and* MADAMOISELLE

Lady Fançy. Well Madamoiselle, 'tis a Prodigious thing, **how**
Women can suffer filthy Fellows to grow so familiar with 'em.

Madamois. Ah Matam, il n'y a rien de si Naturel.

Lady Fancy. Fe, fe, fe. But oh my Heart; O Jealousie, O Torture, I'm upon the rack. What shall I do? my Lover's lost, I ne'er
shall see him Mine. [*Pausing.*] But I may be reveng'd; and that's
the same thing. Ah sweet Revenge. Thou welcome thought, thou
healing Balsam to my wounded Soul. Be but propitious on this
one Occasion, I'll place my Heaven in thee, for all my life to
come.

To Woman how indulgent Nature's kind.
No Blast of Fortune long disturbs her Mind.
Compliance to her Fate supports her still;
If Love won't make her Happy—Mischief will.   [*Exeunt.*

THE END OF THE FOURTH ACT [1]

[1] "The Provok'd Wife" was revived in 1725, and Sir John Vanbrugh
wrote two new scenes for Act IV. These are included in the *Mermaid*
edition of Vanbrugh, and were first published in the 1743 issue of the play.

ACT THE FIFTH

SCENE.—LADY FANCYFULL'S *House*

Enter LADY FANCYFULL *and* MADAMOISELLE.

Lady Fancy. Well, Madamoiselle, Did you Dogg the filthy things?

Madamois. O que Ouy Matam.

Lady Fancy. And where are they?

Madamois. Au Logis.

Lady Fancy. What? Men and All?

Madamois. Tous ensemble.

Lady Fancy. O Confidence! What, carry their Fellows to their own House?

Madamois. C'est que le Mari n'y est pas.

Lady Fanc. No, so I believe, truly. But he shall be there, and quickly too, if I can find him out.
Well, 'tis a Prodigious thing, to see when Men and Women get together, how they fortifie one another in their Impudence. But if that Drunken Fool, her Husband, be to be found in e'er a Tavern in Town, I'll send him amongst 'em. I'll spoil their Sport.

Madamois. En Verite Matam, ce seroit domage.

Lady Fancy. 'Tis in Vain to Oppose it, Madamoiselle; therefore never go about it. For I am the steadiest Creature in the World—when I have determin'd to do Mischief. So, Come along.
                                                              [*Exeunt.*

SCENE.—SIR JOHN BRUTE'S *House*

Enter CONSTANT, HEARTFREE, LADY BRUTE, BELLINDA, *and* LOVEWELL.

Lady B. But are you sure you don't Mistake, Lovewell?

Love. Madam, I saw 'em all go into the Tavern together, and my Master was so drunk he cou'd scarce stand.

Lady B. Then, Gentlemen, I believe we may Venture to let you Stay and Play at Cards with us an Hour or two; for they'll scarce part till Morning.

Bell. I think 'tis pity they shou'd ever part.

Const. The Company that's here, Madam.

Lady B. Then, Sir, the Company that's here must remember to part it self, in time.

Const. Madam, we don't intend to forfeit your future Favours by an indiscreet Usage of this. The moment you give us the Signal, we sha'n't fail to make our Retreat.

Lady B. Upon those Conditions then, Let us sit down to Cards.

Enter LOVEWELL.

Love. O Lord, Madam, here's my Master just staggering in upon you; He has been Quarrelsom yonder, and they have kick'd him out of the Company.

Lady B. Into the Closet, Gentlemen, for Heaven's sake; I'll wheedle him to Bed, if possible.

[CONST. *and* HEART. *run into the Closet.*

Enter SIR JOHN, *all Dirt and Bloody.*

Lady B. Ah—ah—he's all over Blood.

Sir John. What the Plague, do's the Woman—Squall for? Did you never seen a Man in Pickle before?

Lady B. Lord, where have you been?

Sir John. I have been at—Cuffs.

Lady B. I fear that is not all. I hope you are not wounded.

Sir John. Sound as a Roche, Wife.

Lady B. I'm mighty glad to hear it.

Sir John. You know—I think you Lye.

Lady B. I know you do me wrong to think so, then. For Heaven's my Witness, I had rather see my own Blood trickle down, than yours.

Sir John. Then will I be Crucify'd.

Lady B. 'Tis a hard Fate, I shou'd not be believ'd.

Sir John. 'Tis a damn'd Atheistical Age, Wife.

Lady B. I am sure I have given you a Thousand tender Proofs, how great my Care is of you. Nay, spite of all your Cruel Thoughts, I'll still persist, and at this moment, if I can, perswade you to lie down, and Sleep a little.

Sir John. Why,—do you think I am drunk—you Slut, you?

Lady B. Heaven forbid I shou'd: But I'm afraid you are Feaverish. Pray let me feel your Pulse.

Sir John. Stand off and be damn'd.

Lady B. Why, I see your Distemper in your very Eyes. You are all on fire. Pray go to Bed; Let me intreat you.

Sir John.—Come kiss me, then.

Lady B. [*Kissing him.*] There: Now go. [*Aside.*] He stinks like Poison.

Sir John. I see it go's damnably against your Stomach—And therefore—Kiss me again.

Lady B. Nay, now you fool me.

Sir John. Do't, I say.

Lady B. [*Aside.*] Ah Lord, have mercy upon me. Well, There; Now will you go?

Sir John. Now Wife, you shall see my Gratitude. You give me two Kisses—I'll give you—two Hundred.

[*Kisses and tumbles her.*]

Lady B. O Lord: Pray, Sir John, be quiet. Heavens, what a Pickle am I in.

Bell. [*Aside.*] If I were in her Pickle, I'd call my Gallant out of the Closet, and he shou'd Cudgel him soundly.

Sir John. So, Now, you being as dirty and as nasty as my self, We may go Pig together. But first, I must have a Cup of your Cold Tea, Wife. [*Going to the Closet.*]

Lady B. O, I'm ruin'd. There's none there, my Dear.

Sir John. I'll warrant you, I'll find some, my Dear.

Lady B. You can't Open the Door, the Lock's spoil'd. I have been turning and turning the Key this half hour to no purpose. I'll send for the Smith to Morrow.

Sir John. There's ne'er a Smith in Europe can Open a Door with more Expedition than I can do.—As for Example,—Pou. [*He bursts Open the Door with his foot.*]—How now?—What the Devil have we got here?—Constant—Heartfree—And two Whores again, I'gad.—This is the worst Cold Tea—that ever I met with in my Life.—

Enter CONSTANT *and* HEARTFREE.

Lady B. [*Aside.*] O Lord, what will become of us?

Sir John. Gentlemen—I am your very humble Servant—I give you many Thanks—I see you take Care of my Family—I shall do all I can to return the Obligation.

Const. Sir, how odly soever this Business may appear to you, you wou'd have no Cause to be uneasie, if you knew the Truth of all things; your Lady is the most virtuous Woman in the World, and nothing has past, but an Innocent Frolick.

Heart. Nothing else, upon my Honour, Sir.

Sir John. You are both very Civil Gentlemen—And my Wife, there, is a very Civil Gentlewoman; therefore I don't doubt but many Civil things have past between you. Your very humble Servant.

Lady B. [*Aside to* CONST.] Pray be gone; He's so drunk he can't hurt us to Night, and to Morrow Morning you shall hear from us.

Const. I'll Obey you, Madam. Sir, when you are Cool, you'll understand Reason better. So then I shall take the Pains to Inform you. If not—I wear a Sword, Sir, and so good-b'uy to you. Come along, Heartfree.

Sir John.—Wear a Sword, Sir:—And what of all that, Sir?— He comes to my House; Eats my Meat; Lies with my Wife; Dishonours my Family; Gets a Bastard to Inherit my Estate.— And when I ask a Civil Account of all this—Sir, says he, I wear a Sword.—Wear a Sword, Sir? Yes Sir, says he; I wear a Sword —It may be a good Answer at Cross-Purposes; But 'tis a Damn'd One to a Man in my Whimsical Circumstance—Sir, says he, I wear a Sword. [*To* LADY B.] And what do you wear now? ha? tell me. [*Sitting down in a great Chair.*] What? you are Modest and cant?—Why then I'll tell you, you Slut you. You wear—an Impudent Lewd Face.—A Damn'd Designing Heart —And a Tail—and a Tail full of— [*He falls fast asleep, snoaring.*

Lady B. So; Thanks to Kind Heaven, he's fast for some Hours.

Bell. 'Tis well he is so, that we may have time to lay our Story handsomly; for we must Lie like the Devil to bring our selves off.

Lady B. What shall we say, Bellinda?

Bell. [*Musing.*]—I'll tell you: It must all light upon Heartfree and I. We'll say he has Courted me some time, but for Reasons unknown to us, has ever been very earnest the thing might be kept from Sir John. That therefore hearing him upon the Stairs, he ran into the Closet, tho' against our Will, and Constant with him, to prevent Jealousie. And to give this a good Impudent face of Truth, (that I may deliver you from the Trouble you are in:) I'll e'en (if he pleases) Marry him.

Lady B. I'm beholding to you, Cousin; but that wou'd be carrying the Jest a little too far for your Own sake: You know he's a younger Brother, and has Nothing.

Bell. 'Tis true; But I like him, and have Fortune enough to keep above Extremity: I can't say I wou'd live with him in a Cell upon Love and Bread and Butter. But I had rather have the Man I love, and a Middle State of Life, Than that Gentleman in the Chair there, and twice your Ladiship's Splendour.

Lady B. In truth, Neice, you are in the Right on't: for I am very Uneasie with my Ambition. But perhaps, had I married as you'll do, I might have been as Ill us'd.

Bel. Some Risque, I do confess, there always is; But if a Man has the least spark, either of Honour or good Nature, he can never use a Woman Ill, that loves him and makes his Fortune both. Yet I must own to you, some little Struggling I still have, with this teazing Ambition, ours. For Pride, you know, is as Natural to a Woman, as 'tis to a Saint. I can't help being fond of this Rogue; and yet it go's to my Heart to think I must never Whisk to Hide-

Park, with above a Pair of Horses; Have no Coronet upon my Coach, nor a Page to carry up my Train. But above all—that business of Place— Well, Taking Place is a Noble Prerogative.

Lady B. Especially after a Quarrel.

Bell. Or of a Rival. But pray say no more on't, for fear I change my Mind. For o'my Conscience, were't not for your Affair in the ballance, I shou'd go near to pick up some Odious Man of Quality yet, and only take poor Heartfree for a Gallant.

Lady B. Then him you must have, however things go?

Bel. Yes.

Lady B. Why, we may pretend what we will; but 'tis a hard matter to Live without the Man we Love.

Bel. Especially when we are Married to the Man we hate. Pray tell me? Do the Men of the Town ever believe us Virtuous, when they see us do so?

Lady B. O, no: Nor indeed hardly, let us do what we will. They most of 'em think there is no such thing as Virtue consider'd in the strictest notions of it: And therefore when you hear 'em say, Such a one is a Woman of Reputation, They only mean she's a Woman of Discretion. For they consider we have no more Religion than they have, nor so much Morality; and between you and I, Bellinda, I'm afraid the want of Inclination seldom protects any of us.

Bel. But what think you of the fear of being found out?

Lady B. I think that never kept any Woman virtuous long. We are not such Cowards neither. No: Let us once pass Fifteen, and we have too good an Opinion of our own Cunning, to believe the World can penetrate into what we wou'd keep a Secret. And so in short, We cannot reasonably blame the Men for judging of us by themselves.

Bel. But sure we are not so Wicked as they are, after all?

Lady B. We are as Wicked, Child, but our Vice lies another way: Men have more Courage than we, so they commit more Bold, Impudent Sins. They Quarrel, Fight, Swear, Drink, Blaspheme, and the like. Whereas we, being Cowards, only Backbite, tell Lyes, Cheat at Cards and so forth. But 'tis late. Let's end our Discourse for to Night; and out of an excess of Charity, take a small Care of that nasty, drunken thing there—Do but look at him, Bellinda.

Bel. Ah—'tis a Savoury Dish.

Lady B. As Savoury as 'tis, I'm cloy'd with't. Prithee Call the Butler to take it away.

Bel. Call the Butler?—Call the Scavenger.

[*To a* Servant *within.*] Who's there? Call Rasor! Let him take away his Master, Scower him clean with a little Soap and Sand, and so put him to Bed.

Lady B. Come Bellinda, I'll e'en lie with you to Night; and in the Morning we'll send for our Gentlemen to set this Matter even.

Bel. Withal my Heart.

Lady B. Good Night, my Dear.   [*Making a low Curtsy.*

Both. Ha, ha, ha.   [*Exeunt.*

Enter RASOR.

My Lady there's a Wag—My Master there's a Cuckold. Marriage is a slippery thing—Women have deprav'd Appetites:—My Lady's a Wag; I have heard all: I have seen all: I understand all, and I'll tell all; for my little Frenchwoman loves News dearly. This Story'll gain her Heart or nothing will. [*To his Master.*] Come, Sir, Your Head's too full of Fumes at present, to make Room for your Jealousie; but I reckon we shall have Rare work with you, when your Pate's empty. Come; to your Kennel, you Cuckoldly drunken Sot you.   [*Carries him out upon his Back.*

SCENE.—LADY FANCYFULL'S *House*

Enter LADY FANCYFULL *and* MADAMOISELLE.

Lady Fancy. But, why did not you tell me before, Madamoiselle, that Rasor and you were fond?

Madamois. De Modesty hinder me, Matam.

Lady Fancy. Why truly Modesty do's often hinder us from doing things we have an Extravagant Mind to. But do's he love you well enough yet, to do any thing you bid him? Do you think to Oblige you he wou'd speak Scandal?

Madamois. Matam, to Oblige your Ladiship, he shall speak Blasphemy.

Lady Fancy. Why then, Madamoiselle, I'll tell you what you shall do. You shall engage him to tell his Master all that past at Spring-Garden. I have a Mind he shou'd know what a Wife and a Neice he has got.

Madamois. Il le fera, Matam.

Enter a FOOTMAN, *who speaks to* MADAMOISELLE *apart.*

Foot. Madamoiselle; Yonder's Mr. Rasor desires to speak with you.

Madamois. Tell him, I come presently. [*Exit* FOOTMAN.] Rasor be dare, Matam.

Lady Fancy. That's Fortunate: Well, I'll leave you together. And if you find him stubborn, Madamoiselle,—heark you—don't refuse him a few little reasonable Liberties, to put him into humour.

Madamois. Laissez moy faire.   [*Exit* LADY FANCYFULL.

RASOR *peeps in; and seeing* LADY FANCYFULL *gone, runs to* MADAMOISELLE, *takes her about the Neck and kisses her.*

Madamois. How now, Confidence?

Ras. How now, Modesty!

Madamois. Who make you so familiar, Sirrah?

Ras. My Impudence, Hussy.

Madamois. Stand off, Rogue-face.

Ras. Ah—Madamoiselle—great News at our House.

Madamois. Wy, wat be de matter?

Ras. The Matter?—why, Uptails All's the Matter.

Madamois. Tu te mocque de moy.

Ras. Now do you long to know the particulars: The time when: The place where: The manner how; But I won't tell you a Word more.

Madamois. Nay, den dou Kill me, Rasor.

Ras. Come, Kiss me, then.   [*Clapping his hands behind him.*

Madamois. Nay, pridee tell me.

Ras. Good b'wy to ye.   [*Going.*

Madamois. Hold, hold: I will Kiss dee.   [*Kissing him.*

Ras. So: that's Civil: Why now, my pretty Pall; my Goldfinch; My little Waterwagtail—you must know that—Come, Kiss me again.

Madamois. I won't Kiss dee no more.

Ras. Good b'wy to ye.

Madamois. Doucement: Dare: es tu content?   [*Kissing him.*

Ras. So: Now I'll tell thee all. Why the News is, That Cuckoldom in Folio is newly Printed; and Matrimony in Quarto is just going into the Press. Will you Buy any Books, Madamoiselle?

Madamois. Tu Parle comme un Librair; de Devil no Understand dee.

Ras. Why then, that I may make my self intelligible to a Waiting-woman, I'll speak like a Vallet de Chamber. My Lady has Cuckolded my Master.

Madamois. Bon.

Ras. Which we take very ill from her hands, I can tell her that. We can't yet prove Matter of Fact upon her.

Madamois. N'importe.

Ras. But we can prove, that Matter of Fact had like to have been upon her.

Madamois. Ouy da.

Ras. For we have such bloody Circumstances—

Madamois. Sans Doute.

Ras. That any Man of Parts may draw tickling Conclusions from 'em.

Madamois. Fort bien.

Ras. We have found a couple of tight, well-built Gentlemen, stuft into her Ladiships Closet.

Madamois. Le Diable.

Ras. And I, in my particular Person, have discover'd a most Damnable Plot, how to perswade my poor Master, that all this Hide and Seek, this Will in the Wisp, has no other meaning than a Christian Marriage for sweet Mrs. Bellinda.

Madamois. Une Marriage?—Ah, les Droless.

Ras. Don't you interrupt me, Hussy; 'tis Agreed, I say. And my Innocent Lady, to Riggle her self out at the Back-door of the Business, turns Marriage-Bawd to her Neice, and resolves to deliver up her fair Body, to be tumbled and mumbled by that young Liquorish Whipster, Heartfree. Now are you satisfy'd?

Madamois. No.

Ras. Right Woman; Always gaping for more.

Madamois. Dis be all den, dat dou know?

Ras. All? Ay, and a great deal too, I think.

Madamois. Dou be fool, dou know noting. Ecoute mon pauvre Rasor. Dou see des two Eyes?—Des two Eyes have see de Devil.

Ras. The Woman's Mad.

Madamois. In Spring-Garden, dat Rogue Constant meet dy Lady.

Ras. Bon.

Madamois. I'll tell dee no more.

Ras. Nay, prithee, my Swan.

Madamois. Come, Kiss me den.

     [*Clapping her hands behind her, as he had done before.*

Ras. I won't Kiss you, not I.

Madamois. Adieu.

Ras. Hold:—Now proceed.   [*Gives her a hearty Kiss.*

Madamois. A ça—I hide my self in one Cunning place, where I hear all, and see all. First dy drunken Master come mal à propos; But de Sot no know his own dear Wife, so he leave her to her Sport—

     [*As she speaks,* RASOR *still acts the Man, and she the Woman.*
Den de game begin.

De Lover say soft ting.

De Lady look upon de Ground.

He take her by de Hand.

She turn her Head, one oder way.

Den he squeez very hard.

Den she pull—very softly.

Den he take her in his Arm.

Den she give him Leetel pat.

Den he Kiss her Tettons.

Den she say—Pish, nay fee.

Den he tremble.

Den she—Sigh.

Den he pull her into de Arbour.

Den she pinch him.

 Ras. Ay, but not so hard, you Baggage you.

 Madamois. Den he grow Bold.

She grow Weak.

He tro her down.

Il tombe dessu.

Le Diable assiste.

Il emporte tout:

Stand off, Sirrah.

   [RASOR *struggles with her, as if he wou'd throw her down.*

 Ras. You have set me a fire, you Jade you.

 Madamois. Den go to de River and quench dy self.

 Ras. What an unnatural Harlot 'tis.

 Madamois. Rasor.   [*Looking languishingly on him.*

 Ras. Madamoiselle.

 Madamois. Dou no love me.

 Ras. Not love thee!—More than a French-man do's Soupe.

 Madamois. Den dou will refuse noting dat I bid dee?

 Ras. Don't bid me be damn'd then.

 Madamois. No, only tell dy Master all I have tell dee of dy Laty.

 Ras. Why, you little malicious Strumpet, you; shou'd you like to be serv'd so?

 Madamois. Dou dispute den?—Adieu.

 Ras. Hold—But why wilt thou make me be such a Rogue, my Dear?

 Madamois. Voilà un Vrai Anglois: il est Amoureux, et cependant il veut raisoner. Va-t'en au Diable.

 Ras. Hold once more: In hopes thou'lt give me up thy Body, I resign thee up my Soul.

 Madamois. Bon: écoute donc:—if dou fail me—I never see dee more—if dou obey me—je m'abandonne à toy.

  [*She takes him about the Neck, and gives him a smacking Kiss.*

            [*Exit.* MADAMOISELLE.

 Ras. [*Licking his Lips.*] Not be a Rogue?—*Amor Vincit omnia.*

                [*Exit* RASOR.

Enter LADY FANCYFULL *and* MADAMOISELLE.

Lady Fancy. Marry, say ye? Will the two things marry?

Madamois. On le va faire, Matam.

Lady Fancy. Look you, Madamoiselle, in short, I can't bear it—
No; I find I can't—If once I see 'em a-bed together, I shall have
ten thousand Thoughts in my Head will make me run distracted.
Therefore run and call Rasor back immediately, for something
must be done to stop this Impertinent Wedding. If I can but deferr
it four and twenty Hours, I'll make such work about Town, with
that little pert Sluts Reputation, He shall as soon marry a Witch.

Madamois. [*Aside.*] La Voilà bien intentionée. [*Exeunt.*

SCENE.—CONSTANT'S *Lodgings*

Enter CONSTANT *and* HEARTFREE.

Const. But what dost think will come of this Business?

Heart. 'Tis easier to think what will not come on't.

Const. What's that?

Heart. A Challenge. I know the Knight too well for that. His
dear Body will always prevail upon his noble Soul to be quiet.

Const. But tho' he dare not challenge me, perhaps he may venture to challenge his Wife.

Heart. Not if you whisper him in the Ear, you won't have him
do't,—and there's no other way left that I see. For as drunk as he
was, he'll remember you and I were where we shou'd not be; and
I don't think him quite Blockhead enough yet to be perswaded we
were got into his Wife's Closet, only to peep in her Prayer-book.

Enter SERVANT, *with a Letter.*

Servant. Sir, Here's a Letter; a Porter brought it.

Const. O ho, here's Instructions for us.

[*Reads.*] *The Accident that has happen'd has touch'd our Invention to the quick. We wou'd fain come off, without your help; but
find that's impossible. In a word, the whole Business must be
thrown upon a Matrimonial Intrigue between your Friend and
mine. But if the Parties are not fond enough to go quite through
with the Matter, 'tis sufficient for our turn, they own the Design.
We'll find Pretences enough, to break the Match. Adieu.*

—Well, Woman for Invention: How long wou'd my Blockhead
have been a producing this.

—Hey, Heartfree; what, musing, Man? Prithee be cheerful. What
say'st thou, Friend, to this Matrimonial Remedy?

Heart. Why I say, it's worse than the Disease.

Const. Here's a Fellow for you: There's Beauty and Money on her Side, and Love up to the Ears on his; and yet—

Heart. And yet, I think, I may reasonably be allow'd to boggle at marrying the Neice, in the very Moment that you are a debauching the Aunt.

Const. Why truly, there may be something in that. But have not you a good Opinion enough of your own Parts, to believe you cou'd keep a Wife to your self?

Heart. I shou'd have, if I had a good Opinion enough of hers, to believe she cou'd do as much by me. For to do 'em Right, after all, the Wife seldom rambles, till the Husband shews her the way.

Const. 'Tis true; a Man of real Worth, scarce ever is a Cuckold, but by his own Fault. Women are not naturally lewd: there must be something to urge 'em to it. They'll cuckold a Churle, out of Revenge; A Fool, because they despise him; a Beast, because they loath him. But when they make bold with a Man they once had a well grounded Value for, 'tis because they first see themselves neglected by him.

Heart. Nay, were I well assur'd that I shou'd never grow Sir John, I ne'er shou'd fear Bellinda'd play my Lady. But our Weakness, thou know'st my Friend, consists in that very Change we so impudently throw upon (indeed) a steadier and more generous Sex.

Const. Why Faith, we are a little Impudent in that Matter, that's the Truth on't. But this is wonderful, to see you grown so warm an Advocate for those (but t'other Day) you took so much pains to abuse.

Heart. All Revolutions run into Extreams; the Bigot makes the boldest Atheist; and the coyest Saint, the most extravagant Strumpet. But Prithee advise me in this good and Evil, this Life and Death, this Blessing and Cursing, that is set before me. Shall I marry—or die a Maid?

Const. Why Faith, Heartfree, Matrimony is like an Army going to engage. Love's the forlorn Hope, which is soon cut off; the Marriage-Knot is the main Body, which may stand Buff a long, long time; and Repentance is the Rear-Guard, which rarely gives ground, as long as the main Battle has a Being.

Heart. Conclusion then; you advise me to whore on, as you do.

Const. That's not concluded yet. For tho' Marriage be a Lottery in which there are a wondrous many Blanks; yet there is one inestimable Lot, in which the only Heaven on Earth is written. Wou'd your kind Fate but guide your Hand to that, though I were wrapt in all that Luxury it self cou'd cloath me with, I still shou'd envy you.

Heart. And justly too: For to be capable of loving one, doubtless is better than to possess a Thousand. But how far that Capacity's in me, alas I know not.

Const. But you wou'd know?

Heart. I wou'd so.

Const. Matrimony will inform you. Come, one Flight of Resolution carries you to the Land of Experience; where, in a very moderate time, you'll know the Capacity of your Soul and your Body both, or I'm mistaken. [*Exeunt.*

SCENE.—SIR JOHN BRUTE's *House*

Enter LADY BRUTE *and* BELLINDA.

Bel. Well, Madam, what Answer have you from 'em?

Lady B. That they'll be here this Moment. I fansie 'twill end in a Wedding. I'm sure he's a Fool if it don't. Ten Thousand Pound, and such a Lass as you are, is no contemptible Offer to a younger Brother. But are not you under strange Agitations? Prithee how do's your Pulse beat?

Bel. High and low, I have much ado to be Valiant: it must feel very strange to go to Bed to a Man?

Lady B. Um—it do's feel a little odd at first, but it will soon grow easy to you.

Enter CONSTANT *and* HEARTFREE.

Lady B. Good Morrow Gentlemen: How have you slept after your Adventure?

Heart. Some careful Thoughts, Ladies, on your Accounts have kept us waking.

Bel. And some careful Thoughts on your own, I believe, have hindred you from sleeping. Pray how do's this Matrimonial Project relish with you?

Heart. Why Faith, e'en as storming Towns does with Soldiers, where the Hope of delicious Plunder banishes the Fear of being knock'd on the Head.

Bel. Is it then possible after all, That you dare think of downright lawful Wedlock?

Heart. Madam, you have made me so Fool-hardy, I dare do any thing.

Bel. Then Sir, I challenge you; and Matrimony's the Spot where I expect you.

Heart. 'Tis enough; I'll not fail. [*Aside.*] So, Now I am in for
Hobbes's Voyage; a great Leap in the Dark.

Lady B. Well, Gentlemen, this Matter being concluded then,
have you got your Lessons ready? For Sir John is grown such an
Atheist of late, he'll believe nothing upon easie Terms.

Const. We'll find ways to extend his Faith, Madam. But pray
how do you find him this Morning?

Lady B. Most lamentably morose, chewing the Cud after last
Night's Discovery, of which however he had but a confus'd Notion
e'en now. But I'm afraid his Vallet de Chamber has told him all,
for they are very busie together at this Moment. When I told him
of Bellinda's Marriage, I had no other Answer but a Grunt: From
which, you may draw what Conclusions you think fit.
But to your Notes, Gentlemen, He's here.

Enter Sir John *and* Rasor.

Const. Good Morrow, Sir.

Heart. Good Morrow, Sir John. I'm very sorry my Indiscretion
shou'd cause so much Disorder in your Family.

Const. Disorders generally come from Indiscretions, Sir; 'tis
no strange thing at all.

Lady B. I hope, my Dear, you are satisfied there was no wrong
intended you.

Sir John. None, my Dove.

Bel. If not, I hope my Consent to marry Mr. Heartfree will
convince you. For as little as I know of Amours, Sir, I can assure
you, one Intrigue is enough to bring four People together, without
further mischief.

Sir John. And I know too, that Intrigues tend to Procreation of
more kinds than one. One Intrigue will beget another as soon as
beget a Son or a Daughter.

Const. I am very sorry, Sir, to see you still seem unsatisfy'd
with a Lady, whose more than common Vertue, I am sure, were
she my Wife, shou'd meet a better Usage.

Sir John. Sir, If her Conduct has put a trick upon her Vertue,
her Vertue's the Bubble, but her Husband's the Loser.

Const. Sir, You have receiv'd a sufficient Answer already, to
justifie both her Conduct and mine. You'll pardon me for medling
in your Family Affairs; but I perceive I am the Man you are
jealous of, and therefore it concerns me.

Sir John. Wou'd it did not concern me, and then I shou'd not care
who it concern'd.

Const. Well, Sir, if Truth and Reason won't content you, I know
but one way more, which, if you think fit, you may take.

Sir John. Lord, Sir, you are very hasty: If I had been found at Prayers in your Wife's Closet, I shou'd have allow'd you twice as much time to come to your self in.

Const. Nay, Sir, if Time be all you want, We have no Quarrel.

Heart. I told you how the Sword wou'd work upon him.

[SIR JOHN *muzes.*

Const. Let him muze; however, I'll lay Fifty Pound our Foreman brings us in, Not Guilty.

Sir John. [*Aside.*] 'Tis well—'tis very well—In spight of that young Jade's Matrimonial Intrigue, I am a downright stinking Cuckold—Here they are—Boo—[*Putting his Hand to his Forehead.*] Methinks I could Butt with a Bull. What the plague did I marry her for? I knew she did not like me; if she had, she wou'd have lain with me; for I wou'd have done so, because I lik'd her: But that's past, and I have her. And now, what shall I do with her? —If I put my Horns in my Pocket, she'll grow Insolent.—If I don't, that Goat there, that Stallion, is ready to whip me through the Guts.—The Debate then is reduc'd to this: Shall I die a Heroe? or live a Rascal?—Why, Wiser Men than I have long since concluded, that a living Dog is better than a dead Lion.—[*To* CONST. *and* HEART.] Gentlemen, now my Wine and my Passion are governable, I must own, I have never observ'd any thing in my Wife's Course of Life to back me in my Jealousie of her: but Jealousie's a mark of Love; so she need not trouble her head about it, as long as I make no more words on't.

LADY FANCYF. *enters Disguis'd, and Addresses to* BELLINDA *apart.*

Const. I am glad to see your Reason rule at last. Give me your Hand: I hope you'll look upon me as you are wont.

Sir John. Your humble Servant. [*Aside.*] A wheedling Son of a Whore.

Heart. And that I may be sure you are Friends with me too, pray give me your Consent to wed your Neice.

Sir John. Sir, you have it with all my Heart: Damn me if you han't. [*Aside.*] 'Tis time to get rid of her; A young, Pert Pimp; She'll make an incomparable Bawd in a little time.

Enter a SERVANT, *who gives* HEARTFREE *a Letter.*

Bel. Heartfree your Husband, say you? 'tis impossible.

Lady Fancy. Wou'd to kind Heaven it were: but 'tis too true; and in the World there lives not such a Wretch. I'm young; and either I have been flatter'd by my Friends, as well as Glass, or Nature has been kind and generous to me. I had a Fortune too, was greater far than he could ever hope for. But with my Heart,

I am robb'd of all the rest. I'm Slighted and I'm Beggar'd both at once. I have scarce a bare Subsistence from the Villain, yet dare complain to none; for he has sworn, if e'er 'tis known I am his Wife, he'll murder me. [*Weeping.*

Bel. The Traytor.

Lady Fancy. I accidentally was told he Courted you; Charity soon prevail'd upon me to prevent your Misery: And as you see, I'm still so generous even to him, as not to suffer he should do a thing for which the Law might take away his Life. [*Weeping.*

Bel. Poor Creature; how I pity her!

[*They continue talking aside.*

Heart. [*Aside.*] Death and Damnation!—Let me read it again. [*Reads.*] *Though I have a particular Reason not to let you know who I am till I see you; yet you'll easily believe 'tis a faithful Friend that gives you this Advice.—I have lain with Bellinda.* (Good.)—*I have a Child by her,* (Better and Better) *which is now at Nurse;* (Heav'n be prais'd) *and I think the Foundation laid for another:* (Ha!—Old Trupenny!)—*No Rack could have tortur'd this Story from me; but Friendship has done it. I heard of your design to Marry her, and cou'd not see you Abus'd. Make use of my Advice, but keep my Secret till I ask you for't again. Adieu.* [*Exit* Lady Fancyfull.

Const. [*To* B.] Come, Madam, Shall we send for the Parson? I doubt here's no business for the Lawyer: Younger Brothers have nothing to settle but their Hearts, and that I believe my Friend here has already done, very faithfully.

Bel. [*Scornfully.*] Are you sure, Sir, there are no old Mortgages upon it?

Heart. [*Coldly.*] If you think there are, Madam, it mayn't be amiss to deferr the Marriage till you are sure they are paid off.

Bel. [*Aside.*] How the Gall'd Horse Kicks!

[*To* Heart.] We'll deferr it as long as you please, Sir.

Heart. The more Time we take to consider on't, Madam, the less apt we shall be to commit Oversights; Therefore, if you please, we'll put it off for just Nine Months.

Bel. Guilty Consciences make Men Cowards: I don't wonder you want Time to Resolve.

Heart. And they make Women Desperate: I don't wonder you were so quickly Determin'd.

Bel. What does the Fellow mean?

Heart. What do's the Lady mean?

Sir John. Zoons, what do you both mean?

[Heart. *and* Bel. *walk chafing about.*

Ras. [*Aside.*] Here is so much Sport going to be spoil'd, it makes me ready to weep again. A Pox o' this Impertinent Lady Fancyfull, and her Plots, and her French-woman too. She's a Whimsical, Ill natur'd Bitch, and when I have got my Bones broke in her Service, 'tis Ten to One but my Recompence is a Clap; I hear 'em tittering without still. I Cod I'll e'en go lug 'em both in by the Ears, and Discover the Plot, to secure my Pardon. [*Exit* Ras.

Const. Prithee explain, Heartfree.

Heart. A fair Deliverance; thank my Stars and my Friend.

Bel. 'Tis well it went no farther. Ah Base Fellow.

Lady B. What can be the meaning of all this?

Bel. What's his meaning, I don't know. But mine is: That if I had Married him—I had had no Husband.

Heart. And what's her meaning, I don't know. But mine is: That if I had Married her—I had had Wife enough.

Sir John. Your People of Wit have got such Cramp ways of expressing themselves, they seldom comprehend one another. Pox take you both, will you speak that you may be Understood?

Enter Rasor *in Sackcloth, pulling in* Lady Fancyf. *and* Madamois.

Ras. If they won't, here comes an Interpreter.

Lady B. Heavens, what have we here?

Ras. A Villain,—but a Repenting Villain. Stuff which Saints in all Ages have been made of.

All. Rasor.

Lady B. What means this suddain Metamorphose?

Ras. Nothing: without my Pardon.

Lady B. What Pardon do you want?

Ras. Imprimis. Your Ladiships; For a Damnable Lye made upon your Spotless Virtue, and set to the Tune of Spring-Garden. [*To* Sir John.] Next, At my Generous Master's Feet I bend, for Interrupting his more Noble Thoughts with Phantomes of Disgraceful Cuckoldom.

[*To* Const.] Thirdly, I to this Gentleman apply, for making him the Hero of my Romance.

[*To* Heartf.] Fourthly, Your Pardon, Noble Sir, I ask, for Clandestinely Marrying you, without either bidding of Banns, Bishop's Licence, Friends Consent—or your own Knowledge.

[*To* Bel.] And lastly, to my good young Ladies Clemency I come, for pretending the Corn was sow'd in the Ground, before ever the Plough had been in the Field.

Sir John. [*Aside.*] So that after all, 'tis a Moot Point, whether I am a Cuckold or not.

Bel. Well Sir, upon Condition you confess all, I'll Pardon you my self, and try to obtain as much for the rest of the Company. But I must know then, who 'tis has put you upon all this Mischief?

Ras. Sathan, and his Equipage. Woman tempted me, Lust weaken'd me;—And so the Devil overcame me: As fell Adam, so fell I.

Bel. Then pray, Mr. Adam, will you make us acquainted with your Eve?

Ras. [*To* MADAMOIS.] Unmask, for the honour of France.

All. Madamoiselle?

Madamois. Me ask ten tousand Pardon of all de good Company.

Sir John. Why, this Mystery thickens instead of clearing up. [*To* RAS.] You Son of a Whore you, put us out of our pain.

Ras. One moment brings Sun-shine. [*Shewing* MADAMOIS.] 'Tis true, This is the Woman that tempted me. But this is the Serpent that tempted the Woman; And if my Prayers might be heard, her Punishment for so doing shou'd be like the Serpent's of Old. [*Pulls of* LADY F*'s Mask.*] She should lie upon her Face, all the days of her Life.

All. Lady Fancyfull.

Bel. Impertinent.

Lady B. Ridiculous.

All. Ha, ha, ha, ha, ha.

Bel. I hope your Ladiship will give me leave to wish you Joy, since you have own'd your Marriage your self.

Mr. Heartfree: I vow 'twas strangely wicked in you to think of another Wife, when you had one already so Charming as her Ladiship.

All. Ha, ha, ha, ha, ha.

Lady F. [*Aside.*] Confusion seize 'em as it seizes me.

Madamois. Que le Diable étouffe ce Maraud de Rasor.

Bel. Your Ladiship seems disorder'd: A Breeding Qualm, perhaps.

Mr. Heartfree: Your Bottle of Hungary Water to your Lady. Why Madam, he stands as Unconcern'd as if he were your Husband in earnest.

Lady Fancy. Your Mirth's as nauseous as your self Bellinda. You think you triumph o'er a Rival now. Hélas ma pauvre fille. Where e'er I'm Rival, there's no cause for Mirth. No, my poor Wretch; 'tis from another Principle I have acted. I knew that thing there wou'd make so perverse a Husband, and you so impertinent a Wife, that lest your mutual Plagues shou'd make you both run Mad, I charitably wou'd have broke the Match. He, he, he, he, he.

[*Exit laughing affectedly.* MADAMOISELLE *following her*.

Madamois. He, he, he, he, he.

All. Ha, ha, ha, ha, ha.

Sir John. [*Aside.*] Why now this Woman will be married to somebody too.

Bel. Poor Creature, what a Passion she's in: But I forgive her.

Heart. Since you have so much goodness for her, I hope you'll Pardon my Offence too, Madam.

Bel. There will be no great difficulty in that, since I am guilty of an equal Fault.

Heart. Then Pardons being past on all Sides, Pray let's to Church to conclude the Day's Work.

Const. But before you go, let me treat you, pray, with a Song a new married Lady made within this Week; it may be of use to you both.

SONG

I

When yielding first to Damon's flame
I sunk into his Arms,
He swore he'd ever be the same,
Then rifl'd all my Charms.
But fond of what h'ad long desir'd,
Too greedy of his Prey,
My Shepherds flame, alas, expir'd
Before the Virge of Day.

II

My Innocence in Lovers Wars,
Reproach'd his quick defeat.
Confus'd, Asham'd, and Bath'd in Tears,
I mourn'd his Cold Retreat.
At length, Ah Shepherdess, cry'd he,
Wou'd you my Fire renew,
Alas you must retreat like me,
I'm lost if you pursue.

Heart. So Madam; Now had the Parson but done his Business—

Bel. You'd be half weary of your Bargain.

Heart. No sure, I might dispense with one Night's Lodging.

Bel. I'm ready to try, Sir.

Heart. Then Let's to Church:

And if it be our Chance, to disagree—

Bel. Take heed:—The surly Husband's Fate you see.

FINIS

EPILOGUE

By Another Hand

Spoken by Lady Brute *and* Bellinda

Lady B.	*No Epilogue!*
Bell.	*I Swear I know of none.*
Lady	*Lord! How shall we excuse it to the Town?*
Bell.	*Why, we must e'en say something of our own.*
Lady	*Our own! Ay, that must needs be precious stuffe.*
Bell.	*I'll lay my life they'l like well enough.*
	Come Faith begin—
Lady	*Excuse me, after you.*
Bell.	*Nay, pardon me for that, I know my Cue.*
Lady	*O for the World, I would not have Precedence.*
Bell.	*O Lord!*
Lady	*I Swear—*
Bell.	*O Fye!*
Lady	*I'm all Obedience.*
	First then, know all, before our Doom is fixt,
	The Third day is for us—
Bell.	*Nay, and the Sixt.*
Lady	*We speak not from the Poet now, nor is it*
	His Cause—(I want a Rhime.)
Bell.	*That we solicite.*
Lady	*Then sure you cannot have the hearts to be severe*
	And Damm us—
Bell.	*Damm us! Let 'em if they Dare.*
Lady	*Why if they should, what punishment Remains?*
Bell.	*Eternal Exile from behind our Scênes.*
Lady	*But if they're kind, that sentence we'll recal,*
	We can be grateful—
Bell.	*And have wherewithall.*
Lady	*But at grand Treaties, hope not to be Trusted,*
	Before Preliminaries are adjusted.
Bell.	*You know the Time, and we appoint this place;*
	Where, if you please, we'll meet and sign the Peace.

THE WAY OF THE WORLD

by

WILLIAM CONGREVE

Audire est operæ pretium, procedere recte
Qui mœchis non vultis.—HORAT. Lib. i. Sat. 2.

Metuat, doti deprensa.—*Ibid.*[1]

---

[1] "Ye that do not wish well to the proceedings of adulterers, *it* is worth your while to hear how they are hampered on all sides."

COMMENDATORY VERSES

To Mr. CONGREVE, *occasioned by his Comedy called "The Way of the World."*

WHEN pleasure's falling to the low delight,
In the vain joys of the uncertain sight;
No sense of wit when rude spectators know,
But in distorted gesture, farce and show;
How could, great author, your aspiring mind
Dare to write only to the few refined?
Yet though that nice ambition you pursue,
'Tis not in Congreve's power to please but few.
Implicitly devoted to his fame,
Well-dressed barbarians know his awful name.
Though senseless they're of mirth, but when they laugh,
As they feel wine, but when, till drunk, they quaff.
  On you from fate a lavish portion fell
In every way of writing to excel.
Your muse applause to Arabella brings,
In notes as sweet as Arabella sings.
Whene'er you draw an undissembled woe,
With sweet distress your rural numbers flow:
Pastora's the complaint of every swain,
Pastora still the echo of the plain!
Or if your muse describe, with warming force,
The wounded Frenchman falling from his horse;
And her own William glorious in the strife,
Bestowing on the prostrate foe his life:
You the great act as generously rehearse,
And all the English fury's in your verse.
By your selected scenes and handsome choice,
Ennobled Comedy exalts her voice;
You check unjust esteem and fond desire,
And teach to scorn what else we should admire:
The just impression taught by you we bear,
The player acts the world, the world the player;
Whom still that world unjustly disesteems,
Though he alone professes what he seems.

But when your muse assumes her tragic part,
She conquers and she reigns in every heart:
To mourn with her men cheat their private woe,
And generous pity's all the grief they know.
The widow, who, impatient of delay,
From the town joys must mask it to the play,
Joins with your Mourning Bride's resistless moan,
And weeps a loss she slighted when her own:
You give us torment, and you give us ease,
And vary our afflictions as you please.
Is not a heart so kind as yours in pain,
To load your friends with cares you only feign;
Your friends in grief, composed yourself, to leave?
But 'tis the only way you'll e'er deceive.
Then still, great sir, your moving power employ,
To lull our sorrow, and correct our joy.

                                    RICHARD STEELE.

To the Right Honourable

RALPH, EARL OF MONTAGUE, &c.

My Lord,

Whether the world will arraign me of vanity or not, that I have presumed to dedicate this comedy to your Lordship, I am yet in doubt; though, it may be, it is some degree of vanity even to doubt of it. One who has at any time had the honour of your Lordship's conversation, cannot be supposed to think very meanly of that which he would prefer to your perusal; yet it were to incur the imputation of too much sufficiency, to pretend to such a merit as might abide the test of your Lordship's censure.

Whatever value may be wanting to this play while yet it is mine, will be sufficiently made up to it when it is once become your Lordship's; and it is my security that I cannot have overrated it more by my dedication, than your Lordship will dignify it by your patronage.

That it succeeded on the stage, was almost beyond my expectation; for but little of it was prepared for that general taste which seems now to be predominant in the palates of our audience.

Those characters which are meant to be ridiculed in most of our comedies, are of fools so gross, that, in my humble opinion, they should rather disturb than divert the well-natured and reflecting part of an audience; they are rather objects of charity than contempt; and instead of moving our mirth, they ought very often to excite our compassion.

This reflection moved me to design some characters which should appear ridiculous, not so much through a natural folly (which is incorrigible, and therefore not proper for the stage) as through an affected wit; a wit, which at the same time that it is affected, is also false. As there is some difficulty in the formation of a character of this nature, so there is some hazard which attends the progress of its success upon the stage; for many come to a play so overcharged with criticism, that they very often let fly their censure, when through their rashness they have mistaken their aim. This I had occasion lately to observe; for this play had been acted two or three days, before some of these hasty judges could find the leisure to distinguish betwixt the character of a Witwoud and a Truewit.

I must beg your Lordship's pardon for this digression from the true course of this epistle; but that it may not seem altogether impertinent, I beg that I may plead the occasion of it, in part of that excuse of which I stand in need, for recommending this comedy to your protection. It is only by the countenance of your Lordship, and the *few* so qualified, that such who wrote with care and pains can hope to be distinguished; for the prostituted name of *poet* promiscuously levels all that bear it.

Terence, the most correct writer in the world, had a Scipio and a Lælius, if not to assist him, at least to support him in his reputation; and notwithstanding his extraordinary merit, it may be their countenance was not more than necessary.

The purity of his style, the delicacy of his turns, and the justness of his characters, were all of them beauties which the greater part of his audience were incapable of tasting; some of the coarsest strokes of Plautus, so severely censured by Horace, were more likely to affect the multitude; such who come with expectation to laugh at the last act of a play, and are better entertained with two or three unseasonable jests, than with the artful solution of the *fable*.

As Terence excelled in his performances, so had he great advantages to encourage his undertakings; for he built most on the foundations of Menander; his plots were generally modelled, and his characters ready drawn to his hand. He copied Menander, and Menander had no less light in the formation of his characters, from the observations of Theophrastus, of whom he was a disciple; and Theophrastus, it is known, was not only the disciple, but the immediate successor of Aristotle, the first and greatest judge of poetry. These were great models to design by; and the further advantage which Terence possessed, towards giving his plays the due ornaments of purity of style and justness of manners, was not less considerable, from the freedom of conversation which was permitted him with Lælius and Scipio, two of the greatest and most polite men of his age. And indeed the privilege of such a conversation is the only certain means of attaining to the perfection of dialogue.

If it has happened in any part of this comedy, that I have gained a turn of style or expression more correct, or at least, more corrigible, than in those which I have formerly written, I must, with equal pride and gratitude, ascribe it to honour of your Lordship's admitting me into your conversation, and that of a society where everybody else was so well worthy of you, in your retirement last summer from the town; for it was immediately after that this comedy was written. If I have failed in my performance, it is only to be regretted, where there were so many, not inferior either to a Scipio or a Lælius, that there should be one wanting equal in capacity to a Terence.

If I am not mistaken, poetry is almost the only art which has not yet laid claim to your Lordship's patronage. Architecture and painting, to the great honour of our country, have flourished under your influence and protection. In the mean time, poetry, the eldest sister of all arts, and parent of most, seems to have resigned her birthright, by having neglected to pay her duty to your Lordship, and by permitting others of a later extraction, to prepossess that place in your esteem to which none can pretend a better title. Poetry, in its nature, is sacred to the good and great; the relation between them is reciprocal, and they are ever propitious to it. It is the privilege of poetry to address to them, and it is their prerogative alone to give it protection.

This received maxim is a general apology for all writers who consecrate their labours to great men; but I could wish at this time, that this address were exempted from the common pretence of all dedications; and that I can distinguish your Lordship even among the most deserving, so this offering might become remarkable by some particular instance of respect, which should assure your Lordship, that I am, with all due sense of your extreme worthiness and humanity, my Lord, your Lordship's most obedient, and most obliged humble servant,

WILL. CONGREVE.

PROLOGUE

Of those few fools who with ill stars are curst,
Sure scribbling fools, called poets, fare the worst:
For they're a sort of fools which Fortune makes,
And after she has made 'em fools, forsakes.
With Nature's oafs 'tis quite a different case,
For Fortune favours all her idiot-race.
In her own nest the cuckoo-eggs we find,
O'er which she broods to hatch the changeling-kind.
No portion for her own she has to spare,
So much she dotes on her adopted care.

Poets are bubbles, by the town drawn in,
Suffered at first some trifling stakes to win;
But what unequal hazards do they run!
Each time they write they venture all they've won:
The squire that's buttered still, is sure to be undone.
This author heretofore has found your favour;
But pleads no merit from his past behaviour.
To build on that might prove a vain presumption,
Should grants, to poets made, admit resumption:
And in Parnassus he must lose his seat,
If that be found a forfeited estate.

He owns with toil he wrought the following scenes;
But, if they're naught, ne'er spare him for his pains:
Damn him the more; have no commiseration
For dulness on mature deliberation,
He swears he'll not resent one hissed-off scene,
Nor, like those peevish wits, his play maintain,
Who, to assert their sense, your taste arraign.
Some plot we think he has, and some new thought;
Some humour too, no farce; but that's a fault.
Satire, he thinks, you ought not to expect;
For so reformed a town who dares correct?
To please, this time, has been his sole pretence,
He'll not instruct, lest it should give offence.

Should he by chance a knave or fool expose,
That hurts none here, sure here are none of those:
In short, our play shall (with your leave to show it)
Give you one instance of a passive poet,
Who to your judgments yields all resignation;
So save or damn, after your own discretion.

DRAMATIS PERSONÆ

FAINALL, in love with MRS. MARWOOD.

MIRABELL, in love with MRS. MILLAMANT.

WITWOUD, ⎱ Followers of MRS. MILLAMANT.
PETULANT, ⎰

SIR WILFULL WITWOUD, half Brother to WITWOUD, and Nephew
    to LADY WISHFORT.

WAITWELL, Servant to MIRABELL.

LADY WISHFORT, Enemy to MIRABELL, for having falsely pre-
    tended love to her.

MRS. MILLAMANT, a fine Lady, Niece to LADY WISHFORT, and
    loves MIRABELL.

MRS. MARWOOD, Friend to MR. FAINALL, and likes MIRABELL.

MRS. FAINALL, Daughter to LADY WISHFORT, and Wife to FAIN-
    ALL, formerly Friend to MIRABELL.

FOIBLE, Woman to LADY WISHFORT.

MINCING, Woman to MRS. MILLAMANT.

BETTY, Waiting-maid at a Chocolate-house.

PEG, Maid to LADY WISHFORT.

Coachmen, Dancers, Footmen, and Attendants.

SCENE—LONDON.

THE WAY OF THE WORLD

ACT THE FIRST

SCENE I

A Chocolate House

MIRABELL *and* FAINALL, *rising from cards,* BETTY *waiting.*

Mir. You are a fortunate man, Mr. Fainall!

Fain. Have we done?

Mir. What you please: I'll play on to entertain you.

Fain. No, I'll give you your revenge another time, when you are not so indifferent; you are thinking of something else now, and play too negligently; the coldness of a losing gamester lessens the pleasure of the winner. I'd no more play with a man that slighted his ill fortune than I'd make love to a woman who undervalued the loss of her reputation.

Mir. You have a taste extremely delicate, and are for refining on your pleasures.

Fain. Prithee, why so reserved? Something has put you out of humour.

Mir. Not at all: I happen to be grave to day, and you are gay; that's all.

Fain. Confess, Millamant and you quarrelled last night after I left you; my fair cousin has some humours that would tempt the patience of a Stoic. What, some coxcomb came in, and was well received by her, while you were by?

Mir. Witwoud and Petulant; and what was worse, her aunt, your wife's mother, my evil genius: or to sum up all in her own name, my old Lady Wishfort came in.

Fain. O there it is then! She has a lasting passion for you, and with reason.—What, then my wife was there?

Mir. Yes, and Mrs. Marwood, and three or four more, whom I never saw before. Seeing me, they all put on their grave faces, whispered one another; then complained aloud of the vapours, and after fell into a profound silence.

Fain. They had a mind to be rid of you.

Mir. For which reason I resolved not to stir. At last the good old lady broke through her painful taciturnity with an invective against long visits. I would not have understood her, but Millamant joining in the argument, I rose, and, with a constrained smile, told her, I thought nothing was so easy as to know when a visit began to be troublesome. She reddened, and I withdrew, without expecting her reply.

Fain. You were to blame to resent what she spoke only in compliance with her aunt.

Mir. She is more mistress of herself than to be under the necessity of such a resignation.

Fain. What! though half her fortune depends upon her marrying with my lady's approbation?

Mir. I was then in such a humour, that I should have been better pleased if she had been less discreet.

Fain. Now, I remember, I wonder not they were weary of you; last night was one of their cabal nights; they have 'em three times a-week, and meet by turns at one another's apartments, where they come together like the coroner's inquest, to sit upon the murdered reputations of the week. You and I are excluded; and it was once proposed that all the male sex should be excepted; but somebody moved that, to avoid scandal, there might be one man of the community; upon which motion Witwoud and Petulant were enrolled members.

Mir. And who may have been the foundress of this sect? My Lady Wishfort, I warrant, who publishes her detestation of mankind; and full of the vigour of fifty-five, declares for a friend and ratafia; and let posterity shift for itself, she'll breed no more.

Fain. The discovery of your sham addresses to her, to conceal your love to her niece, has provoked this separation; had you dissembled better, things might have continued in the state of nature.

Mir. I did as much as man could, with any reasonable conscience; I proceeded to the very last act of flattery with her, and was guilty of a song in her commendation. Nay, I got a friend to put her into a lampoon, and compliment her with the imputation of an affair with a young fellow, which I carried so far, that I told her the malicious town took notice that she was grown fat of a sudden; and when she lay in of a dropsy, persuaded her she was reported to be in labour. The devil's in't, if an old woman is to be flattered further, unless a man should endeavour downright personally to debauch her; and that my virtue forbade me. But for the discovery of this amour I am indebted to your friend, or your wife's friend, Mrs. Marwood.

Fain. What should provoke her to be your enemy, unless she has made you advances which you have slighted? Women do not easily forgive omissions of that nature.

Mir. She was always civil to me till of late.—I confess I am not one of those coxcombs who are apt to interpret a woman's good manners to her prejudice, and think that she who does not refuse 'em everything, can refuse 'em nothing.

Fain. You are a gallant man, Mirabell; and though you may have cruelty enough not to satisfy a lady's longing, you have too much generosity not to be tender of her honour. Yet you speak with an indifference which seems to be affected, and confesses you are conscious of a negligence.

Mir. You pursue the argument with a distrust that seems to be unaffected, and confesses you are conscious of a concern for which the lady is more indebted to you than is your wife.

Fain. Fy, fy, friend! if you grow censorious I must leave you.—I'll look upon the gamesters in the next room.

Mir. Who are they?

Fain. Petulant and Witwoud.—[*To* BETTY.] Bring me some chocolate.   [*Exit.*

Mir. Betty, what says your clock?

Bet. Turned of the last canonical hour, sir.   [*Exit.*

Mir. How pertinently the jade answers me!—[*Looking on his watch.*]—Ha! almost one o'clock!—O, y'are come!

Enter Footman.

Well, is the grand affair over? You have been something tedious.

Foot. Sir, there's such coupling at Pancras, that they stand behind one another, as 'twere in a country dance. Ours was the last couple to lead up; and no hopes appearing of despatch; besides, the parson growing hoarse, we were afraid his lungs would have failed before it came to our turn; so we drove round to Duke's-place; and there they were rivetted in a trice.

Mir. So, so, you are sure they are married.

Foot. Married and bedded, sir; I am witness.

Mir. Have you the certificate?

Foot. Here it is, sir.

Mir. Has the tailor brought Waitwell's clothes home, and the new liveries?

Foot. Yes, sir.

Mir. That's well. Do you go home again, d'ye hear, and adjourn the consummation till further orders. Bid Waitwell shake his ears, and Dame Partlet rustle up her feathers, and meet me at one o'clock by Rosamond's Pond,[1] that I may see her before she returns to her lady; and as you tender your ears be secret.   [*Exeunt*.

The same

MIRABELL, FAINALL, *and* BETTY.

Fain. Joy of your success, Mirabell; you look pleased.

Mir. Ay; I have been engaged in a matter of some sort of mirth, which is not yet ripe for discovery. I am glad this is not a cabal night. I wonder, Fainall, that you who are married, and of consequence should be discreet, will suffer your wife to be of such a party.

Fain. Faith, I am not jealous. Besides, most who are engaged are women and relations; and for the men, they are of a kind too contemptible to give scandal.

Mir. I am of another opinion. The greater the coxcomb, always the more the scandal: for a woman, who is not a fool, can have but one reason for associating with a man'who is one.

Fain. Are you jealous as often as you see Witwoud entertained by Millamant?

Mir. Of her understanding I am, if not of her person.

Fain. You do her wrong; for, to give her her due, she has wit.

Mir. She has beauty enough to make any man think so; and complaisance enough not to contradict him who shall tell her so.

Fain. For a passionate lover, methinks you are a man somewhat too discerning in the failings of your mistress.

Mir. And for a discerning man, somewhat too passionate a lover; for I like her with all her faults; nay, like her for her faults. Her follies are so natural, or so artful, that they become her; and those affectations which in another woman would be odious, serve but to make her more agreeable. I'll tell thee, Fainall, she once used me with that insolence, that in revenge I took her to pieces; sifted her, and separated her failings; I studied 'em, and got 'em by rote. The catalogue was so large, that I was not without hopes one day or other to hate her heartily: to which end I so used myself to think of 'em, that at length, contrary to my design and expectation, they gave me every hour less and less disturbance; till in a few days it became habitual to me to remember 'em without being dis-

---

[1] Rosamond's Pond was a sheet of water in the south-west corner of St. James's Park, "long consecrated to disastrous love and elegiac poetry." It was filled up in 1770.

pleased. They are now grown as familiar to me as my own frailties; and in all probability, in a little time longer, I shall like 'em as well.

Fain. Marry her, marry her! be half as well acquainted with her charms, as you are with her defects, and my life on't, you are your own man again.

Mir. Say you so?

Fain. Ay, ay, I have experience: I have a wife, and so forth.

Enter Messenger.

Mes. Is one Squire Witwoud here?

Bet. Yes, what's your business?

Mes. I have a letter for him, from his brother Sir Wilfull, which I am charged to deliver into his own hands.

Bet. He's in the next room, friend—that way.

[*Exit* Messenger.

Mir. What, is the chief of that noble family in town, Sir Wilfull Witwoud?

Fain. He is expected to-day. Do you know him?

Mir. I have seen him. He promises to be an extraordinary person; I think you have the honour to be related to him.

Fain. Yes; he is half brother to this Witwoud by a former wife, who was sister to my Lady Wishfort, my wife's mother. If you marry Millamant, you must call cousins too.

Mir. I had rather be his relation than his acquaintance.

Fain. He comes to town in order to equip himself for travel.

Mir. For travel! why, the man that I mean is above forty.

Fain. No matter for that; 'tis for the honour of England, that all Europe should know we have blockheads of all ages.

Mir. I wonder there is not an act of parliament to save the credit of the nation, and prohibit the exportation of fools.

Fain. By no means; 'tis better as 'tis.. 'Tis better to trade with a little loss, than to be quite eaten up with being overstocked.

Mir. Pray, are the follies of this knight-errant, and those of the squire his brother, anything related?

Fain. Not at all; Witwoud grows by the knight, like a medlar grafted on a crab. One will melt in your mouth, and t'other set your teeth on edge; one is all pulp, and the other all core.

Mir. So one will be rotten before he be ripe, and the other will be rotten without ever being ripe at all.

Fain. Sir Wilfull is an odd mixture of bashfulness and obstinacy.—But when he's drunk he's as loving as the monster in the Tempest, and much after the same manner. To give t'other his due, he has something of good-nature, and does not always want wit.

Mir. Not always: but as often as his memory fails him, and his common-place of comparisons. He is a fool with a good memory, and some few scraps of other folks' wit. He is one whose conversation can never be approved, yet it is now and then to be endured. He has indeed one good quality, he is not exceptious; for he so passionately affects the reputation of understanding raillery, that he will construe an affront into a jest; and call downright rudeness and ill language, satire and fire.

Fain. If you have a mind to finish his picture, you have an opportunity to do it at full length. Behold the original!

Enter WITWOUD.

Wit. Afford me your compassion, my dears! pity me, Fainall! Mirabell, pity me!

Mir. I do from my soul.

Fain. Why, what's the matter?

Wit. No letters for me, Betty?

Bet. Did not a messenger bring you one but now, sir?

Wit. Ay, but no other?

Bet. No, sir.

Wit. That's hard, that's very hard.—A messenger! a mule, a beast of burden! he has brought me a letter from the fool my brother, as heavy as a panegyric in a funeral sermon, or a copy of commendatory verses from one poet to another: and what's worse, 'tis as sure a forerunner of the author, as an epistle dedicatory.

Mir. A fool, and your brother, Witwoud!

Wit. Ay, ay, my half brother. My half brother he is, no nearer upon honour.

Mir. Then 'tis possible he may be but half a fool.

Wit. Good, good, Mirabell, *le drôle!* good, good; hang him, don't let's talk of him.—Fainall, how does your lady? Gad, I say anything in the world to get this fellow out of my head. I beg pardon that I should ask a man of pleasure, and the town, a question at once so foreign and domestic. But I talk like an old maid at a marriage; I don't know what I say: but she's the best woman in the world.

Fain. 'Tis well you don't know what you say, or else your commendation would go near to make me either vain or jealous.

Wit. No man in town lives well with a wife but Fainall.— Your judgment, Mirabell.

Mir. You had better step and ask his wife, if you would be credibly informed.

Wit. Mirabell?

Mir. Ay.

Wit. My dear, I ask ten thousand pardons;—gad, I have forgot what I was going to say to you!

Mir. I thank you heartily, heartily.

Wit. No, but prithee excuse me:—my memory is such a memory.

Mir. Have a care of such apologies, Witwoud; for I never knew a fool but he affected to complain, either of the spleen or his memory.

Fain. What have you done with Petulant?

Wit. He's reckoning his money—my money it was.—I have no luck to-day.

Fain. You may allow him to win of you at play: for you are sure to be too hard for him at repartee; since you monopolise the wit that is between you, the fortune must be his of course.

Mir. I don't find that Petulant confesses the superiority of wit to be your talent, Witwoud.

Wit. Come, come, you are malicious now, and would breed debates.—Petulant's my friend, and a very honest fellow, and a very pretty fellow, and has a smattering—faith and troth, a pretty deal of an odd sort of a small wit: nay, I'll do him justice. I'm his friend, I won't wrong him neither.—And if he had any judgment in the world, he would not be altogether contemptible. Come, come, don't detract from the merits of my friend.

Fain. You don't take your friend to be over-nicely bred?

Wit. No, no, hang him, the rogue has no manners at all, that I must own:—no more breeding than a bum-bailiff, that I grant you:—'tis pity, faith; the fellow has fire and life.

Mir. What, courage?

Wit. Hum, faith I don't know as to that, I can't say as to that—Yes, faith, in a controversy, he'll contradict anybody.

Mir. Though 'twere a man whom he feared, or a woman whom he loved.

Wit. Well, well, he does not always think before he speaks; —we have all our failings: you are too hard upon him, you are, faith. Let me excuse him—I can defend most of his faults, except one or two: one he has, that's the truth on't; if he were my brother, I could not acquit him:—that, indeed, I could wish were otherwise.

Mir. Ay, marry, what's that, Witwoud?

Wit. O pardon me!—expose the infirmities of my friend!—No, my dear, excuse me there.

Fain. What, I warrant he's unsincere, or 'tis some such trifle.

Wit. No, no; what if he be? 'tis no matter for that, his wit will excuse that: a wit should no more be sincere, than a woman constant; one argues a decay of parts, as t'other of beauty.

Mir. Maybe you think him too positive?

Wit. No, no, his being positive is an incentive to argument, and keeps up conversation.

Fain. Too illiterate?

Wit. That! that's his happiness:—his want of learning gives him the more opportunities to show his natural parts.

Mir. He wants words?

Wit. Ay: but I like him for that now; for his want of words gives me the pleasure very often to explain his meaning.

Fain. He's impudent?

Wit. No, that's not it.

Mir. Vain?

Wit. No.

Mir. What! he speaks unseasonable truths sometimes, because he has not wit enough to invent an evasion?

Wit. Truths! ha! ha! ha! no, no; since you will have it,—I mean, he never speaks truth at all,—that's all. He will lie like a chambermaid, or a woman of quality's porter. Now that is a fault.

Enter Coachman.

Coach. Is Master Petulant here, mistress?

Bet. Yes.

Coach. Three gentlewomen in a coach would speak with him.

Fain. O brave Petulant! three!

Bet. I'll tell him.

Coach. You must bring two dishes of chocolate and a glass of cinnamon-water.[1]   [*Exeunt* BETTY *and* Coachman.

Wit. That should be for two fasting strumpets, and a bawd troubled with the wind. Now you may know what the three are.

Mir. You are very free with your friend's acquaintance.

Wit. Ay, ay, friendship without freedom is as dull as love without enjoyment, or wine without toasting. But to tell you

---

[1] A mixture of sugar, spirit, powdered cinnamon, and hot water. A favourite drink of Dean Swift, who was a martyr to dyspepsia.

a secret, these are trulls whom he allows coach-hire, and something more, by the week, to call on him once a-day at public places.

Mir. How!

Wit. You shall see he won't go to 'em, because there's no more company here to take notice of him.—Why this is nothing to what he used to do:—before he found out this way, I have known him call for himself.

Fain. Call for himself! what dost thou mean?

Wit. Mean! why he would slip you out of this chocolate-house, just when you had been talking to him—as soon as your back was turned—whip he was gone!—then trip to his lodging, clap on a hood and scarf, and a mask, slap into a hackney-coach, and drive hither to the door again in a trice, where he would send in for himself; that I mean, call for himself, wait for himself; nay, and what's more, not finding himself, some-times leave a letter for himself.

Mir. I confess this is something extraordinary.—I believe he waits for himself now, he is so long a-coming: Oh! I ask his pardon.

Enter PETULANT *and* BETTY.

Bet. Sir, the coach stays.

Pet. Well, well;—I come.—'Sbud, a man had as good be a professed midwife, as a professed whoremaster, at this rate! to be knocked up and raised at all hours, and in all places. Pox on 'em, I won't come!—D'ye hear, tell 'em I won't come:—let 'em snivel and cry their hearts out.

Fain. You are very cruel, Petulant.

Pet. All's one, let it pass:—I have a humour to be cruel.

Mir. I hope they are not persons of condition that you use at this rate.

Pet. Condition! condition's a dried fig, if I am not in humour! —By this hand, if they were your—a—a—your what d'ye-call-'ems themselves, they must wait or rub off, if I want appetite.

Mir. What d'ye-call-'ems! what are they, Witwoud?

Wit. Empresses, my dear:—by your what-d'ye-call-'ems he means sultana queens.

Pet. Ay, Roxolanas.

Mir. Cry you mercy!

Fain. Witwoud says they are—

Pet. What does he say th'are?

Wit. I? fine ladies, I say.

Pet. Pass on, Witwoud.—Hark'ee, by this light his relations:

—two co-heiresses his cousins, and an old aunt, who loves caterwauling better than a conventicle.

Wit. Ha! ha! ha! I had a mind to see how the rogue would come off.—Ha! ha! ha! gad, I can't be angry with him, if he had said they were my mother and my sisters.

Mir. No!

Wit. No; the rogue's wit and readiness of invention charm me. Dear Petulant.

Bet. They are gone, sir, in great anger.

Pet. Enough, let 'em trundle. Anger helps complexion, saves paint.

Fain. This continence is all dissembled; this is in order to have something to brag of the next time he makes court to Millamant, and swear he has abandoned the whole sex for her sake.

Mir. Have you not left off your impudent pretensions there yet? I shall cut your throat some time or other, Petulant, about that business.

Pet. Ay, ay, let that pass—there are other throats to be cut.

Mir. Meaning mine, sir?

Pet. Not I—I mean nobody—I know nothing:—but there are uncles and nephews in the world—and they may be rivals—what then! all's one for that.

Mir. How! hark'ee, Petulant, come hither:—explain, or I shall call your interpreter.

Pet. Explain! I know nothing.—Why, you have an uncle, have you not, lately come to town, and lodges by my Lady Wishfort's?

Mir. True.

Pet. Why, that's enough—you and he are not friends; and if he should marry and have a child, you may be disinherited, ha?

Mir. Where hast thou stumbled upon all this truth?

Pet. All's one for that, why then say I know something.

Mir. Come, thou art an honest fellow, Petulant, and shalt make love to my mistress, thou sha't, faith. What hast thou heard of my uncle?

Pet. I? nothing I. If throats are to be cut, let swords clash! snug's the word, I shrug and am silent.

Mir. Oh, raillery, raillery! Come, I know thou art in the women's secrets.—What, you're a cabalist; I know you stayed at Millamant's last night, after I went. Was there any mention made of my uncle or me? tell me. If thou hadst but good-nature equal to thy wit, Petulant, Tony Witwoud, who is now

thy competitor in fame, would show as dim by thee as a dead
whiting's eye by a pearl of orient; he would no more be seen
by thee, than Mercury is by the sun. Come, I'm sure thou
wo't tell me.

Pet. If I do, will you grant me common sense then for the
future?

Mir. Faith, I'll do what I can for thee, and I'll pray that
Heaven may grant it thee in the meantime.

Pet. Well, hark'ee.   [MIRABELL *and* PETULANT *talk apart.*

Fain. Petulant and you both will find Mirabell as warm a
rival as a lover.

Wit. Pshaw! pshaw! that she laughs at Petulant is plain.
And for my part, but that it is almost a fashion to admire her,
I should—hark'ee—to tell you a secret, but let it go no further
—between friends, I shall never break my heart for her.

Fain. How!

Wit. She's handsome; but she's a sort of an uncertain woman.

Fain. I thought you had died for her.

Wit. Umh—no—

Fain. She has wit.

Wit. 'Tis what she will hardly allow anybody else:—now,
demme, I should hate that, if she were as handsome as Cleopatra. Mirabell is not so sure of her as he thinks for.

Fain. Why do you think so?

Wit. We stayed pretty late there last night, and heard something of an uncle to Mirabell, who is lately come to town—
and is between him and the best part of his estate. Mirabell
and he are at some distance, as my Lady Wishfort has been
told; and you know she hates Mirabell worse than a quaker
hates a parrot, or than a fishmonger hates a hard frost. Whether
this uncle has seen Mrs. Millamant or not, I cannot say, but
there were items of such a treaty being in embryo; and if it
should come to life, poor Mirabell would be in some sort unfortunately fobbed, i'faith.

Fain. 'Tis impossible Millamant should hearken to it.

Wit. Faith, my dear, I can't tell; she's a woman, and a kind
of humourist.

Mir. And this is the sum of what you could collect last night?

Pet. The quintessence. Maybe Witwoud knows more, he staid
longer:—besides, they never mind him; they say anything before him.

Mir. I thought you had been the greatest favourite.

Pet. Ay, *tête-à-tête,* but not in public, because I make
remarks.

Mir. You do?

Pet. Ay, ay; pox, I'm malicious, man! Now he's soft you know; they are not in awe of him—the fellow's well-bred; he's what you call a what-d'ye-call-'em, a fine gentleman; but he's silly withal.

Mir. I thank you, I know as much as my curiosity requires. Fainall, are you for the Mall?[1]

Fain. Ay, I'll take a turn before dinner.

Wit. Ay, we'll walk in the Park; the ladies talked of being there.

Mir. I thought you were obliged to watch for your brother Sir Wilfull's arrival.

Wit. No, no; he comes to his aunt's, my lady Wishfort. Pox on him! I shall be troubled with him too; what shall I do with the fool?

Pet. Beg him for his estate, that I may beg you afterwards: and so have but one trouble with you both.

Wit. O rare Petulant! thou art as quick as fire in a frosty morning; thou shalt to the Mall with us, and we'll be very severe.

Pet. Enough, I'm in a humour to be severe.

Mir. Are you? pray then walk by yourselves: let not us be accessory to your putting the ladies out of countenance with your senseless ribaldry, which you roar out aloud as often as they pass by you; and when you have made a handsome woman blush, then you think you have been severe.

Pet. What, what! then let 'em either show their innocence by not understanding what they hear, or else show their discretion by not hearing what they would not be thought to understand.

Mir. But hast not thou then sense enough to know that thou oughtest to be most ashamed thyself, when thou hast put another out of countenance?

Pet. Not I, by this hand!—I always take blushing either for a sign of guilt, or ill-breeding.

Mir. I confess you ought to think so. You are in the right, that you may plead the error of your judgment in defence of your practice.

Where modesty's ill-manners, 'tis but fit
That impudence and malice pass for wit.

[*Exeunt.*

[1] The Mall was the fashionable lounge where smoking was not allowed.

ACT THE SECOND

Scene I

St. James's Park

Mrs. Fainall and Mrs. Marwood.

Mrs. Fain. Ay, ay, dear Marwood, if we will be happy, we must find the means in ourselves, and among ourselves. Men are ever in extremes; either doating or averse. While they are lovers, if they have fire and sense, their jealousies are insupportable; and when they cease to love (we ought to think at least) they loath; they look upon us with horror and distaste; they meet us like the ghosts of what we were, and as such, fly from us.

Mrs. Mar. True, 'tis an unhappy circumstance of life, that love should ever die before us; and that the man so often should outlive the lover. But say what you will, 'tis better to be left, than never to have been loved. To pass our youth in dull indifference, to refuse the sweets of life because they once must leave us, is as preposterous as to wish to have been born old, because we one day must be old. For my part, my youth may wear and waste, but it shall never rust in my possession.

Mrs. Fain. Then it seems you dissemble an aversion to mankind, only in compliance to my mother's humour?

Mrs. Mar. Certainly. To be free; I have no taste of those insipid dry discourses, with which our sex of force must entertain themselves, apart from men. We may affect endearments to each other, profess eternal friendships, and seem to doat like lovers; but 'tis not in our natures long to persevere. Love will resume his empire in our breasts; and every heart, or soon or late, receive and re-admit him as its lawful tyrant.

Mrs. Fain. Bless me, how have I been deceived! why you profess a libertine.

Mrs. Mar. You see my friendship by my freedom. Come, be sincere, acknowledge that your sentiments agree with mine.

Mrs. Fain. Never!

Mrs. Mar. You hate mankind?

Mrs. Fain. Heartily, inveterately.

Mrs. Mar. Your husband?

Mrs. Fain. Most transcendently; ay, though I say it, meritoriously.

Mrs. Mar. Give me your hand upon it.

Mrs. Fain. There.

Mrs. Mar. I join with you; what I have said has been to try you.

Mrs. Fain. Is it possible? dost thou hate those vipers, men?

Mrs. Mar. I have done hating 'em, and am now come to despise 'em; the next thing I have to do, is eternally to forget 'em.

Mrs. Fain. There spoke the spirit of an Amazon, a Penthesilea!

Mrs. Mar. And yet I am thinking sometimes to carry my aversion further.

Mrs. Fain. How?

Mrs. Mar. Faith, by marrying; if I could but find one that loved me very well, and would be thoroughly sensible of ill usage, I think I should do myself the violence of undergoing the ceremony.

Mrs. Fain. You would not make him a cuckold?

Mrs. Mar. No; but I'd make him believe I did, and that's as bad.

Mrs. Fain. Why, had not you as good do it?

Mrs. Mar. Oh! if he should ever discover it, he would then know the worst, and be out of his pain; but I would have him ever to continue upon the rack of fear and jealousy.

Mrs. Fain. Ingenious mischief! would thou wert married to Mirabell.

Mrs. Mar. Would I were!

Mrs. Fain. You change colour.

Mrs. Mar. Because I hate him.

Mrs. Fain. So do I; but I can hear him named. But what reason have you to hate him in particular?

Mrs. Mar. I never loved him; he is, and always was, insufferably proud.

Mrs. Fain. By the reason you give for your aversion, one would think it dissembled; for you have laid a fault to his charge, of which his enemies must acquit him.

Mrs. Mar. Oh then, it seems, you are one of his favourable enemies! Methinks you look a little pale, and now you flush again.

Mrs. Fain. Do I? I think I am a little sick o' the sudden.

Mrs. Mar. What ails you?

Mrs. Fain. My husband. Don't you see him? He turned short upon me unawares, and has almost overcome me.

Enter FAINALL *and* MIRABELL.

Mrs. Mar. Ha! ha! ha! he comes opportunely for you.

Mrs. Fain. For you, for he has brought Mirabell with him.

Fain. My dear!

Mrs. Fain. My soul!

Fain. You don't look well to-day, child.

Mrs. Fain. D'ye think so?

Mir. He is the only man that does, madam.

Mrs. Fain. The only man that would tell me so at least; and the only man from whom I could hear it without mortification.

Fain. O my dear, I am satisfied of your tenderness; I know you cannot resent anything from me; especially what is an effect of my concern.

Mrs. Fain. Mr. Mirabell, my mother interrupted you in a pleasant relation last night; I would fain hear it out.

Mir. The persons concerned in that affair have yet a tolerable reputation.—I am afraid Mr. Fainall will be censorious.

Mrs. Fain. He has a humour more prevailing than his curiosity, and will willingly dispense with the hearing of one scandalous story, to avoid giving an occasion to make another by being seen to walk with his wife. This way, Mr. Mirabell, and I dare promise you will oblige us both.

[*Exeunt* Mrs. FAINALL *and* MIRABELL.

Fain. Excellent creature! Well, sure if I should live to be rid of my wife, I should be a miserable man.

Mrs. Mar. Ay!

Fain. For having only that one hope, the accomplishment of it, of consequence, must put an end to all my hopes; and what a wretch is he who must survive his hopes! Nothing remains when that day comes, but to sit down and weep like Alexander, when he wanted other worlds to conquer.

Mrs. Mar. Will you not follow 'em?

Fain. Faith, I think not.

Mrs. Mar. Pray let us; I have a reason.

Fain. You are not jealous?

Mrs. Mar. Of whom?

Fain. Of Mirabell.

Mrs. Mar. If I am, is it inconsistent with my love to you that I am tender of your honour?

Fain. You would intimate, then, as if there were a fellow-feeling between my wife and him.

Mrs. Mar. I think she does not hate him to that degree she would be thought.

Fain. But he, I fear, is too insensible.

Mrs. Mar. It may be you are deceived.

Fain. It may be so. I do now begin to apprehend it.

Mrs. Mar. What?

Fain. That I have been deceived, madam, and you are false.

Mrs. Mar. That I am false! what mean you?

Fain. To let you know I see through all your little arts.— Come, you both love him; and both have equally dissembled your aversion. Your mutual jealousies of one another have made you clash till you have both struck fire. I have seen the warm confession reddening on your cheeks, and sparkling from your eyes.

Mrs. Mar. You do me wrong.

Fain. I do not. 'Twas for my ease to oversee and wilfully neglect the gross advances made him by my wife; that by permitting her to be engaged, I might continue unsuspected in my pleasures; and take you oftener to my arms in full security. But could you think, because the nodding husband would not wake, that e'er the watchful lover slept?

Mrs. Mar. And wherewithal can you reproach me?

Fain. With infidelity, with loving another, with love of Mirabell.

Mrs. Mar. 'Tis false! I challenge you to show an instance that can confirm your groundless accusation. I hate him.

Fain. And wherefore do you hate him? he is insensible, and your resentment follows his neglect. An instance! the injuries you have done him are a proof: your interposing in his love. What cause had you to make discoveries of his pretended passion? to undeceive the credulous aunt, and be the officious obstacle of his match with Millamant?

Mrs. Mar. My obligations to my lady urged me; I had professed a friendship to her; and could not see her easy nature so abused by that dissembler.

Fain. What, was it conscience then? Professed a friendship! O the pious friendships of the female sex!

Mrs. Mar. More tender, more sincere, and more enduring than all the vain and empty vows of men, whether professing love to us, or mutual faith to one another.

Fain. Ha! ha! ha! you are my wife's friend too.

Mrs. Mar. Shame and ingratitude! do you reproach me? you, you upbraid me? Have I been false to her, through stric fidelity to you, and sacrificed my friendship to keep my love inviolate? And have you the baseness to charge me with the guilt, unmindful of the merit? To you it should be meritorious, that I have been vicious: and do you reflect that guilt upon me, which should lie buried in your bosom?

Fain. You misinterpret my reproof. I meant but to remind you of the slight account you once could make of strictest ties, when set in competition with your love to me.

Mrs. Mar. 'Tis false, you urged it with deliberate malice! 'twas spoken in scorn, and I never will forgive it.

Fain. Your guilt, not your resentment, begets your rage. If yet you loved, you could forgive a jealousy: but you are stung to find you are discovered.

Mrs. Mar. It shall be all discovered. You too shall be discovered; be sure you shall. I can but be exposed.—If I do it myself I shall prevent your baseness.

Fain. Why, what will you do?

Mrs. Mar. Disclose it to your wife; own what has passed between us.

Fain. Frenzy!

Mrs. Mar. By all my wrongs I'll do't!—I'll publish to the world the injuries you have done me, both in my fame and fortune! With both I trusted you, you bankrupt in honour, as indigent of wealth.

Fain. Your fame I have preserved: your fortune has been bestowed as the prodigality of your love would have it, in pleasures which we both have shared. Yet, had not you been false, I had ere this repaid it—'tis true—had you permitted Mirabell with Millamant to have stolen their marriage, my lady had been incensed beyond all means of reconcilement: Millamant had forfeited the moiety of her fortune; which then would have descended to my wife;—and wherefore did I marry, but to make lawful prize of a rich widow's wealth, and squander it on love and you?

Mrs. Mar. Deceit and frivolous pretence!

Fain. Death, am I not married? What's pretence? Am I not imprisoned, fettered? Have I not a wife? nay a wife that was a widow, a young widow, a handsome widow; and would be again a widow, but that I have a heart of proof, and something of a constitution to bustle through the ways of wedlock and this world! Will you yet be reconciled to truth and me?

Mrs. Mar. Impossible. Truth and you are inconsistent: I hate you, and shall for ever.

Fain. For loving you?

Mrs. Mar. I loathe the name of love after such usage; and next to the guilt with which you would asperse me, I scorn you most. Farewell!

Fain. Nay, we must not part thus.

Mrs. Mar. Let me go.

Fain. Come, I'm sorry.

Mrs. Mar. I care not—let me go—break my hands, do—I'd leave 'em to get loose.

Fain. I would not hurt you for the world. Have I no other hold to keep you here?

Mrs. Mar. Well, I have deserved it all.

Fain. You know I love you.

Mrs. Mar. Poor dissembling!—O that—well, it is not yet—

Fain. What? what is it not? what is it not yet? It is not yet too late—

Mrs. Mar. No, it is not yet too late;—I have that comfort.

Fain. It is, to love another.

Mrs. Mar. But not to loathe, detest, abhor mankind, myself, and the whole treacherous world.

Fain. Nay, this is extravagance.—Come, I ask your pardon—no tears—I was to blame, I could not love you and be easy in my doubts. Pray forbear—I believe you; I'm convinced I've done you wrong; and any way, every way will make amends. I'll hate my wife yet more, damn her! I'll part with her, rob her of all she's worth, and we'll retire somewhere, anywhere, to another world. I'll marry thee—be pacified.—'Sdeath, they come, hide your face, your tears;—you have a mask, wear it a moment.[1] This way, this way—be persuaded. [*Exeunt.*

SCENE II

The same

MIRABELL *and* Mrs. FAINALL.

Mrs. Fain. They are here yet.

Mir. They are turning into the other walk.

Mrs. Fain. While I only hated my husband, I could bear to see him; but since I have despised him, he's too offensive.

Mir. O you should hate with prudence.

---

[1] Masks at this date were generally worn; they were the substitute of the modern veil. A few years later they became associated with disreputable women, and passed out of fashion, giving place to coloured hoods.

Mrs. Fain. Yes, for I have loved with indiscretion.

Mir. You should have just so much disgust for your husband, as may be sufficient to make you relish your lover.

Mrs. Fain. You have been the cause that I have loved without bounds, and would you set limits to that aversion of which you have been the occasion? why did you make me marry his man?

Mir. Why do we daily commit disagreeable and dangerous actions? to save that idol, reputation. If the familiarities of our loves had produced that consequence of which you were apprehensive, where could you have fixed a father's name with credit, but on a husband? I knew Fainall to be a man lavish of his morals, an interested and professing friend, a false and a designing lover; yet one whose wit and outward fair behaviour have gained a reputation with the town enough to make that woman stand excused who has suffered herself to be won by his addresses. A better man ought not to have been sacrificed to the occasion; a worse had not answered to the purpose. When you are weary of him you now your remedy.

Mrs. Fain. I ought to stand in some degree of credit with you, Mirabell.

Mir. In justice to you, I have made you privy to my whole design, and put it in your power to ruin or advance my fortune.

Mrs. Fain. Whom have you instructed to represent your pretended uncle?

Mir. Waitwell, my servant.

Mrs. Fain. He is an humble servant to Foible my mother's woman, and may win her to your interest.

Mir. Care is taken for that—she is won and worn by this time. They were married this morning.

Mrs. Fain. Who?

Mir. Waitwell and Foible. I would not tempt my servant to betray me by trusting him too far. If your mother, in hopes to ruin me, should consent to marry my pretended uncle, he might, like Mosca in the Fox,[1] stand upon terms; so I made him sure beforehand.

Mrs. Fain. So if my poor mother is caught in a contract, you will discover the imposture betimes; and release her by producing a certificate of her gallant's former marriage?

Mir. Yes, upon condition that she consent to my marriage with her niece, and surrender the moiety of her fortune in her possession.

Mrs. Fain. She talked last night of endeavouring at a match between Millamant and your uncle.

[1] *i.e.* Ben Jonson's comedy, *Volpone.*

Mir. That was by Foible's direction, and my instruction, tha
she might seem to carry it more privately.

Mrs. Fain. Well, I have an opinion of your success; for I be
lieve my lady will do anything to get a husband; and when sh
has this, which you have provided for her, I suppose she will submi
to anything to get rid of him.

Mir. Yes, I think the good lady would marry anything that re
sembled a man, though 'twere no more than what a butler could
pinch out of a napkin.

Mrs. Fain. Female frailty! we must all come to it, if we live to
be old, and feel the craving of a false appetite when the true i
decayed.

Mir. An old woman's appetite is depraved like that of a girl—
'tis the green sickness of a second childhood; and, like the fain
offer of a latter spring, serves but to usher in the fall, and wither
in an affected bloom.

Mrs. Fain. Here's your mistress.

Enter Mrs. MILLAMANT, WITWOUD, *and* MINCING.

Mir. Here she comes, i'faith, full sail, with her fan spread and
her streamers out, and a shoal of fools for tenders; ha, no, I cry
her mercy!

Mrs. Fain. I see but one poor empty sculler; and he tows he
woman after him.

Mir. [*To* Mrs. MILLAMANT.] You seem to be unattended
madam—you used to have the *beau monde* throng after you; and
a flock of gay fine perukes hovering round you.

Wit. Like moths about a candle.—I had like to have lost my
comparison for want of breath.

Mrs. Mil. O I have denied myself airs to-day, I have walked a
fast through the crowd.

Wit. As a favourite just disgraced; and with as few followers.

Mrs. Mil. Dear Mr. Witwoud, truce with your similitudes; fo
I'm as sick of 'em—

Wit. As a physician of a good air.—I cannot help it, madam
though 'tis against myself.

Mrs. Mil. Yet, again! Mincing, stand between me and his wit.

Wit. Do, Mrs. Mincing, like a screen before a great fire.—
confess I do blaze to-day, I am too bright.

Mrs. Fain. But, dear Millamant, why were you so long?

Mrs. Mil. Long! Lord, have I not made violent haste; I have
asked every living thing I met for you; I have inquired after you
as after a new fashion.

Wit. Madam, truce with your similitudes.—No, you met her husband, and did not ask him for her.

Mrs. Mil. By your leave, Witwoud, that were like inquiring after an old fashion, to ask a husband for his wife.

Wit. Hum, a hit! a hit! a palpable hit! I confess it.

Mrs. Fain. You were dressed before I came abroad.

Mrs. Mil. Ay, that's true.—O but then I had—Mincing, what had I?.why was I so long?

Min. O mem, your la'ship stayed to peruse a packet of letters.

Mrs. Mil. O ay, letters—I had letters—I am persecuted with letters—I hate letters—Nobody knows how to write letters, and yet one has 'em, one does not know why. They serve one to pin up one's hair.

Wit. Is that the way? Pray, madam, do you pin up your hair with all your letters? I find I must keep copies.

Mrs. Mil. Only with those in verse, Mr. Witwoud, I never pin up my hair with prose.—I think I tried once, Mincing.

Min. O mem, I shall never forget it.

Mrs. Mil. Ay, poor Mincing tift and tift all the morning.

Min. Till I had the cramp in my fingers, I'll vow, mem: and all to no purpose. But when your la'ship pins it up with poetry, it sits so pleasant the next day as anything, and is so pure and so crips.

Wit. Indeed, so crips?

Min. You're such a critic, Mr. Witwoud.

Mrs. Mil. Mirabell, did you take exceptions last night? O ay, and went away.—Now I think on't I'm angry—no, now I think on't I'm pleased—for I believe I gave you some pain.

Mir. Does that please you?

Mrs. Mil. Infinitely; I love to give pain.

Mir. You would affect a cruelty which is not in your nature; your true vanity is in the power of pleasing.

Mrs. Mil. Oh I ask you pardon for that—one's cruelty is one's power; and when one parts with one's cruelty, one parts with one's power; and when one has parted with that, I fancy one's old and ugly.

Mir. Ay, ay, suffer your cruelty to ruin the object of your power, to destroy your lover—and then how vain, how lost a thing you'll be! Nay, 'tis true: you are no longer handsome when you've lost your lover; your beauty dies upon the instant; for beauty is the lover's gift; 'tis he bestows your charms—your glass is all a cheat. The ugly and the old, whom the looking-glass mortifies, yet after commendation can be flattered by it, and discover beauties in it; for that reflects our praises, rather than your face.

Mrs. Mil. O the vanity of these men!—Fainall, d'ye hear him?

If they did not commend us, we were not handsome! Now you must know they could not commend one, if one was not handsome. Beauty the lover's gift!—Lord, what is a lover, that it can give? Why, one makes lovers as fast as one pleases, and they live as long as one pleases, and they die as soon as one pleases; and then, if one pleases, one makes more.

Wit. Very pretty. Why, you make no more of making of lovers, madam, than of making so many card-matches.

Mrs. Mil. One no more owes one's beauty to a lover, than one's wit to an echo. They can but reflect what we look and say; vain empty things if we are silent or unseen, and want a being.

Mir. Yet to those two vain empty things you owe the two greatest pleasures of your life.

Mrs. Mil. How so?

Mir. To your lover you owe the pleasure of hearing yourselves praised; and to an echo the pleasure of hearing yourselves talk.

Wit. But I know a lady that loves talking so incessantly, she won't give an echo fair play; she has that everlasting rotation of tongue, that an echo must wait till she dies, before it can catch her last words.

Mrs. Mil. O fiction!—Fainall, let us leave these men.

Mir. Draw off Witwoud.   [*Aside to* Mrs. FAINALL.

Mrs. Fain. Immediately.—I have a word or two for Mr. Witwoud.   [*Exeunt* Mrs. FAINALL *and* WITWOUD.

Mir. I would beg a little private audience too.—You had the tyranny to deny me last night; though you knew I came to impart a secret to you that concerned my love.

Mrs. Mil. You saw I was engaged.

Mir. Unkind! You had the leisure to entertain a herd of fools; things who visit you from their excessive idleness; bestowing on your easiness that time which is the incumbrance of their lives. How can you find delight in such society? It is impossible they should admire you, they are not capable: or if they were, it should be to you as a mortification; for sure to please a fool is some degree of folly.

Mrs. Mil. I please myself:—besides, sometimes to converse with fools is for my health.

Mir. Your health! is there a worse disease than the conversation of fools?

Mrs. Mil. Yes, the vapours; fools are physic for it, next to assafœtida.

Mir. You are not in a course of fools?

Mrs. Mil. Mirabell, if you persist in this offensive freedom, you'll

displease me.—I think I must resolve, after all, not to have you:
—we shan't agree.

Mir. Not in our physic, it may be.

Mrs. Mil. And yet our distemper, in all likelihood, will be the
same; for we shall be sick of one another. I shan't endure to be
reprimanded nor instructed: 'tis so dull to act always by advice,
and so tedious to be told of one's faults—I can't bear it. Well, I
won't have you, Mirabell—I'm resolved—I think—you may go.
—Ha! ha! ha! what would you give, that you could help loving
me?

Mir. I would give something that you did not know I could not
help it.

Mrs. Mil. Come, don't look grave then. Well, what do you say
to me?

Mir. I say that a man may as soon make a friend by his wit, or
a fortune by his honesty, as win a woman by plain-dealing and
sincerity.

Mrs. Mil. Sententious Mirabell!—Prithee, don't look with that
violent and inflexible wise face, like Solomon at the dividing of
the child in an old tapestry hanging.

Mir. You are merry, madam, but I would persuade you for a
moment to be serious.

Mrs. Mil. What, with that face? no, if you keep your countenance, 'tis impossible I should hold mine. Well, after all, there is
something very moving in a love-sick face. Ha! ha! ha!—well, I
won't laugh, don't be peevish—Heigho! now I'll be melancholy,
as melancholy as a watch-light. Well, Mirabell, if ever you will
win me woo me now.—Nay, if you are so tedious, fare you well;
—I see they are walking away.

Mir. Can you not find in the variety of your disposition one
moment—

Mrs. Mil. To hear you tell me Foible's married, and your plot
like to speed;—no.

Mir. But how came you to know it?

Mrs. Mil. Without the help of the devil, you can't imagine; unless she should tell me herself. Which of the two it may have been
I will leave you to consider; and when you have done thinking of
that, think of me. [*Exit.*

Mir. I have something more.—Gone!—Think of you? to think
of a whirlwind, though 'twere in a whirlwind, were a case of more
steady contemplation; a very tranquillity of mind and mansion.
A fellow that lives in a windmill, has not a more whimsical dwelling than the heart of a man that is lodged in a woman. There is no
point of the compass to which they cannot turn, and by which

they are not turned; and by one as well as another; for motion, not method, is their occupation. To know this, and yet continue to be in love, is to be made wise from the dictates of reason, and yet persevere to play the fool by the force of instinct.—Oh, here come my pair of turtles!—What, billing so sweetly! is not Valentine's day over with you yet?

Enter WAITWELL and FOIBLE.

Sirrah, Waitwell, why sure you think you were married for your own recreation, and not for my conveniency.

Wait. Your pardon, sir. With submission, we have indeed been solacing in lawful delights; but still with an eye to business, sir. I have instructed her as well as I could. If she can take your directions as readily as my instructions, sir, your affairs are in a prosperous way.

Mir. Give you joy, Mrs. Foible.

Foib. O las, sir, I'm so ashamed!—I'm afraid my lady has been in a thousand inquietudes for me. But I protest, sir, I made as much haste as I could.

Wait. That she did indeed, sir. It was my fault that she did not make more.

Mir. That I believe.

Foib. But I told my lady as you instructed me, sir, that I had a prospect of seeing Sir Rowland your uncle; and that I would put her ladyship's picture in my pocket to show him; which I'll be sure to say has made him so enamoured of her beauty, that he burns with impatience to lie at her ladyship's feet, and worship the original.

Mir. Excellent Foible! matrimony has made you eloquent in love.

Wait. I think she has profited, sir, I think so.

Foib. You have seen Madam Millamant, sir?

Mir. Yes.

Foib. I told her, sir, because I did not know that you might find an opportunity; she had so much company last night.

Mir. Your diligence will merit more—in the mean time—

[*Gives money.*

Foib. O dear sir, your humble servant!

Wait. Spouse.

Mir. Stand off, sir, not a penny!—Go on and prosper, Foible:— the lease shall be made good, and the farm stocked, if we succeed.

Foib. I don't question your generosity, sir: and you need not doubt of success. If you have no more commands, sir, I'll be gone; I'm sure my lady is at her toilet, and can't dress till I come.—O dear, I'm sure that [*Looking out*] was Mrs. Marwood that went by in a mask! If she has seen me with you I'm sure she'll tell my lady. I'll make haste home and prevent her. Your servant, sir.— B'w'y, Waitwell. [*Exit.*

Wait. Sir Rowland, if you please.—The jade's so pert upon her preferment she forgets herself.

Mir. Come, sir, will you endeavour to forget yourself, and transform into Sir Rowland?

Wait. Why, sir, it will be impossible I should remember myself. —Married, knighted, and attended all in one day! 'tis enough to make any man forget himself. The difficulty will be how to recover my acquaintance and familiarity with my former self, and fall from my transformation to a reformation into Waitwell. Nay, I shan't be quite the same Waitwell neither; for now, I remember me, I'm married, and can't be my own man again.

Ay there's my grief; that's the sad change of life,
To lose my title, and yet keep my wife. [*Exeunt.*

ACT THE THIRD

Scene I

A Room in LADY WISHFORT'S *House*

LADY WISHFORT *at her toilet,* PEG *waiting.*

Lady Wish. Merciful! no news of Foible yet?

Peg. No, madam.

Lady Wish. I have no more patience.—If I have not fretted myself till I am pale again, there's no veracity in me! Fetch me the red—the red, do you hear, sweetheart?—An arrant ash-colour, as I am a person! Look you how this wench stirs! Why dost thou not fetch me a little red? didst thou not hear me, Mopus?

Peg. The red ratafia does your ladyship mean, or the cherry-brandy?

Lady Wish. Ratafia, fool! no, fool. Not the ratafia, fool—grant me patience!—I mean the Spanish paper,[1] idiot—complexion, darling. Paint, paint, paint, dost thou understand that, changeling, dangling thy hands like bobbins before thee? Why dost thou not stir, puppet? thou wooden thing upon wires!

Peg. Lord, madam, your ladyship is so impatient!—I cannot come at the paint, madam; Mrs. Foible has locked it up, and carried the key with her.

[1] Spanish wool and Spanish paper were favourite cosmetics of the day.

Lady Wish. A pox take you both!—fetch me the cherry-brandy then. [*Exit* PEG.] I'm as pale and as faint, I look like Mrs. Qualmsick, the curate's wife, that's always breeding.—Wench, come, come, wench, what art thou doing? sipping, tasting?—Save thee, dost thou not know the bottle?

Re-enter PEG *with a bottle and china cup.*

Peg. Madam, I was looking for a cup.

Lady Wish. A cup, save thee! and what a cup hast thou brought! —Dost thou take me for a fairy, to drink out of an acorn? Why didst thou not bring thy thimble? Hast thou ne'er a brass thimble clinking in thy pocket with a bit of nutmeg?—I warrant thee. Come, fill, fill!—So—again.—[*Knocking at the door.*]—See who that is.—Set down the bottle first—here, here, under the table.— What, wouldst thou go with the bottle in thy hand, like a tapster? As I am a person, this wench has lived in an inn upon the road, before she came to me, like Maritornes the Asturian in Don Quixote!—No Foible yet?

Peg. No, madam; Mrs. Marwood.

Lady Wish. Oh, Marwood; let her come in.—Come in, good Marwood.

Enter Mrs. MARWOOD.

Mrs. Mar. I'm surprised to find your ladyship in dishabille at this time of day.

Lady Wish. Foible's a lost thing; has been abroad since morning, and never heard of since.

Mrs. Mar. I saw her but now, as I came masked through the park, in conference with Mirabell.

Lady Wish. With Mirabell!—You call my blood into my face, with mentioning that traitor. She durst not have the confidence! I sent her to negotiate an affair, in which, if I'm detected, I'm undone. If that wheedling villain has wrought upon Foible to detect me, I'm ruined. O my dear friend, I'm a wretch of wretches if I'm detected.

Mrs. Mar. O madam, you cannot suspect Mrs. Foible's integrity!

Lady Wish. Oh, he carries poison in his tongue that would corrupt integrity itself! If she has given him an opportunity, she has as good as put her integrity into his hands. Ah, dear Marwood, what's integrity to an opportunity?—Hark! I hear her!—dear friend, retire into my closet, that I may examine her with more freedom.—You'll pardon me, dear friend; I can make bold with you.—There are books over the chimney.—Quarles and Prynne, and "The Short View of the Stage," with Bunyan's works, to entertain you.—[*To* PEG.]—Go, you thing, and send her in.

[*Exeunt* Mrs. MARWOOD *and* PEG.

Enter FOIBLE.

Lady Wish. O Foible, where hast thou been? what hast thou been doing?

Foib. Madam, I have seen the party.

Lady Wish. But what hast thou done?

Foib. Nay, 'tis your ladyship has done, and are to do; I have only promised. But a man so enamoured—so transported!—Well, here it is, all that is left; all that is not kissed away.—Well, if worshipping of pictures be a sin——poor Sir Rowland, I say.

Lady Wish. The miniature has been counted like;—but hast thou not betrayed me, Foible? hast thou not detected me to that faithless Mirabell?—What hadst thou to do with him in the Park? Answer me, has he got nothing out of thee?

Foib. [*Aside.*] So the devil has been beforehand with me. What shall I say?—[*Aloud.*]—Alas, madam, could I help it, if I met that confident thing? was I in fault? If you had heard how he used me, and all upon your ladyship's account, I'm sure you would not suspect my fidelity. Nay, if that had been the worst, I could have borne; but he had a fling at your ladyship too; and then I could not hold; but i'faith I gave him his own.

Lady Wish. Me? what did the filthy fellow say?

Foib. O madam! 'tis a shame to say what he said—with his taunts and his fleers, tossing up his nose. Humph! (says he) what, you are a hatching some plot (says he), you are so early abroad, or catering (says he), ferreting some disbanded officer, I warrant. —Half-pay is but thin subsistence (says he);—well, what pension does your lady propose? Let me see (says he), what, she must come down pretty deep now, she's superannuated (says he) and—

Lady Wish. Odds my life, I'll have him, I'll have him murdered! I'll have him poisoned! Where does he eat?—I'll marry a drawer to have him poisoned in his wine. I'll send for Robin from Locket's immediately.

Foib. Poison him! poisoning's too good for him. Starve him, madam, starve him; marry Sir Rowland, and get him disinherited. Oh you would bless yourself to hear what he said!

Lady Wish. A villain! superannuated!

Foib. Humph (says he), I hear you are laying designs against me too (says he), and Mrs. Millamant is to marry my uncle (he does not suspect a word of your ladyship); but (says he) I'll fit you for that. I warrant you (says he) I'll hamper you for that (says he); you and your old frippery too (says he); I'll handle you—

Lady Wish. Audacious villain! handle me; would he durst!—Frippery! old frippery! was there ever such a foul-mouthed fellow? I'll be married to-morrow, I'll be contracted to-night.

Foib. The sooner the better, madam.

Lady Wish. Will Sir Rowland be here, sayest thou? when, Foible?

Foib. Incontinently, madam. No new sheriff's wife expects the return of her husband after knighthood with that impatience in which Sir Rowland burns for the dear hour of kissing your ladyship's hand after dinner.

Lady Wish. Frippery! superannuated frippery! I'll frippery the villain; I'll reduce him to frippery and rags! a tatterdemalion! I hope to see him hung with tatters, like a Long-lane pent-house [1] or a gibbet thief. A slander-mouthed railer! I warrant the spendthrift prodigal's in debt as much as the million lottery, or the whole court upon a birthday. I'll spoil his credit with his tailor. Yes, he shall have my niece with her fortune, he shall.

Foib. He! I hope to see him lodge in Ludgate [2] first, and angle into Blackfriars for brass farthings with an old mitten.

Lady Wish. Ay, dear Foible; thank thee for that, dear Foible. He has put me out of all patience. I shall never recompose my features to receive Sir Rowland with any economy of face. This wretch has fretted me that I am absolutely decayed. Look, Foible.

Foib. Your ladyship has frowned a little too rashly, indeed, madam. There are some cracks discernible in the white varnish.

Lady Wish. Let me see the glass.—Cracks, sayest thou?—why, I am errantly flayed—I look like an old peeled wall. Thou must repair me, Foible, before Sir Rowland comes, or I shall never keep up to my picture.

Foib. I warrant you, madam, a little art once made your picture like you; and now a little of the same art must make you like your picture. Your picture must sit for you, madam.

Lady Wish. But art thou sure Sir Rowland will not fail to come? or will he not fail when he does come? Will he be importunate, Foible, and push? For if he should not be importunate, I shall never break decorums:—I shall die with confusion, if I am forced to advance.—Oh no, I can never advance!—I shall

---

[1] Long Lane, in West Smithfield, noted for the sale of old clothes and second-hand furniture.

[2] Ludgate was a debtors' prison, "purely for insolvent citizens of London, beneficed clergy, and attorneys at law." It was more comfortable and of a higher class than the Fleet.

swoon if he should expect advances. No, I hope Sir Rowland is better bred than to put a lady to the necessity of breaking her forms. I won't be too coy, neither.—I won't give him despair—but a little disdain is not amiss; a little scorn is alluring.

Foib. A little scorn becomes your ladyship.

Lady Wish. Yes, but tenderness becomes me best—a sort of dyingness—you see that picture has a sort of a—ha, Foible! a swimmingness in the eye—yes, I'll look so—my niece affects it; but she wants features. Is Sir Rowland handsome? Let my toilet be removed—I'll dress above. I'll receive Sir Rowland here. Is he handsome? Don't answer me. I won't know: I'll be surprised, I'll be taken by surprise.

Foib. By storm, madam, Sir Rowland's a brisk man.

Lady Wish. Is he! O then he'll importune, if he's a brisk man. I shall save decorums if Sir Rowland importunes. I have a mortal terror at the apprehension of offending against decorums. O, I'm glad he's a brisk man. Let my things be removed, good Foible.

[*Exit.*

Enter Mrs. FAINALL.

Mrs. Fain. O Foible, I have been in a fright, lest I should come too late! That devil Marwood saw you in the Park with Mirabell, and I'm afraid will discover it to my lady.

Foib. Discover what, madam!

Mrs. Fain. Nay, nay, put not on that strange face, I am privy to the whole design, and know that Waitwell, to whom thou wert this morning married, is to personate Mirabell's uncle, and as such, winning my lady, to involve her in those difficulties from which Mirabell only must release her, by his making his conditions to have my cousin and her fortune left to her own disposal.

Foib. O dear madam, I beg your pardon. It was not my confidence in your ladyship that was deficient; but I thought the former good correspondence between your ladyship and Mr. Mirabell might have hindered his communicating this secret.

Mrs. Fain. Dear Foible, forget that.

Foib. O dear madam, Mr. Mirabell is such a sweet, winning gentleman—but your ladyship is the pattern of generosity.—Sweet lady, to be so good! Mr. Mirabell cannot choose but be grateful. I find your ladyship has his heart still. Now, madam, I can safely tell your ladyship our success; Mrs. Marwood had told my lady; but I warrant I managed myself; I turned it all for the better. I told my lady that Mr. Mirabell railed at her; I laid horrid things to his charge, I'll vow; and my lady is so incensed that she'll be contracted to Sir Rowland to-night, she says; I warrant I worked her up, that he may have her for asking for, as they say of a Welsh maidenhead.

Mrs. Fain. O rare Foible!

Foib. I beg your ladyship to acquaint Mr. Mirabell of his success. I would be seen as little as possible to speak to him:—besides, I believe Madam Marwood watches me.—She has a month's mind; but I know Mr. Mirabell can't abide her.—John!—[*Calls.*] remove my lady's toilet.—Madam, your servant: my lady is so impatient, I fear she'll come for me if I stay.

Mrs. Fain. I'll go with you up the back-stairs, lest I should meet her.   [*Exeunt.*

Scene II

Lady Wishfort's *Closet*

Mrs. Marwood.

Mrs. Mar. Indeed, Mrs. Engine, is it thus with you? are you become a go-between of this importance? yes, I shall watch you. Why this wench is the *passe-partout*, a very master-key to everybody's strong-box. My friend Fainall, have you carried it so swimmingly? I thought there was something in it; but it seems 'tis over with you. Your loathing is not from a want of appetite, then, but from a surfeit. Else you could never be so cool to fall from a principal to be an assistant; to procure for him! a pattern of generosity that, I confess. Well, Mr. Fainall, you have met with your match. —O man, man! woman, woman! the devil's an ass: if I were a painter, I would draw him like an idiot, a driveller with a bib and bells: man should have his head and horns, and woman the rest of him. Poor simple fiend!—"Madam Marwood has a month's mind, but he can't abide her."—'Twere better for him you had not been his confessor in that affair, without you could have kept his counsel closer. I shall not prove another pattern of generosity: he has not obliged me to that with those excesses of himself! and now I'll have none of him. Here comes the good lady, panting ripe; with a heart full of hope, and a head full of care, like any chemist upon the day of projection.

Enter Lady Wishfort.

Lady Wish. O dear, Marwood, what shall I say for this rude forgetfulness?—but my dear friend is all goodness.

Mrs. Mar. No apologies, dear madam, I have been very well entertained.

Lady Wish. As I'm a person, I am in a very chaos to think

should so forget myself:—but I have such an olio of affairs, really I know not what to do.—Foible!—[*Calls.*] I expect my nephew, Sir Wilfull, every moment too.—Why, Foible!—He means to travel for improvement.

Mrs. Mar. Methinks Sir Wilfull should rather think of marrying than travelling at his years. I hear he is turned of forty.

Lady Wish. O he's in less danger of being spoiled by his travels— I am against my nephew's marrying too young. It will be time enough when he comes back, and has acquired discretion to choose for himself.

Mrs. Mar. Methinks Mrs. Millamant and he would make a very fit match. He may travel afterwards. 'Tis a thing very usual with young gentlemen.

Lady Wish. I promise you I have thought on't—and since 'tis your judgment, I'll think on't again. I assure you I will; I value your judgment extremely. On my word, I'll propose it.

Enter FOIBLE.

Lady Wish. Come, come, Foible—I had forgot my nephew will be here before dinner:—I must make haste.

Foib. Mr. Witwoud and Mr. Petulant are come to dine with your ladyship.

Lady Wish. O dear, I can't appear till I'm dressed.—Dear Marwood, shall I be free with you again, and beg you to entertain 'em? I'll make all imaginable haste. Dear friend, excuse me.   [*Exeunt.*

SCENE III

A Room in Lady WISHFORT'S *House*

Mrs. MARWOOD, Mrs. MILLAMANT, *and* MINCING.

Mrs. Mil. Sure never anything was so unbred as that odious man!—Marwood, your servant.

Mrs. Mar. You have a colour; what's the matter?

Mrs. Mil. That horrid fellow, Petulant, has provoked me into a flame:—I have broken my fan.—Mincing, lend me yours; is not all the powder out of my hair?

Mrs. Mar. No. What has he done?

Mrs. Mil. Nay, he has done nothing; he has only talked—nay, he has said nothing neither; but he has contradicted everything that has been said. For my part, I thought Witwoud and he would have quarrelled.

Min. I vow, mem, I thought once they would have fit.

Mrs. Mil. Well, 'tis a lamentable thing, I swear, that one has not the liberty of choosing one's acquaintance as one does one's clothes.

Mrs. Mar. If we had that liberty, we should be as weary of one set of acquaintance, though never so good, as we are of one suit though never so fine. A fool and a doily stuff would now and then find days of grace, and be worn for variety.

Mrs. Mil. I could consent to wear 'em, if they would wear alike; but fools never wear out—they are such *drap de Berri* things! without one could give 'em to one's chambermaid after a day or two.

Mrs. Mar. 'Twere better so indeed. Or what think you of the playhouse? A fine gay glossy fool should be given there, like a new masking habit, after the masquerade is over, and we have done with the disguise. For a fool's visit is always a disguise; and never admitted by a woman of wit, but to blind her affair with a lover of sense. If you would but appear bare-faced now, and own Mirabell, you might as easily put off Petulant and Witwoud as your hood and scarf. And indeed, 'tis time, for the town has found it; the secret is grown too big for the pretence. 'Tis like Mrs. Primly's great belly; she may lace it down before, but it burnishes on her hips. Indeed, Millamant, you can no more conceal it, than my Lady Strammel can her face; that goodly face, which in defiance of her Rhenish wine tea, will not be comprehended in a mask.

Mrs. Mil. I'll take my death, Marwood, you are more censorious than a decayed beauty, or a discarded toast.—Mincing, tell the men they may come up.—My aunt is not dressing here; their folly is less provoking than your malice. [*Exit* MINCING.] The town has found it! what has it found? That Mirabell loves me is no more a secret, than it is a secret that you discovered it to my aunt, or than the reason why you discovered it is a secret.

Mrs. Mar. You are nettled.

Mrs. Mil. You're mistaken. Ridiculous!

Mrs. Mar. Indeed, my dear, you'll tear another fan, if you don't mitigate those violent airs.

Mrs. Mil. O silly! ha! ha! ha! I could laugh immoderately. Poor Mirabell! his constancy to me has quite destroyed his complaisance for all the world beside. I swear, I never enjoined it him to be so coy—If I had the vanity to think he would obey me, I would command him to show more gallantry—'tis hardly well-bred to be so particular on one hand, and so insensible on the other. But I despair to prevail, and so let him follow his own way. Ha! ha! ha! pardon me, dear creature, I must laugh, ha! ha! ha! though I grant you 'tis a little barbarous, ha! ha! ha!

Mrs. Mar. What pity 'tis so much fine raillery, and delivered with so significant gesture, should be so unhappily directed to miscarry!

Mrs. Mil. Ha! dear creature, I ask your pardon—I swear I did not mind you.

Mrs. Mar. Mr. Mirabell and you both may think it a thing impossible, when I shall tell him by telling you—

Mrs. Mil. O dear, what? for it is the same thing if I hear it—ha! ha! ha!

Mrs. Mar. That I detest him, hate him, madam.

Mrs. Mil. O madam, why so do I—and yet the creature loves me, ha! ha! ha! how can one forbear laughing to think of it.— I am a sibyl if I am not amazed to think what he can see in me. I'll take my death, I think you are handsomer—and within a year or two as young—if you could but stay for me, I should overtake you—but that cannot be.—Well, that thought makes me melancholic.—Now, I'll be sad.

Mrs. Mar. Your merry note may be changed sooner than you think.

Mrs. Mil. D'ye say so? Then I'm resolved I'll have a song to keep up my spirits.

Re-enter MINCING.

Min. The gentlemen stay but to comb, madam, and will wait on you.

Mrs. Mil. Desire Mrs. — that is in the next room to sing the song I would have learned yesterday.—You shall hear it, madam—not that there's any great matter in it—but 'tis agreeable to my humour.

SONG.

Love's but the frailty of the mind,
    When 'tis not with ambition joined;
A sickly flame, which, if not fed, expires,
And feeding, wastes in self-consuming fires.

'Tis not to wound a wanton boy
    Or amorous youth, that gives the joy;
But 'tis the glory to have pierced a swain,
For whom inferior beauties sighed in vain.

Then I alone the conquest prize,
When I insult a rival's eyes:
If there's delight in love, 'tis when I see
That heart, which others bleed for, bleed for me.

Enter PETULANT *and* WITWOUD.

Mrs. Mil. Is your animosity composed, gentlemen?

Wit. Raillery, raillery, madam; we have no animosity—we hit off a little wit now and then, but no animosity.—The falling-out of wits is like the falling-out of lovers:—we agree in the main, like treble and bass.—Ha, Petulant?

Pet. Ay, in the main—but when I have a humour to contradict—

Wit. Ay, when he has a humour to contradict, then I contradict too. What, I know my cue. Then we contradict one another like two battledores; for contradictions beget one another like Jews.

Pet. If he says black's black—if I have a humour to say 'tis blue—let that pass—all's one for that. If I have a humour to prove it, it must be granted.

Wit. Not positively must—but it may—it may.

Pet. Yes, it positively must, upon proof positive.

Wit. Ay, upon proof positive it must; but upon proof presumptive it only may.—That's a logical distinction now, madam.

Mrs. Mar. I perceive your debates are of importance, and very learnedly handled.

Pet. Importance is one thing, and learning's another, but a debate's a debate, that I assert.

Wit. Petulant's an enemy to learning; he relies altogether on his parts.

Pet. No, I'm no enemy to learning; it hurts not me.

Mrs. Mar. That's a sign indeed it's no enemy to you.

Pet. No, no, it's no enemy to anybody but them that have it.

Mrs. Mil. Well, an illiterate man's my aversion: I wonder at the impudence of any illiterate man to offer to make love.

Wit. That I confess I wonder at too.

Mrs. Mil. Ah! to marry an ignorant that can hardly read or write!

Pet. Why should a man be any further from being married though he can't read, than he is from being hanged? The ordinary's paid for setting the psalm, and the parish-priest for reading the ceremony. And for the rest which is to follow in both cases, a man may do it without book—so all's one for that.

Mrs. Mil. D'ye hear the creature?—Lord, here's company, I'll be gone. [*Exit.*

Enter Sir WILFULL WITWOUD *in a riding dress, followed by* Footman.

Wit.. In the name of Bartlemew and his fair, what have we here?

Mrs. Mar. 'Tis your brother, I fancy. Don't you know him?

Wit. Not I.—Yes, I think it is he—I've almost forgot him; I have not seen him since the Revolution.

Foot. [*To* Sir WILFULL.] Sir, my lady's dressing. Here's company; if you please to walk in, in the mean time.

Sir Wil. Dressing! what, it's but morning here, I warrant, with you in London; we should count it towards afternoon in our parts, down in Shropshire.—Why then, belike, my aunt han't dined yet, ha, friend?

Foot. Your aunt, sir?

Sir Wil. My aunt, sir! yes, my aunt, sir, and your lady, sir; your lady is my aunt, sir.—Why, what dost thou not know me, friend? why then send somebody hither that does. How long hast thou lived with thy lady, fellow, ha?

Foot. A week, sir; longer than anybody in the house, except my lady's woman.

Sir Wil. Why then belike thou dost not know thy lady, if thou seest her, ha, friend?

Foot. Why, truly, sir, I cannot safely swear to her face in a morning, before she is dressed. 'Tis like I may give a shrewd guess at her by this time.

Sir. Wil. Well, prithee try what thou canst do; if thou canst not guess, inquire her out, dost hear, fellow? and tell her, her nephew, Sir Wilfull Witwoud, is in the house.

Foot. I shall, sir.

Sir Wil. Hold ye, hear me, friend; a word with you in your ear; prithee who are these gallants?

Foot. Really, sir, I can't tell; here come so many here, 'tis hard to know 'em all. [*Exit.*

Sir. Wil. Oons, this fellow knows less than a starling; I don't think a' knows his own name.

Mrs. Mar. Mr. Witwoud, your brother is not behindhand in forgetfulness—I fancy he has forgot you too.

Wit. I hope so—the devil take him that remembers first, I say.

Sir Wil. Save you, gentlemen and lady!

Mrs. Mar. For shame, Mr. Witwoud; why don't you speak to him?—And you, sir.

Wit. Petulant, speak.

Pet. And you, sir.

Sir Wil. No offence, I hope.   [*Salutes* Mrs. MARWOOD.

Mrs. Mar. No sure, sir.

Wit. This is a vile dog, I see that already. No offence! ha! ha! ha! To him; to him, Petulant, smoke him.

Pet. It seems as if you had come a journey, sir; hem, hem.

[*Surveying him round.*

Sir Wil. Very likely, sir, that it may seem so.

Pet. No offence, I hope, sir.

Wit. Smoke the boots, the boots; Petulant, the boots: ha! ha! ha!

Sir Wil. May be not, sir; thereafter, as 'tis meant, sir.

Pet. Sir, I presume upon the information of your boots.

Sir Wil. Why, 'tis like you may, sir: if you are not satisfied with the information of my boots, sir, if you will step to the stable, you may inquire further of my horse, sir.

Pet. Your horse, sir! your horse is an ass, sir!

Sir Wil. Do you speak by way of offence, sir?

Mrs. Mar. The gentleman's merry, that's all sir.—[*Aside.*] S'life, we shall have a quarrel betwixt an horse and an ass before they find one another out.—[*Aloud.*] You must not take anything amiss from your friends, sir. You are among your friends here, though it may be you don't know it.—If I am not mistaken, you are Sir Wilfull Witwoud.

Sir Wil. Right, lady; I am Sir Wilfull Witwoud, so I write myself; no offence to anybody, I hope; and nephew to the Lady Wishfort of this mansion.

Mrs. Mar. Don't you know this gentleman, sir?

Sir Wil. Hum! what, sure 'tis not—yea by'r Lady, but 'tis—s'heart, I know not whether 'tis or no—yea, but 'tis, by the Wrekin. Brother Anthony! what Tony, i'faith! what, dost thou not know me? By'r Lady, nor I thee, thou art so becravated, and so beperiwigged.—S'heart, why dost not speak? art thou overjoyed?

Wit. Odso, brother, is it you? your servant, brother.

Sir Wil. Your servant! why yours, sir. Your servant again—s'heart, and your friend and servant to that—and a—and a—flap-dragon for your service, sir! and a hare's foot and a hare's scut for your service, sir! an you be so cold and so courtly.

Wit. No offence, I hope, brother.

Sir Wil. S'heart, sir, but there is, and much offence!—A pox is this your inns o' court breeding, not to know your friends and your relations, your elders and your betters?

Wit. Why, brother Wilfull of Salop, you may be as short as a Shrewsbury-cake, if you please. But I tell you 'tis not modish to know relations in town: you think you're in the country, where great lubberly brothers slabber and kiss one another when they meet, like a call of serjeants—'tis not the fashion here; 'tis not indeed, dear brother.

Sir Wil. The fashion's a fool; and you're a fop, dear brother. S'heart, I've suspected this—by'r Lady, I conjectured you were a fop, since you began to change the style of your letters, and write on a scrap of paper gilt round the edges, no bigger than a *subpœna.* I might expect this when you left off, "Honoured brother;" and "hoping you are in good health," and so forth —to begin with a "Rat me, knight, I'm so sick of a last night's debauch"—'ods heart, and then tell a familiar tale of a cock and a bull, and a whore and a bottle, and so conclude.—You could write news before you were out of your time, when you lived with honest Pimple Nose the attorney of Furnival's Inn —you could entreat to be remembered then to your friends round the Wrekin. We could have gazettes, then, and Dawks's Letter, and the Weekly Bill, till of late days.[1]

Pet. S'life, Witwoud, were you ever an attorney's clerk? of the family of the Furnival? Ha! ha! ha!

Wit. Ay, ay, but that was but for a while: not long, not long. Pshaw! I was not in my own power then;—an orphan, and this fellow was my guardian; ay, ay, I was glad to consent to that, man, to come to London: he had the disposal of me then. If I had not agreed to that, I might have been bound 'prentice to a felt-maker in Shrewsbury; this fellow would have bound me to a maker of fells.

Sir Wil. S'heart, and better than to be bound to a maker of fops; where, I suppose, you have served your time; and now you may set up for yourself.

Mrs. Mar. You intend to travel, sir, as I'm informed.

Sir Wil. Belike I may, madam. I may chance to sail upon the salt seas, if my mind hold.

Pet. And the wind serve.

Sir Wil. Serve or not serve, I shan't ask licence of you, sir; nor the weathercock your companion: I direct my discourse to the lady, sir.—'Tis like my aunt may have told you, madam— yes, I have settled my concerns, I may say now, and am minded

---

[1] Newspapers of the time. Dawks's News Letter was printed in written characters to look as much like a letter as possible.

to see foreign parts. If an how that the peace holds, whereby that is, taxes abate.

Mrs. Mar. I thought you had designed for France at all adventures.

Sir Wil. I can't tell that; 'tis like I may, and 'tis like I may not. I am somewhat dainty in making a resolution—because when I make it I keep it. I don't stand shill I, shall I, then; if I say't, I'll do't; but I have thoughts to tarry a small matter in town, to learn somewhat of your lingo first, before I cross the seas. I'd gladly have a spice of your French as they say, whereby to hold discourse in foreign countries.

Mrs. Mar. Here's an academy in town for that use.

Sir Wil. There is? 'Tis like there may.

Mrs. Mar. No doubt you will return very much improved.

Wit. Yes, refined, like a Dutch skipper from a whale fishing.

Enter Lady WISHFORT and FAINALL.

Lady Wish. Nephew, you are welcome.

Sir Wil. Aunt, your servant.

Fain. Sir Wilfull, your most faithful servant.

Sir Wil. Cousin Fainall, give me your hand.

Lady Wish. Cousin Witwoud, your servant; Mr. Petulant, your servant—nephew, you are welcome again. Will you drink anything after your journey, nephew; before you eat? dinner's almost ready.

Sir Wil. I'm very well, I thank you, aunt—however, I thank you for your courteous offer. S'heart I was afraid you would have been in the fashion too, and have remembered to have forgot your relations. Here's your cousin Tony, belike, I mayn't call him brother for fear of offence.

Lady Wish. O, he's a railleur, nephew—my cousin's a wit: and your great wits always rally their best friends to choose. When you have been abroad, nephew, you'll understand raillery better. [FAINALL *and* Mrs. MARWOOD *talk apart.*

Sir Wil. Why then let him hold his tongue in the mean time; and rail when that day comes.

Enter MINCING.

Min. Mem, I am come to acquaint your la'ship that dinner is impatient.

Sir Wil. Impatient! why then belike it won't stay till I pull off my boots.—Sweetheart, can you help me to a pair of slippers?—My man's with his horses, I warrant.

Lady Wish. Fy, fy, nephew! you would not pull off your

boots here?—Go down into the hall—dinner shall stay for you. —My nephew's a little unbred, you'll pardon him, madam.— Gentlemen, will you walk?—Marwood—

Mrs. Mar. I'll follow you, madam—before Sir Wilfull is ready.   [*Exeunt all but* Mrs. MARWOOD *and* FAINALL.

Fain. Why then, Foible's a bawd, an arrant, rank, match-making bawd: and I, it seems, am a husband, a rank husband; and my wife a very arrant, rank wife—all in the way of the world. 'Sdeath, to be a cuckold by anticipation, a cuckold in embryo! sure I was born with budding antlers, like a young satyr, or a citizen's child. 'Sdeath! to be out-witted—to be out-jilted—out-matrimony'd!—If I had kept my speed like a stag, 'twere somewhat,—but to crawl after, with my horns, like a snail, and be outstripped by my wife—'tis scurvy wedlock.

Mrs. Mar. Then shake it off; you have often wished for an opportunity to part—and now you have it. But first prevent their plot—the half of Millamant's fortune is too considerable to be parted with, to a foe, to Mirabell.

Fain. Damn him! that had been mine—had you not made that fond discovery—that had been forfeited, had they been married. My wife had added lustre to my horns by that increase of fortune; I could have worn 'em tipped with gold, though my forehead had been furnished like a deputy-lieutenant's hall.

Mrs. Mar. They may prove a cap of maintenance to you still, if you can away with your wife. And she's no worse than when you had her—I dare swear she had given up her game before she was married.

Fain. Hum! that may be.

Mrs. Mar. You married her to keep you; and if you can con-trive to have her keep you better than you expected, why should you not keep her longer than you intended.

Fain. The means, the means.

Mrs. Mar. Discover to my lady your wife's conduct; threaten to part with her!—my lady loves her, and will come to any composition to save her reputation. Take the opportunity of breaking it, just upon the discovery of this imposture. My lady will be enraged beyond bounds, and sacrifice niece, and fortune, and all, at that conjuncture. And let me alone to keep her warm; if she should flag in her part, I will not fail to prompt her.

Fain. Faith, this has an appearance.

Mrs. Mar. I'm sorry I hinted to my lady to endeavour a match between Millamant and Sir Wilfull: that may be an obstacle.

Fain. Oh, for that matter, leave me to manage him: I'll disable him for that; he will drink like a Dane; after dinner, I'll set his hand in.

Mrs. Mar. Well, how do you stand affected towards your lady?

Fain. Why, faith, I'm thinking of it.—Let me see—I am married already, so that's over:—my wife has played the jade with me—well, that's over too:—I never loved her, or if I had, why that would have been over too by this time:—jealous of her I cannot be, for I am certain; so there's an end of jealousy:—weary of her I am, and shall be—no, there's no end of that—no, no, that were too much to hope. Thus far concerning my repose; now for my reputation. As to my own, I married not for it, so that's out of the question;—and as to my part in my wife's—why, she had parted with her's before; so bringing none to me, she can take none from me; 'tis against all rule of play, that I should lose to one who has not wherewithal to stake.

Mrs. Mar. Besides, you forget, marriage is honourable.

Fain. Hum, faith, and that's well thought on; marriage is honourable as you say; and if so, wherefore should cuckoldom be a discredit, being derived from so honourable a root?

Mrs. Mar. Nay, I know not; if the root be honourable, why not the branches?

Fain. So, so, why this point's clear—well, how do we proceed?

Mrs. Mar. I will contrive a letter which shall be delivered to my lady at the time when that rascal who is to act Sir Rowland is with her. It shall come as from an unknown hand—for the less I appear to know of the truth, the better I can play the incendiary. Besides, I would not have Foible provoked if I could help it—because you know she knows some passages—nay, I expect all will come out—but let the mine be sprung first, and then I care not if I am discovered.

Fain. If the worst come to the worst—I'll turn my wife to grass—I have already a deed of settlement of the best part of her estate; which I wheedled out of her; and that you shall partake at least.

Mrs. Mar. I hope you are convinced that I hate Mirabell now; you'll be no more jealous?

Fain. Jealous! no—by this kiss—let husbands be jealous; but let the lover still believe; or if he doubt, let it be only to endear his pleasure, and prepare the joy that follows, when he proves his mistress true. But let husbands' doubts convert to endless jealousy; or if they have belief, let it corrupt to superstition and blind credulity. I am single, and will herd no more with 'em. True, I wear the badge, but I'll disown the order. And since I take my leave of 'em, I care not if I leave 'em a common motto to their common crest:—

> All husbands must or pain or shame endure;
> The wise too jealous are, fools too secure.

[*Exeunt.*

ACT THE FOURTH

Scene I

A Room in Lady Wishfort's *House*

Lady Wishfort *and* Foible.

Lady Wish. Is Sir Rowland coming, sayest thou, Foible? and are things in order?

Foib. Yes, madam, I have put wax lights in the sconces, and placed the footmen in a row in the hall, in their best liveries, with the coachman and postillion to fill up the equipage.

Lady Wish. Have you pulvilled the coachman and postillion, that they may not stink of the stable when Sir Rowland comes by?

Foib. Yes, madam.

Lady Wish. And are the dancers and the music ready, that he may be entertained in all points with correspondence to his passion?

Foib. All is ready, madam.

Lady Wish. And—well—and how do I look, Foible?

Foib. Most killing well, madam.

Lady Wish. Well, and how shall I receive him? in what figure shall I give his heart the first impression? there is a great deal in the first impression. Shall I sit?—no, I won't sit—I'll walk—ay, I'll walk from the door upon his entrance; and then turn full upon him—no, that will be too sudden. I'll lie—ay, I'll lie down—I'll receive him in my little dressing-room, there's a couch—yes, yes, I'll give the first impression on a couch.—I won't lie neither, but loll and lean upon one elbow: with one foot a little dangling off, jogging in a thoughtful way—yes—and then as soon as he appears, start, ay, start and be surprised, and rise to meet him in a pretty disorder—yes—O, nothing is more alluring than a levee from a couch, in some confusion:—it shows the foot to advantage, and furnishes with blushes, and recomposing airs beyond comparison. Hark! there's a coach.

Foib. 'Tis he, madam.

Lady Wish. O dear!—Has my nephew made his addresses to Millamant? I ordered him.

Foib. Sir Wilfull is set in to drinking, madam, in the parlour.

Lady Wish. Odds my life, I'll send him to her. Call her down, Foible; bring her hither. I'll send him as I go—when they are together, then come to me, Foible, that I may not be too long alone with Sir Rowland. [*Exit.*

Enter Mrs. MILLAMANT *and* Mrs. FAINALL.

Foib. Madam, I stayed here, to tell your ladyship that Mr. Mirabell has waited this half hour for an opportunity to talk with you: though my lady's orders were to leave you and Sir Wilfull together. Shall I tell Mr. Mirabell that you are at leisure?

Mrs. Mil. No,—what would the dear man have? I am thoughtful, and would amuse myself—bid him come another time.

    "There never yet was woman made
      Nor shall but to be cursed."

               [*Repeating, and walking about.*

That's hard.

Mrs. Fain. You are very fond of Sir John Suckling [1] to-day, Millamant, and the poets.

Mrs. Mil. He? Ay, and filthy verses—so I am.

Foib. Sir Wilfull is coming, madam. Shall I send Mr. Mirabell away?

Mrs. Mil. Ay, if you please, Foible, send him away—or send him hither—just as you will, dear Foible.—I think I'll see him —shall I? ay, let the wretch come. [*Exit* FOIBLE.

    "Thyrsis, a youth of the inspirèd train."

                      [*Repeating.*

Dear Fainall, entertain Sir Wilfull—thou hast philosophy to undergo a fool, thou art married and hast patience—I would confer with my own thoughts.

Mrs. Fain. I am obliged to you, that you would make me your proxy in this affair; but I have business of my own.

Enter Sir WILFULL.

Mrs. Fain. O Sir Wilfull, you are come at the critical instant. There's your mistress up to the ears in love and contemplation; pursue your point now or never.

Sir Wil. Yes; my aunt will have it so—I would gladly have been encouraged with a bottle or two, because I'm somewhat wary at first before I am acquainted.—[*This while* MILLAMANT

---

[1] Sir John Suckling, poet (born 1609, died 1641).

walks about repeating to herself.]—But I hope, after a time, I shall break my mind—that is, upon further acquaintance—so for the present, cousin, I'll take my leave—if so be you'll be so kind to make my excuse, I'll return to my company—

Mrs. Fain. O fy, Sir Wilfull! what, you must not be daunted.

Sir Wil. Daunted! no, that's not it, it is not so much for that —for if so be that I set on't, I'll do't. But only for the present, 'tis sufficient till further acquaintance, that's all—your servant.

Mrs. Fain. Nay, I'll swear you shall never lose so favourable an opportunity, if I can help it. I'll leave you together, and lock the door.   [*Exit*.

Sir Wil. Nay, nay, cousin—I have forgot my gloves—what d'ye do?—S'heart, a'has locked the door indeed, I think—nay, Cousin Fainall, open the door—pshaw, what a vixen trick is this?—Nay, now a'has seen me too.—Cousin, I made bold to pass through as it were—I think this door's enchanted!

Mrs. Mil. [*Repeating*.]

"I prithee spare me, gentle boy,
    Press me no more for that slight toy."

Sir Wil. Anan? Cousin, your servant.

Mrs. Mil. [*Repeating*.]
            "That foolish trifle of a heart."

Sir Wilfull!

Sir Wil. Yes—your servant. No offence, I hope, cousin.

Mrs. Mil. [*Repeating*.]

    "I swear it will not do its part,   .
        Though thou dost thine, employest thy power and art."

Natural, easy Suckling!

Sir Wil. Anan? Suckling! no such suckling neither, cousin, nor stripling: I thank Heaven, I'm no minor.

Mrs. Mil. Ah, rustic, ruder than Gothic!

Sir Wil. Well, well, I shall understand your lingo one of these days, cousin; in the meanwhile I must answer in plain English.

Mrs. Mil. Have you any business with me, Sir Wilfull?

Sir Wil. Not at present, cousin—yes I make bold to see, to come and know if that how you were disposed to fetch a walk this evening, if so be that I might not be troublesome, I would have sought a walk with you.

Mrs. Mil. A walk! what then?

Sir Wil. Nay, nothing—only for the walk's sake, that's all.

Mrs. Mil. I nauseate walking; 'tis a country diversion; I loathe the country, and everything that relates to it.

Sir Wil. Indeed! ha! look ye, look ye; you do? Nay, 'tis like you may—here are choice of pastimes here in town, as plays and the like; that must be confessed indeed.

Mrs. Mil. Ah *l'étourdi!* I hate the town too.

Sir Wil. Dear heart, that's much—ha! that you should hate 'em both! ha! 'tis like you may; there are some can't relish the town, and others can't away with the country—'tis like you may be one of those, cousin.

Mrs. Mil. Ha! ha! ha! yes, 'tis like I may.—You have nothing further to say to me?

Sir Wil. Not at present, cousin.—'Tis like when I have an opportunity to be more private—I may break my mind in some measure—I conjecture you partly guess—however, that's as time shall try—but spare to speak and spare to speed, as they say.

Mrs. Mil. If it is of no great importance, Sir Wilfull, you will oblige me to leave me; I have just now a little business——

Sir Wil. Enough, enough, cousin: yes, yes, all a case—when you're disposed: now's as well as another time; and another time as well as now. All's one for that—yes, yes, if your concerns call you, there's no haste; it will keep cold, as they say.—Cousin, your servant—I think this door's locked.

Mrs. Mil. You may go this way, sir.

Sir Wil. Your servant; then with your leave I'll return to my company. [*Exit.*

Mrs. Mil. Ay, ay; ha! ha! ha!
"Like Phœbus sung the no less amorous boy."

Enter MIRABELL.

Mir.   "Like Daphne she, as lovely and as coy."
Do you lock yourself up from me, to make my search more curious? or is this pretty artifice contrived to signify that here the chase must end, and my pursuits be crowned? For you can fly no further.

Mrs. Mil. Vanity! no—I'll fly, and be followed to the last moment. Though I am upon the very verge of matrimony, I expect you should solicit me as much as if I were wavering at the grate of a monastery, with one foot over the threshold. I'll be solicited to the very last, nay, and afterwards.

Mir. What, after the last?

Mrs. Mil. Oh, I should think I was poor and had nothing to bestow, if I were reduced to an inglorious ease, and freed from the agreeable fatigues of solicitation.

Mir. But do not you know, that when favours are conferred upon instant and tedious solicitation, that they diminish in their value, and that both the giver loses the grace, and the receiver lessens his pleasure?

Mrs. Mil. It may be in things of common application; but never sure in love. Oh, I hate a lover that can dare to think he draws a moment's air, independent of the bounty of his mistress. There is not so impudent a thing in nature, as the saucy look of an assured man, confident of success. The pedantic arrogance of a very husband has not so pragmatical an air. Ah! I'll never marry, unless I am first made sure of my will and pleasure.

Mir. Would you have 'em both before marriage? or will you be contented with the first now, and stay for the other till after grace?

Mrs. Mil. Ah! don't be impertinent.—My dear liberty, shall I leave thee? my faithful solitude, my darling contemplation, must I bid you then adieu? Ay-h adieu—my morning thoughts, agreeable wakings, indolent slumbers, all ye *douceurs,* ye *sommeils du matin, adieu?*—I can't do't, 'tis more than impossible—positively, Mirabell, I'll lie abed in a morning as long as I please.

Mir. Then I'll get up in a morning as early as I please.

Mrs. Mil. Ah! idle creature, get up when you will—and d'ye hear, I won't be called names after I'm married; positively I won't be called names.

Mir. Names!

Mrs. Mil. Ay, as wife, spouse, my dear, joy, jewel, love, sweetheart, and the rest of that nauseous cant, in which men and their wives are so fulsomely familiar—I shall never bear that—good Mirabell, don't let us be familiar or fond, nor kiss before folks, like my Lady Fadler and Sir Francis: nor go to Hyde-park together the first Sunday in a new chariot, to provoke eyes and whispers, and then never to be seen there together again; as if we were proud of one another the first week, and ashamed of one another ever after. Let us never visit together, nor go to a play together; but let us be very strange and well-bred: let us be as strange as if we had been married a great while; and as well-bred as if we were not married at all.

Mir. Have you any more conditions to offer? Hitherto your demands are pretty reasonable.

Mrs. Mil. Trifles!—As liberty to pay and receive visits to and from whom I please; to write and receive letters, without interrogatories or wry faces on your part; to wear what I please; and choose conversation with regard only to my own taste; to have no obligation upon me to converse with wits that I don't like, because they are your acquaintance: or to be intimate with fools, because they may be your relations. Come to dinner when I please;

dine in my dressing-room when I'm out of humour, without giving a reason. To have my closet inviolate; to be sole empress of my tea-table, which you must never presume to approach without first asking leave. And lastly, wherever I am, you shall always knock at the door before you come in. These articles subscribed, if I continue to endure you a little longer, I may by degrees dwindle into a wife.

Mir. Your bill of fare is something advanced in this latter account.—Well, have I liberty to offer conditions—that when you are dwindled into a wife, I may not be beyond measure enlarged into a husband?

Mrs. Mil. You have free leave; propose your utmost, speak and spare not.

Mir. I thank you.—*Imprimis* then, I covenant, that your acquaintance be general; that you admit no sworn confidant, or intimate of your own sex; no she friend to screen her affairs under your countenance, and tempt you to make trial of a mutual secrecy. No decoy duck to wheedle you a fop-scrambling to the play in a mask—then bring you home in a pretended fright, when you think you shall be found out—and rail at me for missing the play, and disappointing the frolic which you had to pick me up, and prove my constancy.

Mrs. Mil. Detestable *imprimis!* I go to the play in a mask!

Mir. Item, I article, that you continue to like your own face, as long as I shall: and while it passes current with me, that you endeavour not to new-coin it. To which end, together with all vizards for the day, I prohibit all masks for the night, made of oiled-skins, and I know not what—hogs' bones, hares' gall, pigwater, and the marrow of a roasted cat. In short, I forbid all commerce with the gentlewoman in what d'ye call it court. *Item,* I shut my doors against all bawds with baskets, and pennyworths of muslin, china, fans, atlasses, etc.—*Item,* when you shall be breeding—

Mrs. Mil. Ah! name it not.

Mir. Which may be presumed with a blessing on our endeavours.

Mrs. Mil. Odious endeavours!

Mir. I denounce against all strait lacing, squeezing for a shape, till you mould my boy's head like a sugar-loaf, and instead of a man child, make me father to a crooked billet. Lastly, to the dominion of the tea-table I submit—but with proviso, that you exceed not in your province; but restrain yourself to native and simple tea-table drinks, as tea, chocolate, and coffee: as likewise to genuine and authorised tea-table talk—such as mending fashions, spoiling reputations, railing at absent friends, and so forth—but that on no account you encroach upon the men's prerogative, and presume to drink healths, or toast fellows; for prevention of which I banish all foreign forces, all auxiliaries to the tea-table, as orange-brandy, all aniseed, cinnamon, citron, and Barbadoes waters,[1] together with ratafia, and the most noble spirit of clary— but for cowslip wine, poppy water, and all dormitives, those I allow.—These provisos admitted, in other things I may prove a tractable and complying husband.

Mrs. Mil. O horrid provisos! filthy strong-waters! I toast fellows! odious men! I hate your odious provisos.

Mir. Then we are agreed! shall I kiss your hand upon the contract? And here comes one to be a witness to the sealing of the deed.

Enter Mrs. FAINALL.

Mrs. Mil. Fainall, what shall I do? shall I have him? I think I must have him.

Mrs. Fain. Ay, ay, take him, take him, what should you do?

Mrs. Mil. Well then—I'll take my death I'm in a horrid fright— Fainall, I shall never say it—well—I think—I'll endure you.

Mrs. Fain. Fy! fy! have him, have him, and tell him so in plain terms: for I am sure you have a mind to him.

Mrs. Mil. Are you? I think I have—and the horrid man looks as if he thought so too—well, you ridiculous thing you, I'll have you—I won't be kissed, nor I won't be thanked—here kiss my hand though.—So, hold your tongue now, don't say a word.

Mrs. Fain. Mirabell, there's a necessity for your obedience;— you have neither time to talk nor stay. My mother is coming; and in my conscience if she should see you, would fall into fits, and maybe not recover time enough to return to Sir Rowland, who, as Foible tells me, is in a fair way to succeed. Therefore spare your ecstacies for another occasion, and slip down the back-stairs, where Foible waits to consult you.

Mrs. Mil. Ay, go, go. In the mean time I suppose you have said something to please me.

Mir. I am all obedience.   [*Exit.*

Mrs. Fain. Yonder Sir Wilfull's drunk, and so noisy that my mother has been forced to leave Sir Rowland to appease him; but he answers her only with singing and drinking—what they may

---

[1] With these beverages there was always a mixture of alcohol. The poets and satirists were very severe upon the "tasting" of fine ladies. "As soon as she rises she must have a salutary dram to keep her stomach from the colic; a whet before she eats to procure appetite; after eating a plentiful dose for correction; and to be sure a bottle of brandy under her bedside for fear of fainting in the night."

have done by this time I know not; but Petulant and he were upon quarrelling as I came by.

Mrs. Mil. Well, if Mirabell should not make a good husband, I am a lost thing,—for I find I love him violently.

Mrs. Fain. So it seems; for you mind not what's said to you.— If you doubt him, you had best take up with Sir Wilfull.

Mrs. Mil. How can you name that superannuated lubber? foh!

Enter WITWOUD.

Mrs. Fain. So, is the fray made up, that you have left 'em?

Wit. Left 'em? I could stay no longer—I have laughed like ten christnings—I am tipsy with laughing—if I had stayed any longer I should have burst,—I must have been let out and pieced in the sides like an unsized camlet.—Yes, yes, the fray is composed; my lady came in like a *noli prosequi,* and stopped the proceedings.

Mrs. Mil. What was the dispute?

Wit. That's the jest; there was no dispute. They could neither of 'em speak for rage, and so fell a sputtering at one another like two roasting apples.

Enter PETULANT, *drunk.*

Wit. Now, Petulant, all's over, all's well. Gad, my head begins to whim it about—why dost thou not speak? thou art both as drunk and as mute as a fish.

Pet. Look you, Mrs. Millamant—if you can love me, dear nymph—say it—and that's the conclusion—pass on, or pass off— that's all.

Wit. Thou hast uttered volumes, folios, in less than *decimo sexto,* my dear Lacedemonian. Sirrah, Petulant, thou art an epitomiser of words.

Pet. Witwoud—you are an annihilator of sense.

Wit. Thou art a retailer of phrases; and dost deal in remnants of remnants, like a maker of pincushions—thou art in truth (metaphorically speaking) a speaker of shorthand.

Pet. Thou art (without a figure) just one half of an ass, and Baldwin yonder, thy half-brother, is the rest.—A Gemini of asses split would make just four of you.

Wit. Thou dost bite, my dear mustard-seed; kiss me for that.

Pet. Stand off!—I'll kiss no more males—I have kissed your twin yonder in a humour of reconciliation, till he [*Hiccups*] rises upon my stomach like a radish.

Mrs. Mil. Eh! filthy creature! what was the quarrel?

Pet. There was no quarrel—there might have been a quarrel.

Wit. If there had been words enow between 'em to have expressed provocation, they had gone together by the ears like a pair of castanets.

Pet. You were the quarrel.

Mrs. Mil. Me!

Pet. If I have a humour to quarrel, I can make less matters conclude premises.—If you are not handsome, what then, if I have a humour to prove it? If I shall have my reward, say so; if not, fight for your face the next time yourself—I'll go sleep.

Wit. Do, wrap thyself up like a wood-louse, and dream revenge—and hear me, if thou canst learn to write by to-morrow morning, pen me a challenge.—I'll carry it for thee.

Pet. Carry your mistress's monkey a spider!—Go flea dogs, and read romances!—I'll go to bed to my maid. [*Exit.*

Mrs. Fain. He's horridly drunk.—How came you all in this pickle?

Wit. A plot! a plot! to get rid of the night—your husband's advice; but he sneaked off.

Scene II

The Dining-room in Lady Wishfort's *House*

Sir Wilfull *drunk,* Lady Wishfort, Witwoud, Mrs. Millamant, *and* Mrs. Fainall.

Lady Wish. Out upon't, out upon't! At years of discretion, and comport yourself at this rantipole rate!

Sir Wil. No offence, aunt.

Lady Wish. Offence! as I'm a person, I'm ashamed of you—foh! how you stink of wine! D'ye think my niece will ever endure such a Borachio! you're an absolute Borachio.[1]

Sir Wil. Borachio?

Lady Wish. At a time when you should commence an amour, and put your best foot foremost—

Sir Wil. S'heart, an you grutch me your liquor, make a bill—give me more drink, and take my purse— [*Sings.*

"Prithee fill me the glass,
    Till it laugh in my face,
With ale that is potent and mellow;
    He that whines for a lass,
    Is an ignorant ass,
For a bumper has not its fellow."

[1] A receptacle for wine, formed of some animal's skin. A cant term for a drunkard.

But if you would have me marry my cousin—say the word, and I'll do't—Wilfull will do't, that's the word—Wilfull will do't, that's my crest—my motto I have forgot.

Lady Wish. My nephew's a little overtaken, cousin—but 'tis with drinking your health.—O' my word you are obliged to him.

Sir. Wil. In vino veritas, aunt.—If I drunk your health to-day, cousin—I am a Borachio. But if you have a mind to be married, say the word, and send for the piper; Wilfull will do't. If not, dust it away, and let's have t'other round.—Tony!—Odds heart, where's Tony!—Tony's an honest fellow; but he spits after a bumper, and that's a fault.—   [*Sings.*

> "We'll drink, and we'll never ha' done, boys,
>   Put the glass then around with the sun, boys,
> Let Apollo's example invite us;
>   For he's drunk every night,
>   And that makes him so bright,
> That he's able next morning to light us."

The sun's a good pimple, an honest soaker; he has a cellar at your Antipodes. If I travel, aunt, I touch at your Antipodes.—Your Antipodes are a good, rascally sort of topsy-turvy fellows: if I had a bumper, I'd stand upon my head and drink a health to 'em.—A match or no match, cousin with the hard name?—Aunt, Wilfull will do't. If she has her maidenhead, let her look to't; if she has not, let her keep her own counsel in the meantime, and cry out at the nine months' end.

Mrs. Mil. Your pardon, madam, I can stay no longer—Sir Wilfull grows very powerful. Eh! how he smells! I shall be overcome, if I stay.—Come, cousin.

                [*Exeunt* Mrs. MILLAMANT *and* Mrs. FAINALL.

Lady Wish. Smells! he would poison a tallow-chandler and his family! Beastly creature, I know not what to do with him!—Travel, quotha! ay, travel, travel, get thee gone, get thee gone, get thee but far enough, to the Saracens, or the Tartars, or the Turks!—for thou art not fit to live in a Christian commonwealth, thou beastly Pagan!

Sir Wil. Turks, no; no Turks, aunt: your Turks are infidels, and believe not in the grape. Your Mahometan, your Mussulman, is a dry stinkard—no offence, aunt. My map says that your Turk is not so honest a man as your Christian. I cannot find by the map that your Mufti is orthodox—whereby it is a plain case, that orthodox is a hard word, aunt, and [*Hiccups*] Greek for claret.—
                                                          [*Sings.*

"To drink is a Christian diversion,
   Unknown to the Turk or the Persian:
     Let Mahometan fools
     Live by heathenish rules,
And be damned over tea-cups and coffee.
   But let British lads sing,
   Crown a health to the king,
And a fig for your sultan and sophy!"

Ah Tony!

Enter FOIBLE, *who whispers to* Lady WISHFORT.

Lady Wish. [*Aside to* FOIBLE.]—Sir Rowland impatient? Good lack! what shall I do with this beastly tumbril?—[*Aloud.*] Go lie down and sleep, you sot!—or, as I'm a person, I'll have you bastinadoed with broomsticks.—Call up the wenches.

Sir. Wil. Ahey! wenches, where are the wenches?

Lady Wish. Dear Cousin Witwoud, get him away, and you will bind me to you inviolably. I have an affair of moment that invades me with some precipitation—you will oblige me to all futurity.

Wit. Come, knight.—Pox on him, I don't know what to say to him.—Will you go to a cock-match?

Sir. Wil. With a wench, Tony! Is she a shakebag, sirrah? Let me bite your cheek for that.

Wit. Horrible! he has a breath like a bag-pipe!—Ay, ay; come, will you march, my Salopian?

Sir Wil. Lead on, little Tony—I'll follow thee, my Anthony; my Tantony, sirrah, thou shalt be my Tantony, and I'll be thy pig.

                                  [*Sings.*

"And a fig for your sultan and sophy."

               [*Exeunt* Sir WILFULL *and* WITWOUD.

Lady Wish. This will never do. It will never make a match—at least before he has been abroad.

Enter WAITWELL, *disguised as* Sir ROWLAND.

Lady Wish. Dear Sir Rowland, I am confounded with confusion at the retrospection of my own rudeness!—I have more pardons to ask than the pope distributes in the year of jubilee. But I hope, where there is likely to be so near an alliance, we may unbend the severity of decorums, and dispense with a little ceremony.

Wait. My impatience, madam, is the effect of my transport; and till I have the possession of your adorable person, I am tantalised on the rack; and do but hang, madam, on the tenter of expectation.

Lady Wish. You have an excess of gallantry, Sir Rowland, and

press things to a conclusion with a most prevailing vehemence.—
But a day or two for decency of marriage—

Wait. For decency of funeral, madam! The delay will break my
heart—or, if that should fail, I shall be poisoned. My nephew will
get an inkling of my designs, and poison me—and I would willingly starve him before I die—I would gladly go out of the world
with that satisfaction.—That would be some comfort to me, if I
could but live so long as to be revenged on that unnatural viper!

Lady Wish. Is he so unnatural, say you? Truly I would contribute much both to the saving of your life, and the accomplishment of your revenge.—Not that I respect myself, though he has
been a perfidious wretch to me.

Wait. Perfidious to you!

Lady Wish. O Sir Rowland, the hours that he has died away at
my feet, the tears that he has shed, the oaths that he has sworn,
the palpitations that he has felt, the trances and the tremblings,
the ardours and the ecstacies, the kneelings and the risings, the
heart-heavings and the hand-gripings, the pangs and the pathetic
regards of his protesting eyes!—Oh, no memory can register!

Wait. What, my rival! is the rebel my rival?—a' dies.

Lady Wish. No, don't kill him at once, Sir Rowland, starve him
gradually, inch by inch.

Wait. I'll do't. In three weeks he shall be barefoot; in a month
out at knees with begging an alms.—He shall starve upward and
upward, till he has nothing living but his head, and then go out
in a stink like a candle's end upon a save-all.

Lady Wish. Well, Sir Rowland, you have the way—you are no
novice in the labyrinth of love—you have the clue.—But as I am
a person, Sir Rowland, you must not attribute my yielding to any
sinister appetite, or indigestion of widowhood; nor impute my
complacency to any lethargy of continence—I hope you do not
think me prone to any iteration of nuptials—

Wait. Far be it from me—

Lady Wish. If you do, I protest I must recede—or think that I
have made a prostitution of decorums; but in the vehemence of
compassion, and to save the life of a person of so much importance—

Wait. I esteem it so.

Lady Wish. Or else you wrong my condescension.

Wait. I do not, I do not!

Lady Wish. Indeed you do.

Wait. I do not, fair shrine of virtue!

Lady Wish. If you think the least scruple of carnality was an
ingredient—

Wait. Dear madam, no. You are all camphor and frankincense, all chastity and odour.

Lady Wish. Or that—

Enter FOIBLE.

Foib. Madam, the dancers are ready; and there's one with a letter, who must deliver it into your own hands.

Lady Wish. Sir Rowland, will you give me leave? Think favourably, judge candidly, and conclude you have found a person who would suffer racks in honour's cause, dear Sir Rowland, and will wait on you incessantly.   [*Exit.*

Wait. Fy, fy!—What a slavery have I undergone! Spouse, hast thou any cordial; I want spirits.

Foib. What a washy rogue art thou, to pant thus for a quarter of an hour's lying and swearing to a fine lady!

Wait. Oh, she is the antidote to desire! Spouse, thou wilt fare the worse for't—I shall have no appetite to iteration of nuptials this eight-and-forty hours.—By this hand I'd rather be a chairman in the dog-days—than act Sir Rowland till this time to-morrow!

Re-enter Lady WISHFORT, *with a letter.*

Lady Wish. Call in the dancers.—Sir Rowland, we'll sit, if you please, and see the entertainment. [*A Dance.*] Now, with your permission, Sir Rowland, I will peruse my letter.—I would open it in your presence, because I would not make you uneasy. If it should make you uneasy, I would burn it.—Speak, if it does—but you may see the superscription is like a woman's hand.

Foib. [*Aside to* WAITWELL.] By Heaven! Mrs. Marwood's, I know it.—My heart aches—get it from her.

Wait. A woman's hand! no, madam, that's no woman's hand, I see that already. That's somebody whose throat must be cut.

Lady Wish. Nay, Sir Rowland, since you give me a proof of your passion by your jealousy, I promise you I'll make a return, by a frank communication.—You shall see it—we'll open it together—look you here.—[*Reads.*]—"Madam, though unknown to you"—Look you there, 'tis from nobody that I know—"I have that honour for your character, that I think myself obliged to let you know you are abused. He who pretends to be Sir Rowland, is a cheat and a rascal."—Oh Heavens! what's this?

Foib. [*Aside.*] Unfortunate! all's ruined!

Wait. How, how, let me see, let me see!—[*Reads.*] "A rascal, and disguised and suborned for that imposture,"—O villany! O villany!—"by the contrivance of—"

Lady Wish. I shall faint, I shall die, oh!

Foib. [*Aside to* WAITWELL.] Say 'tis your nephew's hand—quickly, his plot, swear it, swear it!

Wait. Here's a villain! madam, don't you perceive it, don't you see it?

Lady Wish. Too well, too well! I have seen too much.

Wait. I told you at first I knew the hand.—A woman's hand! The rascal writes a sort of a large hand; your Roman hand—I saw there was a throat to be cut presently. If he were my son, as he is my nephew, I'd pistol him!

Foib. O treachery!—But are you sure, Sir Rowland, it is his writing?

Wait. Sure! am I here? do I live? do I love this pearl of India? I have twenty letters in my pocket from him in the same character.

Lady Wish. How!

Foib. O what luck it is, Sir Rowland, that you were present at this juncture!—This was the business that brought Mr. Mirabell disguised to Madam Millamant this afternoon. I thought something was contriving, when he stole by me and would have hid his face.

Lady Wish. How, how!—I heard the villain was in the house indeed; and now I remember, my niece went away abruptly, when Sir Wilfull was to have made his addresses.

Foib. Then, then, madam, Mr. Mirabell waited for her in her chamber! but I would not tell your ladyship to discompose you when you were to receive Sir Rowland.

Wait. Enough, his date is short.

Foib. No, good Sir Rowland, don't incur the law.

Wait. Law! I care not for law. I can but die, and 'tis in a good cause.—My lady shall be satisfied of my truth and innocence, though it cost me my life.

Lady Wish. No, dear Sir Rowland, don't fight; if you should be killed I must never show my face; or hanged—O, consider my reputation, Sir Rowland!—No, you shan't fight—I'll go in and examine my niece; I'll make her confess. I conjure you, Sir Rowland, by all your love, not to fight.

Wait. I am charmed, madam, I obey. But some proof you must let me give you; I'll go for a black box, which contains the writings of my whole estate, and deliver them into your hands.

Lady Wish. Ay, dear Sir Rowland, that will be some comfort, bring the black box.

Wait. And may I presume to bring a contract to be signed this night? may I hope so far?

Lady Wish. Bring what you will; but come alive, pray come alive. Oh, this is a happy discovery!

Wait. Dead or alive I'll come—and married we will be in spite of treachery; ay, and get an heir that shall defeat the last remaining glimpse of hope in my abandoned nephew. Come, my buxom widow:—

   Ere long you shall substantial proofs receive,
   That I'm an errant knight—
Foib. [*Aside.*]   Or errant knave.
                  [*Exeunt.*

ACT THE FIFTH

Scene I

A Room in Lady Wishfort's *House*

Lady Wishfort *and* Foible.

Lady Wish. Out of my house, out of my house, thou viper! thou serpent, that I have fostered! thou bosom traitress, that I raised from nothing!—Begone! begone! begone!—go! go!— That I took from washing of old gauze and weaving of dead hair, with a bleak blue nose over a chafing-dish of starved embers, and dining behind a traverse rag, in a shop no bigger than a birdcage!—Go, go! starve again, do, do!

Foib. Dear madam, I'll beg pardon on my knees.

Lady Wish. Away! out! out!—Go, set up for yourself again! —Do, drive a trade, do, with your three-pennyworth of small ware, flaunting upon a packthread, under a brandy-seller's bulk, or against a dead wall by a ballad-monger! Go, hang out an old Frisoneer gorget,[1] with a yard of yellow colberteen [2] again. Do; an old·gnawed mask, two rows of pins, and a child's fiddle; a glass necklace with the beads broken, and a quilted nightcap with one ear. Go, go, drive a trade!—These were your commodities, you treacherous trull! this was the merchandise you dealt in when I took you into my house, placed you next myself, and made you governante of my whole family! You have forgot this, have you, now you have feathered your nest?

Foib. No, no, dear madam. Do but hear me, have but a moment's patience, I'll confess all. Mr. Mirabell seduced me; I am not the first that he has wheedled with his dissembling tongue;

---

[1] A kerchief worn by women over their bosoms.
[2] A kind of lace.

your ladyship's own wisdom has been deluded by him; then how should I, a poor ignorant, defend myself? O madam, if you knew but what he promised me, and how he assured me your ladyship should come to no damage!—Or else the wealth of the Indies should not have bribed me to conspire against so good, so sweet, so kind a lady as you have been to me.

Lady Wish. No damage! What, to betray me, and marry me to a cast-servingman! to make me a receptacle, an hospital for a decayed pimp! No damage! O thou frontless impudence, more than a big-bellied actress!

Foib. Pray, do but hear me, madam; he could not marry your ladyship, madam.—No, indeed, his marriage was to have been void in law, for he was married to me first, to secure your ladyship. He could not have bedded your ladyship; for if he had consummated with your ladyship, he must have run the risk of the law, and been put upon his clergy.—Yes, indeed, I inquired of the law in that case before I would meddle or make.

Lady Wish. What then, I have been your property, have I? I have been convenient to you, it seems!—While you were catering for Mirabell, I have been broker for you! What, have you made a passive bawd of me?—This exceeds all precedent; I am brought to fine uses, to become a botcher of second-hand marriages between Abigails and Andrews!—I'll couple you!—Yes, I'll baste you together, you and your Philanderer! I'll Duke's place you, as I am a person! Your turtle is in custody already: you shall coo in the same cage, if there be a constable or warrant in the parish. [*Exit.*

Foib. Oh that ever I was born! Oh that I was ever married!— A bride!—ay, I shall be a Bridewell-bride.[1]—Oh!

Enter Mrs. FAINALL.

Mrs. Fain. Poor Foible, what's the matter?

Foib. O madam, my lady's gone for a constable. I shall be had to a justice, and put to Bridewell to beat hemp. Poor Waitwell's gone to prison already.

Mrs. Fain. Have a good heart, Foible; Mirabell's gone to give security for him. This is all Marwood's and my husband's doing.

Foib. Yes, yes; I know it, madam: she was in my lady's closet, and overheard all that you said to me before dinner. She sent the letter to my lady; and that missing effect, Mr. Fainall laid this plot to arrest Waitwell, when he pretended to go for the papers; and in the meantime Mrs. Marwood declared all to my lady.

---

[1] Bridewell, situated between Fleet Ditch and Bride Lane. was a House of Correction for the loose and disorderly.

Mrs. Fain. Was there no mention made of me in the letter? My mother does not suspect my being in the confederacy? I fancy Marwood has not told her, though she has told my husband.

Foib. Yes, madam; but my lady did not see that part; we stifled the letter before she read so far,—Has that mischievous devil told Mr. Fainall of your ladyship then?

Mrs. Fain. Ay, all's out—my affair with Mirabell—everything discovered. This is the last day of our living together, that's my comfort.

Foib. Indeed, madam; and so 'tis a comfort if you knew all; —he has been even with your ladyship, which I could have told you long enough since, but I love to keep peace and quietness by my goodwill. I had rather bring friends together, than set 'em at distance: but Mrs. Marwood and he are nearer related than ever their parents thought for.

Mrs. Fain. Sayest thou so, Foible? canst thou prove this?

Foib. I can take my oath of it, madam; so can Mrs. Mincing. We have had many a fair word from Madam Marwood, to conceal something that passed in our chamber one evening when you were at Hyde-park; and we were thought to have gone a-walking, but we went up unawares;—though we were sworn to secrecy too. Madam Marwood took a book and swore us upon it, but it was but a book of poems. So long as it was not a bible-oath, we may break it with a safe conscience.

Mrs. Fain. This discovery is the most opportune thing I could wish.—Now, Mincing!

Enter Mincing.

Min. My lady would speak with Mrs. Foible, mem. Mr. Mirabell is with her; he has set your spouse at liberty, Mrs. Foible, and would have you hide yourself in my lady's closet till my old lady's anger is abated. Oh, my old lady is in a perilous passion at something Mr. Fainall has said; he swears, and my old lady cries. There's a fearful hurricane, I vow. He says, mem, how that he'll have my lady's fortune made over to him, or he'll be divorced.

Mrs. Fain. Does your lady or Mirabell know that?

Min. Yes, mem; they have sent me to see if Sir Wilfull be sober, and to bring him to them. My lady is resolved to have him, I think, rather than lose such a vast sum as six thousand pounds.—O come, Mrs. Foible, I hear my old lady.

Mrs. Fain. Foible, you must tell Mincing that she must prepare to vouch when I call her.

Foib. Yes, yes, madam.

Min. O yes, mem, I'll vouch anything for your ladyship's service, be what it will.

Scene II

Another Room in Lady Wishfort's *House*

Mrs. Fainall, Lady Wishfort, *and* Mrs. Marwood.

Lady Wish. O my dear friend, how can I enumerate the benefits that I have received from your goodness! To you I owe the timely discovery of the false vows of Mirabell; to you I owe the detection of the impostor Sir Rowland. And now you are become an intercessor with my son-in-law, to save the honour of my house, and compound for the frailties of my daughter. Well, friend, you are enough to reconcile me to the bad world, or else I would retire to deserts and solitudes, and feed harmless sheep by groves and purling streams. Dear Marwood, let us leave the world, and retire by ourselves and be shepherdesses.

Mrs. Mar. Let us first despatch the affair in hand, madam. We shall have leisure to think of retirement afterwards. Here is one who is concerned in the treaty.

Lady Wish. Oh, daughter, daughter! is it possible thou shouldst be my child, bone of my bone, and flesh of my flesh, and, as I may say, another me, and yet transgress the most minute particle of severe virtue? Is it possible you should lean aside to iniquity, who have been cast in the direct mould of virtue? I have not only been a mould but a pattern for you, and a model for you, after you were brought into the world.

Mrs. Fain. I don't understand your ladyship.

Lady Wish. Not understand! Why, have you not been naught? have you not been sophisticated? Not understand! here I am ruined to compound for your caprices and your cuckoldoms. I must pawn my plate and my jewels, and ruin my niece, and all little enough——

Mrs. Fain. I am wronged and abused, and so are you. 'Tis a false accusation, as false as hell, as false as your friend there, ay, or your friend's friend, my false husband.

Mrs. Mar. My friend, Mrs. Fainall! your husband my friend! what do you mean?

Mrs. Fain. I know what I mean, madam, and so do you; and so shall the world at a time convenient.

Mrs. Mar. I am sorry to see you so passionate, madam. More temper would look more like innocence. But I have done. I am sorry my zeal to serve your ladyship and family should admit of misconstruction, or make me liable to affronts. You will pardon me, madam, if I meddle no more with an affair in which I am not personally concerned.

Lady Wish. O dear friend, I am so ashamed that you should meet with such returns!—[*To* Mrs. FAINALL.] You ought to ask pardon on your knees, ungrateful creature! she deserves more from you than all your life can accomplish.—[*To* Mrs. MARWOOD.] Oh, don't leave me destitute in this perplexity!— no, stick to me, my good genius.

Mrs. Fain. I tell you, madam, you are abused.—Stick to you! ay, like a leech, to suck your best blood—she'll drop off when she's full. Madam, you shan't pawn a bodkin, nor part with a brass counter, in composition for me. I defy 'em all. Let 'em prove their aspersions; I know my own innocence, and dare stand a trial.   [*Exit.*

Lady Wish. Why, if she should be innocent, if she should be wronged after all, ha?—I don't know what to think;—and I promise you her education has been unexceptionable—I may say it; for I chiefly made it my own care to initiate her very infancy in the rudiments of virtue, and to impress upon her tender years a young odium and aversion to the very sight of men:— ay, friend, she would ha' shrieked if she had but seen a man, till she was in her teens. As I am a person 'tis true;—she was never suffered to play with a male child, though but in coats; nay, her very babies were of the feminine gender. Oh, she never looked a man in the face but her own father, or the chaplain, and him we made a shift to put upon her for a woman, by the help of his long garments, and his sleek face, till she was going in her fifteen.

Mrs. Mar. 'Twas much she should be deceived so long.

Lady Wish. I warrant you, or she would never have borne to have been catechised by him; and have heard his long lectures against singing and dancing, and such debaucheries; and going to filthy plays, and profane music-meetings, where the lewd trebles squeak nothing but bawdy, and the basses roar blasphemy. Oh, she would have swooned at the sight or name of an obscene play-book!—and can I think, after all this, that my daughter can be naught? What, a whore? and thought it excommunication to set her foot within the door of a playhouse! O dear friend, I can't believe it, no, no! as she says, let him prove it, let him prove it.

Mrs. Mar. Prove it, madam! What, and have your name prostituted in a public court! yours and your daughter's reputation worried at the bar by a pack of bawling lawyers! To be ushered in with an O yes of scandal; and have your case opened by an old fumbling lecher in a quoif like a man-midwife; to bring your daughter's infamy to light; to be a theme for legal punsters and quibblers by the statute; and become a jest against a rule of court, where there is no precedent for a jest in any record—not even in doomsday-book; to discompose the gravity of the bench, and provoke naughty interrogatories in more naughty law Latin; while the good judge, tickled with the proceeding, simpers under a grey beard, and fidgets off and on his cushion as if he had swallowed cantharides, or sat upon cow-itch!—

Lady Wish. Oh, 'tis very hard!

Mrs. Mar. And then to have my young revellers of the Temple take notes, like 'prentices at a conventicle; and after talk it over again in commons, or before drawers in an eating-house.

Lady Wish. Worse and worse!

Mrs. Mar. Nay, this is nothing; if it would end here 'twere well. But it must, after this, be consigned by the short-hand writers to the public press; and from thence be transferred to the hands, nay into the throats and lungs of hawkers, with voices more licentious than the loud flounder-man's: and this you must hear till you are stunned; nay, you must hear nothing else for some days.

Lady Wish. Oh, 'tis insupportable! No, no, dear friend, make it up, make it up; ay, ay, I'll compound. I'll give up all, myself and my all, my niece and her all—anything, everything for composition.

Mrs. Mar. Nay, madam, I advise nothing, I only lay before you, as a friend, the inconveniences which perhaps you have overseen. Here comes Mr. Fainall; if he will be satisfied to huddle up all in silence, I shall be glad. You must think I would rather congratulate than condole with you.

Enter FAINALL.

Lady Wish. Ay, ay, I do not doubt it, dear Marwood; no, no, I do not doubt it.

Fain. Well, madam; I have suffered myself to be overcome by the importunity of this lady your friend; and am content you shall enjoy your own proper estate during life, on condition you oblige yourself never to marry, under such penalty as I think convenient.

Lady Wish. Never to marry!

Fain. No more Sir Rowlands;—the next imposture may not be so timely detected.

Mrs. Mar. That condition, I dare answer, my lady will consent to without difficulty; she has already but too much experienced the perfidiousness of men.—Besides, madam, when we retire to our pastoral solitude we shall bid adieu to all other thoughts.

Lady Wish. Ay, that's true; but in case of necessity, as of health, or some such emergency——

Fain. Oh, if you are prescribed marriage, you shall be considered; I will only reserve to myself the power to choose for you. If your physic be wholesome, it matters not who is your apothecary. Next, my wife shall settle on me the remainder of her fortune, not made over already; and for her maintenance depend entirely on my discretion.

Lady Wish. This is most inhumanly savage; exceeding the barbarity of a Muscovite husband.

Fain. I learned it from his Czarish majesty's[1] retinue, in a winter evening's conference over brandy and pepper, amongst other secrets of matrimony and policy, as they are at present practised in the northern hemisphere. But this must be agreed unto, and that positively. Lastly, I will be endowed, in right of my wife, with that six thousand pounds, which is the moiety of Mrs. Millamant's fortune in your possession; and which she has forfeited (as will appear by the last will and testament of your deceased husband, Sir Jonathan Wishfort) by her disobedience in contracting herself against your consent or knowledge; and by refusing the offered match with Sir Wilfull Witwoud, which you, like a careful aunt, had provided for her.

Lady Wish. My nephew was *non compos*, and could not make his addresses.

Fain. I come to make demands—I'll hear no objections.

Lady Wish. You will grant me time to consider?

Fain. Yes, while the instrument is drawing, to which you must set your hand till more sufficient deeds can be perfected: which I will take care shall be done with all possible speed. In the meantime I'll go for the said instrument, and till my return you may balance this matter in your own discretion.   [*Exit.*

Lady Wish. This insolence is beyond all precedent, all parallel; must I be subject to this merciless villain?

Mrs. Mar. 'Tis severe indeed, madam, that you should smart for your daughter's wantonness.

Lady Wish. 'Twas against my consent that she married this barbarian, but she would have him, though her year was not out.—Ah! her first husband, my son Languish, would not have carried it thus. Well, that was my choice, this is hers: she is matched now with a witness.—I shall be mad!—Dear friend, is there no comfort for me? must I live to be confiscated at this

---

[1] Peter the First paid a visit to England in 1697, three years prior to the production of this play.

rebelrate?—Here come two more of my Egyptian plagues too.

Enter Mrs. MILLAMANT, *and* SIR WILFULL WITWOUD.

Sir Wil. Aunt, your servant.

Lady Wish. Out, caterpillar, call not me aunt! I know thee not!

Sir Wil. I confess I have been a little in disguise, as they say.—
S'heart! and I'm sorry for't. What would you have? I hope I have
committed no offence, aunt—and if I did I am willing to make satisfaction; and what can a man say fairer? If I have broke anything
I'll pay for't, an it cost a pound. And so let that content for what's
past, and make no more words. For what's to come, to pleasure
you I'm willing to marry my cousin. So pray let's all be friends, she
and I are agreed upon the matter before a witness.

Lady Wish. How's this, dear niece? have I any comfort? can
this be true?

Mrs. Mil. I am content to be a sacrifice to your repose, madam;
and to convince you that I had no hand in the plot, as you were
misinformed, I have laid my commands on Mirabell to come in
person, and be a witness that I give my hand to this flower of
knighthood: and for the contract that passed between Mirabell
and me, I have obliged him to make a resignation of it in your
ladyship's presence;—he is without, and waits your leave for
admittance.

Lady Wish. Well, I'll swear I am something revived at this testimony of your obedience; but I cannot admit that traitor.—I fear
I cannot fortify myself to support his appearance. He is as terrible
to me as a gorgon; if I see him I fear I shall turn to stone, and
petrify incessantly.

Mrs. Mil. If you disoblige him, he may resent your refusal, and
insist upon the contract still. Then 'tis the last time he will be
offensive to you.

Lady Wish. Are you sure it will be the last time?—If I were
sure of that—shall I never see him again?

Mrs. Mil. Sir Wilfull, you and he are to travel together, are you
not?

Sir Wil. S'heart, the gentleman's a civil gentleman, aunt, let
him come in; why, we are sworn brothers and fellow-travellers.—
We are to be Pylades and Orestes, he and I.—He is to be my
interpreter in foreign parts. He has been over-seas once already;
and with proviso that I marry my cousin, will cross 'em once again,
only to bear me company.—S'heart, I'll call him in,—an I set on
once, he shall come in; and see who'll hinder him.

[*Goes to the door and hems.*

Mrs. Mar. This is precious fooling, if it would pass; but I'll know the bottom of it.

Lady Wish. O dear Marwood, you are not going.

Mrs. Mar. Not far, madam; I'll return immediately.

[*Exit.*

Enter MIRABELL.

Sir Wil. Look up, man, I'll stand by you; 'sbud an she do frown, she can't kill you;—besides—harkee, she dare not frown desperately, because her face is none of her own. S'heart, an she should, her forehead would wrinkle like the coat of a cream-cheese; but mum for that, fellow-traveller.

Mir. If a deep sense of the many injuries I have offered to so good a lady, with a sincere remorse, and a hearty contrition, can but obtain the least glance of compassion, I am too happy.—Ah, madam, there was a time!—but let it be forgotten—I confess I have deservedly forfeited the high place I once held of sighing at your feet. Nay, kill me not, by turning from me in disdain.—I come not to plead for favour;—nay, not for pardon; I am a suppliant only for pity—I am going where I never shall behold you more—

Sir Wil. How, fellow-traveller! you shall go by yourself then.

Mir. Let me be pitied first, and afterwards forgotten.—I ask no more.

Sir Wil. By'r lady, a very reasonable request, and will cost you nothing, aunt! Come, come, forgive and forget, aunt; why you must, an you are a Christian.

Mir. Consider, madam, in reality, you could not receive much prejudice; it was an innocent device; though I confess it had a face of guiltiness,—it was at most an artifice which love contrived; —and errors which love produces have ever been accounted venial. At least think it is punishment enough, that I have lost what in my heart I hold most dear, that to your cruel indignation I have offered up this beauty, and with her my peace and quiet; nay, all my hopes of future comfort.

Sir Wil. An he does not move me, would I may never be o' the quorum!—an it were not as good a deed as to drink, to give her to him again, I would I might never take shipping!—Aunt, if you don't forgive quickly, I shall melt, I can tell you that. My contract went no farther than a little mouth-glue, and that's hardly dry;— one doleful sigh more from my fellow-traveller, and 'tis dissolved.

Lady Wish. Well, nephew, upon your account—Ah, he has a false insinuating tongue!—Well, sir, I will stifle my just resentment at my nephew's request.—I will endeavour what I can to forget,—but on proviso that you resign the contract with my niece immediately.

Mir. It is in writing, and with papers of concern; but I have sent my servant for it, and will deliver it to you, with all acknowledgments for your transcendent goodness.

Lady Wish. [*Aside.*] Oh, he has witchcraft in his eyes and tongue!—When I did not see him, I could have bribed a villain to his assassination; but his appearance rakes the embers which have so long lain smothered in my breast.

Scene III

The same

Lady Wishfort, Mrs. Millamant, Sir Wilfull, Mirabell, Fainall, *and* Mrs. Marwood.

Fain. Your date of deliberation, madam, is expired. Here is the instrument; are you prepared to sign?

Lady Wish. If I were prepared, I am not impowered. My niece exerts a lawful claim, having matched herself by my direction to Sir Wilfull.

Fain. That sham is too gross to pass on me—though 'tis imposed on you, madam.

Mrs. Mil. Sir, I have given my consent.

Mir. And, sir, I have resigned my pretensions.

Sir Wil. And, sir, I assert my right; and will maintain it in defiance of you, sir, and of your instrument. S'heart, an you talk of an instrument, sir, I have an old fox by my thigh that shall hack your instrument of ram vellum to shreds, sir!—it shall not be sufficient for a mittimus or a tailor's measure. Therefore withdraw your instrument, sir, or by'r lady, I shall draw mine.

Lady Wish. Hold, nephew, hold!

Mrs. Mil. Good Sir Wilfull, respite your valour.

Fain. Indeed! Are you provided of your guard, with your single beef-eater there? but I'm prepared for you, and insist upon my first proposal. You shall submit your own estate to my management, and absolutely make over my wife's to my sole use, as pursuant to the purport and tenor of this other covenant.—I suppose, madam, your consent is not requisite in this case; nor, Mr. Mirabell, your resignation; nor, Sir Wilfull, your right.—You may draw your fox if you please, sir, and make a bear-garden flourish somewhere else; for here it will not avail. This, my Lady Wishfort, must be subscribed, or your darling daughter's turned adrift, like a leaky hulk, to sink or swim, as she and the current of this lewd town can agree.

Lady Wish. Is there no means, no remedy to stop my ruin? Ungrateful wretch! dost thou not owe thy being, thy subsistence, to my daughter's fortune?

Fain. I'll answer you when I have the rest of it in my possession.

Mir. But that you would not accept of a remedy from my hands —I own I have not deserved you should owe any obligation to me; or else perhaps I could advise—

Lady Wish. O what? what? to save me and my child from ruin, from want, I'll forgive all that's past; nay, I'll consent to anything to come, to be delivered from this tyranny.

Mir. Ay, madam; but that is too late, my reward is intercepted. You have disposed of her who only could have made me a compensation for all my services; but be it as it may, I am resolved I'll serve you! you shall not be wronged in this savage manner.

Lady Wish. How! dear Mr. Mirabell, can you be so generous at last! But it is not possible. Harkee, I'll break my nephew's match; you shall have my niece yet, and all her fortune, if you can but save me from this imminent danger.

Mir. Will you? I'll take you at your word. I ask no more. I must have leave for two criminals to appear.

Lady Wish. Ay, ay, anybody, anybody!

Mir. Foible is one, and a penitent.

Enter Mrs. FAINALL, FOIBLE, *and* MINCING.

Mrs. Mar. O my shame! [MIRABELL *and* Lady WISHFORT *go to* Mrs. FAINALL *and* FOIBLE.] These corrupt things are brought hither to expose me. [*To* FAINALL.

Fain. If it must all come out, why let 'em know it; 'tis but the way of the world. That shall not urge me to relinquish or abate one tittle of my terms; no, I will insist the more.

Foib. Yes, indeed, madam, I'll take my Bible oath of it.

Min. And so will I, mem.

Lady Wish. O Marwood, Marwood, art thou false? my friend deceive me! hast thou been a wicked accomplice with that profligate man?

Mrs. Mar. Have you so much ingratitude and injustice to give credit against your friend, to the aspersions of two such mercenary trulls?

Min. Mercenary, mem? I scorn your words. 'Tis true we found you and Mr. Fainall in the blue garret; by the same token, you swore us to secrecy upon Messalina's poems. Mercenary! No, if we would have been mercenary, we should have held our tongues; you would have bribed us sufficiently.

Fain. Go, you are an insignificant thing!—Well, what are you the better for this; is this Mr. Mirabell's expedient? I'll be put off no longer.—You thing, that was a wife, shall smart for this! I will not leave thee wherewithall to hide thy shame; your body shall be naked as your reputation.

Mrs. Fain. I despise you, and defy your malice—you have aspersed me wrongfully—I have proved your falsehood—go you and your treacherous—I will not name it, but starve together—perish!

Fain. Not while you are worth a groat, indeed, my dear.— Madam, I'll be fooled no longer.

Lady Wish. Ah, Mr. Mirabell, this is small comfort, the detection of this affair.

Mir. Oh, in good time—your leave for the other offender and penitent to appear, madam.

Enter WAITWELL *with a box of writings.*

Lady Wish. O Sir Rowland!—Well, rascal!

Wait. What your ladyship pleases. I have brought the black box at last, madam.

Mir. Give it me.—Madam, you remember your promise.

Lady Wish. Ay, dear sir.

Mir. Where are the gentlemen?

Wait. At hand, sir, rubbing their eyes—just risen from sleep.

Fain. 'Sdeath, what's this to me? I'll not wait your private concerns.

Enter PETULANT *and* WITWOUD.

Pet. How now? What's the matter? whose hand's out?

Wit. Heyday! what, are you all got together, like players at the end of the last act?

Mir. You may remember, gentlemen, I once requested your hands as witnesses to a certain parchment.

Wit. Ay, I do, my hand I remember—Petulant set his mark.

Mir. You wrong him, his name is fairly written, as shall appear. —You do not remember, gentlemen, anything of what that parchment contains?—

[*Undoing the box.*

Wit. No.

Pet. Not I; I writ, I read nothing.

Mir. Very well, now you shall know.—Madam, your promise.

Lady Wish. Ay, ay, sir, upon my honour.

Mir. Mr. Fainall, it is now time that you should know, that your lady, while she was at her own disposal, and before you had by your insinuations wheedled her out of a pretended settlement of the greatest part of her fortune—

Fain. Sir! pretended!

Mir. Yes, sir. I say that this lady while a widow, having it seems received some cautions respecting your inconstancy and tyranny of temper, which from her own partial opinion and fondness of you she could never have suspected—she did, I say, by the wholesome advice of friends, and of sages learned in the laws of this land, deliver this same as her act and deed to me in trust, and to the uses within mentioned. You may read if you please—[*Holding out the parchment*] though perhaps what is written on the back may serve your occasions.

Fain. Very likely, sir. What's here?—Damnation! [*Reads.*] "A deed of conveyance of the whole estate real of Arabella Languish, widow, in trust to Edward Mirabell."—Confusion!

Mir. Even so, sir; 'tis the Way of the World, sir, of the widows of the world. I suppose this deed may bear an elder date than what you have obtained from your lady.

Fain. Perfidious fiend! then thus I'll be revenged.

[*Offers to run at* Mrs. FAINALL.

Sir Wil. Hold, sir! now you may make your bear-garden flourish somewhere else, sir.

Fain. Mirabell, you shall hear of this, sir, be sure you shall.— Let me pass, oaf!   [*Exit.*

Mrs. Fain. Madam, you seem to stifle your resentment; you had better give it vent.

Mrs. Mar. Yes, it shall have vent—and to your confusion; or I'll perish in the attempt.   [*Exit.*

Lady Wish. O daughter, daughter! 'tis plain thou hast inherited thy mother's prudence.

Mrs. Fain. Thank Mr. Mirabell, a cautious friend, to whose advice all is owing.

Lady Wish. Well, Mr. Mirabell, you have kept your promise— and I must perform mine.—First, I pardon, for your sake, Sir Rowland there, and Foible; the next thing is to break the matter to my nephew—and how to do that—

Mir. For that, madam, give yourself no trouble; let me have your consent. Sir Wilfull is my friend; he has had compassion upon lovers, and generously engaged a volunteer in this action, for our service; and now designs to prosecute his travels.

Sir Wil. S'heart, aunt, I have no mind to marry. My cousin's a fine lady, and the gentleman loves her, and she loves him, and they deserve one another; my resolution is to see foreign parts— I have set on't—and when I'm set on't I must do't. And if these two gentlemen would travel too, I think they may be spared.

Pet. For my part, I say little—I think things are best off or on.

Wit. I'gad, I understand nothing of the matter; I'm in a maze yet, like a dog in a dancing-school.

Lady Wish. Well, sir, take her, and with her all the joy I can give you.

Mrs. Mil. Why does not the man take me? would you have me give myself to you over again?

Mir. Ay, and over and over again; [*Kisses her hand.*] I would have you as often as possibly I can. Well, Heaven grant I love you not too well, that's all my fear.

Sir Wil. S'heart, you'll have time enough to toy after you're married; or if you will toy now, let us have a dance in the mean time, that we who are not lovers may have some other employment besides looking on.

Mir. With all my heart, dear Sir Wilfull. What shall we do for music?

Foib. O sir, some that were provided for Sir Rowland's entertainment are yet within call.   [*A Dance.*

Lady Wish. As I am a person, I can hold out no longer;—I have wasted my spirits so to-day already, that I am ready to sink under the fatigue; and I cannot but have some fears upon me yet, that my son Fainall will pursue some desperate course.

Mir. Madam, disquiet not yourself on that account; to my knowledge his circumstances are such he must of course comply. For my part, I will contribute all that in me lies to a reunion; in the mean time, madam,—[*To* Mrs. FAINALL.] let me before these witnesses restore to you this deed of trust; it may be a means, well-managed, to make you live easily together.

> From hence let those be warned, who mean to wed;
> Lest mutual falsehood stain the bridal bed;
> For each deceiver to his cost may find,
> That marriage-frauds too oft are paid in kind.

[*Exeunt omnes.*

EPILOGUE

After our Epilogue this crowd dismisses,
I'm thinking how this play'll be pulled to pieces.
But pray consider, ere you doom its fall,
How hard a thing 'twould be to please you all.
There are some critics so with spleen diseased,
They scarcely come inclining to be pleased:
And sure he must have more than mortal skill,
Who pleases any one against his will.
Then all bad poets we are sure are foes,
And how their number's swelled, the town well knows:
In shoals I've marked 'em judging in the pit;
Though they're, on no pretence, for judgment fit,
But that they have been damned for want of wit.
Since when, they by their own offences taught,
Set up for spies on plays, and finding fault.
Others there are whose malice we'd prevent;
Such who watch plays with scurrilous intent
To mark out who by characters are meant.
And though no perfect likeness they can trace,
Yet each pretends to know the copied face.
These with false glosses feed their own ill nature,
And turn to libel what was meant a satire.
May such malicious fops this fortune find,
To think themselves alone the fools designed:
If any are so arrogantly vain,
To think they singly can support a scene,
And furnish fool enough to entertain.
For well the learned and the judicious know
That satire scorns to stoop so meanly low,
As any one abstracted fop to show.
For, as when painters form a matchless face,
They from each fair one catch some different grace;
And shining features in one portrait blend,
To which no single beauty must pretend;
So poets oft do in one piece expose
Whole belles-assemblies of coquettes and beaux.

THE BEAUX' STRATAGEM
by
George Farquhar

ADVERTISEMENT

The Reader may find some Faults in this Play, which my Illness prevented the amending of, but there is great Amends made in the Representation, which cannot be match'd, no more than the friendly and indefatigable Care of Mr. *Wilks,* to whom I chiefly owe the Success of the Play.

GEORGE FARQUHAR.

PROLOGUE

Spoken by Mr. Wilks

When Strife disturbs or Sloth Corrupts an Age,
Keen Satyr is the Business of the Stage.
When the Plain-Dealer writ, he lash'd those Crimes
Which then infested most—The Modish Times:
But now, when Faction sleeps and Sloth is fled,
And all our Youth in Active Fields are bred;
When thro' Great Britain's fair extensive Round,
The Trumps of Fame the Notes of Union sound;
When Anna's Scepter points the Laws their Course,
And Her Example gives her Precepts Force:
There scarce is room for Satyr, all our Lays
Must be, or Songs of Triumph, or of Praise:
But as in Grounds best cultivated, Tares
And Poppies rise among the Golden Ears;
Our Products so, fit for the Field or School,
Must mix with Nature's Favourite Plant—A Fool:
A Weed that has to twenty Summer's ran,
Shoots up in Stalk, and Vegetates to Man.
Simpling our Author goes from Field to Field,
And culls such Fools, as may Diversion yield;
And, Thanks to Nature, there's no want of those,
For Rain, or Shine, the thriving Coxcomb grows.
Follies, to Night we shew, ne'er lash'd before,
Yet, such as Nature shews you every Hour;
Nor can the Pictures give a Just Offence,
For Fools are made for Jests to Men of Sense.

DRAMATIS PERSONÆ

MEN

AIMWELL	*Two Gentlemen of broken Fortunes, the first as Master, and the second as Servant*	Mr. Mills
ARCHER		Mr. Wilks

COUNT BELLAIR, *A French Officer, Prisoner at Litchfield* . . . . Mr. Bowman

SULLEN, *A Country Blockhead, brutal to his Wife* . . . . Mr. Verbruggen

FREEMAN, *A Gentleman from London* . . . Mr. Keen

FOIGARD, *A Priest, Chaplain to the French Officers* . . . . Mr. Bowen

GIBBET, *A High-way-man* . . . . . . Mr. Cibber

HOUNSLOW \
BAGSHOT } *His Companions*

BONNIFACE, *Landlord of the Inn* . . . . Mr. Bullock

SCRUB, *Servant to Mr. Sullen* . . . . . Mr. Norris

WOMEN

LADY BOUNTIFUL	*An old civil Country Gentlewoman, that cures all her Neighbours of all Distempers, and foolishly fond of her Son Sullen*	Mrs. Powel

DORINDA, *Lady Bountiful's Daughter* . . . Mrs. Bradshaw

MRS. SULLEN, *Her Daughter-in-law* . . . Mrs. Oldfield

GIPSEY, *Maid to the Ladies* . . . . . Mrs. Mills

CHERRY, *The Landlord's Daughter in the Inn* . Mrs. Bignal

SCENE.—*Litchfield*

THE BEAUX' STRATAGEM

ACT I

SCENE.—*An Inn*

Enter BONNIFACE *running.*

Bon. Chamberlain, Maid, Cherry, Daughter Cherry, all asleep, all dead?

Enter CHERRY *running.*

Cherry. Here, here, Why d'ye baul so, Father? d'ye think we have no Ears?

Bon. You deserve to have none, you young Minx;—The Company of the Warrington Coach has stood in the Hall this Hour, and no Body to shew them to their Chambers.

Cher. And let 'em wait farther; there's neither Red-Coat in the Coach, nor Footman behind it.

Bon. But they threaten to go to another Inn to Night.

Cher. That they dare not, for fear the Coachman should over-turn them to Morrow—Coming, coming: Here's the London Coach arriv'd.

Enter several People with Trunks, Bandboxes, and other Luggage, and cross the Stage.

Bon. Welcome, Ladies.

Cher. Very welcome, Gentlemen—Chamberlain, shew the Lyon and the Rose.   [*Exit with the Company.*

Enter AIMWELL *in riding Habit,* ARCHER *as Footman carrying a Portmantle.*

Bon. This way, this way, Gentlemen.

Aim. Set down the things, go to the Stable, and see my Horses well rubb'd.

Arch. I shall, Sir.   [*Exit.*

Aim. You're my Landlord, I suppose?

Bon. Yes, Sir, I'm old Will. Bonniface, pretty well known upon this Road, as the saying is.

Aim. O Mr. Bonniface, your Servant.

Bon. O Sir—What will your Honour please to drink, as the saying is?

Aim. I have heard your Town of Litchfield much fam'd for Ale, I think I'll taste that.

Bon. Sir, I have now in my Cellar Ten Tun of the best Ale in Staffordshire; 'tis smooth as Oil, sweet as Milk, clear as Amber, and strong as Brandy; and will be just Fourteen Year old the Fifth Day of next March old Stile.

Aim. You're very exact, I find, in the Age of your Ale.

Bon. As punctual, Sir, as I am in the Age of my Children: I'll shew you such Ale.—Here, Tapster, broach Number 1706. as the saying is;—Sir, you shall taste my *Anno Domini;*—I have liv'd in Litchfield Man and Boy above Eight and fifty Years, and I believe have not consum'd Eight and fifty Ounces of Meat.

Aim. At a Meal, you mean, if one may guess your Sense by your Bulk.

Bon. Not in my Life, Sir. I have fed purely upon Ale; I have eat my Ale, drank my Ale, and I always sleep upon Ale.

Enter TAPSTER *with a Bottle and Glass.*

Now, Sir, you shall see [*filling it out*] ; your Worship's Health; ha! delicious, delicious,—fancy it Burgundy, only fancy it, and 'tis worth Ten Shillings a Quart.

Aim. [*Drinks.*] 'Tis confounded strong.

Bon. Strong! It must be so, or how should we be strong that drink it?

Aim. And have you liv'd so long upon this Ale, Landlord?

Bon. Eight and fifty Years, upon my Credit, Sir; but it kill'd my Wife, poor Woman, as the saying is.

Aim. How came that to pass?

Bon. I don't know how, Sir; she would not let the Ale take its natural Course, Sir, she was for qualifying it every now and then with a Dram, as the saying is; and an honest Gentleman that came this way from Ireland, made her a Present of a dozen Bottles of Usquebaugh—But the poor Woman was never well after: But howe're, I was obliged to the Gentleman, you know.

Aim. Why, was it the Usquebaugh that kill'd her?

Bon. My Lady Bountyful said so,—She, good Lady, did what could be done, she cured her of Three Tympanies, but the Fourth carry'd her off; but she's happy, and I'm contented, as the saying is.

Aim. Who's that Lady Bountyful, you mention'd?

Bon. Ods my Life, Sir, we'll drink her Health. [*Drinks.*] My Lady Bountyful is one of the best of Women: Her last Husband Sir Charles Bountyful left her worth a Thousand Pounds a Year; and I believe she lays out one half on't in charitable Uses for the Good of her Neighbours; she cures Rheumatisms, Ruptures, and broken Shins in Men, Green Sickness, Obstructions, and Fits of the Mother in Women;—The Kings-Evil, Chin-Cough, and Chilblains in Children; in short, she has cured more People in and about Litchfield within Ten Years than the Doctors have kill'd in Twenty; and that's a bold Word.

Aim. Has the Lady been any other way useful in her Generation?

Bon. Yes, Sir, She has a Daughter by Sir Charles, the finest Woman in all our Country, and the greatest Fortune. She has a Son too by her first Husband Squire Sullen, who marry'd a fine Lady from London t'other Day; if you please, Sir, we'll drink his Health?

Aim. What sort of a Man is he?

Bon. Why, Sir, the Man's well enough; says little, thinks less, and does—nothing at all, Faith: But he's a Man of a great Estate, and values no Body.

Aim. A Sportsman, I suppose.

Bon. Yes, Sir, he's a Man of Pleasure, he plays at Whisk, and smoaks his Pipe Eight and forty hours together sometimes.

Aim. And marry'd, you say?

Bon. Ay, and to a curious Woman, Sir—But he's a—He wants it, here, Sir. [*Pointing to his Forehead.*

Aim. He has it there, you mean.

Bon. That's none of my Business, he's my Landlord, and so a Man you know, wou'd not—But—I cod, he's no better than—Sir, my humble Service to you. [*Drinks.*] Tho' I value not a Farthing what he can do to me; I pay him his Rent at Quarter day, I have a good running Trade, I have but one Daughter, and I can give her —But no matter for that.

Aim. You're very happy, Mr. Bonniface; pray what other Company have you in Town?

Bon. A power of fine Ladies, and then we have the French Officers.

Aim. O that's right, you have a good many of those Gentlemen: Pray how do you like their Company?

Bon. So well, as the saying is, that I cou'd wish we had as many more of 'em, they're full of Money, and pay double for everything they have; they know, Sir, that we pay'd good round Taxes for the taking of 'em, and so they are willing to reimburse us a little; one of 'em lodges in my House.

Enter ARCHER.

Arch. Landlord, there are some French Gentlemen below that ask for you.

Bon. I'll wait on 'em—Does your Master stay long in Town, as the saying is? [*To* ARCHER.

Arch. I can't tell, as the saying is.

Bon. Come from London?

Arch. No.

Bon. Going to London, may hap?

Arch. No.

Bon. An odd Fellow this. I beg your Worship's Pardon, I'll wait on you in half a Minute. [*Exit.*

Aim. The Coast's clear, I see.--Now my dear Archer, welcome to Litchfield.

Arch. I thank thee, my dear Brother in Iniquity.

Aim. Iniquity! prithee leave Canting, you need not change your Stile with your Dress.

Arch. Don't mistake me, Aimwell, for 'tis still my Maxim, that there is no Scandal like Rags, nor any Crime so shameful as Poverty.

Aim. The World confesses it every Day in its Practice, tho' Men won't own it for their Opinion: Who did that worthy Lord, my Brother, single out of the Side-box to sup with him t'other Night?

Arch. Jack Handycraft, a handsom, well dress'd, mannerly, sharping Rogue, who keeps the best Company in Town.

Aim. Right, and pray who marry'd my Lady Manslaughter t'other Day, the great Fortune?

Arch. Why, Nick Marrabone, a profess'd Pick-pocket, and a good Bowler; but he makes a handsom Figure, and rides in his Coach, that he formerly used to ride behind.

Aim. But did you observe poor Jack Generous in the Park last Week?

Arch. Yes, with his Autumnal Perriwig, shading his melancholly Face, his Coat older than any thing but its Fashion, with one Hand idle in his Pocket, and with the other picking his useless Teeth; and tho' the Mall was crowded with Company, yet was poor Jack as single and solitary as a Lyon in a Desart.

Aim. And as much avoided, for no Crime upon Earth but the want of Money.

Arch. And that's enough; Men must not be poor, Idleness is the Root of all Evil; the World's wide enough, let 'em bustle; Fortune has taken the weak under her Protection, but Men of Sense are left to their Industry.

Aim. Upon which Topick we proceed, and I think luckily hitherto: Wou'd not any Man swear now that I am a Man of Quality, and you my Servant, when if our intrinsick Value were known—

Arch. Come, come, we are the Men of intrinsick Value, who can strike our Fortunes out of our selves, whose worth is independent of Accidents in Life, or Revolutions in Government; we have Heads to get Money, and Hearts to spend it.

Aim. As to our Hearts, I grant'ye, they are as willing Tits as any within Twenty Degrees; but I can have no great opinion of our Heads from the Service they have done us hitherto, unless it be that they have brought us from London hither to Litchfield, made me a Lord, and you my Servant.

Arch. That's more than you cou'd expect already. But what Money have we left?

Aim. But Two hundred Pound.

Arch. And our Horses, Cloaths, Rings, &c. Why we have very good Fortunes now for moderate People; and let me tell you, besides Thousand, that this Two hundred Pound, with the experience that we are now Masters of, is a better Estate than the Ten we have spent.—Our Friends indeed began to suspect that our Pockets were low; but we came off with flying Colours, shew'd no signs of want either in Word or Deed.

Aim. Ay, and our going to Brussels was a good Pretence enough for our sudden disappearing; and I warrant you, our Friends imagine that we are gone a volunteering.

Arch. Why Faith, if this Prospect fails, it must e'en come to that, I am for venturing one of the Hundreds if you will upon this Knight-Errantry; but in case it should fail, we'll reserve the t'other to carry us to some Counterscarp, where we may die as we liv'd in a Blaze.

Aim. With all my Heart; and we have liv'd justly, Archer, we can't say that we have spent our Fortunes, but that we have enjoy'd 'em.

Arch. Right, so much Pleasure for so much Money, we have had our Penyworths, and had I Millions, I wou'd go to the same Market again. O London, London! well, we have had our share, and let us be thankful; Past Pleasures, for ought I know are best, such as we are sure of, those to come may disappoint us.

Aim. It has often griev'd the Heart of me, to see how some inhumane Wretches murther their kind Fortunes; those that by sacrificing all to one Appetite, shall starve all the rest.—You shall have some that live only in their Palates, and in their sense of tasting shall drown the other Four: Others are only Epicures in Appearances, such who shall starve their Nights to make a Figure a Days, and famish their own to feed the Eyes of others: A contrary Sort confine their Pleasures to the dark, and contract their spacious Acres to the Circuit of a Muff-string.

Arch. Right; but they find the Indies in that Spot where they consume 'em, and I think your kind Keepers have much the best on't; for they indulge the most Senses by one Expence, there's the Seeing, Hearing, and Feeling amply gratify'd; and some Philosophers will tell you, that from such a Commerce, there arises a sixth Sense that gives infinitely more Pleasure than the other five put together.

Aim. And to pass to the other Extremity, of all Keepers, I think those the worst that keep their Money.

Arch. Those are the most miserable Wights in being, they destroy the Rights of Nature, and disappoint the Blessings of Providence: Give me a Man that keeps his Five Senses keen and bright as his Sword, that has 'em always drawn out in their just order and strength, with his Reason as Commander at the Head of 'em, that detaches 'em by turns upon whatever Party of Pleasure agreeably offers, and commands 'em to retreat upon the least Appearance of Disadvantage or Danger:—For my part I can stick to my Bottle, while my Wine, my Company, and my Reason holds good; I can be charm'd with Sappho's singing without falling in Love with her Face; I love Hunting, but wou'd not, like Acteon, be eaten up by my own Dogs; I love a fine House, but let another keep it; and just so I love a fine Woman.

Aim. In that last particular you have the better of me.

Arch. Ay, you're such an amorous Puppy, that I'm afraid you'll spoil our Sport; you can't counterfeit the Passion without feeling it.

Aim. Tho' the whining part be out of doors in Town, 'tis still in force with the Country Ladies;—And let me tell you Frank, the Fool in that Passion shall outdoe the Knave at any time.

Arch. Well, I won't dispute it now, you Command for the Day, and so I submit.—At Nottingham you know I am to be Master.

Aim. And at Lincoln I again.

Arch. Then at Norwich I mount, which, I think, shall be our last Stage; for if we fail there, we'll imbark for Holland, bid adieu to Venus, and welcome Mars.

Aim. A Match! [*Enter* BONNIFACE.] Mum.

Bon. What will your Worship please to have for Supper?

Aim. What have you got?

Bon. Sir, we have a delicate piece of Beef in the Pot, and a Pig at the Fire.

Aim. Good Supper-meat, I must confess.—I can't eat Beef, Landlord.

Arch. And I hate Pig.

Aim. Hold your prating, Sirrah, do you know who you are?

Bon. Please to bespeak something else, I have every thing in the House.

Aim. Have you any Veal?

Bon. Veal! Sir, we had a delicate Loin of Veal on Wednesday last.

Aim. Have you got any Fish or Wildfowl?

Bon. As for Fish, truly Sir, we are an inland Town, and indifferently provided with Fish, that's the Truth ont, and then for Wildfowl,—We have a delicate Couple of Rabbets.

Aim. Get me the Rabbets fricasy'd.

Bon. Fricasy'd! Lard, Sir, they'll eat much better smother'd with Onions.

Arch. Pshaw! damn your Onions.

Aim. Again, Sirrah!—Well, Landlord, what you please; but hold, I have a small Charge of Money, and your House is so full of Strangers, that I believe it may be safer in your Custody than mine; for when this Fellow of mine gets drunk, he minds nothing. —Here, Sirrah, reach me the strong Box.

Arch. Yes, Sir.—This will give us a Reputation. [*Aside.*] [*Brings the Box.*]

Aim. Here, Landlord, the Locks are sealed down both for your Security and mine; it holds somewhat above Two hundred Pounds; if you doubt it, I'll count it to you after Supper; but be sure you lay it where I may have it at a Minute's warning; for my Affairs are a little dubious at present, perhaps I may be gone in half an Hour, perhaps I may be your Guest till the best part of that be spent; and pray order your Ostler to keep my Horses always sadled; but one thing above the rest I must beg, that you would let this Fellow have none of your *Anno Domini,* as you call it;—For he's the most insufferable Sot—Here, Sirrah, light me to my Chamber. [*Exit lighted by* ARCHER.

Bon. Cherry, Daughter Cherry?

Enter CHERRY.

Cher. D'ye call, Father?

Bon. Ay, Child, you must lay by this Box for the Gentleman, 'tis full of Money.

Cher. Money! all that Money! why, sure Father the Gentleman comes to be chosen Parliament-man. Who is he?

Bon. I don't know what to make of him, he talks of keeping his Horse ready sadled, and of going perhaps at a minute's warning, or of staying perhaps till the best part of this be spent.

Cher. Ay, ten to one, Father, he's a High-way-man.

Bon. A High-way-man! upon my Life, Girl, you have hit it, and this Box is some new purchased Booty.—Now cou'd we find him out, the Money were ours.

Cher. He don't belong to our Gang?

Bon. What Horses have they?

Cher. The Master rides upon a Black.

Bon. A Black! ten to one the Man upon the black Mare; and since he don't belong to our Fraternity, we may betray him with a safe Conscience; I don't think it lawful to harbour any Rogues but my own.—Look' ye, Child, as the saying is, we must go cunningly to work, Proofs we must have, the Gentleman's Servant loves Drink, I'll ply him that way, and ten to one loves a Wench; you must work him t'other way.

Cher. Father, wou'd you have me give my Secret for his?

Bon. Consider, Child, there's Two hundred Pound to Boot. [*Ringing without*.] Coming, coming.—Child, mind your Business.

Cher. What a Rogue is my Father! my Father! I deny it.—My Mother was a good, generous, free-hearted Woman, and I can't tell how far her good Nature might have extended for the good of her Children. This Landlord of mine, for I think I can call him no more, would betray his Guest, and debauch his Daughter into the bargain,—By a Footman too!

Enter ARCHER.

Arch. What Footman, pray, Mistress, is so happy as to be the Subject of your Contemplation?

Cher. Whoever he is, Friend, he'll be but little better for't.

Arch. I hope so, for I'm sure you did not think of me.

Cher. Suppose I had?

Arch. Why then you're but even with me; for the Minute I came in, I was a considering in what manner I should make love to you.

Cher. Love to me, Friend!

Arch. Yes, Child.

Cher. Child! Manners; if you kept a little more distance, Friend, it would become you much better.

Arch. Distance! good night, Sauce-box.   [*Going*.

Cher. A pretty Fellow! I like his Pride.—Sir, pray, Sir, you see, Sir, [ARCHER *returns*.] I have the Credit to be intrusted with your

Master's Fortune here, which sets me a Degree above his Footman; I hope, Sir, you an't affronted.

Arch. Let me look you full in the Face, and I'll tell you whether you can affront me or no.—S'death, Child, you have a pair of delicate Eyes, and you don't know what to do with 'em.

Cher. Why, Sir, don't I see every body?

Arch. Ay, but if some Women had 'em, they wou'd kill every body.—Prithee, instruct me, I wou'd fain make Love to you, but don't know what to say.

Cher. Why, did you never make Love to any body before?

Arch. Never to a Person of your Figure, I can assure you, Madam, my Addresses have been always confin'd to People within my own Sphere, I never aspir'd so high before.

> *But you look so bright,*
> *And are dress'd so tight, &c.*   [*A Song.*

Cher. What can I think of this Man? [*Aside.*] Will you give me that Song, Sir?

Arch. Ay, my Dear, take it while 'tis warm. [*Kisses her.*] Death and Fire! her Lips are Honey-combs.

Cher. And I wish there had been Bees too, to have stung you for your Impudence.

Arch. There's a swarm of Cupids, my little Venus, that has done the Business much better.

Cher. This Fellow is misbegotten as well as I. [*Aside.*] What's your Name, Sir?

Arch. Name! I gad, I have forgot it. [*Aside.*] Oh! Martin.

Cher. Where were you born?

Arch. In St. Martin's Parish.

Cher. What was your Father?

Arch. St. Martin's Parish.

Cher. Then, Friend, good night.

Arch. I hope not.

Cher. You may depend upon't.

Arch. Upon what?

Cher. That you're very impudent.

Arch. That you're very handsome.

Cher. That you're a Footman.

Arch. That you're an Angel.

Cher. I shall be rude.

Arch. So shall I.

Cher. Let go my Hand.

Arch. Give me a Kiss.   [*Kisses her.*
[*Calls without,* Cherry, Cherry.

Cher. I'mm—My Father calls; you plaguy Devil, how durst you stop my Breath so?—Offer to follow me one step, if you dare.

Arch. A fair Challenge by this Light; this is a pretty fair opening of an Adventure; but we are Knight-Errants, and so Fortune be our Guide.   [*Exit.*

END OF THE FIRST ACT

ACT II

SCENE.—*A Gallery in* LADY BOUNTYFUL'S *House*

MRS. SULLEN *and* DORINDA *meeting.*

Dor. Morrow, my dear Sister; are you for Church this Morning?

Mrs. Sull. Any where to Pray; for Heaven alone can help me: But, I think, Dorinda, there's no Form of Prayer in the Liturgy against bad Husbands.

Dor. But there's a Form of Law in Doctors-Commons; and I swear, Sister Sullen, rather than see you thus continually discontented, I would advise you to apply to that: For besides the part that I bear in your vexatious Broils, as being Sister to the Husband, and Friend to the Wife, your Example gives me such an Impression of Matrimony, that I shall be apt to condemn my Person to a long Vacation all its Life.—But supposing, Madam, that you brought it to a Case of Separation, what can you urge against your Husband? My Brother is, first, the most constant Man alive.

Mrs. Sull. The most constant Husband, I grant 'ye.

Dor. He never sleeps from you.

Mrs. Sull. No, he always sleeps with me.

Dor. He allows you a Maintenance suitable to your Quality.

Mrs. Sull. A Maintenance! do you take me, Madam, for an hospital Child, that I must sit down, and bless my Benefactors for Meat, Drink and Clothes? As I take it, Madam, I brought your Brother Ten thousand Pounds, out of which, I might expect some pretty things, call'd Pleasures.

Dor. You share in all the Pleasures that the Country affords.

Mrs. Sull. Country Pleasures! Racks and Torments! dost think, Child, that my Limbs were made for leaping of Ditches, and clambring over Stiles; or that my Parents wisely foreseeing my future Happiness in Country-pleasures, had early instructed me in the rural Accomplishments of drinking fat Ale, playing at Whisk, and smoking Tobacco with my Husband; or of spreading of Plaisters, brewing of Diet-drinks, and stilling Rosemary-Water with the good old Gentlewoman, my Mother-in-Law.

Dor. I'm sorry, Madam, that it is not more in our power to divert you; I cou'd wish indeed that our Entertainments were a little more polite, or your Taste a little less refin'd: But, pray, Madam, how came the Poets and Philosophers that labour'd so much in hunting after Pleasure, to place it at last in a Country Life?

Mrs. Sull. Because they wanted Money, Child, to find out the Pleasures of the Town: Did you ever see a Poet or Philosopher worth Ten thousand Pound; if you can shew me such a Man, I'll lay you Fifty Pound you'll find him somewhere within the weekly Bills.—Not that I disapprove rural Pleasures, as the Poets have painted them; in their Landschape every Phillis has her Coridon, every murmuring Stream, and every flowry Mead gives fresh Alarms to Love.—Besides, you'll find, that their Couples were never marry'd:—But yonder I see my Coridon, and a sweet Swain it is, Heaven knows.—Come, Dorinda, don't be angry, he's my Husband, and your Brother; and between both is he not a sad Brute?

Dor. I have nothing to say to your part of him, you're the best Judge.

Mrs. Sull. O Sister, Sister! if ever you marry, beware of a sullen, silent Sot, one that's always musing, but never thinks:—There's some Diversion in a talking Blockhead; and since a Woman must wear Chains, I wou'd have the Pleasure of hearing 'em rattle a little.—Now you shall see, but take this by the way—He came home this Morning at his usual Hour of Four, waken'd me out of a sweet Dream of something else, by tumbling over the Tea-table, which he broke all to pieces, after his Man and he had rowl'd about the Room like sick Passengers in a Storm, he comes flounce into Bed, dead as a Salmon into a Fishmonger's Basket; his Feet cold as Ice, his Breath hot as a Furnace, and his Hands and his Face as greasy as his Flanel Night-cap.—Oh Matrimony!—He tosses up the Clothes with a barbarous swing over his Shoulders, disorders the whole Oeconomy of my Bed, leaves me half naked, and my whole Night's Comfort is the tuneable Serenade of that wakeful Nightingale, his Nose.—O the Pleasure of counting the melancholly Clock by a snoring Husband!—But now, Sister, you shall see how handsomely, being a well-bred Man, he will beg my Pardon.

Enter SULLEN.

Sull. My Head akes consumedly.

Mrs. Sull. Will you be pleased, my Dear, to drink Tea with us this Morning? it may do your Head good.

Sull. No.

Dor. Coffee? Brother.

Sull. Pshaw.

Mrs. Sull. Will you please to dress and go to Church with me? the Air may help you.

Sull. Scrub.

Enter SCRUB.

Scrub. Sir.

Sull. What Day o'th Week is this?

Scrub. Sunday, an't please your Worship.

Sull. Sunday! bring me a Dram, and d'ye hear, set out the Venison-Pasty, and a Tankard of strong Beer upon the Hall-Table; I'll go to breakfast.   [*Going*

Dor. Stay, stay, Brother, you shan't get off so; you were very naught last Night, and must make your Wife Reparation; come come, Brother, won't you ask Pardon?

Sull. For what?

Dor. For being drunk last Night.

Sull. I can afford it, can't I?

Mrs. Sull. But I can't, Sir.

Sull. Then you may let it alone.

Mrs. Sull. But I must tell you, Sir, that this is not to be born.

Sull. I'm glad on't.

Mrs. Sull. What is the Reason, Sir, that you use me thus inhumanely?

Sull. Scrub?

Scrub. Sir.

Sull. Get things ready to shave my Head.   [*Exit*

Mrs. Sull. Have a care of coming near his Temples, Scrub, for fear you meet something there that may turn the Edge of your Razor.—Inveterate Stupidity! did you ever know so hard, so obstinate a Spleen as his? O Sister, Sister! I shall never ha' Good of the Beast till I get him to Town; London, dear London is the Place for managing and breaking a Husband.

Dor. And has not a Husband the same Opportunities there for humbling a Wife?

Mrs. Sull. No, no, Child, 'tis a standing Maxim in conjugal Discipline, that when a Man wou'd enslave his Wife, he hurries her into the Country; and when a Lady would be arbitrary with her Husband, she wheedles her Booby up to Town.—A Man dare not play the Tyrant in London, because there are so many Examples to encourage the Subject to rebel. O Dorinda, Dorinda! a fine Woman may do any thing in London: O'my Conscience, she may raise an Army of Forty thousand Men.

Dor. I fancy, Sister, you have a mind to be trying your Power that way here in Litchfield; you have drawn the French Count to your Colours already.

Mrs. Sull. The French are a People that can't live without their Gallantries.

Dor. And some English that I know, Sister, are not averse to such Amusements.

Mrs. Sull. Well, Sister, since the Truth must out, it may do as well now as hereafter; I think one way to rouse my Lethargick sotish Husband, is, to give him a Rival; Security begets Negligence in all People, and Men must be alarm'd to make 'em alert in their Duty: Women are like Pictures of no Value in the Hands of a Fool, till he hears Men of Sense bid high for the Purchase.

Dor. This might do, Sister, if my Brother's Understanding were to be convinc'd into a Passion for you; but I fancy there's a natural Aversion of his side; and I fancy, Sister, that you don't come much behind him, if you dealt fairly.

Mrs. Sull. I own it, we are united Contradictions, Fire and Water: But I cou'd be contented, with a great many other Wives, to humour the censorious Mob, and give the World an Appearance of living well with my Husband, cou'd I bring him but to dissemble a little Kindness to keep me in Countenance.

Dor. But how do you know, Sister, but that instead of rousing your Husband by this Artifice to a counterfeit Kindness, he should awake in a real Fury?

Mrs. Sull. Let him:—If I can't entice him to the one, I wou'd provoke him to the other.

Dor. But how must I behave my self between ye?

Mrs. Sull. You must assist me.

Dor. What, against my own Brother!

Mrs. Sull. He's but half a Brother, and I'm your entire Friend: If I go a step beyond the Bounds of Honour, leave me; till then I expect you should go along with me in every thing; while I trust my Honour in your Hands, you may trust your Brother's in mine. —The Count is to dine here to Day.

Dor. 'Tis a strange thing, Sister, that I can't like that Man.

Mrs. Sull. You like nothing, your time is not come; Love and Death have their Fatalities, and strike home one time or other:— You'll pay for all one Day, I warrant'ye.—But, come, my Lady's Tea is ready, and 'tis almost Church-time. [*Exeunt.*

SCENE.—*The Inn*

Enter AIMWELL *dress'd, and* ARCHER.

Aim. And was she the Daughter of the House?

Arch. The Landlord is so blind as to think so; but I dare swear she has better Blood in her Veins.

Aim. Why dost think so?

Arch. Because the Baggage has a pert *Je ne scai quoi;* she reads Plays, keeps a Monkey, and is troubled with Vapours.

Aim. By which Discoveries I guess that you know more of her.

Arch. Not yet, Faith, the Lady gives her self Airs, forsooth, nothing under a Gentleman.

Aim. Let me take her in hand.

Arch. Say one Word more o'that, and I'll declare my self, spoil your Sport there, and every where else; look'ye, Aimwell, every Man in his own Sphere.

Aim. Right; and therefore you must pimp for your Master.

Arch. In the usual Forms, good Sir, after I have serv'd my self. —But to our Business:—You are so well dress'd, Tom, and make so handsome a Figure, that I fancy you may do Execution in a Country Church; the exteriour part strikes first, and you're in the right to make that Impression favourable.

Aim. There's something in that which may turn to Advantage: The Appearance of a Stranger in a Country Church draws as many Gazers as a blazing Star; no sooner he comes into the Cathedral, but a Train of Whispers runs buzzing round the Congregation in a moment—Who is he? whence comes he? do you know him?— Then I, Sir, tips me the Verger with half a Crown; he pockets the Simony, and Inducts me into the best Pue in the Church, I pull out my Snuff-box, turn my self round, bow to the Bishop, or the Dean, if he be the commanding Officer; single out a Beauty, rivet both my Eyes to hers, set my Nose a bleeding by the Strength of Imagination, and shew the whole Church my concern by my endeavouring to hide it; after the Sermon, the whole Town gives me to her for a Lover, and by perswading the Lady that I am a dying for her, the Tables are turn'd, and she in good earnest falls in Love with me.

Arch. There's nothing in this, Tom, without a Precedent; but instead of riveting your Eyes to a Beauty, try to fix 'em upon a Fortune, that's our Business at present.

Aim. Pshaw, no Woman can be a Beauty without a Fortune.— Let me alone, for I am a Mark'sman.

Arch. Tom.

Aim. Ay.

Arch. When were you at Church before, pray?

Aim. Um—I was there at the Coronation.

Arch. And how can you expect a Blessing by going to Church now?

Aim. Blessing! nay, Frank, I ask but for a Wife.　　　[*Exit.*

Arch. Truly the Man is not very unreasonable in his Demands.
　　　　　　　　　　　　　　　　[*Exit at the opposite Door.*

Enter BONNIFACE *and* CHERRY.

Bon. Well Daughter, as the saying is, have you brought Martin to confess?

Cher. Pray, Father, don't put me upon getting any thing out of a Man; I'm but young you know, Father, and I don't understand Wheedling.

Bon. Young! why you Jade, as the saying is, can any Woman wheedle that is not young? your Mother was useless at five and twenty; not wheedle! would you make your Mother a Whore and me a Cuckold, as the saying is? I tell you his Silence confesses it, and his Master spends his Money so freely, and is so much a Gentleman every manner of way that he must be a Highwayman.

Enter GIBBET *in a Cloak.*

Gib. Landlord, Landlord, is the Coast clear?

Bon. O, Mr. Gibbet, what's the News?

Gib. No matter, ask no Questions, all fair and honourable. Here, my dear Cherry [*Gives her a Bag.*] Two hundred Sterling Pounds, as good as any that ever hang'd or sav'd a Rogue; lay 'em by with the rest, and here—Three wedding or mourning Rings, 'tis much the same you know—Here, two Silver-hilted Swords; I took those from Fellows that never shew any part of their Swords but the Hilts: Here is a Diamond Necklace which the Lady hid in the privatest place in the Coach, but I found it out: This Gold Watch I took from a Pawn-broker's Wife; it was left in her Hands by a Person of Quality: there's the Arms upon the Case.

Cher. But who had you the Money from?

Gib. Ah! poor Woman! I pitied her—From a poor Lady just elop'd from her Husband; she had made up her Cargo, and was bound for Ireland, as hard as she cou'd drive; she told me of her Husband's barbarous Usage, and so I left her half a Crown: But I had almost forgot, my dear Cherry, I have a Present for you.

Cher. What is't?

Gib. A Pot of Cereuse, my Child, that I took out of a Lady's under Pocket.

Cher. What, Mr. Gibbet, do you think that I paint?

Gib. Why, you Jade, your Betters do; I'm sure the Lady that I took it from had a Coronet upon her Handkerchief.—Here, take my Cloak, and go, secure the Premisses.

Cher. I will secure 'em.   [*Exit.*

Bon. But, heark'ye, where's Hounslow and Bagshot?

Gib. They'll be here to Night.

Bon. D'ye know of any other Gentlemen o'the Pad on this Road?

Gib. No.

Bon. I fancy that I have two that lodge in the House just now.

Gib. The Devil! how d'ye smoak 'em?

Bon. Why, the one is gone to Church.

Gib. That's suspitious, I must confess.

Bon. And the other is now in his Master's Chamber; he pretends to be Servant to the other; we'll call him out, and pump him a little.

Gib. With all my Heart.

Bon. Mr. Martin, Mr. Martin?

Enter MARTIN *combing a Perrywig, and singing.*

Gib. The Roads are consumed deep; I'm as dirty as old Brentford at Christmas.—A good pretty Fellow that; who's Servant are you, Friend?

Arch. My Master's.

Gib. Really?

Arch. Really.

Gib. That's much.—The Fellow has been at the Bar by his Evasions:—But, pray Sir, what is your Master's Name?

Arch. Tall, all dall. [*Sings and combs the Perrywig.*] This is the most obstinate Curl—

Gib. I ask you his Name?

Arch. Name, Sir,—*Tall, all dal*—I never ask'd him his Name in my Life, *Tall, all dall.*

Bon. What think you now?

Gib. Plain, plain, he talks now as if he were before a Judge: But, pray, Friend, which way does your Master travel?

Arch. A Horseback.

Gib. Very well again, an old Offender, right—But, I mean does he go upwards or downwards?

Arch. Downwards, I fear, Sir: *Tall, all.*

Gib. I'm afraid my Fate will be a contrary way.

Bon. Ha, ha, ha! Mr. Martin, you're very arch.—This Gentleman is only travelling towards Chester, and wou'd be glad of your Company, that's all.—Come, Captain, you'll stay to Night, I suppose; I'll shew you a Chamber—Come, Captain.

Gib. Farewell, Friend—   [*Exit.*

Arch. Captain, your Servant.—Captain! a pretty Fellow; s'death, I wonder that the Officers of the Army don't conspire to beat all Scoundrels in Red, but their own.

Enter CHERRY.

Cher. Gone! and Martin here! I hope he did not listen; I wou'd have the Merit of the discovery all my own, because I wou'd oblige him to love me. [*Aside.*] Mr. Martin, who was that Man with my Father?

Arch. Some Recruiting Serjeant, or whip'd out Trooper, I sup-pose.

Cher. All's safe, I find.

Arch. Come, my Dear, have you con'd over the Catechise I taught you last Night?

Cher. Come, question me.

Arch. What is Love?

Cher. Love is I know not what, it comes I know not how, and goes I know not when.

Arch. Very well, an apt Scholar. [*Chucks her under the Chin.*] Where does Love enter?

Cher. Into the Eyes.

Arch. And where go out?

Cher. I won't tell'ye.

Arch. What are Objects of that Passion?

Cher. Youth, Beauty, and clean Linen.

Arch. The Reason?

Cher. The two first are fashionable in Nature, and the third at Court.

Arch. That's my Dear: What are the Signs and Tokens of that Passion?

Cher. A stealing Look, a stammering Tongue, Words improb-able, Designs impossible, and Actions impracticable.

Arch. That's my good Child, kiss me.—What must a Lover do to obtain his Mistress?

Cher. He must adore the Person that disdains him, he must bribe the Chambermaid that betrays him, and court the Footman that laughs at him.—He must, he must—

Arch. Nay, Child, I must whip you if you don't mind your Lesson; he must treat his—

Cher. O, ay, he must treat his Enemies with Respect, his Friends with Indifference, and all the World with Contempt; he must suffer much, and fear more; he must desire much, and hope little; in short, he must embrace his Ruine, and throw himself away.

Arch. Had ever Man so hopeful a Pupil as mine? come, my Dear, why is Love call'd a Riddle?

Cher. Because being blind, he leads those that see, and tho' a Child, he governs a Man.

Arch. Mighty well.—And why is Love pictur'd blind?

Cher. Because the Painters out of the weakness or privilege of their Art chose to hide those Eyes that they cou'd not draw.

Arch. That's my dear little Scholar, kiss me again.—And why shou'd Love, that's a Child, govern a Man?

Cher. Because that Child is the end of Love.

Arch. And so ends Love's Catechism.—And now, my Dear, we'll go in, and make my Master's Bed.

Cher. Hold, hold, Mr. Martin—You have taken a great deal of Pains to instruct me, and what d'ye think I have learn't by it?

Arch. What?

Cher. That your discourse and your Habit are Contradictions, and it wou'd be nonsense in me to believe you a Footman any longer.

Arch. 'Oons, what a Witch it is!

Cher. Depend upon this, Sir, nothing in this Garb shall ever tempt me; for tho' I was born to Servitude, I hate it:—Own your Condition, swear you love me, and then—

Arch. And then we shall go make the Bed.

Cher. Yes.

Arch. You must know then, that I am born a Gentleman, my Education was liberal; but I went to London a younger Brother, fell into the Hands of Sharpers, who stript me of my Money, my Friends disown'd me, and now my Necessity brings me to what you see.

Cher. Then take my Hand—promise to marry me before you sleep, and I'll make you Master of two thousand Pound.

Arch. How!

Cher. Two thousand Pound that I have this Minute in my own Custody; so throw off your Livery this Instant, and I'll go find a Parson.

Arch. What said you? A Parson!

Cher. What! do you scruple?

Arch. Scruple! no, no, but—two thousand Pound you say?

Cher. And better.

Arch. S'death, what shall I do—but heark'e, Child, what need you make me Master of your self and Money, when you may have the same Pleasure out of me, and still keep your Fortune in your Hands.

Cher. Then you won't marry me?

Arch. I wou'd marry you, but—

Cher. O sweet, Sir, I'm your humble Servant: you're fairly caught; wou'd you perswade me that any Gentleman who cou'd bear the Scandal of wearing a Livery, wou'd refuse two thousand Pound, let the Condition be what it wou'd—no, no, Sir,—but I hope you'll Pardon the Freedom I have taken, since it was only to inform my self of the Respect that I ought to pay you. [*Going*

Arch. Fairly bit, by Jupiter—hold, hold, and have you actually two thousand Pound.

Cher. Sir, I have my Secrets as well as you—when you please to be more open, I shall be more free, and be assur'd that I have Discoveries that will match yours, be what they will—In the mean while be satisfy'd that no Discovery I make shall ever hurt you, but beware of my Father.—

Arch. So—we're like to have as many Adventures in our Inn, as *Don Quixote* had in his—Let me see,—two thousand Pound! if the Wench wou'd promise to dye when the Money were spent, I gad, one wou'd marry her, but the Fortune may go off in a Year or two, and the Wife may live—Lord knows how long! Then an Inn-keeper's Daughter; ay that's the Devil—there my Pride brings me off.

> *For whatsoe'er the Sages charge on Pride*
> *The Angels fall, and twenty Faults beside,*
> *On Earth I'm sure, 'mong us of mortal Calling,*
> *Pride saves Man oft, and Woman too from falling.* [*Exit.*

END OF THE SECOND ACT

ACT III

SCENE.—*Continues*

Enter MRS. SULLEN, DORINDA.

Mrs. Sull. Ha, ha, ha, my dear Sister, let me embrace thee; now we are Friends indeed! for I shall have a Secret of yours, as a Pledge for mine—now you'll be good for something, I shall have you conversable in the Subjects of the Sex.

Dor. But do you think that I am so weak as to fall in Love with a Fellow at first sight?

Mrs. Sull. Pshaw! now you spoil all; why shou'd not we be as free in our Friendships as the Men? I warrant you the Gentleman has got to his Confident already, has avow'd his Passion, toasted

your Health, call'd you ten thousand Angels, has run over your
Lips, Eyes, Neck, Shape, Air and every thing, in a Description
that warms their Mirth to a second Enjoyment.

Dor. Your Hand, Sister, I an't well.

Mrs. Sull. So,—she's breeding already—come Child up with it
—hem a little—so—now tell me, don't you like the Gentleman
that we saw at Church just now?

Dor. The Man's well enough.

Mrs. Sull. Well enough! is he not a Demigod, a Narcissus, a Star,
the Man i'the Moon?

Dor. O Sister, I'm extreamly ill.

Mrs. Sull. Shall I send to your Mother, Child, for a little of her
Cephalick Plaister to put to the Soals of your Feet, or shall I send to
the Gentleman for something for you?—Come, unlace your Steas,
unbosome your self—the Man is perfectly a pretty Fellow, I saw
him when he first came into Church.

Dor. I saw him too, Sister, and with an Air that shone, methought like Rays about his Person.

Mrs. Sull. Well said, up with it.

Dor. No forward Coquett Behaviour, no Airs to set him off, no
study'd Looks nor artful Posture,—but Nature did it all—

Mrs. Sull. Better and better—one Touch more—come.—

Dor. But then his Looks—did you observe his Eyes?

Mrs. Sull. Yes, yes, I did—his Eyes, well, what of his Eyes?

Dor. Sprightly, but not wandring; they seem'd to view, but
never gaz'd on any thing but me—and then his Looks so humble
were, and yet so noble, that they aim'd to tell me that he cou'd
with Pride dye at my Feet, tho' he scorn'd Slavery any where else.

Mrs. Sull. The Physick works purely—How d'ye find your self
now, my Dear?

Dor. Hem! much better, my Dear—O here comes our Mercury!

Enter SCRUB.

Well, Scrub, what News of the Gentleman?

Scrub. Madam, I have brought you a Packet of News.

Dor. Open it quickly, come.

Scrub. In the first place, I enquir'd who the Gentleman was;
they told me he was a Stranger. Secondly, I ask'd what the Gentleman was; they answer'd and said, that they never saw him before. Thirdly, I enquir'd what Countryman he was; they reply'd
'twas more than they knew. Fourthly, I demanded whence he
came; their Answer was, they cou'd not tell. And Fifthly, I ask'd
whither he went, and they reply'd they knew nothing of the matter
—and this is all I cou'd learn.

Mrs. Sull. But what do the People say, can't they guess?

Scrub. Why some think he's a Spy, some guess he's a Mounte-bank, some say one thing, some another; but for my own part, I believe he's a Jesuit.

Dor. A Jesuit! why a Jesuit?

Scrub. Because he keeps his Horses always ready sadled, and his Footman talks French.

Mrs. Sull. His Footman!

Scrub. Ay, he and the Count's Footman were Gabbering French like two intreaguing Ducks in a Mill-Pond, and I believe they talk'd of me, for thy laugh'd consumedly.

Dor. What sort of Livery has the Footman?

Scrub. Livery! Lord, Madam, I took him for a Captain, he's so bedizen'd with Lace, and then he has Tops to his Shoes, up to his mid Leg, a silver headed Cane dangling at his Nuckles,—he carries his Hands in his Pockets just so—[*Walks in the French Air.*] and has a fine long Perriwig ty'd up in a Bag—Lord, Madam, he's clear another sort of Man than I.

Mrs. Sull. That may easily be—but what shall we do now, Sister?

Dor. I have it—This Fellow has a world of Simplicity, and some Cunning; the first hides the latter by abundance.—Scrub.

Scrub. Madam.

Dor. We have a great mind to know who this Gentleman is, only for our Satisfaction.

Scrub. Yes, Madam, it would be a Satisfaction, no doubt.

Dor. You must go and get acquainted with his Footman, and invite him hither to drink a Bottle of your Ale, because you're Butler to Day.

Scrub. Yes, Madam, I am Butler every Sunday.

Mrs. Sull. O brave, Sister, O my Conscience, you understand the Mathematicks already—'tis the best Plot in the World; your Mother, you know, will be gone to Church, my Spouse will be got to the Ale-house with his Scoundrels, and the House will be our own—so we drop in by Accident and ask the Fellow some Questions our selves. In the Countrey you know any Stranger is Company, and we're glad to take up with the Butler in a Country Dance, and happy if he'll do us the Favour.

Scrub. Oh! Madam, you wrong me; I never refus'd your Lady-ship the Favour in my Life.

Enter GIPSEY.

Gip. Ladies, Dinner's upon Table.

Dor. Scrub, We'll excuse your waiting—Go where we order'd you.

Scrub. I shall.   [*Exeunt*.

SCENE.—*Changes to the Inn*

Enter AIMWELL *and* ARCHER.

Arch. Well, Tom, I find you're a Marksman.

Aim. A Marksman! who so blind cou'd be, as not discern a Swan among the Ravens?

Arch. Well, but heark'ee, Aimwell.

Aim. Aimwell! call me Oroondates, Cesario, Amadis, all that Romance can in a Lover paint, and then I'll answer. O Archer, I read her thousands in her Looks; she look'd like Ceres in her Harvest: Corn, Wine and Oil, Milk and Honey, Gardens, Groves and Purling Streams play'd on her plenteous Face.

Arch. Her Face! her Pocket, you mean; the Corn, Wine and Oil lies there. In short, she has ten thousand Pound, that's the English on't.

Aim. Her Eyes—

Arch. Are Demi-Cannons to be sure, so I won't stand their Battery.   [*Going*.

Aim. Pray excuse me, my Passion must have vent.

Arch. Passion! what a plague, d'ee think these Romantick Airs will do our Business? Were my Temper as extravagant as yours, my Adventures have something more Romantick by half.

Aim. Your Adventures!

Arch. Yes, The Nymph that with her twice ten hundred Pounds
With brazen Engine hot, and Quoif clear starch'd
Can fire the Guest in warming of the Bed—
There's a Touch of Sublime Milton for you, and the Subject but an Inn-keeper's Daughter; I can play with a Girl as an Angler do's with his Fish; he keeps it at the end of his Line, runs it up the Stream, and down the Stream, till at last, he brings it to hand, tickles the Trout, and so whips it into his Basket.

Enter BONNIFACE.

Bon. Mr. Martin, as the saying is—yonder's an honest Fellow below, my Lady Bountiful's Butler, who begs the Honour that you wou'd go Home with him and see his Cellar.

Arch. Do my Baisemains to the Gentleman, and tell him I will do my self the Honour to wait on him immediately.   [*Exit* BON.

Aim. What do I hear? soft Orpheus Play, and fair Toftida sing?

Arch. Pshaw! damn your Raptures, I tell you here's a Pump going to be put into the Vessel, and the Ship will get into Harbour, my Life on't. You say there's another Lady very handsome there?

Aim. Yes, faith.

Arch. I am in love with her already.

Aim. Can't you give me a Bill upon Cherry in the mean time?

Arch. No, no, Friend, all her Corn, Wine and Oil is ingross'd to my Market.—And once more I warn you to keep your Anchorage clear of mine, for if you fall foul of me, by this Light you shall go to the Bottom.—What! make Prize of my little Frigat, while I am upon the Cruise for you!   [*Exit*.

Enter BONNIFACE.

Aim. Well, well, I won't—Landlord, have you any tolerable Company in the House? I don't care for dining alone.

Bon. Yes, Sir, there's a Captain below, as the saying is, that arrived about an Hour ago.

Aim. Gentlemen of his Coat are welcome every where; will you make him a Complement from me, and tell him I should be glad of his Company?

Bon. Who shall I tell him, Sir, wou'd—

Aim. Ha! that Stroak was well thrown in—I'm only a Traveller like himself, and wou'd be glad of his Company, that's all.

Bon. I obey your Commands, as the saying is.   [*Exit*.

Enter ARCHER.

Arch. S'Death! I had forgot, what Title will you give your self?

Aim. My Brother's to be sure; he wou'd never give me any thing else, so I'll make bold with his Honour this bout—you know the rest of your Cue.   [*Exit* BON.

Arch. Ay, ay.

Enter GIBBET.

Gib. Sir, I'm yours.

Aim. 'Tis more than I deserve, Sir, for I don't know you.

Gib. I don't wonder at that, Sir, for you never saw me before, I hope.   [*Aside*.

Aim. And pray, Sir, how came I by the Honour of seeing you now?

Gib. Sir, I scorn to intrude upon any Gentleman—but my Land-lord—

Aim. O, Sir, I ask your Pardon, you're the Captain he told me of.

Gib. At your Service, Sir.

Aim. What Regiment, may I be so bold?

Gib. A marching Regiment, Sir, an old Corps.

Aim. Very old, if your Coat be Regimental. [*Aside.*] You have serv'd abroad, Sir?

Gib. Yes, Sir, in the Plantations; 'twas my Lot to be sent into the worst Service; I wou'd have quitted it indeed, but a man of Honour, you know——Besides 'twas for the good of my Country that I shou'd be abroad——Any thing for the good of one's Country ——I'm a Roman for that.

Aim. One of the first, I'll lay my Life. [*Aside.*] You found the West Indies very hot, Sir?

Gib. Ay, Sir, too hot for me.

Aim. Pray, Sir, han't I seen your Face at Will's Coffee-house?

Gib. Yes, Sir, and at White's too.

Aim. And where is your Company now, Captain?

Gib. They an't come yet.

Aim. Why, d'ye expect 'em here?

Gib. They'll be here to Night, Sir.

Aim. Which way do they march?

Gib. Across the Country——the Devil's in't; if I han't said enough to encourage him to declare——but I'm afraid he's not right, I must tack about.

Aim. Is your Company to quarter in Litchfield?

Gib. In this House, Sir.

Aim. What! all?

Gib. My Company's but thin, ha, ha, ha, we are but three, ha, ha, ha.

Aim. You're merry, Sir.

Gib. Ay, Sir, you must excuse me, Sir, I understand the World, especially, the Art of Travelling; I don't care, Sir, for answering Questions directly upon the Road——for I generally ride with a Charge about me.

Aim. Three or four, I believe.   [*Aside.*

Gib. I am credibly inform'd that there are Highway-men upon this Quarter; not, Sir, that I cou'd suspect a Gentleman of your Figure——But truly, Sir, I have got such a way of Evasion upon the Road, that I don't care for speaking Truth to any Man.

Aim. Your Caution may be necessary——Then I presume you're no Captain?

Gib. Not I, Sir; Captain is a good travelling Name, and so I take it; it stops a great many foolish Inquiries that are generally made about Gentlemen that travel; it gives a Man an Air of something, and makes the Drawers obedient——And thus far I am a Captain, and no farther.

Aim. And pray, Sir, what is your true Profession?

Gib. O, Sir, you must excuse me—upon my Word, Sir, I don't think it safe to tell you.

Aim. Ha, ha, ha, upon my word I commend you. Well, Mr. Bonniface, what's the News?

Enter BONNIFACE.

Bon. There's another Gentleman below, as the saying is, that hearing you were but two, wou'd be glad to make the third Man if you wou'd give him leave.

Aim. What is he?

Bon. A Clergyman, as the saying is.

Aim. A Clergyman! is he really a Clergyman? or is it only his travelling Name, as my Friend the Captain has it?

Bon. O, Sir, he's a Priest and Chaplain to the French Officers in Town.

Aim. Is he a French-man?

Bon. Yes, Sir, born at Brussels.

Gib. A French-man, and a Priest! I won't be seen in his Company, Sir; I have a Value for my Reputation, Sir.

Aim. Nay, but Captain, since we are by our selves—Can he speak English, Landlord?

Bon. Very well, Sir; you may know him, as the saying is, to be a Foreigner by his Accent, and that's all.

Aim. Then he has been in England before?

Bon. Never, Sir, but he's a Master of Languages, as the saying is, he talks Latin, it do's me good to hear him talk Latin.

Aim. Then you understand Latin, Mr. Bonniface?

Bon. Not I, Sir, as the saying is, but he talks it so very fast that I'm sure it must be good.

Aim. Pray desire him to walk up.

Bon. Here he is, as the saying is.

Enter FOIGARD.

Foig. Save you, Gentlemen's, both.

Aim. A French-man! Sir, your most humble Servant.

Foig. Och, dear Joy, I am your most faithful Shervant, and yours alsho.

Gib. Doctor, you talk very good English, but you have a mighty Twang of the Foreigner.

Foig. My English is very vel for the vords, but we Foregners you know cannot bring our Tongues about the Pronunciation so soon.

Aim. A Foreigner! a down-right Teague by this Light. [*Aside.*] Were you born in France, Doctor?

Foig. I was educated in France, but I was borned at Brussels; I am a Subject of the King of Spain, Joy.

Gib. What King of Spain, Sir, speak.

Foig. Upon my Shoul Joy, I cannot tell you as yet.

Aim. Nay, Captain, that was too hard upon the Doctor, he's a Stranger.

Foig. O let him alone, dear Joy, I am of a Nation that is not easily put out of Countenance.

Aim. Come, Gentlemen, I'll end the Dispute.—Here, Landlord, is Dinner ready?

Bon. Upon the Table, as the saying is.

Aim. Gentlemen—pray—that Door—

Foig. No, no fait, the Captain must lead.

Aim. No, Doctor, the Church is our Guide.

Gib. Ay, ay, so it is.—　　　　　　[*Exit foremost, they follow.*

Scene.—*Changes to a Gallery in* Lady Bountyful's *House*

Enter Archer *and* Scrub *singing, and hugging one another,* Scrub *with a Tankard in his Hand,* Gipsey *listning at a distance.*

Scrub. Tall, all dall—Come, my dear Boy—Let's have that Song once more.

Arch. No, no, we shall disturb the Family.—But will you be sure to keep the Secret?

Scrub. Pho! upon my Honour, as I'm a Gentleman.

Arch. 'Tis enough.—You must know then that my Master is the Lord Viscount Aimwell; he fought a Duel t'other day in London, wounded his Man so dangerously, that he thinks fit to withdraw till he hears whether the Gentleman's Wounds be mortal or not: He never was in this part of England before, so he chose to retire to this Place, that's all.

Gip. And that's enough for me.　　　　　　　[*Exit.*

Scrub. And where were you when your Master fought?

Arch. We never know of our Masters Quarrels.

Scrub. No! if our Masters in the Country here receive a Challenge, the first thing they do is to tell their Wives; the Wife tells the Servants, the Servants alarm the Tenants, and in half an Hour you shall have the whole County in Arms.

Arch. To hinder two Men from doing what they have no mind for:—But if you should chance to talk now of my Business?

Scrub. Talk! ay, Sir, had I not learn't the knack of holding my Tongue, I had never liv'd so long in a great Family.

Arch. Ay, ay, to be sure there are Secrets in all Families.

Scrub. Secrets, ay;—But I'll say no more.—Come, sit down, we'll make an end of our Tankard: Here—

· *Arch.* With all my Heart; who knows but you and I may come to be better acquainted, eh?—Here's your Ladies Healths; you have three, I think, and to be sure there must be Secrets among 'em.

Scrub. Secrets! Ay, Friend; I wish I had a Friend—

Arch. Am not I your Friend? come, you and I will be sworn Brothers.

Scrub. Shall we?

Arch. From this Minute.—Give me a kiss—And now Brother Scrub—

Scrub. And now, Brother Martin, I will tell you a Secret that will make your Hair stand on end:—You must know, that I am consumedly in Love.

Arch. That's a terrible Secret, that's the Truth on't.

Scrub. That Jade, Gipsey, that was with us just now in the Cellar, is the arrantest Whore that ever wore a Petticoat; and I'm dying for love of her.

Arch. Ha, ha, ha—Are you in love with her Person, or her Vertue, Brother Scrub?

Scrub. I should like Vertue best, because it is more durable than Beauty; for Vertue holds good with some Women long, and many a Day after they have lost it.

Arch. In the Country, I grant ye, where no Woman's Vertue is lost, till a Bastard be found.

Scrub. Ay, cou'd I bring her to a Bastard, I shou'd have her all to my self; but I dare not put it upon that Lay, for fear of being sent for a Soldier.—Pray, Brother, how do you Gentlemen in London like that same Pressing Act?

Arch. Very ill, Brother Scrub;—'Tis the worst that ever was made for us: Formerly I remember the good Days, when we cou'd dun our Masters for our Wages, and if they refused to pay us, we cou'd have a Warrant to carry 'em before a Justice; but now if we talk of eating, they have a Warrant for us, and carry us before three Justices.

Scrub. And to be sure we go, if we talk of eating; for the Justices won't give their own Servants a bad Example. Now this is my Misfortune—I dare not speak in the House, while that Jade Gipsey dings about like a Fury—Once I had the better end of the Staff.

Arch. And how comes the Change now?

Scrub. Why, the Mother of all this Mischief is a Priest.

Arch. A Priest!

Scrub. Ay, a damn'd Son of a Whore of Babylon, that came over hither to say Grace to the French Officers, and eat up our Provisions—There's not a Day goes over his Head without Dinner or Supper in this House.

Arch. How came he so familiar in the Family?

Scrub. Because he speaks English as if he had liv'd here all his Life; and tells Lies as if he had been a Traveller from his Cradle.

Arch. And this Priest, I'm afraid has converted the Affections of your Gipsey.

Scrub. Converted! ay, and perverted, my dear Friend:—For I'm afraid he has made her a Whore and a Papist.—But this is not all; there's the French Count and Mrs. Sullen, they're in the Confederacy, and for some private Ends of their own to be sure.

Arch. A very hopeful Family yours, Brother Scrub; I suppose the Maiden Lady has her Lover too.

Scrub. Not that I know;—She's the best on 'em, that's the Truth on't: But they take care to prevent my Curiosity, by giving me so much Business, that I'm a perfect Slave.—What d'ye think is my Place in this Family?

Arch. Butler, I suppose.

Scrub. Ah, Lord help you—I'll tell you—Of a Monday, I drive the Coach; of a Tuesday, I drive the Plough; on Wednesday, I follow the Hounds; a Thursday, I dun the Tenants; on Fryday, I go to Market; on Saturday, I draw Warrants; and a Sunday, I draw Beer.

Arch. Ha, ha, ha! if variety be a Pleasure in Life, you have enough on't, my dear Brother.—But what Ladies are those?

Arch. Ours, ours; that upon the right Hand is Mrs. Sullen, and the other is Mrs. Dorinda.—Don't mind 'em; sit still, Man—

Enter Mrs. Sullen *and* Dorinda.

Mrs. Sull. I have heard my Brother talk of my Lord Aimwell, but they say that his Brother is the finer Gentleman.

Dor. That's impossible, Sister.

Mrs. Sull. He's vastly rich, but very close, they say.

Dor. No matter for that; if I can creep into his Heart, I'll open his Breast, I warrant him: I have heard say, that People may be guess'd at by the Behaviour of their Servants; I cou'd wish we might talk to that Fellow.

Mrs. Sull. So do I; for, I think he's a very pretty Fellow: Come this way, I'll throw out a Lure for him presently.

[*They walk a turn towards the opposite side of the Stage.*

Mrs. Sullen *drops her Glove,* Archer *runs, takes it up, and gives it to her.*

Arch. Corn, Wine, and Oil, indeed—But, I think, the Wife has the greatest plenty of Flesh and Blood; she should be my Choice—Ah, a, say you so—Madam—Your Ladyship's Glove.

Mrs. Sull. O, Sir, I thank you—what a handsom Bow the Fellow has!

Dor. Bow! why I have known several Footmen come down from London set up here for Dancing-Masters, and carry off the best Fortunes in the Country.

Arch. [*Aside.*] That Project, for ought I know, had been better than ours, Brother Scrub—Why don't you introduce me?

Scrub. Ladies, this is the strange Gentleman's Servant that you see at Church to Day; I understood he came from London, and so I invited him to the Cellar, that he might show me the newest Flourish in whetting my Knives.

Dor. And I hope you have made much of him?

Arch. O yes, Madam, but the Strength of your Ladyship's Liquour is a little too potent for the Constitution of your humble Servant.

Mrs. Sull. What, then you don't usually drink Ale?

Arch. No, Madam, my constant Drink is Tea, or a little Wine and Water; 'tis prescrib'd me by the Physician for a Remedy against the Spleen.

Scrub. O la, O la!—a Footman have the Spleen.—

Mrs. Sull. I thought that Distemper had been only proper to People of Quality.

Arch. Madam, like all other Fashions it wears out, and so descends to their Servants; tho' in a great many of us, I believe it proceeds from some melancholly Particles in the Blood, occasion'd by the Stagnation of Wages.

Dor. How affectedly the Fellow talks—How long, pray, have you serv'd your present Master?

Arch. Not long; my Life has been mostly spent in the Service of the Ladies.

Mrs. Sull. And pray, which Service do you like best?

Arch. Madam, the Ladies pay best; the Honour of serving them is sufficient Wages; there is a Charm in their looks that delivers a Pleasure with their Commands, and gives our Duty the Wings of Inclination.

Mrs. Sull. That Flight was above the pitch of a Livery; and, Sir, wou'd not you be satisfied to serve a Lady again?

Arch. As a Groom of the Chamber, Madam, but not as a Footman.

Mrs. Sull. I suppose you serv'd as Footman before.

Arch. For that Reason I wou'd not serve in that Post again; for my Memory is too weak for the load of Messages that the Ladies lay upon their Servants in London; my Lady Howd'ye, the last Mistress I serv'd call'd me up one Morning, and told me, Martin, go to my Lady Allnight with my humble Service; tell her I was to wait on her Ladyship yesterday, and left word with Mrs. Rebecca, that the Preliminaries of the Affair she knows of, are stopt till we know the concurrence of the Person that I know of, for which there are Circumstances wanting which we shall accommodate at the old Place; but that in the mean time there is a Person about her Ladyship, that from several Hints and Surmises, was accessary at a certain time to the disappointments that naturally attend things, that to her knowledge are of more Importance.

Mrs. Sull and Dor. Ha, ha, ha! where are you going, Sir?

Arch. Why, I han't half done.—The whole Howd'ye was about half an Hour long; so I hapned to misplace two Syllables, and was turn'd off, and render'd incapable—

Dor. The pleasantest Fellow, Sister, I ever saw.—But, Friend, if your Master be marry'd,—I presume you still serve a Lady.

Arch. No, Madam, I take care never to come into a marry'd Family; the Commands of the Master and Mistress are always so contrary, that 'tis impossible to please both.

Dor. There's a main point gain'd.—My Lord is not marry'd, I find.   [*Aside.*

Mrs. Sull. But, I wonder, Friend, that in so many good Services, you had not a better Provision made for you.

Arch. I don't know how, Madam.—I had a Lieutenancy offer'd me three or four Times; but that is not Bread, Madam—I live much better as I do.

Scrub. Madam, he sings rarely.—I was thought to do pretty well here in the Country till he came; but alack a day, I'm nothing to my Brother Martin.

Dor. Does he? Pray, Sir, will you oblige us with a Song?

Arch. Are you for Passion, or Humour?

Scrub. O le! he has the purest Ballad about a Trifle—

Mrs. Sull. A Trifle! pray, Sir, let's have it.

Arch. I'm asham'd to offer you a Trifle, Madam: But since you command me—

[*Sings to the Tune of Sir Simon the King.*
A trifling Song you shall hear,
Begun with a Trifle and ended, &c.[1]

¹ The song was given in full in the 1721 edition.

A trifling song you shall hear,
Begun with a trifle and ended.
[All trifling people draw near,
And I shall be nobly attended.

Were it not for trifles a few,
That lately have come into play;
The men wou'd want something to do,
And the women want something to say.

What makes men trifle in dressing?
Because the ladies (they know)
Admire, by often possessing,
That eminent trifle a beau.

When the lover his moments has trifled,
The trifle or trifles to gain;
No sooner the virgin is rifled,
But a trifle shall part 'em again.

What mortal man wou'd be able
At White's half an hour to sit?
Or who cou'd bear a tea-table
Without talking of trifles for wit?

The court is from trifles secure;
Gold keys are no trifles, we see:
White rods are no trifles, I'm sure,
Whatever their bearers may be.

But if you will go to the place
Where trifles abundantly breed,
The levee will show you his Grace
Makes promises trifles indeed.

A coach with six footmen behind,
I count neither trifle nor sin:
But, ye gods! how oft do we find
A scandalous trifle within!

A flask of champagne, people think it
A trifle, or something as bad:
But if you'll contrive how to drink it,
You'll find it no trifle, egad!

A parson's a trifle at sea,
A widow's a trifle in sorrow;
A peace is a trifle to-day,
Who knows what may happen to-morrow?

A black coat a trifle may cloak,
Or to hide it the red may endeavour:
But if once the army is broke,
We shall have more trifles than ever.

The stage is a trifle, they say;
The reason, pray, carry along:
Because at ev'ry new play,
The house they with trifles so throng.

But with people's malice to trifle,
And to set us all on a foot:
The author of this is a trifle,
And his song is a trifle to boot.]

Mrs. Sull. Very well, Sir, we're obliged to you.—Something for a pair of Gloves.   [*Offering him Money.*

Arch. I humbly beg leave to be excused: My Master, Madam, pays me; nor dare I take Money from any other Hand without injuring his Honour, and disobeying his Commands.   [*Exit.*

Dor. This is surprising: Did you ever see so pretty a well bred Fellow?

Mrs. Sull. The Devil take him for wearing that Livery.

Dor. I fancy, Sister, he may be some Gentleman, a Friend of my Lords, that his Lordship has pitch'd upon for his Courage, Fidelity, and Discretion to bear him Company in this Dress, and who, ten to one was his Second too.

Mrs. Sull. It is so, it must be so, and it shall be so:—For I like him.

Dor. What! better than the Count?

Mrs. Sull. The Count happen'd to be the most agreeable Man upon the Place; and so I chose him to serve me in my Design upon my Husband.—But I shou'd like this Fellow better in a Design upon my self.

Dor. But now, Sister, for an Interview with this Lord, and this Gentleman; how shall we bring that about?

Mrs. Sull. Patience! you Country Ladies give no Quarter, if once you be enter'd.—Wou'd you prevent their Desires, and give the Fellows no wishing time?—Look'ye, Dorinda, if my Lord Aimwell loves you or deserves you, he'll find a way to see you, and there we must leave it.—My Business comes now upon the Tapis—Have you prepar'd your Brother?

Dor. Yes, yes.

Mrs. Sull. And how did he relish it?

Dor. He said little, mumbled something to himself, promis'd to be guided by me: But here he comes—

Enter SULLEN.

Sull. What singing was that I heard just now?

Mrs. Sull. The singing in you're Head, my Dear; you complain'd of it all Day.

Sull. You're impertinent.

Mrs. Sull. I was ever so, since I became one Flesh with you.

Sull. One Flesh! rather two Carcasses join'd unnaturally together.

Mrs. Sull. Or rather a living Soul coupled to a dead Body.

Dor. So, this is fine Encouragement for me.

Sull. Yes, my Wife shews you what you must do.

Mrs. Sull. And my Husband shews you what you must suffer.

Sull. S'death, why can't you be silent?

Mrs. Sull. S'death, why can't you talk?

Sull. Do you talk to any purpose?

Mrs. Sull. Do you think to any purpose?

Sull. Sister, hark'ye; [*Whispers.*] I shan't be home till it be late.   [*Exit.*

Mrs. Sull. What did he whisper to ye?

Dor. That he wou'd go round the back way, come into the Closet, and listen as I directed him.—But let me beg you once more, dear Sister, to drop this Project; for, as I told you before, instead of awaking him to Kindness, you may provoke him to a Rage; and then who knows how far his Brutality may carry him?

Mrs. Sull. I'm provided to receive him, I warrant you: But here comes the Count; vanish.   [*Exit* DORINDA.

Enter COUNT BELLAIR.

Don't you wonder, Monsieur le Count, that I was not at Church this Afternoon?

Count. I more wonder, Madam, that you go dere at all, or how you dare to lift those Eyes to Heaven that are guilty of so much killing.

Mrs. Sull. If Heaven, Sir, has given to my Eyes with the Power of killing, the Virtue of making a Cure, I hope the one may atone for the other.

Count. O largely, Madam; wou'd your Ladyship be as ready to apply the Remedy as to give the Wound?—Consider, Madam, I am doubly a prisoner; first to the Arms of your General, then to your more conquering Eyes; my first Chains are easy, there a Ransom may redeem me, but from your Fetters I never shall get free.

Mrs. Sull. Alas, Sir, why shou'd you complain to me of your Captivity, who am in Chains my self? you know, Sir, that I am bound, nay, most be tied up in that particular that might give you ease: I am like you, a Prisoner of War—Of War indeed:—

I have given my Parole of Honour; wou'd you break yours to gain your Liberty?

Count. Most certainly I wou'd, were I a Prisoner among the Turks; dis is your Case; you're a Slave, Madam, Slave to the worst of Turks, a Husband.

Mrs. Sull. There lies my Foible, I confess; no Fortifications, no Courage, Conduct, nor Vigilancy can pretend to defend a Place, where the Cruelty of the Governour forces the Garrison to Mutiny.

Count. And where de Besieger is resolv'd to die before de Place—Here will I fix; [*Kneels.*] With Tears, Vows, and Prayers assault your Heart, and never rise till you surrender; or if I must storm—Love and St. Michael—And so I begin the Attack—

Mrs. Sull. Stand off—Sure he hears me not—And I cou'd almost wish he—did not.—The Fellow makes love very prettily. [*Aside.*] But, Sir, why shou'd you put such a Value upon my Person, when you see it despis'd by one that knows it so much better.

Count. He knows it not, tho' he possesses it; if he but knew the Value of the Jewel he is Master of, he wou'd always wear it next his Heart, and sleep with it in his Arms.

Mrs. Sull. But since he throws me unregarded from him—

Count. And one that knows your Value well, comes by, and takes you up, is it not Justice?   [*Goes to lay hold on her.*

Enter SULLEN *with his Sword drawn.*

Sull. Hold, Villain, hold.

Mrs. Sull. [*Presenting a Pistol.*] Do you hold.

Sull. What! Murther your Husband, to defend your Bully!

Mrs. Sull. Bully! for shame, Mr. Sullen; Bullies wear long Swords, the Gentleman has none; he's a Prisoner you know—I was aware of your Outrage, and prepar'd this to receive your Violence, and, if Occasion were, to preserve my self against the Force of this other Gentleman.

Count. O Madam, your Eyes be bettre Fire Arms than your Pistol; they nevre miss.

Sull. What! court my Wife to my Face!

Mrs. Sull. Pray, Mr. Sullen, put up, suspend your Fury for a Minute.

Sull. To give you time to invent an Excuse.

Mrs. Sull. I need none.

Sull. No, for I heard every Sillable of your Discourse.

Count. Ay! and begar, I tink de Dialogue was vera pretty.

Mrs. Sull. Then I suppose, Sir, you heard something of your own Barbarity.

Sull. Barbarity! oons, what does the Women call Barbarity? do I ever meddle with you?

Mrs. Sull. No.

Sull. As for you, Sir, I shall take another time.

Count. Ah, begar, and so must I.

Sull. Look'e, Madam, don't think that my Anger proceeds from any Concern I have for your Honour, but for my own, and if you can contrive any way of being a Whore without making me a Cuckold, do it and welcome.

Mrs. Sull. Sir, I thank you kindly; you wou'd allow me the Sin but rob me of the Pleasure.—No, no, I'm resolv'd never to venture upon the Crime without the Satisfaction of seeing you punish'd for't.

Sull. Then will you grant me this, my Dear? let any Body else do you the Favour but that French-man, for I mortally hate his whole Generation.   [*Exit.*

Count. Ah, Sir, that be ungrateful, for begar, I love some of yours, Madam.—   [*Approaching her.*

Mrs. Sull. No, Sir.—

Count. No, Sir,—Garzoon, Madam, I am not your Husband.

Mrs. Sull. 'Tis time to undeceive you, Sir.—I believ'd your Addresses to me were no more than an Amusement, and I hope you will think the same of my Complaisance, and to convince you that you ought, you must know, that I brought you hither only to make you instrumental in setting me right with my Husband, for he was planted to listen by my Appointment.

Count. By your Appointment?

Mrs. Sull. Certainly.

Count. And so, Madam, while I was telling twenty Stories to part you from your Husband, begar, I was bringing you together all the while.

Mrs. Sull. I ask your Pardon, Sir, but I hope this will give you a Taste of the Vertue of the English Ladies.

Count. Begar, Madam, your Vertue be vera Great, but Garzoon, your Honeste de vera little.

Enter DORINDA.

Mrs. Sull. Nay, now you're angry, Sir.

Count. Angry! fair Dorinda [*Sings Dorinda the Opera Tune, and addresses to* DORINDA.] Madam, when your Ladyship want a Fool, send for me. Fair Dorinda, Revenge, &c.   [*Exit.*

Mrs. Sull. There goes the true Humour of his Nation, Resent-

ment with good Manners, and the height of Anger in a Song.—
Well Sister, you must be Judge, for you have heard the Trial.

Dor. And I bring in my Brother Guilty.

Mrs. Sull. But I must bear the Punishment,—'Tis hard Sister.

Dor. I own it—but you must have Patience.

Mrs. Sull. Patience! the Cant of Custom—Providence sends
no Evil without a Remedy—shou'd I lie groaning under a Yoke
I can shake off, I were accessary to my Ruin, and my Patience
were no better than self-Murder.

Dor. But how can you shake off the Yoke—Your Divisions
don't come within the Reach of the Law for a Divorce.

Mrs. Sull. Law! what Law can search into the remote Abyss
of Nature? what Evidence can prove the unaccountable Disaf-
fections of Wedlock?—Can a Jury sum up the endless Aversions
that are rooted in our Souls, or can a Bench give Judgment upon
Antipathies?

Dor. They never pretended Sister, they never meddle but in
case of Uncleanness?

Mrs. Sull. Uncleanness! O Sister, casual Violation is a transient Injury, and may possibly be repair'd, but can radical
Hatreds be ever reconcil'd?—No, no, Sister, Nature is the first
Lawgiver, and when she has set Tempers opposite, not all the
golden Links of Wedlock, nor Iron Manacles of Law can keep
'um fast.

> *Wedlock we own ordain'd by Heaven's Decree,*
> *But such as Heaven ordain'd it first to be;*
> *Concurring Tempers in the Man and Wife*
> *As mutual Helps to draw the Load of Life.*
> *View all the Works of Providence above,*
> *The Stars with Harmony and Concord move;*
> *View all the Works of Providence below,* ⎫
> *The Fire, the Water, Earth, and Air, we know* ⎬
> *All in one Plant agree to make it grow.* ⎭
> *Must Man the chiefest Work of Art Divine,*
> *Be doom'd in endless Discord to repine?*
> *No, we shou'd injure Heaven by that surmise:*
> *Omnipotence is just, were Man but wise.*

END OF THE THIRD ACT

ACT IV

SCENE.—*Continues*

Enter MRS. SULLEN.

Mrs. Sull. Were I born an humble Turk, where Women have no Soul nor Property there I must sit contented—But in England, a Country whose Women are it's Glory, must Women be abus'd? where Women rule, must Women be enslav'd? nay, cheated into Slavery, mock'd by a Promise of comfortable Society into a Wilderness of Solitude—I dare not keep the Thought about me—O, here comes something to divert me—

Enter a COUNTRY WOMAN.

Wom. I come an't please your Ladyships, you're my Lady Bountiful, an't ye?

Mrs. Sull. Well, good Woman go on.

Wom. I come seventeen long Mail to have a Cure for my Husband's sore Leg.

Mrs. Sull. Your Husband! what, Woman, cure your Husband!

Wom. Ay, poor Man, for his Sore Leg won't let him stir from Home.

Mrs. Sull. There, I confess, you have given me a Reason. Well good Woman, I'll tell you what you must do—You must lay your Husbands Leg upon a Table, and with a Choping-knife, you must lay it open as broad as you can; then you must take out the Bone, and beat the Flesh soundly with a rowling-pin; then take Salt, Pepper, Cloves, Mace and Ginger, some sweet Herbs, and season it very well; then rowl it up like Brawn, and put it into the Oven for two Hours.

Wom. Heavens reward your Ladyship—I have two little Babies too that are pitious bad with the Graips, an't please ye.

Mrs. Sull. Put a little Pepper and Salt in their Bellies, good Woman. I beg your Ladyship's [*Enter* LADY BOUNTIFUL.] Pardon for taking your Business out of your Hands; I have been a tampering here a little with one of your Patients.

L. Boun. Come, good Woman, don't mind this mad Creature. I am the Person that you want, I suppose—What wou'd you have, Woman?

Mrs. Sull. She wants something for her Husband's sore Leg.

L. Boun. What's the matter with his Leg, Goody?

Wom. It come first as one might say with a sort of Dizziness in his Foot, then he had a kind of a Laziness in his Joints, and then his Leg broke out, and then it swell'd, and then it clos'd again, and then it broke out again, and then it fester'd, and then it grew better, and then it grew worse again.

Mrs. Sull. Ha, ha, ha.

L. Boun. How can you be merry with the Misfortunes of other People?

Mrs. Sull. Because my own make me sad, Madam.

L. Boun. The worst Reason in the World, Daughter; your own Misfortunes shou'd teach you to pitty others.

Mrs. Sull. But the Woman's Misfortunes and mine are nothing alike; her Husband is sick, and mine, alas, is in Health.

L. Boun. What! wou'd you wish your Husband sick?

Mrs. Sull. Not of a sore Leg, of all things.

L. Boun. Well, good Woman, go to the Pantrey, get your Belly-full of Victuals, then I'll give you a Receipt of Diet-drink for your Husband—But d'ye hear Goody, you must not let your Husband move too much.

Wom. No, no, Madam, the poor Man's inclinable enough to lye still. [*Exit.*

L. Boun. Well, Daughter Sullen, tho' you laugh, I have done Miracles about the Country here with my Receipts.

Mrs. Sull. Miracles, indeed, if they have cur'd any Body, but, I believe, Madam, the Patient's Faith goes farther toward the Miracle than your Prescription.

L. Boun. Fancy helps in some Cases, but there's your Husband who has as little Fancy as any Body; I brought him from Death's-door.

Mrs. Sull. I suppose, Madam, you made him drink plentifully of Asse's Milk.

Enter DOR., *runs to* MRS. SULL.

Dor. News, dear Sister, news, news.

Enter ARCHER *running.*

Arch. Where, where is my Lady Bountiful—Pray, which is the old Lady of you three?

L. Boun. I am.

Arch. O, Madam, the Fame of your Ladyship's Charity, Goodness, Benevolence, Skill and Ability have drawn me hither to implore your Ladyship's Help in behalf of my unfortunate Master, who is this Moment breathing his last.

L. Boun. Your Master! where is he?

Arch. At your Gate, Madam; drawn by the Appearance of your handsome House to view it nearer, and walking up the

Avenue within five Paces of the Court-Yard, he was taken ill of a sudden with a sort of I know not what, but down he fell, and there he lies.

L. Boun. Here, Scrub, Gipsey, all run, get my easie Chair down Stairs, put the Gentleman in it, and bring him in quickly, quickly.

Arch. Heaven will reward your Ladyship for this charitable Act.

L. Boun. Is your Master us'd to these Fits?

Arch. O yes, Madam, frequently—I have known him have five or six of a Night.

L. Boun. What's his Name?

Arch. Lord, Madam, he's a dying! a Minute's Care or Neglect may save or destroy his Life.

L. Boun. Ah, poor Gentleman! come Friend, show me the way; I'll see him brought in my self.   [*Exit with* ARCHER.

Dor. O Sister, my Heart flutters about strangely; I can hardly forbear running to his Assistance.

Mrs. Sull. And I'll lay my Life, he deserves your Assistance more than he wants it; did not I tell you that my Lord wou'd find a way to come at you. Love's his Distemper, and you must be the Physitian; put on all your Charms, summon all your Fire into your Eyes, plant the whole Artillery of your Looks against his Breast, and down with him.

Dor. O Sister, I'm but a young Gunner; I shall be afraid to shoot, for fear the Piece shou'd recoil and hurt my self.

Mrs. Sull. Never fear, you shall see me shoot before you if you will.

Dor. No, no, dear Sister, you have miss'd your Mark so unfortunately, that I shan't care for being instructed by you.

Enter AIMWELL *in a Chair, carry'd by* ARCHER *and* SCRUB, L. BOUNTIFUL, GIPSEY. AIMWELL *counterfeiting a Swoon.*

L. Boun. Here, here, let's see the Hartshorn-drops—Gipsey a Glass of fair Water, his Fit's very strong—Bless me, how his Hands are clinch'd.

Arch. For shame, Ladies, what d'ye do? why don't you help us—Pray, Madam, [*To* DORINDA] Take his Hand and open it if you can, whilst I hold his Head.   [DORINDA *takes his Hand.*

Dor. Poor Gentleman—Oh—he has got my Hand within his, and squeezes it unmercifully—

L. Boun. 'Tis the Violence of his Convulsion, Child.

Arch. O, Madam, he's perfectly posses'd in these Cases—he'll bite if you don't have a care.

Dor. Oh, my Hand, my Hand.

L. Boun. What's the matter with the foolish Girl? I have got this Hand open, you see, with a great deal of Ease.

Arch. Ay, but, Madam, your Daughter's Hand is somewhat warmer than your Ladyship's, and the Heat of it draws the Force of the Spirits that way.

Mrs. Sull. I find, Friend, you're very learned in these sorts of Fits.

Arch. 'Tis no wonder, Madam, for I'm often troubled with them my self, I find my self extreamly ill at this Minute.

[*Looking hard at* Mrs. Sull.

Mrs. Sull. [*Aside.*] I fancy I cou'd find a way to cure you.

L. Boun. His Fit holds him very long.

Arch. Longer than usual, Madam.—Pray, young Lady, open his Breast, and give him Air.

L. Boun. Where did his Illness take him first, pray?

Arch. To Day at Church, Madam.

L. Boun. In what manner was he taken?

Arch. Very strangely, my Lady. He was of a sudden touch'd with something in his Eyes, which at the first he only felt, but cou'd not tell whether 'twas Pain or Pleasure.

L. Boun. Wind, nothing but Wind.

Arch. By soft Degrees it grew and mounted to his Brain, there his Fancy caught it; there form'd it so beautiful, and dress'd it up in such gay pleasing Colours, that his transported Appetite seiz'd the fair Idea, and straight convey'd it to his Heart. That hospitable Seat of Life sent all its sanguine Spirits forth to meet, and open'd all its sluicy Gates to take the Stranger in.

L. Boun. Your Master shou'd never go without a Bottle to smell to—Oh!—He recovers—The Lavender Water—Some Feathers to burn under his Nose—Hungary-water to rub his Temples—O, he comes to himself. Hem a little, Sir, hem—Gipsey, bring the Cordial-water.

[Aimwell *seems to awake in amaze.*

Dor. How d'ye Sir?

Aim. Where am I? [*Rising.*

Sure I have pass'd the Gulph of silent Death,
And now I land on the Elisian Shore—
Behold the Goddess of those happy Plains,
Fair Proserpine—Let me adore thy bright Divinity.

[*Kneels to* Dorinda *and kisses her Hand.*

Mrs. Sull. So, so, so, I knew where the Fit wou'd end.

Aim. Euridice perhaps—How cou'd thy Orpheus keep his word,
And not look back upon thee;

No Treasure but thy self cou'd sure have brib'd him
To look one Minute off thee.

L. Boun. Delirious, poor Gentleman.

Arch. Very Delirious, Madam, very Delirious.

Aim. Martin's Voice, I think.

Arch. Yes, my Lord—How do's your Lordship?

L. Boun. Lord! did you mind that, Girls.

Aim. Where am I?

Arch. In very good Hands, Sir.—You were taken just now
with one of your old Fits under the Trees just by this good
Lady's House; her Ladyship had you taken in, and has miraculously brought you to your self, as you see—

Aim. I am so confounded with Shame, Madam, that I can now
only beg Pardon—And refer my Acknowledgments for your
Ladyship's Care, till an Opportunity offers of making some
Amends—I dare be no longer troublesome—Martin, give two
Guineas to the Servants.   [*Going.*

Dor. Sir, you may catch cold by going so soon into the Air;
you don't look, Sir, as if you were perfectly recover'd.

    [*Here* ARCHER *talks to* L. BOUNTIFUL *in dumb shew.*

Aim. That I shall never be, Madam, my present Illness is so
rooted, that I must expect to carry it to my Grave.

Mrs. Sull. Don't despair, Sir, I have known several in your
Distemper shake it off, with a Fortnight's Physick.

L. Boun. Come, Sir, your Servant has been telling me that
you're apt to relapse if you go into the Air—Your good Manners
shan't get the better of ours—You shall sit down again, Sir.—
Come, Sir, we don't mind Ceremonies in the Country—Here,
Sir, my Service t'ye—You shall taste my Water; 'tis a Cordial
I can assure you, and of my own making—drink it off, Sir.
[AIMWELL *drinks.*] And how d'ye find your self now, Sir.

Aim. Somewhat better—Tho' very faint still.

L. Boun. Ay, ay, People are always faint after these Fits—Come
Girls, you shall show the Gentleman the House; 'tis but an old
Family Building, Sir, but you had better walk about and cool by
Degrees than venture immediately into the Air—You'll find some
tolerable Pictures—Dorinda, show the Gentleman the way.
[*Exit.*] I must go to the poor Woman below.

Dor. This way, Sir.

Aim. Ladies, shall I beg leave for my Servant to wait on you?
for he understands Pictures very well.

Mrs. Sull. Sir, we understand Originals, as well as he do's Pictures, so he may come along.

        [*Ex.* DOR., MRS. SULL, AIM., ARCH. AIM *leads* DOR.

Enter FOIGARD *and* SCRUB, *meeting.*

Foig. Save you, Master Scrub.

Scrub. Sir, I won't be sav'd your way—I hate a Priest, I abhor the French, and I defie the Devil—Sir, I'm a bold Briton, and will spill the last drop of my Blood to keep out Popery and Slavery.

Foig. Master Scrub, you wou'd put me down in Politicks, and so I wou'd be speaking with Mrs. Shipsey.

Scrub. Good Mr. Priest, you can't speak with her; she's sick, Sir, she's gone abroad, Sir, she's—dead two Months ago, Sir.

Enter GIPSEY.

Gip. How now, Impudence; how dare you talk so saucily to the Doctor? Pray, Sir, dont take it ill; for the Common-people of England are not so civil to Strangers, as—

Scrub. You lie, you lie—'Tis the Common People that are civil-est to Strangers.

Gip. Sirrah, I have a good mind to—Get you out, I say.

Scrub. I won't

Gip. You won't, Sauce-box—Pray, Doctor, what is the Captain's Name that came to your Inn last Night?

Scrub. The Captain! Ah, the Devil, there she hampers me again; —The Captain has me on one side, and the Priest on t'other:— So between the Gown and the Sword, I have a fine time on't.— But, *Cedunt Arma togæ.* [*Going.*

Gip. What, Sirrah, won't you march?

Scrub. No, my Dear, I won't march—But I'll walk—And I'll make bold to listen a little too.

[*Goes behind the side-Scene, and listens.*

Gip. Indeed, Doctor, the Count has been barbarously treated, that's the Truth on't.

Foig. Ah, Mrs. Gipsey, upon my Shoul, now, Gra, his Complainings wou'd mollifie the Marrow in your Bones, and move the Bowels of your Commiseration; he veeps, and he dances, and he fistles, and he swears, and he laughs, and he stamps, and he sings: In Conclusion, Joy, he's afflicted, *à la François,* and a Stranger wou'd not know whider to cry, or to laugh with him.

Gip. What wou'd you have me do, Doctor?

Foig. Noting, Joy, but only hide the Count in Mrs. Sullen's Closet when it is dark.

Gip. Nothing! Is that nothing? it wou'd be both a Sin and a shame, Doctor.

Foig. Here is twenty Lewidores, Joy, for your shame; and I will give you an Absolution for the Shin.

Gip. But won't that Money look like a Bribe?

Foig. Dat is according as you shall tauk it.—If you receive the Money beforehand, 'twill be Logicè, a Bribe; but if you stay till afterwards, 'twill be only a Gratification.

Gip. Well, Doctor, I'll take it Logice.—But what must I do with my Conscience, Sir?

Foig. Leave dat wid me, Joy; I am your Priest, Gra; and your Consciencè is under my Hands.

Gip. But shou'd I put the Count into the Closet—

Foig. Vel, is dere any Shin for a Man's being in a Closhet? one may go to Prayers in a Closhet.

Gip. But if the Lady shou'd come into her Chamber, and go to Bed?

Foig. Vel, and is dere any Shin in going to Bed, Joy?

Gip. Ay, but if the Parties shou'd meet, Doctor?

Foig. Vel den—The Parties must be responsable.—Do you be after putting the Count in the Closet; and leave the Shins wid themselves.—I will come with the Count to instruct you in your Chamber.

Gip. Well, Doctor, your Religion is so pure—Methinks I'm so easie after an Absolution, and can sin afresh with so much security, that I'm resolv'd to die a Martyr to't.—Here's the Key of the Garden-door: come in the back way when 'tis late,—I'll be ready to receive you; but don't so much as whisper; only take hold of my Hand; I'll lead you, and do you lead the Count, and follow me.   [*Exeunt*.

Enter SCRUB.

Scrub. What Witchcraft now have these two Imps of the Devil been a hatching here?—There's twenty Lewidores; I heard that, and saw the Purse: But I must give room to my Betters.

Enter AIMWELL *leading* DORINDA, *and making Love in dumb Show*—MRS. SULL. *and* ARCHER.

Mrs. Sull. Pray, Sir, [*To* ARCHER.] how d'ye like that Piece?

Arch. O, 'tis Leda.—You find, Madam, how Jupiter comes disguis'd to make Love—

Mrs. Sull. But what think you there of Alexander's Battles?

Arch. We want only a Le Brun, Madam, to draw greater Battles, and a greater General of our own.—The Danube, Madam, wou'd make a greater Figure in a Picture than the Granicus; and we have our Ramelies to match their Arbela.

Mrs. Sull. Pray, Sir, what Head is that in the Corner there?

Arch. O, Madam, 'tis poor Ovid in his Exile.

Mrs. Sull. What was he banish'd for?

Arch. His ambitious Love, Madam. [*Bowing.*] His Misfortune touches me.

Mrs. Sull. Was he successful in his Amours?

Arch. There he has left us in the dark.—He was too much a Gentleman to tell.

Mrs. Sull. If he were secret, I pity him.

Arch. And if he were successful, I envy him.

Mrs. Sull. How d'ye like that Venus over the Chimney?

Arch. Venus! I protest, Madam, I took it for your Picture; but now I look again, 'tis not handsome enough.

Mrs. Sull. Oh, what a Charm is Flattery! if you wou'd see my Picture, there it is, over that Cabinet;—How d'ye like it?

Arch. I must admire any thing, Madam, that has the least Resemblance of you——But, methinks, Madam——

> [*He looks at the Picture of* MRS. SULLEN *three or four times, by turns.*

Pray, Madam, who drew it?

Mrs. Sull. A famous Hand, Sir.

> [*Here* AIMWELL *and* DORINDA *go off.*

Arch. A famous Hand, Madam—Your Eyes, indeed, are featur'd there; but where's the sparkling Moisture shining fluid, in which they swim. The Picture indeed has your Dimples; but where's the Swarm of killing Cupids that shou'd ambush there? the Lips too are figur'd out; but where's the Carnation Dew, the pouting Ripeness that tempts the Taste in the Original?

Mrs. Sull. Had it been my Lot to have match'd with such a Man!

Arch. Your Breasts too, presumptuous Man! what! paint Heaven! *Apropo,* Madam, in the very next Picture is *Salmoneus,* that was struck dead with Lightning, for offering to imitate *Jove's Thunder;* I hope you serv'd the Painter so, Madam?

Mrs. Sull. Had my Eyes the power of Thunder, they shou'd employ their Lightning better.

Arch. There's the finest Bed in that Room, Madam; I suppose 'tis your Ladyship's Bed-Chamber.

Mrs. Sull. And what then, Sir?

Arch. I think the Quilt is the richest that ever I saw:—I can't at this Distance, Madam, distinguish the Figures of the Embroidery; will you give me leave, Madam?——

Mrs. Sull. The Devil take his Impudence.—Sure if I gave him an opportunity, he durst not offer it.—I have a great mind to try.—[*Going.*] [*Returns.*] S'death, what am I doing?—And alone too!—Sister, Sister! 　　　　　　　　　　　　　　　[*Runs out.*

Arch. I'll follow her close—

> *For where a French-man durst attempt to storm,*
> *A Briton sure may well the Work perform.*   [*Going.*

Enter SCRUB.

Scrub. Martin, Brother Martin.

Arch. O, Brother Scrub, I beg your Pardon, I was not a going; here's a Guinea, my Master order'd you.

Scrub. A Guinea, hi, hi, hi, a Guinea! eh—by this Light it is a Guinea; but I suppose you expect One and twenty Shillings in change.

Arch. Not at all; I have another for Gipsey.

Scrub. A Guinea for her! Faggot and Fire for the Witch.—Sir, give me that Guinea, and I'll discover a Plot.

Arch. A Plot!

Scrub. Ay, Sir, a Plot, and a horrid Plot.—First, it must be a Plot because there's a Woman in't; secondly, it must be a Plot because there's a Priest in't; thirdly, it must be a Plot because there's French Gold in't; and fourthly, it must be a Plot, because I don't know what to make on't.

Arch. Nor any body else, I'm afraid, Brother Scrub.

Scrub. Truly I'm afraid so too; for where there's a Priest and a Woman, there's always a Mystery and a Riddle—This I know, that here has been the Doctor with a Temptation in one Hand, and an Absolution in the other; and Gipsey has sold her self to the Devil; I saw the Price paid down, my Eyes shall take their Oath on't.

Arch. And is all this bustle about Gipsey?

Scrub. That's not all; I cou'd hear but a Word here and there; but I remember they mention'd a Count, a Closet, a back Door, and a Key.

Arch. The Count! did you hear nothing of Mrs. Sullen?

Scrub. I did hear some word that sounded that way; but whether it was Sullen or Dorinda, I cou'd not distinguish.

Arch. You have told this matter to no Body, Brother?

Scrub. Told! No, Sir, I thank you for that; I'm resolv'd never to speak one word *pro* nor *con,* till we have a Peace.

Arch. You're i'th right, Brother Scrub; here's a Treaty a foot between the Count and the Lady.—The Priest and the Chamber-maid are the Plenipotentiaries.—It shall go hard but I find a way to be included in the Treaty.—Where's the Doctor now?

Scrub. He and Gipsey are this moment devouring my Lady's Marmalade in the Closet.

Aim. [*From without.*] Martin, Martin.

Arch. I come, Sir, I come.

Scrub. But you forget the other Guinea, Brother Martin.

Arch. Here, I give it with all my Heart.

Scrub. And I take it with all my Soul. [*Exeunt severally.*] I'cod, I'll spoil your Plotting, Mrs. Gipsey; and if you shou'd set the Captain upon me, these two Guineas will buy me off.   [*Exit.*

Enter Mrs. Sullen *and* Dorinda *meeting.*

Mrs. Sull. Well, Sister.

Dor. And well, Sister.

Mrs. Sull. What's become of my Lord?

Dor. What's become of his Servant?

Mrs. Sull. Servant! he's a prettier Fellow, and a finer Gentleman by fifty Degrees than his Master.

Dor. O'my Conscience, I fancy you cou'd beg that Fellow at the Gallows-foot.

Mrs. Sull. O'my Conscience, I cou'd, provided I cou'd put a Friend of yours in his Room.

Dor. You desir'd me, Sister to leave you, when you transgress'd the Bounds of Honour.

Mrs. Sull. Thou dear censorious Country-Girl—What dost mean? you can't think of the Man without the Bedfellow, I find.

Dor. I don't find any thing unnatural in that thought; while the Mind is conversant with Flesh and Blood, it must conform to the Humours of the Company

Mrs. Sull. How a little Love and good Company improves a Woman; why, Child, you begin to live—you never spoke before.

Dor. Because I was never spoke to.—My Lord has told me that I have more Wit and Beauty than any of my Sex; and truly I begin to think the Man is sincere.

Mrs. Sull. You're in the right, Dorinda, Pride is the Life of a Woman, and Flattery is our daily Bread; and she's a Fool that won't believe a Man there, as much as she that believes him in any thing else—But I'll lay you a Guinea, that I had finer things said to me than you had.

Dor. Done—What did your Fellow say to ye?

Mrs. Sull. My Fellow took the Picture of Venus for mine.

Dor. But my Lover took me for Venus her self.

Mrs. Sull. Common Cant! had my Spark call'd me a Venus directly, I shou'd have believ'd him a Footman in good earnest.

Dor. But my Lover was upon his Knees to me.

Mrs. Sullen. And mine was upon his Tiptoes to me.

Dor. Mine vow'd to die for me.

Mrs. Sull. Mine swore to die with me.

Dor. Mine spoke the softest moving things.

Mrs. Sull. Mine had his moving things too.

Dor. Mine kiss'd my Hand Ten thousand times.

Mrs. Sull. Mine has all that Pleasure to come.

Dor. Mine offer'd Marriage.

Mrs. Sull. O lard! D'ye call that a moving thing?

Dor. The sharpest Arrow in his Quiver, my dear Sister.—Why, my Ten thousand Pounds may lie brooding here this seven Years, and hatch nothing at last but some ill natur'd Clown like yours:— Whereas, If I marry my Lord Aimwell, there will be Title, Place and Precedence, the Park, the Play, and the drawing-Room, Splendour, Equipage, Noise and Flambeaux—Hey, my Lady Aimwell's Servants there—Lights, Lights to the Stairs—My Lady Aimwell's Coach put forward—Stand by, make room for her Ladyship— Are not these things moving?—What! melancholly of a sudden?

Mrs. Sull. Happy, happy Sister! your Angel has been watchful for your Happiness, whilst mine has slept regardless of his Charge. —Long smiling Years of circling Joys for you, but not one Hour for me!   [*Weeps.*

Dor. Come, my Dear, we'll talk of something else.

Mrs. Sull. O Dorinda, I own my self a Woman, full of my Sex, a gentle, generous Soul,—easie and yielding to soft Desires; a spacious Heart, where Love and all his Train might lodge. And must the fair Apartment of my Breast be made a Stable for a Brute to lie in?

Dor. Meaning your Husband, I suppose.

Mrs. Sull. Husband! no,—Even Husband is too soft a Name for him.—But, come, I expect my Brother here to Night or to Morrow; he was abroad when my Father marry'd me; perhaps he'll find a way to make me easy.

Dor. Will you promise not to make your self easy in the mean time with my Lord's Friend?

Mrs. Sull. You mistake me, Sister—It happens with us, as among the Men, the greatest Talkers are the greatest Cowards; and there's a Reason for it; those Spirits evaporate in prattle, which might do more Mischief if they took another Course;— Tho' to confess the Truth, I do love that Fellow;—And if I met him drest as he shou'd be, and I undrest as I shou'd be—Look'ye, Sister, I have no supernatural Gifts;—I can't swear I cou'd resist the Temptation,—tho' I can safely promise to avoid it; and that's as much as the best of us can do.   [*Ex.* MRS. SULL. *and* DOR.

Enter AIMWELL *and* ARCHER *laughing.*

Arch. And the awkward Kindness of the good motherly old Gentlewoman—

Aim. And the coming Easiness of the young one—S'death, 'tis pity to deceive her.

Arch. Nay, if you adhere to those Principles, stop where you are.

Aim. I can't stop; for I love her to distraction.

Arch. S'death, if you love her a hair's breadth beyond discretion, you must go no farther.

Aim. Well, well, any thing to deliver us from sauntering away our idle Evenings at White's, Tom's, or Will's, and be stinted to bear looking at our old Acquaintance, the Cards; because our impotent Pockets can't afford us a Guinea for the mercenary Drabs.

Arch. Or be oblig'd to some Purse-proud Coxcomb for a scandalous Bottle, where we must not pretend to our share of the Discourse, because we can't pay our Club o' th Reckoning;—dam it, I had rather spunge upon Morris, and sup upon a Dish of Bohee scor'd behind the Door.

Aim. And there expose our want of Sense by talking Criticisms, as we shou'd our want of Money by railing at the Government.

Arch. Or be oblig'd to sneak into the side-Box, and between both Houses steal two Acts of a Play, and because we han't Money to see the other three, we come away discontented, and damn the whole five.

Aim. And Ten thousand such rascally Tricks,—had we outliv'd our Fortunes among our Acquaintance.—But now—

Arch. Ay, now is the time to prevent all this.—Strike while the Iron is hot.—This Priest is the luckiest part of our Adventure;—He shall marry you, and pimp for me.

Aim. But I shou'd not like a Woman that can be so fond of a Frenchman.

Arch. Alas, Sir, Necessity has no Law; the Lady may be in Distress; perhaps she has a confounded Husband, and her Revenge may carry her farther than her Love.—I gad, I have so good an Opinion of her, and of my self, that I begin to fancy strange things; and we must say this for the Honour of our Women, and indeed of our selves, that they do stick to their Men, as they do to their Magna Charta.—If the Plot lies as I suspect,—I must put on the Gentleman.—But here comes the Doctor.—I shall be ready. [*Exit.*

Enter FOIGARD.

Foig. Sauve you, noble Friend.

Aim. O Sir, your Servant; pray Doctor, may I crave your Name?

Foig. Fat Naam is upon me? my Naam is Foigard, Joy.

Aim. Foigard, a very good Name for a Clergyman: Pray, Doctor Foigard, were you ever in Ireland?

Foig. Ireland! No, Joy.—Fat sort of Plaace is dat saam Ireland? dey say de People are catcht dere when dey are young.

Aim. And some of 'em when they're old;—as for Example. [*Takes* FOIGARD *by the Shoulder.*] Sir, I arrest you as a Traytor against the Government; you're a Subject of England, and this Morning shew'd me a Commission, by which you serv'd as Chaplain in the French Army: This is Death by our Law, and your Reverence must hang for't.

Foig. Upon my Shoul, Noble Friend, dis is strange News you tell me! Fader Foigard a Subject of England! de Son of a Burgomaster of Brussels, a Subject of England! Ubooboo—

Aim. The Son of a Bogtrotter in Ireland; Sir, your Tongue will condemn you before any Bench in the Kingdom.

Foig. And is my Tongue all your Evidensh, Joy?

Aim. That's enough.

Foig. No, no, Joy, for I vill never spake English no more.

Aim. Sir, I have other Evidence—Here, Martin, you know this Fellow.

Enter ARCHER.

Arch. [*In a Brogue.*] Saave you, my dear Cussen, how do's your Health?

Foig. Ah! upon my Shoul dere is my Countryman, and his Brogue will hang mine [*Aside.*] *Mynheer, Ick wet neat watt hey zacht, Ick universton ewe neat, sacramant.*

Aim. Altering your Language won't do, Sir; this Fellow knows your Person, and will swear to your Face.

Foig. Faace! fey, is dear a Brogue upon my Faash, too?

Arch. Upon my Soulvation dere ish Joy—But Cussen Mackshane, vil you not put a remembrance upon me.

Foig. Mack-shane! by St. Patrick, dat is Naame, shure enough.
[*Aside.*

Aim. I fancy Archer, you have it.

Foig. The Devil hang you, Joy—By fat Acquaintance are you my Cussen?

Arch. O, de Devil hang your shelf, Joy; you know we were little Boys togeder upon de School, and your foster Moder's Son was marry'd upon my Nurse's Chister, Joy, and so we are Irish Cussens.

Foig. De Devil taak the Relation! vel, Joy, and fat School was it?

Arch. I tinks is vas—Aay—'Twas Tipperary.

Foig. No, no, Joy, it vas Kilkenny.

Aim. That's enough for us—Self-Confession—Come, Sir, we must deliver you into the Hands of the next Magistrate.

Arch. He sends you to Gaol, you're try'd next Assizes, and away you go swing into Purgatory.

Foig. And is it so wid you, Cussen?

Arch. It vil be sho wid you, Cussen, if you don't immediately confess the Secret between you and Mrs. Gipsey—Look'e, Sir, the Gallows or the Secret, take your Choice.

Foig. The Gallows! upon my Shoul I hate that saam Gallow, for it is a Diseash dat is fatal to our Family—Vel den, dere is nothing, Shentlemens, but Mrs. Shullen wou'd spaak wid the Count in her Chamber at Midnight, and dere is no Haarm, Joy, for I am to conduct the Count to the Plash, my shelf.

Arch. As I guess'd—Have you communicated the matter to the Count?

Foig. I have not sheen him since.

Arch. Right agen; why then, Doctor,—you shall conduct me to the Lady instead of the Count.

Foig. Fat, my Cussen to the Lady! upon my Shoul, gra, dat is too much upon the Brogue.

Arch. Come, come, Doctor, consider we have got a Rope about your Neck, and if you offer to squeek, we'll stop your Windpipe, most certainly; we shall have another Job for you in a Day or two, I hope.

Aim. Here's Company coming this way; let's into my Chamber, and there concert our Affair farther.

Arch. Come, my dear Cussen, come along.   [*Exeunt.*

Enter BONNIFACE, HOUNSLOW, *and* BAGSHOT *at one Door,*
GIBBET *at the opposite.*

Gib. Well, Gentlemen, 'tis a fine Night for our Enterprise.

Houns. Dark as Hell.

Bag. And blows like the Devil; our Landlord here has show'd us the Window where we must break in, and tells us the Plate stands in the Wainscot Cupboard in the Parlour.

Bon. Ay, ay, Mr. Bagshot, as the saying is, Knives and Forks, and Cups, and Canns, and Tumblers, and Tankards—There's one Tankard, as the saying is, that's near upon as big as me; it was a Present to the Squire from his Godmother, and smells of Nutmeg and Toast like an East India Ship.

Houns. Then you say we must divide at the Stair-head?

Bon. Yes. Mr. Hounslow, as the saying is—At one end of that

Gallery lies my Lady Bountifull and her Daughter, and at the other Mrs. Sullen—As for the Squire——

Gib. He's safe enough; I have fairly enter'd him, and he's more than half seas over already—But such a Parcel of Scoundrels are got about him now, that I gad I was asham'd to be seen in their Company.

Bon. 'Tis now Twelve, as the saying is—Gentlemen, you must set out at One.

Gib. Hounslow, do you and Bagshot see our Arms fix'd, and I'll come to you presently.

Houns. }
Bag. } We will.   [*Exeunt.*

Gib. Well, my dear Bonny, you assure me that Scrub is a Coward?

Bon. A Chicken, as the saying is—You'll have no Creature to deal with but the Ladies.

Gib. And I can assure you, Friend, there's a great deal of Address and good Manners in robbing a Lady; I am the most a Gentleman that way that ever travell'd th Road—But, my dear Bonny, this Prize will be a Galleon, a Vigo Business—I warrant you we shall bring off three or four thousand Pound.

Bon. In Plate, Jewels and Money, as the saying is, you may.

Gib. Why then, Tyburn, I defie thee! I'll get up to Town, sell off my Horse and Arms, buy my self some pretty Employment in the Household, and be as snug, and as honest as any Courtier of 'um all.

Bon. And what think you then of my Daughter Cherry for a Wife?

Gib. Look'ee, my dear Bonny—Cherry *is the Goddess I adore,* as the Song goes; but it is a Maxim that Man and Wife shou'd never have it in their Power to hang one another, for if they should, the Lord have Mercy on 'um both.   [*Exeunt.*

END OF THE FOURTH ACT

ACT V

Scene.—*Continues. Knocking without*

Enter BONNIFACE.

Bon. Coming, coming —A Coach and six foaming Horses at this time o'Night! Some great Man, as the saying is, for he scorns to ravel with other People.

Enter SIR CHARLES FREEMAN.

Sir Ch. What, Fellow! a Publick-house, and a Bed when other People Sleep.

Bon. Sir, I an't a Bed, as the saying is.

Sir Ch. Is Mr. Sullen's Family a Bed, think'e?

Bon. All but the Squire himself, Sir, as the saying is, he's in the House.

Sir Ch. What Company has he?

Bon. Why, Sir, there's the Constable, Mr. Gage the Exciseman, the Hunchback'd-barber, and two or three other Gentlemen.

Sir Ch. I find my Sister's Letters gave me the true Picture of her Spouse.

Enter SULLEN *Drunk*.

Bon. Sir, here's the Squire.

Sull. The Puppies left me asleep—Sir.

Sir Ch. Well, Sir.

Sull. Sir, I'm an unfortunate Man—I have three thousand Pound ι Year, and I can't get a Man to drink a Cup of Ale with me.

Sir Ch. That's very hard.

Sull. Ay, Sir—And unless you have pitty upon me, and smoke ιne Pipe with me, I must e'en go home to my Wife, and I had rather go the Devil by half.

Sir Ch. But, I presume, Sir, you won't see your Wife to Night; she'll be gone to Bed—you don't use to lye with your Wife in that Pickle?

Sull. What! not lye with my Wife! why, Sir, do you take me for an Atheist or a Rake?

Sir Ch. If you hate her, Sir, I think you had better lye from her

Sull. I think so too, Friend—But I'm a Justice of Peace, and must do nothing against the Law.

Sir Ch. Law! as I take it, Mr. Justice, no Body observes Law for Law's Sake, only for the good of those for whom it was made

Sull. But if the Law orders me to send you to Gaol, you must ly there, my Friend.

Sir Ch. Not unless I commit a Crime to deserve it.

Sull. A Crime! Oons an't I marry'd?

Sir Ch. Nay, Sir, if you call Marriage a Crime, you must dis own it for a Law.

Sull. Eh!—I must be acquainted with you, Sir—But, Sir, shou'd be very glad to know the Truth of this Matter.

Sir Ch. Truth, Sir, is a profound Sea, and few there be that dar wade deep enough to find out the bottom on't. Besides, Sir, I'η afraid the Line of your Understanding mayn't be long enough.

Sull. Look'e, Sir, I have nothing to say to your Sea of Truth but if a good Parcel of Land can intitle a Man to a little Truth, I have as much as any He in the Country.

Bon. I never heard your Worship, as the saying is, talk so much before.

Sull. Because I never met with a Man that I lik'd before—

Bon. Pray, Sir, as the saying is, let me ask you one Question: are not Man and Wife one Flesh?

Sir. Ch. You and your Wife, Mr. Guts, may be one Flesh, because ye are nothing else—but rational Creatures have minds that must be united.

Sull. Minds.

Sir Ch. Ay, Minds, Sir; don't you think that the Mind takes place of the Body?

Sull. In some People.

Sir Ch. Then the Interest of the Master must be consulted before that of his Servant.

Sull. Sir, you shall dine with me to Morrow.—Oons I always thought that we were naturally one.

Sir Ch. Sir, I know that my two Hands are naturally one, because they love one another, kiss one another, help one another in all the Actions of Life; but I cou'd not say so much, if they were always at Cuffs.

Sull. Then 'tis plain that we are two.

Sir Ch. Why don't you part with her, Sir?

Sull. Will you take her, Sir?

Sir Ch. With all my Heart.

Sull. You shall have her to Morrow Morning, and a Venison-pasty into the Bargain.

Sir Ch. You'll let me have her Fortune too?

Sull. Fortune! why, Sir, I have no Quarrel at her Fortune—I only hate the Woman, Sir, and none but the Woman shall go.

Sir Ch. But her Fortune, Sir—

Sull. Can you play at Whisk, Sir?

Sir Ch. No, truly, Sir.

Sull. Nor at All-fours.

Sir Ch. Neither!

Sull. Oons! where was this Man bred. [*Aside.*] Burn me, Sir! I can't go home, 'tis but two a Clock.

Sir Ch. For half an Hour, Sir, if you please—But you must consider 'tis late.

Sull. Late! that's the Reason I can't go to Bed—Come, Sir.—

[*Exeunt.*

Enter CHERRY, *runs across the Stage and knocks at* AIMWELL's *Chamber-door. Enter* AIMWELL *in his Night-cap and Gown.*

Aim. What's the matter? you tremble, Child, you're frighted.

Cher. No wonder, Sir—But in short, Sir, this very Minute a Gang of Rogues are gone to rob my Lady Bountiful's House.

Aim. How!

Cher. I dogg'd 'em to the very Door, and left 'em breaking in.

Aim. Have you alarm'd any Body else with the News?

Cher. No, no, Sir, I wanted to have discover'd the whole Plot, and twenty other things to your Man Martin; but I have search'd the whole House and can't find him; where is he?

Aim. No matter, Child; will you guide me immediately to the House?

Cher. With all my Heart, Sir; my Lady Bountiful is my God-mother; and I love Mrs. Dorinda so well—

Aim. Dorinda! The Name inspires me, the Glory and the Danger shall be all my own—Come, my Life, let me but get my Sword.

[*Exeunt.*

Scene.—*Changes to a Bed-chamber in* LADY BOUNTIFUL'S
House

Enter MRS. SULL., DOR., *undress'd; a Table and Lights.*

Dor. 'Tis very late, Sister; no News of your Spouse yet?

Mrs. Sull. No, I'm condemn'd to be alone till towards four, and then perhaps I may be executed with his Company.

Dor. Well, my Dear, I'll leave you to your rest; you'll go directly to Bed, I suppose.

Mrs. Sull. I don't know what to do? hey'hoe.

Dor. That's a desiring Sigh, Sister.

Mrs. Sull. This is a languishing Hour, Sister.

Dor. And might prove a Critical Minute, if the pretty Fellow were here.

Mrs. Sull. Here! what, in my Bed-chamber, at two a Clock o'th' Morning, I undress'd, the Family asleep, my hated Husband abroad, and my lovely Fellow at my Feet—O gad, Sister!

Dor. Thoughts are free, Sister, and them I allow you—So, my Dear, good Night.

Mrs. Sull. A good Rest to my dear Dorinda—Thoughts free! are they so? why then suppose him here, dress'd like a youthful, gay and burning Bridegroom [*Here* ARCHER *steals out of the Closet.*] with Tongue enchanting, Eyes bewitching, Knees imploring. [*Turns a little o' one side, and sees* ARCHER *in the Posture she describes.*] Ah! [*Shreeks, and runs to the other Side of the Stage.*] Have my Thoughts rais'd a Spirit?—What are you, Sir, a Man or a Devil?

Arch. A Man, a Man, Madam.   [*Rising.*

Mrs. Sull. How shall I be sure of it?

Arch. Madam, I'll give you Demonstration this Minute.

                                  [*Takes her Hand.*

Mrs. Sull. What, Sir! do you intend to be rude?

Arch. Yes, Madam, if you please.

Mrs. Sull. In the Name of Wonder, Whence came ye?

Arch. From the Skies, Madam—I'm a Jupiter in Love, and you shall be my Alcmena.

Mrs. Sull. How came you in?

Arch. I flew in at the Window, Madam; your Cozen Cupid lent me his Wings, and your Sister Venus open'd the Casement.

Mrs. Sull. I'm struck dumb with Admiration.

Arch. And I with wonder.   [*Looks passionately at her.*

Mrs. Sull. What will become of me?

Arch. How beautiful she looks—The teeming Jolly Spring Smiles in her blooming Face, and when she was conceiv'd, her Mother smelt to Roses, look'd on Lilies—

     Lillies unfold their white, their fragrant Charms,
     When the warm Sun thus Darts into their Arms.

                              [*Runs to her.*

Mrs. Sull. Ah!   [*Shreeks.*

Arch. Oons, Madam, what d'ye mean? you'll raise the House.

Mrs. Sull. Sir, I'll wake the Dead before I bear this—What! approach me with the Freedoms of a Keeper; I'm glad on't, your Impudence has cur'd me.

Arch. If this be Impudence [*Kneels.*] I leave to your partial self; no panting Pilgrim after a tedious, painful Voyage, e'er bow'd before his Saint with more Devotion.

Mrs. Sull. Now, now, I'm ruin'd, if he kneels! [*Aside.*] Rise thou prostrate Ingineer, not all thy undermining Skill shall reach my Heart—Rise, and know, I am a Woman without my Sex; I can love to all the Tenderness of Wishes, Sighs and Tears—But go no farther—Still to convince you that I'm more than Woman, I can speak my Frailty, confess my Weakness even for you—But—

Arch. For me!   [*Going to lay hold on her.*

Mrs. Sull. Hold, Sir, build not upon that—For my most mortal hatred follows if you disobey what I command you now—leave me this Minute—If he denies, I'm lost.   [*Aside.*

Arch. Then you'll promise—

Mrs. Sull. Any thing another time.

Arch. When shall I come?

Mrs. Sull. To Morrow when you will.

Arch. Your Lips must seal the Promise.

Mrs. Sull. Pshaw!

Arch. They must, they must! [*Kisses her.*] Raptures and Para-
dice! and why not now, my Angel? the Time, the Place, Silence
and Secrecy, all conspire—And the now conscious Stars have
preordain'd this Moment for my Happiness.

[*Takes her in his Arms.*

Mrs. Sull. You will not, cannot, sure.

Arch. If the Sun rides fast, and disappoints not Mortals of to
Morrow's Dawn, this Night shall crown my Joys.

Mrs. Sull. My Sex's Pride assist me.

Arch. My Sex's Strength help me.

Mrs. Sull. You shall kill me first.

Arch. I'll dye with you.   [*Carrying her off.*

Mrs. Sull. Thieves, Thieves, Murther—

Enter SCRUB *in his Breeches, and one Shoe.*

Scrub. Thieves, Thieves, Murther, Popery.

Arch. Ha! the very timorous Stag will kill in rutting time.

[*Draws and offers to Stab* SCRUB.

Scrub. [*Kneeling.*] O, Pray, Sir, spare all I have and take my
Life.

Mrs. Sull. [*Holding* ARCHER'S *Hand.*] What do's the Fellow
mean?

Scrub. O, Madam, down upon your Knees, your Marrow-bones
—He's one of 'um.

Arch. Of whom?

Scrub. One of the Rogues—I beg your Pardon, Sir, one of
the honest Gentlemen that just now are broke into the House.

Arch. How!

Mrs. Sull. I hope, you did not come to rob me?

Arch. Indeed I did, Madam, but I wou'd have taken nothing
but what you might ha' spar'd; but your crying Thieves has
wak'd this dreaming Fool, and so he takes 'em for granted.

Scrub. Granted! 'tis granted, Sir; take all we have.

Mrs. Sull. The Fellow looks as if he were broke out of Bedlam.

Scrub. Oons, Madam, they're broke in to the House with Fire
and Sword! I saw them, heard them; they'll be here this Minute.

Arch. What, Thieves!

Scrub. Under Favour, Sir, I think so.

Mrs. Sull. What shall we do, Sir?

Arch. Madam, I wish your Ladyship a good Night.

Mrs. Sull. Will you leave me?

Arch. Leave you! Lord, Madam, did not you command me to
be gone just now upon pain of your immortal Hatred?

Mrs. Sull. Nay, but pray, Sir—   [*Takes hold of him.*

Arch. Ha, ha, ha, now comes my turn to be ravish'd.—You see now, Madam, you must use Men one way or other; but take this by the way, good Madam, that none but a Fool will give you the benefit of his Courage, unless you'll take his Love along with it.—How are they arm'd, Friend?

Scrub. With Sword and Pistol, Sir.

Arch. Hush—I see a dark Lanthorn coming thro' the Gallery. —Madam, be assur'd I will protect you, or lose my Life.

Mrs. Sull. Your Life! no, Sir, they can rob me of nothing that I value half so much; therefore, now, Sir, let me intreat you to be gone.

Arch. No, Madam, I'll consult my own Safety for the sake of yours; I'll work by Stratagem: Have you Courage enough to stand the appearance of 'em?

Mrs. Sull. Yes, yes, since I have scap'd your Hands, I can face any thing.

Arch. Come hither, Brother Scrub, don't you know me?

Scrub. Eh! my dear Brother, let me kiss thee. [*Kisses* ARCHER.

Arch. This way—Here—

[ARCHER *and* SCRUB *hide behind the Bed.*

Enter GIBBET *with a dark Lanthorn in one Hand and a Pistol in t'other.*

Gib. Ay, ay, this is the Chamber, and the Lady alone.

Mrs. Sull. Who are you, Sir? what wou'd you have? d'ye come to rob me?

Gib. Rob you! alack a day, Madam, I'm only a younger Brother, Madam; and so, Madam, if you make a Noise, I'll shoot you thro' the Head; but don't be afraid, Madam.

       [*Laying his Lanthorn and Pistol upon the Table.*
These Rings, Madam, don't be concern'd, Madam, I have a profound Respect for you, Madam; your Keys, Madam; don't be frighted, Madam, I'm the most of a Gentleman.

       [*Searching her Pockets.*
This Necklace, Madam, I never was rude to a Lady;—I have a Veneration—for this Necklace—

[*Here* ARCHER *having come round and seiz'd the Pistols, takes* GIBBET *by the Collar, trips up his Heels, and claps the Pistol to his Breast.*

Arch. Hold, profane Villain, and take the Reward of thy Sacrilege.

Gib. Oh! Pray, Sir, don't kill me; I an't prepar'd.

Arch. How many is there of 'em, Scrub?

Scrub. Five and Forty, Sir.

Arch. Then I must kill the Villain to have him out of the way.

Gib. Hold, hold, Sir, we are but three upon my Honour.

Arch. Scrub, will you undertake to secure him?

Scrub. Not I, Sir; kill him, kill him.

Arch. Run to Gipsey's Chamber, there you'll find the Doctor; bring him hither presently. [*Exit* SCRUB *running.*] Come, Rogue, if you have a short Prayer, say it.

Gib. Sir, I have no Prayer at all; the Government has provided a Chaplain to say Prayers for us on these Occasions.

Mrs. Sull. Pray, Sir, don't kill him;—You fright me as much as him.

Arch. The Dog shall die, Madam, for being the Occasion of my disappointment.—Sirrah, this Moment is your last.

Gib. Sir, I'll give you Two hundred Pound to spare my Life.

Arch. Have you no more, Rascal?

Gib. Yes, Sir, I can command Four hundred; but I must reserve Two of 'em to save my Life at the Sessions.

Enter SCRUB *and* FOIGARD.

Arch. Here, Doctor, I suppose Scrub and you between you may manage him.—Lay hold of him, Doctor.

[FOIG. *lays hold of* GIBBET.

Gib. What! turn'd over to the Priest already.—Look 'ye, Doctor, you come before your time; I'ant condemn'd yet, I thank'ye.

Foig. Come, my dear Joy, I vill secure your Body and your Shoul too; I vill make you a good Catholick, and give you an Absolution.

Gib. Absolution! can you procure me a Pardon, Doctor?

Foig. No, Joy.——

Gib. Then you and your Absolution may go to the Devil.

Arch. Convey him into the Cellar, there bind him:—Take the Pistol, and if he offers to resist, shoot him thro' the Head,—and come back to us with all the speed you can.

Scrub. Ay, ay, come, Doctor, do you hold him fast, and I'll guard him.

Mrs. Sull. But how came the Doctor?

Arch. In short, Madam—[*Shreeking without.*] S'death! the Rogues are at work with the other Ladies.—I'm vex'd I parted with the Pistol; but I must fly to their Assistance.—Will you stay here, Madam, or venture your self with me?

Mrs. Sull. O, with you, dear Sir, with you.

[*Takes him by the Arm and Exeunt.*

SCENE.—*Changes to another Apartment in the same House*

Enter HOUNSLOW *dragging in* LADY BOUNTYFULL *and* BAGSHOT
halling in DORINDA; *the* ROGUES *with Swords drawn.*

Houn. Come, come, your Jewels, Mistress.
Bag. Your Keys, your Keys, old Gentlewoman.

Enter AIMWELL *and* CHERRY.

Aim. Turn this way, Villains; I durst engage an Army in such
a Cause.   [*He engages 'em both.*
Dor. O, Madam, had I but a Sword to help the Brave Man!
L. Boun. There's three or four hanging up in the Hall; but
they won't draw. I'll go fetch one however.   [*Exit.*

Enter ARCHER *and* MRS. SULLEN.

Arch. Hold, hold, my Lord, every Man his Bird, pray.
     [*They engage Man to Man; the* ROGUES *are thrown and
          disarm'd.*
Cher. What! the Rogues taken! then they'll impeach my
Father; I must give him timely Notice.   [*Runs out.*
Arch. Shall we kill the Rogues?
Aim. No, no, we'll bind them.
Arch. Ay, ay; here, Madam, lend me your Garter?
                    [*To* MRS. SULLEN *who stands by him.*
Mrs. Sull. The Devil's in this Fellow; he fights, loves, and
banters, all in a Breath.—Here's a Cord that the Rogues brought
with 'em, I suppose.
Arch. Right, right, the Rogue's Destiny, a Rope to hang him-
self.—Come, my Lord,—This is but a scandalous sort of an
Office, [*Binding the* ROGUES *together.*] if our Adventures shou'd
end in this sort of Hangman work; but I hope there is something
in prospect that—[*Enter* SCRUB.] Well, Scrub, have you secur'd
your Tartar?
Scrub. Yes, Sir, I left the Priest and him disputing about Religion.
Aim. And pray carry these Gentlemen to reap the Benefit of
the Controversy.
          [*Delivers the Prisoners to* SCRUB, *who leads 'em out.*
Mrs. Sull. Pray, Sister, how came my Lord here?
Dor. And pray, how came the Gentleman here?
Mrs. Sull. I'll tell you the greatest piece of Villainy—
                              [*They talk in dumb show.*

Aim. I fancy, Archer, you have been more successful in your Adventures than the House-breakers.

Arch. No matter for my Adventure, yours is the principal.—Press her this Minute to marry you,—now while she's hurry'd between the Palpitation of her Fear, and the Joy of her Deliverance; now while the Tide of her Spirits are at High-flood—Throw your self at her Feet; speak some Romantick Nonsense or other;—Address her like Alexander in the height of his Victory, confound her Senses, bear down her Reason, and away with her.—The Priest is now in the Cellar, and dare not refuse to do the work.

Enter LADY BOUNTIFULL.

Aim. But how shall I get off without being observ'd?

Arch. You a Lover! and not find a way to get off—Let me see.

Aim. You bleed, Archer.

Arch. S'death, I'm glad on't; this Wound will do the Business. —I'll amuse the old Lady and Mrs. Sullen about dressing my Wound, while you carry off Dorinda.

L. Boun. Gentlemen, cou'd we understand how you wou'd be gratified for the Services—

Arch. Come, come, my Lady, this is no time for Complements; I'm wounded, Madam.

L. Boun. ⎱
Mrs. Sull. ⎰ How! wounded!

Dor. I hope, Sir, you have receiv'd no Hurt?

Aim. None but what you may cure.

                              [Makes Love in dumb show.

L. Boun. Let me see your Arm, Sir.—I must have some Powder-sugar to stop the Blood—O me! an ugly Gash upon my Word, Sir, you must go into Bed.

Arch. Ay, my Lady a Bed wou'd do very well.—Madam, [*To* MRS. SULL.] Will you do me the Favour to conduct me to a Chamber?

L. Boun. Do, do, Daughter—while I get the Lint and the Probe and the Plaister ready.

        [Runs out one way, AIMWELL *carries off* DORINDA *another.*

Arch. Come, Madam, why don't you obey your Mother's Commands?

Mrs. Sull. How can you, after what is past, have the Confidence to ask me?

Arch. And if you go to that, how can you after what is past, have the Confidence to deny me?—Was not this Blood shed in your Defence, and my Life expos'd for your Protection?—Look 'ye, Madam, I'm none of your Romantick Fools, that fight Gyants and Monsters for nothing; my Valour is down right Swiss; I'm a Soldier of Fortune and must be paid.

Mrs. Sull. 'Tis ungenerous in you, Sir, to upbraid me with your Services.

Arch. 'Tis ungenerous in you, Madam, not to reward 'em.

Mrs. Sull. How! at the Expence of my Honour?

Arch. Honour! can Honour consist with Ingratitude? if you wou'd deal like a Woman of Honour, do like a Man of Honour; d'ye think I wou'd deny you in such a Case?

Enter a SERVANT.

Ser. Madam, my Lady order'd me to tell you that your Brother is below at the Gate.

Mrs. Sull. My Brother? Heavens be prais'd.—Sir, he shall thank you for your Services; he has it in his Power.

Arch. Who is your Brother, Madam?

Mrs. Sull. Sir Charles Freeman.—You'll excuse me, Sir; I must go and receive him.

Arch. Sir Charles Freeman! S'death and Hell!—My old Acquaintance. Now unless Aimwell has made good use of his time, all our fair Machine goes souse into the Sea like the Edistone.

[*Exit.*

SCENE.—*Changes to the Gallery in the same House*

Enter AIMWELL and DORINDA.

Dor. Well, well, my Lord, you have conquer'd; your late generous Action will I hope, plead for my easie yielding, tho' I must own your Lordship had a Friend in the Fort before.

Aim. The Sweets of Hybla dwell upon her Tongue.—Here, Doctor—

Enter FOIGARD *with a Book.*

Foig. Are you prepar'd boat?

Dor. I'm ready: But, first, my Lord, one Word;—I have a frightful Example of a hasty Marriage in my own Family; when I reflect upon't, it shocks me. Pray, my Lord, consider a little—

Aim. Consider! Do you doubt my Honour or my Love?

Dor. Neither: I do believe you equally Just as Brave.—And were your whole Sex drawn out for me to chuse, I shou'd not cast a look upon the Multitude if you were absent.—But my Lord, I'm a Woman; Colours, Concealments may hide a thousand Faults in me.—Therefore know me better first; I hardly dare affirm I know my self in any thing except my Love.

Aim. Such Goodness who cou'd injure; I find my self unequal to the task of Villain; she has gain'd my Soul, and made it honest like her own;—I cannot, cannot hurt her. [*Aside.*] Doctor, retire. [*Exit* FOIGARD.] Madam, behold your Lover and your Proselite, and judge of my Passion by my Conversion.—I'm all a Lie, nor dare I give a Fiction to your Arms; I'm all Counterfeit except my Passion.

Dor. Forbid it Heaven! a Counterfeit!

Aim. I am no Lord, but a poor needy Man, come with a mean, a scandalous Design to prey upon your Fortune:—But the Beauties of your Mind and Person have so won me from my self, that like a trusty Servant, I prefer the Interest of my Mistress to my own.

Dor. Sure I have had the Dream of some poor Mariner, a sleepy image of a welcome Port, and wake involv'd in Storms.— Pray, Sir, who are you?

Aim. Brother to the Man whose Title I usurp'd, but Stranger to his Honour or his Fortune.

Dor. Matchless Honesty—Once I was proud, Sir, of your Wealth and Title, but now am prouder that you want it: Now I can shew my Love was justly levell'd, and had no Aim but Love. Doctor, come in.

Enter FOIGARD *at one Door,* GIPSEY *at another, who whispers* DORINDA.

Your Pardon, Sir, we shannot want you now, Sir, you must excuse me,—I'll wait on you presently.   [*Exit with* GIPSEY.

Foig. Upon my Shoul, now, dis is foolish.   [*Exit.*

Aim. Gone! and bid the Priest depart.—It has an ominous Look.

Enter ARCHER.

Arch. Courage, Tom—Shall I wish you Joy?

Aim. No.

Arch. Oons, Man, what ha' you been doing?

Aim. O, Archer, my Honesty, I fear has ruin'd me.

Arch. How!

Aim. I have discover'd my self.

Arch. Discover'd! and without my Consent? what! have I embark'd my small Remains in the same bottom with yours, and you dispose of all without my Partnership?

Aim. O, Archer, I own my fault.

Arch. After Conviction—'Tis then too late for Pardon.—You may remember, Mr. Aimwell, that you propos'd this Folly—As

you begun, so end it.—Henceforth I'll hunt my Fortune single.
—So farewel.

Aim. Stay, my dear Archer, but a Minute.

Arch. Stay! what, to be despis'd, expos'd and laugh'd at—
No, I wou'd sooner change Conditions with the worst of the
Rogues we just now bound, than bear one scornful Smile from
the proud Knight that once I treated as my equal.

Aim. What Knight?

Arch. Sir Charles Freeman, Brother to the Lady that I had
almost—But no matter for that; 'tis a cursed Night's Work, and
so I leave you to make your best on't.   [*Going.*

Aim. Freeman!—One Word, Archer. Still I have Hopes; methought she receiv'd my Confession with Pleasure.

Arch. S'death! who doubts it?

Aim. She consented after to the Match; and still I dare believe
she will be just.

Arch. To her self, I warrant her, as you shou'd have been.

Aim. By all my Hopes, she comes, and smiling comes.

Enter DORINDA *mighty gay.*

Dor. Come, my dear Lord,—I fly with Impatience to your Arms.
—The Minutes of my Absence was a tedious Year. Where's this
tedious Priest?

Enter FOIGARD.

Arch. Oons, a brave Girl.

Dor. I suppose, my Lord, this Gentleman is privy to our Affairs?

Arch. Yes, yes, Madam, I'm to be your Father.

Dor. Come, Priest, do your Office.

Arch. Make hast, make hast, couple 'em any way. [*Takes* AIM-
WELL'S *Hand*] Come, Madam, I'm to give you—

Dor. My Mind's alter'd, I won't.

Arch. Eh—

Aim. I'm confounded.

Foig. Upon my Shoul, and sho is my shelf.

Arch. What's the matter now, Madam?

Dor. Look'ye, Sir, one generous Action deserves another—This
Gentleman's Honour oblig'd him to hide nothing from me; my
Justice engages me to conceal nothing from him: In short, Sir,
you are the Person that you thought you counterfeited; you are
the true Lord Viscount Aimwell; and I wish your Lordship Joy.
Now, Priest, you may be gone; if my Lord is pleas'd now with the
Match, let his Lordship marry me in the face of the World.

Aim. ⎫
Arch. ⎬ What do's she mean?

Dor. Here's a Witness for my Truth.

Enter Sir Ch. *and* Mrs. Sull.

Sir Charles. My dear Lord Aimwell, I wish you Joy.

Aim. Of what?

Sir Ch. Of your Honour and Estate: Your Brother died the Day before I left London; and all your Friends have writ after you to Brussels; among the rest I did my self the Honour.

Arch. Hark'ye, Sir Knight, don't you banter now?

Sir Ch. 'Tis Truth, upon my Honour.

Aim. Thanks to the pregnant Stars that form'd this Accident.

Arch. Thanks to the Womb of Time that brought it forth; away with it.

Aim. Thanks to my Guardian Angel that led me to the Prize—
[*Taking* Dorinda's *Hand.*

Arch. And double Thanks to the noble Sir Charles Freeman. My Lord, I wish you Joy. My Lady, I wish you Joy.—I Gad, Sir Freeman, you're the honestest Fellow living—S'death, I'm grown strange airy upon this matter—My Lord, how d'ye?—a word, my Lord; don't you remember something of a previous Agreement, that entitles me to the Moyety of this Lady's Fortune, which, I think will amount to Five thousand Pound?

Aim. Not a Penny, Archer; You wou'd ha' cut my Throat just now, because I wou'd not deceive this Lady.

Arch. Ay, and I'll cut your Throat again, if you shou'd deceive her now.

Aim. That's what I expected; and to end the Dispute, the Lady's Fortune is Ten thousand Pound; we'll divide Stakes; take the Ten thousand Pound, or the Lady.

Dor. How! is your Lordship so indifferent?

Arch. No, no, no, Madam, his Lordship knows very well, that I'll take the Money; I leave you to his Lordship, and so we're both provided for.

Enter Count Bellair.

Count. Mesdames, & Messieurs, I am your Servant trice humble: I hear you be rob, here.

Aim. The Ladies have been in some danger, Sir.

Count. And Begar, our Inn be rob too.

Aim. Our Inn! by whom?

Count. By the Landlord, begar—Garzoon, he has rob himself and run away.

Arch. Rob'd himself!

Count. Ay, begar, and me too of a hundre Pound.

Arch. A hundred Pound?

Count. Yes, that I ow'd him.

Aim. Our Money's gone, Frank.

Arch. Rot the Money! my Wench is gone—*Scavez vous quelque chose de Madamoiselle Cherry?*

Enter a FELLOW *with a strong Box and a Letter.*

Fell. Is there one Martin here?

Arch. Ay, ay,—who wants him?

Fell. I have a Box here and Letter for him.

Arch. [*Taking the Box.*] Ha, ha, ha, what's here? Legerdemain! by this Light, my Lord, our Money again; but this unfolds the Riddle. [*Opening the Letter, reads.*] Hum, hum, hum—O, 'tis for the Publick good, and must be communicated to the Company.

MR. MARTIN,

My Father being afraid of an Impeachment by the Rogues that are taken to Night, is gone off, but if you can procure him a Pardon he will make great Discoveries that may be useful to the Country; cou'd I have met you instead of your Master to Night, I wou'd have deliver'd my self into your Hands with a Sum that much exceeds that in your strong Box, which I have sent you, with an Assurance to my dear Martin, that I shall ever be his most faithful Friend until Death.

CHERRY BONNIFACE.

There's a Billet-doux for you—As for the Father I think he ought to be encouraged, and for the Daughter—Pray, my Lord, persuade your Bride to take her into her Service instead of Gipsey.

Aim. I can assure you, Madam, your Deliverance was owing to her Discovery.

Dor. Your Command, my Lord, will do without the Obligation. I'll take care of her.

Sir. Ch. This good Company meets oportunely in favour of a Design I have in behalf of my unfortunate Sister. I intend to part her from her Husband—Gentlemen, will you assist me?

Arch. Assist you! S'Death who wou'd not.

Count. Assist! Garzoon, we all assest.

Enter SULLEN.

Sull. What's all this?—They tell me Spouse that you had like to have been rob'd.

Mrs. Sull. Truly, Spouse, I was pretty near it—Had not these two Gentlemen interpos'd.

Sull. How came these Gentlemen here?

Mrs. Sull. That's his way of returning Thanks you must know.

Count. Garzoon, the Question be a propo for all dat.

Sir Ch. You promis'd last Night, Sir, that you wou'd deliver your Lady to me this Morning.

Sull. Humph.

Arch. Humph. What do you mean by humph?—Sir, you shall deliver her—In short, Sir, we have sav'd you and your Family, and if you are not civil we'll unbind the Rogues, join with 'um and set fire to your House—What do's the Man mean? not part with his Wife!

Count. Ay, Garzoon, de Man no understan Common Justice.

Mrs. Sull. Hold, Gentlemen, all things here must move by consent; Compulsion wou'd Spoil us; let my Dear and I talk the matter over, and you shall judge it between us.

Sull. Let me know first who are to be our Judges—Pray, Sir, who are you?

Sir. Ch. I am Sir Charles Freeman, come to take away your Wife.

Sull. And you, good Sir.

Aim. Charles Viscount Aimwell, come to take away your Sister.

Sull. And you pray, Sir?

Arch. Francis Archer, Esq., come—

Sull. To take away my Mother, I hope—Gentlemen, you're heartily welcome; I never met with three more obliging People since I was born—And now, my Dear, if you please, you shall have the first word.

Arch. And the last for five Pound.

Mrs. Sull. Spouse.

Sull. Ribb.

Mrs. Sull. How long have we been marry'd?

Sull. By the Almanak fourteen Months—But by my Account fourteen Years.

Mrs. Sull. 'Tis thereabout by my reckoning.

Count. Garzoon, their Account will agree.

Mrs. Sull. Pray, Spouse, what did you marry for?

Sull. To get an Heir to my Estate.

Sir Ch. And have you succeeded?

Sull. No.

Arch. The Condition fails of his side—Pray, Madam, what did you marry for?

Mrs. Sull. To support the Weakness of my Sex by the Strength of his, and to enjoy the Pleasures of an agreeable Society.

Sir Ch. Are your Expectations answer'd?

Mrs. Sull. No.

Count. A clear Case, a clear Case.

Sir Ch. What are the Bars to your mutual Contentment?

Mrs. Sull. In the first Place I can't drink Ale with him.

Sull. Nor can I drink Tea with her.

Mrs. Sull. I can't hunt with you.

Sull. Nor can I dance with you.

Mrs. Sull. I hate Cocking and Racing.

Sull. And I abhor Ombre and Piquee.

Mrs. Sull. Your Silence is intollerable.

Sull. Your Prating is worse.

Mrs. Sull: Have we not been a perpetual Offence to each other—
A gnawing Vulture at the Heart?

Sull. A frightful Goblin to the Sight?

Mrs. Sull. A Porcupine to the Feeling?

Sull. Perpetual Wormwood to the Taste?

Mrs. Sull. Is there on Earth a thing we cou'd agree in?

Sull. Yes—To part.

Mrs. Sull. With all my Heart.

Sull. Your Hand.

Mrs. Sull. Here.

Sull. These Hands join'd us, these shall part us—away—

Mrs. Sull. North.

Sull. South.

Mrs. Sull. East.

Sull. West—far as the Poles asunder.

Count. Begar, the Ceremony be vera pretty.

Sir Ch. Now, Mr. Sullen, there wants only my Sister's Fortune
to make us easie.

Sull. Sir Charles, you love your Sister, and I love her Fortune;
every one to his Fancy.

Arch. Then you won't refund?

Sull. Not a Stiver.

Arch. Then I find, Madam, you must e'en go to your Prison
again.

Count. What is the Portion?

Sir Ch. Ten thousand Pound, Sir.

Count. Garzoon, I'll pay it, and she shall go home wid me.

Arch. Ha, ha, ha, French all over—Do you know, Sir, what ten
thousand Pound English is?

Count. No, begar, not justement.

Arch. Why, Sir, 'tis a hundred thousand Livres.

Count. A hundre tousand Livres—A Garzoon! me canno' do't;
your Beauties and their Fortunes are both too much for me.

Arch. Then I will.—This Nights Adventure has prov'd strangely lucky to us all—For Captain Gibbet in his Walk had made bold, Mr. Sullen, with your Study and Escritoire, and had taken out all the Writings of your Estate, all the Articles of Marriage with this Lady, Bills, Bonds, Leases, Receipts to an infinite Value: I took 'em from him, and I deliver them to Sir Charles.

[*Gives him a Parcel of Papers and Parchments.*

Sull. How, my Writings! my Head akes consumedly—Well, Gentlemen, you shall have her Fortune, but I can't talk. If you have a mind, Sir Charles, to be merry, and celebrate my Sister's Wedding, and my Divorce, you may command my House—but my Head akes consumedly—Scrub, bring me a Dram.

Arch. Madam, [*To* Mrs. Sull.] there's a Country Dance to the Trifle that I sung to Day; your Hand, and we'll lead it up.

[*Here a Dance.*

Arch. 'Twou'd be hard to guess which of these Parties is the better pleas'd, the Couple Join'd, or the Couple Parted; the one rejoycing in hopes of an untasted Happiness, and the other in their Deliverance from an experienc'd Misery.

> *Both happy in their several States we find,*
> *Those parted by consent, and those conjoin'd,*
> *Consent, if mutual, saves the Lawyer's Fee,*
> *Consent is Law enough to set you free.*

FINIS.

AN EPILOGUE

If to our Play Your Judgment can't be kind,
Let its expiring Author Pity find.
Survey his mournful Case with melting Eyes,
Nor let the Bard be dam'd before he dies.
Forbear you Fair on his last Scene to frown,
But his true Exit with a Plaudit Crown;
Then shall the dying Poet cease to Fear,
The Dreadful Knell, while your Applause he hears.
At Leuctra so, the Conqu'ring Theban dy'd,
Claim'd his Friend's Praises, but their Tears deny'd:
Pleas'd in the Pangs of Death he greatly Thought
Conquest with loss of Life but cheaply bought.
The Difference this, the Greek was one wou'd fight
As brave, tho' not so gay as Serjeant Kite;
Ye Sons of Will's what's that to those who write?
To Thebes alone the Grecian ow'd his
        Bays,
You may the Bard above the Hero raise,
Since yours is greater than Athenian
        Praise.

THE BEGGAR'S OPERA
by
John Gay

DRAMATIS PERSONÆ

MEN

PEACHUM	Mr. Hippesley
LOCKIT	Mr. Hall
MACHEATH	Mr. Walker
FILCH	Mr. Clark

JEMMY TWITCHER		Mr. H. Bullock
CROOK-FINGER'D JACK		Mr. Houghton
WAT DREARY		Mr. Smith
ROBIN OF BAGSHOT	*Macheath's Gang* .	Mr. Lacy
NIMMING NED		Mr. Pit
HARRY PADINGTON		Mr. Eaton
MAT OF THE MINT		Mr. Spiller
BEN BUDGE		Mr. Morgan

BEGGAR	Mr. Chapman
PLAYER	Mr. Milward

Constables, Drawer, Turnkey, &c.

WOMEN

MRS. PEACHUM	Mrs. Martin
POLLY PEACHUM	Miss Fenton
LUCY LOCKIT	Mrs. Egleton
DIANA TRAPES	Mrs. Martin

MRS. COAXER		Mrs. Holiday
DOLLY TRULL		Mrs. Lacy
MRS. VIXEN		Mrs. Rice
BETTY DOXY	*Women of the Town*	Mrs. Rogers
JENNY DIVER		Mrs. Clarke
MRS. SLAMMEKIN		Mrs. Morgan
SUKY TAWDRY		Mrs. Palin
MOLLY BRAZEN		Mrs. Sallee

INTRODUCTION

BEGGAR, PLAYER

Beggar. If Poverty be a Title to Poetry, I am sure No-body can dispute mine. I own myself of the Company of Beggars; and I make one at their Weekly Festivals at St. Giles. I have a small Yearly Salary for my Catches, and am welcome to a Dinner there whenever I please, which is more than most Poets can say.

Player. As we live by the Muses, 'tis but Gratitude in us to encourage Poetical Merit where-ever we find it. The Muses, contrary to all other Ladies, pay no Distinction to Dress, and never partially mistake the Pertness of Embroidery for Wit, nor the Modesty of Want for Dulness. Be the Author who he will, we push his Play as far as it will go. So (though you are in Want) I wish you Success heartily.

Beggar. This Piece I own was originally writ for the celebrating the Marriage of James Chanter and Moll Lay, two most excellent Ballad-Singers. I have introduc'd the Similes that are in all your celebrated Operas: The Swallow, the Moth, the Bee, the Ship, the Flower, &c. Besides, I have a Prison Scene which the Ladies always reckon charmingly pathetick. As to the Parts, I have observ'd such a nice Impartiality to our two Ladies, that it is impossible for either of them to take Offence. I hope I may be forgiven, that I have not made my Opera throughout unnatural, like those in vogue; for I have no Recitative: Excepting this, as I have consented to have neither Prologue nor Epilogue, it must be allow'd an Opera in all its forms. The Piece indeed hath been heretofore frequently represented by our selves in our great Room at St. Giles's, so that I cannot too often acknowledge your Charity in bringing it now on the Stage.

Player. But I see 'tis time for us to withdraw; the Actors are preparing to begin. Play away the Overture. [*Exeunt*.

THE BEGGAR'S OPERA

ACT I

SCENE I

SCENE.—PEACHUM'S *House*

PEACHUM *sitting at a Table with a large Book of Accounts before him.*

AIR I. An old Woman cloathed in Gray, &c.

Through all the Employments of Life
Each Neighbour abuses his Brother;
Whore and Rogue they call Husband and Wife:
All Professions be-rogue one another.
The Priest calls the Lawyer a Cheat,
The Lawyer be-knaves the Divine;
And the Statesman, because he's so great,
Thinks his Trade as honest as mine.

A Lawyer is an honest Employment, so is mine. Like me too he acts in a double Capacity, both against Rogues and for 'em; for 'tis but fitting that we should protect and encourage Cheats, since we live by them.

SCENE II

PEACHUM, FILCH.

Filch. Sir, Black Moll hath sent word her Tryal comes on in the Afternoon, and she hopes you will order Matters so as to bring her off.

Peach. Why, she may plead her Belly at worst; to my Knowledge she hath taken care of that Security. But as the Wench is very active and industrious, you may satisfy her that I'll soften the Evidence.

Filch. Tom Gagg, Sir, is found guilty.

Peach. A lazy Dog! When I took him the time before, I told him what he would come to if he did not mend his Hand. This is Death without Reprieve. I may venture to Book him. [*Writes.*] For Tom

Gagg, forty Pounds. Let Betty Sly know that I'll save her from Transportation, for I can get more by her staying in England.

Filch. Betty hath brought more Goods into our Lock to-year than any five of the Gang; and in truth, 'tis a pity to lose so good a Customer.

Peach. If none of the Gang take her off, she may, in the common course of Business, live a Twelve-month longer. I love to let Women scape. A good Sportsman always lets the Hen Partridges fly, because the breed of the Game depends upon them. Besides, here the Law allows us no Reward; there is nothing to be got by the Death of Women—except our Wives.

Filch. Without dispute, she is a fine Woman! 'Twas to her I was oblig'd for my Education, and (to say a bold Word) she hath train'd up more young Fellows to the Business than the Gaming-table.

Peach. Truly, Filch, thy Observation is right. We and the Surgeons are more beholden to Women than all the Professions besides.

AIR II.   The bonny grey-ey'd Morn, &c.

> FILCH. *'Tis Woman that seduces all Mankind,*
> *By her we first were taught the wheedling Arts:*
> *Her very Eyes can cheat; when most she's kind,*
> *She tricks us of our Money with our Hearts.*
> *For her, like Wolves by night we roam for Prey,*
> *And practise ev'ry Fraud to bribe her Charms;*
> *For Suits of Love, like Law, are won by Pay,*
> *And Beauty must be fee'd into our Arms.*

Peach. But make haste to Newgate, Boy, and let my Friends know what I intend; for I love to make them easy one way or other.

Filch. When a Gentleman is long kept in suspence, Penitence may break his Spirit ever after. Besides, Certainty gives a Man a good Air upon his Tryal, and makes him risque another without Fear or Scruple. But I'll away, for 'tis a Pleasure to be the Messenger of Comfort to Friends in Affliction.

SCENE III

PEACHUM.

But 'tis now high time to look about me for a decent Execution against next Sessions. I hate a lazy Rogue, by whom one can get nothing 'til he is hang'd. A Register of the Gang, [*Reading.*] Crooked-finger'd Jack. A Year and a half in the Service; Let me see how much the Stock owes to his Industry; one, two, three, four, five Gold Watches, and seven Silver ones. A mighty clean-handed Fellow! Sixteen Snuff-boxes, five of them of true Gold. Six dozen of Handkerchiefs, four silver-hilted Swords, half a dozen of Shirts, three Tye-Perriwigs, and a Piece of Broad Cloth. Considering these are only the Fruits of his leisure Hours, I don't know a prettier Fellow, for no Man alive hath a more engaging Presence of Mind upon the Road. Wat Dreary, alias Brown Will, an irregular Dog, who hath an underhand way of disposing of his Goods. I'll try him only for a Sessions or two longer upon his good Behaviour. Harry Padington, a poor petty-larceny Rascal, without the least Genius; that Fellow, though he were to live these six Months, will never come to the Gallows with any Credit. Slippery Sam; he goes off the next Sessions, for the Villain hath the Impudence to have views of following his Trade as a Taylor, which he calls an honest Employment. Mat of the Mint; listed not above a Month ago, a promising sturdy Fellow, and diligent in his way; somewhat too bold and hasty, and may raise good Contributions on the Publick, if he does not cut himself short by Murder. Tom Tipple, a guzzling soaking Sot, who is always too drunk to stand himself, or to make others stand. A Cart is absolutely necessary for him. Robin of Bagshot, alias Gorgon, alias Bluff Bob, alias Carbuncle, alias Bob Booty.

Scene IV

Peachum, Mrs. Peachum.

Mrs. Peach. What of Bob Booty, Husband? I hope nothing bad hath betided him. You know, my Dear, he's a favourite Customer of mine. 'Twas he made me a Present of this Ring.

Peach. I have set his Name down in the Black-List, that's all, my Dear; he spends his Life among Women, and as soon as his Money is gone, one or other of the Ladies will hang him for the Reward, and there's forty Pound lost to us for-ever.

Mrs. Peach. You know, my Dear, I never meddle in matters of Death; I always leave those Affairs to you. Women indeed are bitter bad Judges in these cases, for they are so partial to the Brave that they think every Man handsome who is going to the Camp or the Gallows.

Air III. Cold and Raw, &c.

If any Wench Venus's Girdle wear,
Though she be never so ugly;
Lillys and Roses will quickly appear,
And her Face look wond'rous smuggly.

Beneath the left Ear so fit but a Cord,
(A Rope so charming a Zone is!)
The Youth in his Cart hath the Air of a Lord,
And we cry, There dies an Adonis!

But really, Husband, you should not be too hard-hearted, for you never had a finer, braver set of Men than at present. We have not had a Murder among them all, these seven Months. And truly, my Dear, that is a great Blessing.

Peach. What a dickens is the Woman always a whimpring about Murder for? No Gentleman is ever look'd upon the worse for killing a Man in his own Defence; and if Business cannot be carried on without it, what would you have a Gentleman do?

Mrs. Peach. If I am in the wrong, my Dear, you must excuse me, for No-body can help the Frailty of an over-scrupulous Conscience.

Peach. Murder is as fashionable a Crime as a Man can be guilty of. How many fine Gentlemen have we in Newgate every Year, purely upon that Article! If they have wherewithal to persuade the Jury to bring it in Manslaughter, what are they the worse for it? So, my Dear, have done upon this Subject. Was Captain Macheath here this Morning, for the Bank-notes he left with you last Week?

Mrs. Peach. Yes, my Dear; and though the Bank hath stopt Payment, he was so cheerful and so agreeable! Sure there is not a finer Gentleman upon the Road than the Captain! If he comes from Bagshot at any reasonable Hour he hath promis'd to make one this Evening with Polly and me, and Bob Booty, at a Party of Quadrille. Pray, my Dear, is the Captain rich?

Peach. The Captain keeps too good Company ever to grow rich. Marybone and the Chocolate-houses are his undoing. The Man that proposes to get Money by Play should have the Education of a fine Gentleman, and be train'd up to it from his Youth.

Mrs. Peach. Really, I am sorry upon Polly's Account the Captain hath not more Discretion. What business hath he to keep Company with Lords and Gentlemen? he should leave them to prey upon one another.

Peach. Upon Polly's Account! What, a Plague, does the Woman mean?—Upon Polly's Account!

Mrs. Peach. Captain Macheath is very fond of the Girl.

Peach. And what then?

Mrs. Peach. If I have any Skill in the Ways of Women, I am sure Polly thinks him a very pretty Man.

Peach. And what then? You would not be so mad to have

the Wench marry him! Gamesters and Highwaymen are generally very good to their Whores, but they are very Devils to their
Wives.

Mrs. Peach. But if Polly should be in love, how should we
help her, or how can she help herself? Poor Girl, I am in the
utmost Concern about her.

AIR. IV. Why is your faithful Slave disdain'd? &c.

> *If Love the Virgin's Heart invade,*
> *How, like a Moth, the simple Maid*
> *   Still plays about the Flame!*
> *If soon she be not made a Wife,*
> *Her Honour's sing'd, and then for Life,*
> *   She's—what I dare not name.*

Peach. Look ye, Wife. A handsome Wench in our way of
Business is as profitable as at the Bar of a Temple Coffee-House,
who looks upon it as her livelihood to grant every Liberty but
one. You see I would indulge the Girl as far as prudently we can.
In any thing, but Marriage! After that, my Dear, how shall we
be safe? Are we not then in her Husband's Power? For a Husband
hath the absolute Power over all a Wife's Secrets but her own.
If the Girl had the Discretion of a Court Lady, who can have
a dozen young Fellows at her Ear without complying with one,
I should not matter it; but Polly is Tinder, and a Spark will at
once set her on a Flame. Married! If the Wench does not know
her own Profit, sure she knows her own Pleasure better than to
make herself a Property! My Daughter to me should be, like a
Court Lady to a Minister of State, a Key to the whole Gang.
Married! If the Affair is not already done, I'll terrify her from
it, by the Example of our Neighbours.

Mrs. Peach. May-hap, my Dear, you may injure the Girl.
She loves to imitate the fine Ladies, and she may only allow the
Captain Liberties in the View of Interest.

Peach. But 'tis your Duty, my Dear, to warn the Girl against
her Ruin, and to instruct her how to make the most of her
Beauty. I'll go to her this moment, and sift her. In the mean
time, Wife, rip out the Coronets and Marks of these dozen of
Cambric Handkerchiefs, for I can dispose of them this Afternoon
to a Chap in the City.

Scene V

Mrs. Peachum.

Never was a Man more out of the way in an Argument than my Husband! Why must our Polly, forsooth, differ from her Sex, and love only her Husband? And why must Polly's Marriage, contrary to all Observation, make her the less followed by other Men? All Men are Thieves in Love, and like a Woman the better for being another's Property.

Air V. Of all the simple Things we do, &c.

A Maid is like the golden Oar,
Which hath Guineas intrinsical in't,
Whose Worth is never known, before
It is try'd and imprest in the Mint.

A Wife's like a Guinea in Gold,
Stampt with the Name of her Spouse;
Now here, now there; is bought, or is sold;
And is current in every House.

Scene VI

Mrs. Peachum, Filch.

Mrs. Peach. Come hither, Filch. I am as fond of this Child, as though my Mind misgave me he were my own. He hath as fine a Hand at picking a Pocket as a Woman, and is as nimble-finger'd as a Juggler. If an unlucky Session does not cut the Rope of thy Life, I pronounce, Boy, thou wilt be a great Man in History. Where was your Post last Night, my Boy?

Filch. I ply'd at the Opera, Madam; and considering 'twas neither dark nor rainy, so that there was no great Hurry in getting Chairs and Coaches, made a tolerable hand on't. These seven Handkerchiefs, Madam.

Mrs. Peach. Colour'd ones, I see. They are of sure Sale from our Warehouse at Redress among the Seamen.

Filch. And this Snuff-box.

Mrs. Peach. Set in Gold! A pretty Encouragement this to a young Beginner.

Filch. I had a fair tug at a charming Gold Watch. Pox take the Taylors for making the Fobs so deep and narrow! It stuck by the way, and I was forc'd to make my Escape under a Coach. Really, Madam, I fear I shall be cut off in the Flower of my

Youth, so that every now and then (since I was pumpt) I have thoughts of taking up and going to Sea.

Mrs. Peach. You should go to Hockley in the Hole, and to Marybone, Child, to learn Valour. These are the Schools that have bred so many brave Men. I thought, Boy, by this time, thou hadst lost Fear as well as Shame. Poor Lad! how little does he know as yet of the Old-Bailey! For the first Fact I'll insure thee from being hang'd; and going to Sea, Filch, will come time enough upon a Sentence of Transportation. But now, since you have nothing better to do, ev'n go to your Book, and learn your Catechism; for really a Man makes but an ill Figure in the Ordinary's Paper, who cannot give a satisfactory Answer to his Questions. But, hark you, my Lad. Don't tell me a Lye; for you know I hate a Lyar. Do you know of any thing that hath past between Captain Macheath and our Polly?

Filch. I beg you, Madam, don't ask me; for I must either tell a Lye to you or to Miss Polly; for I promis'd her I would not tell.

Mrs. Peach. But when the Honour of our Family is concern'd—

Filch. I shall lead a sad Life with Miss Polly, if ever she come to know that I told you. Besides, I would not willingly forfeit my own Honour by betraying any body.

Mrs. Peach. Yonder comes my Husband and Polly. Come, Filch, you shall go with me into my own Room, and tell me the whole Story. I'll give thee a most delicious Glass of a Cordial that I keep for my own drinking.

Scene VII

Peachum, Polly.

Polly. I know as well as any of the fine Ladies how to make the most of my self and of my Man too. A Woman knows how to be mercenary, though she hath never been in a Court or at an Assembly. We have it in our Natures, Papa. If I allow Captain Macheath some trifling Liberties, I have this Watch and other visible Marks of his Favour to show for it. A Girl who cannot grant some Things, and refuse what is most material, will make but a poor hand of her Beauty, and soon be thrown upon the Common.

Aɪʀ VI. What shall I do to show how much I love her, &c.

Virgins are like the fair Flower in its Lustre,
Which in the Garden enamels the Ground;
Near it the Bees in Play flutter and cluster,
And gaudy Butterflies frolick around.
But, when once pluck'd, 'tis no longer alluring,
To Covent-Garden 'tis sent, (as yet sweet,)
There fades, and shrinks, and grows past all enduring,
Rots, stinks, and dies, and is trod under feet.

Peach. You know, Polly, I am not against your toying and trifling with a Customer in the way of Business, or to get out a Secret, or so. But if I find out that you have play'd the fool and are married, you Jade you, I'll cut your Throat, Hussy. Now you know my Mind.

SCENE VIII

PEACHUM, POLLY, MRS. PEACHUM.

Aɪʀ. VII. Oh London is a fine Town

Mʀs. Peachum, *in a very great Passion.*

Our Polly is a sad Slut! nor heeds what we taught her.
I wonder any Man alive will ever rear a Daughter!
For she must have both Hoods and Gowns, and Hoops to swell
her Pride.
With Scarfs and Stays, and Gloves and Lace; and she will have
Men beside;
And when she's drest with Care and Cost, all-tempting, fine
and gay,
As Men should serve a Cowcumber, she flings herself away.
Our Polly is a sad Slut, &c.

You Baggage! you Hussy! you inconsiderate Jade! had you been hang'd, it would not have vex'd me, for that might have been your Misfortune; but to do such a mad thing by Choice! The Wench is married, Husband.

Peach. Married! The Captain is a bold man, and will risque any thing for Money; to be sure he believes her a Fortune. Do you think your Mother and I should have liv'd comfortably so long together, if ever we had been married? Baggage!

Mrs. Peach. I knew she was always a proud Slut; and now the Wench hath play'd the Fool and married, because forsooth she should do like the Gentry. Can you support the expence of a Husband, Hussy, in gaming, drinking and whoring? have you Money enough to carry on the daily Quarrels of Man and Wife about who shall squander most? There are not many Husbands and Wifes, who can bear the Charges of plaguing one another in a handsome way. If you must be married, could you introduce no-body into our Family but a Highwayman? Why, thou foolish Jade, thou wilt be as ill-us'd, and as much neglected, as if thou hadst married a Lord!

Peach. Let not your Anger, my Dear, break through the Rules of Decency, for the Captain looks upon himself in the Military Capacity, as a Gentleman by his Profession. Besides what he hath already, I know he is in a fair way of getting, or of dying; and both these ways, let me tell you, are most excellent Chances for a Wife. Tell me, Hussy, are you ruin'd or no?

Mrs. Peach. With Polly's Fortune, she might very well have gone off to a Person of Distinction. Yes, that you might, you pouting Slut!

Peach. What, is the Wench dumb? Speak, or I'll make you plead by squeezing out an Answer from you. Are you really bound Wife to him, or are you only upon liking?   [*Pinches her.*

Polly. Oh!   [*Screaming.*

Mrs. Peach. How the Mother is to be pitied who hath handsome Daughters! Locks, Bolts, Bars, and Lectures of Morality are nothing to them: They break through them all. They have as much Pleasure in cheating a Father and Mother, as in cheating at Cards.

Peach. Why, Polly, I shall soon know if you are married, by Macheath's keeping from our House.

AIR VIII.   Grim King of the Ghosts, &c.

POLLY. *Can Love be controul'd by Advice?*
Will Cupid our Mothers obey?
Though my Heart were as frozen as Ice,
  At his Flame 'twould have melted away.

When he kist me so closely he prest,
  'Twas so sweet that I must have comply'd:
So I thought it both safest and best
  To marry, for fear you should chide.

Mrs. Peach. Then all the Hopes of our Family are gone for ever and ever!

Peach. And Macheath may hang his Father and Mother-in-Law, in hope to get into their Daughter's Fortune.

Polly. I did not marry him (as 'tis the Fashion) cooly and deliberately for Honour or Money. But, I love him.

Mrs. Peach. Love him! worse and worse! I thought the Girl had been better bred. Oh Husband, Husband! her Folly makes me mad! my Head swims! I'm distracted! I can't support myself—Oh!   [*Faints.*

Peach. See, Wench, to what a Condition you have reduc'd your poor Mother! a Glass of Cordial, this instant. How the poor Woman takes it to Heart!

[POLLY *goes out, and returns with it.*

Ah, Hussy, now this is the only Comfort your Mother has left!

Polly. Give her another Glass, Sir; my Mama drinks double the Quantity whenever she is out of Order. This, you see, fetches her.

Mrs. Peach. The Girl shows such a Readiness, and so much Concern, that I could almost find in my Heart to forgive her.

AIR IX.   O Jenny, O Jenny, where hast thou been

O Polly, you might have toy'd and kist.
By keeping Men off, you keep them on.
POLLY. *But he so teaz'd me,*
         And he so pleas'd me,
What I did, you must have done.

Mrs. Peach. Not with a Highwayman.—You sorry Slut!

Peach. A Word with you, Wife. 'Tis no new thing for a Wench to take Man without consent of Parents. You know 'tis the Frailty of Woman, my Dear.

Mrs. Peach. Yes, indeed, the Sex is frail. But the first time a Woman is frail, she should be somewhat nice methinks, for then or never is the time to make her Fortune. After that, she hath nothing to do but to guard herself from being found out, and she may do what she pleases.

Peach. Make your self a little easy; I have a Thought shall soon set all Matters again to rights. Why so melancholy, Polly? since what is done cannot be undone, we must all endeavour to make the best of it.

Mrs. Peach. Well, Polly; as far as one Woman can forgive another, I forgive thee.—Your Father is too fond of you, Hussy.

Polly. Then all my Sorrows are at an end.

Mrs. Peach. A mighty likely Speech in troth, for a Wench who is just married!

AIR X. Thomas, I cannot, &c.

POLLY. *I, like a Ship in Storms, was tost;*
Yet afraid to put in to Land;
For seiz'd in the Port the Vessel's lost,
Whose Treasure is contreband.
  The Waves are laid,
  My Duty's paid.
O Joy beyond Expression!
  Thus, safe a-shore,
  I ask no more,
My All is in my Possession.

Peach. I hear Customers in t'other Room; Go, talk with 'em, Polly; but come to us again, as soon as they are gone.—But, heark ye, Child, if 'tis the Gentleman who was here Yesterday about the Repeating-Watch; say, you believe we can't get Intelligence of it, till to-morrow. For I lent it to Suky Straddle, to make a Figure with it to-night at a Tavern in Drury-Lane. If t'other Gentleman calls for the Silver-hilted Sword; you know Beetle-brow'd Jemmy hath it on, and he doth not come from Tunbridge till Tuesday Night; so that it cannot be had till then.

SCENE IX

PEACHUM, MRS. PEACHUM.

Peach. Dear Wife, be a little pacified. Don't let your Passion run away with your Senses. Polly, I grant you, hath done a rash thing.

Mrs. Peach. If she had had only an Intrigue with the Fellow, why the very best Families have excus'd and huddled up a Frailty of that sort. 'Tis Marriage, Husband, that makes it a blemish.

Peach. But Money, Wife, is the true Fuller's Earth for Reputations, there is not a Spot or a Stain but what it can take out. A rich Rogue now-a-days is fit Company for any Gentleman; and the World, my Dear, hath not such a Contempt for Roguery as you imagine. I tell you, Wife, I can make this Match turn to our Advantage.

Mrs. Peach. I am very sensible, Husband, that Captain Macheath is worth Money, but I am in doubt whether he hath not two or three Wives already, and then if he should dye in a Session or two, Polly's Dower would come into Dispute.

Peach. That, indeed, is a Point which ought to be consider'd.

AIR XI. A Soldier and a Sailor

A Fox may steal your Hens, Sir,
A Whore your Health and Pence, Sir,
Your Daughter rob your Chest, Sir,
Your Wife may steal your Rest, Sir,
  A Thief your Goods and Plate.
But this is all but picking;
With Rest, Pence, Chest and Chicken,
It ever was decreed, Sir,
If Lawyer's Hand is fee'd, Sir,
  He steals your whole Estate.

The Lawyers are bitter Enemies to those in our Way. They don't care that any Body should get a Clandestine Livelihood but themselves.

SCENE X

MRS. PEACHUM, PEACHUM, POLLY.

Polly. 'Twas only Nimming Ned. He brought in a Damask Window-Curtain, a Hoop-Petticoat, a Pair of Silver Candlesticks, a Perriwig, and one Silk Stocking, from the Fire that happen'd last Night.

Peach. There is not a Fellow that is cleverer in his way, and saves more Goods out of the Fire than Ned. But now, Polly, to your Affair; for Matters must not be left as they are. You are married then, it seems?

Polly. Yes, Sir.

Peach. And how do you propose to live, Child?

Polly. Like other Women, Sir, upon the Industry of my Husband.

Mrs. Peach. What, is the Wench turn'd Fool? A Highwayman's Wife, like a Soldier's, hath as little of his Pay, as of his Company.

Peach. And had not you the common Views of a Gentlewoman in your Marriage, Polly?

Polly. I don't know what you mean, Sir.

Peach. Of a Jointure, and of being a Widow.

Polly. But I love him, Sir: how then could I have Thoughts of parting with him?

Peach. Parting with him! Why, that is the whole Scheme and Intention of all Marriage Articles. The comfortable Estate of Widow-hood, is the only hope that keeps up a Wife's Spirits. Where is the Woman who would scruple to be a Wife, if she had it in her Power to be a widow whenever she pleas'd? If you have any Views of this sort, Polly, I shall think the Match not so very unreasonable.

Polly. How I dread to hear your Advice! Yet I must beg you to explain yourself.

Peach. Secure what he hath got, have him peach'd the next Sessions, and then at once you are made a rich Widow.

Polly. What, murder the Man I love! The Blood runs cold at my Heart with the very Thought of it.

Peach. Fye, Polly! What hath Murder to do in the Affair? Since the thing sooner or later must happen, I dare say, the Captain himself would like that we should get the Reward for his Death sooner than a Stranger. Why, Polly, the Captain knows, that as 'tis his Employment to rob, so 'tis ours to take Robbers; every Man in his Business. So that there is no Malice in the Case.

Mrs. Peach. Ay, Husband, now you have nick'd the Matter. To have him peach'd is the only thing could ever make me forgive her.

Air XII.   Now ponder well, ye Parents dear

> POLLY. *Oh, ponder well! be not severe;*
> *So save a wretched Wife!*
> *For on the Rope that hangs my Dear*
> *Depends poor Polly's Life.*

Mrs. Peach. But your Duty to your Parents, Hussy, obliges you to hang him. What would many a Wife give for such an Opportunity!

Polly. What is a Jointure, what is Widow-hood to me? I know my Heart. I cannot survive him.

Air XIII.   *Le printemps rappelle aux armes*

> *The Turtle thus with plaintive crying,*
> *Her Lover dying,*
> *The Turtle thus with plaintive crying,*
> *Laments her Dove.*
> *Down she drops quite spent with sighing,*
> *Pair'd in Death, as pair'd in Love.*

Thus, Sir, it will happen to your poor Polly.

Mrs. Peach. What, is the Fool in love in earnest then? I hate thee for being particular: Why, Wench, thou art a Shame to thy very Sex.

Polly. But hear me, Mother.—If you ever lov'd—

Mrs. Peach. Those cursed Playbooks she reads have been her Ruin. One Word more, Hussy, and I shall knock your Brains out, if you have any.

Peach. Keep out of the way, Polly, for fear of Mischief, and consider of what is propos'd to you.

Mrs. Peach. Away, Hussy. Hang your Husband, and be dutiful.

Scene XI

Mrs. Peachum, Peachum.

[Polly *listning.*

Mrs. Peach. The Thing, Husband, must and shall be done. For the sake of Intelligence we must take other Measures, and have him peach'd the next Session without her Consent. If she will not know her Duty, we know ours.

Peach. But really, my Dear, it grieves one's Heart to take off a great Man. When I consider his Personal Bravery, his fine Stratagem, how much we have already got by him, and how much more we may get, methinks I can't find in my Heart to have a Hand in his Death. I wish you could have made Polly undertake it.

Mrs. Peach. But in a Case of Necessity—our own Lives are in danger.

Peach. Then, indeed, we must comply with the Customs of the World, and make Gratitude give way to Interest.—He shall be taken off.

Mrs. Peach. I'll undertake to manage Polly.

Peach. And I'll prepare Matters for the Old-Baily.

Scene XII

Polly. Now I'm a Wretch, indeed.—Methinks I see him already in the Cart, sweeter and more lovely than the Nosegay in his Hand!—I hear the Crowd extolling his Resolution and Intrepidity!—What Vollies of Sighs are sent from the Windows of Holborn, that so comely a Youth should be brought to disgrace!—I see him at the Tree! The whole Circle are in Tears! —even Butchers weep!—Jack Ketch himself hesitates to perform his Duty, and would be glad to lose his Fee, by a Reprieve. What then will become of Polly!—As yet I may inform him of their Design, and aid him in his Escape.—It shall be so.—But then he flies, absents himself, and I bar my self from his dear, dear Conversation! That too will distract me.—If he keep out of the way, my Papa and Mama may in time relent, and we may be happy.—If he stays, he is hang'd, and then he is lost for ever!—He intended to lye conceal'd in my Room, 'till the Dusk of the Evening: If they are abroad, I'll this Instant let him out, lest some Accident should prevent him. [*Exit, and returns.*

SCENE XIII

POLLY, MACHEATH.

AIR XIV. Pretty Parrot, say—

MACH. *Pretty Polly, say,*
When I was away,
Did your Fancy never stray
To some newer Lover?
POLLY. *Without Disguise,*
Heaving Sighs,
Doating Eyes,
My constant Heart discover.
Fondly let me loll!
MACH. *O pretty, pretty Poll.*

Polly. And are *you* as fond as ever, my Dear?
Mach. Suspect my Honour, my Courage, suspect any thing but my Love.—May my Pistols miss Fire, and my Mare slip her Shoulder while I am pursu'd, if I ever forsake thee!
Polly. Nay, my Dear, I have no Reason to doubt you, for I find in the Romance you lent me, none of the great Heroes were ever false in Love.

AIR XV. Pray, Fair One, be kind—

MACH. *My Heart was so free,*
It rov'd like the Bee,
'Till Polly my Passion requited;
I sipt each Flower,
I chang'd ev'ry Hour,
But here ev'ry Flower is United.

Polly. Were you sentenc'd to Transportation, sure, my Dear, you could not leave me behind you—could you?
Mach. Is there any Power, any Force that could tear me from thee? You might sooner tear a Pension out of the Hands of a

Courtier, a Fee from a Lawyer, a pretty Woman from a Looking-glass, or any Woman from Quadrille.—But to tear me from **thee** is impossible!

AIR XVI. Over the Hills and far away

Were I laid on Greenland's Coast
And in my Arms embrac'd my Lass;
Warm amidst eternal Frost,
Too soon the Half Year's Night would pass.
POLLY. *Were I sold on Indian Soil,*
Soon as the burning Day was clos'd,
I could mock the sultry Toil,
When on my Charmer's Breast repos'd.
MACH. *And I would love you all the Day,*
POLLY. *Every Night would kiss and play,*
MACH. *If with me you'd fondly stray*
POLLY. *Over the Hills and far away.*

Polly. Yes, I would go with thee. But oh!—how shall I speak it? I must be torn from thee. We must part.

Mach. How! Part!

Polly. We must, we must.—My Papa and Mama are set against thy Life. They now, even now are in Search after thee. They are preparing Evidence against thee. Thy Life depends upon a Moment.

AIR XVII. Gin thou wert mine awn thing—

O what Pain it is to part!
Can I leave thee, can I leave thee?
O what Pain it is to part!
Can thy Polly ever leave thee?
But lest Death my Love should thwart,
And bring thee to the fatal Cart,
Thus I tear thee from my bleeding Heart!
Fly hence, and let me leave thee.

One Kiss and then—one Kiss—begone—farewell.

Mach. My Hand, my Heart, my Dear, is so rivited to thine, that I cannot unloose my Hold.

Polly. But my Papa may intercept thee, and then I should lose the very glimmering of Hope. A few Weeks, perhaps, may reconcile us all. Shall thy Polly hear from thee?

Mach. Must I then go?

Polly. And will not Absence change your Love?

Mach. If you doubt it, let me stay—and be hang'd.

Polly. O how I fear! how I tremble!—Go—but when Safety will give you leave, you will be sure to see me again; for 'till then Polly is wretched.

AIR XVIII. O the Broom, &c.

[Parting, and looking back at each other with fondness; he at one Door, she at the other.

MACH. *The Miser thus a Shilling sees,*
　　Which he's oblig'd to pay,
With Sighs resigns it by degrees,
　　And fears 'tis gone for aye.

POLLY. *The Boy, thus, when his Sparrow's flown,*
　　The Bird in Silence eyes;
But soon as out of Sight 'tis gone,
　　Whines, whimpers, sobs and cries.

ACT II

SCENE I.—*A Tavern near Newgate*

JEMMY TWITCHER, CROOK-FINGER'D JACK, WAT DREARY, ROBIN OF BAGSHOT, NIMMING NED, HENRY PADINGTON, MATT OF THE MINT, BEN BUDGE, *and the rest of the* GANG, *at the Table, with Wine, Brandy and Tobacco.*

Ben. But pr'ythee, Matt, what is become of thy Brother Tom? I have not seen him since my Return from Transportation.

Matt. Poor Brother Tom had an Accident this time Twelve-month, and so clever a made Fellow he was, that I could not save him from those fleaing Rascals the Surgeons; and now, poor Man, he is among the Otamys at Surgeon's Hall.

Ben. So it seems, his Time was come.

Jem. But the present Time is ours, and no Body alive hath more. Why are the Laws levell'd at us? are we more dishonest than the rest of Mankind? What we win, Gentlemen, is our own by the Law of Arms, and the Right of Conquest.

Crook. Where shall we find such another Set of practical Philosophers, who to a Man are above the Fear of Death?

Wat. Sound Men, and true!

Robin. Of try'd Courage, and indefatigable Industry!

Ned. Who is there here that would not dye for his Friend?

Harry. Who is there here that would betray him for his Interest?

Mat. Show me a Gang of Courtiers that can say as much.

Ben. We are for a just Partition of the World, for every Man hath a Right to enjoy Life.

Mat. We retrench the Superfluities of Mankind. The World is avaritious, and I hate Avarice. A covetous fellow, like a Jackdaw, steals what he was never made to enjoy, for the sake of hiding it. These are the Robbers of Mankind, for Money was made for the Free-hearted and Generous, and where is the injury of taking from another, what he hath not the Heart to make use of?

Jem. Our several Stations for the Day are fixt. Good luck attend us all. Fill the Glasses.

AIR I. Fill ev'ry Glass, &c.

MATT. *Fill ev'ry Glass, for Wine inspires us,*
   And fires us
With Courage, Love and Joy.
Women and Wine should Life employ.
Is there ought else on Earth desirous?
CHORUS. *Fill ev'ry Glass, &c.*

SCENE II

To them enter MACHEATH.

Mach. Gentlemen, well met. My Heart hath been with you this Hour; but an unexpected Affair hath detain'd me. No Ceremony, I beg you.

Matt. We were just breaking up to go upon Duty. Am I to have the Honour of taking the Air with you, Sir, this Evening upon the Heath? I drink a Dram now and then with the Stage-Coachmen in the way of Friendship and Intelligence; and I know that about this Time there will be Passengers upon the Western Road, who are worth speaking with.

Mach. I was to have been of that Party—but—

Matt. But what, Sir?

Mach. Is there any man who suspects my Courage?

Matt. We have all been witnesses of it.

Mach. My Honour and Truth to the Gang?

Matt. I'll be answerable for it.

Mach. In the Division of our Booty, have I ever shown the least Marks of Avarice or Injustice?

Matt. By these Questions something seems to have ruffled you. Are any of us suspected?

Mach. I have a fixt Confidence, Gentlemen, in you all, as Men of Honour, and as such I value and respect you. Peachum is a Man that is useful to us.

Matt. Is he about to play us any foul Play? I'll shoot him through the Head.

Mach. I beg you, Gentlemen, act with Conduct and Discretion. A Pistol is your last resort.

Matt. He knows nothing of this Meeting.

Mach. Business cannot go on without him. He is a Man who knows the World, and is a necessary Agent to us. We have had a slight Difference, and till it is accommodated I shall be oblig'd to keep out of his way. Any private Dispute of mine shall be of no ill consequence to my Friends. You must continue to act under his Direction, for the moment we break loose from him, our Gang is ruin'd.

Matt. As a Bawd to a Whore, I grant you, he is to us of great Convenience.

Mach. Make him believe I have quitted the Gang, which I can never do but with Life. At our private Quarters I will continue to meet you. A Week or so will probably reconcile us.

Matt. Your Instructions shall be observ'd. 'Tis now high time for us to repair to our several Duties; so till the Evening at our Quarters in Moor-fields we bid you farewell.

Mach. I shall wish my self with you. Success attend you.

[*Sits down melancholy at the Table.*

AIR II.   March in Rinaldo, with Drums and Trumpet

MATT. *Let us take the Road.*
Hark! I hear the sound of Coaches!
The hour of Attack approaches,
To your Arms, brave Boys, and load.
See the Ball I hold!
Let the Chymists toil like Asses,
Our fire their fire surpasses,
And turns all our Lead to Gold.

[*The* GANG, *rang'd in the Front of the Stage, load their Pistols, and stick them under their Girdles; then go off singing the first Part in Chorus.*

Scene III

Macheath, Drawer.

Mach. What a Fool is a fond Wench! Polly is most confound-edly bit.—I love the Sex. And a Man who loves Money, might as well be contented with one Guinea, as I with one Woman. The Town perhaps hath been as much oblig'd to me, for recruiting it with free-hearted Ladies, as to any Recruiting Officer in the Army. If it were not for us and the other Gentlemen of the Sword, Drury-Lane would be uninhabited.

Air III. Would you have a Young Virgin, &c.

If the Heart of a Man is deprest with Cares,
The Mist is dispell'd when a Woman appears;
Like the Notes of a Fiddle, she sweetly, sweetly
Raises the Spirits, and charms our Ears.
　Roses and Lillies her Cheeks disclose,
　But her ripe Lips are more sweet than those.
　　Press her,
　　Caress her
　　With Blisses,
　　Her Kisses
Dissolve us in Pleasure, and soft Repose.

I must have Women. There is nothing unbends the Mind like them. Money is not so strong a Cordial for the Time, Drawer.

Enter Drawer.

Is the Potter gone for all the Ladies, according to my directions?
Draw. I expect him back every Minute. But you know, Sir, you sent him as far as Hockey in the Hole, for three of the Ladies, for one in Vinegar Yard, and for the rest of them somewhere about Lewkner's Lane. Sure some of them are below, for I hear the Barr Bell. As they come I will show them up. Coming, coming.

Scene IV

Macheath, Mrs. Coaxer, Dolly Trull, Mrs. Vixen, Betty Doxy, Jenny Diver, Mrs. Slammekin, Suky Tawdry, *and* Molly Brazen.

Mach. Dear Mrs. Coaxer, you are welcome. You look charm-ingly to-day. I hope you don't want the Repairs of Quality, and lay on Paint.—Dolly Trull! kiss me, you Slut; are you as amor-ous as ever, Hussy? You are always so taken up with stealing

Hearts, that you don't allow your self Time to steal any thing else.
—Ah Dolly, thou wilt ever be a Coquette!—Mrs. Vixen, I'm
yours, I always lov'd a Woman of Wit and Spirit; they make
charming Mistresses, but plaguy Wives.—Betty Doxy! Come
hither, Hussy. Do you drink as hard as ever? You had better
stick to good Wholesome Beer; for in troth, Betty, Strong-Waters
will in time ruin your Constitution. You should leave those to
your Betters.—What! and my pretty Jenny Diver too! As prim
and demure as ever! There is not any Prude, though ever so
high bred, hath a more sanctify'd Look, with a more mischievous
Heart. Ah! thou art a dear artful Hypocrite.—Mrs. Slammekin!
as careless and genteel as ever! all you fine Ladies, who know
your own Beauty, affect an Undress.—But see, here's Suky
Tawdry come to contradict what I was saying. Every thing she
gets one way she lays out upon her Back. Why Suky, you must
keep at least a dozen Tallymen. Molly Brazen! [*She kisses him.*]
That's well done. I love a free-hearted Wench. Thou hast a most
agreeable Assurance, Girl, and art as willing as a Turtle.—But
hark! I hear musick. The Harper is at the Door. If Musick be
the Food of Love, play on. E'er you seat your selves, Ladies,
what think you of a Dance? Come in.

Enter HARPER.

Play the French Tune, that Mrs. Slammekin was so fond of.
    [*A Dance à la ronde in the French Manner; near the End
    of it this Song and Chorus.*

AIR IV. Cotillon

Youth's the Season made for Joys,
    Love is then our Duty,
She alone who that employs,
    Well deserves her Beauty.
        Let's be gay,
        While we may,
        Beauty's a Flower, despis'd in decay.
Youth's the Season, &c.

Let us drink and sport to-day,
    Ours is not to-morrow.
Love with Youth flies swift away,
    Age is nought but Sorrow.
        Dance and sing,
        Time's on the Wing,
Life never knows the return of Spring.
    CHORUS. *Let us drink, &c.*

Mach. Now, pray Ladies, take your Places. Here Fellow [*Pays the* HARPER.], Bid the Drawer bring us more Wine.

[*Exit* HARPER.

If any of the Ladies chuse Ginn, I hope they will be so free to call for it.

Jenny. You look as if you meant me. Wine is strong enough for me. Indeed, Sir, I never drink Strong-Waters, but when I have the Cholic.

Mach. Just the Excuse of the fine Ladies! Why, a Lady of Quality is never without the Cholic. I hope, Mrs. Coaxer, you have had good Success of late in your Visits among the Mercers.

Coax. We have so many Interlopers—Yet with Industry, one may still have a little Picking. I carried a silver flower'd Lutestring, and a Piece of black Padesoy to Mr. Peachum's Lock but last Week.

Vix. There's Molly Brazen hath the Ogle of a Rattle-Snake. She rivetted a Linnen-draper's Eye so fast upon her, that he was nick'd of three Pieces of Cambric before he could look off.

Braz. Oh dear Madam!—But sure nothing can come up to your handling of Laces! And then you have such a sweet deluding Tongue! To cheat a Man is nothing; but the Woman must have fine Parts indeed who cheats a Woman!

Vix. Lace, Madam, lyes in a small Compass, and is of easy Conveyance. But you are apt, Madam, to think too well of your Friends.

Coax. If any Woman hath more Art than another, to be sure, 'tis Jenny Diver. Though her Fellow be never so agreeable, she can pick his Pocket as cooly, as if Money were her only Pleasure. Now that is a Command of the Passions uncommon in a Woman!

Jenny. I never go to the Tavern with a Man, but in the View of Business. I have other Hours, and other sort of Men for my Pleasure. But had I your Address, Madam—

Mach. Have done with your Compliments, Ladies; and drink about: You are not so fond of me, Jenny, as you use to be.

Jenny. 'Tis not convenient, Sir, to show my Fondness among so many Rivals. 'Tis your own Choice, and not the warmth of my Inclination that will determine you.

AIR V. All in a misty Morning, &c.

Before the Barn-door crowing,
The Cock by Hens attended,
His Eyes around him throwing,
Stands for a while suspended.

Then One he singles from the Crew,
And cheers the happy Hen;
With how do you do, and how do you do,
And how do you do again.

Mach. Ah Jenny! thou art a dear Slut.

Trull. Pray, Madam, were you ever in keeping?

Tawd. I hope, Madam, I ha'n been so long upon the Town, but I have met with some good Fortune as well as my Neighbours.

Trull. Pardon me, Madam, I meant no harm by the Question; 'twas only in the way of Conversation.

Tawd. Indeed, Madam, if I had not been a Fool, I might have liv'd very handsomely with my last Friend. But upon his missing five Guineas, he turn'd me off. Now I never suspected he had counted them.

Slam. Who do you look upon, Madam, as your best sort of Keepers?

Trull. That, Madam, is thereafter as they be.

Slam. I, Madam, was once kept by a Jew; and bating their Religion, to Women they are a good sort of People.

Tawd. Now for my part, I own I like an old Fellow: for we always make them pay for what they can't do.

Vix. A spruce Prentice, let me tell you, Ladies, is no ill thing, they bleed freely. I have sent at least two or three dozen of them in my time to the Plantations.

Jen. But to be sure, Sir, with so much good Fortune as you have had upon the Road, you must be grown immensely rich.

Mach. The Road, indeed, hath done me justice, but the Gaming-Table hath been my ruin.

AIR VI. When once I lay with another Man's Wife, &c.

JEN. *The Gamesters and Lawyers are Jugglers alike,*
If they meddle your All is in danger.
Like Gypsies, if once they can finger a Souse,
Your Pockets they pick, and they pilfer your House,
And give your Estate to a Stranger.

These are the Tools of a Man of Honour.
Cards and Dice are only fit for cowardly
Cheats, who prey upon their Friends.
[*She takes up his Pistol.* TAWDRY *takes up the other.*

Tawd. This, Sir, is fitter for your Hand. Besides your Loss of Money, 'tis a Loss to the Ladies. Gaming takes you off from

Women. How fond could I be of you! but before Company, 'tis ill bred.

Mach. Wanton Hussies!

Jen. I must and will have a Kiss to give my Wine a zest.

　　[*They take him about the Neck, and make Signs to*
　　PEACHUM *and* CONSTABLES, *who rush in upon him.*

SCENE V

To them, PEACHUM *and* CONSTABLES.

Peach. I seize you, Sir, as my Prisoner.

Mach. Was this well done, Jenny?—Women are Decoy Ducks; who can trust them! Beasts, Jades, Jilts, Harpies, Furies, Whores!

Peach. Your Case, Mr. Macheath, is not particular. The greatest Heroes have been ruin'd by Women. But, to do them justice, I must own they are a pretty sort of Creatures, if we could trust them. You must now, Sir, take your leave of the Ladies, and if they have a Mind to make you a Visit, they will be sure to find you at home. The Gentleman, Ladies, lodges in Newgate. Constables, wait upon the Captain to his Lodgings.

AIR VII.　When first I laid Siege to my Chloris, &c.

　　MAC. *At the Tree I shall suffer with pleasure,*
　　At the Tree I shall suffer with pleasure,
　　　　Let me go where I will,
　　　　In all kinds of Ill,
　　I shall find no such Furies as these are.

Peach. Ladies, I'll take care the Reckoning shall be discharg'd.

　　[*Exit* MACHEATH, *guarded with* PEACHUM *and* CONSTABLES.

SCENE VI

The WOMEN *remain.*

Vix. Look ye, Mrs. Jenny, though Mr. Peachum may have made a private Bargain with you and Suky Tawdry for betraying the Captain, as we were all assisting, we ought all to share alike.

Coax. I think Mr. Peachum, after so long an acquaintance, might have trusted me as well as Jenny Diver.

Slam. I am sure at least three Men of his hanging, and in a Year's time too (if he did me justice) should be set down to my account.

Trull. Mrs. Slammekin, that is not fair. For you know one of them was taken in Bed with me.

Jenny. As far as a Bowl of Punch or a Treat, I believe Mrs. Suky will join with me.—As for any thing else, Ladies, you cannot in conscience expect it.

Slam. Dear Madam—

Trull. I would not for the World—

Slam. 'Tis impossible for me—

Trull. As I hope to be sav'd, Madam—

Slam. Nay, then I must stay here all Night—

Trull. Since you command me.

[*Exeunt with great Ceremony.*

SCENE VII.—*Newgate*

LOCKIT, TURNKEYS, MACHEATH, CONSTABLES.

Lock. Noble Captain, you are welcome. You have not been a Lodger of mine this Year and half. You know the custom, Sir. Garnish, Captain, Garnish. Hand me down those Fetters there.

Mach. Those, Mr. Lockit, seem to be the heaviest of the whole sett. With your leave, I should like the further pair better.

Lock. Look ye, Captain, we know what is fittest for our Prisoners. When a Gentleman uses me with Civility, I always do the best I can to please him.—Hand them down I say.—We have them of all Prices, from one Guinea to ten, and 'tis fitting every Gentleman should please himself.

Mach. I understand you, Sir. [*Gives Money.*] The Fees here are so many, and so exorbitant, that few Fortunes can bear the Expence of getting off handsomly, or of dying like a Gentleman.

Lock. Those, I see, will fit the Captain better.—Take down the further Pair. Do but examine them, Sir.—Never was better work.—How genteely they are made!—They will fit as easy as a Glove, and the nicest Man in England might not be asham'd to wear them. [*He puts on the Chains.*] If I had the best Gentleman in the Land in my Custody I could not equip him more handsomly. And so, Sir—I now leave you to your private Meditations.

SCENE VIII

MACHEATH.

AIR VIII. Courtiers, Courtiers think it no harm, &c.

> *Man may escape from Rope and Gun*
> *Nay, some have out-liv'd the Doctor's Pill;*
> *Who takes a Woman must be undone,*
> *   That Basilisk is sure to kill.*

The Fly that sips Treacle is lost in the Sweets,
So he that tastes Woman, Woman, Woman,
He that tastes Woman, Ruin meets.

To what a woful plight have I brought my self! Here must I (all day long, 'till I am hang'd) be confin'd to hear the Reproaches of a Wench who lays her Ruin at my Door.—I am in the Custody of her Father, and to be sure if he knows of the matter, I shall have a fine time on't betwixt this and my Execution.—But I promis'd the Wench Marriage.—What signifies a Promise to a Woman? Does not Man in Marriage itself promise a hundred things that he never means to perform? Do all we can, Women will believe us; for they look upon a Promise as an Excuse for following their own Inclinations.—But here comes Lucy, and I cannot get from her.—Wou'd I were deaf!

SCENE IX

MACHEATH, LUCY.

Lucy. You base Man you,—how can you look me in the Face after what hath past between us?—See here, perfidious Wretch, how I am forc'd to bear about the load of Infamy you have laid upon me.—O Macheath! thou hast robb'd me of my Quiet—to see thee tortur'd would give me pleasure.

AIR IX. A lovely Lass to a Friar came, &c.

Thus when a good Huswife sees a Rat
In her Trap in the Morning taken,
With pleasure her Heart goes pit a pat,
In Revenge for her loss of Bacon.
Then she throws him
To the Dog or Cat,
To be worried, crush'd and shaken.

Mac. Have you no Bowels, no Tenderness, my dear Lucy, to see a Husband in these Circumstances?

Lucy. A Husband!

Mac. In ev'ry respect but the Form, and that, my Dear, may be said over us at any time.—Friends should not insist upon Ceremonies. From a Man of honour, his Word is as good as his Bond.

Lucy. 'Tis the pleasure of all you fine Men to insult the Women you have ruin'd.

AIR X. 'Twas when the Sea was roaring, &c.

> *How cruel are the Traytors,*
> *Who lye and swear in jest,*
> *To cheat unguarded Creatures*
> *Of Virtue, Fame, and Rest!*
> *Whoever steals a Shilling,*
> *Through shame the Guilt conceals:*
> *In Love the perjur'd Villain*
> *With Boasts the Theft reveals.*

Mac. The very first opportunity, my Dear, (have but patience) you shall be my Wife in whatever manner you please.

Lucy. Insinuating Monster! And so you think I know nothing of the Affair of Miss Polly Peachum.—I could tear thy Eyes out!

Mac. Sure Lucy, you can't be such a Fool as to be jealous of Polly!

Lucy. Are you not married to her, you Brute, you?

Mac. Married! Very good. The Wench gives it out only to vex thee, and to ruin me in thy good Opinion. 'Tis true, I go to the House; I chat with the Girl, I kiss her, I say a thousand things to her (as all Gentlemen do) that mean nothing, to divert my self; and now the silly Jade hath set it about that I am married to her, to let me know what she would be at. Indeed, my dear Lucy, these violent Passions may be of ill consequence to a Woman in your condition.

Lucy. Come, come, Captain, for all your Assurance, you know that Miss Polly hath put it out of your power to do me the Justice you promis'd me.

Mac. A jealous Woman believes ev'ry thing her Passion suggests. To convince you of my Sincerity, if we can find the Ordinary, I shall have no scruples of making you my Wife; and I know the consequence of having two at a time.

Lucy. That you are only to be hang'd, and so get rid of them both.

Mac. I am ready, my dear Lucy, to give you satisfaction—if you think there is any in Marriage.—What can a Man of Honour say more?

Lucy. So then it seems, you are not married to Miss Polly.

Mac. You know, Lucy, the Girl is prodigiously conceited. No Man can say a civil thing to her, but (like other fine Ladies) her Vanity makes her think he's her own for ever and ever.

AIR XI. The Sun had loos'd his weary Teams, &c.

> *The first time at the Looking-glass*
> *The Mother sets her Daughter,*
> *The Image strikes the smiling Lass*
> *With Self-love ever after.*
> *Each time she looks, she, fonder grown,*
> *Thinks ev'ry Charm grows stronger.*
> *But alas, vain Maid, all Eyes but your own*
> *Can see you are not younger.*

When Women consider their own Beauties, they are all alike unreasonable in their demands; for they expect their Lovers should like them as long as they like themselves.

Lucy. Yonder is my Father—perhaps this way we may light upon the Ordinary, who shall try if you will be as good as your Word.—For I long to be made an honest Woman.

SCENE X

PEACHUM, LOCKIT *with an Account-Book.*

Lock. In this last Affair, Brother Peachum, we are agreed. You have consented to go halves in Macheath.

Peach. We shall never fall out about an Execution.—But as to that Article, pray how stands our last Year's account?

Lock. If you will run your Eye over it, you'll find 'tis fair and clearly stated.

Peach. This long Arrear of the Government is very hard upon us! Can it be expected that we should hang our Acquaintance for nothing, when our Betters will hardly save theirs without being paid for it? Unless the People in employment pay better, I promise them for the future, I shall let other Rogues live besides their own.

Lock. Perhaps, Brother, they are afraid these matters may be carried too far. We are treated too by them with Contempt, as if our Profession were not reputable.

Peach. In one respect indeed, our Employment may be reckon'd dishonest, because, like Great Statesmen, we encourage those who betray their Friends.

Lock. Such Language, Brother, any where else, might turn to your prejudice. Learn to be more guarded, I beg you.

AIR XII. How happy are we, &c.

> *When you censure the Age,*
> *Be cautious and sage.*

Lest the Courtiers offended should be:
If you mention Vice or Bribe,
'Tis so pat to all the Tribe;
Each crys—That was levell'd at me.

Peach. Here's poor Ned Clincher's Name, I see. Sure, Brother Lockit, there was a little unfair proceeding in Ned's case: for he told me in the Condemn'd Hold, that for Value receiv'd, you had promis'd him a Session or two longer without Molestation.

Lock. Mr. Peachum—This is the first time my Honour was ever call'd in Question.

Peach. Business is at an end—if once we act dishonourably.

Lock. Who accuses me?

Peach. You are warm, Brother.

Lock. He that attacks my Honour, attacks my Livelyhood.—And this Usage—Sir—is not to be born.

Peach. Since you provoke me to speak—I must tell you too, that Mrs. Coaxer charges you with defrauding her of her Information-Money, for the apprehending of curl-pated Hugh. Indeed, indeed, Brother, we must punctually pay our Spies, or we shall have no Information.

Lock. Is this Language to me, Sirrah—who have sav'd you from the Gallows, Sirrah!   [*Collaring each other.*

Peach. If I am hang'd, it shall be for ridding the World of an arrant Rascal.

Lock. This Hand shall do the office of the Halter you deserve, and throttle you—you Dog!—

Peach. Brother, Brother—We are both in the Wrong—We shall be both Losers in the Dispute—for you know we have it in our Power to hang each other. You should not be so passionate.

Lock. Nor you so provoking.

Peach. 'Tis our mutual Interest; 'tis for the Interest of the World we should agree. If I said any thing, Brother, to the Prejudice of your Character, I ask pardon.

Lock. Brother Peachum—I can forgive as well as resent.—Give me your Hand. Suspicion does not become a Friend.

Peach. I only meant to give you occasion to justifie yourself: But I must now step home, for I expect the Gentleman about this Snuff-box, that Filch nimm'd two Nights ago in the Park. I appointed him at this hour.

Scene XI

Lockit, Lucy.

Lock. Whence come you, Hussy?

Lucy. My Tears might answer that Question.

Lock. You have then been whimpering and fondling, like a Spaniel, over the Fellow that hath abus'd you.

Lucy. One can't help Love; one can't cure it. 'Tis not in my Power to obey you, and hate him.

Lock. Learn to bear your Husband's Death like a reasonable Woman. 'Tis not the fashion, now-a-days, so much as to affect Sorrow upon these Occasions. No Woman would ever marry, if she had not the Chance of Mortality for a Release. Act like a Woman of Spirit, Hussy, and thank your Father for what he is doing.

Air XIII. Of a noble Race was Shenkin

Lucy. Is then his Fate decreed, Sir?
Such a Man can I think of quitting?
When first we met, so moves me yet,
O see how my Heart is splitting!

Lock. Look ye, Lucy—There is no saving him.—So, I think you must ev'n do like other Widows—Buy your self Weeds, and be cheerful.

Air XIV

You'll think e'er many Days ensue
This Sentence not severe;
I hang your Husband, Child, 'tis true,
But with him hang your Care.
Twang dang dillo dee.

Like a good Wife, go moan over your dying Husband. That, Child, is your Duty—Consider, Girl, you can't have the Man and the Money too—so make yourself as easy as you can, by getting all you can from him.

Scene XII

Lucy, Macheath.

Lucy. Though the Ordinary was out of the way to-day I hope, my Dear, you will, upon the first opportunity, quiet my Scruples—Oh Sir!—my Father's hard Heart is not to be soften'd, and I am in the utmost Despair.

Mac. But if I could raise a small Sum—Would not twenty Guineas, think you, move him?—Of all the Arguments in the way of Business, the Perquisite is the most prevailing.—Your Father's Perquisites for the Escape of Prisoners must amount to a considerable Sum in the Year. Money well tim'd, and properly apply'd, will do any thing.

Air XV. London Ladies

If you at an Office solicit your Due,
  And would not have Matters neglected;
You must quicken the Clerk with the perquisite too,
  To do what his Duty directed.
Or would you the Frowns of a Lady prevent,
  She too has this palpable Failing
The Perquisite softens her into Consent;
  That Reason with all is prevailing.

Lucy. What Love or Money can do shall be done: for all my Comfort depends upon your Safety.

Scene XIII

Lucy, Macheath, Polly.

Polly. Where is my dear Husband?—Was a Rope ever intended for this Neck!—O let me throw my Arms about it, and throttle thee with Love!—Why dost thou turn away from me?—'Tis thy Polly—'Tis thy Wife.

Mac. Was ever such an unfortunate Rascal as I am!

Lucy. Was there ever such another Villain!

Polly. O Macheath! was it for this we parted? Taken! Imprison'd! Try'd! Hang'd!—cruel Reflection! I'll stay with thee 'till Death—no Force shall tear thy dear Wife from thee now.— What means my Love?—Not one kind Word! not one kind Look! think what thy Polly suffers to see thee in this Condition.

Air XVI. All in the Downs, &c.

Thus when the Swallow, seeking Prey,
  Within the Sash is closely pent,
His Comfort, with bemoaning Lay,
  Without sits pining for th' Event.
Her chatt'ring Lovers all around her skim;
She heeds them not (poor Bird!), her Soul's with him.

Mac. I must disown her. [*Aside.*] The Wench is distracted.

Lucy. Am I then bilk'd of my Virtue? Can I have no Reparation? Sure Men were born to lye, and Women to believe them! O Villain! Villain!

Polly. Am I not thy Wife?—Thy Neglect of me, thy Aversion to me too severely proves it.—Look on me.—Tell me, am I not thy Wife?

Lucy. Perfidious Wretch!

Polly. Barbarous Husband!

Lucy. Hadst thou been hang'd five Months ago, I had been happy.

Polly. And I too—If you had been kind to me 'till Death, it would not have vex'd me. And that's no very unreasonable Request, (though from a Wife) to a Man who hath not above seven or eight Days to live.

Lucy. Art thou then married to another? Hast thou two Wives, Monster?

Mac. If Women's Tongues can cease for an Answer—hear me.

Lucy. I won't.—Flesh and Blood can't bear my Usage.

Polly. Shall I not claim my own? Justice bids me speak.

Aɪʀ XVII. Have you heard of a frolicksome Ditty, &c.

> Mac. *How happy could I be with either,*
> *Were t'other dear Charmer away!*
> *But while you thus teaze me together,*
> *To neither a Word will I say;*
> > *But tol de rol, &c.*

Polly. Sure, my Dear, there ought to be some Preference shown to a Wife! At least she may claim the Appearance of it. He must be distracted with his Misfortunes, or he could not use me thus!

Lucy. O Villain, Villain! thou hast deceiv'd me—I could even inform against thee with Pleasure. Not a Prude wishes more heartily to have Facts against her intimate Acquaintance, than I now wish to have Facts against thee. I would have her Satisfaction, and they should all out.

Aɪʀ XVIII. Irish Trot

Polly. *I'm bubbled.*
Lucy. . . . *I'm bubbled.*
Polly. *Oh how I am troubled!*
Lucy. *Bambouzled, and bit!*
Polly. . . . *My Distresses are doubled.*

LUCY. *When you come to the Tree, should the Hangman refuse,*
These Fingers, with Pleasure, could fasten the Noose.

POLLY. *I'm bubbled, &c.*

Mac. Be pacified, my dear Lucy—This is all a Fetch of Polly's,
to make me desperate with you in case I get off. If I am hang'd, she
would fain have the Credit of being thought my Widow—Really,
Polly, this is no time for a Dispute of this sort; for whenever you
are talking of Marriage, I am thinking of Hanging.

Polly. And hast thou the Heart to persist in disowning me?

Mac. And hast thou the Heart to persist in persuading me that
I am married? Why Polly, dost thou seek to aggravate my Misfortunes?

Lucy. Really, Miss Peachum, you but expose yourself. Besides,
'tis barbarous in you to worry a Gentleman in his Circumstances.

AIR XIX

POLLY. *Cease your Funning;*
Force or Cunning
Never shall my Heart trapan.
All these Sallies
Are but Malice
To seduce my constant Man.
'Tis most certain,
By their flirting
Women oft' have Envy shown;
Pleas'd, to ruin
Others wooing;
Never happy in their own!

Polly. Decency, Madam, methinks might teach you to behave
yourself with some Reserve with the Husband, while his Wife is
present.

Mac. But seriously, Polly, this is carrying the Joke a little too
far.

Lucy. If you are determin'd, Madam, to raise a Disturbance in
the Prison, I shall be oblig'd to send for the Turnkey to show you
the Door. I am sorry, Madam, you force me to be so ill-bred.

Polly. Give me leave to tell you, Madam: These forward Airs
don't become you in the least, Madam. And my Duty, Madam,
obliges me to stay with my Husband, Madam.

AIR XX.   Good-morrow, Gossip Joan

LUCY. *Why how now, Madam Flirt?*
If you thus must chatter;

And are for flinging Dirt,
Let's try for best can spatter;
    Madam Flirt!
POLLY. *Why how now, saucy Jade;*
Sure the Wench is Tipsy!
How can you see me made   [*To him.*
The Scoff of such a Gipsy?
    Saucy Jade!   [*To her.*

SCENE XIV

LUCY, MACHEATH, POLLY, PEACHUM.

Peach. Where's my Wench? Ah Hussy! Hussy!—Come you home, you Slut; and when your Fellow is hang'd, hang yourself, to make your Family some amends.

Polly. Dear, dear Father, do not tear me from him—I must speak; I have more to say to him—Oh! twist thy Fetters about me, that he may not haul me from thee!

Peach. Sure all Women are alike! If ever they commit the Folly, they are sure to commit another by exposing themselves—Away—Not a Word more—You are my Prisoner now, Hussy.

AIR XXI. Irish Howl

POLLY. *No Power on Earth can e'er divide,*
The Knot that Sacred Love hath ty'd.
When Parents draw against our Mind,
The True-love's Knot they faster bind.
Oh, oh ray, oh Amborah—oh, oh, &c.
    [*Holding* MACHEATH, PEACHUM *pulling her.*

SCENE XV

LUCY, MACHEATH.

Mac. I am naturally compassionate, Wife; so that I could not use the Wench as she deserv'd; which made you at first suspect there was something in what she said.

Lucy. Indeed, my Dear; I was strangely puzzled.

Mac. If that had been the Case, her Father would never have brought me into this Circumstance—No, Lucy,—I had rather dye than be false to thee.

Lucy. How happy am I, if you say this from your Heart! For I love thee so, that I could sooner bear to see thee hang'd than in the Arms of another.

Mac. But couldst thou bear to see me hang'd?

Lucy. O Macheath, I can never live to see that Day.

Mac. You see, Lucy, in the Account of Love you are in my debt, and you must now be convinc'd that I rather chuse to die than be another's.—Make me, if possible, love thee more, and let me owe my Life to thee—If you refuse to assist me, Peachum and your Father will immediately put me beyond all means of Escape.

Lucy. My Father, I know, hath been drinking hard with the Prisoners: and I fancy he is now taking his Nap in his own Room —if I can procure the Keys, shall I go off with thee, my Dear?

Mac. If we are together, 'twill be impossible to lye conceal'd. As soon as the Search begins to be a little cool, I will send to thee— 'Till then my Heart is thy Prisoner.

Lucy. Come then, my dear Husband—owe thy Life to me—and though you love me not—be grateful—But that Polly runs in my Head strangely.

Mac. A Moment of time may make us unhappy for-ever.

AIR XXII. The Lass of Patie's Mill, &c.

> LUCY. *I like the Fox shall grieve,*
> *Whose Mate hath left her side,*
> *Whom Hounds, from Morn to Eve,*
> *Chase o'er the Country wide.*
>
> *Where can my Lover hide?*
> *Where cheat the weary Pack?*
> *If Love be not his Guide,*
> *He never will come back!*

ACT III

SCENE I.—*Newgate*

LOCKIT, LUCY.

Lock. To be sure, Wench, you must have been aiding and abetting to help him to this Escape.

Lucy. Sir, here hath been Peachum and his Daughter Polly, and to be sure they know the Ways of Newgate as well as if they had been born and bred in the Place all their Lives. Why must all your Suspicion light upon me?

Lock. Lucy, Lucy, I will have none of these shuffling Answers.

Lucy. Well then—If I know any Thing of him I wish I may be burnt!

Lock. Keep your Temper, Lucy, or I shall pronounce you guilty.

Lucy. Keep yours, Sir,—I do wish I may be burnt. I do—And what can I say more to convince you?

Lock. Did he tip handsomely?—How much did he come down with? Come Hussy, don't cheat your Father; and I shall not be angry with you—Perhaps, you have made a better Bargain with him than I could have done—How much, my good Girl?

Lucy. You know, Sir, I am fond of him, and would have given Money to have kept him with me.

Lock. Ah Lucy! thy Education might have put thee more upon thy Guard; for a Girl in the Bar of an Alehouse is always besieg'd.

Lucy. Dear Sir, mention not my Education—for 'twas to that I owe my Ruin.

Air I. If Love's a sweet Passion, &c.

When young at the Bar you first taught me to score,
And bid me be free of my Lips, and no more;
I was kiss'd by the Parson, the Squire, and the Sot.
When the Guest was departed, the Kiss was forgot.
But his Kiss was so sweet, and so closely he prest,
That I languish'd and pin'd till I granted the rest.

If you can forgive me, Sir, I will make a fair Confession, for to be sure he hath been a most barbarous Villain to me.

Lock. And so you have let him escape, Hussy—Have you?

Lucy. When a Woman loves, a kind Look, a tender Word can persuade her to any thing—And I could ask no other Bribe.

Lock. Thou wilt always be a vulgar Slut, Lucy.—If you would not be look'd upon as a Fool, you should never do any thing but upon the Foot of Interest. Those that act otherwise are their own Bubbles.

Lucy. But Love, Sir, is a Misfortune that may happen to the most discreet Woman, and in Love we are all Fools alike.—Notwithstanding all he swore, I am now fully convinc'd that Polly Peachum is actually his Wife.—Did I let him escape, (Fool that I was!) to go to her?—Polly will wheedle herself into his Money, and then Peachum will hang him, and cheat us both.

Lock. So I am to be ruin'd, because forsooth, you must be in Love!—a very pretty Excuse!

Lucy. I could murder that impudent happy Strumpet:—I gave him his Life, and that Creature enjoys the Sweets of it.—Ungrateful Macheath!

Air II. South-Sea Ballad

My Love is all Madness and Folly,
Alone I lye,
Toss, tumble, and cry,

> *What a happy Creature is Polly!*
> *Was e'er such a Wretch as I!*
> *With Rage I redden like Scarlet,*
> *That my dear inconstant Varlet,*
> >   *Stark blind to my Charms,*
> >   *Is lost in the Arms*
> *Of that Jilt, that inveigling Harlot!*
> >   *Stark blind to my Charms,*
> >   *Is lost in the Arms*
> *Of that Jilt, that inveigling Harlot!*
> *This, this my Resentment alarms.*

Lock. And so, after all this Mischief, I must stay here to be entertain'd with your catterwauling, Mistress Puss!—Out of my sight, wanton Strumpet! you shall fast and fortify yourself into Reason, with now and then a little handsome Discipline to bring you to your Senses.—Go.

SCENE II

LOCKIT.

Peachum then intends to outwit me in this Affair; but I'll be even with him—The Dog is leaky in his Liquor, so I'll ply him that way, get the Secret from him, and turn this Affair to my own Advantage.—Lions, Wolves, and Vulturs don't live together in Herds, Droves or Flocks.—Of all Animals of Prey, Man is the only sociable one. Every one of us preys upon his Neighbour, and yet we herd together.—Peachum is my Companion, my Friend—According to the Customs of the World, indeed, he may quote thousands of Precedents for cheating me—And shall not I make use of the Privilege of Friendship to make him a Return?

AIR III. Packington's Pound

> *Thus Gamesters united in Friendship are found,*
> *Though they know that their Industry all is a Cheat;*
> *They flock to their Prey at the Dice-Box's Sound,*
> *And join to promote one another's Deceit.*
> >   *But if by mishap*
> >   *They fail of a Chap,*
> *To keep in their Hands, they each other entrap.*
> *Like Pikes, lank with Hunger, who miss of their Ends,*
> *They bite their Companions, and prey on their Friends.*

Now, Peachum, you and I, like honest Tradesmen, are to have a fair Tryal which of us two can over-reach the other.—Lucy.

Enter Lucy.

Are there any of Peachum's People now in the House?

Lucy. Filch, Sir, is drinking a Quartern of Strong-Waters in the next Room with Black Moll.

Lock. Bid him come to me.

Scene III

Lockit, Filch.

Lock. Why, Boy, thou lookest as if thou wert half starv'd; like a shotten Herring.

Filch. One had need have the Constitution of a Horse to go through the Business.—Since the favourite Child-getter was disabled by a Mis-hap, I have pick'd up a little Money by helping the Ladies to a Pregnancy against their being call'd down to Sentence.—But if a Man cannot get an honest Livelyhood any easier way, I am sure, 'tis what I can't undertake for another Session.

Lock. Truly, if that great Man should tip off, 'twould be an irreparable Loss. The Vigour and Prowess of a Knight Errant never sav'd half the Ladies in Distress that he hath done.—But, Boy, can'st thou tell me where thy Master is to be found?

Filch. At his [1] Lock, Sir, at the Crooked Billet.

Lock. Very well.—I have nothing more with you. [*Exit* Filch. I'll go to him there, for I have many important Affairs to settle with him; and in the way of those Transactions, I'll artfully get into his Secret.—So that Macheath shall not remain a Day longer out of my Clutches.

Scene IV.—*A Gaming-House*

Macheath *in a fine tarnish'd Coat,* Ben Budge, Matt of the Mint.

Mac. I am sorry, Gentlemen, the Road was so barren of Money. When my Friends are in Difficulties, I am always glad that my Fortune can be serviceable to them. [*Gives them Money.*] You see, Gentlemen, I am not a meer Court Friend, who professes every thing and will do nothing.

---

[1] A Cant Word, signifying a Warehouse where stolen Goods are deposited.

AIR IV. Lillibullero

The Modes of the Court so common are grown,
  That a true Friend can hardly be met;
Friendship for Interest is but a Loan,
  Which they let out for what they can get.
    'Tis true, you find
    Some Friends so kind,
Who will give you good Counsel themselves to defend.
    In sorrowful Ditty,
    They promise, they pity,
But shift you for Money, from Friend to Friend.

But we, Gentlemen, have still Honour enough to break through the Corruptions of the World.—And while I can serve you, you may command me.

Ben. It grieves my Heart that so generous a Man should be involv'd in such Difficulties, as oblige him to live with such ill Company, and herd with Gamesters.

Matt. See the Partiality of Mankind!—One Man may steal a Horse, better than another look over a Hedge—Of all Mechanics, of all servile Handy-crafts-men, a Gamester is the vilest. But yet, as many of the Quality are of the Profession, he is admitted amongst the politest Company. I wonder we are not more respected.

Mach. There will be deep Play to-night at Marybone, and consequently Money may be pick'd up upon the Road. Meet me there, and I'll give you the Hint who is worth Setting.

Matt. The Fellow with a brown Coat with a narrow Gold Binding, I am told, is never without Money.

Mach. What do you mean, Matt?—Sure you will not think of meddling with him!—He's a good honest kind of a Fellow, and one of us.

Ben. To be sure, Sir, we will put our selves under your Direction.

Mach. Have an Eye upon the Money-Lenders.—A Rouleau, or two, would prove a pretty sort of an Expedition. I hate Extortion.

Matt. Those Rouleaus are very pretty Things.—I hate your Bank Bills.—There is such a Hazard in putting them off.

Mach. There is a certain Man of Distinction, who in his Time hath nick'd me out of a great deal of the Ready. He is in my Cash, Ben;—I'll point him out to you this Evening, and you shall draw upon him for the Debt.—The Company are met; I hear the Dice-box in the other Room. So, Gentlemen, your Servant. You'll meet me at Marybone.

SCENE V.—PEACHUM'S *Lock*

A Table with Wine, Brandy, Pipes and Tobacco.

PEACHUM, LOCKIT.

Lock. The Coronation Account, Brother Peachum, is of so intricate a Nature, that I believe it will never be settled.

Peach. It consists indeed of a great Variety of Articles.—It was worth to our People, in Fees of different Kinds, above ten Instalments.—This is part of the Account, Brother, that lies open before us.

Lock. A Lady's Tail of rich Brocade—that, I see, is dispos'd of.

Peach. To Mrs. Diana Trapes, the Tally-woman, and she will make a good Hand on't in Shoes and Slippers, to trick out young Ladies, upon their going into Keeping.—

Lock. But I don't see any Article of the Jewels.

Peach. Those are so well known, that they must be sent abroad—You'll find them enter'd under the Article of Exportation.—As for the Snuff-Boxes, Watches, Swords, &c.—I thought it best to enter them under their several Heads.

Lock. Seven and twenty Women's Pockets compleat; with the several things therein contain'd; all Seal'd, Number'd, and enter'd.

Peach. But, Brother, it is impossible for us now to enter upon this Affair.—We should have the whole Day before us.—Besides, the Account of the last Half Year's Plate is in a Book by it self, which lies at the other Office.

Lock. Bring us then more Liquor.—To-day shall be for Pleasure—To-morrow for Business.—Ah Brother, those Daughters of ours are two flippery Hussies—Keep a watchful Eye upon Polly, and Macheath in a Day or two shall be our own again.

AIR V. Down in the North Country, &c.

LOCK. *What Gudgeons are we Men!*
   Ev'ry Woman's easy Prey.
Though we have felt the Hook, agen
   We bite and they betray.
The Bird that hath been trapt,
   When he hears his calling Mate,
To her he flies, again he's clapt
   Within the wiry Grate.

Peach. But what signifies catching the Bird, if your Daughter Lucy will set open the Door of the Cage?

Lock. If Men were answerable for the Follies and Frailties of their Wives and Daughters, no Friends could keep a good Correspondence together for two Days.—This is unkind of you, Brother; for among good Friends, what they say or do goes for nothing.

Enter a SERVANT.

Serv. Sir, here's Mrs. Diana Trapes wants to speak with you.
Peach. Shall we admit her, Brother Lockit?
Lock. By all means—She's a good Customer, and a fine-spoken Woman—And a Woman who drinks and talks so freely, will enliven the Conversation.
Peach. Desire her to walk in.   [*Exit* SERVANT.

SCENE VI

PEACHUM, LOCKIT, MRS. TRAPES.

Peach. Dear Mrs. Dye, your Servant—One may know by your Kiss, that your Ginn is excellent.
Trapes. I was always very curious in my Liquors.
Lock. There is no perfum'd Breath like it—I have been long acquainted with the Flavour of those Lips—Han't I, Mrs. Dye?
Trapes. Fill it up.—I take as large Draughts of Liquor, as I did of Love.—I hate a Flincher in either.

AIR VI. A Shepherd kept Sheep, &c.

In the Days of my Youth I could bill like a Dove, fa, la, la, &c.
Like a Sparrow at all times was ready for Love, fa, la, la &c.
The Life of all Mortals in Kissing should pass,
Lip to Lip while we're young—then the Lip to the Glass, fa, &c.

But now, Mr. Peachum, to our Business.—If you have Blacks of any kind, brought in of late, Mantoes—Velvet Scarfs—Petticoats—Let it be what it will—I am your Chap—for all my Ladies are very fond of Mourning.
Peach. Why, look ye, Mrs. Dye—you deal so hard with us, that we can afford to give the Gentlemen, who venture their Lives for the Goods, little or nothing.
Trapes. The hard Times oblige me to go very near in my Dealing.—To be sure, of late Years I have been a great Sufferer by the Parliament.—Three thousand Pounds would hardly make me amends.—The Act for destroying the Mint, was a severe Cut upon our Business—'Till then, if a Customer stept out of the way—we

knew where to have her—No doubt you know Mrs. Coaxer—
there's a Wench now ('till to-day) with a good Suit of Cloaths of
mine upon her Back, and I could never set Eyes upon her for three
Months together.—Since the Act too against Imprisonment for
small Sums, my Loss there too hath been very considerable, and it
must be so, when a Lady can borrow a handsome Petticoat, or a
clean Gown, and I not have the least Hank upon her! And, o' my
conscience, now-a-days most Ladies take a Delight in cheating,
when they can do it with Safety.

Peach. Madam, you had a handsome Gold Watch of us t'other
Day for seven Guineas.—Considering we must have our Profit—
To a Gentleman upon the Road, a Gold Watch will be scarce
worth the taking.

Trap. Consider, Mr. Peachum, that Watch was remarkable, and
not of very safe Sale.—If you have any black Velvet Scarfs—they
are a handsome Winter-wear; and take with most Gentlemen who
deal with my Customers.—'Tis I that put the Ladies upon a good
Foot. 'Tis not Youth or Beauty that fixes their Price. The Gentlemen always pay according to their Dress, from half a Crown to
two Guineas; and yet those Hussies make nothing of bilking of
me.—Then, too, allowing for Accidents.—I have eleven fine Customers now down under the Surgeon's Hands,—what with Fees
and other Expences, there are great Goings-out, and no Comings-in,
and not a Farthing to pay for at least a Month's cloathing.—We
run great Risques—great Risques indeed.

Peach. As I remember, you said something just now of Mrs.
Coaxer.

Trap. Yes, Sir.—To be sure I stript her of a Suit of my own
Cloaths about two hours ago; and have left her as she should be,
in her Shift, with a Lover of hers at my House. She call'd him up
Stairs, as he was going to Marybone in a Hackney Coach.—And I
hope, for her own sake and mine, she will perswade the Captain
to redeem her, for the Captain is very generous to the Ladies.

Lock. What Captain?

Trap. He thought I did not know him—An intimate Acquaintance of yours, Mr. Peachum—Only Captain Macheath—as fine
as a Lord.

Peach. To-morrow, dear Mrs. Dye, you shall set your own
Price upon any of the Goods you like—We have at least half a
dozen Velvet Scarfs, and all at your service. Will you give me
leave to make you a Present of this Suit of Night-cloaths for your
own wearing?—But are you sure it is Captain Macheath?

Trap. Though he thinks I have forgot him, no Body knows him
better. I have taken a great deal of the Captain's Money in my

Time at second-hand, for he always lov'd to have his Ladies well drest.

Peach. Mr. Lockit and I have a little business with the Captain;—You understand me—and we will satisfye you for Mrs. Coaxer's Debt.

Lock. Depend upon it—we will deal like Men of Honour.

Trap. I don't enquire after your Affairs—so whatever happens, I wash my Hands on't.—It hath always been my Maxim, that one Friend should assist another—But if you please—I'll take one of the Scarfs home with me. 'Tis always good to have something in Hand.

SCENE VII.—*Newgate*

LUCY.

Jealousy, Rage, Love and Fear are at once tearing me to pieces. How I am weather-beaten and shatter'd with distresses!

AIR VII. One Evening, having lost my Way, &c.

I'm like a Skiff on the Ocean tost,
 Now high, now low, with each Billow born,
With her Rudder broke, and her Anchor lost,
 Deserted and all forlorn.
While thus I lye rolling and tossing all Night,
That Polly lyes sporting on Seas of Delight!
 Revenge, Revenge, Revenge,
Shall appease my restless Sprite.

I have the Rats-bane ready.—I run no Risque; for I can lay her Death upon the Ginn, and so many dye of that naturally that I shall never be call'd in Question.—But say, I were to be hang'd—I never could be hang'd for any thing that would give me greater Comfort, than the poysoning that Slut.

Enter FILCH.

Filch. Madam, here's our Miss Polly come to wait upon you.
Lucy. Show her in.

SCENE VIII

LUCY, POLLY.

Lucy. Dear Madam, your Servant.—I hope you will pardon my Passion, when I was so happy to see you last.—I was so overrun with the Spleen, that I was perfectly out of my self. And really when one hath the Spleen, every thing is to be excus'd by a Friend.

AIR VIII. Now Roger, I'll tell thee, because thou'rt my Son·

When a Wife's in her Pout
(As she's sometimes, no doubt;)
The good Husband as meek as a Lamb,
Her Vapours to still,
First grants her her Will,
And the quieting Draught is a Dram.
Poor Man! And the quieting Draught is a Dram.

—I wish all our Quarrels might have so comfortable a Reconciliation.

Polly. I have no Excuse for my own Behaviour, Madam, but my Misfortunes.—And really, Madam, I suffer too upon your Account.

Lucy. But, Miss Polly—in the way of Friendship, will you give me leave to propose a Glass of Cordial to you?

Polly. Strong-Waters are apt to give me the Head-ache—I hope, Madam, you will excuse me.

Lucy. Not the greatest Lady in the Land could have better in her Closet, for her own private drinking.—You seem mighty low in Spirits, my Dear.

Polly. I am sorry, Madam, my Health will not allow me to accept of your Offer.—I should not have left you in the rude Manner I did when we met last, Madam, had not my Papa haul'd me away so unexpectedly—I was indeed somewhat provok'd, and perhaps might use some Expressions that were disrespectful.— But really, Madam, the Captain treated me with so much Contempt and Cruelty, that I deserv'd your Pity, rather than your Resentment.

Lucy. But since his Escape, no doubt all Matters are made up again.—Ah Polly! Polly! 'tis I am the unhappy Wife; and he loves you as if you were only his Mistress.

Polly. Sure, Madam, you cannot think me so happy as to be the Object of your Jealousy.—A Man is always afraid of a Woman who loves him too well—so that I must expect to be neglected and avoided.

Lucy. Then our Cases, my dear Polly, are exactly alike. Both of us indeed have been too fond.

AIR IX. O Bessy Bell

POLLY.
A Curse attends that Woman's Love,
  Who always would be pleasing.
LUCY.
The Pertness of the billing Dove,
  Like tickling, is but teazing.
POLLY.
What then in Love can Woman do?
LUCY.
  If we grow fond, they shun us.
POLLY.
And when we fly them, they pursue.
LUCY.
  But leave us when they've won us.

Lucy. Love is so very whimsical in both Sexes, that it is impossible to be lasting.—But my Heart is particular, and contradicts my own Observation.

Polly. But really, Mistress Lucy, by his last Behaviour, I think I ought to envy you.—When I was forc'd from him, he did not shew the least Tenderness.—But perhaps, he hath a Heart not capable of it.

AIR X. Would Fate to me Belinda give—

Among the Men, Coquets we find,
Who Court by turns all Woman-kind;
And we grant all their Hearts desir'd,
When they are flatter'd, and admir'd.

The Coquets of both Sexes are Self-lovers, and that is a Love no other whatever can dispossess. I fear, my dear Lucy, our Husband is one of those.

Lucy. Away with these melancholy Reflections,—indeed, my dear Polly, we are both of us a Cup too low.—Let me prevail upon you, to accept of my Offer.

AIR XI. Come, sweet Lass, &c.

Come, sweet Lass,
Let's banish Sorrow
'Till To-morrow;
Come, sweet Lass,
Let's take a chirping Glass.

Wine can clear
The Vapours of Despair;
And make us light as Air;
Then drink, and banish Care.

I can't bear, Child, to see you in such low Spirits.—And I must persuade you to what I know will do you good.—I shall now soon be even with the hypocritical Strumpet.   [*Aside.*

Scene IX

Polly.

Polly. All this wheedling of Lucy cannot be for nothing.— At this time too! when I know she hates me!—The Dissembling of a Woman is always the Fore-runner of Mischief.—By pouring Strong-Waters down my Throat, she thinks to pump some Secrets out of me.—I'll be upon my Guard, and won't taste a Drop of her Liquor, I'm resolv'd.

Scene X

Lucy, *with Strong-Waters.* Polly.

Lucy. Come, Miss Polly.

Polly. Indeed, Child, you have given yourself trouble to no purpose.—You must, my Dear, excuse me.

Lucy. Really, Miss Polly, you are so squeamishly affected about taking a Cup of Strong-Waters as a Lady before Company. I vow, Polly, I shall take it monstrously ill if you refuse me.— Brandy and Men (though Women love them never so well) are always taken by us with some Reluctance—unless 'tis in private.

Polly. I protest, Madam, it goes against me.—What do I see! Macheath again in Custody!—Now every glimm'ring of Happiness is lost.

        [*Drops the Glass of Liquor on the Ground.*

Lucy. Since things are thus, I'm glad the Wench hath escap'd: for by this Event, 'tis plain, she was not happy enough to deserve to be poison'd.   [*Aside.*

Scene XI

Lockit, Macheath, Peachum, Lucy, Polly.

Lock. Set your Heart to rest, Captain.—You have neither the Chance of Love or Money for another Escape,—for you are order'd to be call'd down upon your Tryal immediately.

Peach. Away, Hussies!—This is not a time for a Man to be hamper'd with his Wives.—You see, the Gentleman is in Chains already.

Lucy. O Husband, Husband, my heart long'd to see thee; but to see thee thus distracts me!

Polly. Will not my dear Husband look upon his Polly? Why hadst thou not flown to me for Protection? with me thou hadst been safe.

Air XII. The last time I went o'er the Moor

POLLY.
Hither, dear Husband, turn your Eyes.
LUCY.
Bestow one Glance to cheer me.
POLLY.
Think with that Look, thy Polly dyes.
LUCY. *O shun me not—but hear me.*
POLLY. *'Tis Polly sues.*
LUCY. . . . *'Tis Lucy speaks.*
POLLY. *Is thus true Love requited?*
LUCY. *My Heart is bursting.*
POLLY. . . . *Mine too breaks.*
LUCY. *Must I*
POLLY. . . . *Must I be slighted?*

Mach. What would you have me say, Ladies?—You see, this Affair will soon be at an end, without my disobliging either of you.

Peach. But the settling this Point, Captain, might prevent a Law-suit between your two Widows.

Air XIII. Tom Tinker's my true Love

MACH. *Which way shall I turn me?—How can I decide?*
Wives, the Day of our Death, are as fond as a Bride.
One Wife is too much for most Husbands to bear,
But two at a time there's no Mortal can bear.
This way, and that way, and which way I will,
What would comfort the one, t'other Wife would take ill.

Polly. But if his own Misfortunes have made him insensible to mine—A Father sure will be more compassionate.—Dear, dear Sir, sink the material Evidence, and bring him off at his Tryal—Polly upon her Knees begs it of you.

AIR XIV. I am a poor Shepherd undone

When my Hero in Court appears,
And stands arraign'd for his Life;
Then think of poor Polly's Tears;
For Ah! Poor Polly's his Wife.
Like the Sailor he holds up his Hand,
Distrest on the dashing Wave.
To die a dry Death at Land,
Is as bad as a watry Grave.
And alas, poor Polly!
Alack, and well-a-day!
Before I was in Love,
Oh! every Month was May.

Lucy. If Peachum's Heart is harden'd, sure you, Sir, will have more Compassion on a Daughter.—I know the Evidence is in your Power.—How then can you be a Tyrant to me?

[*Kneeling.*

AIR XV. Ianth the lovely, &c.

When he holds up his Hand arraign'd for his Life,
O think of your Daughter, and think I'm his Wife!
What are Cannons, or Bombs, or clashing of Swords?
For Death is more certain by Witnesses Words.
Then nail up their Lips; that dread Thunder allay;
And each Month of my Life will hereafter be May.

Lock. Macheath's time is come, Lucy.—We know our own Affairs, therefore let us have no more Whimpering or Whining.

Peach. Set your Heart at rest, Polly.—Your Husband is to dye to-day.—Therefore, if you are not already provided, 'tis high time to look about for another. There's Comfort for you, you Slut.

Lock. We are ready, Sir, to conduct you to the Old-Baily.

AIR XVI. Bonny Dundee

MACH. *The Charge is prepar'd; The Lawyers are met,*
The Judges all rang'd (a terrible Show!)
I go, undismay'd.—For Death is a Debt,
A Debt on demand.—So, take what I owe.
Then farewell, my Love—Dear Charmers, adieu.
Contented I die—'Tis the better for you.
Here ends all Dispute the rest of our Lives.
For this way at once I please all my Wives.

Now, Gentlemen, I am ready to attend you.

Scene XII

Lucy, Polly, Filch.

Polly. Follow them, Filch, to the Court. And when the Tryal is over, bring me a particular Account of his Behaviour, and of every thing that happen'd.—You'll find me here with Miss Lucy. [*Exit* Filch.] But why is all this Musick?

Lucy. The Prisoners, whose Tryals are put off till next Session, are diverting themselves.

Polly. Sure there is nothing so charming as Musick! I'm fond of it to distraction!—But alas!—now, all Mirth seems an Insult upon my Affliction.—Let us retire, my dear Lucy, and indulge our Sorrows.—The noisy Crew, you see, are coming upon us.

[*Exeunt.*

[*A Dance of Prisoners in Chains, &c.*

Scene XIII.—*The Condemn'd Hold*

Macheath, *in a melancholy Posture.*

Air XVII. Happy Groves

O cruel, cruel, cruel Case!
Must I suffer this Disgrace?

Air XVIII. Of all the Girls that are so smart

Of all the Friends in time of Grief,
When threatning Death looks grimmer,
Not one so sure can bring Relief,
As this best Friend, a Brimmer. [*Drinks.*

Air XIX. Britons

Since I must swing,—I scorn, I scorn to wince or whine. [*Rises.*

Air XX. Chevy Chase

But now again my Spirits sink;
I'll raise them high with Wine. [*Drinks a Glass of Wine.*

Air XXI. To old Sir Simon the King

But Valour the stronger grows,
The stronger Liquor we're drinking.
And how can we feel our Woes,
When we've lost the Trouble of Thinking? [*Drinks.*

Air XXII. Joy to great Cæsar

If thus—A Man can die
Much bolder with Brandy.　　　　[*Pours out a Bumper of Brandy.*

Air XXIII. There was an old Woman

So I drink off this Bumper.—And now I can stand the Test.
And my Comrades shall see, that I die as brave as the Best.
　　　　　　　　　　　　　　　　　　　　[*Drinks.*

Air XXIV. Did you ever hear of a gallant Sailor

But can I leave my pretty Hussies,
Without one Tear, or tender Sigh?

Air XXV. Why are mine Eyes still flowing

Their Eyes, their Lips, their Busses
Recall my Love.—Ah must I die!

Air XXVI. Green Sleeves

Since Laws were made for ev'ry Degree,
To curb Vice in others, as well as me,
I wonder we han't better Company,
　　Upon Tyburn Tree!
But Gold from Law can take out the Sting;
And if rich Men like us were to swing,
'Twou'd thin the Land, such Numbers to string
　　Upon Tyburn Tree!

Jailor. Some Friends of yours, Captain, desire to be admitted.
—I leave you together.

Scene XIV

Macheath, Ben Budge, Matt of the Mint.

Mach. For my having broke Prison, you see, Gentlemen, I am order'd immediate Execution.—The Sheriffs Officers, I believe, are now at the Door.—That Jemmy Twitcher should peach me, I own surpriz'd me!—'Tis a plain Proof that the World is all alike, and that even our Gang can no more trust one another than other People. Therefore, I beg you, Gentlemen, look well to yourselves, for in all probability you may live some Months longer.

Matt. We are heartily sorry, Captain, for your Misfortune.—But 'tis what we must all come to.

Mach. Peachum and Lockit, you know, are infamous Scoundrels. Their Lives are as much in your Power, as yours are in theirs.—Remember your dying Friend!—'Tis my last Request.—Bring those Villains to the Gallows before you, and I am satisfied.

Matt. We'll do't.

Jailor. Miss Polly and Miss Lucy intreat a Word with you.

Mach. Gentlemen, Adieu.

Scene XV

Lucy, Macheath, Polly.

Mach. My dear Lucy—My dear Polly—Whatsoever hath past between us is now at an end.—If you are fond of marrying again, the best Advice I can give you, is to Ship yourselves off for the West-Indies, where you'll have a fair chance of getting a Husband a-piece; or by good Luck, two or three, as you like best.

Polly. How can I support this Sight!

Lucy. There is nothing moves one so much as a great Man in Distress.

Air XXVII. All you that must take a leap, &c.

Lucy. *Would I might be hang'd!*
Polly. *. . . . And I would so too!*
Lucy. *To be hang'd with you.*
Polly. *. . . My Dear, with you.*
Mach. *O Leave me to Thought! I fear! I doubt!*
I tremble! I droop!—See, my Courage is out.

     [Turns up the empty Bottle.

Polly. *No token of Love?*
Mach. *. . . . See, my Courage is out.*

     [Turns up the empty Pot.

Lucy. *No token of Love?*
Polly. *. . . . Adieu.*
Lucy. *. . . . Farewell.*
Mach. *But hark! I hear the Toll of the Bell.*
Chorus. *Tol de rol lol, &c.*

Jailor. Four Women more, Captain, with a Child a-piece! See, here they come.

Enter Women *and* Children.

Mach. What—four Wives more!—This is too much.—Here—
tell the Sheriffs Officers I am ready.

[*Exit* MACHEATH *guarded.*

SCENE XVI

To them, Enter PLAYER *and* BEGGAR.

Play. But, honest Friend, I hope you don't intend that Macheath shall be really executed.

Beg. Most certainly, Sir.—To make the Piece perfect, I was for doing strict poetical Justice.—Macheath is to be hang'd; and for the other Personages of the Drama, the Audience must have suppos'd they were all either hang'd or transported.

Play. Why then, Friend, this is a down-right deep Tragedy. The Catastrophe is manifestly wrong, for an Opera must end happily.

Beg. Your Objection, Sir, is very just; and is easily remov'd. For you must allow, that in this kind of Drama, 'tis no matter how absurdly things are brought about.—So—you Rabble there —run and cry a Reprieve—let the Prisoner be brought back to his Wives in Triumph.

Play. All this we must do, to comply with the Taste of the Town.

Beg. Through the whole Piece you may observe such a similitude of Manners in high and low Life, that it is difficult to determine whether (in the fashionable Vices) the fine Gentlemen imitate the Gentlemen of the Road, or the Gentlemen of the Road the fine Gentlemen.—Had the Play remain'd, as I at first intended, it would have carried a most excellent Moral. 'Twould have shown that the lower Sort of People have their Vices in a degree as well as the Rich: And that they are punish'd for them.

SCENE XVII

To them, MACHEATH *with* RABBLE, *&c.*

Mach. So, it seems, I am not left to my Choice, but must have a Wife at last.—Look ye, my Dears, we will have no Controversie now. Let us give this Day to Mirth, and I am sure she who thinks herself my Wife will testifie her Joy by a Dance.

All. Come, a Dance—a Dance.

Mach. Ladies, I hope you will give me leave to present a Partner to each of you. And (if I may without Offence) for this time, I take Polly for mine.—And for Life, you Slut,—for we were really marry'd.—As for the rest—But at present keep your own Secret.   [*To* POLLY.

A DANCE

AIR XXVIII. Lumps of Pudding, &c.

Thus I stand like the Turk, *with his Doxies around;*
From all Sides their Glances his Passion confound;
For black, brown, and fair, his Inconstancy burns,
And the different Beauties subdue him by turns:
Each calls forth her Charms, to provoke his Desires:
Though willing to all, with but one he retires.
But think of this Maxim, and put off your Sorrow,
The Wretch of To-day, may be happy To-morrow.
CHORUS. *But think of this Maxim, &c.*

FINIS

ACT I

AIR 1

AIR 2

AIR 3

AIR 4

AIR 5

AIR 6

JOHN GAY

AIR 11

AIR 12

AIR 13

JOHN GAY

AIR 14

AIR 15

AIR 16

AIR 17

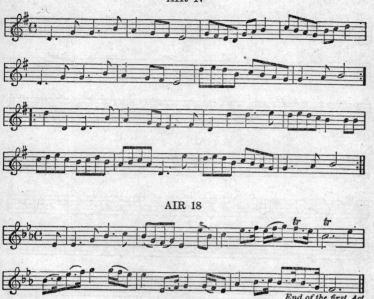

AIR 18

End of the first Act

ACT II

AIR 1

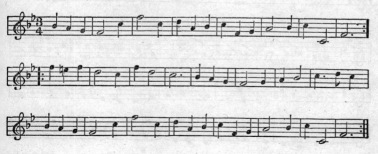

AIR 2

AIR 6

AIR 7

AIR 8

AIR 9

AIR 10

AIR 11

AIR 12

AIR 13

AIR 14

AIR 15

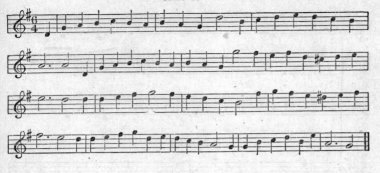

AIR 16

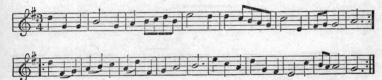

AIR 17

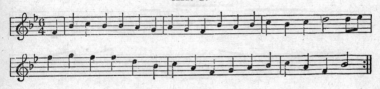

AIR 18

JOHN GAY

AIR 19

AIR 20

AIR 21

AIR 22

End of the second Act

ACT III

AIR 1

AIR 2

JOHN GAY

AIR 3

AIR 7

AIR 8

AIR 9

JOHN GAY

AIR 10

AIR 11

AIR 12

AIR 13

AIR 14

AIR 15

AIR 16

614

AIR 17

AIR 18

AIR 19

AIR 20

AIR 21

AIR 22

AIR 23

AIR 24

AIR 25

AIR 26

AIR 27

AIR 28

THE CLANDESTINE MARRIAGE

by

GEORGE COLMAN, SR., AND DAVID GARRICK

ADVERTISEMENT

Hogarth's MARRIAGE-À-LA-MODE has before furnished Materials to the Author of a Novel, published some Years ago, under the Title of *The Marriage-Act:* But as that Writer pursued a very different Story, and as his Work was chiefly designed for a Political Satire, very little Use could be made of it for the Service of this Comedy.

In Justice to the Person, who has been considered as the sole Author, the Party, who has hitherto lain concealed, thinks it incumbent on him to declare, that the Disclosure of his Name was, by his own Desire, reserved till the Publication of the Piece.

Both the Authors, however, who have before been separately honoured with the Indulgence of the Publick, now beg Leave to make their joint Acknowledgements for the very favourable Reception of the CLANDESTINE MARRIAGE.

PROLOGUE

WRITTEN BY MR. GARRICK. SPOKEN BY MR. HOLLAND

Poets and Painters, who from Nature draw
Their best and richest Stores, have made this Law:
That each should neighbourly assist his Brother,
And steal with Decency from one another.
To-night, your matchless Hogarth gives the Thought,
Which from his Canvas to the Stage is brought.
And who so fit to warm the Poet's Mind,
As he who pictur'd Morals and Mankind?
But not the same their Characters and Scenes;
Both labour for one End, by different Means:
Each, as it suits him, takes a separate Road,
Their one great Object, Marriage-à-la-mode!
Where Titles deign with Cits to have and hold,
And change rich Blood for more substantial Gold!
And honour'd Trade from Interest turns aside,
To hazard Happiness for titled Pride.
The Painter dead, yet still he charms the Eye;
While England lives, his Fame can never die:
But he, who struts his Hour upon the Stage,
Can scarce extend his Fame for Half an Age;
Nor Pen nor Pencil can the Actor save,
The Art, and Artist, share one common Grave.
O let me drop one tributary Tear,
On poor Jack Falstaff's Grave, and Juliet's Bier!
You to their Worth must Testimony give;
'Tis in your Hearts alone their Fame can live.
Still as the Scenes of Life will shift away,
The strong Impressions of their Art decay.
Your Children cannot feel what you have known;
They'll boast of Quins and Cibbers of their own:
The greatest Glory of our happy few,
Is to be felt, and be approv'd by you.

DRAMATIS PERSONÆ

LORD OGLEBY	Mr. King
SIR JOHN MELVIL	Mr. Holland
STERLING	Mr. Yates
LOVEWELL	Mr. Powell
CANTON	Mr. Baddeley
BRUSH	Mr. Palmer
SERJEANT FLOWER	Mr. Love
TRAVERSE	Mr. Lee
TRUEMAN	Mr. Aickin
MRS. HEIDELBERG	Mrs. Clive
MISS STERLING	Miss Pope
FANNY	Mrs. Palmer
BETTY	Mrs. ——
CHAMBERMAID	Miss Plym
TRUSTY	Miss Mills

THE CLANDESTINE MARRIAGE

ACT I

Scene.—*A room in* Sterling's *house*

Miss Fanny *and* Betty *meeting.*

Betty. [*Running in.*] Ma'am! Miss Fanny! Ma'am!

Fanny. What's the matter! Betty!

Betty. Oh, la! Ma'am! as sure as I'm alive, here is your husband—

Fanny. Hush! my dear Betty! if any body in the house should hear you, I am ruined.

Betty. Mercy on me! it has frighted me to such a degree, that my heart is come up to my mouth.—But as I was a saying, Ma'am, here's that dear, sweet—

Fanny. Have a care! Betty.

Betty. Lord! I'm bewitched, I think.—But as I was a saying, Ma'am, here's Mr. Lovewell just come from London.

Fanny. Indeed!

Betty. Yes, indeed, and indeed, Ma'am, he is. I saw him crossing the court-yard in his boots.

Fanny. I am glad to hear it.—But pray, now, my dear Betty, be cautious. Don't mention that word again, on any account. You know, we have agreed never to drop any expressions of that sort for fear of an accident.

Betty. Dear Ma'am, you may depend upon me. There is not a more trustier creature on the face of the earth, than I am. Though I say it, I am as secret as the grave—and if it's never told, till I tell it, it may remain untold till doom's-day for Betty.

Fanny. I know you are faithful—but in our circumstances we cannot be too careful.

Betty. Very true, Ma'am!—and yet I vow and protest, there's more plague than pleasure with a secret; especially if a body mayn't mention it to four or five of one's particular acquaintance.

Fanny. Do but keep this secret a little while longer, and then, I hope you may mention it to any body.—Mr. Lovewell will acquaint the family with the nature of our situation as soon as possible.

Betty. The sooner, the better, I believe: for if he does not tell it, there's a little tell-tale, I know of, will come and tell it for him.

Fanny. Fie, Betty!   [*Blushing.*

Betty. Ah! you may well blush.—But you're not so sick, and so pale, and so wan, and so many qualms—

Fanny. Have done! I shall be quite angry with you.

Betty. Angry!—Bless the dear puppet! I am sure I shall love it, as much as if it was my own.—I meant no harm, heaven knows.

Fanny. Well—say no more of this—It makes me uneasy—All I have to ask of you, is to be faithful and secret, and not to reveal this matter, till we disclose it to the family ourselves.

Betty. Me reveal it!—if I say a word, I wish I may be burned. I wou'd not do you any harm for the world—And as for Mr. Lovewell, I am sure I have loved the dear gentleman ever since he got a tide-waiter's place for my brother—But let me tell you both, you must leave off your soft looks to each other, and your whispers, and your glances, and your always sitting next to one another at dinner, and your long walks together in the evening— For my part, if I had not been in the secret, I shou'd have known you were a pair of lovers at least, if not man and wife, as—

Fanny. See there now! again. Pray be careful.

Betty. Well—well—nobody hears me.—Man and wife—I'll say so no more—what I tell you is very true for all that—

Lovewell. [*Calling within.*] William!

Betty. Hark! I hear your husband—

Fanny. What!

Betty. I say, here comes Mr. Lovewell—Mind the caution I give you—I'll be whipped now, if you are not the first person he sees or speaks to in the family—However, if you chuse it, it's nothing at all to me—as you sow, you must reap—as you brew, so you must bake.—I'll e'en slip down the back-stairs, and leave you together.   [*Exit.*

Fanny. [*Alone.*] I see, I see I shall never have a moment's ease till our marriage is made publick. New distresses croud in upon me every day. The sollicitude of my mind sinks my spirits, preys upon my health, and destroys every comfort of my life. It shall be revealed, let what will be the consequence.

Enter LOVEWELL.

Lovew. My love—How's this?—In tears?—Indeed this is too

much. You promised me to support your spirits, and to wait the determination of our fortune with patience.—For my sake, for your own, be comforted! Why will you study to add to our uneasiness and perplexity?

Fanny. Oh, Mr. Lovewell! the indelicacy of a secret marriage grows every day more and more shocking to me. I walk about the house like a guilty wretch: I imagine myself the object of the suspicion of the whole family; and am under the perpetual terrors of a shameful detection.

Lovew. Indeed, indeed, you are to blame. The amiable delicacy of your temper, and your quick sensibility, only serve to make you unhappy.—To clear up this affair properly to Mr. Sterling, is the continual employment of my thoughts. Every thing now is in a fair train. It begins to grow ripe for a discovery; and I have no doubt of its concluding to the satisfaction of ourselves, of your father, and the whole family.

Fanny. End how it will, I am resolved it shall end soon—very soon. I wou'd not live another week in this agony of mind to be mistress of the universe.

Lovew. Do not be too violent neither. Do not let us disturb the joy of your sister's marriage with the tumult this matter may occasion!—I have brought letters from Lord Ogleby and Sir John Melvil to Mr. Sterling.—They will be here this evening—and, I dare say, within this hour.

Fanny. I am sorry for it.

Lovew. Why so?

Fanny. No matter—Only let us disclose our marriage immediately!

Lovew. As soon as possible.

Fanny. But directly.

Lovew. In a few days, you may depend on it.

Fanny. To-night—or to-morrow morning.

Lovew. That, I fear, will be impracticable.

Fanny. Nay, but you must.

Lovew. Must! why?

Fanny. Indeed, you must.—I have the most alarming reasons for it.

Lovew. Alarming indeed! for they alarm me, even before I am acquainted with them—What are they?

Fanny. I cannot tell you.

Lovew. Not tell me?

Fanny. Not at present. When all is settled, you shall be acquainted with every thing.

Lovew. Sorry they are coming!—Must be discovered!—What

can this mean!—Is it possible you can have any reasons that need be concealed from me?

Fanny. Do not disturb yourself with conjectures—but rest assured, that though you are unable to divine the cause, the consequence of a discovery, be it what it will, cannot be attended with half the miseries of the present interval.

Lovew. You put me upon the rack.—I wou'd do any thing to make you easy.—But you know your father's temper.—Money (you will excuse my frankness) is the spring of all his actions, which nothing but the idea of acquiring nobility or magnificence can ever make him forego—and these he thinks his money will purchase.—You know too your aunt's, Mrs. Heidelberg's, notions of the splendour of high life, her contempt for every thing that does not relish of what she calls Quality, and that from the vast fortune in her hands, by her late husband, she absolutely governs Mr. Sterling and the whole family: now, if they should come to the knowledge of this affair too abruptly, they might, perhaps, be incensed beyond all hopes of reconciliation.

Fanny. But if they are made acquainted with it otherwise than by ourselves, it will be ten times worse: and a discovery grows every day more probable. The whole family have long suspected our affection. We are also in the power of a foolish maid-servant; and if we may even depend on her fidelity, we cannot answer for her discretion.—Discover it therefore immediately, lest some accident should bring it to light, and involve us in additional disgrace.

Lovew. Well—well—I meant to discover it soon, but would not do it too precipitately.—I have more than once sounded Mr. Sterling about it, and will attempt him more seriously the next opportunity. But my principal hopes are these.—My relationship to Lord Ogleby, and his having placed me with your father, have been, you know, the first links in the chain of this connection between the two families; in consequence of which, I am at present in high favour with all parties: while they all remain thus well-affected to me, I propose to lay our case before the old Lord; and if I can prevail on him to mediate in this affair, I make no doubt but he will be able to appease your father; and, being a lord and a man of quality, I am sure he may bring Mrs. Heidelberg into good-humour at any time.—Let me beg you, therefore, to have but a little patience, as, you see, we are upon the very eve of a discovery, that must probably be to our advantage.

Fanny. Manage it your own way. I am persuaded.

Lovew. But in the mean time make yourself easy.

Fanny. As easy as I can, I will.—We had better not remain together any longer at present.—Think of this business, and let me know how you proceed.

Lovew. Depend on my care! But, pray, be chearful.

Fanny. I will.

As she is going out, Enter STERLING.

Sterl. Hey-day! who have we got here?

Fanny. [*Confused*.] Mr. Lovewell, Sir!

Sterl. And where are you going, hussey?

Fanny. To my sister's chamber, Sir!   [*Exit*.

Sterl. Ah, Lovewell! What! always getting my foolish girl yonder into a corner!—Well—well—let us but once see her elder sister fast-married to Sir John Melvil, we'll soon provide a good husband for Fanny, I warrant you.

Lovew. Wou'd to heaven, Sir, you would provide her one of my recommendation!

Sterl. Yourself? eh, Lovewell!

Lovew. With your pleasure, Sir!

Sterl. Mighty well!

Lovew. And I flatter myself, that such a proposal would not be very disagreeable to Miss Fanny.

Sterl. Better and better!

Lovew. And if I could but obtain your consent, Sir—

Sterl. What! you marry Fanny!—no—no—that will never do, Lovewell!—You're a good boy, to be sure—I have a great value for you—but can't think of you for a son-in-law.—There's no *Stuff* in the case, no money, Lovewell!

Lovew. My pretensions to fortune, indeed, are but moderate: but though not equal to splendour, sufficient to keep us above distress.—Add to which, that I hope by diligence to increase it —and have love, honour—

Sterl. But not the *Stuff*, Lovewell!—Add one little round o to the sum total of your fortune, and that will be the finest thing you can say to me.—You know I've a regard for you—would do any thing to serve you—any thing on the footing of friendship —but—

Lovew. If you think me worthy of your friendship, Sir, be assured, that there is no instance in which I should rate your friendship so highly.

Sterl. Psha! psha! that's another thing, you know.—Where money or interest is concerned, friendship is quite out of the question.

Lovew. But where the happiness of a daughter is at stake, you wou'd not scruple, sure, to sacrifice a little to her inclinations.

Sterl. Inclinations! why, you wou'd not persuade me that the girl is in love with you—eh, Lovewell!

Lovew. I cannot absolutely answer for Miss Fanny, Sir; but am sure that the chief happiness or misery of my life depends entirely upon her.

Sterl. Why, indeed now if your kinsman, Lord Ogleby, would come down handsomely for you—but that's impossible—No, no—'twill never do—I must hear no more of this—Come, Lovewell, promise me that I shall hear no more of this.

Lovew. [*Hesitating.*] I am afraid, Sir, I shou'd not be able to keep my word with you, if I did promise you.

Sterl. Why, you wou'd not offer to marry her without my consent? wou'd you, Lovewell!

Lovew. Marry her, Sir! [*Confused.*

Sterl. Ay, marry her, Sir!—I know very well that a warm speech or two from such a dangerous young spark, as you are, will go much farther towards persuading a silly girl to do what she has more than a month's mind to do, than twenty grave lectures from fathers or mothers, or uncles or aunts, to prevent her. —But you wou'd not, sure, be such a base fellow, such a treacherous young rogue, as to seduce my daughter's affections, and destroy the peace of my family in that manner.—I must insist on it, that you give me your word not to marry her without my consent.

Lovew. Sir—I—I—as to that—I—I—I beg, Sir—Pray, Sir, excuse me on this subject at present.

Sterl. Promise then, that you will carry this matter no further without my approbation.

Lovew. You may depend on it, Sir, that it shall go no further.

Sterl. Well—well—that's enough—I'll take care of the rest, I warrant you.—Come, come, let's have done with this nonsense! —What's doing in town?—Any news upon 'Change?

Lovew. Nothing material.

Sterl. Have you seen the currants, the soap, and Madeira, safe in the warehouses? Have you compared the goods with the invoice and bills of lading, and are they all right?

Lovew. They are, Sir!

Sterl. And how are stocks?

Lovew. Fell one and one half this morning.

Sterl. Well—well—some good news from America, and they'll be up again.—But how are Lord Ogleby and Sir John Melvil? When are we to expect them?

Lovew. Very soon, Sir! I came purpose on to bring you their commands. Here are letters from both of them. [*Giving letters.*

Sterl. Let me see—let me see—'Slife, how his Lordship's letter is perfumed!—It takes my breath away.—[*Opening it.*] And French paper too! with a fine border of flowers and flourishes—and a slippery gloss on it that dazzles one's eyes.—*My dear Mr. Sterling.* [*Reading.*]—Mercy on me! His Lordship writes a worse hand than a boy at his exercise—But how's this?—Eh!—*with you to-night*—[*Reading.*]—*Lawyers to-morrow morning*—To-night!—that's sudden indeed.—Where's my sister Heidelberg? she shou'd know of this immediately.—Here John! Harry! Thomas! [*Calling the servants.*] Hark ye, Lovewell!

Lovew. Sir!

Sterl. Mind now, how I'll entertain his Lordship and Sir John—We'll shew your fellows at the other end of the town how we live in the city—They shall eat gold—and drink gold—and lie in gold—Here cook! butler! [*Calling.*] What signifies your birth and education, and titles? Money, money, that's the stuff that makes the great man in this country.

Lovew. Very true, Sir!

Sterl. True, Sir?—Why then have done with your nonsense of love and matrimony. You're not rich enough to think of a wife yet. A man of business shou'd mind nothing but his business.—Where are these fellows? John! Thomas! [*Calling.*]—Get an estate, and a wife will follow of course.—Ah! Lovewell! an English merchant is the most respectable character in the universe. 'Slife, man, a rich English merchant may make himself a match for the daughter of a Nabob.—Where are all my rascals? Here, William!

[*Exit calling.*

Lovewell. [*Alone.*] So!—As I suspected.—Quite averse to the match, and likely to receive the news of it with great displeasure.—What's best to be done?—Let me see!—Suppose I get Sir John Melvil to interest himself in this affair. He may mention it to Lord Ogleby with a better grace than I can, and more probably prevail on him to interfere in it. I can open my mind also more freely to Sir John. He told me, when I left him in town, that he had something of consequence to communicate, and that I could be of use to him. I am glad of it: for the confidence he reposes in me, and the service I may do him, will ensure me his good offices.—Poor Fanny! It hurts me to see her so uneasy, and her making a mystery of the cause adds to my anxiety.—Something must be done upon her account; for at all events, her sollicitude shall be removed.

[*Exit.*

SCENE.—*Changes to another chamber*

Enter MISS STERLING, *and* MISS FANNY.

Miss Sterl. Oh, my dear sister, say no more! This is downright hypocrisy.—You shall never convince me that you don't envy me beyond measure.—Well, after all it is extremely natural—It is impossible to be angry with you.

Fanny. Indeed, sister, you have no cause.

Miss Sterl. And you really pretend not to envy me?

Fanny. Not in the least.

Miss Sterl. And you don't in the least wish that you was just in my situation?

Fanny. No, indeed, I don't. Why should I?

Miss Sterl. Why should you?—What, on the brink of marriage, fortune, title—But I had forgot—There's that dear sweet creature Mr. Lovewell in the case.—You would not break your faith with your true love now for the world, I warrant you.

Fanny. Mr. Lovewell!—always Mr. Lovewell!—Lord, what signifies Mr. Lovewell, sister?

Miss Sterl. Pretty peevish soul!—Oh, my dear, grave, romantick sister!—a perfect philosopher in petticoats!—Love and a cottage! —Eh, Fanny!—Ah, give me indifference and a coach and six!

Fanny. And why not the coach and six without the indifference? —But, pray, when is this happy marriage of yours to be celebrated?—I long to give you joy.

Miss Sterl. In a day or two—I can't tell exactly.—Oh, my dear sister!—I must mortify her a little. [*Aside.*]—I know you have a pretty taste. Pray, give me your opinion of my jewels.—How d'ye like the stile of this esclavage? [*Shewing jewels.*]

Fanny. Extremely handsome indeed, and well fancied.

Miss Sterl. What d'ye think of these bracelets? I shall have a miniature of my father, set round with diamonds, to one, and Sir John's to the other.—And this pair of ear-rings! set transparent! —here, the tops, you see, will take off to wear in a morning, or in an undress—how d'ye like them? [*Shews jewels.*]

Fanny. Very much, I assure you—Bless me; sister, you have a prodigious quantity of jewels—you'll be the very Queen of Diamonds.

Miss Sterl. Ha! ha! ha! very well, my dear!—I shall be as fine as a little queen indeed.—I have a bouquet to come home tomorrow—made up of diamonds, and rubies, and emeralds, and topazes, and amethysts—jewels of all colours, green, red, blue, yellow, intermixt—the prettiest thing you ever saw in your life!—

the jeweller says I shall set out with as many diamonds as any body in town, except Lady Brilliant, and Polly *What d'ye-call-it,* Lord Squander's kept mistress.

Fanny. But what are your wedding-cloaths, sister?

Miss Sterl. Oh, white and silver to be sure, you know.—I bought them at Sir Joseph Lutestring's, and sat above an hour in the parlour behind the shop, consulting Lady Lutestring about gold and silver stuffs, on purpose to mortify her.

Fanny. Fie, sister! how could you be so abominably provoking?

Miss Sterl. Oh, I have no patience with the pride of your city-knights' ladies.—Did you never observe the airs of Lady Lute-string drest in the richest brocade out of her husband's shop, playing crown-whist at Haberdasher's-Hall?—While the civil smirking Sir Joseph, with a smug wig trimmed round his broad face as close as a new-cut yew-hedge, and his shoes so black that they shine again, stands all day in his shop, fastened to his counter like a bad shilling?

Fanny. Indeed, indeed, sister, this is too much—If you talk at this rate, you will be absolutely a bye-word in the city—You must never venture on the inside of Temple-Bar again.

Miss Sterl. Never do I desire it—never, my dear Fanny, I prom-ise you.—Oh, how I long to be transported to the dear regions of Grosvenor-Square—far—far from the dull districts of Aldersgate, Cheap, Candlewick, and Farringdon Without and Within!—My heart goes pit-a-pat at the very idea of being introduced at Court! —gilt chariot!—pyeballed horses!—laced liveries!—and then the whispers buzzing round the circle—"Who is that young Lady! Who is she?"—"Lady Melvil, Ma'am!"—Lady Melvil! my ears tingle at the sound.—And then at dinner, instead of my father perpetually asking—"Any news upon 'Change?"—to cry—"Well, Sir John! any thing new from Arthur's?"—or—to say to some other woman of quality, "Was your Ladyship at the Dutchess of Rubber's last night?—Did you call in at Lady Thunder's? In the immensity of croud I swear I did not see you—scarce a soul at the opera last Saturday—shall I see you at Carlisle-House next Thursday?"—Oh, the dear Beau-Monde! I was born to move in the sphere of the great world.

Fanny. And so, in the midst of all this happiness, you have no compassion for me—no pity for us poor mortals in common life.

Miss Sterl. [*Affectedly.*] You—You're above pity.—You would not change conditions with me—you're over head and ears in love, you know.—Nay, for that matter, if Mr. Lovewell and you come together, as I doubt not you will, you will live very com-fortably, I dare say.—He will mind his business—you'll employ yourself in the delightful care of your family—and once in a season perhaps you'll sit together in a front-box at a benefit play, as we used to do at our dancing-master's, you know—and perhaps I may meet you in the summer with some other citizens at Tunbridge.—For my part, I shall always entertain a proper regard for my relations.—You sha'n't want my countenance, I assure you.

Fanny. Oh, you're too kind, sister!

Enter MRS. HEIDELBERG.

Mrs. Heidel. [*At entring.*] Here this evening!—I vow and pertest we shall scarce have time to provide for them—Oh, my dear! [*To* MISS STERL.] I am glad to see you're not quite in dishabille. Lord Ogleby and Sir John Melvil will be here to-night.

Miss Sterl. To-night, Ma'am?

Mrs. Heidel. Yes, my dear, to-night.—Do, put on a smarter cap, and change those ordinary ruffles!—Lord, I have such a deal to do, I shall scarce have time to slip on my Italian lutestring.— Where is this dawdle of a housekeeper?—[*Enter* MRS. TRUSTY.] Oh, here, Trusty! do you know that people of qualaty are expected here this evening?

Trusty. Yes, Ma'am.

Mrs. Heidel. Well—Do you be sure now that every thing is done in the most genteelest manner—and to the honour of the fammaly.

Trusty, Yes, Ma'am.

Mrs. Heidel. Well—but mind what I say to you.

Trusty, Yes, Ma'am.

Mrs. Heidel. His Lordship is to lie in the chintz bedchamber— d'ye hear?—And Sir John in the blue damask room—His Lordship's valet-de-shamb in the opposite—

Trusty. But Mr. Lovewell is come down—and you know that's his room, Ma'am.

Mrs. Heidel. Well—well—Mr. Lovewell may make shift—or get a bed at the George—But hark ye, Trusty!

Trusty. Ma'am!

Mrs. Heidel. Get the great dining-room in order as soon as possible. Unpaper the curtains, take the civers off the couch and the chairs, and put the china figures on the mantle-piece immediately.

Trusty, Yes, Ma'am.

Mrs. Heidel. Be gone then! fly, this instant!—Where's my brother Sterling—

Trusty. Talking to the butler, Ma'am.

Mrs. Heidel. Very well. [*Exit* TRUSTY.] Miss Fanny!—I pertest I did not see you before—Lord, child, what's the matter with you?

Fanny. With me? Nothing, Ma'am.

Mrs. Heidel. Bless me! Why your face is as pale, and black, and yellow—of fifty colours, I pertest.—And then you have drest yourself as loose and as big—I declare there is not such a thing to be seen now, as a young woman with a fine waist—You all make yourselves as round as Mrs. Deputy Barter. Go, child!— You know the qualaty wil be here by and by—Go, and make your-self a little more fit to be seen. [*Exit* FANNY.] She is gone away in tears—absolutely crying, I vow and pertest.—This ridicalous Love! we must put a stop to it. It makes a perfect nataral of the girl.

Miss Sterl. Poor soul! she can't help it.   [*Affectedly.*

Mrs. Heidel. Well, my dear! Now I shall have an opportunity of convincing you of the absurdity of what you was telling me concerning Sir John Melvil's behaviour to you.

Miss Sterl. Oh, it gives me no manner of uneasiness. But, indeed, Ma'am, I cannot be persuaded but that Sir John is an extremely cold lover. Such distant civility, grave looks, and lukewarm pro-fessions of esteem for me and the whole family! I have heard of flames and darts, but Sir John's is a passion of mere ice and snow.

Mrs. Heidel. Oh, fie, my dear! I am perfectly ashamed of you. That's so like the notions of your poor sister! What you complain of as coldness and indiffarence, is nothing but the extreme gen-tilaty of his address, an exact pictur of the manners of qualaty.

Miss Sterl. Oh, he is the very mirror of complaisance! full of formal bows and set speeches!—I declare, if there was any vio-lent passion on my side, I should be quite jealous of him.

Mrs. Heidel. I say jealus indeed—Jealus of who, pray?

Miss Sterl. My sister Fanny. She seems a much greater favourite than I am, and he pays her infinitely more attention, I assure you.

Mrs. Heidel. Lord! d'ye think a man of fashion, as he is, can't distinguish between the genteel and the wulgar part of the famaly? —Between you and your sister, for instance—or me and my brother?—Be advised by me, child! It is all politeness and good-breeding.—Nobody knows the qualaty better than I do.

Miss Sterl. In my mind the old lord, his uncle, has ten times more gallantry about him than Sir John. He is full of attentions to the ladies, and smiles, and grins, and leers, and ogles, and fills every wrinkle in his old wizen face with comical expressions of tenderness. I think he wou'd make an admirable sweetheart.

Enter STERLING.

Sterl. [*At entring.*] No fish?—Why the pond was dragged but yesterday morning—There's carp and tench in the boat.—Pox on't, if that dog Lovewell had any thought, he wou'd have brought down a turbot, or some of the land-carriage mackarel.

Mrs. Heidel. Lord, brother, I am afraid his lordship and Sir John will not arrive while it's light.

Sterl. I warrant you.—But, pray, sister Heidelberg, let the turtle be drest to-morrow, and some venison—and let the gardener cut some pine-apples—and get out some ice.—I'll answer for wine, I warrant you—I'll give them such a glass of Champagne as they never drank in their lives—no, not at a Duke's table.

Mrs. Heidel. Pray now, brother, mind how you behave. I am always in a fright about you with people of qualaty. Take care that you don't fall asleep directly after supper, as you commonly do. Take a good deal of snuff; and that will keep you awake.— And don't burst out with your horrible loud horse-laughs. It is monstrous wulgar.

Sterl. Never fear, sister!—Who have we here?

Mrs. Heidel. It is Mons. Cantoon, the Swish gentleman, that lives with his Lordship, I vow and pertest.

Enter CANTON.

Sterl. Ah, Mounseer! your servant.—I am very glad to see you, Mounseer.

Canton. Mosh oblige to Mons. Sterling.—Ma'am, I am yours— Matemoiselle, I am yours.   [*Bowing round*

Mrs. Heidel. Your humble servant, Mr. Cantoon!

Canton. I kiss your hands, Matam!

Sterl. Well, Mounseer!—and what news of your good family? —when are we to see his Lordship and Sir John?

Canton. Mons. Sterling! Milor Ogleby and Sir Jean Melvile will be here in one quarter-hour.

Sterl. I am glad to hear it.

Mrs. Heidel. O, I am perdigious glad to hear it. Being so late I was afeard of some accident.—Will you please to have any thing, Mr. Cantoon, after your journey?

Canton. No, I tank you, Ma'am.

Mrs. Heidel. Shall I go and shew you the apartments, Sir?

Canton. You do me great honeur, Ma'am.

Mrs. Heidel. Come then!—come, my dear! [*To* MISS STERLING]   [*Exeunt.*

Manet STERLING.

Sterl. Pox on't, it's almost dark—It will be too late to go round the garden this evening.—However, I will carry them to take a peep at my fine canal at least, I am determined.   [*Exit.*

ACT II

SCENE.—*An ante-chamber to* LORD OGLEBY'S *bedchamber—Table with chocolate, and small case for medicines*

Enter BRUSH, *my Lord's valet-de-chambre, and* STERLING'S *chamber-maid.*

Brush. You shall stay, my dear, I insist upon it.

Ch. Maid. Nay, pray, Sir, don't be so positive; I can't stay indeed.

Brush. You shall take one cup to our better acquaintance.

Ch. Maid. I seldom drinks chocolate; and if I did, one has no satisfaction, with such apprehensions about one—if my Lord should wake, or the Swish gentleman should see one, or Madam Heidelberg should know of it, I should be frighted to death—besides I have had my tea already this morning—I'm sure I hear my Lord. [*In a fright.*

Brush. No, no, Madam, don't flutter yourself—the moment my Lord waits, he rings his bell which I answer sooner or later, as it suits my convenience.

Ch. Maid. But should he come upon us without ringing—

Brush. I'll forgive him if he does—This key [*Takes a phial out of the case.*] locks him up till I please to let him out.

Ch. Maid. Law, Sir! that's potecary's-stuff.

Brush. It is so—but without this he can no more get out of bed —than he can read without spectacles—[*Sips.*] What with qualms, age, rheumatism, and a few surfeits in his youth, he must have a great deal of brushing, oyling, screwing, and winding up to set him a going for the day.

Ch. Maid. [*Sips.*] That's prodigious indeed—[*Sips.*] My Lord seems quite in a decay.

Brush. Yes, he's quite a spectacle [*sips*], a mere corpse, till he is reviv'd and refresh'd from our little magazine here—When the restorative pills, and cordial waters warm his stomach, and get into his head, vanity frisks in his heart, and then he sets up for the lover, the rake, and the fine gentleman.

Ch. Maid. [*Sips.*] Poor gentleman!—but should the Swish gentleman come upon us. [*Frighten'd.*

Brush. Why, then the English gentleman would be very angry —No foreigner must break in upon my privacy. [*Sips.*] But I can assure you Monsieur Canton is otherwise employ'd—He is oblig'd to skim the cream of half a score news-papers for my Lord's breakfast—ha, ha, ha. Pray, Madam, drink your cup peaceably—My

Lord's chocolate is remarkably good, he won't touch a drop but what comes from Italy.

Ch. Maid. [*Sipping.*] 'Tis very fine indeed!—[*sips*] and charmingly perfum'd—it smells for all the world like our young ladies dressing-boxes.

Brush. You have an excellent taste, Madam, and I must beg of you to accept of a few cakes for your own drinking [*Takes 'em out of a drawer in the table.*], and in return, I desire nothing but to taste the perfume of your lips—[*Kisses her.*]—A small return of favours, Madam, will make, I hope, this country and retirement agreeable to both. [*He bows, she curtsies.*] Your young ladies are fine girls, faith: [*sips*] tho' upon my soul, I am quite of my old lord's mind about them; and were I inclin'd to matrimony, I should take the youngest. [*Sips.*

Ch. Maid. Miss Fanny's the most affablest and the most best nater'd creter!

Brush. And the eldest a little haughty or so—

Ch. Maid. More haughtier and prouder than Saturn himself—but this I say quite confidential to you, for one would not hurt a young lady's marriage, you know. [*Sips.*

Brush. By no means, but you can't hurt it with us—we don't consider tempers—we want money, Mrs. Nancy—give us enough of that, we'll abate you a great deal in other particulars—ha, ha, ha.

Ch. Maid. Bless me, here's somebody—[*Bell rings.*]—O! 'tis my Lord—Well, your servant, Mr. Brush—I'll clean the cups in the next room.

Brush. Do so—but never mind the bell—I shan't go this half hour. Will you drink tea with me in the afternoon?

Ch. Maid. Not for the world, Mr. Brush—I'll be here to set all things to rights—but I must not drink tea indeed—and so your servant. [*Exit* MAID *with teaboard.*] [*Bell rings again.*

Brush. It is impossible to stupify one's self in the country for a week without some little flirting with the Abigails: this is much the handsomest wench in the house, except the old citizen's youngest daughter, and I have not time enough to lay a plan for Her—[*Bell rings.*] And now I'll go to my Lord, for I have nothing else to do. [*Going.*

Enter CANTON *with news-papers in his hand.*

Cant. Monsieur Brush—Maistre Brush—My Lor stirra yet?

Brush. He has just rung his bell—I am going to him.

Cant. Depechez vous donc. [*Exit* BRUSH.] [*Puts on spectacles.*] I wish de Deviel had all dese papiers—I forget, as fast as I read—

De Advertise put out of my head de Gazette, de Gazette de Chronique, and so dey all go l'un apres l'autre—I must get some nouvelle for my Lor, or he'll be enragée contre moi—Voyons!— [*Reads in the papers.*] Here is noting but Anti-Sejanus & advertise—

Enter MAID *with chocolate things.*

Vat you vant, child?—
Ch. Maid. Only the chocolate things, Sir.
Cant. O ver well—dat is good girl—and ver prit too!
[*Exit* MAID.

LORD OGLEBY *within.*

Lord Ogle. Canton, he, he—[*Coughs.*]—Canton!
Cant. I come, my Lord—vat shall I do?—I have no news—He vil make great tintamarre!—
Lord Ogle. [*Within.*] Canton, I say, Canton! Where are you?—

Enter LORD OGLEBY *leaning on* BRUSH.

Cant. Here, my Lor; I ask pardon, my Lor, I have not finish de papiers—
Lord Ogle. Dem your pardon, and your papers—I want you here, Canton.
Cant. Den I run, dat is all—
[*Shuffles along*—LORD OGLEBY *leans upon* CANTON *too, and comes forward.*
Lord Ogle. You Swiss are the most unaccountable mixture—you have the language and the impertinence of the French, with the laziness of Dutchmen.
Cant. 'Tis very true, my Lor—I can't help—
Lord Ogle. [*Cries out.*] O Diavolo!
Cant. You are not in pain, I hope, my Lor.
Lord Ogle. Indeed but I am, my Lor—That vulgar fellow Sterling, with his city politeness, would force me down his slope last night to see a clay-colour'd ditch, which he calls a canal; and what with the dew, and the east-wind, my hips and shoulders are absolutely screw'd to my body.
Cant. A littel veritable eau d'arquibusade vil set all to right again—
[*My* LORD *sits down,* BRUSH *gives chocolate.*
Lord Ogle. Where are the Palsy-drops, Brush?
Brush. Here, my Lord!
[*Pouring out.*
Lord Ogle. Quelle nouvelle avez vous, Canton?
Cant. A great deal of papier, but no news at all.

Lord Ogle. What! nothing at all, you stupid fellow?

Cant. Yes, my Lor, I have littel advertise here vill give you more plaisir den all de lyes about noting at all. La voila!

> [*Puts on his spectacles.*

Lord Ogle. Come read it, Canton, with good emphasis, and good discretion.

Cant. I vil, my Lor—[Cant. *reads.*] Dere is no question, but dat de Cosmetique Royale vil utterlie take away all heats, pimps, frecks & oder eruptions of de skin, and likewise de wrinque of old age, *&c. &c.*—A great deal more, my Lor—be sure to ask for de Cosmetique Royale, signed by de Docteur own hand—Dere is more raison for dis caution dan good men vil tink—Eh bien, my Lor!

Lord Ogle. Eh bien, Canton!—Will you purchase any?

Cant. For you, my Lor?

Lord Ogle. For me, you old puppy! for what?

Cant. My Lor?

Lord Ogle. Do I want cosmeticks?

Cant. My Lor?

Lord Ogle. Look in my face—come, be sincere—Does it want the assistance of art?

Cant. [*With his spectacles.*] En verité, non.—'Tis very smoose and brillian—but I tote dat you might take a little by way of prevention.

Lord Ogle. You thought like an old fool, Monsieur, as you generally do—The surfeit-water, Brush! [Brush *pours out.*] What do you think, Brush, of this family, we are going to be connected with?—Eh!

Brush. Very well to marry in, my Lord; but it would not do to live with.

Lord Ogle.—You are right, Brush—There is no washing the Blackamoor white—Mr. Sterling will never get rid of Black-Fryars, always taste of the Borachio—and the poor woman his sister is so busy and so notable, to make one welcome, that I have not yet got over her first reception; it almost amounted to suffocation! I think the daughters are tolerable—Where's my cephalick snuff?   [Brush *gives him a box.*

Cant. Dey tink so of you, my Lor, for dey look at noting else, ma foi.

Lord Ogle. Did they?—Why, I think they did a little—Where's my glass? [Brush *puts one on the table.*] The youngest is delectable.   [*Takes snuff.*

Cant. O, ouy, my Lor—very delect, inteed; she made doux yeux at you, my Lor.

Lord Ogle. She was particular—the eldest, my nephew's lady, will be a most valuable wife; she has all the vulgar spirits of her father, and aunt, happily blended with the termagant qualities of her deceased mother.—Some pepper-mint water, Brush!—How happy is it, Cant, for young ladies in general, that people of quality overlook every thing in a marriage contract but their fortune.

Cant. C'est bien heureux, et commode aussi.

Lord Ogle. Brush, give me that pamphlet by my bed-side— [BRUSH *goes for it.*] Canton, do you wait in the anti-chamber, and let nobody interrupt me till I call you.

Cant. Mush goot may do your Lordship!

Lord Ogle. [*To* BRUSH, *who brings the pamphlet.*] And now, Brush, leave me a little to my studies. [*Exit* BRUSH.

LORD OGLEBY *alone.*

What can I possibly do among these women here, with this confounded rheumatism? It is a most grievous enemy to gallantry and address—[*Gets off his chair.*]—He!—Courage, my Lor! by heav'ns, I'm another creature—[*Hums and dances a little.*] It will do, faith—Bravo, my Lor! these girls have absolutely inspir'd me—If they are for a game of romps—Me voila pret! [*Sings and dances.*] O—that's an ugly twinge—but it's gone—I have rather too much of the lily this morning in my complexion; a faint tincture of the rose will give a delicate spirit to my eyes for the day. [*Unlocks a drawer at the bottom of the glass, and takes out rouge; while he's painting himself, a knocking at the door.*] Who's there! I won't be disturb'd.

Canton. [*Without.*] My Lor, my Lor, here is Monsieur Sterling to pay his devoir to you this morn in your chambre.

Lord Ogle. [*Softly.*] What a fellow!—[*Aloud.*] I am extreamly honour'd by Mr. Sterling—Why don't you see him in, Monsieur? —I wish he was at the bottom of his stinking canal—[*Door opens.*] Oh, my dear Mr. Sterling, you do me a great deal of honour.

Enter STERLING *and* LOVEWELL.

Sterl. I hope, my Lord, that your Lordship slept well in the night—I believe there are no better beds in Europe than I have— I spare no pains to get 'em, nor money to buy 'em—His Majesty, God bless him, don't sleep upon a better out of his palace; and if I had said *in* too, I hope no treason, my Lord.

Lord Ogle. Your beds are like every thing else about you, incomparable!—They not only make one rest well, but give one spirits, Mr. Sterling.

Sterl. What say you then, my Lord, to another walk in the garden? You must see my water by daylight, and my walks, and my slopes, and my clumps, and my bridge, and my flow'ring trees, and my bed of Dutch tulips—Matters look'd but dim last night, my Lord; I feel the dew in my great toe—but I would put on a cut shoe that I might be able to walk you about—I may be laid up to-morrow.

Lord Ogle. I pray heav'n you may!   [*Aside.*

Sterl. What say you, my Lord?

Lord Ogle. I was saying, Sir, that I was in hopes of seeing the young ladies at breakfast: Mr. Sterling, they are, in my mind, the finest tulips in this part of the world—he, he.

Cant. Bravissimo, my Lor!—ha, ha, he.

Sterl. They shall meet your Lordship in the garden—we won't lose our walk for them; I'll take you a little round before breakfast, and a larger before dinner, and in the evening you shall go to the Grand Tower, as I call it, ha, ha, ha.

Lord Ogle. Not a foot, I hope, Mr. Sterling—consider your gout, my good friend—You'll certainly be laid by the heels for your politeness—he, he, he.

Cant. Ha, ha, ha—'tis admirable! en verité!—

[*Laughing very heartily.*

Sterl. If my young man [*To* LOVEWELL.] here, would but laugh at my jokes, which he ought to do, as Mounseer does at yours, my Lord, we should be all life and mirth.

Lord Ogle. What say you, Cant, will you take my kinsman under your tuition? you have certainly the most companionable laugh I ever met with, and never out of tune.

Cant. But when your Lordship is out of spirits.

Lord Ogle. Well said, Cant!—but here comes my nephew, to play his part.

Enter SIR JOHN MELVIL.

Well, Sir John, what news from the island of Love? have you been sighing and serenading this morning?

Sir John. I am glad to see your Lordship in such spirits this morning.

Lord Ogle. I'm sorry to see you so dull, Sir—What poor things, Mr. Sterling, these *very* young fellows are! they make love with faces, as if they were burying the dead—though, indeed, a marriage sometimes may be properly called a burying of the living—eh, Mr. Sterling?—

Sterl. Not if they have enough to live upon, my Lord—Ha, ha, ha.

Cant. Dat is all Monsieur Sterling tink of.

Sir John. [*Apart.*] Prithee, Lovewell, come with me into the garden; I have something of consequence for you, and I must communicate it directly.

Lovew. We'll go together—If your Lordship and Mr. Sterling please, we'll prepare the ladies to attend you in the garden.

[*Exeunt* SIR JOHN *and* LOVEWELL.

Sterl. My girls are always ready, I make 'em rise soon, and to-bed early; their husbands shall have 'em with good constitutions, and good fortunes, if they have nothing else, my Lord.

Lord Ogle. Fine things, Mr. Sterling!

Sterl. Fine things, indeed, my Lord—Ah, my Lord, had not you run off your speed in your youth, you had not been so crippled in your age, my Lord.

Lord. Ogle. Very pleasant, I protest—He, he, he.—

[*Half-laughing.*

Sterl. Here's Mounseer now, I suppose, is pretty near your Lordship's standing; but having little to eat, and little to spend, in his own country, he'll wear three of your Lordship out—eating and drinking kills us all.

Lord Ogle. Very pleasant, I protest—What a vulgar dog!

[*Aside.*

Cant. My Lor so old as me!—He is shicken to me—and look like a boy to pauvre me.

Sterl. Ha, ha, ha. Well said, Mounseer—keep to that, and you'll live in any country of the world—Ha, ha, ha.—But, my Lord, I will wait upon you into the garden: we have but a little time to breakfast—I'll go for my hat and cane, fetch a little walk with you, my Lord, and then for the hot rolls and butter!

[*Exit* STERLING.

Lord Ogle. I shall attend you with pleasure—Hot rolls and butter, in July!—I sweat with the thoughts of it—What a strange beast it is!

Cant. C'est un barbare.

Lord Ogle. He is a vulgar dog, and if there was not so much money in the family, which I can't do without, I would leave him and his hot rolls and butter directly—Come along, Monsieur!

[*Exeunt* LORD OGLEBY *and* CANTON.

SCENE.—*Changes to the Garden*

Enter SIR JOHN MELVIL *and* LOVEWELL.

Lovew. In my room this morning? Impossible.

Sir John. Before five this morning, I promise you.

Lovew. On what occasion?

Sir John. I was so anxious to disclose my mind to you, that I could not sleep in my bed——But I found that you could not sleep neither—The bird was flown, and the nest long since cold.— Where was you, Lovewell?

Lovew. Pooh! prithee! ridiculous!

Sir John. Come now! which was it? Miss Sterling's maid? a pretty little rogue!—or Miss Fanny's Abigail? a sweet soul too!— or—

Lovew. Nay, nay, leave trifling, and tell me your business.

Sir John. Well, but where was you, Lovewell?

Lovew. Walking—writing—what signifies where I was?

Sir John. Walking! yes, I dare say. It rained as hard as it could pour. Sweet refreshing showers to walk in! No, no, Lovewell.— Now would I give twenty pounds to know which of the maids—

Lovew. But your business! your business, Sir John!

Sir John. Let me a little into the secrets of the family.

Lovew. Psha!

Sir John. Poor Lovewell! he can't bear it, I see. She charged you not to kiss and tell.—Eh, Lovewell! However, though you will not honour me with your confidence, I'll venture to trust you with mine.—What d'ye think of Miss Sterling?

Lovew. What do I think of Miss Sterling?

Sir John. Ay; what d'ye think of her?

Lovew. An odd question!—but I think her a smart, lively girl, full of mirth and sprightliness.

Sir John. All mischief and malice, I doubt.

Lovew. How?

Sir John. But her person—what d'ye think of that?

Lovew. Pretty and agreeable.

Sir John. A little grisette thing.

Lovew. What is the meaning of all this?

Sir John. I'll tell you. You must know, Lovewell, that notwith- standing all appearances—[*Seeing* LORD OGLEBY, *&c.*] We are interrupted—When they are gone, I'll explain.

Enter LORD OGLEBY, STERLING, MRS. HEIDELBERG, MISS STERLING, *and* FANNY.

Lord Ogle. Great improvements indeed, Mr. Sterling! wonderful improvements! The four seasons in lead, the flying Mercury, and the basin with Neptune in the middle, are all in the very extreme of fine taste. You have as many rich figures as the man at Hyde-Park Corner.

Sterl. The chief pleasure of a country house is to make improvements, you know, my Lord. I spare no expence, not I.—This is quite another-guess sort of place than it was when I first took it, my Lord. We were surrounded with trees. I cut down above fifty to make the lawn before the house, and let in the wind and the sun—smack-smooth—as you see.—Then I made a green-house out of the old laundry, and turned the brew-house into a pinery.—The high octagon summer-house, you see yonder, is raised on the mast of a ship, given me by an East-India captain, who has turned many a thousand of my money. It commands the whole road. All the coaches and chariots, and chaises, pass and repass under your eye. I'll mount you up there in the afternoon, my Lord. 'Tis the pleasantest place in the world to take a pipe and a bottle,—and so you shall say, my Lord.

Lord Ogle. Ay—or a bowl of punch, or a can of slip, Mr. Sterling! for it looks like a cabin in the air.—If flying chairs were in use, the captain might make a voyage to the Indies in it still, if he had but a fair wind.

Canton. Ha! ha! ha! ha!

Mrs. Heidel. My brother's a little comacal in his ideas, my Lord!—But you'll excuse him.—I have a little gothick dairy, fitted up entirely in my own taste.—In the evening I shall hope for the honour of your Lordship's company to take a dish of tea there, or a sullabub warm from the cow.

Lord Ogle. I have every moment a fresh opportunity of admiring the elegance of Mrs. Heidelberg—the very flower of delicacy, and cream of politeness.

Mrs. Heidel. O my Lord! ⎫
Lord Ogle. O Madam! ⎭   [*Leering at each other.*

Sterl. How d'ye like these close walks, my Lord?

Lord Ogle. A most excellent serpentine! It forms a perfect maze, and winds like a true-lover's knot.

Sterl. Ay—here's none of your strait lines here—but all taste—zig-zag—crinkum-crankum—in and out—right and left—to and again—twisting and turning like a worm, my Lord!

Lord Ogle. Admirably laid out indeed, Mr. Sterling! one can hardly see an inch beyond one's nose any where in these walks.—You are a most excellent œconomist of your land, and make a little go a great way.—It lies together in as small parcels as if it was placed in pots out at your window in Grace-church-Street.

Canton. Ha! ha! ha! ha!

Lord Ogle. What d'ye laugh at, Canton?

Canton. Ah! que cette similitude est drole! So clever what you say, mi Lor.

Lord Ogle. [*To* FANNY.] You seem mightily engaged, Madam. What are those pretty hands so busily employed about?

Fanny. Only making up a nosegay, my Lord!—Will your Lordship do me the honour of accepting it? [*Presenting it.*

Lord Ogle. I'll wear it next my heart, Madam!—I see the young creature doats on me. [*Apart.*

Miss Sterl. Lord, sister! you've loaded his Lordship with a bunch of flowers as big as the cook or the nurse carry to town on Monday morning for a beaupot.—Will your Lordship give me leave to present you with this rose and a sprig of sweet-briar?

Lord Ogle. The truest emblems of yourself, Madam! all sweetness and poignancy.—A little jealous, poor soul! [*Apart.*

Sterl. Now, my Lord, if you please, I'll carry you to see my Ruins.

Mrs. Heidel. You'll absolutely fatigue his Lordship with overwalking, brother!

Lord Ogle. Not at all, Madam! We're in the garden of Eden, you know; in the region of perpetual spring, youth, and beauty.

[*Leering at the women.*

Mrs. Heidel. Quite the man of qualaty, I pertest. [*Apart.*

Canton. Take a my arm, mi Lor! [LORD OGLEBY *leans on him.*

Sterl. I'll only shew his Lordship my ruins, and the cascade, and the Chinese bridge, and then we'll go in to breakfast.

Lord Ogle. Ruins, did you say, Mr. Sterling?

Sterl. Ay, ruins, my Lord! and they are reckoned very fine ones too. You would think them ready to tumble on your head. It has just cost me a hundred and fifty pounds to put my ruins in thorough repair.—This way, if your Lordship pleases.

Lord Ogle. [*Going, stops.*] What steeple's that we see yonder? the parish-church, I suppose.

Sterl. Ha! ha! ha! that's admirable. It is no church at all, my Lord! it is a spire that I have built against a tree, a field or two off, to terminate the prospect. One must always have a church, or an obelisk, or a something, to terminate the prospect, you know. That's a rule in taste, my Lord!

Lord Ogle. Very ingenious, indeed! For my part, I desire no finer prospect, than this I see before me. [*Leering at the women.*]— Simple, yet varied; bounded, yet extensive.—Get away, Canton!

[*Pushing away* CANTON.] I want no assistance—I'll walk with the ladies.

Sterl. This way, my Lord!

Lord Ogle. Lead on, Sir!—We young folks here will follow you. —Madam!—Miss Sterling!—Miss Fanny! I attend you.

[*Exit, after* STERLING, *gallanting the ladies.*

Canton. [*Following.*] He is cock o'de game, ma foy!   [*Exit.*

Manent SIR JOHN MELVIL *and* LOVEWELL.

Sir John. At length, thank heaven. I have an opportunity to unbosom.—I know you are faithful, Lovewell, and flatter myself you would rejoice to serve me.

Lovew. Be assured, you may depend on me.

Sir John. You must know then, notwithstanding all appearances, that this treaty of marriage between Miss Sterling and me will come to nothing.

Lovew. How!

Sir John. It will be no match, Lovewell.

Lovew. No match?

Sir John. No.

Lovew. You amaze me. What should prevent it?

Sir John. I.

Lovew. You! wherefore?

Sir John. I don't like her.

Lovew. Very plain indeed! I never supposed that you was extremely devoted to her from inclination, but thought you always considered it as a matter of convenience, rather than affection.

Sir John. Very true. I came into the family without any impressions on my mind—with an unimpassioned indifference ready to receive one woman as soon as another. I looked upon love, serious, sober love, as a chimæra, and marriage as a thing of course, as you know most people do. But I, who was lately so great an infidel in love, am now one of its sincerest votaries.—In short, my defection from Miss Sterling proceeds from the violence of my attachment to another.

Lovew. Another! So! so! here will be fine work. And pray who is she?

Sir John. Who is she! who can she be? but Fanny, the tender, amiable, engaging Fanny.

Lovew. Fanny! What Fanny?

Sir John. Fanny Sterling. Her sister— Is not she an angel, Lovewell?

Lovew. Her sister? Confusion!—You must not think of it, Sir John.

Sir John. Not think of it? I can think of nothing else. Nay, tell me, Lovewell! was it possible for me to be indulged in a perpetual intercourse with two such objects as Fanny and her sister, and not find my heart led by insensible attraction towards Her?—You seem confounded—Why don't you answer me?

Lovew. Indeed, Sir John, this event gives me infinite concern.

Sir John. Why so?—Is not she an angel, Lovewell?

Lovew. I foresee that it must produce the worst consequences. Consider the confusion it must unavoidably create. Let me persuade you to drop these thoughts in time.

Sir John. Never—never, Lovewell!

Lovew. You have gone too far to recede. A negotiation, so nearly concluded, cannot be broken off with any grace. The lawyers, you know, are hourly expected; the preliminaries almost finally settled between Lord Ogleby and Mr. Sterling; and Miss Sterling herself ready to receive you as a husband.

Sir John. Why the banns have been published, and nobody has forbidden them, 'tis true. But you know either of the parties may change their minds even after they enter the church.

Lovew. You think too lightly of this matter. To carry your addresses so far—and then to desert her—and for her sister too!— It will be such an affront to the family, that they can never put up with it.

Sir John. I don't think so: for as to my transferring my passion from her to her sister, so much the better!—for then, you know, I don't carry my affections out of the family.

Lovew. Nay, but prithee be serious, and think better of it.

Sir John. I have thought better of it already, you see. Tell me honestly, Lovewell! Can you blame me? Is there any comparison between them?

Lovew. As to that now—why that—that is just—just as it may strike different people. There are many admirers of Miss Sterling's vivacity.

Sir John. Vivacity! a medley of Cheapside pertness, and Whitechapel pride.—No—no—if I do go so far into the city for a wedding-dinner, it shall be upon turtle at least.

Lovew. But I see no probability of success; for granting that Mr. Sterling wou'd have consented to it at first, he cannot listen to it now. Why did not you break this affair to the family before?

Sir John. Under such embarrassed circumstances as I have been, can you wonder at my irresolution or perplexity? Nothing but despair, the fear of losing my dear Fanny, cou'd bring me to a declaration even now: and yet, I think I know Mr. Sterling so well, that, strange as my proposal may appear, if I can make it advantageous to him as a money-transaction, as I am sure I can, he will certainly come into it.

Lovew. But even suppose he should, which I very much doubt, I don't think Fanny herself wou'd listen to your addresses.

Sir John. You are deceived a little in that particular.

Lovew. You'll find I am in the right.

Sir John. I have some little reason to think otherwise.

Lovew. You have not declared your passion to her already?

Sir John. Yes, I have.

Lovew. Indeed!—And—and—and how did she receive it?

Sir John. I think it is not very easy for me to make my addresses to any woman, without receiving some little encouragement.

Lovew. Encouragement! did she give you any encouragement?

Sir John. I don't know what you call encouragement—but she blushed—and cried—and desired me not to think of it any more: —upon which I prest her hand—kissed it—swore she was an angel—and I cou'd see it tickled her to the soul.

Lovew. And did she express no surprise at your declaration?

Sir John. Why, faith, to say the truth, she was a little surprised —and she got away from me too, before I cou'd thoroughly explain myself. If I should not meet with an opportunity of speaking to her, I must get you to deliver a letter from me.

Lovew. I!—a letter!—I had rather have nothing—

Sir John. Nay, you promised me your assistance—and I am sure you cannot scruple to make yourself useful on such an occasion.—You may, without suspicion, acquaint her verbally of my determined affection for her, and that I am resolved to ask her father's consent.

Lovew. As to that, I—your commands, you know—that is, if she—Indeed, Sir John, I think you are in the wrong.

Sir John. Well—well—that's my concern—Ha! there she goes, by heaven! along that walk yonder, d'ye see? I'll go to her immediately.

Lovew. You are too precipitate. Consider what you are doing.

Sir John. I wou'd not lose this opportunity for the universe.

Lovew. Nay, pray don't go! Your violence and eagerness may overcome her spirits.—The shock will be too much for her.

[*Detaining him.*

Sir John. Nothing shall prevent me.—Ha! now she turns into another walk.—Let me go! [*Breaks from him.*] I shall lose her.— [*Going, turns back.*] Be sure now to keep out of the way! If you interrupt us, I shall never forgive you.   [*Exit hastily.*

Lovewell. [*Alone.*] 'Sdeath! I can't bear this. In love with my wife! acquaint me with his passion for her! make his addresses before my face!—I shall break out before my time.—This was the meaning of Fanny's uneasiness. She could not encourage him.— I am sure she could not.—Ha! they are turning into the walk, and coming this way. Shall I leave the place?—Leave him to sollicit my wife! I can't submit to it.—They come nearer and nearer—If I stay it will look suspicious—It may betray us, and incense him— They are here—I must go—I am the most unfortunate fellow in the world. [*Exit.*

Enter FANNY *and* SIR JOHN.

Fanny. Leave me, Sir John, I beseech you leave me!—nay, why will you persist to follow me with idle sollicitations, which are an affront to my character, and an injury to your own honour?

Sir John. I know your delicacy, and tremble to offend it: but let the urgency of the occasion be my excuse! Consider, Madam, that the future happiness of my life depends on my present application to you! consider that this day must determine my fate; and these are perhaps the only moments left me to incline you to warrant my passion, and to intreat you not to oppose the proposals I mean to open to your father.

Fanny. For shame, for shame, Sir John! Think of your previous engagements! Think of your own situation, and think of mine!— What have you discovered in my conduct that might encourage you to so bold a declaration? I am shocked that you should venture to say so much, and blush that I should even dare to give it a hearing.—Let me be gone!

Sir John. Nay, stay, Madam! but one moment!—Your sensibility is too great.—Engagements! what engagements have even been pretended on either side than those of family-convenience? I went on in the trammels of matrimonial negotiation with a blind submission to your father and Lord Ogleby; but my heart soon claimed a right to be consulted. It has devoted itself to you, and obliges me to plead earnestly for the same tender interest in yours.

Fanny. Have a care, Sir John! do not mistake a depraved will for a virtuous inclination. By these common pretences of the heart, half of our sex are made fools, and a greater part of yours despise them for it.

Sir John. Affection, you will allow, is involuntary. We cannot always direct it to the object on which it should fix—But when it is once inviolably attached, inviolably as mine is to you, it often creates reciprocal affection.—When I last urged you on this subject, you heard me with more temper, and I hoped with some compassion.

Fanny. You deceived yourself. If I forbore to exert a proper spirit, nay if I did not even express the quickest resentment of your behaviour, it was only in consideration of that respect I wish to pay you, in honour to my sister: and be assured, Sir, woman as I am, that my vanity could reap no pleasure from a triumph, that must result from the blackest treachery to her.   [*Going.*

Sir John. One word, and I have done. [*Stopping her.*]—Your impatience and anxiety, and the urgency of the occasion, oblige me to be brief and explicit with you.—I appeal therefore from your delicacy to your justice.—Your sister, I verily believe, neither entertains any real affection for me, or tenderness for you.—Your father, I am inclined to think, is not much concerned by means of which of his daughters the families are united.—Now as they cannot, shall not be connected, otherwise than by my union with you, why will you, from a false delicacy, oppose a measure so conducive to my happiness, and, I hope, your own?—I love you, most passionately and sincerely love you—and hope to propose terms agreeable to Mr. Sterling.—If then you don't absolutely loath, abhor, and scorn me—if there is no other happier man—

Fanny. Hear me, Sir! hear my final determination.—Were my father and sister as insensible as you are pleased to represent them; —were my heart for ever to remain disengaged to any other—I could not listen to your proposals.—What! You on the very eve of a marriage with my sister; I living under the same roof with her, bound not only by the laws of friendship and hospitality, but even the ties of blood, to contribute to her happiness,—and not to conspire against her peace—the peace of a whole family—and that my own too!—Away! away, Sir John!—At such a time, and in such circumstances, your addresses only inspire me with horror. —Nay, you must detain me no longer.—I will go.

Sir John. Do not leave me in absolute despair!—Give me a glimpse of hope!   [*Falling on his knees.*

Fanny. I cannot. Pray, Sir John!   [*Struggling to go.*

Sir John. Shall this hand be given to another? [*Kissing her hand.*] No—I cannot endure it.—My whole soul is yours, and the whole happiness of my life is in your power.

Enter MISS STERLING.

Fanny. Ha! my sister is here. Rise, for shame, Sir John!

Sir John. Miss Sterling!   [*Rising.*

Miss Sterl. I beg pardon, Sir!—You'll excuse me, Madam!—I have broke in upon you a little unopportunely, I believe—But I did not mean to interrupt you—I only came, Sir, to let you know that breakfast waits, if you have finished your morning's devotions.

Sir John. I am very sensible, Miss Sterling, that this may appear
particular, but——

Miss Sterl. Oh dear, Sir John, don't put yourself to the trouble
of an apology. The thing explains itself.

Sir John. It will soon, Madam!—In the mean time I can only
assure you of my profound respect and esteem for you, and make
no doubt of convincing Mr. Sterling of the honour and integrity
of my intentions. And—and—your humble servant, Madam!

[Exit in confusion.

Manent FANNY *and* MISS STERLING.

Miss Sterl. Respect?—Insolence!—Esteem?—Very fine truly!
—And you, Madam! my sweet, delicate, innocent, sentimental
sister! will you convince my papa too of the integrity of your in
tentions?

Fanny. Do not upbraid me, my dear sister! Indeed, I don't
deserve it. Believe me, you can't be more offended at his behaviour
than I am, and I am sure it cannot make you half so miserable.

Miss Sterl. Make me miserable! You are mightily deceived,
Madam! It gives me no sort of uneasiness, I assure you.—A base
fellow!—As for you, Miss! the pretended softness of your dispo
sition, your artful good-nature, never imposed upon me. I always
knew you to be sly, and envious, and deceitful.

Fanny. Indeed you wrong me.

Miss Sterl. Oh, you are all goodness, to be sure!—Did not I
find him on his knees before you? Did not I see him kiss your sweet
hand? Did not I hear his protestations? Was not I witness of your
dissembled modesty?—No—no, my dear! don't imagine that you
can make a fool of your elder sister so easily.

Fanny. Sir John, I own, is to blame; but I am above the thought
of doing you the least injury.

Miss Sterl. We shall try that, Madam!—I hope, Miss, you'll be
able to give a better account to my papa and my aunt—for they
shall both know of this matter, I promise you.   [*Exit.*

Fanny. [*Alone.*] How unhappy I am! my distresses multiply
upon me.—Mr. Lovewell must now become acquainted with Sir
John's behaviour to me—and in a manner that may add to his
uneasiness.—My father, instead of being disposed by fortunate
circumstances to forgive any transgression, will be previously in
censed against me.—My sister and my aunt will become irrecon
cilably my enemies, and rejoice in my disgrace.—Yet, at all events,
I am determined on a discovery. I dread it, and am resolved to
hasten it. It is surrounded with more horrors every instant, as it
appears every instant more necessary.   [*Exit.*

ACT III

Scene.—A hall

Enter a Servant *leading in* Serjeant Flower, *and* Counsellors Traverse *and* Trueman—*all booted.*

Servant. This way, if you please, gentlemen! my master is at
breakfast with the family at present—but I'll let him know, and
he will wait on you immediately.

Flower. Mighty well, young man, mighty well.

Servant. Please to favour me with your names, gentlemen.

Flower. Let Mr. Sterling know, that Mr. Serjeant Flower, and
two other gentlemen of the bar, are come to wait on him according to his appointment.

Servant. I will, Sir.   [*Going.*

Flower. And harkee, young man! [Servant *returns.*] Desire my
servant—Mr. Serjeant Flower's servant—to bring in my green
and gold saddle-cloth and pistols, and lay them down here in the
hall with my portmanteau.

Servant. I will, Sir.   [*Exit.*

Manent Lawyers.

Flower. Well, gentlemen! the setting these marriage articles
falls conveniently enough, almost just on the eve of the circuits.—
Let me see—the Home, the Midland, and Western,—ay, we can all
cross the country well enough to our several destinations.—
Traverse, when do you begin at Hertford?

Traverse. The day after to-morrow.

Flower. That is commission-day with us at Warwick too.—But
my clerk has retainers for every cause in the paper, so it will be
time enough if I am there the next morning.—Besides, I have
about half a dozen cases that have lain by me ever since the spring
assizes, and I must tack opinions to them before I see my country-
clients again—so I will take the evening before me—and then
currente calamo, as I say—eh, Traverse!

Traverse. True, Mr. Serjeant—and the easiest thing in the
world too—for those country attornies are such ignorant dogs,
that in case of the devise of an estate to A and his heirs for ever,
they'll make a query, whether he takes in fee or in tail.

Flower. Do you expect to have much to do on the Home circuit
these assizes?

Traverse. Not much *nisi prius* business, but a good deal on the crown side, I believe.—The gaols are brimfull—and some of the felons in good circumstances, and likely to be tolerable clients.— Let me see! I am engag'd for three highway robberies, two murders, one forgery, and half a dozen larcenies at Kingston.

Flower. A pretty decent gaol-delivery!—Do you expect to bring off Darkin, for the robbery on Putney-Common? Can you make out your *alibi?*

Traverse. Oh, no! the crown witnesses are sure to prove our identity. We shall certainly be hanged: but that don't signify.— But, Mr. Serjeant, have you much to do?—any remarkable cause on the Midland this circuit?

Flower. Nothing very remarkable,—except two rapes, and Rider and Western at Nottingham, for *crim. con.*—but, on the whole, I believe a good deal of business.—Our associate tells me, there are above thirty *venires* for Warwick.

Traverse. Pray, Mr. Serjeant, are you concerned in Jones and Thomas at Lincoln?

Flower. I am—for the plaintiff.

Traverse. And what do you think on't?

Flower. A nonsuit.

Traverse. I thought so.

Flower. Oh, no manner of doubt on't—*luce clarius*—we have no right in us—we have but one chance.

Traverse. What's that?

Flower. Why, my Lord Chief does not go the circuit this time, and my brother Puzzle being in the commission, the cause will come on before him.

Trueman. Ay, that may do, indeed, if you can but throw dust in the eyes of the defendant's council.

Flower. True.—Mr. Trueman, I think you are concerned for Lord Ogleby in this affair? [*To* TRUEMAN.

Trueman. I am, Sir—I have the honour to be related to his Lordship, and hold some courts for him in Somersetshire,—go the Western circuit—and attend the sessions at Exeter, merely because his Lordship's interest and property lie in that part of the kingdom.

Flower. Ha!—and pray, Mr. Trueman, how long have you been called to the bar?

Trueman. About nine years and three quarters.

Flower. Ha!—I don't know that I ever had the pleasure of seeing you before.—I wish you success, young gentleman!

Enter STERLING.

Sterl. Oh, Mr. Serjeant Flower, I am glad to see you—You

servant, Mr. Serjeant! Gentlemen, your servant!—Well, are all Matters concluded? Has that snail-paced conveyancer, old Ferret of Gray's Inn, settled the articles at last? Do you approve of what he has done? Will his tackle hold? tight and strong?—Eh, Master Serjeant?

Flower. My friend Ferret's slow and sure, Sir—But then, *serius aut citius,* as we say,—sooner or later, Mr. Sterling, he is sure to put his business out of hand as he should do.—My clerk has brought the writings, and all other instruments along with him, and the settlement is, I believe, as good a settlement as any settlement on the face of the earth!

Sterl. But that damn'd mortgage of 60,000l.—There don't appear to be any other incumbrances, I hope?

Traverse. I can answer for that, Sir—and that will be cleared off immediately on the payment of the first part of Miss Sterling's portion—You agree, on your part, to come down with 80,000l.—

Sterl. Down on the nail.—Ay, ay, my money is ready to-morrow if he pleases—he shall have it in India-bonds, or notes, or how he chuses.—Your lords, and your dukes, and your people at the court-end of the town stick at payments sometimes—debts unpaid, no credit lost with them—but no fear of us substantial fellows—eh, Mr. Serjeant?

Flower. Sir John having last term, according to agreement, levied a fine, and suffered a recovery, has thereby cut off the entail of the Ogleby estate for the better effecting the purposes of the present intended marriage; on which above-mentioned Ogleby estate, a jointure of 2000l. per ann., is secured to your eldest daughter, now Elizabeth Sterling, spinster, and the whole estate, after the death of the aforesaid Earl, descends to the heirs male of Sir John Melvil on the body of the aforesaid Elizabeth Sterling lawfully to be begotten.

Traverse. Very true—and Sir John is to be put in immediate possession of as much of his Lordship's Somersetshire estate, as lies in the manors of Hogmore and Cranford, amounting to between two and three thousands per ann., and at the death of Mr. Sterling, a further sum of seventy thousand—

Enter SIR JOHN MELVIL.

Sterl. Ah, Sir John! Here we are—hard at it—paving the road to matrimony—First the lawyers, then comes the doctor—Let us but dispatch the long-robe, we shall soon set Pudding-sleeves to work, I warrant you.

Sir John. I am sorry to interrupt you, Sir—but I hope that both you and these gentlemen will excuse me—having something very particular for your private ear, I took the liberty of following you, and beg you will oblige me with an audience immediately.

Sterl. Ay, with all my heart—Gentlemen, Mr. Serjeant, you'll excuse it—Business must be done, you know.—The writings will keep cold till to-morrow morning.

Flower. I must be at Warwick, Mr. Sterling, the day after.

Sterl. Nay, nay, I shan't part with you to-night, gentlemen, I promise you—My house is very full, but I have beds for you all, beds for your servants, and stabling for all your horses.— Will you take a turn in the garden, and view some of my improvements before dinner? Or will you amuse yourselves on the green, with a game of bowls and a cool tankard?—My servants shall attend you—Do you chuse any other refreshment?—Call for what you please;—do as you please;—make yourselves quite at home, I beg of you.—Here,—Thomas, Harry, William, wait on these Gentlemen!—[*Follows the lawyers out, bawling and talking, and then returns to* SIR JOHN.] And now, Sir, I am entirely at your service.—What are your commands with me, Sir John?

Sir John. After having carried the negotiation between our families to so great a length, after having assented so readily to all your proposals, as well as received so many instances of your chearful compliance with the demands made on our part, I am extremely concerned, Mr. Sterling, to be the involuntary cause of any uneasiness.

Sterl. Uneasiness! what uneasiness?—Where business is transacted as it ought to be, and the parties understand one another, there can be no uneasiness. You agree, on such and such conditions to receive my daughter for a wife; on the same conditions I agree to receive you as a son-in-law; and as to all the rest, it follows of course, you know, as regularly as the payment of a bill after acceptance.

Sir John. Pardon me, Sir; more uneasiness has arisen than you are aware of. I am myself, at this instant, in a state of inexpressible embarrassment; Miss Sterling, I know, is extremely disconcerted too; and unless you will oblige me with the assistance of your friendship, I forsee the speedy progress of discontent and animosity through the whole family.

Sterl. What the deuce is all this? I don't understand a single syllable.

Sir. John. In one word then—it will be absolutely impossible for me to fulfill my engagements in regard to Miss Sterling.

Sterl. How, Sir John? Do you mean to put an affront upon my family? What! refuse to—

Sir John. Be assured, Sir, that I neither mean to affront, nor forsake your family.—My only fear is, that you should desert me; for the whole happiness of my life depends on my being connected with your family by the nearest and tenderest ties in the world.

Sterl. Why, did not you tell me, but a moment ago, that it was absolutely impossible for you to marry my daughter?

Sir John. True.—But you have another daughter, Sir—

Sterl. Well?

Sir John. Who has obtained the most absolute dominion over my heart. I have already declared my passion to her; nay, Miss Sterling herself is also apprized of it, and if you will but give a sanction to my present addresses, the uncommon merit of Miss Sterling will no doubt recommend her to a person of equal, if not superior rank to myself, and our families may still be allied by my union with Miss Fanny.

Sterl. Mighty fine, truly! Why, what the plague do you make of us, Sir John? Do you come to market for my daughters, like servants at a statute-fair? Do you think that I will suffer you, or any man in the world, to come into my house, like the Grand Signior, and throw the handkerchief first to one, and then to t'other, just as he pleases? Do you think I drive a kind of African slave-trade with them? and—

Sir John. A moment's patience, Sir! Nothing but the excess of my passion for Miss Fanny shou'd have induced me to take any step that had the least appearance of disrespect to any part of your family; and even now I am desirous to atone for my transgression, by making the most adequate compensation that lies in my power.

Sterl. Compensation! what compensation can you possibly make in such a case as this, Sir John?

Sir John. Come, come, Mr. Sterling; I know you to be a man of sense, a man of business, a man of the world. I'll deal frankly with you; and you shall see that I do not desire a change of measures for my own gratification, without endeavouring to make it advantageous to you.

Sterl. What advantage can your inconstancy be to me, Sir John?

Sir John. I'll tell you, Sir.—You know that by the articles at present subsisting between us, on the day of my marriage with Miss Sterling, you agree to pay down the gross sum of eighty thousand pounds.

Sterl. Well!

Sir John. Now if you will but consent to my waving that marriage—

Sterl. I agree to your waving that marriage? Impossible, Sir John!

Sir John. I hope not, Sir; as on my part, I will agree to wave my right to thirty thousand pounds of the fortune I was to receive with her.

Sterl. Thirty thousand, d'ye say?

Sir John. Yes, Sir; and accept of Miss Fanny with fifty thousand, instead of fourscore.

Sterl. Fifty thousand—   [*Pausing.*

Sir John. Instead of fourscore.

Sterl. Why,—why,—there may be something in that.—Let me see; Fanny with fifty thousand instead of Betsey with fourscore—But how can this be, Sir John?—For you know I am to pay this money into the hands of my Lord Ogleby; who, I believe —between you and me, Sir John,—is not overstocked with ready money at present; and threescore thousand of it, you know, is to go to pay off the present incumbrances on the estate, Sir John.

Sir John. That objection is easily obviated.—Ten of the twenty thousand, which would remain as a surplus of the fourscore, after paying off the mortgage, was intended by his Lordship for my use, that we might set off with some little *éclat* on our marriage; and the other ten for his own.—Ten thousand pounds therefore I shall be able to pay you immediately; and for the remaining twenty thousand you shall have a mortgage on that part of the estate which is to be made over to me, with whatever security you shall require for the regular payment of the interest, 'till the principal is duly discharged.

Sterl. Why—to do you justice, Sir John, there is something fair and open in your proposal; and since I find you do not mean to put an affront upon the family—

Sir John. Nothing was ever farther from my thoughts, Mr. Sterling.—And after all, the whole affair is nothing extraordinary —such things happen every day—and as the world has only heard generally of a treaty between the families, when this marriage takes place, nobody will be the wiser, if we have but discretion enough to keep our own counsel.

Sterl. True, true; and since you only transfer from one girl to the other, it is no more than transferring so much stock, you know.

Sir John. The very thing.

Sterl. Odso! I had quite forgot. We are reckoning without our host here. There is another difficulty—

Sir John. You alarm me. What can that be?

Sterl. I can't stir a step in this business without consulting my sister Heidelberg.—The family has very great expectations from her, and we must not give her any offence.

Sir John. But if you come into this measure, surely she will be so kind as to consent—

Sterl. I don't know that—Betsey is her darling, and I can't tell how far she may resent any slight that seems to be offered to her favourite niece.—However, I'll do the best I can for you.— You shall go and break the matter to her first, and by that time that I may suppose that your rhetorick has prevailed on her to listen to reason, I will step in to reinforce your arguments.

Sir John. I'll fly to her immediately: you promise me your assistance?

Sterl. I do.

Sir John. Ten thousand thanks for it! and now success attend me!   [*Going.*

Sterl. Harkee, Sir John! [Sir John *returns.*] Not a word of the thirty thousand to my sister, Sir John.

Sir John. Oh, I am dumb, I am dumb, Sir.   [*Going.*

Sterl. You remember it is thirty thousand.

Sir John. To be sure I do.

Sterl. But Sir John!—one thing more. [Sir John *returns.*] My Lord must know nothing of this stroke of friendship between us.

Sir John. Not for the world.—Let me alone! let me alone!

[*Offering to go.*

Sterl. [*Holding him.*]—And when every thing is agreed, we must give each other a bond to be held fast to the bargain.

Sir John. To be sure. A bond by all means! a bond, or whatever you please.   [*Exit hastily.*

Sterl. [*Alone.*] I should have thought of more conditions—he's in a humour to give me every thing—Why, what mere children are your fellows of quality; that cry for a plaything one minute, and throw it by the next; as changeable as the weather, and as uncertain as the stocks.—Special fellows to drive a bargain! and yet they are to take care of the interest of the nation truly!— Here does this whirligig man of fashion offer to give up thirty thousand pounds in hard money, with as much indifference as if it was a china orange.—By this mortgage, I shall have a hold on his *Terra firma*, and if he wants more money, as he certainly will,—let him have children by my daughter or no, I shall have his whole estate in a net for the benefit of my family.—Well; thus it is, that the children of citizens, who have acquired fortunes, prove persons of fashion; and thus it is, that persons of fashion, who have ruined their fortunes, reduce the next generation to cits.   [*Exit.*

SCENE.—*Changes to another apartment*

Enter MRS. HEIDELBERG *and* MISS STERLING.

Miss Sterl. This is your gentle-looking, soft-speaking, sweet-smiling, affable Miss Fanny for you!

Mrs. Heidel. My Miss Fanny! I disclaim her. With all her arts she never could insinuat herself into my good graces—and yet she has a way with her, that deceives man, woman, and child, except you and me, niece.

Miss Sterl. O ay; she wants nothing but a crook in her hand, and a lamb under her arm, to be a perfect picture of innocence and simplicity.

Mrs. Heidel. Just as I was drawn at Amsterdam, when I went over to visit my husband's relations.

Miss Sterl. And then she's so mighty good to servants—*Pray, John, do this—pray, Tom, do that—thank you, Jenny*—and then so humble to her relations—*to be sure, Papa!—as my Aunt pleases—my Sister knows best*—But with all her demureness and humility she has no objection to be Lady Melvil, it seems, nor to any wickedness that can make her so.

Mrs. Heidel. She Lady Melville? Compose yourself, Niece! I'll ladyship her indeed:—a little creepin', cantin'—She shan't be the better for a farden of my money. But tell me, child, how does this intriguing with Sir John correspond with her partiality to Lovewell? I don't see a concatunation here.

Miss Sterl. There I was deceived, Madam. I took all their whisperings and stealing into corners to be the mere attraction of vulgar minds; but, behold! their private meetings were not to contrive their own insipid happiness, but to conspire against mine. —But I know whence proceeds Mr. Lovewell's resentment to me. I could not stoop to be familiar with my father's clerk, and so I have lost his interest.

Mrs. Heidel. My spurrit to a T.—My dear child! [*Kissing her.*]—Mr. Heidelberg lost his election for member of Parliament, because I would not demean myself to be slobbered about by drunken shoemakers, beastly cheese-mongers, and greasy butchers and tallow-chandlers. However, Niece, I can't help diffuring a little in opinion from you in this matter. My experunce and sagucity makes me still suspect, that there is something more between her and that Lovewell, notwithstanding this affair of Sir John—I had my eye upon them the whole time of breakfast. —Sir John, I observed, looked a little confounded, indeed, though I knew nothing of what had passed in the garden. You seemed to sit upon thorns too: but Fanny and Mr. Lovewell made quite another-guess sort of a figur; and were as perfet a pictur of two distrest lovers, as if it had been drawn by Raphael Angelo.— As to Sir John and Fanny, I want a matter of fact.

Miss Sterl. Matter of fact, Madam! Did not I come unexpectedly upon them? Was not Sir John kneeling at her feet, and kissing her hand? Did not he look all love, and she all confusion? Is not that matter of fact? And did not Sir John, the moment that Papa was called out of the room to the lawyer-men, get up from breakfast, and follow him immediately? And I warrant you that by this time he has made proposals to him to marry my sister— Oh, that some other person, an earl, or a duke, would make his addresses to me, that I might be revenged on this monster!

Mrs. Heidel. Be cool, child! you *shall* be Lady Melvil, in spite of all their caballins, if it costs me ten thousand pounds to turn the scale. Sir John may apply to my brother, indeed; but I'll make them all know who governs in this fammaly.

Miss Sterl. As I live, Madam, yonder comes Sir John. A base man! I can't endure the sight of him. I'll leave the room this instant.   [*Disordered.*

Mrs. Heidel. Poor thing! Well, retire to your own chamber, child; I'll give it him, I warrant you; and by and by I'll come, and let you know all that has past between us.

Miss Sterl. Pray do, Madam!—[*Looking back.*]—A vile wretch!   [*Exit in a rage.*

                Enter SIR JOHN MELVIL.

Sir John. Your most obedient humble servant, Madam!
                        [*Bowing very respectfully.*
Mrs. Heidel. Your servant, Sir John.
                    [*Dropping a half-curtsy, and pouting.*
Sir John. Miss Sterling's manner of quitting the room on my approach, and the visible coolness of your behaviour to me, Madam, convince me that she has acquainted you with what past this morning.

Mrs. Heidel. I am very sorry, Sir John, to be made acquainted with any thing that should induce to change the opinion, which I could always wish to entertain of a person of quallaty.
                                    [*Pouting.*
Sir John. It has always been my ambition to merit the best

opinion from Mrs. Heidelberg; and when she comes to weigh all circumstances, I flatter myself—

Mrs. Heidel. You *do* flatter yourself, if you imagine that I can approve of your behaviour to my niece, Sir John.—And give me leave to tell you, Sir John, that you have been drawn into an action much beneath you, Sir John; and that I look upon every injury offered to Miss Betty Sterling, as an affront to myself, Sir John.   [*Warmly.*

Sir John. I would not offend you for the world, Madam! but when I am influenced by a partiality for another, however ill-founded, I hope your discernment and good sense will think it rather a point of honour to renounce engagements, which I could not fulfil so strictly as I ought; and that you will excuse the change in my inclinations, since the new object, as well as the first, has the honour of being your niece, Madam.

Mrs. Heidel. I disclaim her as a niece, Sir John; Miss Sterling disclaims her as a sister, and the whole fammaly must disclaim her, for her monstrus baseness and treachery.

Sir John. Indeed she has been guilty of none, Madam. Her hand and· heart are, I am sure, entirely at the disposal of yourself, and Mr. Sterling.

Enter STERLING *behind.*

And if you should not oppose my inclinations, I am sure of Mr. Sterling's consent, Madam.

Mrs. Heidel. Indeed!

Sir John. Quite certain, Madam.

Sterl. [*Behind.*] So! they seem to be coming to terms already. I may venture to make my appearance.

Mrs. Heidel. To marry Fanny?

[STERLING *advances by degrees.*

Sir John. Yes, Madam.

Mrs. Heidel. My brother has given his consent, you say?

Sir John. In the most ample manner, with no other restriction than the failure of your concurrence, Madam.—[*Sees* STERLING.] Oh, here's Mr. Sterling, who will confirm what I have told you.

Mrs. Heidel. What! have you consented to give up your own daughter in this manner, brother?

Sterl. Give her up! no, not give her up, sister; only in case that you—Zounds, I am afraid you have said too much, Sir John.   [*Apart to* SIR JOHN.

Mrs. Heidel. Yes, yes. I see now that it is true enough what my niece told me. You are all plottin' and caballin' against her.— Pray, does Lord Ogleby know of this affair?

Sir John. I have not yet made him acquainted with it, Madam.

Mrs. Heidel. No, I warrant you. I thought so.—And so his Lordship and myself truly, are not to be consulted 'till the last.

Sterl. What! did not you consult my Lord? Oh, fie for shame, Sir John!

Sir John. Nay, but Mr. Sterling—

Mrs. Heidel. We, who are the persons of most consequence and experunce in the two fammalies, are to know nothing of the matter, 'till the whole is as good as concluded upon. But his Lordship, I am sure, will have more generosaty than to countenance such a perceeding—And I could not have expected such behaviour from a person of your quallaty, Sir John.—And as for you, brother—

Sterl. Nay, nay, but hear me, sister!

Mrs. Heidel. I am perfetly ashamed of you—Have you no spurrit? no more concern for the honour of our fammaly than to consent—

Sterl. Consent?—I consent!—As I hope for mercy, I never gave my consent. Did I consent, Sir John?

Sir John. Not absolutely, without Mrs. Heidelberg's concurrence. But in case of her approbation—

Sterl. Ay, I grant you, if my sister approved.—But that's quite another thing, you know.—   [*To* MRS. HEIDELBERG.

Mrs. Heidel. Your sister approve, indeed!—I thought you knew her better, brother Sterling!—What! approve of having your eldest daughter returned upon your hands, and exchanged for the younger?—I am surprized how you could listen to such a scandalus proposal.

Sterl. I tell you, I never did listen to it.—Did not I say that I would be governed entirely by my sister, Sir John?—And unless she agreed to your marrying Fanny—

Mrs. Heidel. I agree to his marrying Fanny? abominable! The man is absolutely out of his senses.—Can't that wise head of yours foresee the consequence of all this, brother Sterling? Will Sir John take Fanny without a fortune? No.—After you have settled the largest part of your property on your youngest daughter, can there be an equal portion left for the eldest? No.—Does not this overturn the whole systum of the fammaly? Yes, yes, yes. You know I was always for my niece Betsey's marrying a person of the very first quality. That was my maxum. And, therefore, much the largest settlement was of course to be made upon her. —As for Fanny, if she could, with a fortune of twenty or thirty thousand pounds, get a knight, or a Member of Parliament, or a rich common-councilman for a husband, I thought it might do very well.

Sir John. But if a better match should offer itself, why should not it be accepted, Madam?

Mrs. Heidel. What! at the expence of her elder sister! Oh fie, Sir John!—How could you bear to hear of such an indignaty, brother Sterling?

Sterl. I! nay, I shan't hear of it, I promise you.—I can't hear of it indeed, Sir John.

Mrs. Heidel. But you *have* heard of it, brother Sterling. You know you have; and sent Sir John to propose it to me. But if you can give up your daughter, I shan't forsake my niece, I assure you. Ah! if my poor dear Mr. Heidelberg, and our sweet babes, had been alive, he would not have behaved so.

Sterl. Did I, Sir John? nay speak!—Bring me off, or we are ruined.   [*Apart to* SIR JOHN.

Sir John. Why, to be sure, to speak the truth—

Mrs. Heidel. To speak the truth, I'm ashamed of you both. But have a care what you are about, brother! have a care, I say. The lawyers are in the house, I hear; and if every thing is not settled to my liking, I'll have nothing more to say to you, if I live these hundred years.—I'll go over to Holland, and settle with Mr. Vandespracken, my poor husband's first cousin; and my own fammaly shall never be the better for a farden of my money, I promise you.   [*Exit.*

Manent SIR JOHN *and* STERLING.

Sterl. I thought so. I knew she never would agree to it.

Sir John. 'Sdeath, how unfortunate! What can we do, Mr. Sterling?

Sterl. Nothing.

Sir John. What! must our agreement break off, the moment it is made then?

Sterl. It can't be helped, Sir John. The family, as I told you before, have great expectations from my sister; and if this matter proceeds, you hear yourself that she threatens to leave us.—My brother Heidelberg was a warm man; a very warm man; and died worth a Plumb at least; a Plumb! ay, *I* warrant you, he died worth a Plumb and a half.

Sir John. Well; but if I—

Sterl. And then, my sister has three or four very good mortgages, a deal of money in the three per cents, and old South-Sea annuities, besides large concerns in the Dutch and French funds.—The greatest part of all this she means to leave our family.

Sir John. I can only say, Sir—

Sterl. Why, your offer of the difference of thirty thousand, was very fair and handsome to be sure, Sir John.

Sir John. Nay, but I am even willing to—

Sterl. Ay, but if I was to accept it against her will, I might lose above a hundred thousand; so, you see, the ballance is against you, Sir John.

Sir John. But is there no way, do you think, of prevailing on Mrs. Heidelberg to grant her consent?

Sterl. I am afraid not.—However, when her passion is a little abated—for she's very passionate—you may try what can be done: but you must not use my name any more, Sir John.

Sir John. Suppose I was to prevail on Lord Ogleby to apply to her, do you think that would have any influence over her?

Sterl. I think he would be more likely to persuade her to it, than any other person in the family. She has a great respect for Lord Ogleby. She loves a lord.

Sir John. I'll apply to him this very day.—And if he should prevail on Mrs. Heidelberg, I may depend on your friendship, Mr. Sterling?

Sterl. Ay, ay, I shall be glad to oblige you, when it is in my power; but as the account stands now, you see it is not upon the figures. And so your servant, Sir John.   [*Exit.*

Sir John Melvil alone.

Sir John. What a situation am I in!—Breaking off with her whom I was bound by treaty to marry; rejected by the object of my affections; and embroiled with this turbulent woman, who governs the whole family.—And yet opposition, instead of smothering, increases my inclination. I must have her. I'll apply immediately to Lord Ogleby; and if he can but bring over the aunt to our party, her influence will overcome the scruples and delicacy of my dear Fanny, and I shall be the happiest of mankind.   [*Exit.*

ACT IV

Scene.—A room

Enter Sterling, Mrs. Heidelberg, *and* Miss Sterling.

Sterl. What! will you send Fanny to town, sister?

Mrs. Heidel. To-morrow morning. I've given orders about it already.

Sterl. Indeed?

Mrs. Heidel. Positively.

Sterl. But consider, sister, at such a time as this, what an odd appearance it will have.

Mrs. Heidel. Not half so odd, as her behaviour, brother.—This time was intended for happiness, and I'll keep no incendiaries here to destroy it. I insist on her going off to-morrow morning.

Sterl. I'm afraid this is all your doing, Betsey.

Miss Sterl. No indeed, Papa. My aunt knows that it is not.—For all Fanny's baseness to me, I am sure I would not do, or say any thing to hurt her with you or my aunt for the world.

Mrs. Heidel. Hold your tongue, Betsey!—I will have my way.—When she is packed off, every thing will go on as it should do.—Since they are at their intrigues, I'll let them see that we can act with vigur on our part; and the sending her out of the way shall be the purlimunary step to all the rest of my perceedings.

Sterl. Well, but sister—

Mrs. Heidel. It does not signify talking, brother Sterling, for I'm resolved to be rid of her, and I will.—Come along, child! [*To* Miss Sterling.]—The post-shay shall be at the door by six o'clock in the morning; and if Miss Fanny does not get into it, why *I* will, and so there's an end of the matter.

[*Bounces out with* Miss Sterling.

Mrs. Heidelberg *returns.*

Mrs. Heidel. One word more, brother Sterling!—I expect that you will take your eldest daughter in your hand, and make a formal complaint to Lord Ogleby of Sir John Melvil's behaviour.—Do this, brother; shew a proper regard for the honour of your fammaly yourself, and I shall throw in my mite to the raising of it. If not—but now you know my mind. So act as you please, and take the consequences.   [*Exit.*

Sterling *alone.*

Sterl. The devil's in the woman for tyranny—mothers, wives, mistresses, or sisters, they always will govern us.—As to my sister Heidelberg, she knows the strength of her purse, and domineers upon the credit of it.—"I will do this"—and "you shall do that"—and "you must do t'other, or else the fammaly shan't have a farden of"—[*Mimicking.*]—So absolute with her money!—but to say the truth, nothing but money *can* make us absolute, and so we must e'en make the best of her.

SCENE.—*Changes to the garden*

Enter LORD OGLEBY *and* CANTON.

Lord Ogle. What! Mademoiselle Fanny to be sent away!—Why?—Wherefore?—What's the meaning of all this?

Cant. Je ne scais pas.—I know noting of it.

Lord Ogle. It can't be; it shan't be. I protest against the measure. She's a fine girl, and I had much rather that the rest of the family were annihilated than that she should leave us.—Her vulgar father, that's the very abstract of 'Change-Alley—the aunt, that's always endeavouring to be a fine lady—and the pert sister, for ever shewing that she is one, are horrid company indeed, and without her would be intolerable. Ah, la petite Fanchon! She's the thing. Is n't she, Cant?

Cant. Dere is very good sympatie *entre vous,* and dat young lady, mi Lor.

Lord Ogle. I'll not be left among these Goths and Vandals, your Sterlings, your Heidelbergs, and Devilbergs—If she goes, I'll positively go too.

Cant. In de same post-chay, mi Lor? You have no object to dat I believe, nor Mademoiselle neider too—ha, ha, ha.

Lord Ogle. Prithee hold thy foolish tongue, Cant. Does thy Swiss stupidity imagine that I can see and talk with a fine girl without desires?—My eyes are involuntarily attracted by beautiful objects—I fly as naturally to a fine girl—

Cant. As de fine girl to you, my Lor, ha, ha, ha; you always fly togedre like un pair de pigeons.—

Lord Ogle. Like un pair de pigeons—[*Mocks him.*]—*Vous etes un sot, Mons. Canton*—Thou art always dreaming of my intrigues, and never seest me *badiner,* but you suspect mischief, you old fool, you.

Cant. I am fool, I confess, but not always fool in dat, my Lor, he, he, he.

Lord Ogle. He, he, he.—Thou art incorrigible, but thy absurdities amuse one—Thou art like my rappee here [*Takes out his box.*], a most ridiculous superfluity, but a pinch of thee now and then is a most delicious treat.

Cant. You do me great honeur, my Lor.

Lord Ogle. 'Tis fact, upon my soul.—Thou art properly my cephalick snuff, and art no bad medicine against megrims, vertigoes, and profound thinking—ha, ha, ha.

Cant. Your flatterie, my Lor, vil make me too prode.

Lord Ogle. The girl has some little partiality for me, to be sure: but prithee, Cant, is not that Miss Fanny yonder?

Cant. [*Looking with a glass.*] *En verité*, 'tis she, my Lord—'tis. one of de pigeons,—de pigeons d'amour.

Lord Ogle. Don't be ridiculous, you old monkey.   [*Smiling.*

Cant. I am monkeè, I am ole, but I have eye, I have ear, and a little understand, now and den.

Lord Ogle. Taisez vous, bête!

Cant. Elle vous attend, my Lor.—She vil make a love to you.

Lord Ogle. Will she? Have at her then! A fine girl can't oblige me more. Egad, I find myself a little *enjouée*—come along, Cant! she is but in the next walk—but there is such a deal of this damned crinkum-crankum, as Sterling calls it, that one sees people for half an hour before one can get to them—*Allons, Mons. Canton, allons donc!*   [*Exit singing in French.*

Another part of the garden

LOVEWELL *and* FANNY.

Lovew. My dear Fanny, I cannot bear your distress; it overcomes all my resolutions, and I am prepared for the discovery.

Fanny. But how can it be effected before my departure?

Lovew. I'll tell you.—Lord Ogleby seems to entertain a visible partiality for you; and notwithstanding the peculiarities of his behaviour, I am sure that he is humane at the bottom. He is vain to an excess; but withall extremely good-natured, and would do any thing to recommend himself to a lady.—Do you open the whole affair of our marriage to him immediately. It will come with more irresistible persuasion from you than from myself; and I doubt not but you'll gain his friendship and protection at once.— His influence and authority will put an end to Sir John's sollicitations, remove your aunt's and sister's unkindness and suspicions, and, I hope, reconcile your father and the whole family to our marriage.

Fanny. Heaven grant it! Where is my Lord?

Lovew. I have heard him and Canton since dinner singing French songs under the great walnut-tree by the parlour door. If you meet with him in the garden, you may disclose the whole immediately.

Fanny. Dreadful as the task is, I'll do it.—Any thing is better than this continual anxiety.

Lovew. By that time the discovery is made, I will appear to second you.—Ha! here comes my Lord.—Now, my dear Fanny,

summon up all your spirits, plead our cause powerfully, and be
sure of success.—   [*Going*.

Fanny. Ah, don't leave me!

Lovew. Nay, you must let me.

Fanny. Well; since it must be so, I'll obey you, if I have the
power. Oh Lovewell!

Lovew. Consider, our situation is very critical. To-morrow morning is fixt for your departure, and if we lose this opportunity, we
may wish in vain for another.—He approaches—I must retire.—
Speak, my dear Fanny, speak, and make us happy!   [*Exit*.

FANNY *alone*.

Fanny. Good heaven, what a situation am I in! what shall I do?
what shall I say to him? I am all confusion.

Enter LORD OGLEBY *and* CANTON.

Lord Ogle. To see so much beauty so solitary, Madam, is a
satire upon mankind, and 'tis fortunate that one man has broke in
upon your reverie for the credit of our sex.—I say *one*, Madam,
for poor Canton here, from age and infirmities, stands for nothing.

Cant. Noting at all, inteed.

Fanny. Your Lordship does me great honour.—I had a favour
to request, my Lord!

Lord Ogle. A favour, Madam!—To be honoured with your
commands, is an inexpressible favour done to me, Madam.

Fanny. If your Lordship could indulge me with the honour of a
moment's—What is the matter with me?   [*Aside*.

Lord Ogle. The girl's confus'd—he!—here's something in the
wind, faith—I'll have a tete-tete with her—*allez vous en!*
                                              [*To* CANTON.

Cant. I go—ah, *pauvre Mademoiselle!* my Lor, have *pitié* upon
de poor *pigeone!*

Lord Ogle. I'll knock you down, Cant, if you're impertinent.
                                              [*Smiling*.

Cant. Den I mos avay—[*Shuffles along*.]—You are mosh
please, for all dat.   [*Aside, and exit*.

Fanny. I shall sink with apprehension.   [*Aside*.

Lord Ogle. What a sweet girl!—she's a civiliz'd being, and
atones for the barbarism of the rest of the family.

Fanny. My Lord! I—   [*She curtseys, and blushes*.

Lord Ogle. [*Addressing her*.] I look upon it, Madam, to be one
of the luckiest circumstances of my life, that I have this moment
the honour of receiving your commands, and the satisfaction of
confirming with my tongue, what my eyes perhaps have but too

weakly expressed—that I am literally—the humblest of your servants.

Fanny. I think my self greatly honoured, by your Lordship's partiality to me; but it distresses me, that I am obliged in my present situation to apply to it for protection.

Lord Ogle. I am happy in your distress, Madam, because it gives me an opportunity to shew my zeal. Beauty to me, is a religion, in which I was born and bred a bigot, and would die a martyr.— I'm in tolerable spirits, faith!   [*Aside.*

Fanny. There is not perhaps at this moment a more distressed creature than myself. Affection, duty, hope, despair, and a thousand different sentiments, are struggling in my bosom; and even the presence of your Lordship, to whom I have flown for protection, adds to my perplexity.

Lord Ogle. Does it, Madam?—Venus forbid!—My old fault; the devil's in me, I think, for perplexing young women. [*Aside and smiling.*] Take courage, Madam! dear Miss Fanny, explain.— You have a powerful advocate in my breast, I assure you—my heart, Madam—I am attached to you by all the laws of sympathy, and delicacy.—By my honour, I am.

Fanny. Then I will venture to unburthen my mind.—Sir John Melvil, my Lord, by the most misplaced, and mistimed declaration of affection for me, has made me the unhappiest of women.

Lord Ogle. How, Madam! Has Sir John made his addresses to you?

Fanny. He has, my Lord, in the strongest terms. But I hope it is needless to say, that my duty to my father, love to my sister, and regard to the whole family, as well as the great respect I entertain for your Lordship [*curtseying*], made me shudder at his addresses.

Lord Ogle. Charming girl!—Proceed, my dear Miss Fanny, proceed!

Fanny. In a moment—give me leave, my Lord!—But if what I have to disclose should be received with anger or displeasure—

Lord Ogle. Impossible, by all the tender powers!—Speak, I beseech you, or I shall divine the cause before you utter it.

Fanny. Then, my Lord, Sir John's addresses are not only shocking to me in themselves, but are more particularly disagreeable to me at this time, as—as—   [*Hesitating.*

Lord Ogle. As what, Madam?

Fanny. As—pardon my confusion—I am intirely devoted to another.

Lord Ogle. If this is not plain, the devil's in it—[*Aside.*] But tell me, my dear Miss Fanny, for I must know; tell me the how, the when, and the where—Tell me—

Enter CANTON *hastily.*

Cant. My Lor, my Lor, my Lor!—

Lord Ogle. Damn your Swiss impertinence! how durst you interrupt me in the most critical melting moment that ever love and beauty honoured me with?

Cant. I demande pardonne, my Lor! Sir John Melvil, my Lor, sent me to beg you to do him the honour to speak a little to your Lorship.

Lord Ogle. I'm not at leisure—I'm busy—Get away, you stupid old dog, you Swiss rascal, or I'll—

Cant. Fort bien, my Lor.—   [CANT. *goes out tiptoe.*

Lord Ogle. By the laws of gallantry, Madam, this interruption should be death; but as no punishment ought to disturb the triumph of the softer passions, the criminal is pardoned and dismissed—Let us return, Madam, to the highest luxury of exalted minds—a declaration of love from the lips of beauty.

Fanny. The entrance of a third person has a little relieved me, but I cannot go thro' with it—and yet I must open my heart with a discovery, or it will break with its burthen.

Lord Ogle. What passion in her eyes! I am alarmed to agitation. [*Aside.*]—I presume, Madam, (and as you have flattered me, by making me a party concerned, I hope you'll excuse the presumption) that—

Fanny. Do you excuse my making you a party concerned, my Lord, and let me interest your heart in my behalf, as my future happiness or misery in a great measure depend—

Lord Ogle. Upon me, Madam?

Fanny. Upon you, my Lor.   [*Sighs.*

Lord Ogle. There's no standing this: I have caught the infection—her tenderness dissolves me.   [*Sighs.*

Fanny. And should you too severely judge of a rash action which passion prompted, and modesty has long concealed—

Lord Ogle. [*Taking her hand.*] Thou amiable creature—command my heart, for it is vanquished—Speak but thy virtuous wishes, and enjoy them.

Fanny. I cannot, my Lord—indeed, I cannot—Mr. Lovewell must tell you my distresses—and when you know them—pity and protect me!—   [*Exit, in tears.*

LORD OGLEBY *alone.*

Lord Ogle. How the devil could I bring her to this? It is too much—too much—I can't bear it—I must give way to this amiable weakness—[*Wipes his eyes.*] My heart overflows with sympathy, and I feel every tenderness I have inspired.—[*Stifles the tear.*] How blind have I been to the desolation I have made!—How could I possibly imagine that a little partial attention and tender civilities to this young creature should have gathered to this burst of passion! Can I be a man and withstand it? No—I'll sacrifice the whole sex to her.—But here comes the father, quite *apropos*. I'll open the matter immediately, settle the business with him, and take the sweet girl down to Ogleby-house to-morrow morning—But what the devil! Miss Sterling too! What mischief's in the wind now?

Enter STERLING *and* MISS STERLING.

Sterl. My Lord, your servant! I am attending my daughter here upon rather a disagreeable affair. Speak to his Lordship, Betsey!

Lord Ogle. Your eyes, Miss Sterling—for I always read the eyes of a young lady—betray some little emotion—What are your commands, Madam?

Miss Sterl. I have but too much cause for my emotion, my Lord!

Lord Ogle. I cannot commend my kinsman's behaviour, Madam. He has behaved like a false knight, I must confess. I have heard of his apostacy. Miss Fanny has informed me of it.

Miss Sterl. Miss Fanny's baseness has been the cause of Sir John's inconstancy.

Lord Ogle. Nay, now, my dear Miss Sterling, your passion transports you too far. Sir John may have entertain'd a passion for Miss Fanny, but believe me, my dear Miss Sterling, believe me Miss Fanny has no passion for Sir John. She has a passion, indeed a most tender passion. She has opened her whole soul to me, and I know where her affections are placed. [*Conceitedly*

Miss Sterl. Not upon Mr. Lovewell, My Lord; for I have great reason to think that her seeming attachment to him, is, by his consent, made use of as a blind to cover her designs upon Sir John

Lord Ogle. Lovewell! No, poor lad! She does not think of him. [*Smiling*

Miss Sterl. Have a care, my Lord, that both the families are no made the dupes of Sir John's artifice and my sister's dissimulation. You don't know her—indeed, my Lord, you don't know her—a base, insinuating, perfidious!—It is too much—She has been beforehand with me, I perceive. Such unnatural behaviour to me —But since I see I can have no redress, I am resolved that some way or other I will have revenge. [*Exit*

Sterl. This is foolish work, my Lord!

Lord Ogle. I have too much sensibility to bear the tears of beauty.

Sterl. It is touching indeed, my Lord—and very moving for a father.

Lord Ogle. To be sure, Sir!—You must be distrest beyond measure!—Wherefore, to divert your too exquisite feelings, suppose we change the subject, and proceed to business.

Sterl. With all my heart, my Lord!

Lord Ogle. You see, Mr. Sterling, we can make no union in our families by the propos'd marriage.

Sterl. And very sorry I am to see it, my Lord.

Lord Ogle. Have you set your heart upon being allied to our house, Mr. Sterling?

Sterl. 'Tis my only wish, at present, my omnium, as I may call it.

Lord Ogle. Your wishes shall be fulfill'd.

Sterl. Shall they, my Lord!—but how—how?

Lord Ogle. I'll marry in your family.

Sterl. What! my sister Heidelberg?

Lord Ogle. You throw me into a cold sweat, Mr Sterling. No, not your sister—but your daughter.

Sterl. My daughter!

Lord Ogle. Fanny!—now the murder's out!

Sterl. What, *you*, my Lord?—

Lord Ogle. Yes—I, I, Mr. Sterling!

Sterl. No, no, my Lord—that's too much.   [*Smiling.*

Lord Ogle. Too much?—I don't comprehend you.

Sterl. What, you, my Lord, marry my Fanny!—Bless me, what will the folks say?

Lord Ogle. Why, what will they say?

Sterl. That you're a bold man, my Lord—that's all.

Lord Ogle. Mr. Sterling, this may be city wit for ought I know—Do you court my alliance?

Sterl. To be sure, my Lord.

Lord Ogle. Then I'll explain.—My nephew won't marry your eldest daughter—nor I neither—Your youngest daughter won't marry him—I will marry your youngest daughter—

Sterl. What! with a younger daughter's fortune, my Lord?

Lord Ogle. With any fortune, or no fortune at all, Sir. Love is the idol of my heart, and the dæmon Interest sinks before him. So, Sir, as I said before, I will marry your youngest daughter; your youngest daughter will marry me.—

Sterl. Who told you so, my Lord?

Lord Ogle. Her own sweet self, Sir.

Sterl. Indeed?

Lord Ogle. Yes, Sir: our affection is mutual; your advantage double and treble—your daughter will be a Countess directly—I shall be the happiest of beings—and you'll be father to an Earl instead of a Baronet.

Sterl. But what will my sister say?—and my daughter?

Lord Ogle. I'll manage that matter—nay, if they won't consent, I'll run away with your daughter in spite of you.

Sterl. Well said, my Lord!—your spirit's good—I wish you had my constitution!—but if you'll venture, I have no objection, if my sister has none.

Lord Ogle. I'll answer for your sister, Sir. Apropos! the lawyers are in the house—I'll have articles drawn, and the whole affair concluded to-morrow morning.

Sterl. Very well: and I'll dispatch Lovewell to London immediately for some fresh papers I shall want, and I shall leave you to manage matters with my sister. You must excuse me, my Lord, but I can't help laughing at the match—He! he! he! what will the folks say? [*Exit.*

Lord Ogle. What a fellow am I going to make a father of?— He has no more feeling than the post in his warehouse—But Fanny's virtues tune me to rapture again, and I won't think of the rest of the family.

Enter LOVEWELL *hastily.*

Lovew. I beg your Lordship's pardon, my Lord; are you alone, my Lord?

Lord Ogle. No, my Lord, I am not alone! I am in company, the best company.

Lovew. My Lord!

Lord Ogle. I never was in such exquisite enchanting company since my heart first conceived, or my senses tasted pleasure.

Lovew. Where are they, my Lord? [*Looking about.*

Lord Ogle. In my mind, Sir.

Lovew. What company have you there, my Lord? [*Smiling.*

Lord Ogle. My own ideas, Sir, which so croud upon my imagination, and kindle it to such a delirium of extasy, that wit, wine, musick, poetry, all combined, and each perfection, are but mere mortal shadows of my felicity.

Lovew. I see that your Lordship is happy, and I rejoice at it.

Lord Ogle. You shall rejoice at it, Sir; my felicity shall not selfishly be confined, but shall spread its influence to the whole circle of my friends. I need not say, Lovewell, that you shall have your share of it.

Lovew. Shall I, my Lord?—then I understand you—you have heard—Miss Fanny has inform'd you—

Lord Ogle. She has—I have heard, and she shall be happy—'tis determin'd.

Lovew. Then I have reached the summit of my wishes—And will your Lordship pardon the folly?

Lord Ogle. O yes, poor creature, how could she help it?—'Twas unavoidable—Fate and necessity.

Lovew. It was indeed, my Lord—Your kindness distracts me.

Lord Ogle. And so it did the poor girl, faith.

Lovew. She trembled to disclose the secret, and declare her affections?

Lord Ogle. The world, I believe, will not think her affections ill placed.

Lovew. [*Bowing.*]—You are too good, my Lord.—And do you really excuse the rashness of the action?

Lord Ogle. From my very soul, Lovewell.

Lovew. Your generosity overpowers me.—[*Bowing.*]—I was afraid of her meeting with a cold reception.

Lord Ogle. More fool you then.

  Who pleads her cause with never-failing beauty,
  Here finds a full redress.   [*Strikes his breast.*
She's a fine girl, Lovewell.

Lovew. Her beauty, my Lord, is her least merit. She has an understanding—

Lord Ogle. Her choice convinces me of that.

Lovew. [*Bowing.*]—That's your Lordship's goodness. Her choice was a disinterested one.

Lord Ogle. No—no—not altogether—it began with interest, and ended in passion.

Lovew. Indeed, my Lord, if you were acquainted with her goodness of heart, and generosity of mind, as well as you are with the inferior beauties of her face and person—

Lord Ogle. I am so perfectly convinced of their existence, and so totally of your mind touching every amiable particular of that sweet girl, that were it not for the cold unfeeling impediments of the law, I would marry her to-morrow morning.

Lovew. My Lord!

Lord Ogle. I would, by all that's honourable in man, and amiable in woman.

Lovew. Marry her!—Who do you mean, my Lord?

Lord Ogle. Miss Fanny Sterling, that is—the Countess of Ogleby that shall be.

Lovew. I am astonished.

Lord Ogle. Why, could you expect less from me?

Lovew. I did not expect this, my Lord.

Lord Ogle. Trade and accounts have destroyed your feeling.

Lovew. No, indeed, my Lord. [*Sighs.*

Lord Ogle. The moment that love and pity entered my breast, I was resolved to plunge into matrimony, and shorten the girl's tortures—I never do any thing by halves; do I, Lovewell?

Lovew. No, indeed, my Lord—[*Sighs.*]—What an accident!

Lord Ogle. What's the matter, Lovewell? thou seem'st to have lost thy faculties. Why don't you wish me joy, man?

Lovew. O, I do, my Lord. [*Sighs.*

Lord Ogle. She said, that you would explain what she had not power to utter—but I wanted no interpreter for the language of love.

Lovew. But has your Lordship considered the consequences of your resolution?

Lord Ogle. No, Sir; I am above consideration, when my desires are kindled.

Lovew. But consider the consequences, my Lord, to your nephew, Sir John.

Lord Ogle. Sir John has considered no consequences himself, Mr. Lovewell.

Lovew. Mr. Sterling, my Lord, will certainly refuse his daughter to Sir John.

Lord Ogle. Sir John has already refused Mr. Sterling's daughter.

Lovew. But what will become of Miss Sterling, my Lord?

Lord Ogle. What's that to you?—You may have her, if you will.—I depend upon Mr. Sterling's city-philosophy, to be reconciled to Lord Ogleby's being his son-in-law, instead of Sir John Melvil, Baronet. Don't you think that your master may be brought to that, without having recourse to his calculations? Eh, Lovewell!

Lovew. But, my Lord, that is not the question.

Lord Ogle. Whatever is the question, I'll tell you my answer.— I am in love with a fine girl, whom I resolve to marry.

Enter SIR JOHN MELVIL.

What news with you, Sir John?—You look all hurry and impatience—like a messenger after a battle.

Sir John. After a battle, indeed, my Lord.—I have this day had a severe engagement, and wanting your Lordship as an auxiliary, I have at last mustered up resolution to declare, what my duty to you and to myself have demanded from me some time.

Lord Ogle. To the business then, and be as concise as possible; for I am upon the wing—eh, Lovewell?

[*He smiles, and* LOVEWELL *bows.*

Sir John. I find 'tis in vain, my Lord, to struggle against the force of inclination.

Lord Ogle. Very true, Nephew—I am your witness, and will second the motion—shan't I, Lovewell?

[*Smiles, and* LOVEWELL *bows.*

Sir John. Your Lordship's generosity encourages me to tell you —that I cannot marry Miss Sterling.

Lord Ogle. I am not at all surpriz'd at it—she's a bitter potion, that's the truth of it; but as you were to swallow it, and not I, it was your business, and not mine—any thing more?

Sir John. But this, my Lord—that I may be permitted to make my addresses to the other sister.

Lord Ogle. O yes—by all means—have you any hopes there, Nephew?—Do you think he'll succeed, Lovewell?

[*Smiles, and winks at* LOVEWELL.

Lovew. I think not, my Lord. [*Gravely.*

Lord Ogle. I think so too, but let the fool try.

Sir John. Will your Lordship favour me with your good offices to remove the chief obstacle to the match, the repugnance of Mrs. Heidelberg?

Lord Ogle. Mrs. Heidelberg!—Had not you better begin with the young lady first? it will save you a great deal of trouble; won't it, Lovewell?—[*Smiles.*]—but do what you please, it will be the same thing to me—won't it, Lovewell?—[*Conceitedly.*]—Why don't you laugh at him?

Lovew. I do, my Lord. [*Forces a smile.*

Sir John. And your Lordship will endeavour to prevail on Mrs. Heidelberg to consent to my marriage with Miss Fanny?

Lord Ogle. I'll go and speak to Mrs. Heidelberg, about the adorable Fanny, as soon as possible.

Sir John. Your generosity transports me.

Lord Ogle. Poor fellow, what a dupe! he little thinks who's in possession of the town. [*Aside.*

Sir John. And your Lordship is not offended at this seeming inconstancy?

Lord Ogle. Not in the least. Miss Fanny's charms will even excuse infidelity—I look upon women as the *feræ naturæ,*—lawfull game—and every man who is qualified, has a natural right to pursue them; Lovewell as well as you, and I as well as either of you.—Every man shall do his best, without offence to any—what say you, kinsman?

Sir John. You have made me happy, my Lord.

Lovew. And me, I assure you, my Lord.

Lord Ogle. And I am superlatively so—*allons donc*—to horse and away, boys!—you to your affairs, and I to mine—*suivons l'amour!* [*Sings.*] [*Exeunt severally.*

ACT V

SCENE.—FANNY'S *apartment*

Enter LOVEWELL *and* FANNY—*followed by* BETTY.

Fanny. Why did you come so soon, Mr. Lovewell? the family is not yet in bed, and Betty certainly heard somebody listening near the chamber-door.

Betty. My mistress is right, Sir! evil spirits are abroad; and I am sure you are both too good, not to expect mischief from them.

Lovew. But who can be so curious, or so wicked?

Betty. I think we have wickedness, and curiosity enough in this family, Sir, to expect the worst.

Fanny. I do expect the worst.—Prithee, Betty, return to the outward door, and listen if you hear any body in the gallery; and let us know directly.

Betty. I warrant you, Madam—the Lord bless you both! [*Exit.*

Fanny. What did my father want with you this evening?

Lovew. He gave me the key of his closet, with orders to bring from London some papers relating to Lord Ogleby.

Fanny. And why did not you obey him?

Lovw. Because I am certain that his Lordship has open'd his heart to him about you, and those papers are wanted merely on that account—but as we shall discover all to-morrow, there will be no occasion for them, and it would be idle in me to go.

Fanny. Hark!—hark! bless me, how I tremble!—I feel the terrors of guilt—indeed, Mr. Lovewell, this is too much for me.

Lovew. And for me too, my sweet Fanny. Your apprehensions make a coward of me.—But what can alarm you? your aunt and sister are in their chambers, and you have nothing to fear from the rest of the family.

Fanny. I fear every body, and every thing, and every moment—My mind is in continual agitation and dread;—indeed, Mr. Lovewell, this situation may have very unhappy consequences.

[*Weeps.*

Lovew. But it shan't—I would rather tell our story this moment to all the house, and run the risque of maintaining you by the hardest labour, than suffer you to remain in this dangerous perplexity.—What! shall I sacrifice all my best hopes and affections, in your dear health and safety, for the mean, and in such a case, the meanest consideration—of our fortune! Were we to be abandon'd by all our relations, we have that in our hearts and minds, will weigh against the most affluent circumstances.—I should not have propos'd the secrecy of our marriage, but for your sake; and with hopes that the most generous sacrifice you have made to love and me, might be less injurious to you, by waiting a lucky moment of reconciliation.

Fanny. Hush! hush! for heav'n sake, my dear Lovewell, don't be so warm!—your generosity gets the better of your prudence; you will be heard, and we shall be discovered.—I am satisfied, indeed I am.—Excuse this weakness, this delicacy—this what you will.—My mind's at peace—indeed it is—think no more of it, if you love me!

Lovew. That one word has charm'd me, as it always does, to the most implicit obedience; it would be the worst of ingratitude in me to distress you a moment. [*Kisses her.*

Re-enter BETTY.

Betty. [*In a low voice.*] I'm sorry to disturb you.

Fanny. Ha! what's the matter?

Lovew. Have you heard any body?

Betty. Yes, yes, I have, and they have heard *you* too, or I am mistaken—if they had *seen* you too, we should have been in a fine quandary.

Fanny. Prithee don't prate now, Betty!

Lovew. What did you hear?

Betty. I was preparing myself, as usual, to take me a little nap.

Lovew. A nap!

Betty. Yes, Sir, a nap; for I watch much better so than wide awake; and when I had wrap'd this handkerchief round my head, for fear of the ear-ach, from the key-hole I thought I heard a kind of a sort of a buzzing, which I first took for a gnat, and shook my head two or three times, and went so with my hand—

Fanny. Well—well—and so—

Betty. And so, Madam, when I heard Mr. Lovewell a little loud, I heard the buzzing louder too—and pulling off my handkerchief softly—I could hear this sort of noise—
[*Makes an indistinct noise like speaking.*

Fanny. Well, and what did they say?

Betty. Oh! I cou'd not understand a word of what was said.

Lovew. The outward door is lock'd?

Betty. Yes; and I bolted it too, for fear of the worst.

Fanny. Why did you? they must have heard you, if they were near.

Betty. And I did it on purpose, Madam, and cough'd a little too, that they might not hear Mr. Lovewell's voice—when I was silent, they were silent, and so I came to tell you.

Fanny. What shall we do?

Lovew. Fear nothing; we know the worst; it will only bring on our catastrophe a little too soon—but Betty might fancy this noise —she's in the conspiracy, and can make a man of a mouse at any time.

Betty. I can distinguish a man from a mouse, as well as my betters—I am sorry you think so ill of me, Sir.

Fanny. He compliments you, don't be a fool!—Now you have set her tongue a running, she'll mutter for an hour. [*To* Love-well.] I'll go and hearken myself.   [*Exit.*

Betty. I'll turn my back upon no girl, for sincerity and service. [*Half aside, and muttering.*

Lovew. Thou art the first in the world for both; and I will reward you soon, Betty, for one and the other.

Betty. I'm not marcenary neither—I can live on a little, with a good *carreter.*

Re-enter FANNY.

Fanny. All seems quiet—suppose, my dear, you go to your own room—I shall be much easier then—and to-morrow we will be prepared for the discovery.

Betty. You may discover, if you please; but, for my part, I shall still be secret.   [*Half aside, and muttering.*

Lovew. Should I leave you now,—if they still are upon the watch, we shall lose the advantage of our delay.—Besides, we should consult upon to-morrow's business.—Let Betty go to her own room, and lock the outward door after her; we can fasten this; and when she thinks all safe, she may return and let me out as usual.

Betty. Shall I, Madam?

Fanny. Do! let me have my way to-night, and you shall command me ever after.—I would not have you surprized here for the world.—Pray leave me! I shall be quite myself again, if you will oblige me.

Lovew. I live only to oblige you, my sweet Fanny! I'll be gone this moment.   [*Going.*

Fanny. Let us listen first at the door, that you may not be intercepted.—Betty shall go first, and if they lay hold of her—

Betty. They'll have the wrong sow by the ear, I can tell them that.   [*Going hastily.*

Fanny. Softly—softly—Betty! don't venture out, if you hear a noise.—Softly, I beg of you!—See, Mr. Lovewell, the effects of indiscretion!

Lovew. But love, Fanny, makes amends for all.

[*Exeunt all softly.*

SCENE.—*Changes to a gallery, which leads to several bed-chambers*

Enter Miss STERLING, *leading* Mrs. HEIDELBERG *in a night-cap.*

Miss Sterl. This way, dear Madam, and then I'll tell you all.

Mrs. Heidel. Nay, but Niece—consider a little—don't drag me out in this figur—let me put on my fly-cap!—if any of my Lord's fammaly, or the counsellors at law, should be stirring, I should be perdigus disconcarted.

Miss Sterl. But, my dear Madam, a moment is an age, in my situation. I am sure my sister has been plotting my disgrace and ruin in that chamber—O, she's all craft and wickedness!

Mrs. Heidel. Well, but softly, Betsey!—you are all in emotion—your mind is too much flustrated—you can neither eat nor drink, nor take your natural rest—compose yourself, child; for if we are not as warysome as they are wicked, we shall disgrace our selves and the whole fammaly.

Miss Sterl. We are disgrac'd already, Madam—Sir John Melvil has forsaken me; my Lord cares for nobody but himself; or, if for any body, it is my sister; my father, for the sake of a better bargain, would marry me to a 'Change-broker; so that if you, Madam, don't continue my friend—if you forsake me—if I am to lose my best hopes and consolation—in your tenderness—and affect—ions—I had better—at once—give up the matter—and let my sister enjoy—the fruits of her treachery—trample with scorn upon the rights of her elder sister, the will of the best of aunts, and the weakness of a too interested father.

[*She pretends to be bursting into tears all this speech.*

Mrs. Heidel. Don't, Betsey—keep up your spurrit—I hate whimpering—I am your friend—depend upon me in every partickler—but be composed, and tell me what new mischief you have discover'd.

Miss Sterl. I had no desire to sleep, and would not undress myself, knowing that my Machiavel sister would not rest till she had broke my heart:—I was so uneasy that I could not stay in my room, but when I thought that all the house was quiet, I sent my maid to discover what was going forward; she immediately came back and told me that they were in high consultation; that she had heard only, for it was in the dark, my sister's maid conduct Sir John Melvil to her mistress, and then lock the door.

Mrs. Heidel. And how did you conduct yourself in this dalimma?

Miss Sterl. I return'd with her, and could hear a man's voice, though nothing that they said distinctly; and you may depend upon it, that Sir John is now in that room, that they have settled the matter, and will run away together before morning, if we don't prevent them.

Mrs. Heidel. Why the brazen slut! has she got her sister's husband (that is to be) lock'd up in her chamber! at night too?—I tremble at the thoughts!

Miss Sterl. Hush, Madam! I hear something.

Mrs. Heidel. You frighten me—let me put on my fly-cap—I would not be seen in this figur for the world.

Miss Sterl. 'Tis dark, Madam; you can't be seen.

Mrs. Heidel. I protest there's a candle coming, and a man too.

Miss Sterl. Nothing but servants; let us retire a moment!

[*They retire.*

Enter BRUSH *half drunk, laying hold of the* CHAMBERMAID, *who has a candle in her hand.*

Ch. Maid. Be quiet, Mr. Brush; I shall drop down with terror.

Brush. But my sweet, and most amiable chambermaid, if you have no love, you may hearken to a little reason; that cannot possibly do your virtue any harm.

Ch. Maid. But you will do me harm, Mr. Brush, and a great deal of harm too—pray let me go—I am ruin'd if they hear you—I tremble like an asp.

Brush. But they shan't hear us—and if you have a mind to be ruin'd, it shall be the making of your fortune, you little slut, you! —therefore I say it again, if you have no love—hear a little reason!

Ch. Maid. I wonder at your impurence, Mr. Brush, to use me in this manner; this is not the way to keep me company, I assure you.—You are a town rake I see, and now you are a little in liquor, you fear nothing.

Brush. Nothing, by heav'ns, but your frowns, most amiable chambermaid; I am a little electrified, that's the truth on't; I am not used to drink Port, and your master's is so heady, that a pint of it oversets a claret-drinker.

Ch. Maid. Don't be rude! bless me!—I shall be ruin'd—what will become of me?

Brush. I'll take care of you, by all that's honourable.

Ch. Maid. You are a base man to use me so—I'll cry out, if you don't let me go—that is Miss Sterling's chamber, that Miss Fanny's, and that Madam Heidelberg's. [*Pointing.*

Brush. And that my Lord Ogleby's, and that my Lady what d'ye call 'em: I don't mind such folks when I'm sober, much less when I am whimsical—rather above that too.

Ch. Maid. More shame for you, Mr. Brush!—you terrify me—you have no modesty.

Brush. O but I have, my sweet spider-brusher!—for instance, I reverence Miss Fanny—she's a most delicious morsel and fit for a prince—with all my horrors of matrimony, I could marry her myself—but for her sister—

Miss Sterl. There, there, Madam, all in a story!

Ch. Maid. Bless me, Mr. Brush!—I heard something!

Brush. Rats, I suppose, that are gnawing the old timbers of this execrable old dungeon—If it was mine, I would pull it down, and fill your fine canal up with the rubbish; and then I should get rid of two damn'd things at once.

Ch. Maid. Law! law! how you blaspheme!—we shall have the house upon our heads for it.

Brush. No, no, it will last our time—but as I was saying, the eldest sister—Miss Jezabel—

Ch. Maid. Is a fine young lady for all your evil tongue.

Brush. No—we have smoak'd her already; and unless she marries our old Swiss, she can have none of us—no, no, she wont do—we are a little too nice.

Ch. Maid. You're a monstrous rake, Mr. Brush, and don't care what you say.

Brush. Why, for that matter, my dear, I am a little inclined to mischief; and if you won't have pity upon me, I will break open that door and ravish Mrs. Heidelberg.

Mrs. Heidel. [*Coming forward.*] There's no bearing this—you profligate monster!

Ch. Maid. Ha! I am undone!

Brush. Zounds! here she is, by all that's monstrous.   [*Runs off.*

Miss Sterl. A fine discourse you have had with that fellow!

Mrs. Heidel. And a fine time of night it is to be here with that drunken monster.

Miss Sterl. What have you to say for yourself?

Ch. Maid. I can say nothing.—I am so frighten'd, and so asham'd—but indeed I am vartuous—I am vartuous indeed.

Mrs. Heidel. Well, well—don't tremble so; but tell us what you know of this horrable plot here.

Miss Sterl. We'll forgive you, if you'll discover all.

Ch. Maid. Why, Madam—don't let me betray my fellow servants—I shan't sleep in my bed, if I do.

Mrs. Heidel. Then you shall sleep somewhere else to-morrow night.

Ch. Maid. O dear!—what shall I do?

Mrs. Heidel. Tell us this moment,—or I'll turn you out of doors directly.

Ch. Maid. Why, our butler has been treating us below in his pantry—Mr. Brush forc'd us to make a kind of a holiday night of it.

Miss Sterl. Holiday! for what?

Ch. Maid. Nay, I only made one.

Miss Sterl. Well, well; but upon what account?

Ch. Maid. Because, as how, Madam, there was a change in the family they said,—that his honour, Sir John—was to marry Miss Fanny instead of your Ladyship.

Miss Sterl. And so you made a holiday for that.—Very fine!

Ch. Maid. I did not make it, Ma'am.

Mrs. Heidel. But do you know nothing of Sir John's being to run away with Miss Fanny to-night?

Ch. Maid. No, indeed, Ma'am!

Miss Sterl. Nor of his being now locked up in my sister's chamber?

Ch. Maid. No, as I hope for marcy, Ma'am.

Mrs. Heidel. Well, I'll put an end to all this directly—do you run to my brother Sterling—

Ch. Maid. Now, Ma'am!—'Tis so very late, Ma'am—

Mrs. Heidel. I don't care how late it is. Tell him there are thieves in the house—that the house is o'fire—tell him to come here immediately—go, I say!

Ch. Maid. I will, I will, though I'm frighten'd out of my wits.

[*Exit.*

Mrs. Heidel. Do you watch here, my dear; and I'll put myself in order, to face them. We'll plot 'em, and counterplot 'em too.

[*Exit into her chamber.*

Miss Sterl. I have as much pleasure in this revenge, as in being made a countess!—Ha! they are unlocking the door.—Now for it!

[*Retires.*

[FANNY's *door is unlock'd—and* BETTY *comes out with a candle.* MISS STERLING *approaches her.*

Betty. [*Calling within.*] Sir, sir!—now's your time—all's clear. [*Seeing* MISS STERL.] Stay, stay—not yet—we are watch'd.

Miss Sterl. And so you are, Madam Betty!

[MISS STERLING *lays hold of her, while* BETTY *locks the door, and puts the key in her pocket.*

Betty. [*Turning round.*] What's the matter, Madam?

Miss Sterl. Nay, that you shall tell my father and aunt, Madam.

Betty. I am no tell-tale, Madam, and no thief; they'll get nothing from me.

Miss Sterl. You have a great deal of courage, Betty; and considering the secrets you have to keep, you have occasion for it.

Betty. My mistress shall never repent her good opinion of me, Ma'am.

Enter STERLING.

Sterl. What is all this? what's the matter? why am I disturbed in this manner?

Miss Sterl. This creature, and my distresses, Sir, will explain the matter.

Re-enter Mrs. HEIDELBERG, *with another head-dress.*

Mrs. Heidel. Now I'm prepar'd for the rancounter—well, brother, have you heard of this scene of wickedness?

Sterl. Not I—but what is it? Speak!—I was got into my little closet—all the lawyers were in bed, and I had almost lost my senses in the confusion of Lord Ogleby's mortgages; when I was alarm'd with a foolish girl, who could hardly speak; and whether it's fire, or thieves, or murder, or a rape, I am quite in the dark.

Mrs. Heidel. No, no, there's no rape, brother!—all parties are willing, I believe.

Miss Sterl. Who's in that chamber?

        [*Detaining* BETTY, *who seemed to be stealing away.*

Betty. My mistress.

Miss Sterl. And who is with your mistress?

Betty. Why, who should there be?

Miss Sterl. Open the door then, and let us see!

Betty. The door is open, Madam. [MISS STERLING *goes to the door.*] I'll sooner die than peach!   [*Exit hastily.*

Miss Sterl. The door's lock'd; and she has got the key in her pocket.

Mrs. Heidel. There's impudence, brother! piping hot from your daughter Fanny's school!

Sterl. But, zounds! what is all this about? You tell me of a sum total, and you don't produce the particulars.

Mrs. Heidel. Sir John Melvil is lock'd up in your daughter's bed-chamber.—There is the particular!

Sterl. The devil he is!—That's bad!

Miss Sterl. And he has been there some time too.

Sterl. Ditto!

Mrs. Heidel. Ditto! worse and worse, I say. I'll raise the house, and expose him to my Lord, and the whole family.

Sterl. By no means! we shall expose ourselves, sister!—the best way is to insure privately—let me alone!—I'll make him marry her to-morrow morning.

Miss Sterl. Make him marry her! this is beyond all patience!— You have thrown away all your affection; and I shall do as much by my obedience: unnatural fathers make unnatural children.— My revenge is in my own power, and I'll indulge it.—Had they made their escape, I should have been exposed to the derision of the world:—but the deriders shall be derided; and so—help! help, there! thieves! thieves!

Mrs. Heidel. Tit-for-tat, Betsey!—you are right, my girl.

Sterl. Zounds! you'll spoil all—you'll raise the whole family,— the devil's in the girl.

Mrs. Heidel. No, no; the devil's in *you*, brother. I am asham'd of your principles.—What! would you connive at your daughter's being lock'd up with her sister's husband? Help! thieves! thieves! I say.   [*Cries out.*

Sterl. Sister, I beg you!—daughter, I command you.—If you have no regard for me, consider yourselves!—we shall lose this opportunity of ennobling our blood, and getting above twenty per cent. for our money.

Miss Sterl. What, by my disgrace and my sister's triumph! I have a spirit above such mean considerations; and to shew you that it is not a low-bred, vulgar 'Change-Alley spirit—help! help! thieves! thieves! thieves! I say.

Sterl. Ay, ay, you may save your lungs—the house is in an up-roar;—women at best have no discretion; but in a passion they'll fire a house, or burn themselves in it, rather than not be revenged.

Enter CANTON, *in a night-gown and slippers.*

Cant. Eh, diable! vat is de raison of dis great noise, this tinta-marre?

Sterl. Ask those ladies, Sir; 'tis of their making.

Lord Ogleby. [*Calls within.*] Brush! Brush!—Canton! where are you?—What's the matter? [*Rings a bell.*] Where are you?

Sterl. 'Tis my Lord calls, Mr. Canton.

Cant. I com, mi Lor!—
                          [*Exit* CANTON. LORD OGLEBY *still rings.*

Serjeant Flower. [*Calls within.*] A light! a light here!—where are the servants? Bring a light for me, and my brothers.

Sterl. Lights here! lights for the gentlemen!   [*Exit* STERLING.

Mrs. Heidel. My brother feels, I see—your sister's turn will come next.

Miss Sterl. Ay ay, let it go round, Madam! it is the only comfort I have left.

Re-enter STERLING, *with lights, before* SERJEANT FLOWER (*with one boot and a slipper*) *and* TRAVERSE.

Sterl. This way, Sir! this way, gentlemen!

Serjeant Flower. Well, but, Mr. Sterling, no danger I hope.—Have they made a burglarious entry?—Are you prepar'd to repulse them?—I am very much alarm'd about thieves at circuit-time.—They would be particularly severe with us gentlemen of the bar.

Traverse. No danger, Mr. Sterling?—No trespass, I hope?

Sterl. None, gentlemen, but of those ladies making.

Mrs. Heidel. You'll be asham'd to know, gentlemen, that all your labours and studies about this young lady are thrown away—Sir John Melvil is at this moment lock'd up with this lady's younger sister.

Serjeant Flower. The thing is a little extraordinary, to be sure—but, why were we to be frighten'd out of our beds for this? Could not we have try'd this cause to-morrow morning?

Miss Sterl. But, Sir, by to-morrow morning, perhaps, even your assistance would not have been of any service—the birds now in that cage would have flown away.

Enter LORD OGLEBY *in his robe de chambre, night cap, &c.,—leaning on* CANTON.

Lord Ogle. I had rather lose a limb than my night's rest—what's the matter with you all?

Sterl. Ay, ay, 'tis all over!—Here's my Lord too.

Lord Ogle. What is all this shrieking and screaming?—Where's my angelick Fanny? She's safe, I hope!

Mrs. Heidel. Your angelick Fanny, my Lord, is lock'd up with your angelick nephew in that chamber.

Lord Ogle. My nephew! then will I be excommunicated.

Mrs. Heidel. Your nephew, my Lord, has been plotting to run away with the younger sister; and the younger sister has been plotting to run away with your nephew: and if we had not watch'd them and call'd up the fammaly, they had been upon the scamper to Scotland by this time.

Lord Ogle. Look'ee, ladies!—I know that Sir John has conceiv'd a violent passion for Miss Fanny; and I know too that Miss Fanny has conceiv'd a violent passion for another person; and I am so well convinc'd of the rectitude of her affections, that I will support them with my fortune, my honour, and my life.—Eh, shan't I, Mr. Sterling? [*Smiling.*] what say you?—

Sterl. [*Sulkily.*] To be sure, my Lord.—These bawling women have been the ruin of every thing.   [*Aside.*

Lord Ogle. But come, I'll end this business in a trice—if you, ladies, will compose yourselves, and Mr. Sterling will insure Miss Fanny from violence, I will engage to draw her from her pillow with a whisper thro' the keyhole.

Mrs. Heidel. The horrid creatures!—I say, my Lord, break the door open.

Lord Ogle. Let me beg of your delicacy not to be too precipitate!—Now to our experiment!   [*Advancing towards the door.*

Miss Sterl. Now, what will they do?—my heart will beat thro' my bosom.

Enter BETTY, *with the key.*

Betty. There's no occasion for breaking open doors, my Lord; we have done nothing that we ought to be asham'd of, and my mistress shall face her enemies.—   [*Going to unlock the door.*

Mrs. Heidel. There's impudence.

Lord Ogle. The mystery thickens. Lady of the bed-chamber! [*To* BETTY] open the door, and intreat Sir John Melvil (for these ladies will have it that he is there), to appear and answer to high crimes and misdemeanors.—Call Sir John Melvil into the court!

Enter SIR JOHN MELVIL, *on the other side.*

Sir John. I am here, my Lord.

Mrs. Heidel. Heyday!

Miss Sterl. Astonishment!

Sir John. What is all this alarm and confusion? there is nothing but hurry in the house; what is the reason of it?

Lord Ogle. Because you have been in that chamber; *have* been! nay you *are* there at this moment, as these ladies have protested, so don't deny it—

Traverse. This is the clearest Alibi I ever knew, Mr. Serjeant.

Flower. Luce clarius.

Lord Ogle. Upon my word, ladies, if you have often these frolicks, it would be really entertaining to pass a whole summer with you. But come, [*To* BETTY] open the door, and intreat your amiable mistress to come forth, and dispel all our doubts with her smiles.

Betty. [*Opening the door.*] Madam, you are wanted in this room.   [*Pertly.*

Enter FANNY, *in great confusion.*

Miss Sterl. You see she's ready dress'd—and what confusion she's in!

Mrs. Heidel. Ready to pack off, bag and baggage!—her guilt confounds her!—

Flower. Silence in the court, ladies!

Fanny. I *am* confounded, indeed, Madam!

Lord Ogle. Don't droop, my beauteous lily! but with your own peculiar modesty declare your state of mind.—Pour conviction into their ears, and raptures into mine. [*Smiling.*

Fanny. I am at this moment the most unhappy—most distrest —the tumult is too much for my heart—and I want the power to reveal a secret, which to conceal has been the misfortune and misery of my—my— [*Faints away.*

Lord Ogle. She faints; help, help! for the fairest, and best of women!

Betty. [*Running to her.*] O, my dear mistress!— help, help there!—

Sir John. Ha! let me fly to her assistance.

} *Speaking all at once*

LOVEWELL *rushes out from the chamber.*

Lovew. My Fanny in danger! I can contain no longer.—Prudence were now a crime; all other cares are lost in this!—speak, speak to me, my dearest Fanny!—let me but hear thy voice, open your eyes, and bless me with the smallest sign of life!

[*During this speech they are all in amazement.*

Miss Sterl. Lovewell!—I am easy.—

Mrs. Heidel. I am thunderstruck!

Lord Ogle. I am petrify'd!

Sir John. And I undone!

Fanny. [*Recovering.*] O Lovewell!—even supported by thee, I dare not look my father nor his Lordship in the face.

Sterl. What now! did not I send you to London, Sir?

Lord Ogle. Eh!—What!—How's this?—by what right and title have you been half the night in that lady's bed-chamber?

Lovew. By that right that makes me the happiest of men; and by a title which I would not forego, for any the best of kings could give me.

Betty. I could cry my eyes out to hear his magnimity.

Lord Ogle. I am annihilated!

Sterl. I have been choked with rage and wonder; but now I can speak.—Zounds, what have you to say to me?—Lovewell, you are a villain.—You have broke your word with me.

Fanny. Indeed, Sir, he has not—You forbad him to think of me, when it was out of his power to obey you; we have been married these four months.

Sterl. And he shan't stay in my house four hours. What baseness and treachery! As for you, you shall repent this step as long as you live, Madam.

Fanny. Indeed, Sir, it is impossible to conceive the tortures I have already endured in consequence of my disobedience. My heart has continually upbraided me for it; and though I was too weak to struggle with affection, I feel that I must be miserable for ever without your forgiveness.

Sterl. Lovewell, you shall leave my house directly;—and you shall follow him, Madam.   [*To* FANNY.

Lord Ogle. And if they do, I will receive them into mine. Look ye, Mr. Sterling, there have been some mistakes, which we had all better forget for our own sakes; and the best way to forget them is to forgive the cause of them; which I do from my soul.—Poor girl! I swore to support her affection with my life and fortune;—'tis a debt of honour, and must be paid—you swore as much too, Mr. Sterling; but your laws in the city will excuse *you*, I suppose; for you never strike a ballance without errors excepted.

Sterl. I am a father, my Lord; but for the sake of all other fathers, I think I ought not to forgive her, for fear of encouraging other silly girls like herself to throw themselves away without the consent of their parents.

Lovew. I hope there will be no danger of that, Sir. Young ladies with minds, like my Fanny's, would startle at the very shadow of vice; and when they know to what uneasiness only an indiscretion has exposed her, her example, instead, of encouraging, will rather serve to deter them.

Mrs. Heidel. Indiscretion, quoth a! a mighty pretty delicat word to express disobedience!

Lord Ogle. For my part, I indulge my own passions too much to tyrannize over those of other people. Poor souls, I pity them. And you must forgive them too. Come, come, melt a little of your flint, Mr. Sterling!

Sterl. Why, why—as to that, my Lord—to be sure he is a relation of yours, my Lord—what say *you*, sister Heidelberg?

Mrs. Heidel. The girl's ruined, and I forgive her.

Sterl. Well—so do I then.—Nay, no thanks—[*To* LOVEWELL *and* FANNY, *who seem preparing to speak.*] there's an end of the matter.

Lord Ogle. But, Lovewell, what makes you dumb all this while?

Lovew. Your kindness, my Lord—I can scarce believe my own senses—they are all in a tumult of fear, joy, love, expectation, and gratitude; I ever was, and am now more bound in duty to your Lordship; for you, Mr. Sterling, if every moment of my life, spent gratefully in your service, will in some measure compensate the want of fortune, you perhaps will not repent your goodness to me. And you, ladies, I flatter myself, will not for the future suspect me of artifice and intrigue—I shall be happy to oblige, and serve you.—As for you, Sir John—

Sir John. No apologies to me, Lovewell, I do not deserve any. All I have to offer in excuse for what has happened, is my total ignorance of your situation. Had you dealt a little more openly with me, you would have saved me, and yourself, and that lady, (who I hope will pardon my behaviour) a great deal of uneasiness. Give me leave, however, to assure you, that light and capricious as I may have appeared, now my infatuation is over, I have sensibility enough to be ashamed of the part I have acted, and honour enough to rejoice at your happiness.

Lovew. And now, my dearest Fanny, though we are seemingly the happiest of beings, yet all our joys will be dampt, if his Lordship's generosity and Mr. Sterling's forgiveness should not be succeeded by the indulgence, approbation, and consent of these our best benefactors.   .   [*To the audience.*

Finis

EPILOGUE

WRITTEN BY MR. GARRICK

CHARACTERS OF THE EPILOGUE

LORD MINUM	Mr. Dodd
COLONEL TRILL	Mr. Vernon
SIR PATRICK MAHONY	Mr. Moody
MISS CROTCHET	Mrs. ——
MRS. QUAVER	Mrs. Lee
FIRST LADY	Mrs. Bradshaw
SECOND LADY	Miss Mills
THIRD LADY	Mrs. Dorman

SCENE.—*An Assembly*

Several Persons at Cards, at different Tables; among the rest
COL. TRILL, LORD MINUM, MRS. QUAVER, SIR PATRICK
MAHONY.

At the Quadrille Table.

Col. T. Ladies, with Leave—
2nd Lady. Pass!
3d Lady. Pass!
Mrs. Qu. You must do more.
Col. T. Indeed I can't.
Mrs. Qu. I play in Hearts.
Col. T. Encore!
2d Lady. What Luck!
Col. T. To-night at Drury Lane is play'd
      A Comedy, and *toute nouvelle*—a Spade!
      Is not Miss Crotchet at the Play?
Mrs. Qu. My Niece
      Has made a Party, Sir, to damn the Piece.

At the Whist Table.

Lord Min. I hate a Play-house—Trump!—It makes me sick.
1st Lady. We're two by Honours, Ma'am.

Lord Min. And we the odd Trick. Pray do you know the Author, Colonel Trill?

Col. T. I know no Poets, Heaven be prais'd!—Spadille!

1st Lady. I'll tell you who, my Lord!   [*Whispers my Lord.*

Lord Min. What, he again?

"And dwell such daring Souls in little Men?"

Be whose it will, they down our Throats will cram it!

Col. T. O, no.—I have a Club—the best.—We'll damn it.

Mrs. Qu. O Bravo, Colonel! Musick is my Flame.

Lord Min. And mine, by Jupiter!—We've won the Game.

Col. T. What, do you love all Musick?

Mrs. Qu. No, not Handel's. And nasty Plays—

Lord Min. Are fit for Goths and Vandals.

[*Rise from the Table and pay.*

From the Piquette Table.

Sir Pat. Well, faith and troth! that Shakespeare was no Fool!

Col. T. I'm glad you like him, Sir!—So ends the Pool!

[*Pay and rise from Table.*

Song *by the* COLONEL.

I hate all their Nonsense,
  Their Shakespears and Johnsons,
Their Plays, and their Play-house, and Bards:
  'Tis singing, not saying;
  A Fig for all playing,
But playing, as we do, at Cards!
  I love to see Jonas,
  Am pleas'd too with Comus;
Each well the Spectator rewards.
  So clever, so neat in
  Their Tricks, and their Cheating!
Like them we would fain deal our Cards.

Sir Pat. King Lare is touching!—and how fine to see
  Ould Hamlet's Ghost!—"To be, or not to be."—
  What are your Op'ras to Othello's roar?
  Oh, he's an Angel of a Blackamoor!

Lord Min. What, when he choaks his Wife?—

Col. T.   And calls her Whore?

Sir Pat. King Richard calls his Horse—and then Macbeth,
  When e'er he murders—takes away the Breath.
  My Blood runs cold at ev'ry Syllable,
  To see the Dagger—that's invisible.   [*All laugh.*

Sir Pat. Laugh if you please, a pretty Play—
Lord Min.   **Is pretty.**
Sir Pat. And when there's Wit in't—
Col. T.   To be sure 'tis witty.
Sir Pat. I love the Play-house now—so light and gay,
With all those Candles, they have ta'en away!   [*All laugh.*
For all your Game, what makes it so much brighter?
Col. T. Put out the Light, and then—
Lord Min.   'Tis so much lighter.
Sir Pat. Pray do you mane, Sirs, more than you express?
Col. T. Just as it happens—
Lord Min.   Either more, or less.
Mrs. Qu. An't you asham'd, Sir?   [*To* Sir Pat.
Sir Pat.   Me!—I seldom blush.—
For little Shakespeare, faith! I'd take a Push!
Lord Min. News, News!—here comes Miss Crotchet from the
Play.

Enter Miss Crotchet.

Mrs. Qu. Well, Crotchet, what's the News?
Miss Cro.   We've lost the Day.
Col. T. Tell us, dear Miss, all you have heard and seen.
Miss Cro. I'm tired—a Chair—here, take my Capuchin!
Lord Min. And isn't it damn'd, Miss?
Miss Cro. No, my Lord, not quite: But we shall damn it.
Col. T. When?
Miss Cro. To-morrow Night.
      There is a Party of us, all of Fashion,
      Resolv'd to exterminate this vulgar Passion:
      A Play-house, what a Place!—I must forswear it.
      A little Mischief only makes one bear it.
      Such Crowds of City Folks!—so rude and pressing!
      And their Horse-Laughs, so hideously distressing!
      When e'er we hiss'd, they frown'd and fell a swearing,
      Like their own Guildhall Giants—fierce and staring!
Col. T. What said the Folks of Fashion? were they cross?
Lord Min. The rest have no more Judgement than my **Horse.**
Miss Cro. Lord Grimly swore 'twas execrable Stuff.
      Says one, Why so, my Lord?—My Lord took Snuff.
      In the first Act Lord George began to doze,
      And criticis'd the Author—through his Nose;
      So loud indeed, that as his Lordship snor'd,
      The Pit turn'd round, and all the Brutes encor'd.
      Some Lords, indeed, approv'd the Author's Jokes.

Lord Min. We have among us, Miss, *some* foolish Folks.

Miss Cro. Says poor Lord Simper—Well, now to my Mind
The Piece is good;—but he's both deaf and blind.

Sir Pat. Upon my Soul a very pretty Story!
      And Quality appears in all its Glory!—
      There was some Merit in the Piece, no Doubt;

Miss Cro. O, to be sure!—If one could find it out.

Col. T. But tell us, Miss, the Subject of the Play.

Miss Cro. Why, 'twas a Marriage—yes, a Marriage—Stay!
      A Lord, an Aunt, two Sisters, and a Merchant—
      A Baronet—ten Lawyers—a fat Serjeant—
      Are all produc'd—to talk with one another;
      And about something make a mighty Pother;
      They all go in, and out; and to, and fro;
      And talk, and quarrel—as they come and go—
      Then go to Bed, and then get up—and then—
      Scream, faint, scold, kiss,—and go to Bed again.

                                     [All laugh.
      Such is the Play—Your Judgment! never sham it.

Col. T. Oh damn it!

Mrs. Qu.   Damn it!

1st Lady.   Damn it!

Miss Cro.   Damn it!

Lord Min.   Damn it!

Sir Pat. Well, faith, you speak your Minds, and I'll be free—
Good Night! this Company's too good for me.   *[Going.*

Col. T. Your Judgment, dear Sir Patrick, makes us proud.
                                     [All laugh.

Sir Pat. Laugh if you please, but pray don't laugh too loud.
                                       [Exit.

RECITATIVE

Col. T. Now the Barbarian's gone, Miss, tune your Tongue,
And let us raise our Spirits high with Song!

RECITATIVE

Miss Cro. Colonel, *de tout mon Cœur*—I've one in *petto,*
Which you shall join, and make it a *Duetto.*

RECITATIVE

Lord Min. Bello Signora, et Amico mio!
I too will join, and then we'll make a *Trio.*—

Col. T. Come all and join the full-mouth'd Chorus,
And drive all Tragedy and Comedy before us!
> [*All the Company rise, and advance to the Front of the Stage.*

AIR

Col. T. Would you ever go to see a Tragedy?
Miss Cro.   Never, never.
·*Col. T.* A Comedy?
Lord Min.   Never, never,
                                    Live for ever!
> Tweedle-dum and Tweedle-dee!

Col. T., *Lord Min.* and *Miss Cro.* Live for ever!
> Tweedle-dum and Tweedle-dee!

CHORUS

Would you ever go to see, &c.
                                    [*Exit.*

SHE STOOPS TO CONQUER

by

OLIVER GOLDSMITH

To SAMUEL JOHNSON, L.L.D.

DEAR SIR,

By inscribing this slight performance to you, I do not mean so much to compliment you as myself. It may do me some honour to inform the public, that I have lived many years in intimacy with you. It may serve the interests of mankind also to inform them, that the greatest wit may be found in a character, without impairing the most unaffected piety.

I have, particularly, reason to thank you for your partiality to this performance. The undertaking a comedy, not merely senti-mental, was very dangerous; and Mr. Colman, who saw this piece in its various stages, always thought it so. However, I ven-tured to trust it to the public; and though it was necessarily delayed till late in the season, I have every reason to be grateful.

I am, Dear Sir,
Your most sincere friend,
And admirer,
OLIVER GOLDSMITH.

PROLOGUE

By David Garrick, Esq.

Enter Mr. Woodward, *Dressed in Black, and holding a Hand-kerchief to his Eyes.*

> *Excuse me, Sirs, I pray—I can't yet speak—*
> *I'm crying now—and have been all the week!*
> 'Tis not alone this mourning suit, *good masters;*
> I've that within—*for which there are no plaisters!*
> *Pray wou'd you know the reason why I'm crying?*
> *The Comic muse, long sick, is now a dying!*
> *And if she goes, my tears will never stop;*
> *For as a play'r, I can't squeeze out one drop:*
> *I am undone, that's all—shall lose my bread—*
> *I'd rather, but that's nothing—lose my head.*
> *When the sweet maid is laid upon the bier,*
> *Shuter and I shall be chief mourners here.*
> *To* her *a mawkish drab of spurious breed,*
> *Who deals in* sentimentals *will succeed!*
> *Poor Ned and I are dead to all intents,*
> *We can as soon speak Greek as* sentiments!
> *Both nervous grown, to keep our spirits up,*
> *We now and then take down a hearty cup.*
> *What shall we do?—If Comedy forsake us!*
> They'll turn us out, and no one else will take us;
> *But why can't I be moral?—Let me try—*
> *My heart thus pressing—fix'd my face and eye—*
> *With a sententious look, that nothing means,*
> *(Faces are blocks, in sentimental scenes)*
> *Thus I begin—All is not gold that glitters,*
> Pleasure seems sweet, but proves a glass of bitters.
> When ign'rance enters, folly is at hand;
> Learning is better far than house and land.
> Let not your virtue trip, who trips may stumble,
> And virtue is not virtue, if she tumble.
> *I give it up—morals won't do for me;*
> *To make you laugh I must play tragedy.*

One hope remains—hearing the maid was ill,
A doctor *comes this night to shew his skill.*
To cheer her heart, and give your muscles motion,
He in five draughts *prepar'd, presents a potion:*
A kind of magic charm—for be assur'd,
If you will swallow *it, the maid is cur'd:*
But desp'rate the Doctor, and her case is,
If you reject the dose, and make wry faces!
This truth he boasts, will boast it while he lives,
No pois'nous drugs *are mix'd in what he gives;*
Should he succeed, you'll give him his degree;
If not, within he will receive no fee!
The college you, *must his pretensions back,*
Pronounce him regular, *or dub him* quack.

DRAMATIS PERSONÆ

MEN

SIR CHARLES MARLOW	Mr. Gardner
YOUNG MARLOW (*his Son*)	Mr. Lewes
HARDCASTLE	Mr. Shuter
HASTINGS	Mr. Dubellamy
TONY LUMPKIN	Mr. Quick
DIGGORY	Mr. Saunders

WOMEN

MRS. HARDCASTLE	Mrs. Green
MISS HARDCASTLE	Mrs. Bulkley
MISS NEVILLE	Mrs. Kniveton
MAID	Miss Willems

Landlord, Servants, &c., &c.

SHE STOOPS TO CONQUER

OR,

THE MISTAKES OF A NIGHT

ACT I

SCENE.—*A Chamber in an old-fashioned House*

Enter MRS. HARDCASTLE *and* MR. HARDCASTLE.

Mrs. Hardcastle. I vow, Mr. Hardcastle, you're very particular. Is there a creature in the whole country, but ourselves, that does not take a trip to town now and then, to rub off the rust a little? There's the two Miss Hoggs, and our neighbour, Mrs. Grigsby, go to take a month's polishing every winter.

Hardcastle. Ay, and bring back vanity and affectation to last them the whole year. I wonder why London cannot keep its own fools at home. In my time, the follies of the town crept slowly among us, but now they travel faster than a stage-coach. Its fopperies come down, not only as inside passengers, but in the very basket.

Mrs. Hardcastle. Ay, *your* times were fine times, indeed; you have been telling us of *them* for many a long year. Here we live in an old rumbling mansion, that looks for all the world like an inn, but that we never see company. Our best visitors are old Mrs. Oddfish, the curate's wife, and little Cripplegate, the lame dancing-master: And all our entertainment your old stories of Prince Eugene and the Duke of Marlborough. I hate such old-fashioned trumpery.

Hardcastle. And I love it. I love every thing that's old: old friends, old times, old manners, old books, old wine; and, I believe, Dorothy [*taking her hand*], you'll own I have been pretty fond of an old wife.

Mrs. Hardcastle. Lord, Mr. Hardcastle, you're for ever at your Dorothy's and your old wife's. You may be a Darby, but I'll be no Joan, I promise you. I'm not so old as you'd make me, by more than one good year. Add twenty to twenty, and make money of that.

Hardcastle. Let me see; twenty added to twenty, makes just fifty and seven.

Mrs. Hardcastle. It's false, Mr. Hardcastle: I was but twenty when I was brought to bed of Tony, that I had by Mr. Lumpkin, my first husband; and he's not come to years of discretion yet.

Hardcastle. Nor ever will, I dare answer for him. Ay, you have taught *him* finely!

Mrs. Hardcastle. No matter, Tony Lumpkin has a good fortune. My son is not to live by his learning. I don't think a boy wants much learning to spend fifteen hundred a year.

Hardcastle. Learning, quotha! A mere composition of tricks and mischief.

Mrs. Hardcastle. Humour, my dear: nothing but humour. Come, Mr. Hardcastle, you must allow the boy a little humour.

Hardcastle. I'd sooner allow him an horse-pond. If burning the footmens shoes, frighting the maids, and worrying the kittens, be humour, he has it. It was but yesterday he fastened my wig to the back of my chair, and when I went to make a bow, I popt my bald head in Mrs. Frizzle's face.

Mrs. Hardcastle. And am I to blame? The poor boy was always too sickly to do any good. A school would be his death. When he comes to be a little stronger, who knows what a year or two's Latin may do for him?

Hardcastle. Latin for him! A cat and fiddle. No, no, the alehouse and the stable are the only schools he'll ever go to.

Mrs. Hardcastle. Well, we must not snub the poor boy now, for I believe we shan't have him long among us. Any body that looks in his face may see he's consumptive.

Hardcastle. Ay, if growing too fat be one of the symptoms.

Mrs. Hardcastle. He coughs sometimes.

Hardcastle. Yes, when his liquor goes the wrong way.

Mrs. Hardcastle. I'm actually afraid of his lungs.

Hardcastle. And truly, so am I; for he sometimes whoops like a speaking trumpet—[TONY *hallooing behind the Scenes.*]—O, there he goes—A very consumptive figure, truly.

Enter TONY, *crossing the Stage.*

Mrs. Hardcastle. Tony, where are you going, my charmer? Won't you give papa and I a little of your company, lovee?

Tony. I'm in haste, mother, I cannot stay.

Mrs. Hardcastle. You shan't venture out this raw evening, my dear: You look most shockingly.

Tony. I can't stay, I tell you. *The Three Pigeons* expects me down every moment. There's some fun going forward.

Hardcastle. Ay; the ale-house, the old place: I thought so.

Mrs. Hardcastle. A low, paltry set of fellows.

Tony. Not so low neither. There's Dick Muggins the excise-man, Jack Slang the horse doctor, Little Aminadab that grinds the music box, and Tom Twist that spins the pewter platter.

Mrs. Hardcastle. Pray, my dear, disappoint them for one night at least.

Tony. As for disappointing *them,* I should not so much mind; but I can't abide to disappoint *myself.*

Mrs. Hardcastle. [*Detaining him.*] You shan't go.

Tony. I will, I tell you.

Mrs. Hardcastle. I say you shan't.

Tony. We'll see which is strongest, you or I.

[*Exit hawling her out.*

HARDCASTLE, *solus.*

Hardcastle. Ay, there goes a pair that only spoil each other. But is not the whole age in a combination to drive sense and discretion out of doors? There's my pretty darling, Kate; the fashions of the times have almost infected her too. By living a year or two in town, she is as fond of gauze, and French frippery, as the best of them.

Enter MISS HARDCASTLE.

Hardcastle. Blessings on my pretty innocence! Drest out as usual, my Kate. Goodness! What a quantity of superfluous silk hast thou got about thee, girl! I could never teach the fools of this age, that the indigent world could be cloathed out of the trimmings of the vain.

Miss Hardcastle. You know our agreement, Sir. You allow me the morning to receive and pay visits, and to dress in my own manner; and in the evening, I put on my housewife's dress to please you.

Hardcastle. Well, remember, I insist on the terms of our agreement; and, by the bye, I believe I shall have occasion to try your obedience this very evening.

Miss Hardcastle. I protest, Sir, I don't comprehend your meaning.

Hardcastle. Then, to be plain with you, Kate, I expect the young gentleman I have chosen to be your husband from town this very day. I have his father's letter, in which he informs me his son is set out, and that he intends to follow himself shortly after.

Miss Hardcastle. Indeed! I wish I had known something of this before. Bless me, how shall I behave? It's a thousand to one I shan't like him; our meeting will be so formal, and so like a thing of business, that I shall find no room for friendship or esteem.

Hardcastle. Depend upon it, child, I'll never controul your choice; but Mr. Marlow, whom I have pitched upon, is the son of my old friend, Sir Charles Marlow, of whom you have heard me talk so often. The young gentleman has been bred a scholar, and is designed for an employment in the service of his country. I am told he's a man of an excellent understanding.

Miss Hardcastle. Is he?

Hardcastle. Very generous.

Miss Hardcastle. I believe I shall like him.

Hardcastle. Young and brave.

Miss Hardcastle. I'm sure I shall like him.

Hardcastle. And very handsome.

Miss Hardcastle. My dear papa, say no more [*kissing his hand*], he's mine, I'll have him.

Hardcastle. And to crown all, Kate, he's one of the most bashful and reserved young fellows in all the world.

Miss Hardcastle. Eh! you have frozen me to death again. That word *reserved* has undone all the rest of his accomplishments. A reserved lover, it is said, always makes a suspicious husband.

Hardcastle. On the contrary, modesty seldom resides in a breast that is not enriched with nobler virtues. It was the very feature in his character that first struck me.

Miss Hardcastle. He must have more striking features to catch me, I promise you. However, if he be so young, so handsome, and so every thing, as you mention, I believe he'll do still. I think I'll have him.

Hardcastle. Ay, Kate, but there is still an obstacle. It's more than an even wager, he may not have *you*.

Miss Hardcastle. My dear Papa, why will you mortify one so? —Well, if he refuses, instead of breaking my heart at his indifference, I'll only break my glass for its flattery. Set my cap to some newer fashion, and look out for some less difficult admirer.

Hardcastle. Bravely resolved! In the mean time I'll go prepare the servants for his reception; as we seldom see company, they want as much training as a company of recruits, the first day's muster. [*Exit.*

MISS HARDCASTLE, *sola.*

Miss Hardcastle. Lud, this news of Papa's, puts me all in a flutter. Young, handsome; these he put last; but I put them foremost. Sensible, good-natured; I like all that. But then reserved, and sheepish, that's much against him. Yet, can't he be cured of his timidity, by being taught to be proud of his wife? Yes, and can't I—But I vow I'm disposing of the husband, before I have secured the lover.

Enter MISS NEVILLE.

Miss Hardcastle. I'm glad you're come, Neville, my dear. Tell me, Constance, how do I look this evening? Is there any thing whimsical about me? Is it one of my well looking days, child? Am I in face to day?

Miss Neville. Perfectly, my dear. Yet now I look again—bless me!—sure no accident has happened among the canary birds or the gold-fishes. Has your brother or the cat been meddling? Or has the last novel been too moving?

Miss Hardcastle. No; nothing of all this. I have been threatened—I can scarce get it out—I have been threatened with a lover.

Miss Neville. And his name—

Miss Hardcastle. Is Marlow.

Miss Neville. Indeed!

Miss Hardcastle. The son of Sir Charles Marlow.

Miss Neville. As I live, the most intimate friend of Mr. Hastings, *my* admirer. They are never asunder. I believe you must have seen him when we lived in town.

Miss Hardcastle. Never.

Miss Neville. He's a very singular character, I assure you. Among women of reputation and virtue, he is the modestest man alive; but his acquaintance give him a very different character among creatures of another stamp: you understand me.

Miss Hardcastle. An odd character, indeed. I shall never be able to manage him. What shall I do? Pshaw, think no more of him, but trust to occurrences for success. But how goes on your own affair, my dear? has my mother been courting you for my brother Tony, as usual?

Miss Neville. I have just come from one of our agreeable *tête-à-têtes.* She has been saying a hundred tender things, and setting off her pretty monster as the very pink of perfection.

Miss Hardcastle. And her partiality is such, that she actually thinks him so. A fortune like your's is no small temptation. Besides, as she has the sole management of it, I'm not surprized to see her unwilling to let it go out of the family.

Miss Neville. A fortune like mine, which chiefly consists in jewels, is no such mighty temptation. But at any rate, if my dear Hastings be but constant, I make no doubt to be too hard

for her at last. However, I let her suppose that I am in love
with her son, and she never once dreams that my affections are
fixed upon another.

Miss Hardcastle. My good brother holds out stoutly. I could
almost love him for hating you so.

Miss Neville. It is a good natured creature at bottom, and
I'm sure would wish to see me married to any body but himself.
But my aunt's bell rings for our afternoon's walk round the
improvements. *Allons.* Courage is necessary, as our affairs are
critical.

Miss Hardcastle. Would it were bed time and all were well.

[*Exeunt.*

SCENE.—*An Ale-house Room. Several shabby fellows, with Punch
and Tobacco.* TONY *at the head of the Table, a little higher
than the rest: A mallet in his hand.*

Omnes. Hurrea, hurrea, hurrea, bravo!

First Fellow. Now, gentlemen, silence for a song. The 'Squire
is going to knock himself down for a song.

Omnes. Ay, a song, a song.

Tony. Then I'll sing you, gentlemen, a song I made upon this
ale-house, *The Three Pigeons.*

SONG

> *Let school-masters puzzle their brain,*
>   *With grammar, and nonsense, and learning;*
> *Good liquor, I stoutly maintain,*
>   *Gives* genus *a better discerning.*
> *Let them brag of their Heathenish Gods,*
>   *Their Lethes, their Styxes, and Stygians;*
> *Their Quis, and their Quæs, and their Quods,*
>   *They're all but a parcel of Pigeons.*
>   *Toroddle, toroddle, toroll!*
>
> *When Methodist preachers come down,*
>   *A preaching that drinking is sinful,*
> *I'll wager the rascals a crown,*
>   *They always preach best with a skinful.*
> *But when you come down with your pence,*
>   *For a slice of their scurvy religion,*
> *I'll leave it to all men of sense,*
>   *But you, my good friend, are the pigeon.*
>   *Toroddle, toroddle, toroll!*

Then come, put the jorum about,
    And let us be merry and clever,
Our hearts and our liquors are stout,
    Here's the Three Jolly Pigeons for ever.
Let some cry up woodcock or hare,
    Your bustards, your ducks, and your widgeons;
But of all the birds in the air,
    Here's a health to the Three Jolly Pigeons.
      Toroddle, toroddle, toroll!

Omnes. Bravo, bravo.

First Fellow. The 'Squire has got spunk in him.

Second Fellow. I loves to hear him sing, bekeays he never gives us nothing that's *low*.

Third Fellow. O damn any thing that's *low*, I cannot bear it.

Fourth Fellow. The genteel thing is the genteel thing at any time. If so be that a gentleman bees in a concatenation accordingly.

Third Fellow. I like the maxum of it, Master Muggins. What, tho' I am obligated to dance a bear, a man may be a gentleman for all that. May this be my poison if my bear ever dances but to the very genteelest of tunes. *Water Parted,* or the minuet in *Ariadne.*

Second Fellow. What a pity it is the 'Squire is not come to his own. It would be well for all the publicans within ten miles round of him.

Tony. Ecod, and so it would, Master Slang. I'd then shew what it was to keep choice of company.

Second Fellow. O, he takes after his own father for that. To be sure old 'Squire Lumpkin was the finest gentleman I ever set my eyes on. For winding the streight horn, or beating a thicket for a hare, or a wench, he never had his fellow. It was a saying in the place, that he kept the best horses, dogs and girls in the whole county.

Tony. Ecod, and when I'm of age I'll be no bastard, I promise you. I have been thinking of Bett Bouncer and the miller's grey mare to begin with. But come, my boys, drink about and be merry, for you pay no reckoning. Well, Stingo, what's the matter?

Enter LANDLORD.

Landlord. There be two gentlemen in a post-chaise at the door. They have lost their way upo' the forest; and they are talking something about Mr. Hardcastle.

Tony. As sure as can be, one of them must be the gentleman that's coming down to court my sister. Do they seem to be Londoners?

Landlord. I believe they may. They look woundily like Frenchmen.

Tony. Then desire them to step this way, and I'll set them right in a twinkling. [*Exit* LANDLORD.] Gentlemen, as they mayn't be good enough company for you, step down for a moment, and I'll be with you in the squeezing of a lemon.

[*Exeunt* MOB.
TONY, *solus*.

Tony. Father-in-law has been calling me whelp, and hound, this half year. Now if I pleased, I could be so revenged upon the old grumbletonian. But then I'm afraid—afraid of what? I shall soon be worth fifteen hundred a year, and let him frighten me out of that if he can.

Enter LANDLORD, *conducting* MARLOW *and* HASTINGS.

Marlow. What a tedious, uncomfortable day have we had of it! We were told it was but forty miles across the country, and we have come above threescore.

Hastings. And all, Marlow, from that unaccountable reserve of yours, that would not let us enquire more frequently on the way.

Marlow. I own, Hastings, I am unwilling to lay myself under an obligation to every one I meet; and often, stand the chance of an unmannerly answer.

Hastings. At present, however, we are not likely to receive any answer.

Tony. No offence, gentlemen. But I'm told you have been enquiring for one Mr. Hardcastle, in these parts. Do you know what part of the country you are in?

Hastings. Not in the least, Sir, but should thank you for information.

Tony. Nor the way you came?

Hastings. No, Sir; but if you can inform us—

Tony. Why, gentlemen, if you know neither the road you are going, nor where you are, nor the road you came, the first thing I have to inform you is, that—You have lost your way.

Marlow. We wanted no ghost to tell us that.

Tony. Pray, gentlemen, may I be so bold as to ask the place from whence you came?

Marlow. That's not necessary towards directing us where we are to go.

Tony. No offence; but question for question is all fair, you

know. Pray, gentlemen, is not this same Hardcastle a cross,
grain'd, old-fashion'd, whimsical fellow, with an ugly face, a
daughter, and a pretty son?

Hastings. We have not seen the gentleman, but he has the
family you mention.

Tony. The daughter, a tall trapesing, trolloping, talkative may-
pole—The son, a pretty, well-bred, agreeable youth, that every
body is fond of.

Marlow. Our information differs in this. The daughter is said
to be well-bred and beautiful; the son, an awkward booby,
reared up, and spoiled at his mother's apron-string.

Tony. He-he-hem—Then, gentlemen, all I have to tell you is,
that you won't reach Mr. Hardcastle's house this night, I believe.

Hastings. Unfortunate!

Tony. It's a damn'd long, dark, boggy, dirty, dangerous way.
Stingo, tell the gentlemen the way to Mr. Hardcastle's [*Winking
upon the* LANDLORD.] ; Mr. Hardcastle's, of Quagmire Marsh, you
understand me.

Landlord. Master Hardcastle's! Lock-a-daisy, my masters,
you're come a deadly deal wrong! When you came to the bottom
of the hill, you should have cross'd down Squash-lane.

Marlow. Cross down Squash-lane!

Landlord. Then you were to keep streight forward, 'till you
came to four roads.

Marlow. Come to where four roads meet!

Tony. Ay; but you must be sure to take only one of them.

Marlow. O, Sir, you're facetious.

Tony. Then keeping to the right, you are to go side-ways till
you come upon Crack-skull Common: there you must look sharp
for the track of the wheel, and go forward, 'till you come to
farmer Murrain's barn. Coming to the farmer's barn, you are to
turn to the right, and then to the left, and then to the right about
again, till you find out the old mill—

Marlow. Zounds, man! we could as soon find out the longitude!

Hastings. What's to be done, Marlow?

Marlow. This house promises but a poor reception; though
perhaps the Landlord can accommodate us.

Landlord. Alack, master, we have but one spare bed in the
whole house.

Tony. And to my knowledge, that's taken up by three lodgers
already. [*After a pause, in which the rest seem disconcerted.*]
I have hit it. Don't you think, Stingo, our landlady could accommodate the gentlemen by the fire-side, with—three chairs and a
bolster?

Hastings. I hate sleeping by the fire-side.

Marlow. And I detest your three chairs and a bolster.

Tony. You do, do you?—then let me see—what—if you go on a mile further to the Buck's Head; the old Buck's Head on the hill, one of the best inns in the whole county?

Hastings. O ho! so we have escaped an adventure for this night, however.

Landlord. [*Apart to* TONY.] Sure, you ben't sending them to your father's as an inn, be you?

Tony. Mum, you fool you. Let *them* find that out. [*To them.*] You have only to keep on streight forward, till you come to a large old house by the road side. You'll see a pair of large horns over the door. That's the sign. Drive up the yard, and call stoutly about you.

Hastings. Sir, we are obliged to you. The servants can't miss the way?

Tony. No, no: But I tell you though, the landlord is rich, and going to leave off business; so he wants to be thought a Gentleman, saving your presence, he! he! he! He'll be for giving you his company, and, ecod, if you mind him, he'll persuade you that his mother was an alderman, and his aunt a justice of peace.

Landlord. A troublesome old blade, to be sure; but a keeps as good wines and beds as any in the whole country.

Marlow. Well, if he supplies us with these, we shall want no further connexion. We are to turn to the right, did you say?

Tony. No, no; streight forward. I'll just step myself, and shew you a piece of the way. [*To the* LANDLORD.] Mum.

Landlord. Ah, bless your heart, for a sweet, pleasant—damn'd mischievous son of a whore. [*Exeunt.*

END OF THE FIRST ACT

ACT II

SCENE.—*An old-fashioned House*

Enter HARDCASTLE, *followed by three or four awkward* SERVANTS.

Hardcastle. Well, I hope you're perfect in the table exercise I have been teaching you these three days. You all know your posts and your places, and can shew that you have been used to good company, without ever stirring from home.

Omnes. Ay, ay.

Hardcastle. When company comes, you are not to pop out and stare, and then run in again, like frighted rabbits in a warren.

Omnes. No, no.

Hardcastle. You, Diggory, whom I have taken from the barn, are to make a shew at the side-table; and you, Roger, whom I have advanced from the plough, are to place yourself behind *my* chair. But you're not to stand so, with your hands in your pockets. Take your hands from your pockets, Roger; and from your head, you blockhead you. See how Diggory carries his hands. They're a little too stiff indeed, but that's no great matter.

Diggory. Ay, mind how I hold them. I learned to hold my hands this way, when I was upon drill for the militia. And so being upon drill—

Hardcastle. You must not be so talkative, Diggory. You must be all attention to the guests. You must hear us talk, and not think of talking; you must see us drink, and not think of drinking; you must see us eat, and not think of eating.

Diggory. By the laws, your worship, that's perfectly unpossible. Whenever Diggory sees yeating going forward, ecod, he's always wishing for a mouthful himself.

Hardcastle. Blockhead! Is not a belly-full in the kitchen as good as a belly-full in the parlour? Stay your stomach with that reflection.

Diggory. Ecod, I thank your worship, I'll make a shift to stay my stomach with a slice of cold beef in the pantry.

Hardcastle. Diggory, you are too talkative. Then, if I happen to say a good thing, or tell a good story at table, you must not all burst out a-laughing, as if you made part of the company.

Diggory. Then, ecod, your worship must not tell the story of Ould Grouse in the gun-room: I can't help laughing at that— he! he! he!—for the soul of me. We have laughed at that these twenty years—ha! ha! ha

Hardcastle. Ha! ha! ha! The story is a good one. Well, honest Diggory, you may laugh at that—but still remember to be attentive. Suppose one of the company should call for a glass of wine, how will you behave? A glass of wine, Sir, if you please. [*To* Diggory.]—Eh, why don't you move?

Diggory. Ecod, your worship, I never have courage till I see the eatables and drinkables brought upo' the table, and then I'm as bauld as a lion.

Hardcastle. What, will no body move?

First Servant. I'm not to leave this pleace.

Second Servant. I'm sure it's no pleace of mine.

Third Servant. Nor mine, for sartain.

Diggory. Wauns, and I'm sure it canna be mine.

Hardcastle. You numbskulls! and so while, like your betters, you are quarrelling for places, the guests must be starved. O you dunces! I find I must begin all over again.—But don't I hear a coach drive into the yard? To your posts, you blockheads. I'll go in the mean time and give my old friend's son a hearty reception at the gate. [*Exit* HARDCASTLE.

Diggory. By the elevens, my pleace is gone quite out of my head.

Roger. I know that my pleace is to be every where.

First Servant. Where the devil is mine?

Second Servant. My pleace is to be no where at all; and so I'ze go about my business.

[*Exeunt* SERVANTS, *running about as if frighted, different ways.*

Enter SERVANT *with Candles, shewing in* MARLOW *and* HASTINGS.

Servant. Welcome, gentlemen, very welcome. This way.

Hastings. After the disappointments of the day, welcome once more, Charles, to the comforts of a clean room and a good fire. Upon my word, a very well-looking house; antique, but creditable.

Marlow. The usual fate of a large mansion. Having first ruined the master by good housekeeping, it at last comes to levy contributions as an inn.

Hastings. As you say, we passengers are to be taxed to pay all these fineries. I have often seen a good sideboard, or a marble chimney-piece, tho' not actually put in the bill, enflame a reckoning confoundedly.

Marlow. Travellers, George, must pay in all places. The only difference is, that in good inns, you pay dearly for luxuries; in bad inns, you are fleeced and starved.

Hastings. You have lived pretty much among them. In truth, I have been often surprized, that you who have seen so much of the world, with your natural good sense, and your many opportunities, could never yet acquire a requisite share of assurance.

Marlow. The Englishman's malady. But tell me, George, where could I have learned that assurance you talk of? My life has been chiefly spent in a college, or an inn, in seclusion from that lovely part of the creation that chiefly teach men confidence. I don't know that I was ever familiarly acquainted with a single modest woman—except my mother—But among females of another class, you know—

Hastings. Ay, among them you are impudent enough of all conscience.

Marlow. They are of *us,* you know.

Hastings. But in the company of women of reputation I never saw such an ideot, such a trembler; you look for all the world as if you wanted an opportunity of stealing out of the room.

Marlow. Why, man, that's because I *do* want to steal out of the room. Faith, I have often formed a resolution to break the ice, and rattle away at any rate. But I don't know how, a single glance from a pair of fine eyes has totally overset my resolution. An impudent fellow may counterfeit modesty, but I'll be hanged if a modest man can ever counterfeit impudence.

Hastings. If you could but say half the fine things to them that I have heard you lavish upon the bar-maid of an inn, or even a college bed maker—

Marlow. Why, George, I can't say fine things to them, They freeze, they petrify me. They may talk of a comet, or a burning mountain, or some such bagatelle. But to me, a modest woman, drest out in all her finery, is the most tremendous object of the whole creation.

Hastings. Ha! ha! ha! At this rate, man, how can you ever expect to marry!

Marlow. Never, unless, as among kings and princes, my bride were to be courted by proxy. If, indeed, like an Eastern bridegroom, one were to be introduced to a wife he never saw before, it might be endured. But to go through all the terrors of a formal courtship, together with the episode of aunts, grandmothers and cousins, and at last to blurt out the broad staring question of, madam, will you marry me? No, no, that's a strain much above me, I assure you.

Hastings. I pity you. But how do you intend behaving to the lady you are come down to visit at the request of your father?

Marlow. As I behave to all other ladies. Bow very low. Answer yes, or no, to all her demands—But for the rest, I don't think I shall venture to look in her face, till I see my father's again.

Hastings. I'm surprised that one who is so warm a friend can be so cool a lover.

Marlow. To be explicit, my dear Hastings, my chief inducement down was to be instrumental in forwarding your happiness, not my own. Miss Neville loves you, the family don't know you, as my friend you are sure of a reception, and let honour do the rest.

Hastings. My dear Marlow! But I'll suppress the emotion. Were I a wretch, meanly seeking to carry off a fortune, you should be the last man in the world I would apply to for assistance. But Miss Neville's person is all I ask, and that is mine, both from her deceased father's consent, and her own inclination.

Marlow. Happy man! You have talents and art to captivate any woman. I'm doom'd to adore the sex, and yet to converse with the only part of it I despise. This stammer in my address, and this aukward prepossessing visage of mine, can never permit me to soar above the reach of a milliner's 'prentice, or one of the dutch-esses of Drury-lane. Pshaw! this fellow here to interrupt us.

Enter HARDCASTLE.

Hardcastle. Gentlemen, once more you are heartily welcome. Which is Mr. Marlow? Sir, you're heartily welcome. It's not my way, you see, to receive my friends with my back to the fire. I like to give them a hearty reception in the old stile, at my gate. I like to see their horses and trunks taken care of.

Marlow. [*Aside.*] He has got our names from the servants al-ready. [*To him.*] We approve your caution and hospitality, Sir. [*To* HASTINGS.] I have been thinking, George, of changing our travelling dresses in the morning. I am grown confoundedly ashamed of mine.

Hardcastle. I beg, Mr. Marlow, you'll use no ceremony in this house.

Hastings. I fancy, George, you're right: the first blow is half the battle. I intend opening the campaign with the white and gold.

Mr. Hardcastle. Mr. Marlow—Mr. Hastings—gentlemen—pray be under no constraint in this house. This is Liberty-hall, gentle-men. You may do just as you please here.

Marlow. Yet, George, if we open the campaign too fiercely at first, we may want ammunition before it is over. I think to reserve the embroidery to secure a retreat.

Hardcastle. Your talking of a retreat, Mr. Marlow, puts me in mind of the Duke of Marlborough, when we went to besiege Denain. He first summoned the garrison—

Marlow. Don't you think the *ventre dor* waistcoat will do with the plain brown?

Hardcastle. He first summoned the garrison, which might con-sist of about five thousand men—

Hastings. I think not: brown and yellow mix but very poorly.

Hardcastle. I say, gentlemen, as I was telling you, he summoned the garrison, which might consist of about five thousand men—

Marlow. The girls like finery.

Hardcastle. Which might consist of about five thousand men, well appointed with stores, ammunition, and other implements of war. "Now," says the Duke of Marlborough, to George Brooks, that stood next to him—You must have heard of George Brooks; "I'll pawn my Dukedom," says he, "but I take that garrison with-out spilling a drop of blood." So—

Marlow. What, my good friend, if you gave us a glass of punch in the mean time; it would help us to carry on the siege with vigour.

Hardcastle. Punch, Sir! [*Aside*.] This is the most unaccountable kind of modesty I ever met with.

Marlow. Yes, Sir, Punch. A glass of warm punch, after our journey, will be comfortable. This is Liberty-Hall, you know.

Hardcastle. Here's Cup, Sir.

Marlow. [*Aside*.] So this fellow, in his Liberty-hall, will only let us have just what he pleases.

Hardcastle. [*Taking the Cup*.] I hope you'll find it to your mind. I have prepared it with my own hands, and I believe you'll own the ingredients are tolerable. Will you be so good as to pledge me, Sir? Here, Mr. Marlow, here is to our better acquaintance. [*Drinks*.

Marlow. [*Aside*.] A very impudent fellow this! but he's a character, and I'll humour him a little. Sir, my service to you. [*Drinks*.

Hastings. [*Aside*.] I see this fellow wants to give us his company, and forgets that he's an innkeeper, before he has learned to be a gentleman.

Marlow. From the excellence of your cup, my old friend, I suppose you have a good deal of business in this part of the country. Warm work, now and then, at elections, I suppose?

Hardcastle. No, Sir, I have long given that work over. Since our betters have hit upon the expedient of electing each other, there's no business *for us that sell ale*.

Hastings. So, then you have no turn for politics, I find.

Hardcastle. Not in the least. There was a time, indeed, I fretted myself about the mistakes of government, like other people; but finding myself every day grow more angry, and the government growing no better, I left it to mend itself. Since that, I no more trouble my head about Heyder Ally, or Ally Cawn, than about Ally Croaker. Sir, my service to you.

Hastings. So that with eating above stairs, and drinking below, with receiving your friends within, and amusing them without, you lead a good, pleasant, bustling life of it.

Hardcastle. I do stir about a great deal, that's certain. Half the differences of the parish are adjusted in this very parlour.

Marlow. [*After drinking*.] And you have an argument in your cup, old gentleman, better than any in Westminster-hall.

Hardcastle. Ay, young gentleman, that, and a little philosophy.

Marlow. [*Aside*.] Well, this is the first time I ever heard of an innkeeper's philosophy.

Hastings. So then, like an experienced general, you attack them on every quarter. If you find their reason manageable, you attack it with your philosophy; if you find they have no reason, you attack them with this. Here's your health, my philosopher. [*Drinks*.

Hardcastle. Good, very good, thank you; ha! ha! Your Generalship puts me in mind of Prince Eugene, when he fought the Turks at the battle of Belgrade. You shall hear—

Marlow. Instead of the battle of Belgrade, I believe it's almost time to talk about supper. What has your philosophy got in the house for supper?

Hardcastle. For Supper, Sir! [*Aside.*] Was ever such a request to a man in his own house!

Marlow. Yes, Sir, supper, Sir; I begin to feel an appetite. I shall make devilish work to-night in the larder, I promise you.

Hardcastle. [*Aside.*] Such a brazen dog sure never my eyes beheld. [*To him.*] Why really, Sir, as for supper I can't well tell. My Dorothy, and the cook maid, settle these things between them. I leave these kind of things entirely to them.

Marlow. You do, do you?

Hardcastle. Entirely. By-the-bye, I believe they are in actual consultation upon what's for supper this moment in the kitchen.

Marlow. Then I beg they'll admit *me* as one of their privy council. It's a way I have got. When I travel, I always chuse to regulate my own supper. Let the cook be called. No offence, I hope, Sir.

Hardcastle. O, no, Sir, none in the least; yet I don't know how: our Bridget, the cook maid, is not very communicative upon these occasions. Should we send for her, she might scold us all out of the house.

Hastings. Let's see your list of the larder then. I ask it as a favour. I always match my appetite to my bill of fare.

Marlow. [*To* HARDCASTLE, *who looks at them with surprize.*] Sir, he's very right, and it's my way too.

Hardcastle. Sir, you have a right to command here. Here, Roger, bring us the bill of fare for to night's supper. I believe it's drawn out. Your manner, Mr. Hastings, puts me in mind of my uncle, Colonel Wallop. It was a saying of his, that no man was sure of his supper till he had eaten it.

Hastings. [*Aside.*] All upon the high ropes! His uncle a Colonel! We shall soon hear of his mother being a justice of peace. But let's hear the bill of fare.

Marlow. [*Perusing.*] What's here? For the first course; for the second course; for the desert. The devil, Sir, do you think we have brought down the whole Joiners Company, or the Corporation of Bedford, to eat up such a supper? Two or three little things, clean and comfortable, will do

Hastings. But, let's hear it.

Marlow. [*Reading.*] For the first course, at the top, a pig, and pruin sauce.

Hastings. Damn your pig, I say.

Marlow. And damn your pruin sauce, say I.

Hardcastle. And yet, gentlemen, to men that are hungry, pig, with pruin sauce, is very good eating.

Marlow. At the bottom, a calve's tongue and brains.

Hastings. Let your brains be knock'd out, my good Sir; I don't like them.

Marlow. Or you may clap them on a plate by themselves. I do.

Hardcastle. [*Aside.*] Their impudence confounds me. [*To them.*] Gentlemen, you are my guests, make what alterations you please. Is there any thing else you wish to retrench or alter, gentlemen?

Marlow. Item: A pork pie, a boiled rabbet and sausages, a florentine, a shaking pudding, and a dish of tiff—taff—taffety cream!

Hastings. Confound your made dishes, I shall be as much at a loss in this house as at a green and yellow dinner at the French Ambassador's table. I'm for plain eating.

Hardcastle. I'm sorry, gentlemen, that I have nothing you like, but if there be any thing you have a particular fancy to—

Marlow. Why, really, Sir, your bill of fare is so exquisite, that any one part of it is full as good as another. Send us what you please. So much for supper. And now to see that our beds are air'd, and properly taken care of.

Hardcastle. I entreat you'll leave all that to me. You shall not stir a step.

Marlow. Leave that to you! I protest, Sir, you must excuse me, I always look to these things myself.

Hardcastle. I must insist, Sir, you'll make yourself easy on that head.

Marlow. You see I'm resolved on it. [*Aside.*] A very troublesome fellow this, as ever I met with.

Hardcastle. Well, Sir, I'm resolved at least to attend you. [*Aside.*] This may be modern modesty, but I never saw any thing look so like old-fashioned impudence.

[*Exeunt* MARLOW *and* HARDCASTLE.

HASTINGS, *solus.*

Hastings. So I find this fellow's civilities begin to grow troublesome. But who can be angry at those assiduities which are meant to please him? Ha! what do I see? Miss Neville, by all that's happy!

Enter MISS NEVILLE.

Miss Neville. My dear Hastings! To what unexpected good fortune, to what accident am I to ascribe this happy meeting?

Hastings. Rather let me ask the same question, as I could never have hoped to meet my dearest Constance at an inn.

Miss Neville. An inn! sure you mistake! my aunt, my guardian, lives here. What could induce you to think this house an inn?

Hastings. My friend Mr. Marlow, with whom I came down, and I, have been sent here as to an inn, I assure you. A young fellow whom we accidentally met at a house hard by directed us hither.

Miss Neville. Certainly it must be one of my hopeful cousin's tricks, of whom you have heard me talk so often, ha! ha! ha! ha!

Hastings. He whom your aunt intends for you? He of whom I have such just apprehensions?

Miss Neville. You have nothing to fear from him, I assure you. You'd adore him if you knew how heartily he despises me. My aunt knows it too, and has undertaken to court me for him, and actually begins to think she has made a conquest.

Hastings. Thou dear dissembler! You must know, my Constance, I have just seized this happy opportunity of my friend's visit here to get admittance into the family. The horses that carried us down are now fatigued with their journey, but they'll soon be refreshed; and then, if my dearest girl will trust in her faithful Hastings, we shall soon be landed in France, where even among slaves the laws of marriage are respected.

Miss Neville. I have often told you, that though ready to obey you, I yet should leave my little fortune behind with reluctance. The greatest part of it was left me by my uncle, the India Director, and chiefly consists in jewels. I have been for some time persuading my aunt to let me wear them. I fancy I'm very near succeeding. The instant they are put into my possession you shall find me ready to make them and myself yours.

Hastings. Perish the baubles! Your person is all I desire. In the meantime, my friend Marlow must not be let into his mistake. I know the strange reserve of his temper is such, that if abruptly informed of it, he would instantly quit the house before our plan was ripe for execution.

Miss Neville. But how shall we keep him in the deception? Miss Hardcastle is just returned from walking; what if we still continue to deceive him?—This, this way—   [*They confer.*

Enter MARLOW.

Marlow. The assiduities of these good people teize me beyond bearing. My host seems to think it ill manners to leave me alone, and so he claps not only himself but his old-fashioned wife on my back. They talk of coming to sup with us too; and then, I suppose, we are to run the gauntlet thro' all the rest of the family.—What have we got here!—

Hastings. My dear Charles! Let me congratulate you!—The most fortunate accident!—Who do you think is just alighted?

Marlow. Cannot guess.

Hastings. Our mistresses, boy, Miss Hardcastle and Miss Neville. Give me leave to introduce Miss Constance Neville to your acquaintance. Happening to dine in the neighbourhood, they called, on their return, to take fresh horses, here. Miss Hardcastle has just stept into the next room, and will be back in an instant. Wasn't it lucky? eh!

Marlow. [*Aside.*] I have just been mortified enough of all conscience, and here comes something to complete my embarrassment.

Hastings. Well! but wasn't it the most fortunate thing in the world?

Marlow. Oh! yes. Very fortunate—a most joyful encounter— But our dresses, George, you know, are in disorder—What if we should postpone the happiness 'till to-morrow?—To-morrow at her own house—It will be every bit as convenient—And rather more respectful—To-morrow let it be. [*Offering to go.*

Miss Neville. By no means, Sir. Your ceremony will displease her. The disorder of your dress will shew the ardour of your impatience. Besides, she knows you are in the house, and will permit you to see her.

Marlow. O! the devil! how shall I support it? Hem! hem! Hastings, you must not go. You are to assist me, you know. I shall be confoundedly ridiculous. Yet, hang it! I'll take courage. Hem!

Hastings. Pshaw, man! it's but the first plunge, and all's over. She's but a woman, you know.

Marlow. And of all women, she that I dread most to encounter!

Enter MISS HARDCASTLE *as returned from walking, a Bonnet, &c.*

Hastings. [*Introducing him.*] Miss Hardcastle, Mr. Marlow; I'm proud of bringing two persons of such merit together, that only want to know, to esteem each other.

Miss Hardcastle. [*Aside.*] Now, for meeting my modest gentleman with a demure face, and quite in his own manner. [*After a pause, in which he appears very uneasy and disconcerted.*] I'm glad of your safe arrival, Sir—I'm told you had some accidents by the way.

Marlow. Only a few, madam. Yes, we had some. Yes, Madam, a good many accidents, but should be sorry—Madam—or rather glad of any accidents—that are so agreeably concluded. Hem!

Hastings. [*To him.*] You never spoke better in your whole life. Keep it up, and I'll insure you the victory.

Miss Hardcastle. I'm afraid you flatter, Sir. You that have seen so much of the finest company can find little entertainment in an obscure corner of the country.

Marlow. [*Gathering courage.*] I have lived, indeed, in the world, Madam; but I have kept very little company. I have been but an observer upon life, Madam, while others were enjoying it.

Miss Neville. But that, I am told, is the way to enjoy it at last.

Hastings. [*To him.*] Cicero never spoke better. Once more, and you are confirm'd in assurance for ever.

Marlow. [*To him.*] Hem! Stand by me then, and when I'm down, throw in a word or two to set me up again.

Miss Hardcastle. An observer, like you, upon life, were, I fear, disagreeably employed, since you must have had much more to censure than to approve.

Marlow. Pardon me, Madam. I was always willing to be amused. The folly of most people is rather an object of mirth than uneasiness.

Hastings. [*To him.*] Bravo, bravo. Never spoke so well in your whole life. Well! Miss Hardcastle, I see that you and Mr. Marlow are going to be very good company. I believe our being here will but embarrass the interview.

Marlow. Not in the least, Mr. Hastings. We like your company of all things. [*To him.*] Zounds! George, sure you won't go? How can you leave us?

Hastings. Our presence will but spoil conversation, so we'll retire to the next room. [*To him.*] You don't consider, man, that we are to manage a little tête-à-tête of our own.   [*Exeunt.*]

Miss Hardcastle. [*After a pause.*] But you have not been wholly an observer, I presume, Sir: The ladies I should hope have employed some part of your addresses.

Marlow. [*Relapsing into timidity.*] Pardon me, Madam, I—I—I—as yet have studied—only—to—deserve them.

Miss Hardcastle. And that, some say, is the very worst way to obtain them.

Marlow. Perhaps so, madam. But I love to converse only with the more grave and sensible part of the sex.—But I'm afraid I grow tiresome.

Miss Hardcastle. Not at all, Sir; there is nothing I like so much as grave conversation myself; I could hear it for ever. Indeed I have often been surprized how a man of *sentiment* could ever admire those light, airy pleasures, where nothing reaches the heart.

Marlow. It's—a disease—of the mind, Madam. In the variety of tastes there must be some who, wanting a relish—for—um—a—um.

Miss Hardcastle. I understand you, Sir. There must be some, who, wanting a relish for refined pleasures, pretend to despise what they are incapable of tasting.

Marlow. My meaning, Madam, but infinitely better expressed. And I can't help observing—a—

Miss Hardcastle. [*Aside.*] Who could ever suppose this fellow impudent upon some occasions. [*To him.*] You were going to observe, Sir—

Marlow. I was observing, Madam—I protest, Madam, I forget what I was going to observe.

Miss Hardcastle. [*Aside.*] I vow and so do I. [*To him.*] You were observing, Sir, that in this age of hypocrisy—something about hypocrisy, Sir.

Marlow. Yes, Madam. In this age of hypocrisy there are few who upon strict enquiry do not—a—a—a—

Miss Hardcastle. I understand you perfectly, Sir.

Marlow. [*Aside.*] Egad! and that's more than I do myself.

Miss Hardcastle. You mean that in this hypocritical age there are few that do not condemn in public what they practise in private, and think they pay every debt to virtue when they praise it.

Marlow. True, Madam; those who have most virtue in their mouths, have least of it in their bosoms. But I'm sure I tire you, Madam.

Miss Hardcastle. Not in the least, Sir; there's something so agreeable and spirited in your manner, such life and force—pray, Sir, go on.

Marlow. Yes, Madam. I was saying—that there are some occasions—when a total want of courage, Madam, destroys all the—and puts us—upon a—a—a—

Miss Hardcastle. I agree with you entirely: a want of courage upon some occasions assumes the appearance of ignorance, and betrays us when we most want to excel. I beg you'll proceed.

Marlow. Yes, Madam. Morally speaking, Madam—But I see Miss Neville expecting us in the next room. I would not intrude for the world.

Miss Hardcastle. I protest, Sir, I never was more agreeably entertained in all my life. Pray go on.

Marlow. Yes, Madam. I was—But she beckons us to join her. Madam, shall I do myself the honour to attend you?

Miss Hardcastle. Well then, I'll follow.

Marlow. [*Aside.*] This pretty smooth dialogue has done for me.
[*Exit.*

MISS HARDCASTLE, *sola.*

Miss Hardcastle. Ha! ha! ha! Was there ever such a sober, sentimental interview? I'm certain he scarce look'd in my face the whole time. Yet the fellow, but for his unaccountable bashfulness, is pretty well too. He has good sense, but then so buried in his fears, that it fatigues one more than ignorance. If I could teach him a little confidence, it would be doing somebody that I know of a piece of service. But who is that somebody?—that, faith, is a question I can scarce answer.   [*Exit.*

Enter TONY *and* MISS NEVILLE, *followed by* MRS. HARDCASTLE *and* HASTINGS.

Tony. What do you follow me for, Cousin Con? I wonder you're not ashamed to be so very engaging.

Miss Neville. I hope, Cousin, one may speak to one's own relations, and not be to blame.

Tony. Ay, but I know what sort of a relation you want to make me though; but it won't do. I tell you, Cousin Con, it won't do, so I beg you'll keep your distance. I want no nearer relationship.
[*She follows coqueting him to the back scene.*

Mrs. Hardcastle. Well! I vow, Mr. Hastings, you are very entertaining. There's nothing in the world I love to talk of so much as London, and the fashions, though I was never there myself.

Hastings. Never there! You amaze me! From your air and manner, I concluded you had been bred all your life either at Ranelagh, St. James's, or Tower Wharf.

Mrs. Hardcastle. O! Sir, you're only pleased to say so. We Country persons can have no manner at all. I'm in love with the town, and that serves to raise me above some of our neighbouring rustics; but who can have a manner, that has never seen the Pantheon, the Grotto Gardens, the Borough, and such places where the Nobility chiefly resort? All I can do, is to enjoy London at second-hand. I take care to know every tête-à-tête from the *Scandalous Magazine,* and have all the fashions, as they come out, in a letter from the two Miss Rickets of Crooked-lane. Pray how do you like this head, Mr. Hastings?

Hastings. Extremely elegant and *degagée,* upon my word, Madam. Your Friseur is a Frenchman, I suppose?

Mrs. Hardcastle. I protest, I dressed it myself from a print in the *Ladies Memorandum book* for the last year.

Hastings. Indeed. Such a head in a side-box, at the Play-house, would draw as many gazers as my Lady May'ress at a City Ball.

Mrs. Hardcastle. I vow, since inoculation began, there is no such thing to be seen as a plain woman; so one must dress a little particular or one may escape in the crowd.

Hastings. But that can never be your case Madam, in any dress.   [*Bowing.*

Mrs. Hardcastle. Yet, what signifies my dressing when I have such a piece of antiquity by my side as Mr. Hardcastle: all I can say will never argue down a single button from his cloaths. I have often wanted him to throw off his great flaxen wig, and where he was bald, to plaister it over like my Lord Pately, with powder.

Hastings. You are right, Madam; for, as among the ladies, there are none ugly, so among the men there are none old.

Mrs. Hardcastle. But what do you think his answer was? Why, with his usual Gothic vivacity, he said I only wanted him to throw off his wig to convert it into a tête for my own wearing.

Hastings. Intolerable! At your age you may wear what you please, and it must become you.

Mrs. Hardcastle. Pray, Mr. Hastings, what do you take to be the most fashionable age about town?

Hastings. Some time ago, forty was all the mode; but I'm told the ladies intend to bring up fifty for the ensuing winter.

Mrs. Hardcastle. Seriously? Then I shall be too young for the fashion.

Hastings. No lady begins now to put on jewels 'till she's past forty. For instance, Miss there, in a polite circle, would be considered as a child, as a mere maker of samplers.

Mrs. Hardcastle. And yet Mrs. Niece thinks herself as much a woman, and is as fond of jewels as the oldest of us all.

Hastings. Your niece, is she? And that young gentleman,—a brother of yours, I should presume?

Mrs. Hardcastle. My son, Sir. They are contracted to each other. Observe their little sports. They fall in and out ten times a day, as if they were man and wife already. [*To them.*] Well, Tony, child, what soft things are you saying to your Cousin Constance this evening?

Tony. I have been saying no soft things; but that it's very hard to be followed about so. Ecod! I've not a place in the house now that's left to myself but the stable.

Mrs. Hardcastle. Never mind him, Con, my dear. He's in another story behind your back.

Miss Neville. There's something generous in my cousin's manner. He falls out before faces to be forgiven in private.

Tony. That's a damned confounded—crack.

Mrs. Hardcastle. Ah! he's a sly one. Don't you think they're like each other about the mouth, Mr. Hastings? The Blenkinsop mouth to a T. They're of a size too. Back to back, my pretties, that Mr. Hastings may see you. Come Tony.

Tony. You had as good not make me, I tell you.   [*Measuring.*

Miss Neville. O lud! he has almost cracked my head.

Mrs. Hardcastle. O the monster! For shame, Tony. You a man, and behave so!

Tony. If I'm a man, let me have my fortin. Ecod! I'll not be made a fool of no longer.

Mrs. Hardcastle. Is this, ungrateful boy, all that I'm to get for the pains I have taken in your education? I that have rock'd you in your cradle, and fed that pretty mouth with a spoon! Did not I work that waistcoat to make you genteel? Did not I prescribe for you every day, and weep while the receipt was operating?

Tany. Ecod! you had reason to weep, for you have been dosing me ever since I was born. I have gone through every receipt in the complete huswife ten times over; and you have thoughts of coursing me through *Quincy* next spring. But, Ecod! I tell you, I'll not be made a fool of no longer.

Mrs. Hardcastle. Wasn't it all for your good, viper? Wasn't it all for your good?

Tony. I wish you'd let me and my good alone then. Snubbing this way when I'm in spirits. If I'm to have any good, let it come of itself; not to keep dinging it, dinging it into one so.

Mrs. Hardcastle. That's false; I never see you when you're in spirits. No, Tony, you then go to the alehouse or kennel. I'm never to be delighted with your agreeable, wild notes, unfeeling monster!

Tony. Ecod! Mamma, your own notes are the wildest of the two.

Mrs. Hardcastle. Was ever the like? But I see he wants to break my heart, I see he does.

Hastings. Dear Madam, permit me to lecture the young gentleman a little. I'm certain I can persuade him to his duty.

Mrs. Hardcastle. Well! I must retire. Come, Constance, my love. You see, Mr. Hastings, the wretchedness of my situation:

Was ever poor woman so plagued with a dear, sweet, pretty, provoking, undutiful boy.

[*Exeunt* MRS. HARDCASTLE *and* MISS NEVILLE.

HASTINGS, TONY.

Tony. [*Singing.*] *There was a young man riding by, and fain would have his will. Rang do didlo dee.* Don't mind her. Let her cry. It's the comfort of her heart. I have seen her and sister cry over a book for an hour together, and they said, they liked the book the better the more it made them cry.

Hastings. Then you're no friend to the ladies, I find, my pretty young gentleman?

Tony. That's as I find 'um.

Hastings. Not to her of your mother's chusing, I dare answer? And yet she appears to me a pretty, well-tempered girl.

Tony. That's because you don't know her as well as I. Ecod! I know every inch about her; and there's not a more bitter, cantanckerous toad in all Christendom.

Hastings. [*Aside.*] Pretty encouragement this for a lover!

Tony. I have seen her since the height of that. She has as many tricks as a hare in a thicket, or a colt the first day's breaking.

Hastings. To me she appears sensible and silent!

Tony. Ay, before company. But when she's with her playmates, she's as loud as a hog in a gate.

Hastings. But there is a meek modesty about her that charms me.

Tony. Yes, but curb her never so little, she kicks up, and you're flung in a ditch.

Hastings. Well, but you must allow her a little beauty.—Yes, you must allow her some beauty.

Tony. Bandbox! She's all a made up thing, mun. Ah! could you but see Bet Bouncer of these parts, you might then talk of beauty. Ecod, she has two eyes as black as sloes, and cheeks as broad and red as a pulpit cushion. She'd make two of she.

Hastings. Well, what say you to a friend that would take this bitter bargain off your hands?

Tony. Anon.

Hastings. Would you thank him that would take Miss Neville and leave you to happiness and your dear Betsy?

Tony. Ay; but where is there such a friend, for who would take her?

Hastings. I am he. If you but assist me, I'll engage to whip her off to France, and you shall never hear more of her.

Tony. Assist you! Ecod, I will, to the last drop of my blood.

I'll clap a pair of horses to your chaise that shall trundle you off in a twinkling, and may be get you a part of her fortin beside, in jewels, that you little dream of.

Hastings. My dear 'Squire, this looks like a lad of spirit.

Tony. Come along then, and you shall see more of my spirit before you have done with me.   [*Singing.*

> *We are the boys*
> *That fears no noise*
> *Where the thundering cannons roar.*   [*Exeunt.*

END OF THE SECOND ACT

ACT III

Enter HARDCASTLE, *solus.*

Hardcastle. What could my old friend Sir Charles mean by recommending his son as the modestest young man in town? To me he appears the most impudent piece of brass that ever spoke with a tongue. He has taken posssesion of the easy chair by the fire-side already. He took off his boots in the parlour, and desired me to see them taken care of. I'm desirous to know how his impudence affects my daughter.—She will certainly be shocked at it.

Enter MISS HARDCASTLE, *plainly dress'd.*

Hardcastle. Well, my Kate, I see you have changed your dress as I bid you; and yet, I believe, there was no great occasion.

Miss Hardcastle. I find such a pleasure, Sir, in obeying your commands, that I take care to observe them without ever debating their propriety.

Hardcastle. And yet, Kate, I sometimes give you some cause, particularly when I recommended my *modest* gentleman to you as a lover to-day.

Miss Hardcastle. You taught me to expect something extraordinary, and I find the original exceeds the description.

Hardcastle. I was never so surprized in my life! He has quite confounded all my faculties!

Miss Hardcastle. I never saw any thing like it: And a man of the world too!

Hardcastle. Ay, he learned it all abroad,—what a fool was I, to think a young man could learn modesty by travelling. He might as soon learn wit at a masquerade.

Miss Hardcastle. It seems all natural to him.

Hardcastle. A good deal assisted by bad company and a French dancing-master.

Miss Hardcastle. Sure, you mistake, papa! a French dancing-master could never have taught him that timid look,—that aukward address,—that bashful manner—

Hardcastle. Whose look? whose manner? child!

Miss Hardcastle. Mr. Marlow's: his *mauvaise honte,* his timidity struck me at the first sight.

Hardcastle. Then your first sight deceived you; for I think him one of the most brazen first sights that ever astonished my senses.

Miss Hardcastle. Sure, Sir, you rally! I never saw any one so modest.

Hardcastle. And can you be serious! I never saw such a bouncing, swaggering puppy since I was born. Bully Dawson was but a fool to him.

Miss Hardcastle. Surprizing! He met me with a respectful bow, a stammering voice, and a look fixed on the ground.

Hardcastle. He met me with a loud voice, a lordly air, and a familiarity that made my blood freeze again.

Miss Hardcastle. He treated me with diffidence and respect; censured the manners of the age; admired the prudence of girls that never laughed; tired me with apologies for being tiresome; then left the room with a bow, and, "madam, I would not for the world detain you."

Hardcastle. He spoke to me as if he knew me all his life before. Asked twenty questions, and never waited for an answer. Interrupted my best remarks with some silly pun, and when I was in my best story of the Duke of Marlborough and Prince Eugene, he asked if I had not a good hand at making punch. Yes, Kate, he ask'd your father if he was a maker of punch!

Miss Hardcastle. One of us must certainly be mistaken.

Hardcastle. If he be what he has shewn himself, I'm determined he shall never have my consent.

Miss Hardcastle. And if he be the sullen thing I take him, he shall never have mine.

Hardcastle. In one thing then we are agreed—to reject him.

Miss Hardcastle. Yes. But upon conditions. For if you should find him less impudent, and I more presuming; if you find him more respectful, and I more importunate—I don't know—the fellow is well enough for a man—Certainly we don't meet many such at a horse race in the country.

Hardcastle. If we should find him so—But that's impossible. The first appearance has done my business. I'm seldom deceived in that.

Miss Hardcastle. And yet there may be many good qualities under that first appearance.

Hardcastle. Ay, when a girl finds a fellow's outside to her taste, she then sets about guessing the rest of his furniture. With her, a smooth face stands for good sense, and a genteel figure for every virtue.

Miss Hardcastle. I hope, Sir, a conversation begun with a compliment to my good sense won't end with a sneer at my understanding?

Hardcastle. Pardon me, Kate. But if young Mr. Brazen can find the art of reconciling contradictions, he may please us both, perhaps.

Miss Hardcastle. And as one of us must be mistaken, what if we go to make further discoveries?

Hardcastle. Agreed. But depend on't I'm in the right.

Miss Hardcastle. And depend on't I'm not much in the wrong.

[*Exeunt.*

Enter TONY, *running in with a Casket.*

Tony. Ecod! I have got them. Here they are. My Cousin Con's necklaces, bobs and all. My mother shan't cheat the poor souls out of their fortin neither. O! my genus, is that you?

Enter HASTINGS.

Hastings. My dear friend, how have you managed with your mother? I hope you have amused her with pretending love for your cousin, and that you are willing to be reconciled at last? Our horses will be refreshed in a short time, and we shall soon be ready to set off.

Tony. And here's something to bear your charges by the way. [*Giving the casket.*] Your sweetheart's jewels. Keep them, and hang those, I say, that would rob you of one of them.

Hastings. But how have you procured them from your mother?

Tony. Ask me no questions, and I'll tell you no fibs. I procured them by the rule of thumb. If I had not a key to every drawer in mother's bureau, how could I go to the alehouse so often as I do? An honest man may rob himself of his own at any time.

Hastings. Thousands do it every day. But to be plain with you; Miss Neville is endeavouring to procure them from her aunt this very instant. If she succeeds, it will be the most delicate way at least of obtaining them.

Tony. Well, keep them, till you know how it will be. But I know how it will be well enough; she'd as soon part with the only sound tooth in her head.

Hastings. But I dread the effects of her resentment, when she finds she has lost them.

Tony. Never you mind her resentment, leave *me* to manage that. I don't value her resentment the bounce of a cracker. Zounds! here they are. Morrice. Prance. [*Exit* HASTINGS.

TONY, MRS. HARDCASTLE, MISS NEVILLE.

Mrs. Hardcastle. Indeed, Constance, you amaze me. Such a girl as you want jewels? It will be time enough for jewels, my dear, twenty years hence, when your beauty begins to want repairs.

Miss Neville. But what will repair beauty at forty, will certainly improve it at twenty, Madam.

Mrs. Hardcastle. Yours, my dear, can admit of none. That natural blush is beyond a thousand ornaments. Besides, child, jewels are quite out at present. Don't you see half the ladies of our acquaintance, my Lady Kill-day-light, and Mrs. Crump, and the rest of them, carry their jewels to town, and bring nothing but Paste and Marcasites back?

Miss Neville. But who knows, Madam, but somebody that shall be nameless would like me best with all my little finery about me?

Mrs. Hardcastle. Consult your glass, my dear, and then see, if with such a pair of eyes, you want any better sparklers. What do you think, Tony, my dear, does your Cousin Con want any jewels, in your eyes, to set off her beauty?

Tony. That's as thereafter may be.

Miss Neville. My dear aunt, if you knew how it would oblige me.

Mrs. Hardcastle. A parcel of old-fashioned rose and table-cut things. They would make you look like the court of King Solomon at a puppet-shew. Besides, I believe I can't readily come at them. They may be missing, for aught I know to the contrary.

Tony. [*Apart to* MRS. HARDCASTLE.] Then why don't you tell her so at once, as she's so longing for them. Tell her they're lost. It's the only way to quiet her. Say they're lost, and call me to bear witness.

Mrs. Hardcastle. [*Apart to Tony.*] You know, my dear, I'm only keeping them for you. So if I say they're gone, you'll bear me witness, will you? He! he! he!

Tony. Never fear me. Ecod! I'll say I saw them taken out with my own eyes.

Miss Neville. I desire them but for a day, Madam. Just to be permitted to shew them as relicks, and then they may be lock'd up again.

Mrs. Hardcastle. To be plain with you, my dear Constance, if

I could find them, you should have them. They're missing, I assure you. Lost, for aught I know; but we must have patience wherever they are.

Miss Neville. I'll not believe it; this is but a shallow pretence to deny me. I know they're too valuable to be so slightly kept, and as you are to answer for the loss.

Mrs. Hardcastle. Don't be alarm'd, Constance. If they be lost, I must restore an equivalent. But my son knows they are missing, and not to be found.

Tony. That I can bear witness to. They are missing, and not to be found, I'll take my oath on't.

Mrs. Hardcastle. You must learn resignation, my dear; for tho' we lose our fortune, yet we should not lose our patience. See me, how calm I am.

Miss Neville. Ay, people are generally calm at the misfortunes of others.

Mrs. Hardcastle. Now, I wonder a girl of your good sense should waste a thought upon such trumpery. We shall soon find them; and, in the mean time, you shall make use of my garnets till your jewels be found.

Miss Neville. I detest garnets.

Mrs. Hardcastle. The most becoming things in the world to set off a clear complexion. You have often seen how well they look upon me. You *shall* have them. [*Exit.*

Miss Neville. I dislike them of all things. You shan't stir.—Was ever any thing so provoking—to mislay my own jewels, and force me to wear her trumpery.

Tony. Don't be a fool. If she gives you the garnets, take what you can get. The jewels are your own already. I have stolen them out of her bureau, and she does not know it. Fly to your spark, he'll tell you more of the matter. Leave me to manage *her.*

Miss Neville. My dear cousin.

Tony. Vanish. She's here, and has missed them already. [*Exit* Miss Neville.] Zounds! how she fidgets and spits about like a Catharine wheel.

Enter Mrs. Hardcastle.

Mrs. Hardcastle. Confusion! thieves! robbers! We are cheated, plundered, broke open, undone.

Tony. What's the matter, what's the matter, mamma? I hope nothing has happened to any of the good family!

Mrs. Hardcastle. We are robbed. My bureau has been broke open, the jewels taken out, and I'm undone.

Tony. Oh! is that all? Ha! ha! ha! By the laws, I never saw it better acted in my life. Ecod, I thought you was ruin'd in earnest, ha, ha, ha.

Mrs. Hardcastle. Why, boy, I *am* ruin'd in earnest. My bureau has been broke open, and all taken away.

Tony. Stick to that; ha, ha, ha! stick to that. I'll bear witness, you know, call me to bear witness.

Mrs. Hardcastle. I tell you, Tony, by all that's precious, the jewels are gone, and I shall be ruin'd for ever.

Tony. Sure I know they're gone, and I am to say so.

Mrs. Hardcastle. My dearest Tony, but hear me. They're gone, I say.

Tony. By the laws, mamma, you make me for to laugh, ha! ha! I know who took them well enough, ha! ha! ha!

Mrs. Hardcastle. Was there ever such a blockhead, that can't tell the difference between jest and earnest. I tell you I'm not in jest, booby.

Tony. That's right, that's right: You must be in a bitter passion, and then nobody will suspect either of us. I'll bear witness that they are gone.

Mrs. Hardcastle. Was there ever such a cross-grain'd brute, that won't hear me! Can you bear witness that you're no better than a fool? Was ever poor woman so beset with fools on one hand, and thieves on the other?

Tony. I can bear witness to that.

Mrs. Hardcastle. Bear witness again, you blockhead you, and I'll turn you out of the room directly. My poor niece, what will become of *her!* Do you laugh, you unfeeling brute, as if you enjoyed my distress?

Tony. I can bear witness to that.

Mrs. Hardcastle. Do you insult me, monster? I'll teach you to vex your mother, I will.

Tony. I can bear witness to that.

[*He runs off, she follows him.*

Enter Miss Hardcastle *and* Maid.

Miss Hardcastle. What an unaccountable creature is that brother of mine, to send them to the house as an inn, ha! ha! I don't wonder at his impudence.

Maid. But what is more, Madam, the young gentleman as you passed by in your present dress, ask'd me if you were the bar-maid? He mistook you for the bar-maid, Madam.

Miss Hardcastle. Did he? Then as I live, I'm resolved to keep up the delusion. Tell me, Pimple, how do you like my present dress? Don't you think I look something like *Cherry* in the *Beaux' Stratagem?*

Maid. It's the dress, Madam, that every lady wears in the country, but when she visits, or receives company.

Miss Hardcastle. And are you sure he does not remember my face or person?

Maid. Certain of it.

Miss Hardcastle. I vow, I thought so; for though we spoke for some time together, yet his fears were such, that he never once looked up during the interview. Indeed, if he had, my bonnet would have kept him from seeing me.

Mair. But what do you hope from keeping him in his mistake?

Miss Hardcastle. In the first place, I shall be *seen,* and that is no small advantage to a girl who brings her face to market. Then I shall perhaps make an acquaintance, and that's no small victory gained over one who never addresses any but the wildest of her sex. But my chief aim is to take my gentleman off his guard, and, like an invisible champion of romance, examine the giant's force before I offer to combat.

Maid. But are you sure you can act your part, and disguise your voice, so that he may mistake that, as he has already mistaken your person?

Miss Hardcasile. Never fear me. I think I have got the true bar-cant.—Did your honour call?—Attend the Lion there.— Pipes and tobacco for the Angel.—The Lamb has been outrageous this half hour.

Maid. It will do, Madam. But he's here.   [*Exit* MAID.

Enter MARLOW.

Marlow. What a bawling in every part of the house. I have scarce a moment's repose. If I go to the best room, there I find my host and his story. If I fly to the gallery, there we have my hostess with her curtesy down to the ground. I have at last got a moment to myself, and now for recollection.   [*Walks and muses.*

Miss Hardcastle. Did you call, Sir? Did your honour call?

Marlow. [*Musing.*] As for Miss Hardcastle, she's too grave and sentimental for me.

Miss Hardcastle. Did your honour call?

[*She still places herself before him, he turning away.*

Marlow. No, child. [*Musing.*] Besides, from the glimpse I had of her, I think she squints.

Miss Hardcastle. I'm sure, Sir, I heard the bell ring.

Marlow. No, no. [*Musing.*] I have pleased my father, however, by coming down, and I'll to-morrow please myself by returning.

[Taking out his tablets, and perusing.

Miss Hardcastle. Perhaps the other gentleman called, Sir?

Marlow. I tell you, no.

Miss Hardcastle. I should be glad to know, Sir. We have such a parcel of servants.

Marlow. No, no, I tell you. [*Looks full in her face.*] Yes, child, I think I did call. I wanted—I wanted—I vow, child, you are vastly handsome.

Miss Hardcastle. O la, Sir, you'll make one asham'd.

Marlow. Never saw a more sprightly, malicious eye. Yes, yes, my dear, I did call. Have you got any of your—a—what d'ye call it in the house?

Miss Hardcastle. No, Sir, we have been out of that these ten days.

Marlow. One may call in this house, I find, to very little purpose. Suppose I should call for a taste, just by way of trial, of the nectar of your lips; perhaps I might be disappointed in that too.

Miss Hardcastle. Nectar! nectar! That's a liquor there's no call for in these parts. French, I suppose. We keep no French wines here, Sir.

Marlow. Of true English growth, I assure you.

Miss Hardcastle. Then it's odd I should not know it. We brew all sorts of wines in this house, and I have lived here these eighteen years.

Marlow. Eighteen years! Why one would think, child, you kept the bar before you were born. How old are you?

Miss Hardcastle. O! Sir, I must not tell my age. They say women and music should never be dated.

Marlow. To guess at this distance, you can't be much above forty. [*Approaching.*] Yet nearer, I don't think so much. [*Approaching.*] By coming close to some women, they look younger still; but when we come very close indeed—

[Attempting to kiss her.

Miss Hardcastle. Pray, Sir, keep your distance. One would think you wanted to know one's age as they do horses, by mark of mouth.

Marlow. I protest, child, you use me extremely ill. If you keep me at this distance, how is it possible you and I can be ever acquainted?

Miss Hardcastle. And who wants to be acquainted with you? I want no such acquaintance, not I. I'm sure you did not treat Miss Hardcastle that was here awhile ago in this obstropalous manner. I'll warrant me, before her you look'd dash'd, and kept bowing to the ground, and talk'd, for all the world, as if you was before a justice of peace.

Marlow. [*Aside.*] Egad! she has hit it, sure enough. [*To her.*] In awe of her, child? Ha! ha! ha! A mere, aukward, squinting thing, no, no! I find you don't know me. I laugh'd, and rallied her a little; but I was unwilling to be too severe. No, I could not be too severe, curse me!

Miss Hardcastle. O! then, Sir, you are a favourite, I find, among the ladies?

Marlow. Yes, my dear, a great favourite. And yet, hang me, I don't see what they find in me to follow. At the Ladies Club in town, I'm called their agreeable Rattle. Rattle, child, is not my real name, but one I'm known by. My name is Solomons. Mr. Solomons, my dear, at your service. [*Offering to salute her.*]

Miss Hardcastle. Hold, Sir; you are introducing me to your club, not to yourself. And you're so great a favourite there, you say?

Marlow. Yes, my dear. There's Mrs. Mantrap, Lady Betty Blackleg, the Countess of Sligo, Mrs. Langhorns, old Miss Biddy Buckskin, and your humble servant, keep up the spirit of the place.

Miss Hardcastle. Then it's a very merry place, I suppose?

Marlow. Yes, as merry as cards, suppers, wine, and old women can make us.

Miss Hardcastle. And their agreeable Rattle, ha! ha! ha!

Marlow. [*Aside.*] Egad! I don't quite like this chit. She looks knowing, methinks. You laugh, child!

Miss Hardcastle. I can't but laugh to think what time they all have for minding their work or their family.

Marlow. [*Aside.*] All's well; she don't laugh at me. [*To her.*] Do *you* ever work, child?

Miss Hardcastle. Ay, sure. There's not a screen or a quilt in the whole house but what can bear witness to that.

Marlow. Odso! Then you must shew me your embroidery. I embroider and draw patterns myself a little. If you want a judge of your work you must apply to me. [*Seizing her hand.*]

Miss Hardcastle. Ay, but the colours don't look well by candle-light. You shall see all in the morning. [*Struggling.*]

Marlow. And why not now, my angel? Such beauty fires beyond the power of resistance.—Pshaw! the father here! My old luck: I never nick'd seven that I did not throw ames ace three times following. [*Exit* MARLOW.

Enter HARDCASTLE, *who stands in surprize.*

Hardcastle. So, Madam. So I find *this* is your *modest* lover. This is your humble admirer that kept his eyes fixed on the ground, and only ador'd at humble distance. Kate, Kate, art thou not asham'd to deceive your father so?

Miss Hardcastle. Never trust me, dear papa, but he's still the modest man I first took him for; you'll be convinced of it as well as I.

Hardcastle. By the hand of my body, I believe his impudence is infectious! Didn't I see him seize your hand? Didn't I see him hawl you about like a milk-maid? and now you talk of his respect and his modesty, forsooth!

Miss Hardcastle. But if I shortly convince you of his modesty, that he has only the faults that will pass off with time, and the virtues that will improve with age, I hope you'll forgive him.

Hardcastle. The girl would actually make one run mad! I tell you I'll not be convinced. I am convinced. He has scarcely been three hours in the house, and he has already encroached on all my prerogatives. You may like his impudence, and call it modesty. But my son-in-law, madam, must have very different qualifications.

Miss Hardcastle. Sir, I ask but this night to convince you.

Hardcastle. You shall not have half the time, for I have thoughts of turning him out this very hour.

Miss Hardcastle. Give me that hour then, and I hope to satisfy you.

Hardcastle. Well, an hour let it be then. But I'll have no trifling with your father. All fair and open, do you mind me.

Miss Hardcastle. I hope, Sir, you have ever found that I considered your commands as my pride; for your kindness is such, that my duty as yet has been inclination. [*Exeunt.*

END OF THE THIRD ACT

ACT IV

Enter HASTINGS *and* MISS NEVILLE.

Hastings. You surprise me! Sir Charles Marlow expected here this night? Where have you had your information?

Miss Neville. You may depend upon it. I just saw his letter to Mr. Hardcastle, in which he tells him he intends setting out a few hours after his son.

Hastings. Then, my Constance, all must be completed before he arrives. He knows me; and should he find me here, would discover my name, and perhaps my designs, to the rest of the family.

Miss Neville. The jewels, I hope, are safe.

Hastings. Yes, yes. I have sent them to Marlow, who keeps the keys of our baggage. In the meantime, I'll go to prepare matters for our elopement. I have had the Squire's promise of a fresh pair of horses; and, if I should not see him again, will write him further directions.   *[Exit.*

Miss Neville. Well! success attend you. In the meantime, I'll go amuse my aunt with the old pretence of a violent passion for my cousin.   *[Exit.*

Enter MARLOW, *followed by a* SERVANT.

Marlow. I wonder what Hastings could mean by sending me so valuable a thing as a casket to keep for him, when he knows the only place I have is the seat of a post-coach at an Inn-door. Have you deposited the casket with the landlady, as I ordered you? Have you put it into her own hands?

Servant. Yes, your honour.

Marlow. She said she'd keep it safe, did she?

Servant. Yes, she said she'd keep it safe enough; she ask'd me how I came by it? and she said she had a great mind to make me give an account of myself.   *[Exit* SERVANT.

Marlow. Ha! ha! ha! They're safe, however. What an unaccountable set of beings have we got amongst! This little barmaid, though, runs in my head most strangely, and drives out the absurdities of all the rest of the family. She's mine, she must be mine, or I'm greatly mistaken.

Enter HASTINGS.

Hastings. Bless me! I quite forgot to tell her that I intended to prepare at the bottom of the garden. Marlow here, and in spirits too!

Marlow. Give me joy, George! Crown me, shadow me with laurels! Well, George, after all, we modest fellows don't want for success among the women.

Hastings. Some women you mean. But what success has your honour's modesty been crowned with now, that it grows so insolent upon us?

Marlow. Didn't you see the tempting, brisk, lovely little thing that runs about the house with a bunch of keys to its girdle?

Hastings. Well! and what then?

Marlow. She's mine, you rogue you. Such fire, such motion, such eyes, such lips—but, egad! she would not let me kiss them though.

Hastings. But are you so sure, so very sure of her?

Marlow. Why man, she talk'd of shewing me her work above stairs, and I am to improve the pattern.

Hastings. But how can *you*, Charles, go about to rob a woman of her honour?

Marlow. Pshaw! pshaw! we all know the honour of the barmaid of an inn. I don't intend to *rob* her, take my word for it; there's nothing in this house, I shan't honestly *pay* for.

Hastings. I believe the girl has virtue.

Marlow. And if she has, I should be the last man in the world that would attempt to corrupt it.

Hastings. You have taken care, I hope, of the casket I sent you to lock up? It's in safety?

Marlow. Yes, yes. It's safe enough. I have taken care of it. But how could you think the seat of a post-coach at an Inn-door a place of safety? Ah! numbskull! I have taken better precautions for you than you did for yourself.—I have—

Hastings. What!

Marlow. I have sent it to the landlady to keep for you.

Hastings. To the landlady!

Marlow. The landlady.

Hastings. You did!

Marlow. I did. She's to be answerable for its forth-coming, you know.

Hastings. Yes, she'll bring it forth, with a witness.

Marlow. Wasn't I right? I believe you'll allow that I acted prudently upon this occasion?

Hastings. [*Aside.*] He must not see my uneasiness.

Marlow. You seem a little disconcerted though, methinks. Sure nothing has happened?

Hastings. No, nothing. Never was in better spirits in all my life. And so you left it with the landlady, who, no doubt, very readily undertook the charge?

Marlow. Rather too readily. For she not only kept the casket; but, thro' her great precaution, was going to keep the messenger too. Ha! ha! ha!

Hastings. He! he! he! They're safe, however.

Marlow. As a guinea in a miser's purse.

Hastings. [*Aside.*] So now all hopes of fortune are at an end. and we must set off without it. [*To him.*] Well, Charles, I'll leave you to your meditations on the pretty bar-maid, and, he! he! he! may you be as successful for yourself as you have been for me.

[*Exit.*

Marlow. Thank ye, George! I ask no more. Ha! ha! ha!

Enter HARDCASTLE.

Hardcastle. I no longer know my own house. It's turned all topsey-turvey. His servants have got drunk already. I'll bear it no longer, and yet, from my respect for his father, I'll be calm. [*To him.*] Mr. Marlow, your servant. I'm your very humble servant.   [*Bowing low.*

Marlow. Sir, your humble servant. [*Aside.*] What's to be the wonder now?

Hardcastle. I believe, Sir, you must be sensible, Sir, that no man alive ought to be more welcome than your father's son, Sir. I hope you think so?

Marlow. I do from my soul, Sir. I don't want much intreaty. I generally make my father's son welcome wherever he goes.

Hardcastle. I believe you do, from my soul, Sir. But tho' I say nothing to your own conduct, that of your servants is insufferable. Their manner of drinking is setting a very bad example in this house, I assure you.

Marlow. I protest, my very good Sir, that's no fault of mine. If they don't drink as they ought, *they* are to blame. I ordered them not to spare the cellar. I did, I assure you. [*To the side scene.*] Here, let one of my servants come up. [*To him.*] My positive directions were, that as I did not drink myself, they should make up for my deficiencies below.

Hardcastle. Then they had your orders for what they do! I'm satisfied!

Marlow. They had, I assure you. You shall hear from one of themselves.

Enter SERVANT *drunk.*

Marlow. You, Jeremy! Come forward, Sirrah! What were my orders? Were you not told to drink freely, and call for what you thought fit, for the good of the house?

Hardcastle. [*Aside.*] I begin to lose my patience.

Jeremy. Please your honour, liberty and Fleet-street for ever! Tho' I'm but a servant, I'm as good as another man. I'll drink for no man before supper, Sir, dammy! Good liquor will sit upon a good supper, but a good supper will not sit upon—*hiccup*—upon my conscience, Sir.   [*Exit* JEREMY.

Marlow. You see, my old friend, the fellow is as drunk as he can possibly be. I don't know what you'd have more, unless you'd have the poor devil soused in a beer-barrel.

Hardcastle. Zounds! He'll drive me distracted if I contain myself any longer. Mr. Marlow. Sir; I have submitted to your insolence for more than four hours, and I see no likelihood of its coming to an end. I'm now resolved to be master here, Sir, and I desire that you and your drunken pack may leave my house directly.

Marlow. Leave your house!—Sure you jest, my good friend! What, when I'm doing what I can to please you!

Hardcastle. I tell you, Sir, you don't please me; so I desire you'll leave my house.

Marlow. Sure you cannot be serious? At this time o'night, and such a night. You only mean to banter me?

Hardcastle. I tell you, Sir, I'm serious; and, now that my passions are rouzed, I say this house is mine, Sir; this house is mine, and I command you to leave it directly.

Marlow. Ha! ha! ha! A puddle in a storm. I shan't stir a step, I assure you. [*In a serious tone.*] This, your house, fellow! It's my house. This is my house. Mine, while I chuse to stay. What right have you to bid me leave this house, Sir? I never met with such impudence, curse me, never in my whole life before.

Hardcastle. Nor I, confound me if ever I did. To come to my house, to call for what he likes, to turn me out of my own chair, to insult the family, to order his servants to get drunk, and then to tell me *This house is mine, Sir.* By all that's impudent, it makes me laugh. Ha! ha! ha! Pray, Sir [*bantering*], as you take the house, what think you of taking the rest of the furniture? There's a pair of silver candlesticks, and there's a fire-screen, and here's a pair of brazen nosed bellows, perhaps you may take a fancy to them?

Marlow. Bring me your bill, Sir, bring me your bill, and let's make no more words about it.

Hardcastle. There are a set of prints too. What think you of the *Rake's Progress* for your own apartment?

Marlow. Bring me your bill, I say; and I'll leave you and your infernal house directly.

Hardcastle. Then there's a mahogany table, that you may see your own face in.

Marlow. My bill, I say.

Hardcastle. I had forgot the great chair, for your own particular slumbers, after a hearty meal.

Marlow. Zounds! bring me my bill, I say, and let's hear no more on't.

Hardcastle. Young man, young man, from your father's letter to me, I was taught to expect a well-bred, modest man, as a visitor here, but now I find him no better than a coxcomb and a bully; but he will be down here presently, and shall hear more of it. [*Exit*.

Marlow. How's this! Sure I have not mistaken the house? Every thing looks like an inn. The servants cry, Coming. The attendance is aukward; the bar-maid, too, to attend us. But she's here, and will further inform me. Whither so fast, child? A word with you.

Enter Miss Hardcastle.

Miss Hardcastle. Let it be short then. I'm in a hurry. [*Aside*.] I believe he begins to find out his mistake, but it's too soon quite to undeceive him.

Marlow. Pray, child, answer me one question. What are you, and what may your business in this house be?

Miss Hardcastle. A relation of the family, Sir.

Marlow. What! A poor relation?

Miss Hardcastle. Yes, Sir. A poor relation appointed to keep the keys, and to see that the guests want nothing in my power to give them.

Marlow. That is, you act as the bar-maid of this inn.

Miss Hardcastle. Inn. O Law—What brought that in your head? One of the best families in the county keep an inn! Ha, ha, ha, old Mr. Hardcastle's house an inn?

Marlow. Mr. Hardcastle's house? Is this house Mr. Hardcastle's house, child?

Miss Hardcastle. Ay, sure. Whose else should it be?

Marlow. So then all's out, and I have been damnably imposed on. O, confound my stupid head, I shall be laugh'd at over the whole town. I shall be stuck up in caricatura in all the print-shops. The Dullissimo Maccaroni. To mistake this house of all others for an inn, and my father's old friend for an inn-keeper. What a swaggering puppy must he take me for. What a silly puppy do I find myself. There again, may I be hang'd, my dear, but I mistook you for the bar-maid.

Miss Hardcastle. Dear me! dear me! I'm sure there's nothing in my *behaviour* to put me upon a level with one of that stamp.

Marlow. Nothing, my dear, nothing. But I was in for a list of blunders, and could not help making you a subscriber. My stupidity saw every thing the wrong way. I mistook your assiduity for assurance, and your simplicity for allurement. But its over— This house I no more shew *my* face in.

Miss Hardcastle. I hope, Sir, I have done nothing to disoblige you. I'm sure I should be sorry to affront any gentleman who has been so polite, and said so many civil things to me. I'm sure I should be sorry [*pretending to cry*] if he left the family upon my account. I'm sure I should be sorry, people said any thing amiss, since I have no fortune but my character.

Marlow. [*Aside.*] By heaven, she weeps. This is the first mark of tenderness I ever had from a modest woman, and it touches me. [*To her.*] Excuse me, my lovely girl, you are the only part of the family I leave with reluctance. But to be plain with you, the difference of our birth, fortune and education, make an honourable connexion impossible; and I can never harbour a thought of seducing simplicity that trusted in my honour, or bringing ruin upon one, whose only fault was being too lovely.

Miss Hardcastle. [*Aside.*] Generous man! I now begin to admire him. [*To him.*] But I'm sure my family is as good as Miss Hardcastle's, and though I'm poor, that's no great misfortune to a contented mind, and, until this moment, I never thought that it was bad to want fortune.

Marlow. And why now, my pretty simplicity?

Miss Hardcastle. Because it puts me at a distance from one, that if I had a thousand pound I would give it all to.

Marlow. [*Aside.*] This simplicity bewitches me, so that if I stay I'm undone. I must make one bold effort, and leave her. [*To her.*] Your partiality in my favour, my dear, touches me most sensibly, and were I to live for myself alone, I could easily fix my choice. But I owe too much to the opinion of the world, too much to the authority of a father, so that—I can scarcely speak it—it affects me. Farewell. [*Exit.*

Miss Hardcastle. I never knew half his merit till now. He shall not go, if I have power or art to detain him. I'll still preserve the character in which I stoop'd to conquer, but will undeceive my papa, who, perhaps, may laugh him out of his resolution. [*Exit.*

Enter TONY, MISS NEVILLE.

Tony. Ay, you may steal for yourselves the next time. I have done my duty. She has got the jewels again, that's a sure thing; but she believes it was all a mistake of the servants.

Miss Neville. But, my dear cousin, sure you won't forsake us in this distress. If she in the least suspects that I am going off, I shall certainly be locked up, or sent to my Aunt Pedigree's, which is ten times worse.

Tony. To be sure, aunts of all kinds are damn'd bad things. But what can I do? I have got you a pair of horses that will fly like Whistlejacket, and I'm sure you can't say but I have courted you nicely before her face. Here she comes; we must court a bit or two more, for fear she should suspect us.

[*They retire, and seem to fondle.*

Enter MRS. HARDCASTLE.

Mrs. Hardcastle. Well, I was greatly fluttered, to be sure. But my son tells me it was all a mistake of the servants. I shan't be easy, however, till they are fairly married, and then let her keep her own fortune. But what do I see! Fondling together, as I'm alive. I never saw Tony so sprightly before. Ah! have I caught you, my pretty doves? What, billing, exchanging stolen glances, and broken murmurs. Ah!

Tony. As for murmurs, mother, we grumble a little now and then, to be sure. But there's no love lost between us.

Mrs. Hardcastle. A mere sprinkling, Tony, upon the flame, only to make it burn brighter.

Miss Neville. Cousin Tony promises to give us more of his company at home. Indeed, he shan't leave us any more. It won't leave us, Cousin Tony, will it?

Tony. O! it's a pretty creature. No, I'd sooner leave my horse in a pound, than leave you when you smile upon one so. Your laugh makes you so becoming.

Miss Neville. Agreeable cousin! Who can help admiring that natural humour, that pleasant, broad, red, thoughtless [*patting his cheek*], ah! it's a bold face.

Mrs. Hardcastle. Pretty innocence!

Tony. I'm sure I always lov'd Cousin Con's hazle eyes, and her pretty long fingers, that she twists this way and that, over the haspicholls, like a parcel of bobbins.

Mrs. Hardcastle. Ah, he would charm the bird from the tree. I was never so happy before. My boy takes after his father, poor Mr. Lumpkin, exactly. The jewels, my dear Con, shall be your's incontinently. You shall have them. Isn't he a sweet boy, my dear? You shall be married to-morrow, and we'll put off the rest of his education, like Dr. Drowsy's sermons, to a fitter opportunity.

Enter DIGGORY.

Diggory. Where's the 'Squire? I have got a letter for your worship.

Tony. Give it to my mamma. She reads all my letters first.

Diggory. I had orders to deliver it into your own hands.

Tony. Who does it come from?

Diggory. Your worship mun ask that o' the letter itself.

[*Exit* DIGGORY.

Tony. I could wish to know, tho'.

[*Turning the letter, and gazing on it.*

Miss Neville. [*Aside.*] Undone, undone. A letter to him from Hastings. I know the hand. If my aunt sees it, we are ruined for ever. I'll keep her employ'd a little if I can. [*To* Mrs. Hardcastle.] But I have not told you, Madam, of my cousin's smart answer just now to Mr. Marlow. We so laugh'd—You must know, Madam—this way a little, for he must not hear us.

[*They confer.*

Tony. [*Still gazing.*] A damn'd cramp piece of penmanship, as ever I saw in my life. I can read your print-hand very well. But here there are such handles, and shanks, and dashes, that one can scarce tell the head from the tail. *To Anthony Lumpkin, Esquire.* It's very odd, I can read the outside of my letters, where my own name is, well enough. But when I come to open it, it's all—buzz. That's hard, very hard; for the inside of the letter is always the cream of the correspondence.

Mrs. Hardcastle. Ha! ha! ha! Very well, very well. And so my son was too hard for the philosopher.

Miss Neville. Yes, Madam; but you must hear the rest, Madam. A little more this way, or he may hear us. You'll hear how he puzzled him again.

Mrs. Hardcastle. He seems strangely puzzled now himself, methinks.

Tony. [*Still gazing.*] A damn'd up and down hand, as if it was disguised in liquor. [*Reading.*] *Dear Sir.* Ay, that's that. Then there's an *M*, and a *T*, and an *S*, but whether the next be an *izzard* or an *R*, confound me, I cannot tell.

Mrs. Hardcastle. What's that, my dear? Can I give you any assistance?

Miss Neville. Pray, aunt, let me read it. No body reads a cramp hand better than I. [*Twitching the letter from her.*] Do you know who it is from?

Tony. Can't tell, except from Dick Ginger the feeder.

Miss Neville. Ay, so it is. [*Pretending to read.*] Dear 'Squire, Hoping that you're in health, as I am at this present. The gentlemen of the Shake-bag club has cut the gentlemen of Goose-green quite out of feather. The odds—um—odd battle—um—long fighting—um, here, here, it's all about cocks, and fighting; it's of no consequence; here, put it up, put it up.

[*Thrusting the crumpled letter upon him.*

Tony. But I tell you, Miss, it's of all the consequence in the world. I would not lose the rest of it for a guinea. Here, mother, do you make it out. Of no consequence!

[*Giving* MRS. HARDCASTLE *the letter.*

Mrs. Hardcastle. How's this! [*Reads.*] "Dear 'Squire, I'm now waiting for Miss Neville, with a post-chaise and pair, at the bottom of the garden, but I find my horses yet unable to perform the journey. I expect you'll assist us with a pair of fresh horses, as you promised. Dispatch is necessary, as the *hag*, (ay, the hag) your mother, will otherwise suspect us. Your's, Hastings." Grant me patience. I shall run distracted. My rage choaks me.

Miss Neville. I hope, Madam, you'll suspend your resentment for a few moments, and not impute to me any impertinence, or sinister design that belongs to another.

Mrs. Hardcastle. [*Curtesying very low.*] Fine spoken, Madam; you are most miraculously polite and engaging, and quite the very pink of curtesy and circumspection, Madam. [*Changing her tone.*] And you, you great ill-fashioned oaf, with scarce sense enough to keep your mouth shut. Were you too join'd against me? But I'll defeat all your plots in a moment. As for you, Madam, since you have got a pair of fresh horses ready, it would be cruel to disappoint them. So, if you please, instead of running away with your spark, prepare, this very moment, to run off with *me*. Your old Aunt Pedigree will keep you secure, I'll warrant me. You too, Sir, may mount your horse, and guard us upon the way. Here, Thomas, Roger, Diggory! I'll shew you, that I wish you better than you do yourselves.   [*Exit.*

Miss Neville. So now I'm completely ruined.

Tony. Ay, that's a sure thing.

Miss Neville. What better could be expected from being connected with such a stupid fool, and after all the nods and signs I made him.

Tony. By the laws, Miss, it was your own cleverness, and not my stupidity, that did your business. You were so nice and so busy with your Shake-bags and Goose-greens, that I thought you could never be making believe.

Enter HASTINGS.

Hastings. So, Sir, I find by my servant, that you have shewn my letter, and betray'd us. Was this well done, young gentleman?

Tony. Here's another. Ask Miss there who betray'd you. Ecod, it was her doing, not mine.

Enter MARLOW.

Marlow. So I have been finely used here among you. Rendered contemptible, driven into ill manners, despised, insulted, laugh'd at.

Tony. Here's another. We shall have old Bedlam broke loose presently.

Miss Neville. And there, Sir, is the gentleman to whom we all owe every obligation.

Marlow. What can I say to him, a mere boy, an ideot, whose ignorance and age are a protection.

Hastings. A poor contemptible booby, that would but disgrace correction.

Miss Neville. Yet with cunning and malice enough to make himself merry with all our embarrassments.

Hastings. An insensible cub.

Marlow. Replete with tricks and mischief.

Tony. Baw! damme, but I'll fight you both one after the other, —with baskets.

Marlow. As for him, he's below resentment. But your conduct, Mr. Hastings, requires an explanation. You knew of my mistakes, yet would not undeceive me.

Hastings. Tortured as I am with my own disappointments, is this a time for explanations? It is not friendly, Mr. Marlow.

Marlow. But, Sir—

Miss Neville. Mr. Marlow, we never kept on your mistake, till it was too late to undeceive you. Be pacified.

Enter SERVANT.

Servant. My mistress desires you'll get ready immediately, Madam. The horses are putting to. Your hat and things are in the next room. We are to go thirty miles before morning.

[*Exit* SERVANT.

Miss Neville. Well, well; I'll come presently.

Marlow. [*To* HASTINGS.] Was it well done, Sir, to assist in rendering me ridiculous? To hang me out for the scorn of all my acquaintance? Depend upon it, Sir, I shall expect an explanation.

Hastings. Was it well done, Sir, if you're upon that subject, to deliver what I entrusted to yourself, to the care of another, Sir?

Miss Neville. Mr. Hastings. Mr. Marlow. Why will you increase my distress by this groundless dispute? I implore, I intreat you—

Enter SERVANT.

Servant. Your cloak, Madam. My mistress is impatient.

Miss Neville. I come. [*Exit* SERVANT.] Pray be pacified. If I leave you thus, I shall die with apprehension.

Enter SERVANT.

Servant. Your fan, muff, and gloves, Madam. The horses are waiting.

Miss Neville. O, Mr. Marlow! if you knew what a scene of constraint and ill-nature lies before me, I'm sure it would convert your resentment into pity.

Marlow. I'm so distracted with a variety of passions, that I don't know what I do. Forgive me, Madam. George, forgive me. You know my hasty temper, and should not exasperate it.

Hastings. The torture of my situation is my only excuse.

Miss Neville. Well, my dear Hastings, if you have that esteem for me that I think, that I am sure you have, your constancy for three years will but encrease the happiness of our future connexion. If—

Mrs. Hardcastle. [*Within.*] Miss Neville. Constance, why Constance, I say.

Miss Neville. I'm coming. Well, constancy. Remember, constancy is the word. [*Exit.*

Hastings. My heart! How can I support this. To be so near happiness, and such happiness.

Marlow. [*To* TONY.] You see now, young gentleman, the effects of your folly. What might be amusement to you, is here disappointment, and even distress.

Tony. [*From a reverie.*] Ecod, I have hit it. It's here. Your hands. Yours and yours, my poor Sulky. My boots there, ho! Meet me two hours hence at the bottom of the garden; and if you don't find Tony Lumpkin a more good-natur'd fellow than you thought for, I'll give you leave to take my best horse, and Bet Bouncer into the bargain. Come along. My boots, ho!

[*Exeunt.*

END OF THE FOURTH ACT

ACT V

SCENE—*Continues*

Enter HASTINGS *and* SERVANT.

Hastings. You saw the Old Lady and Miss Neville drive off, you say?

Servant. Yes, your honour. They went off in a post coach, and the young 'Squire went on horseback. They're thirty miles off by this time.

Hastings. Then all my hopes are over.

Servant. Yes, Sir. Old Sir Charles is arrived. He and the Old Gentleman of the house have been laughing at Mr. Marlow's mistake this half hour. They are coming this way.

Hastings. Then I must not be seen. So now to my fruitless appointment at the bottom of the garden. This is about the time.

[*Exit.*

Enter SIR CHARLES *and* HARDCASTLE.

Hardcastle. Ha! ha! ha! The peremptory tone in which he sent forth his sublime commands.

Sir Charles. And the reserve with which I suppose he treated all your advances.

Hardcastle. And yet he might have seen something in me above a common inn-keeper, too.

Sir Charles. Yes, Dick, but he mistook you for an uncommon inn-keeper, ha! ha! ha!

Hardcastle. Well, I'm in too good spirits to think of any thing but joy. Yes, my dear friend, this union of our families will make our personal friendships hereditary; and tho' my daughter's fortune is but small—

Sir Charles. Why, Dick, will you talk of fortune to *me.* My son is possessed of more than a competence already, and I can want nothing but a good and virtuous girl to share his happiness and encrease it. If they like each other as you say they do—

Hardcastle. If, man. I tell you they *do* like each other. My daughter as good as told me so.

Sir Charles. But girls are apt to flatter themselves, you know.

Hardcastle. I saw him grasp her hand in the warmest manner myself; and here he comes to put you out of your *ifs,* I warrant him.

Enter MARLOW.

Marlow. I come Sir, once more, to ask pardon for my strange conduct. I can scarce reflect on my insolence without confusion.

Hardcastle. Tut, boy, a trifle. You take it too gravely. An hour or two's laughing with my daughter will set all to rights again. She'll never like you the worse for it.

Marlow. Sir, I shall be always proud of her approbation.

Hardcastle. Approbation is but a cold word, Mr. Marlow; if I am not deceived, you have something more than approbation thereabouts. You take me.

Marlow. Really, Sir, I have not that happiness.

Hardcastle. Come, boy, I'm an old fellow, and know what's what, as well as you that are younger. I know what has past between you; but mum.

Marlow. Sure, Sir, nothing has past between us but the most profound respect on my side, and the most distant reserve on hers. You don't think, Sir, that my impudence has been past upon all the rest of the family?

Hardcastle. Impudence! No, I don't say that—Not quite impudence—Though girls like to be play'd with, and rumpled a little, too, sometimes. But she has told no tales, I assure you.

Marlow. I never gave her the slightest cause.

Hardcastle. Well, well, I like modesty in its place well enough. But this is over-acting, young gentleman. You may be open. Your father and I will like you the better for it.

Marlow. May I die, Sir, if I ever—

Hardcastle. I tell you, she don't dislike you; and as I'm sure you like her—

Marlow. Dear Sir—I protest, Sir,—

Hardcastle. I see no reason why you should not be joined as fast as the parson can tie you.

Marlow. But hear me, Sir—

Hardcastle. Your father approves the match, I admire it, every moment's delay will be doing mischief, so—

Marlow. But why won't you hear me? By all that's just and true, I never gave Miss Hardcastle the slightest mark of my attachment, or even the most distant hint to suspect me of affection. We had but one interview, and that was formal, modest and uninteresting.

Hardcastle. [*Aside.*] This fellow's formal, modest impudence is beyond bearing.

Sir Charles. And you never grasp'd her hand, or made any protestations!

Marlow. As heaven is my witness, I came down in obedience to your commands. I saw the lady without emotion, and parted without reluctance. I hope you'll exact no further proofs of my duty, nor prevent me from leaving a house in which I suffer so many mortifications.   [*Exit.*

Sir Charles. I'm astonish'd at the air of sincerity with which he parted.

Hardcastle. And I'm astonish'd at the deliberate intrepidity of his assurance.

Sir Charles. I dare pledge my life and honour upon his truth.

Hardcastle. Here comes my daughter, and I would stake my happiness upon her veracity.

Enter Miss HARDCASTLE.

Hardcastle. Kate, come hither, child. Answer us sincerely, and without reserve; has Mr. Marlow made you any professions of love and affection?

Miss Hardcastle. The question is very abrupt, Sir! But since you require unreserved sincerity, I think he has.

Hardcastle. [*To* SIR CHARLES.] You see.

Sir Charles. And pray, Madam, have you and my son had more than one interview?

Miss Hardcastle. Yes, Sir, several.

Hardcastle. [*To* SIR CHARLES.] You see.

Sir Charles. But did he profess any attachment?

Miss Hardcastle. A lasting one.

Sir Charles. Did he talk of love?

Miss Hardcastle. Much, Sir.

Sir Charles. Amazing! And all this formally?

Miss Hardcastle. Formally.

Hardcastle. Now, my friend, I hope you are satisfied.

Sir Charles. And how did he behave, Madam?

Miss Hardcastle. As most profest admirers do. Said some civil things to my face, talked much of his want of merit, and the greatness of mine; mentioned his heart, gave a short tragedy speech, and ended with pretended rapture.

Sir Charles. Now I'm perfectly convinced, indeed. I know his conversation among women to be modest and submissive. This forward, canting, ranting manner by no means describes him, and I am confident, he never sate for the picture.

Miss Hardcastle. Then what, Sir, if I should convince you to your face of my sincerity? If you and my papa, in about half an hour, will place yourselves behind that screen, you shall hear him declare his passion to me in person.

Sir Charles. Agreed. And if I find him what you describe, all my happiness in him must have an end. [*Exit.*

Miss Hardcastle. And if you don't find him what I describe— I fear my happiness must never have a beginning. [*Exeunt.*

SCENE.—*Changes to the Back of the Garden*

Enter HASTINGS.

Hastings. What an ideot am I, to wait here for a fellow, who probably takes delight in mortifying me. He never intended to be punctual, and I'll wait no longer. What do I see! It is he, and perhaps with news of my Constance.

Enter TONY, *booted and spattered.*

Hastings. My honest 'Squire! I now find you a man of your word. This looks like friendship.

Tony. Ay, I'm your friend, and the best friend you have in the world, if you knew but all. This riding by night, by the bye, is cursedly tiresome. It has shook me worse than the basket of a stage-coach.

Hastings. But how? Where did you leave your fellow travellers? Are they in safety? Are they housed?

Tony. Five and twenty miles in two hours and a half is no such bad driving. The poor beasts have smoaked for it: Rabbet me, but I'd rather ride forty miles after a fox, than ten with such *varment.*

Hastings. Well, but where have you left the ladies? I die with impatience.

Tony. Left them? Why, where should I leave them, but where I found them?

Hastings. This is a riddle.

Tony. Riddle me this then. What's that goes round the house, and round the house, and never touches the house?

Hastings. I'm still astray.

Tony. Why that's it, mon. I have led them astray. By jingo, there's not a pond or slough within five miles of the place but they can tell the taste of.

Hastings. Ha, ha, ha, I understand; you took them in a round, while they supposed themselves going forward. And so you have at last brought them home again.

Tony. You shall hear. I first took them down Feather-bed-lane, where we stuck fast in the mud. I then rattled them crack over the stones of Up-and-down Hill—I then introduc'd them to the gibbet on Heavy-tree Heath, and from that, with a circumbendibus, I fairly lodged them in the horse-pond at the bottom of the garden.

Hastings. But no accident, I hope.

Tony. No, no. Only mother is confoundedly frightened. She thinks herself forty miles off. She's sick of the journey, and the cattle can scarce crawl. So if your own horses be ready, you may whip off with Cousin, and I'll be bound that no soul here can budge a foot to follow you.

Hastings. My dear friend, how can I be grateful?

Tony. Ay, now its dear friend, noble 'Squire. Just now, it was all ideot, cub, and run me through the guts. Damn *your* way of fighting, I say. After we take a knock in this part of the country, we kiss and be friends. But if you had run me through the guts, then I should be dead, and you might go kiss the hangman.

Hastings. The rebuke is just. But I must hasten to relieve Miss Neville; if you keep the old lady employed, I promise to take care of the young one. [*Exit* HASTINGS.

Tony. Never fear me. Here she comes. Vanish. She's got from the pond, and draggled up to the waist like a mermaid.

Enter MRS. HARDCASTLE.

Mrs. Hardcastle. Oh, Tony, I'm killed. Shook. Battered to death. I shall never survive it. That last jolt that laid us against the quickset hedge has done my business.

Tony. Alack, mama, it was all your own fault. You would be for running away by night, without knowing one inch of the way.

Mrs. Hardcastle. I wish we were at home again. I never met so many accidents in so short a journey. Drench'd in the mud, overturn'd in a ditch, stuck fast in a slough, jolted to a jelly, and at last to lose our way. Whereabouts do you think we are, Tony?

Tony. By my guess we should be upon Crackskull Common, about forty miles from home.

Mrs. Hardcastle. O lud! O lud! the most notorious spot in all the country. We only want a robbery to make a complete night on't.

Tony. Don't be afraid, mama, don't be afraid. Two of the five that kept here are hanged, and the other three may not find us. Don't be afraid. Is that a man that's galloping behind us? No; it's only a tree. Don't be afraid.

Mrs. Hardcastle. The fright will certainly kill me.

Tony. Do you see any thing like a black hat moving behind the thicket?

Mrs. Hardcastle. O death!

Tony. No, it's only a cow. Don't be afraid, mama; don't be afraid.

Mrs. Hardcastle. As I'm alive, Tony, I see a man coming towards us. Ah! I'm sure on't. If he perceives us, we are undone.

Tony. [*Aside.*] Father-in-law, by all that's unlucky, come to take one of his night walks. [*To her.*] Ah, it's a highwayman, with pistils as long as my arm. A damn'd ill-looking fellow.

Mrs. Hardcastle. Good heaven defend us! He approaches.

Tony. Do you hide yourself in that thicket, and leave me to manage him. If there be any danger, I'll cough, and cry hem. When I cough be sure to keep close.

[MRS. HARDCASTLE *hides behind a tree in the back scene.*

Enter HARDCASTLE.

Hardcastle. I'm mistaken, or I heard voices of people in want of help. Oh, Tony, is that you? I did not expect you so soon back. Are your mother and her charge in safety?

Tony. Very safe, Sir, at my Aunt Pedigree's. Hem.

Mrs. Hardcastle. [*From behind.*] Ah death! I find there's danger.

Hardcastle. Forty miles in three hours; sure, that's too much, my youngster.

Tony. Stout horses and willing minds make short journies, as they say. Hem.

Mrs. Hardcastle. [*From behind.*] Sure he'll do the dear boy no harm.

Hardcastle. But I heard a voice here; I should be glad to know from whence it came?

Tony. It was I, Sir, talking to myself, Sir. I was saying that forty miles in four hours was very good going. Hem. As to be sure it was. Hem. I have got a sort of cold by being out in the air. We'll go in, if you please. Hem.

Hardcastle. But if you talk'd to yourself, you did not answer yourself. I am certain I heard two voices, and am resolved [*raising his voice*] to find the other out.

Mrs. Hardcastle. [*From behind.*] Oh! he's coming to find me out. Oh!

Tony. What need you go, Sir, if I tell you? Hem. I'll lay down my life for the truth—hem—I'll tell you all, Sir.

[*Detaining him.*

Hardcastle. I tell you, I will not be detained. I insist on seeing. It's in vain to expect I'll believe you.

Mrs. Hardcastle. [*Running forward from behind.*] O lud, he'll murder my poor boy, my darling. Here, good gentleman, whet your rage upon me. Take my money, my life, but spare that young gentleman, spare my child, if you have any mercy!

Hardcastle. My wife! as I'm a Christian. From whence can she come, or what does she mean?

Mrs. Hardcastle. [*Kneeling.*] Take compassion on us, good Mr. Highwayman. Take our money, our watches, all we have, but spare our lives. We will never bring you to justice, indeed we won't, good Mr. Highwayman.

Hardcastle. I believe the woman's out of her senses. What, Dorothy, don't you know *me?*

Mrs. Hardcastle. Mr. Hardcastle, as I'm alive! My fears blinded me. But who, my dear, could have expected to meet you here, in this frightful place, so far from home. What has brought you to follow us?

Hardcastle. Sure, Dorothy, you have not lost your wits. So far from home, when you are within forty yards of your own door. [*To him.*] This is one of your old tricks, you graceless rogue you. [*To her.*] Don't you know the gate, and the mulberry-tree; and don't you remember the horse-pond, my dear?

Mrs. Hardcastle. Yes, I shall remember the horse-pond as long as I live; I have caught my death in it. [*To* Tony.] And is it to you, you graceless varlet, I owe all this? I'll teach you to abuse your mother, I will.

Tony. Ecod, mother, all the parish says you have spoil'd me, and so you may take the fruits on't.

Mrs. Hardcastle. I'll spoil you, I will.

[*Follows him off the stage. Exit.*

Hardcastle. There's morality, however, in his reply. [*Exit.*

Enter HASTINGS *and* MISS NEVILLE.

Hastings. My dear Constance, why will you deliberate thus? If we delay a moment, all is lost for ever. Pluck up a little resolution, and we shall soon be out of the reach of her malignity.

Miss Neville. I find it impossible. My spirits are so sunk with the agitations I have suffered, that I am unable to face any new danger. Two or three years patience will at last crown us with happiness.

Hastings. Such a tedious delay is worse than inconstancy. Let us fly, my charmer. Let us date our happiness from this very moment. Perish fortune. Love and content will encrease what we possess beyond a monarch's revenue. Let me prevail.

Miss Neville. No, Mr. Hastings; no. Prudence once more comes to my relief, and I will obey its dictates. In the moment of passion, fortune may be despised, but it ever produces a lasting repentance. I'm resolved to apply to Mr. Hardcastle's compassion and justice for redress.

Hastings. But tho' he had the will, he has not the power to relieve you.

Miss Neville. But he has influence, and upon that I am resolved to rely.

Hastings. I have no hopes. But since you persist, I must reluctantly obey you. [*Exeunt.*

SCENE *Changes*

Enter SIR CHARLES *and* MISS HARDCASTLE.

Sir Charles. What a situation am I in. If what you say appears, I shall then find a guilty son. If what he says be true, I shall then lose one that, of all others, I most wish'd for a daughter.

Miss Hardcastle. I am proud of your approbation, and to shew I merit it, if you place yourselves as I directed, you shall hear his explicit declaration. But he comes.

Sir Charles. I'll to your father, and keep him to the appointment. [*Exit* SIR CHARLES.

Enter MARLOW.

Marlow. Tho' prepar'd for setting out, I come once more to take leave, nor did I, till this moment, know the pain I feel in the separation.

Miss Hardcastle. [*In her own natural manner.*] I believe these sufferings cannot be very great, Sir, which you can so easily remove. A day or two longer, perhaps, might lessen your uneasiness, by shewing the little value of what you now think proper to regret.

Marlow. [*Aside.*] This girl every moment improves upon me. [*To her.*] It must not be, Madam. I have already trifled too long with my heart. My very pride begins to submit to my passion. The disparity of education and fortune, the anger of a parent, and the contempt of my equals, begin to lose their weight; and nothing can restore me to myself, but this painful effort of resolution.

Miss Hardcastle. Then go, Sir. I'll urge nothing more to detain you. Tho' my family be as good as her's you came down to visit, and my education, I hope, not inferior, what are these advantages without equal affluence? I must remain contented with the slight approbation of imputed merit; I must have only the mockery of your addresses, while all your serious aims are fix'd on fortune.

Enter HARDCASTLE *and* SIR CHARLES *from behind.*

Sir Charles. Here, behind this screen.

Hardcastle. Ay, ay, make no noise. I'll engage my Kate covers him with confusion at last.

Marlow. By heavens, Madam, fortune was ever my smallest consideration. Your beauty at first caught my eye; for who could see that without emotion? But every moment that I converse with you steals in some new grace, heightens the picture, and gives it stronger expression. What at first seem'd rustic plainness, now appears refin'd simplicity. What seem'd forward assurance, now strikes me as the result of courageous innocence, and conscious virtue.

Sir Charles. What can it mean! He amazes me!

Hardcastle. I told you how it would be. Hush!

Marlow. I am now determined to stay, Madam, and I have too good an opinion of my father's discernment, when he sees you, to doubt his approbation.

Miss Hardcastle. No, Mr. Marlow, I will not, cannot detain you. Do you think I could suffer a connexion, in which there is the smallest room for repentance? Do you think I would take the mean advantage of a transient passion, to load you with confusion? Do you think I could ever relish that happiness, which was acquired by lessening your's?

Marlow. By all that's good, I can have no happiness but what's in your power to grant me. Nor shall I ever feel repentance, but in not having seen your merits before. I will stay, even contrary to your wishes; and tho' you should persist to shun me, I will make my respectful assiduities atone for the levity of my past conduct.

Miss Hardcastle. Sir, I must entreat you'll desist. As our acquaintance began, so let it end, in indifference. I might have given an hour or two to levity; but seriously, Mr. Marlow, do you think I could ever submit to a connexion, where *I* must appear mercenary, and *you* imprudent? Do you think I could ever catch at the confident addresses of a secure admirer?

Marlow. [*Kneeling.*] Does this look like security? Does this look like confidence? No, Madam, every moment that shews me your merit, only serves to encrease my diffidence and confusion. Here let me continue—

Sir Charles. I can hold it no longer. Charles, Charles, how hast thou deceived me! Is this your indifference, your uninteresting conversation!

Hardcastle. Your cold contempt; your formal interview! What have you to say now?

Marlow. That I'm all amazement! What can it mean!

Hardcastle. It means that you can say and unsay things at pleasure. That you can address a lady in private, and deny it in public; that you have one story for us, and another for my daughter.

Marlow. Daughter!—this lady your daughter!

Hardcastle. Yes, Sir, my only daughter. My Kate, whose else should she be?

Marlow. Oh, the devil!

Miss Hardcastle. Yes, Sir, that very identical tall, squinting lady you were pleased to take me for. [*Curtesying.*] She that you addressed as the mild, modest, sentimental man of gravity, and the bold, forward, agreeable Rattle of the Ladies Club; ha, ha, ha.

Marlow. Zounds, there's no bearing this; it's worse than death.

Miss Hardcastle. In which of your characters, Sir, will you give us leave to address you? As the faultering gentleman, with looks on the ground, that speaks just to be heard, and hates hypocrisy; or the loud, confident creature, that keeps it up with Mrs. Mantrap, and old Miss Biddy Buckskin, till three in the morning; ha, ha, ha!

Marlow. O, curse on my noisy head. I never attempted to be impudent yet, that I was not taken down. I must be gone.

Hardcastle. By the hand of my body, but you shall not. I see it was all a mistake, and I am rejoiced to find it. You shall not, Sir, I tell you. I know she'll forgive you. Won't you forgive him, Kate? We'll all forgive you. Take courage, man.

[*They retire, she tormenting him, to the back Scene.*

Enter MRS. HARDCASTLE, TONY.

Mrs. Hardcastle. So, so, they're gone off. Let them go, I care not.

Hardcastle. Who gone?

Mrs. Hardcastle. My dutiful niece and her gentleman, Mr. Hastings, from Town. He who came down with our modest visitor here.

Sir Charles. Who, my honest George Hastings? As worthy a fellow as lives, and the girl could not have made a more prudent choice.

Hardcastle. Then, by the hand of my body, I'm proud of the connexion.

Mrs. Hardcastle. Well, if he has taken away the lady, he has not taken her fortune; that remains in this family to console us for her loss.

Hardcastle. Sure, Dorothy, you would not be so mercenary?

Mrs. Hardcastle. Ay, that's my affair, not your's. But you know if your son, when of age, refuses to marry his cousin, her whole fortune is then at her own disposal.

Hardcastle. Ay, but he's not of age, and she has not thought proper to wait for his refusal.

Enter Hastings *and* Miss Neville.

Mrs. Hardcastle. [*Aside.*] What! returned so soon? I begin not to like it.

Hastings. [*To* Hardcastle.] For my late attempt to fly off with your niece, let my present confusion be my punishment. We are now come back, to appeal from your justice to your humanity. By her father's consent, I first paid her my addresses, and our passions were first founded in duty.

Miss Neville. Since his death, I have been obliged to stoop to dissimulation to avoid oppression. In an hour of levity, I was ready even to give up my fortune to secure my choice. But I'm now recover'd from the delusion, and hope from your tenderness what is denied me from a nearer connexion.

Mrs. Hardcastle. Pshaw, pshaw, this is all but the whining end of a modern novel.

Hardcastle. Be it what it will, I'm glad they're come back to reclaim their due. Come hither, Tony boy. Do you refuse this lady's hand whom I now offer you?

Tony. What signifies my refusing? You know I can't refuse her till I'm of age, father.

Hardcastle. While I thought concealing your age, boy, was likely to conduce to your improvement, I concurred with your mother's desire to keep it secret. But since I find she turns it to a wrong use, I must now declare, you have been of age these three months.

Tony. Of age! Am I of age, father?

Hardcastle. Above three months.

Tony. Then you'll see the first use I'll make of my liberty. [*Taking* Miss Neville's *hand.*] Witness all men by these presents, that I, Anthony Lumpkin, Esquire, of Blank place, refuse you, Constantia Neville, spinster, of no place at all, for my true and lawful wife. So Constance Neville may marry whom she pleases, and Tony Lumpkin is his own man again!

Sir Charles. O brave 'Squire!

Hastings. My worthy friend!

Mrs. Hardcastle. My undutiful offspring!

Marlow. Joy, my dear George, I give you joy sincerely. And could I prevail upon my little tyrant here to be less arbitrary, I should be the happiest man alive, if you would return me the favour.

Hastings. [*To* Miss Hardcastle.] Come, Madam, you are now driven to the very last scene of all your contrivances. I know you like him, I'm sure he loves you, and you must and shall have him.

Hardcastle. [*Joining their hands.*] And I say so too. And Mr. Marlow, if she makes as good a wife as she has a daughter, I don't believe you'll ever repent your bargain. So now to supper; tomorrow we shall gather all the poor of the parish about us, and the Mistakes of the Night shall be crowned with a merry morning; so boy, take her; and as you have been mistaken in the mistress, my wish is, that you may never be mistaken in the wife.

FINIS

EPILOGUE

By Dr. Goldsmith

Well, having stoop'd to conquer with success,
And gain'd a husband without aid from dress,
Still as a Bar-maid, I could wish it too,
As I have conquer'd him to conquer you:
And let me say, for all your resolution,
That pretty Bar-maids have done execution.
Our life is all a play, compos'd to please,
"We have our exits and our entrances."
The first act shews the simple country maid,
Harmless and young, of ev'rything afraid;
Blushes when hir'd, and with unmeaning action,
I hopes as how to give you satisfaction.
Her second act displays a livelier scene,—
Th'unblushing Bar-maid of a country inn,
Who whisks about the house, at market caters,
Talks loud, coquets the guests, and scolds the waiters.
Next the scene shifts to town, and there she soars,
The chop-house toast of ogling connoissieurs.
On 'Squires and Cits she there displays her arts,
And on the gridiron broils her lovers' hearts—
And as she smiles, her triumphs to compleat,
Even Common Councilmen forget to eat.
The fourth act shews her wedded to the 'Squire,
And Madam now begins to hold it higher;
Pretends to taste, at Operas cries caro,
And quits her Nancy Dawson, for Che Faro.
Doats upon dancing, and in all her pride,
Swims round the room, the Heinel *of Cheapside:*
Ogles and leers with artificial skill,
Till having lost in age the power to kill,
She sits all night at cards, and ogles at spadille.
Such, thro' our lives, the eventful history—
The fifth and last act still remains for me.
The Bar-maid now for your protection prays,
Turns Female Barrister, and pleads for Bayes.

791

EPILOGUE

TO BE SPOKEN IN THE CHARACTER OF TONY LUMPKIN [1]

By J. Craddock, Esq.

Well—now all's ended—and my comrades gone,
Pray what becomes of mother's nonly son?
A hopeful blade!—in town I'll fix my station,
And try to make a bluster in the nation.
As for my cousin Neville, I renounce her,
Off—in a crack—I'll carry big Bett Bouncer.
   Why should not I in the great world appear?
I soon shall have a thousand pounds a year;
No matter what a man may here inherit,
In London—'gad, they've some regard to spirit.
I see the horses prancing up the streets,
And big Bet Bouncer bobs to all she meets;
Then hoikes to jiggs and pastimes ev'ry night—
Not to the plays—they say it a'n't polite,
To Sadler's-Wells perhaps, or Operas go,
And once, by chance, to the roratorio.
Thus here and there, for ever up and down,
We'll set the fashions, too, to half the town;
And then at auctions—money ne'er regard,
Buy pictures like the great, ten pounds a yard;
Zounds, we shall make these London gentry say,
We know what's damn'd genteel, as well as they.

[1] This came too late to be Spoken.

THE RIVALS
by
RICHARD BRINSLEY SHERIDAN

PREFACE

A preface to a play seems generally to be considered as a kind of closet-prologue, in which—if his piece has been successful—the author solicits that indulgence from the reader which he had before experienced from the audience: but as the scope and immediate object of a play is to please a mixed assembly in *representation* (whose judgment in the theatre at least is decisive), its degree of reputation is usually as determined by the public, before it can be prepared for the cooler tribunal of the study. Thus any further solicitude on the part of the writer becomes unnecessary at least, if not an intrusion: and if the piece has been condemned in the performance, I fear an address to the closet, like an appeal to posterity, is constantly regarded as the procrastination of a suit, from a consciousness of the weakness of the cause. From these considerations, the following comedy would certainly have been submitted to the reader, without any further introduction than what it had in the representation, but that its success has probably been founded on a circumstance which the author is informed has not before attended a theatrical trial, and which consequently ought not to pass unnoticed.

I need scarcely add, that the circumstance alluded to was the withdrawing of the piece, to remove those imperfections in the first representation which were too obvious to escape reprehension, and too numerous to admit of a hasty correction. There are few writers, I believe, who, even in the fullest consciousness of error, do not wish to palliate the faults which they acknowledge; and, however trifling the performance, to second their confession of its deficiencies, by whatever plea seems least disgraceful to their ability. In the present instance, it cannot be said to amount either to candour or modesty in me, to acknowledge an extreme inexperience and want of judgment on matters, in which, without guidance from practice, or spur from success, a young man should scarcely boast of being an adept. If it be said that under such disadvantages no one should attempt to write a play, I must beg leave to dissent from the position, while the first point of experience that I have gained on the subject is, a knowledge of the candour and judgment with which an impartial public distinguishes between the errors of inexperience and incapacity, and the indulgence which it shows even to a disposition to remedy the defects of either.

It were unnecessary to enter into any further extenuation of what was thought exceptionable in this play, but that it has been said, that the managers should have prevented some of the defects before its appearance to the public—and in particular the uncommon length of the piece as represented the first night. It were an ill return for the most liberal and gentlemanly conduct on their side, to suffer any censure to rest where none was deserved. Hurry in writing has long been exploded as an excuse for an author;—however, in the dramatic line, it may happen, that both an author and a manager may wish to fill a chasm in the entertainment of the public with a hastiness not altogether culpable. The season was advanced when I first put the play into Mr. Harris's hands: it was at that time at least double the length of any acting comedy. I profited by his judgment and experience in the curtailing of it—till, I believe, his feeling for the vanity of a young author got the better of his desire for correctness, and he left many excrescences remaining, because he had assisted in pruning so many more. Hence, though I was not uninformed that the acts were still too long, I flattered myself that, after the first trial, I might with safer judgment proceed to remove what should appear to have been most dissatisfactory. Many other errors there were, which might in part have arisen from my being by no means conversant with plays in general, either in reading or at the theatre. Yet I own that, in one respect, I did not regret my ignorance: for as my first wish in attempting a play was to avoid every appearance of plagiary, I thought I should stand a better chance of effecting this from being in a walk which I had not frequented, and where, consequently, the progress of invention was less likely to be interrupted by starts of recollection: for on subjects on which the mind has been much informed, invention is slow of exerting itself. Faded ideas float in the fancy like half-forgotten dreams; and the imagination in its fullest enjoyments becomes suspicious of its offspring, and doubts whether it has created or adopted.

With regard to some particular passages which on the first night's representation seemed generally disliked, I confess that if I felt any emotion of surprise at the disapprobation, it was not that they were disapproved of, but that I had not before perceived that they deserved it. As some part of the attack on the piece was begun too early to pass for the sentence of *judgment*, which is ever tardy in condemning, it has been suggested to me that much of the disapprobation must have arisen from virulence of malice, rather than severity of criticism: but as I was more apprehensive of there being just grounds to excite the latter than conscious of having deserved the former, I continue not to believe that probable which I am sure must have been unprovoked. However, if it was so, and I could even mark the quarter from whence it came, it would be ungenerous to retort; for no passion suffers more than malice from disappointment. For my own part, I see no reason why the author of a play should not regard a first night's audience as a candid and judicious friend attending, in behalf of the public, at his last rehearsal. If he can dispense with flattery, he is sure at least of sincerity, and even though the annotation be rude, he may rely upon the justness of the comment. Considered in this light, that audience, whose *fiat* is essential to the poet's claim, whether his object be fame or profit, has surely a right to expect some deference to its opinion, from principles of politeness at least, if not from gratitude.

As for the little puny critics, who scatter their peevish strictures in private circles, and scribble at every author who has the eminence of being unconnected with them, as they are usually spleenswoln from a vain idea of increasing their consequence, there will always be found a petulance and illiberality in their remarks, which should place them as far beneath the notice of a gentleman as their original dulness had sunk them from the level of the most unsuccessful author.

It is not without pleasure that I catch at an opportunity of justifying myself from the charge of intending any national reflection in the character of Sir Lucius O'Trigger. If any gentlemen opposed the piece from that idea, I thank them sincerely for their opposition; and if the condemnation of this comedy (however misconceived the provocation) could have added one spark to the decaying flame of national attachment to the country supposed to be reflected on, I should have been happy in its fate, and might with truth have boasted that it had done more real service in its failure than the successful morality of a thousand stage-novels will ever effect.

It is usual, I believe, to thank the performers in a new play for the exertion of their several abilities. But where (as in this instance) their merit has been so striking and uncontroverted as to call for the warmest and truest applause from a number of judicious audiences, the poet's after-praise comes like the feeble acclamation of a child to close the shouts of a multitude. The conduct however, of the principals in a theatre cannot be so apparent to the public. I think it therefore but justice to declare, that from this theatre (the only one I can speak of from experience) those writers who wish to try the dramatic line will meet with that candour and liberal attention which are generally allowed to be better calculated to lead genius into excellence than either the precepts of judgment or the guidance of experience.

THE AUTHOR.

DRAMATIS PERSONÆ

AS ORIGINALLY ACTED AT COVENT-GARDEN THEATRE IN 1775

SIR ANTHONY ABSOLUTE	*Mr. Shuter.*
CAPTAIN ABSOLUTE	*Mr. Woodward.*
FAULKLAND	*Mr. Lewis.*
ACRES	*Mr. Quick.*
SIR LUCIUS O'TRIGGER	*Mr. Lee.*
FAG	*Mr. Lee Lewes.*
DAVID	*Mr. Dunstal.*
THOMAS	*Mr. Fearon.*
MRS. MALAPROP	*Mrs. Green.*
LYDIA LANGUISH	*Miss Barsanti.*
JULIA	*Mrs. Bulkley.*
LUCY	*Mrs. Lessingham.*

Maid, Boy, Servants, &c.

SCENE—BATH.

Time of Action—Five Hours.

PROLOGUE

By the Author

SPOKEN BY MR. WOODWARD AND MR. QUICK

Enter SERJEANT-AT-LAW, *and* ATTORNEY *following, and giving
a paper.*

Serj. What's here!—a vile cramp hand! I cannot see
Without my spectacles.
Att. He means his fee.
Nay, Mr. Serjeant, good sir, try again.   [*Gives money.*
Serj. The scrawl improves! [*more*] O come, 'tis pretty plain.
Hey! how's this? Dibble!—sure it cannot be!
A poet's brief! a poet and a fee!
Att. Yes, sir! though you without reward, I know,
Would gladly plead the Muse's cause.
Serj. So!—So!
Att. And if the fee offends, your wrath should fall
On me.
Serj. Dear Dibble, no offence at all.
Att. Some sons of Phœbus in the courts we meet,
Serj. And fifty sons of Phœbus in the Fleet!
Att. Nor pleads he worse, who with a decent sprig
Of bays adorns his legal waste of wig.
Serj. Full-bottomed heroes thus, on signs, unfurl
A leaf of laurel in a grove of curl!
Yet tell your client, that, in adverse days,
This wig is warmer than a bush of bays.
Att. Do you, then, sir, my client's place supply,
Profuse of robe, and prodigal of tie——
Do you, with all those blushing powers of face,
And wonted bashful hesitating grace,
Rise in the court and flourish on the case.   [*Exit.*
Serj. For practice then suppose—this brief will show it,—
Me, Serjeant Woodward,—counsel for the poet.
Used to the ground, I know 'tis hard to deal
With this dread court, from whence there's no appeal;

No tricking here, to blunt the edge of law,
Or, damn'd in equity, escape by flaw:
But judgment given, your sentence must remain;
No writ of error lies—to Drury-lane!

  Yet when so kind you seem, 'tis past dispute
We gain some favour, if not costs of suit.
No spleen is here! I see no hoarded fury;—
I think I never faced a milder jury!
Sad else our plight! where frowns are transportation,
A hiss the gallows, and a groan damnation!
But such the public candour, without fear
My client waives all right of challenge here.
No newsman from our session is dismiss'd,
Nor wit nor critic we scratch off the list;
His faults can never hurt another's ease,
His crime, at worst, a bad attempt to please:
Thus, all respecting, he appeals to all,
And by the general voice will stand or fall.

PROLOGUE

By the Author

SPOKEN ON THE TENTH NIGHT, BY MRS. BULKLEY

GRANTED our cause, our suit and trial o'er,
The worthy serjeant need appear no more:
In pleasing I a different client choose,
He served the Poet—I would serve the Muse.
Like him, I'll try to merit your applause,
A female counsel in a female's cause.

  Look on this form,[1]—where humour, quaint and sly,
Dimples the cheek, and points the beaming eye;
Where gay invention seems to boast its wiles
In amorous hint, and half-triumphant smiles;
While her light mask or covers satire's strokes,
Or hides the conscious blush her wit provokes.
Look on her well—does she seem form'd to teach?
Should you expect to hear this lady preach?
Is grey experience suited to her youth?
Do solemn sentiments become that mouth?
Bid her be grave, those lips should rebel prove

[1] Pointing to the figure of Comedy.

To every theme that slanders mirth or love.
  Yet, thus adorn'd with every graceful art
To charm the fancy and yet reach the heart——
Must we displace her, and instead advance
The goddess of the woful countenance—
The sentimental Muse?—Her emblems view,
The Pilgrim's Progress, and a sprig of rue!
View her—too chaste to look like flesh and blood—
Primly portray'd on emblematic wood!
There, fix'd in usurpation, should she stand,
She'll snatch the dagger from her sister's hand:
And having made her votaries weep a flood,
Good heaven! she'll end her comedies in blood—
Bid Harry Woodward break poor Dunstal's crown,
Imprison Quick, and knock Ned Shuter down;
While sad Barsanti, weeping o'er the scene,
Shall stab herself—or poison Mrs. Green.
  Such dire encroachments to prevent in time,
Demands the critic's voice—the poet's rhyme.
Can our light scenes add strength to holy laws!
Such puny patronage but hurts the cause:
Fair virtue scorns our feeble aid to ask;
And moral truth disdains the trickster's mask.
For here their favourite stands,[1] whose brow, severe
And sad, claims youth's respect, and pity's tear;
Who, when oppress'd by foes her worth creates,
Can point a poniard at the guilt she hates.

[1] Pointing to Tragedy.

THE RIVALS

ACT I

SCENE I.—*A Street*

Enter THOMAS; *he crosses the Stage;* FAG *follows, looking after him.*

Fag. What! Thomas! Sure 'tis he?—What! Thomas! Thomas!

Thos. Hey!—Odd's life! Mr. Fag!—give us your hand, my old fellow-servant.

Fag. Excuse my glove, Thomas:—I'm devilish glad to see you, my lad. Why, my prince of charioteers, you look as hearty!—but who the deuce thought of seeing you in Bath?

Thos. Sure, master, Madam Julia, Harry, Mrs. Kate, and the postilion, be all come.

Fag. Indeed!

Thos. Ay, master thought another fit of the gout was coming to make him a visit; so he'd a mind to gi't the slip, and whip! we were all off at an hour's warning.

Fag. Ay, ay, hasty in everything, or it would not be Sir Anthony Absolute!

Thos. But tell us, Mr. Fag, how does young master? Odd! Sir Anthony will stare to see the captain here!

Fag. I do not serve Captain Absolute now.

Thos. Why sure!

Fag. At present I am employed by Ensign Beverley.

Thos. I doubt, Mr. Fag, you ha'n't changed for the better.

Fag. I have not changed, Thomas.

Thos. No! Why didn't you say you had left young master?

Fag. No.—Well, honest Thomas, I must puzzle you no farther: —briefly then—Captain Absolute and Ensign Beverley are one and the same person.

Thos. The devil they are!

Fag. So it is indeed, Thomas; and the ensign half of my master being on guard at present—the captain has nothing to do with me.

Thos. So, so!—What, this is some freak, I warrant!—Do tell us, Mr. Fag, the meaning o't—you know I ha' trusted you.

Fag. You'll be secret, Thomas?

Thos. As a coach-horse.

Fag. Why then the cause of all this is—Love,—Love, Thomas, who (as you may get read to you) has been a masquerader ever since the days of Jupiter.

Thos. Ay, ay;—I guessed there was a lady in the case:—but pray, why does your master pass only for an ensign?—Now if he had shammed general indeed——

Fag. Ah! Thomas, there lies the mystery o' the matter. Hark'ee, Thomas, my master is in love with a lady of a very singular taste: a lady who likes him better as a half-pay ensign than if she knew he was son and heir to Sir Anthony Absolute, a baronet of three thousand a year.

Thos. That is an odd taste indeed!—But has she got the stuff, Mr. Fag? Is she rich, hey?

Fag. Rich!—Why, I believe she owns half the stocks! Zounds! Thomas, she could pay the national debt as easily as I could my washerwoman! She has a lap-dog that eats out of gold,—she feeds her parrot with small pearls,—and all her thread-papers are made of bank-notes!

Thos. Bravo, faith!—Odd! I warrant she has a set of thousands at least:—but does she draw kindly with the captain?

Fag. As fond as pigeons.

Thos. May one hear her name?

Fag. Miss Lydia Languish.—But there is an old tough aunt in the way; though, by-the-by, she has never seen my master—for we got acquainted with miss while on a visit in Gloucestershire.

Thos. Well—I wish they were once harnessed together in matrimony.—But pray, Mr. Fag, what kind of a place is this Bath?— I ha' heard a deal of it—here's a mort o' merry-making, hey?

Fag. Pretty well, Thomas, pretty well—'tis a good lounge; in the morning we go to the pump-room (though neither my master nor I drink the waters); after breakfast we saunter on the parades, or play a game at billiards; at night we dance; but damn the place, I'm tired of it: their regular hours stupefy me—not a fiddle nor a card after eleven!—However Mr. Faulkland's gentleman and I keep it up a little in private parties;—I'll introduce you there, Thomas—you'll like him much.

Thos. Sure I know Mr. Du-Peigne—you know his master is to marry Madam Julia.

Fag. I had forgot.—But, Thomas, you must polish a little— indeed you must.—Here now—this wig! What the devil do you do with a wig, Thomas?—None of the London whips of any degree of *ton* wear wigs now.

Thos. More's the pity! more's the pity! I say.—Odd's life!

when I heard how the lawyers and doctors had took to their own hair, I thought how 'twould go next:—odd rabbit it! when the fashion had got foot on the bar, I guessed 'twould mount to the box!—but 'tis all out of character, believe me, Mr. Fag: and look'ee, I'll never gi' up mine—the lawyers and doctors may do as they will.

Fag. Well, Thomas, we'll not quarrel about that.

Thos. Why, bless you, the gentlemen of the professions ben't all of a mind—for in our village now, thoff Jack Gauge, the exciseman, has ta'en to his carrots, there's little Dick the farrier swears he'll never forsake his bob, though all the college should appear with their own heads!

Fag. Indeed! well said, Dick!—but hold—mark! mark! Thomas.

Thos. Zooks! 'tis the captain.—Is that the Lady with him?

Fag. No no, that is Madam Lucy, my master's mistress's maid. They lodge at that house—but I must after him to tell him the news.

Thos. Odd! he's given her money!—Well, Mr. Fag——

Fag. Good-bye, Thomas. I have an appointment in Gyde's porch this evening at eight; meet me there, and we'll make a little party.

[*Exeunt severally.*

SCENE II.—*A Dressing-room in* MRS. MALAPROP'S *Lodgings*

LYDIA *sitting on a sofa, with a book in her hand.* LUCY, *as just returned from a message.*

Lucy. Indeed, ma'am, I traversed half the town in search of it! I don't believe there's a circulating library in Bath I han't been at.

Lyd. And could not you get *The Reward of Constancy?*

Lucy. No, indeed, ma'am.

Lyd. Nor *The Fatal Connexion?*

Lucy, No, indeed, ma'am.

Lyd. Nor *The Mistakes of the Heart?*

Lucy. Ma'am, as ill luck would have it, Mr. Bull said Miss Sukey Saunter had just fetched it away.

Lyd. Heigh-ho! Did you inquire for *The Delicate Distress?*

Lucy. Or, *The Memoirs of Lady Woodford?* Yes, indeed, ma'am. I asked everywhere for it; and I might have brought it from Mr. Frederick's, but Lady Slattern Lounger, who had just sent it home, had so soiled and dog's-eared it, it wa'n't fit for a Christian to read.

Lyd. Heigh-ho! Yes, I always know when Lady Slattern has been before me. She has a most observing thumb; and, I believe, cherishes her nails for the convenience of making marginal notes.—Well, child, what have you brought me?

Lucy. Oh! here, ma'am.—[*Taking books from under her cloak and from her pockets.*] This is *The Gordian Knot,*—and this *Peregrine Pickle.* Here are *The Tears of Sensibility,* and *Humphrey Clinker.* This is *The Memoirs of a Lady of Quality, written by Herself,* and here the second volume of *The Sentimental Journey.*

Lyd. Heigh-ho!—What are those books by the glass?

Lucy. The great one is only *The Whole Duty of Man,* where I press a few blonds, ma'am.

Lyd. Very well—give me the sal volatile.

Lucy. Is it in a blue cover, ma'am?

Lyd. My smelling-bottle, you simpleton!

Lucy. Oh, the drops—here, ma'am.

Lyd. Hold!—here's some one coming—quick! see who it is.—[*Exit* Lucy.] Surely I heard my cousin Julia's voice.

Re-enter Lucy.

Lucy. Lud! ma'am, here is Miss Melville.

Lyd. Is it possible?— [*Exit* Lucy.

Enter Julia.

Lyd. My dearest Julia, how delighted am I!—[*Embrace.*] How unexpected was this happiness!

Jul. True, Lydia—and our pleasure is the greater.—But what has been the matter?—you were denied to me at first!

Lyd. Ah, Julia, I have a thousand things to tell you!—But first inform me what has conjured you to Bath?—Is Sir Anthony here?

Jul. He is—we are arrived within this hour—and I suppose he will be here to wait on Mrs. Malaprop as soon as he is dressed.

Lyd. Then before we are interrupted, let me impart to you some of my distress!—I know your gentle nature will sympathize with me, though your prudence may condemn me! My letters have informed you of my whole connection with Beverley; but I have lost him, Julia! My aunt has discovered our intercourse by a note she intercepted, and has confined me ever since! Yet, would you believe it? she has absolutely fallen in love with a tall Irish baronet she met one night since she has been here, at Lady Macshuffle's rout.

Jul. You jest, Lydia!

Lyd. No, upon my word.—She really carries on a kind of correspondence with him, under a feigned name though, till she chooses to be known to him: but it is a Delia or a Celia, I assure you.

Jul. Then, surely, she is now more indulgent to her niece.

Lyd. Quite the contrary. Since she has discovered her own frailty, she is become more suspicions of mine. Then I must inform you of another plague! That odious Acres is to be in Bath to-day: so that I protest I shall be teased out of all spirits!

Jul. Come, come, Lydia, hope for the best—Sir Anthony shall use his interest with Mrs. Malaprop.

Lyd. But you have not heard the worst. Unfortunately I had quarrelled with my poor Beverley, just before my aunt made the discovery, and I have not seen him since to make it up.

Jul. What was his offence?

Lyd. Nothing at all! But, I don't know how it was, as often as we had been together, we had never had a quarrel, and, somehow, I was afraid he would never give me an opportunity. So, last Thursday, I wrote a letter to myself, to inform myself that Beverley was at that time paying his addresses to another woman. I signed it *your friend unknown,* showed it to Beverley, charged him with his falsehood, put myself in a violent passion, and vowed I'd never see him more.

Jul. And you let him depart so, and have not seen him since?

Lyd. 'Twas the next day my aunt found the matter out. I intended only to have teased him three days and a half, and now I've lost him for ever.

Jul. If he is as deserving and sincere as you have represented him to me, he will never give you up so. Yet, consider, Lydia, you tell me he is but an ensign, and you have thirty thousand pounds.

Lyd. But you know I lose most of my fortune if I marry without my aunt's consent, till of age; and that is what I have determined to do, ever since I knew the penalty. Nor could I love the man who would wish to wait a day for the alternative.

Jul. Nay, this is caprice!

Lyd. What, does Julia tax me with caprice? I thought her lover Faulkland had inured her to it.

Jul. I do not love even his faults.

Lyd. But àpropos—you have sent to him, I suppose?

Jul. Not yet, upon my word—nor has he the least idea of my being in Bath. Sir Anthony's resolution was so sudden, I could not inform him of it.

Lyd. Well, Julia, you are your own mistress (though under the protection of Sir Anthony), yet have you, for this long year, been a slave to the caprice, the whim, the jealousy of this ungrateful Faulkland, who will ever delay assuming the right of a husband, while you suffer him to be equally imperious as a lover.

Jul. Nay, you are wrong entirely. We were contracted before my father's death. That, and some consequent embarrassments, have delayed what I know to be my Faulkland's most ardent wish. He is too generous to trifle on such a point—and for his character, you wrong him there, too. No, Lydia, he is too proud, too noble, to be jealous; if he is captious, 'tis without dissembling; if fretful, without rudeness. Unused to the fopperies of love, he is negligent of the little duties expected from a lover—but being unhackneyed in the passion, his affection is ardent and sincere; and as it engrosses his whole soul, he expects every thought and emotion of his mistress to move in unison with his. Yet, though his pride calls for this full return, his humility makes him undervalue those qualities in him which would entitle him to it; and not feeling why he should be loved to the degree he wishes, he still suspects that he is not loved enough. This temper, I must own, has cost me many unhappy hours; but I have learned to think myself his debtor, for those imperfections which arise from the ardour of his attachment.

Lyd. Well, I cannot blame you for defending him. But tell me candidly, Julia, had he never saved your life, do you think you should have been attached to him as you are?—Believe me, the rude blast that overset your boat was a prosperous gale of love to him.

Jul. Gratitude may have strengthened my attachment to Mr. Faulkland, but I loved him before he had preserved me; yet surely that alone were an obligation sufficient.

Lyd. Obligation! why a water spaniel would have done as much!—Well, I should never think of giving my heart to a man because he could swim.

Jul. Come, Lydia, you are too inconsiderate.

Lyd. Nay, I do but jest—What's here?

Re-enter LUCY *in a hurry.*

Lucy. O ma'am, here is Sir Anthony Absolute just come home with your aunt.

Lyd. They'll not come here.—Lucy, do you watch. [*Exit* LUCY.

Jul. Yet I must go. Sir Anthony does not know I am here, and if we meet, he'll detain me, to show me the town. I'll take another opportunity of paying my respects to Mrs. Malaprop, when she shall treat me, as long as she chooses, with her select words so ingeniously misapplied, without being mispronounced.

Re-enter LUCY.

Lucy. O Lud! ma'am, they are both coming upstairs.

Lyd. Well, I'll not detain you, coz.—Adieu, my dear Julia. I'm sure you are in haste to send to Faulkland.—There, through my room you'll find another staircase.

Julia. Adieu! [*Embraces* LYDIA, *and exit.*

Lyd. Here, my dear Lucy, hide these books. Quick, quick!— Fling *Peregrine Pickle* under the toilet—throw *Roderick Random* into the closet—put *The Innocent Adultery* into *The Whole Duty of Man*—thrust *Lord Aimworth* under the sofa—cram *Ovid* behind the bolster—there—put *The Man of Feeling* into your pocket —so, so—now lay *Mrs. Chapone* in sight, and leave *Fordyce's Sermons* open on the table.

Lucy. O burn it, ma'am! the hair-dresser has torn away as far as *Proper Pride.*

Lyd. Never mind—open at *Sobriety.*—Fling me *Lord Chesterfield's Letters.* Now for 'em. [*Exit* LUCY.

Enter MRS. MALAPROP *and* SIR ANTHONY ABSOLUTE.

Mrs. Mal. There, Sir Anthony, there sits the deliberate simpleton who wants to disgrace her family, and lavish herself on a fellow not worth a shilling.

Lyd. Madam, I thought you once—

Mrs. Mal. You thought, miss! I don't know any business you have to think at all—thought does not become a young woman. But the point we would request of you is, that you will promise to forget this fellow—to illiterate him, I say, quite from your memory.

Lyd. Ah, madam! our memories are independent of our wills. It is not so easy to forget.

Mrs. Mal. But I say it is, miss; there is nothing on earth so easy as to forget, if a person chooses to set about it. I'm sure I have as much forgot your poor dear uncle as if he had never existed—and I thought it my duty so to do; and let me tell you, Lydia, these violent memories don't become a young woman.

Sir Anth. Why sure she won't pretend to remember what she's ordered not!—ay, this comes of her reading!

Lyd. What crime, madam, have I committed, to be treated thus?

Mrs. Mal. Now don't attempt to extirpate yourself from the matter; you know I have proof controvertible of it.—But tell me, will you promise to do as you're bid? Will you take a husband of your friends' choosing?

Lyd. Madam, I must tell you plainly, that had I no preference for any one else, the choice you have made would be my aversion.

Mrs. Mal. What business have you, miss, with preference and aversion? They don't become a young woman; and you ought to know, that as both always wear off, 'tis safest in matrimony to begin with a little aversion. I am sure I hated your poor dear uncle before marriage as if he'd been a blackamoor—and yet, miss, you are sensible what a wife I made!—and when it pleased Heaven to release me from him, 'tis unknown what tears I shed! But suppose we were going to give you another choice, will you promise us to give up this Beverley?

Lyd. Could I belie my thoughts so far as to give that promise, my actions would certainly as far belie my words.

Mrs. Mal. Take yourself to your room. You are fit company for nothing but your own ill-humours.

Lyd. Willingly, ma'am—I cannot change for the worse.   [*Exit.*

Mrs. Mal. There's a little intricate hussy for you!

Sir Anth. It is not to be wondered at, ma'am,—all this is the natural consequence of teaching girls to read. Had I a thousand daughters, by Heaven! I'd as soon have them taught the black art as their alphabet!

Mrs. Mal. Nay, nay, Sir Anthony, you are an absolute misanthropy.

Sir Anth. In my way hither, Mrs. Malaprop, I observed your niece's maid coming forth from a circulating library!—She had a book in each hand—they were half-bound volumes, with marble covers!—From that moment I guessed how full of duty I should see her mistress!

Mrs. Mal. Those are vile places, indeed!

Sir Anth. Madam, a circulating library in a town is as an evergreen tree of diabolical knowledge! It blossoms through the year! —and depend on it, Mrs. Malaprop, that they who are so fond of handling the leaves, will long for the fruit at last.

Mrs. Mal. Fy, fy, Sir Anthony, you surely speak laconically.

Sir Anth. Why, Mrs. Malaprop, in moderation now, what would you have a woman know?

Mrs. Mal. Observe me, Sir Anthony. I would by no means wish a daughter of mine to be a progeny of learning; I don't think so much learning becomes a young woman; for instance, I would never let her meddle with Greek, or Hebrew, or algebra, or simony, or fluxions, or paradoxes, or such inflammatory branches of learning—neither would it be necessary for her to handle any of your mathematical, astronomical, diabolical instruments.—But, Sir Anthony, I would send her, at nine years old, to a boarding-school, in order to let her learn a little ingenuity and artifice. Then, sir, she should have a supercilious knowledge in accounts;—and as she grew up, I would have her instructed in geometry, that she might know something of the contagious countries;—but above all, Sir Anthony, she should be mistress of orthodoxy, that she might not mis-spell, and mis-pronounce words so shamefully as girls usually do; and likewise that she might reprehend the true meaning of what she is saying. This, Sir Anthony, is what I would have a woman know;—and I don't think there is a superstitious article in it.

Sir Anth. Well, well, Mrs. Malaprop, I will dispute the point no further with you; though I must confess that you are a truly moderate and polite arguer, for almost every third word you say is on my side of the question. But, Mrs. Malaprop, to the more important point in debate—you say you have no objection to my proposal?

Mrs. Mal. None, I assure you. I am under no positive engagement with Mr. Acres, and as Lydia is so obstinate against him, perhaps your son may have better success.

Sir Anth. Well, madam, I will write for the boy directly. He knows not a syllable of this yet, though I have for some time had the proposal in my head. He is at present with his regiment.

Mrs. Mal. We have never seen your son, Sir Anthony; but I hope no objection on his side.

Sir Anth. Objection!—let him object if he dare!—No, no, Mrs. Malaprop, Jack knows that the least demur puts me in a frenzy directly. My process was always very simple—in their younger days, 'twas "Jack do this";—if he demurred, I knocked him down—and if he grumbled at that, I always sent him out of the room.

Mrs. Mal. Ah, and the properest way, o' my conscience!—nothing is so conciliating to young people as severity.—Well, Sir Anthony, I shall give Mr. Acres his discharge, and prepare Lydia to receive your son's invocations;—and I hope you will represent her to the captain as an object not altogether illegible.

Sir Anth. Madam, I will handle the subject prudently.—Well, I must leave you; and let me beg you, Mrs. Malaprop, to enforce this matter roundly to the girl.—Take my advice—keep a tight hand; if she rejects this proposal, clap her under lock and key;

and if you were just to let the servants forget to bring her dinner for three or four days, you can't conceive how she'd come about. [*Exit*.

Mrs. Mal. Well, at any rate, I shall be glad to get her from under my intuition. She has somehow discovered my partiality for Sir Lucius O'Trigger—sure, Lucy can't have betrayed me!—No, the girl is such a simpleton, I should have made her confess it.—Lucy!—Lucy!—[*Calls*.] Had she been one of your artificial ones, I should never have trusted her.

Re-enter LUCY.

Lucy.—Did you call, ma'am?

Mrs. Mal. Yes, girl.—Did you see Sir Lucius while you was out?

Lucy. No, indeed, ma'am, not a glimpse of him.

Mrs. Mal. You are sure, Lucy, that you never mentioned——

Lucy. Oh, gemini! I'd sooner cut my tongue out.

Mrs. Mal. Well, don't let your simplicity be imposed on.

Lucy. No, ma'am.

Mrs. Mal. So, come to me presently, and I'll give you another letter to Sir Lucius; but mind, Lucy—if ever you betray what you are entrusted with (unless it be other people's secrets to me), you forfeit my malevolence for ever, and your being a simpleton shall be no excuse for your locality. [*Exit*.

Lucy. Ha! ha! ha!—So, my dear Simplicity, let me give you a little respite.—[*Altering her manner.*] Let girls in my station be as fond as they please of appearing expert, and knowing in their trusts; commend me to a mask of silliness, and a pair of sharp eyes for my own interest under it!—Let me see to what account have I turned my simplicity lately.—[*Looks at a paper.*] For *abetting Miss Lydia Languish in a design of running away with an ensign!—in money, sundry times, twelve pound twelve; gowns, five; hats, ruffles, caps, etc., etc., numberless!—From the said ensign, within this last month, six guineas and a half.*—About a quarter's pay!—Item, *from Mrs. Malaprop, for betraying the young people to her*—when I found matters were likely to be discovered—*two guineas and a black paduasoy.*—Item, *from Mr. Acres, for carrying divers letters*—which I never delivered—*two guineas and a pair of buckles*—Item, *from Sir Lucius O'Trigger, three crowns, two gold pocket-pieces, and a silver snuff-box!*—Well done, Simplicity!—Yet I was forced to make my Hibernian believe that he was corresponding, not with the aunt, but with the niece; for though not over rich, I found he had too much pride and delicacy to sacrifice the feelings of a gentleman to the necessities of his fortune. [*Exit*.

ACT II

Scene I.—Captain Absolute's *Lodgings*

Captain Absolute *and* Fag.

Fag. Sir, while I was there, Sir Anthony came in: I told him you had sent me to inquire after his health, and to know if he was at leisure to see you.

Abs. And what did he say, on hearing I was at Bath?

Fag. Sir, in my life I never saw an elderly gentleman more astonished! He started back two or three paces, rapped out a dozen interjectural oaths, and asked what the devil had brought you here.

Abs. Well, sir, and what did you say?

Fag. Oh, I lied, sir—I forget the precise lie; but you may depend on't, he got no truth from me. Yet, with submission, for fear of blunders in future, I should be glad to fix what has brought us to Bath, in order that we may lie a little consistently. Sir Anthony's servants were curious, sir, very curious indeed.

Abs. You have said nothing to them?

Fag. Oh, not a word, sir,—not a word! Mr. Thomas, indeed, the coachman (whom I take to be the discreetest of whips)——

Abs. 'Sdeath!—you rascal! you have not trusted him!

Fag. Oh, no, sir—no—no—not a syllable, upon my veracity!— He was, indeed, a little inquisitive; but I was sly, sir—devilish sly! My master (said I), honest Thomas (you know, sir, one says honest to one's inferiors), is come to Bath to recruit.—Yes, sir, I said to recruit—and whether for men, money, or constitution, you know, sir, is nothing to him nor any one else.

Abs. Well, recruit will do—let it be so.

Fag. Oh, sir, recruit will do surprisingly—indeed, to give the thing an air, I told Thomas that your honour had already enlisted five disbanded chairmen, seven minority waiters, and thirteen billiard-markers.

Abs. You blockhead, never say more than is necessary.

Fag. I beg pardon, sir—I beg pardon—but, with submission, a lie is nothing unless one supports it. Sir, whenever I draw on my invention for a good current lie, I always forge indorsements as well as the bill.

Abs. Well, take care you don't hurt your credit by offering too much security.—Is Mr. Faulkland returned?

Fag. He is above, sir, changing his dress.

Abs. Can you tell whether he has been informed of Sir Anthony and Miss Melville's arrival?

Fag. I fancy not, sir; he has seen no one since he came in but his gentleman, who was with him at Bristol.—I think, sir, I hear Mr. Faulkland coming down——

Abs. Go tell him I am here.

Fag. Yes, sir.—[*Going.*] I beg pardon, sir, but should Sir Anthony call, you will do me the favour to remember that we are recruiting, if you please.

Abs. Well, well.

Fag. And, in tenderness to my character, if your honour could bring in the chairmen and waiters, I should esteem it as an obligation; for though I never scruple a lie to serve my master, yet it hurts one's conscience to be found out.   [*Exit.*

Abs. Now for my whimsical friend—if he does not know that his mistress is here, I'll tease him a little before I tell him——

Enter FAULKLAND.

Faulkland, you're welcome to Bath again; you are punctual in your return.

Faulk. Yes; I had nothing to detain me when I had finished the business I went on. Well, what news since I left you? how stand matters between you and Lydia?

Abs. Faith, much as they were; I have not seen her since our quarrel; however, I expect to be recalled every hour.

Faulk. Why don't you persuade her to go off with you at once?

Abs. What, and lose two-thirds of her fortune? You forget that, my friend.—No, no, I could have brought her to that long ago.

Faulk. Nay, then, you trifle too long—if you are sure of her, propose to the aunt in your own character, and write to Sir Anthony for his consent.

Abs. Softly, softly; for though I am convinced my little Lydia would elope with me as Ensign Beverley, yet am I by no means certain that she would take me with the impediment of our friends' consent, a regular humdrum wedding, and the reversion of a good fortune on my side: no, no; I must prepare her gradually for the discovery, and make myself necessary to her, before I risk it.—Well, but Faulkland; you'll dine with us to-day at the hotel?

Faulk. Indeed, I cannot; I am not in spirits to be of such a party.

Abs. By heavens! I shall forswear your company. You are the most teasing, captious, incorrigible lover!—Do love like a man.

Faulk. I own I am unfit for company.

Abs. Am I not a lover; ay, and a romantic one too? Yet do I carry everywhere with me such a confounded farrago of doubts, fears, hopes, wishes, and all the flimsy furniture of a country miss's brain!

Faulk. Ah! Jack, your heart and soul are not, like mine, fixed immutably on one only object. You throw for a large stake, but losing, you could stake and throw again:—but I have set my sum of happiness on this cast, and not to succeed were to be stripped of all.

Abs. But, for heaven's sake! what grounds for apprehension can your whimsical brain conjure up at present?

Faulk. What grounds for apprehension, did you say? Heavens! are there not a thousand! I fear for her spirits—her health—her life!—My absence may fret her; her anxiety for my return, her fears for me, may oppress her gentle temper: and for her health, does not every hour bring me cause to be alarmed? If it rains, some shower may even then have chilled her delicate frame! If the wind be keen, some rude blast may have affected her! The heat of noon, the dews of the evening, may endanger the life of her for whom only I value mine. O Jack! when delicate and feeling souls are separated, there is not a feature in the sky, not a movement of the elements, not an aspiration of the breeze, but hints some cause for a lover's apprehension!

Abs. Ay, but we may choose whether we will take the hint or not.—So, then, Faulkland, if you were convinced that Julia were well and in spirits, you would be entirely content?

Faulk. I should be happy beyond measure—I am anxious only for that.

Abs. Then to cure your anxiety at once—Miss Melville is in perfect health, and is at this moment in Bath.

Faulk. Nay, Jack—don't trifle with me.

Abs. She is arrived here with my father within this hour.

Faulk. Can you be serious?

Abs. I thought you knew Sir Anthony better than to be surprised at a sudden whim of this kind.—Seriously, then, it is as I tell you —upon my honour.

Faulk. My dear friend!—Hollo, Du-Peigne! my hat.—My dear Jack—now nothing on earth can give me a moment's uneasiness.

Re-enter FAG.

Fag. Sir, Mr. Acres, just arrived, is below.

Abs. Stay, Faulkland, this Acres lives within a mile of Sir Anthony, and he shall tell you how your mistress has been ever since you left her. Fag, show this gentleman up.   [*Exit* FAG.

Faulk. What, is he much acquainted in the family?

Abs. Oh, very intimate: I insist on your not going: besides, his character will divert you.

Faulk. Well, I should like to ask him a few questions.

Abs. He is likewise a rival of mine—that is, of my other self's, for he does not think his friend Captain Absolute ever saw the lady in question; and it is ridiculous enough to hear him complain to me of one Beverley, a concealed skulking rival, who——

Faulk. Hush!—he's here.

Enter ACRES.

Acres. Ha! my dear friend, noble captain, and honest Jack, how do'st thou? just arrived, faith, as you see.—Sir, your humble servant. Warm work on the roads, Jack!—Odds whips and wheels! I've travelled like a comet, with a tail of dust all the way as long as the Mall.

Abs. Ah! Bob, you are indeed an eccentric planet, but we know your attraction hither.—Give me leave to introduce Mr. Faulkland to you; Mr. Faulkland, Mr. Acres.

Acres. Sir, I am most heartily glad to see you: sir, I solicit your connections.—Hey, Jack—what, this is Mr. Faulkland, who——

Abs. Ay, Bob, Miss Melville's Mr. Faulkland.

Acres. Odso! she and your father can be but just arrived before me?—I suppose you have seen them. Ah! Mr. Faulkland, you are indeed a happy man.

Faulk. I have not seen Miss Melville yet, sir;—I hope she enjoyed full health and spirits in Devonshire?

Acres. Never knew her better in my life, sir,—never better. Odds blushes and blooms! she has been as healthy as the German Spa.

Faulk. Indeed! I did hear that she had been a little indisposed.

Acres. False, false, sir—only said to vex you: quite the reverse, I assure you.

Faulk. There, Jack, you see she has the advantage of me; I had almost fretted myself ill.

Abs. Now are you angry with your mistress for not having been sick?

Faulk. No, no, you misunderstand me: yet surely a little trifling indisposition is not an unnatural consequence of absence from those we love.—Now confess—isn't there something unkind in this violent, robust, unfeeling health?

Abs. Oh, it was very unkind of her to be well in your absence, to be sure!

Acres. Good apartments, Jack.

Faulk. Well, sir, but you were saying that Miss Melville has been so exceedingly well—what then she has been merry and gay, I suppose?—Always in spirits—hey?

Acres. Merry, odds crickets! she has been the belle and spirit of the company wherever she has been—so lively and entertaining! so full of wit and humour!

Faulk. There, Jack, there.—Oh, by my soul! there is an innate levity in woman that nothing can overcome.—What! happy, and I away!

Abs. Have done!—How foolish this is! just now you were only apprehensive for your mistress' spirits.

Faulk. Why, Jack, have I been the joy and spirit of the company?

Abs. No, indeed, you have not.

Faulk. Have I been lively and entertaining?

Abs. Oh, upon my word, I acquit you.

Faulk. Have I been full of wit and humour?

Abs. No, faith, to do you justice, you have been confoundedly stupid indeed.

Acres. What's the matter with the gentleman?

Abs. He is only expressing his great satisfaction at hearing that Julia has been so well and happy—that's all—hey, Faulkland?

Faulk. Oh! I am rejoiced to hear it—yes, yes, she has a happy disposition!

Acres. That she has indeed—then she is so accomplished—so sweet a voice—so expert at her harpsichord—such a mistress of flat and sharp, squallante, rumblante, and quiverante!—There was this time month—odds minums and crotchets! how she did chirrup at Mrs. Piano's concert!

Faulk. There again, what say you to this? you see she has been all mirth and song—not a thought of me!

Abs. Pho! man, is not music the food of love?

Faulk. Well, well, it may be so.—Pray, Mr.——, what's his damned name?—Do you remember what songs Miss Melville sung?

Acres. Not I indeed.

Abs. Stay, now, they were some pretty melancholy purling-stream airs, I warrant; perhaps you may recollect;—did she sing, *When absent from my soul's delight?*

Acres. No, that wa'n't it.

Abs. Or, *Go, gentle dales!*   [*Sings.*

Acres. Oh, no! nothing like it. Odds! now I recollect one of them—*My heart's my own, my will is free.*   [*Sings.*

Faulk. Fool! fool that I am! to fix all my happiness on such a trifler! 'Sdeath! to make herself the pipe and ballad-monger of a circle to soothe her light heart with catches and glees!—What can you say to this, sir?

Abs. Why, that I should be glad to hear my mistress had been so merry; sir.

Faulk. Nay, nay, nay—I'm not sorry that she has been happy—no, no, I am glad of that—I would not have had her sad or sick—yet surely a sympathetic heart would have shown itself even in the choice of a song—she might have been temperately healthy, and somehow, plaintively gay;—but she has been dancing too, I doubt not!

Acres. What does the gentleman say about dancing?

Abs. He says the lady we speak of dances as well as she sings.

Acres. Ay, truly, does she—there was at our last race ball——

Faulk. Hell and the devil!—There!—there—I told you so! I told you so! Oh! she thrives in my absence!—Dancing! But her whole feelings have been in opposition with mine;—I have been anxious, silent, pensive, sedentary—my days have been hours of care, my nights of watchfulness.—She has been all health! spirit! laugh! song! dance!—Oh! damned, damned levity!

Abs. For heaven's sake, Faulkland, don't expose yourself so! —Suppose she has danced, what then?—does not the ceremony of society often oblige——

Faulk. Well, well, I'll contain myself—perhaps as you say—for form sake.—What, Mr. Acres, you were praising Miss Melville's manner of dancing a minuet—hey?

Acres. Oh, I dare insure her for that—but what I was going to speak of was her country dancing. Odds swimmings! she has such an air with her!

Faulk. Now disappointment on her!—Defend this, Absolute; why don't you defend this?—Country-dances! jigs and reels! am I to blame now? A minuet I could have forgiven—I should not have minded that—I say I should not have regarded a minuet —but country-dances!—Zounds! had she made one in a cotillon —I believe I could have forgiven even that—but to be monkeyled for a night!—to run the gauntlet through a string of amorous palming puppies!—to show paces like a managed filly!—Oh, Jack, there never can be but one man in the world whom a truly modest and delicate woman ought to pair with in a country-dance; and, even then, the rest of the couples should be her great-uncles and aunts!

Abs. Ay, to be sure!—grandfathers and grandmothers!

Faulk. If there be but one vicious mind in the set, 'twill spread like a contagion—the action of their pulse beats to the lascivious movement of the jig—their quivering, warm-breathed sighs impregnate the very air—the atmosphere becomes electrical to love, and each amorous spark darts through every link of the chain!—I must leave you—I own I am somewhat flurried—and that confounded looby has perceived it.   [*Going*.

Abs. Nay, but stay, Faulkland, and thank Mr. Acres for his good news.

Faulk. Damn his news!   [*Exit*.

Abs. Ha! ha! ha! poor Faulkland five minutes since—"nothing on earth could give him a moment's uneasiness!"

Acres. The gentleman wa'n't angry at my praising his mistress, was he?

Abs. A little jealous, I believe, Bob.

Acres. You don't say so? Ha! ha! jealous of me—that's a good joke.

Abs. There's nothing strange in that, Bob! let me tell you, that sprightly grace and insinuating manner of yours will do some mischief among the girls here.

Acres. Ah! you joke—ha! ha! mischief—ha! ha! but you know I am not my own property, my dear Lydia has forestalled me. She could never abide me in the country, because I used to dress so badly—but odds frogs and tambours! I shan't take matters so here, now ancient madam has no voice in it: I'll make my old clothes know who's master. I shall straightway cashier the hunting-frock, and render my leather breeches incapable. My hair has been in training some time.

Abs. Indeed!

Acres. Ay—and tho'ff the side curls are a little restive, my hind-part takes it very kindly.

Abs. Oh, you'll polish, I doubt not.

Acres. Absolutely I propose so—then if I can find out this Ensign Beverley, odds triggers and flints! I'll make him know the difference o't.

Abs. Spoke like a man! But pray, Bob, I observe you have got an odd kind of a new method of swearing——

Acres. Ha! ha! you've taken notice of it—'tis genteel, isn't it! —I didn't invent it myself though; but a commander in our militia, a great scholar, I assure you, says that there is no meaning in the common oaths, and that nothing but their antiquity makes them respectable; because, he says, the ancients would never stick to an oath or two, but would say, by Jove! or by Bacchus! or by Mars! or by Venus! or by Pallas, according to the sentiment: so that to swear with propriety, says my little major, the oath should be an echo to the sense; and this we call the *oath referential,* or *sentimental swearing*—ha! ha! 'tis genteel, isn't it.

Abs. Very genteel, and very new, indeed!—and I dare say will supplant all other figures of imprecation.

Acres. Ay, ay, the best terms will grow obsolete.—Damns have had their day.

Re-enter FAG.

Fag. Sir, there is a gentleman below desires to see you.—Shall I show him into the parlour?

Abs. Ay—you may.

Acres. Well, I must be gone——

Abs. Stay; who is it, Fag?

Fag. Your father, sir.

Abs. You puppy, why didn't you show him up directly?

[*Exit* FAG.

Acres. You have business with Sir Anthony.—I expect a message from Mrs. Malaprop at my lodgings. I have sent also to my dear friend, Sir Lucius O'Trigger. Adieu, Jack! we must meet at night, when you shall give me a dozen bumpers to little Lydia.

Abs. That I will with all my heart.—[*Exit* ACRES.] Now for a parental lecture—I hope he has heard nothing of the business that brought me here—I wish the gout had held him fast in Devonshire, with all my soul!

Enter SIR ANTHONY ABSOLUTE.

Sir, I am delighted to see you here; looking so well! your sudden arrival at Bath made me apprehensive for your health.

Sir Anth. Very apprehensive, I dare say, Jack.—What, you are recruiting here, hey?

Abs. Yes, sir, I am on duty.

Sir Anth. Well, Jack, I am glad to see you, though I did not expect it, for I was going to write to you on a little matter of business.—Jack, I have been considering that I grow old and infirm, and shall probably not trouble you long.

Abs. Pardon, sir, I never saw you look more strong and hearty; and I pray frequently that you may continue so.

Sir Anth. I hope your prayers may be heard, with all my heart. Well, then, Jack, I have been considering that I am so strong and hearty I may continue to plague you a long time. Now, Jack, I am sensible that the income of your commission, and what I have hitherto allowed you. is but a small pittance for a lad of your spirit.

Abs. Sir, you are very good.

Sir Anth. And it is my wish, while yet I live, to have my boy make some figure in the world. I have resolved, therefore, to fix you at once in a noble independence.

Abs. Sir, your kindness overpowers me—such generosity makes the gratitude of reason more lively than the sensations even of filial affection.

Sir Anth. I am glad you are so sensible of my attention—and you shall be master of a large estate in a few weeks.

Abs. Let my future life, sir, speak my gratitude; I cannot express the sense I have of your munificence.—Yet, sir, I presume you would not wish me to quit the army?

Sir Anth. Oh, that shall be as your wife chooses.

Abs. My wife, sir!

Sir Anth. Ay, ay, settle that between you—settle that between you.

Abs. A wife, sir, did you say?

Sir Anth. Ay, a wife—why, did not I mention her before?

Abs. Not a word of her, sir.

Sir Anth. Odd so!—I mus'n't forget her though.—Yes, Jack, the independence I was talking of is by marriage—the fortune is saddled with a wife—but I suppose that makes no difference.

Abs. Sir! sir!—you amaze me!

Sir Anth. Why, what the devil's the matter with the fool? Just now you were all gratitude and duty.

Abs. I was, sir—you talked to me of independence and a fortune, but not a word of a wife.

Sir Anth. Why—what difference does that make? Odds life, sir! if you have the estate, you must take it with the live stock on it, as it stands.

Abs. If my happiness is to be the price, I must beg leave to decline the purchase.—Pray, sir, who is the lady?

Sir Anth. What's that to you, sir?—Come, give me your promise to love, and to marry her directly.

Abs. Sure, sir, this is not very reasonable, to summon my affections for a lady I know nothing of!

Sir Anth. I am sure, sir, 'tis more unreasonable in you to object to a lady you know nothing of.

Abs. Then, sir, I must tell you plainly that my inclinations are fixed on another—my heart is engaged to an angel.

Sir Anth. Then pray let it send an excuse. It is very sorry—but business prevents its waiting on her.

Abs. But my vows are pledged to her.

Sir Anth. Let her foreclose, Jack; let her foreclose; they are not worth redeeming; besides, you have the angel's vows in exchange, I suppose; so there can be no loss there.

Abs. You must excuse me, sir, if I tell you, once for all, that in this point I cannot obey you.

Sir Anth. Hark'ee, Jack;—I have heard you for some time with patience—I have been cool—quite cool; but take care—you know I am compliance itself—when I am not thwarted;—no one more easily led—when I have my own way:—but don't put me in a frenzy.

Abs. Sir, I must repeat—in this I cannot obey you.

Sir Anth. Now damn me! if ever I call you Jack again while I live!

Abs. Nay, sir, but hear me.

Sir Anth. Sir, I won't hear a word—not a word! not one word! so give me your promise by a nod—and I'll tell you what, Jack—I mean, you dog—if you don't, by——

Abs. What, sir, promise to link myself to some mass of ugliness! to——

Sir Anth. Zounds! sirrah! the lady shall be as ugly as I choose: she shall have a hump on each shoulder; she shall be as crooked as the crescent; her one eye shall roll like the bull's in Cox's Museum; she shall have a skin like a mummy, and the beard of a Jew—she shall be all this, sirrah!—yet I will make you ogle her all day, and sit up all night to write sonnets on her beauty.

Abs. This is reason and moderation indeed!

Sir Anth. None of your sneering, puppy! no grinning, jackanapes!

Abs. Indeed, sir, I never was in a worse humour for mirth in my life.

Sir Anth. 'Tis false, sir. I know you are laughing in your sleeve; I know you'll grin when I am gone, sirrah!

Abs. Sir, I hope I know my duty better.

Sir Anth. None of your passion, sir! none of your violence, if you please!—It won't do with me, I promise you.

Abs. Indeed, sir, I never was cooler in my life.

Sir Anth. 'Tis a confounded lie!—I know you are in a passion in your heart; I know you are, you hypocritical young dog! but it won't do.

Abs. Nay, sir, upon my word——

Sir Anth. So you will fly out! can't you be cool like me? What the devil good can passion do?—Passion is of no service, you impudent, insolent, overbearing reprobate!—There, you sneer again! don't provoke me!—but you rely upon the mildness of my temper—you do, you dog! you play upon the meekness of my disposition!—Yet take care—the patience of a saint may be overcome at last!—but mark! I give you six hours and a half to consider of this: if you then agree, without any condition, to do everything on earth that I choose, why—confound you! I may in time forgive you.—If not, zounds! don't enter the same hemisphere with me! don't dare to breathe the same air, or use the same light with me; but get an atmosphere and a sun of your own! I'll strip you of your commission; I'll lodge a five-and-threepence in the hands of trustees, and you shall live on the interest.—I'll disown you, I'll disinherit you, I'll unget you! and damn me! if ever I call you Jack again!

[*Exit* SIR ANTHONY.

Abs. Mild, gentle, considerate father—I kiss your hands!—What a tender method of giving his opinion in these matters Sir Anthony has! I dare not trust him with the truth.—I wonder what old wealthy hag it is that he wants to bestow on me!—Yet he married himself for love! and was in his youth a bold intriguer, and a gay companion!

Re-enter FAG.

Fag. Assuredly, sir, your father is wrath to a degree; he comes down stairs eight or ten steps at a time—muttering, growling, and thumping the banisters all the way: I and the cook's dog stand bowing at the door—rap! he gives me a stroke on the head with his cane; bids me carry that to my master; then kicking the poor turnspit into the area, damns us all, for a puppy triumvirate!—Upon my credit, sir, were I in your place, and found my father such very bad company, I should certainly drop his acquaintance.

Abs. Cease your impertinence, sir, at present.—Did you come in for nothing more?—Stand out of the way!

[*Pushes him aside, and exit.*

Fag. So! Sir Anthony trims my master; he is afraid to reply to his father—then vents his spleen on poor Fag!—When one is vexed by one person, to revenge one's self on another, who happens to come in the way, is the vilest injustice! Ah! it shows the worst temper—the basest——

Enter BOY.

Boy. Mr. Fag! Mr. Fag! your master calls you.

Fag. Well, you little dirty puppy, you need not bawl so!—The meanest disposition! the——

Boy. Quick, quick, Mr. Fag!

Fag. Quick! quick! you impudent jackanapes! am I to be

commanded by you too? you little, impertinent, insolent, kitchen-bred—— [*Exit kicking and beating him.*

SCENE II.—*The North Parade.*

Enter LUCY.

Lucy. So—I shall have another rival to add to my mistress's list—Captain Absolute. However, I shall not enter his name till my purse has received notice in form. Poor Acres is dismissed! —Well, I have done him a last friendly office, in letting him know that Beverley was here before him.—Sir Lucius is generally more punctual, when he expects to hear from his *dear Dalia,* as he calls her: I wonder he's not here!—I have a little scruple of conscience from this deceit; though I should not be paid so well, if my hero knew that Delia was near fifty, and her own mistress.

Enter SIR LUCIUS O'TRIGGER.

Sir Luc. Ha! my little ambassadress—upon my conscience, I have been looking for you; I have been on the South Parade this half hour.

Lucy. [*Speaking simply.*] O gemini! and I have been waiting for your lordship here on the North.

Sir Luc. Faith!—may be that was the reason we did not meet; and it is very comical too, how you could go out and I not see you—for I was only taking a nap at the Parade Coffee-house, and I chose the window on purpose that I might not miss you.

Lucy. My stars! Now I'd wager a sixpence I went by while you were asleep.

Sir Luc. Sure enough it must have been so—and I never dreamt it was so late, till I waked. Well, but my little girl, have you got nothing for me?

Lucy. Yes, but I have—I've got a letter for you in my pocket.

Sir Luc. O faith! I guessed you weren't come empty-handed —Well—let me see what the dear creature says.

Lucy. There, Sir Lucius. [*Gives him a letter.*

Sir Luc. [Reads.] *Sir—there is often a sudden incentive impulse in love, that has a greater induction than years of domestic combination: such was the commotion I felt at the first superfluous view of Sir Lucius O'Trigger.*—Very pretty, upon my word. *Female punctuation forbids me to say more; yet let me add, that it will give me joy infallible to find Sir Lucius worthy the last criterion of my affections.* DELIA.

Upon my conscience! Lucy, your lady is a great mistress of language. Faith, she's quite the queen of the dictionary!—for the devil a word dare refuse coming at her call—though one would think it was quite out of hearing.

Lucy. Ay, sir, a lady of her experience——

Sir Luc. Experience! what, at seventeen?

Lucy. O true, sir—but then she reads so—my stars! how she will read off hand!

Sir Luc. Faith, she must be very deep read to write this way —though she is rather an arbitrary writer too—for here are a great many poor words pressed into the service of this note, that would get their *habeas corpus* from any court in Christendom.

Lucy. Ah! Sir Lucius, if you were to hear how she talks of you!

Sir Luc. Oh, tell her I'll make her the best husband in the world, and Lady O'Trigger into the bargain!—But we must get the old gentlewoman's consent—and do everything fairly.

Lucy. Nay, Sir Lucius, I thought you wa'n't rich enough to be so nice.

Sir Luc. Upon my word, young woman, you have hit it:—I am so poor, that I can't afford to do a dirty action.—If I did not want money, I'd steal your mistress and her fortune with a great deal of pleasure.—However, my pretty girl [*Gives her money*], here's a little something to buy you a ribbon; and meet me in the evening, and I'll give you an answer to this. So, hussy, take a kiss beforehand to put you in mind. [*Kisses her.*

Lucy. O Lud! Sir Lucius—I never seed such a gemman! My lady won't like you if you're so impudent.

Sir Luc. Faith she will, Lucy!—That same—pho! what's the name of it?—modesty—is a quality in a lover more praised by the women than liked; so, if your mistress asks you whether Sir Lucius ever gave you a kiss, tell her fifty—my dear.

Lucy. What, would you have me tell a lie?

Sir Luc. Ah, then, you baggage! I'll make it a truth presently.

Lucy. For shame now! here is some one coming.

Sir Luc. Oh, faith, I'll quiet your conscience!

[*Exit humming a tune.*

Enter FAG.

Fag. So, so, ma'am! I humbly beg pardon.

Lucy. O Lud! now, Mr. Fag, you flurry one so.

Fag. Come, come, Lucy, here's no one by—so a little less simplicity, with a grain or two more sincerity, if you please.— You play false with us, madam.—I saw you give the baronet a letter.—My master shall know this—and if he don't call him out, I will.

Lucy. Ha! ha! ha! you gentlemen's gentlemen are so hasty. That letter was from Mrs. Malaprop, simpleton.—She is taken with Sir Lucius's address.

Fag. How! what tastes some people have!—Why, I suppose I have walked by her window a hundred times.—But what says our young lady? any message to my master?

Lucy. Sad news, Mr. Fag.—A worse rival than Acres! Sir Anthony Absolute has proposed his son.

Fag. What, Captain Absolute?

Lucy. Even so—I overheard it all.

Fag. Ha! ha! ha! very good, faith. Good bye, Lucy, I must away with this news.

Lucy. Well, you may laugh—but it is true, I assure you.— [*Going.*] But, Mr. Fag, tell your master not to be cast down by this.

Fag. Oh, he'll be so disconsolate!

Lucy. And charge him not to think of quarrelling with young Absolute.

Fag. Never fear! never fear!

Lucy. Be sure—bid him keep up his spirits.

Fag. We will—we will. [*Exeunt severally.*

ACT III

Scene I.—*The North Parade*

Enter Captain Absolute.

Abs. 'Tis just as Fag told me, indeed. Whimsical enough, faith. My father wants to force me to marry the very girl I am plotting to run away with! He must not know of my connection with her yet awhile. He has too summary a method of proceeding in these matters. However, I'll read my recantation instantly. My conversion is something sudden, indeed—but I can assure him it is very sincere. So, so—here he comes. He looks plaguy gruff. [*Steps aside.*

Enter Sir Anthony Absolute.

Sir Anth. No—I'll die sooner than forgive him. Die, did I say? I'll live these fifty years to plague him. At our last meeting, his impudence had almost put me out of temper. An obstinate, passionate, self-willed boy! Who can he take after? This is my return for getting him before all his brothers and sisters!—for putting him, at twelve years old, into a marching regiment, and allowing him fifty pounds a year, besides his pay, ever since! But I have done with him; he's anybody's son for me. I never will see him more, never—never—never.

Abs. [*Aside, coming forward.*] Now for a penitential face.

Sir Anth. Fellow, get out of my way.

Abs. Sir, you see a penitent before you.

Sir Anth. I see an impudent scoundrel before me.

Abs. A sincere penitent. I am come, sir, to acknowledge my error, and to submit entirely to your will.

Sir Anth. What's that?

Abs. I have been revolving, and reflecting, and considering on your past goodness, and kindness, and condescension to me.

Sir Anth. Well, sir?

Abs. I have been likewise weighing and balancing what you were pleased to mention concerning duty, and obedience, and authority.

Sir Anth. Well, puppy?

Abs. Why, then, sir, the result of my reflections is—a resolution to sacrifice every inclination of my own to your satisfaction.

Sir Anth. Why now you talk sense—absolute sense.—I never heard anything more sensible in my life. Confound you! you shall be Jack again.

Abs. I am happy in the appellation.

Sir Anth. Why, then, Jack, my dear Jack, I will now inform you who the lady really is. Nothing but your passion and violence, you silly fellow, prevented my telling you at first. Prepare, Jack, for wonder and rapture—prepare. What think you of Miss Lydia Languish?

Abs. Languish! What, the Languishes of Worcestershire?

Sir Anth. Worcestershire! no. Did you ever meet Mrs. Malaprop and her niece, Miss Languish, who came into our country just before you were last ordered to your regiment?

Abs. Malaprop! Languish! I don't remember ever to have heard the names before. Yet stay—I think I do recollect something. Languish! Languish! She squints, don't she? A little red-haired girl?

Sir Anth. Squints! A red-haired girl! Zounds! no.

Abs. Then I must have forgot; it can't be the same person.

Sir Anth. Jack! Jack! what think you of blooming, love-breathing seventeen?

Abs. As to that, sir, I am quite indifferent. If I can please you in the matter, 'tis all I desire.

Sir Anth. Nay, but, Jack, such eyes! such eyes! so innocently wild! so bashfully irresolute! not a glance but speaks and kindles some thought of love! Then, Jack, her cheeks! her cheeks, Jack! so deeply blushing, at the insinuations of her tell-tale eyes! Then, Jack, her lips! O, Jack, lips smiling at their own discretion; and if not smiling, more sweetly pouting; more lovely in sullenness.

Abs. That's she, indeed. Well done, old gentleman.   [*Aside.*

Sir Anth. Then, Jack, her neck! O Jack! Jack!

Abs. And which is to be mine, sir; the niece or the aunt?

Sir Anth. Why, you unfeeling, insensible puppy, I despise you! When I was of your age, such a description would have made me fly like a rocket! The aunt, indeed! Odds life! when I ran away with your mother, I would not have touched anything old or ugly to gain an empire.

Abs. Not to please your father, sir?

Sir Anth. To please my father! zounds! not to please—Oh, my father—odd so!—yes—yes; if my father indeed had desired —that's quite another matter. Though he wa'n't the indulgent father that I am, Jack.

Abs. I dare say not, sir.

Sir Anth. But, Jack, you are not sorry to find your mistress is so beautiful?

Abs. Sir, I repeat it—if I please you in this affair, 'tis all I desire. Not that I think a woman the worse for being handsome; but, sir, if you please to recollect, you before hinted something about a hump or two, one eye, and a few more graces of that kind—now, without being very nice, I own I should rather choose a wife of mine to have the usual number of limbs, and a limited quantity of back: and though one eye may be very agreeable, yet as the prejudice has always run in favour of two, I would not wish to affect a singularity in that article.

Sir Anth. What a phlegmatic sot it is! Why, sirrah, you're an anchorite!—a vile, insensible stock. You a soldier!—you're a walking block, fit only to dust the company's regimentals on! Odds life! I have a great mind to marry the girl myself!

Abs. I am entirely at your disposal, sir: if you should think of addressing Miss Languish yourself, I suppose you would have me marry the aunt; or if you should change your mind, and take the old lady—'tis the same to me—I'll marry the niece.

Sir Anth. Upon my word, Jack, thou'rt either a very great hypocrite, or—but, come, I know your indifference on such a subject must be all a lie—I'm sure it must—come, now—damn your demure face!—come, confess, Jack—you have been lying, ha'n't you? You have been playing the hypocrite, hey!—I'll never forgive you, if you ha'n't been lying and playing the hypocrite.

Abs. I'm sorry, sir, that the respect and duty which I bear to you should be so mistaken.

Sir Anth. Hang your respect and duty! But come along with me, I'll write a note to Mrs. Malaprop, and you shall visit the lady directly. Her eyes shall be the Promethean torch to you— come along, I'll never forgive you, if you don't come back stark mad with rapture and impatience—if you don't, egad, I will marry the girl myself! [*Exeunt.*

SCENE II.—*Julia's Dressing-Room*

FAULKLAND *discovered alone.*

Faulk. They told me Julia would return directly; I wonder she is not yet come! How mean does this captious, unsatisfied temper of mine appear to my cooler judgment! Yet I know not that I indulge it in any other point: but on this one subject, and to this one subject, whom I think I love beyond my life, I am ever ungenerously fretful and madly capricious! I am conscious of it—yet I cannot correct myself! What tender honest joy sparkled in her eyes when we met! how delicate was the warmth of her expression! I was ashamed to appear less happy —though I had come resolved to wear a face of coolness and upbraiding. Sir Anthony's presence prevented my proposed expostulations: yet I must be satisfied that she has not been so very happy in my absence. She is coming! Yes!—I know the nimbleness of her tread, when she thinks her impatient Faulkland counts the moments of her stay.

Enter JULIA.

Jul. I had not hoped to see you again so soon.

Faulk. Could I, Julia, be contented with my first welcome— restrained as we were by the presence of a third person?

Jul. O Faulkland, when your kindness can make me thus happy, let me not think that I discovered something of coldness in your first salutation.

Faulk. 'Twas but your fancy, Julia. I was rejoiced to see you —to see you in such health. Sure I had no cause for coldness?

Jul. Nay, then, I see you have taken something ill. You must not conceal from me what it is.

Faulk. Well, then—shall I own to you that my joy at hearing of your health and arrival here, by your neighbour Acres, was somewhat dampened by his dwelling much on the high spirits you had enjoyed in Devonshire—on your mirth—your singing—dancing, and I know not what! For such is my temper, Julia, that I should regard every mirthful moment in your absence as a treason to constancy. The mutual tear that steals down the cheek of parting lovers is a compact, that no smile shall live there till they meet again.

Jul. Must I never cease to tax my Faulkland with this teasing minute caprice? Can the idle reports of a silly boor weigh in your breast against my tried affections?

Faulk. They have no weight with me, Julia: No, no—I am happy if you have been so—yet only say, that you did not sing with mirth—say that you thought of Faulkland in the dance.

Jul. I never can be happy in your absence. If I wear a countenance of content, it is to show that my mind holds no doubt of my Faulkland's truth. If I seemed sad, it were to make malice triumph; and say, that I fixed my heart on one, who left me to lament his roving, and my own credulity. Believe me, Faulkland, I mean not to upbraid you, when I say, that I have often dressed sorrow in smiles, lest my friends should guess whose unkindness had caused my tears.

Faulk. You were ever all goodness to me. Oh, I am a brute, when I but admit a doubt of your true constancy!

Jul. If ever without such cause from you, as I will not suppose possible, you find my affections veering but a point, may I become a proverbial scoff for levity and base ingratitude.

Faulk. Ah! Julia, that last word is grating to me. I would I had no title to your gratitude! Search your heart, Julia; perhaps what you have mistaken for love, is but the warm effusion of a too thankful heart.

Jul. For what quality must I love you?

Faulk. For no quality! To regard me for any quality of mind or understanding, were only to esteem me. And for person—I have often wished myself deformed, to be convinced that I owe no obligation there for any part of your affection.

Jul. Where nature has bestowed a show of nice attention in the features of a man, he should laugh at it as misplaced. I have seen men, who in this vain article, perhaps, might rank above you; but my heart has never asked my eyes if it were so or not.

Faulk. Now this is not well from you, Julia—I despise person in a man—yet if you loved me as I wish, though I were an Æthiop, you'd think none so fair.

Jul. I see you are determined to be unkind! The contract which my poor father bound us in gives you more than a lover's privilege.

Faulk. Again, Julia, you raise ideas that feed and justify my doubts. I would not have been more free—no—I am proud of my restraint. Yet—yet—perhaps your high respect alone for this solemn compact has fettered your inclinations, which else had made a worthier choice. How shall I be sure, had you remained unbound in thought and promise, that I should still have been the object of your persevering love?

Jul. Then try me now. Let us be free as strangers as to what is past: my heart will not feel more liberty!

Faulk. There now! so hasty, Julia! so anxious to be free! If your love for me were fixed and ardent, you would not lose your hold, even though I wished it!

Jul. Oh! you torture me to the heart! I cannot bear it.

Faulk. I do not mean to distress you. If I loved you less I should never give you an uneasy moment. But hear me. All my fretful doubts arise from this. Women are not used to weigh and separate the motives of their affections: the cold dictates of prudence, gratitude, or filial duty, may sometimes be mistaken for the pleadings of the heart. I would not boast—yet let me say, that I have neither age, person, nor character, to found dislike on; my fortune such as few ladies could be charged with indiscretion in the match. O Julia! when love receives such countenance from prudence, nice minds will be suspicious of its birth.

Jul. I know not whither your insinuations would tend:—but as they seem pressing to insult me, I will spare you the regret of having done so.—I have given you no cause for this!

                                                   [Exit in tears.

Faulk. In tears! Stay, Julia: stay but for a moment.—The door is fastened!—Julia!—my soul—but for one moment!—I hear her sobbing!—'Sdeath! what a brute am I to use her thus! Yet stay! Ay—she is coming now:—how little resolution there is in a woman!—how a few soft words can turn them!—No, faith! —she is not coming either.—Why, Julia—my love—say but that you forgive me—come but to tell me that—now this is being too resentful. Stay! she is coming too—I thought she would—no steadiness in anything: her going away must have been a mere trick then—she sha'n't see that I was hurt by it— I'll affect indifference—[*Hums a tune; then listens.*] No— zounds! she's not coming!—nor don't intend it, I suppose.— This is not steadiness, but obstinacy! Yet I deserve it.—What, after so long an absence to quarrel with her tenderness!—'twas barbarous and unmanly!—I should be ashamed to see her now. —I'll wait till her just resentment is abated—and when I distress her so again, may I lose her for ever! and be linked instead to some antique virago, whose gnawing passions, and long hoarded spleen, shall make me curse my folly half the day and all the night.   [*Exit.*

Scene III.—Mrs. Malaprop's *Lodgings*

Mrs. Malaprop, *with a letter in her hand, and* Captain Absolute.

Mrs. Mal. Your being Sir Anthony's son, captain, would itself be a sufficient accommodation; but from the ingenuity of your appearance, I am convinced you deserve the character here given of you.

Abs. Permit me to say, madam, that as I never yet have had the pleasure of seeing Miss Languish, my principal inducement in this affair at present is the honour of being allied to Mrs. Malaprop; of whose intellectual accomplishments, elegant manners, and unaffected learning, no tongue is silent.

Mrs. Mal. Sir, you do me infinite honour! I beg, captain, you'll be seated.—[*They sit.*] Ah! few gentlemen, now-a-days, know how to value the ineffectual qualities in a woman!—few think how a little knowledge becomes a gentlewoman.—Men have no sense now but for the worthless flower of beauty!

Abs. It is but too true, indeed, ma'am;—yet I fear our ladies should share the blame—they think our admiration of beauty so great, that knowledge in them would be superfluous. Thus, like garden-trees, they seldom show fruit, till time has robbed them of more specious blossom.—Few, like Mrs. Malaprop and the orange-tree, are rich in both at once!

Mrs. Mal. Sir, you overpower me with good-breeding.—He is the very pine-apple of politeness!—You are not ignorant, captain, that this giddy girl has somehow contrived to fix her affections on a beggarly, strolling, eaves-dropping ensign, whom none of us have seen, and nobody knows anything of.

Abs. Oh, I have heard the silly affair before.—I'm not at all prejudiced against her on that account.

Mrs. Mal. You are very good and very considerate, captain. I am sure I have done everything in my power since I exploded the affair; long ago I laid my positive conjunctions on her, never to think on the fellow again;—I have since laid Sir Anthony's preposition before her; but, I am sorry to say, she seems resolved to decline every particle that I enjoin her.

Abs. It must be very distressing, indeed, ma'am.

Mrs. Mal. Oh! it gives me the hydrostatics to such a degree.

—I thought she had persisted from corresponding with him; but, behold, this very day, I have interceded another letter from the fellow; I believe I have it in my pocket.

Abs. Oh, the devil; my last note. [*Aside.*

Mrs. Mal. Ay, here it is.

Abs. Ay, my note indeed! Oh, the little traitress Lucy. [*Aside.*

Mrs. Mal. There, perhaps you may know the writing.

[*Gives him the letter.*

Abs. I think I have seen the hand before—yes, I certainly must have seen this hand before——

Mrs. Mal. Nay, but read it, captain.

Abs. [Reads.] *My soul's idol, my adored Lydia!*—Very tender, indeed!

Mrs. Mal. Tender, ay, and profane too, o' my conscience.

Abs. [Reads.] *I am excessively alarmed at the intelligence you send me, the more so as my new rival*——

Mrs. Mal. That's you, sir.

Abs. [Reads.] *Has universally the character of being an accomplished gentleman and a man of honour.*—Well, that's handsome enough.

Mrs. Mal. Oh, the fellow has some design in writing so.

Abs. That he had, I'll answer for him, ma'am.

Mrs. Mal. But go on, sir—you'll see presently.

Abs. [Reads.] *As for the old weather-beaten she-dragon who guards you.*—Who can he mean by that?

Mrs. Mal. Me, sir!—me!—he means me!—There—what do you think now?—but go on a little further.

Abs. Impudent scoundrel!—[Reads.] *it shall go hard but I will elude her vigilance, as I am told that the same ridiculous vanity, which makes her dress up her coarse features, and deck her dull chat with hard words which she don't understand*——

Mrs. Mal. There, sir, an attack upon my language! what do you think of that?—an aspersion upon my parts of speech! was ever such a brute! Sure, if I reprehend any thing in this world it is the use of my oracular tongue, and a nice derangement of epitaphs!

Abs. He deserves to be hanged and quartered! let me see— [Reads.] *same ridiculous vanity*——

Mrs. Mal. You need not read it again, sir.

Abs. I beg pardon, ma'am.—[Reads.] *does also lay her open to the grossest deceptions from flattery and pretended admiration* —an impudent coxcomb!—*so that I have a scheme to see you shortly with the old harridan's consent, and even to make her a go-between in our interview.*—Was ever such assurance!

Mrs. Mal. Did you ever hear anything like it?—he'll elude my vigilance, will he?—Yes, yes! ha! ha! he's very likely to enter these doors;—we'll try who can plot best!

Abs. So we will, ma'am—so we will! Ha! ha! ha! a conceited puppy, ha! ha! ha!—Well, but, Mrs. Malaprop, as the girl seems so infatuated by this fellow, suppose you were to wink at her corresponding with him for a little time—let her even plot an elopement with him—then do you connive at her escape—while I, just in the nick, will have the fellow laid by the heels, and fairly contrive to carry her off in his stead.

Mrs. Mal. I am delighted with the scheme; never was anything better perpetrated!

Abs. But, pray, could not I see the lady for a few minutes now?—I should like to try her temper a little.

Mrs. Mal. Why, I don't know—I doubt she is not prepared for a visit of this kind. There is a decorum in these matters.

Abs. O Lord! she won't mind me—only tell her Beverley——

Mrs. Mal. Sir!

Abs. Gently, good tongue.   [*Aside.*

Mrs. Mal. What did you say of Beverley?

Abs. Oh, I was going to propose that you should tell her, by way of jest, that it was Beverley who was below; she'd come down fast enough then—ha! ha! ha!

Mrs. Mal. 'Twould be a trick she well deserves; besides, you know the fellow tells her he'll get my consent to see her—ha! ha! Let him if he can, I say again. Lydia, come down here!—[*Calling.*] He'll make me a go-between in their interviews!—ha! ha! ha! Come down, I say, Lydia! I don't wonder at your laughing, ha! ha! ha! his impudence is truly ridiculous.

Abs. 'Tis very ridiculous, upon my soul, ma'am, ha! ha! ha!

Mrs. Mal. The little hussy won't hear. Well, I'll go and tell her at once who it is—she shall know that Captain Absolute is come to wait on her. And I'll make her behave as becomes a young woman.

Abs. As you please, madam.

Mrs. Mal. For the present, captain, your servant. Ah! you've not done laughing yet, I see—elude my vigilance; yes, yes; ha! ha! ha!   [*Exit.*

Abs. Ha! ha! ha! one would think now that I might throw off all disguise at once, and seize my prize with security; but such is Lydia's caprice, that to undeceive were probably to lose her. I'll see whether she knows me.

[*Walks aside, and seems engaged in looking at the pictures.*
Enter LYDIA.

Lyd. What a scene am I now to go through! surely nothing can be more dreadful than to be obliged to listen to the loathsome addresses of a stranger to one's heart. I have heard of girls persecuted as I am, who have appealed in behalf of their favoured lover to the generosity of his rival; suppose I were to try it—there stands the hated rival—an officer too;—but oh, how unlike my Beverley! I wonder he don't begin—truly he seems a very negligent wooer!—quite at his ease, upon my word! I'll speak first—Mr. Absolute.

Abs. Ma'am.   [*Turns round.*

Lyd. O heavens! Beverley!

Abs. Hush;—hush, my life! softly! be not surprised!

Lyd. I am so astonished; and so terrified and so overjoyed! —for Heaven's sake! how came you here?

Abs. Briefly, I have deceived your aunt—I was informed that my new rival was to visit here this evening, and contriving to have him kept away, have passed myself on her for Captain Absolute.

Lyd. O charming! And she really takes you for young Absolute.

Abs. Oh, she's convinced of it.

Lyd. Ha! Ha! ha! I can't forbear laughing to think how her sagacity is overreached!

Abs. But we trifle with our precious moments—such another opportunity may not occur; then let me conjure my kind, my condescending angel, to fix the time when I may rescue her from undeserving persecution, and with a licensed warmth plead for my reward.

Lyd. Will you then, Beverley, consent to forfeit that portion of my paltry wealth?—that burden on the wings of love?

Abs. Oh, come to me—rich only thus—in loveliness! Bring no portion to me but thy love—'twill be generous in you, Lydia,— for well you know it is the only dower your poor Beverley can repay.

Lyd. How persuasive are his words!—how charming will poverty be with him!   [*Aside.*

Abs. Ah! my soul, what a life will we then live! Love shall be our idol and support! we will worship him with a monastic strictness; abjuring all worldly toys, to centre every thought and action there. Proud of calamity, we will enjoy the wreck of wealth; while the surrounding gloom of adversity shall make the flame of our pure love show doubly bright. By Heavens! I would fling all goods of fortune from me with a prodigal hand, to enjoy the scene where I might clasp my Lydia to my bosom, and say, the world affords no smile to me but here—[*Embracing her.*] If she holds out now, the devil is in it! [*Aside.*]

Lyd. Now could I fly with him to the antipodes! but my persecution is not yet come to a crisis. [*Aside.*]

Re-enter Mrs. Malaprop, *listening.*

Mrs. Mal. I am impatient to know how the little hussy deports herself. [*Aside.*]

Abs. So pensive, Lydia!—is then your warmth abated?

Mrs. Mal.—Warmth abated!—so!—she has been in a passion, I suppose. [*Aside.*]

Lyd. No—nor ever can while I have life.

Mrs. Mal. An ill-tempered little devil! She'll be in a passion all her life—will she? [*Aside.*]

Lyd. Think not the idle threats of my ridiculous aunt can ever have any weight with me.

Mrs. Mal. Very dutiful, upon my word! [*Aside.*]

Lyd. Let her choice be Captain Absolute, but Beverley is mine.

Mrs. Mal. I am astonished at her assurance!—to his face—this is to his face. [*Aside.*]

Abs. Thus then let me enforce my suit. [*Kneeling.*]

Mrs. Mal. [*Aside.*] Ay, poor young man!—down on his knees entreating for pity!—I can contain no longer.—[*Coming forward.*] Why, thou vixen!—I have overheard you.

Abs. Oh, confound her vigilance! [*Aside.*]

Mrs. Mal. Captain Absolute, I know not how to apologize for her shocking rudeness.

Abs. [*Aside.*] So all's safe, I find.—[*Aloud.*] I have hopes, madam, that time will bring the young lady——

Mrs. Mal. Oh, there's nothing to be hoped for from her! she's as headstrong as an allegory on the banks of Nile.

Lyd. Nay, madam, what do you charge me with now?

Mrs. Mal. Why, thou unblushing rebel—didn't you tell this gentleman to his face that you loved another better?—didn't you say you never would be his?

Lyd. No, madam—I did not.

Mrs. Mal. Good heavens! what assurance!—Lydia, Lydia, you ought to know that lying don't become a young woman!—Didn't you boast that Beverley, that stroller Beverley, possessed your heart?—Tell me that, I say.

Lyd. 'Tis true, ma'am, and none but Beverley——

Mrs. Mal. Hold!—hold, Assurance!—you shall not be so rude.

Abs. Nay, pray, Mrs. Malaprop, don't stop the young lady's speech: she's very welcome to talk thus—it does not hurt me in the least, I assure you.

Mrs. Mal. You are too good, captain—too amiably patient— but come with me, miss.—Let us see you again soon, captain— remember what we have fixed.

Abs. I shall, ma'am.

Mrs. Mal. Come, take a graceful leave of the gentleman.

Lyd. May every blessing wait on my Beverley, my loved Bev——

Mrs. Mal. Hussy! I'll choke the word in your throat!—come along—come along.

[*Exeunt severally;* Captain Absolute *kissing his hand to* Lydia—Mrs. Malaprop *stopping her from speaking.*

Scene IV.—Acres' *Lodgings*

Acres, *as just dressed, and* David.

Acres. Indeed, David—do you think I become it so?

Dav. You are quite another creature, believe me, master, by the mass! an' we've any luck we shall see the Devon monkeyrony in all the print-shops in Bath!

Acres. Dress does make a difference, David.

Dav. 'Tis all in all, I think.—Difference! why, an' you were to go now to Clod Hall, I am certain the old lady wouldn't know you: Master Butler wouldn't believe his own eyes, and Mrs. Pickle would cry, Lard presarve me! our dairy-maid would come giggling to the door, and I warrant Dolly Tester, your honour's favourite, would blush like my waistcoat.—Oons! I'll hold a gallon, there an't a dog in the house but would bark, and I question whether Phillis would wag a hair of her tail!

Acres. Ay, David, there's nothing like polishing.

Dav. So I says of your honour's boots; but the boy never heeds me!

Acres. But, David, has Mr. De-la-grace been here? I must rub up my balancing, and chasing, and boring.

Dav. I'll call again, sir.

Acres. Do—and see if there are any letters for me at the post-office.

Dav. I will.—By the mass, I can't help looking at your head!— if I hadn't been by at the cooking, I wish I may die if I should have known the dish again myself. [*Exit.*

Acres. [*Practising a dancing-step.*] Sink, slide—coupee.—Confound the first inventors of cotillons! say I—they are as bad as algebra to us country gentlemen.—I can walk a minuet easy enough when I am forced!—and I have been accounted a good stick in a country-dance.—Odds jigs and tabors! I never valued your cross-over to couple—figure in—right and left—and I'd foot it with e'er a captain in the county!—but these outlandish heathen allemandes and cotillons are quite beyond me!—I shall never prosper at 'em, that's sure—mine are true-born English legs—they don't understand their curst French lingo!—their *pas* this, and *pas* that, and *pas* t'other!—damn me!—my feet don't like to be called paws! no, 'tis certain I have most Anti-gallican toes!

Enter SERVANT.

Serv. Here is Sir Lucius O'Trigger to wait on you, sir.
Acres. Show him in.   [*Exit* SERVANT.

Enter SIR LUCIUS O'TRIGGER.

Sir Luc. Mr. Acres, I am delighted to embrace you.
Acres. My dear Sir Lucius, I kiss your hands.
Sir Luc. Pray, my friend, what has brought you so suddenly to Bath?
Acres. Faith! I have followed Cupid's Jack-a-lantern, and find myself in a quagmire at last.—In short, I have been very ill-used, Sir Lucius.—I don't choose to mention names, but look on me as on a very ill-used gentleman.
Sir Luc. Pray what is the case?—I ask no names.
Acres. Mark me, Sir Lucius, I fall as deep as need be in love with a young lady—her friends take my part—I follow her to Bath—send word of my arrival; and receive answer, that the lady is to be otherwise disposed of.—This, Sir Lucius, I call being ill-used.
Sir Luc. Very ill, upon my conscience.—Pray, can you divine the cause of it?
Acres. Why, there's the matter; she has another lover, one Beverley, who, I am told, is now in Bath.—Odds slanders and lies! he must be at the bottom of it.
Sir Luc. A rival in the case, is there?—and you think he has supplanted you unfairly?
Acres. Unfairly! to be sure he has. He never could have done it fairly.
Sir Luc. Then sure you know what is to be done!
Acres. Not I, upon my soul!
Sir Luc. We wear no swords here, but you understand me.
Acres. What! fight him?
Sir Luc. Ay, to be sure: what can I mean else?
Acres. But he has given me no provocation.

Sir Luc. Now, I think he has given you the greatest provocation in the world. Can a man commit a more heinous offence against another man than to fall in love with the same woman? Oh, by my soul! it is the most unpardonable breach of friendship.

Acres. Breach of friendship! ay, ay; but I have no acquaintance with this man. I never saw him in my life.

Sir Luc. That's no argument at all—he has the less right then to take such a liberty.

Acres. Gad, that's true—I grow full of anger, Sir Lucius!—I fire apace! Odds hilts and blades! I find a man may have a deal of valour in him, and not know it! But couldn't I contrive to have a little right on my side?

Sir Luc. What the devil signifies right, when your honour is concerned? Do you think Achilles, or my little Alexander the Great, ever inquired where the right lay? No, by my soul, they drew their broad-swords, and left the lazy sons of peace to settle the justice of it.

Acres. Your words are a grenadier's march to my heart! I believe courage must be catching! I certainly do feel a kind of valour rising as it were—a kind of courage, as I may say.—Odds flints, pans, and triggers! I'll challenge him directly.

Sir Luc. Ah, my little friend, if I had Blunderbuss Hall here, I could show you a range of ancestry, in the old O'Trigger line, that would furnish the new room; every one of whom had killed his man!—For though the mansion-house and dirty acres have slipped through my fingers, I thank heaven our honour and the family-pictures are as fresh as ever.

Acres. O, Sir Lucius! I have had ancestors too!—every man of 'em colonel or captain in the militia!—Odds balls and barrels! say no more—I'm braced for it. The thunder of your words has soured the milk of human kindness in my breast:—Zounds! as the man in the play says, *I could do such deeds!*

Sir Luc. Come, come, there must be no passion at all in the case —these things should always be done civilly.

Acres. I must be in a passion, Sir Lucius—I must be in a rage.— Dear Sir Lucius, let me be in a rage, if you love me. Come, here's pen and paper.—[*Sits down to write.*] I would the ink were red! —Indite, I say, indite!—How shall I begin? Odds bullets and blades! I'll write a good bold hand, however.

Sir Luc. Pray compose yourself.

Acres. Come—now, shall I begin with an oath? Do, Sir Lucius, let me begin with a damme.

Sir Luc. Pho! pho! do the thing decently, and like a Christian. Begin now—Sir——

Acres. That's too civil by half.

Sir Luc. To prevent the confusion that might arise——

Acres. Well——

Sir Luc. From our both addressing the same lady——

Acres. Ay, there's the reason—*same lady*—well——

Sir Luc. I shall expect the honour of your company——

Acres. Zounds! I'm not asking him to dinner.

Sir Luc. Pray be easy.

Acres. Well, then, *honour of your company*——

Sir Luc. To settle our pretensions——

Acres. Well.

Sir Luc. Let me see, ay, King's-Mead-Fields will do—*in King's-Mead-Fields.*

Acres. So, that's done—Well, I'll fold it up presently; my own crest—a hand and dagger shall be the seal.

Sir Luc. You see now this little explanation will put a stop at once to all confusion or misunderstanding that might arise between you.

Acres. Ay, we fight to prevent any misunderstanding.

Sir Luc. Now, I'll leave you to fix your own time.—Take my advice, and you'll decide it this evening if you can; then let the worst come of it, 'twill be off your mind to-morrow.

Acres. Very true.

Sir Luc. So I shall see nothing of you, unless it be by letter, till the evening.—I would do myself the honour to carry your message; but, to tell you a secret, I believe I shall have just such another affair on my own hands. There is a gay captain here, who put a jest on me lately, at the expense of my country, and I only want to fall in with the gentleman, to call him out.

Acres. By my valour, I should like to see you fight first! Odds life! I should like to see you kill him, if it was only to get a little lesson.

Sir Luc. I shall be very proud of instructing you. Well for the present—but remember now, when you meet your antagonist, do every thing in a mild and agreeable manner.—Let your courage be as keen, but at the same time as polished, as your sword.

[*Exeunt severally.*

ACT IV

Scene I.—Acres' *Lodgings*

Acres *and* David.

Dav. Then, by the mass, sir! I would do no such thing—ne'er a St. Lucius O'Trigger in the kingdom should make me fight, when

I wasn't so minded. Oons! what will the old lady say, when she hears o't?

Acres. Ah! David, if you had heard Sir Lucius!—Odds sparks and flames! he would have roused your valour.

Dav. Not he, indeed. I hates such bloodthirsty cormorants. Look'ee, master, if you wanted a bout at boxing, quarter-staff, or short-staff, I should never be the man to bid you cry off: but for your curst sharps and snaps, I never knew any good come of 'em.

Acres. But my honour, David, my honour! I must be very careful of my honour.

Dav. Ay, by the mass! and I would be very careful of it; and I think in return my honour couldn't do less than to be very careful of me.

Acres. Odds blades! David, no gentleman will ever risk the loss of his honour!

Dav. I say then, it would be but civil in honour never to risk the loss of a gentleman.—Look'ee, master, this honour seems to me to be a marvellous false friend: ay, truly, a very courtier-like servant.—Put the case, I was a gentleman (which, thank God, no one can say of me); well—my honour makes me quarrel with another gentleman of my acquaintance.—So—we fight. (Pleasant enough that!) Boh;—I kill him—(the more's my luck!) now, pray who gets the profit of it?—Why, my honour. But put the case that he kills me!—by the mass! I go to the worms, and my honour whips over to my enemy.

Acres. No, David—in that case!—odds crowns and laurels! your honour follows you to the grave.

Dav. Now, that's just the place where I could make a shift to do without it.

Acres. Zounds! David, you are a coward!—It doesn't become my valour to listen to you.—What, shall I disgrace my ancestors? —Think of that, David—think what it would be to disgrace my ancestors!

Dav. Under favour, the surest way of not disgracing them, is to keep as long as you can out of their company. Look'ee now, master, to go to them in such haste—with an ounce of lead in your brains—I should think might as well be let alone. Our ancestors are very good kind of folks; but they are the last people I should choose to have a visiting acquaintance with.

Acres. But, David, now, you don't think there is such very, very, very great danger, hey?—Odds life! people often fight without any mischief done!

Dav. By the mass, I think 'tis ten to one against you!—Oons! here to meet some lion-hearted fellow, I warrant, with his damned double-barrelled swords, and cut-and-thrust pistols! Lord bless us! it makes me tremble to think o't—Those be such desperate bloody-minded weapons! Well, I never could abide 'em!—from a child I never could fancy 'em!—I suppose there an't been so merciless a beast in the world as your loaded pistol!

Acres. Zounds! I won't be afraid!—Odds fire and fury! you shan't make me afraid.—Here is the challenge, and I have sent for my dear friend Jack Absolute to carry it for me.

Dav. Ay, i' the name of mischief, let him be the messenger.— For my part I wouldn't lend a hand to it for the best horse in your stable. By the mass! it don't look like another letter! It is, as I may say, a designing and malicious-looking letter; and I warrant smells of gun-powder like a soldier's pouch!—Oons! I wouldn't swear it mayn't go off!

Acres. Out, you poltroon! you han't the valour of a grasshopper.

Dav. Well, I say no more—'twill be sad news, to be sure, at Clod Hall! but I ha' done. How Phillis will howl when she hears of it!—Ah, poor bitch, she little thinks what shooting her master's going after! And I warrant old Crop, who has carried your honour, field and road, these ten years, will curse the hour he was born.

[*Whimpering.*

Acres. It won't do, David—I am determined to fight—so get along, you coward, while I'm in the mind.

Enter SERVANT.

Ser. Captain Absolute, sir.

Acres. Oh! show him up. [*Exit* SERVANT.

Dav. Well, Heaven send we be all alive this time to-morrow.

Acres. What's that?—Don't provoke me, David!

Dav. Good-bye, master. [*Whimpering.*

Acres. Get along, you cowardly, dastardly, croaking raven!

[*Exit* DAVID.

Enter CAPTAIN ABSOLUTE.

Abs. What's the matter, Bob?

Acres. A vile, sheep-hearted blockhead! If I hadn't the valour of St. George and the dragon to boot——

Abs. But what did you want with me, Bob?

Acres. Oh!—There—— [*Gives him the challenge.*

Abs. [*Aside.*] *To Ensign Beverley.*—So, what's going on now? —[*Aloud.*] Well, what's this?

Acres. A challenge!

Abs. Indeed! Why, you won't fight him; will you, Bob?

Acres. Egad, but I will, Jack. Sir Lucius has wrought me to it.

He has left me full of rage—and I'll fight this evening, that so much good passion mayn't be wasted.

Abs. But what have I to do with this?

Acres. Why, as I think you know something of this fellow, I want you to find him out for me, and give him this mortal defiance.

Abs. Well, give it to me, and trust me he gets it.

Acres. Thank you, my dear friend, my dear Jack; but it is giving you a great deal of trouble.

Abs. Not in the least—I beg you won't mention it.—No trouble in the world, I assure you.

Acres. You are very kind.—What it is to have a friend!—You couldn't be my second, could you, Jack?

Abs. Why no, Bob—not in this affair—it would not be quite so proper.

Acres. Well, then, I must get my friend Sir Lucius. I shall have your good wishes, however, Jack?

Abs. Whenever he meets you, believe me.

Re-enter SERVANT.

Ser. Sir Anthony Absolute is below, inquiring for the captain.

Abs. I'll come instantly.—[*Exit* SERVANT.] Well, my little hero, success attend you. [*Going.*

Acres. Stay—stay, Jack.—If Beverley should ask you what kind of a man your friend Acres is, do tell him I am a devil of a fellow—will you, Jack?

Abs. To be sure I shall. I'll say you are a determined dog—hey, Bob?

Acres. Ah, do, do—and if that frightens him, egad, perhaps he mayn't come. So tell him I generally kill a man a week; will you, Jack?

Abs. I will, I will; I'll say you are called in the country Fighting Bob.

Acres. Right—right—'tis all to prevent mischief; for I don't want to take his life if I clear my honour.

Abs. No!—that's very kind of you.

Acres. Why, you don't wish me to kill him—do you, Jack?

Abs. No, upon my soul, I do not. But a devil of a fellow, hey? [*Going.*

Acres. True, true—but stay—stay, Jack,—you may add, that you never saw me in such a rage before—a most devouring rage!

Abe. I will, I will.

Acres. Remember, Jack—a determined dog!

Abs. Ay ay, Fighting Bob! [*Exeunt severally.*

SCENE II.—MRS. MALAPROP'S *Lodgings*

MRS. MALAPROP *and* LYDIA.

Mrs. Mal. Why, thou perverse one!—tell me what you can object to him? Isn't he a handsome man?—tell me that. A genteel man? a pretty figure of a man?

Lyd. [*Aside.*] She little thinks whom she is praising!—[*Aloud.*] So is Beverley, ma'am.

Mrs. Mal. No caparisons, miss, if you please. Caparisons don't become a young woman. No! Captain Absolute is indeed a fine gentleman!

Lyd. Ay, the Captain Absolute you have seen.   [*Aside.*

Mrs. Mal. Then he's so well bred;—so full of alacrity, and adulation!—and has so much to say for himself:—in such good language, too! His physiognomy so grammatical! Then his presence is so noble! I protest, when I saw him, I thought of what Hamlet says in the play:—

> "Hesperian curls—the front of Job himself!—
> An eye, like March, to threaten at command!—
> A station, like Harry Mercury, new—"

Something about kissing—on a hill—however, the similitude struck me directly.

Lyd. How enraged she'll be presently, when she discovers her mistake!   [*Aside.*

Enter SERVANT.

Ser. Sir Anthony and Captain Absolute are below, ma'am.

Mrs. Mal. Show them up here.—[*Exit* SERVANT.] Now, Lydia, I insist on your behaving as becomes a young woman. Show your good breeding, at least, though you have forgot your duty.

Lyd. Madam, I have told you my resolution!—I shall not only give him no encouragement, but I won't even speak to, or look at him.   [*Flings herself into a chair, with her face from the door.*

Enter SIR ANTHONY ABSOLUTE *and* CAPTAIN ABSOLUTE.

Sir Anth. Here we are, Mrs. Malaprop; come to mitigate the frowns of unrelenting beauty,—and difficulty enough I had to bring this fellow.—I don't know what's the matter; but if I had not held him by force, he'd have given me the slip.

Mrs. Mal. You have infinite trouble, Sir Anthony, in the affair. I am ashamed for the cause!—[*Aside to* LYDIA.] Lydia, Lydia, rise, I beseech you!—pay your respects!

Sir Anth. I hope, madam, that Miss Languish has reflected on the worth of this gentleman, and the regard due to her aunt's choice, and my alliance.—[*Aside to* CAPTAIN ABSOLUTE.] Now, Jack, speak to her.

Abs. [*Aside.*] What the devil shall I do!—[*Aside to* SIR ANTHONY.] You see, sir, she won't even look at me whilst you are here. I knew she wouldn't! I told you so. Let me entreat you, sir, to leave us together! [*Seems to expostulate with his father.*

Lyd. [*Aside.*] I wonder I han't heard my aunt exclaim yet! sure she can't have looked at him!—perhaps the regimentals are alike, and she is something blind.

Sir Anth. I say, sir, I won't stir a foot yet!

Mrs. Mal. I am sorry to say, Sir Anthony, that my affluence over my niece is very small.—[*Aside to* LYDIA.] Turn round, Lydia: I blush for you!

Sir Anth. May I not flatter myself, that Miss Languish will assign what cause of dislike she can have to my son!—[*Aside to* CAPTAIN ABSOLUTE.] Why don't you begin, Jack?—Speak, you puppy—speak!

Mrs. Mal. It is impossible, Sir Anthony, she can have any. She will not say she has.—[*Aside to* LYDIA.] Answer, hussy! why don't you answer?

Sir Anth. Then, madam, I trust that a childish and hasty predilection will be no bar to Jack's happiness.—[*Aside to* CAPTAIN ABSOLUTE.] Zounds! sirrah! why don't you speak?

Lyd. [*Aside.*] I think my lover seems as little inclined to conversation as myself.—How strangely blind my aunt must be!

Abs. Hem! hem! madam—hem!—[*Attempts to speak, then returns to* SIR ANTHONY.] Faith! sir, I am so confounded!—and—so—so—confused!—I told you I should be so, sir—I knew it.—The—the—tremor of my passion entirely takes away my presence of mind.

Sir Anth. But it don't take away your voice, fool, does it?—Go up, and speak to her directly!

[CAPTAIN ABSOLUTE *makes signs to* MRS. MALAPROP *to leave them together.*

Mrs. Mal. Sir Anthony, shall we leave them together?—[*Aside to* LYDIA.] Ah! you stubborn little vixen!

Sir Anth. Not yet, ma'am, not yet!—[*Aside to* CAPTAIN ABSOLUTE.] What the devil are you at? unlock your jaws, sirrah, or——

Abs. [*Aside.*] Now Heaven send she may be too sullen to look round!—I must disguise my voice.—[*Draws near* LYDIA, *and speaks in a low hoarse tone.*] Will not Miss Languish lend an ear to the mild accents of true love? Will not——

Sir Anth. What the devil ails the fellow? why don't you speak out?—not stand croaking like a frog in a quinsy!

Abs. The—the—excess of my awe, and my—my—modesty quite choke me!

Sir Anth. Ah! your modesty again!—I'll tell you what, Jack, if you don't speak out directly, and glibly too, I shall be in such a rage!—Mrs. Malaprop, I wish the lady would favour us with something more than a side-front.

[Mrs. Malaprop *seems to chide* Lydia.

Abs. [*Aside.*] So all will out, I see!—[*Goes up to* Lydia, *speaks softly.*] Be not surprised, my Lydia, suppress all surprise at present.

Lyd. [*Aside.*] Heavens! 'tis Beverley's voice! Sure he can't have imposed on Sir Anthony too!—[*Looks round by degrees, then starts up.*] Is this possible?—my Beverley!—how can this be?—my Beverley?

Abs. Ah! 'tis all over.   [*Aside.*

Sir Anth. Beverley!—the devil—Beverley!—What can the girl mean?—this is my son, Jack Absolute.

Mrs. Mal. For shame, hussy! for shame! your head runs so on that fellow, that you have him always in your eyes!—beg Captain Absolute's pardon directly.

Lyd. I see no Captain Absolute, but my loved Beverley!

Sir Anth. Zounds! the girl's mad!—her brain's turned by reading.

Mrs. Mal. O' my conscience, I believe so!—What do you mean by Beverley, hussy?—You saw Captain Absolute before to-day; there he is—your husband that shall be.

Lyd. With all my soul, ma'am—when I refuse my Beverley——

Sir Anth. Oh! she's as mad as Bedlam!—or has this fellow been playing us a rogue's trick!—Come here, sirrah, who the devil are you?

Abs. Faith, sir, I am not quite clear myself; but I'll endeavour to recollect.

Sir Anth. Are you my son or not?—answer for your mother, you dog, if you won't for me.

Mrs. Mal. Ay, sir, who are you? O mercy! I begin to suspect!——

Abs. [*Aside.*] Ye powers of impudence, befriend me!—[*Aloud.*] Sir Anthony, most assuredly I am your wife's son; and that I sincerely believe myself to be yours also, I hope my duty has always shown.—Mrs. Malaprop, I am your most respectful admirer, and shall be proud to add affectionate nephew.—I need not tell my Lydia, that she sees her faithful Beverley, who, knowing the singular generosity of her temper, assumed that name and station, which has proved a test of the most disinterested love, which he now hopes to enjoy in a more elevated character.

Lyd. So!—there will be no elopement after all!　　[*Sullenly.*

Sir Anth. Upon my soul, Jack, thou art a very impudent fellow! to do you justice, I think I never saw a piece of more consummate assurance!

Abs. Oh, you flatter me, sir—you compliment—'tis my modesty, you know, sir—my modesty that has stood in my way.

Sir Anth. Well, I am glad you are not the dull, insensible varlet you pretended to be, however!—I'm glad you have made a fool of your father, you dog—I am. So this was your *penitence,* your *duty* and *obedience!*—I thought it was damned sudden!—*You never heard their names before,* not you!—*what, the Languishes of Worcestershire, hey?—if you could please me in the affair it was all you desired!*—Ah! you dissembling villain!—What!— [*Pointing to* Lydia] *she squints don't she?—a little red-haired girl!*—hey?—Why, you hypocritical young rascal!—I wonder you a'n't ashamed to hold up your head!

Abs. 'Tis with difficulty, sir.—I am confused—very much confused, as you must perceive.

Mrs. Mal. O Lud! Sir Anthony!—a new light breaks in upon me!—hey!—how! what! captain, did you write the letters then?—What—am I to thank you for the elegant compilation of *an old weather-beaten she-dragon*—hey?—O mercy!—was it you that reflected on my parts of speech?

Abs. Dear sir, my modesty will be overpowered at last, if you don't assist me.—I shall certainly not be able to stand it!

Sir Anth. Come, come, Mrs. Malaprop, we must forget and forgive;—odds life; matters have taken so clever a turn all of a sudden, that I could find in my heart to be so good-humoured! and so gallant! hey! Mrs. Malaprop!

Mrs. Mal. Well, Sir Anthony, since you desire it, we will not anticipate the past!—so mind, young people—our retrospection will be all to the future.

Sir Anth. Come, we must leave them together; Mrs. Malaprop, they long to fly into each other's arms, I warrant!—Jack, isn't the cheek as I said, hey?—and the eye, you rogue?—and the lip— hey? Come, Mrs. Malaprop, we'll not disturb their tenderness— theirs is the time of life for happiness!—*Youth's the season made for joy*—[*Sings.*]—hey!—Odds life! I'm in such spirits,—I don't know what I could not do!—Permit me, ma'am—[*Gives his hand to* Mrs. Malaprop.] Tol-de-rol—'gad, I should like to have a little fooling myself—Tol-de-rol! de-rol.

    [*Exit, singing and handing* Mrs. Malaprop.—Lydia *sits sullenly in her chair.*

Abs. [*Aside.*] So much thought bodes me no good.—[*Aloud.*] So grave, Lydia!

Lyd. Sir!

Abs. [*Aside.*] So!—egad! I thought as much!—that damned monosyllable has froze me!—[*Aloud.*] What, Lydia, now that we are as happy in our friends' consent, as in our mutual vows——

Lyd. Friends' consent indeed!   [*Peevishly.*

Abs. Come, come, we must lay aside some of our romance—a little and comfort may be endured after all. And for your fortune, the lawyers shall make such settlements as——

Lyd. Lawyers! I hate lawyers!

Abs. Nay, then, we will not wait for their lingering forms, but instantly procure the license, and——

Lyd. The license!—I hate license!

Abs. Oh, my love! be not so unkind!—thus let me entreat——

                                         [*Kneeling.*

Lyd. Psha!—what signifies kneeling, when you know I must have you?

Abs. [*Rising.*] Nay, madam, there shall be no constraint upon your inclinations, I promise you.—If I have lost your heart—I resign the rest—[*Aside.*] 'Gad, I must try what a little spirit will do.

Lyd. [*Rising.*] Then, sir, let me tell you, the interest you had there was acquired by a mean, unmanly imposition, and deserves the punishment of fraud.—What, you have been treating me like a child!—humouring my romance! and laughing, I suppose, at your success!

Abs. You wrong me, Lydia, you wrong me—only hear——

Lyd. So, while I fondly imagined we were deceiving my relations, and flattered myself that I should outwit and incense them all—behold my hopes are to be crushed at once, by my aunt's consent and approbation—and I am myself the only dupe at last!—[*Walking about in a heat.*] But here, sir, here is the picture—Beverley's picture! [*Taking a miniature from her bosom.*] which I have worn, night and day, in spite of threats and entreaties!—There, sir; [*Flings it to him.*] and be assured I throw the original from my heart as easily.

Abs. Nay, nay, ma'am, we will not differ as to that.—Here, [*Taking out a picture.*] here is Miss Lydia Languish.—What a difference!—ay, there is the heavenly assenting smile that first gave soul and spirit to my hopes!—those are the lips which sealed a vow, as yet scarce dry in Cupid's calendar! and there the half-resentful blush, that would have checked the ardour of my thanks! —Well, all that's past?—all over indeed!—There, madam—in beauty, that copy is not equal to you, but in my mind its merit over the original, in being still the same, is such—that—I cannot find it my heart to part with it.   [*Puts it up again.*

Lyd. [*Softening.*] 'Tis your own doing, sir—I— I, I suppose you are perfectly satisfied.

Abs. O, most certainly—sure, now, this is much better than being in love!—ha! ha! ha!—there's some spirit in this!—What signifies breaking some scores of solemn promises:—all that's of no consequence, you know. To be sure people will say, that miss don't know her own mind but never mind that! Or, perhaps, they may be ill-natured enough to hint, that the gentleman grew tired of the lady and forsook her—but don't let that fret you.

Lyd. There is no bearing his insolence.   [*Bursts into tears.*

Re-enter Mrs. Malaprop *and* Sir Anthony Absolute.

Mrs. Mal. Come, we must interrupt your billing and cooing awhile.

Lyd. This is worse than your treachery and deceit, you base ingrate!   [*Sobbing.*

Sir Anth. What the devil's the matter now?—Zounds! Mrs. Malaprop, this is the oddest billing and cooing I ever heard!—but what the deuce is the meaning of it?—I am quite astonished!

Abs. Ask the lady, sir.

Mrs. Mal. O mercy!—I'm quite analyzed, for my part!—Why, Lydia, what is the reason of this?

Lyd. Ask the gentleman, ma'am.

Sir Anth. Zounds! I shall be in a frenzy!—Why, Jack, you are not come out to be any one else, are you?

Mrs. Mal. Ay, sir, there's no more trick, is there?—you are not like Cerbèrus, three gentlemen at once, are you?

Abs. You'll not let me speak—I say the lady can account for this much better than I can.

Lyd. Ma'am, you once commanded me never to think of Beverley again—there is the man—I now obey you: for, from this moment, I renounce him for ever.   [*Exit.*

Mrs. Mal. O mercy! and miracles! what a turn here is—why, sure, captain, you haven't behaved disrespectfully to my niece?

Sir Anth. Ha! ha! ha!—ha! ha! ha!—now I see it. Ha! ha! ha!—now I see it—you have been too lively, Jack.

Abs. Nay, sir, upon my word——

Sir Anth. Come, no lying, Jack—I'm sure 'twas so.

Mrs. Mal. O Lud! Sir Anthony!—O fy, captain!

Abs. Upon my soul, ma'am——

Sir Anth. Come, no excuse, Jack; why, your father, you rogue, was so before you!—the blood of the Absolutes was always impatient.—Ha! ha! ha! poor little Lydia! why, you've frightened her, you dog, you have.

Abs. By all that's good, sir——

Sir Anth. Zounds! say no more, I tell you, Mrs. Malaprop shall make your peace. You must make his peace, Mrs. Malaprop:—you must tell her 'tis Jack's way—tell her 'tis all our ways—it runs in the blood of our family! Come away, Jack. Ha! ha! ha!—Mrs. Malaprop—a young villain!   [*Pushing him out.*

Mrs. Mal. O! Sir Anthony!—O fy, captain. [*Exeunt severally.*

Scene III.—*The North Parade*

Enter Sir Lucius O'Trigger.

Luc. I wonder where this Captain Absolute hides himself! Upon my conscience! these officers are always in one's way in love affairs:—I remember I might have married Lady Dorothy Carmine, if it had not been for a little rogue of a major, who ran away with her before she could get a sight of me! And I wonder too what it is the ladies can see in them to be so fond of them—unless it be a touch of the old serpent in 'em, that makes the little creatures be caught, like vipers, with a bit of red cloth. Ha! isn't this the captain coming?—faith it is!—There is a probability of succeeding about that fellow, that is mighty provoking! Who the devil is he talking to?   [*Steps aside.*

Enter Captain Absolute.

Abs. [*Aside.*] To what fine purpose I have been plotting! a noble reward for all my schemes, upon my soul!—a little gipsy!—I did not think her romance could have made her so damned absurd either. 'Sdeath, I never was in a worse humour in my life!—I could cut my own throat, or any other person's with the greatest pleasure in the world!

Sir Luc. Oh, faith! I'm in the luck of it. I never could have found him in a sweeter temper for my purpose—to be sure I'm just come in the nick! Now to enter into conversation with him, and so quarrel genteelly.—[*Goes up to* Captain Absolute.] With regard to that matter, captain, I must beg leave to differ in opinion with you.

Abs. Upon my word, then, you must be a very subtle disputant:—because, sir, I happened just then to be giving no opinion at·all.

Sir Luc. That's no reason. For give me leave to tell you, a man may think an untruth as well as speak one.

Abs. Very true, sir; but if a man never utters his thoughts, I should think they might stand a chance of escaping controversy.

Sir Luc. Then, sir, you differ in opinion with me, which amounts to the same thing.

Abs. Hark'ee, Sir Lucius; if I had not before known you to be a gentleman, upon my soul, I should not have discovered it at this interview: for what you can drive at, unless you mean to quarrel with me, I cannot conceive!

Sir Luc. I humbly thank you, sir, for the quickness of your apprehension.—[*Bowing.*] You have named the very thing I would be at.

Abs. Very well, sir; I shall certainly not balk your inclinations. —But I should be glad you would be pleased to explain your motives.

Sir Luc. Pray, sir, be easy; the quarrel is a very pretty quarrel as it stands; we should only spoil it by trying to explain it. However, your memory is very short, or you could not have forgot an affront you passed on me within this week. So, no more, but name your time and place.

Abs. Well, sir, since you are so bent on it, the sooner the better; let it be this evening—here, by the Spring Gardens. We shall scarcely be interrupted.

Sir Luc. Faith! that same interruption in affairs of this nature shows very great ill-breeding. I don't know what's the reason, but in England if a thing of this kind gets wind, people make such a pother, that a gentleman can never fight in peace and quietness. However, if it's the same to you, I should take it as a particular kindness if you'd let us meet in King's-Mead-Fields, as a little business will call me there about six o'clock, and I may despatch both matters at once.

Abs. 'Tis the same to me exactly. A little after six, then, we will discuss this matter more seriously.

Sir Luc. If you please, sir; there will be very pretty small-sword light, though it won't do for a long shot. So that matter's settled, and my mind's at ease!   [*Exit.*

Enter FAULKLAND.

Abs. Well met! I was going to look for you. O Faulkland! all the demons of spite and disappointment have conspired against me! I'm so vex'd, that if I had not the prospect of a resource in being knocked o' the head by-and-by, I should scarce have spirits to tell you the cause.

Faulk. What can you mean?—Has Lydia changed her mind?—
I should have thought her duty and inclination would now have
pointed to the same object.

Abs. Ay, just as the eyes do of a person who squints: when her
love-eye was fixed on me, t'other, her eye of duty, was finely
obliqued: but when duty bid her point that the same way, off
t'other turned on a swivel, and secured its retreat with a frown!

Faulk. But what's the resource you——

Abs. Oh, to wind up the whole, a good-natured Irishman here
has—[*Mimicking* SIR LUCIUS.] begged leave to have the pleasure
of cutting my throat; and I mean to indulge him—that's all.

Faulk. Prithee, be serious!

Abs. 'Tis fact, upon my soul! Sir Lucius O'Trigger—you know
him by sight—for some affront, which I am sure I never intended,
has obliged me to meet him this evening at six o'clock: 'tis on that
account I wished to see you; you must go with me.

Faulk. Nay, there must be some mistake, sure. Sir Lucius shall
explain himself, and I dare say matters may be accommodated.
But this evening did you say? I wish it had been any other time.

Abs. Why? there will be light enough: there will (as Sir Lucius
says) be very pretty small-sword light, though it will not do for a
long shot. Confound his long shots.

Faulk. But I am myself a good deal ruffled by a difference I
have had with Julia. My vile tormenting temper has made me treat
her so cruelly, that I shall not be myself till we are reconciled.

Abs. By heavens! Faulkland, you don't deserve her!

Enter SERVANT, *gives* FAULKLAND *a letter, and exit.*

Faulk. Oh, Jack! this is from Julia. I dread to open it! I fear
it may be to take a last leave!—perhaps to bid me return her
letters, and restore——Oh, how I suffer for my folly!

Abs. Here, let me see.—[*Takes the letter and opens it.*] Ay, a
final sentence, indeed!—'tis all over with you, faith!

Faulk. Nay, Jack, don't keep me in suspense!

Abs. Hear then—[*Reads.*] *As I am convinced that my dear
Faulkland's own reflections have already upbraided him for his last
unkindness to me, I will not add a word on the subject. I wish to
speak with you as soon as possible. Yours ever and truly,* JULIA.
There's stubbornness and resentment for you!—[*Gives him the
letter.*] Why, man, you don't seem one whit happier at this!

Faulk. O yes, I am; but—but——

Abs. Confound your buts! you never hear anything that would
make another man bless himself, but you immediately damn it
with a but!

Faulk. Now, Jack, as you are my friend, own honestly—don't you think there is something forward, something indelicate, in this haste to forgive? Women should never sue for reconciliation: that should always come from us. They should retain their coldness till wooed to kindness; and their pardon, like their love, should "not unsought be won."

Abs. I have not patience to listen to you! thou'rt incorrigible! so say no more on the subject. I must go to settle a few matters. Let me see you before six, remember, at my lodgings. A poor industrious devil like me, who have toiled, and drudged, and plotted to gain my ends, and am at last disappointed by other people's folly, may in pity be allowed to swear and grumble a little; but a captious sceptic in love, a slave to fretfulness and whim, who has no difficulties but of his own creating, is a subject more fit for ridicule than compassion! [*Exit.*

Faulk. I feel his reproaches; yet I would not change this too exquisite nicety for the gross content with which he tramples on the thorns of love! His engaging me in this duel has started an idea in my head, which I will instantly pursue. I'll use it as the touchstone of Julia's sincerity and disinterestedness. If her love proves pure and sterling ore, my name will rest on it with honour; and once I've stamped it there, I lay aside my doubts for ever! But if the dross of selfishness, the alloy of pride, predominate, 'twill be best to leave her as a toy for some less cautious fool to sigh for! [*Exit.*

ACT V

Scene I.—Julia's *Dressing-Room*

Julia *discovered alone.*

Jul. How this message has alarmed me! what dreadful accident can he mean? why such charge to be alone?—O Faulkland!—how many unhappy moments—how many tears have you cost me.

Enter Faulkland.

Jul. What means this?—why this caution, Faulkland?
Faulk. Alas! Julia, I am come to take a long farewell.
Jul. Heavens! what do you mean?
Faulk. You see before you a wretch, whose life is forfeited. Nay, start not!—the infirmity of my temper has drawn all this misery on me. I left you fretful and passionate—an untoward accident drew me into a quarrel—the event is, that I must fly this kingdom instantly. O Julia, had I been so fortunate as to have called you

mine entirely, before this mischance had fallen on me, I should not so deeply dread my banishment!

Jul. My soul is opprest with sorrow at the nature of your misfortune: had these adverse circumstances arisen from a less fatal cause I should have felt strong comfort in the thought that I could now chase from your bosom every doubt of the warm sincerity of my love. My heart has long known no other guardian—I now entrust my person to your honour—we will fly together. When safe from pursuit, my father's will may be fulfilled—and I receive a legal claim to be the partner of your sorrows, and tenderest comforter. Then on the bosom of your wedded Julia, you may lull your keen regret to slumbering, while virtuous love, with a cherub's hand, shall smoothe the brow of upbraiding thought, and pluck the thorn from compunction.

Faulk. O Julia! I am bankrupt in gratitude! but the time is so pressing, it calls on you for so hasty a resolution.—Would you not wish some hours to weigh the advantages you forego, and what little compensation poor Faulkland can make you beside his solitary love?

Jul. I ask not a moment. No, Faulkland, I have loved you for yourself: and if I now, more than ever, prize the solemn engagement which so long has pledged us to each other, it is because it leaves no room for hard aspersions on my fame, and puts the seal of duty to an act of love. But let us not linger. Perhaps this delay——

Faulk. 'Twill be better I should not venture out again till dark. Yet am I grieved to think what numberless distresses will press heavy on your gentle disposition!

Jul. Perhaps your fortune may be forfeited by this unhappy act.—I know not whether 'tis so; but sure that alone can never make us unhappy. The little I have will be sufficient to support us; and exile never should be splendid.

Faulk. Ay, but in such an abject state of life, my wounded pride perhaps may increase the natural fretfulness of my temper, till I become a rude, morose companion, beyond your patience to endure. Perhaps the recollection of a deed my conscience cannot justify may haunt me in such gloomy and unsocial fits, that I shall hate the tenderness that would relieve me, break from your arms, and quarrel with your fondness!

Jul. If your thoughts should assume so unhappy a bent, you will the more want some mild and affectionate spirit to watch over and console you! one who [can,] by bearing your infirmities with gentleness and resignation, may teach you so to bear the evils of your fortune.

Faulk. Julia, I have proved you to the quick! and with this useless device I throw away all my doubts. How shall I plead to be forgiven this last unworthy effect of my restless, unsatisfied disposition?

Jul. Has no such disaster happened as you related?

Faulk. I am ashamed to own that it was pretended; yet in pity, Julia, do not kill me with resenting a fault which never can be repeated: but sealing, this once, my pardon, let me to-morrow, in the face of Heaven, receive my future guide and monitress, and expiate my past folly by years of tender adoration.

Jul. Hold, Faulkland!—that you are free from a crime, which I before feared to name, Heaven knows how sincerely I rejoice! These are tears of thankfulness for that! But that your cruel doubts should have urged you to an imposition that has wrung my heart, gives me now a pang more keen than I can express.

Faulk. By Heavens! Julia——

Jul. Yet hear me,—My father loved you, Faulkland! and you preserved the life that tender parent gave me; in his presence I pledged my hand—joyfully pledged it—where before I had given my heart. When, soon after, I lost that parent, it seemed to me that Providence had, in Faulkland, shown me whither to transfer without a pause, my grateful duty, as well as my affection; hence I have been content to bear from you what pride and delicacy would have forbid me from another. I will not upbraid you, by repeating how you have trifled with my sincerity——

Faulk. I confess it all! yet hear——

Jul. After such a year of trial, I might have flattered myself that I should not have been insulted with a new probation of my sincerity, as cruel as unnecessary! I now see it is not in your nature to be content or confident in love. With this conviction—I never will be yours. While I had hopes that my persevering attention, and unreproaching kindness, might in time reform your temper, I should have been happy to have gained a dearer influence over you; but I will not furnish you with a licensed power to keep alive an incorrigible fault, at the expense of one who never would contend with you.

Faulk. Nay, but, Julia, by my soul and honour, if after this——

Jul. But one word more.—As my faith has once been given to you, I never will barter it with another.—I shall pray for your happiness with the truest sincerity; and the dearest blessing I can ask of Heaven to send you will be to charm you from that unhappy temper, which alone has prevented the performance of our solemn engagement. All I request of you is, that you will yourself reflect upon this infirmity, and when you number up the many true delights it has deprived you of, let it not be your least regret, that it lost you the love of one who would have followed you in beggary through the world! [*Exit.*

Faulk. She's gone—for ever!—There was an awful resolution in her manner, that riveted me to my place.—O fool!—dolt!—barbarian! Cursed as I am, with more imperfections than my fellow-wretches, kind Fortune sent a heaven-gifted cherub to my aid, and, like a ruffian, I have driven her from my side!—I must now haste to my appointment. Well, my mind is tuned for such a scene. I shall wish only to become a principal in it, and reverse the tale my cursed folly put me upon forging here.—O Love!—tormentor!—fiend!—whose influence, like the moon's, acting on men of dull souls, makes idiots of them, but meeting subtler spirits, betrays their course, and urges sensibility to madness! [*Exit.*

Enter Lydia *and* Maid.

Maid. My mistress, ma'am, I know, was here just now—perhaps she is only in the next room. [*Exit.*

Lyd. Heigh-ho! Though he has used me so, this fellow runs strangely in my head. I believe one lecture from my grave cousin will make me recall him. [*Re-enter* Julia.] O Julia, I have come to you with such an appetite for consolation.—Lud! child, what's the matter with you? You have been crying!—I'll be hanged if that Faulkland has not been tormenting you.

Jul. You mistake the cause of my uneasiness!—Something has flurried me a little. Nothing that you can guess at.—[*Aside.*] I would not accuse Faulkland to a sister!

Lyd. Ah! whatever vexations you may have, I can assure you mine surpass them. You know who Beverley proves to be?

Jul. I will now own to you, Lydia, that Mr. Faulkland had before informed me of the whole affair. Had young Absolute been the person you took him for, I should not have accepted your confidence on the subject, without serious endeavour to counteract your caprice.

Lyd. So, then, I see I have been deceived by every one! But I don't care—I'll never have him.

Jul. Nay, Lydia——

Lyd. Why, is it not provoking? when I thought we were coming to the prettiest distress imaginable, to find myself made a mere Smithfield bargain of at last! There, had I projected one of the most sentimental elopements!—so becoming a disguise! —so amiable a ladder of ropes!—Conscious moon—four horses —Scotch parson—with such surprise to Mrs. Malaprop—and such paragraphs in the newspapers!—Oh, I shall die with disappointment!

Jul. I don't wonder at it [!]

Lyd. Now—sad reverse!—what have I to expect, but, after a deal of flimsy preparation, with a bishop's license, and my aunt's blessing, to go simpering up to the altar; or perhaps be cried three times in a country church, and have an unmannerly fat clerk ask the consent of every butcher in the parish to join John Absolute and Lydia Languish, spinster! Oh that I should live to hear myself called spinster!

Jul. Melancholy, indeed!

Lyd. How mortifying, to remember the dear delicious shifts I used to be put to, to gain half a minute's conversation with this fellow! How often have I stole forth, in the coldest night in January, and found him in the garden, stuck like a dripping statue! There would he kneel to me in the snow, and sneeze and cough so pathetically! he shivering with cold and I with apprehension! and while the freezing blast numbed our joints, how warmly would he press me to pity his flame, and glow with mutual ardour!—Ah, Julia, that was something like being in love.

Jul. If I were in spirits, Lydia, I should chide you only by laughing heartily at you; but it suits more the situation of my mind, at present, earnestly to entreat you not to let a man, who loves you with sincerity, suffer that unhappiness from your caprice, which I know too well caprice can inflict.

Lyd. O Lud! what has brought my aunt here?

Enter MRS. MALAPROP, FAG, *and* DAVID.

Mrs. Mal. So! so! here's fine work!—here's fine suicide, parricide, and simulation, going on in the fields! and Sir Anthony not to be found to prevent the antistrophe!

Jul. For Heaven's sake, madam, what's the meaning of this?

Mrs. Mal. That gentleman can tell you—'twas he enveloped the affair to me.

Lyd. Do, sir, will you, inform us?   [*To* FAG.

Fag. Ma'am, I should hold myself very deficient in every requisite that forms the man of breeding, if I delayed a moment to give all the information in my power to a lady so deeply interested in the affair as you are.

Lyd. But quick! quick, sir!

Fag. True, ma'am, as you say, one should be quick in divulging matters of this nature; for should we be tedious, perhaps while we are flourishing on the subject, two or three lives may be lost!

Lyd. O patience!—do, ma'am, for Heaven's sake! tell us what is the matter?

Mrs. Mal. Why, murder's the matter! slaughter's the matter! killing's the matter!—but he can tell you the perpendiculars.

Lyd. Then, prithee, sir, be brief.

Fag. Why, then, ma'am, as to murder—I cannot take upon me to say—and as to slaughter, or manslaughter, that will be as the jury finds it.

Lyd. But who, sir—who are engaged in this?

Fag. Faith, ma'am, one is a young gentleman whom I should be very sorry anything was to happen to—a very pretty behaved gentleman! We have lived much together, and always on terms.

Lyd. But who is this? who? who? who?

Fag. My master, ma'am—my master—I speak of my master.

Lyd. Heavens! What, Captain Absolute!

Mrs. Mal. Oh, to be sure, you are frightened now!

Jul. But who are with him, sir?

Fag. As the rest, ma'am, this gentleman can inform you better than I.

Jul. Do speak, friend   [*To* DAVID.

Dav. Look'ee, my lady—by the mass! there's mischief going on. Folks don't use to meet for amusement with firearms, fire-locks, fire-engines, fire-screens, fire-office, and the devil knows what other crackers beside!—This, my lady, I say, has an angry savour.

Jul. But who is there beside Captain Absolute, friend?

Dav. My poor master—under favour for mentioning him first. You know me, my lady—I am David—and my master of course is, or was, Squire Acres. Then comes Squire Faulkland.

Jul. Do, ma'am, let us instantly endeavour to prevent mischief.

Mrs. Mal. O fy! it would be very inelegant in us:—we should only participate things.

Dav. Ah! do, Mrs. Aunt, save a few lives—they are desperately given, believe me.—Above all, there is that bloodthirsty Philistine, Sir Lucius O'Trigger.

Mrs. Mal. Sir Lucius O'Trigger? O mercy! have they drawn poor little dear Sir Lucius into the scrape? Why how you stand, girl! you have no more feeling than one of the Derbyshire petrifactions!

Lyd. What are we to do, madam?

Mrs. Mal. Why, fly with the utmost felicity, to be sure, to prevent mischief!—Here, friend, you can show us the place?

Fag. If you please, ma'am, I will conduct you.—David, do you look for Sir Anthony.   [*Exit* DAVID.

Mrs. Mal. Come, girls! this gentleman will exhort us.—Come, sir, you're our envoy—lead the way, and we'll precede.

Fag. Not a step before the ladies for the world!

Mrs. Mal. You're sure you know the spot?

Fag. I think I can find it, ma'am; and one good thing is, we shall hear the report of the pistols as we draw near, so we can't well miss them;—never fear, ma'am, never fear.

[*Exeunt, he talking.*

SCENE II.—*The South Parade*

Enter CAPTAIN ABSOLUTE, *putting his sword under his great-coat.*

Abs. A sword seen in the streets of Bath would raise as great an alarm as a mad dog.—How provoking this is in Faulkland! —never punctual! I shall be obliged to go without him at last. —Oh, the devil! here's Sir Anthony! how shall I escape him?

[*Muffles up his face, and takes a circle to go off.*

Enter SIR ANTHONY ABSOLUTE.

Sir Anth. How one may be deceived at a little distance! Only that I see he don't know me, I could have sworn that was Jack! —Hey! Gad's life! it is.—Why, Jack, what are you afraid of? hey—sure I'm right. Why, Jack, Jack Absolute!

[*Goes up to him.*

Abs. Really, sir, you have the advantage of me:—I don't remember ever to have had the honour—my name is Saunderson, at your service.

Sir Anth. Sir, I beg your pardon—I took you—hey?—why, zounds! it is—Stay—[*Looks up to his face.*] So, so—your humble servant, Mr. Saunderson! Why, you scoundrel, what tricks are you after now?

Abs. Oh, a joke, sir, a joke! I came here on purpose to look for you, sir.

Sir Anth. You did! well, I am glad you were so lucky:—but what are you muffled up so for?—what's this for?—hey?

Abs. 'Tis cool, sir, isn't it?—rather chilly somehow:—but I shall be late—I have a particular engagement.

Sir Anth. Stay!—Why, I thought you were looking for me?— Pray, Jack, where is't you are going?

Abs. Going, sir?

Sir Anth. Ay, where are you going?

Abs. Where am I going?

Sir Anth. You unmannerly puppy!

Abs. I was going, sir, to—to—to—to Lydia—sir, to Lydia—

to make matters up if I could; and I was looking for you, sir, to—to—

Sir Anth. To go with you, I suppose.—Well, come along.

Abs. Oh! zounds! no, sir, not for the world!—I wished to meet with you, sir,—to—to—to—You find it cool, I'm sure, sir —you'd better not stay out.

Sir Anth. Cool!—not at all.—Well, Jack—and what will you say to Lydia?

Abs. Oh, sir, beg her pardon, humour her—promise and vow: but I detain you, sir—consider the cold air on your gout.

Sir Anth. Oh, not at all!—not at all! I'm in no hurry.—Ah! Jack, you youngsters, when once you are wounded here [*Putting his hand to* CAPTAIN ABSOLUTE's *breast.*] Hey! what the deuce have you got here?

Abs. Nothing, sir—nothing.

Sir Anth. What's this?—here's something damned hard.

Abs. Oh, trinkets, sir! trinkets!—a bauble for Lydia.

Sir Anth. Nay, let me see your taste.—[*Pulls his coat open, the sword falls.*] Trinkets! a bauble for Lydia!—Zounds! sirrah, you are not going to cut her throat, are you?

Abs. Ha! ha! ha!—I thought it would divert you, sir, though I didn't mean to tell you till afterwards.

Sir Anth. You didn't?—Yes, this is a very diverting trinket, truly!

Abs. Sir, I'll explain to you.—You know, sir, Lydia is romantic, devilish romantic, and very absurd of course: now, sir, I intend, if she refuses to forgive me, to unsheath this sword, and swear—I'll fall upon its point, and expire at her feet!

Sir Anth. Fall upon a fiddlestick's end!—why, I suppose it is the very thing that would please her.—Get along, you fool!

Abs. Well, sir, you shall hear of my success—you shall hear. —*O Lydia!—forgive me, or this pointed steel*—says I.

Sir Anth. O, booby! stay away and welcome—says she.—Get along! and damn your trinkets!　　　[*Exit* CAPTAIN ABSOLUTE.

Enter DAVID, *running.*

Dav. Stop him! stop him! Murder! Thief! Fire!—Stop fire! Stop fire!—O Sir Anthony—call! call! bid'm stop! Murder! Fire!

Sir Anth. Fire! Murder!—Where?

Dav. Oons! he's out of sight! and I'm out of breath for my part! O Sir Anthony, why didn't you stop him? why didn't you stop him?

Sir Anth. Zounds! the fellow's mad!—Stop whom? stop Jack?

Dav. Ay, the captain, sir!—there's murder and slaughter——
Sir Anth. Murder!

Dav. Ay, please you, Sir Anthony, there's all kinds of murder, all sorts of slaughter to be seen in the fields: there's fighting going on, sir—bloody sword-and-gun fighting!

Sir Anth. Who are going to fight, dunce?

Dav. Everybody that I know of, Sir Anthony:—everybody is going to fight, my poor master, Sir Lucius O'Trigger, your son, the captain——

Sir Anth. Oh, the dog! I see his tricks.—Do you know the place?

Dav. King's-Mead-Fields.

Sir Anth. You know the way?

Dav. Not an inch; but I'll call the mayor—aldermen—constables—churchwardens—and beadles—we can't be too many to part them.

Sir Anth. Come along—give me your shoulder! we'll get assistance as we go—the lying villain!—Well, I shall be in such a frenzy!—So this was the history of his trinkets! I'll bauble him!   [*Exeunt.*

SCENE III.—*King's-Mead-Fields*

Enter SIR LUCIUS O'TRIGGER *and* ACRES, *with pistols.*

Acres. By my valour! then, Sir Lucius, forty yards is a good distance. Odds levels and aims!—I say it is a good distance.

Sir Luc. Is it for muskets or small field-pieces? Upon my conscience, Mr. Acres, you must leave those things to me.—Stay now—I'll show you.—[*Measures paces along the stage.*] There now, that is a very pretty distance—a pretty gentleman's distance.

Acres. Zounds! we might as well fight in a sentry-box! I tell you, Sir Lucius, the farther he is off, the cooler I shall take my aim.

Sir Luc. Faith! then I suppose you would aim at him best of all if he was out of sight!

Acres. No, Sir Lucius; but l should think forty or eight and thirty yards——

Sir Luc. Pho! pho! nonsense! three or four feet between the mouths of your pistols is as good as a mile.

Acres. Odds bullets, no!—by my valour! there is no merit in killing him so near; do, my dear Sir Lucius, let me bring him down at a long shot—a long shot, Sir Lucius, if you love me.

Sir Luc. Well, the gentleman's friend and I must settle that.

—But tell me now, Mr. Acres, in case of an accident, is there any little will or commission I could execute for you?

Acres. I am much obliged to you, Sir Lucius, but I don't understand——

Sir Luc. Why, you may think there's no being shot at without a little risk—and if an unlucky bullet should carry a quietus with it—I say it will be no time then to be bothering you about family matters.

Acres. A quietus!

Sir Luc. For instance, now—if that should be the case—would you choose to be pickled and sent home?—or would it be the same to you to lie here in the Abbey? I'm told there is very snug lying in the Abbey.

Acres. Pickled!—Snug lying in the Abbey!—Odds tremors! Sir Lucius, don't talk so!

Sir Luc. I suppose, Mr. Acres, you never were engaged in an affair of this kind before?

Acres. No, Sir Lucius, never before.

Sir Luc. Ah! that's a pity!—there's nothing like being used to a thing. Pray now, how would you receive the gentleman's shot?

Acres. Odds files!—I've practised that—there, Sir Lucius— there. [*Puts himself in an attitude.*] A side-front, hey? Odd! I'll make myself small enough? I'll stand edgeways.

Sir Luc. Now—you're quite out—for if you stand so when I take my aim—— [*Levelling at him.*

Acres. Zounds! Sir Lucius—are you sure it is not cocked?

Sir Luc. Never fear.

Acres. But—but—you don't know—it may go off of its own head!

Sir Luc. Pho! be easy.—Well, now if I hit you in the body, my bullet has a double chance—for if it misses a vital part of your right side, t'will be very hard if it don't succeed on the left!

Acres. A vital part.

Sir Luc. But, there—fix yourself so—[*Placing him.*]—let him see the broad-side of your full front—there—now a ball or two may pass clean through your body, and never do any harm at all.

Acres. Clean through me!—a ball or two clean through me!

Sir Luc. Ay—may they—and it is much the genteelest attitude into the bargain.

Acres. Look'ee! Sir Lucius—I'd just as lieve be shot in an awkward posture as a genteel one; so, by my valour! I will stand edgeways.

Sir Luc. [*Looking at his watch.*] Sure they don't mean to disappoint us—Hah!—no, faith—I think I see them coming.

Acres. Hey!—what!—coming!——

Sir Luc. Ay.—Who are those yonder getting over the stile?

Acres. There are two of them indeed!—well—let them come—hey, Sir Lucius!—we—we—we—we—won't run.

Sir Luc. Run!

Acres. No—I say—we won't run, by my valour!

Sir Luc. What the devil's the matter with you?

Acres. Nothing—nothing—my dear friend—my dear Sir Lucius—but I—I—I don't feel quite so bold, somehow, as I did.

Sir Luc. O fy!—consider your honour.

Acres. Ay—true—my honour. Do, Sir Lucius, edge in a word or two every now and then about my honour.

Sir Luc. Well, here they're coming.   [*Looking.*

Acres. Sir Lucius—if I wa'n't with you, I should almost think I was afraid.—If my valour should leave me! Valour will come and go.

Sir Luc. Then pray keep it fast, while you have it.

Acres. Sir Lucius—I doubt it is going—yes—my valour is certainly going!—it is sneaking off!—I feel it oozing out as it were at the palms of my hands!

Sir Luc. Your honour—your honour.—Here they are.

Acres. O mercy!—now—that I was safe at Clod Hall! or could be shot before I was aware!

Enter FAULKLAND *and* CAPTAIN ABSOLUTE.

Sir. Luc. Gentlemen, your most obedient.—Hah!—what, Captain Absolute!—So, I suppose, sir, you are come here, just like myself—to do a kind office, first for your friend—then to proceed to business on your own account.

Acres. What, Jack!—my dear Jack!—my dear friend!

Abs. Hark'ee, Bob, Beverley's at hand.

Sir Luc. Well, Mr. Acres—I don't blame your saluting the gentleman civilly.—[*To* FAULKLAND.] So, Mr. Beverley, if you'll choose your weapons, the captain and I will measure the ground.

Faulk. My weapons, sir!

Acres. Odds life! Sir Lucius, I'm not going to fight Mr. Faulkland; these are my particular friends.

Sir Luc. What, sir, did you not come here to fight Mr. Acres?

Faulk. Not I, upon my word, sir.

Sir Luc. Well, now, that's mighty provoking! But I hope, Mr. Faulkland, as there are three of us come on purpose for the game, you won't be so cantankerous as to spoil the party by sitting out.

Abs. O pray, Faulkland, fight to oblige Sir Lucius.

Faulk. Nay, if Mr. Acres is so bent on the matter——

Acres. No, no, Mr. Faulkland;—I'll bear my disappointment like a Christian.—Look'ee, Sir Lucius, there's no occasion at all for me to fight; and if it is the same to you, I'd as lieve let it alone.

Sir Luc. Observe me, Mr. Acres—I must not be trifled with. You have certainly challenged somebody—and you came here to fight him. Now, if that gentleman is willing to represent him—I can't see, for my soul, why it isn't just the same thing.

Acres. Why no—Sir Lucius—I tell you, 'tis one Beverley I've challenged—a fellow, you see, that dare not show his face!—if he were here, I'd make him give up his pretensions directly!

Abs. Hold, Bob—let me set you right—there is no such man as Beverley in the case.—The person who assumed that name is before you; and as his pretensions are the same in both characters, he is ready to support them in whatever way you please.

Sir Luc.—Well, this is lucky.—Now you have an opportunity—

Acres. What, quarrel with my dear friend, Jack Absolute?—not if he were fifty Beverleys! Zounds! Sir Lucius, you would not have me so unnatural.

Sir Luc. Upon my conscience, Mr. Acres, your valour has oozed away with a vengeance!

Acres. Not in the least! Odds backs and abettors! I'll be your second with all my heart—and if you should get a quietus, you may command me entirely. I'll get you snug lying in the Abbey here; or pickle you, and send you over to Blunderbuss-hall, or anything of the kind, with the greatest pleasure.

Sir Luc. Pho! pho! you are little better than a coward.

Acres. Mind, gentlemen, he calls me a coward; coward was the word, by my valour!

Sir Luc. Well, sir?

Acres. Look'ee, Sir Lucius, 'tisn't that I mind the word coward —coward may be said in joke.—But if you had called me a poltroon, odds daggers and balls——

Sir Luc. Well, sir?

Acres. I should have thought you a very ill-bred man.

Sir Luc. Pho! you are beneath my notice.

Abs. Nay, Sir Lucius, you can't have a better second than my friend Acres.—He is a most determined dog—called in the country, Fighting Bob.—He generally kills a man a week—don't you, Bob?

Acres. Ay—at home!

Sir Luc. Well, then, captain, 'tis we must begin—so come out, my little counsellor—[*Draws his sword.*]—and ask the gentleman, whether he will resign the lady, without forcing you to proceed against him?

Abs. Come on then, sir—[*Draws.*]; since you won't let it be an amicable suit, here's my reply.

Enter SIR ANTHONY ABSOLUTE, DAVID, MRS. MALAPROP, LYDIA, *and* JULIA.

Dav. Knock 'em all down, sweet Sir Anthony; knock down my master in particular; and bind his hands over to their good behaviour!

Sir Anth. Put up, Jack, put up, or I shall be in a frenzy—how came you in a duel, sir?

Abs. Faith, sir, that gentleman can tell you better than I; 'twas he called on me, and you know, sir, I serve his majesty.

Sir Anth. Here's a pretty fellow; I catch him going to cut a man's throat, and he tells me he serves his majesty!—Zounds! sirrah, then how durst you draw the king's sword against one of his subjects?

Abs. Sir! I tell you, that gentleman called me out, without explaining his reasons.

Sir Anth. Gad! sir, how came you to call my son out, without explaining your reasons?

Sir Luc. Your son, sir, insulted me in a manner which my honour could not brook.

Sir Anth. Zounds! Jack, how durst you insult the gentleman in a manner which his honour could not brook?

Mrs. Mal. Come, come, let's have no honour before ladies—Captain Absolute, come here—How could you intimidate us so?—Here's Lydia has been terrified to death for you.

Abs. For fear I should be killed, or escape, ma'am?

Mrs. Mal. Nay, no delusions to the past—Lydia is convinced; speak, child.

Sir Luc. With your leave, ma'am, I must put in a word here: I believe I could interpret the young lady's silence. Now mark——

Lyd. What is it you mean, sir?

Sir Luc.—Come, come, Delia, we must be serious now—this is no time for trifling.

Lyd. 'Tis true, sir; and your reproof bids me offer this gentleman my hand, and solicit the return of his affections.

Abs. O! my little angel, say you so?—Sir Lucius, I perceive there must be some mistake here, with regard to the affront which you affirm I have given you. I can only say that it could not have been intentional. And as you must be convinced, that I should not fear to support a real injury—you shall now see that I am not ashamed to atone for an inadvertency—I ask your pardon.—But for this lady, while honoured with her approbation, I will support my claim against any man whatever.

Sir Anth. Well said, Jack, and I'll stand by you, my boy.

Acres. Mind, I give up all my claim—I make no pretensions to any thing in the world; and if I can't get a wife without fighting for her, by my valour! I'll live a bachelor.

Sir Luc. Captain, give me your hand: an affront handsomely acknowledged becomes an obligation; and as for the lady, if she chooses to deny her own handwriting, here——

[*Takes out letters.*

Mrs. Mal. O, he will dissolve my mystery!—Sir Lucius, perhaps there's some mistake—perhaps I can illuminate——

Sir Luc. Pray, old gentlewoman, don't interfere where you have no business.—Miss Languish, are you my Delia or not?

Lyd. Indeed, Sir Lucius, I am not.

[*Walks aside with* Captain Absolute.

Mrs. Mal. Sir Lucius O'Trigger—ungrateful as you are—I own the soft impeachment—pardon my blushes, I am Delia.

Sir Luc. You Delia—pho! pho! be easy.

Mrs. Mal. Why, thou barbarous vandyke—those letters are mine.—When you are more sensible of my benignity—perhaps I may be brought to encourage your addresses.

Sir Luc. Mrs. Malaprop, I am extremely sensible of your condescension; and whether you or Lucy have put this trick on me, I am equally beholden to you.—And, to show you I am not ungrateful, Captain Absolute, since you have taken that lady from me, I'll give you my Delia into the bargain.

Abs. I am much obliged to you, Sir Lucius; but here's my friend, Fighting Bob, unprovided for.

Sir Luc. Hah! little Valour—here, will you make your fortune?

Acres. Odds wrinkles! No.—But give me your hand, Sir Lucius, forget and forgive; but if ever I give you a chance of picking me again, say Bob Acres is a dunce, that's all.

Sir Anth. Come, Mrs. Malaprop, don't be cast down—you are in your bloom yet.

Mrs. Mal. O Sir Anthony—men are all barbarians.

[*All retire but* Julia *and* Faulkland.

Jul. [*Aside.*] He seems dejected and unhappy—not sullen; there was some foundation, however, for the tale he told me—O woman! how true should be your judgment, when your resolution is so weak!

Faulk. Julia!—how can I sue for what I so little deserve? I dare not presume—yet Hope is the child of Penitence.

Jul. Oh! Faulkland, you have not been more faulty in your unkind treatment of me than I am now in wanting inclination to resent it. As my heart honestly bids me place my weakness to the account of love, I should be ungenerous not to admit the same plea for yours.

Faulk. Now I shall be blest indeed.

Sir Anth. [*Coming forward.*] What's going on here?—So you have been quarrelling too, I warrant? Come, Julia, I never interfered before; but let me have a hand in the matter at last.—All the faults I have ever seen in my friend Faulkland seemed to proceed from what he calls the delicacy and warmth of his affection for you.—There, marry him directly, Julia; you'll find he'll mend surprisingly!   [*The rest come forward.*

Sir Luc. Come, now I hope there is no dissatisfied person, but what is content; for as I have been disappointed myself, it will be very hard if I have not the satisfaction of seeing other people succeed better.

Acres. You are right, Sir Lucius.—So, Jack, I wish you joy.—Mr. Faulkland the same.—Ladies,—come now, to show you I'm neither vexed nor angry, odds tabors and pipes! I'll order the fiddles in half an hour to the New Rooms—and I insist on your all meeting me there.

Sir Anth. 'Gad! sir, I like your spirit; and at night we single lads will drink a health to the young couples, and a husband to Mrs. Malaprop.

Faulk. Our partners are stolen from us, Jack—I hope to be congratulated by each other—yours for having checked in time the errors of an ill-directed imagination, which might have betrayed an innocent heart; and mine, for having, by her gentleness and candour, reformed the unhappy temper of one, who by it made wretched whom he loved most, and tortured the heart he ought to have adored.

Abs. Well, Jack, we have both tasted the bitters, as well as the sweets of love; with this difference only, that you always prepared the bitter cup for yourself, while I——

Lyd. Was always obliged to me for it, hey! Mr. Modesty?——But come, no more of that—our happiness is now as unalloyed as general.

Jul. Then let us study to preserve it so: and while Hope pictures to us a flattering scene of future bliss, let us deny its pencil those colours which are too bright to be lasting.—When hearts deserving happiness would unite their fortunes, Virtue would crown them with an unfading garland of modest hurtless flowers; but ill-judging Passion will force the gaudier rose into the wreath, whose thorn offends them when its leaves are dropped!

[*Exeunt omnes.*

EPILOGUE

By the Author

SPOKEN BY MRS. BULKLEY

LADIES, for you—I heard our poet say—
He'd try to coax some moral from his play:
"One moral's plain," cried I, "without more fuss;
Man's social happiness all rests on us:
Through all the drama—whether damn'd or not—
Love gilds the scene, and women guide the plot.
From every rank obedience is our due—
D'ye doubt?—The world's great stage shall prove it true

The cit, well skill'd to shun domestic strife,
Will sup abroad; but first he'll ask his wife:
John Trot, his friend, for once will do the same,
But then—he'll just step home to tell his dame.

The surly squire at noon resolves to rule,
And half the day—Zounds! madam is a fool!
Convinced at night, the vanquished victor says,
Ah, Kate! you women have such coaxing ways.

The jolly toper chides each tardy blade,
Till reeling Bacchus calls on Love for aid:
Then with each toast he sees fair bumpers swim,
And kisses Chloe on the sparkling brim!

Nay, I have heard that statesmen—great and wise—
Will sometimes counsel with a lady's eyes!
The servile suitors watch her various face,
She smiles preferment, or she frowns disgrace,
Curtsies a pension here—there nods a place.

Nor with less awe, in scenes of humbler life,
Is view'd the mistress, or is heard the wife.
The poorest peasant of the poorest soil,
The child of poverty, and heir to toil,
Early from radiant Love's impartial light
Steals one small spark to cheer this world of night:
Dear spark! that oft through winter's chilling woes
Is all the warmth his little cottage knows!

871

The wandering tar, who not for years has press'd,
The widow'd partner of his day of rest,
On the cold deck, far from her arms removed,
Still hums the ditty which his Susan loved;
And while around the cadence rude is blown,
The boatswain whistles in a softer tone.

The soldier, fairly proud of wounds and toil,
Pants for the triumph of his Nancy's smile!
But ere the battle should he list her cries,
The lover trembles—and the hero dies!
That heart, by war and honour steel'd to fear,
Droops on a sigh, and sickens at a tear!

But ye more cautious, ye nice-judging few,
Who give to beauty only beauty's due,
Though friends to love—ye view with deep regret
Our conquests marr'd, our triumphs incomplete,
Till polish'd wit more lasting charms disclose,
And judgment fix the darts which beauty throws!
In female breasts did sense and merit rule,
The lover's mind would ask no other school;
Shamed into sense, the scholars of our eyes,
Our beaux from gallantry would soon be wise;
Would gladly light, their homage to improve,
The lamp of knowledge at the torch of love!

THE SCHOOL FOR SCANDAL
by
RICHARD BRINSLEY SHERIDAN

DRAMATIS PERSONÆ

AS ORIGINALLY ACTED AT DRURY LANE THEATRE IN 1777

SIR PETER TEAZLE	*Mr. King.*
SIR OLIVER SURFACE	*Mr. Yates.*
SIR HARRY BUMPER	*Mr. Gawdry.*
SIR BENJAMIN BACKBITE . . .	*Mr. Dodd.*
JOSEPH SURFACE	*Mr. Palmer.*
CHARLES SURFACE	*Mr. Smith.*
CARELESS	*Mr. Farren.*
SNAKE	*Mr. Packer.*
CRABTREE	*Mr. Parsons.*
ROWLEY	*Mr. Aickin.*
MOSES	*Mr. Baddeley.*
TRIP	*Mr. Lamash.*
LADY TEAZLE	*Mrs. Abington.*
LADY SNEERWELL	*Miss Sherry.*
MRS. CANDOUR	*Miss Pope.*
MARIA	*Miss P. Hopkins.*

Gentlemen, Maid, *and* Servants.

SCENE—LONDON.

A PORTRAIT;

ADDRESSED TO MRS. CREWE, WITH THE COMEDY OF THE
SCHOOL FOR SCANDAL.

By R. B. Sheridan, Esq.

TELL me, ye prime adepts in Scandal's school,
Who rail by precept, and detract by rule,
Lives there no character, so tried, so known,
So deck'd with grace, and so unlike your own,
That even you assist her fame to raise,
Approve by envy, and by silence praise!
Attend!—a model shall attract your view—
Daughters of calumny, I summon you!
You shall decide if this a portrait prove,
Or fond creation of the Muse and Love.
Attend, ye virgin critics, shrewd and sage,
Ye matron censors of this childish age,
Whose peering eye and wrinkled front declare
A fix'd antipathy to young and fair;
By cunning, cautious; or by nature, cold,—
In maiden madness, virulently bold;—
Attend, ye skill'd to coin the precious tale,
Creating proof, where inuendos fail!
Whose practised memories, cruelly exact,
Omit no circumstance, except the fact!—
Attend, all ye who boast,—or old or young,—
The living libel of a slanderous tongue!
So shall my theme, as far contrasted be,
As saints by fiends or hymns by calumny.
Come, gentle Amoret (for 'neath that name
In worthier verse is sung thy beauty's fame),
Come—for but thee who seek the Muse? and while
Celestial blushes check thy conscious smile,
With timid grace and hesitating eye,
The perfect model which I boast supply:—
Vain Muse! couldst thou the humblest sketch create
Of her, or slightest charm couldst imitate—
Could thy blest strain in kindred colours trace
The faintest wonder of her form and face—

Poets would study the immortal line,
And Reynolds own his art subdued by thine;
That art, which well might added lustre give
To nature's best and heaven's superlative:
On Granby's cheek might bid new glories rise,
Or point a purer beam from Devon's eyes!
Hard is the task to shape that beauty's praise,
Whose judgment scorns the homage flattery pays?
But praising Amoret we cannot 'err,
No tongue o'ervalues Heaven, or flatters her!
Yet she by fate's perverseness—she alone
Would doubt our truth, nor deem such praise her own!
Adorning fashion, unadorn'd by dress,
Simple from taste, and not from carelessness;
Discreet in gesture, in deportment mild,
Not stiff with prudence, nor uncouthly wild:
No state has Amoret; no studied mien;
She frowns no goddess, and she moves no queen,
The softer charm that in her manner lies
Is framed to captivate, yet not surprise;
It justly suits the expression of her face,—
'Tis less than dignity, and more than grace!
On her pure cheek the native hue is such,
That, form'd by Heaven to be admired so much,
The hand divine, with a less partial care,
Might well have fixed a fainter crimson there,
And bade the gentle inmate of her breast—
Inshrined Modesty—supply the rest.
But who the peril of her lips shall paint?
Strip them of smiles—still, still all words are faint!
But moving Love himself appears to teach
Their action, though denied to rule her speech;
And thou who seest her speak, and dost not hear,
Mourn not her distant accents 'scape thine ear;
Viewing those lips, thou still may'st make pretence
To judge of what she says, and swear 'tis sense:
Clothed with such grace, with such expression fraught,
They move in meaning, and they pause in thought!
But dost thou farther watch, with charm'd surprise,
The mild irresolution of her eyes.
Curious to mark how frequent they repose,
In brief eclipse and momentary close—
Ah! seest thou not an ambush'd Cupid there,
Too tim'rous of his charge, with jealous care

Veils and unveils those beams of heavenly light,
Too full, too fatal else, for mortal sight?
Nor yet, such pleasing vengeance fond to meet,
In pard'ning dimples hope a safe retreat.
What though her peaceful breast should ne'er allow
Subduing frowns to arm her altered brow,
By Love, I swear, and by his gentle wiles,
More fatal still the mercy of her smiles!
Thus lovely, thus adorn'd, possessing all
Of bright or fair that can to woman fall,
The height of vanity, might well be thought
Prerogative in her, and Nature's fault.
Yet gentle Amoret, in mind supreme
As well as charms, rejects the vainer theme;
And, half mistrustful of her beauty's store,
She barbs with wit those darts too keen before:—
Read in all knowledge that her sex should reach,
Though Greville, or the Muse, should deign to teach,
Fond to improve, nor timorous to discern
How far it is a woman's grace to learn;
In Millar's dialect she would not prove
Apollo's priestess, but Apollo's love,
Graced by those signs which truth delights to own,
The timid blush, and mild submitted tone:
Whate'er she says, though sense appear throughout,
Displays the tender hue of female doubt;
Deck'd with that charm, how lovely wit appears,
How graceful science, when that robe she wears!
Such too her talents, and her bent of mind,
As speak a sprightly heart by thought refined:
A taste for mirth, by contemplation school'd,
A turn for ridicule, by candour ruled,
A scorn of folly, which she tries to hide;
An awe of talent, which she owns with pride!
   Peace, idle Muse! no more thy strain prolong,
But yield a theme, thy warmest praises wrong;
Just to her merit, though thou canst not raise
Thy feeble verse, behold th' acknowledged praise
Has spread conviction through the envious train,
And cast a fatal gloom o'er Scandal's reign!
And lo! each pallid hag, with blister'd tongue,
Mutters assent to all thy zeal has sung—
Owns all the colours just—the outline true:
Thee my inspirer, and my model—CREWE!

PROLOGUE

WRITTEN BY MR. GARRICK

A SCHOOL for Scandal! tell me, I beseech you,
Needs there a school this modish art to teach you?
No need of lessons now, the knowing think;
We might as well be taught to eat and drink.
Caused by a dearth of scandal, should the vapours
Distress our fair ones—let them read the papers;
Their powerful mixtures such disorders hit;
Crave what you will—there's *quantum sufficit.*
"Lord!" cries my Lady Wormwood (who loves tattle,
And puts much salt and pepper in her prattle),
Just risen at noon, all night at cards when threshing
Strong tea and scandal—"Bless me, how refreshing!
Give me the papers, Lisp—how bold and free!   [*Sips.*
Last night Lord L. [Sips.] was caught with Lady D.
For aching heads what charming sal volatile!   [*Sips.*
If Mrs. B. will still continue flirting,
We hope she'll DRAW, *or we'll* UNDRAW *the curtain.*
Fine satire, poz—in public all abuse it,
But, by ourselves [*Sips.*], our praise we can't refuse it.
Now, Lisp, read you—there, at that dash and star."
"Yes, ma'am—*A certain Lord had best beware,*
Who lives not twenty miles from Grosvenor Square;
For should he Lady W. find willing,
Wormwood is bitter"——"Oh! that's me! the villain!
Throw it behind the fire, and never more
Let that vile paper come within my door."
Thus at our friends we laugh, who feel the dart;
To reach our feelings, we ourselves must smart.
Is our young bard so young, to think that he
Can stop the full spring-tide of calumny?
Knows he the world so little, and its trade?
Alas! the devil's sooner raised than laid.
So strong, so swift, the monster there's no gagging:
Cut Scandal's head off, still the tongue is wagging.
Proud of your smiles once lavishly bestow'd,
Again our young Don Quixote takes the road;

To show his gratitude he draws his pen,
And seeks his hydra, Scandal, in his den.
For your applause all perils he would through—
He'll fight—that's write—a cavalliero true,
Till every drop of blood—that's ink—is spilt for you.

THE SCHOOL FOR SCANDAL

ACT I

SCENE I.—LADY SNEERWELL'S *Dressing-room*

LADY SNEERWELL *discovered at her toilet;* SNAKE *drinking chocolate.*

Lady Sneer. The paragraphs, you say, Mr. Snake, were all inserted?

Snake. They were, madam; and, as I copied them myself in a feigned hand, there can be no suspicion whence they came.

Lady Sneer. Did you circulate the report of Lady Brittle's intrigue with Captain Boastall?

Snake. That's in as fine a train as your ladyship could wish. In the common course of things, I think it must reach Mrs. Clackitt's ears within four-and-twenty hours; and then, you know, the business is as good as done.

Lady Sneer. Why, truly, Mrs. Clackitt has a very pretty talent, and a great deal of industry.

Snake. True, madam, and has been tolerably successful in her day. To my knowledge, she has been the cause of six matches being broken off, and three sons being disinherited; of four forced elopements, and as many close confinements; nine separate maintenances, and two divorces. Nay, I have more than once traced her causing a *tête-à-tête* in the "Town and Country Magazine," when the parties, perhaps, had never seen each other's face before in the course of their lives.

Lady Sneer. She certainly has talents, but her manner is gross.

Snake. 'Tis very true. She generally designs well, has a free tongue and a bold invention; but her colouring is too dark, and her outlines often extravagant. She wants that delicacy of tint, and mellowness of sneer, which distinguish your ladyship's scandal.

Lady Sneer. You are partial, Snake.

Snake. Not in the least; everybody allows that Lady Sneerwell can do more with a word or look than many can with the most laboured detail, even when they happen to have a little truth on their side to support it.

Lady Sneer. Yes, my dear Snake; and I am no hypocrite to deny the satisfaction I reap from the success of my efforts. Wounded myself, in the early part of my life, by the envenomed tongue of slander, I confess I have since known no pleasure equal to the reducing others to the level of my own injured reputation.

Snake. Nothing can be more natural. But, Lady Sneerwell, there is one affair in which you have lately employed me, wherein, I confess, I am at a loss to guess your motives.

Lady Sneer. I conceive you mean with respect to my neighbour, Sir Peter Teazle, and his family?

Snake. I do. Here are two young men, to whom Sir Peter has acted as a kind of guardian since their father's death; the eldest possessing the most amiable character, and universally well spoken of—the youngest, the most dissipated and extravagant young fellow in the kingdom, without friends or character: the former an avowed admirer of your ladyship, and apparently your favourite; the latter attached to Maria, Sir Peter's ward, and confessedly beloved by her. Now, on the face of these circumstances, it is utterly unaccountable to me, why you, the widow of a city knight, with a good jointure, should not close with the passion of a man of such character and expectations as Mr. Surface; and more so why you should be so uncommonly earnest to destroy the mutual attachment subsisting between his brother Charles and Maria.

Lady Sneer. Then, at once to unravel this mystery, I must inform you that love has no share whatever in the intercourse between Mr. Surface and me.

Snake. No!

Lady Sneer. His real attachment is to Maria or her fortune; but, finding in his brother a favoured rival, he has been obliged to mask his pretensions, and profit by my assistance.

Snake. Yet still I am more puzzled why you should interest yourself in his success.

Lady Sneer. Heavens! how dull you are! Cannot you surmise the weakness which I hitherto, through shame, have concealed even from you? Must I confess that Charles—that libertine, that extravagant, that bankrupt in fortune and reputation—that he it is for whom I am thus anxious and malicious, and to gain whom I would sacrifice everything?

Snake. Now, indeed, your conduct appears consistent; but how came you and Mr. Surface so confidential?

Lady Sneer. For our mutual interest. I have found him out a long time since. I know him to be artful, selfish, and malicious—in short, a sentimental knave; while with Sir Peter, and indeed with all his acquaintance, he passes for a youthful miracle of prudence, good sense, and benevolence.

Snake. Yes; yet Sir Peter vows he has not his equal in England; and, above all, he praises him as a man of sentiment.

Lady Sneer. True; and with the assistance of his sentiment and hypocrisy he has brought Sir Peter entirely into his interest with regard to Maria; while poor Charles has no friend in the house— though, I fear, he has a powerful one in Maria's heart, against whom we must direct our schemes.

Enter SERVANT.

Ser. Mr. Surface.

Lady Sneer. Show him up.—[*Exit* SERVANT.] He generally calls about this time. I don't wonder at people giving him to me for a lover.

Enter JOSEPH SURFACE.

Jos. Surface. My dear Lady Sneerwell, how do you do to-day? Mr. Snake, your most obedient.

Lady Sneer. Snake has just been rallying me on our mutual attachment; but I have informed him of our real views. You know how useful he has been to us; and, believe me, the confidence is not ill-placed.

Jos. Surf. Madam, it is impossible for me to suspect a man of Mr. Snake's sensibility and discernment.

Lady Sneer. Well, well, no compliments now; but tell me when you saw your mistress, Maria—or, what is more material to me, your brother.

Jos. Surf. I have not seen either since I left you; but I can inform you that they never meet. Some of your stories have taken a good effect on Maria.

Lady Sneer. Ah, my dear Snake! the merit of this belongs to you. But do your brother's distresses increase?

Jos. Surf. Every hour. I am told he has had another execution in the house yesterday. In short, his dissipation and extravagance exceed anything I have ever heard of.

Lady Sneer. Poor Charles!

Jos. Surf. True, madam; notwithstanding his vices, one can't help feeling for him. Poor Charles! I'm sure I wish it were in my power to be of any essential service to him; for the man who does not share in the distresses of a brother, even though merited by his own misconduct, deserves——

Lady Sneer. O Lud! you are going to be moral, and forget that you are among friends.

Jos. Surf. Egad, that's true! I'll keep that sentiment till I see Sir Peter. However, it is certainly a charity to rescue Maria from such a libertine, who, if he is to be reclaimed, can be so only by a person of your ladyship's superior accomplishments and understanding.

Snake. I believe, Lady Sneerwell, here's company coming; I'll go and copy the letter I mentioned to you. Mr. Surface, your most obedient.

Jos. Surf. Sir, your very devoted.—[*Exit* SNAKE.] Lady Sneerwell, I am very sorry you have put any farther confidence in that fellow.

Lady Sneer. Why so?

Jos. Surf. I have lately detected him in frequent conference with old Rowley, who was formerly my father's steward, and has never, you know, been a friend of mine.

Lady Sneer. And do you think he would betray us?

Jos. Surf. Nothing more likely: take my word for't, Lady Sneerwell, that fellow hasn't virtue enough to be faithful even to his own villany. Ah, Maria!

Enter MARIA.

Lady Sneer. Maria, my dear, how do you do? What's the matter?

Mar. Oh! there's that disagreeable lover of mine, Sir Benjamin Backbite, has just called at my guardian's, with his odious uncle, Crabtree; so I slipped out, and ran hither to avoid them.

Lady Sneer. Is that all?

Jos. Surf. If my brother Charles had been of the party, madam, perhaps you would not have been so much alarmed.

Lady Sneer. Nay, now you are severe; for I dare swear the truth of the matter is, Maria heard you were here. But, my dear, what has Sir Benjamin done, that you should avoid him so?

Mar. Oh, he has done nothing—but 'tis for what he has said: his conversation is a perpetual libel on all his acquaintance.

Jos. Surf. Ay, and the worst of it is, there is no advantage in not knowing him; for he'll abuse a stranger just as soon as his best friend: and his uncle's as bad.

Lady Sneer. Nay, but we should make allowance; Sir Benjamin is a wit and a poet.

Mar. For my part, I own, madam, wit loses its respect with me, when I see it in company with malice. What do you think, Mr. Surface?

Jos. Surf. Certainly, madam; to smile at the jest which plants a thorn in another's breast is to become a principal in the mischief.

Lady Sneer. Psha! there's no possibility of being witty without

a little ill-nature: the malice of a good thing is the barb that makes
it stick. What's your opinion, Mr. Surface?

Jos. Surf. To be sure, madam; that conversation, where the
spirit of raillery is suppressed, will ever appear tedious and insipid.

Mar. Well, I'll not debate how far scandal may be allowable;
but in a man, I am sure, it is always contemptible. We have pride,
envy, rivalship, and a thousand motives to depreciate each other;
but the male slanderer must have the cowardice of a woman before
he can traduce one.

Re-enter SERVANT.

Ser. Madam, Mrs. Candour is below, and, if your ladyship's at
leisure, will leave her carriage.

Lady Sneer. Beg her to walk in.—[*Exit* SERVANT.] Now, Maria,
here is a character to your taste; for, though Mrs. Candour is a
little talkative, everybody knows her to be the best-natured and
best sort of woman.

Mar. Yes, with a very gross affectation of good nature and
benevolence, she does more mischief than the direct malice of old
Crabtree.

Jos. Surf. I'faith that's true, Lady Sneerwell: whenever I hear
the current running against the characters of my friends, I never
think them in such danger as when Candour undertakes their
defence.

Lady Sneer. Hush!—here she is!

Enter MRS. CANDOUR.

Mrs. Can. My dear Lady Sneerwell, how have you been this
century?—Mr. Surface, what news do you hear?—though indeed
it is no matter, for I think one hears nothing else but scandal.

Jos. Surf. Just so, indeed, ma'am.

Mrs. Can. Oh, Maria! child,—what, is the whole affair off
between you and Charles? His extravagance, I presume—the town
talks of nothing else.

Mar. I am very sorry, ma'am, the town has so little to do.

Mrs. Can. True, true, child: but there's no stopping people's
tongues. I own I was hurt to hear it, as I indeed was to learn,
from the same quarter, that your guardian, Sir Peter, and Lady
Teazle have not agreed lately as well as could be wished.

Mar. 'Tis strangely impertinent for people to busy themselves
so.

Mrs. Can. Very true, child; but what's to be done? People will
talk—there's no preventing it. Why, it was but yesterday I was
told that Miss Gadabout had eloped with Sir Filagree Flirt. But,

Lord! there's no minding what one hears; though, to be sure, I had this from very good authority.

Mar. Such reports are highly scandalous.

Mrs. Can. So they are, child—shameful, shameful! But the world is so censorious, no character escapes. Lord, now who would have suspected your friend, Miss Prim, of an indiscretion? Yet such is the ill-nature of people, that they say her uncle stopped her last week, just as she was stepping into the York mail with her dancing-master.

Mar. I'll answer for't there are no grounds for that report.

Mrs. Can. Ah, no foundation in the world, I dare swear: no more, probably, than the story circulated last month, of Mrs. Festino's affair with Colonel Cassino—though, to be sure, that matter was never rightly cleared up.

Jos. Surf. The license of invention some people take is monstrous indeed.

Mar. 'Tis so; but, in my opinion, those who report such things are equally culpable.

Mrs. Can. To be sure they are; tale-bearers are as bad as the tale-makers—'tis an old observation, and a very true one: but what's to be done, as I said before? how will you prevent people from talking? To-day, Mrs. Clackitt assured me, Mr. and Mrs. Honeymoon were at last become mere man and wife, like the rest of their acquaintance. She likewise hinted that a certain widow, in the next street, had got rid of her dropsy and recovered her shape in a most surprising manner. And at the same time Miss Tattle, who was by, affirmed, that Lord Buffalo had discovered his lady at a house of no extraordinary fame; and that Sir Harry Bouquet and Tom Saunter were to measure swords on a similar provocation. But, Lord, do you think I would report these things! No, no! tale-bearers, as I said before, are just as bad as the tale-makers.

Jos. Surf. Ah! Mrs. Candour, if everybody had your forbearance and good nature!

Mrs. Can. I confess, Mr. Surface, I cannot bear to hear people attacked behind their backs; and when ugly circumstances come out against our acquaintance I own I always love to think the best. By-the-by, I hope 'tis not true that your brother is absolutely ruined?

Jos. Surf. I am afraid his circumstances are very bad indeed, ma'am.

Mrs. Can. Ah!—I heard so—but you must tell him to keep up his spirits; everybody almost is in the same way: Lord Spindle, Sir Thomas Splint, Captain Quinze, and Mr. Nickit—all up, I hear, within this week; so, if Charles is undone, he'll find half his acquaintance ruined too, and that, you know, is a consolation.

Jos. Surf. Doubtless, ma'am—a very great one.

Re-enter SERVANT.

Ser. Mr. Crabtree and Sir Benjamin Backbite.   [*Exit.*

Lady Sneer. So, Maria, you see your lover pursues you; positively you shan't escape.

Enter CRABTREE *and* SIR BENJAMIN BACKBITE.

Crab. Lady Sneerwell, I kiss your hand. Mrs. Candour, I don't believe you are acquainted with my nephew, Sir Benjamin Backbite? Egad, ma'am, he has a pretty wit, and is a pretty poet too. Isn't he, Lady Sneerwell?

Sir Ben. Oh, fie, uncle!

Crab. Nay, egad it's true: I back him at a rebus or a charade against the best rhymer in the kingdom. Has your ladyship heard the epigram he wrote last week on Lady Frizzle's feather catching fire?—Do, Benjamin, repeat it, or the charade you made last night extempore at Mrs. Drowzie's conversazione. Come now; your first is the name of a fish, your second a great naval commander, and——

Sir Ben. Uncle, now—pr'ythee——

Crab. I'faith, ma'am, 'twould surprise you to hear how ready he is at all these sort of things.

Lady Sneer. I wonder, Sir Benjamin, you never publish anything.

Sir Ben. To say truth, ma'am, 'tis very vulgar to print; and, as my little productions are mostly satires and lampoons on particular people, I find they circulate more by giving copies in confidence to the friends of the parties. However, I have some elegies, which, when favoured with this lady's smiles, I mean to give the public.   [*Pointing to* MARIA.

Crab. [*To* MARIA.] 'Fore heaven, ma'am, they'll immortalize you—you will be handed down to posterity, like Petrarch's Laura, or Waller's Sacharissa.

Sir Ben. [*To* MARIA.] Yes, madam, I think you will like them, when you shall see them on a beautiful quarto page, where a neat rivulet of text shall meander through a meadow of margin. 'Fore Gad, they will be the most elegant things of their kind!

Crab. But, ladies, that's true—have you heard the news?

Mrs. Can. What, sir, do you mean the report of——

Crab. No, ma'am, that's not it.—Miss Nicely is going to be married to her own footman.

Mrs. Can. Impossible!

Crab. Ask Sir Benjamin.

Sir Ben. 'Tis very true, ma'am: everything is fixed, and the wedding liveries bespoke.

Crab. Yes—and they do say there were pressing reasons for it.

Lady Sneer. Why, I have heard something of this before.

Mrs. Can. It can't be—and I wonder any one should believe such a story of so prudent a lady as Miss Nicely.

Sir Ben. O Lud! ma'am, that's the very reason 'twas believed at once. She has always been so cautious and so reserved, that everybody was sure there was some reason for it at bottom.

Mrs. Can. Why, to be sure, a tale of scandal is as fatal to the credit of a prudent lady of her stamp as a fever is generally to those of the strongest constitutions. But there is a sort of puny sickly reputation, that is always ailing, yet will outlive the robuster characters of a hundred prudes.

Sir Ben. True, madam, there are valetudinarians in reputation as well as constitution, who, being conscious of their weak part, avoid the least breath of air, and supply their want of stamina by care and circumspection.

Mrs. Can. Well, but this may be all a mistake. You know, Sir Benjamin, very trifling circumstances often give rise to the most injurious tales.

Crab. That they do, I'll be sworn, ma'am. Did you ever hear how Miss Piper came to lose her lover and her character last summer at Tunbridge?—Sir Benjamin, you remember it?

Sir Ben. Oh, to be sure!—the most whimsical circumstance.

Lady Sneer. How was it, pray?

Crab. Why, one evening, at Mrs. Ponto's assembly, the conversation happened to turn on the breeding Nova Scotia sheep in this country. Says a young lady in company, I have known instances of it; for Miss Letitia Piper, a first cousin of mine, had a Nova Scotia sheep that produced her twins. "What!" cries the Lady Dowager Dundizzy (who you know is as deaf as a post), "has Miss Piper had twins?" This mistake, as you may imagine, threw the whole company into a fit of laughter. However, 'twas the next morning everywhere reported, and in a few days believed by the whole town, that Miss Letitia Piper had actually been brought to bed of a fine boy and girl: and in less than a week there were some people who could name the father, and the farm-house where the babies were put to nurse.

Lady Sneer. Strange, indeed!

Crab. Matter of fact, I assure you. O Lud! Mr. Surface, pray is it true that your uncle, Sir Oliver, is coming home?

Jos. Surf. Not that I know of, indeed, sir.

Crab. He has been in the East Indies a long time. You can scarcely remember him, I believe? Sad comfort, whenever he returns, to hear how your brother has gone on!

Jos. Surf. Charles has been imprudent, sir, to be sure; but I hope no busy people have already prejudiced Sir Oliver against him. He may reform.

Sir Ben. To be sure he may; for my part I never believed him to be so utterly void of principle as people say; and though he has lost all his friends, I am told nobody is better spoken of by the Jews.

Crab. That's true, egad, nephew. If the old Jewry was a ward, I believe Charles would be an alderman: no man more popular there, 'fore Gad! I hear he pays as many annuities as the Irish tontine; and that, whenever he is sick, they have prayers for the recovery of his health in all the synagogues.

Sir Ben. Yet no man lives in greater splendour. They tell me, when he entertains his friends he will sit down to dinner with a dozen of his own securities; have a score of tradesmen in the antechamber, and an officer behind every guest's chair.

Jos. Surf. This may be entertainment to you, gentlemen, but you pay very little regard to the feelings of a brother.

Mar. [*Aside.*] Their malice is intolerable!—[*Aloud.*] Lady Sneerwell, I must wish you a good morning: I'm not very well.

[*Exit.*

Mrs. Can. O dear! she changes colour very much.

Lady Sneer. Do, Mrs. Candour, follow her; she may want your assistance.

Mrs. Can. That I will, with all my soul, ma'am.—Poor dear girl, who knows what her situation may be!   [*Exit.*

Lady Sneer. 'Twas nothing but that she could not bear to hear Charles reflected on, notwithstanding their difference.

Sir Ben. The young lady's *penchant* is obvious.

Crab. But, Benjamin, you must not give up the pursuit for that: follow her, and put her into good humour. Repeat her some of your own verses. Come, I'll assist you.

Sir Ben. Mr. Surface, I did not mean to hurt you; but depend on't your brother is utterly undone.

Crab. O Lud, ay! undone as ever man was—can't raise a guinea.

Sir Ben. And everything sold, I'm told, that was movable.

Crab. I have seen one that was at his house. Not a thing left but some empty bottles that were overlooked, and the family pictures, which I believe are framed in the wainscots.

Sir Ben. And I'm very sorry also to hear some bad stories against him. [*Going.*

Crab. Oh, he has done many mean things, that's certain.

Sir Ben. But, however, as he's your brother—— [*Going.*

Crab. We'll tell you all another opportunity.

[*Exeunt* CRABTREE *and* SIR BENJAMIN.

Lady Sneer. Ha, ha! 'tis very hard for them to leave a subject they have not quite run down.

Jos. Surf. And I believe the abuse was no more acceptable to your ladyship than to Maria.

Lady Sneer. I doubt her affections are further engaged than we imagine. But the family are to be here this evening, so you may as well dine where you are, and we shall have an opportunity of observing further; in the meantime, I'll go and plot mischief, and you shall study sentiment. [*Exeunt.*

SCENE II.—*A Room in* SIR PETER TEAZLE'S *House*

Enter SIR PETER TEAZLE.

Sir Pet. When an old bachelor marries a young wife, what is he to expect? 'Tis now six months since Lady Teazle made me the happiest of men—and I have been the most miserable dog ever since! We tift a little going to church, and fairly quarrelled before the bells had done ringing. I was more than once nearly choked with gall during the honeymoon, and had lost all comfort in life before my friends had done wishing me joy. Yet I chose with caution—a girl bred wholly in the country, who never knew luxury beyond one silk gown, nor dissipation above the annual gala of a race ball. Yet she now plays her part in all the extravagant fopperies of fashion and the town, with as ready a grace as if she never had seen a bush or a grass-plot out of Grosvenor Square! I am sneered at by all my acquaintance, and paragraphed in the newspapers. She dissipates my fortune, and contradicts all my humours; yet the worst of it is, I doubt I love her, or I should never bear all this. However, I'll never be weak enough to own it.

Enter ROWLEY.

Row. Oh! Sir Peter, your servant: how is it with you, sir?

Sir Pet. Very bad, Master Rowley, very bad. I meet with nothing but crosses and vexations.

Row. What can have happened since yesterday?

Sir Pet. A good question to a married man!

Row. Nay, I'm sure, Sir Peter, your lady can't be the cause of your uneasiness.

Sir Pet. Why, has anybody told you she was dead?

Row. Come, come, Sir Peter, you love her, notwithstanding your tempers don't exactly agree.

Sir Pet. But the fault is entirely hers, Master Rowley. I am, myself, the sweetest-tempered man alive, and hate a teasing temper; and so I tell her a hundred times a day.

Row. Indeed!

Sir Pet. Ay; and what is very extraordinary, in all our disputes she is always in the wrong! But Lady Sneerwell, and the set she meets at her house, encourage the perverseness of her disposition. Then, to complete my vexation, Maria, my ward, whom I ought to have the power of a father over, is determined to turn rebel too, and absolutely refuses the man whom I have long resolved on for her husband; meaning, I suppose, to bestow herself on his profligate brother.

Row. You know, Sir Peter, I have always taken the liberty to differ with you on the subject of these two young gentlemen. I only wish you may not be deceived in your opinion of the elder. For Charles, my life on't! he will retrieve his errors yet. Their worthy father, once my honoured master, was, at his years, nearly as wild a spark; yet, when he died, he did not leave a more benevolent heart to lament his loss.

Sir Pet. You are wrong, Master Rowley. On their father's death, you know, I acted as a kind of guardian to them both, till their uncle Sir Oliver's liberality gave them an early independence: of course, no person could have more opportunities of judging of their hearts, and I was never mistaken in my life. Joseph is indeed a model for the young men of the age. He is a man of sentiment, and acts up to the sentiments he professes; but, for the other, take my word for't, if he had any grain of virtue by descent, he has dissipated it with the rest of his inheritance. Ah! my old friend, Sir Oliver, will be deeply mortified when he finds how part of his bounty has been misapplied.

Row. I am sorry to find you so violent against the young man, because this may be the most critical period of his fortune. I came hither with news that will surprise you.

Sir Pet. What! let me hear.

Row. Sir Oliver is arrived, and at this moment in town.

Sir Pet. How! you astonish me! I thought you did not expect him this month.

Row. I did not: but his passage has been remarkably quick.

Sir Pet. Egad, I shall rejoice to see my old friend. 'Tis sixteen years since we met. We have had many a day together: but does he still enjoin us not to inform his nephews of his arrival?

Row. Most strictly. He means, before it is known, to make some trial of their dispositions.

Sir Pet. Ah! There needs no art to discover their merits—however, he shall have his way; but, pray, does he know I am married?

Row. Yes, and will soon wish you joy.

Sir Pet. What, as we drink health to a friend in consumption! Ah, Oliver will laugh at me. We used to rail at matrimony together, but he has been steady to his text. Well, he must be soon at my house, though—I'll instantly give orders for his reception. But, Master Rowley, don't drop a word that Lady Teazle and I ever disagree.

Row. By no means.

Sir Pet. For I should never be able to stand Noll's jokes; so I'll have him think, Lord forgive me! that we are a very happy couple.

Row. I understand you:—but then you must be very careful not to differ while he is in the house with you.

Sir Pet. Egad, and so we must—and that's impossible. Ah! Master Rowley, when an old bachelor marries a young wife, he deserves—no—the crime carries its punishment along with it.

[*Exeunt*

ACT II

SCENE I.—*A Room in* SIR PETER TEAZLE'S *House*

Enter SIR PETER *and* LADY TEAZLE.

Sir Pet. Lady Teazle, Lady Teazle, I'll not bear it!

Lady Teaz. Sir Peter, Sir Peter, you may bear it or not, as you please; but I ought to have my own way in everything, and what's more, I will too. What though I was educated in the country, I know very well that women of fashion in London are accountable to nobody after they are married.

Sir Pet. Very well, ma'am, very well; so a husband is to have no influence, no authority?

Lady Teaz. Authority! No, to be sure:—if you wanted authority over me, you should have adopted me, and not married me: I am sure you were old enough.

Sir Pet. Old enough!—ay, there it is! Well, well, Lady Teazle, though my life may be made unhappy by your temper, I'll not be ruined by your extravagance!

Lady Teaz. My extravagance! I'm sure I'm not more extravagant than a woman of fashion ought to be.

Sir Pet. No, no, madam, you shall throw away no more sums on such unmeaning luxury. 'Slife! to spend as much to furnish your dressing-room with flowers in winter as would suffice to turn the Pantheon into a greenhouse, and give a *fête champêtre* at Christmas.

Lady Teaz. And am I to blame, Sir Peter, because flowers are dear in cold weather? You should find fault with the climate, and not with me. For my part, I'm sure I wish it was spring all the year round, and that roses grew under our feet!

Sir Pet. Oons! madam—if you had been born to this, I shouldn't wonder at your talking thus; but you forget what your situation was when I married you.

Lady Teaz. No, no, I don't; 'twas a very disagreeable one, or I should never have married you.

Sir Pet. Yes, yes, madam, you were then in somewhat a humbler style—the daughter of a plain country squire. Recollect, Lady Teazle, when I saw you first sitting at your tambour, in a pretty figured linen gown, with a bunch of keys at your side, your hair combed smooth over a roll, and your apartment hung round with fruits in worsted, of your own working.

Lady Teaz. Oh, yes! I remember it very well, and a curious life I led. My daily occupation to inspect the dairy, superintend the poultry, make extracts from the family receipt-book, and comb my aunt Deborah's lapdog.

Sir Pet. Yes, yes, ma'am, 'twas so indeed.

Lady Teaz. And then, you know, my evening amusements! To draw patterns for ruffles, which I had not the materials to make up; to play Pope Joan with the Curate; to read a sermon to my aunt; or to be stuck down to an old spinet to strum my father to sleep after a fox-chase.

Sir Pet. I am glad you have so good a memory. Yes, madam, these were the recreations I took you from; but now you must have your coach—*vis-à-vis*—and three powdered footmen before your chair; and, in the summer, a pair of white cats to draw you to Kensington Gardens. No recollection, I suppose, when you were content to ride double, behind the butler, on a docked coach-horse?

Lady Teaz. No—I swear I never did that; I deny the butler and the coach-horse.

Sir Pet. This, madam, was your situation; and what have I done for you? I have made you a woman of fashion, of fortune, of rank —in short, I have made you my wife.

Lady Teaz. Well, then, and there is but one thing more you can make me to add to the obligation, that is——

Sir Pet. My widow, I suppose?

Lady Teaz. Hem! hem!

Sir Pet. I thank you, madam—but don't flatter yourself; for, though your ill-conduct may disturb my peace of mind, it shall never break my heart, I promise you: however, I am equally obliged to you for the hint.

Lady Teaz. Then why will you endeavour to make yourself so disagreeable to me, and thwart me in every little elegant expense?

Sir Pet. 'Slife, madam, I say, had you any of these little elegant expenses when you married me?

Lady Teaz. Lud, Sir Peter! would you have me be out of the fashion?

Sir Pet. The fashion, indeed! what had you to do with the fashion before you married me?

Lady Teaz. For my part, I should think you would like to have your wife thought a woman of taste.

Sir Pet. Ay—there again—taste! Zounds! madam, you had no taste when you married me!

Lady Teaz. That's very true, indeed, Sir Peter! and, after having married you, I should never pretend to taste again, I allow. But now, Sir Peter, since we have finished our daily jangle, I presume I may go to my engagement at Lady Sneerwell's?

Sir Pet. Ay, there's another precious circumstance—a charming set of acquaintance you have made there!

Lady Teaz. Nay, Sir Peter, they are all people of rank and fortune, and remarkably tenacious of reputation.

Sir Pet. Yes, egad, they are tenacious of reputation with a vengeance; for they don't choose anybody should have a character but themselves! Such a crew! Ah! many a wretch has rid on a hurdle who has done less mischief than these utterers of forged tales, coiners of scandal, and clippers of reputation.

Lady Teaz. What, would you restrain the freedom of speech?

Sir Pet. Ah! they have made you just as bad as any one of the society.

Lady Teaz. Why, I believe I do bear a part with a tolerable grace. But I vow I bear no malice against the people I abuse: when I say an ill-natured thing, 'tis out of pure good humour; and I take it for granted they deal exactly in the same manner with me. But, Sir Peter, you know you promised to come to Lady Sneerwell's too.

Sir Pet. Well, well, I'll call in just to look after my own character.

Lady Teaz. Then, indeed, you must make haste after me or you'll be too late. So good-bye to ye.　　　　　　[*Exit.*

Sir Pet. So—I have gained much by my intended expostulation! Yet with what a charming air she contradicts everything

I say, and how pleasantly she shows her contempt for my authority! Well, though I can't make her love me, there is great satisfaction in quarrelling with her; and I think she never appears
to such advantage as when she is doing everything in her power
to plague me.   [*Exit.*

SCENE II.—*A Room in* LADY SNEERWELL'S *House*

LADY SNEERWELL, MRS. CANDOUR, CRABTREE, SIR BENJAMIN
BACKBITE, *and* JOSEPH SURFACE, *discovered.*

Lady Sneer. Nay, positively, we will hear it.

Jos. Surf. Yes, yes, the epigram, by all means.

Sir Ben. O plague on't, uncle! 'tis mere nonsense.

Crab. No, no; 'fore Gad, very clever for an extempore!

Sir Ben. But, ladies, you should be acquainted with the circumstance. You must know, that one day last week, as Lady
Betty Curricle was taking the dust in Hyde Park, in a sort of
duodecimo phaeton, she desired me to write some verses on her
ponies; upon which, I took out my pocket-book, and in one moment produced the following:—

> Sure never were seen two such beautiful ponies;
> Other horses are clowns, but these macaronies:
> To give them this title I am sure can't be wrong.
> Their legs are so slim, and their tails are so long.

Crab. There, ladies, done in the smack of a whip, and on horseback too.

Jos. Surf. A very Phœbus, mounted—indeed, Sir Benjamin!

Sir Ben. Oh dear, sir!—trifles—trifles.—

Enter LADY TEAZLE *and* MARIA.

Mrs. Can. I must have a copy.

Lady Sneer. Lady Teazle, I hope we shall see Sir Peter?

Lady Teaz. I believe he'll wait on your ladyship presently.

Lady Sneer. Maria, my love, you look grave. Come, you shall
sit down to piquet with Mr. Surface.

Mar. I take very little pleasure in cards—however, I'll do as
your ladyship pleases.

Lady Teaz. I am surprised Mr. Surface should sit down with
her; I thought he would have embraced this opportunity of
speaking to me before Sir Peter came.   [*Aside.*

Mrs. Can. Now, I'll die; but you are so scandalous, I'll forswear your society.

Lady Teaz. What's the matter, Mrs. Candour?

Mrs. Can. They'll not allow our friend Miss Vermillion to be handsome.

Lady Sneer. Oh, surely she is a pretty woman.

Crab. I am very glad you think so, ma'am.

Mrs. Can. She has a charming fresh colour.

Lady Teaz. Yes, when it is fresh put on.

Mrs. Can. Oh, fie! I'll swear her colour is natural: I have seen it come and go!

Lady Teaz. I dare swear you have, ma'am: it goes off at night, and comes again in the morning.

Sir Ben. True, ma'am, it not only comes and goes; but, what's more, egad, her maid can fetch and carry it!

Mrs. Can. Ha! ha! ha! how I hate to hear you talk so! But surely, now, her sister is, or was, very handsome.

Crab. Who? Mrs. Evergreen? O Lord! she's six-and-fifty if she's an hour!

Mrs. Can. Now positively you wrong her; fifty-two or fifty-three is the utmost—and I don't think she looks more.

Sir Ben. Ah! there's no judging by her looks, unless one could see her face.

Lady Sneer. Well, well, if Mrs. Evergreen does take some pains to repair the ravages of time, you must allow she effects it with great ingenuity; and surely that's better than the careless manner in which the widow Ochre caulks her wrinkles.

Sir Ben. Nay, now, Lady Sneerwell, you are severe upon the widow. Come, come, 'tis not that she paints so ill—but, when she has finished her face, she joins it on so badly to her neck, that she looks like a mended statue, in which the connoisseur may see at once that the head's modern, though the trunk's antique!

Crab. Ha! ha! ha! Well said, nephew!

Mrs. Can. Ha! ha! ha! Well, you make me laugh; but I vow I hate you for it. What do you think of Miss Simper?

Sir Ben. Why, she has very pretty teeth.

Lady Teaz. Yes; and on that account, when she is neither speaking nor laughing (which very seldom happens), she never absolutely shuts her mouth, but leaves it always on ajar, as it were—thus.   [*Shows her teeth.*

Mrs. Can. How can you be so ill-natured?

Lady Teaz. Nay, I allow even that's better than the pains Mrs. Prim takes to conceal her losses in front. She draws her mouth till it positively resembles the aperture of a poor's-box, and all her words appear to slide out edge-wise, as it were—thus: *How do you do, madam? Yes, madam.*

Lady Sneer. Very well, Lady Teazle; I see you can be a little severe.

Lady Teaz. In defence of a friend it is but justice. But here comes Sir Peter to spoil our pleasantry.

Enter SIR PETER TEAZLE.

Sir Pet. Ladies, your most obedient—[*Aside.*] Mercy on me, here is the whole set! a character dead at every word, I suppose.

Mrs. Can. I am rejoiced you are come, Sir Peter. They have been so censorious—and Lady Teazle as bad as any one.

Sir Pet. That must be very distressing to you, Mrs. Candour, I dare swear.

Mrs. Can. Oh, they will allow good qualities to nobody; not even good nature to our friend Mrs. Pursy.

Lady Teaz. What, the fat dowager who was at Mrs. Quadrille's last night?

Mrs. Can. Nay, her bulk is her misfortune; and, when she takes so much pains to get rid of it, you ought not to reflect on her.

Lady Sneer. That's very true, indeed.

Lady Teaz. Yes, I know she almost lives on acids and small whey; laces herself by pulleys; and often, in the hottest noon in summer, you may see her on a little squat pony, with her hair plaited up behind like a drummer's and puffing round the Ring on a full trot.

Mrs. Can. I thank you, Lady Teazle, for defending her.

Sir Pet. Yes, a good defence, truly.

Mrs. Can. Truly, Lady Teazle is as consorious as Miss Sallow.

Crab. Yes, and she is a curious being to pretend to be censorious—an awkward gawky, without any one good point under heaven.

Mrs. Can. Positively you shall not be so very severe. Miss Sallow is a near relation of mine by marriage, and, as for her person, great allowance is to be made; for, let me tell you, a woman labours under many disadvantages who tries to pass for a girl of six-and-thirty.

Lady Sneer. Though, surely, she is handsome still—and for the weakness in her eyes, considering how much she reads by candle-light, it is not to be wondered at.

Mrs. Can. True; and then as to her manner, upon my word I think it is particularly graceful, considering she never had the least education; for you know her mother was a Welsh milliner, and her father a sugar-baker at Bristol.

Sir Ben. Ah! you are both of you too good-natured!

Sir Pet. Yes, damned good-natured! This their own relation! mercy on me! [*Aside.*

Mrs. Can. For my part, I own I cannot bear to hear a friend ill-spoken of.

Sir Pet. No, to be sure.

Sir Ben. Oh! you are of a moral turn. Mrs. Candour and I can sit for an hour and hear Lady Stucco talk sentiment.

Lady Teaz. Nay, I vow Lady Stucco is very well with the dessert after dinner; for she's just like the French fruit one cracks for mottoes—made up of paint and proverb.

Mrs. Can. Well, I will never join in ridiculing a friend; and so I constantly tell my cousin Ogle, and you all know what pretensions she has to be critical on beauty.

Crab. Oh, to be sure! she has herself the oddest countenance that ever was seen; 'tis a collection of features from all the different countries of the globe.

Sir Ben. So she has, indeed—an Irish front——

Crab. Caledonian locks——

Sir Ben. Dutch nose——

Crab. Austrian lips——

Sir Ben. Complexion of a Spaniard——

Crab. And teeth *à la Chinoise*——

Sir Ben. In short, her face resembles a table d'hôte at Spa— where no two guests are of a nation——

Crab. Or a congress at the close of a general war—wherein all the members, even to her eyes, appear to have a different interest, and her nose and her chin are the only parties likely to join issue.

Mrs. Can. Ha! ha! ha!

Sir Pet. Mercy on my life!—a person they dine with twice a week! [*Aside.*

Lady Sneer. Go—go—you are a couple of provoking Toads.

Mrs. Can. Nay, but I vow you shall not carry the laugh off so—for give me leave to say, that Mrs. Ogle——

Sir Pet. Madam, madam, I beg your pardon—there's no stopping these good gentlemen's tongues. But when I tell you, Mrs. Candour, that the lady they are abusing is a particular friend of mine, I hope you'll not take her part.

Lady Sneer. Ha! ha! ha! well said, Sir Peter! but you are a cruel creature—too phlegmatic yourself for a jest, and too peevish to allow wit in others.

Sir Pet. Ah, madam, true wit is more nearly allied to good nature than your ladyship is aware of.

Lady Teaz. True, Sir Peter: I believe they are so near akin that they can never be united.

Sir Ben. Or rather, madam, I suppose them man and wife, because one seldom sees them together.

Lady Teaz. But Sir Peter is such an enemy to scandal, I believe he would have it put down by parliament.

Sir Pet. 'Fore heaven, madam, if they were to consider the sporting with reputation of as much importance as poaching on manors, and pass an act for the preservation of fame, I believe many would thank them for the bill.

Lady Sneer. O Lud! Sir Peter; would you deprive us of our privileges?

Sir Pet. Ay, madam; and then no person should be permitted to kill characters and run down reputations, but qualified old maids and disappointed widows.

Lady Sneer. Go, you monster!

Mrs. Can. But, surely, you would not be quite so severe on those who only report what they hear?

Sir Pet. Yes, madam, I would have law merchant for them too; and in all cases of slander currency, whenever the drawer of the lie was not to be found, the injured parties should have a right to come on any of the indorsers.

Crab. Well, for my part, I believe there never was a scandalous tale without some foundation.

Lady Sneer. Come, ladies, shall we sit down to cards in the next room?

Enter SERVANT, *who whispers* SIR PETER.

Sir Pet. I'll be with them directly.—[*Exit* SERVANT.] I'll get away unperceived. [*Aside.*

Lady Sneer. Sir Peter, you are not going to leave us?

Sir Pet. You ladyship must excuse me; I'm called away by particular business. But I leave my character behind me. [*Exit.*

Sir Ben. Well—certainly, Lady Teazle, that lord of yours is a strange being: I could tell you some stories of him would make you laugh heartily if he were not your husband.

Lady Teaz. Oh, pray don't mind that; come, do let's hear them. [*Exeunt all but* JOSEPH SURFACE *and* MARIA.

Jos. Surf. Maria, I see you have no satisfaction in this society.

Mar. How is it possible I should? If to raise malicious smiles at the infirmities or misfortunes of those who have never injured us be the province of wit or humour, Heaven grant me a double portion of dulness!

Jos. Surf. Yet they appear more ill-natured than they are; they have no malice at heart.

Mar. Then is their conduct still more contemptible; for, in my opinion, nothing could excuse the intemperance of their tongues but a natural and uncontrollable bitterness of mind.

Jos. Surf. Undoubtedly, madam; and it has always been a sentiment of mine, that to propagate a malicious truth wantonly is more despicable than to falsify from revenge. But can you, Maria, feel thus for others, and be unkind to me alone? Is hope to be denied the tenderest passion?

Mar. Why will you distress me by renewing this subject?

Jos. Surf. Ah, Maria! you would not treat me thus, and oppose your guardian, Sir Peter's will, but that I see that profligate Charles is still a favoured rival.

Mar. Ungenerously urged! But, whatever my sentiments are for that unfortunate young man, be assured I shall not feel more bound to give him up, because his distresses have lost him the regard even of a brother.

Jos Surf. Nay, but, Maria, do not leave me with a frown: by all that's honest, I swear—— [*Kneels.*

Re-enter LADY TEAZLE *behind.*

[*Aside.*] Gad's life, here's Lady Teazle.—[*Aloud to* MARIA.] You must not—no, you shall not—for, though I have the greatest regard for Lady Teazle——

Mar. Lady Teazle!

Jos. Surf. Yet were Sir Peter to suspect——

Lady Teaz. [*Coming forward.*] What is this, pray? Do you take her for me?—Child, you are wanted in the next room.— [*Exit* MARIA.] What is all this, pray?

Jos. Surf. Oh, the most unlucky circumstance in nature! Maria has somehow suspected the tender concern I have for your happiness, and threatened to acquaint Sir Peter with her suspicions, and I was just endeavouring to reason with her when you came in.

Lady Teaz. Indeed! but you seemed to adopt a very tender mode of reasoning—do you usually argue on your knees?

Jos. Surf. Oh, she's a child, and I thought a little bombast—— but, Lady Teazle, when are you to give me your judgment on my library, as you promised?

Lady Teaz. No, no; I begin to think it would be imprudent, and you know I admit you as a lover no farther than fashion requires.

Jos. Surf.—True—a mere Platonic cicisbeo, what every wife is entitled to.

Lady Teaz. Certainly, one must not be out of the fashion. However, I have so many of my country prejudices left, that, though Sir Peter's ill humour may vex me ever so, it never shall provoke me to——

Jos. Surf. The only revenge in your power. Well, I applaud your moderation.

Lady Teaz. Go—you are an insinuating wretch! But we shall be missed—let us join the company.

Jos. Surf. But we had best not return together.

Lady Teaz. Well, don't stay; for Maria shan't come to hear any more of your reasoning, I promise you.   [*Exit.*

Jos. Surf. A curious dilemma, truly, my politics have run me into! I wanted, at first, only to ingratiate myself with Lady Teazle, that she might not be my enemy with Maria; and I have, I don't know how, become her serious lover. Sincerely I begin to wish I had never made such a point of gaining so very good a character, for it has led me into so many cursed rogueries that I doubt I shall be exposed at last.   [*Exit.*

SCENE III.—*A Room in* SIR PETER TEAZLE'S *House*

Enter SIR OLIVER SURFACE *and* ROWLEY.

Sir Oliv. Ha! ha! ha! so my old friend is married, hey?—a young wife out of the country. Ha! ha! ha! that he should have stood bluff to old bachelor so long, and sink into a husband at last!

Row. But you must not rally him on the subject, Sir Oliver; 'tis a tender point, I assure you, though he has been married only seven months.

Sir Oliv. Then he has been just half a year on the stool of repentance!—Poor Peter! But you say he has entirely given up Charles—never sees him, hey?

Row. His prejudice against him is astonishing, and I am sure greatly increased by a jealousy of him with Lady Teazle, which he has industriously been led into by a scandalous society in the neighbourhood, who have contributed not a little to Charles's ill name. Whereas the truth is, I believe, if the lady is partial to either of them, his brother is the favourite.

Sir Oliv. Ay, I know there are a set of malicious, prating, prudent gossips, both male and female, who murder characters to kill time, and will rob a young fellow of his good name before he has years to know the value of it. But I am not to be prejudiced against my nephew by such, I promise you! No, no; if Charles has done nothing false or mean, I shall compound for his extravagance.

Row. Then, my life on't, you will reclaim him. Ah, sir, it gives me new life to find that your heart is not turned against him, and that the son of my good old master has one friend, however, left.

Sir Oliv. What! shall I forget, Master Rowley, when I was at his years myself? Egad, my brother and I were neither of us very prudent youths; and yet, I believe, you have not seen many better men than your old master was?

Row. Sir, 'tis this reflection gives me assurance that Charles may yet be a credit to his family. But here comes Sir Peter.

Sir Oliv. Egad, so he does! Mercy on me, he's greatly altered, and seems to have a settled married look! One may read husband in his face at this distance!

Enter Sir Peter Teazle.

Sir Pet. Ha! Sir Oliver—my old friend! Welcome to England a thousand times!

Sir Oliv. Thank you, thank you, Sir Peter! and i'faith I am glad to find you well, believe me!

Sir Pet. Oh! 'tis a long time since we met—fifteen years, I doubt, Sir Oliver, and many a cross accident in the time.

Sir Oliv. Ay, I have had my share. But, what! I find you are married, hey, my old boy? Well, well, it can't be helped; and so—I wish you joy with all my heart!

Sir Pet. Thank you, thank you, Sir Oliver.—Yes, I have entered into—the happy state; but we'll not talk of that now.

Sir Oliv. True, true, Sir Peter; old friends should not begin on grievances at first meeting. No, no, no.

Row. [*Aside to* Sir Oliver.] Take care, pray, sir.

Sir Oliv. Well, so one of my nephews is a wild rogue, hey?

Sir Pet. Wild! Ah! my old friend, I grieve for your disappointment there; he's a lost young man, indeed. However, his brother will make you amends; Joseph is, indeed, what a youth should be—everybody in the world speaks well of him.

Sir Oliv. I am sorry to hear it; he has too good a character to be an honest fellow. Everybody speaks well of him! Psha! then he has bowed as low to knaves and fools as to the honest dignity of genius and virtue.

Sir Pet. What, Sir Oliver! do you blame him for not making enemies?

Sir Oliv. Yes, if he has merit enough to deserve them.

Sir Pet. Well, well—you'll be convinced when you know him. 'Tis edification to hear him converse; he professes the noblest sentiments.

Sir Oliv. Oh, plague of his sentiments! If he salutes me with a scrap of morality in his mouth, I shall be sick directly. But, however, don't mistake me, Sir Peter; I don't mean to defend Charles's errors: but, before I form my judgment of either of them, I intend to make a trial of their hearts; and my friend Rowley and I have planned something for the purpose.

Row. And Sir Peter shall own for once he has been mistaken.

Sir Pet. Oh, my life on Joseph's honour!

Sir Oliv. Well—come, give us a bottle of good wine, and we'll drink the lads' health, and tell you our scheme.

Sir Pet. Allons, then!

Sir Oliv. And don't, Sir Peter, be so severe against your old friend's son. Odds my life! I am not sorry that he has run out of the course a little: for my part, I hate to see prudence clinging to the green suckers of youth; 'tis like ivy round a sapling, and spoils the growth of the tree.   [*Exeunt.*

ACT III

Scene I.—*A Room in* Sir Peter Teazle's *House*

Enter Sir Peter Teazle, Sir Oliver Surface, *and* Rowley.

Sir Pet. Well, then, we will see this fellow first, and have our wine afterwards. But how is this, Master Rowley? I don't see the jet of your scheme.

Row. Why, sir, this Mr. Stanley, whom I was speaking of, is nearly related to them by their mother. He was once a merchant in Dublin, but has been ruined by a series of undeserved misfortunes. He has applied, by letter, since his confinement, both to Mr. Surface and Charles: from the former he has received nothing but evasive promises of future service, while Charles has done all that his extravagance has left him power to do; and he is, at this time, endeavouring to raise a sum of money, part of which, in the midst of his own distresses, I know he intends for the service of poor Stanley.

Sir Oliv. Ah, he is my brother's son.

Sir Pet. Well, but how is Sir Oliver personally to——

Row. Why, sir, I will inform Charles and his brother that Stanley has obtained permission to apply personally to his friends; and, as they have neither of them ever seen him, let Sir Oliver assume his character, and he will have a fair oppor-

tunity of judging, at least, of the benevolence of their dispositions: and believe me, sir, you will find in the youngest brother
one who, in the midst of folly and dissipation, has still, as our
immortal bard expresses it,—

"a heart to pity, and a hand
Open as day, for melting charity."

Sir Pet. Psha! What signifies his having an open hand or purse
either, when he has nothing left to give? Well, well, make the
trial, if you please. But where is the fellow whom you brought
for Sir Oliver to examine, relative to Charles's affairs?

Row. Below, waiting his commands, and no one can give him
better intelligence.—This, Sir Oliver, is a friendly Jew, who, to
do him justice, has done everything in his power to bring your
nephew to a proper sense of his extravagance.

Sir Pet. Pray let us have him in.

Row. Desire Mr. Moses to walk upstairs.   [*Calls to* SERVANT.

Sir Pet. But, pray, why should you suppose he will speak the
truth?

Row. Oh, I have convinced him that he has no chance of
recovering certain sums advanced to Charles but through the
bounty of Sir Oliver, who he knows is arrived; so that you may
depend on his fidelity to his own interests. I have also another
evidence in my power, one Snake, whom I have detected in a
matter little short of forgery, and shall shortly produce to remove some of your prejudices, Sir Peter, relative to Charles
and Lady Teazle.

Sir Pet. I have heard too much on that subject.

Row. Here comes the honest Israelite.

Enter MOSES.

—This is Sir Oliver.

Sir Oliv. Sir, I understand you have lately had great dealings
with my nephew Charles.

Mos. Yes, Sir Oliver, I have done all I could for him; but he
was ruined before he came to me for assistance.

Sir Oliv. That was unlucky, truly; for you have had no
opportunity of showing your talents.

Mos. None at all; I hadn't the pleasure of knowing his distresses till he was some thousands worse than nothing.

Sir Oliv. Unfortunate, indeed! But I suppose you have done
all in your power for him, honest Moses?

Mos. Yes, he knows that. This very evening I was to have
brought him a gentleman from the city, who does not know him,
and will, I believe, advance him some money.

Sir Pet. What, one Charles has never had money from before?

Mos. Yes, Mr. Premium, of Crutched Friars, formerly a broker.

Sir Pet. Egad, Sir Oliver, a thought strikes me!—Charles, you say, does not know Mr. Premium?

Mos. Not at all.

Sir Pet. Now then, Sir Oliver, you may have a better opportunity of satisfying yourself than by an old romancing tale of a poor relation: go with my friend Moses, and represent Premium, and then, I'll answer for it, you'll see your nephew in all his glory.

Sir Oliv. Egad, I like this idea better than the other, and I may visit Joseph afterwards as old Stanley.

Sir Pet. True—so you may.

Row. Well, this is taking Charles rather at a disadvantage, to be sure. However, Moses, you understand Sir Peter, and will be faithful.

Mos. You may depend upon me.—[*Looks at his watch.*] This is near the time I was to have gone.

Sir Oliv. I'll accompany you as soon as you please, Moses—— But hold! I have forgot one thing—how the plague shall I be able to pass for a Jew?

Mos. There's no need—the principal is Christian.

Sir Oliv. Is he? I'm very sorry to hear it. But, then again, an't I rather too smartly dressed to look like a money-lender?

Sir Pet. Not at all; 'twould not be out of character, if you went in your carriage—would it, Moses?

Mos. Not in the least.

Sir Oliv. Well, but how must I talk? there's certainly some cant of usury and mode of treating that I ought to know.

Sir Pet. Oh, there's not much to learn. The great point, as I take it, is to be exorbitant enough in your demands. Hey, Moses?

Mos. Yes, that's a very great point.

Sir Oliv. I'll answer for't I'll not be wanting in that. I'll ask him eight or ten per cent. on the loan, at least.

Mos. If you ask him no more than that, you'll be discovered immediately.

Sir Oliv. Hey! what, the plague! how much then?

Mos. That depends upon the circumstances. If he appears not very anxious for the supply, you should require only forty or fifty per cent.; but if you find him in great distress, and want the moneys very bad, you may ask double.

Sir Pet. A good honest trade you're learning, Sir Oliver!

Sir Oliv. Truly I think so—and not unprofitable.

Mos. Then, you know, you haven't the moneys yourself, but are forced to borrow them for him of a friend.

Sir Oliv. Oh! I borrow it of a friend, do I?

Mos. And your friend is an unconscionable dog: but you can't help that.

Sir Oliv. My friend an unconscionable dog, is he?

Mos. Yes, and he himself has not the moneys by him, but is forced to sell stocks at a great loss.

Sir Oliv. He is forced to sell stocks at a great loss, is he? Well, that's very kind of him.

Sir Pet. I'faith, Sir Oliver—Mr. Premium, I mean—you'll soon be master of the trade. But, Moses! would not you have him run out a little against the annuity bill? That would be in character, I should think.

Mos. Very much.

Row. And lament that a young man now must be at years of discretion before he is suffered to ruin himself?

Mos. Ay, great pity!

Sir Pet. And abuse the public for allowing merit to an act whose only object is to snatch misfortune and imprudence from the rapacious grip of usury, and give the minor a chance of inheriting his estate without being undone by coming into possession.

Sir Oliv. So, so—Moses shall give me further instructions as we go together.

Sir Pet. You will not have much time, for your nephew lives hard by.

Sir Oliv. Oh, never fear! my tutor appears so able, that though Charles lived in the next street, it must be my own fault if I am not a complete rogue before I turn the corner. [*Exit with* Moses.

Sir Pet. So, now, I think Sir Oliver will be convinced: you are partial, Rowley, and would have prepared Charles for the other plot.

Row. No, upon my word, Sir Peter.

Sir Peter. Well, go bring me this Snake, and I'll hear what he has to say presently. I see Maria, and want to speak with her.—[*Exit* Rowley.] I should be glad to be convinced my suspicions of Lady Teazle and Charles were unjust. I have never yet opened my mind on this subject to my friend Joseph—I am determined I will do it—he will give me his opinion sincerely.

Enter Maria.

So, child, has Mr. Surface returned with you?

Mar. No, sir; he was engaged.

Sir Pet. Well, Maria, do you not reflect, the more you converse with that amiable young man, what return his partiality for you deserves?

Mar. Indeed, Sir Peter, your frequent importunity on this subject distresses me extremely—you compel me to declare, that I know no man who has ever paid me a particular attention whom I would not prefer to Mr. Surface.

Sir Pet. So—here's perverseness! No, no, Maria, 'tis Charles only whom you would prefer. 'Tis evident his vices and follies have won your heart.

Mar. This is unkind, sir. You know I have obeyed you in neither seeing nor corresponding with him: I have heard enough to convince me that he is unworthy my regard. Yet I cannot think it culpable, if, while my understanding severely condemns his vices, my heart suggests pity for his distresses.

Sir Pet. Well, well, pity him as much as you please; but give your heart and hand to a worthier object.

Mar. Never to his brother!

Sir Pet. Go, perverse and obstinate! But take care, madam; you have never yet known what the authority of a guardian is: don't compel me to inform you of it.

Mar. I can only say, you shall not have just reason. 'Tis true, by my father's will, I am for a short period bound to regard you as his substitute; but must cease to think you so, when you would compel me to be miserable. [*Exit.*

Sir Pet. Was ever man so crossed as I am, everything conspiring to fret me! I had not been involved in matrimony a fortnight, before her father, a hale and hearty man, died, on purpose, I believe, for the pleasure of plaguing me with the care of his daughter.—[LADY TEAZLE *sings without.*] But here comes my helpmate! She appears in great good humour. How happy I should be if I could tease her into loving me, though but a little!

Enter LADY TEAZLE.

Lady Teaz. Lud! Sir Peter, I hope you haven't been quarrelling with Maria? It is not using me well to be ill humoured when I am not by.

Sir Pet. Ah, Lady Teazle, you might have the power to make me good humoured at all times.

Lady Teaz. I am sure I wish I had; for I want you to be in a charming sweet temper at this moment. Do be good humoured now, and let me have two hundred pounds, will you?

Sir Pet. Two hundred pounds; what, an't I to be in a good humour without paying for it! But speak to me thus, and i'faith

there's nothing I could refuse you. You shall have it; but seal
me a bond for the repayment.

Lady Teaz. Oh, no—there—my note of hand will do as well.
[*Offering her hand.*

Sir Pet. And you shall no longer reproach me with not giving
you an independent settlement. I mean shortly to surprise you;
but shall we always live thus, hey?

Lady Teaz. If you please, I'm sure I don't care how soon we
leave off quarrelling, provided you'll own you were tired first.

Sir Pet. Well—then let our future contest be, who shall be most
obliging.

Lady Teaz. I assure you, Sir Peter, good nature becomes you.
You look now as you did before we were married, when you
used to walk with me under the elms, and tell me stories of what
a gallant you were in your youth, and chuck me under the chin,
you would; and ask me if I thought I could love an old fellow,
who would deny me nothing—didn't you?

Sir Pet. Yes, yes, and you were as kind and attentive——

Lady Teaz. Ay, so I was, and would always take your part,
when my acquaintance used to abuse you, and turn you into
ridicule.

Sir Pet. Indeed!

Lady Teaz. Ay, and when my cousin Sophy has called you a
stiff, peevish old bachelor, and laughed at me for thinking of
marrying one who might be my father, I have always defended
you, and said, I didn't think you so ugly by any means, and that
you'd make a very good sort of a husband.

Sir Pet. And you prophesied right; and we shall now be the
happiest couple——

Lady Teaz. And never differ again?

Sir Pet. No, never—though at the same time, indeed, my dear
Lady Teazle, you must watch your temper very seriously; for
in all our little quarrels, my dear, if you recollect, my love, you
always began first.

Lady Teas. I beg your pardon, my dear Sir Peter: indeed, you
always gave the provocation.

Sir Pet. Now, see, my angel! take care—contradicting isn't
the way to keep friends.

Lady Teaz. Then, don't you begin it, my love!

Sir Pet. There, now! you—you are going on. You don't perceive, my life, that you are just doing the very thing which you
know always makes me angry.

Lady Teaz. Nay, you know if you will be angry without any
reason, my dear——

Sir Pet. There! now you want to quarrel again.

Lady Teaz. No, I'm sure I don't: but, if you will be so peevish——

Sir Pet. There now! who begins first?

Lady Teaz. Why, you, to be sure. I said nothing—but there's no bearing your temper.

Sir Pet. No, no, madam: the fault's in your own temper.

Lady Teaz. Ay, you are just what my cousin Sophy said you would be.

Sir Pet. Your cousin Sophy is a forward, impertinent gipsy.

Lady Teas. You are a great bear, I am sure, to abuse my relations.

Sir Pet. Now may all the plagues of marriage be doubled on me, if ever I try to be friends with you any more!

Lady Teaz. So much the metter.

Sir Pet. No, no, madam: 'tis evident you never cared a pin for me, and I was a madman to marry you—a pert, rural coquette, that had refused half the honest 'squires in the neighbourhood!

Lady Teaz. And I am sure I was a fool to marry you—an old dangling bachelor, who was single at fifty, only because he never could meet with any one who would have him.

Sir Pet. Ay, ay, madam; but you were pleased enough to listen to me: you never had such an offer before.

Lady Teaz. No! didn't I refuse Sir Tivy Terrier, who everybody said would have been a better match? for his estate is just as good as yours, and he has broke his neck since we have been married.

Sir Pet. I have done with you, madam! You are an unfeeling, ungrateful—but there's an end of everything. I believe you capable of everything that is bad. Yes, madam, I now believe the reports relative to you and Charles, madam. Yes, madam, you and Charles are, not without grounds——

Lady Teaz. Take care, Sir Peter! you had better not insinuate any such thing! I'll not be suspected without cause, I promise you.

Sir Pet. Very well, madam! very well! a separate maintenance as soon as you please. Yes, madam, or a divorce! I'll make an example of myself for the benefit of all old bachelors. Let us separate, madam.

Lady Teaz. Agreed! agreed! And now, my dear Sir Peter, we are of a mind once more, we may be the happiest couple, and never differ again, you know: ha! ha! ha! Well, you are going to be in a passion, I see, and I shall only interrupt you—so, bye! bye!   [*Exit.*

Sir Pet. Plagues and tortures! can't I make her angry either!

Oh, I am the most miserable fellow! But I'll not bear her presuming to keep her temper: no! she may break my heart, but she shan't keep her temper.   [*Exit.*

Scene II.—*A Room in* Charles Surface's *House*

Enter Trip, Moses, *and* Sir Oliver Surface.

Trip. Here, Master Moses! if you'll stay a moment; I'll try whether—what's the gentleman's name?

Sir Oliv. Mr. Moses, what is my name?   [*Aside to* Moses.

Mos. Mr. Premium.

Trip. Premium—very well.   [*Exit, taking snuff.*

Sir Oliv. To judge by the servants, one wouldn't believe the master was ruined. But what!—sure, this was my brother's house?

Mos. Yes, sir; Mr. Charles bought it of Mr. Joseph, with the furniture, pictures, &c., just as the old gentleman left it. Sir Peter thought it a piece of extravagance in him.

Sir Oliv. In my mind, the other's economy in selling it to him was more reprehensible by half.

Re-enter Trip.

Trip. My master says you must wait, gentlemen: he has company, and can't speak with you yet.

Sir Oliv. If he knew who it was wanted to see him, perhaps he would not send such a message?

Trip. Yes, yes, sir; he knows you are here—I did not forget little Premium: no, no, no.

Sir Oliv. Very well; and I pray, sir, what may be your name?

Trip. Trip, sir; my name is Trip, at your service.

Sir Oliv. Well, then, Mr. Trip, you have a pleasant sort of place here, I guess?

Trip. Why, yes—here are three or four of us pass our time agreeably enough; but then our wages are sometimes a little in arrear—and not very great either—but fifty pounds a year, and find our own bags and bouquets.

Sir Oliv. Bags and bouquets! halters and bastinadoes! [*Aside.*

Trip. And *à propos*, Moses, have you been able to get me that little bill discounted?

Sir Oliv. Wants to raise money, too!—mercy on me! Has his distresses too, I warrant, like a lord, and affects creditors and duns.   [*Aside.*

Mos. 'Twas not to be done, indeed, Mr. Trip.

Trip. Good lack, you surprise me! My friend Brush has indorsed it, and I thought when he put his name at the back of a bill 'twas the same as cash.

Mos. No, 'twouldn't do.

Trip. A small sum—but twenty pounds. Hark'ee, Moses, do you think you couldn't get it me by way of annuity?

Sir Oliv. An annuity! ha! ha! a footman raise money by way of annuity! Well done, luxury, egad! [*Aside.*

Mos. Well, but you must insure your place.

Trip. Oh, with all my heart! I'll insure my place, and my life too, if you please.

Sir Oliv. It's more than I would your neck. [*Aside.*

Mos. But is there nothing you could deposit?

Trip. Why, nothing capital of my master's wardrobe has dropped lately; but I could give you a mortgage on some of his winter clothes, with equity of redemption before November—or you shall have the reversion of the French velvet, or a post-obit on the blue and silver;—these, I should think, Moses, with a few pair of point ruffles, as a collateral security—hey, my little fellow?

Mos. Well, well. [*Bell rings.*

Trip. Egad, I heard the bell! I believe, gentlemen, I can now introduce you. Don't forget the annuity, little Moses! This way, gentlemen, I'll insure my place, you know.

Sir Oliv. [*Aside.*] If the man be a shadow of the master, this is the temple of dissipation indeed! *Exeunt.*

SCENE III.—*Another Room in the same*

CHARLES SURFACE, SIR HARRY BUMPER, CARELESS, *and* GENTLEMEN, *discovered drinking.*

Chas. Surf. 'Fore heaven, 'tis true!—there's the great degeneracy of the age. Many of our acquaintance have taste, spirit, and politeness; but plague on't they won't drink.

Care. It is so, indeed, Charles! they give in to all the substantial luxuries of the table, and abstain from nothing but wine and wit. Oh, certainly society suffers by it intolerably! for now, instead of the social spirit of raillery that used to mantle over a glass of bright Burgundy, their conversation is become just like the Spa-water they drink, which has all the pertness and flatulency of champagne, without its spirit or flavour.

1 *Gent.* But what are they to do who love play better than wine?

Care. True! there's Sir Harry diets himself for gaming, and is now under a hazard regimen.

Chas. Surf. Then he'll have the worst of it. What! you wouldn't train a horse for the course by keeping him from corn? For my part, egad, I'm never so successful as when I am a little merry: let me throw on a bottle of champagne, and I never lose—at least I never feel my losses, which is exactly the same thing.

2 Gent. Ay, that I believe.

Chas. Surf. And, then, what man can pretend to be a believer in love, who is an abjurer of wine? 'Tis the test by which the lover knows his own heart. Fill a dozen bumpers to a dozen beauties, and she that floats at the top is the maid that has bewitched you.

Care. Now then, Charles, be honest, and give us your real favourite.

Chas. Surf. Why, I have withheld her only in compassion to you. If I toast her, you must give a round of her peers, which is impossible—on earth.

Care. Oh, then we'll find some canonised vestals or heathen goddesses that will do, I warrant!

Chas. Surf. Here then, bumpers, you rogues! bumpers! Maria! Maria—

Sir Har. Maria who?

Chas. Surf. Oh, damn the surname!—'tis too formal to be registered in Love's calendar—but now, Sir Harry, beware, we must have beauty superlative.

Care. Nay, never study, Sir Harry: we'll stand to the toast, though your mistress should want an eye, and you know you have a song will excuse you.

Sir Har. Egad, so I have! and I'll give him the song instead of the lady.   [*Sings.*

> Here's to the maiden of bashful fifteen;
>   Here's to the widow of fifty;
> Here's to the flaunting extravagant quean,
>   And here's to the housewife that's thrifty.
>
> *Chorus.*   Let the toast pass,—
>   Drink to the lass,
> I'll warrant she'll prove an excuse for a glass.
>
> Here's to the charmer whose dimples we prize;
>   Now to the maid who has none, sir;
> Here's to the girl with a pair of blue eyes,
>   And here's to the nymph with but one, sir.

Chorus.   Let the toast pass,—
> Drink to the lass,

I'll warrant she'll prove an excuse for a glass.

> Here's to the maid with a bosom of snow:
>   Now to her that's as brown as a berry:
> Here's to the wife with a face full of woe,
>   And now to the damsel that's merry.

Chorus.   Let the toast pass,—
> Drink to the lass,

I'll warrant she'll prove an excuse for a glass.

> For let 'em be clumsy, or let 'em be slim,
>   Young or ancient, I care not a feather;
> So fill a pint bumper quite up to the brim,
> So fill up your glasses, nay, fill to the brim,
>   And let us e'en toast them together.

Chorus.   Let the toast pass,—
> Drink to the lass,

I'll warrant she'll prove an excuse for a glass.

All. Bravo! Bravo!

Enter TRIP, *and whispers* CHARLES SURFACE.

Chas. Surf. Gentlemen, you must excuse me a little.—Careless take the chair, will you?

Care. Nay, pr'ythee, Charles, what now? This is one of your peerless beauties, I suppose, dropped in by chance?

Chas. Surf. No, faith! To tell you the truth, 'tis a Jew and a broker, who are come by appointment.

Care. Oh, damn it! let's have the Jew in.

1 *Gent.* Ay, and the broker too, by all means.

2 *Gent.* Yes, yes, the Jew and the broker.

Chas. Surf. Egad, with all my heart!—Trip, bid the gentlemen walk in.—[*Exit* TRIP.] Though there's one of them a stranger, I can tell you.

Care. Charles, let us give them some generous Burgundy, and perhaps they'll grow conscientious.

Chas. Surf. Oh, hang 'em, no! wine does but draw forth a man's natural qualities; and to make them drink would only be to whet their knavery.

Re-enter TRIP, *with* SIR OLIVER SURFACE *and* MOSES.

Chas. Surf. So, honest Moses; walk in, pray, Mr. Premium— that's the gentleman's name, isn't it, Moses?

Mos. Yes, sir.

Chas. Surf. Set chairs, Trip.—Sit down, Mr. Premium.—Glasses, Trip.—[TRIP *gives chairs and glasses, and exit.*] Sit down, Moses. —Come, Mr. Premium, I'll give you a sentiment; here's *Success to usury!*—Moses, fill the gentleman a bumper.

Mos. Success to usury! [*Drinks.*

Care. Right, Moses—usury is prudence and industry, and deserves to succeed.

Sir Oliv. Then here's—All the success it deserves! [*Drinks.*

Care. No, no, that won't do! Mr. Premium, you have demurred at the toast, and must drink it in a pint bumper.

1 *Gent.* A pint bumper, at least.

Mos. Oh, pray, sir, consider—Mr. Premium's a gentleman.

Care. And therefore loves good wine.

2 *Gent.* Give Moses a quart glass—this is mutiny, and a high contempt for the chair.

Care. Here, now for't! I'll see justice done, to the last drop of my bottle.

Sir Oliv. Nay, pray, gentlemen—I did not expect this usage.

Chas. Surf. No, hang it, you shan't; Mr. Premium's a stranger.

Sir Oliv. Odd! I wish I was well out of their company. [*Aside.*

Care. Plague on 'em then! if they won't drink, we'll not sit down with them. Come, Harry, the dice are in the next room.—Charles, you'll join us when you have finished your business with the gentlemen?

Chas. Surf. I will! I will!—[*Exeunt* SIR HARRY BUMPER *and* GENTLEMEN; CARELESS *following.*] Careless.

Care. [*Returning.*] Well!

Chas. Surf. Perhaps I may want you.

Care. Oh, you know I am always ready: word, note, or bond, 'tis all the same to me. [*Exit.*

Mos. Sir, this is Mr. Premium, a gentleman of the strictest honour and secrecy; and always performs what he undertakes. Mr. Premium, this is——

Chas. Surf. Psha! have done. Sir, my friend Moses is a very honest fellow, but a little slow at expression: he'll be an hour giving us our titles. Mr. Premium, the plain state of the matter is this: I am an extravagant young fellow who wants to borrow money; you I take to be a prudent old fellow, who has got money to lend. I am blockhead enough to give fifty per cent. sooner than not have it! and you, I presume, are rogue enough to take a hundred if you can get it. Now, sir, you see we are acquainted at once, and may proceed to business without further ceremony.

Sir Oliv. Exceeding frank, upon my word. I see, sir, you are not a man of many compliments.

Chas. Surf. Oh, no, sir! plain dealing in business I always think best.

Sir Oliv. Sir, I like you the better for it. However, you are mistaken in one thing; I have no money to lend, but I believe I could procure some of a friend; but then he's an unconscionable dog. Isn't he, Moses? And must sell stock to accommodate you. Mustn't he, Moses?

Mos. Yes, indeed! You know I always speak the truth, and scorn to tell a lie!

Chas. Surf. Right. People that speak truth generally do. But these are trifles, Mr. Premium. What! I know money isn't to be bought without paying for't!

Sir Olive. Well, but what security could you give? You have no land, I suppose?

Chas. Surf. Not a mole-hill, nor a twig, but what's in the bough-pots out of the window!

Sir Oliv. Nor any stock, I presume?

Chas. Surf. Nothing but live stock—and that's only a few pointers and ponies. But pray, Mr. Premium, are you acquainted at all with any of my connections?

Sir Oliv. Why, to say the truth, I am.

Chas. Surf. Then you must know that I have a devilish rich uncle in the East Indies, Sir Oliver Surface, from whom I have the greatest expectations?

Sir Oliv. That you have a wealthy uncle, I have heard; but how your expectations will turn out is more, I believe, than you can tell.

Chas. Surf. Oh, no!—there can be no doubt. They tell me I'm a prodigious favourite, and that he talks of leaving me everything.

Sir Oliv. Indeed! this is the first I've heard of it.

Chas. Surf. Yes, yes, 'tis just so. Moses knows 'tis true; don't you, Moses?

Mos. Oh, yes! I'll swear to't.

Sir Oliv. Egad, they'll persuade me presently I'm at Bengal.

[*Aside.*

Chas. Surf. Now I propose, Mr. Premium, if it's agreeable to you, a post-obit on Sir Oliver's life: though at the same time the old fellow has been so liberal to me, that I give you my word, I should be very sorry to hear that anything had happened to him.

Sir Oliv. Not more than I should, I assure you. But the bond you mention happens to be just the worst security you could offer me—for I might live to a hundred and never see the principal.

Chas. Surf. Oh, yes, you would! the moment Sir Oliver dies, you know, you would come on me for the money.

Sir Oliv. Then I believe I should be the most unwelcome dun you ever had in your life.

Chas. Surf. What! I suppose you're afraid that Sir Oliver is too good a life?

Sir Oliv. No, indeed I am not; though I have heard he is as hale and healthy as any man of his years in Christendom.

Chas. Surf. There again, now, you are misinformed. No, no, the climate has hurt him considerably, poor uncle Oliver. Yes, yes, he breaks apace, I'm told—and is so much altered lately that his nearest relations would not know him.

Sir Oliv. No! Ha! ha! ha! so much altered lately that his nearest relations would not know him! Ha! ha! ha! egad—ha! ha! ha!

Chas. Surf. Ha! ha!—you're glad to hear that, little Premium?

Sir Oliv. No, no, I'm not.

Chas. Surf. Yes, yes, you are—ha! ha! ha!—you know that mends your chance.

Sir Oliv. But I'm told Sir Oliver is coming over; nay, some say he has actually arrived.

Chas. Surf. Psha! sure I must know better than you whether he's come or not. No, no, rely on't he's at this moment at Calcutta. Isn't he, Moses?

Mos. Oh, yes, certainly.

Sir Oliv. Very true, as you say, you must know better than I, though I have it from pretty good authority. Haven't I, Moses?

Mos. Yes, most undoubted!

Sir Oliv. But, sir, as I understand you want a few hundreds immediately, is there nothing you could dispose of?

Chas. Surf. How do you mean?

Sir Oliv. For instance, now, I have heard that your father left behind him a great quantity of massy old plate.

Chas. Surf. O Lud, that's gone long ago. Moses can tell you how better than I can.

Sir Oliv. [*Aside.*] Good lack! all the family race-cups and corporation-bowls!—[*Aloud.*] Then it was also supposed that his library was one of the most valuable and compact.

Chas. Surf. Yes, yes, so it was—vastly too much so for a private gentleman. For my part, I was always of a communicative disposition, so I thought it a shame to keep so much knowledge to myself.

Sir Oliv. [*Aside.*] Mercy upon me! learning that had run in the family like an heir-loom!—[*Aloud.*] Pray, what has become of the books?

Chas. Surf. You must inquire of the auctioneer, Master Premium, for I don't believe even Moses can direct you.

Mos. I know nothing of books.

Sir Oliv. So, so, nothing of the family property left, I suppose?

Chas. Surf. Not much, indeed; unless you have a mind to the family pictures. I have got a room full of ancestors above: and if you have a taste for old paintings, egad, you shall have 'em a bargain!

Sir Oliv. Hey! what the devil! sure, you wouldn't sell your forefathers, would you?

Chas. Surf. Every man of them, to the best bidder.

Sir Oliv. What! your great-uncles and aunts?

Chas. Surf. Ay, and my great-grandfathers and grandmothers too.

Sir Oliv. [*Aside.*] Now I give him up!—[*Aloud.*] What the plague, have you no bowels for your own kindred? Odd's life! do you take me for Shylock in the play, that you would raise money of me on your own flesh and blood?

Chas. Surf. Nay, my little broker, don't be angry: what need you care, if you have your money's worth?

Sir Oliv. Well, I'll be the purchaser: I think I can dispose of the family canvas.—[*Aside.*] Oh, I'll never forgive him this! never!

Re-enter CARELESS.

Care. Come, Charles, what keeps you?

Chas. Surf. I can't come yet. I'faith, we are going to have a sale above stairs, here's little Premium will buy all my ancestors!

Care. Oh, burn your ancestors!

Chas. Surf. No, he may do that afterwards, if he pleases. Stay, Careless, we want you: egad, you shall be auctioneer—so come along with us.

Care. Oh, have with you, if that's the case. I can handle a hammer as well as a dice box; Going! going!

Sir Oliv. Oh, the profligates!   [*Aside.*

Chas. Surf. Come, Moses, you shall be appraiser, if we want one. Gad's life, little Premium, you don't seem to like the business?

Sir Oliv. Oh, yes, I do, vastly! Ha! ha! ha! yes, yes, I think it a rare joke to sell one's family by auction—ha! ha!—[*Aside.*] Oh, the prodigal!

Chas. Surf. To be sure! when a man wants money, where the plague should he get assistance, if he can't make free with his own relations?   [*Exeunt.*

Sir Oliv. I'll never forgive him; never! never!

ACT IV

SCENE I.—*A Picture Room in* CHARLES SURFACE'S *House*

Enter CHARLES SURFACE, SIR OLIVER SURFACE, MOSES, *and*
CARELESS.

Chas. Surf. Walk in, gentlemen, pray walk in;—here they are, the family of the Surfaces, up to the Conquest.

Sir Oliv. And, in my opinion, a goodly collection.

Chas. Surf. Ay, ay, these are done in the true spirit of portrait-painting; no *volontière grace* or expression. Not like the works of your modern Raphaels, who give you the strongest resemblance, yet contrive to make your portrait independent of you; so that you may sink the original and not hurt the picture. No, no; the merit of these is the inveterate likeness—all stiff and awkward as the originals, and like nothing in human nature besides.

Sir Oliv. Ah! we shall never see such figures of men again.

Chas. Surf. I hope not. Well, you see, Master Premium, what a domestic character I am; here I sit of an evening surrounded by my family. But come, get to your pulpit, Mr. Auctioneer; here's an old gouty chair of my grandfather's will answer the purpose.

Care. Ay, ay, this will do. But, Charles, I haven't a hammer; and what's an auctioneer without his hammer?

Chas. Surf. Egad, that's true. What parchment have we here? Oh, our genealogy in full. [*Taking pedigree down.*] Here, Careless, you shall have no common bit of mahogany, here's the family tree for you, you rogue! This shall be your hammer, and now you may knock down my ancestors with their own pedigree.

Sir Oliv. What an unnatural rogue!—an *ex post facto* parricide!
[*Aside.*

Care. Yes, yes, here's a list of your generation indeed;—faith, Charles, this is the most convenient thing you could have found for the business, for 'twill not only serve as a hammer, but a catalogue into the bargain. Come, begin—A-going, a-going, a-going!

Chas. Surf. Bravo, Careless! Well, here's my great uncle, Sir Richard Ravelin, a marvellous good general in his day, I assure you. He served in all the Duke of Marlborough's wars, and got that cut over his eye at the battle of Malplaquet. What say you, Mr. Premium? look at him—there's a hero! not cut out of his feathers, as your modern clipped captains are, but enveloped in wig and regimentals, as a general should be. What do you bid?

Sir Oliv. [*Aside to* MOSES.] Bid him speak.

Mos. Mr. Premium would have you speak.

Chas. Surf. Why, then, he shall have him for ten pounds, and I'm sure that's not dear for a staff-officer.

Sir Oliv. [*Aside.*] Heaven deliver me! his famous uncle Richard for ten pounds!—[*Aloud.*] Very well, sir, I take him at that.

Chas. Surf. Careless, knock down my uncle Richard.—Here, now, is a maiden sister of his, my great-aunt Deborah, done by Kneller, in his best manner, and esteemed a very formidable likeness. There she is, you see, a shepherdess feeding her flock. You shall have her for five pounds ten—the sheep are worth the money.

Sir Oliv. [*Aside.*] Ah! poor Deborah! a woman who set such a value on herself!—[*Aloud.*] Five pounds ten—she's mine.

Chas. Surf. Knock down my aunt Deborah! Here, now, are two that were a sort of cousins of theirs.—You see, Moses, these pictures were done some time ago, when beaux wore wigs, and the ladies their own hair.

Sir Oliv. Yes, truly, head-dresses appear to have been a little lower in those days.

Chas. Surf. Well, take that couple for the same.

Mos. 'Tis a good bargain.

Chas. Surf. Careless!—This, now, is a grandfather of my mother's, a learned judge, well known on the western circuit.— What do you rate him at, Moses?

Mos. Four guineas.

Chas. Surf. Four guineas! Gad's life, you don't bid me the price of his wig.—Mr. Premium, you have more respect for the wool-sack; do let us knock his lordship down at fifteen.

Sir Oliv. By all means.

Care. Gone.

Chas. Surf. And there are two brothers of his, William and Walter Blunt, Esquires, both members of Parliament, and noted speakers; and, what's very extraordinary, I believe, this is the first time they were ever bought or sold.

Sir Oliv. That is very extraordinary, indeed! I'll take them at your own price, for the honour of Parliament.

Care. Well said, little Premium! I'll knock them down at forty.

Chas. Surf. Here's a jolly fellow—I don't know what relation, but he was mayor of Norwich: take him at eight pounds.

Sir Oliv. No, no; six will do for the mayor.

Chas. Surf. Come, make it guineas, and I'll throw you the two aldermen there into the bargain.

Sir Oliv. They're mine.

Chas. Surf. Careless, knock down the mayor and aldermen. But, plague on't! we shall be all day retailing in this manner; do let us deal wholesale: what say you, little Premium? Give me three hundred pounds for the rest of the family in the lump.

Care. Ay ay, that will be the best way.

Sir Oliv. Well, well, anything to accommodate you; they are mine. But there is one portrait which you have always passed over.

Care. What, that ill-looking little fellow over the settee?

Sir Oliv. Yes, sir, I mean that; though I don't think him so ill-looking a little fellow, by any means.

Chas. Surf. What, that? Oh; that's my uncle Oliver! 'Twas done before he went to India.

Care. Your uncle Oliver! Gad, then you'll never be friends, Charles. That, now, to me, is as stern a looking rogue as ever I saw; an unforgiving eye, and a damned disinheriting countenance! an inveterate knave, depend on't. Don't you think so, little Premium?

Sir Oliv. Upon my soul, sir, I do not; I think it is as honest a looking face as any in the room, dead or alive. But I suppose uncle Oliver goes with the rest of the lumber?

Chas. Surf. No, hang it! I'll not part with poor Noll. The old fellow has been very good to me, and, egad, I'll keep his picture while I've a room to put it in.

Sir Oliv. [*Aside.*] The rogue's my nephew after all!—[*Aloud.*] But, sir, I have somehow taken a fancy to that picture.

Chas. Surf. I'm sorry for't, for you certainly will not have it. Oons, haven't you got enough of them?

Sir Oliv. [*Aside.*] I forgive him everything!—[*Aloud.*] But, sir, when I take a whim in my head, I don't value money. I'll give you as much for that as for all the rest.

Chas. Surf. Don't tease me, master broker; I tell you I'll not part with it, and there's an end of it.

Sir Oliv. [*Aside.*] How like his father the dog is.—[*Aloud.*] Well, well, I have done.—[*Aside.*] I did not perceive it before, but I think I never saw such a striking resemblance.—[*Aloud.*] Here is a draught for your sum.

Chas. Surf. Why, 'tis for eight hundred pounds!

Sir Oliv. You will not let Sir Oliver go?

Chas. Surf. Zounds! no! I tell you, once more.

Sir Oliv. Then never mind the difference, we'll balance that another time. But give me your hand on the bargain; you are an honest fellow, Charles—I beg pardon, sir, for being so free.— Come, Moses.

Chas. Surf. Egad, this is a whimsical old fellow!—But hark'ee, Premium, you'll prepare lodgings for these gentlemen.

Sir Oliv. Yes, yes, I'll send for them in a day or two.

Chas. Surf. But hold; do now send a genteel conveyance for them, for, I assure you, they were most of them used to ride in their own carriages.

Sir Oliv. I will, I will—for all but Oliver.

Chas. Surf. Ay, all but the little nabob.

Sir Oliv. You're fixed on that?

Chas. Surf. Peremptorily.

Sir Oliv. [*Aside.*] A dear extravagant rogue!—[*Aloud.*] Good day!—Come, Moses.—[*Aside.*] Let me hear now who dares call him profligate!   [*Exit with* MOSES.

Care. Why, this is the oddest genius of the sort I ever met with!

Chas. Surf. Egad, he's the prince of brokers, I think. I wonder how the devil Moses got acquainted with so honest a fellow.—Ha! here's Rowley.—Do, Careless, say I'll join the company in a few moments.

Care. I will—but don't let that old blockhead persuade you to squander any of that money on old musty debts, or any such nonsense; for tradesmen, Charles, are the most exorbitant fellows.

Chas. Surf. Very true, and paying them is only encouraging them.

Care. Nothing else.

Chas. Surf. Ay, ay, never fear.—[*Exit* CARELESS.] So! this was an odd old fellow, indeed. Let me see, two-thirds of these five hundred and thirty odd pounds are mine by right. 'Fore Heaven! I find one's ancestors are more valuable relations than I took them for!—Ladies and gentlemen, your most obedient and very grateful servant.   [*Bows ceremoniously to the pictures.*

Enter ROWLEY.

Ha! old Rowley! egad, you are just come in time to take leave of your old acquaintance.

Row. Yes, I heard they were a-going. But I wonder you can have such spirits under so many distresses.

Chas. Surf. Why, there's the point! my distresses are so many, that I can't afford to part with my spirits; but I shall be rich and splenetic, all in good time. However, I suppose you are surprised that I am not more sorrowful at parting with so many near relations; to be sure, 'tis very affecting; but you see they never move a muscle, so why should I?

Row. There's no making you serious a moment.

Chas. Surf. Yes, faith, I am so now. Here, my honest Rowley, here, get me this changed directly, and take a hundred pounds of it immediately to old Stanley.

Row. A hundred pounds! Consider only——

Chas. Surf. Gad's life, don't talk about it! poor Stanley's wants are pressing, and, if you don't make haste, we shall have some one call that has a better right to the money.

Row. Ah! there's the point! I never will cease dunning you with the old proverb——

Chas. Surf. Be just before you're generous.—Why, so I would if I could; but Justice is an old hobbling beldame, and I can't get her to keep pace with Generosity, for the soul of me.

Row. Yet, Charles, believe me, one hour's reflection——

Chas. Surf. Ay, ay, it's very true; but, hark'ee, Rowley, while I have, by Heaven I'll give; so, damn your economy! and now for hazard.   [*Exeunt.*

SCENE II.—*Another room in the same*

Enter SIR OLIVER SURFACE *and* MOSES.

Mos. Well, sir, I think, as Sir Peter said, you have seen Mr. Charles in high glory; 'tis great pity he's so extravagant.

Sir Oliv. True, but he would not sell my picture.

Mos. And loves wine and women so much.

Sir Oliv. But he would not sell my picture.

Mos. And games so deep.

Sir Oliv. But he would not sell my picture. Oh, here's Rowley.

Enter ROWLEY.

Row. So, Sir Oliver, I find you have made a purchase——

Sir Oliv. Yes, yes, our young rake has parted with his ancestors like old tapestry.

Row. And here has he commissioned me to re-deliver you part of the purchase-money—I mean, though, in your necessitous character of old Stanley.

Mos. Ah! there is the pity of all: he is so damned charitable.

Row. And I left a hosier and two tailors in the hall, who, I'm sure, won't be paid, and this hundred would satisfy them.

Sir Oliv. Well, well, I'll pay his debts, and his benevolence too. But now I am no more a broker, and you shall introduce me to the elder brother as old Stanley.

Row. Not yet awhile; Sir Peter, I know, means to call there about this time.

Enter TRIP.

Trip. Oh, gentlemen, I beg pardon for not showing you out; this way—Moses, a word.   [*Exit with* MOSES.

Sir Oliv. There's a fellow for you! Would you believe it, that puppy intercepted the Jew on our coming, and wanted to raise money before he got to his master!

Row. Indeed.

Sir Oliv. Yes, they are now planning an annuity business. Ah, Master Rowley, in my days servants were content with the follies of their masters, when they were worn a little threadbare; but now they have their vices, like their birthday clothes, with the gloss on.

[*Exeunt.*

SCENE III.—*A Library in* JOSEPH SURFACE'S *House*

Enter JOSEPH SURFACE *and* SERVANT.

Jos. Surf. No letter from Lady Teazle?

Ser. No, sir.

Jos. Surf. [*Aside.*] I am surprised she has not sent, if she is prevented from coming. Sir Peter certainly does not suspect me. Yet I wish I may not lose the heiress, through the scrape I have drawn myself into with the wife; however, Charles's imprudence and bad character are great points in my favour.   [*Knocking without.*

Ser. Sir, I believe that must be Lady Teazle.

Jos. Surf. Hold! See whether it is or not, before you go to the door: I have a particular message for you if it should be my brother.

Ser. 'Tis her ladyship, sir; she always leaves the chair at the milliner's in the next street.

Jos. Surf. Stay, stay: draw that screen before the window—that will do;—my opposite neighbour is a maiden lady of so curious a temper.—[SERVANT *draws the screen, and exit.*] I have a difficult hand to play in this affair. Lady Teazle has lately suspected my views on Maria; but she must by no means be let into that secret, —at least, till I have her more in my power.

Enter LADY TEAZLE.

Lady Teaz. What sentiment in soliloquy now? Have you been very impatient? O Lud! don't pretend to look grave. I vow I couldn't come before.

Jos. Surf. O madam, punctuality is a species of constancy very unfashionable in a lady of quality.

[*Places chairs, and sits after* LADY TEAZLE *is seated.*

Lady Teaz. Upon my word, you ought to pity me. Do you know Sir Peter is grown so ill-natured to me of late, and so jealous of Charles too—that's the best of the story, isn't it?

Jos. Surf. I am glad my scandalous friends keep that up.   [*Aside.*

Lady Teaz. I am sure I wish he would let Maria marry him, and then perhaps he would be convinced; don't you, Mr. Surface?

Jos. Surf. [*Aside.*] Indeed I do not.—[*Aloud.*] Oh, certainly I do! for then my dear Lady Teazle would also be convinced how wrong her suspicions were of my having any design on the silly girl.

Lady Teaz. Well, well, I'm inclined to believe you. But isn't it provoking, to have the most ill-natured things said at one? And there's my friend Lady Sneerwell has circulated I don't know how many scandalous tales of me, and all without any foundation, too; that's what vexes me.

Jos. Surf. Ay, madam, to be sure, that is the provoking circumstance—without foundation; yes, yes, there's the mortification, indeed; for, when a scandalous story is believed against one, there certainly is no comfort like the consciousness of having deserved it.

Lady Teaz. No, to be sure, then I'd forgive their malice; but to attack me, who am really so innocent, and who never say an ill-natured thing of anybody—that is, of any friend; and then Sir Peter, too, to have him so peevish, and so suspicious, when I know the integrity of my own heart—indeed 'tis monstrous!

Jos. Surf. But, my dear Lady Teazle, 'tis your own fault if you suffer it. When a husband entertains a groundless suspicion of his wife, and withdraws his confidence from her, the original compact is broken, and she owes it to the honour of her sex to endeavour to outwit him.

Lady Teaz. Indeed! So that, if he suspects me without cause, it follows, that the best way of curing his jealousy is to give him reason for't?

Jos. Surf. Undoubtedly—for your husband should never be deceived in you: and in that case it becomes you to be frail in compliment to his discernment.

Lady Teaz. To be sure, what you say is very reasonable, and when the consciousness of my innocence——

Jos. Surf. Ah, my dear madam, there is the great mistake; 'tis this very conscious innocence that is of the greatest prejudice to you. What is it makes you negligent of forms, and careless of the world's opinion? why, the consciousness of your own innocence. What makes you thoughtless in your conduct, and apt to run into a thousand little imprudences? why, the consciousness of your own innocence. What makes you impatient of Sir Peter's temper, and outrageous at his suspicions? why, the consciousness of your innocence.

Lady Teaz. 'Tis very true!

Jos. Surf. Now, my dear Lady Teazle, if you would but once make a trifling *faux pas,* you can't conceive how cautious you would grow, and how ready to humour and agree with your husband.

Lady Teaz. Do you think so?

Jos. Surf. Oh, I'm sure on't; and then you would find all scandal would cease at once, for—in short, your character at present is like a person in a plethora, absolutely dying from too much health.

Lady Teaz. So, so; then I perceive your prescription is, that I must sin in my own defence, and part with my virtue to preserve my reputation?

Jos. Surf. Exactly so, upon my credit, ma'am.

Lady Teaz. Well, certainly this is the oddest doctrine, and the newest receipt for avoiding calumny?

Jos. Surf. An infallible one, believe me. Prudence, like experience, must be paid for.

Lady Teaz. Why, if my understanding were once convinced——

Jos. Surf. Oh, certainly, madam, your understanding should be convinced. Yes, yes—Heaven forbid I should persuade you to do anything you thought wrong. No, no, I have too much honour to desire it.

Lady Teaz. Don't you think we may as well leave honour out of the argument? [*Rises.*

Jos. Surf. Ah, the ill effects of your country education, I see, still remain with you.

Lady Teaz. I doubt they do, indeed; and I will fairly own to you, that if I could be persuaded to do wrong, it would be by Sir Peter's ill-usage sooner than your honourable logic, after all.

Jos. Surf. Then, by this hand, which he is unworthy of——
[*Taking her hand.*

Re-enter SERVANT.

'Sdeath, you blockhead—what do you want?

Ser. I beg your pardon, sir, but I thought you would not choose Sir Peter to come up without announcing him.

Jos. Surf. Sir Peter!—Oons—the devil!

Lady Teaz. Sir Peter! O Lud! I'm ruined! I'm ruined!

Ser. Sir, 'twasn't I let him in.

Lady Teaz. Oh! I'm quite undone! What will become of me? Now, Mr. Logic—Oh! mercy, sir, he's on the stairs—I'll get behind here—and if ever I'm so imprudent again——
[*Goes behind the screen.*

Jos. Surf. Give me that book.
[*Sits down.* SERVANT *pretends to adjust his chair.*

Enter SIR PETER TEAZLE.

Sir Pet. Ay, ever improving himself. Mr. Surface, Mr. Surface—— [*Pats* JOSEPH *on the shoulder.*

Jos. Surf. Oh, my dear Sir Peter, I beg your pardon. [*Gaping, throws away the book.*] I have been dozing over a stupid book. Well, I am much obliged to you for this call. You haven't been here, I believe, since I fitted up this room. Books, you know, are the only things I am a coxcomb in.

Sir Pet. 'Tis very neat indeed. Well, well, that's proper; and you can make even your screen a source of knowledge—hung, I perceive, with maps.

Jos. Surf. Oh, yes, I find great use in that screen.

Sir Pet. I dare say you must, certainly, when you want to find anything in a hurry.

Jos. Surf. Ay, or to hide anything in a hurry either. [*Aside.*

Sir Pet. Well, I have a little private business——

Jos. Surf. You need not stay. [*To* SERVANT.

Ser. No, sir. [*Exit.*

Jos. Surf. Here's a chair, Sir Peter—I beg——

Sir Pet. Well, now we are alone, there is a subject, my dear friend, on which I wish to unburden my mind to you—a point of the greatest moment to my peace; in short, my good friend, Lady Teazle's conduct of late has made me very unhappy.

Jos. Surf. Indeed! I am very sorry to hear it.

Sir Pet. Yes, 'tis but too plain she has not the least regard for me; but, what's worse, I have pretty good authority to suppose she has formed an attachment to another.

Jos. Surf. Indeed! you astonish me!

Sir Pet. Yes! and, between ourselves, I think I've discovered the person.

Jos. Surf. How! you alarm me exceedingly.

Sir Pet. Ay, my dear friend, I knew you would sympathize with me!

Jos. Surf. Yes, believe me, Sir Peter, such a discovery would hurt me just as much as it would you.

Sir Pet. I am convinced of it. Ah! it is a happiness to have a friend whom we can trust even with one's family secrets. But have you no guess who I mean?

Jos. Surf. I haven't the most distant idea. It can't be Sir Benjamin Backbite!

Sir Pet. Oh, no! what say you to Charles?

Jos Surf. My brother! impossible!

Sir Pet. Oh, my dear friend, the goodness of your own heart misleads you. You judge of others by yourself.

Jos. Surf. Certainly, Sir Peter, the heart that is conscious of its own integrity is ever slow to credit another's treachery.

Sir Pet. True; but your brother has no sentiment—you never hear him talk so.

Jos. Surf. Yet I can't but think Lady Teazle herself has too much principle.

Sir Pet. Ay; but what is principle against the flattery of a handsome, lively young fellow?

Jos. Surf. That's very true.

Sir Pet. And then, you know, the difference of our ages makes it very improbable that she should have any great affection for me; and if she were to be frail, and I were to make it public, why the town would only laugh at me, the foolish old bachelor, who had married a girl.

Jos. Surf. That's true, to be sure—they would laugh.

Sir Pet. Laugh! ay, and make ballads, and paragraphs, and the devil knows what of me.

Jos. Surf. No, you must never make it public.

Sir Pet. But then again—that the nephew of my old friend, Sir Oliver, should be the person to attempt such a wrong, hurts me more nearly.

Jos. Surf. Ay, there's the point. When ingratitude barbs the dart of injury, the wound has double danger in it.

Sir Pet. Ay—I, that was, in a manner, left his guardian: in whose house he had been so often entertained; who never in my life denied him—my advice!

Jos. Surf. Oh, 'tis not to be credited! There may be a man capable of such baseness, to be sure; but, for my part, till you can give me positive proofs, I cannot but doubt it. However, if it should be proved on him, he is no longer a brother of mine— I disclaim kindred with him: for the man who can break the laws of hospitality, and tempt the wife of his friend, deserves to be branded as the pest of society.

Sir Pet. What a difference there is between you! What noble sentiments!

Jos. Surf. Yet I cannot suspect Lady Teazle's honour.

Sir Pet. I am sure I wish to think well of her, and to remove all ground of quarrel between us. She has lately reproached me more than once with having made no settlement on her; and, in our last squarrel, she almost hinted that she should not break heart if I was dead. Now, as we seem to differ in our ideas of expense, I have resolved she shall have her own way, and be her own mistress in that respect for the future; and, if I were to die, she will find I have not been inattentive to her interest while living. Here, my friend, are the drafts of two deeds, which I wish to have your opinion on. By one, she will enjoy eight hundred a year independent while I live; and, by the other, the bulk of my fortune at my death.

Jos. Surf. This conduct, Sir Peter, is indeed truly generous.— [*Aside.*] I wish it may not corrupt my pupil.

Sir Pet. Yes, I am determined she shall have no cause to complain, though I would not have her acquainted with the latter instance of my affection yet awhile.

Jos. Surf. Nor I, if I could help it.   [*Aside.*

Sir Pet. And now, my dear friend, if you please, we will talk over the situation of your hopes with Maria.

Jos. Surf. [*Softly.*] Oh, no, Sir Peter; another time, if you please.

Sir Pet. I am sensibly chagrined at the little progress you seem to make in her affections.

Jos. Surf. [*Softly.*] I beg you will not mention it. What are my disappointments when your happiness is in debate!—[*Aside.*] 'Sdeath, I shall be ruined every way!

Sir Pet. And though you are averse to my acquainting Lady Teazle with your passion, I'm sure she's not your enemy in the affair.

Jos. Surf. Pray, Sir Peter, now oblige me. I am really too much affected by the subject we have been speaking of to bestow a thought on my own concerns. The man who is entrusted with his friend's distresses can never——

Re-enter SERVANT.

Well, sir?

Ser. Your brother, sir, is speaking to a gentleman in the street, and says he knows you are within.

Jos. Surf. 'Sdeath, blockhead, I'm not within—I'm out for the day.

Sir Pet. Stay—hold—a thought has struck me:—you shall be at home.

Jos. Surf. Well, well, let him up.—[*Exit* SERVANT.] He'll interrupt Sir Peter, however.   [*Aside.*

Sir Pet. Now, my good friend, oblige me, I entreat you. Before Charles comes, let me conceal myself somewhere, then do you tax him on the point we have been talking, and his answer may satisfy me at once.

Jos. Surf. Oh, fie, Sir Peter! would you have me join in so mean a trick?—to trepan my brother too?

Sir Pet. Nay, you tell me you are sure he is innocent; if so, you do him the greatest service by giving him an opportunity to clear himself, and you will set my heart at rest. Come, you shall not refuse me: [*Going up*] here, behind the screen will be— Hey! what the devil! there seems to be one listener here already— I'll swear I saw a petticoat!

Jos. Surf. Ha! ha! ha! Well, this is ridiculous enough. I'll tell you, Sir Peter, though I hold a man of intrigue to be a most despicable character, yet you know, it does not follow that one is to be an absolute Joseph either! Hark'ee, 'tis a little French milliner, a silly rogue that plagues me; and having some character to lose, on your coming, sir, she ran behind the screen.

Sir Pet. Ah, a rogue—— But, egad, she has overheard all I have been saying of my wife.

Jos. Surf. Oh, 'twill never go any farther, you may depend upon it!

Sir Pet. No! then, faith, let her hear it out.—Here's a closet will do as well.

Jos. Surf. Well, go in there.

Sir Pet. Sly rogue! sly rogue!   [*Goes into the closet.*

Jos. Surf. A narrow escape, indeed! and a curious situation I'm in, to part man and wife in this manner.

Lady Teaz. [*Peeping.*] Couldn't I steal off?

Jos. Surf. Keep close, my angel!

Sir Pet. [*Peeping.*] Joseph, tax him home.

Jos. Surf. Back, my dear friend!

Lady Teaz. [*Peeping.*] Couldn't you lock Sir Peter in?

Jos. Surj. Be still, my life!

Sir Pet. [*Peeping.*] You're sure the little milliner won't blab?

Jos. Surf. In, in, my dear Sir Peter!—'Fore Gad, I wish I had a key to the door.

Enter CHARLES SURFACE.

Chas. Surf. Holla! brother, what has been the matter? Your fellow would not let me up at first. What! have you had a Jew or a wench with you?

Jos. Surf. Neither, brother, I assure you.

Chas. Surf. But what has made Sir Peter steal off? I thought he had been with you.

Jos. Surf. He was, brother; but, hearing you were coming, he did not choose to stay.

Chas. Surf. What! was the old gentleman afraid I wanted to borrow money of him!

Jos. Surf. No, sir: but I am sorry to find, Charles, you have lately given that worthy man grounds for great uneasiness.

Chas. Surf. Yes, they tell me I do that to a great many worthy men. But how so, pray?

Jos. Surf. To be plain with you, brother, he thinks you are endeavouring to gain Lady Teazle's affections from him.

Chas. Surf. Who, I? O Lud! not I, upon my word.—Ha! ha! ha! ha! so the old fellow has found out that he has got a young wife, has he?—or, what is worse, Lady Teazle has found out she has an old husband?

Jos. Surf. This is no subject to jest on, brother. He who can laugh——

Chas. Surf. True, true, as you were going to say—then, seriously, I never had the least idea of what you charge me with, upon my honour.

Jos. Surf. Well, it will give Sir Peter great satisfaction to hear this.   [*Raising his voice.*

Chas. Surf. To be sure, I once thought the lady seemed to have taken a fancy to me; but, upon my soul, I never gave her the least encouragement. Besides, you know my attachment to Maria.

Jos. Surf. But sure, brother, even if Lady Teazle had betrayed the fondest partiality for you——

Chas. Surf. Why, look'ee, Joseph, I hope I shall never deliberately do a dishonourable action; but if a pretty woman was purposely to throw herself in my way—and that pretty woman married to a man old enough to be her father——

Jos. Surf. Well!

Chas. Surf. Why, I believe I should be obliged to borrow a little of your morality, that's all. But, brother, do you know now that you surprise me exceedingly, by naming me with Lady Teazle; for i'faith, I always understood you were her favourite.

Jos. Surf. Oh, for shame, Charles! This retort is foolish.

Chas. Surf. Nay, I swear I have seen you exchange such significant glances——

Jos. Surf. Nay, nay, sir, this is no jest.

Chas. Surf. Egad, I'm serious! Don't you remember one day, when I called here——

Jos. Surf. Nay, pr'ythee, Charles——

Chas. Surf. And found you together——

Jos. Surf. Zounds, sir, I insist——

Chas. Surf. And another time, when your servant——

Jos. Surf. Brother, brother, a word with you!—[*Aside.*] Gad, I must stop him.

Chas. Surf. Informed, I say, that——

Jos. Surf. Hush! I beg your pardon, but Sir Peter has overheard all we have been saying. I knew you would clear yourself, or I should not have consented.

Chas. Surf. How, Sir Peter! Where is he?

Jos. Surf. Softly, there!   [*Points to the closet.*

Chas. Surf. Oh, 'fore Heaven, I'll have him out. Sir Peter, come forth!

Jos. Surf. No, no——

Chas. Surf. I say, Sir Peter, come into court.—[*Pulls in* SIR PETER.] What! my old guardian!—What!—turn inquisitor, and take evidence, incog.? Oh, fie! Oh, fie!

Sir Pet. Give me your hand, Charles—I believe I have suspected you wrongfully; but you mustn't be angry with Joseph— 'twas my plan!

Chas. Surf. Indeed!

Sir Pet. But I acquit you. I promise you I don't think near so ill of you as I did. What I have heard has given me great satisfaction.

Chas. Surf. Egad, then, 'twas lucky you didn't hear any more. Wasn't it, Joseph?

Sir Pet. Ah! you would have retorted on him.

Chas. Surf. Ah, ay, that was a joke.

Sir Pet. Yes, yes, I know his honour too well.

Chas. Surf. But you might as well have suspected him as me in this matter, for all that. Mightn't he, Joseph?

Sir Pet. Well, well, I believe you.

Jos. Surf. Would they were both out of the room!   [*Aside.*

Sir Pet. And in future, perhaps, we may not be such strangers.

Re-enter SERVANT *and whispers* JOSEPH SURFACE.

Ser. Lady Sneerwell is below, and says she will come up.

Jos. Surf. Gentlemen, I beg pardon—I must wait on you downstairs; here's a person come on particular business.

Chas. Surf. Well, you can see him in another room. Sir Peter and I have not met a long time, and I have something to say to him.

Jos. Surf. [*Aside.*] They must not be left together.—[*Aloud.*] I'll send Lady Sneerwell away, and return directly.—[*Aside to* SIR PETER.] Sir Peter, not a word of the French milliner.

Sir Pet. [*Aside to* JOSEPH SURFACE.] I! not for the world!— [*Exit* JOSEPH SURFACE.] Ah, Charles, if you associated more with your brother, one might indeed hope for your reformation. He is a man of sentiment. Well, there is nothing in the world so noble as a man of sentiment.

Chas. Surf. Psha! he is too moral by half; and so apprehensive of his good name, as he calls it, that I suppose he would as soon let a priest into his house as a wench.

Sir Pet. No, no,—come, come,—you wrong him. No, no, Joseph is no rake, but he is no such saint either, in that respect.— [*Aside.*] I have a great mind to tell him—we should have such a laugh at Joseph.

Chas. Surf. Oh, hang him! he's a very anchorite, a young hermit!

Sir Pet. Hark'ee—you must not abuse him: he may chance to hear of it again, I promise you.

Chas. Surf. Why, you won't tell him?

Sir Pet. No—but—this way.—[*Aside.*] Egad, I'll tell him. [*Aloud.*] Hark'ee, have you a mind to have a good laugh at Joseph?

Chas. Surf. I should like it of all things.

Sir Pet. Then, i'faith, we will! I'll be quit with him for discovering me. He had a girl with him when I called.   [*Whispers.*]

Chas. Surf. What! Joseph? you jest.

Sir Pet. Hush!—a little French milliner—and the best of the jest is—she's in the room now.

Chas. Surf. The devil she is!

Sir Pet. Hush! I tell you.   [*Points to the screen.*]

Chas. Surf. Behind the screen! Odds life, let's unveil her!

Sir Pet. No, no, he's coming:—you shan't, indeed!

Chas. Surf. Oh, egad, we'll have a peep at the little milliner!

Sir Pet. Not for the world!—Joseph will never forgive me.

Chas. Surf. I'll stand by you——

Sir Pet. Odds, here he is!

[CHARLES SURFACE *throws down the screen.*

Re-enter JOSEPH SURFACE.

Chas. Surf. Lady Teazle, by all that's wonderful!

Sir Pet. Lady Teazle, by all that's damnable!

Chas. Surf. Sir Peter, this is one of the smartest French milliners I ever saw. Egad, you seem all to have been diverting yourselves here at hide and seek, and I don't see who is out of the secret. Shall I beg your ladyship to inform me? Not a word!— Brother, will you be pleased to explain this matter? What! is Morality dumb too?—Sir Peter, though I found you in the dark, perhaps you are not so now! All mute! Well—though I can make nothing of the affair, I suppose you perfectly understand one another; so I'll leave you to yourselves.—[*Going.*] Brother, I'm sorry to find you have given that worthy man grounds for so much uneasiness.—Sir Peter! there's nothing in the world so noble as a man of sentiment! [*Exit.*

Jos. Surf. Sir Peter—notwithstanding—I confess—that appearances are against me—if you will afford me your patience—I make no doubt—but I shall explain everything to your satisfaction.

Sir Pet. If you please, sir.

Jos. Surf. The fact is, sir, that Lady Teazle, knowing my pretensions to your ward Maria—I say, sir, Lady Teazle, being apprehensive of the jealousy of your temper—and knowing my friendship to the family—she, sir, I say—called here—in order that—I might explain these pretensions—but on your coming—being apprehensive—as I said—of your jealousy—she withdrew—and this, you may depend on it, is the whole truth of the matter.

Sir Pet. A very clear account, upon my word; and I dare swear the lady will vouch for every article of it.

Lady Teaz. For not one word of it, Sir Peter!

Sir Pet. How! don't you think it worth while to agree in the lie?

Lady Teaz. There is not one syllable of truth in what that gentleman has told you.

Sir Pet. I believe you, upon my soul, ma'am!

Jos. Surf. [*Aside to* LADY TEAZLE.] 'Sdeath, madam, will you betray me?

Lady Teaz. Good Mr. Hypocrite, by your leave, I'll speak for myself.

Sir Pet. Ay, let her alone, sir; you'll find she'll make out a better story than you, without prompting.

Lady Teaz. Hear me, Sir Peter!—I came here on no matter relating to your ward, and even ignorant of this gentleman's pretensions to her. But I came, seduced by his insidious arguments, at least to listen to his pretended passion, if not to sacrifice your honour to his baseness.

Sir Pet. Now, I believe, the truth is coming, indeed!

Jos. Surf. The woman's mad!

Lady Teaz. No, sir; she has recovered her senses, and your own arts have furnished her with the means.—Sir Peter, I do not expect you to credit me—but the tenderness you expressed for me, when I am sure you could not think I was a witness to it, has penetrated so to my heart, that had I left the place without the shame of this discovery, my future life should have spoken the sincerity of my gratitude. As for that smooth-tongued hypocrite, who would have seduced the wife of his too credulous friend, while he affected honourable addresses to his ward—I behold him now in a light so truly despicable, that I shall never again respect myself for having listened to him.   [*Exit.*

Jos. Surf. Notwithstanding all this, Sir Peter, Heaven knows——

Sir Pet. That you are a villain! and so I leave you to your conscience.

Jos. Surf. You are too rash, Sir Peter; you shall hear me. The man who shuts out conviction by refusing to——

    [*Exeunt* Sir Peter *and* Joseph Surface, *talking.*

ACT V

Scene I.—*The Library in* Joseph Surface's *House*

Enter Joseph Surface *and* Servant.

Jos. Surf. Mr. Stanley! and why should you think I would see him? you must know he comes to ask something.

Ser. Sir, I should not have let him in, but that Mr. Rowley came to the door with him.

Jos. Surf. Psha! blockhead! to suppose that I should now be in a temper to receive visits from poor relations!—Well, why don't you show the fellow up?

Ser. I will, sir.—Why, sir, it was not my fault that Sir Peter discovered my lady——

Jos. Surf. Go, fool!—[*Exit* Servant.] Sure Fortune never played a man of my policy such a trick before! My character with Sir Peter, my hopes with Maria, destroyed in a moment! I'm in a rare humour to listen to other people's distresses! I shan't be able to bestow even a benevolent sentiment on Stanley. —So! here he comes, and Rowley with him. I must try to recover myself, and put a little charity into my face, however.   [*Exit.*

Enter Sir Oliver Surface *and* Rowley.

Sir Oliv. What! does he avoid us? That was he, was it not?

Row. It was, sir. But I doubt you are come a little too abruptly. His nerves are so weak, that the sight of a poor relation may be too much for him. I should have gone first to break it to him.

Sir Oliv. Oh, plague of his nerves! Yet this is he whom Sir Peter extols as a man of the most benevolent way of thinking!

Row. As to his way of thinking, I cannot pretend to decide;

for, to do him justice, he appears to have as much speculative
benevolence as any private gentleman in the kingdom, though
he is seldom so sensual as to indulge himself in the exercise of it.

Sir Oliv. Yet he has a string of charitable sentiments at his
fingers' ends.

Row. Or, rather, at his tongue's end, Sir Oliver; for I believe
there is no sentiment he has such faith in as that *Charity begins
at home.*

Sir Oliv. And his, I presume, is of that domestic sort which
never stirs abroad at all.

Row. I doubt you'll find it so;—but he's coming. I mustn't
seem to interrupt you; and you know, immediately as you leave
him, I come in to announce your arrival in your real character.

Sir Oliv. True; and afterwards you'll meet me at Sir Peter's.

Row. Without losing a moment. [*Exit.*

Sir Oliv. I don't like the complaisance of his features.

Re-enter JOSEPH SURFACE

Jos. Surf. Sir, I beg you ten thousand pardons for keeping you
a moment waiting.—Mr. Stanley, I presume.

Sir Olive. At your service.

Jos. Surf. Sir, I beg you will do me the honour to sit down—
I entreat you, sir.

Sir Oliv. Dear sir—there's no occasion.—[*Aside.*] Too civil by
half!

Jos. Surf. I have not the pleasure of knowing you, Mr. Stanley;
but I am extremely happy to see you look so well. You were
nearly related to my mother, I think, Mr. Stanley?

Sir Oliv. I was, sir; so nearly that my present poverty, I fear,
may do discredit to her wealthy children, else I should not have
presumed to trouble you.

Jos. Surf. Dear sir, there needs no apology: he that is in distress, though a stranger, has a right to claim kindred with the
wealthy. I am sure I wish I was one of that class, and had it in
my power to offer you even a small relief.

Sir Oliv. If your uncle, Sir Oliver, were here, I should have a
friend.

Jos. Surf. I wish he was, sir, with all my heart: you should
not want an advocate with him, believe me, sir.

Sir Oliv. I should not need one—my distresses would recommend me. But I imagined his bounty would enable you to become the agent of his charity.

Jos. Surf. My dear sir, you were strangely misinformed. Sir
Oliver is a worthy man, a very worthy man; but avarice, Mr.

Stanley, is the vice of age. I will tell you, my good sir, in confidence, what he has done for me has been a mere nothing; though people, I know, have thought otherwise, and, for my part, I never chose to contradict the report.

Sir Oliv. What! has he never transmitted you bullion—rupees —pagodas?

Jos. Surf. Oh, dear sir, nothing of the kind! No, no; a few presents now and then—china, shawls, congou tea, avadavats, and Indian crackers—little more, believe me.

Sir Oliv. Here's gratitude for twelve thousand pounds!— Avadavats and Indian crackers!   [*Aside.*

Jos. Surf. Then, my dear sir, you have heard, I doubt not, of the extravagance of my brother; there are very few would credit what I have done for that unfortunate young man.

Sir Olive. Not I, for one!   [*Aside.*

Jos. Surf. The sums I have lent him! Indeed I have been exceedingly to blame; it was an amiable weakness; however, I don't pretend to defend it—and now I feel it doubly culpable, since it has deprived me of the pleasure of serving you, Mr. Stanley, as my heart dictates.

Sir Oliv. [*Aside.*] Dissembler!—[*Aloud.*] Then, sir, you can't assist me?

Jos. Surf. At present, it grieves me to say, I cannot; but, whenever I have the ability, you may depend upon hearing from me.

Sir Oliv. I am extremely sorry——

Jos. Surf. Not more than I, believe me; to pity, without the power to relieve, is still more painful than to ask and be denied.

Sir Oliv. Kind sir, your most obedient humble servant.

Jos. Surf. You leave me deeply affected, Mr. Stanley.—William, be ready to open the door.   [*Calls to* Servant.

Sir Oliv. O, dear sir, no ceremony.

Jos. Surf. Your very obedient.

Sir Oliv. Your most obsequious.

Jos. Surf. You may depend upon hearing from me, whenever I can be of service.

Sir Oliv. Sweet sir, you are too good.

Jos. Surf. In the meantime I wish you health and spirits.

Sir Oliv. Your ever grateful and perpetual humble servant.

Jos. Surf. Sir, yours as sincerely.

Sir Oliv. Charles!—you are my heir.   [*Exit.*

Jos. Surf. This is one bad effect of a good character; it invites application from the unfortunate, and there needs no small degree of address to gain the reputation of benevolence without incurring the expense. The silver ore of pure charity is an expensive article in the catalogue of a man's good qualities; whereas the sentimental. French plate I use instead of it makes just as good a show, and pays no tax.

Re-enter ROWLEY.

Row. Mr. Surface, your servant: I was apprehensive of interrupting you, though my business demands immediate attention, as this note will inform you.

Jos. Surf. Always happy to see Mr. Rowley.—[*Aside. Reads the letter.*] Sir Oliver Surface!—My uncle arrived!

Row. He is, indeed: we have just parted—quite well, after a speedy voyage, and impatient to embrace his worthy nephew.

Jos. Surf. I am astonished!—William! stop Mr. Stanley, if he's not gone. [*Calls to* SERVANT.

Row. Oh! he's out of reach, I believe.

Jos. Surf. Why did you not let me know this when you came in together?

Row. I thought you had particular business. But I must be gone to inform your brother, and appoint him here to meet your uncle. He will be with you in a quarter of an hour.

Jos. Surf. So he says. Well, I am strangely overjoyed at his coming.—[*Aside.*] Never, to be sure, was anything so damned unlucky!

Row. You will be delighted to see how well he looks.

Jos. Surf. Oh! I'm overjoyed to hear it.—[*Aside.*]—Just at this time!

Row. I'll tell him how impatiently you expect him.

Jos. Surf. Do, do; pray give my best duty and affection. Indeed, I cannot express the sensations I feel at the thought of seeing him.—[*Exit* ROWLEY.] Certainly his coming just at this time is the cruellest piece of ill fortune. [*Exit.*

SCENE II.—*A Room in* SIR PETER TEAZLE'S *House*

Enter MRS. CANDOUR *and* MAID.

Maid. Indeed, ma'am, my lady will see nobody at present.

Mrs. Can. Did you tell her it was her friend Mrs. Candour?

Maid. Yes, ma'am; but she begs you will excuse her.

Mrs. Can. Do go again; I shall be glad to see her, if it be only for a moment, for I am sure she must be in great distress.—[*Exit* MAID.] Dear heart, how provoking! I'm not mistress of half the circumstances! We shall have the whole affair in the newspapers, with the names of the parties at length, before I have dropped the story at a dozen houses.

Enter Sir Benjamin Backbite.

Oh, dear Sir Benjamin! you have heard, I suppose——

Sir Ben. Of Lady Teazle and Mr. Surface——

Mrs. Can. And Sir Peter's discovery——

Sir Ben. Oh, the strangest piece of business, to be sure!

Mrs. Can. Well, I never was so surprised in my life. I am so sorry for all parties, indeed.

Sir Ben. Now, I don't pity Sir Peter at all: he was so extravagantly partial to Mr. Surface.

Mrs. Can. Mr. Surface! Why, 'twas with Charles Lady Teazle was detected.

Sir Ben. No, no, I tell you: Mr. Surface is the gallant.

Mrs. Can. No such thing! Charles is the man. 'Twas Mr. Surface brought Sir Peter on purpose to discover them.

Sir Ben. I tell you I had it from one——

Mrs. Can. And I have it from one——

Sir Ben. Who had it from one, who had it——

Mrs. Can. From one immediately——But here comes Lady Sneerwell; perhaps she knows the whole affair.

Enter Lady Sneerwell.

Lady Sneer. So, my dear Mrs. Candour, here's a sad affair of our friend Lady Teazle!

Mrs. Can. Ay, my dear friend, who would have thought——

Lady Sneer. Well, there is no trusting to appearances; though indeed, she was always too lively for me.

Mrs. Can. To be sure, her manners were a little too free; but then she was so young!

Lady Sneer. And had, indeed, some good qualities.

Mrs. Can. So she had, indeed. But have you heard the particulars?

Lady Sneer. No; but everybody says that Mr. Surface——

Sir Ben. Ay, there; I told you Mr. Surface was the man.

Mrs. Can. No, no: indeed the assignation was with Charles.

Lady Sneer. With Charles! You alarm me, Mrs. Candour.

Mrs. Can. Yes, yes: he was the lover. Mr. Surface, to do him justice, was only the informer.

Sir Ben. Well, I'll not dispute with you, Mrs. Candour; but, be it which it may, I hope that Sir Peter's wound will not——

Mrs. Can. Sir Peter's wound! Oh, mercy! I didn't hear a word of their fighting.

Lady Sneer. Nor I, a syllable.

Sir Ben. No! what, no mention of the duel?

Mrs. Can. Not a word.

Sir Ben. Oh, yes: they fought before they left the room.

Lady Sneer. Pray let us hear.

Mrs. Can. Ay, do oblige us with the duel.

Sir Ben. "Sir," says Sir Peter, immediately after the discovery, *"you are a most ungrateful fellow."*

Mrs. Can. Ay, to Charles——

Sir Ben. No, no——to Mr. Surface——*"a most ungrateful fellow; and old as I am, sir,"* says he, *"I insist on immediate satisfaction."*

Mrs. Can. Ay, that must have been to Charles; for 'tis very unlikely Mr. Surface should fight in his own house.

Sir Ben. 'Gad's life, ma'am, not at all——*"giving me immediate satisfaction."*——On this, ma'am, Lady Teazle, seeing Sir Peter in such danger, ran out of the room in strong hysterics, and Charles after her, calling out for hartshorn and water; then, madam, they began to fight with swords——

Enter CRABTREE.

Crab. With pistols, nephew——pistols! I have it from undoubted authority.

Mrs. Can. Oh, Mr. Crabtree, then it is all true!

Crab. Too true, indeed, madam, and Sir Peter is dangerously wounded——

Sir Ben. By a thrust in second quite through his left side——

Crab. By a bullet lodged in the thorax.

Mrs. Can. Mercy on me! Poor Sir Peter!

Crab. Yes, madam; though Charles would have avoided the matter, if he could.

Mrs. Can. I knew Charles was the person.

Sir Ben. My uncle, I see, knows nothing of the matter.

Crab. But Sir Peter taxed him with the basest ingratitude——

Sir Ben. That I told you, you know——

Crab. Do, nephew, let me speak!——and insisted on immediate——

Sir Ben. Just as I said——

Crab. Odds life, nephew, allow others to know something too! A pair of pistols lay on the bureau (for Mr. Surface, it seems, had come home the night before late from Salthill, where he had been to see the Montem with a friend, who has a son at Eton), so, unluckily, the pistols were left charged.

Sir Ben. I heard nothing of this.

Crab. Sir Peter forced Charles to take one, and they fired, it seems, pretty nearly together. Charles's shot took effect, as I tell you, and Sir Peter's missed; but, what is very extraordinary, the ball struck against a little bronze Shakspeare that stood over the fireplace, grazed out of the window at a right angle, and wounded the postman, who was just coming to the door with a double letter from Northamptonshire.

Sir Ben. My uncle's account is more circumstantial, I confess; but I believe mine is the true one for all that.

Lady Sneer. [*Aside.*] I am more interested in this affair than they imagine, and must have better information. [*Exit.*

Sir Ben. Ah! Lady Sneerwell's alarm is very easily accounted for.

Crab. Yes, yes, they certainly do say—but that's neither here nor there.

Mrs. Can. But, pray, where is Sir Peter at present?

Crab. Oh! they brought him home, and he is now in the house, though the servants are ordered to deny him.

Mrs. Can. I believe so, and Lady Teazle, I suppose, attending him.

Crab. Yes, yes; and I saw one of the faculty enter just be-fore me.

Sir Ben. Hey! who comes here?

Crab. Oh, this is he: the physician, depend on't.

Mrs. Can. Oh, certainly! it must be the physician; and now we shall know.

Enter Sir Oliver Surface.

Crab. Well, doctor, what hopes?

Mrs. Can. Ay, doctor, how's your patient?

Sir Ben. Now, doctor, isn't it a wound with a small-sword?

Crab. A bullet lodged in the thorax, for a hundred!

Sir Oliv. Doctor! a wound with a small-sword! and a bullet in the thorax?—Oons! are you mad, good people?

Sir Ben. Perhaps, sir, you are not a doctor?

Sir Oliv. Truly, I am to thank you for my degree, if I am.

Crab. Only a friend of Sir Peter's, then, I presume. But, sir, you must have heard of his accident?

Sir Oliv. Not a word!

Crab. Not of his being dangerously wounded?

Sir Oliv. The devil he is!

Sir Ben. Run through the body——

Crab. Shot in the breast——

Sir Ben. By one Mr. Surface——

Crab. Ay, the younger.

Sir Oliv. Hey! what the plague! you seem to differ strangely in your accounts: however, you agree that Sir Peter is dangerously wounded.

Sir Ben. Oh, yes, we agree in that.

Crab. Yes, yes, I believe there can be no doubt in that.

Sir Oliv. Then, upon my word, for a person in that situation, he is the most imprudent man alive; for here he comes, walking as if nothing at all was the matter.

Enter SIR PETER TEAZLE.

Odds heart, Sir Peter! you are come in good time, I promise you; for we had just given you over!

Sir Ben. [*Aside to* CRABTREE.] Egad, uncle, this is the most sudden recovery!

Sir Oliv. Why, man! what do you do out of bed with a small-sword through your body, and a bullet lodged in your thorax?

Sir Pet. A small-sword and a bullet?

Sir Oliv. Ay; these gentlemen would have killed you without law or physic, and wanted to dub me a doctor, to make me an accomplice.

Sir Pet. Why, what is all this?

Sir Ben. We rejoice, Sir Peter, that the story of the duel is not true, and are sincerely sorry for your other misfortune.

Sir Pet. So, so; all over the town already.   [*Aside.*

Crab. Though, Sir Peter, you were certainly vastly to blame to marry at your years.

Sir Pet. Sir, what business is that of yours?

Mrs. Can. Though, indeed, as Sir Peter made so good a husband, he's very much to be pitied.

Sir Pet. Plague on your pity, ma'am! I desire none of it.

Sir Ben. However, Sir Peter, you must not mind the laughing and jests you will meet with on the occasion.

Sir Pet. Sir, sir! I desire to be master in my own house.

Crab. 'Tis no uncommon case, that's one comfort.

Sir Pet. I insist on being left to myself: without ceremony, I insist on your leaving my house directly!

Mrs. Can. Well, well, we are going; and depend on't, we'll make the best report of it we can.   [*Exit.*

Sir Pet. Leave my house!

Crab. And tell how hardly you've been treated.   [*Exit.*

Sir Pet. Leave my house!

Sir Ben. And how patiently you bear it.   [*Exit.*

Sir Pet. Fiends! vipers! furies! Oh! that their own venom would choke them!

Sir Oliv. They are very provoking indeed, Sir Peter.

Enter ROWLEY.

Row. I heard high words: what has ruffled you, sir?

Sir Pet. Psha! what signifies asking? Do I ever pass a day without my vexations?

Row. Well, I'm not inquisitive.

Sir Oliv. Well, Sir Peter, I have seen both my nephews in the manner we proposed.

Sir Pet. A precious couple they are!

Row. Yes, and Sir Oliver is convinced that your judgment was right, Sir Peter.

Sir Oliv. Yes, I find Joseph is indeed the man, after all.

Row. Ay, as Sir Peter says, he is a man of sentiment.

Sir Oliv. And acts up to the sentiments he professes.

Row. It certainly is edification to hear him talk.

Sir Oliv. Oh, he's a model for the young men of the age! But how's this, Sir Peter? you don't join us in your friend Joseph's praise, as I expected.

Sir Pet. Sir Oliver, we live in a damned wicked world, and the fewer we praise the better.

Row. What! do you say so, Sir Peter, who were never mistaken in your life?

Sir Pet. Psha! plague on you both! I see by your sneering you have heard the whole affair. I shall go mad among you!

Row. Then, to fret you no longer, Sir Peter, we are indeed acquainted with it all. I met Lady Teazle coming from Mr. Surface's so humbled, that she deigned to request me to be her advocate with you.

Sir Pet. And does Sir Oliver know all this?

Sir Oliv. Every circumstance.

Sir Pet. What, of the closet and the screen, hey?

Sir Oliv. Yes, yes, and the little French milliner. Oh, I have been vastly diverted with the story! ha! ha! ha!

Sir Pet. 'Twas very pleasant.

Sir Oliv. I never laughed more in my life, I assure you: ha! ha! ha!

Sir Pet. Oh, vastly diverting! ha! ha! ha!

Row. To be sure, Joseph with his sentiments! ha! ha! ha!

Sir Pet. Yes, his sentiments! ha! ha! ha! Hypocritical villain!

Sir Oliv. Ay, and that rogue Charles to pull Sir Peter out of the closet: ha! ha! ha!

Sir Pet. Ha! ha! 'twas devilish entertaining, to be sure!

Sir Oliv. Ha! ha! ha! Egad, Sir Peter, I should like to have seen your face when the screen was thrown down: ha! ha!

Sir Pet. Yes, my face when the screen was thrown down: ha! ha! ha! Oh, I must never show my head again!

Sir Oliv. But come, come, it isn't fair to laugh at you neither, my old friend; though, upon my soul, I can't help it.

Sir Pet. Oh, pray don't restrain your mirth on my account: it does not hurt me at all! I laugh at the whole affair myself. Yes, yes, I think being a standing jest for all one's acquaintance a very happy situation. Oh, yes, and then of a morning to read the paragraphs about Mr. S——, Lady ——, and Sir P——, will be so entertaining!

Row. Without affectation, Sir Peter, you may despise the ridicule of fools. But I see Lady Teazle going towards the next room; I am sure you must desire a reconciliation as earnestly as she does.

Sir Oliv. Perhaps my being here prevents her coming to you. Well, I'll leave honest Rowley to mediate between you; but he must bring you all presently to Mr. Surface's, where I am now returning, if not to reclaim a libertine, at least to expose hypocrisy.

Sir Pet. Ah, I'll be present at your discovering yourself there with all my heart; though 'tis a vile unlucky place for discoveries.

Row. We'll follow.　　　　　[*Exit* Sir Oliver Surface.

Sir Pet. She is not coming here, you see, Rowley.

Row. No, but she has left the door of that room open, you perceive. See, she is in tears.

Sir Pet. Certainly a little mortification appears very becoming in a wife. Don't you think it will do her good to let her pine a little?

Row. Oh, this is ungenerous in you!

Sir Pet. Well, I know not what to think. You remember the letter I found of hers evidently intended for Charles!

Row. A mere forgery, Sir Peter! laid in your way on purpose. This is one of the points which I intend Snake shall give you conviction of.

Sir Pet. I wish I were once satisfied of that. She looks this way. What a remarkably elegant turn of the head she has. Rowley, I'll go to her.

Row. Certainly.

Sir Pet. Though, when it is known that we are reconciled, people will laugh at me ten times more.

Row. Let them laugh, and retort their malice only by showing them you are happy in spite of it.

Sir Pet. I'faith, so I will! and, if I'm not mistaken, we may yet be the happiest couple in the country.

Row. Nay, Sir Peter, he who once lays aside suspicion——

Sir Pet. Hold, Master Rowley! if you have any regard for me, never let me hear you utter anything like a sentiment: I have had enough of them to serve me the rest of my life.

[*Exeunt.*

Scene III.—*The Library in* Joseph Surface's *House*

Enter Joseph Surface *and* Lady Sneerwell.

Lady Sneer. Impossible! Will not Sir Peter immediately be reconciled to Charles, and of course no longer oppose his union with Maria? The thought is distraction to me.

Jos. Surf. Can passion furnish a remedy?

Lady Sneer. No, nor cunning either. Oh, I was a fool, an idiot, to league with such a blunderer!

Jos. Surf. Surely, Lady Sneerwell, I am the greatest sufferer; yet you see I bear the accident with calmness.

Lady Sneer. Because the disappointment doesn't reach your heart; your interest only attached you to Maria. Had you felt for her what I have for that ungrateful libertine, neither your temper nor hypocrisy could prevent your showing the sharpness of your vexation.

Jos. Surf. But why should your reproaches fall on me for this disappointment?

Lady Sneer. Are you not the cause of it? Had you not a sufficient field for your roguery in imposing upon Sir Peter, and supplanting your brother, but you must endeavour to seduce his wife? I hate such an avarice of crimes; 'tis an unfair monopoly, and never prospers.

Jos. Surf. Well, I admit I have been to blame. I confess I deviated from the direct road of wrong, but I don't think we're so totally defeated either.

Lady Sneer. No!

Jos. Surf. You tell me you have made a trial of Snake since we met, and that you still believe him faithful to us?

Lady Sneer. I do believe so.

Jos. Surf. And that he has undertaken, should it be necessary, to swear and prove, that Charles is at this time contracted by vows and honour to your ladyship, which some of his former letters to you will serve to support?

Lady Sneer. This, indeed, might have assisted.

Jos. Surf. Come, come; it is not too late yet.—[*Knocking at the door.*] But hark! this is probably my uncle, Sir Oliver: retire to that room; we'll consult further when he's gone.

Lady Sneer. Well, but if he should find you out too.

Jos. Surf. Oh, I have no fear of that. Sir Peter will hold his tongue for his own credit's sake—and you may depend on it I shall soon discover Sir Oliver's weak side!

Lady Sneer. I have no diffidence of your abilities! only be constant to one roguery at a time.

Jos. Surf. I will, I will!—[*Exit* LADY SNEERWELL.] So! 'tis confounded hard, after such bad fortune, to be baited by one's confederate in evil. Well, at all events, my character is so much better than Charles's, that I certainly—hey!—what—this is not Sir Oliver, but old Stanley again. Plague on't that he should return to tease me just now! I shall have Sir Oliver come and find him here—and—

Enter SIR OLIVER SURFACE.

Gad's life, Mr. Stanley, why have you come back to plague me at this time? You must not stay now, upon my word.

Sir Oliv. Sir, I hear your uncle Oliver is expected here, and though he has been so penurious to you, I'll try what he'll do for me.

Jos. Surf. Sir, 'tis impossible for you to stay now, so I must beg——Come any other time, and I promise you, you shall be assisted.

Sir Oliv. No: Sir Oliver and I must be acquainted.

Jos. Surf. Zounds, sir! then I insist on your quitting the room directly.

Sir Oliv. Nay, sir——

Jos. Surf. Sir, I insist on't!—Here, William! show this gentleman out. Since you compel me, sir, not one moment—this is such insolence. [*Going to push him out.*

Enter CHARLES SURFACE.

Chas. Surf. Heyday! what's the matter now? What the devil have you got hold of my little broker here? Zounds, brother, don't hurt little Premium. What's the matter, my little fellow?

Jos. Surf. So! he has been with you, too, has he?

Chas. Surf. To be sure he has. Why, he's as honest a little—— But sure, Joseph, you have not been borrowing money too, have you?

Jos. Surf. Borrowing! no! But, brother, you know we expect Sir Oliver here every——

Chas. Surf. O Gad, that's true! Noll mustn't find the little broker here, to be sure.

Jos. Surf. Yet, Mr. Stanley insists——

Chas. Surf. Stanley! why his name's Premium.

Jos. Surf. No, sir, Stanley.

Chas. Surf. No, no, Premium.

Jos. Surf. Well, no matter which—but——

Chas. Surf. Ay, ay, Stanley or Premium, 'tis the same thing, as you say; for I suppose he goes by half a hundred names, besides A. B. at the coffee-house.   [*Knocking.*

Jos. Surf. 'Sdeath! here's Sir Oliver at the door. Now I beg, Mr. Stanley——

Chas. Surf. Ay, ay, and I beg, Mr. Premium——

Sir Oliv. Gentlemen——

Jos. Surf. Sir, by heaven you shall go!

Chas. Surf. Ay, out with him, certainly.

Sir Oliv. This violence——

Jos. Surf. Sir, 'tis your own fault.

Chas. Surf. Out with him, to be sure.

[*Both forcing* Sir Oliver *out.*

Enter Sir Peter *and* Lady Teazle, Maria, *and* Rowley.

Sir Pet. My old friend, Sir Oliver—hey! What in the name of wonder!—here are dutiful nephews—assault their uncle at his first visit!

Lady Teaz. Indeed, Sir Oliver, 'twas well we came in to rescue you.

Row. Truly it was; for I perceive, Sir Oliver, the character of old Stanley was no protection to you.

Sir Oliv. Nor of Premium either: the necessities of the former could not extort a shilling from that benevolent gentleman; and with the other I stood a chance of faring worse than my ancestors, and being knocked down without being bid for.

Jos. Surf. Charles!

Chas. Surf. Joseph!

Jos. Surf. 'Tis now complete!

Chas. Surf. Very.

Sir Oliv. Sir Peter, my friend, and Rowley too—look on that elder nephew of mine. You know what he has already received from my bounty; and you also know how gladly I would have regarded half my fortune as held in trust for him? judge, then, my disappointment in discovering him to be destitute of truth, charity, and gratitude!

Sir Pet. Sir Oliver, I should be more surprised at this declaration, if I had not myself found him to be mean, treacherous, and hypocritical.

Lady Teaz. And if the gentleman pleads not guilty to these, pray let him call me to his character.

Sir Pet. Then, I believe, we need add no more: if he knows himself, he will consider it as the most perfect punishment that he is known to the world.

Chas. Surf. If they talk this way to Honesty, what will they say to me, by-and-by? [*Aside.*

[SIR PETER, LADY TEAZLE, *and* MARIA *retire.*

Sir Oliv. As for that prodigal, his brother, there——

Chas. Surf. Ay, now comes my turn: the damned family pictures will ruin me! [*Aside.*

Jos. Surf. Sir Oliver—uncle, will you honour me with a hearing?

Chas. Surf. Now, if Joseph would make one of his long speeches, I might recollect myself a little. [*Aside.*

Sir Oliv. I suppose you would undertake to justify yourself?
[*To* JOSEPH SURFACE.

Jos. Surf. I trust I could.

Sir Oliv. [*To* CHARLES SURFACE.] Well, sir!—and you could justify yourself too, I suppose?

Chas. Surf. Not that I know of, Sir Oliver.

Sir Oliv. What!—Little Premium has been let too much into the secret, I suppose?

Chas. Surf. True, sir; but they were family secrets, and should not be mentioned again, you know.

Row. Come, Sir Oliver, I know you cannot speak of Charles's follies with anger.

Sir Oliver. Odd's heart, no more I can; nor with gravity either. Sir Peter, do you know the rogue bargained with me for all his ancestors; sold me judges and generals by the foot, and maiden aunts as cheap as broken china.

Chas. Surf. To be sure, Sir Oliver, I did make a little free with the family canvas, that's the truth on't. My ancestors may rise in judgment against me, there's no denying it; but believe me sincere when I tell you—and upon my soul I would not say so if I was not—that if I do not appear mortified at the exposure of my follies, it is because I feel at this moment the warmest satisfaction at seeing you, my liberal benefactor.

Sir Oliv. Charles, I believe you. Give me your hand again: the ill-looking little fellow over the settee has made your peace.

Chas. Surf. Then, sir, my gratitude to the original is still increased.

Lady Teaz. [*Advancing.*] Yet, I believe, Sir Oliver, here is one whom Charles is still more anxious to be reconciled to.

                                [*Pointing to* MARIA.

Sir Oliv. Oh, I have heard of his attachment there; and, with the young lady's pardon, if I construe right—that blush——

Sir Pet. Well, child, speak your sentiments.

Mar. Sir, I have little to say, but that I shall rejoice to hear that he is happy; for me, whatever claim I had to his attention, I willingly resign to one who has a better title.

Chas. Surf. How, Maria!

Sir Pet. Heyday! what's the mystery now? While he appeared an incorrigible rake, you would give your hand to no one else; and now that he is likely to reform I'll warrant you won't have him.

Mar. His own heart and Lady Sneerwell know the cause.

Chas. Surf. Lady Sneerwell!

Jos. Surf. Brother, it is with great concern I am obliged to speak on this point, but my regard to justice compels me, and Lady Sneerwell's injuries can no longer be concealed.

                                [*Opens the door.*

Enter LADY SNEERWELL

Sir Pet. So! another French milliner! Egad, he has one in every room in the house, I suppose!

Lady Sneer. Ungrateful Charles! Well may you be surprised, and feel for the indelicate situation your perfidy has forced me into.

Chas. Surf. Pray, uncle, is this another plot of yours? For, as I have life, I don't understand it.

Jos. Surf. I believe, sir, there is but the evidence of one person more necessary to make it extremely clear.

Sir Pet. And that person, I imagine, is Mr. Snake.—Rowley, you were perfectly right to bring him with us, and pray let him appear.

Row. Walk in, Mr. Snake.

Enter SNAKE.

I thought his testimony might be wanted; however, it happens unluckily, that he comes to confront Lady Sneerwell, not to support her.

Lady Sneer. A villain! Treacherous to me at last! Speak, fellow, have you too conspired against me?

Snake. I beg your ladyship ten thousand pardons: you paid

me extremely liberally for the lie in question; but I unfortunately have been offered double to speak the truth.

Lady Sneer. The torments of shame and disappointment on you all!   [*Going.*

Lady Teaz. Hold, Lady Sneerwell—before you go, let me thank you for the trouble you and that gentleman have taken, in writing letters from me to Charles, and answering them yourself; and let me also request you to make my respects to the scandalous college, of which you are president, and inform them, that Lady Teazle, licentiate, begs leave to return the diploma they granted her, as she leaves off practice, and kills characters no longer.

Lady Sneer. You too, madam!—provoking—insolent! May your husband live these fifty years!   [*Exit.*

Sir Pet. Oons! what a fury!

Lady Teaz. A malicious creature, indeed!

Sir Pet. What! not for her last wish?

Lady Teaz. Oh, no!

Sir Oliv. Well, sir, and what have you to say now?

Jos. Surf. Sir, I am so confounded, to find that Lady Sneerwell could be guilty of suborning Mr. Snake in this manner, to impose on us all, that I know not what to say: however, lest her revengeful spirit should prompt her to injure my brother, I had certainly better follow her directly.   [*Exit.*

Sir Pet. Moral to the last drop!

Sir Oliv. Ay, and marry her, Joseph, if you can. Oil and vinegar!—egad, you'll do very well together.

Row. I believe we have no more occasion for Mr. Snake at present?

Snake. Before I go, I beg pardon once for all, for whatever uneasiness I have been the humble instrument of causing to the parties present.

Sir Pet. Well, well, you have made atonement by a good deed at last.

Snake. But I must request of the company, that it shall never be known.

Sir Pet. Hey! what the plague! are you ashamed of having done a right thing once in your life?

Snake. Ah, sir, consider—I live by the badness of my character; and, if it were once known that I had been betrayed into an honest action, I should lose every friend I have in the world.

Sir Oliv. Well, well—we'll not traduce you by saying anything in your praise, never fear.   [*Exit* SNAKE.

Sir Pet. There's a precious rogue!

Lady Teaz. See, Sir Oliver, there needs no persuasion now to reconcile your nephew and Maria.

Sir Oliv. Ay, ay, that's as it should be, and, egad, we'll have the wedding to-morrow morning.

Chas. Surf. Thank you, dear uncle.

Sir Pet. What, you rogue! don't you ask the girl's consent first?

Chas. Surf. Oh, I have done that a long time—a minute ago—and she has looked yes.

Mar. For shame, Charles!—I protest, Sir Peter, there has not been a word——

Sir Oliv. Well, then, the fewer the better: may your love for each other never know abatement.

Sir Pet. And may you live as happily together as Lady Teazle and I intend to do!

Chas. Surf. Rowley, my old friend, I am sure you congratulate me; and I suspect that I owe you much.

Sir Oliv. You do, indeed, Charles.

Row. If my efforts to serve you had not succeeded you would have been in my debt for the attempt—but deserve to be happy—and you over-repay me.

Sir Pet. Ay, honest Rowley always said you would reform.

Chas. Surf. Why as to reforming, Sir Peter, I'll make no promises, and that I take to be a proof that I intend to set about it. But here shall be my monitor—my gentle guide.—Ah! can I leave the virtuous path those eyes illumine?

Though thou, dear maid, shouldst wave thy beauty's sway,
Thou still must rule, because I will obey:
An humble fugitive from Folly view,
No sanctuary near but Love and you: [*To the audience.*
You can, indeed, each anxious fear remove,
For even Scandal dies, if you approve.   [*Exeunt omnes.*

EPILOGUE

By Mr. Colman.

SPOKEN BY LADY TEAZLE

I, who was late so volatile and gay,
Like a trade-wind must now blow all one way,
Bend all my cares, my studies, and my vows,
To one dull rusty weathercock—my spouse!
So wills our virtuous bard—the motley Bayes
Of crying epilogues and laughing plays!
Old bachelors, who marry smart young wives,
Learn from our play to regulate your lives:
Each bring his dear to town, all faults upon her—
London will prove the very source of honour.
Plunged fairly in, like a cold bath it serves,
When principles relax, to brace the nerves:
Such is my case; and yet I must deplore
That the gay dream of dissipation's o'er.
And say, ye fair! was ever lively wife,
Born with a genius for the highest life,
Like me untimely blasted in her bloom,
Like me condemn'd to such a dismal doom?
Save money—when I just knew how to waste it!
Leave London—just as I began to taste it!
    Must I then watch the early crowing cock,
The melancholy ticking of a clock;
In a lone rustic hall for ever pounded,
With dogs, cats, rats, and squalling brats surrounded?
With humble curate can I now retire,
(While good Sir Peter boozes with the squire,)
And at backgammon mortify my soul,
That pants for loo, or flutters at a vole.
Seven's the main! Dear sound that must expire,
Lost at hot cockles round a Christmas fire;
The transient hour of fashion too soon spent,
Farewell the tranquil mind, farewell content!

951

Farewell the plumèd head, the cushion'd tête,
That takes the cushion from its proper seat!
That spirit-stirring drum!—card drums I mean,
Spadille—odd trick—pam—basto—king and queen!
And you, ye knockers, that, with brazen throat,
The welcome visitors' approach denote;
Farewell all quality of high renown,
Pride, pomp, and circumstance of glorious town!
Farewell! your revels I partake no more,
And Lady Teazle's occupation's o'er!
All this I told our bard; he smiled, and said 'twas clear,
I ought to play deep tragedy next year.
Meanwhile he drew wise morals from his play,
And in these solemn periods stalk'd away:—
"Bless'd were the fair like you; her faults who stopp'd,
And closed her follies when the curtain dropp'd!
No more in vice or error to engage,
Or play the fool at large on life's great stage."